POLITICAL TERRORISM

Expanded and updated edition prepared under the auspices of the Center for International Affairs, Harvard University

POLITICAL TERRORISM

Alex P. Schmid
Albert J. Jongman

A New Guide to Actors, Authors, Concepts, Data Bases, Theories, & Literature

Alex P. Schmid and Albert J. Jongman
with the collaboration of Michael Stohl, Jan Brand, Peter A. Flemming, Angela van der Poel, and Rob Thijsse

Foreword by Irving Louis Horowitz

Transaction Publishers
New Brunswick (U.S.A.) and London (U.K.)

First paperback printing 2005

First edition, January 1984.
www.transactionpub.com

This book is printed on acid-free paper that meets the American National Standard for Permanence of Paper for Printed Library Materials.

Library of Congress Catalog Number: 2004062019
ISBN: 0-444-85659-5 (cloth); 1-4128-0469-8 (paper)
Printed in the United States of America

Library of Congress Cataloging-in-Publication Data

Schmid, Alex Peter.

Political terrorism : a new guide to actors, authors, concepts, data bases, theories, and literature / Alex P. Schmid and Albert J. Jongman with the collaboration of Michael Stohl ... [et al.] ; foreword by Irving Louis Horowitz.—Rev., expanded, and updated ed. / prepared under the auspices of the Center for International Affairs, Harvard University.

p. cm.

This edition originally published: 1988.
Includes bibliographical references and index.
ISBN 1-4128-0469-8 (pbk. : alk. paper)

1. Terrorism. 2. Terrorism—Directories. 3. Terrorism—Bibliography. 4. Terrorism—Databases. I. Jongman, A. J. II. Title.

HV6431.S349 2005
303.6'25—dc22 2004062019

CONTENTS

TABLES AND DIAGRAMS

ACKNOWLEDGMENTS

The complete revision of this handbook was accomplished during my stay in Cambridge at the Program on Nonviolent Sanctions of the Center for International Affairs, Harvard University. I am especially grateful to Dr. Gene Sharp, Director of the Program on Nonviolent Sanctions, for his support. I also wish to thank the Albert Einstein Institution for granting me a fellowship. The Department of Political Science of the University of Leiden The Netherlands, was accommodating in letting me pursue this work on the other side of the Atlantic. In particular, I wish to thank Professor A. v. Staden for his assistance in making this sabbatical possible. The Center for the Study of Social Conflicts (C.O.M.T.) at my home university offered much of the infrastructure which made the updating of this handbook possible. Its director, Professor A.J.F. Köbben, in particular, has been a constant source of inspiration and encouragement; other colleagues at the C.O.M.T., especially M. Wildeman and A. v. Tuyll, also went out of their way in assisting me in this work. The contribution of J. Brand and A. v. d. Poel in updating the bibliography has been particularly substantial. This section of the guide also benefitted from the support received from the Social Science Information and Documentation Centre in Amsterdam, where P. de Guchtenaire, the head of the Steinmetz Archives, and Dr. A. Marks, director of SWIDOC, proved especially helpful. At the Steinmetz Archives, Henk Schrik's technical expertise and singular dedication greatly contributed to the realization of the computer-based bibliography. Thanks are also due to Ans Peeters Weem and Suzanne E. Thorin for their bibliographic assistance. Financial support for the updating of the literature section was provided by the Dutch Ministry of Education and Sciences. The Netherlands Organzation for Scientific Research (Z.W.O.) awarded a travel grant to Professor Michael Stohl, which made collaboration possible on the chapter on typologies. For the discussion of the data situation in the field of state terrorism, the help of Laurie Wiseberg from the Human Rights Internet at Harvard University was much appreciated. R. Thysse, from the University of Amsterdam, allowed me to make use of materials from his master's thesis on state violence for the rewriting of the chapter on data bases. A. J. Jongman, who had collaborated on the first edition of this *Research Guide*, has been a source of constant information and is principally responsible for the updated directory of terrorist organizations and protest movements. Finally, I would like to acknowledge the professional editorial assistance of Anne B. Fitzpatrick at the Program on Nonviolent Sanctions.

Like the first *Research Guide*, the present one depends heavily on the contributions of more than fifty authors in the field of terrorism--including many leading theorists--who took the time to answer another lengthy questionnaire with which I attempted to gauge the state of the art in the study of terrorism.[1] A dozen of them prefer to remain anonymous, but their contributions were by no means less than the contributions of those I can mention here by name: F. C. Adams, N. O. Berry, D. Charters, R. R. Corrado, L. A. Costa Pinto, R. Crelinsten, I. Fetscher, N. Friedland, G. Davidson Smith, D. Della Porta, R. Drake, L. C. Green, J. L. Gleason, M. Gunter, T. R. Gurr, W. Hahlweg, J. Harris, H. Hess, Ch. M. Ferguson, Ch. Johnson, P. Kronenberger, A. Merari, E. F. Mickolus, F. M. Ochberg, D. Pipes, W. H. Reid, K. G. Robertson, U. Rosenthal, A. P. Rubin, M. Stohl, D. Szabo, R. Thackrah, Ch. Townshend, M.A.J. Tugwell, C. J. Visser, V. Vasilijevic, B. W. Warner, W. L. Waugh, Jr., P. Wilkinson, J. B. Wolf, M. D. Wolpin, A. Yoder, T. R. Young, and J. K. Zawodny.

While they all helped to make this a richer book, the responsibility for its shortcomings rests with the authors alone.

PREFACE

> Rule by terror, a familiar process in history, has virtually escaped systematic analysis. Working for the modern state, this old scourge of human communities destroys men for the same ends it once achieved as the instrument of immemorial despots. This form of power remains at the edges of rational inquiry, but the experience of recent times, punctuated by terroristic outbreaks and burdened by regimes of terror, makes the world tremble with an awareness that seeks general explanations. *E. V. Walter*[1]

Twenty years ago, when Walter wrote these lines, there were only a handful of studies on political terrorism; today there are many thousands of books, articles, and reports on terrorism. What used to be a rather marginal field of study in the social sciences has moved closer to the center of the stage, paralleling political developments which have seen government administrations rise and fall over controversies arising from terrorist events. As anti-terrorism bureaucracies have emerged--it is estimated that in the United States alone, 18,000 man-years of federal attention are given to combat terrorism[2]--research funds have become available from both governments and foundations to throw light on the root causes of this new wave of violent politics.

Academic researchers from many fields--political science, law, history, sociology, criminology, psychology, communication, and military studies--have entered the field. Together these authors have spilled almost as much ink as the actors of terrorism have spilled blood. Very few actors have been authors and very few authors have been terrorist actors. As one closely examines the literature of terrorism, one often comes away with a feeling of unreality. On the other hand, as one examines the pamphlets of terrorist organizations, one also repeatedly gets a feeling that many of these "true believers" in the righteousness of their cause are fighting a "fantasy war" in which their claimed "victories" are strategically questionable.

In order to increase our sense of reality, we bring actors and authors of political terrorism together in this volume. With regard to the terrorists, we have set up a world directory, describing each organization of some importance. With regard to the authors, we have also been selective. Even so, our bibliography lists close to 6,000 titles. A directory and bibliography alone would not make this a guidebook. Therefore, other parts of this handbook provide information on data bases to guide the reader to sources of information. In order to make sense of the data, we have included chapters dealing with problems of conceptualization and theory formation.

Since no single researcher can survey the field alone any longer, we have drawn on the collected wisdom of the research community studying terrorism. More than fifty other researchers, some of them leaders in the field, have shared their insights and information with us by answering a lengthy questionnaire. This input from the invisible college of fellow researchers has already been a mark of our first *Research Guide* (1984). The fact that it has gone through two printings indicates that it fulfills a need. In the past three years, many new actors and authors have entered the field. By updating, rewriting, and expanding this guide, we hope to continue to serve the needs of those trying to make sense out of seemingly senseless violence.

The reader familiar with the first edition will find that only one part of the book has remained largely unchanged: the chapter on theories. It is our contention that there has been little theoretical progress in the field in the last years. This is probably due to the fact that basic conceptual and data problems have not been solved. However, what progress our sample of the research community feels has been made is recorded in a postscript to the original survey of theories. The chapter on concepts of terrorism has been both expanded and reduced. We have added a new chapter on typologies of terrorism, but we have dropped parts of the discussion that dealt with the relationship between terrorism and political violence, assassination, and anarchism, as well as other sections. The reader will also find that parts of the original material on data bases has been eliminated while at the same time new material, especially on state terrorism, has been added. The bibliography has been expanded by almost 50 percent, although the original twenty-one categories and forty-six subcategories have been retained. To some extent, this will inconvenience the reader: If he wants to find literature on, say, Peru, he will have to turn to "Other Latin American Countries" since only Argentina, Brazil, and Uruguay were specifically subcategorized in the first edition of the bibliography when Sendero Luminoso had not yet gained such prominence. In other respects, however, the quality of the bibliography has been greatly improved, both in layout and in the accuracy of the entries.

The directory of terrorist and other organizations engaged in political protest and violence has also been thoroughly revised. We have no longer included targets of political violence (victim groups) unless these were also violent actors themselves, according to our sources. We have also limited both the number of organizations and the maximum size of the entry for each in order to keep the size of this volume manageable. The decision to exclude a great number of terrorist organizations from the directory has been made on the basis of their relative political importance. Given the fact that we are not equally familiar with the political context in all countries covered, a certain arbitrariness has been unavoidable. However, we have consciously made an effort to avoid political judgments.

If we have made errors of fact and judgment, these shortcomings are ours alone. None of the many contributors to this handbook shares any blame for these, though they contributed greatly in making this work possible.

Foreword by I.L. Horowitz

This new edition of the volume before you delivers precisely what is promised by the subtitle: *A Guide to Actors, Authors, Concepts, Data Bases, Theories and Literature.* Dr. Schmid and Drs. Jongman and their colleagues have made the task of researchers in this area both simpler and devastatingly more complex. It is simpler in the sense that one can now simply go to the present volume for all the basic definitions, conceptual frameworks, paradigmatic formulations, and bibliographic sources which are available. Here then is truly a data base worthy of that much abused phrase. At the same time, the very monumental nature of this undertaking has an intimidating quality to all but the most intrepid scholars. It is almost as if the volume has a sign hanging over it: "All those who enter do so at their own risk."

It is in the nature of contemporary reality, a reality omnipresent in its possibilities and prospects for total nuclear annihilation, that as ordinary human beings we attempt to restore the political act to human proportions by reducing the proportion of actions. It should not be forgotten that in all of its infinite shadings and meanings terrorism permits activities in proportions that can be managed by ordinary individuals. Hence, in some peculiar way the emergence of terrorism as a major global enterprise in our times is not simply a function of the ever-present desire for social change, but a strange back-handed recognition that the channels of social change are much harder to manipulate in a universe of superpowers and totalitarian superstates. In this sense, and without either the brutalization or trivialization of the sentiment for terror, the acute problems terrorism introduces are manageable because of the individual characters and responsibilities of the act.

As one moves through this work, in which terrorism is compared to other forms of political violence, and a number of theories in which terrorism becomes the dependent variable for the further study of imperfect regimes, surrogate warfare, and violence in general, it becomes evident that this political growth industry of the late twentieth century has a long tradition, a history linking it to the late nineteenth century, particularly the 1880's and the 1890's in which the cry of the individual against the state took on similar gargantuan and unmanageable proportions. It is almost as if terrorism has as its latent function, not so much a general political ideology but a specific reminder to the authorities by the anonymous, self-appointed representatives of the masses that those locked outside the political process will be felt, if not heard.

It is a tribute to Dr. Schmid that he both confronts and yet avoids falling prey to ideological definitions of the concept of political terrorism. His work is thoroughly informed by a social scientific attitude, one that appreciates that no given social system has a monopoly on the uses of political terrorism, and therefore no social system can claim virtue in one form of terrorism over another. This is not to say that Dr. Schmid is gratuitously relativistic or blasé. Underneath the careful analysis and attempted balance is a painful realisation on his part of the victims, the innocents, the non-combatants, who bear the price of terror but rarely wear the garments of victory.

It is this carefully understated presumption both of the sense of the sociological and a sense of the humane that raises *Political Terrorism* beyond a data base, into a fundamental effort at understanding in its own right. The temptation to argue the virtues of one form of air piracy or hijacking over another, or left-wing forms of terror over right-wing forms of terror, or the simple-minded change of rhetoric in describing allies vis-a-vis enemies, these convenient linguistic and ideological failings are avoided here. In the very listing and even repetition of the major statements by the leading theorists of terrorism, we have a subtle indication on the part of Dr. Schmid that there must be something beyond the self-serving if we are truly to have a social science recognition of the humanistic potential for cooperation instead of conflict.

So many services are performed by Dr. Schmid and his collaborators, that one can only single them out in a brief foreword. His volume includes the extraordinary collection of information on violent political movements developed chiefly by Drs. A.J. Jongman. For example, the tendency to think of the struggle between the Soviet Union and Afghanistan as a rather simplistic one-to-one relationship is dealt a severe blow when one examines Jongman's tables of Afghanistan political movements: their formation, tendencies, leaders, strenghts, and numbers. The Soviet monolith may be one, their Afghan opponents are diffuse. The word terrorism has a snappy, singular ring to it. But when it is probed with care, the researcher becomes painfully aware of its manifold forms, sizes and shapes. When the reader reaches this level of understanding, he can better appreciate just how complex is the phenomena being studied and collated here. It is thus a simple act of becoming a better citizen to become aware of the materials contained in this truly encyclopedic effort.

The volume also includes a bibliography containing 5831 separate entries that cover the world-wide literature with remarkable thoroughness.

There is almost a quality of putting together the *Oxford English Dictionary* in this compendium. Alex P. Schmid may well turn out to be the James A.H. Murray of this peculiar field of political research. For like Murray, Schmid may not be the first to see the full range and nature of the subject of terrorism (or in Murray's case, language), but he is certainly the first to organize the details, arrange the old materials, and conceptualize the new in a *Scriptorium* that will stand for many years as a quintessential effort to gather the facts, theories and histories of terrorism as an event and ideology. Schmid has done so in a way as not to prejudge outcomes, but make possible new interpretations. This work reverses the ancient Greek maxim that a large book is a great evil. It compels a reverse modern maxim: This is a large book which is in fact a great book.

One is left at the end of this academic journey with a distinct feeling that no matter how hard Schmid and his colleagues tried to isolate and place terrorism under a political microscope, that the fact remains that terrorism is part and parcel of the political process as a whole. Indeed, terrorism forms a seamless web with those dedicated to the maintenance no less than those pledged to the overthrow of established authority. If this compendium does not necessarily bring us any closer to a universal theorem of terrorism, it does bring us much closer to a practical appreciation of terrorism as part of the political process - past and present -, for better or for worse. Before we attempt to celebrate or eradicate this tactic-turned-principle, we would be wise to understand and evaluate. Schmid's volume provides us with an opportunity to just do that.

In the four year interval between the appearance of the first and second editions of this work, I have had the opportunity to prepare several new papers on the broad subject of terrorism, most recently for a compendium of recent work in political psychology being prepared by my colleague at Rutgers University, Professor Roberta Sigel. And I admit that this emphasis on the psychological dimensions has had a sobering effect in redressing a previous imbalance between the structural and personality features characteristic of my work.

The distance between personal motives and political ideologies is murky in that area of terrorism. All too often the therapeutic elements in a terrorist act are seen as either incidental or irrelevant to the analysis of political terror. It should be noted that this is definitely not a shortcoming in the work of Schmid. In point of fact, elements such as personal redemption and the anarchic joy of the act of disruption itself, are very much central to the uses of terror in our age. For terrorism is not simply a means to an end, a mechanism to reform social systems (to be sure, at that level, terror is probably counterproductive). The act of terror is more nearly a mechanism for acting out private rages in an epoch of declining social regimens.

This has made me better appreciate that the subject of terrorism is one that can be addressed at operational levels, i.e., by means of counter-terrorist techniques and technologies, but cannot be resolved in the trenches so to speak. In this sense any guide to political terrorism must be incomplete, since it is an area dependent upon full understanding to allied fields of conflict resolution, normative theory, and societal goals writ large. The resolution of terror, like its instigation, is wrapped tightly about the social intercourse which takes place in everyday life.

Terrorism is an area of study, whose contours and context are made abundantly clear by Schmid's efforts, and whose desperate message is to drive us all into a variety of fields quite beyond theories of terrorism or even acts of terror. This may not be the most joyful outcome of such a work, but the study of this newest entry into the world of the "dismal sciences" does at least move scholarship and research beyond frightening prospects and apocalyptic projections. This serendipitous finding may turn out to be the most lasting benefit of the work of Professor Schmid and his colleagues.

Irving Louis Horowitz
Rutgers University

September 9th, 1987

1

TERRORISM AND RELATED CONCEPTS: DEFINITION

> However certain the facts of any science may be and however just the ideas we may have formed of these facts, we can only communicate false impressions to others while we want words by which these may be properly expressed.
> *A. Lavoisier*[1]

The search for an adequate definition of terrorism is still on. There continues to exist considerable uncertainty about what the right way to think about the problem is. At the same time, many authors seem fatigued about the need to still consider basic conceptual questions. This is a dangerous attitude as it plays into the hands of those experts from the operational antiterrorist camp who have a "we-know-it-when-we-see-it" attitude that easily leads to double standards which produce bad science and also, arguably, bad policies.

While consensus on an adequate social science definition of terrorism as tactic and as doctrine is still lacking, we are, in my estimate, somewhat closer to solutions than we were some years ago. In the first edition of this volume (1984), I devoted more than one hundred pages to conceptual questions of terrorism, citing and discussing more than one hundred definitions. At the end of this exercise I volunteered the following definition:

> Terrorism is a method of combat in which random or symbolic victims serve as an instrumental *target of violence*. These instrumental victims share group or class characteristics which form the basis for their selection for victimization. Through previous use of violence or the

> credible threat of violence other members of that group or class are put in a *state of chronic fear (terror)*. This group or class, whose members' sense of security is purposefully undermined, is the *target of terror*. The victimization of the target of violence is considered extranormal by most observers from the witnessing audience on the basis of its atrocity, the time (e.g., peacetime) or place (not a battlefield) of victimization, or the disregard for rules of combat accepted in conventional warfare. The norm violation creates an attentive audience beyond the target of terror; sectors of this audience might in turn form the main object of manipulation. The purpose of this indirect method of combat is either to immobilize the target of terror in order to produce disorientation and/or compliance, or to mobilize secondary *targets of demands* (e.g., a government) or *targets of attention* (e.g., public opinion) to changes of attitude or behaviour favouring the short or long-term interests of the users of this method of combat.[2]

In a questionnaire which was mailed to some two hundred members of the research community in the field of political terrorism in 1985, respondents were asked to indicate their position vis-à-vis this definition. About one-quarter of those whose judgment was sought were willing to answer the lengthy questionnaire. In the first of thirty questions, they were asked whether they found this definition acceptable. In addition, they were asked to criticize its shortcomings or comment on it if they were answering "no" or "not entirely." The breakdown of the responses is given in Table 1.1.

Table 1.1. "Do you find the above definition acceptable?" (n = 58)

1.1. Yes	19 (33%)*
1.2. Not entirely	28 (48%)*
1.3. No	7 (12%)
No answer	3 (5%)
Other (comment only)	1 (2%)

* One respondent answered both 1.1. and 1.2.

This outcome--that 81 percent of the respondents found this definition partially or fully acceptable--is encouraging in that it indicates a degree of consensus, at least among this (in my estimate, quite representative) sample of respondents. However, the result can also be phrased in more restricted terms: Almost two-thirds of the respondents could not, or not entirely, agree with this definition. One element that links 96 percent of the respondents is that they did not find the definition question so unimportant as not to answer. Yet the one respondent who commented without answering the question had a telling point to make: "Ten years of debates on typologies and definitions have not enhanced our knowledge of the subject to a significant degree." He added "that the study of terrorism can manage with a minimum of theory" (W. Laqueur).

While there is an uncomfortable degree of truth in Laqueur's observation, one can also argue that even a "minimum of theory" requires some consensus about what to theorize about. Laqueur's own, much-quoted, work on terrorism has been criticized by one of the respondents to our first questionnaire for being "a book on an unidentified subject, so that the author can include whatever he sees fit."[3]

Avoiding the question of definition tends to result in an implicit definition of terrorism as "violence of which we do not approve." This is, as two authors who are members of the United States Army observe in an article titled "Terrorism: The Search for Working Definitions," an "operationally valid claim." However, they note one of the drawbacks of such a stand, namely, "the ludicrous situation of governments, referring to totally different activities, accusing each other of terrorism and doing so in good faith." They therefore conclude that "any usable definition must have value-neutrality."[4]

For academic researchers subscribing to a nonpartisan, universalist conception of science rather than, say, a Marxist, Zionist, Islamic, or Liberal one, such a recognition, coming from military quarters, is a welcome one. When it comes to a scientific definition, there is no room for double standards in labeling. This is, as should be noted, something different than saying that similar acts of violence are morally equally condemnable, independent of whether they are perpetrated by a conqueror or by those offering resistance to oppression.[5]

The search for a universalist definition of terrorism is one which scientists cannot give up. Without some solution to the definitional problem, without isolating terrorism from other forms of (political) violence, there can be no uniform data collection and no responsible theory building on terrorism. There is a sound, logical reason for the necessity to define terrorism which is independent from the psychological desire to make sense out of seemingly "senseless" violence. A "universal" definition of terrorism has been offered by R. P. Hoffman, who dedicated an entire doctoral dissertation to this problem. He interviewed experts on terrorism and compiled a dozen discrete factors describing the central characteristics of the subject. Our procedure has been comparable to his, although we used questionnaires rather than interviews and our sample was somewhat broader than his. Some of the definitional elements we identified are the same; we both refer to "fear," "purpose," and "violence." My definition places more stress on "victims" and "target audiences," but then his definition is not as long as mine. Hoffman's conceptual effort led him to the following proposed definition:

> Terrorism is a purposeful human political activity which is directed toward the creation of a general climate of fear, and is designed to influence, in ways desired by the protagonist, other human beings and, through them, some course of events.[6]

This is certainly a more elegant definition than mine, though one might criticize it for a certain vagueness or question whether the climate of fear had to be "general." However, rather than criticize this particular definition, I would like to acquaint the reader with the criticism which my definition evoked. There were several kinds of criticism and also some proposed solutions. Unfortunately, the solutions offered were often contradictory. One of the few aspects many agreed upon was that my definition was too long. A simple definition is unquestionably preferable to a wordy one, yet the price of parsimony should not be a lack of precision.

In the following pages I shall discuss the main reactions of respondents to the definition I proposed in 1984. I shall try to group criticism and comments in a number of clusters, formed by contested issues such as the "narrow" or "broad" definition question, the one-or-several-terrorism(s) question, the guerrilla/terrorism relationship, the terrorism-without-terror problem, the communication function of terrorism, the normative vs. analytical definition question, and the "symbolic" vs. "material" target issue. These are, in our view, the main unsolved conceptual problems. For a broader listing of unsolved conceptual problems--many of them going well beyond the question of definition--the reader is referred to Appendix A. Before we discuss the comments and criticisms on my definition, however, a general word on definitions of terrorism is in place.

ON DEFINING TERRORISM

A definition is basically an equation: a new, unknown, or ill-understood term (the definiendum) is described (defined) by a combination of at least two old, known, understandable terms (the definiens).[7] The question then becomes, how many old, known word elements are necessary to define terrorism? The most primitive, nonscientific definitions use only one element. They are not real definitions but synonyms, translations, tautologies, or mere labels. Examples would be "terrorism = crime" or "terrorism = communism." Definitions with two or three elements are, for instance, "terrorism = political murder," "terrorism = killing of innocents," and "terrorism = violence for political purposes." As one adds more elements, a definition becomes less ambiguous. Gerhard Schmidtchen, for instance, uses five category elements when he defines terrorism as "an action theory of illegal political behaviour."[8] How can we know whether this is a good definition? One way of finding out is by turning it on its head. Ask people, "What is violence for political purposes?" If their most common answer is "war," this is an indication that not enough word elements have been used to differentiate "terrorism" from "war." The definition of Schmidtchen is more likely to elicit the answer "terrorism." However, by implication, it excludes state terrorism as well as nonpolitical terrorism which makes it vulnerable to criticism on other grounds.

In our first *Research Guide*, we identified twenty-two word categories in the 109 definitions we discussed. In declining order of frequency, these were:

Table 1.2. Frequencies of Definitional Elements in 109 Definitions.[9]

Element	*Frequency*
1. Violence, force	83.5%
2. Political	65 %
3. Fear, terror emphasized	51 %
4. Threat	47 %
5. (Psych.) effects and (anticipated) reactions	41.5%
6. Victim-target differentiation	37.5%
7. Purposive, planned, systematic, organized action	32 %
8. Method of combat, strategy, tactic	30.5%

Table 1.2 cont.

Element	*Frequency*
9. Extranormality, in breach of accepted rules, without humanitarian constraints	30 %
10. Coercion, extortion, induction of compliance	28 %
11. Publicity aspect	21.5%
12. Arbitrariness; impersonal, random character; indiscrimination	21 %
13. Civilians, noncombatants, neutrals, outsiders as victims	17.5%
14. Intimidation	17 %
15. Innocence of victims emphasized	15.5%
16. Group, movement, organization as perpetrator	14 %
17. Symbolic aspect, demonstration to others	13.5%
18. Incalculability, unpredictability, unexpectedness of occurrence of violence	9 %
19. Clandestine, covert nature	9 %
20. Repetitiveness; serial or campaign character of violence	7 %
21. Criminal	6 %
22. Demands made on third parties	4 %

On the average, authors used eight categories to define terrorism. Hoffman's definition, cited above, contains five of these elements, while mine contains thirteen of them. The question is whether the above list contains all the elements necessary for a good definition. The answer is probably "no." Some elements overlap, while others might be missing. The more popular elements might not be the most important ones. How can we know? By continuing to argue with each other about what to include and what to exclude from a definition, we can refine our understanding. In the following, I shall enter this friendly quarrel by focusing on some objections raised to my definition.

Before doing so, however, a word of apology is in order. Human beings being what they are, every author is likely to prefer to use his own definition over the one of others, if he can help it. The natural inclination is therefore to reject other definitions when one is "pushed." By repeatedly referring to "my" definition, this "push-rejection effect" is bound to occur and there is little I can do about it except point out that "my" definition is the product of an ongoing dialogue with the research community and thereby becomes somewhat depersonalized. I have no problems with changing it or trading it for a better one. Having said this, we can now turn to substantive criticism of "my" definition.

TERRORISM: SYMBOLIC VIOLENCE OR NOT?

Among the criticisms voiced in the responses to the questionnaire, one topic which was addressed repeatedly centered on an element introduced by Th. P. Thornton in his classic 1964 definition which held that "terror is a symbolic act."[10] One respondent held that my definition "neglects the symbolic quality of terrorist violence." On the other hand, it was pointed out that "Individuals and groups who practice this method may use other terroristic methods which do not fit the precise definition offered here, such as punishment of specific individuals rather than random or symbolic victims. Aldo Moro and the pope were specific targets of terrorists" (Ochberg). Yet another respondent observed, "There is [in your definition] also an emphasis on symbolic victims--yet we know for example in Uruguay many victims (nearly all) of the so-called random terror were in police uniforms. The targets were selected and the wider audience was also selective." This respondent therefore took issue with the "random or symbolic victims" passage in my definition. Another respondent asked ". . . is the killing of a policeman believed to be torturing suspects an example--is the killing of a soldier 'symbolic'?" (Robertson).

In my view there need be no contradiction. A symbol is something that stands for something else, often a *pars pro toto*. The pope is an individual human being, but he is also regarded as representing an important pillar of Western civilization. In the same way that a flag can stand for a nation, one soldier or policeman can stand for the coercive apparatus of a state, given the proper context of an act of violence. The murder of one man can be functional in terms of physically weakening the opposite side, and at the same time be symbolic in terms of psychologically affecting the conception of reality and one's place in it for those identifying with the victim.

Here we are really talking about the difference between assassination and terrorist victimization. Franklin L. Ford defined assassination as ". . . the intentional killing of a specified victim or group of victims, perpetrated for reasons related to his (her, their) public prominence and undertaken with a political purpose in view."[11]

In contrast to assassination victims, the victims of terrorism are often not "specified" and also lack "political prominence"--at least until the moment they become victims of violence. While assassination aims at having the victim dead, terrorism does not care about the victim itself--indeed, the prospective kidnap victim might be released for a price. The behavioral outcome in the aftermath of an assassination is likely to be anger or sadness rather than terror. Thus, while both the assassin and the terrorist commit homicide, the intent is different. However, where political murders occur in series and the intimidation of opponents becomes more important than their physical elimination, we are likely to step into the conceptual space of terrorism.

One American critic who stressed that "the intent of terrorism is psychological and symbolic, not material" complained that the definition "omits terrorism against property." This raises another area of ambiguity. To blow up a piece of property like the Statue of Liberty in New York or the Eiffel Tower in Paris would be a shocking thing for many Americans and Frenchmen, because of the symbolic quality of these objects. Yet it would not "terrorize" anybody. I agree with one respondent (D. A. Charters) who stresses the importance of making a clear distinction between terrorism, assassination, and sabotage.

The fact that some people who are labeled terrorists also engage in other destructive activities should not lead us to place them all in one "terrorist" basket. Soldiers also do different things (attack, demolish, rescue, etc.) as part of their overall mission, and we do not call all of this "war." The assassination of President John F. Kennedy and the attempt to kill Pope John Paul II were not "terrorizing" to anyone, although these acts were profoundly upsetting for various audiences. These acts had the character of tyrannicide, though few would link these particular victims of political murder to the kind of power abuses characteristic of despots. It would appear that terrorist killing--in contrast to murder--intends to send a message to others beyond the immediate victim (though generally these others are from the same group or class), so that these others have reason to fear that they are perhaps the next target. However, to some extent this third-party apprehension is a concomitant of every act of violence, as Leon Trotsky noted:

> A victorious war, generally speaking, destroys only an insignificant part of the conquered army, intimidating the remainder and breaking their will. The revolution works in the same way: it kills individuals, and intimidates thousands. In this sense, the Red Terror is not distinguishable from the armed insurrection of which it is the direct continuation.[12]

What Trotsky, in his attempt to justify mass terrorism, failed to mention is that soldiers are armed and can (as a rule) save their lives by capitulating, while victims of terrorism are generally noncombatants and are granted no "prisoner of war" status when kidnapped or taken hostage.

The answer to the question of whether victims of terrorism have to be symbolic is, in my view, that the case for the victim being labeled a representative (symbol) of a category is quite strong. Why, then, do I in my definition speak of "random or symbolic victims"? Two examples can be helpful in making my case for "random":

- A bomb explosion like the one in the Bologna railway station in August 1980, which indiscriminately killed passers-by, including foreigners and children, is random. Yet it is also symbolic. The contempt for the masses, characteristic of right-wing terrorism, is perfectly expressed in such a blind slaughter; the anonymous victims stand for the people as a whole.

- The bombing campaign launched between September 8 and 17, 1986, in Paris by a "Committee for Solidarity with Arab and Middle Eastern Political Prisoners," which killed eleven people and wounded 161, was largely random, hitting mainly "targets of opportunity." Since anybody could have been a victim, everybody felt threatened. There was symbolism in the very randomness. In other words, even random victims can share group or class characteristics--like being French.

On the basis of the above, I do not see sufficient reason to change the thrust in that part of the definition which refers to "random or symbolic victims." However, I think that there is some theoretical justification for widening the group of victims by a qualifier like "generally" on the basis of objections such as these:

> I disagree with the notion that the targets of the violence (the victims) are necessarily related or of the same identifiable group. Unrelated victims may be more useful in terrorizing a particular target group (Waugh).

> It is not necessarily the case that victims share group or class characteristics; nor is it always true that they are "selected." This ignores the inherently indiscriminate effects of the most characteristic form of terrorism (i.e., bombing), and the fact that terrorists make "mistakes" (Wilkinson).

To accommodate these arguments, a category of "targets of opportunity" will be introducted.

TERRORISM: A NARROW OR BROAD DEFINITION?

Another line of criticism concerned the breadth of the definition. Interestingly, some authors suggested the definition was too narrow while others argued that it was too broad, as illustrated by the following comments:

> This . . . is a good definition of true, pure "terrorism"--i.e., the terror element in what has come to be known as "terrorism." . . . [The popular notion, however, is] generally accepted as including a wider range of pre-revolutionary actions such as accumulation of money, weapons, prestige, legitimacy, recruits, etc., or the sabotage of government assets and weakening of his intelligence and security operations. You would have to reeducate a wide spectrum of opinion (perhaps correctly) to have your rather limited definition accepted (Tugwell).

> I find your definition too narrow (why "instrumental" when murder is murder whether the victim is a primary target or his neighbor!) and too broad (why not restrict the idea to a political context?) (Rubin).

> Too little is said about the structure, logistical possibilities and military shortcomings of the "method of combat" (Visser).

> The definition is too encompassing to be operationally useful and too jargon loaded for theoretical hypothesis (Zawodny).

> The attempt to include elements of the outcome of terrorism in the definition is unnecessary and confusing. The intent or objective of terrorism would suffice. The outcome, in actuality, depends on many variables and it is not necessarily what the terrorists intend to achieve, even as far as emotional response is concerned, let alone the political results (Merari).

Clearly, conflicting demands are made on the definition. Leaving out the outcome because it is too uncertain does indeed make sense for non-state terrorism. With state terrorism, however, the outcome is too often quite predictable, as can be gathered for instance from the--still under-studied--"Document on Terror" from the Communist NKVD (the predecessor of the KGB), which speaks of "amazing results which can be achieved with terror" while warning that it should not be considered "the universal solution for all problems and difficulties."[13]

The paradox of having the definition judged either too narrow or too broad might be linked to the problem of whether terrorism is a unitary concept. It can be argued, as Merari does, that one should make "a clear distinction between terrorism by state and terrorism by individuals or groups, which are not acting as a government." There is much truth in this: the potential and the modus operandi of a terroristic security police forming a state within a state and acting with impunity above the law is very different from the one of small clandestine cells of hit-and-hide gunmen and bombers. However, we use the term "war" for both guerrilla war and nuclear war, though the two are as unalike as state and non-state terrorism. One respondent noted:

> The above definition has the distinct advantage that it does not equate terrorism with the larger field of collective action or political violence. It also has the advantage that it encompasses the political uses of terror irrespective of who initiates them--governments, private intra-national groups, international organizations (Gurr).

My inclination is not to limit the identity of the perpetrator to small groups only but to include individual as well as state actors. I would agree that the outcome can remain unspecified. Yet some indication of the purpose--and thereby the expected outcome--is unavoidable. To take an analogy: it would be difficult to distinguish surgery from mutilation or torture if no purpose were given.

I find it difficult to accommodate Visser's criticism except for the one element of structure, which has also been suggested by Charters: "Emphasize that the act or campaign is usually organized, planned and conducted in a clandestine manner by clandestine political/military group."

It is true for both state and non-state terrorist organizations that they act conspiratorily or in secrecy, for reasons of surprise and/or security. In his own definition, Visser labels terrorism a "strategy or tactic of a (semi-)clandestinely organized group. . . ."[14] This is a useful formulation, though I find other elements of Visser's definition questionable. For example, he characterizes terrorism as a "political-military strategy or tactic, born out of poverty and lack of military potential and political influence. It is the most rudimentary, least costly form which organized political violence can assume."[15]

TERRORISM(S): ONE OR MANY?

Let us now turn to some criticisms which point in the same direction. As this might indicate a certain degree of consensus within the research community, more weight has to be attributed to these. As it turns out, there are only a few such criticisms, and they are never shared by more than a handful respondents.

One criticism is that the definition is biased because it "favors" the state. This has been stated most strongly by Herman:

> The use of the word "combat" is objectionable as the victimization may be systematic and regular as a mode of governance. . . . The choice of "government" as the illustration of type of target is suggestive of bias.

Another respondent holds that I not only leave out state terrorism but also "terrorism exercised by say the possession of atomic weapons" (Harris). In addition to neglecting "terrorism from above" (Costa Pinto), it is also held that the definition does not account for two other forms of terrorism:

> Terrorism can also be a criminal tactic (such as in organized crime) or a strategy of political communication (as in single-issue politics, e.g., bombing abortion clinics) (Crelinsten).

I would hesitate to include the nuclear "balance of terror" and "nuclear deterrence" under terrorism. The balance of terror has arguably prevented the direct use of violence between the superpowers. Deterrence is based on the capacity to inflict unacceptable damage on an opponent. Contrary to widespread beliefs, the nuclear forces of the superpowers are not targetted primarily at the opponents' civilian populations but at their nuclear and conventional military capabilities. Given the proximity of military installations to cities, the collateral civilian damage is bound to be great in any nuclear exchange. Still, the civilian populations of targetted nations are at less risk of being sacrificed than are hostages coercively held in, say, an embassy siege. Deterrence implies that one wishes to prevent the other side from doing something. As long as the other side is doing nothing, nobody is directly threatened. In an embassy siege, however, a third party (not the hostages) is compelled to do something to assure the survival of the hostages. Doing nothing is not enough. While the consequences of consummated nuclear threats are genocidal and beyond anything within the reach of non-state terrorists (that is, until they can get hold of atomic bombs), the record of the first forty years of the superpowers' nuclear diplomacy does not provide any substantial evidence of blackmail and extortion comparable to what is produced by terrorist organizations.[16] The apprehension we feel about the nuclear menace is different from the acute, sharp fear which a campaign of "disappearances," mutilation, torture, and bombings evokes.

On the basis of the above, therefore, I am inclined to exclude "atomic terror." On the other hand, there is enough theoretical ground to justify the retention of nonpolitical categories of terrorism. In my typology I refer to "criminal" and "idiosyncratic" terrorism, but since we are dealing here with only "political" terrorism, there is no need to extend this discussion to these areas.

TERRORISM: A METHOD OF COMBAT?

The criticism of Herman and Crelinsten with regard to terrorism as a "method of combat" is also very valuable. The formulation of terrorism as a "method of combat" was first introduced into the discussion by J.B.S. Hardman in the *Encyclopædia of the Social Sciences* in 1936.[17] His contemporary, J. Waciorsky, used the formulation "method of action" in 1939, which, on reflection, is a more appropriate term.[18] It is, after all, one of the outstanding features of terrorism that there is no battle, that one armed organization commits atrocities against unarmed, unprepared civilians who offer no resistance, against neutrals and mere bystanders. The war metaphor creates a mental image of two armed forces geared for combat, of soldiers in uniform with professional standards of honor fighting each other according to the rules of war, showing restraint toward the nonbelligerents and those taken prisoner. At least, that is the idealized traditional image of war. The reality is less chivalrous and the number of civilian victims in modern war has steadily risen. In the Second World War, the air forces not only attacked their opponents' military forces but also their war industries, thereby killing workers (in some cases forced labor). Ultimately, whole cities, such as Coventry and

Dresden, were targetted. Hiroshima and Nagasaki were different only in that the destruction was brought about by single bombs.

This extension of permissible targetting from military objects (counterforce) to civilian targets (countervalue), from armies to civilians, we find in both conventional and unconventional warfare. "The bomb in the market-place," it has been said, is the "poor man's air force." There is no doubt that both the bomb hidden in the dustbin in a market and the "smart" bomb guided from a fighter-bomber can and do kill people bearing no responsibility for the conflict.

When civilians are deliberately attacked in war, or killed as hostages during war, the term "war crime" is used to describe this conduct. We lack an analogous term for describing a situation in which the perpetrators wear no uniform and do not carry their arms openly, and the conflict is not between two nations but within a nation or across nations.

Several respondents complained that the distinction between terrorism and guerrilla warfare was not clear from my definition. Along the same lines, one might wish to compare terrorism with war, revolution, and some other forms of political violence. For instance, the Syrian Foreign Minister, Farouk al-Shara, called on the United Nations to "draw a clear line between terrorism and resistance."[19] Others might want to distinguish national and liberation struggles from terrorism. I am not sure whether this is the right way to conceptualize the problem. Terrorism is primarily an extremism of means, not one of ends.

Let us concentrate on the guerrilla warfare/terrorism distinction. Urban guerrilla warfare is a term used by some non-state terrorists to describe their own activites. One author, Fritz Rene Allemann, calls this "a semantic trick aimed not only at being recognized as a belligerent party but also masking the essentially criminal nature of their methods."[20] He draws the following distinctions:

> . . . the guerrillero is exclusively or, at least, primarily fighting an armed adversary (the official army and police), even if he does so by unconventional means, while the terrorist attack is fundamentally directed against civilian targets (and tendentially even against persons not at all implied in the actual conflict, such as hostages). Partisan warfare is nothing but an extension of classical warfare; terrorism, on the other hand, amounts to the negation of any notion of "warfare" at all.[21]

It is useful to compare this notion with an "official" Western definition of guerrilla and unconventional warfare. In NATO and United States military terminology, guerrilla warfare is defined as "Military and paramilitary operations conducted in enemy-held or hostile territory by irregular, predominantly indigenous forces. See also unconventional warfare."[22] If we turn to the cross-reference, this is what we read (the definition is by the U.S. Department of Defense):

> A broad spectrum of military and paramilitary operations conducted in enemy-held, enemy-controlled or politically sensitive territory. Unconventional warfare includes, but is not limited to, the interrelated fields of guerrilla warfare, evasion and escape, subversion, sabotage, and other operations of a low visibility, covert or clandestine nature. These interrelated aspects of unconventional warfare may be prosecuted singly or collectively by predominantly indigenous personnel, usually supported and directed by (an) external source(s) during all conditions of war or peace.[23]

Thus, the "official" U.S. and NATO definitions do not consider the issue of targetting and are of little help in corroborating Allemann's observation on non-state terrorism.

If we look at what is going on in reality, we notice that certain groups labeled terrorist do sometimes attack--and in some cases, such as the Basque ETA, even predominantly attack--military personnel. The same is true, though to a lesser degree, for the Provisional Irish Republican Army. Even minuscule terrorist groups like the German Rote Armee Faktion target military personnel.

On the other hand, we find that guerrilla movements like the Afghan resistance fighters engage in both partisan attacks on military forces and attacks in urban areas on representatives of the Afghan Communist government and on Soviet citizens in Kabul. Insurgent guerrilla movements in El Salvador have, when their fortune on the rural battlefield turned in the mid-1980s, turned to urban killings and kidnappings as a means of maintaining a presence on the political scene while they tried to build military strength for new rural campaigns. Ernesto "Ché" Guevara, who had at first condemned terrorism as counterproductive in guerrilla warfare, was also on the point (or even beyond the point) of taking recourse to terrorist tactics when his Bolivian campaign faltered due to the indifference and even hostility of the campesinos he had intended to liberate.[24]

Terrorism, in other words, can take place in a war context, in an insurgency context, and in a "pure" context, that is, in a context where popular support for the struggle is almost completely absent. What matters is the relationship between terror-violence and more civilized conduct in each context. As Douglas Pike put it with regard to war:

> What seems more to the point is not language but thought pattern, world view, philosophy of politics or however you want to charactertize the question which divides us most sharply in the 20th Century: what are the limits of force, irrational violence, terror, in that ascending order, in bringing about social change? All of us fall somewhere along this force-violence-terror continuum. Toward one end are those who believe that less rather than more is justified; toward the other are those who advocate more on grounds of imperative need or as principle. As one looks about at various world societies in various conditions of social pathology, one cannot help but conclude sadly that the drift toward the extreme end, terror, is anything but a diminishing phenomenon. . . . [Even] in warfare certain acts are illegal and may properly be termed terror. This latter point rests on the belief that in all things there are limits, and a limit in warfare is reached at the point of systematic use of death, pain, fear and anxiety among the population (either civilian or military) for the deliberate purpose of coercing, manipulating, intimidating, punishing or simply frightening into helpless submission. Certain acts even in war are beyond the pale and can only be labeled terror.[25]

It can be argued that such methods are exceptional in conventional and guerrilla warfare. In "pure" non-state as well as state terrorism, however, these exceptional tactics have become the rule and are elevated to the level of strategy. In terrorism, certainly in state terrorism but also in much of insurgent terrorism, there is a widening of targets considered to be legitimate objects of threat and destruction, to the point that the unarmed and unprotected often become the main or even sole objects of attack. To the extent that its targetting is countervalue rather than counterforce, its purpose is symbolic rather than material. Military forces might still be attacked, not in order to spare civilian victims but in order to create an image of one military force challenging another. Non-state "pure" terrorists do not control territory because they lack the numerical strength and popular support that would allow them to move as "fish in the water." Their "legitimacy potential" (Ch. Johnson) is often low; even ethnic and nationalist terrorists often enjoy only minority support for their goals.

On the basis of such observations, one could conclude that one reason why terrorist violence is different from other political violence directed against a government or by a government is that it is widely perceived as more inhuman. The victims' guilt or innocence is immaterial to the pure terrorist. Targets of bombings and abductions are generally unable to influence their destiny by a change of attitude or behavior. They are offered no chance to surrender and thereby have their lives spared. It is this kind of cruelty which can make terrorism so devastating in its effects on some target populations. Brian Jenkins's metaphor of "terrorism-as-theatre" alludes to this dimension of terrorism: people are killed not because they deserve it or happen to be in the wrong place, but to make a point with one or another audience. It is violence for effect, in which the victims do not matter as individuals. The particular effect of the terrorist message results from the fact that it is written, as it were, with the blood of people who matter to the addressee, but not to the sender.

This brings us back to our initial question about the difference between terrorism and guerrilla warfare. Edward Kossoy has written:

> To claim that guerrilla is necessarily coupled with terrorism is certainly grossly inaccurate. A number of important guerrilla movements steadily refused to resort to terrorism. . . . And yet if, in popular opinion, the terms "guerrilla" and "terrorism" are often associated or even interchanged, this is not without justification. The fact is that most of the contemporary guerrilla movements either habitually, or at various stages of their activities, use terrorism, at least as a form of revolutionary tactics.[26]

If we take the example of the Nicaraguan Contras who have been hailed by U.S. President Ronald Reagan as "the moral equals of our founding fathers," the terrorist dimension seems to dominate very strongly over the guerrilla dimension. One study labeled the Contras' attacks on military targets "rare." In a chronology of three years of Contra activity, it listed (and selectively documented with sworn affidavits from eyewitnesses) hundreds of incidents in which campesinos were kidnapped, civilians were ambushed, victims were tortured and mutilated. This depressing account of a teacher being assassinated in front of his class, of women being gang-raped or disembowled, of a mother having to watch the beheading of her baby, of a Contra drinking the blood of victims,[27] matches in inhumanity anything which the elite press's front pages, chronicling anti-Western international terrorism, have presented us in their selective attention to human victimization.

The borderline between guerrilla warfare tactics and terrorism is also a fuzzy one when it comes to the notion of guerrillas defending their own people against the repressive government. In the case of Angola, for instance, UNITA's guerrilleros under J. Savimbi largely consist of southern Ovibundu tribesmen. Nevertheless, Savimbi's men appear to target--especially through the use of land mines--their own peasantry as well. This has been interpreted by some observers as "part of a strategy to weaken Angola's already tottering economy, to drive more refugees into the cities, and to eventually force the government to negotiate."[28]

Not all insurgency campaigns are as "dirty" as the ones of the Contras and UNITA. It is also somewhat unfair to single out guerrilla warfare. Terrorism can occur in all armed conflicts where basic human rights are grossly violated. So far, the international community has codified unacceptable conflict behavior only in the context of war. The principles of the law of warfare, which distinguish permissible violent conduct from war crimes, offer some guidelines as to where to look for differences. In the summary of Frits Kalshoven, these are briefly:

> The fundamental principle underlying the whole structure of the international humanitarian law applicable in armed conflicts is that belligerents shall not inflict on their adversaries harm out of proportion to the legitimate goals of warfare. An immediate conclusion from this principle is, for instance, that belligerents shall not kill their prisoners; for, having captured them, they have to that extent weakened the military forces of the enemy, and killing them would add nothing to this result. The basic principle of the law of warfare following out of this most fundamental principle is that the right of the Parties to a conflict to adopt means of injuring the enemy is not unlimited. . . . From this admittedly very general principle, some further, slightly less abstract principles can be deduced. I mention four: (1) distinction shall be made at all times between belligerents and civilian population; (2) the civilian population, as well as objects of civilian character, shall not be made the object of deliberate attacks; (3) in attacking military objectives, any unreasonable damage to the civilian population and objects of civilian character shall be avoided; (4) no weapons or other means and methods of warfare shall be used which are calculated to cause unnecessary or otherwise excessive suffering.[29]

In armed conflicts where such rules of conduct are observed, the unpredictability of violence is lessened and, with this, the degree of terrorization.

TERRORISM WITHOUT TERROR?

This brings us to another problematic area in the defining of terrorism. Several respondents challenged my notion of "terror." F. Ochberg, a psychiatrist, criticized my usage of the term:

> The equation of terror with a state of chronic fear is permissible in lay language, but in psychiatry terror is an extreme form of anxiety, often accompanied by aggression, denial, constricted affect, and followed by frightening imagery and intrusive, repetitive recollection. I would consider a person a terrorist if he attempted the methods you describe so clearly in your definition, even if the targets did not experience terror, as long as they were imperiled or victimized.

This is a significant and accurate observation. It is a fact that non-state terrorist organizations are rarely able to develop a level of activity which places sectors of the public in constant fear of sudden victimization. More often than not, the acts of non-state terrorists are sporadic, producing only episodic increases in the anxiety level of target groups. Yet to remove the element of "massive, overwhelming fear which is designed to act upon the mind of some person other than the immediate victim" (R. P. Hoffman) would be tantamount to abandoning the core concept of terror.[30] The creation of a climate of fear by the calculated "perpetuation of atrocities" (D. C. Rapoport) and the manipulation of the evoked emotional response of those directly and indirectly affected is a distinct method of violent activity which sets it apart from ordinary isolated assassinations where the desired outcome is reached when the murder has been successfully committed. While violence is the key element with murder, it is the combination of the use of violence and the threat of more to come which initiates a terror process. Many extremists might often not be able to produce a prolonged terror effect by unexpected, dramatic acts of violence; however, the fact that the evocation of terror is their intent is sufficient to justify placing them in the same category as those who succeed.

It is worthwhile to dwell on the nature of the terror effect in order to make clear what distinguishes terrorism from other forms of political violence. As illustration, I would like to introduce two statements on terror, one descriptive and the other analytical:

> Terror of any sort shifts the ground strangely, as an earthquake. It removes the underpinnings of the orderly system leaving confusion as much as fear. A civilian

> expects safety and order in his society and when it vanishes he becomes disoriented. Terror isolates. An individual can no longer draw strength from customary social support. He can rely only on himself. Physically he may be untouched by a terror act, but because of it he is suddenly terribly alone and in anguish. A terrorized village, said an American psychiatrist in Viet-Nam, is a case of collective anxiety neurosis, the victim seeking only relief. The victim, in this case the village, stops behaving as a normal social unit; each individual is fragmented within, searching desperately to fix his own personal security.[31]
>
> Terror may be described as a state of mind. Its effect upon individuals cannot always be determined from an objective description of the terrorist act. That which threatens or terrorizes one individual may not affect another in the same way. Essentially, however, the process of terrorism can be viewed in the following manner: The stimulus is the threatening or terroristic act, and the response is the course of action, or inaction, pursued by the individual upon perceiving and interpreting the threat. If the perception of the threat leads to disorganized behavior such as hysteria or panic or the inability to take appropriate action, the individual is said to be in a state of terror. Terror is not a static phenomenon: As threatening acts accumulate or escalate, the degree of terror heightens. A stimulus can be anything from an act of social sanction to threats of physical violence or actual physical attack. The corresponding interpretation of these threatening acts is a heightening state of terror. The response may vary from coerced compliance to acquiescence, from physical flight to psychological immobilization and breakdown. . . . Human response to threat also varies according to the nature of the threatening situation--whether it is specific or uncertain. . . . Some writers emphasize an important distinction between "anxiety" responses and "fear" responses: "fear is apt to produce a prompt reaction either to remove the object of fear from oneself or oneself from the object of fear," whereas anxiety "is chronic and vague . . . one does not know quite what is the cause of his anxiety and, partly for that reason, he does not know quite what to do." Thus, "the more specific the threat, the more fear-inducing it is; the more vague the threat, the more anxiety-inducing it is"--making an individual hypersensitive to ordinarily neutral situations and causing disruptive behavior.[32]

There is, in our view, a solid conceptual core to terrorism, differentiating it from ordinary violence. It consists in the calculated production of a state of extreme fear of injury and death and, secondarily, the exploitation of this emotional reaction to manipulate behavior. The inflation of meanings attached for purposes of rhetoric to the term "terrorism" has opened it up to standing for a whole array of illegal violence manifestations, from bank robberies serving the financing of insurrectional activities by small groups to broadly based popular armed resistance against foreign domination and domestic dictatorship. "Where the corruption of language is an ideological weapon," P. Devine and R. Rafalko have written, "the defense of its integrity is a necessary--though hardly a sufficient--condition of a just and decent approach to human problems."[33]

TERRORISM: THE COMMUNICATION FUNCTION

Several respondents found that the proposed definition did not stress motive and purpose. One of them wrote: "Usually the terrorist group has been excluded forcibly from redress of grievance or access to social justice. . . . To omit this omits the core explanation of terrorism" (Young). Since not all aggrieved parties take recourse to terrorism (some choose other violent means, others engage in nonviolent actions, while most silently endure injustices), and not all terrorists (Stalin, Hitler) lack access to the political process, this particular argument fails to convince me. Neither particular causal grievances nor particular goals "explain" terrorism. It is the intervening means between cause and goals that make terrorism a special problem. These means are of such a nature that they serve as message generators. Terrorist acts are means of communication.

One American respondent holds that the proposed definition "fails to specify that terrorism is related to publicity above all. Terrorism does not exist in the U.S.S.R., for example, for the simple reason that the U.S.S.R. does not publicize it." This argument, too, is based on an implicit identification of terrorism with non-state "violence as communication." As I have pointed out in a book by this title, state terrorism, as it existed in the Soviet Union on a massive scale, generally shuns publicity.[34] Instead it relies on rumors and individual tales of terror to discipline dissidents. Both non-state and state practitioners use terrorism as a "strategy of political communication," to take an expression introduced by R. Crelinsten. In exceptional cases, the audience for the terrorist message might even be fictive, as another respondent pointed out:

> One might note that the constituents, targets, ideals, etc., may or may not be "real." That is, an individual or group may perform acts of terror-violence with/toward an inten-

> ded group, whether or not it is really useful or effective. (Reid)

This is particularly true of groups attracted by the "terrorist chic," who find it fashionable to engage in the currently most conspicuous form of violent protest and utilize it for a wide variety of single-issue causes, as witnessed, for instance, in the recent wave of bombings in the United States of abortion clinics (manifestations which might be termed quasi-terrorist).

In a sense, even terrorism is not what it used to be, as David Rapoport has pointed out, with Robespierre in the back of his mind:

> One of the original justifications for terror was that man would be totally reconstructed; one didn't have to worry about the kinds of means one was using because the reconstruction itself would be total and there would be no lingering after-effects. . . . [Modern] terrorism was initiated by people who had millenial expectations, who expected the world to be utterly transformed. Since the beginning of the twentieth century, terror has been used for very limited political purposes like the separation of a piece of territory from another piece of terrority. . . . Something changed in the nature of terror as people began to see that it can . . . be turned on and off at will.

I cannot refrain from citing another passage of Rapoport's, as it contains one of the most overlooked aspects of terrorism:

> Most people, when they talk about the rise of modern terrorists, are really concerned with the fact that they are dealing with small groups. The effectiveness of small groups has to be explained. . . . What we don't understand is that these people are generating or arousing emotions in us which would not be aroused if we weren't the kind of people that we are. . . . We define it in terms of violence instead of violence that has stirred different kinds of emotions which would not have been stirred in a civilization which was less ambivalent towards the causes that terrorists are associated with. . . . The terrorist acts in an environment where the society has a good deal of ambivalence about the cause the terrorist is concerned with. Society is unwilling to come to grips with the cause that the terrorist is proposing, but will ignore the cause unless it finds it cannot do so. What the terrorist basically does is to direct attention to the cause in ways which indicate that he is willing to die or to sacrifice himself for the cause. It is a cause that most people, in some sense,

> have some sympathies with, but find it impossible to deal with until the terrorist forces them to deal with these sympathies. . . . One problem with contemporary definitions of terrorism, because they focus on the killing, is that they really can't see why somebody like the IRA, for example, would engage in hunger strikes; how that really performs the same kind of functions, and even performs it better than killing does sometimes. . . . Whether the violence is inflicted on oneself or on others, it's the striking character of the act which, first of all, calls attention and secondly, in the process of calling attention, galvanizes latent emotions, which is the critical thing.[35]

Among the respondents to the questionnaire, Crelinsten has, in my view, come closest to stressing this hidden agenda of non-state terrorism when he writes:

> The purpose of terrorism can be more succinctly stated in terms of various allegiances among the various targets identified in your definition. Rather than the phrase "indirect method of combat," I would say the double victimization method (target of violence/threat and target of demands) is designed to affect allegiances between targets of terror and targets of attention, and targets of attention and the terrorists themselves.

One of the tragic ironies of non-state terrorism is that outrages are often committed to gain attention and/or a hearing. Yet the very fact that such a language of blood is used tends to preclude dialogue: the horrified opponent refuses to shake hands with murderers of "innocents." The fact that he usually also refused to listen to the grievances before violence was used, however, makes this response often hypocritical. There is a cruel double-bind in a situation in which violence is deemed a necessary means in order to be taken seriously while at the same time is considered to be an obstacle to communication. The question of whether one should talk or negotiate with terrorists is intensely contested and often polarizes the camp of the opponent--which might be another reason why acts of terrorism are performed or continue to be performed. This, too, points to what Rapoport calls "the peculiar characteristics of terrorism," which he identifies as "the use of violence to provoke consciousness, to evoke certain feelings of sympathy and revulsion."[36]

Here again, Rapoport stresses a point often overlooked: while the terrorist act can evoke "identification with the victim" by large sectors of the public, leading to feelings of helplessness and terror or anger, there are also those who experience an "identification with the aggressor." As another respondent put it: "Terrorism also satisfies personal identification needs and other emotional needs such as revenge and a sense of potency or power" (Corrado).

It should be borne in mind that the picture Rapoport sketches applies only to some groups of terrorists. At least three groups can be distinguished: (1) those who are fully prepared to sacrifice themselves and others for the just cause; (2) those who are prepared to risk their lives for the cause; and (3) those who are not prepared to do so and engage only in low- and no-risk activities like bombings.

Rapoport's remarks refer primarily to the first group. State terrorists, on the other hand, belong to the third group. Yet there are many parallels between state and non-state terrorism even from a communication perspective. The Soviet NKVD's "Documents of Terror," in discussing "enlightened terror" (which is an improved and refined version of general terror), for instance, states:

> The only tool which general terror knows and uses is force. . . . [The] tool used by enlightened terror is any means which is able to produce the planned psychological effect. . . . As has already been frequently emphasized, the aim of any action in the system of enlightened terror is to evoke a psychological process and implant and amplify its effects in the consciousness of the resonant mass. This goal can be attained if one repeats the same action constantly and systematically. But naturally such a method--the repetition of the action--is uneconomical. . . . The same goal can be attained if one is able to cause the resonant mass to experience the same action repeatedly through clever propaganda. It consists of executing a typical, planned action in classic form. Subsequently this action is brought home to the resonant mass through printed statements, the radio, the motion picture, the press--in short, through all the means of propaganda available. Naturally such propaganda cannot be dry and factual reports. . . . Its propaganda must be lively, colorful, dramatic--that is, dynamic. But it is not important that it follow the truth in details.[37]

Even when and where state terrorism does not make use of public mass media (e.g., by means of show trials), communication with the target audience must be established if the desired psychological effects are to be achieved. As de Swaan noted, the victims and their families and friends spread the terrible news through private conversation and personal networks, thereby becoming unwitting collaborators of the terrorist regime.[38]

Having reviewed the main criticisms and comments on my proposed definition, I would like to reformulate the definition. Before doing so, however, it is necessary to look at the relative standing of other definitions currently in use among the research community. After all, it would be of no use to improve a definition which receives limited support if another one has already been found which has a higher chance of being acceptable to a majority of scholars in the field.

Our second question was: "Whose definition of 'terrorism' do you utilize?" There were fifty-two direct responses to this question. No fewer than thirty (58 percent) mentioned their own definition. Of these, two mentioned that their definition followed or was similar to either Crenshaw or Wilkinson, while four respondents said the same with regard to my definition. The twenty-two respondents (42 percent) who utilized another's definition showed little unanimity. Wilkinson received four mentionings, Jenkins two, Wardlaw two, and Schmid two. Among the definitions mentioned only once were official ones such as those by the U.S. State Department or the British Prevention of Terrorism Act. There were a few combined definitions (e.g., "mixture of Thornton and Walter"). In addition, the definitions of Charters, Crozier, Mickolus, Lopez, and Stohl were utilized by individual respondents. For the convenience of the reader, these definitions are reproduced in Appendix B to this chapter, together with a number of other recent definitions. Those thirty respondents who followed their own definitions made some interesting suggestions. A selection of these can also be found in Appendix B.

TERRORISM: THE NORMATIVE QUESTION

A further problem that respondents to our questionnaire raised was whether a reference to norms is appropriate. Martha Crenshaw has proposed a distinction between analytical and normative definitions which I find useful.[39]

My own definition also contains normative elements ("The victimization of the target of violence is considered extranormal by most observers from the witnessing audience. . . . The norm violation. . . ."), as several respondents pointed out. Some authors, like Wilkinson, see this as the fundamental feature of terrorism (he refers to the "amoral and antinomian nature," "rejection of all moral restraints"). Other definitions use elements like "extralegal" or "criminal," or introduce the normative element by referring to the "innocence" of victims or to the fact that it is directed against "political authority" in general or the "government" in particular.

I think that Martha Crenshaw is right in proposing a neutral description in answer to the rhetorical question, "Is the place for [moral] judgment . . . in the construction of a definition?"[40] However, her own 1983 definition (see Appendix B) refers to the "systematic use of unorthodox political violence" which, to my mind, negates this intention. Webster's Dictionary defines "orthodox" as "conforming to the usual beliefs or established doctrines, especially in religion; proper, correct, conventional."[41]

One reason why it is so difficult to find neutral language seems to lie in language itself. Berger and Luckman have noted that "The edifice of legitimations is built upon language and uses language as its principal instrumentality."[42] Language, in this view, is not a neutral vehicle between the brain and the world, but a cultural artifact. As such, it orders the structure of things for those who accept its terminology. In the words of Berger and Luckman:

> It locates all collective events in a cohesive unity that includes past, present and future. With regard to the past, it establishes "memory" that is shared by all individuals socialized within the collectivity.[43]

When groups or individuals have different interests in a situation, how that situation is defined--given the legitimizing function of words--has implications for the situation itself and for its permanence. As the Thomas theorem puts it: "If men define situations as real, they are real in their consequences."[44] This raises the question of the "defining agency," the holder of definitional power in a given situation. He who has this power can, especially if those who utilize his definition are not aware of the origin of the definition, exercise a hegemony in the sense described by the Italian Marxist theorist A. Gramsci:

> An order in which a certain way of life and thought is dominant, in which one concept of reality is diffused throughout society in all its institutional and private manifestations, informing with its spirit all taste, morality, customs, religious and political principles, and all social relations, particularly in their intellectual and moral connotations.[45]

The question of the definition of a term like terrorism cannot be detached from the question of who is the defining agency. A group of authors has written, "The ideal definition is one that both the adherents and abhorrors of terrorism could agree upon."[46] Yet we live not in an ideal world but in a world where people have conflicting interests. With this in mind, a respondent to our first questionnaire held:

> . . . I should like to argue that no commonly agreed definition can in principle be reached, because the very process of definition is in itself part of a wider contestation over ideologies or political objectives. I do not therefore believe that cumulative research on an empiricist scientific model is possible. I do not, however, mean to argue that this means that the subject cannot advance through debate, nor that intellectual frameworks are necessarily so incompatible that everyone must plough his own furrow.

This response came in answer to a question in our first questionnaire: "Do you find that endeavours to come to commonly agreed upon definitions in the field of Political Violence in general and Terrorism in particular are (a) a waste of time; (b) necessary precondition for cumulative research; (c) other?" Twelve percent of the respondents chose the first option, 56 percent the second (though four respondents used some qualifiers), while 26 percent chose the third possibility, with comments such as ". . . it is entirely acceptable to have different schools within the discipline which use different definitions," "desirable but not necessary," or "helps clarify the political character of language and social research and is therefore most useful." From this it would seem that Walter Laqueur's view that ". . . disputes about a comprehensive, detailed definition will . . . make no notable contribution toward the understanding of terrorism" is far from universally shared.[47]

I do not share the pessimism and defeatism of some of the views quoted above. While language has political legitimacy functions--and legal and official definitions of terrorism as well as public discourse reflect this--social science analysts in academia should attempt to create and project their own terminology. There is a good reason for this, as one of our respondents who comes from the quantitative side of social science methodology pointed out:

> There is a need for explicit criteria which can be used to classify events as terroristic in nature. These criteria must be agreed upon and applied evenly by those studying the terrorism problem. We must move away from the idea that "one man's terrorist is another man's freedom fighter."

> Similarly, we must move away from the confusion that we--terrorism researchers--create when one classifies an event as terrorism, and another does not. This latter problem is evidenced, in part, by the difference in data base content (Gleason).

As the reactions to my definition make clear, there is a considerable degree of consensus if not with the wording at least with the thrust of this and similar definitions. My first definition was already an integrative effort, based on an analysis of existing notions among predominantly academic researchers. The feedback obtained through the second questionnaire has, I believe, been very useful in absorbing and meeting some criticism. Therefore, I feel that it is not misplaced to offer another definitional attempt at the end of this conceptual discussion.

TERRORISM: ANOTHER DEFINITIONAL ATTEMPT

"Terrorism is an anxiety-inspiring method of repeated violent action, employed by (semi-)clandestine individual, group, or state actors, for idiosyncratic, criminal, or political reasons, whereby--in contrast to assassination--the direct targets of violence are not the main targets. The immediate human victims of violence are generally chosen randomly (targets of opportunity) or selectively (representative or symbolic targets) from a target population, and serve as message generators. Threat- and violence-based communication processes between terrorist (organization), (imperiled) victims, and main targets are used to manipulate the main target (audience(s)), turning it into a target of terror, a target of demands, or a target of attention, depending on whether intimidation, coercion, or propaganda is primarily sought."

There are sixteen out of the twenty-two elements of Table 1.2 in this definition, three more than in the definition proposed in the first *Research Guide*. The length of this definition is a result of an attempt to accommodate comments and criticism from the research community. That very length will make it vulnerable to criticism since it offers, as it were, a broader flank to the critic than a short one. Some will find this too complex a definition, with too many elements included. The fact that terrorism can be used by almost anyone as a tactic or strategy, for almost any reason and in almost any number of ways, is likely to be a reason why some academic definers will prefer to exclude these elements. The reader searching for alternatives to our proposed definition should consult Appendix B, which offers thirty-five other recent definitions.

APPENDIX A

UNSOLVED CONCEPTUAL PROBLEMS OF TERRORISM

In our second questionnaire we asked, "Which conceptual questions on terrorism are, in your view, not yet adequately solved?" The list of cited problems was long, and included the following:

- "The boundary between terrorism and other forms of political violence" (U.S. author)

- "Whether terrorism can be defined without specifying the intent" (*Ibid.*)

- "Whether government terrorism and resistance terrorism are part of the same phenomenon" (*Ibid.*)

- Separation of "terrorism" from simple criminal acts, from open war between "consenting" groups, and from acts that arise out of clear mental illness (hallucinations, delusions)

- "Is there any one set of 'problems' or 'answers' that may be sought; or is 'terrorism' a very general term?" (Zawodny)

- "Differences between 'bottom-up' and 'top-down' terrorism" (Rosenthal)

- "Political versus other types of terrorism" (Rosenthal)

- "Terrorism as a sub-category of coercion? violence? power? influence?" (Rosenthal)

- "Relation to collective behaviour" (Rosenthal)

- "The 'arbitrariness' dimension" (Rosenthal)

- "Can terrorism be legitimate? What gains justify its use?" (Harris)

- "Relations between guerrilla and terrorism" (Hahlweg)

- "Random, indiscriminate, symbolic, i.e., target selection" (Robertson)

- "International terrorism [as] meaningless phrase" (Robertson)

- "The political distinctions in labeling which make one set of terrorists into freedom fighters and another set into psychopaths" (Young)

- "Whether there is legal utility at all in the word or concept" (Rubin)

- "How it relates to/emerges from larger political conflicts: what are the boundaries between 'terrorism' and 'revolution' or 'violent protest'? Is terrorism when used as a tactic in a larger campaign to suppress opposition, or when used as a tactic in a revolutionary war, conceptually the same as terrorist tactics when used as the exclusive or principal tactic of a group? Second, what's distinctly 'political' about terrorism? Whose uses, in what contexts, are political v. nonpolitical? Third, is 'state terrorism' conceptually the same as 'non-state terrorism'?" (Gurr)

- "The concept of diversity in space and time" (Visser)

- "The problem of value judgments in determining which acts of political violence are legitimate or patriotic and which are terroristic" (Drake)

- "Conceptual bias in favor of incumbent elites" (Waugh)

- "Can one envisage a purely psychic form of terror? Is actual violence necessary?" (Wilkinson)

- "How do we distinguish, in practice, between deliberate promotion of terror and use of war terror in wider conflicts, and the (unintended) epiphenomena of subjective terror experience in war situations?" (Wilkinson)

- "Is 'terrorism' solely the 'terror' element in what may be a wider form of conflict?" (Tugwell)

- "If terror is . . . a narrow subject, what is its relationship with political persuasion?" (Tugwell)

- "Might it not be useful to refer to 'violent politics' rather than 'political violence'?" (Tugwell)

- "Definition--term terrorism is now being widely misapplied to a wide range of violent political/military activities which are not in fact 'terrorist'" (Charters)

- "The distinction between actors and acts; i.e., obviously the commission of a terrorist act does not automatically define the actor as a terrorist. How then are we to define a 'terrorist'?"

- "Legitimacy of violence" (Smith)

- "The relationship between terrorism as a concept and terrorism as a phenomenon is not adequately addressed in the literature" (Crelinsten)

- "Term is too broadly defined" (Wolpin)

- "Distinction between terror and terrorism, respectively their purposes" (Kronenberger)

- "The relationship between crime and terrorism" (Taylor)

- "Degree of violence: often quoted as a main point to define terrorism, never 'measured'" (Della Porta)

APPENDIX B

A SELECTION OF RECENT GOVERNMENTAL AND ACADEMIC DEFINITIONS

A. Governmental Definitions

1. **U.S. Congress (1977)**: "[International terrorism includes any other] . . . unlawful act which results in the death, bodily harm, or forcible deprivation of liberty to any person, or in the violent destruction of property, or an attempt or credible threat to commit any such act, if the act, threat, or attempt is committed or takes effect (A) outside the territory of a state of which the alleged offender is a national; or (B) outside the territory of the state against which the act is directed; or (C) within the territory of the state against which the act is directed and the alleged offender knows or has reason to know that a person against whom the act is directed is not a national of that state; or (D) within the territory of any state when found to have been supported by a foreign state . . . irrespective of the nationality of the alleged offender: provided, that the act of international terrorism is (*i*) intended to damage or threaten the interests of or obtain concessions from a state or an international organization; and (*ii*) not committed in the course of military and paramilitary operations directed essentially against military forces or military targets of a state or an organized armed group."[48]

2. **U.S. Central Intelligence Agency (1980)**: ". . . the threat or use of violence for political purposes by individuals or groups, whether acting for, or in opposition to established governmental authority, when such actions are intended to shock or intimidate a large group wider than the immediate victims."[49]

3. **U.S. Federal Bureau of Investigation (1980)**: "Terrorism is defined as the unlawful use of force or violence against persons or property to intimidate or coerce a government, the civilian population, or any segment thereof, in furtherance of political or social objectives. A terrorist incident is defined as a violent act or an act dangerous to human life in violation of the criminal laws of the United States or of any state to intimidate or coerce a government, the civilian population, or any segment thereof, in furtherance of political or social objectives."[50]

4. **U.S. Department of Justice (1984):** ". . . violent criminal conduct apparently intended: (1) to intimidate or coerce a civilian population; (2) to influence the conduct of a government by intimidation or coercion; or (3) to affect the conduct of a government by assassination or kidnapping."[51]

5. **U.S. Army (and some Commonwealth armies as well) (1983):** "Terrorism (ASCC [= standardized for use by the U.S. Army and the American, Australian, British, Canadian, and New Zealand air forces]): The use or threat of violence in furtherance of a political aim. See also sabotage; subversion."[52]

6. **U.S. Department of Defense (1983):** ". . . the unlawful use or threatened use of force or violence by a revolutionary organization against individuals or property with the intention of coercing or intimidating governments or societies, often for political or ideological purposes."[53]

7. **U.S. Army (1983):** ". . . the calculated use of violence or the threat of violence to attain goals political, religious, or ideological in nature. This is done through intimidation, coercion, or instilling fear. Terrorism involves a criminal act that is often symbolic in nature and intended to influence an audience beyond the immediate victims."[54] [This definition was scheduled to be replaced in 1986 by the following one:]

8. **U.S. Department of Defense (1986):** ". . . the unlawful use or threatened use of force or violence against individuals or property to coerce or intimidate governments or societies, often to achieve political, religious or ideological objectives."[55]

9. **U.S. Department of State (1983):** ". . . premeditated, politically motivated violence perpetrated against noncombatant targets by subnational groups or clandestine state agents."[56]

10. **U.S. Vice President's Task Force (1986):** ". . . the unlawful use or threat of violence against persons or property to further political or social objectives. It is generally intended to intimidate or coerce a government, individuals or groups to modify their behavior or policies."[57]

11. **German Federal Republic, Office for the Protection of the Constitution (1985):** "Terrorism is the enduringly conducted struggle for political goals, which are intended to be achieved by means of

assaults on the life and property of other persons, especially by means of severe crimes as detailed in art. 129a, sect. 1 of the penal law book (above all: murder, homicide, extortionist kidnapping, arson, setting off a blast by explosives) or by means of other acts of violence, which serve as preparation of such criminal acts."[58]

12. **United Kingdom (1974)**: For the purposes of the legislation, terrorism is "the use of violence for political ends, and includes any use of violence for the purpose of putting the public or any section of the public in fear."[59]

B. Academic Definitions

13. **V. K. Anand (1984)**: ". . . terrorism is described as the art of compelling an individual, group, or authority to adopt a particular disposition or accept the imposed demands under conditions of fear created by passive action or violence--demonstrated, threatened or implied."[60]

14. **U. Backes and E. Jesse (1985)**: "Terrorism has a communicative function. By means of a systematic application of acts of violence involving the element of surprise, fear and terror--according to the etymological meaning of the word--are intended to be produced in the social group that is fought; at the same time it is intended to arouse the attention and (in the long run) sympathy of larger sections of the population for certain political purposes."[61]

15. **A. H. Buckelew (1986)**: ". . . terrorism is defined as violent, criminal behavior designed primarily to generate fear in the community, or in a substantial segment of the community, for political purposes."[62]

16. **R. S. Cline and Y. Alexander (1985)**: "It is suggested that state-sponsored terrorism be defined as: 'The deliberate employment of violence or the threat of use of violence by sovereign states (or sub-national groups encouraged or assisted by sovereign states) to attain strategic and political objectives by acts in violation of law intended to create overwhelming fear in a target population larger than the civilian or military victims attacked or threatened.' It is further suggested that recent history indicates: The main goal of this state-sponsored terrorism now at the end of the twentieth century is to undermine selectively the policies, the psycho-social

stability, and political governability of pluralist states with representative governments."[63]

17. **M. Crenshaw (1983)**: ". . . a basic definition would include the following attributes: the systematic use of unorthodox violence by small conspiratorial groups with the purpose of manipulating political attitudes rather than physically defeating an enemy. The intent of terrorist violence is psychological and symbolic, not material. Terrorism is premeditated and purposeful violence, employed in a struggle for political power. As Harold Lasswell defined it: 'Terrorists are participants in the political process who strive for political results by arousing acute anxieties.'"[64]

18. **R. D. Crelinsten (1987)**: ". . . terrorism is conceived as a form of political communication. More specifically, it is the deliberate use of violence and threat of violence to evoke a state of fear (or terror) in a particular victim or audience. The terror evoked is the vehicle by which allegiance or compliance is maintained or weakened. Usually, the use and threat of violence are directed at one group of targets (victims), while the demands for compliance are directed toward a separate group of targets. Hence, we tend to speak of a triangular relationship between the terrorist and two distinct target groups. As for allegiances, the allegiance to be established or maintained is that between the terrorist and one group of targets, while the allegiance to be weakened is that between that same group of targets from whom allegiance is sought and other groups perceived by the terrorist to be enemies to his cause. No matter what the specific end, all terrorism is designed to affect, in some way or another, relationships among people, individuals or groups. In sum, then, terrorism is a tactic involving the use and threat of violence for communicative purposes. How and why it is used varies according to the particular context."[65]

19. **B. Crozier (1974)**: ". . . 'terrorism' means 'motivated violence for political ends' (a definition that distinguishes terrorism from both vandalism and non-political crime). Measures of extreme repression, including torture, used by States to oppress the population or to repress political dissenters, who may or may not be terrorists or guerrillas, are termed 'terror' (the converse of terrorism)."[66]

20. **R. D. Duvall and M. Stohl (1983)**: "Terrorism . . . is action intended to induce sharp fear and through that agency to effect a desired outcome in a conflict situation."[67]

21. **H. Hess (1982)**: "By Terrorism I wish to understand (1) a series of intentional acts of direct physical violence executed (2) at [various] points unpredictably, yet systematically, (3) with the aim of psychic effect on others than the physically affected victim (4) in the framework of a political strategy."[68]

22. **B. M. Jenkins (1975)**: "The threat of violence, individual acts of violence, or a campaign of violence designed primarily to instill fear--to terrorize--may be called terrorism. Terrorism is violence for effect: not only, and sometimes not at all, for the effect on the actual victims of the terrorists. In fact, the victim may be totally unrelated to the terrorists' cause. Terrorism is violence aimed at the people watching. Fear is the intended effect, not the byproduct, of terrorism. That, at least, distinguishes terrorist tactics from mugging and other forms of violent crime that may terrify but are not terrorism."[69]

23. **E. Mickolus (1980)**: ". . . the use, or threat of use, of anxiety-inducing extranormal violence for political purposes by any individual or group, whether acting for or in opposition to established governmental authority, when such action is intended to influence the behavior of a target group wider than the immediate victims and when, through the nationality or foreign ties of its perpetrators, its location, the nature of its institutional or human victims, or the mechanism of its resolution, its ramifications transcend national boundaries."[70]

24. **B. Netanyahu (1986)**: "Terrorism is the deliberate and systematic murder, maiming, and menacing of the innocent to inspire fear for political ends."[71]

25. **A. Schmid and J. de Graaf (1980)**: "Terrorism is the deliberate and systematic use or threat of violence against instrumental (human) targets (C) in a conflict between two (A, B) or more parties, whereby the immediate victims C--who might not even be part of the conflicting parties--cannot, through a change of attitude or behaviour, dissociate themselves from the conflict."[72]

26. **G. Wardlaw (1982)**: "Political terrorism is the use, or threat of use, of violence by an individual or a group, whether acting for or

in opposition to established authority, when such action is designed to create extreme anxiety and/or fear-inducing effects in a target group larger than the immediate victims with the purpose of coercing that group into acceding to the political demands of the perpetrators."[73]

27. **P. Wilkinson (1976)**: "Terrorism is a special mode or process of violence which has at least three basic elements: the terroristic aims of its perpetrators, their modus operandi in deploying particular forms of violence upon the victims and the target audience. . . . I have defined political terrorism as the systematic use of murder and destruction, and the threat of murder and destruction, to terrorise individuals, groups, communities or governments into conceding to the terrorists' political aims."[74]

C. Definitions from Questionnaire

28. **J. Adams**: "A terrorist is an individual or member of a group that wishes to achieve political ends using violent means often at the cost of casualties to innocent civilians and with the support of only a minority of the people they claim to represent."

29. **D. Della Porta**: "Terrorism is the action of clandestine political organisations, of small dimensions, which try to reach political aims through a continuous and almost exclusive use of violent forms of action."

30. **I. Fetscher**: "Application of violence (kidnapping, bombing, killing) in order to intimidate (terrorise) government and/or establishment groups and to impose certain changements (a) in the situation of ethnic minorities (up to independence), (b) in the strength and control of criminality and/or deviating behaviour (right-wing and vigilantism), (c) in the structure of the society (in the direction of more democracy and 'real equality' (left-wing millenarism in developed countries), (d) in the international relations (international terrorism's fight for 'independence' both legal-political and/or economic)."

31. **T. R. Gurr**: "Terrorism is [coercive, life-threatening] action intended to induce sharp fear and through that agency to effect a desired outcome in a conflict situation." (Modified version of a definition used by Raymond Duvall and Michael Stohl.)

32. **A. Merari**: "The systematic use of violence by sub-state groups or individuals in the service of political, social or religious objectives, whose intended psychological impact considerably surpasses the physical results."

33. **R. Thakrah**: "An organized system of extreme and violent intimidation."

34. **Ch. Townsend**: "The use of force by the armed [meaning not merely 'weaponed' but also psychologically prepared] against the unarmed."

35. **A. Yoder**: "Terrorism is the use of violence, usually systematically, to coerce or intimidate a population or government into changing policy."

TERRORISM AND RELATED CONCEPTS: TYPOLOGIES

In collaboration with M. Stohl and P. A. Flemming

INTRODUCTION

While we devoted considerable attention to both concepts and theories of terrorism in our first *Research Guide*, for lack of space we omitted a chapter on typologies. Therefore, we would like to present here a representative selection of current typologies and discuss some of their virtues and shortcomings. While we hope that such a survey of existing typologies will allow us to criticize some features which are illogical, ideological, or ill-fitting for empirical reasons so that some misleading classifications can be disposed of, the general thrust of this chapter is more descriptive than analytical. Its aim is to point out the need for a solution rather than offer a solution which we regard as satisfactory.

WHY TYPOLOGIES?

Typologies order a multitude of objects and/or phenomena and make them manageable for analysis. The ordering criteria can be based on empirical investigation or theoretical considerations. Whether a typology is functional depends on the needs of the user. A distinction between pro- and anti-Western terrorism might be useful for the operational purposes of those involved in responses to terrorism, but its usefulness for social scientists might be nil.

Typologies in the social sciences can be considered as a means of substituting variables for proper names of social systems.[1] In practical terms, typology building involves the categorizing of certain units of study "in accordance with a specified set of characteristics," the object being to compress a good deal of information into a single set of terms.[2] The use of typologies is regarded as essential in that "scientific explantion requires the systematic ordering and classification of empirical data."[3] According to Gregory K. Roberts, typologies can serve "to discover new relationships among the things so ordered, to generate hypotheses, to lead on to the development of theories, and to identify areas for investigation."[4]

TYPOLOGIES OF TERRORISM

Chalmers Johnson noted in 1978 that "there are almost as many typologies of terrorism as there are analysts."[5] While this is a slight exaggeration, the implication that there has been little if any cumulative work remains true. Many researchers bring their own particular concerns to the field, resulting in a whole array of categories. In the literature one finds a multitude of *fundamenta divisionis*, or principles of distinction (see Table 1.3).

Table 1.3. Some Common Bases for Classification.

1. actor-based	6. political-orientation-based
2. victim-based	7. motivation-based
3. cause-based	8. demand-based
4. environment-based	9. purpose-based
5. means-based	10. target-based

Which of these (or other) *fundamenta divisionis* a particular typology uses is dependent on the functions it is meant to serve. In the view of Ezzat A. Fattah:

> Typologies of terrorism are . . . useful in differentiating and categorizing terrorism, in understanding its "causes," manifestations and impact; in controlling its incidence; and in minimizing its effects.[6]

This is a broad agenda, covering both the interests of antiterrorist "firefighters" and the academic "students of combustion" (to use a distinction introduced by T. R. Gurr). While both groups would be served by typologies that could predict future behavior and events, a more realistic research demand which can be made on typologies is that they help social scientists in establishing the types of relationships which exist between a specific category and attributes such as terrorist motivations and behaviors. However, when introducing such a criterion, the number of typologies that can fulfill such a function is very limited. Writing almost decade ago, Richard Shultz noted that:

> . . . one is hard pressed to locate studies aimed at developing typologies that lend themselves to the vigorous analysis of the various forms political terrorism has taken, to depict common linkages and specific differences.[7]

In many ways, the state of typology construction reflects the state of our knowledge about terrorism, which has been described by one of the leading theorists, Martha Crenshaw, in these terms:

> Even the most persuasive statements about terrorism are not cast in the form of testable propositions, nor are they broadly comparable in origin or intent. . . . In general, propositions about terrorism lack logical comparability, specification of the relationship of variables to each other, and a rank ordering of variables in terms of explanatory power.[8]

One has only to consider the category of "international terrorism" (as opposed to "domestic terrorism," "native terrorism," "internal terrorism," or "indigenous terrorism") which we find in many typologies to understand Crenshaw's point about comparability. As long as it is not established what "international terrorism" (IT) stands for, the search for relationships between IT and other variables is likely to be frustrating and confusing. (See Table 1.4 for a number of definitions of "international terrorism.")

Table 1.4. Some Definitions of International Terrorism (IT).

(1) Milbank (1976): "For the purpose of this study, international and transnational terrorism are defined as follows: Common Characteristics: The threat or use of violence for political purposes when (1) such action is intended to influence the attitudes and behavior of a target group wider than its immediate victims, and (2) its ramifications transcend national boundaries (as a result, for example, of the nationality or foreign ties of its perpetrators, its locale, the identity of its institutional or human victims, its declared objectives, or the mechanisms of its resolution).

"International Terrorism: Such action when carried out by basically autonomous non-state actors, whether or not they enjoy some degree of support from sympathetic groups controlled by a sovereign state.

Table 1.4 cont.

"Transnational Terrorism: Such action when carried out by basically autonomous non-state actors, whether or not they enjoy some degree of support from sympathetic states."[9]

(2) A. P. Pierre (1976): IT = ". . . acts of violence across national boundaries, or with clear international repercussions, often within the territory or involving the citizens of a third party to a dispute."[10]

(3) P. Wilkinson (1974): IT = ". . . terrorism committed outside the borders of one or all of the parties to the political conflict . . . when it is motivated by revolutionary objectives."[11]

(4) W. H. Smith (1977): IT = ". . . when the terrorist is of one nationality and at least some of his victims are of another."[12]

(5) B. Jenkins (1975): "The most simple definition of international terrorism comprises acts of terrorism that have clear international consequences: incidents in which terrorists go abroad to strike their targets, select victims or targets because of their connections to a foreign state (diplomats, local executives or officers of foreign corporations), attack airliners in international flights or force airliners to fly to another country. . . . International terrorism may also be defined as acts of violence or campaigns of violence waged outside the accepted rules and procedures of international diplomacy and war."[13]

Depending on which of the above definitions one chooses, an act of violence such as the American raid on Libya in April 1986 can or cannot be classified as a case of international terrorism (was it not "outside the accepted rules and procedures of international diplomacy and war"?). On the other hand, if a hypothetical American citizen hijacks an American aircraft and victimizes U.S. citizens above Beirut in order to get a colleague out of jail, he might or might not be defined as an international terrorist (he might not have been "motivated by revolutionary objectives," or he and all of his victims might have been issued passports by the same country). In one sense, then, "international terrorism" is a meaningless category for social science purposes.

For legal purposes, however, the question of a uniform definition of acts of "international terrorism" does have relevance. A great variety of terms exist. Yehezkel Dror distinguishes, in the area of international terrorism, (1) imported terrorism ("by and on behalf of aliens"); (2) transient terrorism ("by aliens and against aliens"); and (3) extraterritorial terrorism ("against external representatives, properties, and symbols of the democracy").[14]

A legally useful discussion of three types of international terrorism is offered by William L. Waugh, Jr. Basing himself on the responding governments' jurisdiction and responsibilities, Waugh distinguishes (1) spillover terrorism ("the use of violence by foreign nationals against foreign individuals or property"); (2) integrated internal terrorism ("The distinguishing characteristic . . . is the difference in the nationalities of the terrorists and the victims, one group being indigenous to the host state"); and (3) external terrorism ("The distinguishing characteristic . . . is that the terrorists are located or the act is committed outside of the territory of the target government, i.e., in the jurisdiction of another government").[15]

From a social science point of view, however, such a typology is of little utility since it cannot explain or predict terroristic behavior in any way.

Relatively few typologies appear to be interesting in this respect, and our discussion will not systematically cover the ten categories mentioned in Table 1.3.

ACTOR-BASED TYPOLOGIES

The most obvious division which can be found in typologies on terrorism is the one between one group of actors and another. Since the contest in which terrorists are involved invariably affects state power, the state figures as a reference point and usually also as an actor. The terminology introduced by authors thus distinguishes between state and non-state actors, labeling their respective behavior with terms like "enforcement terror" and "agitational terror" (Thornton), or "regime of terror" and "siege of terror" (Walter). These two particular dyads are relatively unproblematical categories. Some authors, however, change the terminology when they refer to different actors. Friedrich Hacker, for instance, uses the term "terror" for a type of state violence, while he reserves "terrorism" for the insurgent variety. This is undesirable as it easily leads to bias. Brian Crozier's usage illustrates this; he uses the term "terror" for violence emanating from insurgents, while "counterterror" is utilized for government acts.[16] This is bound to prejudice the issue as the guilt for committing the first act of terror is attributed to the insurgents. Such usage is reminiscent of the use by some authors of "force" for state activities and "violence" for non-state activities.

In our view, uniformity of terminology is important, and power and differences in power and legitimacy between state and non-state actors do not offer valid grounds for changing terminology. As we put it in our first *Research Guide*:

> . . . those seeking and those holding state power are both involved in a struggle for legitimacy. . . . When the state does not punish those who violate a law, but punishes some people (guilty or not) so that others are deterred to violate repressive laws, then we enter the field of terrorism. Where the law has become unpredictable in its application, because individual guilt is less important to the regime than collective obedience, we are clearly no longer dealing with a legitimate monopoly of violence, but with state terrorism.[17]

Since insurgent terrorists win at least sometimes, their initially smaller power must also have risen, with or without a concomitant rise in legitimacy.

Actor-oriented typologies in which the state is a principal actor might benefit from typologies of states. Distinctions which come readily to mind are between (tribal) developing states, (homogeneous) nation states, and old imperial states (containing a multitude of nations). The distinction between democratic states, authoritarian states, and Communist (or totalitarian) states is one that has gained some currency and might offer a possible basis for classification.

Given that state and non-state actors sometimes act in opposition to as well as in collaboration with each other, a variety of combinations arises which makes individual labeling too cumbersome. To solve this problem, we therefore proposed in 1980 a non-nominal classification. (The theoretically possible configurations and permutations are represented in Table 1.5.)

Table 1.5. Intra-, Inter-, and Transnational Terrorism: An Actor-Based Typology with Two, Three, and Four Actors.[18]

1. A - B	5. A + B - b	11. A + B - a + b
2. A - b	6. A + b - B	12. a + b - A + B
3. a - b	7. A + b - a	13. A + b - a + B
4. a - B	8. A + a - b	14. A + a - B + b
	9. A + a - B	
	10. a + b - A	

Key: A,B means State Actors; a,b means Non-State Actors of Country A,B.

POLITICAL-ORIENTATION-BASED TYPOLOGIES

Once one goes beyond the "terrorism from above"/"terrorism from below" distinction, one finds numerous subdivisions. Loesche, for instance, differentiates between: (1) national or anticolonial liberation movements; (2) regional or separatist movements; (3) social-revolutionary movements in industrialized countries; (4) defensive associations to protect group privileges; and (5) opposition movements in dictatorial systems.[19]

Some typologies distinguish between left-wing and right-wing terrorism directed against the state. Brian Crozier, for instance, implies such a distinction in his six main categories: (1) ethnic, religious, or nationalist groups; (2) Marxist-Leninist groups; (3) anarchist groups; (4) pathological groups or individuals; (5) neofascist groups or individuals; and (6) ideological mercenaries.[20]

Another author, G. Davidson Smith, moving beyond political orientation only distinguishes (1) nationalist-separatist-irredentist (includes ethnic basis); (2) issues; (3) ideological; (4) exile; (5) state and state-sponsored; and (6) religious.[21]

Depending on which typology one uses, one will have to assign right-wing, left-wing, and anarchist groups to different categories. If ideology is seen as a system of beliefs which allows people to order individual and social experiences, it can be argued that nationalism as well as ethnic identity could be subsumed under that category. If categories are not mutually exclusive, the problem of attribution constantly arises for the classifier and renders many typologies of little practical value.

One of the distinctions that does make sense, in our view, is the one between non-state actors who target the state and those who do not. Among the latter, vigilante groups take a prominent position. An example would be the American Ku Klux Klan, which originally defined its objective as "the maintenance of the supremacy of the white man in the Republic by terror and intimidation."[22]

Vigilante terrorism has been an understudied phenomenon and needs more attention. Rosenbaum and Sederberg have defined vigilantism in these terms:

> When individuals or groups identifying with the established order defend that order by resorting to means that violate . . . formal boundaries, they can be usefully classified as vigilantes.[23]

Insofar as vigilante tactics are terroristic, they should be included in any actor-based typology. Rosenbaum and Sederberg distinguish three broad categories:

> (1) crime-control vigilantism: establishment violence directed against persons who are believed to be committing acts proscribed by the establishment legal system;
>
> (2) social-group-control vigilantism: establishment violence directed against groups that are competing for or advocate a redistribution of values within the system; and
>
> (3) regime-control vigilantism: establishment violence to preserve the status quo at times when the formal system of rule enforcement is viewed as ineffective or irrelevant.[24]

The establishment is not always (fully) in control of the state, there might be more than one establishment in one state, or state power might have been usurped by a military coup, depriving the establishment of its main coercive arm. In other situations the state tolerates or even encourages the activities of vigilante death squads. For these reasons it appears useful to introduce more firmly a vigilante category in typologies of terrorism. Needless to say, not all vigilante activities are terroristic, nor are they all directly political, especially if they limit themselves to local crime-control, "order-without-law" types of activities. The term "vigilantism" is usually linked to the defense of the established order. We would plead for a broader usage (or a better term) in which the defense of a group's way of life against challenging groups is more central.

The desirability of an intermediate category of terrorism for "lone-wolf" type individuals, small groups, and organizations aiming at less than maintaining or taking state power has been recognized by several authors. Paul Wilkinson introduced the category "sub-revolutionary terrorism," by which he means groups with "political motives short of revolutionary change." He also proposed a category "epiphenomenal terror," defined as having "no specific aim," being a "by-product of large-scale intra-specific violence."[25]

Richard Shultz, starting from Wilkinson's distinction between revolutionary, sub-revolutionary, and repressive terrorism, offered the following tripartition:

> (1) Revolutionary Terrorism may be defined as the threat and/or employment of extranormal forms of political violence, in varying degrees, with the objective of successfully effecting a complete revolutionary change (change of fundamental political-social processes) within the political system. . . .
>
> (2) Sub-Revolutionary Terrorism may be defined as the threat and/or employment of extranormal forms of political violence, in varying degrees, with the objective of effecting various changes in the structural-functional aspects of the particular political system. The goal is to bring about changes within the body politic, not to abolish it in favor of a complete system change. . . .
>
> (3) Establishment Terrorism may be defined as the threat and/or employment of extranormal forms of political violence, in varying degrees, by an established political system, against both external and internal opposition.[26]

In our own attempt to construct a basic typology, we proposed the category "single-issue terrorism" as one of three subcategories of "insurgent terrorism." Our 1980 typology is reproduced in Table 1.6 with some minor terminological changes (the substitution of "idiosyncratic" for "pathological," and "state" for "repressive") and additions. The typology might be expanded to include categories for "anarchist" and "religious" terrorism. It is no longer a strict "political orientation only" typology, since it also attempts to cover motives (political, criminal, idiosyncratic) and actors. In other words, it is three-dimensional, covering variables 1,

Table 1.6. A Basic Typology of Terrorism (Schmid and de Graaf).[27]

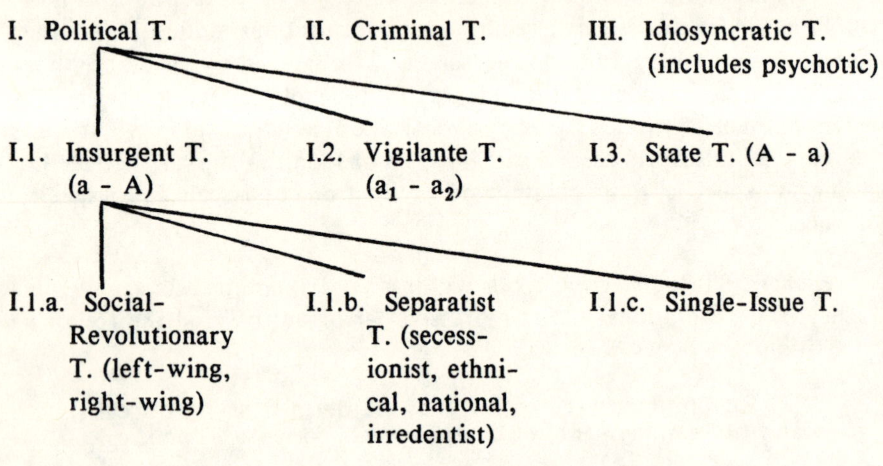

Key: A means State Actor; a_1, a_2 means Non-State Actors.

Table 1.7. Examples of Terrorist Organizations Classified According to Target Population and Base of Operation (Merari).[28]

Terrorist Base	*The Target*	
	Foreigners	*Countrymen*
Domestic	EOKA, FLN, MAU-MAU, FRELIMO	ERP, NWLF, RAF, BR
Abroad	PFLP, PDFLP, ZIPA, FMYO	FNLC, Croatian Revolutionary Brotherhood, United Croats of West Germany

6, and 7 of the ten dimensions in Table 1.3. Many typologies are two-dimensional, and we shall look at some of them in our next section.

MULTIDIMENSIONAL TYPOLOGIES

The 2 x 2 matrix is a very popular form for presenting typologies. Ariel Merari, for instance, takes the dimensions 2 and 10 from Table 1.3 and classifies terrorist groups according to their target population and base of operation. Depending on whether foreigners or nationals are targets of terror violence, he distinguishes between xenofighters and homofighters (see Table 1.7).

Typologies are ideal type classifications, not "true" reflections of the real world which includes impure cases and exceptions. To give a concrete example: the South Moluccan extremists (not the Free Moluccan Youth Organization (FMYO) itself, which is a broad legal youth association, not a terrorist organization), which Merari typifies as "base: Holland; target: Indonesia," has not only targetted Indonesians in the Netherlands, but also Dutch and even moderate South Moluccan people.[29] Unlike the PFLP, which carried out attacks against Israel within its borders, the South Moluccan extremists never got closer than 16,000 kilometers to Indonesia. Perhaps it would be more prudent to introduce a category for "exile terrorists," as Smith proposed in answer to our questionnaire.

The methodological problem illustrated here has been addressed by Harry Eckstein:

> If one can establish how any given case diverges from type, one can also determine to what extent a generalization about a type can apply to it. The most obvious means for assessing degree of divergence from type is of course a close comparison of the elements of the cases involved. One case may have six of the seven elements of a type, another five; one case may [contain] one element of a type in impure form, another two, and so forth. The more such typical elements are present in pure form, the less a theory about the type should need modification to fit the atypical case. And in the world of phenomena there will always be atypical cases to plague the theorist.[30]

PURPOSE-BASED TYPOLOGIES

The purpose of terror, Lenin once said, is to terrify.[31] Yet it is quite evident that not everybody is terrorized and that the sowing of terror is not in most cases an end in itself but a means to a variety of objectives. Thomas P. Thornton, in the single most seminal article on terrorism, has developed a rudimentary typology of the proximate objectives of terrorism:

> (1) morale-building (within the terrorist movement itself as well as in that element of the population that is already sympathetic to the insurgents);
>
> (2) advertising (not only calls attention to the existence of the insurgents but also serves as a reminder of their program and ideals. . . . The advertising function differs from morale-building in that it is directed towards a mass audience);
>
> (3) disorientation (the objective par excellance of the terrorist, removing the underpinnings of the order in which his targets live out their daily lives);
>
> (4) elimination of opposing forces (either physically or by neutralizing their effectiveness. In one sense, this is a by-product of terror, for the aim in itself is not symbolic, it could be accomplished by murder). . . . From elimination of a harmful individual, not only will general disorientation be promoted, but a more specific fear will be instilled into the group to which the victim belongs ("Will I be next?" each will ask);
>
> (5) provocation of countermeasures by the incumbents (in combating an elusive terrorist, the incumbents will be forced to take measures that affect not only the terrorist but also his environment, the society as a whole. Although this result may be incidental to the aims of some terrorists, terroristic acts often are committed with the express purpose of provoking reprisals).[32]

While Thornton's categories fall short of a proper typology, others have built on the foundations he laid. J. Bowyer Bell, whose personal acquaintance with revolutionary actors is unrivaled among the leading authors, expanded Thornton's list and loaded some of the categories differently. He offered a list of six types of revolutionary terror:

> (1) Organizational terror: every revolutionary organization, perhaps without exception, must face the problem of

> maintaining internal discipline, inhibiting penetration, and punishing errant members. . . . To be most effective, punishment must be swift, harsh, and visible. It is therefore often highly formalized, with a trial, defense, sentence, and execution (IRA).
>
> (2) Allegiance terror . . . is a less restrained variant of organizational terror . . . in order to create mass support (Algerian FLN).
>
> (3) Functional terror . . . is employed when in the course of an armed struggle it is necessary to gain strategic advantage through specific action (Bloody Sunday).
>
> (4) Manipulative terror . . . concentrates on exploiting the deed and escalating its impact . . . (Palestine).
>
> (5) Manipulative terror . . . [is employed] to create a bargaining situation, in which the terrorists threaten to destroy seized assets or hostages unless they are granted certain demands.
>
> (6) Symbolic terror . . . must go beyond the organizational and functional and must select as a victim a figure who represents the epitome of the enemy. Yet the deed must be more than simple vengeance (ETA's murder of Carrero Blanco).[33]

Such lists could be expanded. Surveying the purposes and functions attributed to terrorism, we found no fewer than twenty different (though partly overlapping) ones in the literature of terrorism.[34] Strictly speaking, neither Bell nor Thornton offers a typology. Yet they have prepared the ground for others to build on their pioneering efforts. One of those who closely follows the analytical categories introduced by Thornton is Martha Crenshaw (see Table 1.8). Crenshaw stresses that the significance of the terrorist strategy lies in the relationship to the general revolutionary goals that these "proximate objectives" serve. Such a framework, Crenshaw holds, based on a set of general categories, should incorporate the complex detail of reality while emphasizing the common factors of each basic function of terrorism.[35]

The introduction of the "response" and "discrimination" categories is fruitful. Others have also attempted to elaborate on these dimensions. Among them is Philip A. Karber, who views terrorism as the symbolic use of violence and a means of communication. He holds that the message of terrorism varies with the degree of discrimination between the symbolic victim and society. His hypothesis is: "The more indiscriminate and random the terrorist act, the more general the target group and diffuse the message." According to Karber:

> Thus, to communicate a specific message to a particular target, the terrorist must be highly selective in his choice of the symbolic victim. By overlapping the apparent influence and symbolic discrimination, we create a heuristic, if crude, typology of the communicative functions of terrorism.

Table 1.8. Typology of Acts of Terrorism (Crenshaw).

Proximate Objectives	*Tactical Considerations*		
	Target	*Response*	*Discrimination*
Morale building	Sympathizers	Enthusiasm	Irrelevant
Advertising	Mass	Curiosity	High
Disorientation	Mass	Anxiety	Low
Elimination	Victim and identification group	Despair and immobility	High
Provocation	Identification group	Fear	High

Karber distinguishes between the two poles "instrumental influence" (in which the terrorist's message has an immediate effect on the behavior of others against their will due to the induced fear) and "affective influence" (in which the message has a long-range effect on the behavior of others due to their identification with or respect for the transmitter) (see Table 1.9). Another team of authors correlated degree of discrimination with specificity of demands (see Table 1.10). A comparison of these two tables shows identical outcomes in three out of four categories, and, surprisingly, the opposite in the fourth category ("social conscience" vs. "mass casualties"). Such divergencies are potentially fruitful, as they can lead to the testing of rivaling hypotheses.

Table 1.9. A Functional Typology of Terrorism (Karber).[36]

	Instrumental	*Affective*
Discriminate	Coercive Bargaining	Advertisement & Recruiting
Indiscriminate	Social Paralysis	Social Conscience

Table 1.10. Terrorist Means.[37]

Target Selection	*Specificity of Demands*	
	High	*Low*
Discriminate	Bargaining	Political Statement
Random	Social Paralysis	Mass Casualties

At the beginning of this chapter we postulated that a good typology should be able to say something meaningful about the relationship between a particular group of terrorists and its modus operandi. Since the group dynamics of terrorism are still far from fully understood, this is a formidable task. One area in which progress has been made is that in which the terrorist actor is often an individual, which reduces complexity considerably. Table 1.11, a typology of hostage-takers, has been constructed by Irving Goldaber, a sociologist.[38] Table 1.12, a multi-dimensional typology for the broader field of terrorism, or, rather, a framework of a future typology, has been proposed by Richard Shultz.[39] This seven-variable typology is, as Shultz readily admits, only "in its initial stages of development." He adds that "Much work remains to be done before it meets the requirements of a soundly conceptualized typology."[40] Unfortunately, Shultz does not seem to have pursued this

Table 1.11. Typology of Hostage-Takers (Goldaber)

	SUICIDAL PERSONALITY	VENGEANCE SEEKER	DISTURBED INDIVIDUAL	CORNERED PERPETRATOR	AGGRIEVED INMATE	FELONIOUS EXTORTIONIST	SOCIAL PROTESTOR	IDEOLOGICAL ZEALOT	TERRORIST EXTREMIST
	PSYCHOLOGICAL			CRIMINAL			POLITICAL		
WHO IS THE HOSTAGE-TAKER?	An unstable, hopeless, depressed individual in crisis	An otherwise ordinary person who is a disaffected former associate	An acutely or chronically unbalanced individual	Potentially any criminal	A frustrated, desperate leader who can organize other inmates	An unemotional, cunning, professional criminal	An idealistic, educated young person	A fanatic, programmed cultist	An individual willing to sacrifice himself for his political philosophy
WHAT IS HIS DISTINGUISHING CHARACTERISTIC OR SITUATION?	Doesn't care if he is killed	Is driven by an irrational single purpose	Manifest lack of judgment leading to an unsound assessment of reality	Is caught unaware with no prior plan for handling predicament	Is familiar with the setting, prison authority, adversaries, and his victims	Is knowledgeable about and respectful of police power	Is an exuberant celebrant in an uplifting group experience	Is willing to sacrifice himself for his beliefs	Has realistic assessment of impact of act
WHEN DOES HE TAKE THE HOSTAGE?	In a severe emotional, decompensating state	After meticulous planning	When his aberrant mind siezes on the idea as a solution to his problem	In desperation, when victims are available	After considerable planning, or spontaneously when pushed beyond endurance	While executing a carefully prepared plot	When he identifies the need to eliminate a social injustice	After he has sustained a wrong	When publicity potential is greatest
WHERE DOES HE COMMIT THE ACT?	In any place when his defenses fail	In a spot that brings him maximum satisfaction	In any setting	In the area in which he is trapped	In his own environment	In location of his selection	At the site of the unwanted entity or event or where the protest is most visible	Anywhere	Where victim is off guard
WHY DOES HE DO IT?	To cause someone else to fulfill his death wish	To gain revenge	To achieve mastery and to solve his problem	To effectuate escape	To bring about situational change or to obtain freedom	To obtain money	To create social change or social justice	To redress a grievance	To attain political change
HOW DOES HE TAKE THE HOSTAGE?	With irrational taunts	Through overt action or furtive behavior	In an improvised, illogical manner	With weapon and as a reflexive response	With planned, overpowering force	With a weapon, in a calculated manner	In a group by massing a human thrust or blockade	With robot-like violence or nonviolent conduct	With emotional and violent execution of a crafty plot

Table 1.12. Multidimensional Typology (Schultz)

General Categories	Selected Variables: CAUSES	ENVIRONMENT	GOALS	STRATEGY	MEANS	ORGANIZATION	PARTICIPATION
REVOLUTIONARY TERRORISM	Economic, Political, Social, Psychological factors	Internal (urban or rural revolutionary groups) External (autonomous non-state revolutionary actors)	Long Range/ Strategic Objectives Short Term/ Tactical Objectives	Primary or Secondary role in the overall strategy	Various capabilities and techniques employed	Nature – degrees of organizational structures	Participant profiles Leadership style/ attitude
SUB-REVOLUTIONARY TERRORISM	Economic, Political, Social, Psychological factors	Internal (urban-rural non-revolutionary groups) External (non-revolutionary, autonomous, non-state actors)	Long Range/ Strategic Objectives Short Term/ Tactical Objectives	Primary or Secondary role in the overall strategy	Various capabilities and techniques employed	Nature – degrees of organizational structures	Participant profiles Leadership style/ attitude
ESTABLISHMENT TERRORISM	Economic, Political, Social, Psychological factors	Internal (repression of urban or rural opposition) External (aimed at other nation-states or non-state actors)	Long Range/ Strategic Objectives Short Term/ Tactical Objectives	Primary or Secondary role in the overall strategy	Various capabilities and techniques employed	Nature – degrees of organizational structures	Participant profiles Leadership style/ attitude

line of work since the publication of his article in 1978. Nor does it seem that anyone else has done significant typological work recently in the field of terrorism.

In our questionnaire, we asked authors in the field which typologies of terrorism had, in their view, contributed to the four functions mentioned by G. K. Roberts: (1) to discover new relationships among the things so ordered; (2) to generate hypotheses; (3) to lead on to the development of theories; and (4) to identify areas for investigation.[41]

A frequent response was "none" or no answer, indicating low regard for or lack of familiarity with typological efforts in the field. Some typologies cited by our respondents as being useful, apart from those already mentioned, have been authored by Nagel,[42] Schlesinger,[43] Walter,[44] Horowitz,[45] Laqueur,[46] Burton,[47] Gurr,[48] Mazlesh,[49] Cooper,[50] Hubbard,[51] Jenkins,[52] Lasch,[53] Wardlaw,[54] Sloan,[55] and Russell and Miller.[56]

THE PLACE OF TERRORISM IN POLITICAL CONFLICT

One of the problems with typology building is the absence of a commonly agreed-upon definition of terrorism. As long as terrorism is conceptualized as extremism of ends rather than of means, the concept cannot be relieved of its ideological baggage. On the one hand, we must narrow the meaning of terrorism to make it a manageable concept. On the other hand, we must relate it to other forms of social protest and control. In addition, terrorism must be placed in the various contexts of political conflict-waging in general. It makes a great difference whether terrorism is part of a broader insurgency struggle or the work of a small group without any mass constituency. Terrorism in wartime and during revolution must be looked at differently than terrorism in the context of dictatorship and repression. We must stop looking only at the terrorist activities of one party to a conflict and evaluate the interaction between conflict dyads. Only in such a way can we hope to make some typological progress.

In conclusion, we would like to present one typological attempt that does not subdivide terrorism but attempts to classify the place of terrorism--both state and non-state--in the political contest between the forces of order and the forces of change, between power holders and power challengers, between the forces of social control and of social dissent. This mirror scheme of modes of political expression and action has been inspired by Ronald D. Crelinsten,[57] the Canadian criminologist, who views terrorism as "political communication" (see Table 1.13, which, however, uses a partly changed terminology and contains several modifications and additions). This scheme should be regarded as tentative. It can be misleading if taken as a direct depiction of political conflict. The fact that war appears below terrorism indicates a greater lethality but not necessarily that terrorism no longer occurs in war or that war is less rule-guided than terrorism. However, the scheme is illuminating in other ways: for instance, it depicts the "anomaly" of asymmetric conflict-waging when a state actor uses instruments from the repertoire of "force" against non-state actors using conventional opposition techniques like the formation of political parties. Conversely, many perceive it as impermissible when non-state actors use terroristic violence against a political system where alternative modes of participation in the political process are readily available. It can be hypothesized that the legitimacy granted to both government and non-state actors to engage in one of the three forms of conflict-waging is likely to be higher when the other side has resorted to the more severe forms of political conflict-waging at an earlier stage. For instance, the use of violence (force) to prevent (further) harm (e.g., in a hostage liberation situation) can then be judged differently than violence as provocation (e.g., the killing of one hostage to establish credibility for extortionist bargaining over the lives of the others).

Table 1.13. The Spectrum of Political Action.

State of Peace	
State Actor	*Non-State Actor*
Conventional Politics	
I. Rule of law (Routinized rule, legitimated by tradition, customs, constitutional procedures)	I. Opposition politics (Lobbying among powerholders, formation of opposition press and parties, rallies, electoral contests, litigation [use of courts for political struggle])
Unconventional Politics	
II. Oppression (Manipulation of competitive electoral process, censorship, surveillance, harassment, discrimination, infiltration of opposition, (mis-) use of emergency legislation, suspension of constitution and civil liberties)	II. Nonviolent Action (Social protest for political persuasion of rulers and masses; demonstrations to show strength of public support; non-cooperation, civil disobedience, and other forms of nonviolent action)

Table 1.13 cont.

State Actor	*Non-State Actor*
	Violent Politics
III. Violent repression for control of state power	III. Use of violence for contestation challenging state power
III.1. Political justice (Political imprisonment)	III.1. Material destruction
III.2. Assassination	III.2. Assassination (Individuated political murder)
III.3. State terrorism (torture, death squads, disappearances, concentration camps)	III.3. Terrorism (de-individuated political murder)
III.4. Massacres	III.4. Massacres
III.5. Internal war	III.5. Guerrilla warfare
III.6. Ethnocide	III.6. Insurgency, revolution (if successful)
	State of War

2

THEORIES

If theory without policy is for academics, then policy without theory is for gamblers. *J. Mayone Stycos*

This is the only chapter of the *Research Guide* which has not been entirely rewritten for this second edition, because we have not seen enough theoretical development in the past three years to warrant a rewriting. Why has there been so little progress in theory formation? I contend that only when basic conceptual problems are better solved and when the data situation has improved--especially through comparative case studies[1]--can there be major theoretical progress. However, in order to leave the reader of the first edition with at least some added guidance, we have included as a postscript to this chapter a summary of the theory-related answers of our respondents to the second questionnaire.

INTRODUCTION

In our first questionnaire, we asked authors what they thought about the state of development of theories in the field of terrorism and offered them some possible answers (see Table 2.1).

Some of the respondents used very strong language under option F, such as "confused, garbage, irrelevant" (Morris), "confused and confusing, often intentionally" (Lador-Lederer), "hopeless" (Merari). Others noted that "Quantitative research based theory is in its infancy" (Gleason), that things were "coming along slowly" (Ochberg). One author thought that we are still in a state of pre-theory, without cumulativeness and without historical evidence (Crenshaw). Yet another author saw the present state of theory primarily in the sphere of propaganda rather than social science (Young).

Table 2.1. "How would you characterize the state of theory development in the field of political terrorism?"

Answer	*Number of mentionings**
a. Poor	12
b. One-sided, focusing on left-wing terrorism	9
c. One-sided, neglecting state terrorism	7
d. More policy-oriented than scientific	11
e. Not worse than in other areas of social science research	12
f. Other	8
g. No answer, don't know	4

* Some respondents marked more than one category.

Theories of terrorism are, with few exceptions, the result of work done in the past fifteen years. In the following pages, an attempt will be made to review part of this theoretical work with an emphasis on the theories that deal with the etiology of terrorism. It must be stressed from the beginning that the term "theory" is taken more in the sense of current thinking and interpretations than in terms of formal propositions that have been operationalized and tested empirically. Theories in the more rigorous sense of the term, with prognostic power, are nonexistent, as in many other branches of the social sciences.

TERRORISM AND POLITICAL VIOLENCE THEORY

In the 1960s, when counterinsurgency became a government preoccupation in the United States, a sizeable literature on political, collective, and civil violence emerged in answer to this demand, stimulated by a stream of governmental research grants. One of the best-known and most influential works from this period is Ted Gurr's *Why Men Rebel* (Princeton, NJ: Princeton University Press, 1970). In our first questionnaire, we asked authors which of the various theories on the occurrence of political violence they found helpful for understanding (insurgent) terrorism. Gurr's work was mentioned no fewer than eight times, more than any other author.[2]

In one form or another, the Gurr model frequently appears in discussions on the origins of terrorism. For instance, a paper prepared by the United Nations Secretariat, entitled "The Origins and Fundamental Causes of International Terrorism," proclaims:

> It thus appears that the "misery, frustration, grievance and despair" which lead to terrorism have many roots in international and national political, economic and social situations affecting the terrorist, as well as in his personal circumstances. The precise chain of causation of particular acts cannot be traced with scientific exactitude.[3]

The Gurr model is based on Freudian psychoanalysis and is derived from a conceptual framework developed by a group of Yale psychologists in the 1930s. Its principal originator was Dollard, although it has been considerably modified at later stages. Dollard and his Yale associates held:

> . . . that aggression is always a consequence of frustration. More specifically the proposition is that the occurrence of aggressive behavior always presupposes the existence of frustration and, contrariwise, that the existence of frustration always leads to some form of aggression.[4]

Building on these psychological foundations, the political scientist Gurr substituted relative deprivation (RD) for Dollard's frustration-aggression (FA), but also used the terms "deprivation," "discrepancy," and "frustration." In place of aggression, he refers to collective and political violence, and the frustration-aggression nexus applies for Gurr to both individuals and collectives.

The key term, "political violence," is very broad with Gurr, referring to "all collective attacks within a political community against the political regime, its actors--including competing political groups as well as incumbents--or its policies."[5] It not only includes riots and rebellions, but also coups d'état, guerrilla wars, and revolutions.

Gurr's thesis then is:

> "Relative Deprivation" (RD) is the term used . . . to denote the tension that develops from a discrepancy between the

> "ought" and the "is" of collective value satisfaction, that *disposes men to violence. . . .*[6]
>
> The frustration-aggression relationship provides the psychological dynamic for the proposed relationship between intensity of deprivation and the potential for collective violence. . . .[7]

While this model is also supposed to cover (small-scale) terrorism (which Gurr subsumes under "Conspiracy"), together with mutinies, coups d'état, politial assassinations, and small-scale guerrilla wars,[8] there is only one short direct index reference in Gurr's classic work to terrorism.[9] In an article written in 1976 and published in 1979 under the title "Some Characteristics of Political Terrorism in the 1960s," Gurr himself is not invoking RD or elaborating how frustration causes terrorism.[10] The F-A or RD thesis also lies at the basis of the work of many other political scientists (e.g., Davies and Feierabend and Feierabend).

Lee Seechrest commented in 1971: "It is amazing how many people in political science, sociology and anthropology have taken on the frustration-aggression hypothesis for their own use without realizing its still shaky status in psychology."[11]

As to the findings in the field on psychology on the reactive mechanistic F-A thesis, it has been noted by v. d. Dennen:

> More than two decades of research have shown that frustration does not invariably lead to aggression, that frustration can lead to non-aggression, that aggression can occur without frustration, that in some cultures aggression is not a typical response to frustration, that some situations (such as threat and insult) can evoke more aggression than frustration, that the injustice of frustration is more significant than frustration itself, that frustration subsumes a diverse set of conditions, and that the F-A linkage need not be innate and could be learned. The widespread acceptance of the F-A notion is perhaps attributable more to its simplicity than to its predictive power.[12]

Given these shortcomings of the F-A model in psychology, one wonders how much substance can be left after the switch from psychology to sociology, from individual to collective, from aggression to violence, and from frustration to deprivation has been made. At any rate, the operationalization problem of RD has never been satisfactorily solved, as Lawrence C. Hamilton, who made an interesting attempt to develop a synthetic theory of terrorism based on Gurr, has admitted:

"Relative deprivation itself is as elusive of measurement as the psychological state of frustration or beliefs about the effectiveness and justification of political violence."[13]

The expansion of the field to which the model purports to apply, ranging from individual bombing acts to the outbreak of the French Revolution, has also been a major problem.

With regard to terrorism, the RD model has nothing to say on the terrorism of regimes. Nor does it have much to say on the interesting phenomenon that many insurgent terrorists are of upper- and middle-class origin, rather than from the more deprived sectors of society. One of our respondents (M. Crenshaw) has written that she found theories of violence like Gurr's were not relevant to terrorism, and, in a more general vein, Paul Wilkinson has remarked that: "General theories of violence are remarkably unhelpful for the study of terrorism."[14]

While this writer happens to share this view, we nevertheless would like to offer the reader a chance to become acquainted with the work of Lawrence Hamilton, who made a rare effort to test empirically a synthetic theory of what he calls terrorism. In his dissertation, Hamilton took from Gurr's Strive Events Data Set from the period 1961-1970 the conspiracy events "assassinations," "political bombings," "small-scale terrorism," and "small-scale guerrilla war" and declared them to be within his own conceptual definition of terrorism.[15] With this--in our view very questionable--working definition, Hamilton set out to formalize a number of models which he labeled theories of terrorism. Hamilton discussed five such theories, and finally he set out to build a synthetic sixth one. These theories, which he labeled Theories A, B, C, D, and E, can be summarized in the following way:

Theory A: Misery and oppression inspire all types of civil unrest; insurgent terrorism is one of these. Once terrorism occurs, the police are provoked to counterattacks. Under the pressure of these counterattacks, the terrorists cannot hold rallies, make speeches, print newspapers, or otherwise continue political agitation among the masses without exposing both themselves and their supporters to almost certain arrest. However, this is precisely the sort of political work that is necessary to insure that the masses will support the rebels in their confrontations with the regime. Thus, by increasing repression, which in turn precludes political agitation, terrorism makes a successful revolution less likely. According to Hamilton, this is the view of Mao, Lenin, and Guevara on the subject of terrorism, minor disagreements notwithstanding.[16]

Theory B: Terrorism is caused by misery and oppression. Once it occurs, it provokes the regime to intensify oppression. The oppression alienates public support for the regime and increases sympathy for the rebels, who in turn are strengthened and encouraged to provoke the regime even further, and so on. Ultimately, the populace will side with the rebels and revolution will occur.[17] Hamilton lists Marighela as a proponent of this theory, together with the U.S. student leader Tom Hayden.

Theory C: Terrorism is caused by misery and oppression. Once it occurs, however, the government is induced to make reforms that directly remove some of the causes of terrorism. In particular, there is a reduction in the extent of government oppression. A lower level of oppression will, then, cause a lower level of future terrorism, which will reduce oppression even further, and so on. If for some reason initial terrorism failed to reduce oppression, then it might escalate until either reform occurred or the government was overthrown. This theory, which holds that terrorism is, in an important sense, self-reducing, is derived from Hyams.[18]

Theory D: In this view, terrorism is not typically the work of the poor and exploited; it is the work of the idle elites, particularly students and the intelligentia. It arises during periods of unparalleled affluence rather than desperate poverty. Furthermore, it is the most open, democratic, and liberal governments that are most afflicted. Affluence and freedom encourage, allow, or somehow produce terrorism. Once terrorism occurs, it leads to a decrease in freedom (increase in oppression). It also increases the probability of a military coup. Oppressive measures will eventually succeed in suppressing terrorism, thus decreasing the probability of revolution. Since the more oppressive society is relatively stable, prospects for moderate reform are also damaged.[19] Representatives of views containing elements of this chain of causation are, according to Hamilton, Moss, Clutterbuck, and Laqueur.

Theory E: Frustration (caused by relative deprivation), in combination with utilitarian justifications for violence (such as the relative strength of regime and rebel forces, degrees of external support for each, and the historical successes of past insurgencies) and normative justifications (violence as a learned, cultural response) stand at the basis of insurgent violence as well as conservative violence (vigilantism, punitive oppression by the government), the two of which are linked, indirectly, in a positive-feedback relationship. Unlike Theory B, there is no assumption that escalating violence will lead to revolution. This theory is based on some of the views expressed by Gurr, without encompassing the whole of Gurr's intervening variables.[20]

In his attempt to test a synthetic sixth theory of terrorism based on elements of the other five, Hamilton found that revolts were poorly predicted with this set of variables and that their causality was distinct from terrorism and oppression, which he found were linked to each other. Hamilton concluded on the basis of his multivariate analysis:

> 1. Is terrorism most likely under the most oppressive governments, or under the least oppressive? Other things being equal, it is more likely under the least oppressive.
>
> 2. Once terrorism arises, is government oppression more likely to increase or decrease? It is almost certain to increase either temporarily or permanently.
>
> 3. If oppression is increased, will that stimulate terrorism to increase as well? It will further stimulate terrorism *if* the terrorists survive the government countermeasures.
>
> 4. Does terrorism increase the probability of revolution? It increases the probability of wider violence, but apparently does not affect the likelihood of a successful revolution.[21]

Hamilton pointedly added that his findings "are inconsistent with the theoretical rationales most frequently offered to justify terrorism."[22] In his accompanying historical study of terrorism, he admitted that "the causes of terrorism are obscure," adding:

> It has risen among rich and poor, oppressive and relatively unoppressive societies. It has been used to promote causes with no popular support as well as causes endorsed by a large majority. And it has emerged to fight against the overwhelming forces of foreign invaders and has been used, by other invaders, as an extension of interstate war.[23]

Gurr, as noted earlier, also rearranged his old civil strife data. He took the same period as Hamilton (1961-1970) but used fewer countries (87 instead of 115), and his working definition was narrower, excluding small-scale guerrilla war. He took political bombings, kidnappings, and assassinations to constitute "terrorist activity," and carried out a set of bivariate analyses. His conclusions included insights such as:

> . . . the typical terrorist campaign was conducted by tiny groups and was short-lived. Their public motives were not notably different from those of groups using other unconventional methods of political action. More specifically, the perpetrators of terrorist activities seemed more often motivated by hostility towards particular policies and political figures than by revolutionary aspirations. Their actions were more often a social nuisance than a serious threat to life and property, more often a security problem than an imminent revolution.[24]

Such insights, interesting as they are, are quite detached from the original theoretical framework, the relative deprivation model. Gurr himself admitted that his findings for the 1960s did not allow generalizations on terrorism in the 1970s.[25] One could go further and say that the political violence theories from the 1960s, and the data generated to substantiate and test them, are often more of a hindrance than a help to understanding the current wave of insurgent terrorism.

COMMON WISDOM AND COMMON MYTHS ON TERRORISM

Theories usually consist of sets of interconnected propositions. If the interconnections are weak, we are left with isolated propositions. In a state of pre-theory, there are two kinds of propositions: propositions which state what the phenomenon to be studied is not, contrary to widespread assumptions, and propositions which state what a phenomenon positively is. A number of authors have offered such general propositions.

J. B. Bell, for example, offers us a list of points on which the common wisdom is polarized:

> 1. At the very beginning we face the definitional problem: "one man's terrorist is another man's patriot." . . .
>
> 2. Besides the definitional problem there is also the historical problem. Here the conclusion is that the present epidemic of terrorism is either *novel or not*. Some trace the long roots, ideological or tactical, of present day revolutionary terrorists back to the Black Hand or the People's Will or the Carbonari. . . . The advocates of novelty, however, point to differences in kind, not just degree. For one thing, our postindustrial society presents a spectrum of highly vulnerable nodes. . . . And those terrorists

who seek influence rather than to maim now have instant communication to hundreds of millions of people. . . .

3. One of the few firm conclusions emerging from the academic investigations is that *terrorism is the weapon of the weak, but it is a powerful weapon*. . . .

4. How important is terrorism? According to the conventional wisdom, *terrorism is either very important or it is very unimportant*. On the one end of the spectrum stand many of the Union Jack School, who see the terrorist threat as releasing highly undesirable forces within open societies; on the other end are those who insist that terrorism is counterproductive, ineffectual, and unimportant. . . .

5. It is a comfort to know that the common wisdom has accepted the fact that, however defined, terrorism (nonstate variant) *kills relatively few people (but has a great impact)*. . . .

6. Again the specialists have concluded that the "new" terror is either a *transient trend or a growth industry*. . . .

7. In this connection *terrorists are likely to be more effective or else they may not*. . . .

8. What kind of person is the terrorist? *The terrorist is either a psychotic fanatic beyond accommodation or he is a rational rebel*. . . .

9. Then, it is agreed that while nothing can really be done about terrorism in an open society, something must. *The problem is that there is no solution.*[26]

A different set of propositions is offered by Walter Laqueur, one of the most cited authors in the field. He provides a list of seven myths on terrorism:

1. Political terror is a new and unprecedented phenomenon. . . .

2. Terrorism is left-wing and revolutionary in character. . . .

3. Terrorism appears whenever people have genuine, legitimate grievances. Remove the grievance and terror will cease. . . .

4. Terrorism is highly effective. . . .

5. The importance of terrorism will grow enormously in the years to come as the destruction power of its weapons increases. . . .

6. Political terrorists are more intelligent and less cruel than "ordinary" criminals. . . .

7. Terrorists are poor, hungry and desperate human beings.[27]

M. Stohl gives us this list of "eight pervasive myths":

1. Political terrorism is the exclusive province of anti-governmental forces.

2. The purpose of political terrorism is the production of chaos.

3. Political terrorism is the province of madmen.

4. Political terrorism is criminal activity.

5. All insurgent violence is political violence.

6. Governments always oppose nongovernmental terrorism.

7. Terrorism is exclusively a problem relating to internal political conditions.

8. Political terrorism is a strategy of futility.[28]

A different set of hypotheses has been put forward by the Italian political scientist L. Bonanate:

1. Terrorism is a response to the violence of institutions.

2. Terrorism is the desperate (or fanatical) choice of those who lack the patience of the revolutionary.

3. The disintegration of society provokes the formation of terrorist groups.

4. Each terroristic phenomenon has peculiarities which make it incomparable.

5. The global diffusion of terrorism is caused by international conspiracies.

According to the author, all of these hypotheses, except the fifth, could possibly form part of a tentative general interpretation of the significance of terrorism in the contemporary world.[29] Strangely enough, however, it is that fifth hypothesis which is currently one of the most popular and influential in certain political circles, at least in the United States (see Conspiracy Theories of Terrorism, p. 101).

Wilkinson offers us five propositions about "terrorism in a revolutionary context"; the first three are taken from B. Crozier, while the last two are Wilkinson's own generalizations derived from comparative analysis of terrorist movements:

1. Terrorism is generally "the weapon of the weak."

2. It is usually a useful auxiliary weapon rather than a decisive one.

3. Revolutionary terrorism seems to be a strategy most suited to national liberation struggles against foreign rulers used by relatively small conspiratorial movements lacking any power base.

4. Terrorism is highly unpredictable in its effects.

5. Terroristic violence can escalate until it is uncontrollable, with terrible results for society.[30]

Such hypotheses and propositions constitute the basic wisdom in the field. As Bell points out, the minds are divided on several of them and none is properly tested (if it is possible to test them). The originators probably had specific cases in mind when proposing these hypotheses, and the hypotheses might very well hold true for those cases. But those cases themselves might be exceptions to the rule--if there is a rule or law.

Given the absence of a delimitation of the concept of terrorism, it is not surprising that theorizing also shows deficiencies, because the instances of political violence subsumed under the label of terrorism vary.

THEORIES OF REGIME TERRORISM

Terrorism by regimes has a longer history than insurgent terrorism; from this one might expect that theory formation is more advanced and that the number of available theories is greater. But that is not so. Except for the writings on totalitarianism, there is not much to fall back on. Totalitarian states--which have been characterized by the presence of a leader, subversion of the rule of law, control of the private sector, the permanent mobilization of the population, and legitimation through massive popular support--rule not only through terrorism exercised by the state apparatus but also through the party and the official ideology.[31] The link between totalitarian rule and terrorism is in all likelihood much weaker than portrayed by Hannah Arendt, who wrote:

> The extraordinary bloody terror during the initial stage of totalitarian rule serves indeed the exclusive purpose of defeating the opponent and rendering all further opposition impossible; but total terror is launched only after this initial stage has been overcome and the regime no longer has anything to fear from the opposition. In this context it has been frequently remarked that in such a case the means have become the end, but this is after all only an admission, in paradoxical disguise, that the category "the end justifies the means" no longer applies, that terror has lost its "purpose," that it is no longer the means to frighten people.[32]

Arendt, together with Walter and Aron, was one of the authors mentioned more than once in response to our question on the first questionnaire, "Which of the current theories explaining the rise of (various types of) *state terrorism* do you find worthwhile to be subjected to empirical testing?" However, more than half of the respondents either left this question unanswered, answered "none," or said they did not know.[33]

In the following pages we will briefly present the work of Walter, leaving aside Arendt and Aron. In addition, we will point to the studies of Dallin and Breslauer, de Swaan, and Duvall and Stohl.

Eugene V. Walter's *Terror and Resistance* (New York: Oxford University Press, 1969) is an exceptionally original study based on empirical case studies of some tribal African communities. The author attempts to find out why rulers who already have authority nevertheless choose to rule by violence and fear. Unlike some of the authors on totalitarianism, he does not identify organized terror with systems of total power, which, given Walter's nineteenth century data of successive Zulu rulers, is a fallacy more easily avoided than would have been the case with twentieth century subjects. While Walter claimed that his "inquiry is the first systematic effort to develop a general theory of terrorism,"[34] he admitted that his explanations do not cover every typical regime of terror: ". . . revolutionary governments and totalitarian systems, for example, introduce factors that are beyond the scope of the first volume."[35] Unfortunately, Walter never published the promised second volume, in which he wanted to "pursue the analysis in other social conditions and explore the intellectual history of the idea of terror as well as its psycho-dynamics."

Walter's book was a pioneering effort, given that, as he put it, "Rule by terror, a familiar process in history, has virtually escaped systematic analysis."[36] As such, the conclusions he reached about the conditions necessary for the maintenance of a terroristic regime, which he also saw as functional prerequisites for a regime of terror, may not strike the reader as very far-reaching. However, the conditions he lists as necessary for a rule by terror at least show some interdependence which other propositions of terrorism lack. They are:

1. There must be a shared ideology that justifies the violence.

2. The victims in the process of terror must be expendable; that is, their loss cannot affect the system of cooperation.

3. Both the agents and the victims of violence must be dissociated from ordinary social life.

4. Terror must be balanced by working incentives that induce co-operation.

5. Cooperative relationships must survive the effect of the terror.[37]

Seeing terrorism as a "social invention and a political choice within a range of alternatives" by which a regime may overcome the threat of resistance and secure cooperation,[38] Walter's study in fact offers a wealth of insights and is probably the most detached book ever written on terrorism.

A. Dallin's and G. W. Breslauer's *Political Terror in Communist Systems* (Stanford: Stanford University Press, 1970) was published almost simultaneously with Walter's work. Dallin and Breslauer studied, among other things, the Red Terror of the Russian Civil War period (1918-1920) and the Great Terror of the purges in the Soviet Union in the 1930s. Their use of the term "terror" is broader than Walter's. For Walter, all terror is violence designed to control, while for Dallin and Breslauer, terror does not necessarily include violence but can consist of intimidation only. They see political terror as a coercive instrument to effect political control. In their view, there are three systems of sanctions: (1) "normative power," or "positive" or "symbolic" power, commonly called persuasion, and including socialization, education, and the offer of prestige, recognition, or love; (2) "material power," or "technical" or "utilitarian" power, commonly called incentives, and including such forms as wages, rewards, bonuses, bribes, and promotions; and (3) "coercive power," or "negative" or "physical" power, commonly called coercion, and including such forms as fines, penalties, terror, and regulatory and police power.[39] In their study they try to find an answer to the question of when a (Communist) government resorts to terror. They postulate that a Communist party which comes to power by revolution usually lacks the normative and material resources to ensure obedience from the citizens and to satisfy the followers. The turmoil of revolution diminishes the country's material output and the revolutionary ideology as a normative control instrument has yet to be implanted in the masses. With the limited availability of material and normative incentives, the resort to coercion in general and terror in particular in order to eliminate or neutralize resistance becomes mandatory for the survival of the regime. Terror is in fact a sign of the weakness of the regime, as can also be deduced from such a remark as that of Dzerzhinski, the head of the Checka, who was quoted as saying that "the proletariat takes up this weapon [of terror] only when it cannot do without it."[40]

The variations in the amount of terror exercised by Communist regimes after the seizure of power is explained by Dallin and Breslauer with a reference to the pre-takeover conditions:

> If, on the other hand, prior to the takeover of the central government the revolutionary movement is successful in gaining a fair measure of popular support, in penetrating the administrative-organizational system of the country, and in gaining the upper hand over alternative organizations and authorities--whether by guerrilla warfare against domestic or foreign enemies (China, Yugoslavia, Albania) or by administrative manipulation, through front organizations, party and police operations, or other backstage moves (Czechoslovakia, Hungary)--then there is correspondingly less "need" for terror (and no civil war) after the takeover of the central government. The

> equivalent function of terror at this stage will have been substantially fulfilled prior to takeover.[41]

Dallin's and Breslauer's study does not, however, manage to explain the Great Terror of 1936-1939, in which about seven million Russians were said to have been arrested, including half the officer corps of the Red Army, and in which more than two-thirds of the members of the Central Committee, as well as countless others, were liquidated.[42] Yet the authors had to start almost from scratch in their investigation. "We soon discovered," they wrote in their preface, "to our surprise, that the theoretical literature on political terror was not nearly so well developed as we had expected."[43]

Given the ubiquity of rule by terror, the uneven attention given by social scientists to regime terrorism in contrast to insurgent terrorism is depressing. The fact that anti-Communists write on terrorism in Communist regimes and that leftish authors write on terrorism in capitalist societies produces such distortions as the near-automatic linking of the socio-economic system to state terrorist practices. While Dallin and Breslauer are aware of this danger and Walter, because of his subject of inquiry, is removed from it, much of the literature on totalitarianism is poisoned by it.

One study which is not so poisoned is "Terror as a Government Service,"[44] Abram de Swaan's short but highly interesting theoretical sketch of regimes of terror. De Swaan sees torture as a linchpin of such regimes. He observes:

> . . . wherever torture is being practiced on a large scale and over a period of time, the external effects of the system turn out to be foremost: to spread an ever-present fear, of arrest, of ill-treatment, of mutilation, of betrayal, of death. The purpose of all this is that people will ask themselves with every action whether their deeds do not create risks for themselves and for the people around them, that they will not just abstain from what is forbidden, but will avoid whatever has not expressly been allowed. They really most continuously try to imagine what the rulers would want them to do, they must become vicarious rulers for themselves. Only then the completion of the terrorist regime has been achieved.[45]

De Swaan goes on to note that every regime of intimidation and deterrence entails two fundamental contradictions: (1) the contradiction between publicity and secrecy in the practices of intimidation, and (2) the contradiction between predictability and uncertainty as to prosecution and punishment.

With regard to the first contradiction, de Swaan notes:

> This twilight zone is the essential mark of terrorist regimes. This must be so, because, if the existence and manner of operation of the terror apparatus were the subject of public debate, then the citizens would inevitably try the terrorist practices against the confessed ideals of the regime. But if the methods would remain completely unknown, then they would not achieve their intimidating effects. Thus, the system of terror works through a steady system of rumours, through private conversations and personal networks. This has been conceived of as the devilish shrewdness of the set-up: whoever mentions it, himself thereby collaborates with the reign of terror.[46]

It is this internal contradiction, incidentally, which lies at the basis of the success of Amnesty International.

On the second contradiction, de Swaan remarks:

> If everyone would know (for certain) what acts would lead to arrest and torture and which would go unpunished, most people would refrain from the first and, without worrying, commit the others. But the purpose of an intimidation apparatus is precisely to impose so much fear in people that of their own account they will abstain from things that otherwise would be hard for the regime to detect or prevent. Not even a police state can always keep under surveillance all people in all their doings. And because the regime cannot enforce its own commands and prohibitions, fully or even partially, it must create a negative game of chance, which leaves it to the citizens to avoid the risks. Herein lies the unavoidability of a system of prosecution and correction to be unpredictable. . . . In terrorist regimes the unpredictability concerns what may or may not be punished and in the often extreme severity of punishment. Yet, this uncertainty cannot be without limits: if nobody knows anymore what will lead to arrest or ill-treatment, anxious abiding would lose all sense, subjects would become careless or even daring. The point is, therefore, to present the citizens with just enough indications to make them ask themselves continuously what the intentions of the regime are, just enough cues to reconstruct for themselves the desires of the rulers.[47]

This ambivalence has been addressed as well by the Russian writer Ilya Ehrenburg, who wrote of Stalin's terror of the 1930s: "The fate of men was not like a game of chess, but like a lottery."[48]

The last theory we would like to mention has been developed by R. Duvall and M. Stohl.[49] They look beyond the totalitarian state and attempt to find a theory that fits state terrorism in the First World (the developed capitalist states) and the Second World (the socialist countries), as well as the Third World (the developing countries). To accommodate the tremendous variations in the extent, scope, and targeting in these three different settings (see Table 2.2), they had to find a very general model of explanation. They found it in the "Expectancy X Value" theory of motivation,[50] which uses an "expected utility" model. They write:

> The principal feature of this type of model is the assumption that an actor behaves in accordance with a basic rule which consists of three main elements: (1) the benefits, personally defined, that the actor would get from some desired state of affairs; (2) the actor's belief about the probability with which the desired state of affairs would be brought about if the actor were to engage in a particular action; and (3) the actor's belief about the probable costs, or negative consequences, that it would have to bear as a result of its engaging in that action.
>
> A concept of expected reward, or expected utility, is defined from these three elements. It is $U_i = p_iB-C_i$, where U_i is expected utility from engaging in action i, B is the benefit gotten from the desired state of affairs, p_i is the believed probability with which action i will bring about the desired state of affairs, and C_i is the believed probable costs from engaging in action i. In its conventional form, the rule of behaviour is that an actor engages in that action i for which U_i is greatest among the set of variables.[51]

Readapting this rule, they hold that the probability that an actor will engage in an action i increases monotonically with increases in U_i relative to U_j, where j are all alternative actions, including inaction. On the basis of this, they set out to determine the preconditions, or factors p_t, C_t, p_j, and C_j, which explain or predict the recourse to state terrorism if the model is realistic. From this they derive the following principle for a theory of state terrorism:

> If terrorism is to be believed to be a relatively more effective means of governance, then, the government must estimate that terrorism will perform better than alternative

means in eliminating or quieting some actual or perceived potential challenge or threat.[52]

Table 2.2. Major Aspects of Contextual Variation in State Terrorism, According to Duvall and Stohl.[53]

Context	*State Terrorism Used*	*Social Scope of State Terrorism*	*Characteristics of Target Population*
First World	Some, but generally little.	Very limited.	Socially isolated groups, distrusted by the general population.
Second World	Previously extremely high; now relatively little.	Previously pervasive; now quite limited.	Previously nonrevolutionary classes and members of revolutionary party; now dissident intelligentsia.
Third World	Quite variable, but very high in many societies.	Pervasive where it occurs extensively.	Potential political opposition in general, especially "the left" as amorphous category.

Duvall and Stohl find that their model is able not only to explain why weak governments engage in terrorism (for this, the Dallin and Breslauer explanation for the Red Terror of the period 1918-1920 is also a satisfactory explanation), but they also manage to solve the seeming paradox why a strong regime in a situation of confident strength can also find it attractive to engage in terrorism.

The thrust of their explanation for the "weak" state terrorist lies in the believed *relative* effectiveness of terrorism which depends less on the perception of terror as highly efficacious but in the belief that other available means of rule are quite *inefficacious*.[54] Strong states, on the other hand, are likely to engage in terrorism, according to Duvall and Stohl, when they are reclusive states with low vulnerability to international pressure and domestic retribution or when they show features of either a *militaristic-state* or an *ideological-mission* syndrome. They write:

> This is the syndrome of the policy with highly developed informational and organizational networks through which the regime penetrates society, and in which the government perceives itself in actual or potential conflict with some socially marginal group that is poorly integrated into . . . the rest of society. In this syndrome, one would expect state terror to be limited in scope and generally of fairly low intensity--sufficient only to "win" the conflict with the marginal social group. At the same time, one would expect terror in this situation to be used more regularly, and perhaps with greater intensity, by governments who have learned its utility for rule through past experience.[55]

The model which these authors sketch, in which the expected relative effectiveness, the expected costs of producing terrorism, and the expected response costs to terrorism are key variables, can in principle also be applied to explanations of insurgent terrorism, as Duvall and Stohl point out,[56] but only if terrorism remains a rational strategy with predictable results. As to the latter, it is perhaps worthwhile recalling that Stalin in effect admitted later that the Great Terror exceeded in scope what he had planned.[57]

This brings us to the question of whether the terrorists themselves have a theory.

TERRORIST THEORIES OF TERRORISM

Brian Jenkins has written in his article "International Terrorism: A New Mode of Conflict": "There is a theory of terrorism, and it often works. . . . Unless we try to think like terrorists we are liable to miss the point. . . ."[58] What this theory is Jenkins fails to make explicit, unless we take his following section on "The Purposes of Terror" as explaining the "theory." But the point Jenkins makes is well taken. The acts of violence do not stand by themselves but form part of a strategy, however rudimentary. Take for instance the statement of a student involved in the November 1979 occupation of the U.S. Embassy in Tehran. The U.S. Marines guarding the embassy did not use their weapons when the storming took place, something which the right-wing students could not be certain of beforehand. About the gamble they took, one of them commented: "If the Marines don't shoot, we take over. If they do, we have our martyr. Either way, we win." This statement is reminiscent of a dictum of the Russian terrorist Stepniak: "The terrorist is beautiful, terrible and irresistably fascinating because he reunites two types of human grandeur: the martyr and the hero."[59] One of the commanders of the so-called "Stern gang" which fought the British in Palestine in the 1940s wrote: "A man who goes forth to kill another whom he does not know must believe only one thing--that by his act he will change the course of history."[60]

The Russian terrorists of the late 1870s and thereafter were the first to develop a "theory" of terrorism. In the party program of the Narodnaya Volya ("People's Will") of 1879, the terrorist strategy was outlined in this manner:

> Terroristic activity, consisting in destroying the most harmful person in the government, in defending the party against espionage, in punishing the perpetrators of the notable cases of violence and arbitrariness on the part of the government and the administration, aims to undermine the prestige of the government's power, to demonstrate steadily the possibility of struggle against the government, to arouse in this manner the revolutionary spirit of the people and their confidence in the success of the cause, and finally, to give shape and direction to the forces fit and trained to carry on the fight.[61]

In the following year, Nicholas Morozov, a theorist of Narodnaya Volya, published a "theory" of terrorism, wherein he stated:

> . . . terroristic struggle has exactly this advantage that *it can act unexpectedly* and find means and ways which no one anticipates. All that the terroristic struggle really needs is a *small number of people* and large material means. This presents really a new form of struggle. It replaces by *a series of individual and political assassinations*, which always hit their target, the massive revolutionary movements, where people often rise against each other because of misunderstanding and where a nation kills off its own children, while the enemy of the people watches from a secure shelter and sees to it that the people of the organization are destroyed. The movement punishes

> only those who are really responsible for the evil deed. Because of this the terroristic revolution is the only just form of revolution. At the same time it is also the most convenient form of revolution Using insignificant forces it had an opportunity to restrain all the efforts of tyranny which seem to be undefeated up to this time. "Do not be afraid of the Tsar, do not be afraid of despotic rulers, because all of them are weak and helpless against *secret, sudden assassination*," it says to mankind. Never before in history were there such convenient conditions for the existence of a revolutionary party and for such successful methods of struggle.[62]

Stepniak, another theorist of the Russian Underground, writing more than a decade later, made less exaggerated claims for the new method of combat, but nevertheless saw it as an effective asymmetric strategy:

> In a struggle against an invisible, impalpable, omnipresent enemy, *the strong is vanquished not by arms of his own kind*, but by the continuous exhaustion of his own strength, which ultimately exhausts him, more than he would be exhausted by defeat. . . . The terrorists cannot overthrow the government, cannot drive it from St. Petersburg and Russia; but having compelled it, for many years running, to neglect everything and to do nothing but struggle with them . . . they will render its position untenable.[63]

While power in Tsarist Russia was concentrated in a few hands, the diffusion of authority in West European and American societies probably also led to a widening of the potential targets of terroristic violence.

The disappearance of discrimination in target selection becomes even more pronounced in cases of state terrorism. Martin Latsis, a leading Cheka official, reflects this in the following statement:

> Do not seek in your accusations proof whether the prisoner has rebelled against the soviets with guns or by word. You must ask him, first, what class he belongs to, what his social origin is, what his education was, and his profession. The answer must determine the fate of the accused. That is the meaning of Red Terror.[64]

To hold individuals responsible for the deeds of their group or class without looking at the personal involvement of the target of terroristic violence leads to vicarious intimidation if the "punishment" meted out against one or a few becomes known.

In a sense, the use of torture by governments also serves the same function. While torture is connived in or defended mostly as "a minor intensification of interrogation practices,"[65] its latent meaning often becomes the frightening and intimidation of the population or certain sectors of the population. Amnesty International has collected many examples of evidence which show that torture is consciously used to inculcate a climate of fear in order to discourage dissent. One Amnesty International report states:

> For those who govern without the consent of the governed this [torture] has proved to be an effective means of maintaining power. To set torture as the price of dissent is to be assured that only a small minority will act. With the majority neutralized by fear, the well-equipped forces of repression can concentrate on an isolated minority.

The Amnesty report on torture makes reference to a victim of the Greek Colonels, whose interrogator told the victim that he should tell people he was being tortured so that "all who entered military police quarters would tremble."[66]

This element of meting out cruel treatment against one to produce reverberations with others we find both in state terrorism and insurgent terrorism. An example from the other side would be the hanging of two British soldiers from a tree by Irgun terrorists, which demoralized all British soldiers in Palestine. Menachem Begin, the Irgun leader, later commented on the effects of such needlepoint attacks: "In the end, the nervous system of the British resembled an old broken piano. It was sufficient to attack one camp to make all others resound from fear, day and night."[67] After another attack on the King David Hotel, which was blown up by explosives smuggled into the British headquarters in milk cans, the mere sight of a milk can could evoke suspicion and fear.[68]

The same kind of tactics--perhaps a shade more indiscriminate--was also encountered by the British in Cyprus, where General Grivas started the struggle for independence with a small group of insurgents. He defended the primarily terroristic form of struggle in these words:

> The truth is that our form of war, in which a few hundred fell in four years, was more selective than most, and I speak as one who has seen battlefields covered with dead. We did not strike, like the bomber, at random. We shot only British servicemen who would have killed us, if they could have fired first, and civilians who were traitors or intelligence agents. To shoot down your enemies in the street may be unprecedented, but I was looking for results,

> not precedents. How did Napoleon win his victories? He took his opponents in the flank or rear; and what is right on the grand scale is not wrong when the scale is reduced and the odds against you are a hundred to one.[69]

With such strategy--which incidentally was less discriminating than this apologetic passage makes the reader believe--the few hundred EOKA fighters managed to tie down 30,000 British troops for four and one-half years, killing 600 and wounding 1,300 on both sides before independence from Britain was achieved. The second terrorist campaign of the EOKA-B in the early 1970s--this time for *enosis*, union of the island with Greece--badly backfired, producing 280,000 Cypriot refugees when the Turkish army intervened.[70]

The practice of urban guerrilla warfare in Latin America has also shown increasing elements of terrorism. While Ché Guevara had rejected terrorism in all but his Bolivian writings because he believed that "terrorism is of negative value, that it by no means produces the desired effects, that it can bring a loss of lives to its agents out of proportion to what it produces,"[71] Carlos Marighela, the Brazilian Communist, thought differently. In his *Mini-Manual* he states:

> There are two main ways in which revolutionary organizations can grow. One is through propaganda and ideology--by convincing people and arguing over documents and programmes. . . . The other way . . . is not through proselytism but by unleashing revolutionary action and calling for extreme violence and radical solutions. . . . Since our way is through violence, radicalism and terrorism (the only effective weapons against the dictators' violence), anyone joining our organization will not be deluded as to its real nature and will join because he has himself chosen violence. . . .
>
> The basic principle of revolutionary strategy in a context of permanent political crisis is to unleash, in urban and rural areas, a volume of revolutionary activity which will oblige the enemy to transform the country's political situation into a military one. The discontent will spread to all social groups and the military will be held exclusively responsible for failures. . . .
>
> When we use revolutionary terrorism we know that such activities alone will not win us power. All acts of revolutionary terrorism, punishment of spies or sabotage are tactical operations designed to demoralize the authorities and North American imperialism, reduce its capacity for repression, break its communication system,

> and damage the government, supporter of latifundio property. Revolutionary terrorist acts and sabotage are not designed to kill members of the common people, or upset or intimidate them in any way. The tactic of revolutionary terrorism and sabotage must be used to combat the terrorism used by the dictatorship against the Brazilian people.[72]

The allegation made by Marighela that the terrorist acts were not meant to upset or intimidate the common people was hypocritical since his strategy depended on the state reaction against common people, and he admits this in another passage: "The government has no alternative except to intensify repression. . . . [The] problems in the lives of people become truly catastrophic. . . . In their vain attempt to prevent revolutionary activity through violent laws, the enemy has become more cruel than ever, using police terror indistinguishable from that used by the Nazis. . . . In such a climate our revolution is gaining ground."[73] The counterterrorism of the government in this way becomes an integral part of the terrorist strategy. This dual function of terrorism--propaganda for the masses on the one hand, and repression, or extra repression, of the masses by the adversary to force them to become participants on the other--we also find by the numerous imitators of the Latin American urban guerrillas. The West German Red Army Faction's theorist, Horst Mahler, later admitted:

> The strategy of the terrorist nuclei was aimed at provoking the overreaction of the state in the hope to stir the flames of hate against the state and to channel new recruits into the armed underground.[74]

The weakness of such a strategy in a noncolonial context is evident: the overreaction of the state and the siding of the masses with the terrorists are taken for granted. Overreaction can in fact crush the terrorist movement whether or not the masses side with the terrorists. Alternatively, the government might make some concessions that satisfy the masses but not the terrorists, and thus effectively separate the one from the other. The historical evidence does not bear out the simplistic theory of Marighela, the Tupamaros, and their imitators.

Trying to make a revolution with a bad theory or an outdated or inapplicable blueprint to bring about social change is not the exclusive privilege of urban terrorists in noncolonial or industrialized societies. Chalmers Johnson has offered the suggestion that each age has its own "revolutionary paradigm."[75] In his view, the Chinese model of the "People's War" was such a new paradigm. In the Latin American context, the Cuban experience produced the "foquismo" paradigm. Like the Chinese-style guerrilla war it was primarily a rural model, but in contrast to it "foquismo" did not postulate a liberated territory from which action against the power holder was to be conducted.

Urban guerrilla warfare evolved from the "foco" concept. The Guevara experience had shown that it was more difficult to mobilize the Latin American campesinos than the Chinese peasants. The urban setting, on the other hand, was much more familiar to middle-class revolutionaries. The growth of urbanization, with its dissatisfied new proletariat, together with the proximity of the enemy in the urban centers, made the temptation to rely on a predominantly urban strategy of insurrection great. In a way, it was a return to the classic insurrection strategy of the nineteenth century, a strategy which had failed in the Paris Commune. However, the increased fire-power of the urban guerrillas, together with the contemporary communications infrastructure and the anonymity of metropolitan life seemed to favor again this approach, all the more because the population density made the use of heavy weapons by the power holder impracticable. At the same time, the visibility of the armed actions of the insurgents is greatly increased in the cities.[76]

The urban scene imposed a number of rules on the armed men, such as secrecy, structuring in small cells, hit-and-run operations which in effect separated them from the masses. Their contact with the population was dependent to a large degree on the cooperation of the media. The freedom of the press, however, was one of the first things to go in the clash between the militants and the security forces. And with the arrival of censorship, the watchdog function of the media on governmental actions also ceased, allowing the power holders to engage in repressive crimes of a magnitude completely unexpected beforehand. Torture became the order of the day, and with the cell structure of the terrorist underground far from perfected, it was relatively easy to produce whole chain reactions of arrests following the capture of one terrorist. All those suspected as potential or actual sympathizers of the urban guerrilla had to endure governmental repression, and thousands of potential leaders from the trade unions, the universities, and the political parties were forced into exile. The masses did not rise, but either withdrew themselves into private life or went abroad. Driven by paranoia, hate, and despair, the urban guerrillas often lost sight of what they originally stood for. Abraham Guillén, one of the fathers of the "urban guerrilla" model, heavily criticized the Tupamaros, saying that they were "perilously close to resembling a political Mafia."[77] Referring to the killing of hostages, he held:

> In a country where the bourgeoisie has abolished the death penalty, it is self-defeating to condemn to death even the most hated enemies of the people. . . . The Tupamaros' "prisoners of the people" do more harm than benefit to the cause of national liberation. . . . Moreover, it is intolerable to keep anyone hostage for a long time. To achieve a political or propaganda victory through this kind of tactic, the ransom terms must be moderate and capable of being met; in no event should the guerrillas be pressed into executing a prisoner because their demands are excessive and accordingly rejected. A hostage may be usefully executed only when a government refuses to negotiate on any terms after popular pressure has been applied; for then it is evident to everyone that the government is ultimately responsible for the outcome.[78]

The question of *responsibility*, referred to in the above quotation, is often a central issue in the terrorist strategy. Terrorists "claim" or "take" responsibility for some acts of violence and deny or shift responsibility to the adversary in other cases. Take a statement like the following one from Leila Khaled, the notorious Arab skyjacker:

> If we throw bombs, it is not our responsibility. You may care for the death of a child, but the whole world ignored the death of Palestinian children for 22 years. We are not responsible.[79]

The implication is that the apathy of the whole world is to blame for the terrorists' violent actions and that if the world redresses the just grievances of the terrorists it will no longer be subjected to attacks of this nature.

This transfer of responsibility to other parties, which are only indirectly or not at all involved in their conflict, is a form of blackmail. Where hostages are threatened with death and their survival is made conditional upon the fulfillment of demands by a third party, this third party is placed in a no-win situation of either capitulating to terrorist demands or becoming, through inaction, an accomplice to murder.

Perhaps it was such a theory of compellance that Brian Jenkins had in mind when he wrote, as we quoted at the beginning of this chapter: "There is a theory of terrorism, and it often works." At any rate, if terrorists have a theory of blackmail, it might be worthwhile to put some thought into a "theory of whitemail," which would aim at attacking their strategy, rather than play the no-win role in their strategy.[80]

PSYCHOLOGICAL THEORIES

If it is assumed that nonviolent behavior in society is normal, then those who engage in violence, criminal or other, are necessarily "abnormal," deviating from the rules of society. Flowing from this assumption are the many theories that regard the terrorist as a peculiar personality with clearly identifiable character traits. An example of this approach in the preventive field has been the construction of a behavioral profile of the hijacker. This profile, developed by psychiatrists and social scientists on behalf of the U.S. Federal Aviation Administration, is still classified.[81]

If we look at profiles that are not secret, they strike us by their lack of details. Charles A. Russell and his associates, for instance, have constructed such a profile on the basis of information on some 350 known terrorists from eighteen different groups involving eleven nationalities:

> One can draw a general composite into which fit the great majority of those terrorists from the 18 urban guerrilla groups examined here. To this point, they have been largely single men aged 22 to 24, with exceptions as noted, who have some university education, if not a college degree. The women terrorists, except for the West German groups and an occasional leading figure in the IRA, JRA and PFLP, are preoccupied with support rather than operational roles. More often than not, these urban terrorists come from affluent, urban, middle-class families, many of whom enjoy considerable social prestige. Like their fathers, many of the older terrorists have been trained for the professions and may have practiced these occupations prior to their commitment to a terrorist life. Whether having turned to terrorism as a university student or later, most were provided an anarchistic or Marxist world view as well as recruited into terrorist operations while in the university. In the universities, these young products of an affluent society were confronted with and provided anarchistic or Marxist ideological underpinnings for their otherwise unstructured frustrations and idealism.[82]

While this is more a sociological than a psychological profile, some of the data assembled by Russell and Miller immediately raise fundamental psychological issues. How, for instance, can one explain the relatively prominent role of women in insurgent left-wing terrorism as compared to the smaller share of women in violent crime in general? In the cases of the German RAF and the June 2nd Movement, the women constituted one-third of the operational personnel. Nearly 60 percent of the known terrorists at large from these movements in 1976 were female.[83] This high percentage has been explained as being the result of the excesses of women's liberation on the one hand, and as an "excess of female (self) sacrifice" for a cause on the other.[84]

An interesting profile has been extracted from fifty biographies by the sociologist I. L. Horowitz. It takes the form of twelve propositions:

> 1. A terrorist is a person engaged in politics who makes little if any distinction between strategy and tactics on one hand, and principles on the other. . . .
>
> 2. A terrorist is a person prepared to surrender his own life for a cause considered transcendent in value. . . .
>
> 3. A terrorist is a person who possess both a self-fulfilling prophetic element and a self-destructive element. . . .
>
> 4. A terrorist is a person for whom all events are volatile and none are determined. . . .
>
> 5. A terrorist is a person who is (a) young; (b) most often of middle class family background; (c) usually male; and (d) economically marginal. . . .
>
> 6. A terrorist performs his duties as an avocation. . . .
>
> 7. The terrorist distinguishes himself from the casual homicide in several crucial respects: he murders systematically rather than at random; he is symbolic rather than passionate . . . and his actions are usually well planned rather than spontaneous. Terrorism is thus primarily a sociological phenomenon; whereas homicide can more easily be interpreted in psychological terms. . . .
>
> 8. The terrorist by definition is a person who does not distinguish between coercion and terrorism because he lacks access to the coercive mechanisms of the state.
>
> 9. A terrorist is a person who, through the act of violence, advertises and dramatizes a wider discontent. . . .
>
> 10. A terrorist believes that the act of violence will encourage the uncommitted public to withdraw support from a regime or institution, and hence

make wider revolutionary acts possible by weakening the resolve of the opposition.

11. A terrorist may direct his activities against the leadership of the opposition by assassinating presidents and power holders. . . . Other terrorists may direct their activities against the symbols of establishment and agencies. . . .

12. A terrorist does not have a particularly well-defined ideological persuasion.[85]

These observations will not strike the reader as psychological in the narrow sense of the term. We will list a number of more directly psychological theories in the following enumeration, which is rather summary and only intended to indicate the main thrust of a theory.

1. Inconsistent mothering plays a role in the making of a terrorist. (Jonas)[86]

2. Terrorists suffer from faulty vestibular functions of the middle ear, which correlates with a history of learning to walk late, dizzy spells, visual problems, and general clumsiness. (Hubbard)[87]

3. Grave political violence can be found especially in those countries where fantasies of cleanliness are frequent. (Frank)[88]

4. Terrorists are zealots who seek aggressive confrontations with authority in the name of social justice. Zealotry is thereby defined as "low rule attunement, high social sensitivity, and low self-awareness," and is contrasted to moral realism and moral enthusiasm as the two other basic moral attitudes. (Hogan)[89]

5. The terrorists (in Québec) generally reject the father and the values he represents, are impatient with the constitutional process and accepted morality, and combine an above-average intelligence with emotional immaturity. Their affective qualities seem to be replaced by instincts--sexual lust, craving for notoriety, and thirst for power. (Morf)[90]

6. Neither politics nor ideology makes terrorists: the politics of sex are more influential in terrorism than the politics of Mao, Trotsky, or Ho Chi Minh. It is just that the latter, as a rationalization, seems so much more respectable and the terrorist, above all, craves respect. (Cooper)[91]

7. Terrorism arises periodically when the persons who are predisposed to violent actions are stimulated more strongly than before. The contemporary epidemic of psychological disorders started in 1963 with the assassination of President Kennedy. Indicators of group unrest and violence as well as of mental disorders, drug addiction, criminality, etc., were rising before that time. Craze (délire, Wahn, rabbia), a cognitive disorder, is noticeable in the ideas which motivate and dominate terrorism. An epidemic of terrorism occurs when increasing numbers of action groups are constituted and held together and when they are capable of executing series of operations. (Possony)[92]

8. Terrorists show three main character traits: (a) Their handling of their own emotions is disturbed, which shows itself in fear to engage in real commitments. The fear of love leads them to choose violence. (b) Their attitude toward authority is disturbed, whereby a principally negative attitude toward the "old authorities" is combined with an uncritical subjection under the new counter-authorities. (c) They have a disturbed relationship with their own identity. Having failed to develop an identity of their own, they try to get one by the use of violence. (Salewski)[93]

9. Terrorism is an urge to destroy oneself and others born out of radical despair, a new form "disease unto death," which manifests itself by way of the inability to be part of the community, the loss of the capacity to understand reality, and an aimlessness due to "methodological atheism." (Kasch)[94]

10. Terrorism might in part be due to a failure of the socialization process, especially resulting from a lack of felt authority or an antiauthoritarian education. Education has to restrain, forbid, and suppress in order to adapt children to prosocial behavior. Education as it is presently practiced often favors the achievement of personal advantage which can result in blindness toward the community. The failure is not only one of the families but also of the universities and certain publishers who spread anarchist literature in cheap editions. (Schwind)[95]

11. Characteristic for the terrorist is the need to pursue absolute ends. The meaning of the terrorist act is localized in the violence. (The victim of the act is a sacrifice, and the ultimate sacrifice is oneself.) The social matrix which produced this kind of behavior

is one in which alienation, a sense of helplessness, and a general lack of purpose and personal worth are widespread. (Kaplan)[96]

12. The driving forces behind terrorism include these four: (a) the assertion of masculinity (or femininity in the case of women); (b) the desire for depersonalization, that is, to get outside or away from oneself, as a result of chronic lack of self-esteem; (c) the desire for intimacy; and (d) the belief in the magic of violence and blood. (Harris)[97]

13. Terrorists tend to resemble each other, regardless of their cause. Most of them are individuals for whom terrorism provides profound personal satisfaction, a sense of fulfillment through total dedication, to the point of self-sacrifice, a sense of power through inflicting pain and death upon other human beings. (Berger)[98]

14. Almost always, insecurity and risk-seeking behavior, and the suicidal intentions linked to it, are present in varying mixtures in the terrorist. Out of this insecurity arises the need for self-realization and ego-inflation. Thus, the interpersonal relations of terrorists are always disturbed, resulting in an instrumental use of the fellow human being. This deficiency is compensated by the strong dedication to the idealistic cause the terrorist purports to fight for. (Mulder)[99]

The chief assumption underlying most of these "theories" is that the terrorist is in one way or the other not normal and that the insights from psychology and psychiatry are adequate keys to understanding. Some terrorists are certainly psychotics, but whether all criminal and political terrorists fall under this lable is questionable. Some authors see little prospect in the search for the terrorist personality and question whether a profile analogous to the "authoritarian personality" is possible at all. Walter Laqueur, for instance, holds that the search for a "terrorist personality" is a fruitless one,[100] but a few pages earlier he notes that "Terrorists are fanatics and fanaticism frequently makes for cruelty and sadism."[101] Paul Wilkinson is also ambiguous. On the one hand, he maintains that "We already know enough about terrorist behaviour to discount the crude hypothesis of a 'terrorist personality' or 'phenotype',"[102] but at the same time he admits that "I do not believe we really understand much about the inner motivations of those who readily enunciated terrorist techniques."[103]

It seems certain that with the relatively limited empirical evidence presently available,[104] caution should be observed to declare "the terrorist" prematurely insane. There are, indeed, some intriguing pieces of evidence to the contrary. Psychiatrists who examined the sole surviving Japanese terrorist of the Lydda airport massacre certified that Koza Okamoto was absolutely sane and rational.[105] An examination of some members of the German Rote Armee Faktion by a German psychiatrist led him to the conclusion that they were "intelligent" and "humorous," and showed no symptoms of psychosis or neurosis and "no particular personality type."[106]

The possible nonexistence of a "terrorist personality" does not of course devalue a psychological approach to the problem of terrorism. It is a necessary complement to a sociological approach. Brian Crozier put it well when he said:

> . . . men do not necessarily rebel merely because their conditions of life are intolerable: it takes a rebel to rebel. Look at it another way: some men or groups of men will tolerate more than others. If one describes conditions of life as intolerable, one begs the question: "To whom?"[107]

Materials for an Identification Theory of Insurgent Terrorism

In the following pages we would like to offer some materials which in the view of this writer (a layman in the field of psychology) provide a psychological explanation for why some individuals choose terrorism. The theoretical concept utilized is one of *identification.* This term is used in social psychology to refer to the more or less lasting influence one person can exert on the behavior of another. The term has a variety of meanings in the literature.

For our purposes, we take as our point of departure a passage from Karmela Liebknecht, who bases herself on the work of Weinreich:

> Identification can mean at least two different things: a wish to become or remain like the other (individual or group), or a recognition of existing similarities, good or bad, between the self and the object of identification. In the first sense, the other (individual or group) represents highly valued qualities, and the issue is about the acquisition or preservation of these desired attributes. In the latter case, a person simply recognizes that the other (individual or group) shares the same desired or undesired qualities with his own experienced self.

> Correspondingly, the contrast of the first instance would be a negative identification, a desire to deviate as much as possible from the other person or group, who has many undesirable features. The contrast of the latter instance would denote only a recognition of differences, or a lack of identification. The difference between the two meanings of identification thus encompasses this difference between how people perceive things to be as opposed to how they would like them to be. The former meaning is an assessment of the present state of affairs, while the latter is connected to future goals and aspirations. Often enough these meanings tend, deliberately or not, to be mixed with each other. . . .
>
> In a definition of a person's overall identity both of these meanings of identification have to be incorporated: "A person's identity is defined as the totality of his self-construal, in which how he construes himself in the present expresses the *continuity between* how he construes himself as he was in the past and as he aspires to be in the future."[108]

With this in mind, we can return to the study of terrorism. There, the use of identification is generally confined to the "identification with the aggressor" as manifesting itself in the positive attitude some hostages show toward their captors, which has also been referred to as the "Stockholm syndrome." Yet other identification processes are at work as well. The tremendous public interest in acts of hostage taking seem to be due to the fact that most members of the audience identify with the fate of the victim and share his sufferings in an act of empathy. Yet not all members of an audience will automatically show compassion for the victim. Some will identify with the terrorist, because he represents for them the awful power of one who can destroy life at his whim. If the spectator considers the victim guilty, he may even derive pleasure from the victim's humiliation and suffering. Depending on the way the identification goes--with the victim or with the inflictor of pain--the attitudinal outcome may be either empathy or cruelty. The direction of the identification can be determined by several factors, but one or two key factors like class, race, nationality, or party can be decisive for the majority of spectators.

We can illustrate this by a reference to the assassinations of John F. Kennedy and Martin Luther King and the public reactions to them. Hearing that the (Democrat) Kennedy had been murdered in Dallas, 64 percent of the Democrats in a sample said that they "felt as if the whole world was caving in," while only 5 percent of the Republican voters in the sample had the same feeling. The violent death of the Negro leader in 1968 led 96 percent of the black people in the sample to say that they were "shocked, grieved, saddened or angry," while only 41 percent of the white people in the sample felt the same. Fifty-nine percent of the whites in the sample were indifferent or even had a feeling of satisfaction, which applied to only 4 percent of the black people. No less than 41 percent of the whites in the sample felt that King himself was to blame for his own death (because he started riots, etc.).[109] Such data indicate that a polarization is taking place in the audience, depending on whether the identification is weak or strong with the victim or perpetrator of violence. The media provide us daily with polarizing acts which make us more or less consciously take sides wherever conflict and violence along lines relevant to our own context occurs. The "good guy/bad guy" dichotomy, the "in group/out group" dichotomy, and a number of similar cleavages play a role in this. The strength of our emotional reaction to such a polarizing act depends on the psychological distance, the spatial distance, and other factors between the event and one's own situation. Identification with the aggressor can make us feel vicariously powerful, while identification with the victim can make us feel weak or revengeful.

This process of taking sides whenever a polarizing act occurs can stir some members of the passive audience so deeply that they emerge as actors themselves engaging in new polarizing acts. Leon Trotsky has given us a description of how in this way terrorists can be made:

> Before it is elevated to the level of a method of political struggle terrorism makes its appearance in the form of individual acts of revenge. So it was in Russia, the classic land of terrorism. The flogging of political prisoners impelled Vera Zasulich to give expression to the general feeling of indignation by an assassination attempt on General Trepov. Her example was imitated in the circles of the revolutionary intelligentsia, who lacked any mass support. What began as an act of unthinking revenge was developed into an entire system in 1879-81. The outbreaks of anarchist assassination attempts in Western Europe and North America always come after some atrocity committed by the government--the shooting of strikers or executions of political opponents. The most important psychological source of terrorism is always the feeling of revenge in search of an outlet.[110]

The role that vengeance based on identification with the victim can play *in the making* of the terrorist has also been stressed by M. Crenshaw and, with a reference to Fromm, by P. Wilkinson. What *keeps them going afterward* cannot be explained by revenge alone.[111]

A few more examples will stress the role of revenge:

- The beating of two anarchists by the police and their subsequent sentencing induced Ravachol to avenge these "martyrs of Clichy" by bombing the homes of judges and magistrates in 1892. In court he declared: "It has been my intention to terrorize in order to force the present society to pay attention to those who suffer."[112]

- The execution of Ravachol made him a martyr and a cult developed which led to further revenge acts, including the assassination of the French President Sadi Carnot by the Italian anarchist, S. Caserio, who was also taking revenge for the execution of Emil Henry for throwing a bomb in the Café Terminus of Gare St. Lazare in Paris in 1894.[113]

- The unprovoked killing of a student demonstrator on 2 June 1967 by a policeman during a visit of the Shah of Iran in Berlin (for which the policeman was not punished) created feelings of revenge in many participants and led to the naming of a group "June 2nd Movement." Michael Baumann, for instance, the author of *How It All Began*, sees in this episode a key experience which turned him into a terrorist.[114]

- Renato Curcio, the founder of the Italian Red Brigades, was, in all likelihood, converted to violence in reaction to the events of 2 December 1968 in Aola. Farm laborers held a procession and occupied the state highway leading to Siracusa. The police fired on them for twenty-five minutes, leaving two dead and many wounded, including some children.[115]

One of the most traumatic collective experiences crying for revenge in recent times was the slaughter of peasant people in Vietnam by the U.S. war machine. Horst Mahler, the co-founder of the German RAF, noted that the massacres in Vietnam and the passivity of the German government vis-à-vis the atrocities committed by its ally drove the RAF to resistance and revenge:

> It was our moralism which led us to terrorism. Many of us (in any case Ulrike Meinhof and Gudrun Enslin) came the same way. The German nation again was passive. How could we escape from the . . . society which once again

> mixed itself in a war: that of Vietnam? *We had nothing to identify with the West, so we identified with the Third World*. . . . From that time on we no longer felt like Germans; we were the fifth column of the Third World in Europe. . . .
>
> From now on we observed the simple antithesis: we were on this side, the police were on the other. We did not see by which lines of communication the people identified with the state.[116]

On another occasion Mahler said:

> He who also shows empathy with distant suffering will find revolutionary promises more plausible and will easier become morally exalted. The young life which is demotivated by a sense of the absurd seeks in the commitment to a revolutionary movement--and be it only as a Fifth Column of the militants in the Third World--the salvation from nihilism and desperation. . . . If you think of it, it is a terrible thing if you cannot identify with your own people. . . . However, "the heartbeat for the welfare of humanity," to use Hegel's phrase, "turns into the fury of self-conceit." These people have constructed their own--you might call it private--moral. Since I was part of them I know it. The world is bad, every day there is untold suffering, murder, killing. This we have to change. This can only be done by violence, which also causes victims; but all told it will cause fewer victims than the continuation of the present state of affairs.[117]

The switch from love for mankind to destruction of human beings is apparently facilitated by adolescents who find it difficult to identify with their fathers or their nations. Mahler admitted that he was ashamed of being a German at a very young age.[118] Arthur Koestler offers some useful insights for this context: "The longing to belong left without appropriately mature outlets, manifested itself mostly in primitive or perverted forms." The act of identification which enables us to empathize with others is also capable of leading to vicarious emotions, to anger and aggressiveness toward the apparent source of the misery of the person or group we have love and compassion for. Koestler adds:

> The total identification of the individual with the group makes him unselfish in more than one sense. . . . It makes him perform comradly, altruistic, heroic actions--to the point of self-sacrifice--and at the same time behave with ruthless cruelty towards the enemy or victim of the group. . . . In other words, the self-assertive behaviour of the

> group is based on the self-transcending behaviour of its members, which often entails sacrifice of personal interests and even of life in the interest of the group. To put it simply: the egotism of the group feeds on the altruism of its members.[119]

These remarks by Koestler, written in a different context, offer, in our view, some insights into the dynamics of a terrorist movement. This identification mechanism might also be helpful in explaining the high percentage of women and intellectuals in insurgent terrorism. It might be that women experience other people's suffering and humiliation more strongly than men, since they recognize it more easily in their own existence because of their domination in a male society. The sacrificial spirit which women manifest vis-à-vis their children might reinforce this. As to the intellectuals' role in revolutionary and terrorist movements--Lenin called terrorism "a specific kind of struggle practised by the intelligentsia"[120]--it might be that the middle- or upper-class terrorist has become alienated from his class by the very university education which his parents made possible. This leads him to search for a new reference group. Unwilling to take up the cause of his own class, he chooses another class or group for which he wants to care and by which he wants to be appreciated. His self-styled role as liberator of the masses and champion of another class's assumed interests is, however, not always accepted in gratitude by the people in need of "liberation." The experience of Ché Guevara in Bolivia is a case in point. In another case in Istanbul, members of the Turkish People's Liberation Army had kidnapped a fourteen-year-old girl and were engaged in a shootout with the police. One of the terrorists shouted to the watching crowd, "We are doing this for you." The crowd, however, showed little sympathy and subsequently attempted to lynch the single surviving terrorist.[121] That the crowd identified with the victim and not with the terrorists in this particular case was to be expected, given the age and sex of the victim, not to mention other, less concrete, reasons.

The strategy of insurgent terrorism involves the production of identification processes. The Brazilian urban guerrilla leader, Ladislas Dowbor, elaborated on this theme. Speaking in 1970, he said that political explanations did not create revolutionary consciousness of the population, but military actions could do this. While discontent among the population was widespread, the people "have not yet reached the stage of holding the system responsible." Terrorists therefore "attack the targets they [the people] consciously identify, their visible enemies--the farm overseer, or the shop foreman, or the landowner who throws squatters off his land. . . . [This] provokes a reaction of the system. . . . [We] provoke the army, the police, the press and the clergy into taking positions against us and in support of the visible enemy. It is then that the workers are able to identify the system as the enemy. . . ."[122]

While the insurgent terrorist wants the people to identify with him, he also makes use of the identification mechanism to bring home the terror to a target group by stimulating the identification between the instrumental victim and the victim's reference group. In his *Blueprint for Revolution*, R. M. Momboisse has stressed the role this identification process plays:

> Thus if the victim is a police officer or an occupying soldier, others belonging to that class will identify themselves as members of a marked group. This group will probably be both "terrorized" and subjected to disorientation effects.[123]

Identification, in this writer's view, is a key mechanism in the process of terrorism. How identification operates in a variety of contexts, how it is utilized to generate support, are questions that require attention.

The foregoing remarks should not be taken for more than they are intended to be, namely, an invitation by a layman to psychologists to look more closely at what might be a fertile area for theory building--more fertile, at any rate, than the search for the "terrorist personality."

TERRORISM AS SURROGATE WARFARE

Many authors see terrorism as a form of war. In the 1960s, terrorism was generally placed into the context of internal war. Today, terrorism is often treated as a form of international war, or rather, as its substitute. With the internationalization of national conflicts, the two often overlap. Col. Roger Trinquier had already noted in 1954 in his book *Modern Warfare* that:

> The goal of modern warfare is control of the population, and terrorism is a particularly appropriate weapon, since it aims directly at the inhabitant. In the street, at work, at home, the citizen lives continually under the threat of violent death. . . . The fact that public authority and the police are no longer capable of ensuring his security adds to his distress. . . . He is more and more drawn to the side of the terrorists, who alone are able to protect him.[124]

Another French author, R. Gaucher, was the first to suggest that the nuclear balance of terror, which made direct war between great powers more difficult, favored the rise of terrorism:

> The truth is, at a time when it is difficult to mobilize great masses of people without provoking a global conflict with irreparable damage, terrorism tends to become more and more a substitute for war.[125]

This thought was also reiterated by the British counterinsurgency specialist, Robert Thompson, who, however, used the term "revolutionary warfare," by which he meant a "form of warfare which enables a small ruthless minority to gain control by force over the people of a country and thereby to seize power by violent and unconstitutional means."[126] Thompson held:

> The great advantage of revolutionary war as an instrument of policy in the nuclear age was to be that it avoided direct [superpower] confrontation.[127]

Brian Jenkins, a Vietnam veteran who now heads the Rand Corporation's research on terrorism, has brought the concept of terrorism as surrogate warfare firmly into the literature of terrorism. Speculating about the future direction terrorism will take, he offered three scenarios: (1) an international conspiracy whereby all terrorists in the world are members of a single organization; (2) a move toward new weapons and mass destruction by, for instance, nuclear terrorism; and (3) surrogate war. About the latter, he wrote:

> A third possible trend is that national governments will recognize the achievements of terrorists and begin to employ them or their tactics as a means of surrogate warfare against other nations. . . . The alternative to modern conventional war is low-level protracted war, debilitating military contests, in which staying power is more important than fire power, and military victory loses its traditional meaning. . . . Terrorism, though now rejected as a legitimate mode of warfare by most conventional military establishments, could become an accepted form of warfare in the future. Terrorists could be employed to provoke international incidents, create alarm in an adversary's country, compel it to divert valuable resources to protect itself, destroy its morale, and carry out specific acts of sabotage. Governments could employ existing terrorist groups to attack their opponents, or they could create their own terrorists.[128]

What Jenkins postulated as a future possibility in 1975 has become increasingly plausible in the years since to a number of authors. Paul Wilkinson of the University of Aberdeen has noted:

> I believe the most significant underlying causes of the recent upsurge in international terrorism to be political and strategic. As has already been emphasized, international war has increasingly become a less attractive option for states in the nuclear age. There is the grave risk that limited war might involve intervention by one or more nuclear powers with the inevitable consequential dangers of escalation to the nuclear threshold and beyond. . . . But the effect of these strategic constraints is likely to be . . . that violence in the international system will increasingly take the form of guerrilla warfare and terrorism. . . . The Soviets have also encouraged their client states to share in the tasks of training, financing and assisting terrorist activity. . . . One of the major underlying political causes of terrorism, however, cannot be placed solely at the door of the Soviet Union or her allies. It is the Palestinian problem.[129]

The impossibility of normal war-waging in the present age is also one of the elements used by H. W. Tromp of the University of Groningen to explain the increase of political terrorism.[130] He finds it difficult to distinguish political terrorism from war on the basis of qualitative criteria:

> Terrorism as well as war constitutes a form of use of violence for political purposes, directed mainly at people who cannot defend themselves and who often are not even a party to the political conflict, the aim being to force the opposing party in the conflict to a certain behavior.[131]

Rather than viewing contemporary terrorism as a series of separate incidents, Tromp is inclined to see it as "surrogate warfare," "camouflaged war," or "war by proxy."[132] Tromp offers the suggestion that terrorism might have already partly taken over the place of classical warfare in the international system, that it might express a trend toward a "global civil war":

> It could be that it is a "Third World War" which has assumed the completely unexpected form of a "protracted warfare" by terroristic methods, but without clear front lines, without clear goals, and above all without two clearly distinguishable parties, a war which cannot be charted on a map since the parties are nonterritorial and their aim is also not the conquest of territory.[133]

The "Third World War" perspective, first developed in the French "guerre revolutionnaire" literature, has gained some support from many policy makers who are alarmed by Soviet activities in the area of détente. It blends into conspiracy theories of terrorism.

CONSPIRACY THEORIES OF TERRORISM

Terrorism, often characterized by dramatic actions staged by clandestine groups aiming at prominent targets whose connection to the professed conflict remains obscure to many, seems to lend itself particularly well to conspiracy theories. At the end of the nineteenth century, the press and some police chiefs were already speaking of a "great international Anarchist conspiracy," even though such a conspiracy did not exist. Individual anarchists, motivated as much by feelings of personal revenge and the wish to be in the limelight as by revolutionary dreams, bombed and assassinated with some regularity but with no instructions or co-ordination from an "anarchist party."[134]

It is tempting for police chiefs to blame acts they cannot prevent or solve on international forces because it will then appear that they are in fact engaged in a fight against a well-orchestrated campaign backed by foreign powers, which makes failure explicable and even forgiveable. In this vein, Francesco Cossiga, the then Italian Minister of the Interior, claimed that both right- and left-wing terrorism in Italy was part of an international movement.[135]

This perspective has also been increasingly adopted by people less in need of scapegoats. Walter Laqueur, chairman of the Research Council of the Center for Strategic and International Studies in Washington, D.C., and one of the most influential writers on terrorism, wrote in 1977:

> Modern terrorism, with its ties to Moscow and Havana, with its connections with Libya and Algeria, bears a certain resemblance to the anonymous character of a multinational corporation: whenever multinational enterprises sponsor patriotic causes, caution is called for. . . .
>
> Multinational terrorism reached its climax in the early 1970s, involving close cooperation between small terrorist groups in many countries, with the Libyans, the Algerians, the North Koreans and the Cubans acting as paymasters, suppliers of weapons and other equipment as well as coordinators. . . . The Soviet Union supported a number of terrorist movements such as some Palestinians and African groups and the exile Croats; mostly such assistance

> would be given through intermediaries so that its origins would be difficult to prove and any charges of complicity could be indignantly denied. . . . This new multinational terrorism was, however, for all practical purposes, surrogate warfare between governments.[136]

Other authors, such as Beres, Demaris, and Possony and Bouchey, carry this line of reasoning further. In 1978, for instance, Possony and Bouchey published *International Terrorism: The Communist Connection*,[137] in which they state:

> There is virtually no terrorist operation or guerrilla movement anywhere in the world today, whether communist, semicommunist or non-communist, from the Irish Republican Army to the Palestinian Liberation Organization to our own Weather Underground, with which communists of one sort or another have not been involved. This includes non-communist operations and movements, for communist parties and governments always stand ready to exploit disorder in Europe, the Middle East, Latin America and elsewhere, however and by whomever it is fomented. Because Moscow, Peking, Havana and other communist centers are linked to so many terrorist and guerrilla groups and organizations and because so many of the groups look to those centers not simply for support and assistance but also for ideological inspiration, the groups often seem to be connected to one another. They are certainly in cooperation with one another more and more, as if they constituted a Terrorist International controlled and directed by some central authority. *This study does not make that claim* because the facts do not warrant that conclusion. But it does recognize--and will show--that a significant degree of coordination of terrorist activities does exist, and that it is mainly communists who are doing the coordinating. Put differently, if communist governments and political groupings, of one ideological emphasis or another, were to cease terrorist activity and assistance, the present wave of international terrorism would be squashed.[138]

American congressional committees had looked for the nexus between terrorism and communism in the first half of the 1970s, and by the early 1980s this connection had become the official view of the White House and the U.S. Department of State, and was echoed on Capitol Hill. S. T. Francis, for instance, a national security and intelligence analyst working for a U.S. senator, published a book titled *The Soviet Strategy of Terror*,[139] in which he states:

> Some terrorism is indeed carelessly planned and executed by amateurs or mentally unstable elements, but the kind of terrorism that has become a threat to the public order of Western societies--the kind of terrorism that the Soviets and their allies support--is not. . . . The Soviets, of course, do not generally call terrorism by that name; they refer to it as "armed struggle," "guerrilla war," or "liberation struggle."
>
> The small terrorist cadres that have existed in Western Europe for the last ten years are not under formal Soviet control either, and their ideologies are often at odds with Soviet orthodoxy yet . . . there is considerable evidence to indicate many clandestine links between these terrorists and the Soviet, East German, Czechoslovak, or Cuban intelligence services as well as with Libyan and Middle Eastern surrogates. . . . [The] European terrorist network, then, may not be under Soviet control, but certainly it appears to be in de facto alliance with the Soviet Union and its satellites.[140]

Francis goes on to quote approvingly a leading figure at the Georgetown University Center for Strategic and International Studies, the former deputy director of the CIA, Ray S. Cline, who held:

> What they [the Soviets] do is supply the infrastructure of terror: the money, the guns, the training, the background information, the communications, the propaganda that will inspire individual terrorist groups.[141]

The breakthrough of the Soviet conspiracy theory occurred with the publication of Claire Sterling's book, *The Terror Network: The Secret War of International Terrorism* (New York: Holt, Rinehart and Winston, 1980), which became a bestseller in Italy (where the author has worked as a U.S. foreign correspondent since the 1950s), as well as in other countries, most notably the United States. Secretary of State Alexander Haig even distributed excerpts from it to a congressional committee. Haig, who blamed the U.S.S.R. publicly "for training, funding and equipping international terrorists,"[142] gave her theory the aura of legitimacy.[143]

The Sterling thesis is not substantially different from what Francis and Possony and Bouchey state. Her chief thesis is that: "The heart of the Russians' strategy is to provide the terrorist network with the goods and services necessary to undermine the industrialized democracies of the West."[144] The conspiracy started, in her view, on orders of Moscow, in 1966 at Fidel Castro's "Tricontinental Conference" in Havana, where the

"Guerrilla International" was founded. The first big success of this conspiracy, she implies, were the revolutionary events of 1968. Some of her main witnesses happen to be advisers of Alexander Haig, while at other times she refers to "confidential sources" or "police information" for other "proofs." According to her, the role of the KGB is not an object of speculation, but a documented fact. The documents she refers to were found by the Belgian police in a car which had been made to have an "accident." These documents, which had come from a KGB post in the International Atomic Energy Commission in Vienna, stated that the KGB was planning to engage in assassination activities in Western Europe. For Claire Sterling, there is apparently no doubt that these documents refer to current terrorism rather than wartime Spetsnaz operations.[145]

The fact that her work could be labeled a "plausible analysis" by a quality paper like *Neue Zürcher Zeitung* says more about the political climate in the early 1980s than about the quality of the book. In this political climate, the suggestion had been offered that those who did not believe that the Soviet Union was behind it all (or almost all) were brainwashed by the "disinformation" campaigns from Moscow. The fact that they could not see the evidence was proof that Soviet propaganda had successfully subverted the disbelievers.[146] Among the disbelievers, however, or at least among those who do not believe in the quality of the evidence, are important sectors of the U.S. government.

While the Pentagon thought that the Soviets were deeply involved in the support of international terrorism, the CIA, though hard-pressed by the Reagan administration, could find only indications but no hard evidence.[147] The assertion by the Reagan administration that the Soviet Union was directly helping terrorists was based essentially on the testimony of a Czechoslovak defector, Maj. Gen. Jan Sejna, a close associate of Antonin Novotny who had fled his country when Alexander Dubçek came to power in 1968. Not only was his "evidence" more than a decade old, it must also be kept in mind that defectors generally try to sell the best possible stories as an entry ticket into the host camp and they often overstate their case.[148] Nontheless, this did not constrain Alexander Haig--himself a near victim of a terrorist attack on 25 June 1979 in Belgium--from blaming the Soviets for having a "conscious policy" of "training, funding and equipping" international terrorists.[149] Haig declared that "International terrorism will take the place of human rights in our concern because it is the ultimate abuse of human rights."[150]

Brian M. Jenkins, director of the Rand Corporation's Research Program on Political Violence and Subnational Conflict and a leading researcher in the field of terrorism, has written on the Sterling book:

> . . . the author's theme that the Soviet Union is behind much of today's terrorism coincides with and could reinforce the attitudes of Reagan administration officials who are inclined to blame Moscow for most of the unrest in the world. A friend of mine recently observed that at the moment there are three kinds of people in Washington: those who have always believed the Soviet Union is responsible for terrorism; those who want to believe that it is; and those who, in order to maintain their influence in government, must pretend to believe. Because the book could have major implications for U.S. policy, its arguments merit a careful examination. . . . Sterling suggests that the Soviet Union and its East European, Cuban and Palestinian proxies are behind the "terror network." She implies forethought on the part of the Soviet Union and its satellites. She never actually states it as a fact. She implies. She insinuates. Like a magician she conjures up the impression that there is a Moscow Master Plan, leaving the audience to flesh out the illusion. . . . [If] the "Sterling thesis" is meant to . . . imply--as many are taking it to imply--a Soviet blueprint, Soviet instigation, Soviet direction or Soviet control, then the book offers no new evidence, and what is offered does not make its case.[151]

Another insider, who works for the CIA, found the book "poorly researched" and called the "use of evidence flawed," with "quotations taken out of context," "biases creeping in on every page," and "data impossible to reproduce."[152]

Yet the "Sterling thesis"--that terrorists are Lenin's children--has gained widespread currency due to forces interested in reviving the Cold War. It is the thesis, for instance, of a "strikingly authentic thriller" written by Arnaud de Borchgrave, a veteran foreign correspondent for *Newsweek*, and Robert Moss, formerly of *The Economist*, who are known as the authors of a study on Chile which was allegedly subsidized by the CIA.[153] In their roman à clef, *The Spike*, which was advertised as "the secret history of our times," they unveil a Red Plot in which the Kremlin plays the terrorists and the media in a drive to gain global supremacy.[154]

There is, of course, no denying that some of the "friends" of the Soviet Union use terrorist tactics, but the important point to note is that nongovernmental friends of many big powers do so and that secret services are also deeply involved. This is nothing new. The murder of

Archduke Franz Ferdinand in July 1914 at Sarajewo was masterminded by secret services, and in the interwar period Hitler and Mussolini meddled with terrorists in the Balkan. There is also no dispute about the fact that many terrorist movements of ideologically diverse orientations fighting for ethnic and revolutionary causes cooperate with each other, trading training for weapons and helping each other out with hiding places and money. But if the KGB stands behind it all, why, for instance, should the Red Brigades have had to risk their lives in bank robberies and kidnappings to raise the $10 million a year necessary to function?[155] Or why should it be that European terrorists have to steal most of their weapons from U.S. Army depots in Europe? In the 1970s, the U.S. depots in Miesau and Weilerback in the German Federal Republic lost so many explosives, ammunition, and weapons through theft that "almost a whole battalion" could be equipped, according to a police report cited by a study by the Centre for Contemporary Studies on "The International Arms Trade and the Terrorists."[156] And if it were true that the Soviet Union equips and trains terrorists through intermediaries like Libya, why then should Colonel Gaddafi hire ex-CIA agents and have U.S. explosives, electronic equipment, and terrorist weapons brought to his country? With the help of two ex-CIA agents, Edwin Wilson and Frank E. Terpil, Libya obtained all sorts of exotic and deadly technology and materials from the United States which in turn ended up in the German Federal Republic, Italy, Japan, and Ireland, according to the testimony of another ex-CIA agent, Kevin Mulcahy, before the FBI. Why should Wilson and Terpil have had to bring in exile Cubans, formerly employed by the CIA, for assassination missions against enemies of Colonel Gaddafi, or why should several dozen Green Berets from the JFK Training Center at Fort Bragg have instructed Libyan soldiers and mercenaries, as the Mulcahy testimony revealed, if the Russians were behind it all, as the "Sterling thesis" suggests?[157] The evidence available to the public indicates that the Soviet Union has given rhetorical support to movements using terrorism. There is also some evidence of logistical support and training of members of "national liberation" movements. However, hard evidence of operational support is thin. The amateurish attempt to kill the pope does not look like a KGB operation to this writer.

The conspiracy theory also exists in the reverse form, with the CIA rather than the KGB pulling most of the strings. Philip Agee, who worked for the CIA for twelve years, has described the close collaboration of the Central Intelligence Agency with right-wing regimes and vigilante groups in his *CIA Diary*, which reconstructs agency involvement in Latin America. On Uruguay, for instance, his entry for 22 March 1964 states that some of the CIA operations "were designed to take control of the streets away from Communists and other leftists, and our squads, often with the participation of off-duty policemen, would break up their meetings and generally terrorize them."[158] At that period, the Tupamaros were still in their infancy and it might very well be that some CIA tactics were partly responsible for driving young militants along the road to terrorism. The most complete work on U.S. involvement in international terrorism is Noam Chomsky's and Edward S. Herman's massive study, *The Political Economy of Human Rights* (Nottingham: Spokesman, 1979). The first volume, titled *The Washington Connection and Third World Fascism*, lays out the anti-thesis to Sterling et al.:

> The military juntas of Latin America and Asia are our juntas. Many of them were directly installed by us or are the beneficiaries of our direct intervention, and most of the others came into existence with our tacit support, using military equipment and training supplied by the United States. . . . Terror in these states is functional, improving the "investment climate," at least in the short run, and U.S. aid to terror-prone states . . . is *positively related to terror and improvement of investment climate and negatively related to human rights*. . . . It turns out, therefore, that if we cut through the propaganda barrage, *Washington has become the torture and political murder capital of the world*. . . . [The] United States is the power whose quite calculated and deliberate policy and strategy choices have brought about a system of clients who consistently practice torture and murder on a terrifying scale. . . . It is convenient to pretend that Guatemala, South Korea and the Philippines are "independent" in contrast to Rumania, Poland and Hungary. In this manner U.S. responsibility for terror in its sphere can be dismissed, while the Soviet Union's imposition of tyranny and crushing of freedom in its sphere can be sanctimoniously deplored. Given our role in creating and sustaining our terror-prone clients . . . their alleged independence and our posture of innocent and concerned bystander must be taken simply as principles of state propaganda.[159]

Which of the two conspiracy theories of terrorism one wishes to believe is a question of political choice. It is safe to assume that both theories contain elements of truth. From the point of view of documented hard evidence, the Chomsky/Herman book is, however, qualitatively different and superior to Sterling's work. The reader interested in the present state of the debate should consult C. Sterling, *The Time of the Assassins: Anatomy of an Investigation* [into the assassination attempt on Pope John Paul II] (New York: Holt, Rinehart and Winston, 1985); and

E. S. Herman and F. Brodhead, *The Rise and Fall of the Bulgarian Connection* (New York: Sheridan Square Publications, 1986).

COMMUNICATION THEORY OF TERRORISM

In discussions on the purposes of insurgent terrorism, a prominent and sometimes even paramount place is reserved by analysts of terrorism to the communication aspect. Martha Crenshaw, for instance, writes, "The most basic reason for terrorism is to gain recognition or attention. . . ."[160] J. Bowyer Bell also sees the advertising function of terrorism as the most important one. Brian Jenkins uses the metaphor of terrorism-as-theatre to express the notion that "Terrorists want a lot of people watching and a lot of people listening and not a lot of people dead."[161]

While many authors view terrorism as either a form of internal warfare or, when state-supported, as surrogate war, there has always been some uneasiness about the appropriateness of the "war model" or "war paradigm" to terrorism. The notion that there was more to terrorism than visible and atrocious violence is expressed by many authors. Stephen T. Hosmer, in *Viet Cong Repression and Its Implications for the Future*, holds that terrorism is "the violent act for psychological rather than military reasons."[162] Paul Wilkinson contends that "the richest theoretical insights into political terrorism are to be gained from an analysis of terrorism as a distinctive mode of unconventional psychological warfare aimed ultimately at bringing about a climate of fear and collapse in an incumbent regime or target group."[163] In the same vein, Francis M. Watson holds that "terrorism must not be defined only in terms of violence, but also in terms of propaganda. The two are both in operation together."[164]

This theme also played a role in Nazi politics. One Nazi theorist, Eugen Hadamovsky, for instance, noted in 1933 in his *Propaganda and National Power* that "Propaganda and violence are never contradictions. Use of violence can be part of the propaganda."[165] Goebbels, the Nazi Minister of Propaganda, shifted the emphasis even further in the direction of communication on the war/communication axis when in the spring of 1942 he gave orders to slant the news: "News is a weapon of war. Its purpose is to wage war and not to give out information."[166]

Some theorists of terrorism have gone even further in emphasizing the communication aspect over the war/violence aspect of terrorism. Returning to the sources of modern insurgent terrorism in the 1870s, one finds that the concepts of the "exemplary deed" or "propaganda by the deed" primarily referred to attempts by an intellectual elite to communicate with the masses, who seemed to lack revolutionary fervor and were therefore in need of "education." Peter Kropotkin, the "Anarchist Prince," wrote:

> By actions which compel general attention, the new idea seeps into people's minds and wins converts. One such act may, in a few days, make more propaganda than thousands of pamphlets. Above all, it awakens the spirit of revolt; it breeds daring. . . . Soon it becomes apparent that the established order does not have the strength often supposed. One courageous act has sufficed to upset in a few days the entire governmental machinery, to make the colossus tremble. . . . The people observe that the monster is not so terrible as they thought . . . [and] hope is born in their hearts.[167]

Another revolutionary theorist, the German-American Johan Most, put it more explicitly:

> Everyone now knows, for example, that the more highly placed the one shot or blown up, and the more perfectly executed the attempt, the greater the propagandistic effect. . . .[168]

In the 1960s, the Brazilian Carlos Marighela rediscovered "armed propaganda" and the symbolic use of violence as a means of communication, and he recommended it in his *Mini-Manual of the Urban Guerrilla.* In an attempt to explain the basically nonrevolutionary bombings in the United States during the Vietnam War, Philip A. Karber offered the communication dimension as an alternative framework for conceptualizing terrorism. Rather than treating bombings as urban guerrilla warfare, he treated them as a form of social protest.[169] Karber describes his conceptual framework in these terms:

> As a symbolic act, terrorism can be analyzed much like other mediums of communication, consisting of four basic components: transmitter (terrorist), intended recipient (target), message (bombing, ambush) and feed-back (reaction of target). The terrorist's message of violence necessitates a victim, whether personal or institutional, but the target or intended recipient of the communication may not be the victim. . . .
>
> Terrorism is subject to many of the same pathologies and disruptions suffered by more conventional means of communication. These include lack of fidelity in the medium of transmission (the choice of victim conveys

> wrong message to target), background noise (competing events obscure the message), target distortion (recipient misinterprets the meaning of the one signal and fails to regulate output to changing circumstances or target feedback). . . .
>
> However, if terrorism is to be conceived of as "propaganda of the deed," we must devise a content analysis of symbolic violence.[170]

Other authors have treated terrorism in terms of communication without directly building on Karber. Franz Wördemann, a former editor-in-chief of a German newspaper, noted that "communication is not alone the goal, but a necessary part of the terrorist act."[171] Martha Crenshaw also stresses the role of violence as communication to various audiences, without giving up the terrorism-as-revolution model.[172] She quotes, for instance, one revolutionary leader, Ramdane Abane, as saying: "We must have blood in the headlines of all the newspapers."[173] The spread of television and the increase in audiences made possible by the use of satellite transmission have been judged by several authors (Clutterbuck, Jenkins, and Wördemann) as permissive causes which have made terrorism an attractive strategy and contributed to its spread to societies where local preconditions were largely absent. Amy Sands Redlick concludes that transnational information-flows from mass media (but also from international travel or intellectual exchanges) has benefitted militants in four main ways:

1. The information flow can be a propaganda tool.

2. The flow of information may expose societies to information that will inspire and justify an individual's or group's use of violence.

3. In providing information concerning specific terrorist tactics and strategies, the international communication system has often supplied discontented groups sufficient technological knowledge and ideological justification to support their use of violence.

4. The flow of information resulting from a successful terrorist attack may provide the utilitarian inspiration needed to cause a contagion of similar events elsewhere in the world.[174]

One behavioral expert, the Austrian-American psychiatrist F. Hacker, put the role of mass communication as a causal agent especially high, offering the suggestion: "If one could cut out publicity, I would say you could cut out 75% of the national and international terrorism."[175] An attempt to assess the influence of publicity on future terroristic incidents by means of coding the amount of publicity has been undertaken by Ralph William Connally in his master's thesis, "Third Party Involvement in International Terrorist Extortion."[176]

The role of the media as instruments of terrorism, as agents in the spread of terroristic acts, and as tools for manipulation by both terrorists and their adversaries has recently been analyzed by Silj, de la Haye, Clutterbuck, Schlesinger, and Schmid and de Graaf. In the latter's studies, an attempt has been made to link the rise of mass communication to the rise of insurgent terrorism and to portray some forms of insurgent terrorism as a violent reaction to problems of access to newsmaking in the present information order. In our study titled *South Moluccan Terrorism, the Media and Public Opinion*, an attempt is made to assess the effects of terrorism on various audiences, including the terrorists themselves, their reference group, the hostages, and the Dutch public.[177] The communication model lends itself particularly well to an effect analysis, although the Lasswellian formula for communication process analysis--"Who says what, through what channel, to whom, with what effect?"--was found to be insufficient. The elements "with what intention?", "by what message generator?", and "in what social context?" must be introduced, and the "to whom?" must be differentiated to account for the variety of audiences to terrorism--the terrorist himself, his movement, his sympathizers, the enemy, and local, national, and foreign publics.

The study of shifts in public opinion as a result of terroristic acts, related to an assessment of the degree of harmony or disharmony of interest between the goals of the terrorists and particular sectors in society, is one of the most crucial research desiderata at the present time.

SOCIOLOGICAL THEORIES AND MODELS

If one rejects the thesis that a terrorist is born endowed with certain personality traits accounting for a lack of moral restraint, the root cause of terrorism is sought in influences emanating from environmental factors. Such explanations focus on different environments conducive to the rise of terrorism, such as the international or national environment, or the subcultural environment (the universities, for example). Having identified one or another particular terror-genetic environment, authors generally proceed by distinguishing between *precipitants* (the almost always unique and ephemeral phenomena which start the outbreak of violence) and *preconditions* (those circumstances which make it possible for the precipitants to bring about the violence).[178] Preconditions have been further subdivided into *permissive factors*, which enable a terrorist strategy and make it attractive to political actors, and *direct situational factors*, which motivate terrorists.[179]

Surveying the literature, one notes again that the theories and models pertain mainly to insurgent terrorism, not state terrorism, and that the actions of the state are often ignored or neglected in explaining the occurrence of terrorism. Walter Laqueur has noted that "any analysis of terrorism is incomplete unless it considers those against whom terror is directed."[180]

In the following pages some models, theories, and theses will be presented.

International Environment Theories

Emphasis on international terrorism has produced analyses stressing regional and global etiological factors. Brian M. Jenkins has pointed to the failure of rural guerrilla movements in Latin America, which pushed the rebels into the cities; the defeat of the Arab armies in the 1967 Six-Day War, which caused the Palestinians to abandon hope for a conventional military solution to their problem; and the reactions of students in Europe, Japan, and the United States to the Vietnam War, which led to the formation of small extremist groups dedicated to armed struggle.[181]

The same set of factors with different accentuation can be found in the work of Edward Heyman, whose speciality is the mapping of the diffusion of transnational terrorism:

> Student activism was a global phenomenon. Student leaders met at international conferences to discuss the problems of capitalism, and to debate alternative strategies for action. They believed that economic resurgence in the quarter century since the end of World War II had not closed the gap between the rich and the poor and that Western society had discarded human values in the search for economic well being. The appeal of nationalism seemed increasingly powerful, and as Walter Laqueur notes, "conditions that had been accepted for centuries became intolerable." In Latin America, the rural model of guerrilla warfare collapsed in Bolivia with the death of Ché Guevara, and the guerrillas moved to the cities where they believed their struggles would have more impact. . . .

> The guerrillas tapped the pool of student activism and adopted labor unrest and urban poverty as rallying causes. But the move to the cities also led to radical changes in tactics. The range, number, and vulnerability of urban targets led to the adoption of terrorism, a tactic that the theorists of rural guerrilla warfare had eschewed. . . . Transnational terrorism was born of the marriage between the urban guerrilla and the student activist. The emigrant guerrilla fed on the latent violence of the student movement, exploited the student's causes and contacts, and learned new tactics. . . . The qualitative move to transnational terrorism required only a determination to use tested techniques against new targets to exploit the weaknesses of the international system.[182]

Jenkins's and Heyman's explanations beg many questions. Jenkins basically explains international terrorism out of national terrorism without explaining the latter's domestic causes. Heyman's hidden cause lies in the minds of the guerrillas and students who meet and "marry." We find the same explanatory mechanism in J. D. Elliott, a political-military officer at the U.S. Army Concepts Analysis Agency, who explains one level of terrorism by the other:

> Terrorists have maintained the offensive role and governments have had to react to their innovations. During this action-reaction cycle, terrorists have been forced to cross new thresholds of violence to retain their momentum. This has resulted in three transitions that will be discussed here: First, the transition to *urban guerrilla warfare* in the sixties, in which guerrillas moved their tactics from their traditional battleground to ambush the government in the cities. Second, a consideration of *transnational terrorism* in the early seventies, during which political violence migrated via skyjacked jumbo jets to the industrialized societies. And, finally, the emerging transition to *international terrorism* in which terrorism will be controlled by sovereign states.[183]

Such a theory is less notable for its insights (note the dubious broadening of terrorism to political violence and the reification of terrorism in the hijacking of a jet) than for the status and influence accorded to those who maintain and spread terrorism and apparently also (re)act on the basis of such models.

We find a more balanced view in Henk Leurdijk's summary of the proceedings of an international conference:

> The 1960s saw two kinds of revolutionary violence in particular: first, "national liberation" movements--each of which was unique--in every case the main target being the foreign countries which dominated their territory or were at least seen as dominating them; secondly, "guerrilla movements" which erupted mostly in Latin American countries and whose main targets were originally their oppressive domestic governments.
>
> The distinction between the two types is sometimes difficult to make, but it certainly is true that in recent years we have seen a dramatic increase in international terrorism as a result of the failure of both types of warfare to achieve their desired goals. The unifying idea of the various types of terrorism is to put their cause before the world audience and their means of doing that is to engage in dramatic acts of transnational violence, mainly directed against those whom they consider to be especially responsible for their ill-fortune. Acts of individual physical violence are often carried out against innocent persons; but in a broader context they may be regarded as small-scale reprisals for the acts of some Western governments, which, in resisting revolutionary warfare in the Third World, have allegedly engaged in deliberate killing of whole villages of innocent civilians--acts which Western governments have for the most part condemned. Some participants asked how one can persuade Third World international terrorists, who have practically no other means at their disposal, to agree to the outlawing of acts of small-scale terrorism while some Western governments, controlling enormous potential for violence, perpetuate acts of terrorism on a much larger scale.[184]

The cause of terrorism in this view is twofold: it is caused on the one hand by colonialism and neocolonialism, and on the other hand by the lack of other suitable methods of struggle. It is quite true that the international structure, with its power blocs, its satellite and dominant states, is a powerful source of conflicts. But not all conflicts are fought out violently and not all violence is terroristic.

The international system is subject to many tensions. Conflicts seem to stem frequently from two main factors: (1) conquests in some historical past and ongoing attempts to undo them, and (2) modern revolutions and counterrevolutions.[185] The first relates not only to colonies or former colonies, but also to ethnically distinct regions within old nation states, such as the Basque region and Spain, Corsica and France, or Northern Ireland and Great Britain. Moreover, some of the conflicts presently waged by means of terrorism have a very long history.

The Arab-Israeli conflict can be traced back more than two thousand years and both the chief opponents, the Jews and the Palestinians, were conquerors of the land they now claim as being rightfully theirs. The terrorism in the early 1970s in Québec, in turn, can be traced back to the year 1759 when the British conquered Québec Province and began their dominion over the French-Canadian Québecois.

In both the colonial situations in Africa and Asia and the older states caught by the resurgence of ethnicism, the key issue seems to be the reassertion of one's identity, whether national or ethnic. However, we have no good explanation why, for instance, Basques in Spain take recourse to terrorism, while the French Basques do not and seem not to desire a national identity of their own.

The second set of circumstances in which terrorism is likely to occur is revolution. Revolution generally has its origin within a national context, but given the struggle for markets and influence which characterizes the international system, few national conflicts are not to some degree internationalized, partly because the parties in a civil war often attempt to maintain or improve their position by involving previously uninvolved foreign actors, both state and non-state. Holy (and not-so-holy) alliances of Haves and of Have-Nots increasingly cross national borders. Equality and identity motives underlying revolt often coincide and reinforce each other, while at times they clash. In ideological terms, the main expressions of these dimensions have been nationalism and socialism. Nationalism (or ethnicism), however, seems to predominate whenever the two are at cross-purposes, because most people seem to reject more that they are exploited by foreigners than that they are exploited at all.

But while these forces in the international system go some way toward explaining international conflict, they do not account for the choice of terrorism as a tactic. Some national liberation struggles involved a great deal of terrorism (as in Algeria), while in others (such as Indonesia) terrorism hardly played a role. Martha Crenshaw, who has provided an excellent account of the Algerian independence struggle, offers this rationale for the choice of tactic:

> In the case of the FLN, the dominant reason for choosing terrorism appears to have been its expected utility in achieving the insurgents' goals, despite the unquestionable influences of psychological, social and organizational factors. . . . The key motivation for terrorism in a context in which the normal means of access to government

> (elections, political parties, interest groups, strikes or demonstrations) were denied was a willingness by the FLN to accept high risks and a considerable inequality of power between the revolutionary movement and the French regime. The absolute determination of the revolutionary elite was based on the intrinsic merit of the goal of independence as well as the fact that its expected benefits were obtainable only through violence. . . . Struggles for freedom elsewhere, particularly in neighboring Tunisia and Morocco, served as inspiration to the FLN and also as a challenge. . . . Terrorism, a low-cost and easily implemented strategy, was the only feasible alternative for the new nationalist organization because the FLN lacked *both* the necessary material resources (money, arms, soldiers) *and* active popular support. When a committed core of leaders agreed that violence was the only solution to the impasse in which they found themselves, their inability to push the mass of the Algerian people into open opposition or to mount large-scale guerrilla warfare encouraged them to adopt a strategy of terrorism. It is in this sense that terrorism is the weapon of the weak, the result of desperation and despair. Terrorism was an attempt to acquire political power through unusual means. Its users accepted risk and danger, because of the importance of their goal and the absence of choice.[186]

Behind the Algerian strategy of terrorism stood the desire to manipulate the international situation. Stated more concretely, part of the strategy was to alienate the French population from the French government by increasing the price it had to pay for controlling a territory which was not worth much to the average Frenchman, and to drive a wedge between France and the United States, which considered colonialism outdated and, as France's Vietnam legacy illustrated, a breeding ground for anti-capitalist forces if not satisfied on the issue of nationalism.

In her study, Crenshaw distinguished between direct and indirect audiences of terrorism, the first consisting of potential victims and the second of spectators. She then notes:

> The FLN's use of terrorism demonstrated that the responses of the indirect audiences were as important to the revolutionary cause as the reactions of the direct audiences. The need to reach indirect audiences may be the reason for the adoption of increasingly spectacular violence by modern terrorist groups. Present-day terrorists rely more extensively on the tactics of pressure and manoeuvre, or influencing third parties to compel their opponent to concede, than the FLN did. Terrorists with

> such an imperative demand the attention of the world audience, of people who are unsympathetic to, or unaware of, their cause.[187]

An important goal of insurgent terrorist movements operating internationally is "the projection of an image of strength and determination abroad," to use another phrase of Crenshaw's. The Palestinians, for instance, who took their inspiration from the success of the FLN and who have been unable to achieve much on the borders of Israel, have been masters in this, attracting first the attention and money of the rich Arab nations and then the attention and votes of many non-Arab states in the United Nations. However, they have been unable to make a credible step from violence back into politics after having gained status by violent means.

A precondition for the manipulation of the international environment is the existence of a global infrastructure permitting it. Among the permissive causes of international and transnational terrorism figure, as many authors point out, *urbanization* (which provides anonymity, targets, and audiences for the terrorist act), *transportation* (which makes possible kidnappings in private transport and hostage taking in public transport as well as escape to safe havens, that is, nations sharing the goals of the terrorists), and *communication* (which allows threat communication by telephone or the public media, the delivery of letter bombs, and the gaining of attention of mass audiences through the creation of newsworthy events).[188]

Another factor is the availability of *weapons*. The huge arsenals assembled by big powers, the replacement of older weapons with new ones, and the dumping of the old weapons in the Third World or on the black market, as well as the willingness of secret services to support foreign clients, have led to a "democratization of violence" (H. W. Tromp). The weapons of terrorists are generally not very advanced ones. The standard weapons are the machine pistol and the plastic bomb, and only in a tiny percentage of cases are more sophisticated weapons like anti-tank or man-portable guided missles utilized by insurgent terrorists.

A third permissive cause mentioned in the literature is the toleration that many governments show toward certain types of terrorists when it is a question of "my enemy's enemy is my friend," when goal consonance makes for "understanding" no matter how abominable the means, or when the host country of terrorist actors is compliant because it is too weak or too intimidated by the terrorists on its soil, as in the case of Lebanon both before and after 1982.[189]

A fourth permissive cause, at least in the beginning of a terrorist campaign, is the absence of security measures,[190] as illustrated by the ease with which skyjacking could be arranged before the screening of handbaggage and the physical search of passengers became mandatory.

Most of the elements mentioned in the preceding pages deal with situational and permissive factors in the international environment, primarily because precipitants for acts of international terrorism are basically unique and do not lend themselves to generalizations in the way that preconditions do. This is probably not as serious a deficiency as one might at first think. After all, World War I was not caused primarily by the assassination of Archduke Franz Ferdinand in 1914, but by national rivalries, alliance policies, militarism, and the like. Terrorist outrages have more often been a pretext for going to war than a principal cause.

Theories of Domestic Causation

Quételet, the Belgian philosopher, once wrote: "Society contains in herself all the crimes which will be committed; in a sense, it's she who commits them."[191] Explanations along this line of thinking have been offered by Hannah Arendt, who suggested that acts of extreme revolutionary violence in contemporary industrialized societies may be a revolt against the anonymity of the bureaucratic state, against the "Rule of Nobody." Bernard Crick has likewise suggested that "in an age of bureaucrats, tyrannicide is plainly less useful than terror."[192]

Others have denied that terrorism rises out of the domestic situation. The German political scientist, Peter Graf Kielmansegg, for instance, maintains:

> What can be said about social-revolutionary terrorism in a society like the West German one, in a state like the German Federal Republic, is that it has--except in its effects--no relationship with reality; the terrorists are assaulting a world which exists only in their heads. The consequence is: explanations do not fall into the province of political science but, at best, in psychology.[193]

And, slightly less far-going, Gerhard Schmidtchen observes:

> The scandal of German terrorism consists exactly in the fact that it is situated in an absurd, paradoxical relationship to the societal development in the Federal Republic.[194]

One problem in the sociological analysis of insurgent terrorism in industrialized societies is the fact that the terrorist movements are very small. In political and social science, it is much easier to explain the behavior of majorities than of minorities. For example, it is next to impossible to explain satisfactorily the actions of the twelve people who comprised the Symbionese Liberation Army (SLA) by looking at U.S. society as a whole.

Sociological explanations sometimes also reflect political guilt-attributions. The terrorism debate in West Germany illustrates this. Thus, the two main lines of reasoning reflect the political positions of the Christian-Democratic party and the Social Democrats. The Christian Democrats saw in the 1970s the causes of terrorism in excessive civil liberty, tolerance, democratization, and freedom in almost all social spheres, while the Social Democrats took the contrary view, putting the blame on intolerance and resistance to social reforms, on the curtailment of freedom of expression and the premature criminalization of nonviolent extra-parliamentarian strategies of action at the beginning of the student revolt.[195]

A representative of the first line of thinking is Hermann Lübbe, professor of political theory, who blames the politicians for not having acted in time to stop the left from creating a crisis of legitimacy of the state.[196] Ernst Topitsch, professor of sociology, blames the proponents of the permissive society in the media and the universities for preparing the ground for the attack on the democratic order.[197]

On the other side of the German ideological divide, we find causal interpretations like those of Fetscher and Hess. Iring Fetscher has presented some social-psychological theses to explain the road which some of the (mainly academic) young people took from protest to terrorism. His five-step model takes this form:

1. Point of departure is an extreme dissatisfaction with society. Life is experienced as absurd, notwithstanding the growing wealth and perhaps in part even because of it.

2. For some years, left-wing students in the SDS had been searching for an exit through the study of Marxist theorists.

3. Intellectual dissatisfaction and impatience found their expression in mass events and mass demonstrations.

4. The death of the student Benno Ohnesorg (2 June 1967) and the assassination attempt on the student leader Rudi Dutschke raise the anger and militancy of numerous students and other young people.

5. It is no accident that psychologically disturbed people (like the patients' collective in Heidelberg) discover, as it were, that one can temporarily get rid of painful symptoms of one's own sickness by way of armed aggression. Many former members of this collective have since joined the terrorist groups.

Fetscher also refers to the brutalities of the Vietnam War as a factor contributing to the readiness to engage openly in armed aggression.[198]

The Hess model lists ten steps on the road to terrorism and covers the rise of both German and Italian insurgent left-wing terrorism. In abbreviated form, these steps are:

1. Point of departure is a broad social protest movement. In Germany and Italy, this was the antiauthoritarian student movement, the causes and contents of which were in turn extraordinarily multiple: the end of the postwar reconstruction period; the mass university; the alienation of youth from the political system of the parties and trade unions which were perceived as offering no possibilities for opposition and change (in Germany, the great coalition; in Italy, the reformist turn of the Communist party); a categoric rejection of achievement compulsions, which are seen as absurd, of mass manipulation (especially the Springer press imperium), and of the compulsion to consume; the demand for participatory democracy in the political and economic field; a new directness in private life; the accusation of fascism against the older generation; the experience of the Vietnam War, which led to the charge of imperialism against the old system and to identification with the liberation movements of the Third World.

2. The members of the protest movement undergo key experiences of repressive violence during the course of conflict with their adversaries. In Germany, these were a visit by the Shah to Berlin (police violence) and the assassination attempt on Dutschke ("violence" of the Springer press); in Italy, the bomb explosion in the agricultural bank on the Piazza Fontana in Milan which marked the beginning of a strategy of tension, by which neofascist terror groups and parts of the state apparatus were preparing a right-wing coup d'état. Add to these the experiences of

everyday police violence on less important occasions. These experiences produce a radicalization and a consideration of counterviolence.

3. Due to the lack of response from those sectors of the population which are addressed by the movement as potential carriers for social change, the members of the movement experience frustration. The movement deteriorates. As one of the products of deterioration, small groups are formed in which the use of violence as a tactical means is discussed for achieving the aspired goals despite all.

4. Factors of individual biography have to be consulted in order to explain the reasons why certain persons choose to engage in counterviolence and in aggressive violence. Both in Germany and in Italy, high moral engagement, a product of class- and family-specific socialization as well as a product of isolation in a small group with high internal and low external contact, seems to play an important role.

5. Models are available for the decision to use violence. With regard to Germany, these were primarily foreign groups such as the Tupamaros and the Palestinians; with regard to Italy, there was in addition an autonomous tradition of revolutionary violence and above all the antifascist partisan movement of the period 1943-1945.

6. The first violent actions have more the character of a test in order to see how far one's own energy goes and what freedom of action is available. The arsonist attempt on a shopping center and the liberation of Baader as first actions of what was to become the RAF, as well as the conspiratorial game of Feltrinelli and the first arsonist actions of the Collettivo Politico Metropolitano, from which the Brigate Rosse emerged, appear as a sort of primary deviation which most definitely is not yet serious terrorism.

7. Further development is determined by the interplay of internal dynamics and the experience of prosecution by the state, both of which produce escalation. On the one hand, successful actions affirm the chosen tactic and its elaboration; on the other hand, police persecution forces them to live in the illegal underground, which furthers isolation and the sizeable concomitant criminality. Much of mature terrorism is secondary, police-control-induced

deviance, but nevertheless the motivation which produced the original primary deviance is not at all lost at this later stage.

8. Existing terroristic groups function as crystallization points which attract additional persons who are predestined in the sense of point 4. The attraction effect occurs by means of the mass media.

9. The life span of a social-revolutionary terrorist group is determined not only by the effectiveness of the police, but primarily by the resonance and support which it obtains from certain sectors of society. The quantitative size as well as the qualitative element of the willingness to use violence on the part of such sectors, which on the basis of historical experience have been receptive to anarchism, social-revolutionary theory, and praxis, plays a role in this. The greater virulence of the terrorism in Italy can in part be explained by the existence of a significantly larger lumpen-proletariat, a declassé petty and medium bourgeoisie, more unemployed young people, more students in a critical economic situation, and a more sizeable so-called academic proletariat.

10. Certainly not to be underestimated, but difficult to pinpoint, is the role which covert provocation plays with regard to the success and life span of social-revolutionary terrorist groups. The agent provocateur is a well-known figure, and especially in Italy the thesis of a conspiracy between the right and the pseudo-left is fervently discussed.[199]

Some of the elements which Hess offers can also be found in the explanations of other authors, although the emphasis is often different. Alessandro Silj, author of books on the Red Brigades, for instance, places rather more emphasis on the strategy of tension of the neofascist MSI party and the "black conspiracy" as causes for the emergence of a left reaction. Yet Silj also concludes that, on the whole, "it is fairly obvious that urban guerrillas in Italy are the product of a combination of indigenous political, economic and social conditions."[200]

Franco Ferrarotti, the eminent Italian sociologist, places strong emphasis on the immobility of politics in Italy:

> Terrorism is a response to the lack of political education in Italy. It is a tragic response to an overabundance of political stability. I know it sounds paradoxical, but you have to remember that the Italian government almost never changes. The Christian-Democrats are in power and stay

> in power--always the same faces, 38 years of Andreotti, Fanfani and so on. The country is a democracy, but its institutions are not run according to democratic criteria. Youth and the new urban classes are cut off from power. Political parties and trade unions carry a heavy responsibility for the birth and growth of terrorism since they have neglected the energy and the demands of the young ones.[201]

A variation on the immobility thesis is offered by L. Bonanate:

> A society that knows terrorism is a *blocked society*, incapable of answering the citizens' requests for change, but nevertheless capable of preserving and reproducing itself. . . . A situation seems blocked when there seems no innovation capable of bringing about a new situation. . . . When a political system is capable of rejecting the requests it receives without giving them any answer and still does not lose its stability, then a block occurs which in time produces a terrorist answer. . . . When a Communist party collaborates with a middle-class government or actually agrees to share government responsibilities with the latter, how much room is there for an autonomous mass initiative by a "revolutionary"? . . . This would be our final corollary: terrorism appears whenever and wherever the masses lose their role as protagonists of history.[202]

The Bonanate thesis resembles in some ways the "lack of alternative" thesis, which is not only a favorite argument of terrorist practitioners themselves but also is found with some authors. E. Hyams, for instance, concludes:

> I can find no single case in which recourse to terrorism was not forced on the organization in question by denial of all other means of fighting against social injustice. Whenever I have seemed to come upon such a case, it has turned out that although other means exist in theory, they have been found useless in practice--a common case in the great oligarchies called parliamentary democracies, and the invariable case in the great bureaucracies called Communist or People's Republics.[203]

If this thesis were to hold true, however, then there should be--other things being equal--a great number of insurgent terrorists in Communist societies, which is manifestly not true.

It is probably a good idea to differentiate the causation of insurgent terrorism in democratic societies from such terrorism in more autocratic societies. Feliks Gross has made such an attempt in his study of terror and political assassination in Eastern Europe and Russia. Gross sees two different sets of causes at work: where domestic autocracy or foreign conquerors are the terrorist target, *oppression* is a causal factor; where individual terrorism is directed against representatives of democracy or against members of the revolutionary organization itself, a growing *anomie* takes the place of oppression (see Diagrams 2.1 and 2.2).[204]

Diagram 2.1. Causation of Tactical Terrorist Acts Against Foreign Rule or Autocracy, According to Gross.

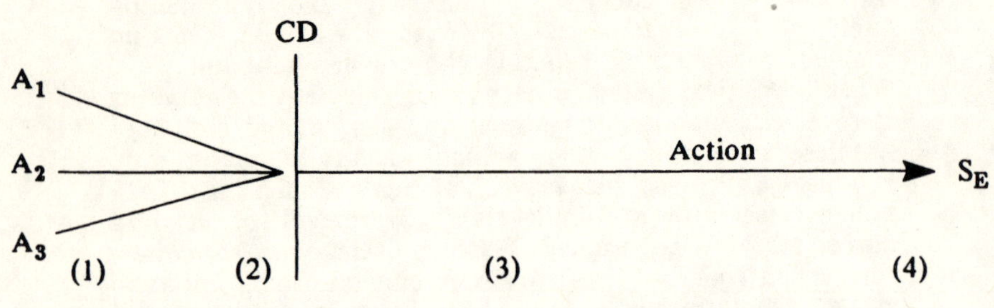

Systematic terrorist acts (S_E) were sequences (effects) of the following process:

(1) Presence of three antecedents was seminal:

A_1 (Antecedent 1): Existence of a political party with an ideology and tactics of direct action;

A_2 (Antecedent 2): Perception of social-political conditions as oppression;

A_3 (Antecedent 3): Presence of activist personality types willing to make political choice of and respond with direct action and violence to conditions of oppression.

(2) Choice and decision (CD) was made within conditions which were a result of an interplay of A_1, A_2, and A_3, and terroristic action was chosen.

(3) Action: Terroristic action followed.

(4) S_E (sequence-effect): The terroristic act was accomplished.

Briefly, the interplay of three causal factors--A_1, A_2, and A_3--was necessary in cases discussed here to result in an effect: individual, tactical terror.

Diagram 2.2. Causation of Individual Violence as Tactic Against Democratic Institutions, According to Gross.

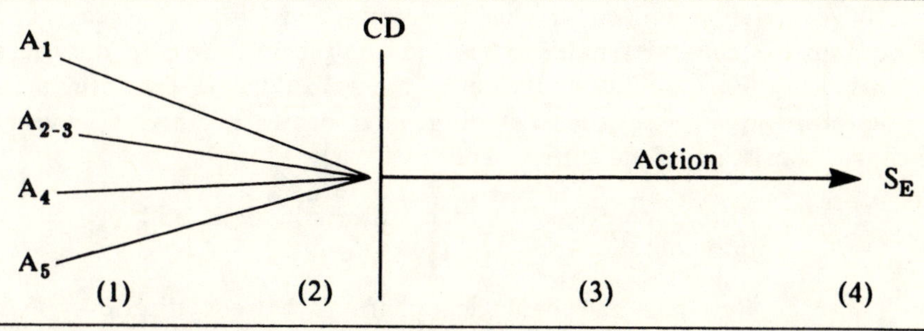

Political assassination in this case is a sequence (S_E) of the following antecedents:

(1) A_1: Social-political determinant; weakening of shared democratic values and/or crisis of democratic institutions;

A_{2-3}: Pre-assassination process of defamation and actions of the party directed against democratic institutions;

A_4: Existence of a party, temporary conspiracy with ideology and tactics of direct violence;

A_5: Presence of certain personality types, with propensities toward overt aggression once antecedents are present.

(2) Choice and decision (CD) is made by the terrorist group or terrorist party.

(3) Action is organized and released against target-person.

(4) Assassination (S_E) follows, which is the sequence and effect of antecedents and decisions.

Antecedents form a contributing but not sufficient set of causal variables. The will, which reflects the personality of the decision makers and affects the choice and decision of tactics, is the necessary causal variable.

The terrorist action may be planned by the party, but in the past the parties were frequently inspired, supported, or even directed by an outside government.

Paul Wilkinson adds to Gross's list of antecedent conditions of terrorism the following:

- the diffusion of knowledge concerning terrorist "successes," methods and technologies which facilitate emulation;

- the existence of a tradition of terrorism; and

- the intensification of hatred and the desires for vengeance which characterizes communal violence.[205]

A recurring problem in the literature is whether the causes of revolution, the causes of political violence in general, are also the causes of terrorism. For Wilkinson, the latter are embedded in the former and he therefore gives us a checklist of general causes of internal political violence, consisting of eleven elements:

1. Ethnic conflicts, hatreds, discrimination, and oppression;
2. Religious and ideological conflicts, hatreds, discrimination, and oppression;
3. Socio-economic relative deprivation;
4. Stresses and strains of rapid modernization tending to accentuate such relative deprivation;
5. Perceived political inequities, infringements of rights, injustice, or oppression;
6. Lack of adequate channels for peaceful communication of protests, grievances, and demands (e.g., denial of franchise or other rights of participation, representation, or access to media);
7. Existence of a tradition of violence, disaffection, and popular turbulence;
8. The availability of a revolutionary leadership equipped with a potentially attractive ideology;
9. Weakness and ineptness of the government, police, and judicial organs (e.g., under-reaction, over-reaction);
10. Erosion of confidence in the regime and its values and institutions afflicting all levels of the population, including the government;
11. Deep divisions within governing elites and leadership groups.[206]

Similar checklists can be found with other authors as well,[207] but they add little that is not already present in the enumerations presented above. The fact that enumerations of elements appear relatively frequently can be taken as an indication that theory formation has not yet reached a stage where important and less important variables are grouped into a hierarchy.

In the view of this writer, sociological approaches to the study of terrorism would probably benefit if they do not take society and its "sick" condition as the point of departure, but if they instead begin by studying the terrorist movement or organization: its internal structure, the recruiting and desertion of members, its preterroristic phase, its non-terroristic activities, its internal dynamics, and its external links. Unfortunately, such an analytical approach is generally only possible for movements and organizations which are no longer active and no longer in the underground or in secrecy, but given the short life cycles of many movements and the high turnover of members of many of these organizations, the problem is perhaps less serious than would appear at first sight. In fact, there is no shortage of study objects, as can be gathered from these figures on the European scene:

> . . . terrorist groups tend to proliferate in certain regions and countries. For example, 217 terrorist groups existed in Europe between 1970 and 1980. In the past two years alone, 128 groups were counted there. In Italy some 60 groups are active, while in Spain some 25 groups were operating in recent years.[208]

From the above quote, one can deduce that eighty-nine terrorist groups have either changed names or ceased to exist. If the latter, that would mean that they are potentially accessible for social science analysis based on, for instance, interviews with ex-members.

CONCLUSION

The reader might at this point rightfully ask: Is that all there is? This survey has naturally been sketchy but nevertheless it gives, in this writer's view, a fairly broad overview of what is presently available in the *open* literature on the etiology of terrorism. A number of authors are writing classified studies and there might be some "golden eggs" there which are of a higher calibre than the "theories" presented here. A glance at that other side can be gained from some of the responses we received to our first questionnaire, in answer to the question: "Do you know any areas where theoretical contributions on terrorism have produced policy changes?" Here are some answers:

- "Yes, but I am not at liberty to say [which]."

- "My own with regard to the . . . government and its security authorities."

- "I must admit that my own general theory of the hardline liberal democratic response has been increasingly adopted in Western countries. This has brought cumulative policy changes over 5-6 years."

- "Of course: everywhere in Europe, North America and South America, Asia . . . but those changes can't be identified, demonstrated by 'positivistic' research methods. The results are in the repression, disappearance or increasing of terrorist activities."

Another respondent soberly remarked that "Significant policy changes are normally dictated by expediency rather than theory or even empirical evidence. Theoreticians end up in ivory towers, not the White House" (Monday). The first part of this statement can be true even when the second is not. Some theoreticians do end up at high levels of policy making. T. P. Thornton, for instance, the author of one of the most perceptive articles on terrorism, ended up in the White House's National Security Council. Some areas where policy changes have become visible are hostage negotiation techniques or screening procedures for identifying potential hijackers. These, however, are not directly linked to the main thrust of this survey, which was on the etiology of terrorism.

If we return from applied theories to social science theories, the question is, what ought to be done next? We put the question, "Where do you see the most fruitful areas for theory construction in the field of terrorism?" to the respondents to our first questionnaire. Much pessimism emerged from the answers. Merari, for instance, simply answered "Nowhere." Sederberg made some very sensible remarks:

> I find it hard to see how we can go about "constructing theories" when there seems so little consensus on the boundaries of the subject about which we are "theorizing." I see the descriptive studies as contributing to our understanding of past events. I see the typological and definitional disputes as (optimistically) contributing to the gradual emergence of a common sense of what we are talking about. The character of terroristic acts (their secrecy, relative infrequency, emotional nature, etc.) reinforce all the ambiguities that generally afflict all social science theorizing. I think the quest for "terrorist" theory, at least in the narrow sense of the word (as opposed to heuristic speculation, analytical frameworks, etc.) is otiose.

It would seem that satisfactory solutions to the definition and data problems would have to be found first, before much progress is possible. Charles Wilber placed special emphasis on this aspect, writing:

> We need more precise and extensive data (not conjecture) on the various terrorist episodes plus voluminous data on practitioners. If we could then extract some common elements we might be able to begin on theory construction. I suggest that the epidemiological approach or the natural history format might give us a preliminary base for *hypothesis* construction.

Several authors pleaded for interdisciplinary approaches or comparative case studies, both contemporary and historical, as a means to advance the state of thinking. An interesting avenue for theory construction has been suggested by Mark Monday, who wrote:

> Terrorism should be studied in *relationship* to all other forms of social/political violence and non-violent insurgency. It is the intensities and the relationships of one to the other where the theories can be best tested.

Not infrequently, terrorist groups are splinter groups from broader political movements (like the student movement) and it might be that the life cycle of these movements--e.g., when such a movement stagnates and the choice is between giving up or radicalization--can tell us something about the decision to opt for terrorist techniques. Such an option is often justified by the argument that there is no alternative to terrorism to advance one's cause. Such self-justifications by those engaging in terrorism are in themselves worthy study objects and a content analysis of terrorist texts can potentially reveal much on the cosmology of the violent actors. If such texts reveal different criteria for what constitutes a successful action or campaign than others utilize, it is important to know their reference system. The perceptions of terrorist actors, their justifications for what they are doing, the validity of their strategic assumptions, should not be dismissed lightly as ideology and propaganda, but deserve serious attention and evaluation. After all, those who engage in terrorist violence--if they are not psychopaths or mere imitators--have some sort of theory which determines their terrorist practice. The "theories" of the terrorists themselves are, in a sense, the most important theories in the field, and social scientists would do well to absorb them thoroughly before proceeding to construct their own theories. While terrorist writings are harder to study than terrorist incidents, it is an area which promises greater progress than mere bomb counts.

POSTSCRIPT

In our second questionnaire we asked members of the research community three questions on theory:

1. "Which theory on non-state terrorism written since 1975 do you find most fruitful--and why?"

2. "Which theory on state(-supported/sponsored) terrorism written since 1975 do you find most fruitful--and why?"

3. "Which theoretical questions on terrorism are, in your view, not yet adequately approached/solved?"

In this postscript we shall provide a brief summary of the answers. The answers were generally somber, echoing the tenor of answers to the first questionnaire. One of the leading theorists in the field (in the view of the other respondents), who preferred not to be mentioned by name, wrote with regard to the first question: "There are no theories--some random hypotheses only. Most are untestable."

This view was echoed by others. Mickolus, for instance, wrote: "I have yet to find such a theory, and I am not convinced one is needed." Gurr held that "in fact most writings on the subject are not 'theory' in any rigorous sense." Paul Wilkinson also did "not really find any one theory/theorist sufficiently satisfying to pick out a 'leader.'"

It all depends, of course, on what one calls a "theory." Perhaps there will never be a mature sociological theory of terrorism, independent of a theory of conflict and coercion. However, there might be partial theories like a psychological theory of why young idealists *join* a terrorist organization. Another (social-)psychological theory might help us explain why they *stay* in such an organization. In this area, Zawodny, Ferracuti, Post, and the German authors writing for the Ministry of the Interior have done useful work. Some of this work is based on the classic frustration-aggression hypothesis. In the shorthand of one respondent:

1. Frustration of political needs; no other effective outlet within the social system (at least not perceived);

2. Frustration of emotional needs (e.g., for protest or angry criticism) (at least none perceived);

3. Usefulness/rewards of terrorist methods (gain ends, status, feeling of strength, publicity, feeling of being in control of one's own destiny);

4. Being part of an accepting group (identifying with and working for the terrorist group in return for a feeling of acceptance, love, strength, etc.);

5. Psychologically infantile needs and impulses, such as to get attention or to show strength to oneself and the "parent" (country, government). Dangerous situation of a child's fantasies/impulses in an adult's body;

6. To maintain a situation of chaos, so that no stable condition can be reached (cf. Trotsky's "continuous revolution").

Among the authors cited as being "good" theorists, Crenshaw is one of the most appreciated. Her dissertation and articles are, as one respondent put it, "amenable to Social Science analysis and lack the ideological baggage common in the policy literature" (Waugh). Other favorites are Ferracuti, Laqueur, Merari, Miller, Wardlaw, Wilkinson, and the team of German authors working on the ideology, biographical background, group dynamics processes, and action and reaction between dissident political groups and the police on behalf of the West German Ministry of the Interior (Baeyer-Katte, Claessens, Feger, Fetscher, Jaeger, Matz, Neidhardt, Rohrmoser, Schmidtchen, and Suellwold).

Turning to the theories and theorists of state terrorism, our respondents were not any more satisfied than with regard to non-state terrorism. Mickolus held that "The literature is too new--and, alas, too involved in name-calling--to have developed a set of concepts that deserve the name." Several authors had to fall back on a pre-1975 publication to come up with a good name. Wilkinson finds "the late Hannah Arendt's *The Origins of Totalitarianism* the most provocative and large-scale exploration of the development of modern systems of state terror," adding that "It is based on enormous erudition and a passionate commitment to human rights and dignity." Another respondent finds that Arendt's approach highlights "some important commonalities between state and insurgent terrorism," which, in his view, makes it "conducive to the development of an integrative theory of terrorism" (Friedland). However, one author, in comparing insurgent terrorism to state-supported terrorism, warns that such an integration could be misleading, "because it [state-supported terrorism] is not a civilian organization self-generating its values, finances and tactics and personnel. Here is the problem: State may use terrorism as a tactic--but it should not be identified with the dynamics, process and structures of genuine terrorism."

The problem of terrorist states exporting terrorism abroad--either directly through their own agency, or indirectly through non-state actors or proxies--is one which has only recently become a major topic for research. Brian M. Jenkins was the first, in the 1970s, to draw our attention to the attractiveness of "proxy or surrogate warfare" as an inexpensive, "cost-effective" method of achieving one's state ends. The events in Lebanon and the use of Western Europe as a theatre for Middle East proxy warfare have borne out Jenkins's original hypothesis as to the direction terrorism might take in the 1980s.

The explanation of domestic state terrorism in terms of an "expected utility model" offered by Stohl and his various coauthors (e.g., Duvall and Stohl's "Governance by Terror" (1983)) has received some acceptance. The policy effectiveness of terrorism as an explanation for its occurrence is certainly a more powerful variable for state terrorism than for non-state terrorism. Lately, Ted Gurr has also taken up the topic of state terrorism and, building on Stohl's work, he has developed a synthetic theory of the causes of state terrorism which looks promising. Some of the recent work on genocide, like Barbara Harff's "Anticipating Genocides: A Theory with Applications" (paper presented at the March 1985 annual meeting of the International Studies Association in Washington, D.C.), is also deemed relevant. By explaining why some states in some circumstances use genocide, she tried to unravel the causal conditions of state violence in a systematic manner. The question of choice--why some actors in conflict situations choose nonconventional terrorist (rather than merely violent) or nonviolent or conventional political means to further their interests--is, after all, the basic question of research on terrorism. T. R. Gurr put it well when he said:

> 1. Too much research assumes "terrorism" is either nonrational or an instrument of someone else's foreign policy. There should be more analysis based on the premise that "terrorism" is a tactic taken by groups based on a rationalistic analysis of their political circumstances. Why, under what conditions, do particular leaders (decision makers) estimate that terror tactics are likely to be cost-effective?
>
> 2. What are the consequences of campaigns of terrorism, both state and non-state? Are there any em-

pirically grounded generalizations to be made about their success or lack of it (from the perpetrators' perspective), or about their larger socioeconomic and political effects?

3. To what extent are tactics of terror (both by states and non-state actors) modeled on others' uses and perceived successes? Modelling and diffusion approaches seem fruitful.

Many of these questions had been posed already by E. V. Walter in the 1960s. It is a tribute to his fertile mind and a humbling testimony to those who came after him that his *Terror and Resistance: A Study of Political Violence* (1969) is still unsurpassed.

The perception of terrorism as an appropriate problem-solving mechanism is but one open question. There are many others, e.g., with regard to the causation, patterns, and peculiarities of terrorist violence and outcomes. In order to answer them we need to elaborate, as Corrado points out, "a multi-level variable model to explain terrorism. Individual, group and macro-level variables need to be identified and linked in various combinations to begin to understand the different types of terrorism."

Terrorism is, as should be clear from the above, still in search of a theory. This is certainly true for those who study and write about terrorism; it might also be true for (some of) the actors who confuse the dead bodies and headlines they create with a workable recipe for socio-political transformations in a direction they desire. However, there are some signs that social-revolutionary terrorism by young people in search of a role and on behalf of somebody else's goal is declining, at least in Western Europe. On the other hand, however, we notice an increase in single-issue terrorism (e.g., environmental issues, abortion, animal rights, anti-gay activity) in Western Europe and the United States. Several other new trends in terrorism require theoretical explanation. Our respondents noticed several new tendencies:

- decrease in middle- and upper-class terrorists and growing appeal to criminal and mercenary elements;

- growing interconnections between terrorist groups on logistical and operational level;

- increased magnitude of casualties per terrorist incident;

- increasing absence of claims of responsibility for terrorist acts;
- increasing use of terrorist free-lancers and groups by state intelligence agencies in pursuance of foreign policy objectives;
- shift from bombings to other forms of assassination;
- increase in suicidal terrorist attacks by faceless true believers;
- increase in random killings of targets of opportunity;
- stronger increase of ethnically and religiously motivated terrorism as compared to ideologically motivated terrorism;
- stronger anti-United States, anti-NATO terrorism;
- increase of right-wing and vigilante terrorism in the United States and elsewhere;
- generally increased number of incidents of terrorist acts;
- spread of terrorism into formerly unaffected countries;
- increased number of groups using terrorism;
- wider range of issues serving as inspiration for terrorism;
- increased cooperation between political terrorist groups and criminal underworld (especially related to narcotics);
- increased use of sophisticated equipment by terrorists;
- increased use of torture by states;
- increased use of terrorism in civil war conflicts.

The task of integrating these trends into a theory is a difficult one. In a way, it is harder to develop a theory of terrorism than a theory of assassination or war. Both war and assassination we can "understand." Terrorism is more absurd since it does not give the victim a "deserved" place but dehumanizes him by not even granting him the possibility of capitulation. Hence, "innocence is irrelevant," as E. V. Walter has written.[209] In his many insights, he has also noted a paradox of political terror: a terroristic government destroys part of a community in order to control the rest. In insurgent terrorism we find the related notion of destroying, if necessary, innocent people to create a better world. The destruction that terrorists bring about is real; the better world they strive for is an uncertain gamble with history. Ultimately, it remains a mystery why men should choose to rule by terror when they could, once they are in control of the state, rule by consent. It is equally hard to comprehend why nonrulers who wish to humanize society should strive for this goal by inhuman means. Perhaps a theory of terrorism must also be a theory of the absurd, which would go some way toward explaining why we have been so unsuccessful in theory building so far.

At any rate, we need more knowledge of why terrorists, both state and non-state, choose terrorist tactics and strategies over other methods of waging conflict (both violent and nonviolent). In order to gain this knowledge, we need to go beyond the study of terrorist incidents and campaigns. We need to know more about the nonterroristic and non-violent activities of social movements and organizations prior to their decision to go terrorist. We need to know more about the relationship between social protest and social control, and in particular about the role that authorities' responses play in the escalation of terrorist activity. Equally important, however, is the study of the role of ideology in justifying the use of terrorist violence, and in particular the study of the neutralization and rationalization processes used by terrorists to defend their deeds. We need to know more about (potential) alternative strategies open to social movements and organizations who presently and in the past have used terrorism, and the obstacles standing in the way of opting for these. We need to know more about why some terrorist campaigns have ended and whether the conditions which brought campaigns of terrorism to a halt are reproducible.

When we are on more solid ground with regard to these questions, a specific theory of terrorism might then come within reach and might be linked to a general theory of conflict and coercion.

3

DATA AND DATA BASES ON STATE AND NON-STATE TERRORISM

In collaboration with R. Thysse

INTRODUCTION

The data situation in the field of terrorism is paradoxical: on the one hand, there is a scarcity of data on terrorist organizations due to the (semi-)clandestine nature of terrorist activities; on the other, there is an abundance of data on "terrorist atrocities" since these meet so well the news gathering practices of the Western press. There is a large quantity of data on what Chomsky and Herman term "retail terror," the political violence engaged in by "insurgents," as compared to the "wholesale terror" practiced by "terror states."[1] The question is how relevant the available data are for scholarly analysis. In this chapter we will look at some of the data and data bases in the areas of non-state and state terrorism respectively.

Before we turn to the various data bases, let us look at the data commonly used by scholars in the field of terrorism. In answer to our questionnaire, the respondents showed a marked preference for certain types of data. (See Table 3.1.) There are several noteworthy aspects to this table: the authors' strong reliance on each others' published work might indicate a certain lack of individual data generation and research. This conclusion is reinforced by the answers to another question: "Have you generated data of your own in the field of terrorism?" Fewer than half (twenty-three out of fifty respondents) answered in the affirmative. The strong reliance on the press by authors is a sobering fact. It means that, to some extent, they cannot rise above what journalists have already unearthed. The strong reliance on government documents, compounded by the influence of a largely progovernment press, might indicate that non-state terrorism is probably viewed (too) narrowly through the eyes of the establishment.

Table 3.1. "Where do you obtain your information on terrorism? Please rank in declining order of usefulness (as applicable to yourself)."

	Number of mentionings		*Rank*	
	Total	*Ranked*		
	A	B	A	B
1. Interviews with government officials	23	[18]	IV	IV
2. Classified government documents	13	[8]	V	VI
3. Open government documents	46	[33]	IIa	IIa
4. Interviews with terrorists	12	[10]	VI	V
5. Documents originating from terrorists/sympathizers	29	[23]	III	III
6. The press/news services	46	[33]	II	II
7. Scholarly books and articles	50	[35]	I	I
8. Other	10	[7]	VII	VII

NB: Since not all respondents ranked the categories they checked, two counts have been made: total mentionings (unranked) under A, and ranked mentionings (between brackets) under B.

Philip Schlesinger has distinguished four perspectives on terrorism: (1) the official; (2) the alternative; (3) the populist; and (4) the oppositional.[2] It would seem that the official perspective and the populist (governmental and mass media) perspective have a lead over the other two perspectives. At any rate, it is remarkable how little use is made of interviews with "oppositional" terrorists and documents emanating from them. It is also noteworthy, however, that about equally few of our respondents use interviews with government officials and classified information as sources of information. This could mean that the large majority of respondents are bona fide academic scholars, in principle capable of taking a detached view of terrorism that can be an "alternative" to the "official" line.

DATA AND DATA BASES ON NONGOVERNMENTAL TERRORISM

In the following section, we shall first describe a number of important aggregate data bases in the field of terrorism, and then look at some institutes and journals which serve the research community.

Aggregate Data

In the 1960s, aggregate data analyses on comparative (cross-nation) political violence were first undertaken. The primary, and in many cases only, source of information was *The New York Times Index*. However, for the purpose of retrieving data on terrorism, this particular computerized source remained "silent" because the *Index* did not carry an entry under the heading "terrorism" until 1969.[3] There were, however, event entries under such headings as "bombings" or "assassination" in this *Index* so that researchers looking for readily available data could take these for "terrorism," depending on their work definitions.

Some of the best-known data sets based primarily on *The New York Times Index* are T. R. Gurr's *Strife Events Data Sets* (like all the other sets described below, these can be obtained from the Inter-University Consortium for Political and Social Indicators, P.O. Box 1248, Ann Arbor, MI 48106, USA, citing the ICPSR identification number). They can be briefly identified as:

(1) *Causal Model on Civil Strife, 1961-1965* (ICPSR 5009). This data set on 114 polities for the period 1961-1965 contains variables on conspiracy, internal war, turmoil, and total strife. These are related to measures of deprivation. Mediating variables refer to legitimacy, coercive potential, past strife levels, etc.

(2) *Civil Strife Events, 1955-1970* (ICPSR 7531). Gurr's general data collection on civil strife events includes non-state terrorist events and is used to study some aspect of such events. The data cover 86/87 countries for the 1961-1970 period (10 of these countries have data sets extending back to 1955, 18 for 1961-1965, and 87 for 1961-1970). The coded information covers the "who, what, why, what targets, what coercive response" of each event or set of related events. Each event is coded for approximately 90 characteristics (including type and number of partici-

pants, location, type of event, motives of actors, and amounts of violence).

(3) *Conflict and Society* (ICPSR 7452). This set contains data for 86 countries. There are 136 variables, covering regime coercion, social rigidities, dissident group characteristics, etc.

(4) *Civil Strife Conflict Magnitudes, 1955-1970* (ICPSR 7485). The two files of data in this set cover 115 countries for the period 1955-1970 (not all countries have data for all years). One file contains annual data, while the other consists of five-year aggregates. The purpose of the files is to measure the magnitude and intensity of civil conflict. Conflict types covered include domestic, antiforeign, violent, and nonviolent conflict.

Some other data sets of comparable format which are useful for the study of terrorism are the following:

(5) *Domestic Conflict Behavior, 1919-1966* (ICPSR 5003). This cross-polity time series data set, generated by Arthur S. Bank, contains information for 111 countries. For the twenty years before and the twenty years after the Second World War there are incomplete data for 59 countries, while the whole period is covered for 52 countries. Variable occurrences like guerrilla wars, revolutions, purges, etc., are recorded.

(6) *Political Events Project, 1948-1965* (ICPSR 5206). This data collection was developed by Ivo and Rosalind Feierabend and Betty Nesvold. It covers 8,000 domestic events in 84 countries, and measures the amount of conflict directed by groups and individuals against other groups and individuals in the prevailing political system. This macro-quantitative data set distinguishes 28 categories of events. It is based on the *Encyclopedia Britannica Yearbook* and *Deadline Data on World Affairs*.

(7) *Systemic Conditions of Political Aggression (SCOPA) Project, 1955-1964* (ICPSR 5207). Developed by the same team as above, this data set covers approximately 35,000 events in all countries. It is based on *The New York Times*, *The New York Times Index*, and *Facts on File*, and the data reflect the geographical priorities of these sources. Two categories of events are covered: (1) turmoil initiated by non-state actors against other non-state actors and the government, and (2) coercion and conciliation by the government. Dimensions covered include amount of violence and level of repressive force. One subset of events covers minority-group tensions.

(8) *Data Bank of Assassinations, 1948-1967* (ICPSR 5208). Another Feierabend and Feierabend effort (in collaboration with F. M. Jagger). This set, based on *The New York Times Index*, covers assassination attempts (409 cases) in 84 countries during two decades. For perspective, the user might wish to consult Franklin L. Ford's *Political Murder: From Tyrannicide to Terrorism* (Cambridge, MA: Harvard University Press, 1985).

(9) *Data Bank of Minority Group Conflict, 1955-1965* (ICPSR 5209). Also a product of the Feierabends (together with Rose Kelly), this collection covers conflicts between linguistic, religious, racial, and ethnic minorities and the majority. Forty-three countries are covered on the basis of *Deadline Data on World Affairs*. Some 60 different types of events are recorded.

(10) *Conflict and Peace Data Bank* (*COPDAB*), *1948-1978: Daily Events File* (ICPSR 7767). These daily aggregations of dyadic domestic and international conflict events cover 135 countries and are based on 70 international sources. Besides conflict manifestations, cooperative events are also recorded by Edward E. Azar (University of Maryland) and his associates. A description of this body of data by the chief author can be found in *Journal of Conflict Resolution* 24, no. 1 (1980).

Probably the best accessible international data set is to be found in:

(11) *World Handbook of Political and Social Indicators* (ICPSR 5306 update). Developed by Charles L. Taylor et al., it contains domestic and international events data for the period 1948-1982. For Europe, the computer tape is available from the Zentralarchiv fuer empirische Sozialforschung in Cologne (GFR), while for the United States the ICPSR serves this function. It is also published (in part) in two volumes under the title *World Handbook of Political and Social Indicators*, 3d ed., by Ch. L. Taylor and D. A. Jodice (New Haven: Yale University Press, 1983) (the second edition was dated 1972 and brought data up to 1967). Like other data bases, *The New York Times Index* is the chief source of information. However, in order to balance the uneven attention which the United States' leading newspaper gives to the world's regions (". . . *The New York Times* covers the Middle East, Latin America, Asia, and Africa in descending order of attention," Taylor (1983), p. 179), a second source is used for each region, which increased considerably the number of reported events over other data bases. Presently there are 87,333 cases, divided into 34 categories, for 156 countries over the period 1948-1982,

which makes the file the largest and broadest data collection in this field. Therefore, we shall devote more detailed attention to it here.

What is an "event"? The compilers of the *World Handbook* define it in the following way:

> An event is a noteworthy occurrence that represents a substantial departure from a previous pattern of behavior by a state and its constituent agencies, groups or individuals. (*World Handbook*, 3d ed., vol. 2 (1983), p. 8.)
>
> . . . we make no claims to have coded all events that happened and . . . the following indicators would be more accurately thought of as "event reports" than as simple "events." (Ch. L. Taylor and M. C. Hudson, *World Handbook of Political and Social Indicators*, 2d ed. (New Haven: Yale University Press, 1972), p. 16.)

As indicated in the quote, this data base is very much dependent on its mother sources. Adding sources changes the number of events. The authors of the *World Handbook* second edition estimated that going beyond a "two-sources approach" by adding a third source ". . . would have increased the total number of events by perhaps as much as 15 percent. . . ." (p. 422). However, even a fuller use of *The New York Times* would have markedly increased the number of (certain categories of) events. The *World Handbook* is based on *The New York Times Index* rather than the daily *New York Times*, with its fuller coverage. If we take the categories "government sanctions" and "armed attacks," there would be a sixfold increase in the number of events in the first category and a near doubling of the number of events in the second category, as the editors of the third edition admit (p. 185).

If we suppose for the moment that "armed attacks" refer mainly to nongovernmental violence and that "government sanctions" refer mainly to state actions, it becomes plausible to assume that this source covers non-state terrorism more thoroughly than state terrorism. In other words, the *World Handbook* is likely to be a better data base for non-state terrorism than for state terrorism. However, as far as "terrorism" is concerned, the *World Handbook* does not list it as a separate category. The codebook of the third edition of the *World Handbook* contains the following related categories: 702, Demonstration Met by Police Violence; 705, Armed Attack; 706, Attack by Insurgents; 707, Attack by the State; 708, Unsuccessful Assassination; 709, Assassination; 712, Other Forms of Protest; 713, Deaths from Domestic Violence; 728, Political Executions; 731, Arrest (added 1978); 740, Bombings (including defused bombs, bomb threats); 741, Ambushes. In addition, the third edition features variables for Actor Groups for the period 1968-1982: V-30, Government; V-31, Political Party; V-32, Political Group; V-38, Minorities; V-39, Revolutionaries.[4]

In principle, the combination of variables like "government" (as actor) and "assassination" (as act) should allow us to link acts to actors. However, it turns out that in about 98 percent of the cases, the variable "government = actor" is missing in the data base for this particular combination. Nevertheless, the *World Handbook* is probably the least biased and most scientific data base in the field in terms of spacial and temporal coverage, differentiation of variables, and reliability. This says something about the difficulties in creating good data bases as well as the quality of some other data bases.

Some older but still important data bases are:

(12) *Cascon Project: Local Conflict Data, 1945-1969* (ICPSR 5301). Developed by Lincoln Bloomfield and Robert R. Beattie. Over 400 "factors" are coded for 52 local conflicts since 1945. "Factors" are conditions or situations which might influence the course of local conflict toward or away from increased violence.

(13) *Middle East Event/Interaction Data, 1949-1969* (ICPRS 5201) and *Middle East Military Event Data, 1949-1969* (ICPSR 5202). Both created by Barry Blechman (Brookings Institution, Washington, D.C.), these describe 10,000 and 3,800 events, respectively, on the basis of *The New York Times Index* and other sources such as *The New York Times* and *Jerusalem Post*. They cover, in varying degrees of detail, events in which Israel, Egypt, Syria, Jordan, Lebanon, and Iraq were actors and targets. For a detailed description, see Barry Blechman, "A Quantitative Description of Arab-Israeli Interactions, 1949-1969: Data Sets and Processor," Professional Paper 78 (Washington, D.C.: Center for Naval Analyses, September 1971). See also the author's dissertation, "The Consequences of Israeli Reprisals: An Assessment" (Georgetown University, 1971).

Undoubtedly the best-known data set for terrorism in recent years has been:

(14) *International Terrorism: Attributes of Terrorist Events, 1968-1977* (*ITERATE 2*) (ICPSR 7947). Created by Edward F. Mickolus, this four-part study contains data on 3,329 international terrorist attacks from 1968 through 1977. It is unquestionably the most widely used public data set;

scores of universities use it and dozens of dissertations have been based on it. It allows the study of terrorism as a global phenomenon as well as on the basis of single cases. No fewer than 150 variables per case are computer-coded. The Common File (A) has 37 variables. The Hostage File has 52 variables and 315 cases. The Fate File, which provides more detailed information on the fates and characteristics of hostages and terrorists, has 415 cases and counts 19 variables. The Skyjack File has 617 cases with 24 variables. All subfiles can be linked to the Common File, which includes data on location, beginning and end of incidents, type of attack, name of the terrorist group involved, and number of casualties and fatalities resulting from the incidents. The author, formerly associated with the U.S. Central Intelligence Agency, is presently updating *ITERATE 2* for the 1980s. Like the present file, it will be available both as a computer dataset and as a book.

ITERATE has been described in:

1. E. F. Mickolus, "*ITERATE*: International Terrorism: Attributes of Terrorist Events," *Data Codebook* (Ann Arbor: ICPSR, 1976), 57 pp.

2. E. F. Mickolus, *ITERATE 2 Codebook* (Ann Arbor: ICPSR, 1982), 203 pp.

3. E. F. Mickolus, *International Terrorism in the 1980s: Data Codebook for Microcomputers* (Ann Arbor: ICPSR, in preparation).

4. E. F. Mickolus and Edward Heyman, "*ITERATE*: Monitoring Transnational Terrorism." In Yonah Alexander and John M. Gleason (eds.), *Behavioral and Quantitatve Perspectives on Terrorism* (New York: Pergamon, 1981), pp. 153-174.

Among Mickolus's *ITERATE*-based publications, the following are the most prominent:

1. *Transnational Terrorism: A Chronology of Events, 1968-1979* (Westport, CT: Greenwood Press, 1980), 967 pp.

2. *Combatting International Terrorism: A Quantitative Analysis* (New Haven: Yale University, Department of Political Science, Ph.D. dissertation, 1981), 600 pp., forthcoming from Greenwood Press.

3. *International Terrorism in the 1980s: A Chronology* (Westport, CT: Greenwood Press, forthcoming).

4. *Who's Who in Terrorism: A Directory of the World's Revolutionaries* (in preparation).

5. "Tracking the Growth and Prevalence of Terrorism." In George S. Roukis and Patrick J. Montana (eds.), *Managing Terrorism: Strategies for the Corporate Executive* (Westport, CT: Greenwood Press, 1983), p. 3-22.

ITERATE has demonstrated that one can use quantitative computer-resident data to make sense out of huge amounts of seemingly unrelated information on terrorism. Together with John Gleason and John Wolf, he has also been one of the pioneers in showing us how this can be accomplished. Originally, this data base was developed from two Rand chronologies and from press accounts in *The New York Times*, *The Washington Post*, and other media. By 1980, it listed more than 200 sources.[5] *ITERATE* has been utilized for a variety of purposes, including the study of the global diffusion patterns of transnational terrorism over time (Heyman); terrorist trends analysis; comparison of terrorist campaigns (CIA); evaluation of policy prescriptions for crisis management (CIA); evaluation of deterrence possibilities of terrorism (CIA); to improve hostage negotiation techniques (Mickolus, Miller); and evaluation of the effects of publicity on terrorist behavior.[6]

Like other data sets, Mickolus's *ITERATE* has flaws. There seems to be a discrepancy between the explicit operational definition of terrorism and a number of the categories of incidents listed in the narrative description published in 1980. While some types of incidents--such as kidnappings, barricade-hostage situations, explosive and incendiary bombings, letter bombings, assassinations and murders, and aerial hijackings--fit the general notion of terrorism and are compatible with the working definition, other types of incidents--such as sabotage, arms smuggling, shootouts with police, occupations, thefts or break-ins, conspiracies, and snipings--are not. Given the process character of terrorism, particular incidents might or might not fall within the notion of terrorism, depending on the context. Yet the fact remains that there is a strained relationship between many of the 3,329 cases of *ITERATE 2* and Mickolus's operational definition. Given the fact that *ITERATE* is often considered an authoritative data base, it is worth being extra critical toward it. Given the CIA background of its principal developer, its inherent American establishment perspective should not be forgotten. However, the merit of *ITERATE* is that its results can be controlled and reproduced because the coding procedures are publicly available through the ICPSR.

Another data base of potential interest to social scientists is the one operated by the Control Risk Group. Formed in 1975, the Group has its head office in London and branch offices in the U.S. and Australia. It serves the security requirements of business companies and multinational executives. The political risks facing business personnel and assets are detailed for 70 countries, while risk summaries are available for a total of 144 countries. Country files contain data on terrorist and criminal organizations, chronologies of violence, risk trends, and forecasts. Updated monthly, the *Datasolve* information system from Control Risks Information Services (CRIS) is available in several formats, including on-line on videotex miniterminals or personal computers. The price of the various services offered, however, is on the high side for the average budgets of academic researchers. Research Director is Peter Janke. Control Risks is located at 83 Victoria Street, London, and at 4350 East West Highway, Suite 900, Bethesda, Maryland, in the United States.

A number of academic researchers have developed or are in the process of developing computer-based data banks on terrorism. At the Jaffee Center for Strategic Studies (Tel Aviv University, Ramat-Aviv, 69978 Tel Aviv, Israel), Ariel Merari, the head of the Project on Terrorism, maintains a data base covering both international and domestic terrorism worldwide. The data collection started in 1979, and by 1980 over 1,100 events and about 200 "real groups" (not ad hoc names) were included in this information system. The data have been computerized since November 1983. Three main categories are covered in detail: terrorist events, terrorist groups, and countries' attitudes to terrorism. This project seems to be part of an emerging international data base in which the Rand Corporation and the University of Aberdeen are participating. For a description, see A. Merari, S. Elad, and D. Ball, *A Data Base of International Terrorism in 1980* (Tel Aviv: The Center for Strategic Studies, 1981) (307 pp., in Hebrew).

At the University of Aberdeen, Scotland, Paul Wilkinson, is presently putting incident chronologies and dossiers on terrorist organizations into a computer data bank, while country files on trends in specific nation states are held in traditional form. The aim of this effort (which apparently is coordinated with Rand and the Jaffe Center for Strategic Studies) is fourfold: (1) to develop precise and full incident data; (2) to produce a chronology of events; (3) to arrive at profiles of terrorist movements; and (4) to monitor the laws and measures adopted by governments and international bodies that deal with terrorism.

On the basis of his ambitious research program, Wilkinson and his team address themselves to such topics as the impact of different types and intensities of terrorism on specific political systems and societies; the effects of terrorism on international relations, with particular reference to its role in triggering or exacerbating conflict or military intervention; the spread of terrorism in Third World countries, with particular reference to the relationship between terror violence and wider insurgencies and conflicts; terrorism as an issue in foreign and security policies of Western states (policies, resources, capabilities); the threat of terrorism, low-level conflict, and piracy to the civilian maritime industry and offshore facilities; terrorist movements; and political extremism in Western Europe. The Terrorism Research Unit is part of the Department of Politics and International Relations, University of Aberdeen, Edward Wright Building, Old Aberdeen, Scotland.

Wilkinson's research program is unique in size in Western Europe. In the United States, there are comparable efforts taking place at the Center for Strategic and International Studies (CSIS), Georgetown University, Washington, D.C., and at the Rand Corporation, Santa Monica, California.

The Rand Corporation, an independent, nonprofit think tank which performs contract research for various sponsors, primarily branches of the federal government, has been a pioneer in quantitative analyses of terrorism. Under the direction of Brian M. Jenkins, it has been conducting wide-ranging studies on subnational and low-intensity conflict and international terrorism. Beginning with the establishment of chronologies of incidents of terrorism, Rand laid out in 1980 *An Agenda for Quantitative Research on Terrorism* (Rand Publication P-6591) by William W. Fowler; see also, by the same author, *Terrorism Data Bases: A Comparison of Missions, Methods, and Systems* (N-1503-RC) (Santa Monica: Rand, 1981). A recent description of Rand's attempt to organize information about terrorism into data bases identifies 150 attributes of terrorist groups in ten major categories. On the basis of the attribute list, a codebook was developed to elicit codified responses. This resulted in the breakdown of the attributes into a total of 281 data-specific queries. This effort is described in Bonnie Cordes, Brian M. Jenkins, and Konrad Kellen, with Gail Bass, Daniel Relles, William Sater, Mario Juncosa, William Fowler, and Geraldine Petty, *A Conceptual Framework for Analyzing Terrorist Groups* (Santa Monica: Rand, June 1985) (R-3151).

Although Rand's work is very policy-oriented, some of the best social science work on terrorism has been done there. Rand studies in the field of terrorism combine original methodology with originally developed data and have been a stimulation to other researchers in the field. Among Rand's publications in the field of terrorism, the following are noteworthy:

- R-3351-DOE, *Terrorism in the United States and the Potential Threat to Nuclear Facilities*, by Bruce Hoffman, January 1986 (56 pp.)

- N-2391-RC, *Court Depositions of Three Red Brigadists*, edited by Sue Ellen Moran, February 1986 (269 pp.)

- N-2412-USDP, *Countering Covert Aggression*, by Stephen T. Hosmer and George K. Tanham, January 1986 (28 pp.)

- R-3302-AF, *International Terrorism: The Other World War*, by Brian M. Jenkins, November 1985 (29 pp.)

- R-3183-SL, *Trends in International Terrorism, 1982 and 1983*, by Bonnie Cordes, Bruce Hoffman, Brian M. Jenkins, Konrad Kellen, Sue Moran, and William Sater, August 1984 (54 pp.)

- N-2178-RC, *Military Countermeasures to Terrorism in the 1980s*, by Thomas C. Tompkins, August 1984 (38 pp.)

- P-7076, *Recent Trends in Palestinian Terrorism: II*, by Bruce Hoffman, March 1985 (19 pp.)

- P-7124, *Generational Changes in Terrorist Movements: The Turkish Case*, by Sabrei Sayari, July 1985 (16 pp.)

- R-3009-DNA, *New Modes of Conflict*, by Brian M. Jenkins, January 1983 (20 pp.)

- N-1942-RC, *On Terrorists and Terrorism*, by Konrad Kellen, December 1982 (54 pp.)

- R-2714-DOE/DOJ/DOS/RC, *Terrorism and Beyond: An International Conference on Terrorism and Low-Level Conflict*, by Brian M. Jenkins, December 1982 (287 pp.)

- N-1856-AF, *Right-Wing Terrorism in Europe*, by Bruce Hoffman, March 1982 (31 pp.)

- P-6750, *Talking to Terrorists*, by Brian M. Jenkins, March 1982 (15 pp.)

- N-1901/1902-DOJ, *Intelligence Constraints of the 1970s and Domestic Terrorism*, vol. 1, *Effects on the Incidence, Investigation, and Prosecution of Terrorist Activity*, by Sorrel Wildhorn, Brian M. Jenkins, and Marvin M. Lavin (179 pp); vol. 2, *A Survey of Legal, Legislative, and Administrative Constraints*, by Marvin M. Lavin (155 pp.), December 1982

- P-6627, *The Psychological Implications of Media-Covered Terrorism*, by Brian M. Jenkins, 1981

- R-2842-DOC, *The Problems of U.S. Businesses Operating Abroad in Terrorist Environments*, by Susanna W. Purnell and Eleanor S. Wainstein, November 1981 (103 pp.)

- P-6474, *Terrorism in the United States*, by Brian M. Jenkins, 1980 (17 pp.)

- R-2651-RC, *Embassies Under Siege: A Review of 48 Embassy Takeovers*, by Brian M. Jenkins, 1981

- P-5627, *Numbered Lives: Some Statistical Observations from 77 International Hostage Episodes*, by Brian M. Jenkins, M. Johnson, and D. Ronfeldt, 1977

- N-1300-SL, *Terrorists: What Are They Like? How Some Terrorists Describe Their World and Actions*, by Konrad Kellen, 1977 (67 pp.)

- P-5830, *U.S. Preparations for Future Low-Level Conflict*, by Brian M. Jenkins, 1977 (20 pp.)

- P-5969, *Rand's Research on Terrorism*, by Brian M. Jenkins, 1977 (13 pp.)

- P-5217, *Terrorism Works--Sometimes*, by Brian M. Jenkins, 1974 (9 pp.)

These and other Rand publications are available to the public. A list of Rand publications (*Selected Rand Abstracts, 1965-*) in the field of terrorism is available from Rand East, 2100 M Street, N.W., Washington, D.C. 20037. Rand publications are directly available in subscribing libraries throughout the Western world. In Great Britain, for instance, there are three such libraries (Boston Spa, London, and Oxford), in The Netherlands there is one (Delft), as there is in Denmark (Aarhus), Belgium (Sint-Niklaas), Norway (Trondheim), Spain (Madrid), Sweden (Stockholm), Switzerland (Zurich), and Israel (Haifa), while there are ten libraries in West Germany. The Rand Corporation is located at 1700 Main Street, P.O. Box 2138, Santa Monica, California 90406, USA.

More modest data banks on terrorist incidents are maintained by academic researchers. John B. Wolf, Chairman of the Department of Criminal Justice at New York's John Jay College, maintains a computerized file which is available on request against a work-based fee. It is based on over 20,000 5" x 8" cards containing information on terrorism from press clippings, and is now cross-indexed. Wolf's work reflects a police/crime-control perspective and is published regularly in *Update Report: A Technical and Background Intelligence Data Service* (Clandestine Tactics and Technology Service, International Association of Chiefs of Police, Inc., 11 Firstfield Road, Gaithersburg, Maryland 20760, USA). Wolf's data-gathering effort was first described in his article "Analytical Framework for the Study and Control of Agitational Terrorism," *The Police Journal* 49 (July-September 1976): 165-171. For its utility, see the author's *Fear of Fear: A Survey of Terrorist Operations and Controls in Open Societies* (New York: Plenum Press, 1981).

William L. Waugh, Jr. (Georgia State University, Atlanta, Georgia, USA) has developed a dataset on approximately 100 hostage incidents between 1968 and 1980 with 30 to 35 variables identified on the nature of the terrorist organization, the type of event, and the governmental response and its effect. For details, see the author's *International Terrorism: How Nations Respond to Terrorists* (Salisbury, NC: Documentary Publications, 1982).

NON-COMPUTER-BASED DATA BASES

Facts on File has also published a number of useful surveys on terrorism under the editorship of Lester A. Sobel: *Palestinian Impasse: Arab Guerrillas and International Terror* (New York: Facts on File, 1977) (282 pp.); *Political Terrorism*, vol. 1 (Oxford: Clio Press, 1975) (309 pp.), covers the period from the late 1960s on through the first half of the 1970s; *Political Terrorism*, vol. 2, *1974-78* (Oxford: Clio Press, 1978) (279 pp.).

Giving regional and country-by-country accounts of developments, these well-indexed volumes form basic handbooks for anyone trying to monitor insurgent terrorism. Drawing from the weekly records compiled by Facts on File, Inc., these volumes provide detailed incident descriptions, and add enough information to place terrorist events into political contexts. Where there are conflicting versions of an incident, alternative interpretations are offered to the reader in the volume on Palestinian terrorism.

In 1982, J. L. Scherer began to compile *Terrorism: An Annual Survey.* He based his work on a wide variety of news media, generally consulting a country x source for a country x event. Unfortunately, only two volumes of this promising work were published. It featured a chronology, a survey of groups, a country survey, and general information, and contained numerous statistics and graphics on international and domestic terrorism, drawing from a variety of official and other sources. In 1986, Scherer resumed this work, this time in the form of a quarterly report. Each issue of *Terrorism* consists of fifteen to twenty pages in a computer printout format inside a plastic binder. The first two of the four 1986 issues dealt with, among other things, Libyan terrorism, attacks against U.S. military bases worldwide with particular emphasis on the German Federal Republic, and attacks in Spain and the United States. The quarterly is available from J. L. Scherer, 4900 18th Avenue South, Minneapolis, Minnesota 55417, USA.

In France, the Polemological Institute has been assembling political violence data since the late 1960s. Between 1968 and 1970, these were published as "Chronologie de la Violence Mondiale" in the journal *Guerre et Paix*, and since then (with an interruption from June 1976 to December 1977) in *Etudes Polemologiques* (*EP*). Based mainly on media accounts, data on macro- and microconflicts have been gathered, with terrorism being one of several categories. However, the data are not very specific and the coverage is uneven for many countries. This data base is important because it covers France well, which is not done by many other data bases. A recent edition of the journal (*EP* 37, le Trimestre 1986:13-42), for instance, contained a statistical analysis of terrorism in France by the editor-in-chief, Daniel Hermant, and Didier Bigo, as well as case studies on political violence in Corsica, the Bretagne, and Guadeloupe-Martinique. The Institute Français de Polemologie is located at the Hotel National des Invalides, rue de Grenelle, 75007 Paris.

For up-to-date French political data, the researcher can turn to *The Documentation Française Political Data Base* from BIPA (Banque d'Information Politique et d'Actualites). The *Logos Data Base* draws from government reports, monographs, press cuttings, and speeches of the

General Secretariat of the French government. Founded in 1979, it had some 185,000 references by 1986. In late 1986, *Logos* contained 256 references on the domestic terrorist organization Action Directe, while 217 references dealt with antiterrorist measures. Its on-line search is in the hands of Telesystems Questel (83-85 Boulevard V. Auriol, 75013 Paris). In the United States, its vendor is Questel, Inc. (1626 Eye Street, Suite 719, Washington, D.C. 20006).

More broadly based than the French Polemological Institute is the British Institute for the Study of Conflict (ISC). It was founded as an educational charitable organization in June 1970 by Brian Crozier, a right-of-center journalist-turned-scholar. The scope of the ISC's data collection is broader than terrorism. The institute, now directed by Michael Goodwin, publishes a monthly monograph under the title *Conflict Studies*, each about 12,000 words long. So far about 200 titles have been published. The ISC's publishing division, the Centre for Security and Conflict Studies (CSCS) issues occasional Special Reports and *Conflict Bulletin*. Until 1982, the ISC also produced a sizeable *Annual of Power and Conflict*. It included country-by-country reports, chronologies, and regional surveys. Part of its function seems to have been taken over by Control Risks International. Indeed, a senior researcher of the ISC is now the research director of CRIS. The aims of the Institute for the Study of Conflict (which is supported by donations from corporations and foundations) is threefold. In its own description, it aims to research into the causes, manifestations, and likely trends of political instability worldwide; to identify and analyze threats posed by Soviet expansionism to the security of the Western democracies; and to highlight the terrorist and subversive activities of political extremist organizations, whether or not they be Soviet-inspired, and trace their international links.

The ISC has a close association in the United States with the Center for Security Studies in Washington, D.C. Its recent publications on terrorism include the following *Conflict Studies* (*CS*): *Patterns of Protest in Western Europe* (no. 189); *Northern Ireland: An Anglo-Irish Dilemma?* (no. 185); *Living with Terrorism: The Problem of Air Piracy* (no. 184); *Diplomatic Immunities and State-Sponsored Terrorism* (no. 164); *Terrorism: International Dimensions* (no. 113); *Protest and Violence: The Police Response* (no. 75); *Terrorism versus Liberal Democracy: The Problems of Response* (no. 67); and *Libya's Foreign Adventures* (no. 41).

Some of the *Conflict Studies* have also been compiled into book form. Recently, William Gutteridge edited for the ISC *The New Terror-*

ism (London: Mansell, 1986). The Institute for the Study of Conflict is located at 12/12A Golden Square, London W1R 3AF, United Kingdom.

JOURNALS AND INSTITUTES IN THE FIELD OF TERRORISM

Since data bases are usually established at research centers and such institutes often publish journals or bulletins of one sort of another, some of the entries in this section have already been mentioned.

One of the more widely read journals in the field is *Terrorism: An International Journal* edited by Yonah Alexander. It has been published since 1977 by Crane Russak & Company (3 East 44th Street, New York, NY 10017), four times a year. The editor is associated with the Center for Strategic and International Studies, Georgetown University (1800 K Street N.W., Washington, D.C. 20006). He is also the director of the Institute for Studies in International Terrorism at the State University of New York in Oneonta, NY 13820. The purpose of the journal is, according to its own description, to "offer dialogue on definitional, historical, biological, sociological, psychological, philosophical, political, strategic, legal, economic, and future perspectives on the subject for the purpose of advancing the cause of peace with justice." While its editorial board is international, U.S. perspectives clearly dominate and one would be surprised to find an article criticizing the "official" line (in the sense of Philip Schlesinger) in its pages, despite its stated commitment to observe no "restrictions on the ideological or political approach of contributors." The journal has its critics; it has been said that it is poorly edited and that little of substance is published. The journal sometimes serves as an outlet for official documents and conference papers. *Terrorism: An International Journal* undoubtedly fulfills a forum function through its interdisciplinary setup. The Institute for Studies in International Terrorism has organized conferences, workshops, and seminars since its founding in the spring of 1977, and many of these conference proceedings were subsequently edited by Professor Alexander. Some typical themes are: Eli Tavin and Yonah Alexander (eds.), *Terrorists or Freedom Fighters?* (Arlington, VA: Hero, 1986); Y. Alexander and Allan S. Nanes (eds.), *Legislative Responses to Terrorism* (Dordrecht: Martinus Nijhoff, 1986); Ray S. Cline and Y. Alexander (eds.), *Terrorism as Covert Warfare* (Arlington, VA: Hero, 1985).

Yonah Alexander is also director of The Institute of Social and Behavioral Pathology (1755 Massachusetts Avenue, N.W., Suite 324, Washington, D.C. 20036), whose chairman is Lawrence Z. Freedman (who is also an associate editor of *Terrorism*, together with L. C. Green, B. M.

Jenkins, J. Toman, and P. Wilkinson). The ISBP performs research in human conflict and policy analysis incorporating methods and insights of political science and psychological inquiry. Lawrence Z. Freedman and Yonah Alexander edit its *Journal of Social and Behavioral Pathology.* This quarterly publishes research on terrorism, the epidemiology of violence, policy analysis, behavioral and criminal studies, and interdisciplinary studies in psychiatry, law, and the social sciences. In addition, the ISBP issues *The Bulletin of the Institute of Social and Behavioral Pathology* (edited by Paul M. Lin), a report on the activities of the Fellows and Research Associates of ISBP. Its content reflects the confluence of biology, psychology, political science, and policy analysis as methodological tools for approaching the study of conflict and conflict resolution.

A second journal edited by Yonah Alexander is *Political Communication and Persuasion: An Interdisciplinary Journal.* It has been published since 1983, also by Crane Russak. It examines the roles of nongovernmental, intergovernmental, and governmental organizations as political communicators. The journal presents original research on propaganda and psychological warfare and on peacekeeping, peacemaking, and peacebuilding assignments of political communicators, according to an editorial statement. Many articles could as well be published in *Terrorism: An International Journal.*

While Alexander's journals are linked to the Center for Strategic and International Studies, other journals are associated with Rand. George K. Tanham, the Rand representative in Washington, has edited *Conflict* since 1978, a journal devoted to "All Warfare Short of War." This quarterly focuses on informal wars, including guerrilla warfare, insurgency, revolution, and terrorism. The journal also covers nonphysical conflicts, such as those of an economic, social, political, and psychological nature. It is also published by Crane Russak in New York and looks very much the same and covers very much the same ground as the two journals cited above.

Rather different in format and readership is the *TVI Journal.* Founded in 1980 in San Diego by the journalist Mark Monday (*TVI* is an acronym for Terrorism, Violence, Insurgency), its original target readership were probably fellow journalists and corporate executives rather than counterinsurgency officials. Since it was taken over in 1985 by Brian M. Jenkins, the Rand director for studies on subnational conflict, it has also served as an outlet for the well-researched studies produced by this quasigovernmental think tank. Its target audience includes law enforcement officials, the military, corporate directors of security, and diplomats. Its contributors are academic experts in the field of terrorism and officials with direct responsibilities and firsthand experiences in dealing with the problems they address. The *TVI Journal* is available from the managing editor, William F. Sater (P.O. Box 1055, Beverly Hills, California 90213).

Beginning in 1987, a new journal called *VAT* (for Violence, Aggression, and Terrorism) started publication. It is edited by Stanley Einstein, an Israeli psychotherapist who has already successfully launched four other journals. It is an interdisciplinary, international forum with a broad editorial board. *VAT* is designed to embrace a broad spectrum of issues, areas, and concerns and to serve as a central platform for researchers in social, biomedical, and other sciences. Some of the articles in the first volume address themselves to the relationship between crime and terrorism; state violence and terror; mythologizing terrorism; infrastructures of terrorist organizations; and sociological analysis of anti-terrorist legislation in Western Europe. *VAT: An Interdisciplinary International Forum* is available from DIA, Inc., 259 Carol Street, Danbury, Connecticut 06810, USA. While these journals focus chiefly on terrorism and related phenomena, a number of other journals also regularly feature articles on that subject. Prominent among these are *Conflict Quarterly*, the *Journal of Conflict Resolution*, *World Politics*, *Comparative Politics*, the *Journal of Political and Military Sociology*, and the *Journal of Peace Research*.

In addition to these major journals, there are a number of newsletters devoted to terrorism. We have already mentioned Scherer's *Terrorism*, which began publication in 1986. A monthly newsletter, edited since 1979 by Charles M. Hellebusch, is called *The International Terrorism Newsletter* (P.O. Box 22425, Louisville, Kentucky 40222). Its usefulness for the academic researcher is more limited than Scherer's quarterly. Highly useful are the special editions of the *Current News* by the News Clipping and Analysis Service of the U.S. Air Force, acting as agent for the Department of Defense. This service regularly reproduces, *in toto*, worthwhile newspaper and periodical articles, using sources like the *FBI International Report*, the *Congressional Quarterly Weekly Report*, etc. This is a first-rate source of information. However, it is very difficult to obtain outside the United States and it does not seem to be available on the basis of private subscription.

Another clipping service which is very valuable is the Knipsel-krant/Resistance *Documents and Analysis [for?] the Illegal Front*. This is a weekly photocopying service with forty-five issues per year, totaling about 1,900 pages annually. This trilingual (Dutch, English, and German) service is primarily meant to serve as a forum for proviolent elements of the revolutionary left in Western Europe. Academic subscribers might be charged a "revolutionary tax" for subscribing. While its clippings from about 175 Belgian, British, Dutch, German, Irish, and other daily and weekly press are like those of any other specialist service, it is the grey literature from terrorist sympathizers and terrorist movements that makes this weekly service valuable. The Knipselkrant serves as a post office box for claims of responsibility, communiques, and other literature from the revolutionary underground. In addition, it covers government countermeasures and right-wing activities. It translates statements from French and French-speaking Belgian sources, as well as from Italian and occasionally Spanish sources. For the academic researcher without links to government sources, the Knipselkrant is an important and, in some cases, unique source for studying firsthand the thinking in circles with close affinities to terrorist actors. Apart from the Knipselkrant, the editors also produce special volumes dedicated to the pamphlets and other output of movements like Action Directe, CCC, Red Brigades, Rote Armee Faktion, etc. The publications can be ordered from De Knipselkrant, P.O. Box 7001, 9701 JA Groningen, The Netherlands.

Finally, the newsletter *Terrorism and the News Media*, published by the Terrorism and the News Media Research Project, deserves mentioning. Under the direction of Robert G. Picard (Manship School of Journalism, Louisiana State University, Baton Rouge, LA) and Lowndes Stephens (College of Journalism, University of South Carolina, Columbia, SC), this newsletter provides updates on the contents of its program repository (which contains more than 500 studies, both published and unpublished, and articles on terrorism and the media). It also serves as liaison between the approximately forty researchers from universities, government agencies, and other institutions taking part in this research program. In August 1986, the project began issuing a series of papers featuring the work of the participating researchers. Since then, papers on issues and research findings on terrorism and communication have been published at a rate of one per month. A catalog of the materials in the repository is scheduled for publication in June 1987. The project, under the auspices of the Association for Education in Journalism and Mass Communication, Mass Communication and Society Division, intends, according to its statement of objectives,

> . . . to produce substantive evidence about the roles of media in the planning, implementation, and conclusion of

> acts of terrorism, the methods employed in covering such acts, the content of coverage, and the effects of coverage on official responses to terrorism and public perceptions of organizations engaged in political terrorism. In addition, the project is seeking significant information about the historic and ethical contexts of coverage of violence. Topics for consideration include the content of news coverage of acts of political violence, manipulation of news coverage, the role of staged and unstaged acts of terrorism, the effects of coverage on outcomes of incidents, differences in coverage in various types of media, the legitimacy of coverage, and the role of coverage in inducing subsequent acts of terrorism.

This three-year project, which brings together researchers from journalism, sociology, criminal justice, the armed forces, and political science, represents one of the few clear academic research programs in the field and is one of the most significant developments in the study of terrorism in recent years. A presentation of the results of the nearly forty studies is expected to take place in a major national academic conference. The address is Terrorism and the News Media Research Project, Prof. R. G. Picard, School of Journalism, Louisiana State University, Baton Rouge, Louisiana, 70803-7202.

Beyond these journals and newsletters, there are many others that cover terrorism from an operational rather than social science point of view. They include *Security Management*, *Journal of Security Administration*, *Executive Risk Assessment*, *Police Chief*, *Military Law Enforcement Journal*, *Asset Protection*, and *Risk Management*. In the field of social and political science, there are scores of journals that regularly cover terrorism, and it is impossible to list them all. An example would be the *Journal of Palestinian Studies: A Quarterly on Palestinian Affairs and the Arab-Israeli Conflict*, which has been published since 1972 by Kuwait University and the Institute for Palestine Studies, 3501 M Street N.W., Washington, D.C. 20007. To identify relevant periodicals and articles, the researcher will have to consult indexes, such as: *Air University Library Index to Military Periodicals* (Maxwell Air Force Base, Alabama, 1965-); *Alternative Press Index* (Baltimore, Maryland, Alternative Press Center, 1969-); *Communication Abstracts* (Beverly Hills, California, Sage, 1978-); *Criminal Justice Periodicals Index* (Ann Arbor, Michigan, University Microfilms International, 1975-); *Criminology and Penology Abstracts* (Amstelveen, The Netherlands, Kugler, 1965-); *Historical Abstracts* (Santa Barbara, California, ABC-Clio, 1965-); *Index to Jewish Periodicals* (Cleveland Heights, Ohio, Index to Jewish Periodicals, 1964-); *Index to Legal Periodicals* (New York, H. W. Wilson,

1965-); *Index to U.S. Government Periodicals* (Chicago, Illinois, Infordata International, 1974-); *International Political Science Abstracts* (Paris, IPSA, 1965-); *The Middle East: Abstracts and Indexes* (Pittsburgh, Pennsylvania, Northumberland Press, 1978-); *Peace Research Abstracts Journal* (Dundas, Ontario, Canadian Peace Research Institute, 1964-); *Police Science Abstracts* (Amstelveen, The Netherlands, Kugler, 1973-); *Political Science Abstracts* (New York, IFL-Plenum, 1966-); *Psychological Abstracts* (Arlington, Virginia, American Psychological Association, 1965-); *Social Sciences Index* (New York, H. W. Wilson, 1965-); and *Sociological Abstracts* (San Diego, California, Sociological Abstracts, 1965-).

More and more of these indexes and abstracts are computerized and available through on-line services (see introduction to bibliography for details).

CHRONOLOGIES

One of the unfortunate features of the literature on terrorism is that there are more chronologies of terrorist acts than good case studies of terrorist movements. The listing of terrorist deeds is the most simple form of scientific activity. In many cases, there is a covert political purpose behind it, with the citing involving only the atrocities committed by one side, without regard for context and preceding provocative events. More often than not, newspaper accounts form the only basis of such surveys, which are presented without efforts at double-checking. For many objectives, chronologies form a dubious basis for scientific inquiry. The origin and quality of the information is often forgotten as chronology data are incorporated in a computer file and correlated against each other, producing "hard" statistical findings. Unfortunately, few other researchers seem willing to replicate such research with other, better data, and "scientific findings" obtained in such a manner sometimes go unchallenged for years, if not forever.

In the following, we will simply list some chronologies, commenting only occasionally on their features and merits.

Northern Ireland

Richard Deutsch and Vivien Magowan, *Northern Ireland, 1968-1973: A Chronology of Events* (Belfast: Blackstaff Press, 1973), 2 vols. This is one of the finest chronologies written on any recent conflict, going well beyond a simple time line based on newspaper accounts. The authors have carefully evaluated their sources, screened private papers and official publications, and arrived at a factual record which is hard to improve on. It is worth quoting the authors themselves in order to give an idea of the kind of detachment that is still possible in a situation that invites polarized perspectives:

> In this chronology we are naturally not concerned with drawing conclusions from events, but with the presentation of an accurate sequence of happenings. In order to arrive at a true picture we have constantly questioned and double-checked sources and have questioned them yet again. After determining, on a balance of reason and probability, what did or did not take place on a given day at a given time, we make no claims to be completely successful, but we do feel that we made a fair effort. It has been said that impartiality consists of doing justice to everybody: in the final analysis, however, one man's fact is another's falsehood and no human being--not even any "official source"--can claim a monopoly of "absolute truth." . . . We tried to show the life of the Province as it really was--not as any single person or individual imagined it to be. . . .[7]

None of the other chronologies which we surveyed matches the quality of this one. Some other chronologies on Northern Ireland are to be found in Pauline M. Chakeres, *Developments in Northern Ireland, 1968-1976* (Washington, D.C.: Library of Congress, Congressional Research Service, 1976); William D. Griffin (ed.), *Ireland: A Chronology and Fact Book* (Dobbs Ferry, NY: Oceana, 1973).

Federal Republic of Germany

Official Calender of Events (in German), compiled by the working group Oeffentlichkeitsarbeit gegen Terrorismus (Public Information Against Terrorism) of the Ministry of the Interior, printed as an approximately 70-page appendix in A. Jeschke and W. Malanowski (eds.), *Der Minister und der Terrorist: Gespraeche zwischen Gerhard Baum und Horst Mahler* (Reinbek (bei Hamburg): Rowohlt, 1980): Covers the period 1967-1980, citing left- and right-wing "terroristic" events, using a rather wide definition ranging from sabotage to armed robberies by political groups. For each event, data, location, type of act, and name of perpetrating group are given. For updates, the annual *Verfassungschutzberichte* (reports by the Office for the Protection of the Constitution, edited by the Ministry of the Interior, Graurheindorfer Strasse 198, 5300 Bonn, FRG) should be consulted.

United States

Chronology of Incidents of Terroristic, Quasi-Terroristic, and Political Violence in the United States: January 1965-March 1976: Compiled by Marcia McKnight-Trick and printed as Appendix 6 of the *Task Force Report on Disorders and Terrorism*, issued by the U.S. National Advisory Committee on Criminal Justice Standards and Goals (Washington, D.C.: Government Printing Office, 1976). This 80-page chronology covers incidents of a terroristic nature, violence with political implications, hijackings, and acts of hostage taking. It is based mainly on newspaper accounts, supplemented by information from the Federal Bureau of Investigation (FBI) and the Federal Aviation Administration (FAA). It is prefaced by a "Who's Who," describing eighteen left-wing and ten right-wing movements responsible for many of the incidents listed in the chronology. What is striking is how many incidents are unclaimed. (According to a Rand study published in 1985, "nearly half of all terrorist attacks are unclaimed,"[8] which is probably indicative of a structural change in terrorism as we know it.) For updates, the reader can turn to "FBI Analysis of Terrorist Incidents in the United States: 1982," in *Terrorism: An International Journal* 7, no. 1 (1984). See also Scherer's *Terrorism* newsletter, Rand publications, and Congressional reports.

More specialized chronologies of incidents in the United States or against U.S. targets can be found in:

- "Chronology of Transnational Terrorist Attacks upon American Business People, 1968-1978," a 21-page survey in Y. Alexander and Robert A. Kilmark (eds.), *Political Terrorism and Business* (New York: Praeger, 1979).

- "Threats and Acts of Violence Against U.S. Nuclear Facilities." This list of more than 200 incidents of hoaxes and more disturbing events forms Appendix 2 in A. R. Norton and M. H. Greenberg, *Studies in Nuclear Terrorism* (Boston: G. K. Hall & Co., 1979).

- "Incidents of Terrorism and Hijackings in the United States 1980-1983," *TVI Journal* 5, no. 1 (1984): 30-39.

- United States Department of State, *Chronology of Significant Terrorist Incidents Involving U.S. Diplomatic Official Personnel, 1963-1975* (Washington, D.C.: GPO, 1976).

- United States Department of State, *Chronology of Attacks upon Non-Official American Citizens, 1971-1975* (Washington, D.C.: Department of State, 1976).

- United States Department of State, Office of Combatting Terrorism, *Terrorist Hijackings, January 1968 Through June 1982* (Washington, D.C.: Department of State, 1982), 26 pp.

- United States Department of Transportation, Federal Aviation Administration, Civil Aviation Security Service, *Domestic and Foreign Aircraft Hijackings (1931-1979)* (Washington, D.C.: FAA, 1979), 77 pp.

Skyjacking

The U.S. Department of Transportation, Federal Aviation Administration, periodically issues a *Master List of All Hijacking Attempts, Worldwide, Air Carrier and General Aviation.* See also Federal Aviation Administration, *Significant Worldwide Criminal Acts Involving Civil Aviation* (Washington, D.C.: FAA, 1974) and Federal Aviation Administration, Civil Aviation Security Service, *Domestic and Foreign Aircraft Hijackings (1931-1979)* (Washington, D.C.: FAA, 1979), 77 pp. However, these lists are not complete and should be supplemented with other sources, such as Appendix A in James A. Arey, *The Sky Pirates* (London: Ian Allan, 1973). This list uses, in addition to the FAA data, information provided by the International Civil Aviation Organization, the International Air Transport Association, the American Air Transport Association, and news clippings referring to non-American and foiled hijacking attempts as well. For more recent data, see United States Department of State, Office of Combatting Terrorism, *Terrorist Skyjackings, January 1968 Through June 1982* (Washington, D.C.: Department of State, 1982), 26 pp.

General

International Terrorism: A Chronology, 1968-1974, by B. M. Jenkins and J. Johnson (Santa Monica: Rand, 1975), 58 pp. (R-1597). This is one of the earlier chronologies and covers 507 incidents in the March 1975 version for the period 9 January 1968 to 26 April 1974. Since then, the chronology has been greatly expanded. It was originally based on press accounts and data from the London-based fortnightly, *Arab Report and Record*, as well as chronologies prepared by various United States congressional committees and government agencies. Some seminal data analysis work has been done by Brian M. Jenkins on the basis of expanded versions of this chronology. This Rand chronology includes incidents that had "clear international repercussions . . . --incidents in which terrorists went abroad to strike their targets, selected victims or targets that had connections with a foreign state (e.g., diplomats, foreign businessmen, officers of foreign corporations) or created international incidents by attacking airline passengers, personnel and equipment." Not included were incidents in the course of wars such as in Vietnam and along the border of Israel. However, the original list, at least, contains a congeries of acts of political violence and destruction which stretch the concept of terrorism too much. While it is a common (though deplorable) practice to treat hijackings for escape as well as hijackings for blackmail as if they belonged to the same type of action, we also find in the chronology incidents of mere vandalism, sabotage, and theft. The original Rand chronology has been updated: Brian M. Jenkins, *International Terrorism: A Chronology, 1974 Supplement* (Santa Monica: Rand, 1976), 23 pp. (R-1909-1). For an "unofficial" update of the Rand chronology for the period January 1975 through December 1985, see Suzanne Robitaille Ontiveros, *Global Terrorism: A Historical Bibliography* (Santa Barbara: ABC-Clio, 1986), pp. 145-168. The advent of Edward F. Mickolus's massive *Transnational Terrorism: A Chronology of Events, 1968-1979* (Westport, CT: Greenwood Press, 1980), 967 pp. (an update for the 1980s is forthcoming) has reduced the use of Rand's chronology by social scientists. For Mickolus's chronology, see *ITERATE*, discussed above.

"Worldwide Chronology of Terrorism: 1981," *Terrorism: An International Journal* 6, no. 2 (1982), whole issue. This 280-page chronology covers 88 countries and regions individually for one year.

The U.S. Central Intelligence Agency in 1976 began publication of an annual unclassified report on inter- and transnational terrorism: *International and Transnational Terrorism: Diagnosis and Prognosis* (Washington, D.C.: CIA, 1976), 58 pp.

U.S. Central Intelligence Agency, *International Terrorism in 1976* (Washington, D.C.: CIA, 1977), 19 pp.

These CIA publications, while based on a chronology, are basically statistical analyses. In the early 1980s, the CIA discontinued the publication of these reports in line with the new administration's desire to reduce its public profile. Since then, the Department of State's Office of Combatting Terrorism has issued an annual report which includes a chronology of significant events. The *Department of State Bulletin*, a monthly publication, and the *Foreign Service Journal* also contain relevant materials.

The U.S. Congress and the Library of Congress are among the most prolific and informative sources on international as well as domestic terrorism. See, for instance:

- The Library of Congress, Congressional Research Service, *Terrorist Incidents Involving U.S. Citizens or Property 1981-1986: A Chronology* (updated 08/16/86), by James P. Wootten (Washington, D.C.: CRS, 1986), 13 pp.

- The Library of Congress, *International Terrorism: Issue Brief: Chronology of Events*, by Marjorie Brown and Allan Nanes (09/04/1969 - 04/04/1978). In U.S. Senate, Committee on Governmental Affairs, *An Act to Combat International Terrorism*. Report (no. 95-908) to accompany S.2236, 23 May 1978, 95th Congress, 2d Session (Washington, D.C.: GPO, 1978), pp. 105-135.

Middle East

- "A Chronology of Significant Attacks on Israel and Israeli Reprisal Operations," *TVI Journal* 5, no. 4 (1985): 26-30.

- "Arab Terrorism: A Chronology (1968-1973)," *United States Congressional Record* (22 December 1973), pp. 43427-43428.

- "Chronology of Zionist and Israeli Terrorism," *Palestine Digest* 2 (January 1973): 3-8.

- "Record of Arab Terrorism, 1967-1975," *United States Congressional Record* (25-27 February 1975), pp. 4306-4307, 4521-4522, 4753-4754.

- *Savage Kinship: A Chronology of the Use of Violence for Political Ends in Arab Countries* (Jerusalem: Carta, 1973), 32 pp.

- United States Library of Congress, Congressional Research Service, *Iran Hostage Crisis: A Chronology of Daily Development Reports* (Rockville, MD: National Criminal Justice Reference Service, 1981), 425 pp. (The NCJRS, which is operated by the Law Enforcement Assistance Administration of the U.S. Department of Justice, is located at P.O. Box 6000, Rockville, Maryland 20850, USA.)

Latin America

- "Urban Guerrilla Warfare: Argentina: Chronology." In James Kohl and J. Litt (eds.), *Urban Guerrilla Warfare in Latin America* (Cambridge, MA: MIT Press, 1974), pp. 339-364.

- "Urban Guerrilla Warfare: Brazil: Chronology." In *ibid*., pp. 196-226.

- "Chronology of Contra Attacks on Civilians: December 1, 1981 - November 30, 1984." In Reed Brody, *Contra Terror in Nicaragua: Report of a Fact Finding Mission: September 1984 - January 1985* (Boston: South End Press, 1985), pp. 153-183.

Spain

For a chronology of a decade of ETA and GRAPO terrorism, the most extensive published source is:

- *Equipo "D": 1973-1983: La Decada del Terror (Datos para una Causa General)* (Madrid: Ediciones Dyrsen, 1984), approximately 1,000 pp.

- For an update, see J. L. Scherer, "Selected Terrorist Incidents in Spain, 1983 - June 1986," *Terrorism* 1, no. 3 (July 1986): 1-11.

DATA ON STATE TERRORISM AND REGIME REPRESSION

Just as most researchers in the field of terrorism shy away from the past, the majority also avoid dealing with state terrorism. While insurgent terrorists and the media often seek each other out, state terrorists generally avoid publicity and attempt to conceal the regime's repressive activities by media censorship and/or disinformation. Nonconforming journalists are often primary targets of state violence, which also contributes to a fear of investigating charges of state abuses of power. The disproportionately small amount of media attention to terrorism from above, as opposed to terrorism from below, is not compensated by the data-gathering efforts of social scientists. It is a difficult field and not one where careers are to be made. Therefore, there is woefully little material on regime terrorism. As Michael Stohl, one of the few American scholars devoting consistent attention to this area, put it: "To our knowledge there is no systematic data set on state terrorism, nor is there likely to be one."[9]

"Proving" state terrorism is usually more difficult than proving insurgent terrorism. Except in very unusual circumstances (such as the Nuremberg and Tokyo trials), there are no courts collecting evidence that would lead to the conclusion that a particular regime is or has been engaged in certain action in order "to induce sharp fear, and through that agency to effect a desired outcome in a conflict situation," to use Duvall and Stohl's definition of terrorism.[10]

States usually have definition power, and they also commission most of the statistical data on terrorism. Depending on who defines and who counts, the outcome can vary greatly. An example is provided in Table 3.2. As this table indicates, there are several sources of information for a particular country like El Salvador, but they are not sources that are interested in terrorism from a scientific point of view. These sources often serve to make a political point; there is a tendency to downplay human rights violations in one's own camp and to emphasize those in the other.

Among the various sources which monitor human rights abuses by governments, there is only one that is global in scope. It also uses conservative, low estimates of casualties in order to guard itself against charges of partisanship. This source is the human rights organization Amnesty International (AI) (its international secretariat is located at 1 Easton Street, London WC1 8DJ, United Kingdom). Amnesty International has its own research department, which collects information on human rights violations from a wide range of sources, including governments, local organizations, official and unoffical news media, and independent observers and fact-finding missions. In this way, Amnesty International accumulates a rich variety of information which it publishes in various forms. Its purpose is to assist people detained for their beliefs, color, sex, ethnic origin, language, or religion who have not used or advocated violence (prisoners of conscience), and to see that those who are detained without charge or trial receive fair and prompt trials (political prisoners). In addition, AI opposes the death penalty (which is still in force in more than 100 countries) and torture or other cruel, inhuman, or degrading treatment or punishment of all prisoners without reservations as to whether they have used or advocated violence.

Table 3.2. Number of Persons Killed in El Salvador in 1983, According to Various Sources.[11]

Source	*Civilian deaths attributable to various govt. agents and right-wing death squads*	*Civilian deaths attributable to guerrilla forces*
El Salvador government (official Human Rights Commission)	1,239	346
U.S. Embassy	ca. 1,464	ca. 216
Tutela Legal	5,142	67
CDHES	5,654	46
SJC	5,670	---

Tutela Legal (Legal Assistance): The Archbishopric's official monitoring office

CDHES (Comisión de Derechos Humanos de El Salvador) (Commission of Human Rights of El Salvador)

SJC (Socorro Jurídico) (Legal Aid)

In its research, AI makes a clear distinction between facts and allegations, carefully assesses the credibility of sources, and assures the impartiality of the research by disqualifying staff with a vested interest in a country (e.g., citizenship) from making decisions concerning that country. While these procedures are comparable to scientific procedures, AI's goal is not to contribute to our scientific knowledge but to protect the rights of prisoners based on the principles set forth in the United Nations Universal Declaration of Human Rights. Therefore, AI does not compare one country with another or grade governments according to their human rights records. The various country reports on human rights violations issued by Amnesty International differ from country to country and period to period and according to the nature and quality of data available. The desire of social scientists to utilize AI as a data gatherer has so far been resisted:

> Amnesty International is often asked to compare and contrast human rights records of different countries or of successive governments. It does not and cannot do this. Government secrecy and intimidation from many countries can impede efforts to corroborate allegations; this fact alone makes it impossible to establish a reliable and consistent basis for comparison. Furthermore, prisoners are subjected to widely differing forms of harassments, ill treatment and punishment, taking place in diverse contexts and affecting the victims and their families in different ways; this fact would render any statistical or other generalized comparison meaningless as a real measure of the impact of human rights abuses.[12]

This is of course true as far as it goes, but it also applies to all other sources that deal with political violence and its effects. Social scientists will continue to press Amnesty International to make its data collection and publication more uniform and therefore more useable for scientific purposes. Given that AI has been gathering data for a quarter of a century and that its data are among the most reliable available under given circumstances, researchers who wish to increase their knowledge about state violence and terrorism cannot do without them.

The following is a partial list of the main publications of Amnesty International (for a complete record of all published AI material, consult *Amnesty International in Print*, available from the secretariat in London). Except where noted, all publications were published in London by Amnesty International.

1. *Amnesty International Report 1985* (1986), available in six languages;

2. *Amnesty International Report 1984* (1985), 382 pp., available in English, French, and Spanish;

3. *Amnesty International Reports, 1962-1983*, until 1979 available in English only, since then also in French and Spanish;

4. *Amnesty International on Microfiche*, Inter-Documentation Company AG (Poststrasse 14, 6300 Zug, Switzerland). A major collection of published and unpublished research materials recording human rights abuses in 105 countries, accompanied by a printed catalog. Updated annually;

5. *Political Killings by Governments* (1983), 120 pp., available in English, French, and Spanish;

6. *Torture in the Eighties* (1984), 263 pp., in English, French, and Spanish;

7. *The "Disappeared" of Argentina* (1976, 1982), in English. A computer list of more than 3,600 documented cases of "disappearances" known to AI since 1976, updated in 1982. This should be compared with *Nunca Mas: A Report by Argentina's National Commission on Disappeared People* (London: Faber and Faber, 1986), which documents 8,960 cases of "disappearances";

8. *El Salvador: Extrajudicial Executions* (1983), 48 pp., in English, French, and Spanish;

9. *Guatemala: A Government Program of Political Murder* (1981), 32 pp., in English and Spanish;

10. *China: Violations of Human Rights* (1984), 132 pp., in English and French;

11. *Pakistan: Human Rights Violations and the Decline of the Rule of Law* (1981), 51 pp., in English;

12. *Northern Ireland: Report of an Amnesty International Mission* (1978), 72 pp.;

13. *Spain: The Question of Torture* (1985), 60 pp., in English and Spanish;

14. *Prisoners of Conscience in the USSR: Their Treatment and Conditions*, 2d ed. (1980), in English, French, and Spanish;

15. *Israel: Report and Recommendations of an Amnesty International Mission* (1980), 71 pp., in English and French;

16. *Law and Human Rights in the Islamic Republic of Iran* (1980), 216 pp., in English and French;

17. *Syria: Report to the Government* (1983), 68 pp., in English and French;

18. *Nicaragua: The Human Rights Record* (1986), 36 pp., in English and Spanish.

In addition to these reports, Amnesty International publishes a monthly *Newsletter* and the journal, *Chronicle of Current Events*, a collection of translated Soviet Samizat documents, so far more than sixty, also available on microfiche.

While it remains true, as Ekhart Zimmermann has said, that probably no other variable of political violence is as unsatisfactorily measured as state repression[13]--a statement that can be extended to state terrorism--it can be argued that Amnesty International data can be usefully employed for approximate measurements. "Torture," one of AI's central concerns, almost invariably involves more than information gathering by applying physical force; it usually also serves de facto as an instrument of intimidation. This makes it coextensive with some forms of terrorism. While Amnesty International operates an in-house computer data base to monitor the investigation of political prisoners' cases, this information is confidential and not available to academic researchers. However, there is some hope that in the future some country offices of AI might become less rigorous in their policy of keeping bona fide social scientists at a distance.

While Amnesty International's raw data are probably superior to those of the *World Handbook*, these are not the only sources. At the University of Utrecht, The Netherlands Institute of Human Rights (Studieen Informatiecentrum Mensenrechten, or SIM) is in the process of creating a data base as an outflow of the deliberations of a Working Group on Human Rights Information and Documentation System (HURIDOCS), which was established in 1982. This European working group has stressed the importance of developing common formats for data entry in different human rights documentation centers.[14] SIM issues a *Newsletter*, and is located at Domplein 24, 3512 JE Utrecht, The Netherlands.

One of the most important human rights monitoring efforts is the Human Rights Internet (HRI), located at the Harvard Law School, Pound Hall, Cambridge, Massachusetts 02138, USA. Founded in 1976 in Washington, D.C., HRI is a nonpartisan, nonprofit organization open to all who subscribe to the Universal Declaration of Human Rights. HRI is an international communications network and clearinghouse on human rights, with universal coverage. Over 2,000 individuals and organizations contribute to the network. HRI services the information needs of the human rights community and stimulates communication and coordination between activists, policy makers, and scholars concerned with the promotion and protection of internationally recognized human rights. The HRI regards accurate information as a precondition to effective action, and it is building a computerized data base to continually update bibliographical and organizational indexes and to facilitate information retrieval. The HRI also serves as an informal depository for the documentation of many nongovernmental human rights organizations, and it maintains a multilingual library of grey literature--fugitive materials like tracts, pamphlets, unpublished papers, newsletters, documents, reports, etc.--and edits an annual series of this material on microfiche (these are available through Inter-Documentation AG, Poststrasse 14, 6300 Zug, Switzerland). While its computer files are not yet available for on-line research, they can be searched at a public terminal on the premises with Boolean operators (the software is BRS Search and the hardware is a Fortune multiuser system). The file features subject indexing terms such as "Terrorism," "State terror," "Violence (political)," "War (counter-insurgency)," "War (insurgency)," "Movements (of armed resistance)," "Guerrillas," etc.

HRI issues the *Human Rights Internet Reporter* five times a year (editor: Laurie S. Wiseberg). Each issue of the *Reporter* contains about 250 pages of information on the human rights activities of organizations worldwide; key human rights developments in the Americas, Africa, Asia, Europe, and the Middle East; responses to significant human rights violations; human rights conferences; human rights bibliographies with detailed abstracts; scholarly research and publications; and book reviews. The *HRI Reporter*, published since 1976, is in all likelihood the most current, comprehensive reference work in the field of human rights. It updates J. P. Martin's *Human Rights: A Topical Bibliography* (Boulder, CO: Westview Press, 1983) and supplements the *Human Rights Quarterly*, and performs a number of other unrivaled functions. The Human Rights Internet has consultative status with the United Nations (ECOSOC and UNICEF).

The United Nations is also a source of data on state repression. The U.N. Human Rights Commission has set up a working group and two rapporteurs (S. Amos Wako and P. Kooijmans). Within rather narrow "rules of the game," a number of reports have been produced on specific topics and countries which are useful:

- United Nations (ECOSOC), *Report of the Working Group on Enforced or Involuntary Disappearances* (New York: United Nations, 24 January 1986) (E/CN.4/1986/18); for earlier reports, see E/CN.4/1985/15/Add.1 (14 February 1985), E/CN.4/1984/21 (for 1984), E/CN.4/1983/14 (for 1983); E/CN.4/1492 (for 1982), and E/CN.4/1435 (for 1981).

- United Nations (ECOSOC), *Summary or Arbitrary Executions: Report by the Special Rapporteur, Mr. S. Amos Wako, Appointed Pursuant to Resolution 1982/35 of May 1982 of the Economic and Social Council* (New York: United Nations, 31 January 1983) (E/CN.4/1983/16); see also E/CN.4./1984/29 (21 February 1984) and E/CN.4/1985/17 (12 February 1985).

As far as country reports are concerned, the researcher should also keep in mind the U.S. Department of State's "Country Reports on Human Rights," which are based on embassy materials. Under the Foreign Assistance Act of 1961 (section 502(B)(b)), these reports must be presented to Congress by the Secretary of State if security assistance is requested. While the embassies are instructed to present their reports according to uniform guidelines, the country reports are even less uniform than the country sections in the *Amnesty International Yearbook*, presumably because keeping friendly local ruling elites happy and the U.S. Congress cooperative are overriding considerations.[15]

As a conclusion to this survey on data bases about state terrorism, we would like to draw attention to the annual Freedom House surveys compiled by Raymond D. Gastil since 1973.[16] He defines political terror as

> . . . an attempt by a government or private group to get its way through the use of murder, torture, exile, prevention of departure, police controls, or threats against the family. These weapons are usually directed against the expression of civil liberties. . . . In fact political terror is a tool of revolutionary repression of the right and left. When that repression is no longer necessary to achieve the suppression of civil liberties, then political terror is replaced by implacable and well-organized but often less general and

> newsworthy controls. Of course, there is a certain unfathomable terror in the sealed totalitarian state, yet life can be lived with a normality in these states that is impossible in the more dramatically terrorized.

Gastil juxtaposes to some extent political terror and civil liberties. He then distinguishes between seven levels of civil liberties and political rights, judging the 167 sovereign nations and 54 related territories as being "free" (ranks 1 or 2), "partly free" (ranks 3, 4, and 5), and "not free" (ranks 6 and 7), depending on the combined scores they receive:

> (1) In political rights, states rated (1) have a fully competitive electoral process and those elected clearly rule. Most West European democracies belong here. . . . Turning to the scale for civil liberties, in countries rated (1) publications are not closed because of the expression of rational political opinion, especially when the intent of the expression is to affect the legitimate political process. No major media are simply conduits for government propaganda. The courts protect the individual; persons are not imprisoned for their opinions; private rights and desires in education, occupation, religion, residence and so on, are generally respected; law-abiding persons do not fear for their lives because of their rational political activities. States at this level include most traditional democracies. There are, of course, flaws in the liberties of all of these states, and these flaws are significant when measured against the standards these states set themselves.
>
> (2) Relatively free states may receive a (2) because, although the electoral process works and the elected rule, there are factors which cause us to lower our rating of the effective equality of the process. These factors may include extreme income inequality, illiteracy, or intimidating violence. They also include the weakening of effective competition that is implied by the absence of periodic shifts in rule from one group or party to another. . . . Moving down from (2) to (7) represents a steady loss of the civil freedoms we have detailed. Compared to (1) the police and courts of states at (2) have more authoritarian traditions. In some cases they may simply have a less institutionalized or secure set of liberties, such as in Portugal or Greece.
>
> (3) and (4) Below [the 2nd level], political ratings of (3) through (5) represent successively less effective implementation of democratic processes. . . . Those rated (3) or below may have political prisoners and generally varying

> forms of censorship. Too often their security services practice torture.
>
> (5) Governments of states rated (5) sometimes have no effective voting processes at all, but strive for consensus among a variety of groups in society in a way weakly analogous to those of the democracies.
>
> (6) States at (6) do not allow competitive electoral processes that would give the people a chance to voice their desire for a new ruling party or for a change in policy. The rulers of states at this level assume that one person or a small group has the right to decide what is best for the nation, and that no one should be allowed to challenge that right. Such rulers do respond, however, to popular desire in some areas, or respect (and therefore are constrained by) belief systems (e.g., Islam) that are the general property of the society as a whole. . . . [At] (6) there still may be relative freedom in private conversation, especially in the home; illegal demonstrations do take place; underground literature is published; and so on.
>
> (7) At (7) the political despots at the top appear by their sanctions to feel little constraint from either public opinion or popular tradition. . . . [There] is pervading fear, little independent expression takes place even in private, almost no public expressions of opposition emerge in the police-state environment, and imprisonment or execution is often swift and sure.[17]

Matching his data (presumably journalistic) for 1985 with this typology, Gastil arrived at the conclusions outlined in Table 3.3. Such a survey can be challenged on several grounds; nevertheless it is helpful in providing some perspective. Even if we assume that state terrorism is only present in categories 6 and 7, the sheer magnitude of the populations and countries affected should be a matter for great concern. There is every reason for researchers to look not only into non-state terrorism but also, increasingly, into state terrorism.

Table 3.3. Freedom in the World: 1985.[18]

	No. of Nations (n = 167) (= 100%)	*No. of Territories (n = 54) (= 100%)*	*No. of People in millions 4,795.9 (= 100%)*
Free (1, 2)	53 (32%)	32 (59%)	1,671.4 (34.85%)
Partly Free (3, 4, 5)	59 (35%)	19 (35%)	1,117.4 (23.30%)
Not Free (6, 7)	55 (33%)	3 (6%)	2,007 (41.85%)

DATA REQUIREMENTS

This survey of some of the existing data bases might create the impression that there is a substantial body of information to work with. Unfortunately, this is not true. Reviewing the empirical literature on political terrorism, T. R. Gurr, one of the leading data specialists in the field, recently concluded:

> I am convinced . . . that many, perhaps most of the important questions being raised cannot be answered adequately with the kinds of information now generally available to scholars. . . . The . . . problem is the lack of enough reliable data for the analysis of the entire range of questions about terrorism: etiology, processes, and outcomes. . . . Let me highlight the principal omission in the publicly available data:
>
> There are no comprehensive, current datasets on incidents of domestic [as opposed to "international"] terrorism. . . . There are no datasets which provide systematic information about the identities and characteristics of groups which use terrorist strategies. . . . There are no broadly based datasets with coded information on the outcomes of terrorist campaigns or on government responses to episodes of domestic terrorism. . . . There is no systematic compilation of information from case studies about ideologies,

> recruitment practices, organization, decision-making, or command and control in violent political groups. . . . There is no system or common framework for cumulating information on the psychological characteristics, recruitment, and careers of members of terrorist movements.[19]

In addition, Gurr pleads for a systematic collection of coded information on internal state terrorism, including types, targets, and effects. He suggests that such a collection could build on the *World Handbook*'s ongoing data collection, using the category "government sanctions" as a starting point, differentiating those that are terrorist and those that are not.

Other researchers who answered our questionnaire had overlapping data requirements. There were those who called for more detailed, comparative, high-quality case studies of terrorist movements (Berry, Merari, Robertson). Others called for case studies relating to specific instances of decision making in conflict situations involving governmental authorities and terrorists (Rosenthal). Yet others found that the psychology of terrorism remains *terra incognita* and called for biographical analyses of terrorists comparable to the research program commissioned by the German Ministry of the Interior, which produced the best single set of studies on any contemporary domestic terrorist situation, including a detailed biographical analysis of 250 terrorists (Drake).[20] Yet others called for content analyses of texts by state and non-state terrorists which would make clear the political use of language in justifying and legitimizing or condemning and attacking the use of terrorist strategies and tactics in social and political affairs (Crelinsten).

While the complaint about lack of data is a recurring theme, both in the literature and among our respondents, this is only true to a point. In many cases, the data are somewhere but cannot be retrieved either because of government secrecy, because researchers lack imagination (e.g., the glaring under-utilization of court testimonies by terrorists), or because researchers lack the courage to seek out and talk to terrorists and their sympathizers and supporters. The net result has been that there is a large and superficial literature on terrorism based on a small data base.

4

THE LITERATURE OF TERRORISM

The literature of terrorism is young: more than 85 percent of all books on the topic have been written since 1968. In terms of output, the growth was explosive in the late 1970s; since then there has been less dramatic, steady growth. Despite the volume of the literature--more than 6,000 titles, not counting fictional and ephemeral journalistic titles--its substance is less than impressive. Much of the writing in the crucial areas of terrorism research (areas 2 and 3.1, 3.4 of Table 4.1) is impressionistic, superficial, and at the same time often also pretentious, venturing far-reaching generalizations on the basis of episodal evidence. The subject matter is not one which invites dispassion, and the sense of moral outrage and resulting eagerness to condemn has often hindered authors from coming to a deeper understanding of terrorism. Practically all authors who write on the subject of terrorism today are opposed to terrorism and have not practiced terrorism themselves. Therefore, the literature is characterized by a certain lack of "first-hand" experience with the subject. From the point of view of an intellectual discourse on the subject, this is regrettable. Most of us would find it strange if all books on war were written by pacifists, and we therefore welcome at least some books by soldiers and generals. But the fact is that advocates of terrorism have gone underground, and their theoretical writings--if they produce any--are generally inaccessible. Works like Leon Trotsky's *The Defence of Terrorism: Terrorism and Communism, A Reply to Karl Kautsky* have become rare in our time.

The literature of terrorism is not the product of a single discipline. Rather, scholars from such different fields as psychology, criminology, law, political science, sociology, history, and the military and communication sciences have contributed to it. Terrorism has become a fashionable phenomenon to study, despite the fact that it is such a depressing subject.

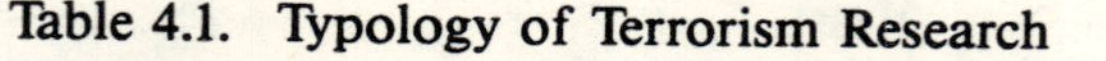
Table 4.1. Typology of Terrorism Research

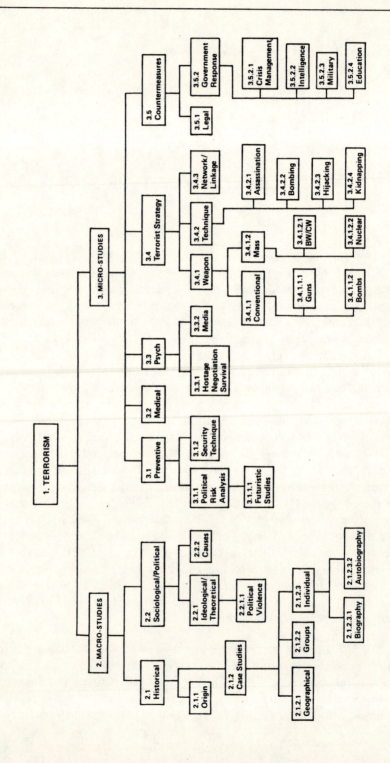

- 1. TERRORISM
  - 2. MACRO-STUDIES
    - 2.1 Historical
      - 2.1.1 Origin
      - 2.1.2 Case Studies
        - 2.1.2.1 Geographical
        - 2.1.2.2 Groups
        - 2.1.2.3 Individual
          - 2.1.2.3.1 Biography
          - 2.1.2.3.2 Autobiography
    - 2.2 Sociological/Political
      - 2.2.1 Ideological/Theoretical
        - 2.2.1.1 Political Violence
      - 2.2.2 Causes
  - 3. MICRO-STUDIES
    - 3.1 Preventive
      - 3.1.1 Political Risk Analysis
        - 3.1.1.1 Futuristic Studies
      - 3.1.2 Security Technique
    - 3.2 Medical
    - 3.3 Psych
      - 3.3.1 Hostage Negotiation Survival
      - 3.3.2 Media
    - 3.4 Terrorist Strategy
      - 3.4.1 Weapon
        - 3.4.1.1 Conventional
          - 3.4.1.1.1 Guns
          - 3.4.1.1.2 Bombs
        - 3.4.1.2 Mass
          - 3.4.1.2.1 BW/CW
          - 3.4.1.2.2 Nuclear
      - 3.4.2 Technique
        - 3.4.2.1 Assassination
        - 3.4.2.2 Bombing
        - 3.4.2.3 Hijacking
        - 3.4.2.4 Kidnapping
      - 3.4.3 Network/Linkage
    - 3.5 Countermeasures
      - 3.5.1 Legal
      - 3.5.2 Government Response
        - 3.5.2.1 Crisis Management
        - 3.5.2.2 Intelligence
        - 3.5.2.3 Military
        - 3.5.2.4 Education

One of the most experienced researchers, Ariel Merari, has commented in this regard:

> Terrorism is a study area which is very easy to approach but very difficult to cope with in a scientific sense. Easy to approach--because it has so many angles, touching upon all aspects of human behaviour. Difficult to cope with--because it is so diverse. As terrorism is not a discipline, there can hardly be a general theory of terrorism. . . . There are few social scientists who specialize in this study area. Most contributions in this field are ephemeral. Precise and extensive factual knowledge is still grossly lacking. Much effort must still be invested in the very first stage of scientific inquiry with regard to terrorism--the collection of data.

There are probably few areas in the social science literature in which so much is written on the basis of so little research. Perhaps as much as 80 percent of the literature is not research-based in any rigorous sense; instead, it is too often narrative, condemnatory, and prescriptive. Even the prescriptive literature is very one-sided: Almost all recommendations on how to cope with terrorism and how to deal with terrorists focus on non-state, mainly left-wing and minority-group opponents. There is a conspicuous absence of literature that addresses itself to the much more serious problem of state terrorism.

Ideally, the scientific literature of terrorism should be apolitical and amoral. The research should not take a "top-down" perspective, looking at the phenomenon of terrorism through the eyes of the power holders; nor should the researcher look at terrorism from a "revolutionary" or "progressive" perspective, identifying with one "just" cause or another. As a citizen or member of a group, he should take a stand on the issues of the day; as a scientist, however, he should not judge in-group and out-group by different standards. Moreover, the researcher should not confuse his roles. His role is not to "fight" the terrorist fire; rather than a "firefighter," he should be a "student of combustion," to use a distinction introduced by T. R.. Gurr. Such a neutral researcher might be less popular with political parties attempting to win allies to bolster their perspective. However, the quality of his research might improve and ultimately his prescriptions for dealing with terrorism might be more valuable if they are not built on the ideological foundations of one or another party to the conflict. Terrorist organizations must be studied within their political context, and the study of the terrorists' opponent and his (re-)actions are mandatory for a fuller understanding of the dynamics of terrorism. This sounds almost trivial, but the absence of such even-handedness is nevertheless the chief deficiency of the literature of terrorism.

The academic literature on terrorism has depended heavily on data provided by governments or think tanks contracted by government agencies. Many authors have also sought to give advice and guidance to antiterrorist agencies of governments. The result has not been a happy one. As one of our respondents, R. Crelinsten, put it:

> The perception of political terrorism as a practical problem requiring urgent solution has led to poorly defined, ideologically biased, conceptually skewed research. As Jerome Ravetz (1971) has pointed out, policy-oriented research tends to impede sound theoretical work because of urgent social need (real or perceived) to achieve concrete results in the real world.

Ironically, the operative community has not made much use of academic authors. One of our respondents--a practitioner of violence who yet had enough detachment to write about the dynamics of terrorist groups--concluded that "there is a tremendous amount of nonsense written in this field." In his judgment, there are "about 5 [authors who] really know what they are talking about--[the] rest are integrators of literature (which also is a very useful job)." Another respondent (Smith) held that "too many authors create the impression that they are merely using the 'popularity' of the phenomenon [of terrorism] as a means to promote their own image." Many authors have never written more than one article about terrorism; few have dedicated most of their research time to this field of study. Real specialists in academia are still few.

Who are the leading authors in the field? We asked this question in our 1982 questionnaire and again in 1985. The answers of our respondents were rather consistent. Table 4.2 provides a citation index. The thirty-three respondents to this question cited 166 different names out of a total of 373 names. On the average, they each cited 11.3 names. (In answer to the first questionnaire, there were 520 citations of 199 different names, with an average of 10 names cited by each respondent.) Within the five categories above, authors are listed in order of the number of citations they received, with those cited first receiving more citations than those toward the end.

Table 4.2. Leading Authors in the Field of Terrorism, Based on Frequency of Citation by Our Respondents.*

25-20 citations	*Jenkins*, *Wilkinson*
19-15 citations	*Bell*, *Alexander*
14-10 citations	*Crenshaw*, *Laqueur*
9-5 citations	Schmid,** *Clutterbuck*, *Mickolus*, *Friedlander*, *Kupperman*, *Miller*, *Sterling*, *Stohl*, Wardlaw, *Arendt*, *Bassiouni*
4-3 citations	Carlton, Ferracuti, *Merari*, Sloan, *Thornton*, Wolf, Cline, *Cooper*, *Crozier*, Dobson (+ Payne), E. Evans, *Gurr*, *Hacker*, Horowitz, Livingston, *Paust*, *Walter*

* Names printed in italics were also cited as leading authors in the first *Research Guide* on the basis of the same question.
** May indicate a bias, as people knowing Schmid were more likely to answer the questionnaire.

Among the authors receiving the most citations are several who are to varying degrees associated with research institutions and with government agencies. Alexander and Laqueur are associated with the Georgetown University Center for Strategic and International Studies in Washington, D.C. Laqueur's contribution is generally appreciated because he has placed terrorism in an historical context. His work on terrorism is only part of his enormous productivity in many areas. Alexander is credited with creating a forum for the debate on terrorism, and has edited more works on terrorism than anyone else. Jenkins, a Vietnam veteran, is the chief specialist at the Rand Corporation in California, which conducts much contract research for various U.S. government agencies. While very policy-oriented and narrow in its focus, Jenkins's empirical research is appreciated for its skillful operationalization even by those who do not share his perspective. To a lesser extent, this also appears to be true of

Wilkinson. His contribution is considered lucid and logical by many critics, while some hold that his work is not of the same quality as that of Thornton and Walter. Wilkinson appears to have had considerable influence on British and West European governmental thinking on how to deal with terrorism in a liberal state. As one of our respondents, Ch. Johnson, put it, Wilkinson "shows how control of terrorism itself is not a problem; the problem arises within the liberal state," i.e, the real problem is containing terrorism without paying the high price of closing open societies. Kupperman and Mickolus have been associated with the U.S. Arms Control and Disarmament Agency and the CIA. With one foot in the academic sector and the other in the operative sector, they each have had the opportunity to integrate the best insights from both worlds. Clutterbuck is a retired British general with extensive counterinsurgency experience in the Third World, a practitioner-turned-scholar whose work is considered to be well-informed and focused on the real issues. Crenshaw, on the other hand, is a purely academic scholar (though with Congressional experience in Washington). Her dissertation on the use of terrorism as a revolutionary tactic in the Algerian struggle for independence is one of the truly outstanding case studies. In her subsequent work, she has aimed at synthetic, interdisciplinary analysis guided by theoretical principles. She is presently working on a book on causes and effects of terrorism. J. B. Bell, on the other hand, is more journalistic in his writings. He is the maverick among the leading authors, someone who takes the trouble to go to Ireland, the Middle East, and the Third World to talk to revolutionaries and terrorists. This gives his work a rare authenticity. Probably only E. V. Walter, the author of the anthropological classic *Terror and Resistance*, receives as much praise as Bell for his work. However, in contrast to Bell, Walter's wonderful case study is based on a very strong conceptualization. Both Bell and Walter show a humane understanding for their topic which stands in marked contrast to the emotionalism of some of the American literature. European respondents to our first questionnaire were generally often critical of the dominant trends in the literature. One of them wrote: "Most of the American and English study . . . is one-sided and concentrated on insurgent terrorism without referring to social causes," a view echoed by an American respondent who characterized this literature as "Primarily an exercise in condemnation of resistance and an apology for state repression." These are summary judgments that do no justice to the diversity and richness of the American output. However, the basic truth of these statements is not affected since some of the most prominent authors who are closest to the centers of power are the ones whose writings at times are dangerously close to "counterinsurgency masquerading as political science," to use a phrase from one of our respondents.

Ronald D. Crelinsten, one of our present respondents, offers good advice as to where to look for the advancement of our knowedge:

> Perhaps a "unified field theory" of terrorism will prove as elusive as one in physics, but I am convinced that the resort to violence and terrorism can only be explained by analyzing the intimate relationship between social protest and social control, insurgency and repression, revolution and oppression.

A more widespread adoption of a two-dimensional perspective on terrorism would be a great improvement over the present situation in which the majority of authors focus mainly on revolutionary, left-wing movements while a small minority of authors point to the evils of imperialism, state repression, fascism, communism, or religious fanaticism. However, the "spiral of violence" is, as Dom Helder Camara, the Roman Catholic archbishop of Recife, Brazil, points out, one that moves through three levels or forms which feed on each other:[1]

- Violence No. 1: Injustice. In the tradition of St. Thomas Aquinas, who wrote that unjust laws "are acts of violence rather than laws," Dom Helder identifies injustice as the prime source of violence. This idea can be found as well in President Johnson's Commission on the Causes and Prevention of Violence report entitled *To Establish Justice, To Ensure Domestic Tranquillity*, which states: "To make violence unnecessary, our institutions must be capable of providing justice for all who live under them."

- Violence No. 2: Revolt. When the injustice becomes too oppressive, the second level of violence, which Dom Helder calls revolt, bursts forth. The important thing to note in connection with insurgent terrorism is that those who revolt by means of acts of terrorism are generally not those who are most oppressed but instead those who identify with and subsequently act on behalf of those who suffer from injustice. Their identification with the victims of injustice moves them to act against the perceived source of the injustice. They are often rebels for somebody else's cause. Their empathy with those who suffer turns them into "self-appointed spokesmen" (Köbben)[2] of the oppressed. They perceive themselves as unelected representatives of the "people's will" (the name of the first modern terrorist movement in Russia) and revenge the injustices, usually real but sometimes imagined, committed against their reference group by acts of violence against the agents of the state, who are, rightly or wrongly, held responsible for a particular state of affairs.

- Violence No. 3: Repression. Confronted with revolt, those who hold state power attempt to quell the revolt by repressive means, sometimes including terroristic means, to ensure the continuation of their rule. The power holders cite the overt violence of revolt as justification for their repression, while the advocates of revolt cite the violence of injustice and, subsequently, the violence of repression as legitimation for the violence of revolt. The "process(es) of legitimation and delegitimation of violence" (Crelinsten) is then played out for domestic and foreign audiences in a struggle of mutual guilt attribution. Audiences determine their allegiances on the basis of selected evidence, become polarized, and empathize with the sufferings of one side to the struggle while remaining much more insensitive to the victims of the other side. Each side has its own "facts" to support its opinions, each side is "right" within the parameters of its own "facts," and the spiral of violence continues. Attempts to break out of the spiral are generally unsuccessful because those who stray from the "righteous" course are likely to be considered traitors or appeasers and become likely targets of violence from within their own ranks. Perhaps only an alliance of direct and indirect victims of the violence of both sides can ever bridge the gap between the poles of conflict and restore a fragile peace, although the root causes of violence would remain unaddressed. In the few cases where the revolt is successful and a new society is erected atop the ruins of the old, the spiral of violence remains. The habit of solving conflict by violence has become established and the former victims or their spokesmen often become victimizers, consolidating their new regime with a level of violent repression equaling or even surpassing that of the previous regime, thereby legitimizing new revolts. With both regime and insurgents looking for foreign allies to maintain or strengthen their positions, the stage is set for subversion, intervention, and international terrorism.

Such a frame of reference, rather than a conspiratorial one in which certain nations (the Soviet Union, Libya, Iran, Syria, Nicaragua) are rather arbitrarily placed on and taken off lists of practitioners and supporters of international terrorism, might be scientifically more helpful in bringing the literature of terrorism to greater maturity. The role of academic research and writing on terrorism should not, even in democracies, be confined to providing intellectual support to consolidate the rule of those in power. Rather, social scientists should seek to "speak truth to power" as well as to "speak truth to the powerless" and those who identify with and fight for their causes. As members of a "theory class" rather than a ruling or other class, social scientists have the freedom to criticize and to construct new frameworks for conceptualizing and transforming realities.

THE STATE OF THE ART

The last item in our questionnaire was the question, "Where do you see elements of cumulativeness and maturation in the literature on terrorism?" The answers were generally pessimistic, ranging from "virtually none" (Townshend) to "not really--not yet" (Della Porta), with more than twenty others finding reason not to answer at all. Yet another (Warner) wrote: "I have to say that after 10 years of a veritable avalanche of literature there are few signs of maturation or cumulativeness outside of a handful of authors. . . . For example, discounting the monograph *The New Fascists* (1981) Wilkinson has turned out nothing major since *Terrorism and the Liberal State* (1977)."

Another respondent (Crelinsten) held: "The most heartening signs of cumulativeness and maturation are the appearance of books . . . which directly address and include in their collections both insurgent and official forms of terrorism. At least different forms and conceptions of terrorism are getting between the same two covers of certain books. On the whole, however, the preponderance of work is still based on truncated definitions or is merely polemical in nature. The word 'terrorism' is a political label with derogatory overtones and this still colours academic and scientific discourse. At least certain books, such as Herman's *The Real Terror Network*, are effecting a sort of balance in the ideological debate."

What are the few hopeful signs in the view of our respondents? One is the gradual emergence of an "invisible college" of data crunchers, policy experts, and victimologists (Mickolus). Some scholars, such as Y. Alexander, B. Jenkins, R. Kupperman, A. Merari, D. Szabo, and P. Wilkinson, are credited with creating the basis for an international community of scholars in the field (Ochberg). However, others complain that "research is too diffuse and communication among scholars limited" (Ferracuti). A German scholar (Fetscher) agreed, writing that "With the exception of the working group [organized by the German Ministry of the Interior], there is a considerable lack of inter-relatedness and communication between legal, social, political, ideological, psychological, etc., studies in the field."

Several authors (including Drake, Robertson, and Wilkinson) saw some slow progress on the case-study level, e.g., in the work of David Rapoport, Bernard Lewis, Clark, and Ivianski. Progress was seen to have taken place also in the legal area by some scholars (Robertson, Wolf, and Wilkinson).

In the area of psychological research, one respondent sees a "lack in rigor" (Taylor). One American psychiatrist interested in the comparative psychology of terrorism finds that there has been little work of real substance over the last decade: "All too often the papers state and restate trends." On the other hand, one respondent sees progress in the area of "personality inventory of terrorists" (Szabo), while another (Johnson) points to progress in "negotiation techniques." Another, cited earlier, holds that "We badly need more work on the psychological determinants and aspects of terrorism" (Taylor).

Another respondent concludes that "We have moved beyond simple typologies and ideological positions to develop more sophisticated theories and data sets. There is greater diversity in policy studies as well" (Corrado). One author agrees with this as far as "classifications" are concerned, but at the same time takes issue with the rather meaningless category of "international" terrorism (Robertson). Yet others keep despairing about the "intense subjectivity of the word terrorism" (Drake) and the fact that "too many works confuse terror with political violence, guerrilla warfare and military issues" (Thakrah).

Whom should one believe? The literature on terrorism is now so large that no single reader can absorb it all. Individual respondents might be right with regard to the material they have surveyed. For an authoritative judgment, it would be necessary to have an informed panel evaluating the same body of essential works. Yet, how should we determine what the essential works are?

ESSENTIAL WORKS ON TERRORISM

Every newcomer to the field of terrorism, facing a literature list of 6,000 titles, will be uncertain as to where to begin his study. To provide him with some guidance we have constructed this short literature list. It is based on the assessment of the respondents to our questionnaire in answer to the question of whose work they value most. Some works were cited many times, others only a few times.

Conceptual and Theoretical Works

Alexander, Yonah, and John M. Gleason, eds. *Behavioral and Quantitative Perspectives on Terrorism*. Elmsford, NY: Pergamon Press, 1981.

Arendt, Hannah. *On Violence*. Collected in *Crises of the Republic*. Harmondsworth: Penguin, 1972.

Baeyer-Katte, Wanda von, Dieter Claessens, Hubert Feger, and Friedhelm Neidhardt, with the collaboration of Karen de Ahna and Jo Groebel. *Gruppenprozesse*. Vol. 3, Bundesministerium des Innern, *Analysen zum Terrorismus*. Opladen: Westdeutscher Verlag, 1982 (525 pp.).

Bell, J. B. *Transnational Terrorism*. Washington, D.C.: American Enterprise Institute, 1975 (91 pp.).

Cline, Ray S., and Yonah Alexander. *State-Sponsored Terrorism: Report Prepared for the Subcommittee on Security and Terrorism for the Use of the Committee on the Judiciary, United States Senate*. 99th Congress, 1st Session. Washington, D.C.: GPO, June 1985 (186 pp.).

Clutterbuck, Richard. *Living with Terrorism*. New York: Arlington House Publishers, 1975.

Crenshaw, M. "The Causes of Terrorism." *Comparative Politics* (July 1981): 379-399.

De Nardo, James. *Power in Numbers: The Political Strategy of Protest and Rebellion*. Princeton, NJ: Princeton University Press, 1985 (267 pp.).

Evans, Alona E., and John F. Murphy, eds. *Legal Aspects of International Terrorism*. Lexington, MA: Lexington Books, 1978 (690 pp.).

Ferracuti, F. "Theories of Terrorism." In *International Terrorism and the Drug Connection*. Ankara: Ankara University Press, 1984, pp. 225-239.

Ferrari, Maurizio, et al. *I terrorismi in Italia.* Milano, 1980.

Guillaume, Gilbert, and George Levasseur. *Terrorisme international.* Paris, 1977.

Gurr, T. R. "Some Characteristics of Political Terrorism in the 1960s." In M. Stohl, ed. *The Politics of Terrorism.* 2d ed. New York: Dekker, 1983, pp. 23-49.

Hacker, Frederick J. *Crusaders, Criminals, Crazies: Terror and Terrorism in Our Time.* New York: W. W. Norton, 1977 (355 pp.).

Herman, Edward S. *The Real Terror Network: Terrorism in Fact and Propaganda.* Boston: South End Press, 1982 (252 pp.).

Jenkins, Brian M. "The Study of Terrorism: Definitional Problems." In Y. Alexander and J. M. Gleason, eds. *Behavioral and Quantitative Perspectives on Terrorism.* New York: Pergamon Press, 1981, pp. 3-10.

Laqueur, Walter. *Terrorism.* Boston: Little, Brown, 1977 (277 pp.).

Merari, Ariel. "A Classification of Terrorist Groups." *Terrorism: An International Journal* 1 (1978): 167-175.

O'Brien, Connor Cruise. "Liberty and Terrorism." *International Security* 2 (Fall 1977): 56-67.

Price, H. Edward. "The Strategy and Tactics of Revolutionary Terrorism." *Comparative Studies in Society and History* 19:1.

Salert, Barbara. *Revolutions and Revolutionaries.* New York: Elsevier, 1976 (161 pp.).

Schmid, A. P. *Political Terrorism: A Research Guide to Concepts, Theories, Data Bases and Literature.* Amsterdam: North-Holland Publishing Company, 1984 (585 pp.).

Schmid, A. P., and J. de Graaf. *Violence as Communication: Insurgent Terrorism and the Western News Media.* Beverley Hills: Sage, 1982 (283 pp.).

Stohl, M. *The Politics of Terrorism.* 2d ed. New York: Dekker, 1983.

Thornton, Thomas Perry. "Terror as a Weapon of Political Agitation." In H. Eckstein, ed. *Internal War: Problems and Approaches*. New York: The Free Press of Glencoe, 1964, pp. 71-99.

Tomasevska, K. *Challenges of Terrorism*. Beograd, 1983.

Walter, E. V. "Violence and the Process of Terror." *American Sociological Review* 29, no. 2 (April 1964): 248-257.

Wardlaw, Grant. *Political Terrorism: Theory, Tactics, and Countermeasures*. Cambridge: Cambridge University Press, 1982 (218 pp.).

Wilkinson, Paul. *Terrorism and the Liberal State*. 2d ed. New York: New York University Press, 1986 (322 pp.).

Case Studies

Aust, Stefan. *Der Baader Meinhof Komplex*. Hamburg: Hoffmann and Campe, 1985 (592 pp.).

Bell, J. B. *The Secret Army: A History of the IRA, 1916-1979*. Cambridge, MA: MIT Press, 1980.

Clark, Robert P. *The Basque Insurgents: ETA, 1952-1980*. Madison: The University of Wisconsin Press, 1984 (328 pp.).

Cobban, Helena. *The Palestinian Liberation Organisation: People, Power and Politics*. Cambridge: Cambridge University Press, 1984 (305 pp.).

Crenshaw Hutchinson, M. *Revolutionary Terrorism: The FLN in Algeria, 1954-1962*. Stanford: Hoover Institution Press, 1978 (178 pp.).

Fournier, Louis. *FLQ: The Anatomy of an Underground Movement*. Toronto: N.C. Press, 1984 (372 pp.).

Horne, Alistair. *A Savage War of Peace: Algeria, 1954-1962*. Harmondsworth: Penguin, 1986.

Kerkvliet, J. Benedict. *The Huk Rebellion: A Study of Peasant Revolt in the Philippines*. Berkeley: University of California Press, 1977.

Manconi, Luigi. *Vivere con il terrorismo*. Milano, 1980.

Sack, Fritz, and Heinz Steinert, with the collaboration of Uwe Berlit, Horst Dreier, Henner Hess, Susanne Karstedt-Henke, Martin Moerings, Dieter Paas, Sebastian Scheerer, and Hubert Treiber. *Protest und Reaktion.* Vol. 4, pt. 2, Bundesministerium des Innern, *Analysen zum Terrorismus.* Opladen: Westdeutscher Verlag, 1984 (603 pp.).

Silj, Alessandro. *Never Again Without a Rifle: The Origins of Italian Terrorism.* New York: Karz Publishers, 1979 (233 pp.).

Soskis, David A., and Frank M. Ochberg. "Concepts of Terrorist Victimization." In F. M. Ochberg and D. A. Soskis, eds. *Victims of Terrorism.* Boulder, CO: Westview Press, 1982, pp. 105-136.

Sterling, Claire. *The Terror Network: The Secret War of International Terrorism.* New York: Holt, Rinehart and Winston, 1980 (357 pp.).

Townshend, Charles. *Political Violence in Ireland: Government and Resistance since 1848.* London: Oxford University Press, 1984.

Managing and Controlling Terrorism

Alexander, Yonah, and S. M. Finger, eds. *Terrorism: Interdisciplinary Perspectives.* New York: John Jay Press, 1977 (377 pp.).

Alexander, Y., and Robert Kilmarx, eds. *Political Terrorism and Business: The Threat and the Response.* New York: Praeger, 1979.

Bell, J. B. *Transnational Terrorism.* Washington, D.C.: American Enterprise Institute, 1985.

Bell, J. B. *A Time of Terror: How Democratic Societies Respond to Terrorism.* New York: Basic Books, 1978.

Bobrow, Davis. "Preparing for Unwanted Events: Instances of International Political Terrorism." In R. D. Crelinsten, ed. *Research Strategies for the Study of International Political Terrorism.* Montreal: International Centre for Comparative Criminology, 1977, pp. 35-60.

Bundesministerium des Innern. *Bericht über ein Seminar . . . veranstaltet vom Bundesministerium des Innern: Auseinandersetzung mit dem*

Terrorismus-Möglichkeiten der politischen Bildungsarbeit. Bonn, 1981 (229 pp.).

Crenshaw, Martha, ed. *Terrorism, Legitimacy, and Power: The Consequences of Political Violence*. Essays by I. L. Horowitz, Y. Dror, Conor Cruise O'Brien, P. Wilkinson, R. Cox, and A. Quainton. Middletown, CT: Wesleyan University Press, 1983 (162 pp.).

Friedlander, Robert A. *Terrorism: Documents of International and Local Control*. 4 vols. Dobbs Ferry, NY: Oceana, 1979-1984.

Hassel, Conrad. "Terror: The Crime of the Privileged: An Examination and Prognosis." *Terrorism: An International Journal* 1 (1978): 1-16.

Jenkins, Brian M., ed. *Terrorism and Personal Protection*. Stoneham, MA: Butterworth, 1985 (451 pp.).

Kupperman, Robert, and Darrell Trent. *Terrorism: Threat, Reality, Response*. Stanford: Hoover Institution Press, 1979 (450 pp.).

Livingston, Neil C. *The War Against Terrorism*. Lexington, MA: Lexington Books, 1982 (291 pp.).

Livingston, Neil C., and T. E. Arnold, eds. *Fighting Back: Winning the War Against Terrorism*. Lexington, MA: Lexington Books, 1985 (268 pp.).

Merari, A. "Berlin Conference Statement." *Terrorism: An International Journal* 3, nos. 3-4 (1980): 279-283.

Miller, Abraham H. *Terrorism: The Media and the Law*. Dobbs Ferry, NY: Transnational Publishers, 1982 (221 pp.).

Schmid, A. P. *Political Terrorism: A Research Guide to Concepts, Theories, Data Bases and Literature*. Amsterdam: North-Holland Publishing Company, 1984 (585 pp.).

Wardlaw, Grant. *Political Terrorism: Theory, Tactics, and Counter-measures*. Cambridge: Cambridge University Press, 1982 (218 pp.).

Wilkinson, Paul. *Terrorism and the Liberal State*. 2d ed. New York: New York University Press, 1986 (322 pp.).

Strategy of Terrorism

Alexander, Yonah, David Carlton, and Paul Wilkinson, eds. *Terrorism: Theory and Practice.* Boulder, CO: Westview Press, 1979.

Aron, Raymond. *Peace and War.* London: Weidenfeld and Nicolson, 1966.

Ascensio, Diego. *Our Man Is Inside.* Boston: Little, Brown, 1983.

Bundesministerium des Innern. *Analysen zum Terrorismus.* 4 vols. Opladen: Westdeutscher Verlag, 1981-1984.

Crenshaw, M. "The Concept of Revolutionary Terrorism." *Journal of Conflict Resolution* 16, no. 3 (September 1972): 383-396.

Fetscher, Iring, and Guenther Rohrmoser. *Ideologien und Strategien.* Vol. 1, Bundesministerium des Innern, *Analysen zum Terrorismus.* Opladen: Westdeutscher Verlag, 1981 (346 pp.).

Funke, M., ed. *Terrorismus: Untersuchungen zur Struktur und Strategie revolutionärer Gewaltpolitik.* Düsseldorf: Droste und Athenäum, 1977 (391 pp.).

Gamson, William A. *The Strategy of Social Protest.* Homewood, IL: Dorsey Press, 1975.

Guevara, Ernesto. *Guerrilla Warfare.* New York: Random House, 1961.

Hacker, Frederick J. *Crusaders, Criminals, Crazies: Terror and Terrorism in Our Time.* New York: W. W. Norton, 1976.

Herman, Edward S. *The Real Terror Network: Terrorism in Fact and Propaganda.* Boston: South End Press, 1982 (252 pp.).

Kupperman, R. H. *Terrorism: Threat, Reality and Response.* Stanford: Hoover International Press, 1979.

Laqueur, Walter Z., ed. *The Terrorism Reader: From Aristotle to the IRA and the PLO: A Historical Anthology.* New York: New American Library, 1978 (291 pp.).

Leites, Nathan. "Understanding the Next Act." *Terrorism: An International Journal* 3, nos. 1-2:1-46.

Marighela, Carlos. *For the Liberation of Brazil.* Harmondsworth: Penguin, 1970 [includes the *Mini-Manual of Guerrilla Warfare*].

Moss, Robert. *Urban Guerrillas: The New Face of Political Violence.* London: Maurice Temple Smith, Ltd., 1972 (288 pp.).

Price, H. Edward. "The Strategy and Tactics of Revolutionary Terrorism." *Comparative Studies in Society and History* 19, no. 1 (January 1977): 52-66.

Silj, Alessandro. *Never Again Without a Rifle: The Origins of Italian Terrorism.* New York: Karz Publishers, 1979 (233 pp.).

Stohl, M., ed. *The Politics of Terrorism.* 2d ed. New York: Dekker, 1983 (473 pp.).

Wardlaw, Grant. *Political Terrorism: Theory, Tactics, and Countermeasures.* Cambridge: Cambridge University Press, 1982 (218 pp.).

Wiberg, Hakan. "Are Urban Guerrillas Possible?" In J. Niezing, ed. *Urban Guerrilla.* Rotterdam: Rotterdam University Press, 1974.

Wilkinson, Paul. *Terrorism and the Liberal State.* 2d ed. New York: New York University Press, 1986 (322 pp.).

State and State-Supported Terrorism

Arendt, H. *The Origins of Totalitarianism.* New York: Harcourt Brace Jovanovich, 1973.

Chomsky, Noam, and Edward S. Herman. *The Washington Connection and Third World Fascism.* Boston: South End Press, 1979.

Conquest, R. *The Great Terror: Stalin's Purges of the Thirties.* London: Macmillan, 1971 (633 pp.).

Dallin, A., and G. W. Breslauer. *Political Terror in Communist Systems.* Stanford: Stanford University Press, 1970.

Duvall, R., and M. Stohl. "Governance by Terror." In M. Stohl, ed. *The Politics of Terrorism.* 2d ed. New York: Dekker, 1983, pp. 179-219.

Goren, Roberta. *The Soviet Union and Terrorism.* London: George Allen & Unwin, 1984 (232 pp.).

Herman, Edward S. *The Real Terror Network: Terrorism in Fact and Propaganda.* Boston: South End Press, 1982.

Horowitz, I. L. *Taking Lives: Genocide and State Power.* 3d ed. New Brunswick, NJ: Transaction Books, 1980.

Koestler, Arthur. *Darkness at Noon.* New York: Bantam, 1970.

McClintock, Michael. *The American Connection.* Vol. 1, *State Terror and Popular Resistance in El Salvador* (400 pp.). Vol. 2, *State Terror and Popular Resistance in Guatemala* (327 pp.). London: Zed Press, 1985.

Merleau-Ponty, Maurice. *Humanism and Terror: An Essay on the Communist Problem.* Boston: Beacon Press, 1969.

Schmid, A. P. *Political Terrorism: A Research Guide to Concepts, Theories, Data Bases and Literature.* Amsterdam: North-Holland Publishing Company, 1984 (585 pp.).

Solzhenitsyn, A. *The Gulag Archipelago, 1918-1956.* London: Book Club Associates, 1974.

Stohl, Michael, and George Lopez. *The State as Terrorist: The Dynamics of Governmental Violence and Repression.* Westport, CT: Greenwood Press, 1984 (202 pp.).

Timerman, Jacobo. *Prisoner Without a Name, Cell Without a Number.* New York: Random House, 1982.

Timerman, Jacobo. *The Longest War: Israel and Lebanon.* New York: Random House, 1983 (167 pp.).

Trotsky, Leon. *The Defence of Terrorism: Terrorism and Communism.* London: George Allen & Unwin, 1935.

International Terrorism

Alexander, Y. *International Terrorism: National, Regional and Global Perspectives.* New York: Praeger, 1976 (414 pp.).

Bassiouni, M. Cherif. *International Terrorism and Political Crimes.* Springfield, IL: Charles C. Thomas, 1975 (594 pp.).

Bell, J. B. *Transnational Terror.* Washington, D.C.: American Enterprise Institute, 1975.

Bonanate, Luigi, ed. *Dimensioni del terrorismo politico.* Milano: Franco Angeli, Editore, 1979.

Carlton, D., and C. Schaerf, eds. *International Terrorism and World Security.* New York: Wiley, 1975 (332 pp.).

Crenshaw, Martha. "Transnational Terrorism and World Politics." *Jerusalem Journal of International Relations* 1 (1975): 109-129.

Dobson, Christopher, and Ronald Payne. *The Terrorists: Their Weapons, Leaders, and Tactics.* New York: Facts on File, 1979 (224 pp.).

Evans, Alona, and John Murphy, eds. *Legal Aspects of International Terrorism.* Lexington, MA: Lexington Books, 1978.

Gross, Feliks. *The Seizure of Political Power.* New York: Philosophical Library, 1957 (398 pp.).

Hardman, J.B.S. "Terrorism." In *Encyclopaedia of the Social Sciences.* Vol. 14. New York: Macmillan, 1936, pp. 575-576.

Kellett, Anthony. *International Terrorism: A Prospective and Retrospective Examination.* Ottawa: ORAE, DND, 1981.

Mickolus, Edward F. *Transnational Terrorism: A Chronology of Events, 1968-1979.* London: Aldwych Press, 1980 (967 pp.).

Sterling, Claire. *The Terror Network: The Secret War of International Terrorism.* New York: Holt, Rinehart and Winston, 1980 (357 pp.).

Wilkinson, Paul. *Terrorism and the Liberal State.* 2d ed. New York: New York University Press, 1986 (322 pp.).

Wolfgang, Marvin E. "Surveying Violence Across Nations: A Review of the Literature, With Research and Policy Recommendations." *International Review of Criminal Policy* 37 (1981): 62-95.

Etiology of Terrorism

Alexander, Y., and S. M. Finger. *Terrorism: Interdisciplinary Perspectives.* New York: John Jay Press, 1977 (377 pp.).

Alexander, Y., and J. M. Gleason. *Behavioral and Quantitative Perspectives in Terror.* New York: Pergamon Press, 1981.

Arendt, Hannah. *The Origins of Totalitarianism.* New York: Harcourt Brace Jovanovich, 1973.

Baeyer-Katte, Wanda von, Dieter Claessens, Hubert Feger, and Friedhelm Neidhardt, with the collaboration of Karen de Ahna and Jo Groebel. *Gruppenprozesse.* Vol. 3, Bundesministerium des Innern, *Analysen zum Terrorismus.* Opladen: Westdeutscher Verlag, 1982 (525 pp.).

Bell, J. Bowyer. *A Time of Terror: How Democratic Societies Respond to Revolutionary Violence.* New York: Basic Books, 1978.

Bundesministerium des Innern. *Analysen zum Terrorismus.* 4 vols. Opladen: Westdeutscher Verlag, 1981-1984.

Camus, Albert. *L'homme revolte.* Paris: Gallimard, 1951.

Crenshaw, Martha. "The Concept of Revolutionary Terrorism." *Journal of Conflict Resolution* 16, no. 3 (September 1972).

Crenshaw, Martha. "The Causes of Terrorism." *Comparative Politics* 13 (July 1981): 379-399.

Dostoyevsky, Fyodor. *The Possessed.* New York: Modern Library, 1986.

Fall, Bernard. *Street Without Joy: Insurgency in Indo-China, 1946-1963.* London: Pall Mall, 1964.

Fromm, Erich. *The Anatomy of Human Destructiveness.* London: Cape, 1974.

Gross, Feliks. *The Seizure of Political Power.* New York: Philosophical Library, 1958 (398 pp.).

Gurr, T. R. *Why Men Rebel.* Princeton: Princeton University Press, 1970.

Hyams, E. *Terrorists and Terrorism.* London: J. M. Dent & Sons, 1975.

Jackson, Geoffrey. *Surviving the Long Night: An Autobiographical Account of a Political Kidnapping.* New York: Vanguard Press, 1974 (226 pp.).

Jaeger, Herbert, Berhard Schmidtchen, and Liselotte Suellwold, with the collaboration of Lorenz Boellinger. *Lebenslaufanalysen.* Vol. 2, Bundesministerium des Innern, *Analysen zum Terrorismus.* Opladen: Westdeutscher Verlag, 1981 (243 pp.).

Leauté, Jacques. "Violence de guerre et violence de paix." *Revue de science criminelle et de droit penal compare* 4 (1978).

Mannheim, Karl. *Ideology and Utopia.* London: Routledge and Kegan Paul, 1936.

Matz, Ulrich, and Gerhard Schmidtchen, with the collaboration of Hans-Martin Uehlinger. *Gewalt und Legitimität.* Vol. 4, pt. 1, Bundesministerium des Innern, *Analysen zum Terrorismus.* Opladen: Westdeutscher Verlag, 1983 (437 pp.).

Norton, A. R., and M. H. Greenberg. *Studies in Nuclear Terror.* Boston: G. K. Hall, 1979.

Rosenbaum, H. J., and P. C. Sederberg, eds. *Vigilante Politics.* Philadelphia: University of Pennsylvania Press, 1977.

Salert, Barbara. *Revolutions and Revolutionaries.* New York: Elsevier, 1976 (161 pp.).

Schmid, A. P. *Political Terrorism: A Research Guide to Concepts, Theories, Data Bases and Literature.* Amsterdam: North-Holland Publishing Company, 1984 (585 pp.).

Schmid, A. P., and J. de Graaf. *Violence as Communication: Insurgent Terrorism and the Western News Media.* Beverley Hills: Sage, 1982 (283 pp.).

Thornton, Thomas Perry. "Terror as a Weapon of Political Agitation." In H. Eckstein, ed. *Internal War: Problems and Approaches.* New York: The Free Press of Glencoe, 1964, pp. 71-99.

Townshend, Charles. *Political Violence in Ireland: Government and Resistance since 1848.* London: Oxford University Press, 1983.

Walter, E. V. *Terror and Resistance: A Study of Political Violence.* London: Oxford University Press, 1969 (395 pp.).

Wilkinson, Paul. *Political Terrorism.* New York: Wiley, 1975 (159 pp.).

Wilkinson, Paul. "Social Scientific Theory and Civil Violence." In Y. Alexander, D. Carlton, and P. Wilkinson, eds. *Terrorism: Theory and Practice.* Boulder, CO: Westview Press, 1979, pp. 45-72.

Bibliographies

Bonanate, L., et al. *Political Violence in the Contemporary World.* Milan: Angeli, 1979 (253 pp.). Selected bibliography for period 1945-1978, in Italian and English.

Janke, Peter. *Guerrilla and Terrorist Organizations: A World Directory and Bibliography.* Brighton: Harvester Press, 1983 (531 pp.).

Jenkins, B. M., J. Johnson, and I. Long. *International Terrorism: An Annotated Bibliography.* Santa Monica: Rand Corporation, 1977.

Kress, Lee Bruce. "Selected Bibliography." In Marius H. Livingston et al. *International Terrorism in the Contemporary World.* Westport, CT: Greenwood Press, 1978, pp. 469-502.

Lakos, Amos. *International Terrorism: A Bibliography.* Boulder, CO: Westview Press, 1986 (481 pp.). The most extensive bibliography (5,622 items) of English-language materials published since the late 1960s, by a professional librarian.

Mickolus, Edward F. *The Literature of Terrorism: A Selectively Annotated Bibliography.* Westport, CT: Greenwood Press, 1980 (553 pp.). One of the best bibliographies in the field, presently being updated by the author.

Norton, A. R., and M. H. Greenberg. *International Terrorism: An Annotated Bibliography and Research Guide.* Boulder, CO: Westview Press, 1979 (218 pp.).

Schmid, A. P. *Political Terrorism: A Research Guide to Concepts, Theories, Data Bases and Literature. With a Bibliography by the*

Author and a World Directory of "Terrorist" Organizations by A. J. Jongman. Amsterdam: North-Holland Publishing Company, 1984 (585 pp.). A 4,091-item bibliography, partly annotated, covering more non-English-language material than other bibliographies.

Smith, M. J., Jr. *The Secret Wars: A Guide to Sources in English.* Vol. 3, *International Terrorism, 1968-1980.* Santa Barbara: ABC-Clio, 1980 (237 pp.). Journalistic articles form the main category in this bibliography.

Tutenberg, V., and Ch. Pollak. *Terrorismus: Gestern, Heute, Morgen: Eine Auswahlbibliographie.* München: Bernard & Graefle Verlag für Wehrwesen, 1978 (298 pp.). Especially strong for American and German military literature on terrorism.

United States Army Military Police School. *Terrorism: A Selected Bibliography.* Fort McClellan, AL: Army Military Police School, 1984 (238 pp.).

COMPUTER DATA BASES FOR BIBLIOGRAPHIC SEARCHES ON TERRORISM

Printed books are gradually becoming obsolete. The serious researcher will have to take recourse to up-to-date on-line data services. There has been an enormous expansion in the number of computer on-line data bases over the past two decades. By the end of 1982, there were approximately 1,150 data bases on-line,[3] and it is likely that this figure has doubled since then. The reader should consult Gale's *Online Database Search Services Directory* (1985 and updates) for specifics about data base specialities throughout Canada and the United States. The international edition of the *Encyclopedia of Information Systems and Services* (4th edition, Anthony T. Kruzas and John Schmittroth, Jr., eds. (Detroit: Gale, ca. 1984), available from Gale Research Company (Book Tower, Detroit, Michigan 48226, USA), lists European and other non-American data bases as well. Updates to the *Encyclopedia* are available in the form of the periodical publication *New Information Systems and Services*, also issued by Gale. European users might wish to subscribe to *Information Market* (I'M) (incorporating Euronet and Diane News), which is published by the Directorate General of the Commission of the European Communities (I'M, 177 Route d'Esch, L-1471 Luxembourg). Users interested in particular national on-line information centers can also obtain lists from this address. For the German Federal Republic, for instance, they can turn to GID (Gesellschaft für Information und

Dokumentation) mbH, Lyoner Strasse 44048, D-6000 Frankfurt 71. This society would be able to direct the researcher to, say, the German bibliographic service Biblio-Data, the on-line service of the Deutsch Bibliothek, Frankfurt am Main. Their holdings include over one million books, theses, and other university papers, conference proceedings, reports, and journals accumulated since 1966. The user equipped with a personal computer, a modem, and an access number can conduct subject-related searches on terrorism in the German Federal Republic from his desk.

Advantages of On-Line Searches

An example will illustrate the advantages of on-line searches. Staying with the German example from above, the Biblio-Data user can propose key words which can be arranged to make the search as narrow or as broad as desired. By combining key words (e.g., RAF, WOMEN, 1980-), he might find books and articles that deal with the question of why women are so prominent in this left-wing organization. By conducting a contrasting literature search on the role of women in right-wing extremist organizations or among common violent criminals, he might be able to assemble in one hour interdisciplinary materials which would take days to gather if he were to search through many volumes of traditional bibliographic indexes. In many cases, such topics as women and political violence are not indexed anywhere in printed form, and one of the advantages of ex-machina is that key words and multiple concepts can be searched from titles, abstracts, and in some cases the entire texts of articles in many journals across disciplines. Certain sources of information, such as recent conference papers, working papers, and grey literature, can be tapped by on-line searches only. However, if the researcher is not assisted by a reference librarian in his initial attempts to find relevant literature, he might despair at the amount of "noise"--nonrelevant literature--he gets. He might also be shocked at the price he has to pay. The cost of a particular search will depend on the data base(s) chosen, the complexity of the search (i.e., amount of time spent on-line), and the number of references retrieved and displayed. One way of saving money is to have the citations printed off-line and mailed. Especially when abstracts and not mere citations are wanted, this might save a great deal of precious time.

Major On-Line Data Bases for Political Terrorism

It is only since the mid-1960s that computer-based data bases have come into existence, and most institutions have never found the time and resources to store their pre-1965 holdings in computer-readable form.

My own experience with on-line bibliographic searches is primarily with the services available at the Library of Congress in Washington, D.C., and the Widener Library at Harvard University. These are, respectively, the largest library and the largest university library in the world. Before introducing a number of other services, I would like to dwell on the Library of Congress holdings.

Library of Congress Systems

The Library of Congress (LC) collection includes almost 80 million items. About 20 million of them are books and pamphlets in some sixty languages. Approximately 75,000 serial titles are received annually, and 1,200 newspapers are subscribed to. These items are cataloged by MARC (Machine-Readable Cataloging), the system used for creating the majority of LC on-line files. Material prior to 1968 was not cataloged by the Library of Congress in machine-readable form, but some Pre-MARC (PREM) records for the period since 1898 are available for books in English before 1968, in French before 1973, in German, Spanish, and Portuguese before 1975, and for serials before 1973. However, these files are incomplete and the citations are short (usually only the author's name, title, basic publication information, subject headings, and LC call and card numbers).

The two main subsystems of MARC are SCORPIO and MUMS. These sets of computer programs are written in ALC and PL1 languages. The library uses IBM 3033 and 3084 computers to process on-line requests.

SCORPIO (Subject-Content-Oriented Retriever for Processing Information Online) contains five types of files: books, selected periodical articles since 1976, federal legislation since 1973, copyright registrations since 1978, and organizations. Some files have more commands than others. Basic search results can be refined by a variety of techniques, including combinations of groups of responses and specification of such elements as language, date of publication, and geographic area of coverage. Files are updated daily (for Congressional legislative information (CG)), biweekly (for the Library of Congress Computerized

Catalog (BOOKSM/LCCC) which contains books, and for the National Referral Center Master File (NRCM), a list of organizations doing research or providing information to the public in various areas), and weekly (for the Bibliographic Citation File (BIBL), which lists periodical articles, government publications, pamphlets, etc., on current affairs, and for copyright documents and registrations (COHM)).

MUMS (Multiple Use MARC System) is a subsystem that provides access to information in BOOKSM/LCCC and Pre-MARC as well as nine other files. Most of the books in the LC that have been cataloged since 1968 and serials cataloged since 1973 are in this file. It is broader than SCORPIO, providing information about newer books not yet acquired by the Library. Under "Serials" it lists not only Library of Congress cataloged publications but also those from some other major research libraries, including series not in the LC. Under APIF (Automated Process Information File), MUMS lists preliminary cataloging for all books, minimal-level cataloging for low-priority books, romanized records for nonroman script language items, microforms, etc. Under LOIS (Library Order Information System), books and serials to be purchased (rather than being given, as most items are) are listed. Another advantage of MUMS is that through Component Word Search MUMS provides more access points to bibliographic records than is possible in SCORPIO.

While these searches are free for the bona fide researcher who uses on-site terminals and printers, outside users can obtain citations from the MARC Retriever Service on a fee basis. Through this service, a bibliographic listing can be produced by accessing any data found in the system. Listings from SCORPIO and MUMS can be produced in printed form, on magnetic tape, or on-line. In practice, the researcher interested in terrorism will be chiefly interested in the LCCC (Library of Congress Computerized Catalog for books) and BIBL (Bibliographic Citation File, for articles, including abstracts) files. The standard fee is $20 per file searched, plus an eight-cent charge for each record retrieved. (Customer Service Section, Cataloging Distribution Service, Library of Congress, Washington, D.C. 20541, USA.)[4]

Other On-Line Data Bases

DIALOG, a data base company in Palo Alto, California, owns the largest data bases in the world and serves hundreds of thousands of subscribers every year. DIALOG Information Services provides access to more than 170 data bases in all subject areas. These can be searched with full-text retrieval software and Boolean operators. Its bibliographic and factual files are based on publishers' information, government agencies, and other sources. Through DIALOG, the researcher can obtain access to the following files which are of interest for the study of terrorism:

- Biography Master Index (BMI), annual;

- Books in Print, 1900- ;

- Congressional Record Abstracts, 1981- ;

- Criminal Justice Periodicals Index, 1975- ;

- Dissertation Abstracts Online, 1891- ;

- U.S. Federal Index, 1976- ;

- U.S. Government Printing Office Monthly Catalog, 1976- ;

- Historical Abstracts, 1973- (articles, books, dissertations in the field of world history, 1450 to present, excluding the United States and Canada);

- Legal Resource Index, 1980- ;

- Magazine Index, 1959- (broad coverage of general-interest magazines in areas of current events, etc.);

- Middle East: Abstracts and Index, 1980- (an interdisciplinary index to English-language articles, books, dissertations, documents, speeches, etc., including abstracts);

- NCJRS (National Criminal Justice Reference System), 1972- (one of the best sources on terrorism. The NCJRS also conducts personalized searches for a fee of $48, with extensive abstracts of the items, including summaries of non-English-language publications, conference information, etc. Address: NCJRS, Box 6000, Rockville, MD 20850, USA);

- Public Affairs Information Service (PAIS) International, 1976- (indexes articles, books, pamphlets, government publications, reports, etc., in all fields of social science. Coverage from 1976 for English-language materials, and from 1972 for non-English-language materials);

- PSYCHINFO, 1967- (abstracts of articles, books, dissertations, technical reports, etc., in psychology and related behavioral sciences. Includes all material from *Psychological Abstracts* (index table) as well as other sources);

- SOCIAL SCISEARCH, 1972- (indexes articles by title words, authors, journal names, corporate sources, and cited references in area of social and behavioral sciences; corresponds to Social Science Citation Index);

- Sociological Abstracts, 1963- (covers articles, reviews, books, conference reports, discussions, case studies, etc., in sociology and related social and behavioral sciences);

- World Affairs Report, 1980- .

Another major seller of electronic information is Mead Data Central, an electronic information firm with 190,000 users. Under the name LEXIS, it sells electronically stored information on U.S. federal and state case law. LEXIS also provides on-line full-text information on British and French law. The data base contains about two million items, with some 150,000 new items added annually, and is continually updated. Mead Data Central also hosts the Defense and Foreign Affairs Handbook file.

NEXIS, which is also owned by Mead Data Central, sells information on business, medical, scientific, and commercial subjects. It also contains a massive library of newspaper articles. The full text of more than fifty publications and wire services are stored electronically. Among these are *The New York Times*, *The Washington Post*, the *Christian Science Monitor*, and the *Manchester Guardian*, which are added with only one day's delay after the date of publication. Wire services such as AP, UPI, Reuters, and Kyodo English Language Service are available between twelve and forty-eight hours after they first go over the wire. Magazines are available one week after publication. NEXIS has also acquired The New York Times Company's Infobank, whose files include *The Abstract*, which covers articles selected from more than sixty publications in addition to *The New York Times*, since 1969. NEXIS also stores the full text of other sources such as newsletters, directories, government documents, etc.[5] The names of some of the NEXIS files are: NEXIS Associated Press Political Service; NEXIS Code of Federal Regulations; NEXIS Federal Register; NEXIS Magazines; NEXIS Newsletters; NEXIS Newspapers; NEXIS Wire Services.

The information provided here on on-line data bases is only eclectic. There are dozens of interesting files available from various hosts. These include: Africa News Service; American History and Life, 1964- ; Applied Science and Technology Index; Australian Public Affairs Information service (APAI); Book Review Digest; Canadian Business and Current Affairs; Cumulative Book Index; Federal (U.S.) Research in Progress; Middle East File; National (U.S.) Newspaper Index, 1979- ; National (U.S.) Technical Information Service; Mental Health Abstracts; Readers' Guide to Periodical Literature; Religion Index, 1975- ; and U.S. Political Science Documents.

A word about the costs of data bases might be useful. Costs will vary from place to place, depending on whether the channel one uses has special rates. At the Widener Reference Department in Cambridge, MA, Harvard affiliates could, in late 1986, obtain the following rates for some specific services:

- Dissertation Abstracts Online: $1.50/minute on-line; $0.25/record typed on-line; $0.25/record printed off-line.

- Middle East: Abstracts and Index: $1.15/minute on-line; $0.25/record printed off-line.

- National Newspaper Index: $1.75/minute on-line; $0.20/record printed off-line; $0.10/record typed on-line.

- PAIS International: $1.45/minute on-line; $0.30/record printed off-line; $0.20/record typed on-line.

- SOCIAL SCISEARCH: $1.45/minute on-line; $0.30/record printed off-line; $0.20/record typed on-line.

- Sociological Abstracts: $1.25/minute on-line; $0.30/record printed off-line; $0.20/record typed on-line.

NOTES

ACKNOWLEDGMENTS

1. Altogether, fifty-eight replies were received to the approximately 200 questionnaires mailed out in 1985. Three of the responses contained only minimal information, five were very incomplete, and the rest were reasonably complete. Seven respondents did not want to be quoted directly and intended their information for background only; two wanted to be quoted without direct attribution; and three did not indicate their wishes with regard to the status of their replies. Approximately half of the respondents had answered the first questionnaire. For various reasons, no use could be made of this coincidence for longitudinal analysis. All but two respondents were male. In terms of origin (country of present residence), the breakdown was as follows (figures in parentheses indicate number of respondents to the first questionnaire from that country): United States 27 (21); United Kingdom 10 (9); Canada 6 (3); West Germany 3 (3); The Netherlands 2 (4); Israel 2 (3); Switzerland 2 (0); Finland 1 (0); Yugoslavia 1 (3); Republic of Ireland 1 (0); France 1 (0); Italy 2 (1); Australia, Sweden, South Africa 0 (1). When asked to state their main interest in terrorism (multiple entries were allowed), the respondents most often mentioned social science (37 entries), followed by law enforcement (18 entries), counterinsurgency (17 entries), intelligence (16 entries), public opinion (15 entries), deviance (6 entries), journalism (6 entries), victimology (5 entries). "Other" received 11 entries. The academic specializations of the respondents broke down as follows (again, multiple entries were allowed; percentages refer to proportion of total number of citations):

Political Science	32%	History	12%
Military	14%	Psychology	10%
Sociology	12%	Law	6%
Criminology	8%	Other	10%

Fifty-one of the respondents were institutionally affiliated with a university, one with a military college, one with a newspaper, and four with think tanks. Their research on terrorism was primarily academic. In answer to a question about their sources of financing, forty referred to "unsupported academic research," nineteen to "scholarly grants research," and eleven to "government-supported contract research" (multiple entries were possible). In order to obtain an impression of how long the respondents had been interested in terrorism, we asked them for the date of publication of their first article in this field. The earliest entry was 1950; two more respondents had entered the field by 1960; by 1965 three more had joined them. In 1970 two more joined the field; between 1971 and 1975 nine entered; between 1976 and 1980 twenty-two entered; and since 1980 another eighteen have entered the field. How representative is this sample of authors who answered our questionnaire? There is no easy way of measuring that exactly. My feeling is that this sample is a good cross section of the field and that the academic and geographic distribution reflects the research production distribution of the field. In our first questionnaire, we asked the respondents to name the twenty leading authors in the field. A list of 199 different authors emerged out of a total of 520 names mentioned. Forty-three authors were most often cited according to an index. Ten of our present respondents belong to this group of forty-three. Repeating the question in the second questionnaire produced a list of 166 different authors out of a total of 373 mentionings. Approximately 10 percent of these names were in our sample. Among the thirty-four leading authors (those mentioned most often; see Table 4.2), ten were in our sample.

PREFACE

1. E. V. Walter, *Terror and Resistance: A Study of Political Violence* (London: Oxford University Press, 1969), p. 3.

2. Vice President of the United States, *Public Report of the Vice President's Task Force on Combatting Terrorism* (Washington, D.C.: GPO, February 1986), p. 10, figure for 1985. In financial terms, it is estimated that $2 billion were spent for (1) research and development, (2) administration and support, (3) command, control, and communications, (4) intelligence, (5) personnel security, (6) physical security, (7) counterterrorist operations, and (8) education and training. Within these categories, more than 150 specific activities to combat terrorism are carried out by various federal departments and agencies.

CHAPTER 1. TERRORISM AND RELATED CONCEPTS: DEFINITION

1. Cited in *Veritas Reconsidered* (Harvard), special edition, September 1986, p. 9.

2. Alex P. Schmid, *Political Terrorism: A Research Guide to Concepts, Theories, Data Bases and Literature, With a Bibliography by the Author and a World Directory of "Terrorist" Organizations by A. J. Jongman* (Amsterdam: North-Holland Publishing Company, 1984), p. 111.

3. Cited in *ibid.*, p. 420.

4. Lt. Col. Donald B. Vought, U.S. Army (Ret.), and Lt. Col. James H. Fraser, Jr., U.S. Army, "Terrorism: The Search for Working Definitions," *Military Review* (July 1986), ca. p. 71; quoted from reprint in *Current News*, special edition (25 September 1986), *Terrorism*, no. 1493, U.S. Department of Defense (SAF/AA).

5. Lawrence Davidson, "Terrorism in Context: The Case of the West Bank," *Journal of Palestinian Studies* 15, no. 3 (Spring 1986): 121-122.

6. R. P. Hoffman, "Terrorism: A Universal Definition" (Ph.D. dissertation, Claremont Graduate School, 1984), p. 181.

7. Helmut Seifert, *Einführung in die Wissenschaftstheorie*, vol. 1 (München: Verlag C. H. Beck, 1971), pp. 33-34.

8. G. Schmidtchen, "Jugend und Staat: Übergänge von der Bürger-Aktivität zur Illegalität: Eine empirische Untersuchung zur Sozialpsychologie der Demokratie." In Ulrich Matz and Gerhard Schmidtchen, with the collaboration of Hans-Martin Uelinger, *Gewalt und Legitimität*, vol. 4, pt. 1 of Bundesministerium des Innern, *Analysen zum Terrorismus* (Opladen: Westdeutscher Verlag, 1983), quoted from questionnaire response.

9. A. P. Schmid, *op. cit.*, pp. 76-77.

10. Th. P. Thornton, "Terror as a Weapon of Political Agitation." In H. Eckstein (ed.), *Internal War: Problems and Approaches* (New York: The Free Press of Glencoe, 1964), p. 73.

11. Franklin L. Ford, *Political Murder: From Tyrannicide to Terrorism* (Cambridge, MA: Harvard University Press, 1985), p. 2.

12. Leon Trotsky, *Against Individual Terrorism* (New York: Pathfinder Press, 1974), pp. 3-4.

13. Reprinted in David C. Rapoport and Yonah Alexander (eds.), *The Morality of Terrorism: Religious and Secular Justifications* (New York: Pergamon Press, 1983), p. 189. The authenticity of this document, which reached the West in the early 1950s, has not been fully established; however, even if the NKVD was not the originator, it provides profound insights into Communist practices.

14. C. Visser, *Terrorisme en Westeuropa* (The Hague: Clingendael, 1986), p. 13.

15. *Ibid.*, p. 12.

16. For an inventory of Soviet nuclear threats, see Alex P. Schmid, *Social Defence and Soviet Military Power: An Inquiry into the Relevance of an Alternative Defence Concept* (The Hague: Government Printing Office, 1986), Appendix, pp. 185-206. For more detailed analyses, including the American record, see the forthcoming works of Richard Betts and Milton Leitenberg.

17. *Encyclopædia of the Social Sciences* (New York: Macmillan, 1936), pp. 575-576.

18. J. Waciorsky, *Le terrorisme politique* (Paris: A. Pedone, 1939), p. 98.

19. Cited in *The New York Times*, 2 October 1986, p. A12.

20. F. R. Allemann, "Terrorism: Definitional Aspects." *Terrorism: An International Journal* 3, nos. 3/4:185.

21. *Ibid.*, p. 188.

22. The Joint Chiefs of Staff, U.S. Department of Defense, *Dictionary of Military and Associated Terms (Incorporating the NATO and IADB Dictionaries)* (Washington, D.C., 1 April 1984), p. 164.

23. *Ibid.*, p. 383.

24. F. R. Allemann, *op. cit.*, p. 188.

25. Douglas Pike, "The Viet-Cong Strategy of Terror," monograph prepared for the U.S. Mission, Viet Nam, n.d., pp. 2-3.

26. Edward Kossoy, *Living with Guerrilla: Guerrilla as a Legal Problem and a Political Fact* (Geneva: Librarie Droz, 1976), p. 328.

27. Reed Brody (former Assistant Attorney General of the State of New York), *Contra Terror in Nicaragua: Report of a Fact-Finding Mission, September 1984-January 1985* (Boston: South End Press, 1985), pp. 153-183.

28. James Brooke, "Angolan War Taking Toll on Civilians," *The New York Times*, 23 November 1986, p. A26.

29. Frits Kalshoven, *The Law of Warfare: A Summary of its Recent History and Trends in Development* (Leiden: A. W. Sijthoff, 1973), pp. 27-29.

30. R. P. Hoffman, *op. cit.*, p. 181.

31. Douglas Pike, *op. cit.*, p. 21.

32. Andrew R. Molnar, in collaboration with Jerry M. Tinker and John D. LeNoir, *Human Factor Considerations of Undergrounds in Insurgencies* (Washington, D.C.: Special Operations Research Office, 1965), pp. 169n, 170.

33. Philip E. Devine and Robert J. Rafalko, "On Terror," *The Annals of The American Academy of Political and Social Science* 463 (September 1982): 40.

34. Alex P. Schmid and Janny de Graaf, *Violence as Communication: Insurgent Terrorism and the Western News Media* (Beverly Hills: Sage, 1982), p. 176.

35. Cited in interview with Robert Paul Hoffman, *op. cit.*, pp. 172-180.

36. Cited in *ibid.*, p. 171.

37. *Document on Terror*, *op. cit.*, pp. 213-214.

38. Abram de Swaan, "Terror as a Government Service." In M. Hoefnagels (ed.), *Repression and Repressive Violence* (Amsterdam: Swets and Zeitlinger, 1977), pp. 44-45.

39. Martha Crenshaw, "Introduction: Reflections on the Effects of Terrorism." In M. Crenshaw (ed.), *Terrorism, Legitimacy, and Power: The Consequences of Political Violence* (Middletown, CT: Wesleyan University Press, 1983), p. 1.

40. *Ibid.*, p. 2.

41. *Webster's New Unabridged Dictionary*, 2d ed. (New York: Simon & Schuster, 1979), p. 1264.

42. P. L. Berger and Th. Luckman, *The Social Construction of Reality: A Treatise on the Sociology of Knowledge* (Garden City, NY: Doubleday, 1966), p. 64.

43. P. L. Berger and Th. Luckman, as cited in J. Veenma and L. G. Jansma, "Molukkers in Nederland: beleid en onderzoek," *Mens en Maatschappij* 53, no. 2 (1978): 217.

44. W. I. Thomas, *The Child in America* (New York, 1928), p. 572; cited in Veenma and Jansma, *op. cit.*, p. 221.

45. Cited in G. A. Williams, "Gramsci's Concept of Egemonia," *Journal of the History of Ideas* 21, no. 4 (1960): 487; as cited in R. Miliband, *State and Capitalist Society* (1972), p. 180n.

46. Charles A. Russell, Leon J. Banker, J. Bouman, and H. Miller, "Out-Inventing the Terrorist." In Yonah Alexander, David Carlton, and Paul Wilkinson (eds.), *Terrorism: Theory and Practice* (Boulder, CO: Westview Press, 1979), p. 37n.

47. W. Laqueur, *Terrorism* (London: Weidenfeld and Nicolson, 1977), p. 79n.

48. U.S. Congress, Senate Committee on Governmental Affairs, *Report to Accompany S.2236*, 95th Congress, 2d Session (Washington, D.C.: GPO, 1978), pp. 91-92.

49. U.S. Central Intelligence Agency, *Patterns of International Terrorism* (1980 edition), p. *ii*; as quoted in U.S. Congress, Senate Committee on the Judiciary, Subcommittee on Security and Terrorism, *Report: State-Sponsored Terrorism*, 99th Congress, 1st Session (Washington, D.C.: GPO, 1985), p. 109.

50. U.S. Federal Bureau of Investigation, *FBI Analysis of Terrorist Incidents in the U.S., 1983*, by Terrorism Research and Analytical Center, Terrorism Section, Criminal Investigative Division; as quoted in U.S. Congress, Senate, *op. cit.*, p. 110.

51. U.S. Department of Justice, Testimony by Victoria Toensing, Deputy Assistant Attorney General, Criminal Division, U.S. Department of Justice, before the Senate Subcommittee on Security and Terrorism, 5 June 1984; as quoted in U.S. Congress, Senate, *op. cit.*, p. 110.

52. Headquarters, Department of the Army, *Dictionary of United States Army Terms* (Army Regulation 310-25, Effective 15 November 1983) (Washington, D.C.: Military Publication, 15 October 1983), p. 260.

53. U.S. Department of Defense, *Directive 2000.12*, quoted in *Report of the DOD Commission on Beirut International Airport Terrorist Act, October 23, 1983* (20 December 1983), p. 1220; as reproduced in U.S. Congress, Senate, *op. cit.*, p. 109.

54. U.S. Army, 1983 definition, *Army Regulation 190-52*; as quoted by D. B. Vought and J. H. Fraser, Jr., *op. cit.*, ca. p. 71.

55. U.S. Department of Defense, ca. 1986, as quoted by D. B. Vought and J. H. Fraser, Jr., *op. cit.*, ca. p. 71.

56. U.S. Department of State, *Patterns of Global Terrorism: 1983* (U.S. Department of State, September 1984).

57. Vice President of the United States, *Public Report of the Vice President's Task Force on Combatting Terrorism* (Washington, D.C.: GPO, February 1986), p. 1.

58. Ministry of the Interior, *Verfassungschutzbericht 1984* (Bonn: Bundesministerium des Innern, 1985), p. 17n.

59. *Prevention of Terrorism (Temporary Provisions) Act of 1974*; cited in E. F. Mickolus, *The Literature of Terrorism* (Westport, CT: Greenwood Press, 1980), p. 295.

60. V. K. Anand, *Terrorism and Security* (New Delhi, 1984), p. 19.

61. Uwe Backes and Eckhard Jesse, *Totalitarismus, Extremismus, Terrorismus: Ein Literaturführer und Wegweiser zur Extremismusforschung in der Bundesrepublik Deutschland*, 2d ed. (Opladen: Leske & Budrich, 1985), pp. 245-246.

62. Alvin H. Buckelew, *Terrorism and the American Response* (San Rafael: Mira Academic Press, 1986), p. 18.

63. Ray S. Cline and Yonah Alexander, *State-Sponsored Terrorism: Report Prepared for the Subcommittee on Security and Terrorism for the Use of the Committee on the Judiciary*, United States Senate, 99th Congress, 1st Session (S.Prt.99-56), June 1985 (Washington, D.C.: GPO, 1985), pp. 39-40.

64. Martha Crenshaw, *op. cit.*, pp. 2-3.

65. Ronald D. Crelinsten, "Terrorism as Political Communication: The Relationship between the Controller and the Controlled." In P. Wilkinson (ed.), *Contemporary Research on Terrorism* (Aberdeen: Aberdeen University Press, forthcoming) (quoted from ms.).

66. B. Crozier, "Aid for Terrorism." In *Annual of Power and Conflict, 1973-1974: A Survey of Political Violence and International Influence* (London: Institute for the Study of Conflict, 1974), p. 4.

67. Raymond D. Duvall and Michael Stohl, "Governance by Terror." In M. Stohl (ed.), *The Politics of Terrorism*, 2d ed. (New York: M. Dekker, Inc., 1983), p. 182.

68. H. Hess, "Terrorismus und Terrorismus-Diskurs," *Kriminologisches Journal* 15 (1983): 92.

69. Brian Jenkins, "International Terrorism: A New Mode of Conflict," Research Paper no. 48, California Seminar on Arms Control and Foreign Policy (Los Angeles: Crescent Publications, 1975), p. 1.

70. E. F. Mickolus, *Transnational Terrorism: A Chronology of Events, 1968-1979* (London: Aldwych Press, 1980), pp. *xiii-xiv*.

71. Benjamin Netanyahu, "Defining Terrorism." In B. Netanyahu (ed.), *Terrorism: How the West Can Win* (New York: Farrar, Straus, Giroux, 1986), p. 9.

72. Alex P. Schmid and Janny de Graaf, *Insurgent Terrorism and the Western News Media: An Exploratory Analysis with a Dutch Case Study* (Leiden: C.O.M.T., 1980), p. 8.

73. Grant Wardlaw, *Political Terrorism: Theory, Tactics, and Counter-measures* (Cambridge: Cambridge University Press, 1982), p. 16.

74. Paul Wilkinson, *Terrorism and the Liberal State*, 2d ed. (New York: New York University Press, 1986), pp. 54, 56.

CHAPTER 1. TERRORISM AND RELATED CONCEPTS: TYPOLOGIES

1. Adam Przeworski and Henry Teune, *The Logic of Comparative Social Inquiry* (New York: Wiley-Interscience, 1970), p. 25.

2. Betty Zisk, *Political Research: A Methodological Sampler* (Lexington, MA: D. C. Heath and Company, 1981), p. 332.

3. Eugene J. Meehan, *The Theory and Method of Political Analysis* (Homewood, IL: Dorsey Press, 1965), p. 40.

4. G. K. Roberts, *A Dictionary of Political Analysis* (London: Longman, 1971), p. 216.

5. Chalmers Johnson, "Perspectives on Terrorism." Reprinted in W. Laqueur (ed.), *The Terrorism Reader* (New York: American Library, 1978), p. 276.

6. Ezzat A. Fattah, "Terrorist Activities and Terrorist Targets." In Yonah Alexander and John M. Gleason (eds.), *Behavioral and Quantitative Perspectives on Terrorism* (New York: Pergamon Press, 1981), p. 11.

7. Richard Shultz, "Conceptualizing Political Terrorism: A Typology." *Journal of International Affairs* 32, no. 1 (1978): 7.

8. Martha Crenshaw, "The Causes of Terrorism," *Comparative Politics* 13 (July 1981): 380.

9. David L. Milbank, *Research Study: International and Transnational Terrorism: Diagnosis and Prognosis* (Washington, D.C.: CIA Political Research Department, April 1976), p. 1.

10. A. Pierre, "The Politics of International Terrorism." *Orbis* 19, no. 4 (1976): 1252.

11. P. Wilkinson, *Political Terrorism* (London: Macmillan, 1974), pp. 38-39.

12. W. H. Smith, "International Terrorism: A Political Analysis." In *The Year Book of World Affairs*, vol. 31 (London: Stevens, 1977), pp. 140-141.

13. B. M. Jenkins, "International Terrorism: A New Mode of Conflict." In D. Carlton and C. Schaerf (eds.), *International Terrorism and World Security* (London: Croom Helm, 1975), pp. 20-21.

14. Yehezkel Dror, "Terrorism as a Challenge to the Democratic Capacity to Govern." In M. Crenshaw (ed.), *Terrorism, Legitimacy, and Power: The Consequences of Political Violence* (Middletown, CT: Wesleyan University Press, 1983).

15. William L. Waugh, Jr., *International Terrorism: How Nations Respond to Terrorists* (Salisbury, NC: Documentary Publications, 1982), pp. 56-67.

16. B. Crozier, before the U.S. Senate Subcommittee on Internal Security, 14 May 1975; cited in L. A. Sobel (ed.), *Political Terrorism*, vol. 2 (Oxford: Clio, 1978), p. 3.

17. A. P. Schmid, *Political Terrorism: A Research Guide to Concepts, Theories, Data Bases and Literature* (Amsterdam: North-Holland Publishing Company, 1984), p. 105.

18. A. P. Schmid and J. de Graaf, *Violence as Communication: Insurgent Terrorism and the Western News Media* (Beverly Hills: Sage, 1982), p. 61 (Dutch edition published in 1980).

19. P. Loesche, "Terrorismus und Anarchismus." In M. Funke (ed.), *Extremismus im demokratischen Rechtsstaat* (Bonn: Bundeszentrale fuer politische Bildung, 1978), pp. 83-84.

20. Cited in L. A. Sobel (ed.), *Political Terrorism*, vol. 2 (Oxford: Clio, 1978), pp. 4-5.

21. In response to questionnaire, quoting from his unpublished Ph.D. thesis.

22. Cited in R. Moss, *Urban Guerrillas: The New Face of Political Violence* (London: Temple Smith, 1972), p. 35.

23. H. Ron Rosenbaum and Peter C. Sederberg, "Vigilantism." *Comparative Politics* 6, no. 4 (1974): 542.

24. George W. Nowell, reviewing H. J. Rosenbaum and P. C. Sederberg (eds.), *Vigilante Politics* (Philadelphia: University of Pennsylvania Press, 1977), in *Stanford Journal of International Studies* 12 (Spring 1977): 186.

25. P. Wilkinson, *Terrorism and the Liberal State* (London: Macmillan, 1977), pp. 56-57.

26. Richard Shultz, "Conceptualizing Political Terrorism: A Typology." *Journal of International Affairs* 32, no. 1 (1978): 9-10.

27. A. P. Schmid and J. de Graaf, *op. cit.*, p. 60.

28. A. Merari, "Classification of Terrorist Groups." *Terrorism: An International Journal* 1, nos. 3-4 (1978): 333.

29. See A. P. Schmid et al., *Zuid-Moluks terrorisme, de media en de publieke opinie* (Amsterdam: Intermediair, 1982).

30. Harry Eckstein, *Internal War: Problems and Approaches* (London: Free Press, 1964), pp. 20-21.

31. Cited in Robert Taber, *The War of the Flea: Guerrilla Warfare Theory and Practice* (St. Albans: Paladin, 1972), p. 92.

32. Thomas Perry Thornton, "Terror as a Weapon of Political Agitation." In Harry Eckstein (ed.), *Internal War: Problems and Approaches* (New York: The Free Press of Glencoe, 1964), pp. 82-88.

33. J. Bowyer Bell, *Transnational Terror* (Washington, D.C.: American Enterprise Institute, 1975), p. 15.

34. See Table VI of Schmid, *Research Guide* (1984), pp. 97-99.

35. M. Crenshaw, *Revolutionary Terrorism* (Stanford: Hoover Institution, 1979), pp. 36-37.

36. Philip A. Karber, "Urban Terrorism: Baseline Data and a Conceptual Framework." *Social Science Quarterly* 52 (December 1971): 528-529.

37. U.S. National Advisory Committee on Criminal Justice Standards and Goals, *Disorders and Terrorism: Report of the Task Force on Disorders and Terrorism* (Washington, D.C.: GPO, 1976), p. 453.

38. Irving Goldaber, "A Typology of Hostage-Takers." *The Police Chief* (June 1979): 21-23; cited in James B. Motley, *U.S. Strategy to Counter Domestic Political Terrorism* (Washington, D.C.: The National Defense University, 1983), p. 90.

39. Richard Shultz, *op. cit.*, p. 11.

40. *Ibid.*, pp. 13-15.

41. See note 4.

42. W. H. Nagel, "A Socio-Legal View on the Suppression of Terrorists." *International Journal of the Sociology of Law* 8:213-226.

43. Philip Schlesinger, Graham Murdock, and Philip Elliott, *Televising "Terrorism": Political Violence in Popular Culture* (London: Comedia Publishing Group, 1984).

44. E. V. Walter, *Terror and Resistance* (London: Oxford University Press, 1969), especially chapters 1 and 2.

45. I. L. Horowitz, "Transnational Terror, Civil Liberties and Social Science." In Y. Alexander and S. Finger (eds.), *Terrorism: Interdisciplinary Perspectives* (New York: John Jay Press, 1977).

46. W. Laqueur, *Terrorism* (New York: Little, Brown & Co., 1977).

47. Anthony M. Burton, *Urban Terrorism: Theory, Practice and Response* (New York: The Free Press, 1976), pp. 246-247.

48. Ted Gurr, *Why Men Rebel* (Princeton: Princeton University Press, 1970).

49. Bruce Mazlesh, *The Revolutionary Ascetic* (New York: McGraw-Hill, 1976).

50. H.H.A. Cooper, "Psychopath or Terrorist." *Legal Medical Quarterly* (1978).

51. D. Hubbard, "Terrorism and Protest." *Legal Medical Quarterly* (1978).

52. B. Jenkins, *The Terrorist Mindset and Terrorist Decisionmaking: Two Areas of Ignorance* (Santa Monica: Rand Corporation, June 1979).

53. C. Lasch, *The Culture of Narcisism* (New York: W. W. Norton, 1979).

54. G. Wardlaw, *Political Terrorism: Theory, Tactics, and Countermeasures* (Cambridge: Cambridge University Press, 1982).

55. S. Sloan, "Conceptualizing Political Terror." *Journal of International Affairs* 32 (1978).

56. Charles A. Russell and Bowman H. Miller, "Profile of a Terrorist." *Military Review* (August 1977): 27.

57. R. D. Crelinsten, "Terrorism as Political Communication: The Relationship between the Controller and the Controlled." Conference paper published in P. Wilkinson (ed.), *Contemporary Research on Terrorism* (Aberdeen: University of Aberdeen Press, 1987), quoted from manuscript.

CHAPTER 2. THEORIES

1. Despite the quantity of writings on terrorism, we still lack in-depth study of most terrorist organizations. While there are hundreds of major terrorist movements, we have adequate case studies on only a small number of them. Among the well-covered ones figure ASALA, BR, ETA, FLN, FLQ, IRA, Irgun, NAP, PIRA, and the PLO.

2. Twenty-eight authors received one mentioning; Laqueur and Arendt, three; Fromm, Wilkinson, and Young, two.

3. Study prepared by the U.N. Secretariat in accordance with the decision taken by the Sixth Committee at its 1314th meeting on 27 September 1972. Reprinted in M. Ch. Bassiouni, *International Terrorism and Political Crimes* (Springfield, IL: Charles C. Thomas, 1975), p. 10.

4. J. Dollard, L. W. Miller, N. E. Mowrer, O. H. Sears, and R. R. Sears, *Frustration and Aggression* (New Haven: Yale University Press, 1939). Cited in J.M.G. v. d. Dennen, *Problems in the Concepts and Definitions of Aggression, Violence and some Related Terms* (Groningen: Polemological Institute, 1980), p. 21.

5. Ted Robert Gurr, *Why Men Rebel* (Princeton, NJ: Princeton University Press, 1970), p. 21.

6. *Ibid*., pp. 3-4.

7. *Ibid*., p. 23. (Emphasis added.)

8. *Ibid.*, p. 11.

9. *Ibid.*, pp. 212-221.

10. See pp. 23-45, in M. Stohl (ed.), *The Politics of Terrorism* (New York: M. Dekker, 1979).

11. Cited in M. Stohl, *War and Domestic Political Violence: The American Capacity for Repression and Reaction* (Beverly Hills: Sage, 1976), p. 32.

12. J.M.G. v. d. Dennen, *op. cit.*, basing himself on R. J. Rummel, *Conflict in Perspective: Understanding Conflict and War*, vol. 3 (Beverly Hills: Sage, 1977). Also see Richard de Ridder, "De Frustratie Voorbij," *Psychologie* (September 1981): 23-30, for a critique of the Frustration-Aggression model.

13. Lawrence C. Hamilton, "Ecology of Terrorism: A Historical and Statistical Study" (Ph.D. dissertation, University of Colorado, Boulder, 1978), pp. 91-92.

14. P. Wilkinson, *Terrorism and the Liberal State* (London: Macmillan, 1977), p. 96.

15. L. C. Hamilton, *op. cit.*, pp. 187-188.

16. *Ibid.*, pp. 70-71.

17. *Ibid.*, p. 76.

18. *Ibid.*, pp. 78-79.

19. *Ibid.*, pp. 79, 84.

20. *Ibid.*, pp. 86, 89.

21. *Ibid.*, p. 180.

22. *Ibid.*

23. *Ibid.*, p. 62.

24. Ted Robert Gurr, "Some Characteristics of Political Terrorism in the 1960s." In M. Stohl (ed.), *The Politics of Terrorism* (New York: M. Dekker, 1979), pp. 24-25.

25. *Ibid.*, p. 24.

26. J. B. Bell, *A Time of Terror: How Democratic Societies Respond to Revolutionary Violence* (New York: Basic Books, 1978), pp. 95-104. (Enumeration added.)

27. W. Laqueur, "The Futility of Terrorism," *Harper's* 252 (March 1976): 99-105. Reprinted in J. D. Elliott and L. K. Gibson (eds.), *Contemporary Terrorism: Selected Readings* (Gaithersburg, MD: IACP, 1978), pp. 287-290. (Enumeration added.)

28. Michael Stohl, "Myths and Realities of Political Terrorism." In M. Stohl (ed.), *The Politics of Terrorism* (New York: M. Dekker, 1979), p. 2; 2d ed. (1983), pp. 5-17. (Author's enumeration.)

29. L. Bonanate, "Dimensioni del terrorismo politico." In L. Bonanate (ed.), *Dimensioni del Terrorismo Politico: Aspetti interni e internazionali, politici e giuridici* (Milano: Franco Angeli, Editore, 1979), pp. 169-175. (Enumeration added.)

30. P. Wilkinson, *Political Terrorism* (London: Macmillan, 1974), p. 126. (Enumeration added.)

31. L. Shapiro, *Totalitarianism* (London, 1972). Cited in B. Tromp, "Theorie en totalitarianisme," *Amsterdam Sociologisch Tijdschrift* 6, no. 2 (1979): 333.

32. Hannah Arendt, *The Origins of Totalitarianism* (New York: Harcourt Brace Jovanovich, 1973), p. 440.

33. Other authors mentioned only once (the three mentioned in the text were listed twice) were: Rubinstein (*The Cunning of History*), Young (*A Theory of Underground Structures*), Hess (*Repressives Verbrechen*), Taylor (*Beating the Terrorists*), Dallin and Breslauer (*Political Terror in Communist Systems*), and Friedrich and Brzezinski (*Totalitarian Dictatorship and Democracy*).

34. E. V. Walter, *Terror and Resistance* (New York: Oxford University Press, 1969), p. *vii*.

35. *Ibid*., p. *viii*.

36. *Ibid*., p. 3.

37. *Ibid*., pp. 341-344.

38. *Ibid*., pp. 340-343.

39. A. Dallin and G. W. Breslauer, *Political Terror in Communist Systems* (Stanford: Stanford University Press, 1970), p. 2.

40. Cited in *ibid*., p. 22n.

41. *Ibid.*, p. 17.

42. *Ibid.*, p. 29.

43. *Ibid.*, p. *ix*.

44. In M. Hoefnagels (ed.), *Repression and Repressive Violence* (Amsterdam: Swets and Zeitlinger, 1977).

45. *Ibid.*, p. 44.

46. *Ibid.*, pp. 44-45.

47. *Ibid.*, p. 45.

48. Cited in Dallin and Breslauer, *op. cit.*, p. 56.

49. Raymond D. Duvall and Michael Stohl, "Governance by Terror." In M. Stohl (ed.), *The Politics of Terrorism*, *op. cit.* The quotes here are from the draft manuscript.

50. *Ibid.*, p. 34.

51. *Ibid.*, pp. 36-37.

52. *Ibid.*, p. 38.

53. *Ibid.*, p. 34 (Table 1).

54. *Ibid.*, p. 39. (Author's emphasis.)

55. *Ibid.*, pp. 43-44.

56. *Ibid.*, p. 49.

57. Dallin and Breslauer, *op. cit.*, p. 40.

58. In D. Carlton and C. Schaerf (eds.), *International Terrorism and World Security* (London: Croom Helm, 1975), p. 15.

59. Cited in *Time* (European edition), 19 November 1979, p. 23.

60. Cited in E. Hyams, *Terrorists and Terrorism* (London: J. M. Dent & Sons Ltd., 1975), p. 143.

61. *Programma Ispolnitelnago Komiteta.* Cited in *Encyclopaedia of the Social Sciences*, vol. 14 (New York: Macmillan, 1936), p. 578.

62. Nicolas Morozov, "Terroristic Struggle" (London, 1880). Reprinted fully in Feliks Gross, *Violence in Politics: Terror and Political*

Assassination in Eastern Europe and Russia (The Hague: Mouton, 1972), p. 106. (Emphasis added.)

63. Stepniak, *Underground Russia* (New York: Scribner's Sons, 1892). Cited in R. Moss, *Urban Guerrillas: The New Face of Political Violence* (London: Temple Smith, 1972), p. 39. (Emphasis added.)

64. M. Latsis, "Zakony Grazhdanskoi voiny ne pisany." Cited in Dallin and Breslauer, *op. cit.*, p. 22n.

65. Abram de Swaan, "Terror as a Government Service." In M. Hoefnagels, *op. cit.*

66. Cited in Carol Ackroyd, Karen Margolis, Jonathan Rosenhead, and Tim Shallice, *The Technology of Political Control* (Harmondsworth: Pelican, 1977), pp. 233-234.

67. M. Begin, *La Révolt d'Israel* (Paris, 1953). Cited in R. Gaucher, *Les Terrorists* (1965), p. 254.

68. *Ibid.*

69. *The Memoirs of General Grivas* (New York: Praeger, 1964). Cited in Robert Taber, *The War of the Flea: Guerrilla Warfare, Theory and Practice* (Frogmore: Paladin, 1974), p. 106.

70. Albert Parry, *Terrorism: From Robespierre to Arafat* (New York: Vanguard Press, 1976), pp. 414-415.

71. Cited in Harold Jacobs (ed.), *Weatherman* (San Francisco: Ramparts Press, 1970), p. 438.

72. Carlos Marighela, *For the Liberation of Brazil* (Harmondsworth: Penguin Books, 1971), pp. 34-35, 46, 112.

73. Carlos Marighela, *Mini-Manual of the Urban Guerrilla.* Reprinted in Robert Moss, *Urban Guerrilla Warfare*, Adelphi Papers no. 79 (London: International Institute for Strategic Studies, 1971), pp. 40, 33-34. The wording in the Penguin edition (see note 72) is less sanguine.

74. Spiegel Gespräch, "Wir müssen raus aus den Schützengräben: Bundesminister Gerhart Baum und Ex-Terrorist Horst Mahler über das Phänomen Terrorismus," *Der Spiegel* 33, no. 53 (31 December 1979): 47.

75. *Autopsy of People's War* (Berkeley: University of California Press, 1973). Cited in H. E. Price, Jr., "The Strategy and Tactics of Revolutionary Terrorism," *Comparative Studies in Society and History* 19, no. 1 (January 1977): 63.

76. J. Kohl and J. Litt (eds.), *Urban Guerrilla Warfare in Latin America* (Cambridge, MA: MIT Press, 1974), pp. 15-19.

77. Donald C. Hodges (ed.), *Philosophy of the Urban Guerrilla: The Revolutionary Writings of Abraham Guillén* (New York: Morrow, 1973), p. 271.

78. *Ibid.*, p. 267.

79. *Time*, 2 November 1970. Cited in L. Sobel (ed.), *Political Terrorism*, vol. 1 (Oxford: Clio Press, 1975), p. 3.

80. For some ideas, see H.J.N. Horsburgh, "Moral Black- and Whitemail," *Inquiry* 18, no. 1 (Spring 1975): 23-38.

81. E. F. Mickolus, *Transnational Terrorism: A Chronology of Events, 1968-1979* (London: Aldwych Press, 1980), p. *xxxvii*.

82. Charles A. Russell and Bowman H. Miller, "Profile of a Terrorist," *Military Review* 58, no. 8 (August 1977): 33.

83. *Ibid.*, p. 25.

84. Susanne von Paczensky, "Ohnmächtige Wut gegen Gewaltandrohung." In A. Jeschke and W. Malanowski (eds.), *Der Minister und der Terrorist* (Reinbek: Rowohlt, 1980), p. 128. See also W. Jubelius, "Frauen und Terror: Erklärungen, Scheinerklärungen, Diffamierungen," *Kriminalistik* (June 1981): 247-255.

85. I. L. Horowitz, "Political Terrorism and State Power," *Journal of Political and Military Sociology* 1 (1973): 147-157.

86. E. F. Mickolus, *The Literature of Terrorism* (Westport, CT: Greenwood Press, 1980), p. 361.

87. D. Hubbard and F. G. Harris, cited in *ibid.*, p. 361.

88. R. S. Frank, "The Prediction of Political Violence from Objective and Subjective Social Indicators," paper presented at IPSA Conference, Edinburgh, 1976, as quoted by Gerhard Schmidtchen, "Bewaffnete Heilslehren." In H. Geissler (ed.), *Der Weg in die Gewalt* (München: Olzog, 1978), p. 49.

89. R. T. Hogan, J. A. Johnson, and N. P. Emler, "A Socioanalytical Theory of Moral Development," *New Directions for Child Development*, no. 2 (1978): 1-18.

90. Gustave Morf, *Le terrorisme québecois* (Montreal: Editions de l'Homme, 1970), as quoted by R. Moss, *Urban Guerrillas*, *op. cit.*, p. 118.

91. H.H.A. Cooper, Testimony Before the U.S. Senate on 21 July 1977, as quoted in L. A. Sobel (ed.), *Political Terrorism*, vol. 2 (Oxford: Clio, 1978), p. 6.

92. Stefan T. Possony, "Kaleidoscopic View on Terrorism," *Terrorism: An International Journal* 4:90-93.

93. W. Salewski, quoted in Zdenek Zofka, *Denkbare Motive und mögliche Aktionsformen eines Nukleärterrorismus* (Essen: AUGE, 1981), p. 27.

94. Wilhelm Kasch, quoted by Walter Laqueur in "Foreword" to R. Kupperman and D. Trent, *Terrorism* (Stanford: Hoover Institution Press, 1979), p. *xvi*. See also Wilhelm F. Kasch, "Terror: Bestandteil einer Gesellschaft ohne Gott?" In H. Geissler (ed.), *Der Weg in die Gewalt* (München: Olzog, 1978), pp. 52-68.

95. Hans-Dieter Schwind, "Meinungen zu den 'ursachen' des Terrorismus." In Hans-Dieter Schwind, *Ursachen des Terrorismus in der Bundesrepublik Deutschland* (Berlin: Walter de Gruyter, 1978), pp. 55-57.

96. Abraham Kaplan, "The Psychodynamics of Terrorism." In J. Alexander and J. M. Gleason (eds.), *Behavioral and Quantitative Perspectives on Terrorism* (New York: Pergamon, 1981), pp. 41-50.

97. F. Gentry Harris, Testimony Before the U.S. House of Representatives Committee on Internal Security, *Terrorism*, pt. 4, 93d Congress, 2d session (Washington, D.C.: GPO, 1974), p. 4429. Cited in M. Stohl, "Myths and Realities of Political Terrorism," chapter 1 of the revised edition of *The Politics of Terrorism* (New York: M. Dekker, 1983), as quoted from manuscript, p. 12.

98. Peter L. Berger, in *Worldview* (May 1976). Cited in L. A. Sobel (ed.), *Political Terrorism*, vol. 2, *op. cit.*, p. 8.

99. D. Mulder, "Terrorism." In J. Bastiaans, D. Mulder, W. K. van Dijk, and H. M. v. d. Ploeg, *Mensen bij Gijzelingen* (Alphen aan de Rijn: Sijthoff, 1981), pp. 124-126.

100. W. Laqueur, *Terrorism* (London: Weidefeld and Nicolson, 1977), p. 129.

101. *Ibid.*, p. 125.

102. P. Wilkinson, *Terrorism and the Liberal State*, *op. cit.*, p. 193.

103. *Ibid.*

104. F. Hacker, *Crusaders, Criminals, Crazies: Terror and Terrorism in Our Time* (New York: W. W. Norton, 1976), p. 105; J. Sundberg, in R. D. Crelinsten (ed.), *Research Strategies for the Study of International Political Terrorism* (Montreal: International Centre for Comparative Criminology, 1977), p. 177.

105. L. Paine, *The Terrorists* (London: Robert Hale & Co., 1975), p. 142.

106. From the account of the proceedings of a conference on terrorism held in Berlin in December 1978, see *Science*, no. 203 (5 January 1979): 34, as quoted in M. Crenshaw, "The Causes of Terrorism," *Comparative Politics* 13 (July 1981): 390.

107. B. Crozier, *The Rebels: A Study of Post-war Insurrections* (London: Chatto & Windus, 1960), p. 9.

108. Karmela Liebkind, *The Social Psychology of Minority Identity: A Case Study of Intergroup Identification: Theoretical Refinement and Methodological Experimentation* (Helsinki: University of Helsinki Department of Social Psychology, 1979); P. Weinreich, *Identity Development: Extensions of Personal Construct Theory and Application to Ethnic Identity Conflict and Redefinition of Gender Roles* (1979).

109. William J. Crotty (ed.), *Assassination and the Political Order* (New York: Harper and Row, 1971), pp. 290-306.

110. Leon Trotsky, "On Terrorism," *Der Kampf* (November 1911), reprinted in L. Trotsky, *Against Individual Terrorism* (New York: Pathfinder Press, 1974), p. 8.

111. M. Crenshaw, "The Causes of Terrorism," *Comparative Politics* 13 (July 1981): 394; P. Wilkinson, "Social Scientific Theory and Civil Violence." In Y. Alexander et al., *Terrorism: Theory and Practice* (Boulder, CO: Westview Press, 1979), pp. 67-68.

112. Cited in P. Wurth, *La répression internationale du terrorisme* (Lausanne: Imprimerie la Concorde, 1941), p. 18n.

113. M. Crenshaw, "The Causes of Terrorism," *op. cit.*, p. 394.

114. Cited in Z. Zofka, *Denkbare Motive und mögliche Aktionsformen eines Nukleärterrorismus* (Essen: AUGE, 1981), p. 30.

115. A. Silj, *Never Again Without a Rifle* (New York: Karz, 1979), p. 207.

116. Horst Mahler, in interview with Luciana Catelina in the Italian newspaper *Il Manifesto* (1977). Cited in W. H. Nagel, "A Socio-Legal View on the Suppression of Terrorism," *International Journal of Sociology of Law* 8 (1980): 221-222.

117. Spiegel Gespräch, "Wir müssen raus aus den Schützengräben: Bundesminister Baum und Ex-Terrorist Horst Mahler über das Phänomen Terrorismus," *Der Spiegel* 33, no. 53 (31 December 1979): 37.

118. *Ibid.*, p. 14.

119. Arthur Koestler, *The Ghost in the Machine* (London: Hutchinson, 1967), pp. 243, 251. The fact that compassion on the one hand and cruelty on the other can go hand in hand might seem paradoxical. Anatol Rapoport has suggested in his book *Conflict in Man-Made Environment* (Harmondsworth: Penguin, 1974) that aggression and empathy are two sides of the same coin, being nearer to each other than either is to indifference. The latter is a lack of identification while the former are positive and negative identifications with the object of suffering (Anatol Rapoport, *Conflict in sociale systemen* (Utrecht: Het Spectrum, 1976), p. 128). The fact that violence is done to human beings can be rationalized away by the terrorist and those who identify with him in several ways. Terrorists have a need to justify what they are doing. There are a variety of "neutralization techniques" that terrorists can use to justify to themselves and to others that they are not "murderers." Some of these techniques are: (1) denial of the victim; (2) denial of responsibility; (3) condemnation of the condemner; (4) appeal to higher loyalties; and (5) denial of the injury itself (G. M. Sykes and D. Matza, "Techniques of Neutralization: A Theory of Delinquency," *American Sociological Review* (22 December 1957): 664-670).

120. Cited in W. Laqueur, *Terrorism*, *op. cit.*, p. 66.

121. Robert Moss, *Urban Guerrilla Warfare*, Adelphi Papers no. 79 (London: International Institute for Strategic Studies, 1971), p. 2.

122. In interview with Sanche de Gramont, *The New York Times Magazine*, 15 November 1970. Cited in L. A. Sobel, *Political Terrorism*, vol. 1, *op. cit.*, pp. 5-6.

123. R. M. Momboisse, *Blueprint for Revolution* (Springfield, IL: Charles C. Thomas, 1970). Cited in E. A. Fattah, "Terrorist Activities and Terrorist Targets." In Y. Alexander and J. M. Gleason, *op. cit.*, p. 24.

124. Cited in L. A. Sobel (ed.), *Political Terrorism*, vol. 1, *op. cit.*, pp. 2-3.

125. R. Gaucher, *Les Terroristes* (Paris, 1965), p. 359.

126. Robert Thompson, *Revolutionary War in World Strategy 1945-1969* (London: Seeker & Warburg, 1970), p. 4.

127. *Ibid*., p. 32.

128. Brian M. Jenkins, "International Terrorism: A New Mode of Conflict." In D. Carlton and C. Schaerf (eds.), *International Terrorism and World Security* (London: Croom Helm, 1975), pp. 30-31.

129. P. Wilkinson, *Terrorism and the Liberal State*, *op. cit*., pp. 181-184.

130. H. W. Tromp, "Politiek Terrorisme," *Transaktie* 7, no. 1 (March 1978): 13.

131. *Ibid*., p. 5.

132. *Ibid*., p. 2.

133. Hylke Tromp, "Politiek terrorisme: de derde wereldoorlog in een volstrekt onverwachte vorm?" *Universiteitskrant* (Groningen) 8, no. 5 (28 September 1978): 11.

134. W. Laqueur, *Terrorism*, *op. cit*., p. 53.

135. Cited in *Volkskrant*, 17 November 1977, p. 5.

136. W. Laqueur, *Terrorism*, *op. cit*., pp. 216, 115-116.

137. S. T. Posony and L. F. Bouchey, *International Terrorism: The Communist Connection, With a Case Study of West German Terrorist Ulrike Meinhof* (Washington, D.C.: American Council for World Freedom, 1978).

138. *Ibid*., p. 1.

139. S. T. Francis, *The Soviet Strategy of Terror* (Washington, D.C.: The Heritage Foundation, 1981).

140. *Ibid*., pp. 2-3, 41-42.

141. Cited in *ibid*., p. 42.

142. In a news conference on 28 January 1981. *Current Policy*, no. 258, U.S. Department of State, p. 5.

143. The official Soviet attitude toward international terrorism has been expressed by V. Terekhov: "Marxism-Leninism rejects individual

terror as a method of revolutionary action since it weakens the revolutionary movement by diverting the working people away from the mass struggle. 'The first and chief lesson,' Lenin wrote, 'is that only the revolutionary struggle of the masses is capable of achieving any serious improvement in the life of the workers. . . .' International terrorism is radically different from the revolutionary movement of the people's masses, whose aim is to effect changes in society and which alone is capable of so doing. The terrorist act, however, even if its main point is to awaken public opinion and force it to pay attention to a particular political situation, can only have limited consequences: say, lead to the release of a group of prisoners, increase the financial assets of an organization. . . ." V. Terekhov, "International Terrorism and the Struggle Against It," *Novove Vremva*, 15 March 1975, pp. 20-22, in Foreign Broadcast Information Service, *USSR International Affairs III*, 28 March 1975, as quoted in W. Scott Thompson, "Political Violence and the 'Correlation of Forces'," *Orbis* (1976): 1284.

144. Claire Sterling, *The Terror Network: The Secret War of International Terrorism* (New York: Holt, Rinehart and Winston, 1980), p. 54. Cited in M. Stohl, "Fashions and Fantasies in the Study of Political Terrorism," unpublished paper, Inter-University Center, Dubrovnik (1981), p. 15.

145. Michael Haller, reviewing *Das internationale Terror-Netz* (München: Scherz Verlag, 1982) in *Der Spiegel* 39, no. 8 (22 February 1982): 206-208.

146. M. Stohl, "Fashions and Fantasies in the Study of Political Terrorism," *op. cit*., p. 14.

147. *Ibid*., p. 12; "CIA rapport valt beleid-Haig af," *Volkskrant*, 30 March 1981, p. 1.

148. Leslie H. Gelb, "Soviet Terror Charge Based on Old U.S. Data," *International Herald Tribune*, 19 October 1981, p. 6.

149. Cited in *ibid*.

150. Cited in *The Guardian*, 30 and 31 January 1981, as quoted in Philip Elliott, Graham Murdock, and Philip Schlesinger, "The State and 'Terrorism' on British Television," paper presented as Festival dei Popoli, Florence, 6-7 December 1981, pp. 56ff. See also "Moskau: Quelle allen Terrors," *Der Spiegel* 35, no. 22 (25 May 1981): 124.

151. Review by B. M Jenkins, *The Washington Post*, reprinted in *International Herald Tribune*, 28 May 1981.

152. Private information.

153. *More* (May 1978), p. 26.

154. A. de Borchgrave and R. Moss, *The Spike* (New York: Avon Books, 1980).

155. C. Sterling, *op. cit.*, p. 302.

156. Contemporary Affairs Briefing no. 7 (London, 1981), revealing that the United States was the main source of terrorist arms. *Der Spiegel* 35, no. 31 (27 July 1981): 89.

157. *Der Spiegel* 35, no. 26 (22 June 1981): 110-114. See also Joseph C. Goulden and A. W. Raffio, *The Death Merchant: The Rise and Fall of Edwin P. Wilson* (New York: Simon and Schuster, 1984), and Peter Maas, *Manhunt: The Incredible Pursuit of a CIA Agent Turned Terrorist* (New York: Random House, 1986).

158. Philip Agee, *Inside the Company: CIA Diary* (Harmondsworth: Penguin, 1974), p. 337.

159. Noam Chomsky and E. S. Herman, *The Political Economy of Human Rights*, vol. 1, *The Washington Connection and Third World Fascism* (Nottingham: Spokesman, 1979), pp. 16-17. (Emphasis added.)

160. M. Crenshaw, "The Causes of Terrorism," *op. cit.*, p. 386.

161. Brian M. Jenkins, "International Terrorism: A New Mode of Conflict," *op. cit.*, p. 15.

162. Santa Monica: Rand Corporation, 1970, p. 8. Cited in Geoffrey Fairbairn, *Revolutionary Guerrilla Warfare: The Countryside Version* (Harmondsworth: Penguin, 1974), p. 353.

163. P. Wilkinson, *Terrorism and the Liberal State*, *op. cit.*, p. 110.

164. Francis M. Watson, *Political Terrorism: The Threat and the Response* (Washington, D.C.: Robert B. Luce Co., 1976), p. 15.

165. Eugen Hadamovsky, *Propaganda und nationale Macht* (1933), p. 22. Cited in Hannah Arendt, *The Origins of Totalitarianism* (New York: Harcourt Brace Jovanovich, 1971), p. 341.

166. Cited in David M. Abshire, *International Broadcasting: A New Dimension of Western Diplomacy* (Beverly Hills: Sage, 1976), p. 20.

167. Peter Kropotkin, "The Spirit of Revolt." In *Revolutionary Pamphlets* (New York, 1968). Cited in Ze'ev Iviansky, "Individual Terror: Concept and Typology," *Journal of Contemporary History* 12, no. 1 (1977): 45.

168. *Freiheit*, 13 September 1884. Reprinted in W. Laqueur (ed.), *The Terrorism Reader* (New York: New American Library, 1978), p. 100.

169. See Philip A. Karber, "Terrorism as Social Protest," unpublished paper, 1971.

170. Philip A. Karber, "Urban Terrorism: Baseline Data and a Conceptual Framework," *Social Science Quarterly* 52 (December 1971): 527-533.

171. Franz Wördemann, *Terrorismus: Motive, Täter, Strategien* (München: Piper, 1977), p. 141.

172. M. Crenshaw Hutchinson, *Revolutionary Terrorism: The FLN in Algeria, 1954-1962* (Stanford: Hoover Institution Press, 1978), especially pp. 88-101.

173. Cited in *ibid*., p. 94.

174. Amy Sands Redlick, "The Transnational Flow of Information as a Cause of Terrorism." In Y. Alexander et al., *Terrorism: Theory and Practice* (Boulder, CO: Westview Press, 1979), p. 91.

175. Statement of Dr. Frederick Hacker to U.S. House of Representatives Committee on Internal Security, *Terrorism*, pt. 4, 93d Congress, 2d session, 14 August 1974 (Washington, D.C.: GPO, 1974), p. 3039. Cited in R. H. Kupperman and Darell M. Trent, *Terrorism* (Stanford: Hoover Institution Press, 1979), p. 42.

176. Naval Graduate School (1976). Cited in E. F. Mickolus, *The Literature of Terrorism*, *op. cit*., p. 12.

177. *Violence as Communication: Insurgent Terrorism and the Western News Media* (London: Sage, 1982); A. P. Schmid et al., *Zuidmoluks terrorisme, de media en de publieke opinie* (Amsterdam: Intermediair Bibliotheek, 1982).

178. This distinction was first introduced by Harry Eckstein, "On the Etiology of Internal Wars." In Ivo K. Feierabend, Rosalind L. Feierabend, and Ted Robert Gurr (eds.), *Anger, Violence and Politics: Theories and Research* (Englewood Cliffs, NJ: Prentice-Hall, 1972), p. 15.

179. Chalmers Johnson, "Perspectives on Terrorism." Reprinted in W. Laqueur (ed.), *The Terrorism Reader* (New York: New American Library, 1978), p. 278; M. Crenshaw, "The Causes of Terrorism," *op. cit*., p. 381.

180. W. Laqueur, *Terrorism*, *op. cit*., p. 80.

181. Brian M. Jenkins, "Terrorists at the Threshold." In E. Nobles Lowe and Harry D. Shargel (eds.), *Legal and Other Aspects of Terrorism* (New York, 1979), pp. 74-75.

182. E. S. Heyman, *Monitoring the Diffusion of Transnational Terrorism* (Gaithersburg, MD: IACP, 1980), pp. 2-3.

183. John D. Elliott and Leslie K. Gibson (eds.), *Contemporary Terrorism: Selected Readings* (Gaithersburg, MD: IACP, 1978), pp. 1-2. See also Elliott's "Transitions of Contemporary Terrorism," *Military Review* 57, no. 5 (May 1977): 3.

184. J. Henk Leurdijk, "Summary of Proceedings: Our Violent Future." In David Carlton and Carlo Schaerf (eds.), *International Terrorism and World Security* (London: Croom Helm, 1975), p. 2.

185. Imanuel Geiss, "Sources of Contemporary Conflicts and Political Revolutions: A Preliminary Survey," *Co-existence* 14:11.

186. M. Crenshaw Hutchinson, *op. cit.*, pp. 133-135.

187. *Ibid.*, p. 139.

188. The communication, transportation, and urbanization aspects as permissive factors are stressed by Evans, Grabosky, Wördemann, and Chalmers Johnson.

189. Chalmers Johnson, *op. cit.*, p. 281.

190. M. Crenshaw, "The Causes of Terrorism," *op. cit.*, pp. 382-383.

191. Cited in E. Hyams, *Terrorists and Terrorism* (London: J. M. Dent & Sons, 1975), p. 173.

192. Hannah Arendt, "On Violence." In *Crises of the Republic* (Harmondsworth: Penguin, 1972), p. 233. Both quoted from P. Wilkinson, *Political Terrorism* (London: Macmillan, 1974), p. 130.

193. "Politikwissenschaft und Gewaltproblematik." In H. Geissler (ed.), *Der Weg in die Gewalt* (München: Olzog, 1978), p. 74.

194. "Bewaffnete Heilslehren." In H. Geissler, *ibid.*, p. 40.

195. Egbert Jahn, "Was heisst geistige Auseinandersetzung mit dem Terrorismus?" Zusammenfassende Thesen zum Vortrag in Groningen, September 1980, mimeo, p. 1.

196. Herman Lübbe, *Endstation Terror: Rückblick auf lange Märsche* (Stuttgart, 1978), p. 99. Cited in Hans Dieter Schwind (ed.),

Ursachen des Terrorismus in der Bundesrepublik Deutschland (Berlin: Walter de Gruyter, 1978), p. 49.

197. Cited in Schwind, *ibid*., p. 51.

198. Iring Fetscher, *Terrorismus und Reaktion* (Köln: Europäische Verlagsanstalt, 1977), pp. 20-22.

199. H. Hess, "Terrorismus und Terrorismus-Diskurs," *Tijdschrift voor Criminologie*, no. 4 (1981): 181-184.

200. A. Silj, *op. cit*., p. *xii*.

201. Gaither Stewart, "Italië: De traditie van het terrorisme," *Haagse Post*, no. 44 (31 October 1981): 51.

202. L. Bonanate, "Some Unanticipated Consequences of Terrorism," *Journal of Peace Research* 16, no. 3 (1979): 205-209.

203. Edward Hyams, *Terrorists and Terrorism*, *op. cit*., p. 170.

204. F. Gross, *Violence in Politics* (The Hague: Mouton, 1972), pp. 89-92.

205. P. Wilkinson, *Terrorism and the Liberal State*, *op. cit*., p. 96.

206. *Ibid*., p. 37.

207. For instance in Anthony Burton, *Urban Terrorism: Theory, Practice and Response* (New York, 1975), p. 248.

208. Y. Alexander and John M. Gleason (eds.), *Behavioral and Quantitative Perspectives on Terrorism*, *op. cit*., p. *xiv*.

209. E. V. Walter, *Terror and Resistance: A Study of Political Violence* (London: Oxford University Press, 1969), p. 26.

CHAPTER 3. DATA AND DATA BASES

1. N. Chomsky and E. S. Herman, *The Washington Connection and Third World Fascism* (Nottingham: Spokesman, 1979), p. 6.

2. Philip Schlesinger, Graham Murdock, and Philip Elliott, *Televising "Terrorism": Political Violence in Popular Culture* (London: Comedia Publishing Group, 1983).

3. J. B. Bell, *A Time of Terror* (New York: Basic Books, 1978), p. 38. For *The New York Times* as source, see J. Rothman, *The New York Times Information Bank* (New York: NYT Library and

Information Services, n.d.). Indexes exist to other papers as well: e.g., the *Christian Science Monitor Index* (Boston), the (London) *Times Index*, the *Newspaper Index* (for *The Washington Post*, *The Los Angeles Times*, *The Chicago Tribune*, and *The New Orleans Picayune*). For the German Federal Republic, the *Spiegel Index* (Hamburg) is useful.

4. Charles Lewis Taylor, *Domestic Political Events Data 1948-1982, Codebook World Handbook of Political and Social Indicators*, computer tape (Cologne: Zentralarchiv für empirische Sozialforschung, 1985).

5. For a survey of various uses of *ITERATE* and other aggregate data, see "Appendix B: Statistical and Mathematical Approaches to the Study of Terrorism: A Study of Current Work," in Y. Alexander and S. M. Finger (eds.), *Terrorism: Interdisciplinary Perspectives* (New York: John Jay Press, 1977), pp. 253-256.

6. E. S. Heyman, *Monitoring the Diffusion of Transnational Terrorism* (Gaithersburg, MD: IACP, 1980), p. 8.

7. R. Deutsch and V. Magowan, *Northern Ireland, 1968-1973: A Chronology of Events*, vol. 1 (Belfast: Blackstaff Press, 1973), p. *ix*.

8. Bonnie Cordes et al., *A Conceptual Framework for Analyzing Terrorist Groups* (Santa Monica: Rand, 1985), quoted from unpaged abstract.

9. M. Stohl (ed.), *The Politics of Terrorism*, 2d ed. (New York: Marcel Dekker, 1983), p. 181.

10. R. Duvall and M. Stohl, "Governance by Terror." In *ibid*., p. 182.

11. D. Elsen and B. Verstappen, "Counting Human Rights Violations: El Salvador in Statistics," *SIM Newsletter*, no. 6 (May 1984): 3-14.

12. Amnesty International, *Annual Report 1984* (London: AI Publications, 1984), p. 4.

13. E. Zimmermann, *Soziologie der Politischen Gewalt* (Stuttgart: Enke Verlag, 1977), p. 131.

14. Laurie S. Wiseberg, *Research Manual on Human Rights* (Cambridge, MA: Harvard Law School, 1984) (quoted from unpublished manuscript).

15. United States Department of State, *Country Reports on Human Rights: Practices for 1981: A Report Submitted to the Committee on Foreign Affairs, U.S. House of Representatives, and the*

Committee on Foreign Relations, U.S. Senate, 97th Congress, 2d Session, February 1982 (Washington, D.C.: GPO, 1982).

16. The survey is published in the January issue of *Freedom at Issue*, a bi-monthly published by Freedom House, 20 West 40th Street, New York, NY 10018. The surveys also appear annually in a more complete (book) form: Raymond D. Gastil, *Freedom in the World: Political Rights and Civil Liberties* (New York: Freedom House, 1978, 1979, 1980; and Westport, CT: Greenwood Press, 1981, 1982, 1983-84, and 1984-85).

17. Raymond D. Gastil, "The Comparative Survey of Freedom," *Freedom at Issue*, no. 82 (January-February 1985): 7.

18. *Ibid*., p. 5.

19. T. R. Gurr, "Empirical Research on Political Terrorism: The State of the Art and How It Might Be Improved." In Robert O. Slater and Michael Stohl (eds.), *Current Perspectives on International Terrorism* (New York: St. Martin's Press, 1987) (quoted from manuscript).

20. Bundesministerium des Innern, *Analysen zum Terrorismus*, 4 vols. (Opladen: Westdeutscher Verlag, 1981-1983).

CHAPTER 4. THE LITERATURE OF TERRORISM

1. Edna Ferguson Reid, "An Analysis of Terrorism Literature: A Bibliometric and Content Analysis Study" (Ph.D. dissertation, University of Southern California, 1983), p. 21.

2. Helder Camara, *Spiral of Violence* (Denville, NJ: Dimension Books, 1981); as quoted in Robert McAfee Brown, *Religion and Violence: A Primer for White Americans* (Philadelphia: The Westminster Press, 1973), pp. 8-13.

3. A.J.F. Koebben, *De Zaakwaarnemer* (Deventer: Van Logum Slaterus, 1983).

4. Sharon Logsdon Yoder, "Searching for News: Computer On-Line Data Bases," *Freedom of Information Center Report*, no. 490 (March 1984); cited in Laurie S. Wiseberg, *Research Manual on Human Rights* (Cambridge, MA: Harvard Law School, 1984), unpublished manuscript.

5. Library of Congress, *Introducing MUMS*, *Introducing SCORPIO*, and other leaflets.

6. Laurie S. Wiseberg, *op. cit.*; *The Boston Sunday Globe*, 30 November 1986, p. 13.

A BIBLIOGRAPHY OF POLITICAL TERRORISM

INTRODUCTION

The present bibliography is, to our knowledge, the most comprehensive printed general bibliography on terrorism currently available. It has grown to its present size as a by-product of this writer's research in the field of terrorism since 1977. A compilation by a researcher rather than a professional bibliographer has both drawbacks and advantages. The advantage is a great familiarity with the subject matter and a selection of titles on the basis of qualitative criteria. The major drawback is that it reflects the preferences of an author with a background in history, sociology, and political science. Another drawback is that uniformity of all citations could not be achieved since the systematic search for missing publication details for all titles would have been too time-consuming and boring. The present bibliography, like its 1984 predecessor, is more Europe-centered than most of the existing American bibliographies. However, at the same time, the author collected most of the titles while doing research in the United States. The New York Public Library, the Library of Congress in Washington, D.C., and the Widener Library at Harvard University have been important sources of bibliographic information, as has the British Library in London and the University Library of Leiden, The Netherlands.

For certain types of titles, the reader should consult other bibliographies which are superior in certain areas. Those interested in journalistic articles on terrorism will find more citations in Smith's work. Those interested in military perspectives on terrorism should consult primarily Tutenberg and Pollak. Those interested in terrorism in fiction should consult Mickolus's excellent bibliography, which is also stronger in the field of legal literature than the present work. Those interested primarily in Italian, French, and Spanish books and articles would do well to consult Bonanate. Those whose language skills are confined to the

English language should turn to the truly outstanding Lakos bibliography, which covers United States dissertations as well as conference papers, U.S. government documents, and reports more thoroughly than our work. Lakos's work is also superior to this one in its coverage of the Middle East.

The present bibliography is divided into twenty major categories (plus one for Varia and Related Studies) and forty-six subcategories. Three categories have been subdivided: (1) Terroristic Activities by Region and Country, (2) Countermeasures Against Terrorism, and (3) Special Forms of Terrorism. Each title is placed in only one category or subcategory; there are no duplicate listings even when a title could be rightfully assigned to two or more categories. A particular title is cited under the category judged to be most appropriate by this writer.

It is our intention to keep this computer-based bibliography up-to-date and to publish periodical supplements to it. The bibliographic information is stored on magnetic tape at the Social Science Information and Documentation Centre (SWIDOC) in Amsterdam (Herengracht 410, 1017 BX Amsterdam, The Netherlands). Comments, additions, and criticism should be directed to the authors of the bibliography, A. P. Schmid and J. Brand, C.O.M.T., State University of Leiden, Hooigracht 15, 2312 KM Leiden, The Netherlands.

BIBLIOGRAPHY

Table of contents

A. BIBLIOGRAPHIES ON TERRORISM AND RELATED FORMS OF VIOLENCE

1. Backes, U. * Jesse, E. Totalitarismus, Extremismus, Terrorismus : Ein Literaturfuehrer und Wegweiser im Lichte deutscher Erfahrungen. Leske und Budrich, 1984. p. 351. Analysen. ; 38.

2. Bander, E.J. * Ryan, M.T. * (comp.) Bibliography on disorders and terrorism. - Washington D.C. : GPO, 1976. p. 597-634.
In: National Advisory Committee on Criminal Justice Standards and Goals, "Disorders and terrorism." Report of the task force on disorders and terrorism
Ca. 1250 items, partly annotated.

3. Bettini, L. Bibliografia dell'anarchismo. - Firenze : C.P.Editrice, 1972.

4. Blackey, R. Modern revolution and revolutionists : A bibliography. - Santa Barbara, Calif. : ABC-Clio, 1976. 257 p. War/Peace Series

5. Blackstock, P.W. * Schaf, F.L. Intelligence, espionage, counterespionage, and covert operations : A guide to information sources. - Detroit : Gala Research Co., 1978. 255 p

6. Bock, H.M. Bibliographischer Versuch zur Geschichte des Anarchismus und Anarcho-Syndikalismus in Deutschland. - Frankfurt : 1973. p. 295-334. Jahrbuch der Arbeiterbewegung. ; 1.
Bibliography on anarchism in Germany.

7. Bonanate L. * (ed.) La violenza politica nel mondo contemporaneo. - Milano : F. Angeli editore, 1979. 253 p

8. Bonanate, L. * et al. * (eds.) Political violence in the contemporary world : International bibliography on terrorism, movements of rebellion, guerilla warfare, anti-imperialistic struggles, the map of terrorism in the contemporary world. - Milan : F. Angeli editore, 1979. 253 p
Covers period 1945 to 1977, with some later addenda. Consists of 3 major parts. I: Politics of terrorism; II: Terrorism and law; III: Bibliography of terrorism.

9. Boston, G.D. * O'Brien, K. * Palumbo, J. Terrorism - A selected bibliography. - 2nd ed. - Washington D.C. : National Institute of Law Enforcement and Criminal Justice, 1976. 69 p
168 annotated citations of items published in the period 1969-1976.

10. Boulding, E. * Passmore, J.R. * Gassler, R.S. Bibliography on world conflict and peace. - 2nd ed. - Boulder, Colo. : Westview Press., 168 p
One of the 26 major categories covers terrorism.

11. Bourdet, Y. * Brohm, J.M. * Dreyfus, M.R. Bibliographie de la revolution. - Paris : Editions du Jour, 1975. 262 p. Que lire? Etudes et documentations internationales

12. Bracher, K.D. * Jacobson, H.A. * Funke, M. * (eds.) Bibliographie zur Politik in Theorie und Praxis. - New revised edition. - Bonn : 1976.
Bibliography with items on Notstand, Widerstand, Gewalt, Terror.

13. Chilcote, R.H. Revolution and structural change in Latin America: a bibliography on ideology, development and the radical left, 1930 1965. - 2 vols. - Stanford : Hoover Institution, 1970.

14. Condit, D.M. * et al. A counter-insurgency bibliography. - Washington, D.C. : American University (SORO), 1963. 269 p
A series of 6 supplements was published until 1965.

15. Cornog, D. Unconventional warfare: a bibliography of bibliographies. - Washington, D.C. : 1964.
Prepared by the Information Technology Division of the National Bureau of Standards. Deals with unconventional warfare including counterinsurgency, guerrilla warfare, special warfare, and psychological operations.

16. Cosyns-Verhaegen, R. Actualite du terrorisme: selection bibliographique. - Warre : Centre d'Information et de Documentation de la L.I.L., 1973. 21 p
Lists 131 items, most of them in French.

17. Cosyns-Verhaegen, R. Guerres revolutionnaires et subversives: selection bibliographique. - Brussels : Les Ours, 1967.

18. Coxe, B. * (comp.) Terrorism. - Colorado : USAFA, 1977. 47 p. United States Air Force Academy Library, Special Bibliograpy Series. ; No. 57.
Ca. 600 items, most of them newspaper articles. Not annotated.

19. Deutsch, R. Northern Ireland 1921-1974: a selected bibliography. - New York : Garland Publishing, 1975. 142 p

20. Duncan, J.T.S. * et al. Arson : A selected bibliography. - Washington, D.C. : National Institute of Law Enforcement and Criminal Justice, 1979. 94 p

21. Eckert, W.G. * (ed.) International terrorism. - Wichita, Kansas : The Milton Helpern International Center for the Forensic Sciences, 1977. 23 p
Unannotated bibliography under 27 subject headings listing 515 items, predominantly legal.

22. Felsenfeld, L. * Jenkins, B.M. International terrorism: an annotated bibliography. - Santa Monica, Calif. : RAND, Sept. 1973.
Lists a great deal of ephemeral journalism and non-English literature.

23. Goehlert, R. Anarchism: a bibliography of articles, 1900-1975. 1976. Political Theory. ; 4:113.

24. Guth, D.J. * Wrone, D.R. The assassination of John F. Kennedy : A comprehensive historical and legal bibliography, 1963-1979. - Westport, Conn. : Greenwood Press, 1980.

25. Hoerder, D. Protest - direct action - repression : Dissent in American society from colonial times to the present. A bibliography. - Muenchen : Verlag Dokumentation, 1977. 434 p

26. Jenkins, B.M. * Johnson, J. * Long, L. International terrorism: an annotated bibliography. - Santa Monica, Calif. : RAND, 1977.
Concentrates on journalistic articles.

27. Kelly, M.J. * Mitchell, T.H. Violence, internal war and revolution : A select bibliography. - Ottawa : The Norman Paterson School of International Affairs, Carleton University, 1976.
496 items bibliography.

28. Kenton, Ch. Terrorism or civil disorders. - Bethesda, Maryland : National Library of Medicine, 1979. 6 p

29. Kornegay jr, F.A. A bibliographic essay on comparative guerilla warfare and social change in Southern Africa. 1970. p. 5-20. A current bibliography on African affairs. ; 111 (new series): 2.
Covers scholarly works published since 1966 on Union of South Africa, Southwest Angola, Mozambique and Rhodesia.

30. Kress, L.B. Selected bibliography. - Westport, Conn. : Greenwood Press, 1978. p. 469-503.
In: M.H. Livingston (ed.), International terrorism in the contemporary world

31. Lakos, A. International terrorism bibliography. - Boulder : Westview Press, 1986.

32. Lakos, A. Terrorism in the Middle East : A Bibliography. - Monticello, Ill. : Vance Bibliographies, 1986. 39 p

33. Lakos, A. Terrorism, 1970-1978 : A bibliography. - Waterloo : University of Waterloo Library, 1979.

34. Lakos, A. The nuclear terrorism threat : A bibliography. - Monticello, Ill. : Vance Bibliographies, 1985. 20 p

35. Longolius, A. * (comp.) Auswahlbibliographie zu Anarchismus, Radikalismus und Terrorismus. - Berlin : Bibliothek des Abgeordnetenhauses von Berlin, 1976. 16 p

36. Manheim, J.B. * Wallace, M. Political violence in the United States, 1875-1974: a bibliography. - New York : Garland Publishers, 1975. 116 p

37. Mayans, E. * (ed.) Tupamaros: antologia documental. - Cuernavaca : Centro intercultural de documentacion, 1971.
The best reference work on the Tupamaros with a 250 titles bibliography.

38. Mickolus, E.F. Annotated bibliography on transnational and international terrorism. - Washington D.C. : CIA, Dec. 1976. 225 p
1277 items, mostly in English.

39. Mickolus, E.F. Scholarship and international terrorism : A bibliography. - Westport, Conn. : Greenwood Press, in preparation.

40. Mickolus, E.F. The literature of terrorism: a selectively annotated bibliography. - Westport, Conn. : Greenwood Press, 1980. 553 p

41. Miller, H. * Lybrand, W.A. * Brokheim, H. A selected bibliography on unconventional warfare. - Washington, D.C. : American University (SORO), 1961. 137 p

42. Monroe, J.L. Prisoners of war and political hostages : A selected bibliography. - Springfield, Virg. : The Monroe Corporation, 1973. 45 p
Not annotated, drawing from many sources.

43. Nettlau, M. Bibliographie de l'anarchie. - Brussels : 1897.

44. Norton, A.R. * Greenberg, M.H. International terrorism: an annotated bibliography and research guide. - Boulder, Colo. : Westview Press, 1979. 200 p

45. Norton, A.R. Terror-violence : A critical commentary and selective annotated bibliography. - Gaithersburg, Md. : IACP., 16 p

46. Novotny, E.J.S. * Whitley, J.A.G. A select bibliography on the terrorist threat to the commercial nuclear industry. - Vienna, Virg. : The BDM Corporation, 1975. ; Draft working paper D

47. O'Brien, A. * (comp.) Hijacking : Selected references, 1961-1969. - Washington, D.C. : Library Services Division, Federal Aviation Administration, 1969. 22 p

48. Ontiveros, S.R. Global terrorism. - Santa Barbara, Calif. : ABC-CLIO, 1986. 168 p
Historical bibliography based on journals, with 598 abstracts. Includes incidents chronology, 1975-.

49. Osanka, F.M. * (ed.) Der Krieg aus dem Dunkel. - Koeln : 1963.
pp. 625-681: bibliography on guerrilla warfare and unconventional warfare.

50. Overholt, W.H. Revolution : A bibliography. - Croton-on-Hudson, N.Y. : Hudson Institute, 1975. 43 p

51. Overholt, W.H. Sources of radicalism and revolution : A survey of the literature. - Boulder, Colo. : Westview Press, 1977. p. 293-335. In: S. Bialer and S. Sluzar (eds.), Radicalism in the contemporary age. Vol. 1. Sources of contemporary radicalism

52. Piasetzki, J.P. Urban guerrilla warfare and terrorism - a selected bibliography. - Monticello, Ill. : Council of Planning Librarians, 1976. 16 p
Bibliography with more than 100 listings of articles, pamphlets and books.

53. Ramirez Mitchell, R.A. Terrorismo. - Buenos Aires : Abstracts of Military Bibliography, 1983. 27 p

54. Rao, D.N. Terrorism and law : A selected bibliography of articles, 1980-1985. - Monticello, Ill. : Vance Bibliographies, 1986. 10 p

55. Roemelingh, H.E. Literatuur over terroristen en verzet. March 1977. p.124-133. Tijdschrift voor de Politie. ; 39:3.

56. Rose, R. Ulster politics: a select bibliography of political discord. 1972. p. 206-212. Political Studies. ; 20:2.

57. Russell, Ch.A. * Miller, J.A. * Hildner, R.E. The urban guerrilla in Latin America : A selected bibliography. 1974. p. 37-79. Latin American Research Review. ; 9:1.
Annotated, 261 titles.

58. Russell, Ch.A. * Schenkel, J.F. * Miller, J.A. Urban guerillas in Argentina: a select bibliography. 1974. p. 53-89. Latin American Research Review. ; 9:3.
Mostly newspaper article citations.

59. Sabetta, A.R. Annotated bibliography on international terrorism. 1977. p. 157-164. Stanford Journal of International Studies. ; 12:1.

60. Sable, M.H. The guerrilla movement in Latin America since 1950 : A bibliography. - Madison : University of Wisconsin, 1977.

61. Schmid, A.P. * Graaf, J.F.A.de. Bibliography on terrorism. - The Hague : Advisory Group on Research into Non-violent Conflict Resolution, 1977. 33 pp. (appendix pp. 63-96.).
In: A.P. Schmid and J.F.A.de Graaf, A pilot-study on polical terrorism

62. Schmid, A.P. Political terrorism : A research guide to concepts, theories, data bases and literature, with a bibliography by the author and a world directory of "Terrorist" organizations by A.J. Jongman. - Amsterdam * New Brunswick, N.J. : North-Holland Publishing Company * Transaction Books, 1984. 585 p

63. Sherman, J. * (ed.) The Arab-Israeli conflict 1945-1971: a bibliography. - New York : Garland, 1978. 419 p

64. Smirnoff, M. Bibliographie internationale sur le probleme de la piraterie aerienne. 1971. p. 191-199. Revue generale de l'air et de l'espace. ; 34:2.

65. Smith, M.J. The secret wars : A guide to sources in English. - 3 vols. - Santa Barbara, Calif. : ABC-Clio, 1980-1981.

66. Smith, M.J. The secret wars : International terrorism, 1968-1980. - New York : ABC-Clio, 1980.

67. Symser, W.M. * et al. Annotated bibliography on internal defense. - Washington, D.C. : 1968.
Selected books, periodicals, reports, and articles rela'ing to internal defense. Prepared by the Center for Research in Social Systems. Much of the material listed deals with the problems of insurgency and urban guerilla warfare.

68. Tutenberg, V. * Pollak, Chr. Terrorismus - gestern, heute, morgen. Eine Auswahlbibliographie. - Muenchen : Bernard & Graefe Verlag fuer Wehrwesen, 1978. 298 p
Unannotated bibliography, ca. 3600 titles, country by country and under headings such as espionage, psychological warfare, territorial defence, emergency law etc. Since the authors do not distinguish between terrorism and guerilla warfare, resistance against occupation, and revolutions, this book is of limited usefulness for research on political terrorism.

69. Watson, F.M. The textbook of political violence : A selected bibliography. - Gaithersburg, Md. : IACP., 20 p

70. White, A.G. Recent military views of terrorism : A selected bibliography. - Monticello, Ill. : Vance Bibliographies, 1986. 9 p

71. Whitehouse, J.E. A police bibliography : Published and unpublished sources through 1976. - New York : AMS Press, 1976.
pp. 397-407 cover terrorism; emphasis on U.S. magazine articles.

72. Wilcox, L.M. Bibliography on terrorism and assassination. - Kansas City, Mo. : Editorial Research Service, 1980.
Partially annotated, with more than 400 entries.

73. _____ A select bibliography on international terrorism. 25 Oct. 1972.
United Nations. ; List no. 5/rev. 1.

74. _____ A select bibliography on aerial piracy. 20 Nov. 1972.
United Nations. ; List no. 6.

75. _____ Amnesty International in print, 1962-1978. - London : Jan. 1979.
Amnesty International
A.I. Index doc. 06/01/79.

76. _____ Annotated bibliography on transnational terrorism. - Fort Bragg, N.C. : 1975. 27 p.
U.S. Army Institute for Military Assistance ; 7th security assistance symposium of the Foreign Area Officer Course
With emphasis on journalistic accounts.

77. _____ Bibliografia guerra revolucionaria y subversion en el continente. - Washington D.C. : 1973.
Library of the Inter-American Defence College
Bibliography on Latin American revolution and counterrevolution.

78. _____ Bibliografie selective sur la violence et les actes de terrorisme. - Geneve : 1975.
Institut Henry-Dunant * (ed.)

79. _____ Hijacking: selected references. - Washington, D.C. : 1969. 22 p.
U.S. Department of Transportation. Federal Aviation Administration. Bibliographical List. ; No. 18.
Lists 206 items, mostly journalistic articles.

80. _____ Hijacking: selected readings. - Washington, D.C. : 1971. 53 p.
U.S. Department of Transportation. Bibliographic List. ; No. 5.
Lists 268 articles published between Febr. 1969 and Dec. 1970; annotated; mostly from newspapers and magazines.

81. _____ Hostage situations. - Quantico, Virg. : FBI Academy, Learning Resource Center, Jan. 1975. 11 p.
FBI Academy
130 items, not annotated, mostly from U.S. magazines.

82. _____ Hostage situations. - Quantico, Virg. : 1975. 35 p.
FBI Academy

83. _____ Hostage situations: bibliography. - Quantico, Virg. : 1973. 8 p.
FBI Academy
Ca. 100 citations on ground and air hostage situations.

84. _____ Hostages. - Quantico, Virg. : FBI Academy Library, June 1980. 8 p.
FBI Academy
A bibliography on books, periodicals, films, video cassettes and other materials on the subject.

85. _____ International terrorism : A select bibliography. - New York : 1973. 10 p.
United Nations, Dag Hammerskjold Library

86. _____ International terrorism and revolutionary warfare: library booklist. 1976. p. 1-4.
U.S. Department of State. Library. Reader's Advisory Service. ; 3:4.

87. _____ Kidnapping. - Quantico, Virg. : FBI Academy Library, June 1980. 7 p.
FBI Academy
Lists books, periodicals, articles, governmental documents, films on the subject.

88. _____
Nuclear related terrorist bibliography. - Washinton, D.C. : Inscom (CID/DNA), 1979.
Unannotated bibliography on nuclear-related terrorist incidents, scenarios and tactics.

89. _____ Radical militants - an annotated bibliography of empirical research on campus unrest. - Lexington, Mass. : Heath Lexington Books, 1973. 241 p
On U.S. student radicalism since 1945.

90. _____ Terrorism. - Quantico, Virg. : FBI Academy Library, June 1980. 12 p.
FBI Academy ; Mimeo
A bibliography on books, periodicals, newspapers, movies and other material on the subject.

91. _____ Terrorism. - Colorado : USAFA, 1977. 47 p.
U.S. Air Force Academy library. Special bibliography series. ; No. 57.
Ca. 600 items, many of them newspaper articles. Not annotated.

92. _____ Terrorism : A selective bibliography. - Washington, D.C. : Pentagon Library, 1984. 30 p

93. _____ Terrorism : Bibliography. - Rockville, Md. : National Institute of Law Enforcement and Criminal Justice, 1978.
U.S. Department of Justice. Law Enforcement Assistance Administration

94. _____ Terrorism : An annotated bibliography. - Washington, D.C. : 1977-78.
U.S. Department of Justice. Law Enforcement Assistance Administration
Bibliography names agency or publisher but rarely author of an item.

95. _____ Terrorism: a selective bibliography : Supplement 3. - Washington, D.C. : 1982. 11 p.
U.S. Army Library

96. _____ Terrorismus und Gewalt. Auswahlbibliographie mit Annotationen. - Bonn : July 1975. 86 p. Deutscher Bundestag. Wissenschaftliche Dienste. Bibliographien. ; 43.
38 of the ca. 1100 titles are annotated.

97. _____ Terrorismus und Gewalt, 1975-1977. Auswahlbibliographie. - Bonn : Febr. 1978. 53 p.
Deutscher Bundestag. Wissenschaftliche Dienste. Bibliographien. ; 49.
Few of the ca. 600 titles are annotated.

98. _____ Terroristic activities. - Quantico, Virg. : FBI Academy, Learning Resource Center, Jan. 1975. 79 p.
FBI Academy ; Mimeo
Ca. 1200 items, not annotated, mostly journalistic articles.

99. _____ The Palestine question : A select bibliography. - New York : 1976. 63 p.
United Nations, Dag Hammerskjold Library. Bibliography Series. ; 22.

B. CONCEPTUAL, DEFINITORY AND TYPOLOGICAL ASPECTS OF TERRORISM

100. Ake, C. A definition of political stability. Jan. 1975. p. 271-283. Comparative Politics. ; 7:2.

101. Amann, p. Revolution : A redefinition. March 1962. p. 36-53. Political Science Quarterly. ; 77:1.

102. Andreski, S. Terror. - New York : Free Press of Glencoe, 1964. p. 179.
In: J. Gould and W.L. Kolb (eds.), A dictionary of the social sciences

103. Arblaster, A. Terrorism: myths, meaning and morals. Sept. 1977. p. 413-424. Political Studies. The Journal of the Political Studies Association of the U.K. ; 25:3.
Reviews several books on terrorism.

104. Baeyer-Katte, W.von * Grimm, T. Terror. - Freiburg i.Br. : 1972. p. 341 ff. Sowjetsystem und demokratische Gesellschaft. ; 6.

105. Bell, J.B. Trends on terror : The analysis of political violence. April 1977. p. 476-488. World Politics. ; 29:3.

106. Berger, P.L. Elements of terrorism. 1976. p. 29-30. Worldview. ; 19:5.

107. Bonanate, L. Il teorema del terrorismo. 1978. p. 574-595. Il Mulino. ; 27:258.

108. Bonanate, L. Some unanticipated consequences of terrorism. 1979. p. 197-211. Journal of Peace Research. ; 16:3.

109. Bonanate, L. Terrorism: an international political analysis. 1979. Terrorism. ; 3:1-2.

110. Bonanate, L. Terrorismo, lotta politica e violenza. 1978. p. 23-38. Biblioteca della liberta. ; 15:68.

111. Bouthoul, G. Definitions of terrorism. - London : Croom Helm, 1975. p. 50-59.
In: D. Carlton and C. Schaerf (eds.), International terrorism and world security

112. Bracher, K.D. Der umstrittene Totalitarismus : Erfahrung und Aktualitaet. - 5th ed. - Muenchen : 1984. p. 33-61.
In: K.D. Bracher, Zeitgeschichtliche Kontroversen. Um Faschismus, Totalitarismus, Demokratie

113. Bracher, K.D. Zeitgeschichtliche Kontroversen : Um Faschismus, Totalitarismus, Demokratie. - 4th ed. - Muenchen : R. Piper Verlag, 1980. 159 p. Serie Piper. ; 142.

114. Brainerd jr, G.R. Terrorism : The theory of differential effects. 1984. p. 233-244. Conflict. ; 5:3.

115. Buckley, A.D. * Olson, D.D. International terrorism : Current research and future directions. - New York : Avery Publications.

116. Chandler, D.B. Toward a classification of violence. 1973. p. 63-83. Sociological Symposion. ; 9.

117. Cooper, H.H.A. Terrorism: the problem of the problem of definition. March 1978. p.105-108. Chitty's Law Journal. ; 26.

118. Cordes, B.J. * et al. A conceptual framework for analyzing terrorist groups. - Santa Monica, Calif. : RAND, 1985. 114 p

119. Crenshaw, M. An organizational approach to the analysis of political terrorism. 1985. p. 465-487. Orbis. ; 29:3.

120. Crenshaw, M. The concept of revolutionary terrorism. Sept. 1972. p. 383-396. The Journal of Conflict Resolution. ; 16:3.
A thoughtful conceptual attempt.

121. Crozier, B. Anatomy of terrorism. 1959. p. 250-252. Nation. ; 188.

122. Dahrendorf, R. Ueber einige Probleme der soziologischen Theorie der Revolution. - Frankfurt a.M. : Athenaeum Fischer, 1974.
In: U. Jaeggi and S. Papcke (eds.), Revolution und Theorie. Vol. 1

123. David, E. Definition et repression du terrorisme. 1973. p. 861-864. Revue de droit penal et de criminologie. ; 52:9.

124. Dennen, J.M.G.van der Problems in the concepts and definitions of aggression, violence and some related terms. - Groningen : Polemological Institute, 1980. 154 p

125. Dugard, J. An ideal definition of terrorism : International terrorism: problems of definition. Jan. 1974. p. 67-81. International Affairs. ; 50:1.

126. Dugard, J. Towards the definition of international terrorism. 1973. p. 94-100. American Journal of International Law. ; 67:5.

127. Edmonds, M. Civil war, internal war, and intrasocietal conflict: a taxonomy and typology. - Lexington : The University Press of Kentucky, 1972. p. 11-26.
In: R. Higham (ed.), Civil wars in the twentieth century

128. Faleroni, A.D. What is an urban guerrilla?. 1969. p. 94. Military Review. ; 47.

129. Farrell, W.R. Terrorism is ...?. 1980. p. 64-72. Naval War College Review. ; 32:3.

130. Fattah, E.A. Terrorist activities and terrorist targets: a tentative typology. - New York : Pergamon Press, 1981. p. 11-32.
In: Y. Alexander and J.M. Gleason (eds.), Behavioral and quantitative perspectives on terrorism

131. Finer, S.E. Terrorism. 1976. p. 168-169. New Society. ; 35:694.

132. Flechtheim, O.K. Radikalismus contra Extremismus. 1974. p. 485-493. Neues Hochland. ; 66.

133. Fowler, W.W. An agenda for quantitative research on terrorism. - Santa Monica, Calif. : RAND, 1980. 11 p. RAND Paper Series. ; P-6591.

134. Fowler, W.W. Terrorism data bases : A comparison of missions, methods, and systems. - Santa Monica, Calif. : RAND, 1981. 42 p. RAND Paper Series. ; N-1503-RC.

135. Friedlander, R.A. Terrorism and political violence: some preliminary observations. 1976. International Studies Notes. ; 2.

136. Galtung, J. On violence in general and terrorism in particular. - Geneva : U.N. University, 1978. 27 p ; Mimeo

137. Goldaber, I. A typology of hostage terror. June 1979. p. 21-23. Police Chief

138. Gove, W.R. * (ed.) The labelling of deviance : Evaluating a perspective. - New York : John Wiley & Sons, 1975.

139. Govea, R.M. Terrorism as a political science offering. - Cleveland : 1980. p. 3-19. Teaching Political Science. ; 8:1.

140. Gransow, V. Konzeptionelle Wandlungen der Kommunismusforschung : Vom Totalitarismus zur Immanenz. - Frankfurt a.M./New York : Campus Verlag, 1980. 234 p. Campus Forschung. ; 177.

141. Grebing, H. Linksradikalismus gleich Rechtsradikalismus : Eine falsche Gleichung. - Stuttgart : 1971.

142. Greenstein, F.I. * Polsby, N.W. * (eds.) Handbook of political science. - 8 vols. - Reading, Mass. : Addison-Wesley, 1975.
See entries "Political terror"and "Terrorism" in cumulative index, p.80.

143. Groom, A.J.R. Coming to terms with terrorism. April 1978. p.62-77. British Journal of International Studies. ; 4:1.
Review abstracts on books by: Burton, Carlton, Clutterbuck, Jenkins, Sobel, Walter, Wilkinson and others.

144. Groth, A. A typology of revolution. - Belmont, Calif. : Duxbury Press, 1972. In: C.E. Welch and M.B. Taintor (eds.), Revolution and political change

145. Guenther, J. Terror und Terrorismus. 1972. p. 32. Neue Deutsche Hefte. ; 19:4.

146. Gurr, T.R. * Grabosky, P.N. * Hula, R.C. * et al. The politics of crime and conflict : A comparative history of four cities. - Beverly Hills : Sage, 1977. 792 p

147. Gurr, T.R. * Ruttenberg, Ch. Cross-national studies of civil violence. - Washington : The American University, Center for Research in Social Systems, 1968. 208 p

148. Hardman, J.B.S. Terrorism. - New York : MacMillan, 1937. p. 575-579. In: E.R. Seligman * (ed.), Encyclopaedia of the social sciences. Vol. 14 The first serious attempt of defining the subject.

149. Herpen, M.van Terrorisme zonder terreur : Een poging tot een sociologische definitie van de begrippen terrorisme en terreur. - Nijmegen : Studiecentrum voor Vredesvraagstukken, 1978. 13 p ; Unpubl. paper

150. Hess, H. Repressive crime and criminal typologies. 1977. p. 91-108. Contemporary Crises. ; 1. Orig. in German: Repressives Verbrechen: 1976. Kriminologisches Journal. 8:1.

151. Hess, H. Terrorismus und Terrorismus-Diskurs. 1981. p. 171-188. Tijdschrift voor Criminologie. ; 4. A lucid and original conceptualization.

152. Heyman, E.S. * Mickolus, E.F. Imitation by terrorists : Quantitative approaches to the study of diffusion patterns in transnational terrorism. - New York : Pergamon Press, 1981. p. 175-228. In: Y. Alexander and J.M. Gleason (eds.), Behavioral and quantitative perspectives on terrorism

153. Heyman, E.S. Monitoring the diffusion of transnational terrorism. - Gaithersburg, Md. : IACP, 1980. 36 p

154. Hoffman, R.P. Terrorism : A universal definition. Claremont Graduate School, 1984. ; Ph.D. dissertation

155. Holmes, R.L. The concept of physical violence in moral and political affairs. 1973. p. 387-409. Social Theory and Practice. ; 2:4.

156. Horowitz, I.L. Unicorns and terrorists. - Washington, D.C. : U.S. Department of State, 1976. 13 p ; Paper. Conference on international terrorism, March 1976

157. Ivianski, Z. Individual terror : Concept and typology. 1977. p. 44-63. Journal of Contemporary History. ; 12:1.

158. Ivianski, Z. Individual terror as a phase in revolutionary violence in the late nineteenth and the beginning of the twentieth century. - Jerusalem : 1973. ; Doctoral diss. In Hebrew.

159. Jaszi, O. * Lewis, J.D. Against the tyrant; the tradition and theory of tyrannicide. - Glencoe, Ill. : Free Press, 1957.

160. Jenkins, B.M. Terrorism works - sometimes. - Santa Monica, Calif. : RAND, 1974. 9 p. RAND Paper. ; p. 5217.

161. Jenkins, B.M. The study of terrorism: definitonal problems. - New York : Pergamon Press, 1981. p. 3-10. In: Y. Alexander and J.M. Gleason (eds.), Behavioral and quantitative perspectives on terrorism

162. Jenkner, S. Totalitarismus. - Muenchen : 1983. p. 521-524. In: W.W. Mickel (ed.), Handlexikon zur Politikwissenschaft

163. Jesse, E. Renaissance der Totalitarismuskonzeption? : Zur Kontroverse um einen strittigen Begriff. 1983. p. 459-492. NPL. ; 28.

164. Johnson, Ch. Perspectives on terrorism. - New York : New American Library, 1978. p. 267-285. In: W. Laqueur (ed.), The terrorism reader. A historical anthology Discusses definitions and typologies debated at a Dept. of State-sponsored conference on terrorism in March 1976.

165. Kader, O.M. Contemporary political terror : Comparing the use of violence by national liberation and ideological groups. University of Southern California, 1981. ; Ph.D. dissertation

166. Kahn, M.W. * Kirk, W.E. The concepts of aggression : A review and reformulation. 1969. p. 559-573. Psychological Record. ; 18.

167. Kalshoven, F. "Guerrilla" and "terrorism" in internal armed conflict. Fall 1983. p. 67-81. American University Law Review. ; 33.

168. Karanovic, M. The concept of terrorism. - vol. 3. - Rockville, Md. : National Criminal Justice Reference Service, Law Enforcement Assistance Administration, U.S. Depart, 1979. p. 81-88. In: M. Kravitz (ed.), International summaries. A collection of selected translations in law enforcement and criminal justice

169. Karber, Ph.A. Urban terrorism : Baseline data and conceptual framework. Dec. 1971. p. 521-533. Social Science Quarterly. ; 52.
Author stresses the symbolic quality of political terrorism and suggests that it can be analysed in much the same fashion as other forms ofcommunication.

170. Kasturi, D.G. A typological analysis of collective political violence. Louisiana State University, 1979. 285 p ; Unpubl. Ph.D

171. Kessler, H. Terreur, Ideologie und Nomenklatur der revolutionaere Gewaltanwendung in Frankreich von 1770 bis 1794. - Muenchen : W. Fink, 1973. 195 p

172. Laqueur, W. Coming to terms with terror. 2 April 1976. p. 262-263. The Times Literary Supplement. ; 3864.

173. Laqueur, W. Interpretations of terrorism - fact, fiction and political science. 1977. p. 1-42. Journal of Contemporary History. ; 12:1.

174. Leach, E.R. Custom, law and terrorist violence. - Edinburgh : University Press, 1977. 37 p

175. Loesche, p. Anarchismus. Versuch einer Definition und historischen Typologie. 1974. Politische Vierteljahresschrift. ; 1.

176. Lopez, G.A. A scheme for the analysis of governments as terrorists. - Milwaukee, Wisc. : Midwest Political Science Association, 1982. ; Conference paper

177. Lopez, G.A. Terrorism and alternative worldviews. - San Antonio, Texas : Southwest International Studies Association, 1981. 19 p ; Conference paper

178. Mars, P. Nature of political violence. - Kingston, Jamaica : June 1975. p. 221-238. Social and Economic Studies. ; 24:5.
Activities associated with political violence are defined and arranged on a rank-orderscale to measure the intensity of political violence in a particular country. Attempts definition of political violence.

179. McCamant, J.F. Governance without blood : Social science antiseptic view of rule or the neglect of political repression. - Milwaukee, Wisc. : Midwest Political Science Association, 1982. 57 p ; Conference paper

180. Merari, A. A classification of terrorist groups. 1978. p. 331-346. Terrorism. ; 1.

181. Mickolus, E.F. Reflections on the study of terrorism.
In: Th. Harries (ed.), Complexity: a challenge to the adaptive capacity of American society ; Proceedings of a conference sponsored by the Society for General Systems Research, Columbia. Md, 24-26 March 1977

182. Mickolus, E.F. Studying terrorist incidents: issues in conceptualization and data acquisition. 1980. ; Paper presented to the annual convention of the International Studies Association, Los Angeles, March 1980

183. Monday, M. Insurgent war : A backgrounder book for reporters. - San Diego : TVI, 1980. 34 p ; Mimeo

184. Muenkler, H. Guerillakrieg und Terrorismus. 1980. p. 299-326. Neue Politische Literatur. ; 25:3.

185. Nardin, T. Conflicting conceptions of political violence. - Vol. 4. - Indianapolis : Bobbs-Merrill, 1973. p. 75-126.
In: p. Cotter (ed.), Political Science Annual, an international review

186. O'Brien, C.C. On violence and terror. 1977. Dissent. ; 24:4.

187. O'Neill, B.E. Towards a typology of political terrorism: the Palestinian resistance movement. 1978. p. 17-42. Journal of International Affairs. ; 32.

188. Paust, J.J. Some thougts on "Preliminary thougts" on terrorism. July 1974. p. 502-503. American Journal of International Law. ; 68.

189. Ponsaers, p. Terrorisme: aktie-reaktie-interaktie : Deel 1: theoretisch kader (poging tot algemene duiding van het begrip terrorisme). - Leuven : Katholieke Universiteit, 1976. 153 p ; Master's thesis

190. Pontara, G. Violenza e terrorismo. Il problema della definizione e della giustificazione. - Milano : F. Angeli Editore, 1979. p. 25-98.
In: L. Bonanate (ed.), Dimensioni del terrorismo politico

191. Ranly, E.W. Defining violence. 1972. p. 415-427. Thought. ; 47.

192. Reid, E.F. An analysis of terrorism literature : A bibliometric and content analysis study. University of Southern California, 1983. ; Ph.D. dissertation

193. Roettgers, K. * Saner, H. * (eds.) Gewalt : Grundlagenprobleme in der Diskussion der Gewaltphaenomene. - Basel : Schwabe Verlag, 1978.

194. Rosenthal, U. Terreur: een hinderlijke analyse van stellige uitspraken. 1978. p. 429-438. Tijdschrift voor de Politie

195. Roucek, J.S. Sociological elements of a theory of terror and violence. 1962. p. 165-172. American Journal of Economics and Sociology. ; 21.

196. Ruitenberg, H. Politiek en misdaad. June 1978. p. 3. Wordt Vervolgd. Berichten van Amnesty International
On the distinction between political and criminal delinquents.

197. Sarhan, A. Definition de terrorisme international et fixation de son contenue. 1973. p. 173-178. Revue egyptienne de droit international. ; 29.

198. Schlangen, W. Die Totalitarismus Theorie : Entwicklung und Probleme. - Stuttgart etc. : Verlag W. Kohlhammer, 1976. 176 p

199. Schmid, A.P. * Graaf, J.F.A.de A pilot study on political terrorism. - The Hague : Advisory Group on Research into Non-violent Conflict Resolution, 1977. 62 p

200. Schmid, A.P. * Graaf, J.F.A.de Internationaal terrorisme : Begripsbepaling, structuur en strategieen. 19 May 1978. p. 1-11. Intermediair

201. Schultz, G. Phaenomenologie und Theorie des Totalitarismus. - Frankfurt a.M. : 1974. p. 138-147.
In: G. Schulz, Nationalsozialismus. Versionen und theoretische Kontroversen 1922-1972

202. Schuyt, C.J.M. Denken en discussieren over terreur. Oct. 1977. p. 529-542. Delikt en delinkwent. ; 7:8.

203. Sederberg, P.C. Defining terrorism. - Columbia : University of South Carolina, 1981. 5 p ; Mimeo

204. Seidel, B. * Jenkner, S. * (ed.) Wege der Totalitarismus-Forschung. - 3rd ed. - Darmstadt : 1974.

205. Singh, B. Political terrorism : Some third world perspectives. Michigan State University, 1977. ; Unpubl. paper

206. Stohl, M. Fashions and phantasies in the study of political terrorism. - Dubrovnik : Inter-University Center, 1981. 18 p ; Unpubl. paper

207. Stohl, M. Three worlds of terrorism. - Dubrovnik : Inter-University Center, 1981. 20 p ; Unpubl. paper

208. Stoll, A. Die Totalitarismuskonzeption von C.J. Friedrich in Kritik und Gegenkritik. - Bayreuth : 1980. 457 p ; Diss. Bayreuth

209. Tatsis, N.C. Phenomenology : The methodology of conceptual terrorism: a sociological analysis and critique. Syracuse University, 1975. ; Ph.D. dissertation

210. Taylor, R.W. * Vanden, H.E. Defining terrorism in El Salvador : 'La matanza'. Sept. 1982. p. 106-118. Annals of the American Academy of Political and Social Science. ; 463.

211. Thackrah, R. A dictionary of terrorism and political violence. - London : Routledge and Kegan Paul, 1986.

212. Thamer, H.U. * Wippermann, W. Faschistische und Neofaschistische Bewegungen : Probleme der Faschismusforschung. - Darmstadt : 1977.

213. Tromp, H.W. Politiek terrorisme. March 1978. p. 1-19. Transaktie. ; 7:1.

214. Tromp, H.W. Politiek terrorisme: de derde wereldoorlog in een volstrekt onverwachte vorm. 28 Sept. 1978. p. 9-11. Universiteitskrant Groningen. ; 8:5.

215. Vought, D.B. * Fraser jr, J.H. Terrorism : The search for working definitions. July 1986. p. 70-76. Military Review. ; 66.

216. Waciorski, J. Le terrorisme politique. - Paris : A. Pedone, 1939.

217. Waldmann, p. Terror. - Muenchen : 1976. p. 305-307.
In: p. Noack and Th. Stammen (eds.), Grundbegriffe der politischen Fachsprache

218. Walter, E.V. Violence and the process of terror. - New York : Aldine, Atherton, 1971.
In: J.V. Bondurant (ed.), Conflict: violence and nonviolence

219. Walter, E.V. Violence and the process of terror. April 1964. p. 248-257. American Sociological Review. ; 29:2.

220. Walzer, M. * Bell, J.B. * Morris, R. Terrorism: a debate. 22 Dec. 1975. p. 12. New Republic

221. Weber, H.von Terrorismus. - Berlin : 1962. p. 439-440.
In: Woerterbuch des Voelkerrechts. Begruendet von K. Strupp. Neu hrsg. von H.J. Schlochauer. Bd.3

222. Weimann, G. Terrorists or freedom fighters? : Labeling terrorism in the Israeli press. 1985. p. 433-445. Political Communication and Persuasion. ; 2.

223. Wilkinson, p. A fatality of illusions. 1976. ; Paper presented at the U.S.

State Department conference on international terrorism in retrospect and prospect, March 1976, in Washington, D.C

224. **Wilkinson, p.** Can a state be 'terrorist'?. 1981. p. 467-472. International Affairs. ; 57:3.

225. **Wilkinson, p.** Political terrorism. - London : MacMillan, 1974. 160 p Conceptually one of the basic works on the subject.

226. **Wilkinson, p.** Three questions on terrorism. 1973. p. 290-312. Government and Opposition. ; 8:3.

227. **Wippermann, W.** Faschismustheorien : Zum Stand der gegenwaertigen Diskussion. - 4th ed. - Darmstadt : 1980.

228. **Wolf, J.B.** An analytical framework for the study and control of agitational terrorism. July 1976. p. 165-171. The Police Journal. ; 49:3.

229. **Young, R.** Revolutionary terrorism, crime and morality. 1977. p. 287-302. Social Theory and Practice. ; 4:3.

230. _____ Reflexions sur la definition et la repression du terrorisme. - Bruxelles : Ed. de l'Universite, 1974. 292 p. Centre de droit internationale et association belge de juristes democrates ; Actes du colloque, Universite Libre de Bruxelles

231. _____ Terror, reign of; terrorism. 1976. p. 904. In: The New Encyclopaedia Brittanica (micropaedia). Vol. 9

C. GENERAL WORKS ON TERRORISM

232. **Alexander, Y. * (ed.)** International terrorism; national, regional and global perspectives. - New York : Praeger, 1976. 414 p
Contents: L.C. Green, Terrorism - the Canadian perspective; B.K. Johnpoll, Perspectives on political terrorism in the U.S.; R.E. Butler, Terrorism in Latin America; J. Bowyer Bell, Strategy, tactics, and terror: an Irish perspective; T.E. Hackey, Political terrorism: the British experience; R.O. Freedman, Soviet policy toward international terrorism; S. Qureshi, Political violence in the South Asian subcontinent; E.S. Efrat, Terrorism in South Africa; Y. Alexander, From terrorism to war: the anatomy of the birth of Israel; E. Weisband and D. Roguly, Palestinian terrorism: violence, verbal strategy and legitimacy; S.M. Finger, International terrorism and the United Nations.

233. **Alexander, Y. * Carlton, D. * Wilkinson, p. * (eds.)** Terrorism : Theory and practice. - Boulder, Colo. : Westview Press, 1978. 275 p
analyses the use of sporadic political and ideological violence by nongovernmental groups, with a view toward understanding current challenges and implications for the future.

234. **Alexander, Y. * Finger, S.M. * (eds.)** Terrorism: interdisciplinary perspectives. - New York : The John Jay Press, 1977. 377 p
Contents: B. Singh, An overview; J.J. Paust, A definitional focus; R.A. Friedlander, The origins of international terrorism; D. Rapoport, The politics of atrocity; J.A. Miller, Political terrorism and insurgency: an interrogative approach; J. Mallin, Terrorism as a military weapon; E. Evans, American policy response to international terrorism: problems of deterrence; A.P. Rubin, International terrorism and international law; A.E. Evans, The realities of extradition and prosecution; H.H.A. Cooper, Terrorism and the media; B. Johnpoll, Terrorism and the media in the United States; Y. Alexander, Terrorism and the media in the Middle East; E.F. Mickolus, Statistical approaches to the study of terrorism; J. Margolin, Psychological perspectives in terrorism; I.L. Horowitz, Transnational terrorism, civil liberties, and social science; M. Crenshaw, Defining future threats: terrorists and nuclear proliferation.

235. **Alexander, Y.** Super-terrorism. - New York : Pergamon, 1980. In: Y. Alexander and J.M. Gleason (eds.), Terrorism, behavioral perspectives

236. **Argiolas, T.** La guerriglia : Storia e dottrina. - Firenze : Sansoni, 1967.

237. **Astorg, B.d'** Introduction au monde de la terreur. - Paris : Editions du Seuil, 1945.

238. **Bar-Zohar, M. * Haber, E.** The quest for the Red Prince. - London : Weidenfeld and Nicolson, 1983.

239. **Bassiouni, M.C. * (ed.)** International terrorism and political crimes : Third conference on terrorism and political crimes, held in Syracuse, Sicily. - Springfield, Ill. : Thomas, 1974.

240. **Bassiouni, M.C.** Prolegomenon to terror violence. 1979. p. 745-779. Creighton Law Review. ; 12.

241. Bell, J.B. Terror: an overview. - Westport, Conn. : Greenwood Press, 1978. p. 36-43.
In: M.H. Livingston (ed.), International terrorism in the contemporary world

242. Beloff, M. Terrorism and the people. - New York : Crane-Russak, 1979. p. 109-127.
In: J. Shaw, E.F. Gueritz and A.E. Younger (eds.), Ten years of terrorism: collected views

243. Benewick, R. Political violence and public order. - Harmondsworth : Penguin, 1969.

244. Bennett, R.K. Terrorists among us: an intelligence report. Oct. 1971. p. 115-120. Reader's Digest,

245. Bite, V. International terrorism. - Washington, D.C. : Library of Congress, CRS, 31 Oct. 1975. Issue Brief. ; 1 B 74042.

246. Bonanate, L. * (ed.) Dimensioni del terrorismo politico. - Milano : F. Angeli editore, 1979. 347 p

247. Bonanate, L. * Gastaldo, p. * (eds.) Il terrorismo nell'ETA contemporanea. - Firenze : Le Monnier, 1981.

248. Bonanate, L. Terrorismo politico. - Torino : Utet, 1976. p. 1034-1037.
In: N. Bobbio and N. Matteucci (eds.), Dizionario di politica

249. Bouthoul, G. La guerra : Guerriglia, guerra urbana e terrorismo. - Roma : Armando, 1975.

250. Bracher, K.D. Terrorismus in der demokratischen Gesellschaft. - Hamburg : Bergedorfer Gespraechskreis zu Frag der Freien Industriellen Gesellschaft, 1978. 15 p. Protokoll. ; 59.

251. Bradshaw, J. The dream of terror. 18 July 1978. p. 24-50. Esquire

252. Bravo, G.M. Critica dell'estremismo. - Milano : Il Saggiatore, 1977.

253. Brewer, G.D. Existing in a world of institutionalized danger. - New Haven, Conn. : School of Organization and Management, Yale University, March 1976. p. 339-387. Technical Report. ; 102. Published in Yale Studies in World Public Order 3, 1977.

254. Broche, F. Alexandre 1er - Louis Barthou. - Paris : Balland, 1977.

255. Brown, G. * Wallace, M. * (eds.) Terrorism. - New York : The New York Times Arno Press, 1979. 378 p

256. Brown, L.C. Transnational terrorism and foreign policy: a summary of workshop deliberation. - Fort Bragg, N.C. : U.S. Army Institute for Military Assistance, Dec. 1977. p. 46-54.
In: Proceedings of the 13th International Affairs Symposium of the Foreign Area Officers Course

257. Browne, M.A. * Nanes, A.S. International terrorism. - Washington, D.C. : Library of Congres Congressional Research Service, 10 March 1978. Issue Brief. ; 74042.

258. Buckman, p. The limits of protest. - London : Panther, 1970. 286 p

259. Burnham, J. Notes on terrorism. 13 Oct. 1972. p. 1116. National Review

260. Butter, H. * et al. Blutspur der Gewalt : Bilanz eines Jahrzehnts des Terrorismus. - Zuerich : Verlag Neue Zuercher Zeitung, 1980. 185 p

261. Calvert, J.M. The pattern of guerrilla warfare. 1966. Military Review. ; 46:7.

262. Camus, A. L'homme revolte. - Paris : Gallimard, 1951.

263. Carlton, D. * Schaerf, C. * (eds.) Violence at substate level. - London : MacMillan, 1978.

264. Carlton, D. The future of political substate violence. - Boulder, Colo. : Westview Press, 1979. p. 201-230.
In: Y. Alexander, D. Carlton and p. Wilkinson (eds.), Terrorism, theory and practice

265. Carmichael, D.J.C. Terrorism: some ethical issues. Sept. 1976. p. 233-239. Chitty's Law Journal. ; 24.

266. Carrere, R. * Valat-Morio, p. Mesure du terrorisme de 1968 a 1972. 1973. p. 47-58. Etudes polemologiques. ; 3:8.

267. Carson, J. * (ed.) Terrorism in theory and practice : Proceedings of a colloquium. - Toronto : Atlantic Council of Canada, 1978.

268. Cerqueira, M. Cadaver barato : Um retrato do terrorismo. - Rio de Janeiro : Pallas, 1982.

269. Chairoff, p. Dossier B...comme Barbouzes. - Paris : Alain Moreau, 1975.

270. Charters, D.A. Wet affairs. 1986. In: D.A. Charters and M. Tugwell (eds), The tangled web: deception in East-West relations

271. Cheason, J.M. Terrorist risk exposure: a bayesian approach. ; Paper, Academy of Criminal Justice Sciences National Meeting, Oklahoma City, Oklahoma, March 1980

A less mathematical version of this paper was presented under the title of "A bayesian framework for the determination of terrorist risk exposure in world countries", Third Annual Third World Conference, Omaha, Nebraska, October 1979.

272. Clutterbuck, R.L. * (ed.) The future of political violence : Destabilization, disorder and terrorism. - London : MacMillan, 1986. 232 p. RUSI Defence Studies Series

273. Clutterbuck, R.L. Kidnap and ransom : The response. - London : Faber & Faber, 1978. 192 p

274. Clutterbuck, R.L. Living with terrorism. - London : Faber & Faber, 1975. 160 p

275. Coblentz, S.A. The militant dissenters. - South Brunswick : A.S. Barnes & Co, 1970. 291 p

276. Connelly, R.W. Third party involvement in international terrorist extortion. Naval Postgraduate School, 1976. ; Master's thesis

277. Cooper, H.H.A. Menace of terrorism. 6 p ; Paper for the International Symposium on terrorism in the contemporary world, Glassboro, N.J., April 1976

278. Cooper, H.H.A. Terrorism and the intelligence function. - Westport, Conn. : Greenwood Press, 1978. p. 287-296. In: M.H. Livingston (ed.), International terrorism in the contemporary world

279. Cooper, H.H.A. The international experience with terrorism. - Washington, D.C. : National Advisory Committee on Criminal Justice Standards and Goals, Dec. 1976. p. 419-442.
In: Report of the Task Force on Disorders and Terrorism

280. Cormier, R. After the first death. - New York : Pantheon Books, 1979.

281. Costa Pinto, L.A. Religion and rebellion : A sociological analysis of the theology of liberation. ; Paper to be presented in the session Dialectical Sociology of Religion, World Congress of Sociology, New Delhi, August 1986

282. Crelinsten, R.D. Prepared statement for international scientific conference on terrorism. - Berlin : Nov. 1978. p. 203-214. Terrorism. ; 3.

283. Crenshaw, M. * (ed.) Terrorism, legitimacy, and power : The consequences of political violence. - Middletown, Conn, : Wesleyan University Press, 1983. 162 p
Essays by I.L. Horowitz, Y. Dror, C.C. O'Brien, p. Wilkinson, R. Coxand A. Quainton.

284. Crenshaw, M. The meaning of terrorism for world order. ; Paper presented to the International Studies Association, Mexico City, April 1983

285. Davies, T.R. Feedback processes and international terrorism. Florida State University, 1977. ; Ph.D.dissertation

286. Davies, T.R. The terrorists : Youth, biker and prison violence. - San Diego, Calif. : Grossmont Press, 1978.

287. Denton, F.H. * Phillips, W. Some patterns in the history of violence. June 1968. p. 182-195. Journal of Conflict Resolution. ; 12.

288. Derrer, D.S. Terrorism. May 1985. p. 190, 192-203. United States Naval Institute proceedings. ; 111.

289. Desjardins, T. Les rebelles d'aujourd'hui. - Paris : Presses de la Cite, 1977.

290. Devine, P.E. * Refalko, R.J. On terror. 1982. p. 39-53. Annals of the American Academy of Political and Social Science. ; 463.

291. Diaz Silva, E. Los secretos de Niehous. - Caracas, Venezuela : Publicaciones Seleven, 1979.

292. Dittrich, Z.R. Terrorisme : Terugblikken en vooruitzien. - The Hague : 1979. p. 21-24. Liberaal Reveil. ; 19:4. Compares Russian terrorism around 1880 with present-day terrorism. Article forms introduction to a series of articles on terrorism in this issue.

293. Dobson, Chr. * Payne, R. Terror : The West fights back. - London : MacMillan, 1982.

294. Dobson, Chr. * Payne, R. The new terrorists. - Lexington, Mass. : Lexington Books, 1986. 256 p

295. Dobson, Chr. * Payne, R. The terrorists : Their weapons, leaders, and tactics. - New York : Facts on File, 1979.
Simultaneously published as 'Weapons of terror', London: MacMillan, 1979.

296. Dollinger, H. Schwarzbuch der Weltgeschichte : 5000 Jahre der Mensch des Menschenfeind. - Munich : Suedwest Verlag, 1973.
Blackbook of world history. 5000 years of human hostility towards humans.

297. Dreher, E.T. * Magner, J.W. Investigation of terrorist activities. - Gaithersburg, Md. : IACP., 25 p

298. Drew, p. Domestic political violence: some problems of measurement. 1974. p. 5-25. Sociological Review. ; 22:1.

299. Eichelman * Soskis, D. * Reid, W. Terrorism : Interdisciplinary perspectives. American Psychiatric Press, 1983. 186 p

300. Elliott, J.D. * Gibson, L.K. * (eds.) Contemporary terrorism: selected readings. - Gaithersburg, Md. : IACP, 1978. 306 p

301. Elliott, J.D. Primers on terrorism. Oct. 1976. Military Review

302. Ellul, J. Terrorisme et violence psychologique. - Bruxelles : Desclee de Brouwer, 1968. p. 43-62.
In: La violence dans le monde actuel

303. Evron, Y. * (ed.) International violence: terrorism, surprise and control. - Jerusalem : Hebrew University, Leonard Davis Institute for International Relations, 1979.

304. Farhi, D. The limits to dissent : Facing the dilemmas posed by terrorism. - Palo Alto, Calif. : Aspen Institute for Humanistic Studies, 1978.

305. Fearey, R.A. Introduction to international terrorism. - Westport, Conn. : Greenwood Press, 1978. p. 25-35.
In: M.H. Livingston (ed.), International terrorism in the contemporary world

306. Feierabend, I.K. * Feierabend, R.L. Aggressive behaviors within politics 1948-1962 : A cross-national study. - New York : The Free Press, 1971.
In: J.C. Davies (ed.), When men revolt and why

307. Fishman, W.J. The insurrectionists. - New York : Barnes and Noble, 1970.

308. Freedman, L.Z. * Alexander, Y. Perspectives on terrorism. - Wilmington, Del. : Scholarly Resources, 1983.

309. Freiberg, J.W. The dialectics of violence : Repression and rebellion. - Los Angelos : University of California, 1971. ; Ph.D. dissertation

310. Friedlander, R.A. Terrorism and the law : What price safety?. - Gaithersburg, Md. : IACP, 1980. 22 p

311. Gallet, M. Genesi del terrorismo e mito della violenza. 1975. p. 61-71. La Destra. ; 1.

312. Gaucher, R. The terrorists, from tsarist Russia to the O.A.S. - London : Secker & Warburg, 1968. 325 p
Orig.: Les terroristes. Paris: A. Michel, 1965.

313. Geismar, A. L'engrenage terroriste. - Paris : Fayard, 1981.

314. Gerlach, L.P. Movements of revolutionary change: some structural characteristics. 1971. p. 812-836. American Behavioral Scientist. ; 14.

315. Gleason, J.M. * Lily, C. The impact of terrorism on investment decisions in the third world: a framework for analysis. ; Paper to the Second national conference on the third world, Omaha, Nebraska, 1978

316. Gleason, J.M. Third world terrorism: perspectives for quantitative research. - New York : Pergamon Press, 1980. p.242-255.
In: Y. Alexander and J.M. Gleason (eds.), Behavioral and quantitative perspectives of terrorism

317. Gonzales-Mata, L.M. Terrorismo internacional: la extreme derecha la extrema izquierda, y los crimenes del estado. - Barcelona : Libreria Editorial Argos, 1978.

318. Grammens, M. Enige beschouwingen over het terrorisme. Dec. 1977. p. 195-202. Tijdschrift voor Diplomatie. ; 4.

319. Green, L.C. Aspects of terrorism. 1982. p. 373-400. Terrorism. ; 5:4.
Review article, concentrating on books by Rapoport, Dobson, Payne, Sterling, Schmid & De Graaf.

320. Greisman, H.C. Social meanings of terrorism: reification, violence, and social control. 1977. p. 308-318. Contemporary Crises. ; 1:3.

321. Gribble, L. I terroristi. - Milano : Sugar, 1961.

322. Gros, B. Le terrorisme. - Paris : Hatier, 1976. Ca. 80 p

323. Guenther, J. Terror und Terrorismus. 1972. p. 32-42. Neue Deutsche Hefte. ; 19:4.

324. Gurr, T.R. * Duvall, R. Civil conflict in the 1960's : A reciprocal theoretical system with parameter estimates. July 1973. p. 135-170. Comparative Political Studies. ; 6.

325. Gurr, T.R. * Duvall, R. Introduction to a formal theory of conflict within social systems. - New York : The Free Press, 1976. p. 139-154.
In: L.A. Coser and O.N. Larsen (eds.), The uses of controversy in sociology

326. Gurr, T.R. Burke and the modern theory of revolution : A reply to Freeman. Aug. 1978. p. 299-312. Political Theory. ; 6:3.

327. Gurr, T.R. Contemporary crime in historical perspective : A comparative study of London, Stockholm and Sydney. Nov. 1977. p. 114-136. Annals of the American Academy of Political and Social Science. ; 334.

328. Gurr, T.R. Handbook of political conflict : Theory and research. - New York : The Free Press, 1980.

329. Gurr, T.R. Persisting patterns of repression and rebellion : Foundations for a general theory of political coercion. - New York : Praeger, 1986. In: M.P. Karns (ed.), Persistent patterns and emergent structures in a waning century

330. Gurr, T.R. The calculus of civil conflict. 1972. p. 27-48. Journal of Social Issues. ; 1.

331. Gurr, T.R. The faces of violence. April 1973. p. 2-8. Event. ; 13.

332. Gurr, T.R. Theories of violence and the control of intervention. Johns Hopkins Press, 1975. p. 70-91. In: W. Friedman and J.N. Moore (eds.), Law and civil war in the modern world

333. Gurr, T.R. Urban disorder : Perspectives from the comparative study of civil strife. March 1968. p. 50-55. American Behavioral Scientist. ; 11.

334. Gurr, T.R. Vergleichende Analyse von Krisen und Rebellionen. - Bonn : Westdeutscher Verlag, 1973. p. 64-89. In: M. Janicke (ed.), Herrschaft und Krise

335. Gurr, T.R. Violence and politics : Some conclusions on the uses of force in society. 6-9 March 1970. Princeton Alumni Weekly

336. Gutteridge, W. * (ed.) Contemporary terrorism. - New York : Facts on File, 1986. 225 p

337. Gutteridge, W. * (ed.) The new terrorism. - London : ISC, 1986. 240 p

338. Hamilton, L.C. * Hamilton, J.D. Dynamics of terrorism. March 1983. p. 39-54. International Studies Quarterly. ; 27:1.

339. Hamilton, p. Espionage, terrorism and subversion. - Surrey : Peter A. Helms, 1979.

340. Harris, J. Violence and responsibility. - London : Routledge and Kegan Paul, 1980.

341. Heer, F. Sieben Kapitel aus der Geschichte des Schreckens. - Zuerich : M. Niehaus, 1957. 162 p

342. Herman, E.S. The real terror network : Terrorism in fact and propaganda. - Boston : South End Press, 1982. 240 p

343. Heyman, E.S. * Mickolus, E.F. Observations on "Why violence spreads". June 1982. p. 299-305. International Studies Quarterly. ; 24:2.

344. Higham, R. * (ed.) Civil wars in the twentieth century. - Lexington : The University Press of Kentucky, 1972.

345. Hobsbawn, E.J. An appraisal of terrorism. Winter 1972. p. 11-14. Canadian Dimension. ; 9.

346. Hoffmann, p. Widerstand, Staatsstreich, Attentat. - Muenchen : R. Piper Verlag, 1969.

347. Honderich, T. Political violence : A philosophical analysis of terrorism. - Ithaca, N.Y. : Cornell University Press, 1976.

348. Hondt, J.d' Terrorism and politics. 1973. p. 72-77. Etudes internationales de psycho-sociologie criminelle. ; 24.

349. Horner, Ch. The facts about terrorism. June 1980. p. 40-45. Commentary. ; 69:6.

350. Horowitz, I.L. The routinization of terrorism and its unanticipated consequences. - Middletown, Conn. : Wesleyan University Press, 1983. p. 38-64. In: M. Crenshaw (ed.), Terrorism, legitimacy and power

351. Housman, L. Terrorism by ordinance. - London : The India League.,

352. Howard, B. Living with terrorism. 18 July 1976. p. C1, C4. Washington Post

353. Howe, I. The return of terror. 1975. p. 227-237. Dissent. ; 22.

354. Hyams, E. Terrorists and terrorism. - New York : St. Martin's, 1974. 200 p

355. Ingwell, M. The war of the entrails. 12 July 1981. Birmingham News

356. Iredynski, I. Ottarz wzniesiony sobie : Terroysci. - Warshaw : Czytelnik, 1985. 200 p

357. Janos, A.C. The seizure of power : A study of force and popular consent. - Princeton, N.J. : 1964., On various types of coups d'etat.

358. Jenkins, B.M. * (ed.) Terrorism and beyond : An international conference on terrorism and low-level conflict. - Santa Monica, Calif. : RAND, 1982. 287 p

359. Jenkins, B.M. * Johnson, J. International terrorism: a chronology, 1974 supplement. - Santa Monica, Calif. : RAND, Febr. 1976. ; R-1909-1-ARPA.

360. Jenkins, B.M. International terrorism: a new mode of conflict. - London : Croom Helm, 1975. p.13-49.

In: D. Carlton and C. Schaerf (eds.), International terrorism and world security

361. Jenkins, B.M. International terrorism: trends and potentialities : A summary. 1978. p. 115-124. Journal of International Affairs. ; 32.
Orig: RAND, Oct. 1977.

362. Jenkins, B.M. New modes of conflict. - Santa Monica, Calif. : RAND, 1983. 20 p

363. Jenkins, B.M. RAND's research on terrorism. - Santa Monica, Calif. : RAND, Aug. 1977. ; P-5969.
Repr. in: Terrorism 1, 1977, pp. 85-95.

364. Jenkins, B.M. Statements about terrorism. Sept. 1982. p. 11-23. Annals of the American Academy of Political and Social Science. ; 463.

365. Jenkins, B.M. Terrorism in the 1980s. - Santa Monica, Calif. : RAND, 1980. 13 p. RAND Paper Series. ; P-6564.

366. Jenkins, B.M. Testimony before the Senate Governmental Affairs Committee regarding Senate bill against terrorism. - Santa Monica, Calif. : RAND, 1981. 16 p

367. Johnson, Ch. Hypotheses and assumptions. 1980. p. 251-255. Terrorism. ; 3.

368. Johnson, Ch. Revolutionary change. - 2nd ed. - Palo Alto, Calif. : Stanford University Press and Longman, 1982.

369. Johnson, Ch. Terror. Nov. 1977. p. 48-52. Society. ; 15:1.

370. Johnson, Ch. Theory and practice of clandestine warfare. 29 May 1966. p. 4-6. The Asia Magazine

371. Johnson, p. The seven deadly sins of terrorism. 15 Sept. 1979. p. 19-21. New Republic. ; 181.

372. Jonsson, p. * (ed.) Political terrorism. - Stockholm : Natur och Kultur, 1978. 235 p
With contributions by Lennart Geijer, Walter Laqueur, et al.

373. Kaaden, J.J.van der Terrorisme. 1975. p. 1. Justitiele Verkenningen. ; 4.

374. Kemov, A.V. * et al. Terrorizm : Orudie imperializma. - Moscow : Znanie, 1982.

375. Klarin, M. Terorizam. - Beograd : Nin, 1978. 127 p

376. Kravitz, M. * (ed.) International summaries: a collection of selected translations in law enforcement and criminal justice. - Vol. 3. - Rockville, Md. : U.S. Department of Justice, National Criminal Justice Reference Service, April 1979. 172 p

377. Kritzer, H.M. Political protest and political violence: a nonrecursive causal model. March 1977. p. 630-640. Social Forces. ; 55:3.

378. Kupperman, R.H. * Trent, D.M. Terrorism threat, reality, response. - Stanford, Calif. : Hoover Institution Press, 1979. 450 p

379. Lador-Lederer, J.J. On certain trivialities written on terrorism. 1973. p. 25-28. International Problems. ; 12:3-4.

380. Lagorio, L. Appunti, 1978-1981 : Difesa dello stato moderno. - Firenze : Le Monnier, 1981.

381. Lallemand, R. Terrorisme et democratie. - Brussels : Institut Emile Vandervelde, 1979. 74 p

382. Landazabal, R.F. Conflicto social. - Medellin, Republica de Colombia : Beta, 1982.

383. Laqueur, W. * (ed.) The guerrilla reader : A historical anthology. - New York : New American Library, 1977. 246 p
Part 5: Guerrilla doctrine today, also deals with urban guerrilla strategy.

384. Laqueur, W. * (ed.) The terrorism reader : A historical anthology. - New York : New American Library, 1978. 291 p
Part I: Tyrannicide; Part II: The origins of modern terrorism; Part III: Terrorism in the twentieth century; Part IV: Interpretations of terrorism.

385. Laqueur, W. Fehlgedeuteter Terrorismus. Oct. 1976. p. 567-576. Schweizer Monatshefte. ; 156.

386. Laqueur, W. Guerrilla : A historical and critical study. - Boston : Little, Brown & Co, 1976.
pp. 343-352: philosophy of the urban guerrilla; pp. 321-325: on urbanterrorism; pp. 352-358: the uses of terror.

387. Laqueur, W. Karl Heinzen: the origins of modern terrorism. Aug. 1977. p. 23-27. Encounter. ; 49.

388. Laqueur, W. Terrorism. - London : Weidenfeld and Nicolson, 1977. 277 p
On the historical evolution of the doctrine of systematic terrorism. The author views terrorism not as a new stage of guerrilla warfare butas a development of tyrannicide.

389. Laqueur, W. The anatomy of terrorism. - New York : Crane, Russak, 1979. p. 7-21.

In: J. Shaw, E.F. Gueritz and A.E. Younger (eds.), Ten years of terrorism

390. Laqueur, W. The continuing failure of terrorism. Nov. 1976. p. 69-74. Harper's. ; 253.

391. Laqueur, W. The futility of terrorism. March 1976. p. 99-105. Harper's. ; 252.

392. Larteguy, J. Tout l'or du diable: guerre, petrole et terrorisme. - Paris : Presses de la Cite, 1974.

393. Lasswell, H.D. Terrorism and the political process. 1978. p. 255-264. Terrorism. ; 1.

394. Leff, A. * Roos, J.V. The transformation of terrorism : Three characteristics of the new terrorism. 1977.
p. 179-184. Stanford Journal of International Studies. ; 12.

395. Leiden, C. * Schmitt, K.M. * (eds.) The politics of violence. - Englewood Cliffs, N.J. : Prentice-Hall, 1968. 244 p

396. Lentner, H.H. * Lewis, T.J. Revolutionary terrorism in democratic society. May 1971. p. 3-19. Freedom at Issue. ; 7.

397. Lipovetsky, G. * (comp.) Territoires de la terreur. - Grenoble : 1978. 172 p. Silex. ; 10.
Various articles dealing with both state and nonstate terrorism in the widest sense of the word.

398. Liston, R.A. Terrorism. - Nashville : Thomas Nelson Inc., 1977. 158 p

399. Livingstone, N. The war against terrorism. - Lexington, Mass. : Lexington Books, 1982.

400. Lodge, J. * (ed.) Terrorism : A challenge to the state. - Oxford : Martin Robertson, 1981. 247 p

401. Lowe, E.N. * Shargel, H.D. * (eds.) Legal and other aspects of terrorism. - New York : Practicing Law Institute, 1979. 862 p
Includes an extensive bibliography by E.F. Mickolus.

402. Luebbe, H. Die Politik, die Wahrheit und die Moral. Dec. 1984. p. 288-304. Geschichte und Gegenwart. Vierteljahreshefte fur Zeitgeschichte, Geschellschafts-Analyse. ; 3:4.

403. Luebbe, H. Leichen als Ruhmesblatt : Was einen zum Mittater bei politischen Grossverbrechen macht. - Wien : 6 Febr. 1985. p. 5. Die Furche Unabhaengige Wochenzeitung fur Politiek, Gesellschaft, Kultur. ; 41:6.

404. Luebbe, H. Protest und Verweigerung : Ursachen und politische Konsequenzen. - Hamburg : 1982. p. 95-114. Hamburger Jahrbuch fur Wirtschafts- und Gesellschaftspolitiek. ; 27.

405. Maffesioli, M. La violence totalitaire. - Paris : Presses Universitaires, 1979.

406. Marshall, J. The business of terrorism. Jan. 1982. p. 48-51. Dial. ; 3.

407. May, W.G. Terrorism as strategy and ecstasy. 1974. p. 277-298. Social Research

408. McClure, B. The dynamics of terrorism. - Gaithersburg, Md. : IACP., 31 p

409. Medem, V. On terror. 1975. p. 189-190. Dissent. ; 22:2.

410. Merari, A. Berlin conference statement. 1980. p. 279-283. Terrorism. ; 3:3-4.

411. Mickolus, E.F. An events data base for studying transnational terrorism. - Boulder, Colo. : Westview Press, 1978. p. 127-163.
In: R.J. Heuer jr (ed.), Quantitative approaches to political intelligence: the CIA experience

412. Mickolus, E.F. Codebook: ITERATE (International Terrorism: Attributes of Terrorist Events). - Ann Arbor, Mich. : Inter-University Consortium for Political and Social Research, University of Michigan, 1976. 47 p

413. Mickolus, E.F. Statistical approaches to the study of terrorism. - New York : John Jay Press, 1977. p. 209-269.
In: S.M. Finger and Y. Alexander (eds.), Terrorism: interdisciplinary perspectives
Orig. paper presented to the Ralph Bunche Institute's conference on international terrorism, June 9-11, 1976.

414. Mickolus, E.F. Transnational terrorism. - New York : Dekker, 1979. p. 147-190.
In: M. Stohl (ed.), The politics of terrorism

415. Miller, Ch.A. * Miller, B.H. Transnational terrorism: terrorist tactics and techniques. - Gaithersburg, Md. : IACP, 1977. Clandestine Tactics and Technology, Group and Area Studies

416. Miller, J.A. Political terrorism and insurgency: an interrogative approach. - New York : John Jay Press, 1977. p. 64-91.
In: S.M. Finger and Y. Alexander (eds.), Terrorism, interdisciplinary perspectives

417. Modzhorian, L.A. Terrorizmi : Pravda i vymysel. - 2nd ed. - Moscow : lurid. lit., 1986. 239 p

418. Mommsen, W.J. * Hirschfeld, G. * (eds.) Sozialprotest, Gewalt, Terror : Gewaltanwendung durch politische und gesellschaftliche Randgruppen im 19. und 20. Jahrhundert. - Stuttgart : Klett-Cotta, 1982. 476 p. Publications of the German Historical Institute London. ; 10.

419. Montovio, I.G. Derechos humanos y terrorismo. - Buenos Aires : Ed. Depalma, 1980.

420. Moodie, M. Political terrorism: a unique kind of tyranny. 1978. p. 27-38 ; Paper presented to the 19th Annual convention of the International Studies Association, February 22-25, 1978, at Washington, D.C. Oesterreichische Zeitschrift fuer Aussenpolitik. ; 18.

421. Morander, G. FNL terror eller befrielse. - Lund : Studentlitteratur, 1972.

422. Nielsen, T. Terror. - Kopenhagen : Lademann, 1977. 269 p

423. O'Brien, C.C. Liberty and terror : Illusions of violence, delusions of liberation. Oct. 1977. p. 34-41. Encounter. ; 44:4.

424. O'Brien, C.C. Reflections on terrorism. 16 Sept. 1976. p. 44-48. New York Review

425. Osmond, R.L. Transnational terrorism 1968-1974 : A quantitative analysis. Syracuse University, 1979. ; Ph.D.dissertation

426. Paine, L. The terrorists. - London : Robert Hale & Co., 1975. 176 p

427. Parry, A. Terrorism: from Robespierre to Arafat. - New York : Vanguard, 1976. 624 p

428. Paul, L. The age of terror. - London : Faber, 1950.

429. Pierson-Mathy, p. Formes nouvelles de la lutte revolutionnaire et cooperation internationale dans le combat contre-revolutionnaire. - Brussels : Editions de l'Universite de Bruxelles, 1974. p. 59-94. In: Reflexions sur la definition et la repression du terrorisme

430. Pisapia, C.V. Terrorismo: delitto politico o delitto comune?. 1975. p. 257-271. La giustizia penale. ; 80:2.

431. Plastrik, S. On terrorism. 1974. p. 143. Dissent. ; 21.

432. Quester, G.H. World tolerance for terrorisme. - Jerusalem : Hebrew University, Leonard Davis Institute for International Relations, 1979. p. 166-181. In: Y. Evron (ed.), International violence: terrorism, surprise and control

433. Roucek, J.S. Terrorism in its sociological aspects. 1980. p. 97-110. Sociologica Internationalis. ; 18.

434. Russell, Ch.A. Terrorism: an overview 1970-1978. - New York : Praeger, 1979. p. 491-498. In: Y. Alexander and R.A. Kilmarx (eds.), Political terrorism and business, the threat and response

435. Santoro, V. Disruptive terrorism. Loompanics, 1984. 135 p

436. Schmid, A.P. Political terrorism : A research guide to concepts, theories, data bases and literature. - New Brunswick, N.J. : Transactions Books, 1984. 585 p
Also: Amsterdam: North Holland Publishing Comp., 1984.

437. Schreiber, M. * Birkl, R. Zwischen Sicherheit und Freiheit. - Muenchen-Wien : G. Olzog, 1977.

438. Servier, J. Le terrorisme. - Paris : Presses universitaires, 1979. 127 p

439. Shaffer, H.B. Political terrorism. 1970. p. 341-360. Editorial Research Reports. ; 1.

440. Shaw, J. * Gueritz, E.F. * Younger, A.E. * (eds.) Ten years of terrorism: collected views. - New York : Crane, Russak, 1979. 192 p

441. Shultz, R. Conceptualizing political terrorism: a typology and application. 1978. p. 7-16 ; Paper presented to the 19th Annual convention of the International Studies Association, Febr. 22-25, 1978, at Washington, D.C. Journal of International Affairs. ; 32.

442. Sloan, S. * Kearney, R. Non-territorial terrorism: an empirical approach to policy formation. 1978. p. 131-144. Conflict. ; 1.

443. Sobel, L.A. * (ed.) Political terrorism. - New York : Facts on File, 1975. 309 p
Gives a narrative survey of terrorist activity as reported in the world press from 1968 through 1974.

444. Sobel, L.A. * (ed.) Political terrorism : Vol. 2: 1974-1978. - New York : Facts on File, 1978.

445. Stencel, S. Terrorism: an idea whose time has come. Jan. 1976. Skeptic. ; 11.

446. Stiles, D.W. Sovereignty and the new violence. - Gaithersburg, Md. : IACP,

1978. p. 261-267.
In: J.D. Elliott and L.K. Gibson (eds.), Contemporary terrorism: selected readings

447. Stohl, M. * (ed.) The politics of terrorism. - 2nd. revised and expanded edition. - New York : Marcel Dekker, 1983. 473 p

448. Stohl, M. Myths and realities of political terrorism. - New York : Dekker, 1979. p. 1-19.
In: M. Stohl (ed.), The politics of terrorism

449. Tomasevski, K. Terrorism in the contemporary world. - Zagreb : Institute for Social Research, 1979. 257 p ; Mimeographed monograph
In Croatian.

450. Tomasevski, K. The challenge of terrorism. - Rijeka : Liburnia, 1981.
In Croatian.

451. Trick, M.M. Chronology of incidents of terroristic, quasi-terroristic, and political violence in the U.S.: January 1965 to March 1976. - Washington D.C. : National Advisory Committee on Criminal Justice Standards and Goals, Dec. 1976. p. 507-595.
In: Report of the task force on disorders and terrorism

452. Troncoso de Castro, A. Terrorismo y estado moderno. - Burgos : Ediciones Aldecoa, 1975.

453. Villemarest, P.F.de * Faillant, D. Histoire secrete des organisations terroristes. - 4 vols. - Geneva : Famot, 1976.
Secret history of terrorist organizations.

454. Wallace, M. * (ed.) Terrorism. - New York : Arno Press, 1979.

455. Walter, E.V. Theories of terrorism and the classical tradition. - New York : Atherton Press, 1967. p. 133-160.
In: D. Spitz (ed.), Political theory and social sciences

456. Wardlaw, G. Political terrorism : Theory, tactics and countermeasures. - Cambridge, N.Y. : Cambridge University Press, 1982. 218 p

457. Watson, F.M. Political terrorism: the threat and the response. - Washington, D.C. : Robert B. Luce, 1976. 248 p
Includes chronology of significant terroristic incidents, 1968-1975, and lists 97 organizations using terrorism.

458. Wijgaerts, D. Facetten van het politiek terrorisme. Dec. 1980. p. 195-204. Tijdschrift voor Diplomatie. ; 7:4.

459. Wilkinson, p. * (ed.) British perspectives on political terrorism. - London : George Allen and Unwin, 1981.

460. Wilkinson, p. A question of ransom. 12 July 1979. The Listener

461. Wilkinson, p. After Tehran. 1981. p. 5-14. Conflict Quarterly

462. Wilkinson, p. Die Droehung des Terrorismus. - Vol.11. - Stuttgart : Klett, Cotta, 1979.
In: W. Hennis, P.G. Kielmansegg and U. Matz (eds.), Regiebarkeit Studies zu ihrer Problematisierung

463. Wilkinson, p. Diplomacy under siege. 3 April 1980. The Listener

464. Wilkinson, p. El problema del terrorismo. 1985. p. 24-31. Ideas. ; 2.

465. Wilkinson, p. Terrorism and the liberal state. - Revised and enlarged ed. - London : MacMillan, 1985.
Also: New York, NYUP, 1985.

466. Woerdemann, F. * Loeser H.J. Terrorismus : Motive, Taeter, Strategien. - Muenchen : Piper, 1977. 394 p

467. Wolf, J.B. * Kaufman, L. Hotel-room-interviewing-anxiety and suspicion. Spring 1982. p. 57-61. Sloan Management Review. ; 23:3.

468. Wolf, J.B. Aspects of contemporary terrorism in the Americas. - Gaithersburg, Md. : IACP, 1979. Update Report. ; 5:2.

469. Wolf, J.B. Economic aspects of terroristic threats. - Gaithersburg, Md. : IACP, 1979. Update Report. ; 5:1.

470. Wolf, J.B. Fear of fear : A survey of terrorist operations and controls in open societies. - New York : Plenum Press, 1981. 235 p

471. Wolf, J.B. Terrorism : An unabating menace. - Gaithersburg, Md. : IACP, 1980.

472. Wolf, J.B. Terrorism, the scourge of the 1980's. - Gaithersburg, Md:. : IACP, 1980. Update Report. ; 6:1.

473. Wolf, J.B. Terrorist manipulation of the democratic process. - Westport, Conn. : Greenwood Press, 1978. p. 197-306.
In: M.H. Livingston et al. (eds.), International terrorism in the contemporary world

474. Wright, C.D. Terrorism. - Fayetteville, Ark. : Lost Roads Publ., 1979.

475. _____ Annual of Power and Conflict. - Vol. 1-11. - London : 1970-1982.

Provides annual overviews of terroristic trends and events.

476. _____ Disorder and terrorism. - Washington, D.C. : GPO, 1977. 661 p. U.S.National Advisory Committee on Criminal Justice Standards and Goals A study of the growth of terrorism in the United States with a list of almost 2000 incidents from 1965 to spring 1976. Serves as a police manual on how to deal with terrorism and disorders.

477. _____ Focus on terrorism. Winter 1976. p. 1251-1343. Orbis. ; 19.

478. _____ Gewalt-Terrorismus. - Berlin : 1975. p. 102-150. Kommunitaet. ; 19:76.

479. _____ Het vraagstuk van het politiek terrorisme. Sept. 1978. Civis Mundi. ; 17.
Whole number, pp. 193-234, on terrorism. Contents: J. Niezing, Politiek terrorisme en oorlog; J.W. Schneider, Politiek terrorisme als internationaal en volkenrechtelijk vraagstuk; B. Tromp, Sociologie van het terrorisme; J.S.van der Meulen, Terrorisme en krijgsmacht; R.P.B. van der Laan Bouma and J. Wiersma, Terrorisme en burgerlijke grondrechten; C.N. Peijster, Politiek terrorisme en de verdediging van de demokratische rechtsstaat; H. Bianchi, Politiek terrorisme en kriminaliteit; D. Wijgaerts, Het politiek terrorisme: een bondig literatuuroverzicht.

480. _____ Le siecle de tous les terrorismes. Oct.-Nov. 1984. Esprit. ; 94-95. Whole number on terrorism.

481. _____ Le terrorisme. Febr. 1979. Apres-demain. ; 211.
Series of articles in the monthly published by the League of the Rights of Man.

482. _____ Political violence and terror. - Berkeley : University of California Press, 1986.

483. _____ Proceedings of the Conference on terrorism held under auspices of Glassboro State College, Glassboro, N.J. - Westport, Conn. : Greenwood Press, 1978.

484. _____ Sondeo sobre terrorismo y secuestros. Oct. 1972. p. 221-249. Revista espanola de la opinion publica. ; no. 30.

485. _____ Terrorism. 1976. Military Police Law Enforcement Journal. ; 3. Whole issue.

486. _____ Terrorism. Jan. 1976. Skeptic. ; 11.
Contains a.o. an interview with Sean MacBride; I. Howe, The ultimate price of random terror; R. Ridenour, Who are the terrorists - and whatdo they want?; W. Laqueur, Can terrorism succeed?; The Weather Underground, Prairie Fire; Institute for the Study of Conflict, Terrorism can be stopped.

487. _____ Terrorism. - Washington, D.C. : 1981. 74 p.
U.S. Department of Defense. Current News, Special Edition. ; 773.

488. _____ Terrorism: what should we do? : A "This World" symposium. Fall 1985. p. 31-84. This World. ; 12.

489. _____ Terrorisme. - Groningen : Pamflet, 1975. De As. ; 13.
Whole issue of this anarcho-socialist journal.

490. _____ Terrorisme als vorm van politiek geweld. - Tilburg : 1977. 242 p.
Buro Buitenland der Katholieke Hogeschool ; Informatiemap bij de cyclus Concentrating mainly on Germany; containing lecture transcripts and articles.

491. _____ Worldwide chronology of terrorism - 1981. 1982. Terrorism. ; 6:2. Whole issue.

D. REGIME TERRORISM AND REPRESSION

492. Accattatis, V. Capitalismo e repressione. - Milano : 1977.
Discusses Italian anti-terrorist legislation.

493. Agee, Ph. Inside the company: CIA diary. - New York : Bantam Books, 1975.

494. Ahn, B.J. Chinese politics and the cultural revolution : Dynamics of policy processes. - Seattle : University of Washington Press, 1976.

495. Aizcorbe, R. Argentina, the peronist myth : An essay on the cultural decay in Argentina after the Second World war. - Hicksville, N.Y. : Exposition Press, 1975. 313 p

496. Alesevich, E. Police terrorism. - Westport, Conn. : Greenwood Press, 1978. p. 269-275.
In: M.H. Livingston et al. (eds.), International terrorism in the contemporary world

497. Allen, F.A. The crimes of politics. - Cambridge, Mass. : Harvard University Press, 1974.

498. Almond, G.A. The struggle for democracy in Germany. - Chapel Hill : University of North Carolina Press, 1949.
On nazi-terror.

499. Ames, B. Rhetoric and reality in a militarized regime : Brazil since 1964. - Beverly Hills : Sage, 1973. Sage Professional-
Paper in Comparative Politics Series. ; No. 01-042.

500. Anders, K. Murder to order. - New York : Devin-Adair, 1967. 127 p
By a former KGB assassin.

501. Andics, H. Rule of terror. - New York : Holt, Rinehart & Winston, 1969.
State terror in Russia until 1953.

502. Arendt, H. The origins of totalitarianism. - New York : Harcourt, Brace and World, 1951.

503. Arens, R. Terrorism from above: genocide. - Chicago : University of Chicago, Nov. 1979. ; Paper presented to the Conference on psychopathology and political violence

504. Aron, R. Frieden und Krieg : Eine Theorie der Staatengewalt. - Frankfurt a.M. : Fischer-Verlag, 1963.
Also contains a perceptive discussion of terrorism.

505. Baeyer-Katte, W.von Terrorism. - New York : Harder and Harder, 1973.
In: C.D. Kerning (ed.), Marxism, communism and Western society

506. Baldwin, R.N. * (ed.) Kropotkin's revolutionary pamphlets. - Dover : 1970.

507. Barron, J. * Paul, A. Murder of a gentle land. - New York : Reader's Digest Press, 1977. 240 p
On post-1975 government terror in Cambodia.

508. Barron, J. K.G.B.: the secret work of Soviet secret agents. - New York : Reader's Digest Press, 1974.

509. Baynac, J. * (ed.) La terreur sous Lenin 1917-1924. - Paris : Le Sagittaire, 1975.
An anthology with an introduction by the editor.

510. Beck, J. * (ed.) Terror und Hoffnung in Deutschland, 1933-1945 : Leben im Faschismus. - Reinbek : Rowohlt, 1980. 526 p

511. Becker, p. Rule of fear: the life and times of Dingane, king of the Zulu. - London : 1964.

512. Becker, Th.L. * Murray, V.G. * (eds.) Government lawlessness in America. - New York : Oxford University Press, 1971.

513. Beria di Argentine, A. Giustizia, anni difficili. - Milano : Rusconi, 1985. 313 p

514. Berman, J.J. * Halperin, M.H. * (eds.) The abuses of the intelligence agencies. - Washington D.C. : Center for National Security Studies, 1975. 185 p
Covers FBI, NSA, IRS, CIA and White House activities against alleged dissidents, some of which come close to terrorism.

515. Berman, M.R. * Clark, R.S. State terrorism : Disappearances. Spring 1982. p. 531-577. Rutgers Law Journal. ; 13.

516. Bicudo, H. My testimony on the death squad. - Sao Paulo, Brazil : Sao Paulo Justice and Peace Commission, Oct. 1976.

517. Biocca, E. Strategia del terrore: il modelo brasiliano. - Bari : De Donato, 1974. 251 p
Government terror in Brazil.

518. Blackstock, N. COINTELPRO. - New York : Vintage, 1976.

519. Block, S. * Reddaway, p. Psychiatric terror : How Soviet psychiatry is used to suppress dissent. - New York : Basic Books, 1977.

520. Borcke, A.von Die Urspruenge des Bolschewismus : Die jakobinische Tradition in Russland und die Theorie der revolutionaeren Diktatur. - Muenchen : Berchmans, 1977. 646 p

521. Borneman, E. Der Staat, die Herrscher, der Terror : Semantische Notizen eines alten Socialisten. 1975. Frankfurter Hefte. ; 30:10.

522. Bousquet, J. Les "folles" de la Place de Mai. - Paris : Stock, 1982. 258 p

523. Bramstedt, E.K. Dictatorship and political police : The technique of control by fear. - London : Kegan Paul, 1956. 275 p

524. Branch, T. The Letelier investigation. 16 July 1978. Section 6, pp. 26-39. The New York Times Magazine
On DINA's, CIA's and exile Cubans' network of trained terrorists.

525. Brune, J.M. Die Papageienschankel : Diktatur und Folter in Brasilien. - Duesseldorf : 1971.
Dictatorship and torture in Brazil.

526. Buchheim, H. * et al. Anatomie des SS-Staates. - 2 vols. - Muenchen :

DTV, 1967. 231 p
527. Buhrer, J.C. Repression et luttes populaires en Amerique Centrale. Sept. 1978. Le monde diplomatique
Repression and resistance in Central America.

528. Byas, H. Government by assassination. - London : 1943.
An anti-Japanese tract.

529. Cancogni, M. Gli squadristi... - Milano : Longanesi, 1972. 188 p
On fascism in Italy.

530. Carlton, D. * Schaerf, C. * (eds.) Contemporary terror : Studies in sub-state violence. - London : McMillan, 1981. 202 p ; Proceedings of the International School on Disarmament and Research on Conflicts, 7th annual meeting, Ariccia Italy 1978

531. Carmichael, J. Stalin's masterpiece : The show trials and purges of the thirties, the consolidation of the Bolshevist dictatorship. - New York : St. Martin's Press, 1976. 238 p

532. Carranza, M.E. Fuerzas armadas y estado de excepcion en America Latina. - 2nd ed. - Mexico City : Editores Siglo 21, 1978.

533. Chamberlain, W.H. Beyond containment. - Chicago : Henry Regnery, 1953. 406 p
On USSR government strategies of repression.

534. Chapman, R.D. State terrorism. 1982. p. 283-298. Conflict. ; 3:4.

535. Chomsky, N. * Herman, E.S. The political economy of human rights : Vol.2. After the cataclysm: postwar Indochina and the reconstruction of imperial ideology. - Nottingham : Spokesman, 1979. 392 p

536. Chomsky, N. * Herman, E.S. The political economy of human rights : Vol.1. The Washington connection and third world fascism. - Nottingham : Spokesman, 1979. 441 p
A work long suppressed in the U.S.A.

537. Chossudovsky, M. Capital accumulation and state violence in the third world. - Unpubl. paper. - Oaxtepec : IPRA, 1977. 27 p

538. Clements, J.M. Repression: beyond the rhetoric. p. 1-31. Issues in Criminology. ; 6:1.

539. Cohen, S.F. Bukharin and the bolshevik revolution. - New York : Vintage, 1975.
On stalinist terrorism.

540. Cohn, W. Perspectives on communist totalitarianism. 1980. p. 68-73. Problems of Communism. ; 29:5.

541. Conquest, R. The great terror : Stalin's purge of the thirties. - London : MacMillan, 1968. 633 p

542. Conquest, R. The Soviet police system. - New York : Praeger, 1968.

543. Corradi, J.E. The mode of destruction : Terror in Argentina. Winter 1982-1983. p. 61-75. Telos. ; 54.

544. Crankshaw, E. Gestapo - instrument of tyranny. - London : Putnam, 1956. 275 p
On Nazi government terrorism during World War 2.

545. Crassweller, D. Trujillo : The life and times of a Caribbean dictator. - London : 1966.

546. Crawley, E. Dictators never die. - London : 1979.

547. Curtis, M. Totalitarianism. - 2nd ed. - New Brunswick, N.J. : Transaction Books, 1980. 128 p

548. Da Silva, R. * et al. Evidence of terror in Chile. - Merli : 1974.,
Transl. from the Swedish.

549. Dadrian, V.N. Factors of anger and aggression in genocide in Turkey. 1971. p. 394-417. Journal of Human Relations. ; 19.

550. Dadrian, V.N. The common features of the Armenian and Jewish cases of genocide : A comparative victimological perspective. - Lexington, Mass. : Lexington Books, 1975. p. 99-120.
In: I. Drapkin and E. Viano (eds.), Victimology

551. Dadrian, V.N. The structural-functional components of genocide: a victimological approach to the Armenian case. - Lexington, Mass. : Lexington Books, 1975. p. 123-136.
In: I. Drapkin and E. Viano (eds.), Victimology

552. Dallin, A. * Breslauer, G.W. Political terror in communist systems. - Stanford : Stanford University Press, 1970. 172 p

553. Danske, H. Terror, sabotage och annat dagligt liv i Danmark. - Stockholm : Blocks Forlag, 1943. 111 p

554. Dehghani, A. Torture and resistance in Iran. - London : Iran Committee, 1977. 153 p

555. Denemark, R.A. * Lehman, A.S. South African state terror :
The costs of continuing repression. - Milwaukee, Wisc. : Midwest Political Science Association, 1982. 55 p ;

Conference paper
556. Dror, Y. Crazy states: a counter-conventional strategic issue. - Lexington, Mass. : D.C. Heath, 1971. 118 p

557. Duhalde, E.L. El estado terrorista argentino. - Barcelona : Argos Vergara, 1983. 265 p

558. Duncan, p. South Africa's rule of violence. - London : Methuen, 1964.

559. Enzensberger, H.M. Politik und Verbrechen. - Frankfurt a.M. : 1964.

560. Fainsod, M. How Russia is ruled. - Cambridge, Mass. : Harvard University Press, 1964.
Orig. edition 1953.

561. Federn, E. The terror as a system: the concentration camp. 1948. Psychiatry Quarterly Supplement. ; 22.

562. Fest, J.C. Das Gesicht des Dritten Reiches. - Muenchen : 1963.
Nazi Germany.

563. Fields, R.M. A society on the run : A psychology of Northern Ireland. - Harmondsworth : Penguin, 1973.
This book was censored, than withdrawn from the British market and 10.000 copies were shredded. An expanded version under the title 'Society under siege' was published in the U.S. by Temple University Press in1977.

564. Frame, W.V. Dialectical historicism and the terror in Chinese communism. University of Washington, 1969. 401 p ; Unpubl. dissertation

565. Frazier, H. * (ed.) Uncloaking the C.I.A. - New York : Free Press, 1978.

566. Freed, D. * Landis, F. Death in Washington : The murder of Orlando Letelier. - London : Zed Press, 1980.

567. Friedrich, C.J. * (ed.) Totalitarianism. - New York : Grosset & Dunlap, 1954. 386 p
A collection of essays which analyse communist and fascist movements.

568. Friedrich, C.J. * Brzezinski, S.K. Totalitarian dictatorship and autocracy. - 2nd revised ed. - Cambridge, Mass. : Harvard University Press, 1965.
Original ed. 1956.

569. Friedrich, C.J. * et al. Totalitarianism in perspective. - New York : Praeger, 1969.

570. Friedrich, C.J. Opposition and government by violence. Jan. 1972. p. 3-19. Government and Opposition. ; 7.

571. Friedrich, C.J. Uses of terror. Nov. 1970. p. 46. Problems of Communism. ; 19.

572. Funke, M. * (ed.) Terrorismus : Untersuchungen zur Struktur und Strategie revolutionaerer Gewaltpolitik. - Duesseldorf : Droste und Athenaeum, 1977. 391 p
Deals mainly with the German scene.

573. Funke, M. * (ed.) Totalitarismus : Ein Studien-Reader zur Herrschaftsanalyse moderner Diktaturen. - Duesseldorf : Droste Verlag, 1978. 195 p. Bonner Schriften zur Politik und Zeitgeschichte. ; 14.

574. Galeano, E. Guatemala: occupied country. - New York : Monthly Review Press, 1969.
On post-1954 government terror.

575. Gall, N. Santo Domingo: the politics of terror. 22 July 1971. p. 15-10. New York Review of Books
On police terror in the Dominican Republic.

576. Gall, N. Slaughter in Guatemala. 20 May 1971. p. 13-17. New York Review of Books
On government terrorism via death squadrons.

577. Garling, M. The human rights handbook. - New York : Facts on File, 1979. 229 p

578. George, A. * Lall, D. * Simons, W. The limits of coercive diplomacy. - Boston : Little, Brown, 1971.

579. Glicksman, W.M. Violence and terror: the Nazi German conception of killing and murder. - Westport, Conn. : Greenwood Press, 1978. p. 423-429.
In: M.H. Livingston et al. (eds.), International terrorism in the contemporary world

580. Gliksman, J. Social prophylaxis as a form of Soviet terror. - New York : Grosset and Dunlap, 1963.
In: C.J. Friedrich (ed.), Totalitarianism

581. Goldstein, R.J. Political repression in modern America from 1870 to the present. - Boston : G.K. Hall & Co., 1978. 682 p
Covers red scare of the 1920s; Mc-Carthyism and the 'dirty tricks' of the Nixon administration.

582. Grishaev, p. I. * et al. Rezkim terrora : Bezzakoniva: Zakonodatel stro: praktika chiliiskoi khunty. - Moscow : Mezhdunar, 1979. 255 p

583. Gundersheim, A. Terror and political control in communist China. - Chicago : University of Chicago, Center for Social Organization Studies, 1966. ; Unpubl. paper

584. Gurr, T.R. * Bishop, V.F. Violent

nations, and others. 1976. p. 79-110. Journal of Conflict Resolution. ; 20:1.

585. Gurr, T.R. The political origins of state terror : A theoretical analysis. - Westport, Conn. : Greenwood Press, 1986.
In: G. Lopez and M. Stohl (eds.), Yearbook of state violence and state terrorism

586. Gutierrez, C.M. The Dominican Republic: rebellion and repression. - New York : Monthly Review Press, 1972.
On post-1965 government terror which claimed at least 2000 lives and drove over 150.000 people into exile.

587. Gwyn, D. Idi Amin : Death-light of Africa. - Boston : Little & Brown, 1977. 240 p

588. Halperin, M. * et al. The lawless state. - New York : Penguin, 1976.

589. Handler, B. Death squad ties to Brazil's regime. 26 Dec. 1976. p. A38-A39. Washington Post
Review of H. Bicudo, My testimony on the death squad, Sao Paulo, 1976.

590. Hendel, S. The price of terror in the U.S.S.R. - Westport, Conn. : Greenwood Press, 1978. p. 122-130.
In: M.H. Livingston et al. (eds.), International terrorism in the contemporary world

591. Henkys, R. Die national-sozialistischen Gewaltverbrechen : Geschichte und Gericht. - Stuttgart : 1964.

592. Herrnleben, H.G. Totalitaere Herrschaft : Faschismus-Nationalsozialismus-Stalinismus. - Freiburg/Wurzburg : Verlag Ploetz, 1978. 100 p. Ploetz Arbeitsmaterialen

593. Heynowski, W. * et al. * (eds.) Operacion Silencio: Chile nach Salvador Allende : Dokumentation. - Berlin : Verlag der Nation, 1974. 237 p

594. Hill, W. Terrorismus und Folter. April 1976. Merkur. Deutsche Zeitschrift fuer europaeisches Denken. ; 4.

595. Hills, D.C. Horror in Uganda : Amin's subjects. 16 Sept. 1976. p. 21-23. The New York Review of Books

596. Hoefnagels, M. * (ed.) Repression and repressive violence. - Amsterdam : Swets & Zeitlinger, 1977. 194 p
Contains a.o. an article by the editor with the title: Political violence and peace research.

597. Homer, F.D. Government terror in the U.S : An exploration of containment policy. 1982. 26 p ; Unpubl. paper

598. Horkheimer, M. * Eisenberg, E. * Jacoby, R. The authoritarian state. 1973. p. 3-20. Telos. ; 15.

599. Horowitz, I.L. Democracy and terrorism. - 3rd rev. ed. - New Brunswick, N.J. : Transaction Books, 1980.
In: I.L. Horowitz, Taking lives: genocide and state power

600. Horowitz, I.L. Genocide: state power and mass murder. - New Brunswick, N.J. : Transaction Books, 1976.

601. Huckenbeck, E. Terror, Verfolgung, Kirchenkampf : Zur Geschichte Hildens im Dritten Reich. - Hilden : Verlag Stadtarchiv Hilden, 1981. 233 p

602. Ignotus, p. The AVH : Symbol of terror. Sept. 1957. Problems of Communism. ; 6:5.
On secret police in Hungary.

603. Jones, S. * McCaughan, E. * Sutherland Martinez, E. * (eds. and transl.) Guatemala: tyranny on trial : Testimony of the Permanent People's Tribunal. - San Francisco : Synthesis Publications, 1984. 301 p

604. Kalme, A. Total terror: an expose of genocide in the Baltics. - New York : Appleton-Century-Croft, 1951. 310 p
Documents German and Soviet state terrorism, 1940 1951.

605. Kassof, A. The administered society - totalitarianism without terror. July 1964. p. 558-575. World Politics. ; 16.

606. Kataja, S. Der Terror der Bourgeoisie in Finnland. - Amsterdam : Verlag Bef, 1920. 47 p

607. Katsh, A.I. Terror, holocaust and the will lo live. - Westport, Conn. : Greenwood Press, 1978. p. 430-435.
In: M.H. Livingston et al. (eds.), International terrorism in the contemporary world
On Nazi Germany.

608. Khrushchev, N.S. The anatomy of terror : Relevations about Stalin's regime. - Washinton, D.C. : Rabbie Affairs Press, 1956.

609. Kirchheimer, O. Political Justice. - Princeton, N.J. : Princeton University Press, 1961.

610. Klare, M.T. * Arnson, C. Exporting repression : US support for authoritarianism in Latin America. - Stanford, Calif. : Stanford University Press, 1979.
In: R. Fagen (ed.), Capitalism and the state in US-Latin American relations

611. Klare, M.T. * Arnson, C. Supplying repression : US support for authoritarian regimes abroad. - Washington, D.C. :

Institute for Policy Studies, 1981.
612. Klare, M.T. * Stein, N. Police terrorism in Latin America : Secret U.S. bomb school exposed. - New York : NACLA, Jan. 1974. p. 19-23. NACLA's Latin American and empire report. ; 8:1.

613. Koch, E. Gewalt und Militaer : Ueber die staatlichen Repressionen in drei sudamerikanischen Militaerregimen. - Koeln : Bohlau Verlag, 1978.
In: R. Kontzke et al. (eds.), Jahrbuch fuer Geschichte von Staat, Wirtschaft und Gesellschaft Lateinamerikas. Vol. 15

614. Kogon, E. De SS-staat : Het systeem der Duitse concentratiekampen. - Amsterdam : Amsterdam Boek N.V., 1976. 406 p
Orig.: Der SS-Staat. Muenchen: Kindler, 1974. The first chapter, "De terreur als machtssysteem", was written in 1948 for the German sociologists' congress.

615. Kogon, E. Staatsterror als Ordnungsfaktor. 1976. Frankfurter Hefte. ; 31:6.

616. Korbonski, S. Terror and counterterror in nazi occupied Poland, 1939-1945. - New York, N.Y. : John Jay School of Criminal Justice, Oct. 1976. ; Paper presented to the Conference on terror: the man, the mind and the matter

617. Kren, G.M. * Rapoport, L. S.S. atrocities: a psychohistorical perspective. 1975. History of Childhood Quarterly. ; 3.

618. Kren, G.M. * Rapoport, L. The Waffen SS. Nov. 1976. Armed Forces and Society

619. Kren, G.M. The SS: a social and psychohistorical analysis. - Westport, Conn. : Greenwood Press, 1978. p. 436-443.
In: M.H. Livingston et al. (eds.), International terrorism in the contemporary world

620. Kropotkin, P.A. The terror in Russia. - London : Methuen, 1909.

621. Kuehnl, R. Faschismustheorien. - Reinbek bei Hamburg : 1979.

622. Labrousse, A. La terreur blanche et les chemins de l'armee. Nov. 1974. Le Monde diplomatique

623. Langguth, A.J. Hidden terrors. - New York : Pantheon, 1978. 339 p
U.S. aid to Latin American repressive regimes.

624. Leggett, G.H. Lenin, terror and the political police. 1975. Survey. ; 21:4.

625. Leonhard, W. Terror in the Soviet system : Trends and portents. Nov. 1958. p. 1-7. Problems of Communism. ; 7.

626. Levytsky, B. * (comp.) The Stalinist terror in the thirties; : Documentation from the Soviet press. - Stanford, Calif. : Hoover Institution Press, 1974. 521 p

627. Levytsky, B. The uses of terror: the Soviet secret service, 1917-1970. - London : Sidgwick and Jackson, 1971. 349 p
On Cheka, GPU and NKVD.

628. Levytsky, B. Vom roten Terror zur sozialistischen Gesetzlichkeit. - Muenchen : Nymphenburger Verlag, 1961.

629. Linz, J.J. Totalitarian and authoritarian regimes. - Reading, Mass. : 1975. p. 175-411.
In: F.I. Greenstein and N.W. Polsby (ed.), Handbook of political science. Vol.3. Macropolitical theory

630. Locicero, S.L. Government in France during the first terror. University of Washington, 1975. ; Unpubl. dissertation

631. Loomis, S. Paris in the Terror, June 1793-July 1794. - Philadelphia : Lippincott, 1964. 415 p

632. Lopez, G.A. * Stohl, M. * (eds.) Government violence and repression. - Westport, Conn. : Greenwood Press, 1986.

633. Lorenz, R. Politischer Terror in der UdSSR waehrend der dreissiger Jahre. March 1979. p. 224-233. Das Argument. ; 21:114.
Stalinist terror in 1930's.

634. Ludwig, G. Massenmorde im Weltgeschehen. - Stuttgart : 1951.
Mass murder in world history.

635. Luebbe, H. Totalitarismus : Anmerkungen zu George Orwell's "1984". - Freiburg i.Br. : 1983. p. 99-107.
In: H. Neumann and H. Scheer (eds.), Plus Minus 1984. George Orwells Vision in heutiger Sicht

636. Maestre Alfonso, J. Guatemala : Unterentwicklung und Gewalt. - Frankfurt a.M. : 1971.

637. Maksimov, G.P. The guillotine at work; twenty years of terror in Russia : Data and documents. - 2 vols. - Brooklyn, N.Y. : Revisionist Press, 1975. 624 p
Reprint of the 1940 edition.

638. Marks, J. The C.I.A., Cuba and terrorism. 28 June 1977. p. 31. The New York Times
On U.S. government use of terrorism as instrument of foreign policy.

639. Martin, D. Horror in Uganda : Amin's butchery. 16 Sept 1976. p. 24-26. The New York Review of Books. ; 23:14.

640. Materne, Y. Au Bresil, le commissaire Fleury et l'Escadron de la mort. March 1978. Le monde diplomatique

641. Maulnier, T. La face de Meduse du communisme. - Paris : Gallimard, 1951. 236 p
Communist state terrorism.

642. Medvedev, R.A. Let history judge. - New York : Vintage, 1973.
Stalinist terrorism.

643. Melady, T. * Melady, M. Idi Amin: Hitler. Febr. 1978. p. 63-63, 66, 104, 107-108. Penthouse. ; 9.
Firsthand account by U.S. ambassador to Uganda.

644. Melgounov, S.P. The red terror in Russia. - London : Dent, 1925. 271 p

645. Menze, E.A. Totalitarianism reconsidered. - New York/London : Kennikat Press, 1981. 272 p

646. Merleau-Ponty, M. Humanism and terror: an essay on the communist problem. - Boston : Beacon, 1969.
Orig. publ. in French, 1947.

647. Moffit, R.E. Equatorial Guinea : The shame of Africa. Summer 1979. p. 67-85. Lincoln Review. ; 1.

648. Moody, P.R. Law and heaven : The evolution of Chinese totalitarianism. 1979. p. 116-132. Survey. ; 24.

649. Moore jr, B. Terror and progress in the U.S.S.R. - Cambridge, Mass. : Harvard University Press, 1954.

650. Moreira Alves, M. El despertar de la revolucion brasilena. - Mexico, D.F. : Diogenes, 1972.
On government terror and torture in Brazil.

651. Morley, M. * Petras, B. Chile: terror for capital's sake. 1974. p. 36-50. New Politics. ; 11.

652. Neumann, F. The democratic and the authoritarian state. - New York : Free Press, 1957.

653. Nordlinger, E. Soldiers in politics : Military coups and governments. - Englewood Cliffs : Prentice-Hall, 1977.

654. O'Higgins, p. Unlawful seizure of persons by states. - Springfield, Ill. : Thomas, 1975. p. 336-342.
In: M.C. Bassiouni (ed.), International terrorism and political crimes

655. Oppenheimer, M. * Canning, J.C. The national security state : Repression within capitalism. 1978. p. 349-365. Berkeley Journal of Sociology. ; 23.

656. Orlov, A. The secret history of Stalin's crimes. - New York : Random House, 1953.

657. Pabst, W. Du sollst schon langsam sterben : Der Terror des jugoslawischen Regimes gegen kroatische Buerger. - Herne : M.C. Wolf, 1982. 194 p

658. Palmer, G. God's underground in Asia. - New York : Appleton-Century-Crofts, 1953. 376 p
On Red Chinese policy towards the churches.

659. Pierre-Charles, G. Dominacion politica y terrorismo de estado. Universidad Nacional Autonoma de Mexico, 1978. Revista Mexicana de Sociologia. ; 40:3.

660. Pierre-Charles, G. El terror como condicionante social en Haiti. 1975. p. 963ff. Revista Mexicana de Sociologia. ; 37:4.

661. Pierremont, E. Tche-Ka : Materiaux et documents sur la terreur bolcheviste. Recueilles par le Bureau Central du Parti Socialiste Revolutionnaire Russe. - Paris : J. Povalozky & Cie., 1922.
Bolschevik terrorism 1918-1922.

662. Pirkes, Th. * (ed.) Die Moskauer Schauprozesse, 1936-1938. - Muenchen : 1963. 295 p
The Moscow show trials, 1936-1938.

663. Plaidy, J. The Spanish inquisition. - London : Book Club Associates, 1978. 544 p

664. Ponchaud, F. Cambodge, annee zero. - Paris : Julliard, 1977.

665. Premo, D.L. Political assassination in Guatemala : A case of institutionalized terror. Nov. 1981. p. 429-456. Journal of Interamerican Studies and World Affairs. ; 23.

666. Psinakis, S. Two "terrorists" meet. - San Francisco, Calif. : Alchemy Books, 1981. 346 p

667. Randle, M. Militarism and repression. 1981. p. 61-144. Alternatives. ; 7:1.

668. Reifer, A. Design for terror. - New York : Exposition Press, 1962. 82 p
Analyses 1932-41 German and 1918-58 USSR government repression.

669. Renzo, F.de Fascism : An informal introduction to its theory and practice. - New Brunswick, N.J. : Transaction

Books, 1976.
670. Resnick, D.P. The white terror and the political reaction after Waterloo. - Cambridge, Mass. : Harvard University Press, 1966. 152 p
France 1815-1816.

671. Reyes, J.G. Terrorism and redemption : Japanese atrocities in the Philippines. - Manila : 1945. 91 p
1939-1945.

672. Roman, N.E. * O'Mara, R. The juntas of Chile and Argentina: studies in government by terror. 2 April 1977. p. 12-18. Saturday Review

673. Roman, W. Imperialismo y dictadura : Crisis de una formacion social. - Mexico City : 1975.

674. Rotcage, L. Going for a ride with Brazil's guerrilleros. Aug. 1970. Atlas
On government torture.

675. Rubin, B. Paved with good intentions. - New York : Penguin, 1981.
Repression in Iran and U.S. relations with the Shah.

676. Rudel, Ch. Guatemala : Terrorisme d'etat. - Paris : Karthala, 1981. 183 p

677. Runes, D.D. Despotism : A pictoral history of tyranny. - New York : 1963.

678. Salvemini, G. La terreur fasciste : 1922-1926. - Paris : 1938.
State terrorism in Mussolini's Italy.

679. Sartre, J.P. * (ed.) Griechenland. Der Weg in den Faschismus. - Frankfurt a.M. : Melzer, 1970. 255 p
Orig.: Aujourd'hui la Grece.

680. Savater, F. * Fresneda, G.M. Teoria y presencia de la tortura en Espana. - Barcelona : Anagrama, 1982. 91 p

681. Schapiro, L.B. Totalitarianism. - London : 1972.

682. Schapiro, L.B. Totalitarianism. - London :
1972.
683. Schieder, W. * (ed.) Faschismus als soziale Bewegung : Deutschland und Italien im Vergleich. - 2nd ed. - Goettingen : 1983.

684. Schwab, p. * Frangor, G.D. Greece under the junta. - New York : Facts on File Inc., 1970.

685. Selznick, p. The organizational weapon: a study of Bolshevik strategy and tactics. - New York : The Free Press of Glencoe, 1960.
Also treats use of terror.

686. Six, F.A. Die politische Propaganda der NSDAP im Kampf um die Macht. 1936.
On Nazi's use of violence as political propaganda in Germany.

687. Snyder, D. Theoretical and methodological problems in the analysis of government coercion and collective violence. 1976. p. 277-294. Journal of Political and Military Sociology. ; 4:2.

688. Solzhenitsyn, A. A world split apart. - New York : Harper and Row, 1979.

689. Solzhenitsyn, A. Gulag Archipelago 1918-1956: an experiment in literary investigation. - New York : Harper and Row, 1973. 660 p
On Soviet state repression. Also: London, Book Club Associates, 1974.

690. Soudiere, E.de la Republique Dominicaine: le neo-trujillisme s'appuie sur le terrorisme militaire. March 1972. Le Monde diplomatique
Dominican Republic.

691. Southall, A. Social disorganisation in Uganda : Before, during, and after Amin. 1980. p. 627-656. Journal of Modern African Studies. ; 18:4.

692. Steinberg, I.N. Gewalt und Terror in der Revolution : Oktober-Revolution oder Bolschewismus. - Berlin : Rowohlt, 1931. 338 p

693. Stohl, M. * Lopez, G. A. * (eds.) The state as terrorist : The dynamics of governmental violence and repression. - Westport, Conn. : Greenwood Press, 1984.

694. Stohl, M. International dimension of state terrorism. - Westport, Conn. : Greenwood Press, 1984.
In: M. Stohl and G. Lopez (eds.), The state as terrorist

695. Stohl, M. National interest and state terrorism. - West Lafayette : Purdue University, March 1982. 28 p ; Unpubl. paper

696. Stohl, M. War and domestic political violence : The American capacity for repression and reaction. - Beverly Hills : Sage, 1976. 153 p

697. Stowe, L. Conquest by terror. - New York : Random House, 1952. 300 p
Study of the use of terrorism in both theory and practice.

698. Swaan, A.de Terreur als overheidsdienst. 1975. p. 176-184. De Gids. ; 3.

699. Tanin, O. * Yohan, A. Militarism and fascism in Japan. - London : 1934.

700. Tavares, F. Pan de arara : La violencia militar en el Brazil. - Mexico,

D.F. : Siglo Veintiuno, 1972.
701. Taylor, T. * et al. Courts of terror : Soviet criminal justice and jewish emigration. - New York : Vintage Books, 1976. 187 p

702. Terry, J.P. State terrorism : A juridical examination in terms of existing international law. 1980. p. 94-117. Journal of Palestine Studies. ; 10:1.

703. Thomas, M. * (ed.) The politics of anti-politics : The military in Latin America. - Lincoln, Na. : University of Nebraska Press, 1978.

704. Thompson, J.M. Robespierre and the French revolution. - London : English University Press, 1952.

705. Tiltman, H.H. The terror in Europe. - New York : Frederick A.Stokes Company, 1932. 413 p

706. Timmerman, J. Prisoner without a name, cell without a number. - New York : Alfred A. Knopf, 1981.
By jewish victim of Argentinian state terrorism.

707. Timperley, H.J. * (comp.) What war means: the Japanese terror in China. - London : 1938.

708. Timperley, H.J. Japanese terror in China. - Calcutta : Thacher, Spink & Co., 1938. 222 p
On Japanese army's treatment of the Chinese civilian population in North China, 1937-38.

709. Tobagi, W. Gli anni del manganello. - Milano : Fratelli Fabbri, 1973. 166 p

710. Torres Sanchez, J. * et al. Colombia represioni 1970-1981. - 2 vols. - Bogota : Centro de Investigacion y Educacion Popular, 1982.

711. Toynbee, A.J. El terrorismo aleman en Belgica. - London : Hayman, Christy & Lilly, 1917. 166 p
German atrocities in Belgium, 1914-.

712. Treaster, J.B. Argentina: a state of fear. Nov. 1977. p. 16, 18, 20, 24-26. Atlantic Monthly. ; 240.

713. Trotsky, L. Stalin. - New York : Harper, 1941.

714. Tutino, S. La violenza di stato in America Latina : L'escempio argentino. 1978. p. 43-49. Problemi di Ulisse. ; 14:86.

715. Valenzuela, A. The breakdown of democratic regimes : Chile. - Baltimore : Johns Hopkins University Press, 1978.

716. Vieille, p. * Banisadr, A.H. * (eds.) Petrole et violence: terreur blanche et resistance en Iran. - Paris : Editions Anthropos, 1974. 346 p
717. Wagner, H. Die Rolle des Terrors und des Persoenlichkeitskultes in der Sovietunion. 1967. Osteuropa. ; 10-11.

718. Walsh, R. Terror and greed in Argentina: a writer bears witness. 1978. Dissent. ; 25:1.

719. Walter, E.V. Terror and resistance: a study of political violence. - New York : Oxford University Press, 1969.
A seminal work on regime terrorism.

720. Wehr, p. Nonviolence and nuclear terrorism. - Uppsala : 1978. ; ISA paper
Argues that a nation's manufacture, deployment and threats to use nuclear weapons can be seen as, in effect, state terrorism.

721. Weil, C. * et al. * (eds.) The repressive state : Brazilian studies documents. - Toronto : 1976.

722. Wilkinson, p. American terrorism. p. 344-350. The World Today. ; 39:9.

723. Wise, D. The American police state. - New York : Random House, 1976.

724. Wittfogel, K.A. Oriental despotism: a comparative study of total power. - New Haven : Yale University Press, 1957.

725. Wolfe, A. The seamy side of democracy : Repression in America. - New York : Langman, 1978.

726. Wolin, S. * Slusser, R.M. * (eds.) The Soviet secret police. - New York : Praeger, 1957.

727. Wolpin, M. Militarism and social revolution in the third world. - Totowa, N.J. : Alanheld, Osmuns, Oct. 1981.

728. Wolpin, M. State terrorism and repression in the third world : Parameters and prospects. - Oslo : 1983. ; PRIO Report
Rev. version: Westport, Conn.: Greenwood Press, 1985.

729. Woolf, S.J. * (ed.) European fascism. - London : 1968.

730. Wriggins, H. The rulers imperative. - New York : Columbia University, 1969.
How to do it suggestions for state terrorists.

731. _____ A collection of reports on bolshevism in Russia. - London : HMSO, April 1919.
A rather unreliable account on bolshevist atrocities.

732. _____ A summary of interviews with former inmates of Soviet labor camps. - New York : International

Public Opinion Research, 1952.
733. _____ Allegations of torture in Brazil. - London : 1972.
Amnesty International

734. _____ Anexos del informe de la Comision Nacional sobre la Desaparicion de Persona. - Buenos Aires, : EUDEBA, 1984. 485, 140, 15 p

735. _____ Definitivamente - nunca mas. - Buenos Aires : Foro de Estudios sobre la Administracion de Justicia, 1985. 127 p

736. _____ Desaparecidos en la Argentina. - Sao Paulo : Comite de Defensa de Derechos Humanos en el Cono Sur, 1982. 416 p

737. _____ Document on terror. March 1952. p. 43-57. News from behind the Iron Curtain. ; 1:3.
Purported NKVD document assessing the various effects of Stalinist terror. Surfaced originally in German. Theoretically interesting independent of autorship question.

738. _____ Guatemala: its state terrorism, its refugees, ideology and aid. 10 Feb. 1984. p. 76-81. Commonweal. ; 140.

739. _____ How many millions perished from 1930-1938?. 1983. p. 3-26. Russia. ; 7-8.

740. _____ Human rights and the phenomenon of disappearances. - 96th Cong., 1st sess. - Washington, D.C. : GPO, 1980. 636 p.
U.S. Congress. House. Committee on Foreign Affairs. Subcommittee on International Organizations ; Hearings,

741. _____ Konterrevolution in Chile : Analysen und Dokumente zum Terror. - Reinbek : Rowohlt, 1973. 202 p.
Komitee "Solidaritaet mit Chile". * (ed.)

742. _____ Le proces du Centre Terroriste Trotskiste-Zinovieviste devant le tribunal militaire de la Court Supreme de l'U.R.S.S. Contre: Zinoviev, G.E.; Kamenev, L.B.; Evdokimov, G.E.;. Compte rendu des debats [19 aout-24 aout 1936]. - Milano : 1967. 183 p
Stalin's show trials 1936, reprint of text published in Moscow.

743. _____ Nazi conspiracy and aggression. - Washington, D.C. : 1946.
U.S. Office of the U.S. Chief of Counsel for the Prosecution of Axis Criminality

744. _____ Nazi plans for dominating Germany and Europe : The attitude of the NSDAP toward political terror. - Washington : 1945.
U.S. Office of Strategic Services. Research and Analysis Branch

745. _____ Nunca mas. - Buenos Aires : EUDEBA, 1984. 490 p.
Argentina, Comision Nacional sobre la Desaparicion de Personas

746. _____ One year of the rule of terror in Chile : Documents adopted by the International commission of enquiry into the crimes of the military junta in Chile at the Secretariat's meeting held in Stockholm, House of Parliaments, Sept. 7th, 1974. - Helsinki : 1974. 32 p

747. _____ Raise your voice against landlord-police terror in Andhra Pradesh. - Calcutta : 1968.
Communist Party of India

748. _____ Rechtsstaat en staatsterreur. - Utrecht : 1975.
Medisch-Juridisch Comite Politieke Gevangenen
On German Federal Republic.

749. _____ Report on torture. - New York : Farrar, Strauss, and Giroux, 1975. 295 p.
Amnesty International
Mainly on state terrorism.

750. _____ Represion y tortura en Colombia : Informes internacionales y testimonios nacionales. - Bogota : Fondo Editorial Suramerica, 1980. 368 p.
Comite Permanente por la Defensa de los Derechos Humanos

751. _____ Situation of human rights in El Salvador. - New York : United Nations, 1983. 51 p.
United Nations, Secretary-General ; Note

752. _____ Terror and state terrorism. Winter 1982-1983. p. 2-154. Telos. ; 54.

753. _____ Terror in Brazil : A dossier. - New York : April 1970.
American Committee for Information on Brazil
On government terror.

754. _____ Terror in Tete : A documentary report of Portuguese atrocities in Tete District, Mozambique, 1971-72. - London : International Defence and Aid Fund, 1973. 48 p

755. _____ Terrorismen i Soedra Afrika. - Stockholm : 1974. 54 p.
Amnesty International. Svenska sektionen
South Africa.

756. _____ Terrorist raids and fascist laws in South Vietnam : Documents. - Hanoi : Foreign Languages Publ. House, 1959. 88 p

757. _____ The death penalty. - London : 1979. 209 p.
Amnesty International
Chapter 4 (pp. 182-198): "Murder committed or acquiesced by governments", deals with Argentina, Ethiopia, Guate-

mala and Uganda.
758. _____ The treatment of Armenians in the Ottoman Empire 1915-16 : Documents presented to Viscount Grey of Fallodon by Viscount Bryce. Presented to both Houses of Parliament by command of His Majesty, October 1916. - London : HMSO, 1916. Turkey.

759. _____ The trial of the major war criminals : Nuremberg, 1947-1948. - 42 vols.

760. _____ Torture and oppression in Brazil : Hearings. - Washington, D.C. : GPO, 1975. U.
S. Congress, House. Committee on Foreign Affairs

761. _____ Trials of war criminals before the Nuremberg military tribunals. - 15 vols. - Washington D.C. : 1949.

E. INSURGENT TERRORISM

762. Aaron, H.R. The anatomy of guerrilla terror. March 1967. p. 14-18. Infantry. ; 58.

763. Alexander, Y. * Friedlander, R.A. Self-determination : National, regional and global dimensions. - Boulder, Colo. : Westview Press, 1980. 392 p

764. Allemann, F.R. Macht und Ohnmacht der Guerilla. - Muenchen : Piper, 1974. 340 p

765. Arendt, H. On revolution. - London : Faber & Faber, 1963.

766. Armstrong, R. * Shenk, J. El Salvador : A revolution brews. July-Aug. 1980. p. 1-36. NACLA (North American Congress on Latin America) Report on the Americas. ; 14.

767. Arnold, Th. Der revolutionaere Krieg. - Pfaffenhofen : Ilmgau Verlag, 1961.

768. Asprey, R.B. War in the shadows. - 2 vols. - London : MacDonald and Jane's, 1975. 1615 p
Also: New York: Doubleday & Co., 1975.

769. Berger, P.L. * Heuhaus, R.J. Movement and revolution. - Garden City, N.Y. : Doubleday, 1970.

770. Bernard, A. Strategia terroryzmu. Vol. 1. - Washaw : Wydaw, Min. Obrony Marodowei, 1978. 221 p

771. Bertelsen, J.S. * (ed.) Non-state nations in international politics: comparative system analyses. - New York : Praeger, 1977. 272 p

772. Beyme, K.von * (ed.) Empirische Revolutionsforschung. - Opladen : Westdeutscher Verlag, 1973.

773. Bialer, S. * (ed.) Radicalism in the contemporary age : Vol. 3: Strategies and impact of contemporary radicalism. - Boulder, Colo. : Westview Press, 1977.

774. Burton, A.M. Urban terrorism. - New York : MacMillan, 1975. 259 p

775. Cappel, R. The S.W.A.T. term manual. - Boulder, Colo. : Paladin Press., 159 p

776. Casteran, C. Continents dynamites par les minorites violentes. - Paris : Denoel, 1973.

777. Chaliand, G. Revolution in the third world : Myths and prospects. - Hassocks : The Harvester Press, 1977. 195 p

778. Chaliand, G. Terrorismes et guerillas. - Paris : Flammarion, 1985. 185 p

779. Charters, D.A. Terrorism and the 1984 Olympics. Summer 1983. Conflict Quarterly

780. Clines, Th.G. The urban insurgents. - Newport, Rhode Island : Naval War College, 1972.

781. Clutterbuck, R.L. Guerrillas and terrorists. - London : Faber & Faber, 1977. 125 p

782. Clutterbuck, R.L. Protest and the urban guerrilla. - London : Abelard-Schuman, 1973. 277 p

783. Clutterbuck, R.L. Terrorism and urban violence. 1982. p. 165-175. Proceedings of the Academy of Political Science. ; 34.

784. Condit, D.M. Modern revolutionary warfare. - Kensington, Md. : American Institute for Research, 1973.

785. Constandse, A.L. Het anarchisme van de daad. - Groningen : 1978. 190 p

786. Coyle, D.J. Minorities in revolt : Political violence in Ireland, Italy and Cyprus. - Rutherford, N.J. * London : Fairleigh Dickinson University Press * Associated University Presses, 1982. 253 p

787. Crozier, B. The rebels : A study of post-war insurrections. - London : Chatto & Windus, 1960. 256 p

788. Dimitrijevic, V. Terorizam kao sredstvo borbe antikolonija-listickih i narodnooslobodi-lackih pokreta. 1973. p. 44-61. Medjunarodni Radnicki Pokret. ; 4.

789. Dixon, C.A. * Heilbrunn, D. Communist guerrilla warfare. - New York : Praeger, 1954.

790. Drinnon, R. Rebels in paradise. - Chicago : 1961.
Anarchist terrorism.

791. Edwards, L.P. The natural history of revolution. - New York : Russell & Russell, 1965. 229 p

792. Evenhuis, J.R. De conscientie van rechtsstaten en het caesarcomplex van gewelddadige minderheden. Mei 1981. p. 221-230. Militaire Spectator

793. Fairbairn, G. Revolutionary guerrilla warfare : The countryside version. - Harmondsworth : Penguin, 1974. 400 p
pp. 348-357 on terrorism. Appendix 3 on the Palestinians.

794. Footman, D. Red prelude. - Westport, Conn. : Hyperion Press, 1979.

795. Forster, A. Violence on the fanatical left and right. March 1966. p. 141. Annals of the American Academy of Political and Social Science. ; 364.

796. Freymond, J. * (ed.) La premiere internationale. - 3 vols. - Geneva : 1971.

797. Friedmann, W. Terrorist and subversive activities. 1956. p. 475. American Journal of International Law. ; 50.

798. Fromkin, D. Strategy of terrorism. 1975. p. 683-698. Foreign Affairs. ; 53:4.

799. Gamson, W.A. Power and discontent. - Homewood, Ill. : Dorsey, 1968.

800. Garin, J. L'anarchie et les anarchistes. - Paris : 1885.

801. Garrigan, T.B. * Lopez, G.D. Terrorism: a problem of political violence. Ohio State Consortium for International Studies Education, 1980.

802. Gatti, A. Kleines Handbuch der Stadtguerilla : Vier Stuecke. - Muenchen : Deutscher Taschenbuch Verlag, 1971. 160 p. Sonderreihe DTV. ; 96.
Germany.

803. Gellner, J. Bayonets in the streets: urban guerrilla at home and abroad. - Ontario : Collier-MacMillan, 1974. 196 p

804. Genaste, M. The terrible strategy of terror. 1979. Strategic Review

805. Goode, S. Guerrilla warfare and terrorism. - New York : Franklin Watts, Inc., 1977.
Juvenile literature.

806. Grabosky, P.N. The urban context of political terrorism. - New York : Marcel Dekker, 1979. p. 51-76.
In: M. Stohl (ed.), The politics of terrorism

807. Gross, F. The seizure of political power in a century of revolutions. - New York : New Philosophical Library, 1958. 398 p

808. Guillen, A. La rebellion del tercer mundo. - Montevideo : Ed. Andes, 1969.

809. Hagopian, M. The phenomenon of revolution. - New York : Dodd, Mead & Company, 1974.

810. Hamilton, L.C. Dynamics of insurgent violence : Preliminary findings. - San Francisco : American Sociological Association, 1978. 12 p
Unpubl. conference paper on effects of terrorism.

811. Harsch, J.C. * et al. Revolution and social change: toward an urban guerrilla movement. 1970. p. 13-26. Current. ; 118.

812. Hayes, D. Terrorists and freedom fighters. - London : Wayland, 1980. 96 p

813. Heilbrunn, O. When the counter-insurgents cannot win. - London : 1969. p. 55-58. Journal of the Royal United Service Institution. ; 114:653.

814. Hodges, D.C. * Abu-Shanab, R.E. National liberation fronts 1960-1970 : Essays, documents, interviews. - New York : William Morrow and Co., 1972. 350 p

815. Hodges, D.C. * Guillen, A. Revaloracion de la guerrilla urbana. - Mexico : Ediciones El Caballito, 1977. 130 p
Mainly on Latin American urban guerrilla experience.

816. Horowitz, I.L. Left-wing fascism : An infantile disorder. May-June 1981. Transaction/Society. ; 18:4.

817. Horowitz, I.L. Political terrorism and state power. Spring 1973. p. 147-157. Journal of Political and Military Sociology. ; 1.

818. Horowitz, I.L. Toward a qualitative micropolitics of terror. - Washington, D.C. : U.S. Department of State, 1976. 11 p ; Paper to the Conference on international terrorism, March 1976

819. Howard, A.J. Urban guerrilla warfare in a democratic society. Oct. 1972. p. 231-243. Medicine Science and the Law. ; 12:4.

820. Huntington, S.P. Civil violence and the process of development. - London : IISS, 1972. Adelphi Papers. ; 89.

821. Hyams, E. A dictionary of modern revolution. - New York : Taplinger

Publishing Co., 1973.

822. Jay, M. Politics of terror. 1971. p. 95-103. Partisan Review. ; 38.

823. Jenkins, B.M. An urban strategy for guerrillas and governments. - Santa Monica, Calif. : RAND, 1972. 13 p. RAND-Paper. ; P-4670/1.

824. Jenkins, B.M. The five stages of urban guerrilla warfare: challenge of the 1970's. - Santa Monica, Calif. : RAND, 1971. 18 p

825. Johnson, Ch. Civilian loyalties and guerrilla conflicts. July 1962. p. 46-61. World Politics. ; 14.

826. Johnson, Ch. Revolution and the social system. - Palo Alto, Calif. : Stanford University, Hoover Institution on War, Revolution and Peace, 1964. 75p

827. Johnson, Ch. The third generation of guerrilla warfare. June 1968. p. 435-447. Asian Survey. ; 8:6.

828. Johnson, p. De zeven doodzonden van het terrorisme. Oct. 1980. p. 28-33. NAVO Kroniek. ; 5.

829. Jones, W.H.M. Perspectives on political violence. - London : Institute of Commonwealth,

830. Justice, B. Violence in the city. - Fort Worth, Tex. : Texas Christian University Press, 1973.

831. Kautsky, K. Terrorismus und kommunismus : Ein Beitrag zur Naturgeschichte der Revolution. - Berlin : Verlag Neues Vaterland, 1919. 154 p

832. Kelly, G.A. * Brown jr, C.W. * (eds.) Struggles in the state : Sources and patterns of world revolution. - New York : John Wiley & Sons, 1970.

833. Kittrie, N. * Friedlander, R. Terrorism and national liberation movements : Dialogue. Spring 1981. p. 281-313. Case Western Reserve Journal of International Law. ; 13.

834. Krippendorff, E. Minorities, violence and peace research. 1974. p. 27-40. Journal of Peace Research. ; 16:1.

835. Kuiper, R.L. Theory and practice of insurgency. - Maxwell Air Force Base, Alabama : Air Force R.O.T.C. Air University, Sept. 1974. Educational Journal

836. Lamberg, R.F. La guerrilla urbana: condiciones y perspectivas de la 'segunda ola guerrillera'. 1973. p. 431-443. Foro Internacional. ; 11:3.

837. Laqueur, W. Continuing failure of terrorism. 1976. p. 69. Harpers. ; 253:1518

838. Lederer, H. Kommunisten und individueller Terror - alte Wahrheiten zur aktuellen Lage. - Frankfurt a.M. : 1972. p. 73-80. Marxistische Blaetter. ; 10:4.

839. Leiser, B.M. Terrorism, guerrilla warfare, and international morality. 1977. p. 39-65. Stanford Journal of International Studies. ; 12.

840. Leurdijk, D.A. In de ban van de terreur : Politiek geweld komt nooit van een kant. 11 April 1975. p. 1-13. Intermediair. ; 11:15.

841. Livingstone, N.C. Is terrorism effective?. Fall 1981. p. 387-409. International Security Review. ; 6.

842. Mack, A. Non-strategy of urban guerrilla warfare. - Rotterdam : Rotterdam University Press, 1974. p. 22-45. In: J. Niezing (ed.), Urban guerrilla: studies on the theory, strategy and practice of political violence in modern societies

843. Mack, A. The non-strategy of urban guerrilla warfare. - Rotterdam : University of Rotterdam Press, 1974. p. 22-45.
In: J. Niezing (ed.), Urban guerrilla: studies on the theory, strategy and practice of political violence in modern societies

844. Mallin, J. * (ed.) Terror and urban guerrillas: a study of tactics and documents. - Coral Gables, Fla. : University of Miami Press, 1971.

845. Mallin, J. * (ed.) Terrorism as a political weapon. 1971. p. 45-52. Air University Review. ; 22.
Mainly on Vietnam and Latin America.

846. Mansbach, R.W. * Ferguson, Y.H. * Lampert, D.E. The web of world politics : Nonstate actors in the global system. - Englewood Cliffs, N.J. : Prentice-Hall, 1976. 326 p

847. Mathu, M. The urban guerrilla. - Richmond, B.C. : LSM Information Center, 1974. 94 p

848. Methvin, E.H. The riot makers: the technology of social demolition. - New Rochelle, N.Y. : Arlington House, 1970. 586 p. Editor of the Reader's Digest on terrorists.

849. Miahofer, W. The strategy of terrorism. 1977. p. 16. Polizei. ; 68.

850. Mickolus, E.F. Growth and prevalence of terrorism. - Westport, Conn. : Greenwood Press, 1982.
In: G.S. Roukis and P.J. Montana (eds.), Managing terrorism: strategies for the corporate executive

851. Miller, A.H. The evolution of terrorism. 1985. p. 5-16. Conflict quarterly. ; 5:4.

852. Miller, J.A. Terrorism and guerrilla warfare : A model for comparative analysis. - Washington, D.C. : American University., ; Ph.D. dissertation

853. Miller, N. * Aya, R. * (eds.) National liberation : Revolution in the third world. - New York : Free Press, 1971.

854. Momboisse, R.M. Riots, revolts and insurrections. - Springfield, Ill. : Charles C. Thomas, 1967.

855. Moss, R. The collapse of democracy. - London : Abacus, 1977.

856. Moss, R. The war for the cities. - New York : Coward, McCann and Geoghegan, 1972. 288 p
Published in the U.K. under the title: Urban guerrillas: the new face of political violence. London, Temple Smith, 1971.

857. Moss, R. Urban guerilla warfare. - London : IISS, 1971. Adelphi Papers. ; 79.
In the appendix: Minimanual of the urban guerilla, by Carlos Marighella.

858. Moss, R. Urban guerrilla warfare. - New York : AMS, 1974. p. 405-427.
In: J. Susman (ed.), Crime and justice, 1971-1972; an A.M.S. anthology

859. Motley, J.B. Terrorist warfare : A reassessment. June 1985. p. 45-57. Military Review. ; 65:6.

860. Mucchielli, R. La subversion. - Paris : CLC, 1976.

861. Mueller-Borchert, H.J. Guerilla im Industriestaat : Ziele, Ansatzpunkte und Erfolgsaussichten. - Hamburg : Hoffmann und Campe, 1973. 182 p

862. Nettlau, M. Geschichte der Anarchie. - 3 vols. - Bremen : 1978.
Orig. 1925.

863. Nieburg, H.L. Political violence: the behavioral process. - New York : St. Martin's Press, 1969.

864. Niezing, J. * (ed.) Urban guerrilla: studies on the theory, strategy and practice of political violence in modern societies. - Rotterdam : Rotterdam University Press, 1974. 154 p

865. O'Neill, B.E. * Alberts, D.J. * Rossetti, S.J. * (eds.) Political violence and insurgency: a comparative approach. - Arvade, Colo. : Phoenix Press, 1974. 518 p

866. O'Neill, B.E. * Heaton, W.R. * Alberts, D.J. Insurgency in the modern world. - Boulder, Colo. : Westview Press, 1980.

867. Oppenheimer, M. The urban guerrilla. - Chicago : Quadrangle, 1969. 188 p

868. Orlansky, J. The state of research on internal war. - Arlington, Va. : Institute for Defense Analyses, 1970.

869. Osanka, F.M. Social dynamics of revolutionary guerilla warfare. - Beverly Hills : Sage Publications, 1971. p. 399-416.
In: R.W. Little (ed.), Handbook of military institutions

870. Paret, p. * Shy, J.W. Guerrillas in the 1960's. - Rev. ed. - New York : Praeger, 1962. 98 p

871. Portes, A. * Ross, A. A model for the prediction of leftist radicalism. 1974. p. 33-56. Journal of Political and Military Sociology. ; 2:1.

872. Price jr, H.E. The strategy and tactics of revolutionary terrorism. Jan. 1977. p. 52-66. Comparative Studies in Society and History. ; 19:1.

873. Rocquigny, Col. de Urban terrorism. 1969. p. 93-99. Military Review. ; 38:11.
Orig. in: Revue Militaire d'Information, Feb. '68; discusses the nature of urban terrorism as an arm of psychological warfare.

874. Roucek, J.S. Guerrilla warfare: its theories and strategies. March 1974. p. 57-80. International Behavorial Scientist. ; 6.

875. Roucek, J.S. Partisanenkampf als Mittel revolutionaerer Politik : Bedeutung, Methoden, Gegenmassnahmen. Jan. 1972. p. 69-78. Europa Archiv. ; 27:2.
'Guerrilla warfare as a means of revolutionary politics. Meaning, methods, countermeasures.'

876. Schissler, J. Gewalt und gesellschaftliche Entwicklung : Die Kontroverse ueber die Gewalt zwischen Sozialdemokratie und Bolschewismus. - Meisenheim am Glan : Anton Hain, 1976.

877. Schumann, H. Der verdeckte Kampf. - Heidelberg : 1969.

878. Selzer, M. Terrorist chic : An exploration of violence in the seventies. - New York : Hawthorne, 1979. 224 p

879. Smart, I.M.H. The power of terror. 1975. p. 225-237. International Journal. ; 30:2.

880. Snodgrass, T. Urban insurgency: observations based on the Venezuelan experience, 1960 to 1964. - Austin, Texas : 1972. ; Unpublished M.A. thesis

881. Snyder, D. Collective violence : A research agenda and some strategic considerations. 1978. p. 499-534. Journal of Conflict Resolution. ; 22:3.

882. Sola Pool, I.de * Yates, D.J. * Laquain, A. * Blum, R. * Weatlake, M. Report on urban insurgency studies. - New York : Simulmatics Corp., 1966.

883. Sorenson, J.L. Urban insurgency cases. - Santa Barbara, Calif : Defense Research Corp., 1965.

884. Sorokin, p. Sociology of revolution. - New York : Howard Fertig, 1967. Orig. ed. Philadelphia: J.B. Lippincott, 1925.

885. Sperber, M. Ueber die Gewalt von unten. 1971. Merkur. Zeitschrift fuer europaeisches Denken. ; 25:3.

886. Strother, R.S. * Methvin, E.H. Terrorism on the rampage. Nov. 1975. p. 73-77. Reader's Digest. ; 107.

887. Stupach, R.J. * Booher, D.C. Guerrilla warfare : A strategic analysis in the superpower context. 2 Nov. 1970. p. 181-196. Journal of Southeast Asia and the Far East. ; 1.

888. Teitler, G. The urban guerrilla, as a revolutionary phenomenon and as a recruiting problem. - Rotterdam : Rotterdam University Press, 1974. p. 111-127. In: J. Niezing (ed.), Urban guerrilla: studies on the theory, strategy, and practice of political violence in modern societies

889. Thornton, T.P. Terror as a weapon of political agitation. - New York : Free Press, 1964. p. 71-99. In: H. Eckstein (ed.), Internal war One of the most seminal articles.

890. Veen, Th.W.van Delicten plegen om de wereld te veranderen. Sept. 1971. p. 176-181. Maandblad voor Berechtiging en Reclassering. ; 50:9.

891. Veen, Th.W.van Het plegen van delicten uit politieke motieven. Nov. 1971. p. 232-235. Maandblad voor Berechtiging en Reclassering. ; 50:11.

892. Veenaskay. Terrorism and political destabilization. - Bombay : Advance Research Enterprise, 1984. 156 p

893. Verhegge, G. Bedenkingen bij een aktueel fenomeen : Het verzetsterrorisme. 18 Nov. 1978. p. 753-786. Rechtskundig Weekblad

894. Walzer, M. The new terrorists. 30 Aug. 1975. New Republic

895. Wiberg, H. Are urban guerilla's possible?. - Rotterdam : University Press, 1974.

896. Wilkinson, D. Revolutionary civil war. - Palo Alto, Calif. : Page-Ficklin, 1975.

897. Wittke, C.F. Against the current. - Chicago : 1945. Biography of Heinzen.

898. Wohlstetter, R. Terror on a grand scale. May 1976. p. 98-104. Survival. ; 18.

899. Wolf jr, Ch. Insurgency and counterinsurgency : New myths and old realities. 1966. p. 225-241. Yale Review. ; 56:2. Orig. Santa Monica, Calif.: RAND, 1965.

900. Wolf, J.B. Appraising the performance of terrorist organizations. - Gaithersburg, Md. : IACP, 1978.

901. Wolf, J.B. Ethnic, religious and racial dimensions of contemporary terrorist activity: ETA, IRA and the KKK. - Gaithersburg, Md. : IACP, 1979. Update Report. ; 5:4.

902. Wolf, J.B. Terrorist manipulation of the democratic process. April 1975. p. 102-112. Police Journal (United Kingdom). ; 48:2.

903. Zawodny, J.K. Unconventional warfare. 1962. p. 384-394. American Scholar. ; 31:3.

904. _____ El terrorismo anarquista. - Mexico, D.F. : Siglo Veintiuno, 1983. 250 p

905. _____ Guerrilla warfare. - Boulder, Colo. : Paladin Enterprises, 1965. U.S. Army

906. _____ Subnational conflict. Winter 1983-1984. World Affairs. ; 146. Whole issue.

907. _____ Terror and political violence : Forum. Spring 1984. p. 5-52. Orbis. ; 28.

908. _____ Terror gangs. Is anyone safe?. 22 May 1978. p. 30-35 ; Special report. U.S. News and World Report With individual reports on Italy, the Middle East, Japan, Ireland and Germany.

909. _____ Trends in urban guerrilla tactics. July 1973. p. 3-7. FBI Law Enforcement Bulletin. ; 42:7.

910. _____ Urban warfare. - Gaithersburg, Md. : IACP., 35 p.
IACP

F. VIGILANTE TERRORISM

911. Alexander, Ch.C. The Ku Klux Klan in the South West. - Lexington : University of Kentucky Press, 1965.

912. Brown, R.M. Legal and behavioral perspectives on American vigilantism : Perspectives in America. 1971. p. 106-116. History. ; 5.

913. Brown, R.M. Strain of violence: historical studies of American violence and vigilantism. - London : Oxford University Press, 1975.

914. Chalmers, D.M. Hooded Americanism : The first century of the Ku Klux Klan 1865-1965. - Chicago : Quadrangle Books, 1968. 420 p

915. Cutler, J.E. Lynch-law : An investigation into the history of lynching in the United States. - Westport, Conn. : Greenwood Press, 1978.
Reprint of 1905 edition.

916. Fortuny, J.M. Guatemala: the political situation and revolutionary politics. Febr. 1967. World Marxist Review
Discusses U.S. involvement in the establishment of Guatemalan death squads.

917. Horn, F.S. Invisible empire: the story of the Ku Klux Klan, 1866-1871. - Boston : Houghton Mifflin, 1939.

918. Huie, W.B. Die weissen Ritter des Ku-Klux-Klan. - Wien-Hamburg : Zsolnay, 1969. 226 p
Orig.: Three lives for Mississippi.

919. Kennedy, S. I rode with the Ku Klux Klan. - London : 1954.

920. Krueger, G. Die Brigade Ehrhardt. - Berlin : 1932.
Interwar Germany: Free Corps.

921. Lipset, S.M. * Raab, E. The politics of unreason: right-wing extremism in America, 1790-1970. - 2nd ed. - Chicago : University of Chicago Press, 1978.

922. Lopes, A. L'escadron de la mort : Sao Paulo 1968-1971. - Paris : 1973.
923. Madison, A. Vigilantism in America. - New York : Seabury Press, 1973.

924. Meltzer, M. The truth about the Ku Klux Klan. - New York : F. Watts, 1982.

925. Nicolosi, A.S. The rise and fall of the New Jersey vigilant societies. 1968. New Jersey History. ; 86.

926. Randel, W.P. The Ku Klux Klan - a century of infamy. - London : Hamish Hamilton, 1965. 269 p

927. Rice, A.S. The Ku Klux Klan in American politics. - Washington, D.C. : Public Affairs Press, 1962.

928. Rosenbaum, H.J. * et al. * (eds.) Vigilante politics. - Philadelphia : University of Pennsylvania Press, 1976.

929. Rosenbaum, H.J. * Sederberg, P.C. Vigilantism: an analysis of establishment violence. 1974. p. 541-570. Comparative Politics. ; 6.

930. Steinmetz, S.R. Selbsthilfe. - Stuttgart : Ferd. Enke Verlag, 1931. p. 518-522.
In: A. Vierkandt (ed.), Handwoerterbuch der Soziologie
On private justice.

931. Steward, G.R. Committee of vigilance: revolution in San Francisco, 1851. - Boston : Houghton Mifflin Co., 1964.

932. Trelease, A.W. White terror: the Ku Klux Klan conspiracy and southern reconstruction. - New York : Harper & Row, 1971. 557 p

933. _____ Thirty years of lynching in the United States 1889-1918. - Westport, Conn. : Greenwood Press, 1978.
National Association for the Advancement of Colored People
Reprint of 1919 edition.

G. OTHER TYPES OF TERRORISM

934. Blok, A. The mafia of a Sicilian village, 1860-1960. - Oxford : A. Blackwell, 1974.
Also: New York: Harper & Row, 1975.

935. Bugliosi, V. * Gentry, C. Helter skelter. - New York : Bantam Books, 1975.
On Manson "family" atrocities in California.

936. Cohen, N. The pursuit of the millenium : Revolutionary messianism in medieval and reformation Europe and its bearing on modern totalitarian movements. - New York : Harper, 1961.

937. Gale, W. The compound. - New York : Rawson Associates Publishers, 1977. 252 p

938. Guiraud, J. Histoire de l'Inquisition au Moyen Age. - Paris : 1935.

939. Holt, S. Terror in the name of God: the story of the Sons of Freedom Doukhobors. - Toronto : McClelland and Steward, 1964. 312 p
On Canadian anti-authoritarian religious immigrant group.

940. Kamen, H. Die spanische Inquisition. - Munich : 1969.
The Spanish Inquisition.

941. Maisonneuve, H. Etude sur les origines de l'Inquisition. - Paris : 1960.

942. McLean, G.R. Terror in the streets : The inside story of a growing menace. The juvenile gangs of America's cities. - Minneapolis : Bethany Fellowship, 1977. 188 p

943. Pantelone, M. The mafia and politics. - New York : 1966.

944. Sabatini, R. Torquemada and the Spanish Inquisition. - Boston : Houghton Mifflin, 1924.

H. TERRORISTIC ACTIVITIES, BY REGION AND COUNTRY

945. Bagley, C. The Dutch plural society : A comparative study in race relations. - London : Oxford University Press, 1973.
Contains material on South Moluccans.

946. Bravo, G.M. Zur Funktion des Terrorismus in der politischen Entwicklung Italiens. 1979. p. 705-725. Blaetter fuer Deutsche und Internationale Politik. ; 24:6.

947. Eucken-Erdsiek, E. Die Macht der Minderheit : Eine Auseinandersetzung mit dem neuen Anarchismus. - Freiburg : Herder, 1971. 123 p

948. Hederberg, H. Operation Leo. - Stockholm : Raben & Sjogren Boktorlag Ab.,
On German RAF.

949. Itote, W. Mau Mau general. - Nairobi : East African Publishing House, 1967. 297 p

950. Jean. Vom Freiheitskampf der Korsen. - Munich : Trikont, 1978. 161 p
Corsic terrorism.

951. Norton, A.R. Moscow and the Palestinians. - Miami : Center for Advanced International Studies, University of Miami, 1974.

952. Sanders, E. The Family : The story of Charles Manson's dune buggy attack battalion. - New York : E.P. Dutton, 1971. 383 p

953. Sciascia, L. Affaire Moro : Verite officielle et verite tout court. Nov. 1978. Le monde diplomatique

954. _____ Schwarzer September : Dokumente, Kommuniques. - Frankfurt a.M. : Verlag Roter Stern, 1973. 60 p

H.1. Western Europe, General

955. Alexander, Y. * Myers, K.A. * (eds.) Terrorism in Europe. - London : Croom Helm, 1982. 183 p

956. Aston, C.C. A contemporary crisis : Political hostage-taking and the experience of Western Europe. - Westport, Conn. : Greenwood Press, 1982.

957. Aston, C.C. Political hostage-taking in Western Europe. - London : ISC, 1984. 21 p. Conflict Studies. ; 157.

958. Bok, R.de * Rijn, A.van Europa opnieuw in de ban van terreur. Feb. 1986. p. 32-34. Elseviers Magazine. ; 41:6.

959. Bracher, K.D. Geschichte und Gewalt : Zur Politik im 20 Jahrhundert. - Berlin : 1981.

960. Clutterbuck, R.L. Terrorism and the security forces in Europe. Jan. 1981. p. 12-29. Army Quarterly and Defence Journal. ; 111.

961. Corrado, R.R. Ethnic and student terrorism in Western Europe. - New York : Dekker, 1979. p. 191-257.
In: M. Stohl (ed.), The politics of terrorism

962. Crozier, B. Terrorism: the problem in perspective. - London : ISC, Febr. 1976.

963. Di Biase, B. * (ed.) Terrorism today in Italy and Western Europe. - Sidney : Circolo G. di Vittorio, 1978.

964. Esman, M.J. * (ed.) Ethnic conflict in the western world. - Ithaca, N.Y. : Cornell University Press, 1977.

965. Fletcher-Cooke, C. Terrorism and the European Community. - London : European Conservative Group, 1979.

966. Freestone, D. * Lodge, J. The European Community and terrorism : Political and legal aspects. - London : Croom Helm, 1982. p. 79-101.
In: Y. Alexander and K.A. Myers (eds.), Terrorism in Europe

967. Freestone, D. The EEC Treaty and common action on terrorism. Oxford University Press, 1985.
In: 1984 Yearbook of European Law

968. Goodman jr, R.W. * Hoffman, J.C. * McClanahan, J.R. * Tompkins, T.C. A compendium of European theater terrorist groups. - Maxwell Air Force Base, Alabama : Air War College, Air University, 1976. 218 p

969. Guillaume, J. * (ed.) l'Internationale : Documents et souvenirs, 1864-1887. - Paris : 1910.
Anarchist terrorism.

970. Harmon, C.C. The red and the black : Collusion between leftist and rightist terrorists in Europe. Claremont Graduate School, 1984. ; Ph.D. dissertation

971. Hayes, B. The effects of terrorism in society : An analysis with particular reference to the United Kingdom and the European Economic Community. 1979. p. 4-10. Political Studies. ; 2:3.

972. Hess H. Entwickling des Terrorismus in Italien, Frankreich und den Niederlanden. - Muenster : Polizei-Fuehrungsakademie, 1984. p. 225-246.
In: H. Hess, Schlussbericht ueber die Arbeitstagung Terrorismus

973. Hoffman, B. Right-wing terrorism in Europe. 1984. p. 185-210. Conflict. ; 5:3.

974. Husbands, Chr. T. Contemporary right-wing extremism in Western European democracies : A review article. March 1981. p. 75-100. European Journal of Political Research. ; 9.

975. Krejci, J. Ethnic problems in Europe. - London : Routledge & Kegan Paul, 1978. p. 124-171.
In: S. Giner and M.S. Archer (eds.), Contemporary Europe: social structures and cultural patterns

976. Langguth, G. Ursprung und Ziele des Terrorismus in Europa. 1986. p. 162-174. Aussenpolitik. ; 37:2.

977. Melander, G. Terroristlagen-ett onodigt ont. - Stockholm : Norstedts, 1975. 141 p

978. Offergeld, J. * Souris, Chr. Euro-terrorisme : La Belgique etranglee. - Montigny-le-Tilleul : Scaillet, 1985. 250 p

979. Pilat, J.F. Demons, demigods, and democrats : European images of European revolutionary terrorism. - 2 vols. Georgetown University, 1982. ; Ph.D. dissertation

980. Pilat, J.F. Euroright extremism. 1981. p. 48-63. Wiener Library Bulletin. ; 53:4.

981. Pilat, J.F. Research note : European terrorism and the Euromissiles. 1984. p. 63-70. Terrorism. ; 7:1.

982. Pisano, V.S. Euroterrorism and NATO. - Gaithersburg, Md. : International Association of Chiefs of Police, 1985. 6 p

983. Raufer, X. Euroterrorisme : Comprendre pour combattre. 1985-86. p. 251-263. Politique Internationale. ; 30.

984. Russell, Ch.A. Europe : Regional view. 1979-80. p. 157-171. Terrorism. ; 3.

985. Salas, J.T.de Responsibility of the press and other information media with regard to terrorism. - Strasbourg, France : Nov. 1980. ; Paper presented to the Council of Europe

986. Salvi, S. Le nazioni proibite : Guida a dieci colonie interne dell'Europa Occidentale. - Firenze : Vallecchi, 1973.

987. Statera, G. Death of a utopia : The development and decline of student movements in Europe. - New York : Oxford University Press, 1975.

988. Sterling, C. The terrorist war for

Europe. Dec. 1978. p. 92-96. Reader's Digest. ; 63.

989. Venohr, W. * (ed.) Europas ungeloeste Fragen : Die Probleme nationaler und religioeser Minderheiten. - Reinbek : Rowohlt, 1971. 119 p

990. Visser, C.J. Oorlogsverklaring aan de NAVO : Het Westeuropese terrorisme. 24 mei 1985. p. 19-31. Intermediair. ; 21:21.

991. Visser, C.J. Terrorisme en West-europa. - The Hague : 1986. 83 p. Clingendael-Cahier. ; 1.

992. Vitiuk, V.V. Leftist terrorism. - Moscow : 1985. 235 p
American edition, Chicago Progress Publishers.

993. Wilkinson, p. Still working for the extinction of mankind; an assessment of the significance of the resurgence of fascist terrorism in Western Europe. Jan. 1981. p. 27-31. Across the Board

994. Wolf, J.B. Agitational terrorism in Europe : Part 2: Jan. 1980 - Febr. 1981. - Gaithersburg, Md. : IACP, 1981. Update Report. ; 7:3.

995. Wolf, J.B. European neo-fascist groups. - Gaithersburg, Md. : IACP, 1980. Update Report. ; 6:6.

996. Wolf, J.B. Police confrontations with terrorists in Western Europe. - Gaithersburg, Md. : IACP, 1983. Update Report. ; 9:3.

997. _____ Conference on the defence of democracy against terrorism in Europe : Tasks and problems, Strasbourg, 12-14 Nov. 1980. - Strasbourg : 1981. Council of Europe ; Compendium of Documents

998. _____ Developments in Europe, June 1984. - Washington, D.C. : GPO, 1984. 100 p.
U.S. Congress. House. Committee on Foreign Affairs. Subcommittee on Europe and the Middle East ; Hearing, 98th Cong., 2nd sess., 25 June 1984

999. _____ Political violence and civil disobedience in western Europe. - London : Institute for the Study of Conflict, 1983. 31 p

1000. _____ Social protest, violence and terror in nineteenth- and twentieth-century Europe. - New York : St. Martin's Press, 1982. 411 p
Published for the German Historical Institute, London.

1001. _____ Storia delle nueve sinistre in Europa. - Bologna : Malino, 1976. 694 p

H.1.1. German Federal Republic

1002. Althammer, W. * Rombach, B. Gegen den Terror : Texte - Dokumente. - Muenchen : Hanns Seidel-Stiftung, 1978. 213 p
CSU-publication, with chronology of terroristic acts up to Nov. 1977.

1003. Amerongen, M.van * (comp.) De Baader-Meinhofgroep : Een documentaire. - Groningen : Xenos, 1975. 101 p

1004. Backer, H.J. * Mahler, H. Die Linke und der Terrorismus : Gespraeche mit Stefan Aust. - Berlin : 1979. p. 174-204.
In: Die Linke im Rechtsstaat. Vol. 2. Bedingungen sozialistischer Politik 1965 bis heute

1005. Backes, U. Der neue Rechtsextremismus in der Bundesrepublik Deutschland. 1982. p. 147-201. Neue Politische Literatur. ; 17.

1006. Bartsch, G. Anarchismus in Deutschland. - Bd. 2-3: 1965-1973. - Hannover : 1973.

1007. Bauss, G. Die Studentenbewegung der sechziger Jahre in der Bundesrepublik und Westberlin : Handbuch. - Koeln : Pahl-Rugenstein, 1977. 353 p
On German student movement in the 60s.

1008. Becker, J. Hitler's children. - London : Panther, 1978. 415 p
On Baader-Meinhof group.

1009. Benz, W. * (ed.) Rechtsradikalismus : Randerscheinung oder Renaissance?. - Frankfurt a.M. : Fischer Taschenbuch Verlag, 1980. 283 p

1010. Binder, S. Terrorismus : Herausforderung und Antwort. - Bonn : 1978.

1011. Blei, H. Terrorism, domestic and international: the West German experience. - Washington, D.C. : National Advisory Committee on Criminal Justice Standards and Goals, Dec. 1976. p. 497-506.
In: Report of the Task Force on Disorders and Terrorism

1012. Bock, H.M. Geschichte des linken Radikalismus in Deutschland. - Frankfurt a.M. : Suhrkamp, 1976.

1013. Boeden, G. Politisch motivierte Gewaltkriminalitaet. Zwischenbilanz und Prognose : Ein Beitrag zum gegenwartigen Stand des Terrorismus. 1976.
On terrorism in the German Federal Republic.

1014. Boehme, W. * (ed.) Terrorismus und Freiheit. - Heidelberg : Kriminalistik Verlag, 1978. 85 p

1015. Bosch, M. Antisemitismus, Nationalsozialismus und Neonazismus. - Duesseldorf : Paedogischer Verlag Schwann, 1979. 152 p

1016. Botzat, T. * et al. Ein deutscher Herbst : Zustaende, Berichte, Kommentare. - Frankfurt : Verlag Neue Kritik, 1978. 205 p
Compilation of articles and analyses of media coverage of Schleyer incident, 1977.

1017. Bracher, K.D. Gewalt in der Weimarer Republik und in der Bundesrepublik : Vergleiche und Kontraste. - Berlin : 1981. p. 106-112.
In: K.D. Bracher, Geschichte und Gewalt. Zur Politik im 20. Jahrhundert

1018. Brudigam, H. Das Jahr 1933. - Frankfurt a.M. : Roderberg Verlag, 1978. 136 p

1019. Brueckner, P. * Sichtermann, B. Gewalt und Solidaritaet : Zur Ermordung Ulrich Schmueckers durch Genossen: Dokumente und Analysen. - Berlin : Wagenbach, 1974. 103 p
On public reaction to Buback murder.

1020. Brueckner, P. Die Mescalero Affaere : Ein Lehrstueck fuer Aufklaerung und politische Kultur. - Hannover : Internationalismus Buchladen und Verlagsgesellschaft, 1977. 80 p

1021. Brueckner, P. Ulrike Marie Meinhof und die deutschen Verhaeltnisse. - Berlin : Wagenbach, 1977. 191 p

1022. Carlson, A.R. Anarchism in Germany. - New York : 1972.

1023. Chorus, B. Als op ons geschoten wordt. : Gewapend verzet in de BRD. - Groningen : Pamflet, 1978. 147 p
On RAF in German Federal Republic.

1024. Conley, M.C. Proteste, Subversion und Stadtguerilla. - Koeln : 1974. p. 71-87. Beitraege zur Konfliktforschung. ; 4.

1025. Cook, S. Germany : From protest to terrorism. - London : Croom Helm, 1982. p. 154-178.
In: Y. Alexander and K.A. Myers (ed.), Terrorism in Europe

1026. Corves, E. Terrorism and criminal justice operations in the FRG. - Lexington, Mass. : Lexington Books, 1978.
In: R.D. Crelinsten, D. Laberge-Altmejd and D. Szabo (eds.), Terrorism and criminal justice: an international perspective

1027. Crijnen, A.J. De Baader-Meinhof groep. - Utrecht : Spectrum, 1975. 125 p

1028. Croissant, K. A propos du proces Baader Meinhof Fraction Armee Rouge : La torture dans les prisons en RFA. - Paris : 1975.

1029. Deppe, F. * (ed.) 2. Juni 1967 und die Studentenbewegung heute. - Dortmund : Weltkreis-Verlag, 1977. 153 p

1030. Dressen, W. * (ed.) Ueber die Organisation des Befreiungskaempfes. - Berlin : Wagenbach, 1970. 271 p. Rotbuch. ; 20.

1031. Dudek, P. * Jaschke, H.G. Jugend rechtsaussen : Essays, Analysen, Kritik. - Bensheim : Paed. Extra Buchverlag, 1982. 165 p

1032. Dudek, P. * Jaschke, H.G. Revolte von Rechts : Anatomie einer neuen Jugendpresse. - Frankfurt a.M./New York : Campus Verlag, 1981. 191 p

1033. Dyson, K.H.F. Left-wing political extremism and the problem of tolerance in Western Germany. 1975. p. 330. Government and Opposition. ; 10.

1034. Eckstein, G. Germany: democracy in trouble : Coping with terrorism. 1978. Dissent. ; 25:1.

1035. Elliott, J.D. Action and reaction: West Germany and the Baader-Meinhof guerrillas. 1976. p. 60-67. Strategic Review. ; 4.

1036. Elliott, J.D. West Germany's political response to contemporary terrorism. - Gaithersburg, Md. : IACP, 1978.

1037. Fach, W. Souveraenitaet und Terror. 1978. p. 333-353. Leviathan. ; 6:3.
On public reaction to terrorism.

1038. Faina, G. * et al. * (eds.) La guerriglia urbana nella Germania Federale. - Genova : Collectivo Editoriale, 1976.

1039. Fetscher, I. * Rohrmoser, G. Ideologien und Strategien. - Bonn : Westdeutscher Verlag, 1981. 346 p. Analysen zum Terrorismus. ; 1.

1040. Fetscher, I. Terrorismus und Reaktion. - Frankfurt a.M. : Europaeische Verlagsanstalt, 1977. 148 p

1041. Fetscher, I. Terrorismus und Rechtsstaat. 1977. Neue Rundschau. ; 88:4.

1042. Fichter, T. * Loennendonker, S. Kleine Geschichte der SDS : Von 1946 bis zur Selbstaufloesung. - Berlin : Rotbuch, 1977.
History of German student movement.

1043. Funke, M. * (ed.) Extremismus im demokratischen Rechtsstaat : Ausgewaehlte Texte und Materialien zur aktuellen Diskussion. - Bonn : 1978. 612 p. Schriftenreihe der Bundeszentrale fuer politische Bildung. ; 122.

1044. Funke, M. Terrorismus - Ermittlungsversuch zu einer Herausforderung. 1977. Aus Politik und Zeitgeschichte. ; 41.

1045. Gemmer, K. Problems, means and methods of police action in the Federal Republic of Germany. - Lexington, Mass. : Lexington Books, 1979. p. 119-126.
In: R. Crelinsten and D. Szabo (eds.), Hostage-taking

1046. Gerhard, P. * Schossig, B. * (ed.) Jugend und Neofaschismus : Provokation oder Identifikation?. - Frankfurt a.M. : Europaeische Verlagsanstalt, 1979. 232 p

1047. Ginzel, G.B. Hitlers (ur)-enkel : Neonazis. Ihre Ideologien und Aktionen. - 3rd ed. - Duesseldorf : Droste Verlag, 1983. 155 p

1048. Glaser, H. Die Diskussion ueber den Terrorismus : Ein Dossier. 24 June 1978. Aus Politik und Zeitgeschichte, Beilage zur Wochenzeitung Das Parlament. ; 25.

1049. Glaser, H. Jugend zwischen Aggression und Apathie : Diagnose der Terrorismus-Diskussion. Ein Dossier. - Heidelberg/Karlsruhe : C.F. Muller Juristischer Verlag, 1980. 172 p. Recht - Justiz - Zeitgeschehen. ; 32.

1050. Goote, T. Kameraden die Rotfront und Reaktion erschossen. - Berlin : 1934.

1051. Goyke, E. Terror. - Bonn : Bundeszentrale fuer politische Bildung, Sept. 1975. Zeitlupe. ; 2.

1052. Grossarth-Maticek, R. Revolution der Gestoerten? : Motivationsstrukturen, Ideologien und Konflikte bei politisch engagierten Studenten. - Heidelberg : Quelle & Meyer, 1975. 360 p

1053. Gruetzbach, F. * (comp.) Heinrich Boell: Freies Geleit fuer Ulrike Meinhof : Ein Artikel und seine Folgen. - Koeln : Kiepenheuer und Witsch, 1972. 192 p
Documentation on reactions to Boell's 10 Jan.1972 article in Der Spiegel dealing with Bild-Zeitung's coverage of German terrorists.

1054. Gude, M. * et al. Zur Verfassung unserer Demokratie : 4 republikanische Reden. - Reinbek : Rowohlt, 1978. 98 p

1055. Guggenberger, B. Guerilla in Deutschland? : Schwierigkeiten und Gefahren in der Demokratie. - Bonn : 1976. p. 45-65. Die Politische Meinung. ; 21:166.

1056. Gumbel, E.J. Vier Jahre politischer Mord. - Berlin : 1922.
Germany, 1918-1922.

1057. Habermas, J. Die Buehne des Terrors : Ein Brief an Kurth Sontheimer. 1977. p. 944-959. Merkur. ; 31.

1058. Habermehl, W. Sind die Deutschen faschistoid? : Ergebnisse einer empirischen Untersuchung die Verbreitung rechter und rechtsextremer Ideologien in der Bundesrepublik Deutschland. - Hamburg : Hoffmann und Campe Verlag, 1979. 253 p

1059. Haller, M. * (ed.) Aussteigen oder rebellieren : Jugendliche gegen Staat und Gesellschaft. - Hamburg : 1981.

1060. Heckelmann, G. * Heumann, L. Herbert Marcuse und die Szene 1978 : Studentenrevolte und Terror-Eskalation. 1978. p. 55-69. Die Politische Meinung. ; 23:181.

1061. Herb, H. * Peter, J. * Thesen, M. Der Neue Rechtsextremismus : Fakten und Trends. - Lohra-Rodenhausen : Winddruck Verlag, 1980. 194 p

1062. Herold, H. Erscheinungsformen des Terrors und anarchistischer Bewegung in Deutschland. Deutsche IPA-Sektion, 1976. IPA-Zeitschrift (Internat. Polizei-Ass.). ; 1.

1063. Herold, H. Taktische Wandlungen des deutschen Terrorismus. Dec. 1976. p. 401-405. Die Polizei, Zentralorgan fuer das Sicherheits- und Ordnungswesen. ; 67:12.

1064. Hessler, K. Brief an einen Freund, den mutmasslichen Terroristen D. - Hamburg : Hoffmann und Campe, 1978. 188 p

1065. Hillmayr, H. Roter und weisser Terror in Bayern nach 1818. - Muenchen : Nasser, 1976. 224 p

1066. Hoffken, H.W. * Sattler, M. Rechtsextremismus in der Bundesrepublik : Die "Alte", die "Neue" Rechte und der Neonazismus. Leske Verlag & Budrich GmbH, 1980. 117 p

1067. Horchem, H.J. Die Rote Armee Fraktion : Analyse und Bewertung einer extremistischen Gruppe in der Bundesrepublik Deutschland. 1974. p. 83-110. Beitraege zur Konfliktforschung. ; 4:2.

1068. Horchem, H.J. European terrorism : A German perspective. 1982. p. 27-51. Terrorism. ; 6:1.

1069. Horchem, H.J. Extremisten in einer selbstbewussten Demokratie : Rote Armee Fraktion - Rechtsextremismus - der lange Marsch durch die Institutionen. - Freiburg i.Br. : Herder, 1975.
A police officer's account.

1070. Horchem, H.J. Right-wing extremism in Western Germany. - London : ISC, 1975. 11 p. Conflict Studies. ; 65.

1071. Horchem, H.J. Terrorismus in der Bundesrepublik Deutschland : Eine Uebersicht und Einschaetzung der verschiedenen Gruppen. 1986. p. 5-23. Beitraege zur Konfliktforschung. ; 16:1.

1072. Horchem, H.J. The urban guerrilla in West Germany : Origins and perspectives. - Washington, D.C. : March 1976. ; Unpubl. paper presented at the U.S.Department of State conference on terrorism

1073. Horchem, H.J. West Germany's Red Army anarchists. - London : ISC, 1974. Conflict Studies. ; 46.

1074. Horchem, H.J. Wurzeln des Terrorismus in Deutschland. 1976. p. 70-73. Die Neue Gesellschaft. ; 26:1.
Roots of terrorism in the German Federal Republic.

1075. Kahl, W. Akteure und Aktionen waehrend der Formationsphase des Terrorismus. - Bonn : 1977. p. 272. Terror, Schriftenreihe des Bundeszentrale fuer politische Bildung

1076. Kaltenbrunner, G-K. Die Wiederkehr der Woelfe : Die Progression des Terrors. - Freiburg i.Br. : Herder, 1978.

1077. Kepplinger, H.M. Statusdevianz und Meinungsdevianz : Die Sympathisanten der Baader-Meinhof-Gruppe. 1976. p. 770-800. Koelner Zeitschrift fuer Psychologie und Sozialpsychologie. ; 26:4.

1078. Klein, J.K. Der deutsche Terrorismus in den Perspektiven der Konfliktforschung. 1977. p. 139-168. Beitraege zur Konfliktforschung. ; 7:4.

1079. Kogon, E. * (ed.) Terrorismus und Gewaltkriminalitaet : Herausforderung fuer den Rechtsstaat. - Frankfurt a.M. : Aspekte, 1975. 114 p

1080. Krause, Ch. * Lehnert, D. * Scherer, K.J. Zwischen Revolution und Resignation : Alternativkultur, politische Grundstromingen und Hochschulaktivitaeten in der Studentenschaft. Eine Empirische Untersuchung ueber die politischen Einstellungen von Studenten. - Bonn : 1980.

1081. Langguth, G. Die Protestbewegung in der Bundesrepublik Deutschland 1968-1976. - Koeln : Verlag Wissenschaft und Politik, 1976. 363 p

1082. Langguth, G. Protestbewegung : Entwicklung - Niedergang - Renaissance. Die neue Linke seit 1968. - Koeln : Verlag Wissenschaft und Politik, 1983. 374 p. Bibliothek Wissenschaft und Politik. ; 30.

1083. Langguth, G. Protestbewegung am Ende : Die Neue Linke als Vorhut der DKP. - Mainz : 1971.

1084. Lasky, M.J. Ulrike Meinhof and the Baader-Meinhof-gang. June 1975. p. 9-23. Encounter. ; 44:6.

1085. Lersch, P. * (ed.) Die verkannte Gefahr : Rechtsradikalismus in der Bundesrepublik. - Hamburg : Rowohlt Taschenbuch Verlag, 1981. 288 p

1086. Luebbe, H. Endstation Terror : Rueckblick auf Lange Marsche. - Muenchen : Olzog Verlag, 1978. p. 96-108. In: H. Geissler (ed.), Der Weg in die Gewalt. Geistige und gesellschaftliche Ursachen des Terrorismus und seine Folgen

1087. Luebbe, H. Freiheit und Terror. 1977. Merkur. ; 31:9.

1088. Mahler, H. * et al. Bewaffneter Kampf: Texte der RAF : Auseinandersetzung und Kritik. - Graz : Verlag Rote Sonne, 1973.

1089. Mahler, H. Ausbruch aus einem Missverstaendnis. 1977. p. 77-98. Kursbuch. ; 48.

1090. Mahler, H. Erklaerungen von -. - Berlin : Rote Hilfe, 1974.

1091. Mahler, H. Horst Mahlers Erklaerung zum Prozessbeginn am 9.10.72 vor dem 1. Strafsenat des Westberliner Kammergerichts. 1972.

1092. Mahler, H. Interview with - on terrorism. - Amsterdam : Febr. 1978. 't Kan anders

1093. Mahler, H. Terrorism in West-Germany: interview with Horst Mahler. May 1978. p. 118-123. Socialist Review. ; 39.
Cover title for: Die Luecken der revolutionaeren Theorie schliessen - die Rote Armee aufbauen; later published as: Der bewaffneter Kampf in Westeuropa.

1094. Mahler, H. Verkehrsrechts- und Verkehrsaufklaerungs-Heft : Die neue Strassenverkehrs-Ordnung mit den neuen Verkehrszeichen und Hinweisschildern sowie Bussgeldkatalog. 1971.

1095. Marenssin, E. * (ed.) La bande a Baader ou la violence revolutionnaire. - Paris : Edition Champ Libre, 1977.

1096. Marenssin, E. * Zahl, P.P. * (eds.) Die 'Baader Meinhof Bande' oder revolutionaere Gewalt. - Haarlem : Editora Oneimada, 1974. 210 p
RAF texts.

1097. Matz, U. * Schmidtchen, G. Gewalt und Legitimitaet. - Bonn : Westdeutscher Verlag, 1983. 437 p. Analysen zum Terrorismus. ; 4.

1098. Meier-Bergfeld, P. Hitlers spaete Erben : Die rechte Vegetation in der

Bundesrepublik. 1981. p. 54-62. Die Politische Meinung. ; 26:199.

1099. **Meinhof, U.** Dem Volke dienen - Rote Armee Fraktion: Stadtguerilla und Klassenkampf. 24 April 1972. Der Spiegel. ; 18.

1100. **Meinhof, U.** Dokumente einer Rebellion : 10 Jahre "Konkret"-Kolumnen. - Hamburg : Konkret-Buchverlag, 1972. 111 p

1101. **Meinhof, U.** Pequena antologia. - Barcelona : Anagram, 1976. 109 p

1102. **Merten, K.** Terreur uit gevangeniscellen. 6 June 1978. p. 305-310. Tijdschrift voor de Politie. ; 40. On RAF in Germany.

1103. **Meyer, A. * Rabe, K.K.** Unsere Stunde, die wird kommen : Rechtsextremismus unter jugendlichen. - Bornheim-Merten : Lamuv Verlag, 1979. 286 p

1104. **Meyer, T.** Am Ende der Gewalt : Der deutsche Terrorismus - Protokol eines Jahrzehnts. - Frankfurt, Berlin, Wien : 1980.

1105. **Mueller-Borchert, H.J.** Grossstadtguerilla. p. 337-340, pp. 77-79, 363-36. Die Polizei. ; 61:9; 62.

1106. **Nassi, E.** La banda Meinhoff. - Milano : Fabbri, 1974.

1107. **Negt, O. * Grossman, I. * (eds.)** Die Auferstehung der Gewalt : Springerblockade und politische Reaktion in der Bundesrepublik. - Frankfurt a.M. : EVA, 1968.

1108. **Oestreicher, P.** Roots of terrorism - West Germany: special case. 1978. p. 75-80. Round Table. ; 269.

1109. **Otto, K.A.** Vom Ostenmarsch zur APO : Geschichte der aussenparlementarischen Opposition in der BRD 1960-1970. - Frankfurt : 1977.

1110. **Paul, G.** Irgendwie hat jeder seinen Platz : Zur Faszination des Faschismus bei jugendlichen. 1981. p. 2-8. Medien und Erziehung. ; 25:1.

1111. **Peter, J. * (ed.)** Nationaler "Sozialismus" von rechts. - Berlin : Verlag Klaus Guhl, 1980. 269 p

1112. **Peukert, D.** Volksgenossen und Gemeinschaftsfremde : Anpassung, Ausmerze und Aufbegehren unter dem Nationalsozialismus. - Koln : Bund-Verlag, 1982.

1113. **Philip, U.** Combatting terrorism in Federal Germany. 1979. p. 999-1001. International Defence Review. ; 12:6.

1114. **Pifuger, P.M. * (ed.)** Die Notwendigkeit des Bosen : Aggression und Depression in der Gesellschaft. - Stuttgart : Bonz, 1979. 150 p

1115. **Possony, S.T. * Bouchey, L.F.** International terrorism: the communist connection : With a case study of the West German terrorist Ulrike Meinhof. - New York : American Council for World Freedom, 1978. 172 p

1116. **Pridham, G.** Terrorism and the state in West Germany during the 1970s : A threat to stability or a case of political overreaction?. - Oxford : Martin Robertson, 1981. p. 11-56. In: J. Lodge (ed.), Terrorism. A challenge to the state

1117. **Prohuber, K.K.** Die nationalrevolutionaere Bewegung in West-Deutschland. - Hamburg : Verlag Deutsch-Europaeischer Studien, 1980. 288 p

1118. **Rabe, K.K. * (ed.)** Rechtsextreme Jugendliche : Gespraeche mit Verfuehrer und Verfuehrten. - Bornheim-Merten : Lamuv Verlag, 1980. 252 p

1119. **Rammstedt, O.H.** Die Instrumentalisierung des Baader-Meinhof Gruppe. 1975. p. 27-38. Frankfurter Hefte. ; 30:3.

1120. **Rauball, R. * (ed.)** Die Baader-Meinhof-Gruppe: aktuelle Dokumente de Gruyter. - Berlin : Walter de Gruyter, 1973. 265 p

1121. **Richter, C. * (ed.)** Die ueberfluessige Generation : Jugend zwischen Apathie und Aggression. - Konigstein/Ts. : 1979.

1122. **Rinser, L. * et al.** Terroristen Sympathisanten? Im Weltbild der Rechten : Eine Dokumentation. - Sonderheft 1. - Muenchen : Pressedienst demokrat. Initiative., 1977.

1123. **Robbe, M.** Verlockung der Gewalt : Linksradikalismus - Anarchismus - Terrorismus. - East Berlin : Verlag Neues Leben, 1981. 192 p. Konkret. ; 49.

1124. **Roehl, K.R.** Die Genossin. - Muenchen : Molden, 1975. 324 p A novel written by the ex-husband of Ulrike Meinhof, giving an unflattering picture of her.

1125. **Roehl, K.R.** Fuenf Finger sind keine Faust. - Koeln : Kiepenheuer & Witsch, 1974. 456 p A history of Konkret, by Meinhof's ex-husband.

1126. **Roemel, G.** Die anarchistische Gewaltkriminalitaet in der BRD. 1975. Kriminalistiek. ; 29:12.

1127. Rohrmoser, G. Krise der politischen Kultur. - Mainz : V. Hase & Koehler, 1983. 412 p

1128. Rupprecht, R. Entwickelt sich in der Bundesrepublik ein rechtsextremer Terrorismus?. 1979. p. 285ff. Kriminalistik. ; 6.

1129. Salomon, E.von Die Geaechteten. - Berlin : 1932.
On post-World War 1 'Freikorps'.

1130. Schaefer, G. Rote Armee-Fraktion und Baader-Meinhof-Gruppe. Jan. 1972. Links

1131. Schelsky, H. Die Arbeit tun die anderen : Klassenkampf und Priesterherrschaft der Intellektuellen. - Opladen : Westdeutscher Verlag, 1975. 447 p
pp. 342-363 deal with relationship between German intellectuals (esp.H.Boehl) and terrorism.

1132. Schiller, D.Th. Germany's other terrorists. 1986. p. 87-99. Terrorism. ; 9:1.

1133. Schmid, A.P. De RAF op het psychologische oorlogspad. 12 July 1985. p. 19-27. Intermediair. ; 21:28.

1134. Schneider, R. Die SS ist ihr Vorbild : Neonazistische Kampfgruppen und Aktionskreise in der Bundesrepublik. - Frankfurt a.M. : Roderberg Verlag, 1981. 208 p

1135. Schubert, A. * (ed.) Stadtguerilla. Tupamaros in Uruguay. Rote Armee Fraktion in der Bundesrepublik. - Berlin : Wagenbach, 1971. 129 p

1136. Schwarz, H. Der Fahndungsskandal Schleyer. - Bonn : Eigenverlag, 1978.

1137. Schwinge, E. Terroristen und ihre Verteidiger. 1975. p. 35-49. Politische Meinung. ; 20:158.

1138. Sochaczewski, J. "Demokratischer Terror" in der Bundesrepublik. Vorstufe oder Abart des verdeckten Kampfes?. - Muenchen : 1968. p. 187-192. Wehrkunde. ; 17:4.

1139. Sontheimer, K. Gewalt und Terror in der Politik. 1977. Neue Rundschau. ; 88:1.

1140. Sperber, M. Sieben Fragen zur Gewalt : Leben in dieser Zeit. Deutscher Taschenbuch Verlag.,

1141. Stommeln, H. Neonazismus in der Bundesrepublik Deutschland : Eine Bestandsaufnahme. - Bonn : Hochwacht Verlag, 1979. 93 p. Reihe Demokratische Verantwortung. ; 1.

1142. Stuberger, U.G. * (ed.) In der Strafsache gegen Andreas Baader, Ulrike Meinhof, Jan- Carl Raspe, Gudrun Ensslin wegen Mordes u.a : Dokumente aus dem Prozess. - Frankfurt : Syndikat, 1972. 280 p

1143. Stumper, A. Considerations a propos de l'affaire Baader-Meinhof. Oct. 1973. p. 33. Revue de droit penal et de criminologie. ; 54.

1144. Thadden, A.von Die Schreibtischtaeter. Das geistige Umfeld des Terrorismus. - Hannover : Greifen Verlag, 1977. 148 p

1145. Tophoven, R. * (ed.) Politik durch Gewalt : Guerilla und Terrorismus heute. - Bonn : Wehr und Wissen, 1976. 173 p
Papers on historical, political, social-psychological and military aspects and causes of subversive warfare.

1146. Vinke, H. Mit zweierlei Mass : Die deutsche Reaktionen auf den Terror von rechts. Eine Dokumentation. - Reinbek bei Hamburg : 1981.

1147. Volck, H. Rebellen um Ehre. - Berlin : 1932.

1148. Volker, B. L'affaire Schleyer : La guerre d'Andreas Baader. Heure par heure. Documentation de Michel Vey. Menges, 1977. 224 p

1149. Wagenlehner, G. Motivation for political terrorism in Germany. - Westport, Conn. : Greenwood Press, 1978. p. 195-203.
In: M.H. Livingston et al. (eds.), International terrorism in the contemporary world

1150. Wassermann, R. * (ed.) Terrorismus contra Rechtsstaat. - Darmstadt : Luchterhand, 1976. 266 p

1151. Wassermann, R. * (ed.) Terrorismus und Rechtsstaat. 1978. Gewerkschaftliche Monatshefte. ; 29:2.

1152. Wellner, A. Terrorismus und Gesellschaftskritik. - Frankfurt : 1979.
In: J. Habermas, Stichworte zur 'Geistigen Situation der Zeit'

1153. Werner, G. * (ed.) Wenn ich die Regierung waere.. : Die rechtsradikale Bedrohung. - Berlin/Bonn : 1984.

1154. Winn, G.F.T. * Witt, G.W. German terrorists : A profile. University of Southern California, 1980. ; Unpubl. paper

1155. Winn, G.F.T. Terrorism, alienation and German society. - New York : Pergamon Press, 1981. p. 256-282.
In: Y. Alexander and J.M. Gleason (eds.), Behavioral and quantitative perspectives on terrorism

1156. Wit, J.de * Ponsaers, P. On facts and how to use them. 1978. p. 363-375. Terrorism. ; 1.

1157. Wolff, F. * Windaus, E. Studentenbewegung 67-69. - Frankfurt a.M. : Roter Stern, 1977. 254 p

1158. Wolfgang, B. * (ed.) Rechtsextremismus in der Bundesrepublik : Voraussetzungen, Zusammenhaenge, Wirkungen. - Frankfurt a.M. : 1984.

1159. _____ Analysen zum Terrorismus. - 5 vols. - Bonn : Westdeutscher Verlag, 1981-1984. 229 p.
Bundesministerium des Inneren
Bd.1: I. Fetscher and G. Rohrmoser, Ideologien und Strategien; Bd.2:H. Jager, G. Schmidtchen and L. Sullwolda, Lebenslaufanalysen; Bd.3:W. von Baeyer-Katte, D. Claessens, H. Feger and F. Neidhardt, Gruppenprozesse; Bd.4: U. Matz and G. Schmidtchen, Gewalt und Legitimitat; Bd.5: F. Sack and H. Syteinert, Protest und Reaktion.

1160. _____ Andreas Baader? Er ist ein Feigling! : Peter Homann vor seiner Verhaftung ueber die Baader-Meinhof-Gruppe. 1971. p. 47-61. Der Spiegel. ; 25:48.

1161. _____ Aus der Krankheit eine Waffen machen : Eine Agitationsschrift des Sozialistischen Patientenkollektivs an der Universitaet Heidelberg. - Muenchen : Trikont, 1972. 136 p.
SPK

1162. _____ Auseinandersetzung mit dem Terrorismus : Moeglichkeiten der politischen Bildungsarbeit. - Bonn : Bundesministerium des Inneren, 1981. 229 p

1163. _____ Bericht ueber ein Seminar : Auseinandersetzung mit dem Terrorismus - Moeglichkeiten der politischen Bildungsarbeit. - Bonn : Westdeutscher Verlag, 1981.
Bundesministerium des Inneren

1164. _____ Bericht ueber neonazistische Aktivitaeten 1978 : Eine Dokumentation. - Muenchen : Information Verlagsgesellschaft, 1979. 208 p.
Presseausschuss Demokratische Initiative (PDI). PDI Taschenbuch. ; 1.

1165. _____ Bericht ueber neonazistische Aktivitaeten 1979 : Eine Dokumentation. - Muenchen : Information Verlagsgesellschaft, 1980. 239 p.
Presseausschus Demokratische Initiative (PDI). PDI-Taschenbuch

1166. _____ Bomben in der Bundesrepublik : Die Guerilla kaempft aus dem Hinterhalt. 1972. p. 24-34. Der Spiegel. ; 26:23.

1167. _____ Buback - ein Nachruf : Wer sich nicht wehrt lebt verkehrt, Dokumentation der Auseinandersetzung um die Dokumentation 'Buback - ein Nachruf'. - Berlin : Das politische Buch, 1977.

1168. _____ Der Baader-Meinhof-Report : Dokumente, Analysen, Zusammenhaenge. - Mainz : Von Hase und Koehler Verlag, 1972. 245 p ; Aus den Akten des Bundeskriminalamtes, der "Sonderkommission Bonn" und dem Bundesamt fuer Verfassungsschutz

1169. _____ Der Kampf gegen die Vernichtungshaft. 1975.
Komitees gegen Folter an politischen Gefangenen in der BRD * (ed.)

1170. _____ Der Ueberfall auf die israelische Olympiamannschaft 19 Sept. 1974 : Dokumentation der Bundesregierung und des Freistaates Bayern. - Bonn : Bundesdruckerei, 1972. 63 p.
Presse- und Informationsamt der Bundesregierung

1171. _____ Die Aktion des Schwarzen September in Muenchen. 1973.
RAF

1172. _____ Die Berliner Presse, die Studentenschaft und die Polizei. - Muenchen : 1968. p. 176-182. Vorgaenge. ; 3.

1173. _____ Die Erschiessung des Georg Rauch. - Berlin : Wagenbach, 1976. 153 p

1174. _____ Die Zeitbombe der Gegenwart : Terrorismus in Deutschland. - Worms : 1977. 95 p

1175. _____ Dokumentation der Bundesregierung zur Entfuehrung von Hanns Martin Schleyer : Ergebnisse und Entscheidungen im Zusammenhang mit der Entfuehrung von H.M. Schleyer und der Lufthansa-Maschine "Landshut". - Muenchen : Goldmann, 1977. 384 p
Government documentation following the Schleyer murder.

1176. _____ Dokumentation ueber Aktivitaeten anarchistischer Gewalttaeter in der Bundesrepublik Deutschland. - Bonn : Innenministerium, 1975. 165 p
A compendium of confiscated Baader-Meinhof writings seized during raids on terrorists' cells in July 1973 and on Febr. 4, 1974. Publishedby the German Interior Ministry.

1177. _____ Dokumentation zu den Ereignissen und Entscheidungen im Zusammenhang mit der Entfuehrung von Hanns Martin Schleyer und der Lufthansa Machine 'Landshut'. - Bonn : Nov. 1977.
German Federal Press and Information Office

1178. _____ Dokumentation zum Hunger- und Durststreik der politischen Gefangenen. - Frankfurt a.M. : S. Lissner, Aug. 1977.

1179. _____ Dossier terrorisme en Allemagne. 1975. p. 29-191. Documents. ; 2-3.
With extensive bibliography.

1180. _____ Erklaerung der Bundesregierung zu Fragen der inneren Sicherheit : Abgegeben von H.D. Genscher vor dem deutschen Bundestag am 7. Juni 1972. 1972. p. 1155-1161.
Deutsche Bundestag. Bulletin. Presse- und Informationsamt der Bundesregierung. ; 84.

1181. _____ Erklaerung der Bundesregierung zur inneren Sicherheit : Abgegeben von Bundeskanzler Schmidt vor dem deutschen Bundestag am 13. Maerz 1975. 1975. p. 341-348.
Deutsche Bundestag. Bulletin. Presse- und Informationsamt der Bundesregierung. ; 35.

1182. _____ Erklaerung der Bundesregierung zur inneren Sicherheit und zur Terrorismus Bekaempfung : Abgegeben von Bundeskanzler Schmid. 22 April 1977. p. 361-365.
Deutsche Bundestag. Bulletin. Presse- und Informationsamtes der Bundesregierung. ; 40.

1183. _____ Erklaerung der Bundesregierung zum Terroranschlag auf die deutsche Botschaft in Stockholm : Abgegeben von Bundeskanzler Schmidt vor dem deutschen Bundestag am 25. April 1975. 1975. p. 517-520. Bulletin. Presse - und Informationsamt der Bundesregierung. ; 55.

1184. _____ Extremismus - Terrorismus - Kriminalitaet. - Bonn : 1978. Schriftenreihe der Bundeszentrale fuer politische Bildung. ; 38.

1185. _____ Geschichte der politischen Kriminalitaet in Deutschland : Eine Studie zu Justiz und Staatsverbrechen. - Frankfurt a.M. : 1983.

1186. _____ Holger. Der Kampf geht weiter : Dokumente und Beitraege zum Konzept Stadtguerilla. - Gaiganz : 1975.

1187. _____ In die Bank und durchgeladen! : Baader-Meinhof-Prozess gegen Ruhland. Horst Mahler ueber Stadtguerilla. D. Poser antwortet Heinrich Boell. 1972. p. 28-47. Der Spiegel. ; 26:5.

1188. _____ Kommen sie raus. Ihre Chance ist gleich null : Gefasst: Baader. 1972. p. 19-32. Der Spiegel. ; 26:24.

1189. _____ La morte di Ulrike Meinhof : Rapporto commissione internazionale d'inchiestra. - Napels : Libreria Tullio Pirouti, 1979.
'The death of Ulrike Meinhof', Report of the International Commission of Inquiry.

1190. _____ Leben gegen Gewalt. March 1978. 186 p. Kursbuch
Special issue dedicated to RAF in Germany.

1191. _____ Les crimes politiques en Allemagne. - Paris : 1931.

1192. _____ Letzte Texte von Ulrike. June 1976.
Internationales Kommittee zur Verteidigung politischer Gefangener in Westeuropa. * (eds.)

1193. _____ Nicht heimlich und nicht kuehl : Entgegungen an Dienst U.S. Herren. - Berlin : 1978. 135 p

1194. _____ Pfarrer, die dem Terror dienen? Bischof Scharf und der Berliner Kirchenstreit 1974, eine dokumentation. - Reinbek : Rowohlt, 1975. 137 p

1195. _____ Pflasterstrand. 1977. Unabhaengige Stadtzeitung Frankfurt/M. ; 11, 18.

1196. _____ Politische Unterdrueckung in der BRD und Westberlin. - Koeln : Verlag Rote Fahne, 1976. 159 p.
Kommunistische Partei Deutschland

1197. _____ R.A.F.-boek. - 2 vols. - Groningen : Stichting Pamflet, 1978. Ca 300 p.
RAF
58 RAF texts.

1198. _____ RAF-teksten. 280 p.
RAF

1199. _____ Rechtsextremismus in der Bundesrepublik nach 1960 : Dokumentation und Analyse von Verfassungsschutzberichten. - Muenchen : Information Verlagsgesellschaft, 1982. 78 p.
Presseausschus Demokratische Initiative (PDI). PDI-Sonderheft. ; 18.

1200. _____ Stadsguerilla in de BRD; de revolutionaere Zelle. - Groningen : Stichting Pamflet, 1977.

1201. _____ Terror. - Hamburg : 1970. p. 29-74. Der Monat. ; 267.

1202. _____ Terror dient der Reaktion : Kritische Texte. - Gelsenkirchen : 1977.
Jungsozialisten NRW

1203. _____ Terrorism and politics in West-Germany. - Cambridge, U.K. : CAPG., 160 p

1204. _____ Terrorisme en Allemagne. 1975. p. 31-191. Documents. Revue mensuelle des questions allemandes. ; 30:2-3.

1205. _____ Texte der R.A.F. - Malmoe : Verlag Bo Cavefors, 1977.
RAF

1206. _____ The West German guerilla : Interviews with H.J. Klein and members of the June 2nd group. - Orkney : Cienfuegos, 1981.

1207. _____ Ueber den bewaffneten Kampf in Westeuropa. - Berlin : Wagenbach, 1971. 70 p.
RAF. Rotbuch. ; 29.
"Strassenverkehrs-Ordnung", ascribed to Horst Mahler, banned in Germany.

1208. _____ Vorbereitung der RAF-Prozesse durch Presse, Polizei und Justiz. - Berlin : 1975. 192 p

1209. _____ Wiederkehr der Woelfe. - Freiburg i.B. : Herder, 1978. 192 p

1210. _____ Zur Frage des Verhaeltnisses von Marx zu Blanqui. - Graz : 1973.
RAF
RAF texts; the title is deliberately misleading to evade censorship.

H.1.2. France

1211. Bruun, G. Saint-Just, apostle of the terror. 1966.
Orig. ed. 1932.

1212. Buonarotti, P. History of Baboeuf's conspiracy for equality. - London : 1836.

1213. Chatelain, D. * Tafani, P. Qu'est-ce qui fait courir les autonomistes?. - Paris : Stock, 1976. 312 p

1214. Cobb, R. Terreur et subsistances, 1793-1795. - Paris : Librairie Clavreuil, 1964.

1215. Cubberly, R.E. The committee of general security during the Reign of Terror. - Madison : University of Wisconsin, 1969. 371 p ; Ph.D. dissertation

1216. Curtis, W.N. Saint-Just, colleague of Robespierre. 1935.

1217. Daudet, E. La terreur blanche. - Paris : 1978.
On the excesses of the monarchist restauration in post-1815 France

1218. Deniel, A. Le mouvement breton, 1918-1945. - Paris : Maspero, 1976. 456 p

1219. Dispot, L. Le machine a terreur. - Paris : Grasset, 1975.
Philosophical contemplation on interrelationship of 'terror' and French political history; Dutch ed.: De terreurmachine, Wereldvenster, 1980, 221 pp.

1220. Dubois, F. Le peril anarchiste. - Paris : 1894.

1221. Dutcher, G.M. The deputies on mission during the Reign of Terror. - Ph.D. thesis. - Ithaca, N.Y. : Cornell University, 1903. 104 p

1222. Fouere, Y. Histoire resumee du mouvement Breton. - Quimper : 1977.

1223. Garraud, R. L'anarchie et la repression. - Paris : 1895.

1224. Gershoy, L. Bertrand Barere, A reluctant terrorist. 1962.
French revolution.

1225. Greer, D. The incidence of the terror during the French revolution : A statistical interpretation. - Cambridge, Mass. : Harvard University Press, 1935. 196 p

1226. Hampson, N. The terror in the French revolution. - London : 1981.

1227. Harrington, D.B. French historians and the terror : The origins, developments and present-day fate of the 'these du complot' and the 'these des circumstances'. University of Connecticut, 1970. 315 p ; Ph.D. dissertation

1228. Hentig, H.von Terror : Zur Psychologie der Machtergreifung. Robespierre, Saint-Just, Fouche. - Frankfurt a.M. : Ullstein, 1970.

1229. Holitscher, A. Ravachol und die pariser Anarchisten. - Berlin : 1925.

1230. Ikor, R. Lettre ouverte a des gentils terroristes. - Paris : A. Michel, 1976.

1231. Jacob, J.E. The Basques and occitans of France: a comparative study in ethnic militancy. - Ithaca, N.Y. : Cornell University, 1979. ; Ph.D. dissertation

1232. Kerr, W.B. The Reign of Terror, 1793-1794. 1927.

1233. Labin, S. La violence politique. - Paris : Ed. France-Empire, 1978. 317 p

1234. Landorf, S. Legalisme et violence dans le Mouvement Autonomiste Corse: l'annee 1976. 1977. p. 1270-1305. Les temps modernes. ; 23:367.

1235. Laurent, F. L'orchestre noir. - Paris : Stock, 1978. 439 p

1236. Lefebvre, G. La premiere terreur.

CDU, 1953.
On French revolution, 1792.

1237. Lefebvre, G. The Thermidorians and the Directory. - New York : Random House, 1964.

1238. Levergeois, P. J'ai choisi la D.S.T. - Paris : Flammarion, 1978.

1239. Loesch, A. OAS Parle. - Paris : Julliard, 1964. 353 p

1240. Louie, R. The incidence of the Terror : A critique of a statistical interpretation. 1964. p. 379-389. French Historical Studies. ; 3.

1241. Lucas, C. The structure of the Terror: the examples of Javogues and the Loire. - London : Oxford University Press, 1972.

1242. Maitron, J. Histoire du mouvement anarchiste en France, 1880-1914. - Paris : 1955.

1243. Maitron, J. Le mouvement anarchiste en France : Vol.1: Des origins a 1914. - 2nd ed. 1978. 191 p

1244. Maitron, J. Le mouvement anarchiste en France : Vol.2: De 1914 a nos jours. - 2nd ed. 1978. 440 p

1245. Maitron, J. Ravachol et les anarchistes. - Paris : Ed. Julliard, 1964.

1246. Marcellin, R. L'ordre public et les groupes revolutionnaires. - Paris : Plon, 1969.

1247. Mathiez, A. La revolution francaise : Vol. 1: La chute de la royaute. Vol. 2: La Gironde et la Montagne. Vol. 3: La terreur. - 2nd ed. - Paris : Librairie Armand Colin, 1925;1927;1928.
American ed.: The French revolution. New York: Grosset & Dunlap.

1248. Mathiez, A. La vie chere et le mouvement social sous la Terreur. - Paris : 1927.

1249. McNamara, Ch.B. The Hebertists: study of a French revolutionary "faction" in the Reign of Terror, 1793-1794. Fordham University, 1974. 491 p ; Unpubl. dissertation

1250. Moxon-Browne, E. Terrorism in France. - London : ISC, 1983. 26 p. Conflict Studies. ; 144.

1251. Pisano, V.S. France as a setting for domestic and international terrorism. - Gaithersburg, Md. : International Association of Chiefs of Police, 1985. 26 p

1252. Pisano, V.S. Terrorism is as French as champagne : Bloodstains along the Seine. Febr. 1982. p. 8-13. TVI Journal. ; 3.

1253. Plumyene, J. * Lassiera, R. Les fascismes francais. - Paris : 1963.

1254. Raufer, X. Terrorisme, violence. - Issy-les-Moulineaux : Carrere Paris, Editions 13, 1984. 23 p

1255. Raufer, X. Terrorisme: maintenant la France? : La guerre des Partis Communistes Combattants. - Paris : Garnier, 1982. 336 p

1256. Savigear, P. Separatism and centralism in Corsica. Sept. 1980. p. 351-355. World Today. ; 36.

1257. Scott, W. Terror and repression in revolutionary Marseilles. - New York : Barnes & Noble, 1973. 385 p 1789-1799.

1258. Shapiro, G. * Markoff, J. The incidence of the Terror : Some lessons for quantitative history. 1975. p. 193-218. Journal of Social History. ; 9:2.
Reviews Donald Greer's work and others on late 18th century France.

1259. Shepard, W.F. Prize control and the Reign of Terror: France, 1793-1795. 1953.

1260. Stagnara, V. Le sens de la revolution Corse. 1976. p. 1670-1686. Les temps modernes. ; 31:357.

1261. Ternaux, M. Histoire de la terreur. - 7 vols. - Paris : M. Levy, 1862.
On French revolution.

1262. True, W.M. The dechristianizing movement during the Terror, 1793-1794. - Cambridge, Mass. : Harvard University Press, 1939. ; Ph.D. thesis

1263. Varenne, H. De Ravachol a Caserio. - Paris : 1895.

1264. Wallon, H La terreur. - 2 vols. - Paris : Hachette, 1873.
On French revolution.

1265. Walter, G. Histoire de la Terreur 1793-1795. - Paris : A. Michel, 1937.

1266. _____ Die Terroristen : Unsere Partner, die Geheimdienste. Dossier B... wie Barbouzes. - Tuebingen : Initiative Verlagsanstalt, 1977. 224 p

1267. _____ Responses a la violence. - 2 vols. - Paris : Presses-pocket, 1977.
Peyrefitte Commission
On French govt. response to political violence.

1268. _____ The revolutionary committees in the departments of France during the Reign of Terror. - Cambridge, Mass. : Harvard University Press, 1943.

1269. _____ Volkskrieg in Frankreich? Strategie und Taktik der proletarischen Linken : Texte zusammengest. von den Genossen der GP. - Berlin : Wagenbach, 1972. 137 p.
Gauche proletarienne

H.1.3. Ireland

1270. Alexander, Y. * O'Day, A. * (eds.) Terrorism in Ireland. - London : Croom Helm, 1984.
Also: New York: St. Martin's Press, 1984.

1271. Bakker, J. Noord-Ierland. - Den Haag : Staatsuitgeverij, 1980. NIVV-reeks. ; 24.

1272. Barritt, D.F. * Carter, C.F. The Northern Ireland problem. - London : Oxford University Press, 1972.

1273. Barry, T.B. Guerrilla days in Ireland: a first hand account of the Black Tan war, 1919-1921. - New York : Devin-Adair, 1956.

1274. Bayce, D.G. Englishmen and Irish troubles, 1918-1922. - Cambridge : Cambridge University Press, 1972.

1275. Beasley, P.S. Michael Collins and the making of a new Ireland. - London : 1926.

1276. Beckett, J.C. Northern Ireland. 1971. p. 121-134. Journal of Contemporary History. ; 6:1.

1277. Bell, G. The protestants of Ulster. - London : Pluto, 1976. 159 p

1278. Bell, J.B. Societal lessons and patterns: the Irish case. - Lexington : University of Kentucky Press, p. 217-228.
In: R. Higham (ed.), Civil war in the twentieth century

1279. Bell, J.B. Strategy, tactics, and terror: an Irish perspective, 1969-1974. - New York : Praeger, 1976. p. 65-89.
In: Y. Alexander (ed.), International terrorism. National, regional and global perspectives

1280. Bell, J.B. The chroniclers of violence in Northern Ireland revisited: the analysis of tragedy. 1974. p. 521-544. Review of Politics. ; 36:4.

1281. Bell, J.B. The chroniclers of violence in Northern Ireland: a tragedy in endless acts. 1976. p. 510-533. Review of Politics. ; 38:4.

1282. Bell, J.B. The chroniclers of violence in Northern Ireland: the first wave interpreted. 1972. p. 147-157. Review of Politics. ; 34:2.

1283. Bell, J.B. The secret army: the I.R.A. 1916-1974. - Cambridge, Mass. : Massachusetts Institute of Technology Press, 1974. 434 p

1284. Bennett, R.L. The Black and Tans. - Boston : Houghton Mifflin, 1960.

1285. Bew, P. * Patterson, H. The protestant-catholic conflict in Ulster. Fall-Winter 1982-198. p. 223-234. Journal of International Affairs. ; 36.

1286. Blundy, D. The army's secret war in Northern Ireland. 13 March 1977. Sunday Times

1287. Borrell, C. Crime in Britain today. - London : Routledge and Kegan Paul, 1975. 212 p

1288. Boulton, D. The UVF 1966-73. - Dublin : 1973.

1289. Boulton, D. UVF (Ulster Volunteer Force) 1966-73; an anatomy of loyalist rebellion. - Dublin : Gill and MacMillan, 1973. 188 p

1290. Bowden, T. The breakdown of public security: the case of Ireland 1916- 1921 and Palestine 1936-1939. - London and Beverly Hills : Sage Publ., 1977. 342 p

1291. Bowden, T. The IRA and the changing tactics of terrorism. Oct. 1976. p. 425-437. Political Quarterly (London). ; 47.

1292. Boyd, A. Holy war in Belfast. - Tralee : Anvil Press, 1969.

1293. Boyle, K. * et al. Law and state : The case of Northern Ireland. - London : Martin Robertson, 1975.

1294. Boyle, K. * Hadden, T. * Hillyard, P. Ten years on in Northern Ireland. - Nottingham : England Cobden Trust, 1980. 119 p

1295. Breen, D. My fight for Irish freedom. - Kerry : 1964.

1296. Brown, T.N. Irish American nationalism. - New York : 1966.

1297. Budge, I. * O'Leary, C. Belfast : Approach to crisis: a study of Belfast politics, 1613-1970. - London : MacMillan/St. Nartin's Press, 1973.

1298. Carlton, Ch. Bigotry and blood: documents on the Ulster troubles. - Chicago : Nelson-Hall, 1977. 160 p

1299. Carlton, Ch. Judging without consensus : the Diplock courts in Northern Ireland. April 1981. p. 225-242. Law and Policy Quarterly. ; 3.

1300. Carroll, T.G. Regulating conflicts : The case of Ulster. Oct.-Dec. 1980. p. 451-463. Political Quarterly. ; 51.

1301. Chakeres, P.M. Developments in Northern Ireland, 1968-1976. - Washington, D.C. : Congressional Research Service, Library of Congress, 1976. 40 p

1302. Charters, D.A. Changing forms of conflict in Northern Ireland. Fall 1980. Conflict Quarterly

1303. Charters, D.A. Intelligence and psychological warfare operations in Northern Ireland. Sept. 1977. p. 22-27. Journal of the Royal United Services Institute for Defense Studies. ; 122.

1304. Charters, D.A. Northern Ireland. - Ottawa : Department of National Defense, 1981.
In: D.A. Charters, D. Graham and M. Tugwell, Trends in low intensity conflict

1305. Charters, D.A. Provisional IRA. - Ottawa : Department of National Defense, 1981.
In: D.A. Charters, D. Graham and M. Tugwell, Trends in low intensity conflict
Also in: P. Wilkinson, British perspectives on terrorism. London: Allen and Unwin, 1981.

1306. Chilton, A. Urban guerrilla tactics : Are they likely to be employed in Britain. 1976. p. 9-18. Police College Magazine. ; 14.

1307. Clark, D. Terrorism in Ireland: renewal of a tradition. - London : Greenwood Press, 1978. p. 77-83.
In: M.H. Livingston et al. (eds.), International terrorism in the contemporary world

1308. Clark, D. Which way the I.R.A.?. 1973. p. 294-297. Commonweal. ; 13.

1309. Clutterbuck, R.L. Britain in agony : The growth of political violence. - London : Faber and Faber, 1978. 335 p

1310. Clutterbuck, R.L. Intimidation of witnesses and juries. April 1974. p. 285-294. Army Quarterly. ; 104.

1311. Clutterbuck, R.L. Northern Ireland : Is there a way?. April 1978. p. 52-64. Washington Review of Strategic and International Studies. ; 1:2.

1312. Clutterbuck, R.L. Threats to public order in Britain. July 1977. p. 279-290. Army Quarterly. ; 107.

1313. Collins, M. The path to freedom. - Dublin : Talbot, 1922.

1314. Connolly, J. Revolutionary warfare. - Dublin : 1968.

1315. Coogan, T.P. The I.R.A. - New York : Praeger, 1970.

1316. Cooper, G.L.C. Some aspects of conflict in Ulster. Sept. 1973. p. 86-95. Military Review. ; 53:9.

1317. Corte, T. The Phoenix murders : Conflict, compromise and tragedy in Ireland 1879-1882. - London : 1967.

1318. Crenshaw, M. The persistence of IRA terrorism. - London * New York : Croom Helm * St.Martin's, 1984. p. 246-271.
In: A. O'Day and Y. Alexander (eds), Terrorism in Ireland

1319. Cross, D. * Sweet, W. Prospects for peace in Northern Ireland. 1982. p. 739-756. Washington Congressional Quarterly

1320. Crozier, B. Ulster: politics and terrorism. - London : ISC, 1973. 20 p. Conflict Studies. ; 36.
Deals with provisional and official wing of IRA as well as the Ulster Defense Association and the Ulster Volunteer Force.

1321. Crozier, F.P. Ireland forever. - London : Jonathan Cape, 1932.

1322. Darby, J. Conflict in Northern Ireland: the development of a polarized community. - New York : Barnes & Noble Books, 1976. 268 p

1323. Denieffe, J. A personal narrative of the Irish Revolutionary Brotherhood. - Cambridge : Houghton Mifflin, 1906.

1324. Deutsch, R.L. * Magowan, V. Northern Ireland, 1968-1973 : A chronology of events. Vol.2: 1972-1973. - Belfast : Blackstaff Press, 1974.

1325. Deutsch, R.L. * Magowan, V. Northern Ireland, 1968-1973 : A chronology of events. Vol.1: 1968-1971. - Belfast : Blackstaff Press, 1973.
An indispensable reference work.

1326. Devlin, B. The price of my soul?. - London : Andre Deutsch/Pan Books, 1969.

1327. Devoy, J. Recollections of an Irish rebel. - Shannon : 1969.
Account of the Irish nationalist movement, including description of the Fenian William Mackey Lomasney.

1328. Dillon, M. * Lehane, D. Political murder in Northern Ireland. - Baltimore : Penguin Books, 1973. 318 p

1329. Dutter, L.E. Northern Ireland and theories of ethnic politics. Dec. 1980. p. 613-640. Journal of Conflict Resolution. ; 24.

1330. Edwards, O.D. * Pyle, F. * (eds.) The Easter Rising. - London : 1968.

1331. Elliot, R.S.P. Ulster : A case study in conflict theory. - New York : St. Martin's Press, 1972. 180 p

1332. Elliott, Ph. Reporting Northern Ireland: a study of news in Britain, Ulster and the Irish Republic. - Leicester : Centre for Mass Communication Research, University of Leicester, 1976.
Also published by UNESCO in a book titled: Ethnicity and the media.

1333. Enloe, C.H. Police and military in Ulster: peacekeeping or peace- subverting forces?. March 1978. p. 253-258. Journal of Peace Research. ; 15.

1334. Faligot, R. Nous avons tue Mountbatten. - Paris : J. Picollec, 1981. 227 p

1335. Farrel, M. Northern Ireland : The Orange State. - London : Pluto Press, 1977.

1336. Fisk, R. The effect of social and political crime on the police and British army in Northern Ireland. - Westport, Conn. : Greenwood Press, 1978. p. 84-93.
In: M.H. Livingston et al. (eds.), International terrorism in the contemporary world

1337. Fisk, R. The point of no return. - London : Deutsch, 1975.
On Northern Ireland and media, by Times correspondent.

1338. Fitzgibbon, C. Problems of the Irish revolution : Can the IRA meet the challenge?. - New York : Pathfinder, 1972.

1339. Fitzgibbon, C. Red Hand: the Ulster colony. - Garden City, N.Y. : Doubleday, 1972.

1340. Foley, Th.P. Public security and individual freedom : The dilemma of Northern Ireland. Spring 1982. p. 284-324. Yale Journal of World Public Order. ; 8.

1341. Gleason, J.J. Bloody sunday. - London : Davies, 1962. 212 p

1342. Goulding, L. Entwicklung und Ziele der Irish Republican Army (IRA). 1973. p. 415-427. Blaetter fuer Deutsche und Internationale Politik. ; 18:4.

1343. Greaves, C.D. The Irish crisis. - London : Lawrence and Wishart, 1972.

1344. Haggerty, J.J. Northern Ireland : The wound that never stopped bleeding. 1979. p. 7-14. Monthly Review. ; 59:6.

1345. Hall, R.A. Violence and its effects on the community. 1975. p. 89-100. Medical Legal Journal. ; 43.

1346. Hamilton, I. * Moss, R. The spreading Irish conflict : Part 1: From liberalism to extremism. Part 2: The security of Ulster. - London : ISC, 1971. Conflict Studies. ; 17.

1347. Hamilton, I. The Irish tangle. - London : ISC, 1970. Conflict Studies. ; 6.

1348. Hanson, R.P.C. It is a religious issue : Some drastic proposals for an end to the miseries of Irish sectarianism. Oct. 1980. p. 11-20. Encounter. ; 55.

1349. Harmon, M. Fenians and fenianism. - Dublin : 1968.

1350. Hart, W. Waging peace in Northern Ireland. May 1980. p. 22-32. Police Magazine. ; 3.

1351. Holt, E. Protest in arms : The Irish troubles, 1916-1923. - New York : Coward-McCan, 1960.

1352. Houston, J. The Northern Ireland economy: a special case?. 16 Aug. 1976. p. 274-288. Politics Today. ; 16.
On impact of terrorism on economy.

1353. Hull, R.H. The Irish triangle : Conflict in Northern Ireland. - Princeton, N.J. : Princeton University Press, 1978. 312 p

1354. Janke, P. * Price, D.L. Ulster: consensus and coercion. - London : ISC, August 1974. 20 p. Conflict Studies. ; 50.

1355. Kee, R. The Green Flag: a history of Irish nationalism. - New York : Delacorte Press, 1972.

1356. Kelly, K. The longest war : Dingle, Kerry, Brandon. - Westport, Conn. : Lawrence Hill, 1982. 364 p

1357. Kramer, G. Mord und Terror. Britischer Imperialismus: Nordirland. - Frankfurt a.M. : Fischer, 1972. 286 p

1358. Krumpach, R. Terrorismus in Nordirland; ein Ueberblick. 1978. p. 21-25; 65-68. Kriminalistik. ; 32:1-2.

1359. Lebow, R.N. Civil war in Ireland: a tragedy in endless acts?. 1973. p. 247-260. Journal of International Affairs. ; 26.

1360. Lebow, R.N. The origins of sectarian assassination: the case of Belfast. Spring-Summer 1978. p. 43-61. Journal of International Affairs. ; 32.

1361. Lee, A.M. Insurgent and "peace keeping" violence in Northern Ireland. 1973. p. 532-546. Social Problems. ; 20:4.

1362. Lee, A.M. Terrorism in Northern Ireland. - Bayside, N.Y. : General Hall, 1983. 253 p

1363. Lee, A.M. The dynamics of terrorism in Northern Ireland, 1968-1980. 24 June 1985. p. 100-134. Social Research. ; 48.

1364. Lieberson, G. The Irish uprising, 1916-1922. - New York : Hinkhouse, 1964.

1365. Lijphart, A. The Northern Ireland problem; cases, theories and solutions. 1975. p. 83-106. British Journal of Political Science. ; 5:1.

1366. Lynch, J. The Anglo-Irish problem. July 1972. p. 601-617. Foreign Affairs. ; 50.

1367. MacDonald, M.D. Children of wrath : Political violence in Northern Ireland. University of California, 1984. ; Ph.D. dissertation

1368. Manhattan, A. Religious terror in Ireland. - 4th ed. - London : Paravision Publications, 1970. 246 p

1369. McCaffery, L.J. The Irish question: 1800-1922. - Lexington : University of Kentucky Press, 1968.

1370. McFee, T. Ulster through a lens. 17 March 1978. New Statesman

1371. McKeown, M. The first five hundred. - Belfast : Irish News, 1972. On the first 500 dead in Northern Ireland due to ethnic strife, 385 of whom were casualties of terrorism.

1372. Mealing, E.T. Ulster, some causes and effects of low intensity operations, 1969-1972. - Carlisle Barracks, Penn. : Army War College, 23 Dec. 1972.

1373. Middleton, R. Urban guerrilla warfare and the IRA. 1971. p. 72-75. Journal of the Royal United Services Institute for Defense Studies. ; 116:664.

1374. Miller, D.W. Queen's rebels : Ulster loyalism in historical perspective. - New York : Harper & Row, 1979. 194 p

1375. Milnor, A. Politics, violence, and social change in Northern Ireland. - Ithaca, N.Y. : Cornell University, 1976. 73 p

1376. Monday, M. A summer of sunshine : Interviews with Irish paramilitary leaders. - Phoenix : Joseph Davidson Co., 1976.

1377. Moodie, M. The patriot game: the politics of violence in Northern Ireland. - Westport, Conn. : Greenwood Press, 1978. p. 94-110.
In: M.H. Livingston et al. (eds.), International terrorism in the contemporary world

1378. Moody, T.W. * Martin, F.Y. * (eds.) The course of Irish history. - New York : Weybright & Tally, 1967.

1379. Murray, R. Killings of local security forces in Northern Ireland 1969- 1981. 1984. p. 11-52. Terrorism. ; 7:1.

1380. O'Ballance, E. Terror in Ireland : The heritage of hate. - Novato, Calif. : Presidio Press, 1981.

1381. O'Brien, C.C. Herod: reflections on political violence. - London : Hutchinson, 1978. 236 p

1382. O'Brien, C.C. States of Ireland. - London : Panther, 1974.

1383. O'Brien, L. Revolutionary underground: the story of the Irish Republican Brotherhood 1858-1924. - London : Gill and MacMillan, 1976.

1384. O'Broin, L. Dublin Castle and the 1916 rising. - New York : New York University Press, 1971.

1385. O'Callaghan, S. Execution. - London : Frederick Muller, 1974.

1386. O'Callaghan, S. The Easter Lily: the story of the IRA. - New York : Roy, 1938.

1387. O'Connor, U. * (ed.) Irish liberation - an anthology. - New York : Grove Press, 1974.

1388. O'Day, A. Northern Ireland, terrorism, and the British state. - Boulder, Colo. : Westview, 1979. p. 121-135.
In: Y. Alexander, D. Carlton, and P. Wilkinson (eds.), Terrorism: theory and practice

1389. O'Donnell, P. The Irish faction fighters of the nineteenth century. - Dublin : 1975.

1390. O'Farrell, P. Ireland's English question. - London : Batesford, 1971.

1391. O'Riordan, M. * Sinclair, B. Irish communists and terrorism. Oct. 1976. p. 87-97. World Marxist Review. ; 10.

1392. O'Sullivan, P.M. Patriot graves: resistance in Ireland. - Chicago : Follett, 1972.

1393. Paor, L.de Divided Ulster. - Harmondsworth : Penguin, 1970.

1394. Patrick, D. Fetch Felix : The fight against the Ulster bombers, 1976-1977. - London : Hamish Hamilton, 1981. 184 p

1395. Pell, C. Some thoughts on the situation in Northern Ireland. - Washington, D.C. : GPO, 1981. 14 p ; Report to the Committee on Foreign Relations, US Senate

1396. Peroff, K. * Hewitt, Chr. Rioting in Northern Ireland : The effects of different policies. Dec. 1980. p. 593-612. Journal of Conflict Resolution. ; 24.

1397. Phillips, W.A. The revolution in Ireland, 1906-1923. - London : Longmans and Green, 1927.

1398. Pollard, H.B.C. The secret societies of Ireland. - London : Philip Allan, 1922.

1399. Power, J. Can the peace people bring an Irish peace. March 1977. p. 9-17. Encounter. ; 68.

1400. Power, P.F. Violence, consent and the Northern Ireland problem. July 1976. p. 119-140. Journal of Commonwealth and Comparative Politics. ; 14.

1401. Reed, D. Nordirland: Anatomie eines Buergerkrieges. June 1975. p. 146-191. Das Beste aus Reader's Digest (Swiss ed.)

1402. Rose, R. Governing without consensus: an Irish perspective. - London : Faber & Faber, 1971.

1403. Rose, R. Northern Ireland: a time of choice. - London : MacMillan, 1976.

1404. Rothstein, A. Terrorism : Some plain words. Sept. 1973. p. 413-417. Labour Monthly. ; 55.

1405. Ryan, D. Fenian memoirs. - Dublin : 1945.

1406. Ryan, D. James Connolly. - Dublin : 1924.

1407. Ryan, D. The Phoenix flame. - London : 1937.

1408. Ryan, D. The rising. - Dublin : 1957.

1409. Schellenberg, J.A. Area variations of violence in Northern Ireland. Jan. 1977. p. 67-78. Sociological Focus. ; 10.

1410. Schmitt, D. Violence in Northern Ireland: ethnic conflict and radicalization in an international setting. - Morristown, N.J. : General Learning Press, 1974.

1411. Scott, M. Conflict regulation vs. mobilization: the dilemma of Northern-Ireland. Columbia University, 1976. ; Ph.D. dissertation

1412. Shearman, H. Conflict in Northern Ireland. - New York : Praeger, 1970. p. 40-53.
In: G.W. Keeton and G. Schwarzenberg (eds.), Yearbook of world affairs 1970

1413. Skidelsky, R. The Irish problem: an historical perspective. - Boulder, Colo : Westview, 1979.
In: Y. Alexander, D. Carlton and P. Wilkinson (eds.), Terrorism: theory and practice

1414. Smith, W.B. Terrorism : The lessons of Northern Ireland. Winter 1982. p. 29-50. Journal of Contemporary Studies. ; 5.

1415. Stetler, R. Northern Ireland : From civil rights to armed conflict. Nov. 1970. p. 12-29. Monthly Review. ; 22.

1416. Stewart, A.T.Q. The Ulster crisis. - London : Faber & Faber, 1967.

1417. Tansill, C.C. America and the fight for Irish freedom. - New York : Devin-Adair, 1957.

1418. Taylor, R. Michael Collins. - London : Hutchinson, 1958.

1419. Terchek, R.J. Conflict and cleavage in Northern Ireland. Sept. 1977. p. 47-60. Annals of the American Academy of Political and Social Science. ; 433.

1420. Townsend, C. Bloody sunday : Michael Collins speaks. 1979. European Studies Review

1421. Townsend, C. British civil wars : Counterinsurgency in the twentieth century. - London : Faber & Faber, forthcoming.

1422. Townsend, C. Political violence in Ireland : Government and resistance since 1848. - Oxford : Oxford University Press, 1983-1984.

1423. Townsend, C. The British campaign in Ireland 1919-1921. - Oxford : 1975.

1424. Townsend, C. The function of terror in Ireland. - Brighton : Whedsheaf Press, forthcoming.
In: N. O'Sullivan (ed.), Ideology and Revolution

1425. Townsend, C. The Irish Republican Army and the development of guerilla warfare. 1979. English Historical Review

1426. Tugwell, M. Politics and propaganda of the provisional IRA. - London : Allen and Unwin, 1981.
In: P. Wilkinson (ed.), British perspectives on terrorism

1427. Turner, M. Social democrats and Northern Ireland, 1964-1970 : The origins of the present struggle. June 1978. p. 30-45. Monthly Review. ; 30.

1428. Tynan, P.J.F. The Irish invincibles. - New York : 1894.

1429. Utley, T.E. The politico-military campaign in Northern Ireland, 1975. - Boulder, Colo. : Westview Press, 1976. p. 210-224.
In: Royal United Service Institution for Defence Studies (eds.), RUSI and Brassey's defence yearbook, 1976-1977

1430. Van Voris, W.H. The Provisional I.R.A. and the limits of terrorism. Summer 1975. p. 413-428. Massachusetts Review. ; 16.

1431. Waterworth, P. Northern Ireland : The administration of justice in the light of civil disorder and sectarian violence. University of Durham, 1978. ; B.A. dissertation

1432. Whyte, J. Why is the Northern Ireland problem so intractable?. Autumn 1981. p. 422-435. Parliamentary Affairs. ; 34.

1433. Wilkinson, P. Murder incorporated : A sketch of the PIRA. - London : Central Office of Information, Jan. 1982.

1434. Wilkinson, P. Orange extremism and terrorism in Northern Ireland. - London : Central Office of Information, Jan. 1982.

1435. Wilkinson, P. The Orange and the Green. - Middletown : Wesleyan University Press, 1983. p. 105-123.
In: M. Crenshaw (ed.), Terrorism legitimacy and power

1436. Wilkinson, P. The Provisional IRA in the wake of the 1981 hunger-strike. Spring 1982. p. 140-156. Government and Opposition

1437. Williams, D. The Irish struggle. - London : Routledge and Kegan Paul, 1966.

1438. Williams, T.D. Secret societies in Ireland. - Dublin : 1973.

1439. Winchester, S. In holy terror : Reporting the Ulster troubles. - London : Faber & Faber, 1975.

1440. Winchester, S. Northern Ireland in crisis. - New York : Holmes and Meier, 1974.

1441. Wolf, J.B. British antiterrorist policy in Northern Ireland : Legal aspects. April 1983. p. 36-40. Police Chief

1442. Wolf, J.B. Provos versus the Crown : A review of contemporary terrorist and anti-terrorist operations in Northern Ireland. - Gaithersburg, Md. : IACP, 1982. Update Report. ; 8:7.

1443. Wright, S. A multivariate time series analysis of the Northern Irish conflict 1969-1976. - New York : Pergamon, 1981. p. 283-321.
In: Y. Alexander and J.M. Gleason (eds.), Behavioral and quantitative perspectives on terrorism

1444. Younger, C. Ireland's civil war. - New York : Tapplinger Co., 1969.

1445. _____ Assessment of the British government white paper "Northern Ireland - a framework for devolution" and the "Northern Ireland Bill, 1982". - London : 1982. 36, 11, 3 p.
Irish National Council

1446. _____ Die I.R.A. spricht: die I.R.A. in den 70-er Jahren. - Berlin : 1972. p. 131-142. Sozialistisches Jahrbuch. ; 4.

1447. _____ Editorial: Ulster catharsis. 2 March 1974. p. 343-344. Lancet

1448. _____ Freedom struggle by the provisional IRA. - London : Red Books, 1973.
IRA, Provisional

1449. _____ Handbook for the Irish Republican Army. - Boulder, Colo. : Paladin Press, 1979. 40 p.
IRA, Provisional

1450. _____ In the 70's the IRA speaks. - London : 1970.
IRA, Official

1451. _____ Ireland against the United Kingdom of Great Britain and Northern Ireland : Annexes I and II to the report of the commission [on] application 5310.71. - London : Council of Europe, 1976. 123 p.
European Commission of Human Rights

1452. _____ Ireland against the United Kingdom of Great Britain and Northern Ireland : Report of the commission [on] application 5310-71. - London : Council of Europe, 1976. 564 p.
European Commission of Human Rights

1453. _____ Ireland's terrorist dilemma. - Dordrecht * Boston : M. Nijhoff, 1986.

1454. _____ Measures to deal with terrorism in Northern Ireland. - London : HMSO, 1975. 78 p.
Gardiner Committee

1455. _____ Northern Ireland : Hearings. - 92nd Cong., 2nd sess. - Washington, D.C. : GPO, 1972. 639 p.
U.S. Congress, House, Committee on Foreign Affairs, Subcommittee on Europe

1456. _____ Northern Ireland. - New York : H.W. Wilson Company, 1983. 167 p

1457. _____ Northern Ireland : Problems and perspectives. - London : 1982. 48 p ISC. Conflict Studies. ; 135.

1458. _____ Northern Ireland - A role for the United States? : Report. - 95th Cong., 2nd sess. - Washington, D.C. : GPO, 1979. 675 p.
U.S. Congress, House, Committee on the Judiciary

1459. _____ Northern Ireland: a report on the conflict. - New York : Vintage Books, 1972.
Sunday Times Insight Team

1460. _____ Report to the Commission to consider legal procedures to deal with terrorist activities in Northern Ireland. - London : HMSO, 1972.

1461. _____ Small screen = smoke screen : Response to Annan. - London : 1977.
Campaign for Free Speech on Ireland

1462. _____ The campaign for social justice in Northern Ireland - the mailed fist : A record of army and police brutality from August 9-November 9, 1971. - Dungannon : 1972. 71 p

1463. _____ The escalation of insurgency: the experience of the Provisional IRA. July 1973. p. 398-411. Review of Politics. ; 35:3.

1464. _____ The protection of human rights by law in Northern Ireland. - London : H.M. Stationary Off., 1977. 141 p.
Great Britain. Standing Advisory Commission on Human Rights

1465. _____ The terror and the tears: the facts about IRA brutality and the suffering of victims. - Belfast : Government of Northern Ireland, Information Service, 1972.

1466. _____ The Ulster debate : Report of a study group. - London : Bodley Head, 1972. 160 p.
ISC

1467. _____ The Ulster yearbook. - Belfast : H.M. Stationery Office, 1968-.
Northern Ireland, Information Service

1468. _____ Tribunal appointed to inquire into the events of Sunday, 30th January 1972, which led to the loss of life in connection with the procession in Londonderry on that day : Report. - London : HMSO, 1972. 45 p
Great Britain, Parliament

H.1.4. Italy

1469. Acquaviva, S.S. * Santuccio, M. Social structure in Italy : Crisis of a system. - Boulder, Colo. : Westview Press, 1976. 236 p

1470. Acquaviva, S.S. Guerriglia e guerra rivoluzionaria in Italia. - Milano : Rizzoli Editore, 1979.

1471. Acquaviva, S.S. Terrorismo e guerriglia in Italia : La cultura della violenza. - Roma : Citta nuova, 1979. 222 p

1472. Allegretti, P. Terrorismo politico italiano. - Fasano : Grafischena, 1982. 97 p

1473. Allum, P. L'Italie de la violence : Les deux vagues du terrorisme. April 1978. p. 1-2. Le monde diplomatique. ; 289.

1474. Allum, P. Political terrorism in Italy. August 1978. p. 75-84. Contemporary Review. ; 233.

1475. Ascari, O. Accusa, reato distrage : La storia di Piazza Fontana. - Milano : Editoriale Nuova, 1979.

1476. Asor Rosa, A. * et al. Sulla violenze: politica e terrorismo : Un dibattito nella sinistra. - Roma : Savelli, 1978. 169 p

1477. Asor Rosa, A. Le due societa : Ipotesi sulla crisi italiana. - Turin : 1977.

1478. Bandinelli, A. * Vecellio, V. * (ed.) Una inutile strage : Da via rasella lle fosse ardeatine. - Napoli : T. Poronti, 1982. 155 p

1479. Banfi, A. Terrorismo fuori e dentro lo stato. 1978. p. 311-328. Ponte. ; 34:3-4.
On 20th century terrorism, emphasis on Italy.

1480. Barbieri, D. Agenda nera : Trent'anni di neofascismo in Italia. - Roma : Coines, 1976.

1481. Bell, J.B. Violence and Italian politics. 1978. p. 49-69. Conflict. ; 1:1.

1482. Berner, W. Italiens APO : Ausser- und anti-parlementarische Gruppen der italienischen Linken und Ultralinken. - Koeln : 1973. 174 p. Berichte des Bundesinstituts fuer Ostwissenschaftliche und Internationale Studien

1483. Bertini, B. * Franchi, P. * Spagnoli, U. Estremismo, terrorismo, ordine democratico. - Rome : Editori Riuniti, 1978.

1484. Bocca, G. Il caso 7 aprile : Toni Negri e la grande inquisizione. - Milano : Feltrinelli, 1980. 181 p

1485. Bocca, G. Il terrorismo in Italia. - Milano : Ed. Rizzoli, 1978.

1486. Bocca, G. Il terrorismo italiano 1970-1978. - Milano : Rizzoli, 1979.

1487. Bocca, G. Moro, una tragedia italiana. - Milano : Bompiani, 1978.
Instant history on the seven weeks between the kidnapping of Aldo Moro and the death of the ex-prime minister by the Red Brigades.

1488. Boccarossa, L. La violenza e la politica. - Roma : Savelli, 1979. 144 p

1489. Bologna, S. La tribu delle talpe. - Milano : Feltrinelli, 1978.

1490. Bonanza, A.M. Del terrorismo, di alcuni imbecile e di altre cose. - Catania : Edizzioni di Anarchismo, 1979. 36 p

1491. Bufalini, P. Terrorismo e democrazia. - Rome : Editori Riuniti, 1978.

1492. Buonarotti, F. Scritti politici. - Turin : Einaudi, 1976. 101 p

1493. Campa, R. * (ed.) Estremismo e radicalismo. - Rome : Edizione della Nuova Antologia, 1969.

1494. Cantore, R. * Rossella, C. * Valentini, C. Dall'interno della guerriglia. - Milano : Arnoldo Mondadori, 1978. 207 p
From within the guerrilla.

1495. Carli, G. Italy's malaise. July 1976. p. 708-718. Foreign Affairs. ; 54.

1496. Casalegno, C. Il nostro stato. - Milano : Bompiani, 1978. 312 p

1497. Caserta, J. The Red Brigades: Italy's agony. - New York : Manor, 1978. 240 p

1498. Cattani, A. Italiens dilemma. June 1978. Schweizer Monatshefte. ; 58:6.

1499. Cavallini, M. Il terrorismo in fabbrica : Interviste. - Roma : Editori riuniti, 1978. 245 p

1500. Cederna, C. Pinelli : Una finestra sulla strage. - Milano : 1971.

1501. Cervone, V. Ho fatto di tutto per salvare Moro. - Torino : Marietti, 1979. 191 p

1502. Charters, D.A. Italian terrorist groups. - Ottawa : Department of National Defense, 1981.
In: D.A. Charters, M. Tugwell and D. Graham, Trends in low intensity conflict

1503. Charters, D.A. Italy. - Ottawa : Department of National Defense, 1981.
In: D.A. Charters, D. Graham and M. Tugwell, Trends in low intensity conflict

1504. Chierici, M. I guerriglieri della speranza. - Milano : Arnoldo Mondadori, 1978.

1505. Cowan, S. Terrorism and the Italian left. - London : MacMillan, 1980.
In: C. Boggs and D. Plotke (eds.), The politics of eurocommunism, socialism in transition

1506. Degli Incerti, D. * (ed.) La sinistra rivoluzionaria in Italia. - Roma : Savelli, 1977.

1507. Della Porta, D. Terrorismi in Italia. - Bologna : Il mulino, 1984. 353 p

1508. Drake, R. The Red and the Black : Terrorism in contemporary Italy. 1984. p. 274-295. International Political Science Review. ; 5:3.

1509. Farago, J. Az olasz helyzet : Valsag terrorizmus, alternativak. - Budapest : Kossuth konyykiado, 1978. 220 p

1510. Ferracuti, F. * Bruno, F. Italy : A systems perspective. - New York : Pergamon, 1983. p. 287-312.
In: A.P. Goldstein and M.H. Segall (eds.), Agression in global perspective

1511. Ferracuti, F. * Bruno, F. Psychiatric aspects of terrorism in Italy. - Lexington, Mass. : 1981. p. 179-213.
In: J.L. Barak and C.R. Huff (eds.), The mad, the bad and the different

1512. Ferrari, M. * et al. Il terrorismo in Italia. - Milano : 1984.

1513. Ferrarotti, F. La ypnosi della violenza. - Milano : 1980.
On political violence in Italy.

1514. Fini, M. * Barberi, A. Valpreda - processo del processo. - Milano : Feltrinelli, 1972.

1515. Fini, M. La forza della tensione in Italia 1969-1976. - Torino : Einaudi, 1977.
On the Italian process of the alleged 1969 bomber of a bank in Milan.

1516. Fiorillo, E. Terrorism in Italy: analysis of a problem. 1979. p. 261-270. Terrorism. ; 2.

1517. Flamini, G. Il partito del goipe : Le strategie della tensione e del, terrore dal primo centrosinistra organico al sequestro Moro. - Ferrara : Bovolenta, 1981.

1518. Galli, G. La destra italiana e la

crisi internazionale. - Milano : Mondadori, 1974.

1519. Galli, G. La tigre di carta e il drago scarlatto. - Bologna : 1970.

1520. Georgel, J. Un an apres l'affaire Moro : L'Italie entre terrorisme et politique ou un art de survivre. 1979. p. 54-74. Revue politique et parlementaire. ; 80:879.

1521. Ghezzi, G. Processo al sindacato : Una svolta nelle relazioni industriali, i 61 licenziamenti FIAT. - Bari : De Donato, 1981.

1522. Guiso, G. La condanna di Aldo Moro. - Milano : Sugar Co., 1979.

1523. Harmon, C.C. Left meets right in terrorism : A focus on Italy. Winter 1985. p. 40-51. Strategic Review. ; 13.

1524. Hess H. Mafia : Centrale Herrschaft und lokale Gegenwart. - Tuebingen : Mohr, 1970.
English ed.: Mafia and Mafiosi: the structure of power. Lexington, Mass.: Heath, 1973.

1525. Hess, H. Italien : Die ambivalente Revolte. - Frankfurt : Suhrkamp Verlag, 1986. 250 p.
In: H. Hess et al. (eds.), Das Jahrzehnt des Terrorismus: Ein socialhistorischer Rueckblick

1526. Katz, R. Day of wrath : The ordeal of Aldo Moro, the kidnapping, the execution, the aftermath. - Garden City, N.Y. : Doubleday, 1980.

1527. Ledeen, M.A. Italy in crisis. - Beverly Hills, Calif. : Sage, 1977. 76 p. Washington Papers. ; 5:43.
On Red Brigades alleged infiltration of Italian communist party.

1528. Ledeen, M. Inside the Red Brigades : An exclusive report. 1 May 1978. p. 36-38. New York. ; 11.

1529. Lojacono, V. Alto adige Suedtirol : Dal pangermanismo al terrorismo. - Milano : Mursia, 1968. 293 p

1530. Lojacono, V. I dossier di Septembre Nero. - Milano : Bietto, 1974.

1531. Lotringer, S. * Marazzi, C. Italy : Autonomia. - New York : Colombia University, 1980.

1532. Mancini, F. Terroristi e riformisti. - Bologna : Il Mulino, 1981.

1533. Manconi, L. Vivere con il terrorismo. - Milano : 1980.

1534. Mantovani, V. Mazurka blu : La strage del Diana. - Milano : Rusconi, 1979. 682 p

1535. Mariel, P. Les carbonari : Idealisme et la revolution. - Paris : 1971.

1536. Martigoni, G. * Morandini, S. Il diritto al odio. - Verona : Bertani, 1977.
On the Italian autonomists.

1537. Martines, L. * (ed.) Violence and civil disorder in Italian cities. - Berkeley : University of California Press, 1972.

1538. Mazzetti, R. Genesi e sviluppo del terrorismo in Italia. - Milano : A. Armando, 1979. 141 p

1539. McHale, V. Economic development, political extremism and crime in Italy. p. 59-79. Western Political Quarterly. ; 31:1.

1540. Melucci, A. New movements, terrorism, and the political system : Reflections on the Italian case. March-April., p. 97-136. Socialist Review. ; 11.

1541. Minucci, A. Terrorismo e crisi italiana. - Rome : Editore riuniti, 1978. 117 p

1542. Monicelli, M. L'ultrasinistra in Italia. - Rome-Bari : Laterza, 1978. 237 p

1543. Natta, A. L' uso politico de caso Moro e la crisi d'Oggi : Intervista con A. Natta. Febr. 1979. Rinascita. ; 36:3.

1544. Negri, A. Il dominio e il sabotaggio. - Milano : Feltrinelli, 1978.
By alleged leader of the Italian autonomists.

1545. Negri, A. Partito operaio contra il lavoro. - Milano : Feltrinelli, 1974.
Negri, allegedly the leader of the Italian autonomists, argues against the historical compromise of the communist party

1546. Negri, A. Proletari e stato. - Milano : Feltrinelli.,
'Proletarians and the state'.

1547. Neppi Modona, G. di * Rodota, S. Attacco allo stato : Dossier 7 aprile: dalla illegalita di massa al terrorismo: calogero F. Amato, Palombarini: atti, documenti, testimonianze. - Roma : Napoleone, 1982. 160 p

1548. Orlando, F. La P.38. - Milan : Editoriale Nuova, 1978. 253 p

1549. Orlando, F. Siamo in guerra : Documenti per la storia dell'Italia d'Oggi. - Roma : A. Armando, 1980.

1550. Ottolini, A. La Carboneria, dalle origini ai primi tentativi insurrezionali. - Modena : 1946.
18th and 19th century insurrectional movement.

1551. Padellaro, A. Il delitto Moro. IVI, 1979.

1552. Padovani, M. Vivre avec le terrorisme : Le modele italien. - Paris : Calman-Levy, 1982.

1553. Pallotta, G. Obiettivo Moro : Un attacco al cuore dello stato. - Roma : Newton Compton, 1978. 126 p

1554. Panebiance, A. Italie: terrorisme et strategie non-violente. - Lyon : 1978. p. 53-57. Alternatives non-violentes. ; 28.

1555. Pansa, G. Storie italiane di violenza e terrorismo. - 2nd ed. - Roma * Bari : Laterza, 1980. 279 p

1556. Perelli, L. di Il terrorismo e lo stato nel i secolo a.c. - Palermo : Palumbo, 1981. 132 p

1557. Pesenti, R. * Sassano, M. Fiasconaro e Allessandrino accusano : La requisitoria su la strage di Piazza Fontana e le bombe del '69. - Venice : Marsilio, 1974. 287 p

1558. Pisano, V.S. A survey of terrorism of the left in Italy: 1970-78. 1979. p. 171-212. Terrorism. ; 2.

1559. Pisano, V.S. Contemporary Italian terrorism. - Washington D.C. : Library of Congress Law Library, 1979. 190 p

1560. Pisano, V.S. Terrorism and security : The Italian experience. - Washington, D.C. : GPO, 1984. 96 p ; Report of the Subcommittee on security and terrorism of the committee on the judiciary, U.S. Senate

1561. Pisano, V.S. Terrorism in Italy : An update report, 1983-1985. - Washington, D.C. : GPO, 1985. 36 p ; Report of the Subcommittee on Security and Terrorism, for the use of the Committee on the Judiciary, U.S. Senate

1562. Pisano, V.S. Terrorism in Italy : The "Dozier affair". April 1982. p. 38-41. Police Chief. ; 49.

1563. Pisano, V.S. Terrorism of the right in Italy : Facts and allegations. Summer 1985. p. 20-23. TVI Journal. ; 6.

1564. Pisano, V.S. The Red Brigades : A challenge to Italian democracy. - London : ISC, July 1980. 19 p. Conflict Studies. ; 120.

1565. Pisano, V.S. The structure and dynamics of Italian terrorism. - Gaithersburg, Md. : IACP., 33 p

1566. Possony, S.T. Giangiacomo Feltrinelli : The millionaire dinamitero. 1979. p. 213-230. Terrorism. ; 2:3-4.

1567. Quarantotto, C. Il terrorismo in Italia, 1968-1975. 1975. p. 19-46. La destra. ; 1.

1568. Ricci, A. Giovani non sono piante. - Milano : Sugar Co., 1978.

1569. Richards, V. * (ed.) Enrico Malatesta. - London : 1965.

1570. Roggi, E. * Gambescia, P. * Gruppi, L. * (eds.) Terrorismo : Come opera, a che cosa mira, come sconfiggerlo. - Roma : PCI, 1978.

1571. Ronchey, A. Accadde in Italia, 1968-1977. - Milano : 1977.

1572. Ronchey, A. Guns and gray matter: terrorism in Italy. 1979. p. 921-940. Foreign Affairs

1573. Ronchey, A. Libro bianco sull' ultima generazione. - Milano : Garzanti, 1978.
'Whitebook on the last generation'.

1574. Ronchey, A. Terror in Italy, between red and black. 1978. p. 150-156. Dissent. ; 25:2.

1575. Rosa, A. * et al. Politica terrorismo, un dibattito nella sinistra. - Roma : Savelli, 1978. 169 p

1576. Rosenbaum, P. Il nuovo fascismo da salo ad almirante : Storia del MSI. - Milan : Feltrinelli, 1975.

1577. Rosenbaum, P. Neofaschismus in Italien. - Frankfurt a.M. : Europaeische Verlagsanstalt, 1975. 117 p

1578. Rossanda, R. * (comp.) Il manifesto : Analyses et theses de la nouvelle extreme-gauche italienne. - Paris : Seuil, 1971. 429 p

1579. Rossani, O. L'industria dei sequestri. Longanesi & Co., 1978.
On kidnapping industry in Italy.

1580. Rossetti, C.G. La politica della violenza e la crisi della legittimita razionale dello stat. July 1980. Studi de soziologia. ; 18:3.

1581. Rubini, W. Il segreto dell repubblica. - Milano : FLAN, 1978. 146 p

1582. Russell, Ch.A. Terrorist incidents - Italy 1978. 1979. p. 297-300. Terrorism. ; 2.

1583. Sanguinetti, G. Du terrorisme et de l'etat : La theorie et la pratique du terrorisme divulguees pour la pemiere fois. - Paris : 1980.
Dutch ed.: Baarn: Wereldvenster, 1982.

1584. Sartre, J.P. Critique de la raison dialectique : La theorie et la practique du terrorisme divulguees pour la

premiere fois. - Paris : 1960.
Dutch ed.: Baarn: Wereldvenster, 1982.

1585. Scianna, F. Mafia et terrorisme : Lois d'exception en Italie. Febr. 1980. Le monde diplomatique

1586. Sciascia, L. I pugnalatori. - Torino : Einaudi, 1976. 95 p

1587. Sciascia, L. L'affaire Moro. - Palermo : Sellerio ed., 1978.
Dutch ed.: De zaak Aldo Moro. Antwerp: Lotus, 1979.

1588. Selva, G. * Marcucci, E. Il martirio di Moro. - Bologna : Cappelli, 1978.

1589. Sernicoli, E. L'anarchia. - 2 vols. - Milano : 1894.

1590. Sheehan, T. Italy : Terror on the right. 22 Jan. 1981. New York Review of Books

1591. Sheehan, T. Italy behind the ski mask : The Red Brigades. 16 Aug. 1979. p. 20-26. New York Review of Books. ; 26.

1592. Silj, A. Brigate rosse-stato : La scontro spettacolo nella regia della stampa quotidiana. - Firenze : Vallecchi, 1978. 243 p
Analyzes news treatment of Moro kidnapping in five Italian dailies.

1593. Silj, A. Never again without a rifle. - New York : Karz Publishers, 1979. 256 p
Reconstructs the emergence of student protest in Italy and the escalation of violence after 1968; the Italian edition 'Mai piu senza fugile' was published in Florence: Vallecchi, 1977.

1594. Sofri, A. * Mea, L.della Zur strategie und Organisation von "Lotta Continua". - Berlin : Merve Verlag, 1971. 119 p

1595. Sole, R. Le defi terroriste : Lecons italiennes a l'usage de l'Europe. - Paris : Le Seuil, 1979. 288 p
By Le Monde correspondent in Rome, placing Italian terrorism againstpolitical background.

1596. Solinas, S. Macondo e P38. - Milano : Il falco, 1980. 99 p

1597. Stajano, C. * Fini, F. La forza della democrazia : La strategia della tensione in Italia 1969-1976. - Torino : Einaudi, 1977.
Transcript of Italian TV-program.

1598. Statera, G. * et al. Violenze sociale e violenza politica nell'Italia degli anni '70 : Analisi e interpretazioni sociopolitiche, giurdiche della stampa quatidiana. - Milano : F. Angeli editore, 1983.

1599. Sterling, C. Italy: the Feltrinelli case. July 1972. p. 10-18. Atlantic Monthly. ; 230.

1600. Stoppa, P. Revolutionary culture Italian style. Spring 1981. p. 100-113. Washington Quarterly. ; 4.

1601. Tessandori, V. B.R. Cronaca e documenti delle Brigate Rosse. - Milano : Garzanti, 1977.
On Italy's Red Brigades.

1602. Tessandori, V. B.R. Imputazione: banda armata. - Milano : Garzanti, 1977. 414 p
B.R.= Brigate Rosse, Italy's Red Brigades.

1603. Visser, C.J. De belegerde staat : Terrorisme in Italie. Dec. 1981. p. 748-756. Internationale Spectator. ; 35:12.

1604. Visser, C.J. Een Italiaanse polemiek : Recente literatuur over links politiek geweld in Italie. 1983. p. 356-382. Transaktie. ; 12:4.

1605. Visser, C.J. Rechts politiek geweld in Italie : Een polemiek. 1985. Transaktie. ; 14:2.

1606. Visser, C.J. Rechts terrorisme : Een Italiaanse polemiek. 1985. p. 146-162. Transaktie. ; 14:2.

1607. Vittorio, G.D. Four months of terrorism in Italy. - Sydney : 1978.

1608. Wagner-Pacifici, R. Negotiation in the Aldo Moro affair : The suppressed alternative in a case of symbolic politics. 1983. p. 487-517. Politics & Society. ; 12:4.

1609. Weinberg, L. Patterns of neo-fascist violence in Italian politics. 1979. 231-259. Terrorism. ; 2.

1610. Whetten, L.L. Italian terrorism: record figures and political dilemmas. 1978. p. 377-395. Terrorism. ; 1.

1611. Wolf, J.B. Italy's year of terror. - Gaithersburg, Md. : IACP, 1978. Update report. ; 4:6.

1612. _____ Al di la del 7 aprile : Discorso anonimo alla ricerca di autori. - Brescia : Shakespeare and Co., 1980. ; Microfilm

1613. _____ Brigate rosse : Che cosa hanno fatto, che cosa hanno detto, che cosa se ne e detto. - Milano : 1976. Soccorso Rosso. * (ed.)

1614. _____ Can Italy survive?. 22 May 1978. p. 35, 36, 38. Newsweek
Effect of Moro kidnapping on Italian political system.

1615. _____ Eine Chance fuer Aussteiger : Das Beispiel Peter-Jurgen Boock:

Dokumentation des Komitees fur Grundrechte und Demokratie zu einem noch schwebenden Verfahren. - Sensbachtal : 1982. 44 p

1616. _____ Feltrinelli, il guerrigliero impotente. - Rome : Ed. Documenti.,

1617. _____ Germania e germanizzazione. - Napoli : Pironti, 1977.

1618. _____ I NAP: storia politica dei Nuclei Armati Proletari e requisitoria del tribunale di Napoli. - Milano-Napoli : Collettivo Editoriale Libri Rossi, 1976. 249 p.
Soccorso Rosso Napoletano
On the armed proletarian nuclei.

1619. _____ Il caso Coco. - Milano : Collectivo Editoriale Libri Rossi, 1978. 99 p.
Soccorso Rosso Napoletano

1620. _____ L'affare Feltrinelli : Con testimonianza di Carlo Ripa di Meana. - Milano : Stampa Club, 1972.

1621. _____ L'hypothese revolutionnaire : Documents sur les luttes etudiantes a Trente, Turin, Naples, Pise, Milan et Rome. - Paris : Mercure de France, 1968. 267 p

1622. _____ Le complot terroriste en Italie. 1970. p. 1264-1285.
Groupe Anarchiste-Libertaire (Clandestin) "22 mars". Les temps modernes. ; 26:283.

1623. _____ Le radici di una rivolta - il movimento studentesco a Roma. - Milano : Feltrinelli, 1977.
Collettivo Nostra Assemblea

1624. _____ Le straghe di stato. - Roma : Savelli, 1970.

1625. _____ Memorie : Dalla clandestinita un terrorista non pentito si racconta. - Roma : Savelli, 1981.

1626. _____ Nehmen wir uns die Stadt. Klassenanalyse, Organisationspapier, Kampfprogramm : Beitraege der Lotta Continua zur Totalisierung der Kaempfe. - Muenchen : Trikont, 1972. 138 p.
Lotta Continua

1627. _____ Phenomenological and dynamic aspects of terrorism in Italy. 1979. p. 159-170. Terrorism. ; 2.

1628. _____ Primavalie : Incendio a porte chiuse. - Roma : La nuova sinistra, 1974. 284 p

1629. _____ Risk assessment for Italy. - Washington, D.C. : 1978. 143 p.
Blackstone Associates

1630. _____ Risoluzione della direzione strategica (febr. 1978). July 1978. p. 76-95.
Brigate Rossi. Controinformazione. ; 5:11-12.

1631. _____ Sulla guerriglia urbana. - Verona : 1972. p. 157-183.
In: Formare l'Armata Rossa - i Tupamaros d'Europa?

1632. _____ The Red Brigades. - New York : Manor Books, 1978.
Red Brigades

1633. _____ The Red Brigades and the Italian political tradition : Drake, R. - New York : St. Martin's Press, 1982.

1634. _____ The story of the bloodiest skyacking : Terrorism in the Rome airport. Dec. 1973. p. 16-17. U.S. News and World Report. ; 75.

H.1.5. Spain

1635. Alonso, A.M. El terrorismo en Espana. - Barcelona : Planeta, Instituto de Estudios Economicos, 1982. 279 p

1636. Arenillas, J.M. The Basque country, the national question and the socialist revolution. - Leeds : I.L.P. Square One Publications, 1973.

1637. Ayerra, R. Los terroristas. - Barcelona : Planeta, 1980.

1638. Batista, J. Le antitesis de la paz. - Madrid : St. Martin, 1981. 295 p

1639. Benegas, J.M. Euskadi. - Barcelona : ARgos Vergara, 1984. 218 p

1640. Bereciartu, G.J. Ideologia y estrategia politica de ETA 1959-1968. - Madrid : 1981.

1641. Bookchin, M. The Spanish anarchists. - New York : 1977.

1642. Brenan, G. The Spanish labyrinth : An account of the social and political background of the civil war. - Cambridge : 1960.
Orig. publ. in 1943.

1643. Campo Vidal, M. La Espana que hereda Felipe Gonzalez. - Barcelona : Argos Vergara, 1983. 223 p

1644. Clark, R.P. The Basques : The Franco years and beyond. - Reno : University of Nevada Press, 1979.

1645. Cuadrat, X. Socialismo y anarquismo en Catalunya : Los origenes de la CNT. - Madrid : Revista del Trabaja, 1976. 682 p

1646. Enzensberger, H.M. Der kurze Sommer der Anarchie. - Frankfurt : 1972.

1647. Frey, P. Widerstand in Euskadi. - Zuerich : 28 Aug. 1976. Tagesanzeiger Magazin
On Basque ETA.

1648. Garcia Damborenea, R. La encrucijada vasca. - Barcelona : Editorial Argos Vergara, 1984. 250 p

1649. Gurriaran, J.A. La bomba. - Barcelona : Planeta, 1982. 310 p

1650. Heiberg, M. Insiders/outsiders : Basque nationalism. Spring 1975. p. 169-193. European Journal of Sociology. ; 16.

1651. Herzog, W. * (ed.) Terror in Baskenland : Gefahr fuer Spaniens Demokratie?. - Reinbek : Rowohlt, 1979. 140 p
On ETA terrorism.

1652. Ibarzabal, E. 50 anos de nacionalismo vasco. - San Sebastian : Ed. Vascas, 1978.

1653. Janke, P. Spanish separatism : ETA's threat to Basque democracy. - London : ISC, 1980. Conflict Studies. ; 123.

1654. Kaufmann, J. Mourir au Pays Basque, la lutte impitoyable de l'E.T.A. - Paris : Plon, 1976.

1655. Letamendia, F. Les basques. Un peuple contre les etats. - Paris : Le Seuil, 1977.

1656. Lida, C.E. Anarquismo y revolucion en la Espana del XIX. - Madrid : 1972.

1657. Lorenzo, C.M. Les anarchistes espagnols et le pouvoir 1868-1969. - Paris : Ed. du Seuil, 1969. 429 p

1658. Maura, R. Terrorism in Barcelona and its impact on Spanish politics 1904-1919. Dec. 1968. Past and Present

1659. Meaker, G.H. The revolutionary left in Spain, 1914-1923. - Stanford : 1974.

1660. Mella, R. * Prat, J. La barbarie gubernamental en Espana. - Brooklyn (in fact Barcelona) : 1897.

1661. Menges, C.C. Spain : The struggle for democracy today. - Beverly Hills, Calif. : Sage, 1978. 80 p. Washington Papers. ; 58.

1662. Mohedano, J.M. * Pena, M. Constitucion, cuenta atras : ETA-operacion Galaxia y otros terrorismos. - Madrid : Casa de Campo, 1978.

1663. Nunez, L.C. La sociedad vasca actual. - San Sebastian : 1977.

1664. Orrantia, M. Euskadi, pacificacion? : Documentos sobre el 28 de octubre de 1978. - Madrid : Ediciones Libertarias, 1980. 235 p

1665. Ortzi (pseud. of F. Letamendia). Historia de Euskadi. - Barcelona : Ruedo Iberico, 1978.
Basque history.

1666. Padilla Bolivar, A. El movimento anarquista espanol. - Barcelona : Planeta, 1976. 358 p

1667. Payne, S.G. Basque nationalism. - Reno : University of Nevada Press, 1975.

1668. Payne, S.G. Catalan and Basque nationalism. 1971. p. 15-51. Journal of Contemporary History. ; 6:1.

1669. Payne, S.G. Madrid: ETA - Basque terrorism. 1979. p. 109-113. Washington Quarterly. ; 2:2.

1670. Pestana, A. El terrorismo en Barcelona : Seguido de principios medios y finos del sindicalismo communista. - Barcelona : J.J. de Olamela, 1978. 75 p

1671. Pestana, A. Lo que apprendi en la vida. - Madrid : 1933.

1672. Pisano, V.S. Spain faces the extremists : Cannons to the left and cannons to the right. July 1981. p. 10-16. TVI Journal. ; 2.

1673. Portell, J.M. Euskadi: amnistia avrancada. - Barcelona : Dopesa, 1977.

1674. Portell, J.M. Los hombres de ETA. - Barcelona : Dopesa, 1976. 280 p

1675. Preston, P. * (ed.) Spain in crisis. - New York : Barnes & Noble, 1976. 341 p

1676. Reguant, J.M. 1941 - Marcelino Massana : Terrorismo o resistancia. - Barcelona : Dopesa, 1979. 219 p

1677. Tellez, A. Sabate. Stadtguerilla in Spanien nach dem Buergerkrieg, 1945--1960. - Muenchen : Trikont, 1974. 154 p
On Francisco Sabate Leopart.

1678. Thomas, H. The Spanish civil war. - New York : 1961.

1679. Visser, C.J. Spanje en de Baskische ETA : Terrorisme van dictatuur tot democratie. - Den Haag : Staatsuitgeverij, 1982. 94 p. NIVV-reeks. ; 37.

1680. Waldmann, P. Mitgliederstruktur, Sozialisationsmedien und gesellschaftlicher Rueckhalt : Der baskischen ETA. 1981. p. 45-66. Politische Vierteljahresschriften. ; 1.

1681. _____ ETA. - San Sebastian : 1978.

1682. _____ Ontwikkelingen op het gebied van het terrorisme sinds de algemene verkiezingen van oktober 1982. 4 April 1985. p. 216-221. Keesings Historisch Archief. ; 54:2785.
Developments in Spain since 1982.

1683. _____ Spain : Bandas armadas y elementos terroristas. - Madrid : Academia Editorial Lamruja, 1985. 141 p

1684. _____ Spanje : Ontwikkelingen op het gebied van het terrorisme. 2 May 1985. p. 275-282. Keesings Historisch Archief

1685. _____ Spanje : Ontwikkelingen op het gebied van het terrorisme sinds eind 1983. 18 April 1985. p. 294-254. Keesings Historisch Archief

1686. _____ Spanje : Ontwikkelingen op het gebied van het terrorisme sinds medio 1984. 25 April 1985. p. 260-265. Keesings Historisch Archief

1687. _____ Terrorismo y justicia en Espana. - Madrid : Centro Espanol de Documentacion, 1975.

H.1.6. The Netherlands

1688. Abspoel, J.J. Requisitoir in de zaak van het Openbaar Ministerie tegen J.R. en zes anderen; bezetting Indonesisch consulaat Amsterdam. June 1976. p. 304-337. Delikt en delinkwent. ; 6:6.

1689. Amersfoort, J.M.M.van De sociale positie van de Molukkers in Nederland. - Den Haag : Staatsuitgeverij, 1971. 74 p

1690. Barker, R. Not here, but in another place. - New York : St.Martin's, 1979.
On South Moluccan terrorist acts in the Netherlands; 1975, 1977.

1691. Boomen, G.van den * Metekohy, R. * (eds.) Maluku Selatan; : Zuid-Molukken, Een vergeten vrijheidsstrijd.. - Amsterdam : De Populier, 1977. 96 p

1692. Bouman, P.J. Vrijheidshelden en terroristen : Vijf eeuwen geweld in Europa. - Amsterdam : Elsevier, 1977. 192 p
Chapter deals with 1st South Moluccan train incident.

1693. Cuperus, J. * Klijnsma, R. Onderhandelen of bestormen : Het beleid van de Nederlandse overheid inzake terroristische acties. - Groningen : Polemologisch Instituut, 1980. 98 p
Negotiate or storm. The Dutch government's policy during terroristicactions.

1694. Decker, G. Republik Maluku Selatan. - Goettingen : O. Schwartz and Co., 1957.

1695. Drevan, W.P.van Came the dawn: South Moluccan terror in the Netherlands. Sept. 1977. p. 15-21. Counterforce. ; 1.

1696. Droesen, H.W.J. Pleitaantekeningen in de zaak tegen J.R. en zes anderen; bezetting Indonesisch consulaat Amsterdam. Oct. 1976. p. 447-458. Delikt en delinkwent. ; 6:8.

1697. Egter van Wissekerke, F. Terreur anno 1977. Dec. 1977. Carre. Maandblad voor de Nederlandse Officieren Vereniging

1698. Ellemers, J.E. Minderheden en beleid in Nederland : Molukkers en enkele andere categorieen allochtonen in vergelijkend perspectief. March 1978. p. 20-40. Transaktie. ; 7:1.

1699. Graaf, H.J.de De geschiedenis van Ambon en de Zuid-Molukken. - Franeker : Wever, 1977.

1700. Hulsman, L.H.C. Juni 1976; gewelddadigheid, terrorisme en strafrechtelijke normen. June 1976. p. 299-303. Delikt en delinkwent. ; 6:6.

1701. Jong, J.J.P.de Het Zuid-Molukse radicalisme in Nederland: een emancipatiebeweging?. Sept. 1971. p. 413-416. Sociologische Gids. ; 18:5.

1702. Kaam, B.van Ambon door de eeuwen. - Baarn : In den Toren, 1977.

1703. Kaam, B.van The South Moluccans : Background to the train hijackings. - London : 1980.

1704. Kamsteeg, A. De Zuidmolukse bezetting in Wassenaar. - Dordrecht : G.P.V., 1970.

1705. Knot, G. * Weltje, H.G. * Kamsteeg, A. Wat moeten ze hier? : Zuidmolukkers op weg naar vrijheid. - Groningen : De Vuurbaak, 1975. 96 p

1706. Knot, G. Balans van 'Wassenaar'. - Eindhoven : Oct. 1970. Zelfbeschikking. ; 1:2.

1707. Koebben, A.J.F. De gijzelingsakties van Zuid-Molukkers en hun effekten op de samenleving. - Groningen : June 1979. p. 147-154. Transaktie. ; 8:2.
South Moluccan hostage-taking actions and their social effects.

1708. Kraker, W.A.de * Groot, F.C.V.de Analyseverslag van de gijzeling in de Franse ambassade van 13-17 september 1974. - Den Haag : 1975. 45 p

1709. Kranenburg, F.J. Gijzeling, rechtsorde, openbare orde; een verstoorde samenleving. 10 Apr. 1976. p. 195-201.

Algemeen Politieblad. ; 125:8.
Also published in: De Nederlandse Gemeente 30:10, 1976, pp. 109-116.

1710. Kruijs, P.W.van der Kanttekeningen bij een requisitoir. Oct. 1976. p. 459-462. Delikt en delinkwent. ; 6:8.
On South Moluccan incident in Indonesian consulate in Amsterdam.

1711. Kuijer, K.de De weg van de Zuidmolukkers. - Nijmegen : 1973.

1712. Maarseveen, H.Th.J.F.van De verbeelding aan de macht; opmerkingen naar aanleiding van de gijzelingen. 13 Aug. 1977. p. 697-698. Nederlands Juristenblad. ; 52.

1713. Manusama, J.A. Om recht en vrijheid : Geschiedenis van de strijd om de onafhankelijkheid der Zuid- Molukken. - Utrecht : Libertas, 1951. 85 p

1714. Marien, M.H. Actuele beschouwingen. Het Zuid-Molukse radicalisme in Nederland : Nationalistische of emancipatiebeweging?. Jan. 1971. p. 62-76. Sociologische Gids

1715. Marien, M.H. De Zuidmolukkers in Nederland : Migranten tegen wil en dank in de minderheidssituatie. - Amsterdam : 1968.

1716. Meulen, E.I.van der Dossier Ambon 1950 : De houding van Nederland ten opzichte van Ambon en de RMS. - Den Haag : Staatsuitgeverij, 1981. 327 p
Historical background of South Moluccan terrorism.

1717. Oen, K.L. Balans van 25 jaar R.M.S.-ideaal Zuidmolukkers; en onvrede Zuidmolukkers verklaard met het begrip "relatieve deprivatie". - Amsterdam : Sociologisch Instituut, 1975. 55 p

1718. Orie, A.M.M. * Verburg, J.J.I. De koningin bedreigd. Oct. 1975. p. 475-489. Delikt en delinkwent. ; 5:8.

1719. Penonton, B. De Zuidmolukse republiek : Schets voor een beschrijving van de nieuwste geschiedenis van het Zuidmolukse volk. - Amsterdam : Buijten & Schipperheijn, 1977. 299 p
Title of the original 1970 edition: Wat er gebeurde na 1950.

1720. Persijn, J. Uit de schaduw van het verleden : Legende en realiteit in het Molukse vraagstuk. Febr. 1976. p. 103-110. Internationale Spectator. ; 30:2.

1721. Praag, C.S.van Molukse jongeren in botsing met de Nederlandse maatschappij : De gevolgen van een beleid. Dec. 1975. p. 342-348. Beleid en Maatschappij. ; 2:12.

1722. Reijntjes, J.M. Samenspanning. July 1977. p. 418-432. Delikt en delinkwent. ; 7:7.
On South Moluccan terrorist incidents.

1723. Rijken, A.G.L. De actie van Zuidmolukkers op 31 augustus 1970 te Wassenaar. 1971. p. 153-157; 185-192; 211-215;. Algemeen Politieblad. ; 120:7-11.

1724. Rinsampessy, E. De mogelijke gronden van agressie onder Molukse jongeren. - Utrecht : 1975. 76 p. Pattimura Special. ; 2.

1725. Rinsampessy, E. De RMS-strijd als emancipatiestrijd. 1975, 1976. Madjalah Pattimura. ; 3:1, 4:1.

1726. Rinsampessy, E. Gewapende propaganda. Jan. 1975. Madjalah Pattimura. ; 1.

1727. Ritzema Bos, J.H. Dies ater (een zwarte dag) : Opgedragen aan 33 Zuidmolukkers. - Doetinchem : 1970.

1728. Rosenthal, U. Rampen, rellen, gijzelingen : Crisisbesluitvorming in Nederland. - Amsterdam-Dieren : De Bataafsche Leeuw, 1984.

1729. Sahetapy, A. Minnestrijd voor de R.M.S. - Amsterdam : J. Ririmasse, 1981. 128 p
'Love struggle for the R.M.S.', by one of the trainhijackers of 1975

1730. Schmid, A.P. * Graaf, J.F.A. de * Bovenkerk, F. * Bovenkerk- Teerink, L.M. * Brunt, L. Zuidmoluks terrorisme, de media en de publieke opinie. - Amsterdam : Intermediair Bibliotheek, 1982. 204 p
"South Moluccan terrorism, the media and public opinion", two COMT studies.

1731. Siahaya, T. Mena-muria. Wassenaar '70: Zuidmolukkers slaan terug. - Amsterdam : De Bezige Bij, 1972. 182 p
On a South Moluccan action against the Indonesian embassy in Wassenaar, 1970, by a participant.

1732. Utrecht, E. Ambon : Kolonisatie, dekolonisatie en neo-kolonisatie. - Amsterdam : Van Gennep, 1972.

1733. Verwey-Jonker, H. * (ed.) Allochtonen in Nederland : Beschouwingen over de: gerepatrieerden, Molukkers, Surinamers, Antillianen, buitenlandse studenten in onze samenleving. - 2nd ed. - Den Haag : 1973. 267 p

1734. Wittermans, T. * Gist, N.P. The Ambonese nationalist movement in the Netherlands : A study in status deprivation. 1962. p. 309-317. Social Forces. ; 40:4.

1735. _____ Ambonezen in Nederland. - Den Haag : Staatsdrukkerij, 1959. 111p.

Commissie Verwey-Jonker ; Rapport

1736. _____ Bovensmilde, hoe verder? : Voorlopige voorstellen voor een nader beleid. - Smilde : 1978. 59 p. Begeleidingscommissie Voorbereiding Projekt Sociaal- Kultureel Werk
On the life in a Dutch community after terroristic violence.

1737. _____ De gijzeling in de Franse ambassade. 9 Nov. 1974. p. 582-588. Algemeen Politieblad. ; 123:10.
Occupation of French embassy in The Hague by Japanese terrorists.

1738. _____ De gijzelingen in Bovensmilde en Vries(mei-juni 1977). - Den Haag : Staatsuitgeverij, 1977. ; 2e Kamer 14610, nrs. 1-2

1739. _____ De Molukkers. Wat brengt hen tot gijzelingsakties? : Achtergronden, geschiedenis. - Rotterdam : Ordeman, Dec. 1975. 32 p
Short and superficial instant-history that does not deal with terrorist actions.

1740. _____ Evolucion de la delincuencia terrorista en la Argentina. - Buenos Aires : Poder Ejecutivo Nacional, 1979. 424 p

1741. _____ Gijzeling Assen, 13-14 maart 1978. - Den Haag : 1978. 296 p. Rijksvoorlichtingsdienst

1742. _____ Gijzelingen 2-19 december 1975; : Persoverzicht deel A: ANP-berichten. - Den Haag : 1975. 422 p. Ministerie van Justitie, Stafbureau Voorlichting

1743. _____ Salawaku RMS; de Zuidmolukse jongeren en hun eisen. - Den Haag : 1970.
Vrije Zuidmolukse Jongeren

1744. _____ Terrorisme (in Nederland). 20 feb. 1986. 13 p. Beleid Beschouwd. ; 5292.

1745. _____ Treinkaping te Beilen - Overval op het Indonesisch consulaat-generaal te Amsterdam : Regeringsverslag., 1976. p. 109-120, 140-152. Algemeen Politieblad. ; 125:5-6.

1746. _____ Verslag van de gebeurtenissen rond de treinkaping te Beilen en de overval op het Indonesische consulaat-generaal te Amsterdam (dec. 1975). - Den Haag : Staatsuitgeverij, 1976.
Ministerie van justitie ; 2e Kamer 13756 nrs. 1-3

1747. _____ Verslag van de gebeurtenissen rond de gijzeling van 22 personen in het Penitentiair Centrum te 's-Gravenhage. 21 Dec. 1974. p. 650-652. Algemeen Politieblad. ; 123:26.

H.1.7. Other West European countries

1748. Bloomfield jr, L.P. Anarchy in Turkey : The growing pains of a young democracy. 1980. p. 31-56. Conflict. ; 2:1.

1749. Botz, G. Gewalt in der Politik : Attentate, Zusammenstosse, Putschversuche, Unruhe in Oesterreich, 1918 bis 1934. - Muenchen : Fink, 1976.

1750. Brown, G. The red paper on Scotland. - Nottingham : 1975.

1751. Burns, A. The Angry Brigade. - London : Quartet, 1973.
On British terrorist group.

1752. Carr, G. The Angry Brigade, a history of Britain's first urban guerrilla group. - London : Gollancz, 1975.

1753. Carvalho, J.M. O terror goncalvista. - Lisbon : Livraria populas de F. Franco, 1976. 67 p

1754. Clissold, S. * (ed.) A short history of Yugoslavia: from early times to 1966. - Cambridge : Cambridge University Press, 1966.
Also deals with Croatian terrorists.

1755. Engels, F. Die Bakunisten an der Arbeit. - Berlin : 1969.
In: Marx/Engels Werke. Bd 18

1756. Firth, C.E. Urban guerrillas in Athens. 1972. p. 52-56. Journal of the Royal United Service Institution. ; 117:165.

1757. Goodhart, Ph. The climate of collapse: the terrorist threat to Britain and her allies. - Richmond : Foreign Affairs Publ. Co., 1975. 15 p

1758. Gunter, M.M. "Pursuing the just cause of their people.". - Westport, Conn. : Greenwood Press, 1986.
On Armenian terrorists.

1759. Gunter, M.M. Contemporary Armenian terrorism. 1986. p. 213-252. Terrorism. ; 8:3.

1760. Gunter, M.M. The Armenian terrorist campaign against Turkey. Summer 1983. p. 447-477. Orbis. ; 27.

1761. Gunter, M.M. The historical origins of contemporary Armenian terrorism. Fall 1985. p. 77-96. Journal of South Asian and Middle Eastern Studies. ; 9:1.

1762. Gunter, M.M. Transnational sources of support for Armenian terrorism. Fall 1985. p. 31-51. Conflict Quarterly. ; 5.

1763. Haeggman, B. Sweden's maoist 'subversives' - a case study. - London

: ISC, 1975. 20 p. Conflict Studies. ; 58.
1764. Harris, G.S. The left in Turkey. July-Aug. 1980. p. 26-41. Problems of Communism. ; 29.

1765. Hearne, D. The rise of the Welsh republic. - Wales : Talybont, 1975.

1766. Hewsen, R.H. Who speaks today of the Armenians?. - Westport, Conn. : Greenwood Press, 1978. p. 444-446. In: M.H. Livingston et al. (eds.), International terrorism in the contemporary world

1767. Larsson, J.E. Politisk terror i Sverige. - Goeteborg : Zinderman-Solna, Seelig, 1968. 8
2 p

1768. Orlow, D. Political violence in 7pre-coup Turkey. 1982. p. 53-71. Terrorism. ; 6:1.

1769. Philip, A.B. The Welsh question. - Cardiff : 1975.

1770. Schwarz, J.E. The Scottish national party: nonviolent separatism and theories of violence. 1970. p. 496-517. World Politics. ; 22:4.

1771. Shipley, P. Revolutionaries in modern Britain. - London : Bodley Head, 1976. 255 p

1772. Stafford, D. Anarchists in Britain today. 1970. Government and Opposition. ; 5.

1773. Stafford, D. Anarchists in Britain today. 1971. p. 346-353. Government and Opposition. ; 6:3.

1774. Szaz, Z.M. Armenian terrorists and the East-West conflict. Winter 1983. p. 386-394. Journal of Social, Political and Economic Studies. ; 8.

1775. Thomas, N. The Welsh extremist. - London : 1971.

1776. Wilkinson, P. Armenian terrorism. Sept. 1983. p. 344-350. World Today. ; 39.

1777. _____ "Dossier" terrorismo. - Lisboa : Avante, 1977. 179 p
On Portuguese right-wing terrorism 1975-1977.

1778. _____ Armenian terrorism. - Antalya : Akdeniz University, Research Center for the Study of Ataturk Reforms and Principles, 1985. 12 p

1779. _____ International terrorism and the drug connection : Symposium. - Ankara : Information and Public Relations Office, Ankara University, 1984. 294 p

1780. _____ Turkey. 1982. p. 108-137. Wilson Quarterly. ; 6.

H.2. Eastern Europe and Russia, General

1781. Gross, F. Political violence and terror in 19th and 20th century Russia and Eastern Europe. - Washington, D.C. : GPO, 1969. p. 421-476.
In: J.F. Kirkham, S.G. Levy and W.J. Crotty (eds.), A report to the National Commission on the Causes and Prevention of Violence. Vol. 8: Assassination and political violence

1782. Gross, F. Violence in politics : Terror and political assassination in Eastern Europe and Russia. - The Hague * Paris : Mouton, 1972. 139 p

H.2.1. Eastern Europe, excl. Russia and the Balkan

1783. Lacko, M. Arrow-cross men, national socialists. - Budapest : 1969.

1784. Maerker, R. Angst vor dem Ueberschwappen des Terrorismus? Die DDR und der Terrorismus in der Bundesrepublik. 1977. p. 1248. Deutschland Archiv. ; 10.

1785. Nagorski, R. Historique du mouvement anarchiste en Pologne. - London : Slienger, 1976. 22 p

1786. Pilsudski, J. The memoirs of a Polish revolutionary and soldier. - London : 1931.

H.2.2. Russia

1787. Ascher, A. Lessons of Russian terrorism. Nov.-Dec. 1980. p. 70-74. Problems of Communism. ; 29.

1788. Avrich, P. The Russian anarchists. - New York : W.W. Norton & Co., 1978.
Orig. ed.: 1967.

1789. Bernstein, L. L'affaire Azeff. - Paris : 1910.

1790. Bernstein, L. Le terrorisme en Russie. - Paris : 1910.

1791. Bogucharski, V. Aktivnoe narodnichestvo. - Moscow : 1912.

1792. Borovoj, A. Michailu Bakuninu- (1876-1926): ocerk istorii anarchiceskogo dvizenija v rossii. - Moscow : 1926.

1793. Burtsev, V. Koruzhyu. - London : 1903.

1794. Burtsev, V. Za sto let. - London : 1897.
On Russian terrorists, 1880's.

1795. Cannac, R. Aux sources de la revolution russe: Netchaiev : Du nihilisme au terrorisme. - Paris : 1961.

1796. Cassinelli, C.W. Total revolution : A comparative study of Germany under Hitler, the Soviet Union under Stalin and China under Mao. - Santa Barbara, Calif. : Clio Press, 1976.

1797. Chernov, V.M. Pered burei. - New York : 1953.

1798. Confino, M. * (ed.) Daughter of a revolutionary, Natalie Herzen and the Bakunin/Nechayev circle. - London : Alcove Press, 1974.

1799. Daix, P. Marxismus. Die Doktrin des Terrors. - Graz-Wien-Koeln : Verlag Styria, 1976.

1800. Dragomanov, M.P. La tyrannicide en Russie et l'action de l'Europe Occidentale. - Geneva : 1883.

1801. Dragomanov, M.P. Terrorism i Svoboda. - Geneva : 1880.

1802. Faure, Ch. Terre, terreur, liberte. - Paris : Maspero, 1979. 250 p

1803. Figner, V. Nacht ueber Russland. - Berlin : Guhl, 1928. 590 p
Russian terrorism against the tsarist regime, 1880's ff.

1804. Geierhos, W. Vera Zasulic und die russische revolutionaere Bewegung. - Munich : Oldenbourg, 1977.

1805. Gerassimoff, A. Der Kampf gegen die erste russische Revolution. - Berlin : 1933.

1806. Gerassimoff, A. Tsarisme et terrorisme. - Paris : 1934.

1807. Gorev, B. Anarchizm v Rossii: ot Bakunina do Machno. - Moscow : 1930.

1808. Gribin, N.P. Tragediia Olstera. - Moskva : Mezhdunar, otnosheniia, 1983. 220 p

1809. Hildermeier, M. Zur Sozialstruktur der Fuehrungsgruppen und zur terroristischen Kampfsmethode der Sozial-Revolutionaeren Partei Russlands 1917. Dec.1972. Jahrbuecher fuer Geschichte Osteuropas. ; 20:4.

1810. Hingley, R. Nihilists. - London : Weidenfeld and Nicolson, 1967.
On Russian terrorists of the 1880's.

1811. Itenberg, B.S. Dvizhenie revoliutsonnove narodnichestva. - Moscow : 1965.
On narodnaya volya in Russia, 1870's and 1880's.

1812. Jansen, M. A show trial under Lenin : the trial of the socialist revolutionaires, Moscou, 1922. - The Hague * Boston : M. Nijhoff * Hingham * Kluwer Boston, 1982.

1813. Knight, A. Female terrorists in the Russian socialist revolutionary party. p. 139-159. Russian Review. ; 39:2.

1814. McDaniel, J.F. Political assassination and mass execution: terrorism in revolutionary Russia, 1918-1938. University of Michigan, 1976. 402 p ; Unpubl. dissertation

1815. Metzl, L. Communist political terror: a behaviorist interpretation. 1970. p. 769-772. Orbis. ; 14:3.

1816. Millard, M.B. Russian revolutionary emigration, terrorism and the political struggle. University of Rochester, 1973. 217 p ; Unpubl. dissertation

1817. Morozov, N.A. Povest moei zhizni. - Moscow : 1965.

1818. Naimark, N.M. Terrorists and the social democrats : The Russian revolutionary movement under Alexander 3. - Cambridge : Harvard University Press, 1983. 308 p

1819. Naimark, N.M. The workers' section and the challenge of the young : Narodnaia Volnia 1881-1884. July 1978. p. 273-297. Russian Review. ; 37:3.

1820. Nestroev, G. Iz dnevnik maksimalista. - Paris : 1910.

1821. Nettlau, M. Anarchisten und Sozialrevolutionaere. - Berlin : 1914.

1822. Newell, D.A. The Russian Marxist response to terrorism; 1878-1917. Stanford University, 1981. ; Ph.D. dissertation

1823. Nicolaevsky, B. 1887-1966. Istoria odngo predatelia : Terroristy i politicheskaia polisiia. - New York : Russica Publishers, 1980. 372 p

1824. Payne, P.S.R. The terrorists: the story of the forerunners of Stalin. - New York : Funk & Wagnalls, 1967.

1825. Payne, P.S.R. Zero: the story of terrorism. - New York : Day, 1950. 270 p
On Nechayev and his alleged influence on Hitler and Lenin.

1826. Resh, R.E. The employement of terror in the Soviet Union and Eastern Europe : A changing concept. 1973. p. 81-103. Revue de droit international de sciences diplomatiques et politiques. ; 51.

1827. Savinkov, B. Souvenirs d'un terroriste. - Paris : 1931.
Also publ. as "Memoirs of a terrorist", New York: A.& C. Boni, 1931.

1828. Savinkov, B. The pale horse. - London : Allen & Unwin, 1981.
Publ. under pseud. V. Ropsin.

1829. Schmiedling, W. Aufstand der Toechter : Russische Revolutionaerinnen im 19. Jahrhundert. - Munich : Kindler, 1979. 270 p
Russian 19th century terrorism and the role of women.

1830. Stepniak, S. (pseud. for S.M. Kravcinskij). Le tsarisme et la revolution. - Paris : 1886.

1831. Stepniak, S. (pseud. for S.M. Kravcinskij). Underground Russia : Revolutionary profiles and sketches from life. - New York : Scribner's, 1892.

1832. Sternberg, L. Politicheski terror v Rossii. 1884.

1833. Talmon, J.L. The origins of totalitarian democracy. - London : Secker and Warburg, 1952.

1834. Tarnovski, G. Terrorizm i rutina. - Geneva : 1880.
On Russian terrorism; author's real name is Romaneko.

1835. Ulam, A.B. In the name of the people : Prophets and conspirators in prerevolutionary Russia. - New York : Viking Press, 1977.
Russia 1870's ff.

1836. Venturi, F. Il populismo russo : Vol.3: Dall'andata nel popolo al terrorismo. - 2nd ed. - Torino : Einaudi, 1972.
Orig. 1952.

1837. Volk, S.S. Narodnaya volya. - Moscow : 1966.

1838. Wolf, J.B. Islam in the Soviet Union. March 1969. p. 161-166. Current History

1839. Wolf, J.B. Soviet intelligence operations. - Gaithersburg, Md. : IACP, 1981. Update Report. ; 7:5.

1840. _____ Histoire du terrorisme russe. - Paris : Payot, 1930.

1841. _____ Historical antecedents of Soviet terrorism. - Washington, D.C. : GPO, 1981. 83 p.
U.S. Congress. Senate. Committee on the Judiciary. Subcommittee on Security and Terrorism

1842. _____ Literatura social 'no-revoljucionnoj partii "Narodnoj Voli". - Leipzig : Zentralantiquariat, 1977. 978 p
; Reprint
Orig. ed.: Paris: 1905.

1843. _____ Women against the tsar : The memoirs of five revolutionaries of the 1880's. - London : 1976.
Five sisters

H.2.3. Balkan, excl. Greece

1844. Christowe, St. Heroes and assassins. - New York : Holt, 1935.
On the Inner Macedonian Revolutionary Organization (IMRO). Established in the 1890s to fight the Turks and achieve independence for Macedonia. Later it became a tool of the Bulgarian government; 1890-1930.

1845. Clissold, S. Croat separatism : Nationalism, dissidence and terrorism. - London : ISC, 1979. 21 p. Conflict Studies. ; 103.

1846. Codreanu, C.Z. Pentru legionari. - Bucharest : 1936.

1847. Davies, D. The Ustasha in Australia. - Sidney : Communist Party of Australia, April 1972.

1848. Dedijer, V. The road to Serajevo. - New York : 1966.

1849. Doolard, D. Quatre mois chez les Comitadjis. - Paris : 1932.

1850. Fatu, M. * Spalatelu, I. Garda de fier. - Bucharest : 1971.

1851. Frey, C.W. Yugoslav nationalism and the question of limited sovereignty. Winter 1977. p. 79-108. East European Quarterly. ; 10.

1852. Jurjevic, M. Ustasha under the southern cross. - Melbourne : Jurjevic, 1973. 71 p

1853. Kovacevic, S. Hronologija anti-jugoslovenskog terorizma 1960-1980. - Beograd : ISRO "Privredno finansijski vodic", 1981. 151 p
On Croat terrorism in Jugoslavia.

1854. Lespart, M. Les Oustachis : Terroristes de l'ideal. - Paris : Editions de la pensee moderne, 1976. 282 p
On Croat terrorism.

1855. Londres, A...Les Comitadjis; ou, le terrorisme dans les Balkans. - Paris : A. Michel, 1932. 250 p
English ed.: Terror in the Balkans, London: Constable, 1935.

1856. Maslic, A. Terrorism by fascist emigration of Yugoslav origin. March 1981. p. 49-64. Socialist Thought and Practice. ; 21.

1857. Neuweiler, M. Zwischen Galgen und Kreuz : Das Leben des rumanischen Freiheitskampfers Oliviu Beideanu. Schweizerisches Ost-Institut, 1979. 294 p

1858. Papanace, C. La genesi ed il martirio del Movimento Legionario Rumenio. 1959.

1859. Sburlati, C. Codreanu, il capitano. - Roma : 1970.

1860. Tomasic, D. The Ustasha movement. - New York : Kennicat Press, 1949. p. 1337-1341.
In: Slavonic Encyclopedia

1861. Vidovic, M. La face cachee de la lune : Ou, cinq ans dans les prisons de Tito. - Paris : Nouvelles Editions Latines, 1983.

1862. Wuerthe, F. Die Spur fuehrt nach Belgrad. - Vienna : Molden Verlag, 1975.
On Sarajewo, 1914 and Serbian secret service behind the student terrorists.

1863. Zwerin, M. A case for the balkanization of practically everyone. The new nationalism. - London : Wildwood House, 1976. 188 p

H.3. Middle East

1864. Al-Khashaf. Arab terrorism, American style. - Gaithersburg, Md. : IACP, 1974.

1865. Alexander, Y. Terrorism in the Middle East: a new phase?. 1978. p. 115-117. Washington Quarterly. ; 1.

1866. Barakak, H. Lebanon in strife. - London : University of Texas Press, 1977.

1867. Bassiouni, M.C. * Fisher, E.M. An Arab-Israeli conflict: real and apparent issues : An insight into its future from the lessons of the past. 1970. p. 399-465. St. John's Law Review. ; 44.

1868. Bulloch, J. Death of a country : Civil war in Lebanon. - London : Weidenfeld and Nicolson, 1977.

1869. Chomsky, N. Middle East terrorism and the American ideological system. Summer 1986. p. 1-28. Class. ; 28:1.

1870. Crawshaw, N. The Cyprus revolt : The origins, development and aftermath of an international dispute. - London : Allen and Unwin, 1978.

1871. Dam, N.van The struggle for power in Syria. - London : 1981.

1872. Dan, U. Etsba elohim : Sodot ha-milbaham ba-terror. - Ramat Gan : Masadah, 1976. 231 p

1873. DeVore, R.M. The Arab-Israeli conflict : A historical, political, social and military bibliography. - Santa Barbara, Calif. : ABC-Clio, 1976. 273 p. War/Peace Series

1874. Ehrlich, T. Cyprus, the warlike isle: origins and elements of the current crisis. 1966. p. 1021-1098. Stanford Law Review. ; 18:5.

1875. Fisher, E.M. * Bassiouni, M.C. Storm over the Arab world. - Chicago : Follett, 1972.

1876. Habash, G. Perche dirottiamo gli aeri. Nov. 1970. Quaderni del Medio Oriente. ; 8.

1877. Halliday, F. Arabia without sultans. - Harmondsworth : Penguin, 1979.

1878. Jansen, G.H. Militant Islam. - London : 1979.

1879. Kazziha, W.W. Revolutionary transformation in the Arab world : Habash and his comrades from nationalism to marxism. - London : Charles Knight, 1975.

1880. Kosut, H. Cyprus, 1946-68. - New York : Facts on File, 1970.

1881. Laffin, J. Fedayeen : The Arab-Israeli dilemma. - New York : The Free Press, 1974. 160 p

1882. Laqueur, W. Confrontation: the Middle East and world politics. - New York : Bantam Books, 1974.

1883. Merari, A. Political terrorism and Middle Eastern instability. - New York : Praeger, 1981. p. 101-112.
In: N. Novik and J. Starr (eds.), Challenges in the Middle East

1884. Miller, L.B. Cyprus: the law and politics of civil strife. - Cambridge : Harvard University Press, 1968.

1885. Mitchell, R. The society of the muslim brothers. - London : 1969.

1886. Mortimer, E. Faith and power : The politics of Islam. - London : 1982.

1887. O'Ballance, E. Language of violence : The blood politics of terrorism. - San Rafael, Calif. : Presidio Press, 1979. 365 p
Concentrating on Fedayeen and Zionist terrorism and their international ramifications.

1888. Osmond, A. Saladin!. - New York : Doubleday, 1976.

1889. Sansing, J. No man is told by God

what is the right way. March 1981. p. 69-70, 73, 75-77. Washingtonian. ; 16. On Hanafi muslims.

1890. Schmidt, D.A. Armageddon in the Middle East. - New York : John Jay, 1974.

1891. Stephens, R. Cyprus: a place of arms. - London : Pall Mall Press, 1966.

1892. Wolf, J.B. Middle Eastern death squads. - Gaithersburg, Md. : IACP, 1980. Update Report. ; 6:4.

1893. Wolf, J.B. The Arab refugee problem. Dec. 1967. p. 352-358. Current History

1894. Wright, R.B. Sacred rage : The crusade of modern Islam. - New York : Linden Press, Simon and Schuster, 1985. 315 p

1895. Yodfat, A. The Soviet Union and the Palestine guerrillas. Febr. 1969. p. 8-17. Mizan

1896. _____ Accessories to terror : The responsibility of Arab governments for the organization of terrorist activities. - Jerusalem : 1973. 47 p. Israel Ministry of Foreign Affairs, Information Division. Middle East Information Series. ; 25.

1897. _____ Arab terrorism : A chronology [1968-1973]. 22 Dec. 1973. p. 43427-43428. Congressional Record. ; 119.

1898. _____ Attentats terroristes et repression : Vague d'agitation confessionelle en Syrie. Oct. 1979. p. 7. Le monde diplomatique
Terrorist assassinations and repression. Wave of religious agitationin Syria.

1899. _____ Chronology: activities of Arab guerrillas since 1968. 1973. p. 43427. Congressional Record. ; 119.

1900. _____ Record of Arab terrorism. 25-27 Febr. 1975. p. 4306-4307, 4521-4522, 4753. Congressional Record. ; 121.

1901. _____ Terrorism in the Middle East. 1974. p. 373-421. Akron Law Review. ; 7.

1902. _____ The Soviet attitude to the Palestine problem. 1972. p. 187-212. Journal of Palestine Studies. ; 2.

H.3.1. Israel

1903. Aines, R.C. The Jewish underground against the British mandate in Palestine. - Schenectady, N.Y. : Union College, 1973. ; Thesis

1904. Bauer, Y. From diplomacy to resistance: a history of jewish Palestine, 1939-1945. - Philadelphia : Jewish Publication Society, 1970.

1905. Bell, J.B. The long war: Israel and the Arabs since 1946. - Englewood Cliffs, N.J. : Prentice Hall, 1969.

1906. Blechman, B.M. The impact of Israel's reprisals on behavior of the bordering Arab nations directed at Israel. June 1972. p. 155-191. Journal of Conflict Resolution. ; 16.

1907. Borisov, J. Palestine underground; the story of Jewish resistance. - New York : Judea Publ., 1947.

1908. Breener, Y.S. The Stern gang 1948. Oct. 1965. Middle Eastern Studies

1909. Chomsky, N. A proposito di Entebbe. Il terrorismo civilizzato. 1976. p. 731-734. Il ponte. ; 32:7-8.

1910. Clarke, T. By blood and fire : The attack on the King David Hotel. - New York : Putnam, 1981.

1911. Cohen, G. Women of violence: memoirs of a young terrorist, 1943-1948. - London : Hart-Davis, 1966.
On Lehi.

1912. Davis, M. Jews fight too!. - New York : Jordan, 1945.

1913. Dekel, E. (pseud. Krasner). Shai: historical exploits of Haganah intelligence. - New York : Yoseloff, 1959.

1914. Dinstein, Y. Terrorism and wars of liberation: an Israeli perspective of the Arab-Israeli conflict. - Springfield, Ill. : Thomas, 1975. p. 155-172.
In: M.C. Bassiouni (ed.), International terrorism and political crimes

1915. Downing, D. * Herman, G. War without end, peace without hope. Thirty years of the Arab-Israeli conflict. - London : New English Library, 1978. 288 p

1916. Eisenberg, D. * Dan, U. * Landau, E. The Mossad - inside stories : Israel's secret intelligence service. - New York : Paddington Press, 1978. 272 p

1917. Frank, G. Le groupe Stern attaque. - Paris : Laffont, 1963.

1918. Frank, G. The deed : The assassination in Cairo during World War II of Lord Moyne. - New York : Simon and Schuster, 1963. 319 p
On Stern gang.

1919. Frank, G. The Moyne case: a tragic history. Dec. 1945. p. 64-71. Commentary

1920. Friedman, R.I. In the realm of perfect faith : Israel's Jewish terrorists. 12 Nov. 1985. p. 16-22. Village Voice. ; 30.

1921. Gazit, S. Risk, glory and the rescue operation. Summer 1981. p. 111-135. International Security. ; 6. On Entebbe.

1922. Goldberg, Y. Haganah or terror. - New York : Hechalutz, 1947.

1923. Groussard, S. The blood of Israel : The massacre of the Israeli athletes, the Olympics, 1972. - New York : Morrow, 1975.

1924. Hirst, D. The gun and the olive branch : The roots of violence in the Middle East. - New York : Harcourt Brace Jovanovich, 1979. 357 p
Traces events from 1921 onwards.

1925. Horowitz, I.L. Israeli ecstasies/-jewish agonies. - New York : Oxford University Press, 1974. 272 p

1926. Horsley, R.A. The Sicarii : Ancient Jewish 'Terrorists'. October 1979. p. 435-458. Journal of Religion. ; 59.

1927. Howe, I. * Gershma, C. Israel, the Arabs and the Middle East. - New York : Quadrangle, 1972.

1928. Inbar, E. Israel and Lebanon: 1975-1982. Spring 1983. p. 39-80. Crossroads. ; 10.

1929. Kanaan, H. Gardomim bi-Netanyah : Parashat shene ha-serjentim ha-Britiyim she-nitly bi-fekudat ha-Irgun hatseva i ha-le umi. - Tel Aviv : Hadar, 1976. 103 p

1930. Katz, D. The lady was a terrorist : During Israel's war of liberation. - New York : Shiloni, 1953. 192 p
On Irgun.

1931. Katz, S. Days of fire : The secret history of the Irgun Zvai Leumi. - Garden City, N.Y. : Doubleday, 1968. 317 p
Memoirs of a member of the Irgun.

1932. Khalidi, W. From haven to conquest. - Beirut : Institute for Palestine Studies, 1971.
Anthology of readings on the history of zionism 1897-1948.

1933. Langer, F. La repressione di Israele contro i Palestinesi. - Milano : Teti, 1976.

1934. Lorch, N. Israels war of independence 1947-1949. - New York : G.P. Putman's Sons, 1961.

1935. Lorch, N. The edge of the sword : Israel's war of independence 1947-1949. - New York : Putnam, 1961. 475 p

1936. Mardor, M. Haganah. - New York : New American Library, 1966.

1937. McCormick, D. The Israeli secret service. - New York : Taplinger, 1978. 318 p

1938. Meridor, Y. Long road to freedom. - New York : United Zionists Revisionists, 1961.

1939. Monteil, V. Secret dossier on Israeli terrorism. - Paris : Guy Authier, 1978. 450 p

1940. Mor, N.Y. Lokame herut Israel. - 2 vols. - Tel Aviv : 1974.
On jewish terrorism in Palestine, 1940s.

1941. Niv, D. Ma'arakhot ha'irgun hazvai halevmi. - 5 vols. - Tel Aviv : 1977.

1942. Nolin, T. La Haganah: l'armee secrete d'Israel. - Paris : Ballard, 1971.

1943. O'Neill, B.E. Israel's counter-insurgency and the Fedayeen. July 1973. p. 452-460. Army Quarterly. ; 53.

1944. O'Neill, B.E. Revolutionary warfare in the Middle East: the Israelis versus the Fedayeen. - Boulder, Colo. : Paladin, 1974. 140 p

1945. Paust, J.J. Selected terroristic claims arising from the Arab-Israeli context. 1974. Akron Law Review. ; 7.

1946. Peeke, J.L. Jewish-zionist terrorism and the establishment of Israel. Naval Postgraduate School, 1977. ; Master's thesis

1947. Rokach, L. Israel's sacred terrorism. - Belmont, Mass. : Association of Arab-American University Graduates Press, 1980.

1948. Sacher, H. Israel: the establishment of a state. - London : Weidenfeld, 1952.

1949. Simon, U. Jewish terror - how did we get it? : An interview with Uriel Simon. Dec. 1984. p. 31-34. Midstream. ; 30.

1950. Slater, L. The pledge. - New York : Simon & Schuster, 1970. 343 p
On Haganah, Irgun.

1951. Stern, A. Bedamai lead tikhi. - Tel Aviv : 1976.

1952. Sykes, C. Cross roads to Israel. - London : 1965.

1953. Yishai, Y. The Jewish Terror Organization : Past or future danger?. 1986. p. 307-332. Conflict. ; 6:4.

1954. _____ Arab thinking on: solving the problem of Israel, terrorism, international relations, human rights, domestic problems. - Jerusalem : 1969. 221 p.
Israel Ministry of Foreign Affairs, Research Division

1955. _____ Chronology of zionist and Israeli terrorism. p. 3-8. Palestine Digest. ; 2.

1956. _____ Dir yassin. 1969. p. 27-30. West Asia Affairs

1957. _____ Israel police annual report. - Jerusalem : 1968-.
Israel Police Headquarters

1958. _____ Israel's counter-terror. March 1973. p. 1-9. Israel and Palestine. ; 19.

1959. _____ Israeli policy towards the Palestinians : 25 years of terrorism. Jan. 1975. p. 23-32. Arab Palestinian Resistance

1960. _____ Israeli terror, 1967-72. 1973. p. 6-22. Arab Palestinian Resistance. ; 5:1.

1961. _____ Tension, terror and blood in the Holy Land. - Damascus : 1955. Palestine Arab Refugees Institution

1962. _____ Terrorism's targets : Democracy, Israel and jews. - New York : Anti-Defamation League of B'nai B'rith, 1981. 36 p. ADL special report

1963. _____ The Palestine Liberation Organization : Liberation of liquidation?. - Jerusalem : 1979.
Israel Information Centre

1964. _____ Who are the terrorists? : Aspects of zionist and Israeli terrorism. - Beirut : Institute for Palestine Studies and the Arab Women's Information Committee., 1972. Monograph Series. ; 33.

1965. _____ Zionist terrorism. - New York : 22 Nov. 1972.
United Nations. United Nations Doc. ; A/c.6/c.876.

H.3.2. Palestine

1966. Abu Lughad, I. Altered realities : The Palestinians since 1967. Autumn 1973. p. 648-669. International Journal. ; 28.

1967. Al-Azm, S.J. Dirasa naqdiya li fikr al-muqawama al-filastiniya. - Beirut : Dar al-auda, 1973.
A critical study of the thought of the Palestinian resistance.

1968. Alexander, Y. * Kittrie, N.N. Crescent and star: Arab-Israeli perspectives on the Middle East conflict. - New York : AMS Press, 1972.

1969. Alexander, Y. The legacy of Palestinian terrorism. - Tel Aviv : 1976. p. 57-64. International Problems. ; 15:3-4.

1970. Aloush, N. Al thawra al filistiniya. - Beirut : 1970.

1971. Ashab, N. To overcome the crisis of the Palestinian resistance. 1972. p. 71-78. World Marxist Review. ; 15:5.

1972. Avineri, S. * (ed.) Israel and the Palestinians: reflections on the clash of two national movements. - New York : St. Martin's, 1971.

1973. Bell, J.B. Arafat's man in the mirror: the myth of the Fedayeen. - London : April 1970. p. 19-24. New Middle East. ; 19.

1974. Bell, J.B. Bab el Mandeb, strategic troublespot. 1973. p. 975-989. Orbis. ; 16.

1975. Bell, J.B. Terror out of Zion: Irgun, Lehi, and the Palestine underground, 1929-1949. - New York : St. Martin's Press, 1977. 359 p

1976. Ben Amon, S. Be-akvot ha-chavlanim. - Tel Aviv : Madim, 1970. 198 p
Following the Arab terrorist.

1977. Ben Porath, Y. Revolution and terror in the Palestinian Communist Party (P.C.P.) 1929-1939. 1968. p. 246-269. Hamizrah hehadash. ; 18:3-4.

1978. Ben Porath, Y. The Palestinian Arab national movement : 1929-1939. Frank Cass, 1977.

1979. Ben-Dor, G. The strategy of terrorism in the Arab-Israel conflict: the case of the Palestinian guerrillas. - Jerusalem : Hebrew University, Leonard Davis Institute for Inter-national Relations, 1979. p. 126-165.
In: Y. Evron (ed.), International violence: terrorism, surprise and control

1980. Bishop, V.F. The role of political terrorism in the Palestinian resistance movement: June 1967-October 1973. - New York : Dekker, 1979. p. 323-350.
In: M. Stohl (ed.), The politics of terrorism

1981. Brown, N. Palestinian nationalism and the Jordanian state. Sept. 1970. p. 370-378. World Today. ; 26.

1982. Bruzousky, M.A. The P.L.O. and Israel. August 1976. p. 64-71. Contemporary Review. ; 229.

1983. Cetiner, Y. El-Fatah. - Istanbul : May Yazinlari, 1970.

1984. Chailand, G. The Palestinian resistance. - Baltimore : Penguin, 1972.

1985. Charters, D.A. Insurgency and counter-insurgency in Palestine 1945-1947. University of London, 1980. ; Unpubl. Ph.D. dissertation

1986. Churba, J. Fedayeen and the Middle East crisis. - Maxwell, Ala. : Air University, 1969.

1987. Cobban, H. The Palestinian Liberation Organisation. California University Press, 1984.

1988. Colebrook, J. Israel with terrorists. July 1974. p. 30. Commentary. ; 58:1.

1989. Cooley, J.K. China and the Palestinians. 1972. p. 19-34. Journal of Palestinian Studies. ; 1:2.

1990. Cooley, J.K. Green March, Black September: the story of the Palestinian Arabs. - London : Frank Cass, 1973. 263 p
Author is correspondent for the Christian Science Monitor and ABC inBeirut.

1991. Cooley, J.K. Moscow faces a Palestinian dilemma. 1970. p. 32-35. Mid East. ; 11:3.

1992. Curtis, M. * Neyer, J. * Waxman, C.I. * Pollack, A. The Palestinians: people, history, politics. - New Brunswick, N.J. : Transaction Books, 1975. 27 7 pContains a chronology of Arab terrorist acts.

1993. Davis, U. * Mack, A. * Javal-Davis, N. * (eds.) Israel and the Palestinians. - London : 1975.

1994. Denoyan, G. El-Fatah parle: les palestiniens contre Israel. - Paris : Albin Michel, 1970.

1995. Dethoor, N. Le reveil de la Palestine. 1969. p. 13-16. Croissance de jeunes nations

1996. Diskin, A. Trends in intensity variation of Palestinian military activity: 1967-1978. June 1983. p. 335-348. Canadian Journal of Political Science. ; 16.

1997. Dobson, Chr. Black September: its short, violent history. - New York : MacMillan, 1974.

1998. Dyad, A. My home, my land : A narrative of the Palestinian struggle. - New York : 1981.

1999. Ellenberg, E.S. The PLO and its place in violence and terror. - Westport, Conn. : Greenwood Press, 1976. p. 165-176.
In: M.H. Livingston et al. (eds.), International terrorism in the contemporary world

2000. Francos, A. Les palestiniens. - Paris : Julliard, 1970.

2001. Franjieh, S. How revolutionary is the Palestinian resistance? : A marxist interpretation. 1972. p. 52-60. Journal of Palestine Studies. ; 1.

2002. Ganahl, J. Time, trial, and terror: an analysis of the Palestinian guerrilla revolution. - Maxwell, Ala. : Air War College, 1975. 87 p

2003. Guldescu, S. Behind the scenes of the Jordanian civil strife. Summer 1971. p. 250-260. Queen's Quarterly. ; 78.

2004. Hamid, R. What is the P.L.O.?. Summer 1975. p. 90-109. Journal of Palestine Studies. ; 4.

2005. Harkabi, Y. Fedayeen action and Arab strategy. - London : IISS, 1968. 23 p. Adelphi Papers. ; 53.

2006. Harkabi, Y. Palestinians and Israel. - Jerusalem : Keter Publishing House, 1974.

2007. Heradstveit, D. A profile of the Palestine guerrillas. 1972. p. 13-36. Cooperation and Conflict. ; 7:1.

2008. Heradstveit, D. Nahost-Guerillas : Eine politikologische Studie. - Berlin : Verlag Arno Spitz, 1973. 261 p

2009. Hoffman, B. Recent trends in Palestinian terrorism. - Santa Monica, Calif. : RAND, 1985. 19 p

2010. Hoffman, B. The plight of the Phoenix : The PLO since Lebanon. Spring 1985. p. 5-17. Conflict Quarterly. ; 5.

2011. Howley, D.C. The U.N. and the Palestinians. - New York : Exposition Press, 1975. 168 p

2012. Hudson, M.C. Developments and setbacks in the Palestinian resistance movement. Spring 1972. p. 64-84. Journal of Palestine Studies. ; 1.

2013. Hudson, M.C. The Palestinian Arab resistance movement: its significance in the Middle East crisis. Summer 1969. p. 291-301. Middle East Journal. ; 23.

2014. Hudson, M.C. The Palestinian factor in the Lebanese civil war. Summer 1978. p. 261-278. Middle East Journal. ; 32.

2015. Hudson, M.C. The Palestinian resistance movement since 1972. -

Albany : State University of New York Press, 1973. p. 101- 125.
In: A.B. Willard (ed.), the Middle East; quest for an American policy

2016. Hurewitz, J.C. The struggle for Palestine. - New York : Greenwood, 1968.

2017. Hurni, F. Terrorism and the struggle for Palestine. Febr. 1979. p. 14-23. Swiss Review of World Affairs. ; 28.

2018. Hussain, M. The Palestine Liberation Organization: a study in ideology and tactics. - New York : International Publications Service, 1975. 156 p

2019. Hussaini, H.I. * El-Boghdady, F. * (eds.) The Palestinians : Selected essays. - Washington D.C. : Arab Information Centre, 1976.

2020. Hussaini, H.I. The Palestinian problem : An annotated bibliography, 1967-1974. - New York : Arab Information Center, 1974. 81 p

2021. Ibrahim, S. Zur Genesis des palestinensischen Widerstandes 1882-1972. 1973. p. 517-537. Blaetter fuer deutsche und internationale Politik. ; 18:5.

2022. Ijad, A. Heimat oder Tod : Der Freiheitskampf der Palaestinenser. - Econ : 1978. 320 p
By the chief of intelligence of the P.L.O.

2023. Ismael, T.Y. The Arab left. - Syracuse, N.Y. : Syracuse University Press, 1976. 204 p

2024. Issa, M. Je suis un Fedayin. - Paris : Stock, 1976.

2025. Ittayem, M. The Palestine national struggle: the PFLP and the transformation of ideology. - Washington : American University, 1977. ; Ph.D.dissertation

2026. Jabber, F. The Arab regimes and the Palestinian revolution, 1967-71. 1973. p. 79-101. Journal of Palestinian Studies. ; 2:2.

2027. Jabber, F. The Palestinian resistance and inter-Arab politics. - Santa Monica, Calif. : RAND, 1971. 34 p. RAND-paper. ; P-4653.

2028. Jureidini, P.A. * et al. The Palestinian movement in politics. - Lexington, Mass. : Lexington Books, 1976.

2029. Jureidini, P.A. The Palestinian revolution: its organization, ideologies, and dynamics. - Washington, D.C. : American Institute for Research, 1972.

2030. Jureidini, P.A. The relationship of the Palestinian guerrilla movement with the government of Jordan: 1967-70. - Washington : American University, 1975. ; Ph.D. dissertation

2031. Kadi, L.S. * (ed.) Basic political documents: documents of the armed Palestinian resistance movement. - Beirut : Palestine Liberation Organization Research Center, 1969.

2032. Katz, S. Battleground : Fact and fantasy in Palestine. - London-New York : W.H. Allen, 1973. 271 p

2033. Kelidar, A. The Palestine guerrilla movement. Oct. 1976. p. 412-420. World Today. ; 29.

2034. Khader, B. * Khader, N. * (eds.) Textes de la revolution palestinienne, 1968-1974. - Paris : Sindbad, 1975. 350 p

2035. Khalidi, W. * Khadduri, J. * (eds.) Palestine and the Arab-Israeli conflict : An annotated bibliography. - Oxford, Pa. : Institute for Palestine Studies, 1974. 736 p
Bibliography numbering over 4500 entries.

2036. Koestler, A. Promise and fulfilment : Palestine 1917-1949. - London : MacMillan, 1949.

2037. Krosney, H. The PLO's Moscow connection. 24 Sept. 1979. p. 64-72. New York

2038. Kuroda, Y. Young Palestinian commandos in political socialization perspective. Summer 1972. p. 253-270. Middle East Journal. ; 26.

2039. L'Heureux, R.J. Syria and the Palestinian resistance movement 1965-1975. - Wright-Patterson Air Force Base, Ohio : Air Force Institute of Technology, 11 May 1976.

2040. Lagerwist, F.A. Israel and the politics of terrorism in the Middle East. 1981. 143 p

2041. Leibstone, M. Palestine terror : Past present and future: some observations. - Gaithersburg, Md. : IACP., 27 p

2042. Lewis, B. The Palestinians and the PLO: a historical approach. Jan. 1975. p. 32-48. Commentary. ; 59:1.

2043. Lilienthal, A.M. Middle East terror : The double standard. 15 Feb. 1986. p. 277-282. Vital Speeches of the Day. ; 52.

2044. Little, T. The nature of the Palestinian resistance movement. June 1970. p. 157-169. Asian Affairs. ; 57.

2045. Little, T. The new Arab extremists: a view from the Arab world. - London : ISC, May 1970. Conflict Studies. ; 4.

2046. Ma'oz, M. Soviet and Chinese relations with the Palestinian guerilla organizations. - Jeruzalem : The Hebrew University, 1974.
Jerusalem paper on peace problems.

2047. MacIntyre, R.R. The Palestine Liberation Organization : Tactics, strategies and options toward the Geneva peace conference. Summer 1975. p. 65-89. Journal of Palestine Studies. ; 4.

2048. Mark, C.F. Palestinians and Palestine. - Washington, D.C. : Library of Congres, Congressional Research Service, Major Issues System, Foreign Affairs and Nation, 15 Oct. 1976.

2049. Mark, C.F. The Palestine resistance movement. - Washington, D.C. : Legislative Reference Service to the Library of Congress, 17 June 1970. ; Report

2050. Matekolo, I. Droit vers la mort: Septembre Noir. 1974. p. 121-131. Historama. ; 270.

2051. Merari, A. PLO. - Jerusalem : Carta, 1983. 31 p

2052. Moore, J.N. * (ed.) The Arab-Israeli conflict : Readings and documents. - 2 vols. - Princeton, N.J. : Princeton University Press, 1974.

2053. Moshe, B. * (ed.) Issues and analysis : Arab terror vs. pioneering. - Jerusalem : World Zionist Organization.,

2054. Mury, G. Schwarzer September : Analysen, Aktionen und Dokumente. - Berlin : Wagenbach, 1974. 127 p

2055. Muslik, M.Y. Moderates and rejectionists within the Palestine Liberation Organization. Spring 1976. p. 127-140. Middle East Journal. ; 30.

2056. Nakleh, E.A. The anatomy of violence: theoretical reflections of Palestinian resistance. Spring 1971. p. 180-200. Middle East Journal. ; 25.

2057. Nisan, M. PLO messianism : Diagnosis of a modern gnostic sect. 1984. p. 299-312. Terrorism. ; 7:3.

2058. O'Ballance, E. Arab guerrilla power, 1967-1972. - London : Faber, 1972. 246 p

2059. O'Neill, B.E. Armed struggle in Palestine : An analysis of the Palestinian guerrilla movement. - Boulder, Colo. : Westview Press, 1978. 320 p

2060. O'Neill, B.E. Revolutionary warfare in the Middle East : An analysis of the Palestinian guerrilla movement 1967-1972. University of Denver, 1972. ; Unpublished Ph.D. dissertation

2061. Pachter, H. Who are the Palestinians?. 1975. p. 387-395. Dissent. ; 22:4.

2062. Peled, M. The question of Arab terrorism. 1970. p. 18-24. Commentary. ; 20:6.

2063. Pipes, D. How important is the PLO?. April 1983. p. 17-25. Commentary

2064. Plascov, A. A Palestinian state? : Examining the alternatives. - London : IISS, 1981.

2065. Poupard, O. La revolution palestinienne et l'etat palestinien. 1975. p. 475-492. Politique etrangere. ; 40:5.

2066. Price, D.L. Jordan and the Palestinians : The P.L.O.'s prospects. - London : ISC, Dec. 1975. p. 1-20. Conflict Studies. ; 66.

2067. Pryce-Jones, D. The face of defeat: Palestinian refugees and guerrillas. - London : Weidenfeld & Nicholson, 1972. 179 p

2068. Quandt, W.B. Palestinian nationalism : Its political and military dimensions. - Santa Monica, Calif. : RAND, 1971. 132 p. RAND report. ; R-782-ISA.

2069. Quandt, W.D. * Jabber, F. * Lesch, A.M. The politics of Palestinian nationalism. - Berkeley : University of California Press, 1973. 234 p

2070. Ribet, S. Il nodo del conflitto libanese. Tra resistenza palestinese e destra maronita. - Torino : Claudiana, 1977.

2071. Rouleau, E. Abou Iyad: palestinien sans patrie : Entretiens avec Eric Rouleau. - Paris : Fayolle, 1978. 360 p

2072. Rubner, M. * (comp.) Middle East conflict from October 1973 to July 1976 : A selected bibliography. - Los Angeles : Center for the Study of Armament and Disarmament, California State University, 1977. 82 p. Political Issues Series. ; 4:4.

2073. Said, E.W. The question of Palestine. - New York : Times Books, 1979. 256 p

2074. Sayegh, A. Palestine and Arab nationalism. - Beirut : Palestine Liberation Organization Research Center.,

2075. Sayigh, R. Palestinians, from peasants to revolutionaries : A people's history recorded from interviews with camp Palestinians in Lebanon. - London : Zed, 1979. 206 p

2076. Schiff, Z. * Rothstein, R. Fedayeen: guerrillas against Israel. - New York : David McKay, 1972. 246 p

2077. Scully, E. The PLO's growing

Latin American base. - Washington, D.C. : Heritage Foundation, 1983. 8 p

2078. Sharabi, H. Liberation or settlement : The dialects of the Palestinian struggle. Winter 1973. p. 33-48. Journal of Palestine Studies. ; 2.

2079. Sharabi, H. Palestinian guerrillas: their credibility and effectiveness. - Washington, D.C. : Georgetown University Center for Strategic and Internal Studies, 1970. Ca. 55 p ; Supplementary Papers

2080. Sherman, A. The Palestinians : A case of mistaken national identity?. March 1971. p. 104-114. World Today. ; 27.

2081. Sobel, L.A. * (ed.) Palestinian impasse: Arab guerrillas and international terror. - New York : Facts on File, 1977.

2082. Staieh, E. The Jordanian-Palestinian civil war 1970. Jan.-March 1974. p. 42-59. India Quarterly. ; 30.

2083. Stanley, B. Fragmentation and national liberation movements : The P.L.O. Winter 1979. p. 1033-1055. Orbis. ; 22.

2084. Stetler, R. * (ed.) Palestine: the Arab-Israeli conflict. - Palo Alto, Calif. : Ramparts Press, 1974.

2085. Stol, A. Zwarte September : Het relaas van de mysterieuze organisatie die bloedige terreuracties ondertekent met de naam Zwarte September. - Baarn : Meulenhoff, 1974.
On Black September.

2086. Syrkin, M. Political terrorism - or plain murder?. Nov. 1972. p. 3-11. Midstream. ; 18:9.

2087. Tophoven, R. Fedayin - Guerilla ohne Grenzen : Geschichte, soziale Struktur und politische Ziele der palaestinensischen Widerstands-Organisationen. Die israelische Konter-Guerilla. - Muenchen : Bernard & Graefe, 1975. 159 p

2088. Tophoven, R. Guerillas in Nahost : Aufstieg und Schicksal der palaestinensischen Widerstands- Organisationen. 1972. p. 3-45. Aus Politik und Zeitgeschichte. ; 8.

2089. Tophoven, R. The Palestinians and the network of international terrorism. - Rockville, Md. : National Criminal Justice Reference Service, Law Enforcement Assistance Administration, Department, 1979. p. 37-44.
In: M. Kravitz (ed.), International summaries. A collection of selected translations in law enforcement and criminal justice, vol. 3

2090. Wilson, B.A. Conflict in the Middle East: the challenge of the Palestinian movement. - Washington, D.C. : American University, Center for Research in Social Systems, Jan. 1969.

2091. Wilson, B.A. Palestinian guerrilla movements. - Washington, D.C. : American University, Center for Research in Social Systems, 1969.

2092. Wilson, R.D. Cordon and search. - Aldershot : Gale and Polden, 1949.

2093. Wise, C.D. The impact of Palestinian terrorism on the Arab/Israeli conflict. The University of Oklahoma, 1980. ; Ph.D. dissertation

2094. Wolf, J.B. A Mideast profile: the cycle of terror and counterterror. Nov. 1972. International Perspectives

2095. Wolf, J.B. Black September : A description of an international terrorist organization and an assessment of its implications for urban law enforcement agencies of the United States. - New York : John Jay College of Criminal Justice, 1974. ; Master's thesis no. 395

2096. Wolf, J.B. Black September: militant Palestinianism. 1973. p. 8-37. Current History. ; 64:377.

2097. Wolf, J.B. Palestinian resistance movement. Jan. 1971. p. 26-31. Current History

2098. Woods jr, S.R. The Palestinian guerrilla organization : Revolution or terror as an end. - Carlisle Barracks, Pa. : U.S. Army War College, 1973. 80 p

2099. Yaari, E. Strike terror : The story of Fatah. - New York : Sabra Books, 1970

2100. Yaari, E. The decline of Al-Fatah. May 1971. p. 3-12. Midstream

2101. Yahalom, D. File on Arab terrorism. - Jerusalem : Carta, 1973.

2102. Yahalom, Y. Arab terror. - Tel Aviv : World Labour Zionist Movement, 1969.

2103. Yaniv, A. P.L.O.: a profile. - Jerusalem : Israel Universities Study Group for Middle East Affairs, 1974. 39 p

2104. Yedlin, R. The manifesto of the Popular Democratic Front of the Liberation of Palestine. 1971. p. 30-37. Hamizrah Hehadash. ; 21:1.

2105. _____ Aims of the Palestinian resistance movement with regard to the jews. - Beirut : Palestine Research Center, 1970. 14 p.
Fifth of June Society

2106. _____ Arab documents on Pales-

2106. _____ Arab documents on Palestine and the Arab-Israeli conflict. Spring 1977. p. 178-197. Journal of Palestine Studies. ; 6.

2107. _____ Arab terrorism. 1969. p. 13-16. Jewish Frontier. ; 36.

2108. _____ De PLO en terreur in Europa. - Den Haag : CIDI, 1981.

2109. _____ Europe and the PLO. - New York : Anti-defamation League of B'nai B'rith, 1980. 37 p

2110. _____ La revolution palestinienne et les juifs. - Paris : Editions de Minuit, 1970.
El Fath

2111. _____ Nassers terror gangs: the story of the Fedayeen. - Jerusalem : Ministry for Foreign Affairs, 1956.

2112. _____ P.L.O. and Palestinian-inspired terrorism, 1982-1985 : Th continuing record of violence. - New York : Anti-defamation League of B'nai B'rith, 1985. ca. 32 p

2113. _____ Palestine : Crisis and liberation. - Havanna : Tricontinental, 1970. 223 p

2114. _____ Periodicals and pamphlets published by the Palestinian Commando Organizations. Autumn 1971. p. 136-151. Journal of Palestine Studies. ; 1.

2115. _____ Resistance issue. May 1969. p. 3-55. Arab World. ; 15.

2116. _____ Scope and limit of a Fedayeen consensus. 1970. p. 1-8. Wiener Library Bulletin

2117. _____ Since Jordan: the Palestinian Fedayeen. - London : Sept. 1973. ISC. Conflict Studies. ; 38.

2118. _____ Terrorism, settlements and Palestinians. Autumn 1984. p. 6-22. Present Tense. ; 12.

2119. _____ The activities of the Hagana, Irgun and Stern bands. - New York : Palestine Liberation Organization.,

2120. _____ The Palestinian issue in the Middle East effort : Hearings. - 94t Cong., 1st sess. - Washington, D.C. : GPO, 1975. 293 p.
U.S. Congress, House, Committee on International Relations, Subcommittee on Investigation

2121. _____ The Sandinistas and Middle Eastern radicals. - Washington, D.C. : U.S. Dept. of State, 1985. 19 p

2122. _____ The savage kinship: a chronology of the use of violence for political ends in Arab countries. - Jerusalem : Carta, 1973.

H.3.3. Middle East, other countries

2123. Ahmed, F. The Turkish guerrillas : Symptoms of a deeper malaise. 1973. New Middle East. ; 55.

2124. Al-Kubeissi, B. Storia del movimento dei nazionalisti arabi. - Milan : Jaca, 1977.

2125. Alastos, D. Cyprus guerillas: Grivas, Makarios, and the British Doros Alastos. - London : Heinemann, 1960.

2126. Alexander, Y. * Nanes, A. * (eds.) The United States and Iran : A documentary history. - Frederick, Md. : University Publications of America, 1980.

2127. Batatu, H. The old social classes and the revolutionary movements in Iraq : A study of Iraq's old landed and commercial classes and of its communists, Ba'thists, and free officers. - Princeton : Princeton University Press, 1978.

2128. Benazech, Y. Les terroristes de l'esperance : Chroniques de la resistance dans le Iran. - Albi : 1985.

2129. Berberoglu, B. Turkey : The crisis of the neo-colonial system. Winter 1981. p. 277-291. Race and Class. ; 22.

2130. Byford-Jones, W. Grivas and the story of EOKA. - London : Robert Hayle, 1959.

2131. Chamie, J. The Lebanese civil war : An investigation into the causes. Winter 1976-1977. p. 171-188. World Affairs. ; 139.

2132. Chamoun, C. Crise au Libanon. - Beirut : 1977.

2133. Crouzet, F. Le conflict de Cypre, 1946-1959. - 2 vols. - Bruxelles : Brylant, 1973. 1187 p. Etudes de cas de conflicts internationaux. ; 4.

2134. Deeb, M. The Lebanese civil war. - New York : Praeger, 1979. 150 p

2135. Desjardins, T. Le martyre du Liban. - Paris : Librairie Plon-SAS Production, 1976.

2136. Durrell, L. Bitter lemons. - London : 1959.
Cyprus, 1950's EOKA.

2137. Fay, J.R. Terrorism in Turkey : Threat to NATO's troubled ally. April 1981. p. 16-26. Military Review. ; 61.

2138. Foley, Ch. * Scoble, W.I. The struggle for Cyprus. - Stanford, Calif. : Hoover Institution Press, 1975. 193 p
Journalistic narrative of the Grivas campaign, 1955-1960, and aftermath.

2139. Foley, Ch. Island in revolt. - London : Longmans, 1962. 248 p
Cyprus 1955-1959.

2140. Foley, Ch. Legacy of strife : Cyprus from rebellion to civil war. - Harmondsworth : Penguin, 1964.

2141. Franzius, E. History of the order of assassins. - New York : Funk & Wagnalls, 1969.
On 11th century terrorist movement of Hasan Sabba in northwest Persia.

2142. Gabriel, P. In the ashes : The story of Lebanon. - Ardmore, Pa. : Whitmore Publishing, 1978. 259 p

2143. Gavin, R.J. Aden under British rule, 1839-1967. - London : C. Hurst and Co., 1975. 472 p

2144. Gourlay, B.I.S. Terror in Cyprus. 1959. Marine Corps Gazette. ; 8/9.

2145. Haley, E. * Snider, L. * Cooley, J. Lebanon in crisis. Syracuse University, 1979.

2146. Heikal, M. The return of the ayatollah. - London : 1982.

2147. Hodgson, M.G.S. The order of assassins. - The Hague : 1955.
On 11th century islamic sect.

2148. Ismail, A.F. How we liberated Aden. April 1976. Gulf Studies

2149. Jazani, B. Armed struggle in Iran. - London : Iran Committee, 1977. 143 p
By a member of the marxist-leninist Siahkal killed in 1975.

2150. Johnson, H.O. Recent opposition movements in Iran. - Salt Lake City : University of Utah, 1975. ; Unpubl. master's thesis

2151. Kelidar, A. * Burrell, M. Lebanon: the collapse of a state. Regional dimensions of the struggle. - London : ISC, 1976. Conflict Studies. ; 74.

2152. Khalidi, W. Conflict and violence in the Lebanon. - Cambridge, Mass. : Harvard University Press, 1979.

2153. Krahenbuhl, M. Political kidnappings in Turkey 1971-72. - Santa Monica, Calif. : RAND, 1977.

2154. Kurz, A. * Merari, A. ASALA : Irrational terror or political tool. - Tel Aviv : Tel Aviv University, 1985. 118 p. Jaffee Center for Strategic Studies. ; 2.
On Armenian terrorism.

2155. Landau, J.M. Radical politics in modern Turkey. - Leiden : E.J. Brill, 1974.

2156. Lewis, B. The assassins : A radical sect in islam. - London : Weidenfeld & Nicholson, 1967.
On the 11th century order of assassins.

2157. Mackenzie, K. Turkey after the storm and Turkey under the generals. - London : ISC, 1974.

2158. Mackenzie, K. Turkey under the generals. - London : ISC, 1981. 31 p. Conflict Studies. ; 126.

2159. Markides, K. The rise and fall of the Cyprus republic. - New Haven, Conn. : Yale University Press, 1977.

2160. Motley, J.B. Beirut : A terrorist nightmare revisited. 1986. Terrorism

2161. Nalbadian, L. The Armenian revolutionary movement. - Berkeley : 1963.

2162. Ottaway, D.B. Syria connection to terrorism probed : 'New and very disturbing' links emerge. 1 June 1986. A1, A24. Washington Post

2163. Owen, R. * (ed.) Essays on the crisis in Lebanon. - London : Ithaka Press, 1976.

2164. Paget, J. Last post Aden, 1964-67. - London : Faber, 1969.
On terrorist campaign which forced Great Britain out of South Jemen.

2165. Pipes, D. Death to America in Lebanon. March/April 1985. p. 3-9. Middle East Insight. ; 4.

2166. Pipes, D. Hostages are snarled in Iran's factionalism. 8 Oct. 1980. Los Angeles Times

2167. Pipes, D. More Americans may die in Lebanon. 27 Jan. 1985. New York Times

2168. Pipes, D. Undeclared war : Iranian terrorism hijacks US influence. 7 and 14 Jan. 1985. New Republic

2169. Price, D.L. Oman : Insurgency and development. - London : ISC, 1975.

2170. Reilly, D.E. Urban guerrillas in Turkey: causes and consequences. - Carlisle Barracks, Penn. : Army War College, 1972. 62 p

2171. Roth, J. * Taylan, Y. Die Turkei : Republik unter Wolfen. - Bornheim : Lamuv-Verlag, 1981. 212 p

2172. Said, E.W. Iran. March-April 1980. p. 23-33. Columbia Journalism Review

2173. Salibi, K. Cross roads to civil war : Lebanon 1958-76. - New York/London

: 1976.

2174. Salinger J. America held hostage : The secret negotiations. - Garden City, N.Y. : Doubleday, 1981. Iran 1978-1981.

2175. Schiller, D.Th. Der Buergerkrieg in Libanon : Entstehung, Verlauf, Hintergrunde. - Munich : 1979.

2176. Sick, G. All fall down : America's tragic encounter with Iran. - New York : Random House, 1985. 366 p

2177. Sim, R. Kurdistan : The search for recognition. - London : ISC, 1980. Conflict Studies. ; 124.

2178. Stempel, J.D. Inside the Iranian revolution. Indiana University Press, 1981.

2179. Szyliowicz, J. A political analysis of student activism : The Turkish case. - Beverly Hills, Calif. : 1972.

2180. Toynbee, A.J. Armenian atrocities : The murder of a nation. - London : 1915. 119 p

2181. Trelford, D. * (ed.) Siege: six days at the Iranian embassy. - London : MacMillan, 1980.

2182. Vallaud, P. Le Liban au bout du fusil. - Paris : Hachette, 1976.

2183. Vocke, H. The Lebanese civil war : Its origins and political dimensions. - London : C. Hurst and Co., 1978. 100 p On 1975-1976 civil war. U.S.ed.: New York, St. Martin's.

2184. Volsky, D. The Beirut crime. 1973. p. 12-13. New Times. ; 16.

2185. Wolf, J.B. Lebanon : The politics of survival. Jan. 1972. p. 20-25. Current History

2186. Zabih, S. Aspects of terrorism in Iran. Sept. 1982. p. 39-53. Annals of the American Academy of Political and Social Science. ; 463.

2187. _____ Armenian terrorism and the Paris trial : Views and evaluation of Ankara University. - Ankara : Directorate of Press and Information of Ankara University, 1984. 48 p

2188. _____ Armenian terrorism, its supporters, the narcotic connection, the distortion of history. - Ankara : Press, Information, and Public Relations Office, Ankara University, 1984. 294 p ; Symposium on International Terrorism

2189. _____ Griechenland und der Terrorismus auf Zypern. 1957. p. 1-7. British Information. ; 351.

2190. _____ Report of the DOD Commission on Beirut International Airport terrorist act. - Washington : 1983. 141 p ; U.S. Department of Defense,

H.4. Asia

2191. Harrison, S. In Afghanistan's shadow. - New York : 1981.

2192. Shaplen, R. A turning wheel : Three decades of the Asian revolution. - New York : 1979.

H.4.1. Indian Subcontinent

2193. Alles, A.C. Insurgency. - Colombo, Ceylon : 1976.

2194. Anand, V.S. Dhananjay keer veer savarkar. - London : 1967. Indian terrorism.

2195. Bayley, D.H. Violent protests in India: 1900-1960. July 1963. The Indian Journal of Political Science

2196. Camper, F. The Sikh terror plot. April and May 1986. p. 40-42, 62, 64-66, 161; p. Penthouse. ; 17.

2197. Chanda, B. The revolutionary terrorists in Northern India in the 1920's. - Delhi : 1972. In: B.R. Nanda (ed.), Socialism in India

2198. Chatterji, J.C. Indian revolutionaries in conference. - Calcutta : Mukkopadhyay.,

2199. Chopra, P. Three waves of Indian terrorism : A first-hand report on the Naxalite movement. 1970. p. 433-438. Dissent. ; 17:5.

2200. Dasgupta, B. Naxalite armed struggles and the annihilation campaign in rural areas. - Bombay : 1973. p. 4-6. Economic and Political Weekly

2201. Dasgupta, B. The Naxalite movement. - New Delhi : Allied Publishers, 1974.

2202. Gopal, R. How India struggled for freedom. - Bombay : 1967.

2203. Gordon, L.A. Bengal: the nationalist movement, 1876-1940. - New York : Columbia University Press, 1974.

2204. Hale, H.W. Political trouble in India, 1917-1937. - Allahabad : Chugh Publ., 1974. 285 p

2205. Hale, H.W. Terrorism in India, 1917-1936. - Columbus, Ohio : Southern Asia, 1974. Orig. ed.: Simla: Government of India Press, 1937.

2206. Hula, R.C. Political violence and terrorism in Bengal. - New York : Dekker, 1979. p. 351-372. In: M. Stohl (ed.), The politics of terrorism

2207. Indira Devi, M.G. Terrorist movement in South India. - Trivandrum : Kercila Historical Society, 1977.

2208. Kearney, R. Language and the rise of Tamil separatism. May 1978. Asian Survey

2209. Khaleque, A. Terrorism's menace: how to combat it. - Jalpaiguri : A. Wadubat: Jalpaiguri Kohinoor Printing Works, 1932.

2210. Kini, N.G.S. Terrorist world-outlook in the 19th century Western India. 1972. p. 68ff. Political Science Review. ; 11:1.

2211. Lambrick, H.T. The terrorist. - London : Benn, 1972. 246 pIndia: Hur r ebellion 1942-1947.

2212. Laushey, D.M. Bengal terrorism and the marxist left. - Calcutta : Firma K.L. Mukhopadhyay, 1975.

2213. Laushey, D.M. The Bengal terrorists and their conversion to marxism: aspects of regional nationalism in India, 1905-1942. University of Virginia, 1969. 276 p ; Unpubl. dissertation

2214. Manoranjan, M. Revolutionary violence: a study of the maoist movement in India. - New Delhi : Sterling, 1977.

2215. Mitchell, K.L. India without fable. - New York : Alfred A. Knopf, 1942. On 1919ff. Gandhi's Satyagraha and terrorism.

2216. Nath, S. Terrorism in India. - New Delhi : National Publ.House, 1980. 350 p

2217. Nayar, B.R. Violence and crime in India: a quantitative study. - Delhi : MacMillan Co of India, 1975.

2218. Ram, M. Shift in Naxalite tactics. 21 Aug. 1971. Economic and Political Weekly

2219. Ram, M. The urban guerrilla movement in Calcutta. Jan. 1972. Institute for Defence Studies and Analyses Journal

2220. Roy, S. Bharatera baiplabika samgramera itihasa. - Karachi : 1955. India. In Bengali.

2221. Sen, N. Bengal's forgotten warriors. - Bombay : 1945.

2222. Singh, K. A history of the Sikhs. - London : 1966.

2223. Sleeman, J.L. La secte secrete des Thugs. - Paris : Ed. Payot, 1934.

2224. Tapaua, G. The Gandhi murder trial. - London : 1973. 336 p

2225. Vajpeyi, J.N. The extremist movement in India. - Allahabad : 1974.

2226. Weiner, M. Violence and politics in Calcutta. May 1961. p. 275-281. Journal of Asian Studies. ; 20.

2227. Wickramanayake, D. Harijan terror in India. 1971. p. 17-20. Plural Societies. ; 6:3.

2228. Williams, L.F.R. Pakistan under challenge. - London : 1975.

2229. _____ Report. - Calcutta : Superintendent Government Printing Office, 1918. Sedition Committee Gives a narrative of the major terroristic events in Bengal, 1906-1916.

2230. _____ Terror in East Pakistan. Karachi Publications, 1971.

H.4.2. South-East Asia and China

2231. Aerker, S.R. * Krause, J.R. Communist terrorist campaign: Thailand-Malaysian frontier. 1966. p. 39-46. Military Review. ; 4:6.

2232. Averch, H. * Koehler, J. The HUK rebellion in the Philippines : A quantitative approache. - Santa Monica, Calif. : RAND, 1970.

2233. Baclagon, U.S. The Huk campaign in the Philippines. - Manila : 1960.

2234. Barber, N. The war of the running dogs. - London : 1971.

2235. Brass, P. * Franda, M. * (eds.) Radical politics in South Asia. - Cambridge, Mass. : M.I.T. Press, 1973.

2236. Caldwell, M. * (ed.) Ten years' military terror in Indonesia. - Nottingham : Spokesman Books, 1975.

2237. Chesneaux, J. * (ed.) Popular movements and secret societies in China, 1840-1950. - Stanford : 1972.

2238. Clutterbuck, R.L. Riots and revolution in Singapore and Malaya 1945-1963. - London : Faber and Faber, 1973.

2239. Clutterbuck, R.L. The long, long war : The emergency in Malaya 1948-1960. - New York : Praeger, 1966.

2240. Davison, W.Ph. Some observations on Viet Cong operations in the villages. Sept. 1968. p. 2. RAND Abstracts. ; RM 5367.

2241. Dentan, R.K. The Semai : A nonviolent people of Malaya. - New York : Rinehart & Winston, 1968.

2242. Duke, W.D.H. Operation Metcalff : The story of a raid on a terrorist camp in Malaya. 1953. p. 28-32. Army Quarterly. ; 67:1.

2243. Dunn, J.S. Notes on the current situation in East Timor. Parliament of Australia Legislative Research Service, March 1979.

2244. Fairbairn, G. Revolutionary and communist strategy : The threat to South-East Asia. - London : Faber and Faber, 1968.

2245. Fall, B.B. Street without joy : Insurgency in Indo-China 1946-1963. - London : Pall Mall, 1964.

2246. Fall, B.B. The two Vietnams: a political and military analysis. - New York : Praeger, 1964.

2247. George, T.J.S. Revolt in Mindanao : The rise of islam in Philippine politics. - Oxford : 1980.

2248. Gregor, A.J. * Chang, M.H. Terrorism : The view from Taiwan. 1981. p. 233-264. Terrorism. ; 5:3.

2249. Hanrahan, G.Z. * (ed.) Chinese communist guerrilla warfare tactics. - Boulder, Colo. : Paladin Press, 1974.

2250. Herman, E.S. Atrocities in Vietnam : Myths and realities. Pilgrim Press, 1970.

2251. Hill, H. The Timor story. - Melbourne : 1976.

2252. Hiniker, P.J. Revolutionary ideology and Chinese reality : Dissonance under Mao. - Beverly Hills : 1977.

2253. Jacoby, E.H. Agrarian unrest in Southeast Asia. - New York : 1949.

2254. Joiner, C.A. The politics of massacre : Political processes in South Vietnam. - Philadelphia : Temple University Press, 1974.

2255. Jolliffe, J. East Timor, nationalism and colonialism. University of Queensland Press, 1978.

2256. Jones, A. * et al. Study of threats and terror. - Washington, D.C. : American University, Cress, 1966. Vietnam.

2257. Kerkvliet, J.B. The Huk rebellion: a study of peasant revolt in the Philippines. - Berkeley : University of California Press, 1977.

2258. Kodikara, S.V. The separist Eelam movement in Sri Lanka : An overview. April-June 1981. p. 194-212. India Quarterly. ; 37.

2259. Kohen, A. * Taylor, J. An art of genocide : Indonesia's invasion of East Timor. - London : 1979.

2260. Komer, R.W. Impact of pacification on insurgency in South Vietnam. 1971. p. 48-69. Journal of International Affairs. ; 25:1.

2261. Lobe, T. United States national security policy and aid to the Thai police. University of Denver, 1977.

2262. Mallin, J. * (ed.) Terror in Viet Nam. - Princeton, N.J. : D. van Nostrand, 1966.

2263. Moody, P.R. Opposition and dissent in contemporary China. - Stanford, Calif. : 1977.

2264. Muros, R.L. Communist terrorism in Malaya. 1961. p. 51-57. United States Naval Institute Proceedings. ; 87:10.

2265. Noble, L.G. The Moro National Liberation Front in the Philippines. 1976. p. 405-424. Pacific Affairs. ; 49.

2266. Nuechterlein, D.E. Thailand and the struggle for Southeast Asia. - New York : 1965.

2267. O'Ballance, E. Malaya; the communist insurgent war, 1948-1960. - London : Faber & Faber, 1966.

2268. Pike, D. The kind of war that is Vietnam: people's war with terror as the tool. June 1970. Air Force and Space Digest

2269. Pike, D. The Viet Cong strategy of terror. - Saigon : U.S. Mission, 1970.

2270. Pike, D. Viet Cong: the organization and techniques of the National Liberation Front of South Vietnam. - Cambridge, Mass. : M.I.T. Press, 1966.

2271. Pye, L. Guerrilla communism in Malaya. - Princeton, N.J. : Princeton University Press, 1956.

2272. Randolph, R.S. The Thai insurgency in the later 1970s' conflict. 1980. Conflict. ; 1:2.

2273. Rees, D. North Korea's growth as a subversive center. - London : ISC, . Conflict Studies. ; 28.

2274. Renick, R.O. The emergency regulations of Malaya : Cause and effect. Sept. 1965. p. 1-39. Journal of Southeast Asian History. ; 6:2.

2275. Reynolds, J.A.C. Terrorist activity in Malaya. Nov. 1961. Marine Corps Gazette

2276. Seymour, W.N. Terrorism in Malaya. April 1949. Army Quarterly. ; 17).

2277. Short, A. The communist insurrection in Malaya, 1948-1960. - London : Frederick Muller Ltd., 1975.

2278. Shuja, S.M. Political violence in Southeast Asia : A critical analysis of some models. 1977. p. 48-64. Pakistan Horizon

2279. Shultz, R. The limits of terrorism in insurgency warfare: the case of the Vietcong. Fall 1978. p. 67-91. Polity. ; 11:1.

2280. Tanham, G.K. Communist revolutionary warfare : From Vietminh to the Viet Cong. - New York : 1961.

2281. Tanham, G.K. Trial in Thailand. - New York : 1974.

2282. Thompson, R. Defeating communist insurgency. - New York : Praeger, 1970. Orig. London: Chatto & Windus, 1966.

2283. Turpin, A. New society's challenges in the Philippines. - London : ISC, 1980. Conflict Studies. ; 122.

2284. Yap-Diango, R.T. The Filipino guerrilla tradition. - Manila : 1971.

2285. Zasloff, J.J. Origins of the insurgency in South Vietnam 1954-1960 : The role of the southern Vietminh cadres. - Santa Monica, Calif. : RAND, 1967.

2286. _____ A Viet Cong directive on "repression". - Coral Gables, Florida : University of Miami Press, 1971. p. 31-43.
In: J. Mallin (ed.), Terror and urban guerrillas

2287. _____ La terreur, instrument de pouvoir revolutionaire. April 1971. p. 1-124. l'Ordre francais

2288. _____ Viet Cong use of terror : A study by the United States Mission in Vietnam. - Saigon : 1967. 84 p. U.S. government. Agency for International Development

2289. _____ Vietnam Terrorist Incident Reporting System (TIRS). - Saigon : Military Assistance Command.,

H.4.3. Japan

2290. Beraud, B. La gauche revolutionnaire au Japon. - Paris : Seuil, 1970. 157 p

2291. Boyd jr, J.A. The Japanese Red Army. - Maxwell, Ala. : Air Command and Staff College, Air university, April 1978. Research Report. ; 0200-78. Available as FAR 29106-N AD B028 137L.

2292. Duvila, J. Au Japon la violence sert le pouvoir. July 1972. p. 1069-1084. Revue de defense nationale. ; 28.

2293. Iwakawa, T. Making of a terrorist: suicidal fanaticism of the Japanese Red Army. Jan. 1976. p. 33. Atlas. ; 23.

2294. Kuriyama, Y. Terrorism at Tel Aviv airport and a "New Left" group in Japan. March 1973. p. 336-346. Asian Survey. ; 13:3.
On United Red Army, Japan.

2295. Nishio, H.K. Extraparliamentary activities and political unrest in Japan. - Toronto : 1968. p. 122-137. International Journal. ; 24:1.

2296. Otsuka, B. Rengo sekigun: sono seiritsu kara hokai made. - Tokyo : May 1972. The Shokun. ; 4:5.
On the founding and disintegration of the United Red Army.

2297. Seiffert, J.E. Zengakuren : Universitaet und Widerstand in Japan. - Muenchen : Trikont, 1969. 149 p

2298. Tachibara, T. Chukaku us kakumaru. - 2 vols. - Tokyo : 1975.
On United Red Army and other Japanese terrorist groups.

2299. Takagi, M. Rengo sekigun to shin sayoku undo. - Tokyo : 14 April 1972. Asahi Journal
On the United Red Army and the "New Left".

2300. Taylor, R.W. * Kim, B.S. Violence and change in postindustrial societies : Student protest in America and Japan in the 1960's. - Westport, Conn. : Greenwood Press, 1978. p. 204-222.
In: M.H. Livingston et al. (eds.), International terrorism in the contemporary world

2301. _____ Hijackings by Japan's Red Army. Jan. 1978. p. 8-11. Japan Quarterly

2302. _____ Sekigun. - Tokyo : 1975. Sasho Henshu Committee
pp. 361-484 contain a detailed bibliography on the Japanese United Red Army.

2303. _____ Terror : Behind the Red Army. 26 Nov. 1976. p. 26-31. Asia Week A summary article on the Japanese Red Army.

2304. _____ Tokushu: rengo sekigun jiken no imi suru mono-ningen, kakumei, skukusei. 14 April 1972. p. 4-17. Asahi Journal
Special: the meaning of the U.R.A. incident - man, revolution, and purge.

2305. _____ Uchi geba no rouri. - Tokyo : 1974.
Symposium on United Red Army terrorists.

H.5. Africa, General

2306. **Bozeman, A.B.** Conflict in Africa : Concepts and realities. - Princeton : Princeton University Press, 1976.

2307. **Chaliand, G.** Armed struggle in Africa. - New York/London : 1969.

2308. **Cohen * Jacopetti** Africa addio. - Munich : 1966.
Accounts of violence in Africa, based on documentary movie.

2309. **Grundy, K.W.** Guerrilla struggle in Africa : An analysis and preview. - New York : Grossmann Publ., 1971. 204 p

2310. **Henderson, I * Goodhart, P.** The hunt for Kimathi. - London : 1958.

2311. **Jenkins, B.M.** Urban violence in Africa. 1968. p. 37. American Behavioral Scientist. ; :4.

2312. **Legum, C. * (ed.)** Africa contemporary record. - vol. 1-. - New York : Holmes & Meier, 1969-.

2313. **Mazrui, A.A.** The Third World and international terrorism : Preliminary reflections. April 1985. p. 348-364. Third World Quarterly. ; 7.

2314. **Mazrui, A.A.** Thoughts on assassination in Africa. March 1968. p. 40-58. Political Science Quarterly. ; 83:1.

2315. **Mazrui, A.A.** Violence and thought : Essays on social tensions in Africa. - London : 1969.

2316. **Mitchell, P.** African afterthoughts. - London : 1954.

2317. **Oruka, H.O.** Punishment and terrorism in Africa. - Kampala : East African Literature Bureau, 1976.

2318. _____ Terrorisme en Afrique. - Moscou : Editions du Progres, 1984. 134 p

H.5.1. Northern Africa

2319. **Abbas, F.** Guerre et revolution d'Algerie. - Paris : Julliard, 1962.

2320. **Alleg, H.** Die Folter. - Munich : 1958.
On torture during the French-Algerian war, 1954- 1962, by one of itsvictims, a communist journalist from Algiers.

2321. **Bell, J.B.** Endemic insurgency and international order. The Eritrean experience. Summer 1974. p. 427-450. Orbis. ; 17.

2322. **Beyssade, P.** La guerre d'Algerie 1954-1962. - Paris : Editions Planete 1968. 263 p

2323. **Boutang, P.** La terreur en question. - Paris : Fasquelle, 1958.

2324. **Boyce, F.** The internationalizing of internal war: Ethiopia, the Arabs, and the case of Eritrea. 1972. p. 51-73. Journal of International and Comparative Studies. ; 5.

2325. **Bromberger, S.** Les rebelles algeriens. - Paris : Plon, 1958.

2326. **Buchard, R.** Organisation Armee Secrete. - Paris : Albin Michel, 1963. 203 p

2327. **Campbell, J.F.** Rumblings along the Red Sea: the Eritrean question. April 1970. p. 537-548. Foreign Affairs. ; 48.

2328. **Clark, M.K.** Algeria in turmoil : A history of the rebellion, 1954-58. - New York : Praeger, 1959. 466 p

2329. **Courriere, Y.** La guerre d'Algerie. - 4 vols. - Paris : Fayard, 1968.

2330. **Crenshaw, M.** Revolutionary terrorism : The FLN in Algeria, 1954-1962. - Stanford : Hoover Institution Press, 1978. 178 p

2331. **Duchemin, J.** Histoire du FLN. - Paris : La Table Ronde, 1962. 331 p

2332. **Dumas, A.** Der Krieg in Algerien. - Zollikon : Evang. Verl., 1958. 148 p

2333. **Elsenhans, H.** Frankreichs Algerienkrieg, 1954-1962 : Entkolonisierungsversuch einer kapitalistischen Metropole. Zum Zusammenbruch der Kolonialreiche. - Muenchen : Hanser, 1974. 908 p

2334. **Fanon, F.** Sociologie d' une revolution : L'an V de la revolution algerienne. - Paris : Maspero, 1978. Orig. published in 1959.

2335. Favrod, C.H. La revolution algerienne. - Paris : Maspero, 1959.

2336. Feret, A. * Huy, C. La question de l'Erythree. - Paris : 1979.

2337. Gorce, P.M. de la Histoire de l'O.A.S. en Algerie. Oct. 1962. La Nef

2338. Hamilton, D. Ethiopia's embattled revolutionaries. - London : ISC, 1977. Conflict Studies. ; 82.

2339. Heggoy, A.A. Insurgency and counterinsurgency in Algeria. - Bloomington : Indiana University Press, 1972. 327 p

2340. Henissart, P. Wolves in the city. - New York : Simon & Schuster, 1970. 508 p
Detailed history of the O.A.S.

2341. Horne, A. A savage war of peace: Algeria, 1954-1962. - New York : Viking Press, 1978. 604 p

2342. Humbaraci, A. Algeria : A revolution that failed: a political history since 1954. - London : Pall Mall Press, 1966.

2343. Joesten, J. The Red Hand; the sinister account of the terrorist arm of the French right-wing Ultras" - in Algeria and on the continent. - New York : Abelard-Schuman, 1962. 200 p

2344. Julien, Ch.A. l'Afrique du Nord en marche : Nationalismes musulmans et souverainete francaise. - 3rd ed. - Paris : Julliard, 1972.

2345. Jureidini, P.A. Case studies in insurgency and revolutionary warfare: Algeria 1954-1962. - Washington : American University, 1963.

2346. Keramane, H. La pacification : Livre noir de six annees de guerre en Algerie. - Lausanne : La Cite, 1960. Trad. it.: Milano, Feltrinelli, 1960.

2347. Kessel, P. * Pirelli, G. Le peuple Algerien et la guerre : Lettres et temoignages d'algeriens, 1954-1962. - Paris : Maspero, 1962. 757 p

2348. Khelifa, L. Manuel du militant algerien. Vol. 1. - Lausanne : La Cite Editeur, 1962.

2349. Lebjaoui, M. Bataille d'Alger ou bataille d'Algerie?. - Paris : Gallimard, 1972. 303 p

2350. Lebjaoui, M. Verites sur la revolution algerienne. - Paris : Gallimard, 1970.

2351. Loesch, A. La valise et le cercueil. - Paris : Plon, 1963. 267 p
On O.A.S.

2352. Massu, J. La vraie bataille d'Alger. - Paris : Plon, 1971.

2353. Morlaud, B. * Morlaud, M. Histoire de l'Organisation de l'Armee Secrete. - Paris : Julliard, 1964. 605 p

2354. Nicol, A. La bataille de l'O.A.S. - Paris : Ed. des Sept Couleurs, 1963. 224 p

2355. O'Ballance, E. The Algerian insurrection, 1954-1962. - Hamden : Shoestring, 1967.

2356. Ouzagane, A. Le meilleure combat. - Paris : Julliard, 1962. 307 p
F.L.N.; the revolutionary movement in Algeria.

2357. Plumyene, J. O.A.S. et guerre d'Algerie. - Paris : 1963. p. 261-298. In: J. Plumyene, Les fascismes francais

2358. Quandt, W.B. Revolution and political leadership: Algeria, 1954-1968. - Cambridge, Mass. : MIT-Press, 1969. 313 p

2359. Roy, J. La guerre d'Algerie. - Paris : Julliard, 1960. 215 p
Engl. ed.: The war in Algeria. New York: Grove Press, 1961.

2360. Soustelle, J. Aimee et souffrante Algerie. - Paris : Plon, 1956.
By the French governor-general of Algeria.

2361. Tillion, G. Les ennemis complementaires. - Paris : Minuit, 1960.
On terrorism and counterterrorism in Algeria 1954ff.

2362. Tournoux, J.R. l'Histoire secrete. - Paris : Plon, 1962.
Algeria, OAS.

2363. Wales, G.E. Algerian terrorism. 1969. p. 26-42. Naval War College Review. ; 22:26.

2364. Yacef, S. Souvenirs de la bataille d'Alger. - Paris : Julliard, 1962.

H.5.2. Sub-Saharan Africa

2365. Barnett, D. Karari njama: Mau Mau from within. - London-New York : MacGibbon and Kee, 1966.

2366. Berman, B.J. Bureaucracy and incumbent violence: colonial administration and the origin of the 'Mau Mau' emergency in Kenya. 1976. p. 143-175. British Journal of Political Science. ; 6:2.

2367. Brom, K.L. Blutnacht ueber Afrika. - Frankfurt a.M. : Ammelburg, 1957. 198 p

2368. Buijtenhuijs, R. Le mouvement Mau-Mau, une revolte paysanne et anticoloniale en Afrique noire. - Paris-Den Haag : Mouton, 1971.

2369. Buijtenhuijs, R. Mau-Mau twenty years after : The myth and the survivors. - Paris-Den Haag : Mouton, 1973.

2370. Cabral, A. Die Revolution der Verdammten : Der Befreiungskampf in Guinea-Bissao. - Berlin : Rotbuch Verlag, 1974. 142 p

2371. Corfield, F.D. Historical survey of the origin and growth of Mau Mau. - New York-London : British Information Service-HMSO, 1960.

2372. Efrat, E.S. * (ed.) Introduction to Sub-Saharan Africa. - Lexington-Toronto : Xerox College Publishing, 1973.

2373. Hempstone, I. Rebels, mercenaries, and dividends: the Katanga story. - New York : Praeger, 1962.

2374. Henderson, I. * Goos, Ph. Man hunt in Kenya. - New York : Doubleday, 1958.
On hunt for the Mau Mau leader Dedan Kimathi in Kenya.

2375. Holman, D. Menschenjagd : Der Mau-Mau-Aufstand in Kenia. - Muenchen : Bechtle, 1966. 246 p

2376. Horne, N.S. On patrol against Mau Mau terrorists. 1955. Forces Magazine. ; 3.

2377. Kariuku, J. Mau Mau detainee. - London : Oxford University Press, 1963.

2378. Kenyatta, J. Suffering without bitterness : The founding of the Kenya nation. - Nairobi : East African Publishing House, 1968. 348 p

2379. Krug, W.G. Terror und Gegenterror in British-Ostafrika. 1953. p. 589-594. Aussenpolitik. ; 4:9.

2380. Leakey, L.S.M. Mau Mau and the Kikuyu. - London : Methuen, 1954.

2381. Leigh, I. In the shadows of Mau Mau. - London : 1954.

2382. Maier, F.X. Revolution and terrorism in Mozambique. - New York : American African Affairs Association, 1974. 60 p

2383. Majdalani, F. State of emergency: the full story of Mau Mau. - Boston : Houghton Mifflin, 1963.

2384. Mojekwu, Chr.C. From protest to terror-violence: the African experience. - Westport, Conn. : Greenwood Press, 1978. p. 177-181.
In: M.H. Livingston et al. (eds.), International terrorism in the contemporary world

2385. Moufflet, C. Otages a Kampala. - Paris : Presses de la Cite, 1976.

2386. Muehlmann, W.E. Die Mau Mau Bewegung in Kenya. 1961. p. 56-87. Politische Vierteljahresschrift. ; 2:1.

2387. Reed, D. 111 days in Stanleyville. - New York : Harper & Row, 1965.
Violence in the Congo, 1964.

2388. Rosberg, C.G. * Nottingham, J. The myth of "Mau Mau": nationalism in Kenya. - New York : Praeger, 1966. 427 p

2389. Rothberg, R. * Mazrui, A.A. Protest and power in black Africa. - London : 1970.

2390. Sundiata, I.K. Integrative and disintegrative terror: the case of Equatorial Guinea. - Westport, Conn. : Greenwood Press, 1978. p. 182-194.
In: M.H. Livingston et al (eds.), International terrorism in the contemporary world

2391. Thompson, B. Ethiopia, the country that cut off its head : A diary of the revolution. - London : Robson, 1975.

2392. Wagoner, F.E. Dragon Rouge : The rescue of hostages in the Congo. - Washington : National Defence University, 1980.

2393. Welfling, M.B. Terrorism in Sub-Sahara Africa. - New York : Dekker, 1979. p. 259-300.
In: M. Stohl (ed.), The politics of terrorism

2394. _____ A handbook of anti Mau Mau operations. - Nairobi : Government Printer, 1954.
Kenya, General Headquarters

2395. _____ Repression, violence et terreur : Rebellions au Congo. - Bruxelles : Institut d'Etudes Africaines, 1969.
Centre de Recherche et d'Information socio-politiques

2396. _____ The Mau Mau insurgency : A guerrilla and counter-guerrilla study. 1967. p. 193-222. Columbia Essays in Internal ?. ; 2.

H.5.3. Southern Africa

2397. Ackermann, M.F. Terrorisme in Suid-Afrika. - Pretoria : Instituut vir Strategiese Studies, Universiteit van Pretoria, 1983. 82 p

2398. Brigham, D.T. Blueprint for conflict. - New York : American-African Affairs Association, 1969. 34 p
On terrorism in southern Africa - Rhodesia, South Africa, Mozambique, Angola.

2399. Costa Pinto, L.A. Further research needed to support more effectiviness in combatting Apartheid. 1968. ; U.N.Paper

2400. Davidson, B. * Slovo, J. * Wilkinson, A.R. Southern Africa: the new politics of revolution. - Harmondsworth : Penguin, 1976.

2401. Dorabji, E.V. South African National Congress: change from non-violence to sabotage between 1952 and 1964. University of California, 1979. ; Ph.D. dissertation

2402. Felgas, H.A.E. Os movimentos terroristas de Angola, Guine, Mocambique : Influencia externa. - Lisboa : 1966. 93 p

2403. Felt, E. Urban revolt in South Africa 1960-1964: a case study. - Evanston, Ill. : Northwestern University Press, 1971.

2404. Gibson, R. African liberation movements : Contemporary struggles against white minority rule. - London : Oxford University Press, 1972. 350 p

2405. Gifford, T. South Africa's record of international terrorism. - London : Anti-Apartheid Movement, Stop the War Against Angola and Mozambique, 1981. 15 p

2406. Horrell, M. Terrorism in Southern Africa. - Johannesburg : South African Institute of Race Relations, 1968.

2407. Humbaraci, A. * Mucknik, N. Portugal's African wars: Angola, Guinea Bissao, Mozambique. - London : MacMillan, 1974.

2408. Jacobs, W.D. * et al. Terrorism in Southern Africa : Portents and prospects. - New York : American-African Affairs Association, 1973.

2409. Jakonya, T.J.B. The effects of the war on the rural population of Zimbabwe. April 1980. p. 133-147. Journal of South African Affairs. ; 5.

2410. Janke, P. Southern Africa : New horizons. - London : ISC, 1976.

2411. Kuper, L. The pity of it all : Polarization of racial and ethnic relations. - Minneapolis : University of Minnesota Press, 1979. 302 p

2412. Legum, C. * Modges, T. After Angola: the war over Southern Africa. - London : Rex Collings, 1976.

2413. Lejeune, A. * (comp.) The case for South West Africa. - London : Tom Stacey, 1971.

2414. Mathews, A.S. Terrors of terrorism. Aug. 1974. p. 381. South African Law Journal. ; 91.

2415. Meridor, Y. Long is the road to freedom. - Johannesburg : 1955.

2416. Metrowich, F.R. Communism and terrorism in Southern Africa. - Pretoria : 1969. Occasional Papers of the African Institute of South Africa. ; 25.

2417. Metrowich, F.R. Terrorism in Southern Africa. - Pretoria : African Institute of South Africa, 1973. 79 p

2418. Mondlane, E. The struggle for Mozambique. - Baltimore : Penguin, 1969.

2419. Morris, M. Armed conflict in Southern Africa: a survey of regional terrorisms from their beginnings to the present : With a comprehensive examination of the Portuguese position. - Cape Town : Jeremy Spence, 1974. 371 p

2420. Morris, M.S.L. South African political violence and sabotage, 1 July-31 December 1982. June 1981. - Cape Town, South Africa. : Terrorism Research Centre, 1981. 49 p

2421. Morris, M. Terrorism; the first full account in detail of terrorism and insurgency in Southern Africa. - Cape Town : H. Timmins, 1971. 249 p

2422. Neves, A. Razes do terrorismo em Angola e Mocambique, 1969. - Lisboa : 1970.

2423. Passos, I.de Mocambique a escalada do terror. - Queluz : Literal, 1977. 190 p

2424. Raeburn, M. Black fire : Accounts of the guerrilla war in Rhodesia. - London : J. Friedmann, 1978. 243 p

2425. Rich, P. Insurgency, terrorism and the apartheid system in South Africa. March 1984. p. 68-85. Political Studies. ; 32.

2426. Rudolph, H. Security, terrorism, and torture. - Cape Town : Juta, 1984. 270 p

2427. Shay, R. * Vermaak, Ch. The silent war. - Salisbury : Galaxy Press, 1971. 267 p

2428. Sitte, F. Flammenherd Angola. - Vienna : 1972.

2429. Teixeira, B. The fabric of terror: three days in Angola. - New York : Devin-Adair, 1965.

2430. Venter, A.J. Africa at war. - Old Greenwich, Conn. : Devin-Adair, 1974.

2431. Venter, A.J. Portugal's guerrilla war : The campaign for Africa. - Capetown : John Malherbe, 1973. 220 p

2432. Venter, A.J. The terror fighters. - Capetown-Johannesburg : Purnell, 1969.

2433. Wilkinson, A. Insurgency and counter-insurgency in Rhodesia 1957-73. - London : IISS, 1973.

2434. Wilkinson, A.R. Insurgency in Rhodesia, 1957-1963 : An account and assessment. - London : IISS, 1973.

2435. _____ A harvest of fear : Diary of terrorist atrocities in Rhodesia. - Salisbury : RGPO, 1976.
Rhodesia. Ministry of Information

2436. _____ South African political violence & sabotage, 1 July 1984 - 30 June 1985. - Cape Town : Terrorism Research Associates, 1985. 154 p

2437. _____ South West Africa : Measures taken to combat terrorism. - Cape Town : 1968.
South Africa. Department of Foreign Affairs

H.6. Latin America, General

2438. Adler, H.G. Revolutionaeres Lateinamerika : Eine Dokumentation. - Paderborn : Schoeningh, 1970. 216 p

2439. Anderson, T.P. Political violence and cultural patterns in Central America. - Westport, Conn. : Greenwood Press, 1978. p. 153-159.
In: M.H. Livingston et al. (eds.), International terrorism in the contemporary world

2440. Anderson, T.P. Politics in Central America : Guatemala, El Salvador, Honduras and Nicaragua. - New York : 1982.

2441. Baenziger, A. * Berger, R. * Buehrer, J.C. Lateinamerika : Widerstand und Befreiung. - Freiburg : Imba Verlag, 1973.

2442. Baenziger, A. * Berger, R. * Buehrer, J.C. Lateinamerika : Abhaengigkeit und Gewalt. - Freiburg : Imba Verlag, 1973.

2443. Bambirra, V. * (ed.) Diez anos de insurreccion. - 2 vols. - Santiago : Prensa Latino-Americana, 1971.
Documents of struggle and analysis on guerrilla warfare in various Latin American nations by participants.

2444. Barreiro, J. Violencia y politica en America Latino. - 2nd ed. - Mexico City : Editorial Siglo 21, 1974.

2445. Baudouin, L.R. La guerra de guerrillas en America Latina entre 1960 y 1969 : El refuerzo de una ideologia y el debilitamento de un movimiento. Febr. 1972. p. 105-126. Boletin uruguayano de sociologia. ; 19-20.

2446. Boeckh, A. Analytische Ebenen und Kausalanalysen. - Koeln : Bohlau Verlag, 1978.
In: R. Konetzke et al. (eds.), Jahrbuch fuer Geschichte von Staat, Wirtschaft und Gesellschaft Lateinamerikas. Vol. 15

2447. Boils Morales, G. Experiencas teorico-metodologicas en la elaboracion de una cronologia de violencia politica en America Latina 1945-1970. 1975. Revista Mexicana de Sociologia. ; 37:4.

2448. Brummer, J. Gewalt in den aussenpolitischen Beziehungen Lateinamerikas. - Koeln : Bohlau Verlag, 1978.
In: R. Konetzke et al. (eds.), Jahrbuch fuer Geschichte von Staat, Wirtschaft und Gesellschaft Lateinamerikas, Vol. 15

2449. Butler, R.E. Terrorism in Latin America. - New York : AMS, 1976. p. 46-61.
In: Y. Alexander (ed.), International terrorism: national, regional and global perspectives

2450. Castano, C. Und sei es mit Gewalt. - Wuppertal : Hammer Verlag, 1968.
On Latin American political violence.

2451. Chilcote, R.H. The radical left and revolutions in Latin America. Stanford : Hoover Institution Press, 1970.

2452. Chrenko, W. Probleme des revolutionaeren Kampfes in Lateinamerika. - Berlin : Dietz Verlag, 1977.

2453. Craig, A. Urban guerrilla in Latin America. 1971. p. 112-128. Survey. ; 17:3.

2454. Davis, J. A study in political violence in Latin America. - Washington, D.C. : IISS, 1972. Adelphi Papers

2455. Davis, J. Political violence in Latin America. - London : IISS, 1972. Adelphi Papers. ; 85.

2456. Deas, M. Guerrillas in Latin America. 1968. p. 72-78. World Today. ; 24:2.

2457. Debray, R. Revolution in the revolution? : Armed struggle and political struggle in Latin America. - New York : Grove Press, 1967. 126 p
An influental book on guerrilla warfare and revolution.

2458. Detrez, C. Les mouvements revolutionnaires en Amerique latine. - Bruxelles : Ed. Vie Ouvriere, 1972. 147 p

2459. Dubois, J. Freedom is my beat. - New York : Bobbs-Merrill, 1959. A.o. on 1958 kidnapping.

2460. Duff, E.A. * McCamant, J.F. * Morales, W.Q. Violence and repression in Latin America: a quantitative and historical analysis. - New York : Free Press, 1976.

2461. Francis, S.T. Latin American terrorism: the Cuban connection. - Washington, D.C. : Heritage Foundation, 9 Nov. 1979. 23 p. Backgrounder Series

2462. Garcia Ponce, G. Terrorismo. - Caracas : Editorial Domingo-Fuentes, 1984. 159 p

2463. Gerhardt, H.P. Guerillas: Schicksalsfrage fuer den Westen : Die lateinamerikanische Revolutionsbewegung. - Stuttgart-Degerloch : Seewald, 1971. 168 p

2464. Goldenberg, B. The Cuban revolution and Latin America. - New York : Praeger, 1965.

2465. Gonzales Lapeyre, E. Violencia y terrorismo. - Santo Domingo, : Alfa y Omega, 1980. 399 p

2466. Gonzales, C.P. La violence latino-americaine dans les enquetes empiriques nord-americaines. Jan. 1970. p. 159-181. L'homme et la societe. ; 15.

2467. Goodsell, J.N. Terrorism in Latin America. March 1966. Commentator. ; 9.

2468. Gott, R. Guerrilla movements in Latin America. - Garden City, N.Y. : Doubleday, 1971. 629 p
Orig. ed.: Guerrillas en America Latina. Santiago de Chile: Editorial universitario, 1971.

2469. Halperin, E. Terrorism in Latin America. - Beverly Hills : Sage, 1975. 90 p. The Washington Papers. ; 33.

2470. Hennessy, A. The new radicalism in Latin America. Jan. 1972. p. 1-26. Journal of Contemporary History. ; 7.

2471. Herrera, A. Pusimos la bomba - y que. - Mexico, D.F. : Presencia Latinoamericana, 1981. 210 p

2472. Herreros, A.Y. El anarquismo como doctrina y movimiento. 1978. p. 99-114. Rivista de estudios politicos. ; 1.

2473. Hoagland, J.H. Changing patterns of insurgency and American response. 1971. p. 120-141. Journal of International Affairs. ; 25.

2474. Hobsbawn, E.J. Guerrillas in Latin America. - London : Merlin Press, 1970. p. 51-61.
In: R. Miliband and J. Saville (eds.), Socialist register, 1970

2475. Hodges, D.C. The Latin American revolution: politics and strategy from apro-marxism to guevarism. - New York : Morrow, 1974.

2476. Horowitz, I.L. * Castro, J.de * Gerassi, J. * (eds.) Latin American radicalism 1969. - London : Jonathan Cape, 1969. 656 p

2477. Huberman, L. * Sweezy, P.M. * (eds.) Regis Debray and the Latin American revolution; a collection of essays. - New York : Monthly Review Press, 1968. 138 p

2478. Huizer, G. Peasant rebellion in Latin America: the origins : Forms of expression and potential of Latin American peasant unrest. - Harmondsworth : Penguin, 1973.

2479. Jaquett, J.S. Women in revolutionary movements in Latin America. May. 1973. p. 344-354. Journal of Marriage and the Family. ; 35.

2480. Jarrin, E.M. Insurgency in Latin America : Its impact on political and military strategy. March 1969. p. 10-20. Military Review. ; 49.

2481. Kling, M. Violence and politics in Latin America. - New York : Random House, 1969.
In: I.L. Horowitz et al. (eds.), Latin American radicalism

2482. Kohl, J. * Litt, J. Urban guerrilla warfare in Latin America. - Cambridge, Mass. : MIT-Press, 1974. 425 p
A collection of texts with introductory comments.

2483. Lamberg, R.F. Die castristische Guerilla in Lateinamerika : Theorie und Praxis eines revolutionaeres Modells. - Hannover : Verlag fuer Literatur und Zeitgeschehen, 1971. 173 p. Vierteljahresberichte des Forschungsinstituts der Friedrich- Ebert-Stiftung. ; 7.

2484. Lamberg, R.F. Die Guerilla in Lateinamerika. - Stuttgart : Deutscher Taschenbuch Verlag, 1972. 250 p

2485. Lamberg, V.B.de La guerrilla castrista en America Latina : Bibliografia selecta, 1960-1970. 1970. p. 95-111. Foro internacional. ; 21:1.

2486. Landazabal Reyes, F. La subversion y el conflicto social. - Bogota, Colombia : Ediciones Tercer Mundo, 1980. 157 p

2487. Landazabal, R.F. Politica y tactica de la guerra revolucionaria. Bogota : 1966

2488. Larteguy, J. Les guerilleros. - Paris : R. Solar, 1967. 443 p

2489. Larteguy, J. The guerrillas; new patterns in revolution in Latin America. - New York : Signet Books, 1972. 237 p

2490. Levi, G. * (ed.) Il fascismo dipendente in America Latina: una nuova fase dei rapporti fra oligarchia e imperialismo. - Bari : De Donato, 1976.

2491. Lora, G. Revolucion y foquismo : Balance de la discusion sobre la desviacion "guerrillerista". - Buenos Aires : El Yunque editorial, 1975.

2492. Martinez Codo, E. The urban guerrilla. 1971. p. 3-10. Military Review. ; 51:8.

2493. Max, A. Guerrillas in Latin America. - The Hague : International Documentation and Information Centre, 1971.

2494. McDonald, L.P. Terrorism and subversion in Latin America : In extension of remarks of Larry McDonald. 13 July 1977. p. E4425-E4437. Congressional Record (daily ed.). ; 123.

2495. Mercier Vega, L. * (ed.) Guerrillas in Latin America. - New York : Praeger, 1969.

2496. Mercier Vega, L. Bilancio della guerriglia in America Latina. 1970. p. 481-494. Annali della Fondazione Luigi Einaudi. ; 4.

2497. Molina, A. * (ed.) Ensayos revolucionarios de America Latina. - New York : A.L. Ediciones, 1974.

2498. Moreno, F.J. * Mitrani, B. * (eds.) Conflict and violence in Latin American politics. - New York : Thomas Y. Cromwell & Co., 1971.

2499. Moss, R. Urban guerrillas in Latin America. - London : ISC, Oct. 1970. 15 p. Conflict Studies. ; 8.

2500. Petras, J. Guerrilla movements in Latin America. Spring 1970. p. 40-41. Time. ; 6.

2501. Ribeiro, D. Il dilemma dell' America Latina : Strutture di potere e forze insorgenti. - Milano : Il saggiatore, 1976.

2502. Ronfeldt, D.E. * Einaudi, L.R. Prospects for violence. - New York : Crane, Russak, 1974.
In: L.R. Einaudi (ed.), Beyond Cuba: Latin America takes charge of its future

2503. Russell, Ch.A. * Hildner, R.E. Urban insurgency in Latin America: its implications for the future. 1971. p. 55-64. Air University Review. ; 22.

2504. Russell, Ch.A. Latin America : Regional review. 1980. p. 277-292. Terrorism. ; 4.

2505. Sloan, J.W. Political terrorism in Latin America: a critical analysis. - New York : Dekker, 1979. p. 301-322.
In: M. Stohl (ed.), The politics of terrorism

2506. Stokes, W.S. Violence as a power factor in Latin America. - Garden City, N.Y. : Anchor Books, 1966.
In: R.D. Tomasek (ed.), Latin American politics. Studies of the contemporary scene

2507. Tarabocchia, A. Cuba : The technology of subversion, espionage and terrorism. - Gaithersburg, Md. : IACP, 1976.

2508. Uschner, M. Lateinamerika: Schauplatz revolutionaerer Kaempfe. - Berlin : Staatsverlag der DDR, 1975. 345 p

2509. Warth, H. Sterben fuer die Indios - Literaturbericht zur lateinamerikanischen Revolutionsbewegung. May 1973. p. 297-309. Politische Studien. ; 209.

2510. West, G.T. The dimensions of political violence in Latin America, 1949- 1964 : An empirical study. University of Pennsylvania, 1973. ; Ph.D. dissertation

2511. _____ Cuba et le castrisme en Amerique latine. 1971. p. 112-128. Survey. ; 17:3.

2512. _____ Les guerrillas d'Amerique Latine : Revolutionnaires des maquis et des villes. - Lausanne : Editions Rencontre, 1971.

2513. _____ Movimientos revolucionarios de America Latina : Documentacion propia, 1. - Haverlee-Louvain : Informacion documental de America Latina, 1972.

H.6.1. Argentina

2514. Barcia, P.A. Las guerrillas en Argentina. June 1975. p. 30-60. Interrogations. ; 3.

2515. Barkey, D.W. * Eitzen, D.S. Toward an assesment of multinational corporate social expenditures in relation to political stability and terrorist activity : The Argentine case. Spring 1981. p. 77-90. Inter-American Economic Affairs. ; 34.

2516. Barrett, R. El terror argentino. - Buenos Aires : Editorial Proyeccion, 1971. 123 p

2517. Belloni, A. Del anarquismo : Historia del movimiento obrero argentino. - Buenos Aires : A. Pena Lillo, 1960. 72 pp. Coleccion "La Siringa"

2518. Cooke, J.W. La lucha por la liberacion nacional. - Buenos Aires : 1973.

2519. Craig, A. Urban guerrilla in Argentina. 1975. p. 19-27. Canadian Defence Quarterly. ; 4.

2520. David, P.R. Profile of violence in Argentina: 1955-1976. - Washington, D.C. : National Advisory Committee on Criminal Justice Standards and Goals, Dec. 1976. p. 474-478.
In: Report of the Task Force on disorders and terrorism

2521. Escobar, J. Examen de la violencia argentina. - Mexico : Fonda de Cultura Economica, 1985. 186 p

2522. Geze, F. * Labrousse, A. Argentine, revolution et contrarevolution. - Paris : 1975.

2523. Heyman, E.S. Background to human rights violations in Argentina. - Washington, D.C. : Library of Congress, Congressional Research Service, Foreign Affairs and National Defense Division, 29 July 1977.

2524. Janke, P. Terrorism in Argentina. Sept. 1974. Journal of the Royal United Services Institute

2525. Johnson, K.F. Guerrilla politics in Argentina. - London : ISC, 1975. 21 p. Conflict Studies. ; 63.

2526. Marin, J.C. Argentina 1973-1976 : Armed events and democracy. - Toronto : Latin American Research Unit, 1970. 61 p

2527. Muenster, A. Argentinien: Guerilla und Konterrevolution : Arbeiterkaempfe gegen oligarchische Diktatur und Gewerkschafts-Buerokratie. - Muenchen : Trikont, 1977. 246 p

2528. Petric, A. Asi sangraba la Argentina : Sallustro, quijada, larrdbure. - Buenos Aires : Ediciones Depalma, 1980. 208 p

2529. Piacentini, P. Terror in Argentina. March 1977. p. 3-7. Index on Censorship. ; 6.

2530. Rock, D. Revolt and repression in Argentina. June 1977. p. 215-222. World Today. ; 33.

2531. Romero Carranza, A. El terrorismo en al historia universal y en la Argentina. - Buenos Aires : Ed. Depalma, 1980.

2532. Sofer, E.F. Terror in Argentina: jews face new dangers. 1977. p. 19-25. Present Tense. ; 5.

2533. Villemarest, P.F.de Les strateges de la peur : Vingt ans de guerre revolutionnaire en Argentine. - Geneve : Vox mundi, 1981. 231 p ; Des archives du Centre Europeen d'Information

2534. Villemarest, P.F.de The strategists of fear : Twenty years of revolutionary war in Argentina. - Geneva : 1981.

2535. Waldmann, P. El peronismo. - Buenos Aires : 1981.

2536. Waldmann, P. Las cuatro fases del gobierno peronista. Jan. 1971. Aportes. ; 19.

2537. Waldmann, P. Terror-Organisationen in Argentinien. Marz 1977. p. 10-22. Berichte zur Entwicklung Spanien, Portugal und Lateinamerika. ; 2:10.

2538. Waldmann, P. Ursachen der Guerrilla in Argentinien. - Koeln : Bohlau Verlag, 1978.
In: R. Konetzke (ed.), Jahrbuch fuer Geschichte von Staat, Wirtschaft und Gesellschaft Lateinamerikas. Vol. 15

2539. _____ Argentina and Peron 1970-75. - New York : Facts on File, Inc., 1975.

2540. _____ Argentine: organizations revolutionaires armees. 1971. p. 18-43. Tricontinental. ; 6:59.

2541. _____ Cronica de la subversion en la Argentina : Con un estudio preliminar de Armando Alonso Pineiro. - Buenos Aires : Depalma, 1980.

2542. _____ Per la rivoluzione in Argentina. - Roma : Samona & Savelli, 1975.
Montoneros

2543. _____ Terrorism in Argentina. - Buenos Aires : 1980.
Argentine Government

H.6.2. Brazil

2544. Costa Pinto, L.A. Lutas de familias no Brasil. - 3rd ed. - Sao Paulo : Co. Ed. Nacional, 1980.

2545. Costa Pinto, L.A. O negro no Rio de Janiero : Relaciones de raca numa sociedade em mudanca. - Sao Paulo : Co. Ed. Nacional, 1953.

2546. Fragoso, H. Terrorismo e criminalidade politica. - Rio de Janeiro : Forense, 1981. 136 p

2547. Lima, D. M.de Os senhores da direita. - Rio de Janeiro : Antares, 1980. 168 p

2548. Martin, B. The politics of violence: the urban guerrilla in Brazil. Oct. 1970. Ramparts

2549. Moreira Alves, M. A grain of mustard seed : The awakening of the Brazilian revolution. - Garden City, N.Y. : Doubleday Anchor Press, 1973. 194 p

2550. Moreira Alves, M. Bresil: etat terroriste et guerilla urbaine. - Paris : July 1971. p. 89-101. Politique aujourd'hui. ; 7-8.
On state terrorism in Brazil and urban guerrilla warfare.

2551. Pinheiro, P.S. * (comp.) Crime, violencia e poder. - Sao Paulo, Brasil : Brasiliense, 1983. 277 p

2552. Quartim, J. Dictatorship and armed struggle in Brazil. - London : New Left Books, 1971.

2553. Quartim, J. La guerrilla urbaine au Bresil. p. 839-874. Les temps modernes. ; 27:292.

2554. Quartim, J. Regis Debray and the Brazilian revolution. Jan. 1970. p. 61-82. New Left Review

2555. Truskier, A. The politics of violence : The urban guerrillas in Brazil. 1970. p. 30-34, 39. Ramparts. ; 9.

2556. Wedge, B. The case study of student political violence : Brazil, 1964 and Dominican Republic, 1965. 1969. p. 183-206. World Politics. ; 21:2.

2557. _____ Focus und Freiraum: Debray, Brasilien, Linke in den Metropolen. - Berlin : Wagenbach, 1970. 138 p

2558. _____ L'activite terroriste au Brasil. - Paris : 26 Oct. 1969. p. 3-24. America Latina

2559. _____ La lutte armee au Bresil. 1969. p. 590-635. Les temps modernes. ; 25:280.

H.6.3. Uruguay

2560. Alsina, G. The war and the Tupamaros. Aug. 1972. p. 29-42. Bulletin Tricontinental

2561. Aznares, C.A. * Canar, J.E. Los Tupamaros: fracaso del Che?. - Buenos Aires : Orbe, 1969.

2562. Biedma, F. * Minello, F. Experiencias de la crisis y de la guerra urbana en el Uruguay. April 1972. p. 180-226. Cuadernos de la realidad nacional. ; 12.

2563. Cardillo, L.M. The Tupamaros : A case of power duality in Uruguayan politics. Fletcher School of Law and Diplomacy, 1975. ; Unpubl. manuscript

2564. Clutterbuck, R.L. Two typical guerrilla movements: the IRA and the Tupamaros. 1972. p. 17-29. Canadian Defense Quarterly. ; 24.

2565. Connolly, S. * Druehl, G. The Tupamaros: the new focus in Latin America. 1971. p. 59-68. Journal of Contemporary Revolutions. ; 3:3.

2566. Costa, O. Los Tupamaros. - Mexico, D.F. : Coleccion Andro Mundo, 1971. 282 p

2567. Costa-Gavras, C. * Solinas, F. State of siege. - New York : Ballantine, 1973.
Movie based on Tupamaros and Dan Mitrione incident.

2568. Debray, R. Apprendre d'eux. - Milano : Feltrinelli, 1972.
Italian edition.

2569. Debray, R. La critique des armes. - Paris : Le Seuil, 1974.
A.o. on Tupamaros.

2570. Debray, R. Was wir von den Tupamaros lernen koennen. 1972. p. 144-175. Sozialistisches Jahrbuch. ; 4.

2571. Duenas Ruiz, O. * Rugnon de Duenas, M. Tupamaros, libertad o muerte. - Bogota : Ediciones Mundo Andino, 1971.

2572. Faraone, R. El Uruguay en que vivimos. - Montevideo : 1969.

2573. Gerassi, M.N. Uruguay's urban guerrillas. 1969. p. 306-310. Nation. ; 209:10.

2574. Gilio, M.E. The Tupamaros guerrillas. - New York : Ballantine, 1970. 242 p

2575. Ginneken, J.van De Tupamaros : Bevrijdingsbeweging in Uraquay. - Odijk : Sjaloom, 1977.

2576. Gutierrez, C.M. Tupamaros : Neue Methoden. Stadtsguerilla. 1969.
In: Cuba. Kursbuch 18. Beilage

2577. Jackson, G. "Halte uns nicht fuer dumm, Amigo!" : Bericht aus der Gefangenschaft bei den Tupamaros in Uruguay. 1973. Der Spiegel. ; 27: 48-50.

2578. Labrousse, A. The Tupamaros: urban guerrillas in Uruguay. - Harmondsworth : Penguin, 1973. 168 p

2579. Lopez Silveira, J.J. * Bengochea, A. Guerra de guerrillos. - Montevideo : 1970.

2580. Madruga, L. Interview with a Tupamaros using the pseudonym "Urbane". - Havana : 8 Oct. 1970. Granma

2581. Martinez Anzorena, G. Los Tupamaros. - Mendoza : Editorial la Tecla.,

2582. Max, A. Tupamaros: a pattern for urban guerrilla warfare in Latin America. - The Hague : International Documentation and Information Centre, 1970.

2583. Mercader, A. * Vega, J.de Tupamaros: estrategia y accion. - Montevideo : Editorial Alfa, 1971.

2584. Miller, J.A. The Tupamaro insurgents of Uruguay. - Arvada, Colo. : Phoenix, 1974. p. 199-283.
In: B.E. O'Neill, D.J. Alberts and S.J. Rossetti (eds.), Political violence and insurgency: a comparative approach

2585. Moss, R. Urban guerrillas in Uruguay. 1971. p. 14-23. Problems of Communism. ; 20:5.

2586. Moss, R. Uruguay: terrorism versus democracy. - London : ISC, 1971. Conflict Studies. ; 14.

2587. Nunez, C. Los Tupamaros: vanguardia armada en el Uruguay. - Montevideo : Ediciones Provincias Unidas, 1969.
English edition: The Tupamaros: urban guerrillas of Uruguay. New York: Times Change Press, 1970.

2588. Oliveira, S.L.d' Uruguay and the Tupamaro myth. April 1973. p. 25-36. Military Review. ; 53:4.

2589. Porzecanski, A.C. Uruguay's Tupamaros: the urban guerrilla. - New York : Praeger, 1973.

2590. Rovira, A. Subversion, terrorismo, guerra revolucionaria : La experiencia uruguaya. - Montevideo : 1981. 29 p ;
Conferencia dictada el 17 de fabrero de 1981 a una delegacion de representantes de organizaciones norteamericanas interesadas en problemas de seguri

2591. Suarez, C. * Sarmiento, R.A. Los Tupamaros. - Mexico, D.F. : Editorial extemporaneas, 1971. 247 p

2592. Vorwerck, E. Tupamaros : Entstehung und Entwicklung der Stadtsguerillas. 1971. p. 403-409. Wehrkunde. ; 20:8.

2593. Wilson, C. The Tupamaros: the unmentionables. - Boston : Branden, 1973.

2594. _____ Actas Tupamaros. - Buenos Aires : Schapire, 1971. 248 p.
Movimiento de Liberacion Nacional
A participant's account on past actions.

2595. _____ Generals and Tupamaros : The struggle for power in Uruguay, 1969-1973. - London : Latin America Review of Books, 1974. 77 p

2596. _____ La accion terrorista en Uruquay. - Montevideo : Direccion Nacional de Relacionas Publicas, 1980. ; Microfilm

2597. _____ La guerrilla urbaine en Uruguay : Les Tupamaros. 1970. p. 20-24. Est et Ouest. ; 22:439.

2598. _____ La subversion: las fuerzas armadas al pueblo oriental. - Montevideo : 1977. 777 p.
Uruguay, Junta de Commandantes en Jefe

2599. _____ The Tupamaros : Urban guerrilla warfare in Uruguay. - New York : Liberated Guardian, 1970.
A paperback pamphlet containing articles reprinted from Tricontinental.

2600. _____ Tupamaros. - Havana : Dec. 1970. Revolucion y cultura. ; 26.
Special issue devoted to the Tupamaros.

2601. _____ Tupamaros in azione : Testimonianze dirette dei guerriglieri. - Milano : Feltrinelli, 1971.

2602. _____ Wir die Tupamaros : Von den Tupamaros selbst verfasste Berichte und Analysen ueber ihre Aktionen mit aktuellen Dokumenten. - Frankfurt a.M. : Roter Stern, 1974. 155 p

H.6.4. Other Latin American countries

2603. Aguilera Peralta, G. El proceso del terror en Guatemala. April 1972. p. 116-138. Aportes. ; 24.

2604. Aguilera Peralta, G. * Edgardo, G. La violencia en Guatemala como fenomeno politico. - Guatemala City : Universidad de San Carlos de Guatemala, 1970.

2605. Alexander, R. The tragedy of Chile. - London/Westport, Conn. : 1978.

2606. Alman, T.D. Rising to rebellion. March 1981. p. 31-35, 38-47, 50. Harper's Magazine. ; 262.
El Salvador, Honduras.

2607. Anderson, T.P. The ambiguities of political terrorism in Central America. 1980. p. 267-276. Terrorism. ; 4:1-4.

2608. Arenas, J. Colombie : Guerillas du peuple. - Paris : Editions Sociales, 1969.

2609. Armstrong, R. El Salvador - beyond elections. March-April 1982. p. 2-31. NACLA (North American Congress on Latin America) report on the Americas. ; 16.

2610. Armstrong, R. El Salvador, the face of revolution. - Boston : South End Press, 1982. 283 p

2611. Aroche Parra, M. Los secuestros de Figueros Zuno y la muerte de Lucio Cabanes. - Mexico : Editorial de los Estados, 1976. 226 p

2612. Asencio, D. * Asencio, N. Our man is inside. - Boston : Atlantic, Little Brown, 1983. 244 p

2613. Assman, H. Teoponte : Una experiencia guerrilla. - Oruro, Bolivia : CEDI, 1971.

2614. Ayala, T. * Cesar, J. Colombia, una posicion democratica frente a la violencia. - Bogota : Secretaria de Informacion y Prensa de la Presidencia de la Republica, 1980.

2615. Bastos, R.R. El Paraguay, entre el terror y la revolucion. 1970. Cuadernos americanas. ; 3.

2616. Bejar, H. Peru 1965: notes on a guerrilla experience. - New York : Modern Reader, 1971.
Orig. ed.: Las guerrillas de 1965: balance y perspectiva. Lima: Ediciones peisa, 1973.

2617. Blanco Munoz, A. Modelos de violencia en Venezuela. - Caracas : Ediciones Desorden, 1974.

2618. Bonachea, R.L. * San Martin, M. The Cuban insurrection, 1952-1959. - New Brunswick, N.J. : Transaction Books, 1974.

2619. Bonner, R. The agony of El Salvador. 22 Febr. 1981. p. 26-31, 35-36, 38, 40, 42-4. New York Times Magazine

2620. Bouchey, L.F. * Piedra, A.M. Quatemala, a promise in peril. - Washington D.C. : Council for Inter-American Security, 1980.

2621. Bravo, D. La guerriglia nel Venezuela. - Milano : Feltrinelli, 1967.

2622. Brody, R. Contra terror in Nicaragua : Report of a fact-finding mission, September 1984-January 1985. - Boston, Mass. : South End Press, 1985. 206 p

2623. Callanan, E.F. Terror in Venezuela, 1960-64. Febr.1969. p. 49-56. Military Review. ; 49:2.

2624. Campbell, L.G. The historiography of the Peruvian guerrilla movement 1960- 65. 1973. p. 45-70. Latin American Research Review. ; 8:1.

2625. Casas, U. Origen y desarrollo del movimiento revolucionarion colombiano. - Bogota : 1980.

2626. Castaneda, J. Nicaragua : Contradicciones en la revolucion. - Mexico City : 1980.

2627. Castro Rojas, G. Como secuestramos a Niehous. - Caracas : Editorial Fuentes, 1979. 249 p. Ediciones Tres Continentes

2628. Castro, G. Del ELN al M-19: once anos de lucha guerrilla. - Bogota : 1980.

2629. Chanatry, F.I. A study of insurgency in Venezuela. - Maxwell Air Force Base, Ala. : Air War College, 1967. 94 p
Post-1959 insurgency.

2630. Charters, D.A. Guatemalan, Honduran, Salvadoran terrorists groups. - Ottawa : Operational Research and Analysis Establishment/Department of Defense, 1983.
In: D.A. Charters and M. Tugwell, Insurgency in Central America

2631. Corro, A.del Guatemala : La violencia. - Cuernavaca : 1968. ; Working paper

2632. Corro, A.del Venezuela : La violencia. - Cuernavaca : 1968.

2633. Costa Pinto, L.A. Transicion social en Colombia. - Bogota, Colombia : Ed. Tercer Mundo, 1970.

2634. Costa Pinto, L.A. Voto e cambio social. - Bogota, Colombia : Ed. Tercer Mundo, 1971.

2635. Didion, J. Salvador. - New York : Simon and Schuster, 1982-1983. 108 p

2636. Dios Marin, J.de Inside a Castro 'terror school'. Dec. 1964. p. 119-123. Reader's digest

2637. Fajardo, J. * Roldan, M. "Soy el Comandante 1". - Bogota, Colombia : Editorial la Oveja Negra, 1980. 220 p

2638. Fernandez Salvatteci, J.A. Terrorismo de quien?. - Lima : Editorial Venceremos EIRL, 1983. 108 p
On Peru.

2639. Funes de Torres, L. Los derechos humanos en Honduras. - Tegucigalpa, Honduras : Centro de Documentacion de Honduras, 1984.

2640. Garcia, A.M. Paraguay: il paternalismo terrorista. - Bari : De Donato, 1976.
In: G. Levi (ed.), Il fascismo dipendente in America Latina

2641. Gude, E.W. Political violence in Venezuela: 1958-1964. - New York : The Free Press, 1971. p. 259-273.
In: J.C. Davies (ed.), When men revolt and why

2642. Guevara, E. (Che). Boliviaans dagboek. - Amsterdam : Polak & Van Gennep, 1968.
Guevara, in his last phase, unable to win over the peasants, tried to neutralize them through terrorizing Bolivian campesinos.

2643. Guevara, E. (Che). Episodes of the revolutionary war. - New York : International Publishers, 1968. 144 p

2644. Guzman, G. La violencia en Columbia. - Bogota : National University, 1962. Monografias Sociologias. ; 12.

2645. Harding, T.F. * Landau, S. Terrorism, guerrilla warfare and the democratic left in Venezuela. 1964. p. 118-128. Student Left. ; 4:4.

2646. Herrera Campins, L. Introduccion a la violencia. - Caracas : Monte Avila, 1972.
In: G. Boscan Yepes (ed.), Violencia y politica

2647. Ingwell, M. Insurgency and counterinsurgency in Central-America. - Ottawa : Department of National Defense, 1983. ORAE Extra-Mural Paper

2648. Johnson, K.F. Guatemala: from terrorism to terror. - London : ISC, 1973. 17 p. Conflict Studies. ; 23.

2649. Johnson, K.F. On the Guatemalan political violence. 1973. Politics and Society. ; 4.

2650. Kiracofe, C.A. The Soviet network in Central America. June 1981. p. 3-6. Midstream. ; 27.

2651. Kruger, A. El Salvador's Marxist revolution. - Fairfax, Va. : Council for Economic Studies, Mason University., 1981. Journal of Social, Political and Economic Studies. ; 6:2.

2652. Lacey, T. Violence and politics in Jamaica 1960-70. - Manchester : Manchester University Press, 1976.

2653. Lamberg, R.F. Die Guerrilla in Guatemala. 1969. p. 57-174. Vierteljahres-Berichte des Forschungsinstituts der Friedrich-Ebert-Stiftung

2654. Lara, P. M-19 : Siembra vientos y recogeras tempestades. - Bogota : 1982.

2655. Lopez, J. 10 anos de guerrillas en Mexico, 1964-1974. - Mexico : Ed. Posada, 1974.

2656. Lora, G. Sobre Sendero Luminoso. - La Paz : 1984. 27 p
On Peruvian "Shining Path".

2657. Lovera, V. Tiempo de guerrilleros : Prisionero en Bogota. - Bogota : Ediciones Tercer Mundo, 1981. 151 p
On M-19 in Columbia.

2658. Maullin, R. Soldiers, guerrillas and politics in Columbia. - Lexington, Mass. : Lexington Books, 1973. 168 p

2659. Medina Ruiz, F. El terror en Mexico. - Mexico : Editores Asociades, 1974. 159 p

2660. Mercado, R. * (comp.) Algo mas sobre sendero : Teoria y tactica, violencia, represion y desaparecidos: documentos. - Lima, Peru : Ediciones de Cultura Popular, 1983. 104 p

2661. Mercado, R. El partido communista del Peru : Sendero luminoso. - Lima : Ediciones de Cultura Popular, 1982.

2662. Moleiro, M. El mir de Venezuela. - Havana : 1967.

2663. Nairn, A. Reagan administration links with Guatemalan terrorist government. April 1981. p. 16-21. Covert Action. ; 12.

2664. Ortega, H. Cincuenta anos de lucha sandinista. - Colombia : Medellin, 1979.

2665. Parejo Pflucker, P. Terrorismo y sindicalismo en Ayacucho. - Lima : Empresa Editora Ital Peru, 1981. 198 p

2666. Preston, J. Guatemala : The muffled scream. Nov. 1981. p. 40-49. Mother Jones. ; 8.

2667. Ramirez, R. El movimiento estudiantil de Mexico. - Mexico : Ediciones Era, 1969.

2668. Rashenbush, R. The terrorist war in Guatemala. - Washington, D.C. : Council for Intern-American Security Educational Institute, 1983.

2669. Roberts, K.E. * Munger, M.D. Urban guerrillas in the Americas. - Carlisle Barracks, Penn. : Army War College, Strategic Studies Institute, Dec. 1976.

2670. Rodriguez, E. La crise du mouvement revolutionnaire latino-americain et l'experience du Venezuela. 1970. p. 74-99. Les temps modernes. ; 27:288.

2671. Stevens, E.P. Protest and response in Mexico. - Cambridge, Mass. : MIT-press, 1974.

2672. Townley, R. Covering the war in El Salvador. 9 and 16 May 1981. p. 6-8, 10; 36-37, 39-40. TV Guide. ; 29.

2673. Valsalice, L. Guerriglia e politica : L'esemplo del Venezuela. - Florence : Valmartina, 1973.
On first Latin American guerrilla movement.

2674. Valsalice, L. Guerrilla y politica : Curso de accion en Venezuela 1962-1969. - Buenos Aires : Editores Pleamar, 1975.

2675. Velez, M.M. Cuadernos de campana. - Colombia : Abejo Mono, 1973.

2676. Werlich, D.P. Peru: the shadow of the shining path. Feb. 1984. p. 78-82, 90. Current History. ; 83.

2677. Williamson, R.C. Toward a theory of political violence : The case of rural Columbia. March 1965. p. 35-44. Western Political Quarterly. ; 18:1.

2678. Wolf, J.B. The arrest of William Morales in Mexico : Inferences and implications. - Gaithersburg, Md. : IACP, 1983. Update Report. ; 9:4.

2679. _____ Chile and Allende. - New York : Facts on File, Inc., 1974.

2680. _____ Economismo y terrorismo : Linea politica para la revolucion colombiana?. - Bogota : Ediciones Ideas Proletarias, 1978. 51 p

2681. _____ Terroristic activity, part 5 : The Cuban connection in Puerto Rico - hearings. - 94th Cong., 1st sess. - Washington, D.C. : GPO, 1975. 177 p. U.S. Congress, Senate, Committee on the Judiciary, Subcommittee to investigate the administration of the internal security act and other internal security laws

H.7. North America

H.7.1. Canada

2682. Baril, M. L'image de la violence au Quebec : Recherche exploratoire qualitative. - Montreal : Centre International de Criminologie Comparee, 1977.

2683. Beaton, L. Crisis in Quebec. 1971. p. 147-152. Round Table. ; 241.

2684. Bergeron, L. The history of Quebec: a patriot's handbook. - Toronto : New Canada Press, 1971.

2685. Breton, R. The socio-political dynamics of the October events. - Toronto : McClelland and Stewart, 1973. p. 213-238.
In: D.C. Thompson (ed.), Quebec society and politics: views from the inside

2686. Cameron, D. Self-determination and the Quebec question. - Ontario : MacMillan of Canada, 1974.

2687. Chodos, R. * Auf der Maur, N. Quebec : A chronicle 1968-1972. - Toronto : Canadian Journalism Foundation, 1972.

2688. Crelinsten, R.D. Collective violence in Canada. 1979. ; Report for the research division of the Department of the Sollicitor General of Canada

2689. Daniels, D. Quebec, Canada and the October crisis. - Montreal : Black Rose, 1973.

2690. Drache, D. * (ed.) Quebec - only the beginning: the Manifestos of the Common Front. - Toronto : New Press, 1972.

2691. Fournier, L. F.L.Q : Histoire d'un movement clandestin. - Montreal : 1982.

2692. Frank, J.A. * Kelly, M. Etude preliminaire sur la violence collective en Ontario et au Quebec, 1963-1973. 1977. p. 145-157. Revue canadienne de Science Politique. ; 10:1.

2693. Golden, A.E. * Haggart, R. Rumours of war : Canada and the kidnap crisis. - Toronto : New Press, 1971. Also: Chicago: Follett, 1971.

2694. Green, L.C. Terrorism: the Canadian perspective. - New York : AMS Press, 1976. p. 3-29.
In: Y. Alexander (ed.), International terrorism: national, regional, and global perspectives

2695. Grosman, B.A. Dissent and disorder in Canada. - Washington, D.C. : National Advisory Committee on Criminal Standards and Goals, Dec. 1976. p. 479-496.
In: Report of the Task Force on disorders and terrorism

2696. Hagy, J.W. Quebec separatists: the first twelve years. - Toronto : McGraw-Hill, 1971.
In: N. Sheffe (ed.), Issues for the seventies

2697. Ingwell, M. Low-intensity violence in Canada : The myth, the reality, the prospects. 1981. Laurentian University Review. ; 14:1.

2698. Lacoursiere, J. Alarme citoyens. - Ottawa : Les Editions de la Presse, 1972. 438 p
On FLQ and Cross-Laporte kidnappings.

2699. Latouche, D. Violence, politique et crise dans la societe Quebecoise. - Toronto : McClelland and Stewart, 1971. p. 175-199.
In: L. Lapierre et al. (eds.), Essays on the left: essays in honour of T.C. Douglas

2700. Laurendeau, M. Les Quebecois violents. Oct. 1974. Canadian Journal of Criminology and Corrections

2701. Manzer, R. Canada: a social-political report. - New York : McGraw-Hill, 1974.
Also deals with the 6 deaths resulting from FLQ terrorism.

2702. McKinsey, L.S. Dimensions of national political integration and disintegration: the case of Quebec separatism, 1960-1975. Oct. 1976. p. 335-360. Comparative Political Studies. ; 9.

2703. Milner, S.M. * Milner, H. The decolonization of Quebec: an analysis of left wing nationalism. - Toronto : McClelland and Stewart, 1973.

2704. Moore, B. The revolution script. - New York : Holt, Rinehart & Winston, 1971. 261 p
Semi-fictionalized account on the James Cross kidnapping by the FLQ.

2705. Pellentier, G. The October crisis. - Toronto : McClelland & Stewart, 1971.

2706. Radwanski, G. * Windeyer, K. No mandate but terror. - Richmond Hill, Ontario : Simon and Schuster, 1970.

2707. Redlick, A.S. Transnational factors affecting Quebec separatist terrorism. ; Paper to the 17th annual convention of the International Studies Association, Febr. 1976 in Toronto, Canada

2708. Regush, N.M. Pierre Vallieres: the revolutionary process in Quebec. - New York : Dial, 1973.

2709. Reid, M. The shouting signpainters : A literary and political account of Quebec revolutionary nationalism. - Toronto : McClelland & Stewart, 1972.

2710. Reilly, W.G. Canada, Quebec and theories of internal war. 1973. p. 67-75. American Review of Canadian Studies. ; 3.

2711. Rioux, M. Quebec in question. - Toronto : James Lewis and Samuel, 1971.

2712. Rotstein, A. * (ed.) Power corrupted: the October crisis and the repression of Quebec. - Toronto : New Press, 1971.

2713. Ryan, C. Le devoir et la crise d'Octobre 70. - Ottawa : Lemeac, 1971.

2714. Savoie, C. La veritable histoire du FLQ. - Montreal : Les editions du jour, 1963.

2715. Saywell, J.T. Quebec 70: a documentary narrative. - Toronto : University of Toronto Press, 1971.

2716. Singer, H.L. Institutionalization of protest: the Quebec seperatist movement. Department of Political Science, New York University, 1976. ; Ph.D.dissertation

2717. Smith, D. Bleeding hearts... bleeding country: Canada and the Quebec crisis. - Edmonton : Hurtig, 1971.

2718. Stewart, J. The FLQ: seven years of terrorism : Special report by the Montreal Star. - Richmond Hill, Ontario : Simon & Schuster, 1970.

2719. Torrance, J. The response of Canadian governments to violence. Sept. 1977. p. 473-496. Canadian Journal of Political Science. ; 10.

2720. Trait, J.C. FLQ 70: offensive d'automne. - Ottawa : Les Editions de l'Homme, 1970. 230 p
On Cross and Laporte kidnappings.

2721. Vallieres, P. Negres blancs d'Amerique. - Montreal : Editions Parti Pris, 1969.
Chief terrorist of FLQ, radical journalist. The book is an attempt to justify political terrorism (a la Fanon) - an English edition, 'White nigger of America', was published in 1968 in New York.

2722. Vallieres, P. The assassination of Pierre Laporte : Behind the October '70 scenario. - Toronto : James Lorimer, 1977.

2723. Vallieres, P. The impossible Quebec. - Montreal : 1980.

2724. Woodcock, G. * Avakunovec, J. The Doukhobors. - Toronto : Oxford University Press, 1968.

H.7.2. United States

2725. Adamic, L. Dynamite: the story of class violence in America. - New York : Viking, 1934.

2726. Adelson, A. S.D.S.: a profile. - New York : Scribner's, 1972.
U.S. student violence, Weather Movement.

2727. Amendt, G. * (ed.) Black Power : Dokumente und Analysen. - Frankfurt a.M. : Suhrkamp, 1970. 234 p

2728. Avrich, P. The modern school movement : Anarchism and education in the United States. - Princeton, N.J. : 1980.
Uncovers preparations for assassination attempts by A. Berkman and others on John D. Rockefeller in 1913-14.

2729. Bacciocco, E.J. The New Left in America : Reform to revolution, 1956

to 1970. - Stanford, Calif. : Hoover Institution, 1974. 300 p

2730. Baker, M. * Brompton, S. Exclusive! : The inside story of Patty Hearst and the SLA. - New York : MacMillan, 1974.

2731. Belcher, J. * West, D. Patty - Tania. - New York : Pyramid Books, 1975.

2732. Bell, J.B. * Gurr, T.R. Terrorism and revolution in America. - Revised ed. - Beverly Hills : Sage, 1979. p. 329-347.
In: H.D. Graham and T.R. Gurr (eds.), Violence in America: historical and comparative perspectives. A report submitted to the National Commission on the causes and prevention of violence

2733. Boulton, D. The making of Tania Hearst. - London : New English Library, 1975. 224 p
A narrative about the workings of the SLA with some emphasis on their drive for publicity.

2734. Boulton, D. The Symbionese Liberation Army. - Amsterdam : Editions Rodopi NV, 1974.

2735. Broehl, W.G. The Molly Maguires. - Cambridge, Mass. : Harvard University Press, 1964.
U.S. labor struggles, 19th century.

2736. Brown, R.M. The American vigilante tradition. - New York : Signet Books, 1969.
In: H.D. Graham and T.R. Gurr (eds.), Violence in America

2737. Burrows, W.E. Vigilante. - New York : Harcourt, Brace, Jovanovich, 1976.

2738. Cohen, M. * Hale, D. The new student left. - Boston : Beacon Press, 1967.

2739. Collier, P. * Horowitz, D. Doing it: the inside story of the rise and fall of the Weather Underground. 30 Sept. 1982. p. 19, 21-24, 26, 29-30, 35-3. Rolling Stone. ; 379.

2740. Conant, R. The prospects for revolution: a study of riots, civil disobedience and insurrection in contemporary America. - New York : Harper's Magazine Press, 1971.

2741. Courtright, J.A. Rhetoric of the gun: an analysis of the rhetorical modifications of the Black Panther Party. 1974. p. 249-268. Journal of Black Studies. ; 4:3.

2742. Cunningham, B. On bended knees : The night rider story. - Nashville, Tenn. : McClanahan Publ. House, 1983. 224 p

2743. Daigon, A. Violence - U.S.A. - New York : Bantam, 1975.

2744. Daley, R. Target blue. - New York : Delacorte Press, 1973.
On Black Liberation Army's attacks on the blue- uniformed New York City Police.

2745. Daniels, S. The Weathermen. Jan. 1974. p. 430-459. Government and Opposition. ; 9:1.

2746. David, H. The history of the Haymarket affair : A study of the American social-revolutionary and labor movements. - New York : 1936.

2747. Davis, A. An autobiography. - New York : Random House, 1974.

2748. Dawson, H.B. The Sons of Liberty. - New York : 1859.
On the Sons of Liberty who struck at Tory sympathizers during the 18th century American war of independence.

2749. Deakin, T.J. Legacy of Carlos Marighella. Oct. 1974. p. 19-25. FBI Law Enforcement Bulletin. ; 43:10.
On U.S. disciples of Marighella: Weathermen, Black Panthers, and theSLA.

2750. Derber, M. Terrorism and the movement. Febr. 1971. p. 36. Monthly Review. ; 22.

2751. Fainstein, N.I. * Fainstein, S.S. Urban political movements: the search for power by minority groups in American cities. - Englewood Cliffs, N.J. : Prentice Hall, 1974.

2752. Farren, M. * Barker, E. * et al. Watch our kids. - London : Open Gate Books, 1972.

2753. Foner, P.S. Black Panthers speak. - Philadelphia : J.B. Lippincott, 1970.

2754. Forman, J. The making of black revolutionaries. - New York : MacMillan, 1972.

2755. Foster, J. * Long, D. Protest: student activism in America. - New York : William Morrow, 1970.

2756. Francis, S.T. * Poole, W.T. Terrorism in America: the developing internal security crisis. - Washington, D.C. : Heritage Foundation, 2 June 1978. 23 p. Backgrounder. ; 59.

2757. Francis, S.T. The terrorist underground in the United States. - Washington, D.C. : Nathan Hale Institute, 1985. 30 p

2758. Franks, L. The seeds of terror. 22 Nov. 1981. p. 24-28, 44, 46, 54,

58-59,. New York Times Magazine Weather Underground.

2759. Frye, Ch.A. * (ed.) Values in conflict : Blacks and the American ambivalence toward violence. - Washington, D.C. : University Press of America, 1980. 169 p

2760. Gerassi, J. Lutte armee aux Etats-Unis. 1970. p. 1779-1810. Les temps modernes. ; 26:286.

2761. Gilman, I. Philsophy of terrorism. Oct. 1918. p. 294-305. Unpopular Review. ; 6.

2762. G
itlin, T. White heat underground. 19 Dec. 1981. p. 657, 669-674. Nation. ; 233. Weather Underground, 1969 to 1981.

2763. Glantz, O. New left radicalism and punitive moralism. Spring 1975. p. 281-303. Polity. ; 7.

2764. Goode, S. Affluent revolutionaries : A portrait of the New Left. - New York : New Viewpoints, 1974.

2765. Grathwohl, L. Bringing down America. An FBI informer with the Weathermen : Larry Grathwohl as told to Frank Reagan. - New Rochelle, N.Y. : Arlington House, 1976. 191 p

2766. Greisman, H.C. Terrorism in the U.S.: a social impact projection. ; Paper presented at the Annual meeting of the American Sociological Association, New York, Aug. 1976

2767. Gurr, T.R. * Chong-Soo Tai * Peterson, E. Internal vs. external sources of anti-Americanism : Two comparative studies. Sept. 1973. p. 455-488. Journal of Conflict Resolution. ; 17.

2768. Gurr, T.R. * Graham, H.D. Violence in America. - Beverly Hills : Sage, 1979. 528 p ; Revised college edition Revised edition: Beverly Hills: Sage Publications. 1979.

2769. Gurr, T.R. Dissent and protest in America : A brief history. 1971. p. 769-778. Reader's Digest Almanac 1971

2770. Gurr, T.R. Political protest and rebellion in the 1960s : The United States in world perspective. - New York : Praeger, 1969. p. 49-76.
In: H.D. Graham and T.R. Gurr (eds.), Violence in America: historical and comparative perspectives. A report submitted to the National Commission on the causes and prevention of violence

2771. Gurr, T.R. Politiche di coercizione e conflitti negli Stati Uniti : Usi e consequenze della violenza politica e del terrorismo. - Bologna : Il Mulino, 1983. p. 91-160.
In: D. della Porta and G. Pasquino (eds.), Terrorismo e violenza politica, tre casi a confronto: Stati Uniti, Germania e Giappone
Orig.: New York: Praeger, 1969.

2772. Hayden, T. Rebellion and repression. - New York : World Publishing Co., 1970.

2773. Heath, G.L. * (ed.) Vandals in the bomb factory : The history and literature of the Students for a Democratic Society. - Metuchen, N.J. : Scarecrow Press, 1976. 485 p

2774. Hinckle, W. * et al. Guerrilla-verzet in de VS : Een documentaire. - Amsterdam : Van Gennep, 1971. 204 p

2775. Hofstadter, R. * Wallace, M. * (eds.) American violence: a documentary history. - New York : Knopf, 1970.

2776. Homer, F.D. Terror in the United States: three perspectives. - New York : Dekker, 1979. p. 373-405.
In: M. Stohl (ed.), The politics of terrorism

2777. Hoover, J.E. The revolutionary-guerilla attacks law enforcement and democratic society : Analysis of the destructive power of the fanatical few. Albany Law Review. ; 35:4.

2778. Hopkins, Ch.W. The deradicalization of the Black Panther Party: 1967-1973. University of North Carolina, 1978. ; Ph.D. dissertation

2779. Horowitz, I.L. The struggle is the message : The organization and ideology of the anti-war movement. - Berkeley : The Glendessary Press, 1970.

2780. House, A. The Carasso tragedy : Eleven days of terror in the Huntsville prison. - Waco, Texas : Texian p ress, 1975. On hostage episode.

2781. Howell, A.Ch. Kidnapping in America. - Ann Arbor, Mich. : Xerox University Microfilm, 1975. ; Ph.D. Temple University

2782. Hunter, R. Violence and the labor movement. - New York : 1914.

2783. Jackson, G. Blood in my eye. - London : Faber and Faber, 1975.

2784. Jacobs, H. * (ed.) Weatherman. - Berkeley, Calif. : Ramparts Press, 1970. 519 p

2785. James, D. Puerto Rican terrorists also threaten Reagan assassination. 19 Dec. 1981. p. 1,8,19. Human Events. ; 41.

2786. Jenkins, B.M. * Sorrel, W. * Lavin, M.M. Intelligence constraints of the 1970s and domestic terrorism :

Executive summary. - Santa Monica, Calif. : RAND, 1982. 22 p ; Prepared for the U.S. Department of Justice

2787. Jenkins, B.M. Terrorism in the United States. - Santa Monica, Calif. : RAND, 1980.

2788. Johnpoll, B.K. Perspectives on political terrorism in the United States. - New York : AMS, 1976. p. 30-45. In: Y. Alexander (ed.), International terrorism: national, regional and global perspectives

2789. Jones, J.H. The Minutemen. - Garden City, N.Y. : Doubleday, 1968.

2790. Karasek, H. * (ed.) 1886 Haymarket : Die deutsche Anarchisten von Chicago. Reden und Lebenslaeufe. - Berlin : Wagenbach, 1977. 190 p

2791. Karber, Ph.A. * Novotny, E.J.S. Radical bombings in the United States: what happened to the revolution?. Jan. 1973. Bomb Incident Bulletin

2792. Kedward, R. The anarchists: the men who shocked an era. - New York : American Heritage, 1971. Reprint 1975; Dutch ed.: Leiden: Sijthof, 1970. 125 pp.

2793. Keniston, K. The young radicals : Notes on committed youth. - New York : Harcourt, Brace and World, 1968.

2794. Lasch, Chr. The agony of the American left. - Har mondsworth : Pelican, 1973.

2795. Lawrence, R. Guerrilla warfare in the United States. - Canoga Park, Calif. : Weiss Day, 1970.

2796. Lens, S. Radicalism in America. - New York : Thomas Y. Cromwell, 1966.

2797. Lerner, M. Anarchism and the American counter-culture. 1970. p. 430-455. Government and Opposition. ; 5.

2798. Lewis, G.K. Notes on the Puerto Rican revolution: an essay on American dominance and Caribbean resistance. - New York : Monthly Review, 1975. 288 p

2799. Luce, Ph.A. The New Left. - New York : David McKay, 1965.

2800. Luce, Ph.A. The New Left today. - Washington, D.C. : Capitol Hill Press, 1972.

2801. Lum, D.D. A concise history of the great trial of the Chicago anarchists. - Chicago : Socialistic Publishing Co., 1887.

2802. Marine, G. The Black Panthers. - New York : New American Library, 1969.

2803. Martin, J.J. Men against the state : The expositors of individualist anarchism in America 1827- 1908. - 2nd ed. - Colorado Springs : Col. Ralph Myles, 1970. 332 p

2804. Martinelli, A. * Cavalli, A. * (eds.) Il Black Panther Party. - Turin : 1971.

2805. Masotti, L.H. * Corsi, J.R. Shoot-out in Cleveland, black militants and the police. - Washington, D.C. : GPO, 1969.

2806. Maurer, M. The Ku Klux Klan and the National Liberation Front: terrorism applied to achieve diverse goals. - Westport, Conn. : Greenwood Press, 1978. p. 131-152. In: M. Livingston et al. (eds.), International terrorism in the contemporary world

2807. McCartney, J. Black Power: past, present, and future. - St. Louis : Forum Press, 1973.

2808. McDonald, L.P. Trotskyisme and terror: the strategy of revolution. - Washington, D.C. : ACU Education and Research Institute, 1977. 109 p On the U.S. Socialist Workers Party and the Fourth International involvement with terrorism.

2809. McLellan, V. * Avery, P. The voices of guns : The definitive and dramatic story of the 22-month career of the Symbionese Liberation Army. - New York : Putnam, 1976. 544 p

2810. Motley, J.B. * et al. American political culture, Vietnam and implications for future US national security planning. - Baltimore Md. : The John Hopkins University, forthcoming. ; Proceedings 1985 West Point seminar conference: Vietnam - did it make a difference?

2811. Motley, J.B. The domestic terrorist threat : A growing danger. - Gaithersburg, Md. : IACP, May 1984.

2812. Muhammad, A. Civil war in islamic America : Behind the Washington siege. 11 June 1977. p. 721-724. Nation. ; 224. On March 1977 takeover of three buildings in Washington, D.C., by Hanafis.

2813. Newton, H.P. Revolutionary suicide. - London : Wildwood House, 1974.

2814. Newton, H.P. To die for the people: the writings of Huey P. Newton. - New York : Random House, 1972. 232 p Black Power.

2815. Novack, G. Marxism versus neo-anarchist terrorism. July 1970. p. 14-19. International Socialist Review. ; 31:4.

2816. Overstreet, H. * Overstreet, B. The strange tactics of extremism. - New York : Norton, 1964. 315 p
On extreme right in USA: John Birch Society et al.

2817. Parker, T.F. * (ed.) Violence in the United States. - New York : Facts on File, 1974. 248 p

2818. Payne, L. * Findley, T. The life and death of the SLA. - New York : Ballantine Books, 1976.

2819. Pearsall, R.B. * (ed.) The Symbionese Liberation Army : Documents and communications. - Atlantic Highlands, N.J. : Humanities Press, 1974.

2820. Pinkney, A. The American way of violence. - New York : Random House, 1972. 235 p

2821. Popov, M.I. The American extreme left: a decade of conflict. - London : ISC, Dec. 1972. 19 p. Conflict Studies. ; 29.
On 1962-1972 period, analysing various leftist groups, both 'orthodox' and new left.

2822. Powers, T. Diana: the making of a terrorist. - Boston : Houghton-Mifflin, 1971. 225 p

2823. Powers, T. The war at home. - New York : Grossman, 1973. 348 p

2824. Raskin, J. * (ed.) The Weather eye : Communiques from the Weather Underground, May 1970-May 1974. - New York : 1974. 124 p

2825. Reeves, K.J. The trial of Patty Hearst. - San Francisco : Great Fidelity Press, 1976.

2826. Reisz, J.B. A theory on terrorist activity in America and its effect on the United States Army. U.S. Army Command and General Staff College, 1979. ; Master's thesis

2827. Ritz, R. The lady and the laywers. - San Francisco : Anthelion Press, 1976.
On Patty Hearst.

2828. Rose, G.F. The terrorists are coming. July 1978. p. 22-54. Politics Today. ; 5.

2829. Rose, T. * (ed.) Violence in America: a historical and contemporary reader. - New York : Vintage, 1970. 381 p

2830. Rubenstein, R.E. Rebels in Eden: mass political violence in the United States. - Boston : Little Brown, 1970.

2831. Russell, D. Little Havana's reign of terror. - New York : 29 Oct. 1976. p. 36-37, 40-45. New Times. ; 7.
On terrorism among the 450.000 Cuban exiles in the Miami area.

2832. Sale, K. S.D.S. - New York : Random House, 1973.

2833. Sater, W. Puerto Rican terrorists : A possible threat to US energy installations?. - Santa Monica, Calif. : RAND, 1981. 30 p

2834. Schang, G. * Rosenbaum, R. From the Capitol's bombers. Nov. 1976. More. ; 6:11.
On Weather Underground.

2835. Seale, B. Seize the time : The story of the Black Panther Party, and H.P. Newton. - New York : Random House, 1970. 429 p

2836. Sears, D.D. * McConahay, J.B. Politics of violence: the new urban blacks and the Watts riot. - Boston : Houghton Mifflin, 1973.

2837. Sederberg, P.C. The phenomenology of vigilantism in contemporary America: an interpretation. 1978. p. 287-305. Terrorism

2838. Spichal, D. Die Black Panther Party : Ihre revolutionaere Ideologie und Strategie in Beziehung zur Geschichte und Situation der Afro-Amerikaner, zur 'Dritten Welt' und zum Marxismus-Leninismus. - Osnabrueck : Biblio Verlag, 1974. 268 p

2839. Stanford, M. Black guerrilla warfare: strategy and tactics. - San Francisco : Nov. 1970. The Black Scholar

2840. Stein, D.L Living the revolution: the Yippies in Chicago. - New York : Bobbs-Merrill, 1969.

2841. Taft, Ph. * Ross, Ph. American labor violence: its causes, characters and outcome. - New York : Signet Books, 1969.
In: H.D. Graham and T.R. Gurr (eds.), Violence in America

2842. Thayer, G. The farther shores of politics: the American political fringe today. - New York : Simon and Schuster, 1967. 616 p

2843. Tierney jr, J.J. Terror at home: the American revolution and irregular warfare. 1977. p. 1-20. Stanford Journal of International Studies. ; 12.

2844. Trautman, F. The voice of terrorism : A biography of Johann Most. - Westport, Conn. : Greenwood Press, 1980.

2845. Useem, M. Protest movements in America. - Indianapolis : Bobbs-Merrill, 1975.

2846. Vestermark, S.D. Extremist groups in the U.S. - Gaithersburg, Md. : IACP, 1975.

2847. Walton, P. The case of the Weathermen: social reaction and radical commitment. - Harmondsworth : Penguin, 1973. p. 157-181.
In: I. Taylor and L. Taylor (eds.), Politics and deviance

2848. Wicker, T. A time to die. 1975.
On 1971 prison uprising at Attica, New York, where hostages were taken.

2849. Widener, A. The detonators : Their total break with America. - New York : U.S.A. Publishing Co., 1969.
Discussion of radical leftist groups of the 1960's and their demonstrations and terrorism.

2850. Williams, R.F. * Rigg, R.F. Grossstadtguerilla. - Berlin : Voltaire, 1969. 35 p

2851. Wolf, J.B. * Kaufman, L. An inspection system to monitor White House subordinates compliance with presidential directives. Winter 1981. p. 92-98. Presidential Studies Quarterly. ; 9:1.

2852. Wolf, J.B. * Zoffer, G.R. The menace of terrorism in the United States. 3 Jan. 1981. p. 10-15. Human Events: the National Conservative Weekly. ; 41:3.

2853. Wolf, J.B. Domestic terrorist movements. - New York : Praeger, 1979. p. 18-63. In:
Y. Alexander and R.A. Kilmarx (eds.), Political terrorism and business: the threat and response

2854. Wolf, J.B. Domestic terrorist organizations confront the police. - Gaithersburg, Md. : IACP, 1982. Update Report. ; 8:2.

2855. Wolf, J.B. Resurgence of terrorism in the United States. - Gaithersburg, Md. : IACP, 1982. Update Report. ; 8:1.

2856. Wolf, J.B. Terrorism in the United States : 1982. - Gaithersburg, Md. : IACP, 1983. Update Report. ; 9:1.

2857. Wolf, J.B. Terrorist death squad activity in the United States. - Gaithersburg, Md. : IACP, 1980. Update Report. ; 6:5.

2858. _____ "Guerrilla warfare and terrorism.". Jan. 1971. Scanlon's Magazine. ; 8.
Lists 1404 incidents covering the period 12 Febr. 1965 to 7 Sept. 1970.

2859. _____ Anti-Soviet zionist terrorism in the U.S. 1971. p. 6-8. Current Digest of the Soviet Press. ; 23.

2860. _____ Cuban extremists in U.S. - a growing terror threat. Dec. 1976. p. 29-32. U.S. News and World Report. ; 81:23.
On anti-Castro Cubans.

2861. _____ Domestic terrorism : Superintendent of documents. 1979.
U.S. National Governors' Association
Overview of U.S. laws and local ordinaces relating to terrorists incidents.

2862. _____ Extremist groups in the United States : A curriculum guide. - New York : Anti-Defamation League of B'nai B'rith, 1982. 315 p

2863. _____ FBI analysis of terrorist incidents in the United States - 1982. 1984. Terrorism. ; 7:1.

2864. _____ FBI Domestic Terrorist Digest. 1970-1974 weekly, th.
FBI
Originally called the Summary of Extremist Activities; classified until 1972, recently released under the Freedom of Information Act.

2865. _____ Manifeste des Weathermen. 1970. p. 1811-1836. Les temps modernes. ; 26:286.

2866. _____ Meir Kahane: a candid conversation with the militant leader of the Jewish Defense League. Oct. 1972. p. 69. Playboy

2867. _____ Outlaws of America : Communiques from the Weather Underground. - New York : 1971.

2868. _____ Report: the Weather Underground. - 94th Congr., 1st sess., Jan. 1975. - Washington, D.C. : GPO, 1975. 169 p.
U.S. Congress, Senate. Committee on the judiciary

2869. _____ State Department bombing by Weathermen Underground : Hearings. - Washington, D.C. : GPO, 1975.
U.S. Congress, Senate. Committee on the judiciary

2870. _____ Terrorism : Hearings. - 93rd Congr., 2nd sess., 27 Febr.-20 Aug. - Washington, D.C. : GPO, 1974.
U.S. Congress, House. Committee on internal security

2871. _____ Terrorism in California. July 1974. p. 1-8. Criminal Justice Digest. ; 2.

2872. _____ Terrorism: its tactics and techniques : An FBI special study. - Washington, D.C. : U.S. Department of Justice, 12 Jan. 1973.
FBI

2873. _____ Terroristic activity :

Terrorism in the Miami area. - 94th Cong. 2nd sess. Part 8. - Washington, D.C. : GPO, 1976. p. 607-662.
U.S. Congress. Senate. Committee on the Judiciary. Subcommittee to Investigate the Administration of the Internal Security Act and Other Internal Security Laws ; Hearings, 6 May 1976

2874. _____ Terroristic activity : Hearings. Part 2. Inside the Weathermen movement. - 93rd Congr., 2nd sess., 18 Oct. 1974. - Washington, D.C. : GPO, 1975.
U.S. Congress, Senate. Committee on the judiciary

2875. _____ Terroristic activity : Hearings. Part 3. Testimony of dr. Frederick C. Schwarz. - 93rd Congr., 2nd sess., 5 July 1974. - Washington, D.C. : GPO, 1975.
U.S. Congress, Senate. Committee on the judiciary

2876. _____ Terroristic activity : Hearings. Part 8. Terrorism in the Miami area. - 94th congr., 2nd sess., 6 May 1976. - Washington, D.C. : GPO, 1976.
U.S. Congress, Senate. Committee on the judiciary

2877. _____ Terroristic activity : Hearings. Part 1. - 93rd Congr., 2nd sess., 2 Sept. 1974. - Washington, D.C. : GPO, 1974. 96 p.
U.S. Congress, Senate. Committee on the judiciary

2878. _____ The interrelationship of terrorism and the politics of Hispanic groups in the United States. - Gaithersburg, Md. : IACP, 1979. Update Report. ; 5:3.

2879. _____ The Symbionese Liberation Army: a study. - Washington, D.C. : GPO, 1974.
U.S. Congress, House. Committee on Internal Security ; 93rd Cong., 2nd sess., 18 Febr. 1974

2880. _____ The Symbionese Liberation Army in Los Angeles : A report to Mayor Tom Bradley. - Los Angeles : LAPD, 1974.
Los Angeles Board of Police Commissioners

2881. _____ The Weather Underground. - Washington, D.C. : GPO, 1975.
The history and political theory plus a chronology of events involving the Weathermen to June 1974 are discussed.

2882. _____ Toward people's war for independence and socialism in Puerto Rico. - San Juan : Committee on Solidarity with Puerto Rican Independence, 1979. 94 p

I. INTER- AND TRANSNATIONAL TERRORISM

2883. Adams, N.M. Iran's ayatollahs of terror : A Reader's Digest special report. Jan. 1985. p. 36-42. Reader's Digest. ; 126.

2884. Adie, W.A.C. China, Israel and the Arabs. - London : ISC, 1971. 18 p. Conflict Studies. ; 12.

2885. Ahmadzadeh, M. Armed struggle : A strategy and a tactic. - New York : 1976.

2886. Alexander, Y. * Kilmarx, R.A. International network of terrorist movements. - New York : Praeger, 1979. p. 64-105.
In: Y. Alexander and R.A. Kilmarx (eds.), Political terrorism and business: the threat and response

2887. Alexander, Y. Network of international terrorism. - Boulder, Colo. : Westview, 1978.
In: Y. Alexander, D. Carlton and P. Wilkinson (eds.), Terrorism: theory and practice

2888. Alexander, Y. Some perspectives on international terrorism. - Tel Aviv : 1975. p. 24-29. International Problems. ; 14:3-4.
Overview of worldwide manifestations of terrorism and attempts to counter them.

2889. Anable, D. Terrorism : Loose net links diverse groups: no central plot. - Gaithersburg, Md. : IACP, 1978. p. 247-259.
In: J.D. Elliott and L.K. Gibson (eds.), Contemporary terrorism: selected readings

2890. Astin, A. * Astin, H.S. * Bayer, A.E. * Bisconti, A.S. The power of protest. - San Francisco : Jossey-Bass, 1975.

2891. Banks, A.S. Patterns of domestic conflict : 1919-1939 and 1946-1966. March 1972. p. 41-50. Journal of Conflict Resolution. ; 1.

2892. Bartos, M. International terrorism. April 1972. p. 25. Review of International Affairs. ; 23.

2893. Bauman, C.E. * (ed.) International terrorism : Proceedings of an intensive panel at the 15th Annual convention of the International Studies Association, March 23, 1974. - Milwaukee : Institute of World Affairs, 1974. 96 p

2894. Becker, J. The Soviet connection : State sponsorship of terrorism. - London : Institute for European Defence and Strategic Studies, 1985. 55 p. Occasional Paper. ; 13.

2895. Beichman, A. Quaddafi's safe house for terrorism. Febr. 1982. p. 164-166, 187. National Review. ; 34.

2896. Bell, J.B. Transnational terror and world order. 1975. p. 404-417. South Atlantic Quarterly. ; 74.

2897. Bell, J.B. Transnational terror. - Washington, D.C. : American Enterprise Institute for Public Policy Research, 1975. 91 p

2898. Beres, L.R. Guerillas, terrorists, and polarity: new structural models of world politics. Dec. 1974. p. 624-636. Western Political Quarterly. ; 27:4.

2899. Bergier, J. La troisieme guerre mondiale est commencee. - Paris : Albin Michel, 1976. 183 p
On rise of terrorism, with focus on Western Europe and north-south conflict.

2900. Bergquist, M. Surrogatkrigets uppsving : S.K. terroristgrupper som aktoerer i internationell politik. Oct. 1977. Internasjonal Politik. ; 3.
The increase of surrogate wars: so-called terrorist groups as actorsin international politics.

2901. Bite, V. International terrorism in its historical depth and present dimension, 1968-1975. - Washington, D.C. : Department of State, 1976. 36 p

2902. Bodunescu, I. Flagelui terrorismului international. - Bukarest : Editura Militara, 1978. 274 p

2903. Bouthoul, G. International terrorism in its historical depth and present dimension, 1968-1975. - Washington, D.C. : U.S. Department of State, 1976. 36 p

2904. Braungart, R.C. * Braungart, M.M. International terrorism : Background and response. 1981. p. 263-288. Journal of political and military sociology. ; 9:2.

2905. Briant, E. Het internationale terrorisme en zijn bestrijding. June 1976. p. 413-428. Kultuurleven. ; 5.

2906. Brown, M.A. Terrorism. - 96th Cong., 1st sess. - Washington, D.C. : GPO, 1979. p. 225-248.
In: U.S. Congress, Joint Economic Committee, The U.S. role in a changing world political economy - major issues for the 96th congress. A compendium of papers

2907. Carlton, D. * Schaerf, C. * (eds.) International terrorism and world security. - London : Croom Helm, 1975. 332 p
Volume contains papers presented at the Urbino (Italy) 1974 Conference of the International School on Disarmament and Research on Conflicts. Articles on terrorism by B. Jenkins, G. Bouthoul, S.J. Rosen, R. Frank, G. Sliwowski, J. Bowyer Bell and D. Heradstveit.

2908. Casey, W.J. International terrorism. 15 Sept. 1985. p. 713-717. Vital Speeches of the Day. ; 51.

2909. Charters, D.A. * Tugwell, M. Trends in international terrorism. Centre for Conflict Studies, 1980. ; Unpubl. study

2910. Cleveland, R.H. * et al. A global perspective on transnational terrorism; a case study of Libya. - Maxwell Air Force Base, Ala. : Air War College, 1977. 66 p. U.S. Air War College Research Report. ; 25.

2911. Cline, R.S. * Alexander, Y. State-sponsored terrorism : Report. - Washington, D.C. : GPO, 1985. 186 p

2912. Cline, R.S. * Alexander, Y. Terrorism : The Soviet connection. - New York : Crane Russak, 1984. 162 p

2913. Clutterbuck, R.L. Terrorist international. - London : Jan. 1974. p. 154-159. The Army Quarterly and Defense Journal. ; 104.

2914. Copeland, M. Beyond cloak and dagger: inside the CIA. - New York : Pinnacle Books, 1975.

2915. Copson, R.W. Libya : US relations. Nov.-Dec. 1983. p. 5-7. Congressional Research Service Review

2916. Cordes, B.J. * et al. Trends in international terrorism, 1982-1983. - Santa Monica, Calif. : RAND, 1984. 54 p

2917. Crenshaw, M. The international consequences of terrorism. ; Paper presented to the American Political Science Association, Chicago, Sept. 1983

2918. Crenshaw, M. Transnational terrorism as a policy issue. ; Paper delivered at the 1974 meeting of the American Political Science Association, Chicago

2919. Crenshaw, M. Transnational terrorism and world politics. 1975. p. 109-129. Jerusalem Journal of International Relations. ; 1:2.

2920. Crozier, B. Aid for terrorism. - London : ISC, 1974. p. 2-11.
In: Annual of Power and Conflict. Vol. 1973-1974

2921. Crozier, B. The surrogate forces of the Soviet Union. - London : ISC, 1978. Conflict Studies. ; 92.

2922. Crozier, B. Transnational terrorism. - London : ISC, 1973. p. 2-12.
In: Annual of Power and Conflict, 1972-1973

2923. Crozier, B. Transnational terrorism. - Gaithersburg, Md. : IACP., 98 p

2924. Demaris, O. Brothers in blood : The international terrorist network. - New York : Charles Scribner's Sons, 1977. 441 p
The last section includes a discussion of the threat of nuclear terrorism.

2925. Deutsch, R.L. Dealing with Quaddafy. March-April 1982. p. 47-53. Africa Report. ; 27.

2926. Dobson, Chr. * Payne, R. The Carlos complex : A pattern of violence. - London : Hodder & Stoughton, 1977. 254 p

2927. Dobson, Chr. * Payne, R. The weapons of terror : International terrorism at work. - London : MacMillan, 1979. 216 p

2928. Dobson, Chr. The Carlos complex : A study in terror. - Fully rev. and ext. version of 1977 ed. - Seven Oaks : Coronet, 1978. 304 p

2929. Doherty, D.A. Carlos from 1970 to 1976 : A lesson in transnational terrorism. Summer 1981. p. 70-79. Joint Perspectives. ; 2.

2930. Dugard, J. International terrorism and the just war. 1977. p. 21-38. Stanford Journal of International Studies. ; 12:1.

2931. Dunn, A.M. International terrorism : Targets, responses and the role of law. - Charlotteville, Va. : John Bassell Moore Society of International Law., 1977. 195 p

2932. East, J.P. Does the USSR really support international terrorism?. 13 June 1981. p. 12-13, 21. Human Events. ; 41.

2933. Eckstein, H. Incidence of internal wars 1946-59. - Princeton : Center of International Studies, 1962.

2934. Eisenberg, D. * Landau, E. Carlos: terror international. - London : Corgi, 1976. 285 p

2935. Elad, Sh. * Merari, A. The Soviet bloc and world terrorism. - Tel Aviv : Tel Aviv University, 1984. 81 p. Jaffee Center for Strategic Studies. ; 26.

2936. Elliott, J.D. Transitions of contemporary terrorism. May 1977. p. 3-15. Military Review. ; 57.

2937. Farahani, A.A.S. What a revolutionary must know. - London : 1973.

2938. Fearey, R.A. International terrorism. March 1976. p. 394-403. Department of State Bulletin. ; 74:1918.

2939. Flores, D.A. Export controls and the US effort to combat international terrorism. 1981. p. 521-590. Law and Policy in International Business. ; 13:2.

2940. Foster, C. Nations without a state. - New York : 1980.

2941. Francis, S.T. The Soviet strategy of terror. - Washington, D.C. : The Heritage Foundation., 1981. 78 p
Sees the Soviet Union supporting international terrorist movements.

2942. Francis, S.T. The terrorist international and Western Europe. - Washington, D.C. : The Heritage Foundation, 21 Dec. 1977. 18 p. Backgrounder Series. ; 47.

2943. Freedman, R.O. Soviet policy toward international terrorism. - New York : Praeger, 1976. p. 115-147.
In: Y. Alexander (ed.), International terrorism: national, regional and global perspectives

2944. Friedlander, R.A. Reflections on terrorist havens. March-April 1976. p. 59-67. Naval War College Review. ; 32.

2945. Ginsburg, H.J. Khadaffi en het terrorisme. 31 Jan. 1986. p. 11-15. Intermediair. ; 22:5.

2946. Glaser, S. Le terrorisme international et ses divers aspects. 1973. p. 825-850. Revue internationale de droit compare. ; 25:4.

2947. Gleason, J.M. A poisson model of incidents of international terrorism in the United States. 1980. p. 259-265. Terrorism. ; 4.

2948. Golan, G. The Soviet Union and the PLO. - London : IISS, 1976.

2949. Gonzales, P. Carlos, la internacional del terrorismo. - Madrid : A.Q. Ediciones, 1976. 254 p

2950. Goren, R. The Soviet Union and terrorism. - London : Allen & Unwin, 1984. 232 p

2951. Green, L.C. The nature and control of international terrorism. -

Atlanta : University of Atlanta, Department of Political Science, 1974. 56 p. Occasional paper. ; 1.

2952. Guillaume, G. * Levasseur, G. Terrorisme international. - Paris : Institute des Hautes Etudes Internationales de Paris, 1977. 134 p

2953. Han, H.H. * (ed.) Terrorism, political violence, and world order. - Lanham, Maryland : University Press of America, 1984. 767 p

2954. Hannay, W.A. International terrorism: the need for a fresh perspective. 1974. p. 268-284. International Lawyer. ; 8:2.

2955. Harden, B. Terrorism. 15 March 1981. p. 14-16, 18-22. Washington Post Magazine
Questions USSR involvement.

2956. Heradstveit, D. The role of international terrorism in the Middle East conflict and its implication for conflict resolution. - London : Croom Helm, 1975. p. 93-103.
In: D. Carlton and C. Schaerf (eds.), International terrorism and world security

2957. Hersh, S.M. The Qaddafi connection. 14 and 21 June 1981. New York Times Magazine

2958. Holley, Ch. Why Libya exports chaos: the anatomy of an international terror network. Nov. 1976. p. 14-16. Atlas. ; 23.
Alleged role of Muammar el Qadaffi.

2959. Holton, G. Reflections on modern terrorism. 1977. p. 96-104. The Jerusalem Journal of International Relations. ; 3:1.

2960. Hunter, J.D. The terror alliance. - London : Seven House, 1981. 318 p

2961. Hutton, J.B. The subverters. - New Rochelle, N.Y. : Arlington House, 1972. 266 p
By a former member of the Czech Communist Party.

2962. Huyn, H. Sieg ohne Krieg. - Muenchen : Universitas, 1985. 407 p

2963. Imberger, H. Die Terrormultis. - Wien-Muenchen : Jugend und Volk Verlag, 1976. 330 p

2964. Irish, J. Terrorismo internacional. - Barcelona : Producciones Editoriales, 1975. 226 p

2965. Jacquard, R. Les dossiers secrets du terrorisme. - Paris : A. Michel, 1985. 322 p

2966. Jarach, A. Terrorismo internazionale. - Firenze : Vallecchi, 1979.

2967. Javits, J.K. International terrorism: apathy exacerbates the problem. 1978. p. 111-117. Terrorism. ; 1:2.

2968. Jazani, B. Armed struggle : The road to the mobilisation of the masses. - London : 1976.

2969. Jenkins, B.M. * Johnson, J. International terrorism: a chronology, 1968-1974. - Santa Monica, Calif. : RAND, 1975. 65 p

2970. Jenkins, B.M. Embassies under siege : A review of 48 embassy takeovers, 1971-1980. - Santa Monica, Calif. : RAND, 1981. 38 p

2971. Jenkins, B.M. International terrorism: trends and potentialities. - Washington, D.C. : GPO, 1978. 139 p.
In: U.S. Congress, Senate. Committee on Governmental Affairs. Report to accompany S.2236 (An act to combat terrorism). 95th Congres, 2nd session

2972. Jenkins, B.M. International terrorism. - Santa Monica, Calif. : RAND, 1975. 58 p

2973. Jenkins, B.M. International terrorism: a balance sheet. July 1975. p. 158-164. Survival. ; 17:4.

2974. Jenkins, B.M. The future course of international terrorism. - Santa Monica, Calif. : Rand, 1985. 13 p

2975. Jenkins, B.M. Trends in international terrorism. Spring 1984. p. 40-48. World Affairs Journal. ; 3.

2976. Kaldos, M. * Anderson, P. * (eds.) Mad dogs : The U.S. raids on Libya. Pluto Press, 172 p

2977. Kaufmann, J. L'internationale terroriste. - Paris : Plon, 1977. 231 p

2978. Kellett, A. International terrorism : A prospective and retrospective examination. - Ottawa : Operational Research and Analysis Establishment, Department of Defense, 1981.

2979. Kemp, A. A computer model of international violence. 1977. p. 51-62. International Interactions. ; 3:1.

2980. Kemp, A. A path analytical model of international violence. 1978. p. 63-85. International Interactions. ; 4:1.

2981. Ketelsen, D. Moskaus Haltung zum internationalen Terrorismus. Nov. 1978. p. 965-977. Osteuropa. ; 28.
Moscow and international terrorism.

2982. Kreis, K.M. Der Internationale Terrorismus. - Frankfurt a.M. : 1977. p. 390-403.
In: Sicherheitspolitik vor neuen Ausgaben

2983. Kreis, K.M. International terrorism - unsolved problem of international community. 1976. p. 367-375. Europa Archiv. ; 31:11.

2984. Kumamoto. R.D. International terrorism and American foreign relations, 1945- 1976. University of California, 1984. ; Ph.D. dissertation

2985. Kupperman, R.H. * Smith, H.A. Waiting for terror. 1978. p. 50-61. The Washington Review of Strategic and International Studies. ; 1:2.

2986. Kupperman, R.H. * Trent, D.M. The terrorist international. Feb. 1980. p. 50-68. Across the Board. ; 17.

2987. Kurkjian, S. * Bradlee jr, B. The Americans who are training and supplying Libyan terrorists. 22 March 1981. p. D1, D5. Washington Post

2988. Laffin, J. Murder incorporated. 30 Aug. 1975. Spectator
On Libyian and other support for Palestinian terrorists.

2989. Lagoni, R. United Nations and international terrorism. 1977. p. 171-189. Europa Archiv. ; 32:6.

2990. Laqueur, W. Terrorism : A study in national and international political violence. - Boston : Little Brown, 1977.

2991. Laurent, R. L'internationale terroriste demasquee. - Nice : A. Lefeuvre, 1981. 300 p

2992. Leber, J.R. International terrorism: criminal or political?. 1973. p. 129ff. Towson State Journal of International Affairs. ; 7:2.

2993. Leichter, O. Die Vereinigten Nationen und der internationale Terrorismus. Febr. 1973. Vereinigte Nationen. ; 21:1.

2994. Leonard, L.L. Global terrorism confronts the nations. - New York : New York University Press, 1979. 186 p

2995. Leoni Houssay, L.A. La conexion internacional del terrorismo. - Buenos Aires : Ediciones Depalma, 1980.

2996. Lillich, R.B. * (ed.) Transnational terrorism, conventions and commentary : A compilation of treaties, agreements and declarations of especial interest to the United States. - Charlottesville : 1982.

2997. Lillich, R.B. * Paxman, J.M. State responsibility for injuries to aliens occasioned by terrorist activities. 1977. p. 217-313. American University Law Review. ; 26:2.

2998. Livingston, M.H. * et al. * (eds.) International terrorism in the contemporary world. - Westport, Conn. : Greenwood Press, 1978. 522 p

2999. Matekolo, I. Les dessous du terrorisme international. - Paris : Julliard, 1973. 221 p
Mysteries of international terrorism.

3000. Medzini, R. China and the Palestinians. 1971. p. 34-40. The New Middle East. ; 32.

3001. Mickolus, E.F. * Heyman, E.S. ITERATE: monitoring transnational terrorism. - New York : Pergamon Press, 1981. p. 153-174.
In: Y. Alexander and J.M. Gleason (eds.), Behavioral and quantitative perspectives on terrorism
The ITERATE data were developed by Edward Mickolus; they are available through the Inter-University Consortium for Political and Social Research, University of Michigan.

3002. Mickolus, E.F. Chronology of transnational attacks upon American businessmen, 1968-1978. - New York : Praeger, 1979. p. 499-521.
In: Y. Alexander and R.A. Kilmarx (eds.), Political terrorism and business: the threat and response

3003. Mickolus, E.F. Chronology of transnational terrorist attacks upon American business people, 1968-1976. 1978. p. 217-235. Terrorism. ; 1:2.

3004. Mickolus, E.F. International terrorism in the 1980's : A chronology. - Westport, Conn. : Greenwood Press, in preparation.

3005. Mickolus, E.F. International terrorism in the 1980's : Data codebook for microcomputers. - Ann Arbor, Mich. : Inter-University Consortium for Political and Social Research, in preparation.

3006. Mickolus, E.F. International terrorism : Attributes of terrorist events, 1968-1977. - Ann Arbor, Mich. : Inter-University Consortium for Political and Social Research, 1982. 203 p
Iterate 2 data codebook.

3007. Mickolus, E.F. International terrorism : Review and projection. 51 p ; Address to the Conference on terrorism and the American Corporation, sponsored by Probe International Inc., held in New York City, Sept. 14-15, 1976

3008. Mickolus, E.F. International terrorism in 1979. 1980. ; Paper presented to the Annual convention of the Academy of Criminal Justice Sciences, Oklahoma City, Oklahoma, March 1980

3009. Mickolus, E.F. International terrorism : Attributes of terrorist events (ITERATE). - Ann Arbor, Mich. : Inter-University Consortium for Political and Social Research, 1976. 41 p Codebook for data on 539 transnational terrorist events from Jan. 1970 to July 1973

3010. Mickolus, E.F. Project ITERATE: quantitative studies of transnational terrorism. 1976. 49 p ; Paper presented to the Annual convention of the North-east Political Science Association, Nov. 1976, at the Jug End, South Egremont, Massachusetts
Reprinted by the US Department of State, INR/XR as FAR 26105-N.

3011. Mickolus, E.F. Transnational terrorism : A chronology of events 1968-1979. - London : Aldwych Press, 1980. 967 p
The material in this volume forms the data that comprises the 'International terrorism: attributes of terrorist events' (ITERATE) computer system.

3012. Mickolus, E.F. Trends in transnational terrorism. - Westport, Conn. : Greenwood Press, 1978. p. 44-73.
In: M.H. Livingston et al. (eds.), International terrorism in the contemporary world

3013. Milbank, D.L. International and transnational terrorism: diagnosis and prognosis. - Washington, D.C. : CIA, 1976. 58 p
Includes surveys of terrorist organisations and a breakdown of different types of terrorism.

3014. Milbank, D.L. International terrorism in 1976. - Washington, D.C. : CIA, 1977. 19 p
Unlike the author's previous study, this one no longer distinguishesbetween international terrorism (government backed) and transnational terrorism (without direct government support).

3015. Moayedoddin, M. International terrorism : Three case studies. Claremont Graduate School, 1982. ; Ph.D. dissertation

3016. Momtaz, D. Rapport de Monsieur D.M. sur le terrorisme internationale. 1974. p. 172-190. Revue egyptienne de droit international. ; 30.

3017. Moss, R. International terrorism and Western societies. 1973. p. 418-430. International Journal. ; 28:3.
Evaluates the motives and means of a number of terrorists and evaluates the techniques used by governments to cope with them.

3018. Moss, R. Terror: a Soviet export. 2 Nov. 1980. p. 42, 46, 48, 50, 52, 58. New York Times Magazine

3019. Motley, J.B. Coping with state-supported international terrorism : An undeclared war. - Lexington, Mass. : D.C. Health and Co., forthcoming.
In: N. Livingstone and T. Arnold (eds.), Figthing Back

3020. Mueller-Borchert, H.J. Zum Problem des internationalen Terrorismus - Flugzeug- Entfuehrungen, Menschenraub, Kaderguerrilla. 1976. Kriminalistik. ; 30.

3021. Mumcu, U. The Pope, the Mafia, and Agca. - Washington, D.C. : Foreign Broadcast Information Service, 1985. 225 p

3022. Muszynskiego, J. * (ed.) Terroryzm politiczny. - Warshaw : Paristwowe Wydawn Nanki, 1981. 353 p

3023. Netanyahu, B. * (ed.) International terrorism : Challenge and response. - New Brunswick, N.J. : Transaction Books, 1981. ; Proceedings of the Jerusalem conference on international terrorism

3024. Norton, A.R. International terrorism. 1981. p. 597-628. Armed Forces and Society. ; 7:4.

3025. Oots, K.L. Transnational terrorism : A political approach. Northern Illinois University, 1984. ; Ph.D. dissertation

3026. Palchev, I. The assassination attempt against the Pope and the roots of terrorism. - Sofia : Sofia Press, 1985. 106 p

3027. Petersen, R.W. * Chrisman, W.G. International terrorism threat analysis. - Monterey, Calif. : Naval Postgraduate School, 1977. 96 p ; Master's thesis

3028. Pierre, A.J. The politics of international terrorism. 1976. p. 1251-1269. Orbis. ; 19.

3029. Pipes, D. No one likes the colonel : From the shores of Tripoli to the airstrip in Fua'amotu. March 1981. p. 363-371. American Spectator

3030. Pipes, D. Qaddafi's little Libya plays great power games. 19 Febr. 1981. Wall Street Journal

3031. Pisano, V.S. Clandestine operations in Italy : The Bulgarian connection. Winter 1984. p. 28-38. Conflict Quarterly. ; 4.

3032. Pisano, V.S. Communist bloc covert action : The Italian case. - Gaithersburg, Md. : IACP, 1981. 26 p

3033. Pisano, V.S. Libya's foothold in Italy. Spring 1982. p. 179-182. Washington Quarterly. ; 5.

3034. Pisano, V.S. Libya's multifaceted foreign policy : The Italian application. 15 Dec. 1981. Congressional Record (daily ed.). ; 127.

3035. Possony, S.T. Terrorism : A global concern. Jan. 1973. p. 4-5. Defense and Foreign Affairs Digest. ; 2.

3036. Prevost, J.F. Les aspects nouveaux du terrorisme international. 1973. p. 579-600. Annuaire francais de droit international. ; 19.

3037. Ra'anan, U. * Pfaltzgraff, R.L. * Schultz, R.H. * et al. * (eds.) Hydra of carnage : International linkages of terrorism. The witnesses speak. - Lexington, Mass. : Lexington Books, 1986. 656 p

3038. Radovanovic, L. The problem of international terrorism. Oct. 1972. p. 5. Review of International Affairs. ; 23.

3039. Reagan, R. The new network of terrorist states. Aug. 1985. p. 7-12. Dept. of State Bulletin. ; 85.

3040. Reisman, W.M. Private armies in a global war system: prologue to decision. 1973. p. 1. Virginia Journal of International Law. ; 14.

3041. Revesz, L. Christian peace conference: church funds for terrorists. - London : ISC, 1978.

3042. Romaniecki, L. Arab terrorists in the Middle East and the Soviet Union. - Jerusalem : Soviet and East European Research Center, Hebrew University, 1973. Research Paper. ; 4.

3043. Romaniecki, L. The Soviet Union and international terrorism. July 1974. p. 417-440. Soviet Studies. ; 26:3.

3044. Romerstein, H. Soviet support for international terrorism. - Washington, D.C. : Foundation for Democratic Education, 1981. 40 p

3045. Rosenau, J.N. Internal war as an international event. - Princeton, N.J. : Princeton University Press, 1964.
In: J.N. Rosenau (ed.), International aspects of civil strife

3046. Russell, Ch.A. Transnational terrorism. Jan. 1976. p. 26-35. Air University Review. ; 27:2.

3047. Sablier, E. Le fil rouge : Histoire secrete du terrorisme international. - Paris : Plon, 1983.

3048. Sandler, T. * Tschirhart, J.T. * Cauley J. A theoretical analysis of transnational terrorism. March 1983. p. 36-54. American Political Science Review. ; 77:1.

3049. Shultz jr, R.H. International terrorism : Operations and R&D measurements. - Gaithersburg, Md. : IACP., 22 p

3050. Shultz, G.P. Terrorism and the modern world. Dec. 1984. p. 12-17. Dept. of State Bulletin. ; 84.

3051. Skolnick jr, J.M. An appraisal of studies of the linkage between domestic and international conflict. 1974. p. 485-509. Comparative Political Studies. ; 6:4.

3052. Sloan, S. * Wise, Ch. International terrorism. Nov. 1977. ADL Bulletin. ; 34:9.

3053. Sloan, S. The anatomy of non-territorial terrorism. - Gaithersburg, Md. : IACP, 1978.
In: Ch.T. Whittier and S. Sloan (eds.), The conduct of businessmen overseas, an Oklahoma perspective

3054. Smith, W.H. International terrorism : A political analysis. - London : Stevens & Sons, 1977. p. 138-157.
In: the Year Book of World Affairs 1977, London Institute of World Affairs

3055. Sottile, A. Le terrorisme international. 1938. p. 87-184. Recueil des cours de l'Academie de Droit International de La Haye. ; 3.

3056. St.John, P. Analysis and response of a decade of terrorism. Sept.-Oct. 1981. p. 2-5. International Perspectives

3057. St.John, R.B. Terrorism and Libyan foreign policy, 1981-1986. July 1986. p. 111-115. World Today. ; 42.

3058. Steelman, H. International terrorism vis-a-vis air hijacking. 1977. p. 85-110. Southwestern University Law Review. ; 9.

3059. Stencel, S. International terrorism. 1977. p. 911-932. Washington Editorial Research Reports. ; 2:21.

3060. Sterling, C. Qaddafi spells chaos. 7 March 1981. p. 15-20. New Republic. ; 184.

3061. Sterling, C. Terrorism tracing the international network. 1 March 1981. p. 16-19, 24, 54-56, 58-60. New York Times Magazine

3062. Sterling, C. The great Bulgarian cover-up. 27 May 1985. p. 16-18, 20-21. New Republic. ; 192.

3063. Sterling, C. The plot to murder the Pope. Sept. 1982. p. 71-84. Reader's Digest. ; 121.

3064. Sterling, C. The strange case of Henri Curiel. 15 March 1981. p. 26-30, 38-39. Washington Post Magazine

3065. Sterling, C. The terror network : The secret war of international terrorism. - New York : Holt, Rinehart & Winston/Reader's Digest, 1980. 357 p

3066. Sterling, C. The terrorist network. Nov. 1978. p. 37-47. Atlantic Monthly. ; 242.

3067. Sterling, C. The time of the assassins. - New York : Holt, Rinehart, and Winston, 1984. 264 p

3068. Stohl, M. The nexus of civil and international conflict. - New York : Free Press, 1980. p. 297-330.
In: T.R. Gurr (ed.), Handbook of political conflict. Theory and research

3069. Styles, G. Terrorism: the global war of the seventies. Aug. 1976. p. 594-596. International Defense Review. ; 9.

3070. Thompson, J. Rejsende i terror : En dokumentarbog om Carlos, PFLP, Japans Rode Haer, Baader- Meinhof Gruppen og andre. - Lynge : Bogan, 1977. 136 p

3071. Thompson, W.S. Political violence and the correlation of forces. 1976. p. 1270-1288. Orbis. ; 19:34.

3072. Tinnin, D.B. Terror, Inc. 1977. p. 152-154, 158, 166, 170, 17. Playboy. ; 24.

3073. Tobon, N. Carlos: terrorist or guerrilla?. - Barcelona : Ediciones Grijalbo, 1978. 217 p

3074. Vasquez de Martinez, M. del Valle El terrorismo internacional. - Caracas : Publicaciones S.A. Venetesa, 1981. 506 p

3075. Vitiuk, V.V. Toward an analysis and evaluation of the evolution of terrorism. Winter 1980-1981. p. 85-106. Soviet review. ; 21.

3076. Walker, W. The bear at the back door. - Richmond, Surrey : Foreign Affairs Publ. Co., 1978. 246 p

3077. Wilkinson, P. Terrorism - international dimensions. - London : ISC, 1979.

3078. Wilkinson, P. Uncomfortable thruths about international terrorism. Jan. 1982. p. 78-84. Across the Board. ; 19.

3079. Williams, S.G. Insurgency terrorism : Attitudes, behavior and response and national policies. The City University of New York, 1980. ; Ph.D. dissertation

3080. Williams, S.G. The transnational impact of insurgency terrorism: a quantitative approach. City University of New York, Queens College, Department of Political Science, 1978. ; Ph.D. dissertation

3081. Wohlstetter, R. International terrorism: kidnapping to win friends and influence people. 1974. p. 1-40. Survey. ; 20:4.

3082. Wolf, J.B. Assessing the performance of a terrorist and an anti-terrorist organization. - New York : John Jay Press, 1982. p. 72-102.
In: D.E.J. MacNamara and P.J. Stead (eds.), New dimensions in transnational crime

3083. Wolf, J.B. Cuban and Soviet involvement in international terrorism. - Gaithersburg, Md. : IACP, 1981. Update Report. ; 7:6.

3084. Wolf, J.B. Global terrorist coalition: its incipient stage. Oct. 1977. p. 328-339. Police Journal (England). ; 50.

3085. Wolf, J.B. International terrorism : Statement of Dr.J.B. Wolf, chairman of the Department of Criminal Justice at Union College. - Washington, D.C. : GPO, 1975. p. 48-73 ; Hearings before the Subcommittee on the Near East and South Asia of the Committee on Foreign Affairs, House of Representatives, 39th Cong., 2nd sess

3086. Wolf, J.B. The Cuban connections and involvements. - Gaithersburg. Md. : IACP, 1979. Update Report. ; 5:5.

3087. Yonay, E. The PLO underground in California. 26 Febr. 1979. ppp. 22-31. New West

3088. Zlataric, B. History of international terrorism and its legal control. - Springfield, Ill. : Thomas, 1975. p. 474-484.
In: M.C. Bassiouni (ed.), International terrorism and political crimes
Discusses league of nations attemps to come to an antiterrorist convention.

3089. _____ Chronology of attacks upon non-official American citizens, 1971-1975. - Washington, D.C. : 20 Jan. 1976.
U.S. Department of State

3090. _____ Chronology of significant terrorist incidents involving U.S. diplomatic official personnel, 1963-1975. - Washington, D.C. : 20 Jan. 1976.
U.S. Department of State

3091. _____ Civil violence and the international system. - 2 vols. - London : 1971.
IISS. Adelphi Papers. ; 82-83.

3092. _____ Firearm felonies by foreign diplomats. - Washington, D.C. : GPO, 1985. 150 p.
U.S. Congress. Senate. Committee on the Judiciary. Subcommittee on Security and Terrorism

3093. _____ Hearings. Terrorist activity. Part 6 : The Cuban connection in Puerto Rico; Castro's hand in Puerto Rican and U.S. terrorism. - 94th Cong., 1st sess., 30 July, 1975. - Washington, D.C. : GPO, 1975.
U.S. Congress, Senate. Committee on the judiciary

3094. _____ Hearings. Terroristic activity. Part 9 : Interlocks between communism and terrorism. - 94th Cong., 2nd sess., 7 May 1976. - Washington, D.C. : GPO, 1976. p. 663-749.
U.S. Congress, Senate. Committee on the judiciary
pp. 720-747 are a reprint of Scanlan's vol. 1, No. 8, Jan. 1971 listof guerrilla acts of sabotage and terrorism in the United States, 1965-1970.

3095. _____ Hearings. Terroristic activity. Part 4 : International terrorism. - 94th Cong., 1st sess., 14 May 1975. - Washington, D.C. : GPO, 1975. p. 177-260.
U.S. Congress, Senate. Committee on the judiciary

3096. _____ Het netwerk van terreur. - Naarden : 1981. De Kern

3097. _____ International terorrism. - Moscow : Novosti Press Agency Pub. House, 1981. 71 p

3098. _____ International terrorism and the CIA : Documents, eyewitness, reports, facts. - Moscow : Progress, 1983. 263 p

3099. _____ International terrorism. June 1981.
U.S. Department of State, Bureau of Public Affairs. Current Policy,. ; 285.

3100. _____ International terrorism : Hearings. - 95th Cong., 1st sess. - Washington, D.C. : GPO, 1978. 93 p.
U.S. Congress, Senate, Committee on Foreign Relations, Subcommittee on Foreign Assistance

3101. _____ International terrorism : Hearings. - 95th Cong., 2nd sess. - Washington, D.C. : GPO, 1978. 392 p.
U.S. Congress, Senate, Committee on Public Works and Transportation, Subcommittee on Aviation

3102. _____ International terrorism in 1976. - Washington, D.C. : CIA, National Foreign Assessments Center, July 1977.
CIA. ; RP 77-10034U.

3103. _____ International terrorism in 1977. - Washington, D.C. : CIA, National Foreign Assessments Center, Aug. 1978.
CIA. ; RP 78-10255U.

3104. _____ International terrorism. 1983. p. 389-499. Terrorism. ; 6:3.
Whole issue.

3105. _____ International terrorism. - Washington, D.C. : GPO, 1985. 29 p.
U.S. Congress. Senate. Committee on Appropriations. Subcommittee on Foreign Operations

3106. _____ International terrorism, insurgency, and drug trafficking: present trends in terrorist activity. - Washington, D.C. : GPO, 1986. 426 p.
U.S. Congress. Senate. Committee on Foreign Relations, and Committee on the Judiciary ; Joint hearings, 13-15 may 1985

3107. _____ International terrorism. - Washington, D.C. : GPO, 1981. 94 p.
U.S. Congress. Senate. Committee on Foreign Relations ; Hearing, 97th Cong., 1st sess., on S. 873, 10 June 1981,

3108. _____ International terrorism. - Philadelphia : American Academy of Political and Social Science, 1982. 206 p

31
09. _____ International terrorism: 1985. - Washington, D.C. : GPO, 1985. 339 p.
U.S. Congress. House. Committee on Foreign Affairs. Subcommittee on Arms Control, International Security and Science ; Hearings and markup before the Committee on Foreign Affairs and its Subcommittees on Arms Control, International Security and Science and on Interna

3110. _____ International terrorism. Aug. 1986. p. 1-16. Dept. of State Bulletin. ; 86.

3111. _____ International terrorism : Proceedings of the 3rd Annual conference of the Canadian Council on International Law, 18-19 Oct. 1974.
Canadian Council on International Law
Reviewed by A. Beichman in: Canadian Journal of Political Science 9:3, 1976, pp. 521-522.

3112. _____ International terrorism in 1978. - Washington, D.C. : CIA National Foreign Assessment Center, March 1979.
CIA. Rp. ; 79-10149.

3113. _____ International terrorism. 1977. Stanford Journal of International Studies. ; 12.
Whole issue. Contains a.o.: J. Tierney jr., Terror at home: the American revolution and irregular warfare; J. Paust, Responses to terrorism: a prologue to decisions concerning private measures of sanction; J. Dugard, International terrorism and the just war.

3114. _____ International terrorism. 1978. Journal of International Affairs (Columbia University). ; 32:1.
On international terrorism with articles by Y. Alexander, B.M. Jenkins, R.N. Lebow, R.K. Mullen, B.E. O'Neill, R.

Shultz, S. Sloan and P.A. Thorp jr.

3115. ______ International terrorism : Hearings. - 93rd Cong., 2nd sess., 11, 18, 19 and 24. - Washington, D.C. : GPO, 1974. 219 p.
U.S. Congress, House. Committee on foreign affairs

3116. ______ International terrorism. - Washington, D.C. : GPO, 1978. 392 p.
U.S. Congress, House. Committee on public works and transportation

3117. ______ International terrorism. - Washington, D.C. : GPO, 1978. 201 p.
U.S. Congress, House. Committee on the judiciary

3118. ______ International terrorism : Hearings. - 95th Congr., 1st sess., 14 Sept. 1977. - Washington, D.C. : GPO, 1977. 90 p.
U.S. Congress, Senate. Committee on foreign relations

3119. ______ International terrorism. 29 March 1976. p. 394-403.
U.S. Department of State. Department of State Bulletin. ; 74:1918.

3120. ______ Latin America's terrorist international. 23 March 1977. p. 1-4.
Economist Foreign Report

3121. ______ Libie : Terreur. 7 Feb. 1986. p. 1-6. Atlantisch Nieuws. ; 1:2.

3122. ______ Libie en het terrorisme. 16 Jan. 1986. p. 33-38. Keesings Historisch Archief. ; 2826.

3123. ______ Libya under Qadhafi : A pattern of aggression. - Washington, D.C. : U.S. Dept. of State, Bureau of Public Affairs, 1986. 8 p

3124. ______ Libya's foreign adventures. - London : 1973.
ISC. Conflict Studies. ; 41.

3125. ______ Libya: still a threat to Western interests. - London : ISC, 1984. 25 p

3126. ______ Libyan activities. - Washington, D.C. : GPO, 1981. 18 p.
U.S. Congress. Senate. Committee on Foreign Relations. Subcommittee on African Affairs ; Hearing before the Subcommittee on African Affairs and the Subcommittee on Near Eastern and South Asian Affairs of the Committee on Foreign Relation

3127. ______ Observations of states submitted in accordance with General Assembly resolution 3034 (XXVII). - New York : 22 June 1973. 22 p.
United Nations, General Assembly. Ad hoc committee on international terrorism ; Analytic study prepared by the secretary-general

3128. ______ Patterns of global terrorism: 1984. - Washington, D.C. : Dept. of State, Office of the Ambassador at Large for Counter-Terrorism, 1985. 29 p

3129. ______ Patterns of international terrorism 1980 : A research paper. - Washington, D.C. : Library of Congress, 1981. 22 p.
National Foreign Assessment Center

3130. ______ Report. - New York : 1977. 51 p.
United Nations, General Assembly. Ad hoc committee on international terrorism. United Nations Document. ; A/32/37.

3131. ______ Report on international terrorism. - Strasbourg : 1972.
Council of Europe

3132. ______ Review of the Presidential certification of Nicaragua's connection to terrorism. - Washington, D.C. : GPO, 1980. 50 p.
U.S. Congress. House. Committee on Foreign Affairs. Subcommittee on Inter-American Affairs

3133. ______ Significant non-Fadayeen international terrorist incidents, January 1970-March 1974.
Available from the London International Institute for Strategic Studies.

3134. ______ Strategic survey, 1985-1986. - London : International Institute for Strategic Studies, 1986. 238 p

3135. ______ Symposium on international terrorism. Spring 1982. p. 453-605.
Rutgers Law Journal. ; 13.

3136. ______ Symposium: international terrorism in the Middle East. 1974.
Akron Law Review. ; 7.

3137. ______ Terrorism. Summer 1983.
World Affairs. ; 146.
Whole issue.

3138. ______ Terrorism : A staff study. - 93rd Cong., 2nd sess., 1 Aug. 1974. - Washington, D.C. : GPO, 1974. 246 p.
U.S. Congress, House. Committee on internal security

3139. ______ Terrorism. - Washington, D.C. : The Pentagon, 1984. 78 p

3140. ______ Terrorism. Aug. 1982. p. 1-35. Department of State Bulletin. ; 82.

3141. ______ Terrorism : Worldwide report. - Washington, D.C. : Foreign Broadcast Information Service, 1984. 104 p

3142. ______ Terrorism as a phenomenon of the late 20th century : Colby College conference report. 1985. p. 79-112. Terrorism. ; 8:1.

3143. _____ Terrorism, the role of Moscow and its subcontractors. - Washington, D.C. : GPO, 1982. 55 p.
U.S. Congress. Senate. Committee on the Judiciary. Subcommittee on Security and Terrorism

3144. _____ Terrorism: vital part of Moscow's foreign policy. Feb. 1984. p. 6-17. Conservative Digest. ; 10.

3145. _____ Terrorismo internacional. - Madrid : Instituto de Cuestiones Internationales, 1984. 364 p

3146. _____ Terroristic activity, part 9 : Interlocks between communism and terrorism - hearings. - 94th Cong., 2nd sess. - Washington, D.C. : GPO, 1976. 97 p.
U.S. Congress, Senate, Committee on the Judiciary, Subcommittee to investigate the administration of the internal security act and other internal security laws

3147. _____ The boss of the terrorist support networks. - Paris : 21 June 1976. p. 7-13. Le point
On the alleged Curiel apparatus.

3148. _____ The disposition of persons involved in international terrorism. - Washington, D.C. : 1976.
U.S. Department of state. Office to combat terrorism
On release of political international terrorists by governments.

3149. _____ The International implications of the papal assassination attempt. - Washington, D.C. : Center for Strategic and International Studies, Georgetown University, 1985. 23 p

3150. _____ The role of Cuba in international terrorism and subversion. - Washington, D.C. : GPO, 1982. 273 p.
U.S. Congress. Senate. Committee on the Judiciary. Subcommittee on Security and Terrorism

3151. _____ The role of the Soviet Union, Cuba, and East Germany in fomenting terrorism in Southern Africa. - 2 vols. - Washington, D.C. : GPO, 1982.
U.S. Congress. Senate. Committee on the Judiciary. Subcommittee on Security and Terrorism

3152. _____ Toenemend internationaal terrorisme. 11 April 1986. p. 3-6. Atlantisch Nieuws. ; 3.

3153. _____ Trotskyite terrorist international : Hearings. - 94th Cong., 1st sess., 24 July 1975. - Washington, D.C. : GPO, 1975.
U.S. Congress, Senate. Committee on the judiciary

3154. _____ Turkey : Investigative profile of Agca's activities, 1978-1984. - Washington, D.C. : Foreign Broadcast Information Service, 1985. 39 p

3155. _____ Understanding Libya's role in world politics. - Washington, D.C. : People's Committee for Students of the Socialist People's Libyan Arab Jamahiriya, 1985. 55 p

3156. _____ War powers, Libya, and state-sponsored terrorism. - Washington, D.C. : GPO, 1986. 382 p.
U.S. Congress. House. Committee on Foreign Affairs. Subcommittee on Arms Control, International Security and Science ; Hearings, 99th Cong., 2nd sess

J. THE TERRORIST PERSONALITY AND ORGANIZATION

3157. Abel, Th. The nazi movement: why Hitler came into power. - New York : 1966.
See Peter H. Merkl's book for a secondary analysis.

3158. Adam, F.C. Saints or sinners : A selective and political study of certain nonstate terrorists. University of Alberta, 1979. ; Ph.D. dissertation

3159. Agostini, P. Cagol Mara : Una donna nelle prime brigate rosse. - Venezia etc. : Temi, 1980. 163 p

3160. Allerbeck, K.R. Soziologie radikaler Studentenbewegungen : Eine vergleichende Untersuchung in der BRD und den Vereinigten Staaten. - Muenchen-Wien : Oldenbourg, 1973. 272 p

3161. Alpert, J. I bombed the Federal building. 23 July 1981. p. 20-23, 62-63. Rolling Stone. ; 348.

3162. Avner (pseud.). Memoirs of an assassin. - New York : Yoseloff, 1959. 200 p
Description by a former member of Lehi of some of the organization'sactivities.

3163. Avrich, P. Bakunin and Nechaev. - London : 1974.

3164. Baeyer-Katte, W.von * Claessens, D. * Feger, H. * Neidhardt, F. Gruppenprozesse. - Bonn : Westdeutscher Verlag, 1982. 525 p. Analysen zum Terrorismus. ; 3.

3165. Bakounine, M. Oeuvres completes. Vol. 5 : Michel Bakounine et ses relations avec Serge Netchaieff. 1870-1872. - Paris : Editions Champ Libre, 1977.

576 p

3166. Barker, D. Grivas. Portrait of a terrorist. - New York : Harcourt, Brace, 1960. 202 pCypr
us.

3167. Barrue, J. Bakounine et Nechaiev. - Paris : 1971.

3168. Bartoldi. Memoirs of the secret societies of the south of Italy. - London : 1821.
On Carbonari.

3169. Baumann, M. Terror or love : Personal account of a West German urban guerrilla. - London : Calder, 1979. 136 p

3170. Begin, M. The revolt : Story of the Irgun. - Revised ed. - New York : Dell Publishing Co., 1977.
Orig. ed.: New York: Schumann, 1951.

3171. Bell, J.B. Assassination in international politics: Lord Moyne, Count Bernadotte, and the Lehi. 1972. p. 59-82. International Studies Quarterly. ; 16:1.
On personality traits of terrorists.

3172. Bell, J.B. Contemporary revolutionary organizations. - Cambridge, Mass. : Harvard University Press, 1973. p. 153-168.
In: R.O. Keokane and J.S. Nye jr. (eds.), Transnational relations and world politics
Notes the national character of the majority of revolutionary groupsprofessing internationalism.

3173. Bell, J.B. Revolutionary organizations : Special cases and imperfect models. - New York : Wiley, 1975. p. 78-92.
In: D. Carlton and C. Schaerf (eds.), International terrorism and world security
Also: London: Croom Helm, 1975.

3174. Bell, J.B. The profile of a terrorist. - New York : Columbia Institute of War and Peace Studies.,

3175. Bergman, J. Vera Zasulich : A biography. - Stanford : Stanford University Press, 1983.

3176. Berkman, A. Prison memoirs of an anarchist. - New York : Schocken, 1970. Orig. published in 1912.

3177. Betancourt, L.A. Por que Carlos?. - New York : Distribuido por Ediciones Vitral, 1981. 167 p

3178. Billig, O. The lawyer terrorist and his comrades. March 1985. p. 29-46. Political Psychology. ; 6.

3179. Bocca, G. Noi terroristi. - Milano : Garzanti, 1985. 292 p

3180. Broido, V. Apostles into terrorists : Women in the revolutionary movement in the Russia of Alexander II. - New York : Viking Press, 1977. 238 p

3181. Bryan, J. This soldier still at war. - New York : Harcourt, Brace, Jovanovich, 1975. 341 p
On Joseph Michael Remiro, SLA.

3182. Calvert, M. The characteristics of guerrilla leaders and their rank and file. - London : Dec. 1973. The Practitioner
Historical survey of 55 guerrilla leaders.

3183. Caso, A. * (ed.) Los subversivos. - Havana : 1973.
On L.A. (urban) guerrilleros.

3184. Chard, J.la The mind of the terrorist. 5 June 1975. p. 722-723. Listener. ; 93.

3185. Clark, R.P. Patterns in the lives of ETA members. 1983. p. 423-454. Terrorism. ; 6:3.

3186. Daly, W.T. The revolutionary : A review and synthesis. - Beverly Hills : Sage, 1972. 40 p

3187. Danto, A.C. Logical portrait of the assassin. Aug. 1974. p. 426-438. Social Research. ; 41.

3188. Debray, R. La guerrilla du Che. - Paris : Editions du Seuil, 1974.

3189. Delarne, J. Geschichte der Gestapo. - Duesseldorf : 1964.

3190. Deutscher, I. Stalin : Eine politische Biographie. - Stuttgart : Kohlhammer, 1962. 648 p

3191. Di Lorenzo, G. Stefan, 22, deutscher Rechtsextremist : Mein Traum ist der Traum von vielen. - Reinbek bei Hamburg : 1984.
Portrait of a German extremist on the right.

3192. Dicks, H.V. Licensed mass murder : A socio-psychological study of some SS killers. - London : Chatto/Heidemann, 1972. 283 p

3193. Donovan, W.J. * Roucek, J.S. Secret movements. - New York : Cromwell, 1958.

3194. Downton, J.V. Rebel leadership; commitment and charisma in the revolutionary process. - New York : Free Press, 1973. 306 p
Socio-psychological study of four movements; among them the Nazi andBolsheviks.

3195. Drif, Z. La mort de mes freres. - Paris : Maspero, 1960.
Memoirs of an Algerian woman terrorist.

3196. Drooz, D.B. Carlos. Nov. 1976. p. 12-17. Movement

3197. El-Rayyes, R. * Nahas, D. Guerrillas for Palestine : A study of the Palestinian Commando Organisation. - London : Croom Helm, 1976.

3198. Emerson, R.Q. Who's who in terrorism, 1984. R.Q. Emerson, 1984. 56 p

3199. Erikson, E.H. Identity : Youth and crisis. - London : Faber & Faber, 1968.

3200. Falcionelli, A. Les societes secretes italiennes. - Paris : 1969.

3201. Falk, C. Psychologie der Guerillas. 1970. Allgemeine Schweizerische Militaerzeitschrift. ; 7.

3202. Fallaci, O. A leader of Fedayeen: 'We want a war like the Vietnam war' : Interview with Georg Habash. 12 June 1970. p. 32-34. Life

3203. Fare, I. * Spirito, F. Mara e le altre : Le donne e la lotta armata: storie, interviste, riflessioni. - 3. ed. - Milano : Feltrinelli, 1979. 184 p

3204. Ferreira, J.C. Carlos Marighella. - Havana : Tricontinental, 1970.

3205. Figner, V. Memoirs of a revolutionist. - New York : 1927.
By a member of the Russian "People's Will".

3206. Foley, Ch. * (ed.) The memoirs of general Grivas. - London : Longmans, 1964. 226 p
On Cyprus and EOKA.

3207. Forni, D. Storia di uno di noi : Diario di una segregazione. - Venezia : Marsillio, 1980. 183 p

3208. Gall, S.N. Teodoro Petkoff : The crisis of the professional revolutionary. Part 1: Years of insurrection. - Hannover, N.H. : American University, 1972. Field Staff Reports. ; 1.

3209. Geschwender, J.A. Explorations in the theory of social movements and revolutions. Dec. 1968. p. 127-135. Social Forces

3210. Giacomoni, P.D. J'ai tue pour rien : Un Commando Delta a Alger. - Paris : Fayard, 1974. 313 p
On OAS 1961-62 in Algeria, personal observations.

3211. Godfrey, J.R. Revolutionary justice : A study of the organization, personnel, and procedure of the Paris tribunal, 1793-1795. 1951.

3212. Goldman, E. Living my life. - New York : 1931.

3213. Goulden, J.C. * Raffio, A.W. The death merchant : The rise and fall of Edwin P. Wilson. - New York : Simon and Schuster, 1984. 455 p

3214. Gramont, S.de How a pleasant, scholarly young man from Brazil became a kidnapping, gun-toting, bombing revolutionary. 15 Nov 1970. New York Times Magazine

3215. Greene, T.H. Comparative revolutionary movements. - Englewood Cliffs, N.J. : Prentice-Hall, 1974. 172 p

3216. Greig, I. Today's revolutionaries : A study of some prominent modern revolutionary movements and methods of sedition in Europe and the United States. - Richmond, Surrey : Foreign Affairs Publ., 1970. 120 p

3217. Gross, F. The revolutionary party : Essays in the sociology of politics. - Westport, Conn. : Greenwood Press, 1974. 280 p

3218. Guttmacher, M.S. The mind of the murderer. - New York : Farrar, Strauss & Cudahy, 1960. 244 p

3219. Hamon, A. Psychologie de l'anarchist-socialiste. - Paris : 1895.

3220. Hampden-Turner, C. Radical man: the process of psycho-social development. - Cambridge : Schenkman, 1970. 433 p

3221. Heller, M. Lenin and the Cheka: the real Lenin. Spring 1979. p. 175-192. Survey. ; 24.

3222. Hildermeier, M. Sozialstruktur und Kampfmethode der Sozial-Revolutionaeren Partei. Dec. 1972.
In: Jahrbuecher fuer Geschichte Osteuropas
Russia before 1914.

3223. Hills, D.C. Rebel people. - New York : Africana Publ., 1978. 248 p

3224. Hobsbawn, E.J. Bandits. - New York : Delacorte, 1969. 128 p

3225. Hobsbawn, E.J. Primitive rebels: studies in archaic forms of social movements in the 19th and 20th centuries. - Manchester : Manchester University Press, 1959. 208 p

3226. Hobsbawn, E.J. Revolutionaries. - New York : Pantheon, 1973. 278 p

3227. Hodde, L.de la Histoire de societes secretes. - Paris : 1850.
Repr. New York, 1964, as 'History of secret societies'. The author, a French police spy, lists what sort of people joined revolutionary movements in the 1830s and 1840s.

3228. Hoess, R. Commandant of Auschwitz. - New York : 1960.

3229. Hoffner, E. Der Fanatiker : Eine Pathologie des Parteigaengers. - Reinbek : Rowohlt, 1965.
Orig.: The true believer. Thoughts on the nature of mass movements.

3230. Hollstein, W. Der Untergrund : Zur Soziologie jugendlicher Protestbewegungen. - Neuwied : Luchterhand, 1969. 180 p

3231. Hopper, R.D. The revolutionary process: a frame of reference for the study of revolutionary movements. March 1950. p. 28. Social Forces

3232. Hubbard, D.G. The skyjackers. - New York : Collier Books, 1973. 317 p

3233. Ijad, A. Un palestien sans patrie. - Paris : Afrique Biblio Club, 1978.
Reminicenses of a co-founder of El Fatah and chief of intelligence of the PLO, compiled by Eric Rouleau, the Near- East specialist of Le Monde.

3234. Iskenderow, A.A. Die nationale Befreiungsbewegung : Probleme, Gesetzmaessigkeiten, Perspektiven. - East-Berlin : Staatsverlag der Deutschen Demokratischen Republik, 1972. 414 p

3235. Jaeger, H. * et al. Lebenslaufanalysen. - Opladen : Westdeutscher Verlag, 1981. 243 p

3236. Jaeger, H. * Schmidtchen G. * Sullwolda, L. Lebenslaufanalysen. - Bonn : Westdeutscher Verlag, 1981. 243 p. Analysen zum Terrorismus. ; 2.
Biographies of German extremists.

3237. Janke, P. Guerilla and terrorist organisations : A world directory and bibliography. - Brighton : The Harvester Press, 1983. 531 p
Also: New York: MacMillan.

3238. Kaplan, J. The assassins. May 1967. p. 1110-1151. Stanford Law Review. ; 10.

3239. Kellen, K. Terrorists what are they like? : How some terrorists describe their world and actions. - Santa Monica, Calif. : RAND, 1979.

3240. Kelly, C.M. Terrorism : A phenomenon of sick men. - Clarmont, Calif. : Clarmont Men's College, 1974. Res-Publica. ; 2:3.

3241. Khaled, L. My people shall live : The autobiography of a revolutionary. - London : Hodder and Stoughton, 1973. 223 p
Memoirs of a PLO terrorist. Also: New York: Bantam Books, 1974.

3242. Kiernan, T. Arafat: the man and the myth. - New York : Norton, 1976. 281 p
Biography of the PLO leader.

3243. Killinger, M.von Ernstes und heiteres aus dem Putschleben. - Munich : 1934.

3244. Klein, H.J. Rueckkehr in die Menschlichkeit : Appell eines ausgestiegenen Terroristen. - Reinbek : Rowohlt, 1979. 331 p
Return to humanity. Appeal of a drop-out terrorist.

3245. Korte-Pucklitsch, I. Warum werden Frauen zu Terroristen?. 1978. p. 178-187. Merkur. ; 32.

3246. Kreml, W.P. The vigilante personality. - Philadelphia : University of Philadelphia Press, 1976. p. 45-63. In: H.J. Rosenbaum and P.C. Sederberg (eds.), Vigilante politics

3247. Kulman, B.G. Eliminating the political offense exception for violent crimes : The proposed United States-United Kingdom supplementary extradition treaty. Spring 1986. p. 755-783. Virginia Journal of International Law. ; 26.

3248. Lasswell, H.D, * Lerner, D. * (eds.) World revolutionary elites: studies in coercive ideological movements. - Cambridge, Mass. : Massachusetts Institute of Technology Press, 1965.
4 studies on communists in Russia and China, and fascists in Italy and Germany.

3249. Lennhoff, E. Politische Geheimbuende. - Muenchen-Wien : Langen-Mueller, 1968. 139 p

3250. Levine, I.D. The mind of an assassin. - New York : Farrar, Straus, Cudahy, 1959. 232 p
On the assassin of Leon Trotsky, Ramon Mercader.

3251. Lombroso, C. Die Anarchisten : Eine kriminal-psychologische und soziologische Studie. - Hamburg : Richter, 1895. 139 p

3252. Long, S. Carlos. Nov. 1977. p. 62-66. High Times

3253. Mac Stiofain, S. (pseud. for J.E.D. Stephenson) Revolutionary in Ireland. - Farnborough : Gordon Cremonesi, 1975. 372 p
Autobiography of the chief of staff of the IRA Provisionals.

3254. Macbride, S. Interview with -. Jan. 1976. p. 8-11, 54-57. Skeptic. ; 11.

3255. Mahler, H. Per la critica del terrorismo. - Bari : De Donato, 1980. 155 p

3256. Manzini, G. Indagino su un Brigatista Rosso : La storia di Walter Alasia. - Torino : Einaudi, 1978.
Investigations on a member of the Red Brigades (Italy).

3257. Maser, W. Studien zum Typus revolutionaerer Organisation. - Darmstadt : Wittmann, 1976. 100 p

3258. Mathiez, A. Robespierre : L'histoire et la legende. 1977. p. 3-31. Ann. Hist. de la revolution francaise. ; 49:1.
Robespierre: history and legend.

3259. May, E. Che Guevara. - Hamburg : Rowohlt Verlag, 1978.

3260. Mazlish, B. The revolutionary ascetic : Evolution of a political type. - New York : Basic Books, 1976.

3261. McGuire, M. To take arms: my years with the IRA provisionals. - New York : Viking, 1973. 159 p
Memoirs of an ex-IRA-member who left the movement when the indiscriminate bombing campaign began in 1972.

3262. McKnight, G. The mind of the terrorist. - London : Michael Joseph, 1974. 182 p
Based on interviews with terrorists.

3263. Melman, Y. The master terrorist : The true story behind Abu Nidal. - New York : Adama Books, 1986. 215 p

3264. Meltzer, M. The terrorists. - New York : Harper and Row, 1983. 216 p

3265. Melucci, A. * (ed.) Movimenti di rivolta. - Milano : 1976.
'Revolting movements'.

3266. Merkl, P.H. Political violence under the Swastica : 581 early Nazis. - Princeton, N.J. : Princeton University Press, 1975. 735 p
Based on sample of 581 "alte Kaempfer", first analysed in 1934 by Theodore Abel.

3267. Middendorff, W. Die Persoenlichkeit des Terroristen : Ins besondere die Frau als Terroristin. 1976. p. 289-296. Kriminalistik. ; 30.

3268. Middendorff, W. Neue Erscheinungsformen der Gewaltkriminalitaet - zugleich Versuch einer Taetertypologie. Nov. 1973. p. 481-493. Kriminalistik. ; 27:11.

3269. Middendorff, W. The personality of the terrorist. - Vol. 3. - Rockville, Md. : National Criminal Justice Reference Service, Law Enforcement Assistance Administration, Department, 1979. p. 89-98.
In: M. Kravitz (ed.), International summaries. A collection of selected translations in law enforcement and criminal justice

3270. Miksche, F.O. Secret forces : The technique of underground movements. - 3rd impr. - London : Faber & Faber, 1951. 181 p

3271. Miller, J.A. Political violence movements : An interrogative, integrative systems approach. - Washington : American University, 1976. ; Unpubl. Ph.D. dissertation

3272. Molnar, A.R. * et al. Undergrounds in insurgent, revolutionary, and resistance warfare. - Washington, D.C. : The American University Special Operations Research Office, 1963.

3273. Momboisse, R.M. Blueprint for revolution - the rebel, the party, the techniques of revolt. - Springfield, Ill. : Charles C. Thomas, 1970. 336 p

3274. Moran, S.E. Court depositions of three Red Brigadists. - Santa Monica, Calif. : RAND, 1986. 269 p
Testimony of P. Peci, M. Cianfanelli and E. Fenzi.

3275. Morf, G. Terror in Quebec. - Toronto-Vancouver : Clark, Irwin, 1970.
The French edition "Le terrorisme quebecois" was published in Montreal, Editions de l'Homme, 1970. - the author, a psychiatrist practicing in Montreal, interviewed captured members of the F.L.Q.

3276. Mueller, M.A. Revolutionary terrorist : A character analysis. Fall 1976. p. 38-43. Military Police Law Enforcement Journal. ; 3.

3277. Mukerjee, D. The terrorist. - New York : Vintage, 1980.

3278. Nass, G. Anarcho-Terroristen in Untersuchungs- und Strafhaft. 1973. p. 36-41. Zeitschrift fuer Strafvollzug,. ; 22:1.

3279. Neuhauser, P. The mind of a German terrorist : Interview with M.C. Baumann. Sept. 1978. p. 81-88. Encounter. ; 51.

3280. O'Flaherty, L. The terrorist. - London : Archer, 1926.

3281. O'Neill, T. The autobiography of Terence O'Neill. - London : Hart-Davis, 1972. 160 p

3282. Oots, K.L. A political organization approach to transnational terrorism. - New York : Greenwood Press, 1986. 174 p

3283. Paczensky, S.von * (ed.) Frauen und Terror : Versuche, die Beteiligung von Frauen an Gewalttaten zu erklaeren. - Reinbek : Rowohlt, 1978.

3284. Paine, L. The assassins' world. - New York : Taplinger Publishing Co.,

1975.
Case studies of assassins.

3285. Palmer, R.R. Twelve who ruled: the Committee of Public Safety during the Terror. - Princeton, N.J. : Princeton University Press, 1941.
Reissued 1970. France 1792-3.

3286. Parsons, T. Some sociological aspects of the fascists movements. - Glencoe, Ill. : Free Press, 1954.
In: T. Parsons, Essays in sociological theory

3287. Peci, P. Io, l'infame. - Milano : A. Mondadori, 1983. 222 p
Confessions of an Italian ex-terrorist.

3288. Pellicani, L. I revoluzionari di proffessioni. - Firenze : Vallechi, 1975.
'The professional revolutionaries'.

3289. Prawdin, M. The unmentionable Nechaev. - London : 1961.

3290. Rayfield, G.E. The righteous executioners : A comparative analysis of Jewish terrorists of the 1940s and Palestinian terrorists of the 1970s. City University of New York, 1980. ; Ph.D. dissertation

3291. Rejai, M. * Philips, K. Leaders of revolutions. - Beverly Hills : Sage Publications, 1979.

3292. Renshon, S.A. Psychological needs and political behavior : A theory of personality and political efficacy. - New York : Free Press, 1974.

3293. Ronfeldt, D. * Sater, W. The mind sets of high technology terrorists : Future implications from a historical analogue. - Santa Monica, Calif. : RAND, 1981.

3294. Rosie, G. The directory of international terrorism. - New York : Paragon House, 1986.

3295. Rubin, A.P. Terrorism and the laws of war. Spring 1983. p. 219-235. Denver Journal of International Law and Policy. ; 12.

3296. Rude, G. Robespierre : Portrait of a revolution democrat. - London : Collins, 1975.

3297. Russell, Ch.A. * et al. Profile of a terrorist. Nov. 1977. p. 17-34. Terrorism. ; 1:1.
Based on information on some 350 known terrorists from 18 different groups involving 11 nationalities.

3298. Salert, B. Revolutions and revolutionaries : Four theories. - New York : 1976. 160 p

3299. Sanchez, G. The great rebel : Che Guevara in Bolivia. - New York : Grove Press, 1969.

3300. Sayari, S. Generational changes in terrorist movements : The Turkish case. - Santa Monica, Calif. : RAND, 1985. 16 p

3301. Scott, S. * Schultz D.O. The subversive. - Springfield, Ill. : Thomas, 1973. 107 p

3302. Silbersky, L. Portraett av terrorister: intervjuer med terrorister i israeliska faengelser. - Stockholm : Aldus/Bonniers, 1977. 124 p
Transcripts of interviews with terrorists in Israel.

3303. Slote, W.H. Case analysis of a revolutionary. - Cambridge, Mass. : The MIT Press, 1967.
In: F. Bomilla and J.S. Michelena (eds.), A strategy for research on social policy
By a psychologist who interviewed revolutionaries outside prison.

3304. Smith, C.L. Carlos: portrait of a terrorist. - London : Deutsch, 1976. 304 p

3305. Soto Guerrero, A. Carlos, el terror de unil rostros. - Jerusalem : Semana Publ. Co., 1976. 286 p

3306. Soto Guerrero, A. El chacal venezolano, Carlos. - Caracas : El Cid Editor, 1976. 286 p

3307. Stajano, C. L'Italia nichilista : Il caso di Marco Donat Cattin, la rivolta, il potere. - Milano : Mondadori, 1982. 266 p

3308. Standing, P.D. Guerrilla leaders of the world. - London : Cassell.,

3309. Steck, P. Ueber die Beziehung zwischen Persoenlichkeitsmerkmalen und politischen Einstellungen : Ein empirischer Beitrag zur politischen Psychologie. - Wuerzburg : 1974. ; Dissertation

3310. Steinhoff, P.G. Portrait of a terrorist: an interview with Kozo Okamoto. Sept. 1976. p. 830-845. Asian Survey. ; 16.

3311. Stepniak, S. (pseud. for S.M. Kravcinskij). Kozkukhov : The career of a nihilist. - London : 1889.

3312. Stern, S. With the Weathermen: a personal journal of a revolutionary woman. - New York : Doubleday, 1975.

3313. Struyker Boudier, C.E.M. * et al. Politieke dissidenten. - Bilthoven : 1974. 141 p

3314. Taintor, Z.C. Assessing the revolutionary personality. - North Scituate, Mass. : Duxbury Press, 1972. p. 239-249.

In: C.E. Welch jr and M.B. Taintor (eds.), Revolution and political change

3315. Thompson, J.M. Robespierre. - 2 vols. 1936.
Reissued 1968.

3316. Todoroff, K. The Macedonian organization yesterday and today. 1928. p. 473-482. Foreign Affairs. ; 6.

3317. Tromp, B. Sociologie van het terrorisme. Sept. 1978. p. 200-203. Civis Mundi. ; 5.

3318. Trotsky, L. My life. - Gloucester, Mass. : P. Smith, 1970.

3319. Truby, J.D. Women as terrorists. - Gaithersburg, Md. : IACP., 47 p

3320. VonLaue, Th.H. Stalin in focus. Fall 1983. p. 373-389. Slavic Review. ; 42.

3321. Wagner, J. Politischer Terrorismus und Strafrecht im Deutschen Kaiserreich von 1871. - Heidelberg-Hamburg : v. Decker, 1981. 448 p

3322. Watson, P. * Moynahan, B. The mind of the terrorist. 19 Aug. 1973. p. 8ff. Sunday Times-Spectrum

3323. Waugh, W.L. The values in violence : Organisation and political objectives of terrorist groups. Summer 1983. p. 1-19. Conflict Quarterly

3324. Wijne, J.S. Terreur in de politiek : Politieke geheime genootschappen in deze tijd. - Den Haag : Kruseman, 1967. 157 p
On: Mafia, OAS, Ku Klux Klan, John Birch Society, Black Moslims.

3325. Wilkinson, P. The new fascists. - London : Grant MacIntyre, 1981. 179 p

3326. Wilson, C. Order of assassins : The psychology of murder. - London : Rupert Hart-Davis, 1972. 242 p
Concentrates on psychological motivations of assassins.

3327. Wolf, J.B. Appraising the performance of terrorist organizations : Selected European separatist groups, Fall 1978 to Summer 1979. - Gaithersburg, Md. : IACP, 1979. 25 p

3328. Wolf, J.B. Organization and management practices of urban terrorist groups as revealed by the Brinks robbery inquiry. - Gaithersburg, Md. : IACP, 1983. Update Report. ; 9:2.

3329. Wolf, J.B. Organization and management practices of urban terrorist groups. 1978. p. 169-186. Terrorism. ; 1:2.

3330. Wolf, J.B. Organizational and operational aspects of contemporary terrorist groups. - Gaithersburg, Md. : IACP, 1980. Update Report. ; 6:3.

3331. Wolfenstein, E. The revolutionary personality. - Princeton, N.J. : Princeton University Press, 1967. 330 p

3332. Worthy, W. Bombs blast a message of hate: an interview with an admitted bomber. 27 March 1970. p. 24-32. Life. ; 68.

3333. Yablonski, L. The violent gang. - Middlesex : Pelican Books, 1967.

3334. Zawodny, J.K. Internal organizational problems and the sources of tensions of terrorist movements as catalysts of violence. 1978. p. 277-286. Terrorism. ; 1.

3335. _____ Abu Nidal and his Palestinian terrorists : An ADL background report. - New York : Anti-defamation League of B'nai B'rith, 1986. 6 p

3336. _____ Bakounine et les autres: esquisses et portraits contemporains d'un revolutionnaire. - Paris : Union Generale d'Editions, 1976. 432 p

3337. _____ Crimes by women are on the rise all over the world. 22 Dec. 1975. p. 49-51. U.S. News and World Report. ; 79.

3338. _____ Diario de un guerrillero colombiano. - Buenos Aires : Freeland, 1968.
Also published as: Diario de un guerrillero latinoamericano. Montevideo, Sandoni, 1968; a series of vignettes.

3339. _____ Interview mit Andreas Baader, Ulrike Meinhof, Gudrun Ensslin, Jan-Carl Raspe. 20 Jan. 1975. Der Spiegel. ; 29:4.

3340. _____ Jugend und Terrorismus : Ein Hearing des Bundesjugend-Kuratoriums. - Muenchen : Juventa-Verlag, 1979. 128 p

3341. _____ On organizing urban guerilla units. - Gaithersburg, Md. : 36 p. IACP

3342. _____ Portrait of a terrorist. June 1974. p. 70. Science Digest. ; 75.

3343. _____ Testimony of H.H.A. Cooper: the terrorist and his victim : Hearing. - 95th Cong., 1st sess., July 21, 1977. - Washington, D.C. : GPO, 1977. 33 p.
U.S.Congress, Senate. Committee on the judiciary. Subcommittee on criminal law and procedures
Includes reprint of Cooper's article: What is a terrorist: a psychological perspective.

3344. _____ What makes a skyjacker?. 1972. p. 21-22. Science Digest. ; 71.

3345. _____ Yassir Arafat : An interview. April 1986. p. 399-410. Third World Quarterly. ; 8.

3346. _____ Yassir Arafat. March 1971. p. 3-5. Current Biography. ; 32.

K. VICTIMOLOGICAL ASPECTS

3347. Appley, M.H. * Trumbull, R. Psychological stress. - New York : Appleton-Century-Crofts, 1967. Hostage and victim aspects.

3348. Bakels, F. Nacht und Nebel : Mijn verhaal uit Duitse gevangenissen en concentratiekampen. - Amsterdam : Elsevier, 1977. 344 p On concentration camp experience.

3349. Baker, G.W. * Chapman, D.W. * (eds.) Man and society in disaster. - New York : Basic Books, 1962.

3350. Barton, A.H. Communities in disaster : A social analysis of collective stress situations. - Garden City, N.Y. : Doubleday, 1970.

3351. Bastiaans, J. * Mulder, D. * Dijk, W.K.van * Ploeg, H.M.van der Mensen bij gijzelingen. - Alphen aan den Rijn : Sijthoff, 1981. 304 p Four accounts of psychiatrists involved with the aftercare of Dutch victims of acts of hostage taking.

3352. Bastiaans, J. Guidance and treatment of victims of terrorism. 1979. ; Paper presented to World Congress of Psychiatry, Honolulu, 1977

3353. Bastiaans, J. Het KZ-syndroom en de menselijke vrijheid. 1974. Nederlands Tijdschrift voor Geneeskunde. ; 118:31. On concentration camp experience.

3354. Bastiaans, J. Psychosomatische gevolgen van onderdrukking en verzet. - Amsterdam : Noord-Hollandse Uitgevers Mij., 1957. ; Dissertatie

3355. Bastiaans, J. Von Menschen in KZ und KZ in Menschen. - Amsterdam : 1973. In: Essays ueber Naziverbrechen, Simon Wiesenthal gewidmet On concentration camp experience.

3356. Batigne, J. Nous sommes tous des hotages. - Paris : Plon, 1973. 253 p

3357. Belz, M. * et al. Is there a treatment for terror?. Oct. 1977. p. 54-56, 61, 108, 111-112, 1. Psychology Today. ; 11. Description of group therapy sessions provided to 50 hostages of theWashington-March 1977- Hanafi incident.

3358. Berkowitz, L. * Cottingham, D.R. The interest value and relevance of fear-arousing communications. 1960. p. 37-43. Journal of Abnormal and Social Psychology. ; 60.

3359. Bettelheim, B. Individual and mass behavior in extreme situations. 1943. p. 417-452. Journal of Abnormal and Social Psychology. ; 38.

3360. Bloch, H.A. The personality of inmates of concentration camps. 1946. p. 335-341. American Journal of Sociology. ; 52.

3361. Bluhm, H.O. How did they survive? : Mechanisms of defense in Nazi concentration camps. - New York : MacMillan, 1964. In: B. Rosenberg et al., Mass society in crisis

3362. Bowlby, J. Separation, anxiety and anger. - London : Hogarth Press, 1973. On hostage experience.

3363. Bristow, A.P. Police disaster operations. - Springfield, Ill. : Thomas, 1973. 240 p

3364. Brockman, R. Notes while being hijacked : Croation terrorists. Dec. 1976. p. 68-75. Atlantic. ; 238.

3365. Brooks, M. Hostage survival. April 1976. ; Paper presented to the Conference organized by Glanboro State College on 'Terrorism in the contemporary world'

3366. Cohen, E.A. Human behavior in the concentration camp. - New York : Norton, 1953. Medical and psychological aspects.

3367. Cohen, S. * Taylor, L. Psychological survival: the experience of long term imprisonment. - Harmondsworth : Pelican, 1972.

3368. Cooper, H.H.A. The terrorist and his victims. June 1976. Victimology. ; 1:2.

3369. Crelinsten, R.D. * (ed.) The dimensions of victimization in the context of terroristic acts. - Montreal : ICCC, 1977. 220 p ; Final report of seminar

3370. Cressy, D.L. * Krassowski, W. Inmate organization and anomie in American prisons and Soviet labor camps. 1958. p. 217-230. Social Problems. ; 5.

3371. Dortzbach, K. * Dortzbach, D. Kidnapped. - New York : Harper & Row, 1975. 177 p
On kidnapping experience in Eritrea.

3372. Drapkin, I. * Viano, E. * (eds.) Victimology: a new focus. - 5 parts. - Lexington, Mass. : D.C. Heath, 1975.
Material from the first international symposium on victimology, Jerusalem 1973.

3373. Eggers, W. Terrorism: the slaughter of innocents. - Chatsworth, Calif. : Major Books, 1975.

3374. Eitinger, L. Concentration camp survivors in Norway and Israel. - London : Allen and Unwin, 1964.

3375. Eitinger, L. The stress of captivity. - Montreal : International Center for Comparative Criminology, 1977. p. 71-85.
In: R.D. Crelinsten (ed.), Dimensions of victimization in the context of terroristic acts

3376. Elbrick, Ch.B. The diplomatic kidnappings: a case study. - Milwaukee : Institute of World Affairs, 1974. p. 45-56.
In: International terrorism: proceedings of an intensive panel at the 15th Annual convention of the ISA
U.S. ambassador's account of his being kidnapped in Sept. 1969 in Brazil.

3377. Erskine, H. Fear of violence and crime. 1974. p. 131-145. Public Opinion Quarterly. ; 38:1.

3378. Fenyvesi, Ch. Living with a fearful memory. Oct. 1977. p. 61ff. Psychology Today

3379. Fenyvesi, Ch. Looking into the muzzle of terrorists. 1977. p. 16-18. The Quill
Hostage experience, Hanafi incident 1977.

3380. Fields, R.M. Psychological sequelae of terrorization. - New York : Pergamon Press, 1981. p. 51-72.
In: Y. Alexander and J.M. Gleason (eds.), Behavioral and quantitative perspectives on terrorism
Summary of findings on hostage experience, Hanafi incident, and Northern Ireland prisons.

3381. Fields, R.M. Victims of terrorism : The effects of prolonged stress. 1980. p. 76-83. Eval. and change
Special issue based on research conducted in Northern Ireland and the United States.

3382. Figley, Ch.R. Mobilization I: the Iranian crisis : Final report of the Task Force on families of catastrophe. - West Lafayette : Purdue University, 1980.
The experience of families of hostage victims.

3383. Fly, C.L. No hope but God. - New York : Hawthorne Books Inc., 1973. 220 p
Author, an American agronomist, was held for 208 days as hostage by Tupamaros in 1971; relates his experience.

3384. Fromm-Reichmann, F. Psychiatric aspects of anxiety. - New York : Free Press, 1960.
In: M.R. Stein (ed.), Identity and anxiety

3385. Fuentes Mohr, S.A. Sequestro y prision : Dos caras de la violencia en Guatemala. - San Jose (Costa Rica) : 1971.
Recollections of the foreign minister of Guatemala who was kidnappedin 1970.

3386. Graham-Yooll, A. A matter of fear : Portrait of an Argentinian exile. - Westport, Conn. : L. Hill, 1982. 128 p

3387. Grey, A. Hostage in Peking. 1970.
A foreign correspondent's account of his two years imprisonment in China.

3388. Grosser, G.H. * Wechsler, H. * Greenblatt, M. * (eds.) The threat of impending disaster: contributions to the psychology of stress. - Cambridge, Mass. : MIT Press, 1964. 335 p

3389. Hirshleifer, J. Some thoughts on the social structure after a bombing disaster. 1956. p. 206-227. World Politics. ; 8.

3390. Holkers, A. * Bijlsma, J. Nazorg gegijzelden. 1978.
On Dutch ex-hostage treatment and experiences.

3391. Hulsman, L.H.C. Terrorism and victims. - Montreal : International Center for Comparative Criminology, 1977. p. 149-16
3. In: R.D. Crelinsten (ed.), Dimensions of victimization in the context of terroristic acts

3392. Israel, Ch.E. The hostages. - Toronto : MacMillan of Canada, 1966. 319 p

3393. Istha, D. * Smit, N.W.de Crisis-interventie: therapie of strategie. - Alphen aan den Rijn : Samsom, 1977.

3394. Jackson, G. Surviving the long nights: an autobiographical account of a political kidnapping. - New York : Vanguard, 1974. 222 p
Hostage experience in a "people's prison" of the Tupamaros by a British diplomat.

3395. Jacobson, S. Leadership patterns and stress adaptations among hostages in three terrorists-captured planes. - Tel Aviv : Jan. 1975. ; Paper presented at the international conference on psychological stress and adjustment in time of war and peace

3396. Jong, L.de Het Koninkrijk der Nederlanden in de Tweede Wereldoorlog. Deel 8 : Gevangenen en gedeporteerden. - 2 vols. - Den Haag : 1978. 1014 p

3397. Jost, W. Rufzeichen: Haifa : Ein Passagier erlebt die Entfuehrung des Swissair DC-8 "Nidwalden" und als Geisel den Krieg der Fedayin. - Zuerich : Schweizer Verlag Haus, 1972. 317 p
Hostage account of the 1970 multiple-hijacking ending on Dawson Field, Jordan.

3398. Kelman, H.C. Violence without moral restraint : Reflections on the dehumanization of victims and victimizers. 1973. p. 25-61. Journal of Social Issues. ; 29:4.

3399. Kent, G. The effects of threats. - Columbus : Ohio State University Press, 1967.

3400. Kho-So, Chr. Naar een diagnose van het gijzelingssyndroom en psychotherapie van gegijzelden. 1977. p. 206-213. Tijdschrift voor Psychotherapie. ; 3:5.
On experiences of the 36 hostages in the siege at the Indonesian consulat in Amsterdam, 4-19 Dec.1979.

3401. Kits, T.P. De opvang van de familieleden van de gegijzelden in de trein bij De Punt. 1977. p. 683-687. Maandblad Geestelijke Volksgezondheid. ; 32.

3402. Lador-Lederer, J.J. 'Victims'law, jus cogens and national law. - Tel Aviv : 1978. p. 267-295. Israel Yearbook on Human Rights

3403. Lang, D. A reporter at large: the bank drama. 25 Nov. 1974. p. 56-126. New Yorker Magazine. ; 49.
On the hostage-terrorist interaction during an incident in a Swedishbank resulting in the victim's identification with the aggressor - "the Stockholm syndrome".

3404. Lazarus, R. Psychological stress and the coping process. - New York : McGraw-Hill, 1966.
Victim aspects in hostage situations.

3405. Leventhal, H. * et al. Effects of fear and specificity of recommendation upon attitudes and behavior. 1965. p. 20-29. Journal of Personality and Social Psychology. ; 2.

3406. Lincoln, A. * Leirgner, G. Observers' evaluations of the victim and the attacker in an aggressive incident. May 1972. p. 202-210. Journal of Personality and Social Psychology. ; 22.

3407. Lindroth, K. Het bankdrama in Norrmalmstorg (Stockholm). May 1974. p. 153-165. Tijdschrift voor de Politie. ; 36:5.
On "Stockholm syndrome".

3408. Lyons, H.A. Violence in Belfast: a review of the psychological effects. - Bristol : Nov. 1973. p. 163-168. Community Health. ; 5:3.

3409. McCreary, A. Survivors : A documentary account of the victims of Northern Ireland. - New York : Beekman Books, 1977. 280 p

3410. Meeuwisse, E.Th.F. * Ploeg, H.M.van der Gijzelingen en media : Een kritische beschouwing van kranten-publikaties over de hulpverlening bij de gijzelingen van De Punt en Bovensmilde in mei/juni 1977. - Leiden : AZL, 1978. 20 p
On ex-hostage treatment as mirrored in Dutch press.

3411. Middendorff, W. Viktimologie der Geiselnahme. April 1974. p. 145-148. Kriminalistik. ; 28:4.

3412. Mierlo, G.H.J.van * et al. Huisarts en gijzeling : Suggesties voor opvang en begeleiding. 1977. Medisch Contact. ; 32.

3413. Milgram, S. Research on victimization. - Montreal : International Center for Comparative Criminology, 1977. p. 177-180.
In: R.D. Crelinsten (ed.), Dimensions of victimization in the context of terroristic acts

3414. Mills, R.T. Nazorg gegijzelden : Verslag van het projekt nazorg gegijzelden van de treinen bij Wijster en De Punt. - Assen : Drents Centrum voor Geestelijke Gezondheidszorg, 1979. 81 p
On aftercare of 1975 and 1977 Dutch train hostages.

3415. Moore, R. Psychiatric sequelae of the Belfast riots. April 1972. p. 47ff. British Journal of Psychiatry. ; 120.

3416. Murphy, J.R. Political terrorism: means to an end?. Sept. 1974. Encore
Author was kidnapped by the "American Revolutionary Army" in an incident modelled after the Patty Hearst kidnapping.

3417. Nagel, W.H. Het viktimologisch aspekt in de penologische benadering van terrorisme. 1976. p. 26-53. Ars Aequi Libri
The victimological aspect in the penological approach to terrorism.

3418. Ochberg, F.M. * et al. * (eds.) Post traumatic therapy. APA Press, 1986.

3419. Ochberg, F.M. * Soskis, D.A. * (ed.) Victims of terrorism. - Boulder, Colo. : Westview Press, 1982. 201 p

3420. Ochberg, F.M. Hostages in Teheran. May 1980. Psychological Annals. ; 10:5.

3421. Ochberg, F.M. Preparing for terrorist victimization. - New York : Praeger, 1979. p. 201-218.
In: Y. Alexander and R.A. Kilmarx (eds.), Political terrorism and business: the threat and response

3422. Ochberg, F.M. The victim of terrorism: psychiatric considerations. 1978. p. 147-168. Terrorism. ; 1.

3423. Ochberg, F.M. Victims of terrorism. March 1980. Journal for Clinical Psychiatry. ; 41:3.

3424. Odling-Smee, W. Victims of Belfast's violence. 6 Sept. 1973. p. 1143-1146. Nursing Times

3425. Oren, U. 99 days in Damascus: the story of professor Shlomo Samueloff and the hijack of TWA flight 848. - London : Weidenfeld and Nicolson, 1970.
Victim's experience of skyjacking.

3426. Ovazza, C. 5 ciliege rosse. - Milano : Mursia Editore, 1977.
By the mother-in-law to Giovanni Agnelli's daughter (of FIAT) on kidnapping experience.

3427. Pascal, F. * Pascal, J. The strange case of Patty Hearst. - New York : American Library, 1974.

3428. Pepitone, A. * Kleiner, R. The effects of threat and frustration on group cohesiveness. 1957. p. 192-199. Journal of Abnormal and Social Psychology. ; 54.

3429. Pepper, C.B. Kidnapped. 20 Nov. 1977. p. 42-46, 126, 128, 131-132,. New York Times Magazine
Factual account of the kidnapping victim Paolo Lazzaroni, Italy.

3430. Pereira, O.G. Effects of violence on military personnel in the Portugese colonies. - Washington, D.C. : Sept. 1976. ; Paper presented to the Symposium on the effects of institutional coercion by law, government, and violence, of the 94th annual convention of the Psy

3431. Pinto Flores, A. Yo fui rehen del M-19 : 61 dias en la embajada de la Republica Dominicana. - Bogota : Canal Ramirez-Antares, 1980. 225 p
Columbian hostage experience.

3432. Ploeg, H.M.van der * Meeuwisse, E.Th.F. Deskundigen aan het woord.. : Beschouwingen van perspublikaties over het voorspellen van gevolgen van gijzelingen. - Leiden : AZL, 1978. 12 p
On ex-hostage experiences as predicted in the Dutch press.

3433. Pres, T.des An anatomy of life in the death camps. - New York : Oxford University Press, 1976.

3434. Queen, R. * Hass, R. Inside and out : Hostage to Iran, hostage to myself. - New York : Putnam, 1981.

3435. Rauter, E.A. Folter-Lexikon : Die Kunst der verzoegerten Humanschlachtung vom Nero bis Westmoreland. - Hamburg : Konkret Verlag, 1969.

3436. Rossi di Montelera, L. Racconto di un sequestro. - Torino : Societa Editrice Internazionale, 1977.
Account of the heir of the Martini and Rossi vermouth business on his kidnapping experience.

3437. Rueckerl, A. * (ed.) Nationalsozialistische Vernichtungslager im Spiegel deutscher Strafprozesse. Deutscher Taschenbuch Verlag, 1977.

3438. Salewski, W. Luftpiraterie. - Muenchen : 1976.
By a Munich psychologist commissioned by Lufthansa to interview passengers and crew members involved in various skyjacking incidents. Hisreport "Luftpiraterie" was the basis for a training film made by Lufthansa to prepare crew members on how to cope with hijack situations.

3439. Schneider, H.J. Viktimologie - Wissenschaft vom Verbrechensopfer. - Tuebingen : 1975.

3440. Schultz, D.P. Panic behavior. - New York : Random House, 1964.

3441. Scott, P.D. Victims of violence. 4 July 1970. p. 1036-1037. Nursing Times

3442. Sebastian, R.J. Immediate and delayed effects of victims suffering on the attacker's aggression. Sept. 1978. p. 312-328. Journal of Research on Personality. ; 12:3.

3443. Segal, J. * Hunter, E.J. * Segal, Z. Universal consequences of captivity: stress reactions among divergent populations of prisoners of war and their families. 1976. International Social Science Journal. ; 28:3.

3444. Silverstein, M.E. The medical survival of victims of terrorism. - Stanford : Hoover, 1979. p. 349-392.
In: R.H. Kupperman and D.M. Trent (eds.), Terrorism

3445. Silverstein, M. Surviving terrorism. Autumn 1982. p. 175-180. Washington Quarterly. ; 5.

3446. Simpson, J. * Bennett, J. The disappeared and the Mothers of the Plaza. - New York : St. Martin's Press, 1985. 416 p

3447. Soskis, D.A. * Ayalon, O. A six-year follow-up of hostage victims. 1985. p. 411-415. Terrorism. ; 7:4.

3448. Sossi, M. Nella prigione delle BR. - Milano : Editoriale nuova, 1979. 254 p

3449. Svirski, G. Hostages. - New York : Knopf, 1976. 305 p

3450. Swart, Ch. * Berkowitz, L. Effects of a stimulus associated with a victim's pain on later aggression. 1976. p. 623-631. Journal of Personality and Social Psychology. ; 33:5.

3451. Szabo, D. * (ed.) Dimensions of victimization in the context of terroristic acts. - Montreal : ICCC, 1977. 218 p
Hostage experience and treatment of after effects.

3452. Szymusiak, M. The stoner cry out : A Cambodian childhood, 1975-1980. - New York : Hill and Wang, 1986. 245 p

3453. Tarantini, D. La democrazia totalitaria : Il moro necessario, potere e rivoluzione: le lettere di Moro. - Verona : Bertani, 1979. 165 p

3454. Thompson, C. Identification with the enemy and loss of the sense of the self. 1940. p. 15-21. Psychoanalytic Quarterly. ; 8.

3455. Vaders, G. Strangers on a train: the diary of a hostage. 1976.

3456. Van Voris, W.H. Violence in Ulster: an oral documentary. - Amherst : University of Massachusetts Press, 1975. 326 p
Based on hundreds of interviews with Ulstermen.

3457. Wallace, A.F.C. Human behavior in extreme situations. - Washington, D.C. : National Academy of Sciences, National Research Council, 1956. ; Publication no.390.

3458. Weed, S. * Swanton, S. My search for Patty Hearst. - London : Secker & Warburg, 1976. 343 p
By her ex-fiancee.

3459. Wells, T. 444 days : The hostage remembers. - New York : Harcourt Brace Jovanovich, 1985. 469 p
Iran hostage crisis '79-'81.

3460. Wolfenstein, M. Disaster: a psychological essay. - Glencoe, Ill. : Free Press, 1957.

3461. _____ H.R. 1956 and H.R. 2019, benefits to federal employees who are victims of terrorism. - Washington, D.C. : GPO, 1985. 195 p.
U.S. Congress. House. Committee on Post Office and Civil Service. Subcommittee on Civil Service

3462. _____ Kidnapping victims: tragic aftermaths. April 1976. p. 62-65, 106-107, 113, 116. Saturday Evening Post. ; 248.

3463. _____ Rapport psychologisch onderzoek naar de gevolgen van gijzelingen in Nederland. - Den Haag : Staatsuitgeverij, 1979. 359 p
Psychological research on the effects of hostage experiences in theNetherlands 1974-1977.

3464. _____ The medical survival of the victims of terrorism. 1976.
U.S. Arms Control and Disarmament Agency ; Prepared for the office of the chief scientist

L. TERRORISM FROM A PSYCHOLOGICAL PERSPECTIVE

3465. Ax, A.F. The physiological differentiation between fear and anger in humans. 1953. p. 433-442. Psychosomatic Medicine. ; 15.

3466. Baeyer-Katte, W.von Agitatorischer Terror und dessen Wirkung in sozialpsychologischer Sicht. - Mainz : 1979. p. 15-46.
In: H. Maier (ed.), Terrorismus. Beitraege zur geistigen Auseinandersetzung

3467. Bandura, A. * Underwood, B. * Fromson, M.E. Disinhibition of aggression through diffusion of responsibility and dehumanization of victims. Dec. 1975. p. 253-269. Journal of Research in Personality. ; 9:4.

3468. Bandura, E. * (ed.) Psychological modeling : Conflicting theories. - Chicago : Aldine-Atherton, 1971.

3469. Baron, R.A. Aggression as a function of magnitude of victim's pain cues, level of prior anger arousal and aggressor-victim similarity. April 1971. p. 48-54. Journal of Personality and Social Psychology. ; 18:1.

3470. Baron, R.A. Human aggression. - New York : Plenum, 1977.

3471. Batselier, S.de Sadomasochisme: antropologisch interpretatiemodel van de terreur van minderheden als secundair aktiepatroon op het strukturele geweld. - Utrecht : Ars Aequi, 1976. p. 12-25. In: L.G.H. Gunther Moor (ed.), Terreur. Criminologische en juridische aspecten van terrorisme

3472. Bieber, L.E. Gewalt und Identitaetssuche : Sozialpsychologische Aspekte der Lateinamerikanischen Guerrilla-Bewegung. - Koeln : Bohlau Verlag, 1978. In: R. Konetzke et al. (eds.), Jahrbuch fuer Geschichte von Staat, Wirtschaft und Gesellschaft Lateinamerikas. Vol. 15

3473. Bossle, L. Soziologie und Psychologie des Radikalismus-Phaenomens in der Politik. - Muenchen : 1975. Politische Studien. ; 220.

3474. Brueckner, P. Politisch-psychologische Anmerkungen zur Roten-Armee-Fraktion. - Berlin : 1973. p. 73-100. In: W. Dressen (ed.), Socialistisches Jahrbuch, Vol. 5

3475. Calvi, G. * Martini, M. L'estremismo politico : Richerche psichologiche sul terrorismo e sugli attegiamenti radicali. - Milano : F. Angeli, 1982. 159 p

3476. Cooper, H.H.A. What is a terrorist: a psychological perspective. 1977. Legal Medical Quarterly. ; 1:1.

3477. Cooper, M.R. * et al. Factor analysis of air passenger reactions to skyjacking and airport security measures as related to personal characteristic and alternatives to flying. June 1974. p. 365-368. Applied Psychology. ; 59.

3478. Crawford, T.J. * Naditch, M. Relative deprivation, powerlessness, and militancy: the psychology of social protest. May 1970. p. 208-223. Psychiatry. ; 33.

3479. Crelinsten, R.D. A case-study of a terrorism game : Implications for research and policy. 1979. ; Report for the International Society of Political Psychology

3480. Crelinsten, R.D. The study of the effects of isolation in the laboratory and in the prison : A critical review. 1981. ; Report for Amnesty International

3481. Crenshaw, M. The psychology of political terrorism. - 2nd. ed. - San Francisco : Jossey-Bass, 1985. In: M. Hermann (ed), Handbook of political psychology

3482. Daniels, D.N. * Gigula, M.F. * Ochberg, F.M. * (eds.) Violence and the struggle for existence. - Boston : Stanford University School of Medicine, Committee on violence of the Department of Psychiatry, 1970. 451 p

3483. Davies, J.C. Aggression, violence, revolution and war. - San Francisco : Jossey-Bass, 1973. In: J.N. Knutson (ed.), Handbook of political psychology

3484. Dowling, J.A. Prolegomena to a psychohistorical study of terrorism. - Westport, Conn. : Greenwood Press, 1978. p. 223-230. In: M.H. Livingston, M.H. et al. (eds.), International terrorism in the contemporary world

3485. Duster, T. Conditions for guilt-free massacre. - San Francisco : 1971. p. 25-36. In: N. Sanford et al. (eds.), Sanctions for evil

3486. Ferencz, B.B. When one person's terrorism is another person's heroism. Summer 1981. p. 39-42, 55-56. Human Rights. ; 9.

3487. Ferracuti, F. A sociopsychiatric interpretation of terrorism. 1982. p. 129-140. The Annals of AAPSS

3488. Ferracuti, F. Consecuencias morales, sociales y politicas del terrorismo. - Madrid : 1984. p.33-40 and passim. Terrorismo Internacional

3489. Fields, R.M. Psychological genocide: the children of Northern Ireland. 1975. p. 201-224. History of Childhood Quarterly. ; 3.

3490. Frank, J.D. Some psychological determinants of violence and its control. Sept. 1972. p. 158-164. Australian and New Zealand Journal of Psychiatry. ; 6.

3491. Freedman, L.Z. Why does terrorism terrorize?. 1983. p. 389-401. Terrorism. ; 6:3.

3492. Fromm, E. The anatomy of human destructiveness. - New York : Holt, Rinehart & Winston, 1973.

3493. Gamson, W.A. Violence and political power : The meek don't make it. July 1974. p. 35-41. Psychology Today. ; 8.

3494. Geen, R.G. * Stoner, D. Context effects in observed violence. Jan. 1973. p. 145-150. Journal of Personal and Social Psychology. ; 25.

3495. Glaser, H. Radikalitaet und Scheinradikalitaet - Spielraum : Zur Sozialpsychologie und Sozialpathologie des jugendlichen Protests. 1969. p. 1-32. Aus Politik und Zeitgeschichte. ; 12.

3496. Goldman, E. Anarchism and other essays. - New York : 1910.
Includes an essay on: The psychology of political violence.

3497. Guggenberger, B. Kulturkritik und Guerilla-Mythos : Die Dritte Welt als Identifikations-Objekt. - Koeln : p. 91-108. Beitraege zur Konfliktforschung. ; 3:4.

3498. Guiness, O. Violence - crisis or catharsis?. - Revised ed. - Downers Grove, Ill. : Intervarsity, 1974.

3499. Gurr, T.R. Psychological factors in civil violence. 1968. p. 245-278. World Politics. ; 20:2.

3500. Hacker, F.J. Aggression : Die Brutalisierung der moderne Welt. - Wien : 1971.

3501. Hacker, F.J. Contagion and attraction of terror and terrorism. - New York : Pergamon Press, 1981. p. 73-85.
In: Y. Alexander and J.M. Gleason (eds.), Behavioral and quantitative perspectives on terrorism

3502. Hacker, F.J. Crusaders, criminals, crazies : Terror and terrorism in our time. - New York : Norton, 1976. 371 p

3503. Hassel, C.V. Political assassin. Dec. 1974. p. 399-403. Journal of Police Science and Administration. ; 2.

3504. Hebb, D.O. On the nature of fear. 1946. p. 259-276. Psychological Review. ; 53.

3505. Heilman, M.E. Threats and promises: reputational consequences and transfer of credibility. 1974. p. 310-324. Journal of Experimental Social Psychology. ; 10.

3506. Heskin, K. Northern Ireland, a psychological analysis. - New York : Columbia University Press, 1980. 174 p

3507. Horn, M. Sozialpsychologie des Terrorismus. - Frankfurt a.M./ New York : Campus Verlag, 1982. 196 p

3508. Hubbard, D.G. A glimmer of hope: a psychiatric perspective. - Springfield, Ill. : Thomas, 1975. p. 27-32.
In: M.C. Bassiouni (ed.), International terrorism and political crimes

3509. Hubbard, D.G. A story of inadequacy: hierarchical authority vs. the terrorist. - New York : Praeger, 1979. p. 187-200.
In: Y. Alexander and R.A. Kilmarx (eds.), Political terrorism and business: the threat and response

3510. Hubbard, D.G. Extortion threats: the possibility of analysis. 1975. p. 17-19. Assets Protection. ; 1.

3511. Hubbard, D.G. Organic factors underlying the psychology of terror. - New York : Pergamon Press, 1981.
In: Y. Alexander and J.M. Gleason (eds.), Behavioral and quantitative perspectives on terrorism

3512. Hubbard, D.G. The skyjacker: his flights of fantasy. - New York : MacMillan, 1971. 262 p
On pathological elements in terrorism; the author, a psychologist, concludes that a majority of the skyjackers were motivated not by politics but by personal frustrations.

3513. Hubbard, D.G. The terrorist mind. April 1971. p. 12-13. Counterforce

3514. Ingwell, M. Guilt transfer. - New York : Pergamon Press, 1982.
In: D. Rapoport and Y. Alexander (eds.), The morality of terrorism

3515. Janis, I.L. Air war and emotional stress. - New York : McGraw-Hill, 1951.

3516. Janis, I.L. Effects of fear arousal on attitude change. - New York : 1961.
In: L. Berkowitz (ed.), Advances in social psychology

3517. Janis, I.L. Group identification under conditions of external danger. - New York : Harper and Row, 1968.
In: D. Cartwright and A. Zander (eds.), Group dynamics: research and theory

3518. Janis, I.L. Psychological effects of warnings. - New York : Basic Books, 1962.
In: G.W. Baker and D.W. Chapman (eds.), Man and society in disaster

3519. Jaspers, J.P.C. Gijzelingen in Nederland : Een onderzoek naar de psychiatrische, psychologische en andragologische aspecten. - Lisse : Swets & Zeitlinger, 1980. 475 p
Largely identical with J. Bastiaans et al., 1979.

3520. Kaplan, A. The psychodynamics of terrorism. - New York : Pergamon Press, 1981. p. 35-50.
In: Y. Alexander and J.M. Gleason (eds.), Behavioral and quantitative perspectives on terrorism

3521. Karber, Ph.A. Some psychological effects of terrorism as protest. Aug. 1973. ; Paper presented before the Annual convention of the American Psychological Association

3522. Karber, Ph.A. The psychological dimensions of bombing motivations. - Gaithersburg, Md. : IACP, June 1973. p. 24-32. Bomb Incident Bulletin. ; Tab 02: Targets and tacti.

3523. Kelman, H.C. Israelis and Palestinians : Psychological prerequisites for mutual acceptance. Summer 1978. p. 162-186. Internal Security. ; 3.

3524. Knutson, J.N. Toward a United States policy on terrorism. June 1984. p. 287-294. Political Psychology. ; 5.

3525. Leloup, J.J.H. Vliegtuigkapingen, terreurdaden, gijzelingen: een psychiatrische visie. 20 June 1975. p. 11-13. Intermediair

3526. Lichter, S.R. Psychopolitical models of student radicals : A methodological critique and West German case study. Harvard University, 1977. ; Ph.D. dissertation

3527. Lichter, S.R. Young rebels : A psychological study of West German male radical students. Oct. 1979. p. 29-48. Comparative Politics. ; 12:1.

3528. Liebert, R. Radical and militant youth: a psychiatrist's report. - New York : Praeger, 1971.

3529. Lowenthal, L. Crisis of the individual: terror's atomization of man. 1946. p. 1-8. Commentary

3530. Lyons, H.A. Terrorists bombing and the psychological sequelae. 12 Jan. 1974. p. 15-19. Journal of the British Medical Association. ; 67.

3531. MacDonald, J.M. * Whittacker, L. Psychiatry and the criminal. - Springfield, Ill. : Charles C. Thomas, 1969.

3532. Margolin, J. Psychological perspectives. - New York : John Jay Press, 1977. p. 270-282.
In: S.M. Finger and Y. Alexander (eds.), Terrorism: interdisciplinary perspectives

3533. Merari, A. * Friedland, N. Negotiating with terrorists. Springer, in press.
In: W. Stroebe, A. Kruglanski and D. Barital (eds.), The social psychology and international conflict: theory, research and application

3534. Merari, A. * Friedland, N. Social psychological aspects of political terrorism. - Beverly Hills : Sage, 1985.
In: S. Oskamp (ed.), Applied social psychology annual

3535. Milburn, Th.W. The nature of threat. 1977. p. 126-139. Journal of Social Issues. ; 33.

3536. Miller, L. Identity and violence in pursuit of the causes of war and organized violence. March 1972. p. 71-77. Israeli Annals of Psychiatry. ; 10.

3537. Milte, K.L. Terrorism : Political and psychological considerations. June 1976. p. 89-94. Australian and New Zealand Journal of Criminology. ; 9.

3538. Miron, M.S. Psycholinguistic analysis of the SLA. 1976. Assets Protection. ; 1.

3539. Nass, G. Psychologische Ursachen des Anarchoterrorismus. - Kassel : Ges. fuer Vorbeugende Verbrechensbekampfung, 1978. 198 p

3540. Oots, K.L. * Wiegele, T.C. Terrorist and victim : Psychiatric and physiological approaches from a social science perspective. 1985. p. 1-32. Terrorism. ; 8:1.

3541. Pepitone, A. The social psychology of violence. 1972. International Journal of Group Tensions. ; 2:19.

3542. Peterson, R.A. Aggression as a function of expected retaliation and aggression level of target and aggressor. 1971. p. 161-66. Developmental Psychology. ; 5:1.

3543. Petzel, T.P. * Michaels, E.J. Perception of violence as a function of levels of hostility. August 1973. p. 35-36. Journal of Consulting Clinical Psychology. ; 41.

3544. Pisano, R. * Taylor, S.P. Reduction of physical aggression : The effects of four strategies. Aug. 1971. p. 237-242. Journal of Personality and Social Psychology. ; 19.

3545. Post, J.H. Individual and group dynamics of terrorist behavior. 1983. ; Proceedings of the 7th world congress of psychiatry

3546. Post, J.H. Notes on a psychodynamic theory of terrorist behavior. 1984. Terrorism. ; 7:3.

3547. Post, J.H. Rewarding fire with fire? : Effects of retaliation on terrorist group dynamics. Jaffee Center for Strategic Studies, University of Tel Aviv, 1985. ; Proceedings of an international conference on current trends in world terrorism

3548. Riezeler, K. The social psychology of fear. 1944. p. 489-498. American Journal of Sociology. ; 49.

3549. Roth, W. Psychosomatic implications of confinement by terrorists. - Montreal : International Center for Comparative Criminology, 1977. p. 41-60.
In: R.D. Crelinsten (ed.), Dimensions of victimization in the context of terroristic acts

3550. Scharff, W.H. * Schlottman, R.S. The effects of verbal reports of violence on aggression. July 1973. p. 283-290. Journal of Psychology. ; 84.

3551. Schmidt-Mummendey, A. * Schmidt, H.D. * (eds.) Aggressives Verhalten :

Neue Ergebnisse der psychologischen Forschung. - 3rd ed. - Muenchen : Juventa Verlag, 1975.

3552. Schmidtchen, G. Die Motive des Uebergangs zu illegaler Politik. - Bonn : 1984.
In: Extremismus und Schule. Schriftenreihe der Bundeszentrale fur politische Bildung. ; Band 121.

3553. Schmidtchen, G. Jugend und Staat : Uebergange von der Burger-Aktivitaet zur Illegalitaet, eine empirische Untersuchung zur Socialpsychologie der Democratie. - Bonn : Westdeutscher Verlag, 1983.
In: U. Matz and G. Schmidtchen (eds.), Gewalt und Legitimitat

3554. Schmidtchen, G. Terroristische Karrieren : Sociologische Analyse an Hand von Fahndungsunterlagen und Prozessakten. - Bonn : Westdeutscher Verlag, 1981.
In: H. Jager, G. Schmidtchen and L. Sullwold, Lebenslaufanalysen. Reihe Analysen zum Terrorismus. ; 2.

3555. Sewell, A.F. Political crime: a psychologist's perspective. - Springfield, Ill. : Thomas, 1975. p. 11-26.
In: M.C. Bassiouni (ed.), International terrorism and political crimes

3556. Silverman, S.M. A symbolic element in the PFLP hijackings. 1973. International Journal of Social Psychiatry

3557. Slomich, S.J. * Kantor, R.E. Social psychopathology of political assassination. March 1969. p. 9-12. Bulletin of the Atomic Scientists. ; 25:3.

3558. Sperber, M. The psychology of terror. 1969. p. 91-107. Survey. ; 15:72.

3559. Spiegel, J.P. The dynamics of violent confrontation. Sept. 1972. p. 93-108. International Journal of Psychiatry. ; 10.

3560. Storr, A. Sadism and paranoia. - Westport, Conn. : Greenwood Press, 1978. p. 231-239.
In: M. Livingston (ed.), International terrorism in the contemporary world

3561. Strentz, Th. The terrorist organizational profile: a psychological role model. - New York : Pergamon Press, 1981. p. 86-104.
In: Y. Alexander and J.M. Gleason (eds.), Behavioral and quantitative perspectives on terrorism

3562. Toch, H.H. Violent men : An inquiry into the psychology of violence. - Chicago, Ill. : Aldine Publishing Co., 1969. 268 p

3563. Turner, Ch. * Berkowitz, L. Identification with film aggressor (covert role taking) and reactions to film. 1972. p. 256-264. Journal of Personality and Social Psychology. ; 21:2.

3564. Weinstein, E.A. * Lyerly, O.G. Symbolic aspects of presidential assassination. Febr. 1969. p. 1-11. Psychiatry. Journal for the study of interpersonal processes. ; 32:1.

3565. Wiesbrock, H. * (ed.) Die politische und gesellschaftliche Rolle der Angst. - Frankfurt a.M. : Europaeische Verlagsanstalt, 1967. 297 p

3566. Wilkins, J.L. * Scharff, W.H. * Schlottman, R.S. Personality type, reports of violence, and aggressive behavior. Aug. 1973. p. 243-247. Journal of Personality and Social Psychology. ; 30.

3567. Wykert, J. Psychiatry and terrorism. 2 Febr. 1979. p. 1, 12-14. Psychiatric News. ; 14.

3568. Zillmann, D. Hostility and aggression. - Hillsdale : Lawrence Erlbau Associates, 1979.

3569. _____ Belfast syndrome: Irish violence damages psyches. p. 26-27. Science Digest. ; 74.

3570. _____ Terror: Psychologie der Taeter und der Opfer. 1978. Psychologie Heute. ; 1.

3571. _____ The Belfast syndrome : Irish violence damages psyches. Sept. 1973. p. 26-27. Science Digest. ; 74.

M. TERRORISM FROM A CRIMINOLOGICAL PERSPECTIVE

3572. Baudouin, J.L. * Fortin, J. * Szabo, D. Terrorisme et justice : Entre la liberte et l'ordre: le crime politique. - Montreal : Editions du Jour, 1970. 175 p

3573. Beristain, A. Terrorism and aircraft hijackings. Nov. 1974. p. 347-389. International Journal of Criminology and Penology. ; 2:4.

3574. Bianchi, H. Politiek terrorisme en kriminaliteit. Sept. 1978. p. 227-231. Civis Mundi. ; 17:5.

3575. Clinard, M.B. * Abbott, D.J. Crime in developing countries. - New York : John Wiley and Sons, 1973.

3576. Clinard, M.B. * Meier, R.F. Sociology of deviant behavior. - 5th ed. - New York : Holt, Rinehart & Winston, 1979. 613 p

3577. Crelinsten, R.D. * (ed.) Research strategies for the study of international political terrorism. - Montreal : International Centre for Comparative Criminology, 1977. 218 p ; Final report of a conference held in Evian from May 30-June 1, 1977

3578. Crelinsten, R.D. * Laberge-Altmejd, D. * Szabo, D. Terrorism and criminal justice. - Lexington, Mass. : Lexington Books, 1978. 131 p

3579. Crelinsten, R.D. International political terrorism : A challenge for comparative research. 1978. p. 107-126. International Journal of Comparative and Applied Criminal Justice. ; 2.

3580. Cullinane, M.J. Terrorism - a new era of criminality. 1978. p. 119-124. Terrorism. ; 1:2.

3581. Davidson, E. The Nuremberg fallacy : Wars and war crimes since World War II. - New York : 1973. 331 p

3582. Dessaur, C.I. Foundations of theory-formation in criminology. - The Hague : Mouton & Co., 1971.

3583. Dessaur, C.I. Golven van terreur. Febr. 1978. Delikt en Delinkwent

3584. Dietrich, P. Terroristische und erpresserische Gewaltkriminalitaet. 1973. p. 190-201. Kriminalistik. ; 5:4.

3585. Fishman, G. Criminological aspects of international terrorism: the dynamics of the Palestinian movement. - New York : Praeger, 1974. p. 103-113. In: M. Riedel and T.P. Thornberry (eds.), Crime and delinquency: dimensions of deviance

3586. Gunther Moor, L.H.G. * (ed.) Terreur : Criminologische en juridische aspecten van terrorisme. - Utrecht : Ars Aequi, 1976.

3587. Gurr, T.R. * et al. Rogues, rebels, and reformers : A political history of urban crime and conflict. - Beverly Hills : Sage, 1976. 192 p

3588. Gurr, T.R. Crime : A retrospective view. Center for the Study of Democratic Institutions., Jan-Febr. 1978. p. 74-79. The Center Magazine. ; 11.

3589. Gurr, T.R. Crime trends in modern democracies since 1945. 1977. p. 41-86. International Annals of Criminology. ; 16:1-2.

3590. Gurr, T.R. Historical trends in violent crimes : A critical review of evidence. University of Chicago Press, 1981. p. 295-353. Crime and Justice. ; 3.

3591. Hassel, C.V. Terror: the crime of the privileged : An examination and prognosis. 1977. p. 1-16. Terrorism. ; 1:1.

3592. Hippchen, L.J. * Yim. Y.S. Terrorism, international crime, and arms control. - Springfield, Ill. : Thomas, 1982. 293 p

3593. Kelly, C.M. Statement on terrorism. - Washington, D.C. : N.C.J.R.S. Microfiche Program, 31 May 1974.
By FBI director.

3594. Kelly, R.J. New political crimes and the emergence of revolutionary nationalist ideology. - Chicago : Rand-McNally, 1973.
Includes treatment of terroristic activities of Palestinian nationalist groups.

3595. Kittrie, N.N. In search of political crime and political criminals. April 1975. p. 202-209. New York University Law Review. ; 50.

3596. Langemann, H. Das Attentat : Eine kriminalwissenschaftliche Studie zum politischen Kapitalverbrechen. - Hamburg : 1956.

3597. Leaute, J. Notre violence. - Paris : Editions Denoel, 1977.

3598. Lombroso, C. * Laschi, R. Le delitto politico e rivoluzionari. - Torino : Bocca, 1890.
The German edition "Der politische Verbrecher und die Revolution in anthropologischer, juridischer und staatswissenschaftlicher Beziehung" was published in two volumes in Hamburg, 1891-1892.

3599. Mednick, S.A. * Shoham, S.G. * (eds.) New paths in criminology. - Lexington : Lexington Books, 1979.

3600. Middendorff, W. Das kleine Uebel oder: das Ansehen des Staates; historisch- kriminologische Betrachtung zu Geiselnahme und Kidnapping. 1973. p. 71-82. Kriminalistik. ; 5:2.

3601. Middendorff, W. Die Gewaltkriminalitaet unserer Zeit : Geschichte, Erscheinungsformen, Lehren. - Stuttgart : 1976. Polizei Aktuell. ; 19.

3602. Middendorff, W. Politische Kriminalitaet am Beispiel des Terrorismus. - Zuerich : 1981. p. 402-418.
In: H.J. Schneider (ed.), Die Psychologie des 20. Jahrhunderts. Vol. 14. Auswirkungen auf die Kriminologie. Delinquenz und Gesellschaft

3603. Milte, K.L. Terrorism and international order. June 1975. p. 101-111. The Australian and New Zealand Journal of Criminology. ; 8:2.

3604. Minor, W.W. Political crime, political justice and political prisoners. Feb. 1975. p. 385-398. Criminology. ; 12.

3605. Nagel, W.H. A socio-legal view on the suppression of terrorism. 1980. p. 213-226. International Journal of the Sociology of Law. ; 8.

3606. Nagel, W.H. Devil's advocate on the question of terrorism. 1971. p. 15-17. Etudes internationales de psycho-sociologie criminelle. ; 20-23.

3607. Nagel, W.H. Terrorisme. - Den Haag : Ministerie van Justitie, 1975. p. 150-156. Justitiele Verkenningen. ; 4. Conceptual analysis of the phenomenon of terrorism from a criminological point of view.

3608. Nagel, W.H. Terrorisme. Jan. 1978. p. 17-25. Tijdschrift voor Criminologie. ; 20:1.

3609. Schafer, S. The political criminal : The problem of morality and crime. - New York : Free Press, 1974. 179 p

3610. Sousa Santos, B.de * Scheerer, S. * Schwinghammer, T. * et al. Terrorism and the violence of the state. - Hamburg : European Group for the Study of Deviance and Social Control, 1979. Working Papers in European Criminology. ; 1.

3611. Springer, W. Kriminalitaets-Theorien und ihr Realitaetsgehalt. - Stuttgart : Ferd. Enke Verlag, 1973.

3612. Stanciu, V.V. Macrocriminologie : Psychologie des Terroristes. 1973. p. 189-198. Revue internationale de criminologie et de police technique. ; 26:2.

3613. Stanciu, V.V. Terrorisme et crime politique. 1972. p. 28-37. Revue politique et parlementaire. ; 74:832.

3614. Stinson, J.L. * Heyman, E.S. Analytic approaches for investigating terrorist crimes. - Gaithersburg, Md. : IACP., 43 p

3615. Szabo, M.O. Political crimes : A historical perspective. 1972. Denver Journal of International Law and Politics. ; 2:7.

3616. Taylor, D.L. Terrorism and criminology: the application of a perspective. - West Lafayette, Ind. : Institute for the Study of Social Change, Purdue University, 1978.

3617. Taylor, I. * Taylor, L. * (eds.) Politics and deviance. - Harmondsworth : Penguin, 1973.

3618. Taylor, I. * Walton, P. * Young, J. The new criminology : For a social theory of deviance. - London : Routledge & Kegan Paul, 1973.

3619. Turk, A.T. Political criminality : The defiance and defense of authority. - London : Sage, 1982. 232 p

3620. Wilkinson, P. Assassination. - London : Routledge and Kegan Paul., p. 12-13. In: A dictionary of criminology

3621. Wilkinson, P. Emergency laws. - London : Routledge and Kegan Paul., p. 80-82. In: A dictionary of criminology

3622. Wilkinson, P. Hijacking. - London : Routledge and Kegan Paul., p. 103-104. In: A dictionary of criminology

3623. Wilkinson, P. Kidnapping. - London : Routledge and Kegan Paul., p. 125-126. In: A dictionary of criminology

3624. Wilkinson, P. Political crime/terrorism. - London : Routledge and Kegan Paul., p. 168-170. In: A dictionary of criminology

3625. Wilson, J.Q. Thinking about crime. - New York : Basic Books, 1975.

3626. _____ Changes in forms and dimensions of criminality - transnational and national. - Geneva : 1975. United Nations ; Working paper, Fifth congress on prevention of crime and the treatment of offenders

N. TERRORISM FROM A MILITARY PERSPECTIVE

3627. Allemann, F.R. Wie wirksam ist Terrorismus?. 25 June 1978. p. 343-358. Europa-Archiv. ; 33:12. Discusses effectiveness of urban guerrillas in Latin America, Europeand Israel.

3628. Aron, R. Peace and war. - London : Weidenfeld and Nicolson, 1966.

3629. Avery, W.P. Terrorism and the international transfer of conventional armaments. - New York : Pergamon Press, 1981. p. 329-342. In: Y. Alexander and J.M. Gleason (eds.), Behavioral and quantitative perspectives on terrorism

3630. Bayo, A. 150 questions to a guerrilla. - Boulder, Colo. : Panther, 1963.
A Spanish civil war veteran general who trained Castro gives his experience on how to wage a guerrilla.

3631. Beaufre, A. La guerre revolutionnaire : Les formes nouvelles de la guerre. - Paris : Fayard, 1972.
Also deals with terrorism.

3632. Bigney, R.E. * Crancer, J.W. * Hamlin, T.M. * Hetrick, B.W. * Munger, M.D. Exploration of the nature of future warfare. - Carlisle Barracks, Pa. : Army War College, June 1974. 106 p

3633. Black, R.J. A change in tactics? : The urban insurgent. Jan. 1972. ppp. 50-58. Air University Review. ; 23.

3634. Blaufarb, D.S. The counter-insurgency era. - New York : Free Press, 1977.

3635. Bouthoul, G. Le terrorisme. April 1973. p. 37-46. Etudes polemologiques. ; 3.

3636. Browne, M.W. The new face of war. - Indianapolis : Bobbs-Merrill Co., 1965.

3637. Cabral, A. La pratique revolutionnaire. - Paris : Maspero, 1975. 309 p

3638. Caine, P.D. Urban guerrilla warfare. 1970. p. 73-78. Military Review. ; 50:2.

3639. Chisholm, H.J. The function of terror and violence in revolution. - Washington, D.C. : Georgetown University, 1948. 202 p ; Unpubl. M.A. thesis

3640. Cline, R.S. * Alexander, Y. Terrorism as a covert warfare. Hero Books, 1986. 128 p

3641. Cobb, R. Les armees revolutionnaires : Instrument de la terreur dans les departements. - 2 vols. - Paris : Mouton, 1964.

3642. Dach, H.von Total resistance. - Boulder, Colo. : Panther, 1965.

3643. Dalen, H.van Terror as a political weapon. 1975. p. 21-26. Military Police Law Enforcement Journal. ; 2:1.

3644. Delmas, C. La guerre revolutionnaire. - Paris : 1965. Que sais-je? Le point des connaissances actuelles. ; 826.

3645. Eldridge, A. Images of conflict. - New York : St. Martin's Press, 1979. 229 p

3646. Elliott-Bateman, M. * Ellis, J. * Bowden, T. Revolt to revolution : Studies in the 19th and 20tn century European experience. Manchester University Press, 1974. 373 p. The fourth dimension of warfare. ; Vol. 2.

3647. Elliott-Bateman, M. * (ed.) The fourth dimension of warfare. - Manchester : 1970.

3648. Ellis, J. A short history of guerrilla warfare. - New York : St. Martin's, 1976.

3649. Esson, D.M.R. The secret weapon - terrorism. 1959. p. 167. Army Quarterly. ; 78.

3650. Gablonski, E. Terror from the sky: airwar. - Garden City, N.Y. : Doubleday, 1971.

3651. Gann, L.H. Guerrillas in history. - Stanford : Hoover Institution Press, 1971. 99 p

3652. Garthoff, R.L. Unconventional warfare in communist strategy. 1962. p. 566-575. Foreign Affairs. ; 40.

3653. Giap, V.N. Big victory, great task. - London : Pall Mall Press, 1968.

3654. Giap, V.N. La guerre de liberation et l'armee populaire. - Hanoi : 1950.

3655. Giap, V.N. People's war, people's army: the Viet-Cong insurrection manual for underdeveloped countries. - New York : Praeger, 1962. 217 p

3656. Giap, V.N. Recits de la resistance vietnamienne 1925-1945. - Paris : 1966.

3657. Giap, V.N. The military art of people's war : Selected writings. - New York-London : Monthly Review Press, 1970. 332 p

3658. Giap, V.N. The South Vietnam people will win. - Hanoi : Foreign Languages Publishing House, 1966.

3659. Grivas-Dighenis, G. Guerrilla warfare and EOKA's struggle : A politico-military study. - London : Longmans, Green, 1964.

3660. Guevara, E. (Che). Obra revolucionaria. - 4th ed. - Mexico : Ediciones Era, 1971.

3661. Guevara, E. (Che) Guerrilla warfare. - New York : Random House, 1961.

3662. Haeggman, B. Terrorism: var tids krigfoering. - Malmoe : Bergh, 1978. 236 p

3663. Hahlweg, W. Guerilla - Krieg ohne Fronten. - Stuttgart etc. : Kohlhammer, 1968.

3664. Hahlweg, W. Theoretische Grundlagen der modernen Guerilla und des

Terrorismus. - Bonn : Wehr und Wissen, 1976.
In: R. Tophoven (ed.), Politik durch Gewalt. Guerilla und Terrorismus heute

3665. Hahlweg, W. Typologie des modernen Kleinkrieges. - Wiesbaden : Steiner, 1967. 74 p

3666. Heilbrunn, O. Partisan warfare. - New York : Praeger, 1962.
British ed.: London: Allen and Unwin, 1962.

3667. Heilbrunn, O. Warfare in the enemy's rear. - New York : Praeger, 1963.

3668. Jacobs, W.D. Urban guerilla warfare. 1971. p. 62-70. NATO's Fifteen Nations. ; 16:6.

3669. Janos, A.C. Unconventional warfare: framework and analysis. 1963. p. 636-646. World Politics. ; 15.

3670. Jender, D. Urban guerrilla warfare in western countries. 1971. p. 12-20. Army Journal. ; 260.

3671. Jenkins, B.M. High technology terrorism and surrogate war: the impact of new technology on low-level violence. - Santa Monica, Calif. : RAND, 1975. RAND Paper. ; P-5339.

3672. Jenkins, B.M. International terrorism : The other world war. - Santa Monica, Calif. : RAND, 1985. 29 p

3673. Jenkins, B.M. International terrorism: a new kind of warfare. - Santa Monica, Calif. : RAND, June 1974. RAND Paper. ; P-5261.

3674. Johnson, Ch. Autopsy on people's war. - Berkeley : University of California Press, 1973. 118 p

3675. Kaufman, E. La estrategia de los guerrillos. 1973. p. 12-27. Problemas internacionales. ; 20:1.

3676. Kern, J.W. Terrorism and gunrunning. - Gaithersburg, Md. : IACP., 15 p

3677. Klonis, N.I. Guerrilla warfare: analysis and projections. - New York : Speller, 1972.

3678. Knorr, K. Unconventional warfare: strategy and tactics in internal political strife. May 1962. p. 346. The Annals of the American Academy of Political and Social Science

3679. Laqueur, W. Guerrillas and terrorists. Oct. 1974. p. 40-48. Commentary. ; 54:4.

3680. Latey, M. Violence as a political weapon. Dec. 1971; Jan. 1972. p. 65-71. NATO's Fifteen Nations. ; 16.

3681. Mallin, J. Terrorism as a military weapon. Jan. 1977. p. 54-64. Air University Review. ; 28.
Revised version in: M.H. Livingston et al. (eds.), International terrorism in the contemporary world, pp. 389-401. Westport, Conn.: Greenwood Press, 1978.

3682. Mallin, J. Terrorism is revolutionary warfare. 1974. p. 48-55. Strategic Review. ; 2.
Mainly on Tupamaros.

3683. Mao Tse-tung. Basic tactics. - New York : Praeger, 1966.

3684. Mao Tse-tung. On guerrilla warfare. - New York : Praeger, 1961.

3685. Mao Tse-tung. On the protected war. - Peking : 1954.

3686. Mao Tse-tung. Theorie des Guerillakrieges oder Strategie der Dritten Welt. - Reinbek : Rowohlt, 1966. 203 p
Selected military writings.

3687. Marighella, C. Urban guerrilla minimanual. - Vancouver : Pulb Press, 1974. 37 p

3688. Martinez-Codo, E. Guerrilla warfare after Guevara. July 1969. p. 24-30. Military Review. ; 49.

3689. Miller, D.M.O. Insurgency : The theory and practice of contemporary insurgencies. 1966. p. 33-46. Army Quarterly and Defence. ; 91:1-2.

3690. Minnery, J. * Truby, J.D. Improvised modified firearms. - Boulder, Colo. : Paladin Press, 1975.

3691. Moss, R. Urban guerrilla war. - 3rd ed. - Baltimore : Johns Hopkins Press, 1973. p. 242-259.
In: R.G. Head and E.J. Rokke (eds.), American defence policy

3692. Most, J. Revolutionaere Kriegswissenschaft : Ein Handbuechlein zur Anleitung betreffend Gebrauches und Herstellung von Nitroglycerin, Dynamit, Schiessbaumwolle, Knallquecksilber, Bomben, Brandsaetzen, Giften, usw. - 3rd ed. - London : Slienger, 1976. 74 p. Bibliotheca Historico Militaris. ; 3.
The orig. edition in English was titled: Science of revolutionary war; manual for instruction in the use and preparation of nitro- glycerine, dynamite, guncotton, fulminating mercury, bombs, fuses, and poisons, etc. New York, Internationale Zeitung Verein, 1884.

3693. Motley, J.B. * et al. Global terrorism : What should the US do?. National Defense University Press, 1981. ; The 1980's: Decade of confrontation? Proceedings of the Eigth annual national security affairs conference, 13-15 July 1981

3694. Motley, J.B. If terrorism hits home, will the army be ready?. April 1984. Army

3695. Motley, J.B. International terrorism : A new mode of warfare. May 1981. p. 93-123. International Security Review. ; 6.

3696. Motley, J.B. Terrorism. Jan. 1985. National Defense

3697. Motley, J.B. Terrorist warfare : Formidable challenges. Summer 1985. p. 295-306. Fletcher Forum. ; 9.

3698. Munger, M.D. Growing utility of political terrorism. - Springfield, Virg. : National Technical Information Service, 1977.
Counts approximately 300 identifiable terrorist groups.

3699. Nasution, A.H. Fundamentals of guerrilla warfare. - New York : Praeger, 1965.

3700. Neale, W.D. Oldest weapon in the arsenal: terror. Aug. 1973. p. 10. Army

3701. Ney, V. Guerrilla warfare and propaganda. - Washington, D.C. : Georgetown University, 1958. 106 p ; Unpubl. M.A. thesis

3702. Niezing, J. Politiek terrorisme en oorlog. Sept. 1978. p. 193-196. Civis Mundi. ; 5.

3703. Nkrumah, K. * (ed.) Handbook of revolutionary warfare : A guide to the armed phase of the African revolution. - 2nd ed. - New York : International Publishers, 1969. 122 p

3704. O'Ballance, E. Terrorism : The new growth form of warfare. - Westport, Conn. : Greenwood Press, 1978. p. 415-423.
In: M.H. Livingston (ed.), International terrorism in the contemporary world

3705. Ohanna, Y.A. Strategy and tactics. - London : 1981.

3706. Osanka, F.M. Modern guerilla warfare : Fighting communist guerrilla movement, 1941-1961. - Glencoe, Ill. : The Free Press, 1962.

3707. Peters, C.C.M. Urban guerrillas. 1975. p. 21-48. Army Journal. ; 311.

3708. Peterson, H.C. Urban guerrilla warfare. 1972. p. 82-89. Military Review. ; 52:3.

3709. Qualter, T.H. Propaganda and psychological warfare. - New York : Random House, 1962.

3710. Quintero Morente, F. Empleo de la violencia urbana por la subversion (I-IV). p. 23-28; 28-33; 7-16; 57-66. Ejercito. ; 33:394; 33:395; 34:398; 3.

3711. Quintero Morente, F. Terrorism. 1965. p. 55. Military Review. ; 45.

3712. Roberts, K.E. The terror trap : Military issues research memorandum. - Carlisle Barracks, Pa. : Strategic Studies Institute, U.S. Army War College, 1975. 20 p

3713. Roetter, Ch. Psychological warfare. - London : Faber, 1974.

3714. Ruiz Molina, J. De la guerrilla urbana (I-II). 1973. p. 35-42; 27-35. Ejercito. ; 34:404; 34-405.

3715. Ryter, S.L. Terror as a psychological weapon. May-June 1966. p. 21, 145-146, 149-150. The Review

3716. Schamis, G.J. War and terrorism in international affairs. - New Brunswick, N.J. : Transaction Books, 1980. 89 p

3717. Schmitt, C. Theorie der Partisanen. - Berlin : Duncker und Humbolt, 1963.

3718. Schreiber, J. The ultimate weapon: terrorists and world order. - New York : Morrow, 1978. 218 p

3719. Scott, A.M. * Hill, C. Insurgency. - Chapel Hill : University of North Carolina Press, 1970. 139 p

3720. Short, K. The dynamite war. - Atlantic Highlands, N.J. : Humanities Press, 1979.

3721. Shultz, R. Study of the selective use of political terrorism in process of revolutionary warfare : N.L.F. of South Vietnam. 1976. p. 43-77. International Behavioral Scientist. ; 8:2.

3722. Silverman, J.M. * Jackson, P.M. Terror in insurgency warfare. 1970. p. 61-70. Military Review. ; 50:10.

3723. Simpson, H.R. Terror. 1970. p. 65-69. U.S. Naval Institute Proceedings. ; 19:4.

3724. Singh, B. Theory and practice of modern guerrilla warfare. - New York : Asia Publishing House, 1971.

3725. Spengele, R. Terrorism in unconventional warfare. University of California Press, 1964. ; Unpubl. M.A. thesis

3726. Taber, R. The war of the flea : A study of guerrilla warfare. Theory and practice. - New York : Citadel, 1970.

3727. Thayer, Ch.W. Guerrillas und Partisanen : Wesen und Methoden der irregulaeren Kriegsfuehrung. - Muenchen : 1964.

3728. Thompson, R. * Fuchs, N.L. * Kloppenberg, R.E. * Stokreef, J. * Wegener, U. Terrorism and security force requirements. - New York : Crane, Russak, 1979. p. 128-146. In: J. Shaw, E.F. Gueritz and A.E. Younger (eds.), Ten years of terrorism

3729. Thompson, R. Revolutionary war in world strategy, 1945-1969. - London : Seeker & Warburg, 1970.

3730. Toynbee, A.J. The German terror in France. - London : 1917. 212 p

3731. Trinquier, R. Modern warfare : A french view of counterinsurgency. - New York : Praeger, 1964.

3732. Truby, J.D. Improvised/modified small arms used by terrorists. - Gaithersburg, Md. : IACP., 16 p

3733. Walter, H. Terror by satellite. - London : Faber, 1980.

3734. Weisl, W.von Terror als Methode moderner Kriegsfuehrung. 1969. p. 437-447. Allgemeine Schweizerische Militaerzeitschrift. ; 135:8.

3735. Wilkinson, P. Terrorism - weapon of the weak. 1979. p. 128-137. Encyclopaedia Britannica Book of the Year. ; 1979.

3736. Wohlstetter, A. The delicate balance of terror. Jan. 1959. Foreign Affairs. ; 38.
On East-West conflict.

3737. Wright, J.W. Terrorism : A mode of warfare. Oct. 1984. p. 35-45. Military Review. ; 64:10.

3738. Zawodny, J.K. Guerrilla and sabotage: organization, operations, motivations, escalation. May 1962. Annals of the American Academy of Political and Social Science. ; 341.
Special edition on "unconventional warfare".

3739. Zawodny, J.K. Guerrilla warfare and subversion as a means of political change. - Stanford : Stanford University Press, 1961.

3740. _____ Le defi de la guerre : Deux siecles de guerres et de revolutions. - Paris : Presse Universitaire., 1976.

3741. _____ The international arms trade and the terrorist. - London : 1981.
Center for Contemporary Studies. * (ed.). Contemporary Affairs Briefing. ; 7.
Shows U.S. armed forcessin Germany to be chief supply source by thefts.

O. JURIDICAL ASPECTS OF TERRORISM

3742. Abu-Lughad, I. Unconventional violence and international politics. Nov. 1973. ppp. 100-104. American Journal of International Law. ; 67.

3743. Agrawala, S.K. Aircraft hijacking and international law. - Dobbs Ferr, N.Y. : Oceana Publ., 1973.

3744. Ajomo, M.A. The Entebbe affair : Intervention in international law. ; A public lecture delivered under the auspices of the Nigerian Institute of International Affairs, Victoria Island, Lagos, on Monday Oct. 25, 1976

3745. Akehurst, M. Arab-Israeli conflict and international law. 1973. p. 231. New Zealand Universities Law Review. ; 5.

3746. Argoustis, A. Hijacking and the controller. 1978. p. 91-95. Air Law. ; 111:2.
Legal, representing a position of a member of the International Federation of Air Traffic Controllers' Association (IFATCA).

3747. Atala, Ch. * Groffier, E. Terrorisme et guerilla: la revolte armee devant les nations. - Ottawa : Dossiers Interlex, les Editions Lemeac, 1973. 181 p

3748. Bailey, S.D. Prohibitions and restraints in war. - London : Oxford University Press, 1972. 194 p

3749. Bakker-Schut, P.H. * Prakken, T. * Hartkamp, D. * Mols, G. Kanttekeningen bij een anti-terrorismeverdrag. 13 Aug. 1977. Nederlands Juristenblad. ; 52:28.

3750. Barrie, G.N. Crimes committed aboard aircraft. 1968. p. 203-208. South African Law Journal. ; 83.

3751. Bassiouni, M.C. Methodological options for international legal control of terrorism. 1974. p. 388-396. Akron Law Review. ; 7.

3752. Bauer, E.F. Die voelkerrechtswidrige Entfuehrung. - Berlin : 1968. 208 p

3753. Baxter, R.R. A skeptical look at the concept of terrorism. 1974. p. 380-387. Akron Law Review. ; 7.

3754. Bemmelen, J.M.van Terrorisme. Sept. 1972. p. 945-949. Nederlands Juristenblad. ; 33.

3755. Blishchenko, I.P. Terrorism and international law. - Moscow : Progress, 1984. 286 p

3756. Bloomfield, L.M. * Fitzgerald, G.F. Crimes against internationally protected persons: prevention and punishment : An analysis of the U.N. convention. - New York : Praeger, 1975. 273 p

3757. Bolle, P.H. Le droit et la repression du terrorisme. April 1977. p. 121-128. Revue internationale de criminologie et de police technique. ; 30:2.

3758. Bond, J.E. Application of the law of war to internal conflicts. 1973. p. 345. Georgia Journal of International and Comparative Law. ; 3.

3759. Bond, J.E. The rules of riot: internal conflict and the law of war. - Princeton, N.J. : Princeton University Press, 1974. 280 p

3760. Bradford, A.L. Legal ramifications of hijacking airplanes. 1962. p. 1034-1039. American Bar Association Journal. ; 48.

3761. Bravo, N.M. Apoderamiento ilicito de aeronaves en vuelo. 1969. p. 788-809. Revista espanola de derecho internacional. ; 22.

3762. Breton, J.M. Piraterie aerienne et droit international public. 1971. p. 392-445. Revue generale de droit international public. ; 75.

3763. Buchheit, L.C. Secession : The legacy of self-determination. - New Haven, Conn. : Yale University Press, 1978.

3764. Caloyanni, M.A. Deux conventions: prevention et repression du terrorisme - creation d'une cour penale internationale. 1930. p. 403-420. Revue de science criminelle et de droit penal compare. ; 2.

3765. Cassandro, G. * et al. Unione giucisti cattolici italiani : Violenza e diritto. - Milano : Giuffre, 1982. 184 p ; Atti del xxxi Convegno nazionale di studio, Roma, 6-8 dicembre 1980

3766. Cassandro, G. * et al. Violenza e diritto. - Milano : Giuffre, 1982. ; Atti del 31 Convegno Nazionale di Studio, Roma, 6-8 dicembre 1980

3767. Cautrell, Ch.L. Political offence exemption in international extradiction : A comparison of the United States, Great Britain and the Republic of Ireland. 1977. op. 777-824. Marquette Law Review. ; 60:3.

3768. Chandam, K.S. Le terrorisme devant la S.D.N. - Paris : Publications Contemporaines., 1935.

3769. Chaturvedi, S.C. Hijacking and the law. 1971. p. 89-105. Indian Journal of International Law. ; 11.

3770. Chung, D.Y. Some legal aspects of aircraft hijacking in international law. University of Tennessee, 1976. ; Ph.D. dissertation

3771. Crelinsten, R.D. * Laberge-Altmejd, D. * (eds.) The impact of terrorism and skyjacking on the operations of the criminal justice system. - Montreal : ICCC, 1976. 348 p
Final report on basic issue seminar.

3772. Daetwyler, G. Der Terrorismus und das internationale Strafrecht. - Zurich : W. Schneider, 1981. 353 p

3773. David, E. Le terrorisme en droit international. - Bruxelles : Editions de l'Universite de Bruxelles, 1974. p. 103-173.
In: Reflexions sur la definition et la repression du terrorisme; actes du Colloque sous la presidence d'honneur de Henri Rolin, 19 et 20 mars 1973

3774. DeNaro, J.M. In-flight crimes, the Tokyo convention and federal judicial jurisdiction. 1969. p. 171-203. Journal of Air Law and Commerce. ; 35.

3775. Dimitrijevic, V. Aktuelna pitanja medjunarodnog terorizma. 1974. p. 55-63. Jugoslovenska Revija za Medjunarodno Pravo

3776. Dimitrijevic, V. Internationaler Terrorismus und Auslieferungsrecht. - Stuttgart : W. Kohlhammer, 1979. p. 63-83.
In: T. Berberich, W. Holl, K.J. Maass (eds.), Neue Entwicklungen im offentlichen Recht

3777. Dinstein, Y. Criminal jurisdiction over aircraft hijacking. 1972. p. 195-206. Israel Law Review. ; 7.

3778. Dominguez, C.H. El terrorismo en el estado de derecho. - Buenos Aires : Editorial Abaco de Rodolfo Depalma, 1983. 290 p

3779. Draper, Th. The ethical and juridical status of constraints in war. 1972. p. 169. Military Law Review. ; 55.

3780. Emanuelli, C. Legal aspects of aerial terrorism : The piecemeal vs. the comprehensive approach. 1975. p. 503-518. Annual of International Law and

Economics. ; 10.

3781. Enzensberger, H.M. * (ed.) Freisprueche : Revolutionaere vor Gericht. - Frankfurt a/M : 1970.

3782. Evans, A.E. * Murphy, J.F. * (eds.) Legal aspects of international terrorism. - Lexington, Mass. : Lexington Books, 1978. 696 p
Also contains a compilation of hijacking incidents between 1.1.1960 and 31.7.1977.

3783. Evans, A.E. Report on aircraft hijacking in the U.S : Law and practice. Sept. 1974. p. 589-604. Criminal Law Bulletin. ; 10.

3784. Evans, A.E. Terrorism and political crimes in international law. p. 87-110.
In: Proceedings, 67th Annual meeting of the American Society of International Law, 12-14 April 1973

3785. Falk, R.A. * (ed.) The international law of civil war. - Baltimore : 1971. 452 p

3786. Falk, R.A. * Blum, Y.Z. The Beirut raid and the international law of retaliation. July 1969; Jan. 1970. p. 415-443; 73-105. American Journal of International Law. ; 63;64.

3787. Falk, R.A. * Kolko, G. * Lifton, R.J. * (eds.) Crimes of war. - New York : Random House, 1971. 590 p

3788. Falk, R.A. Terror, liberation movements, and the process of social change. 1969. p. 423-427. American Journal of International Law. ; 63.

3789. Faller, E.W. Gewaltsame Flugzeugentfuehrungen aus voelkerrechtlicher Sicht. - Berlin : Dunker & Humbolt, 1972. 212 p

3790. Farrell, W.R. Military involvement in domestic terror incidents. July-Aug. 1981. p. 53-66. Naval War College Review. ; 34.

3791. Feller, S.Z. Comment on criminal jurisdiction over aircraft hijacking. 1972. p. 207-214. Israel Law Review. ; 7.

3792. Fenwick, C.G. "Piracy" in the Caribbean. 1961. p. 426-428. American Journal of International Law. ; 55.

3793. Fitzgerald, G.F. Development of international rules concerning offences and certain other acts committed on board aircraft. 1963. p. 230-251. Canadian Yearbook of International Law. ; 1.

3794. Flores Castro Altomirano, E. El delito de terrorismo. - Mexico : 1963. 110 p

3795. Francke, H. Flugzeugentfuehrungen als Weltverbrechen : Zum Haager Abkommen vom 16.12.1970. - Goettingen : 1973. p. 301-327. Jahrbuch fuer Internationales Recht. ; 16.

3796. Freestone, D. Legal responses to terrorism : Towards European cooperation?. - Oxford : Martin Robertson, 1981. p. 195-224.
In: J. Lodge (ed.), Terrorism, a challenge to the state

3797. Friedlander, R.A. Terrorism and international law : Recent developments. Spring 1982. p. 493-511. Rutgers Law Journal. ; 13.

3798. Friedlander, R.A. Terrorism and international law: what is being done?. 1977. p. 383-392. Rutgers Camden Law Journal. ; 8.

3799. Gaay Fortman, W.F.de Rechtsstaat en terrorisme. - Alphen aan den Rijn : Samsom, 1979. 26 p

3800. Galyean, T.E. Acts of terrorism and combat by irregular forces: an insurance 'war risk'. 1974. p. 314. California Western International Law Journal. ; 4.

3801. Garcia-Mora, M.R. International responsibility for hostile acts of private persons against foreign states. - The Hague : Martinus Nijhoff, 1962.

3802. Garcia-Mora, M.R. The nature of political offenses: a knotty problem of extradition law. 1962. p. 122. Virginia Law Review. ; 48.

3803. Gjidara, M. La "piraterie aerienne" en droit international et en droit compare. 1972. p. 791-844. Revue internationale en droit compare. ; 24:4.

3804. Gonzales Lapeyre, E. Aspectos juridicas del terrorismo. - Montevideo : Fernandez, 1972. 125 p

3805. Green, L.C. Double standards in the United Nations : The legislation of terrorism. 1979. p. 129-148. Archiv der Voelkerrechts. ; 18:2.

3806. Green, L.C. Extradition and asylum for aerial hijackers. 1975. p. 207-224. Israel Yearbook of Human Rights. ; 5.

3807. Green, L.C. Hijacking and the right of asylum. - New York : Oceana, 1971. p. 124-146.
In: E. McWhinney (ed.), Aerial piracy and international law

3808. Green, L.C. Hijacking, extradition and asylum. 1974. p. 135-143. Chitty's Law Journal. ; 22.

3809. Green, L.C. Humanitarian intervention - 1976 version. 1976. p. 217-225. Chitty's Law Journal. ; 24.

3810. Green, L.C. International law and the control of terrorism. 1983. p. 136-156. Dalhouse Law Journal. ; 7.

3811. Green, L.C. International terrorism and its legal control. 1973. p. 389-301. Chitty's Law Journal. ; 21.

3812. Green, L.C. Piracy of aircraft and the law. 1972. p. 72-88. Alberta Law Review. ; 10.

3813. Green, L.C. Rescue at Entebbe : Legal aspects. 1976. p. 312-324. Israel Yearbook of Human Rights. ; 6.

3814. Green, L.C. Terrorism and international law. 1981. 17 p. Research Reports of the Institute of Jewish Affairs. ; 13-14.

3815. Green, L.C. Terrorism and the courts. 1981. p. 333-358. Manitoba Law Journal. ; 11.

3816. Green, L.C. Terrorism and the law. 1982. p. 107-112. Chitty's Law Journal

3817. Green, L.C. The Tehran embassy incident : Legal aspects. 1980. p. 1-22. Archiv des Volkenrechts. ; 19.

3818. Gross, L. International terrorism and international criminal jurisdiction. July 1973. p. 508-511. American Journal of International Law. ; 67:3.

3819. Heilbronner, K. Luftpiraterie in rechtlicher Sicht. - Hannover : 1972.

3820. Hennings, A. Die Unabhangigkeit der Strafverteidigung im Spannungsfeld von Rechtsstaatlichkeit und Terroristen-Bekaempfung. 1978. p. 31-42. Gegenwartskunde. ; 27:1.

3821. Hewitt, W.E. Respect for human rights in armed conflict. 1971. p. 41. New York University Journal of International Law and Politics. ; 4.

3822. Horlick, G.N. The developing law of air hijacking. 1971. p. 33-70. Harvard International Law Journal. ; 12.

3823. Ingwell, M. Tugwell's terrorist. 16 Nov. 1982. Canadian Lawyer

3824. Jenkins, B.M. Should corporations be prevented from paying ransom?. - Santa Monica, Calif. : RAND, 1974.

3825. Joyner, N.D. Aerial hijacking as an international crime. - Dobbs Ferry, N.Y. : Oceana Publ., 1974. 352 p

3826. Khan, R. Guerrilla warfare and international law. - New Delhi : 9 Oct. 1967. International Studies

3827. Khan, R. Hijacking and international law. 1971. p. 398-403. Africa Quarterly. ; 10.

3828. Kipling, R.E. Is terrorism ever justified?. Jan.-Febr. 1976. p. 34-36, 61-62. Skeptic. ; 11.

3829. Kossoy, E. Living with guerrilla : Guerrilla as a legal problem and a political fact. - Geneva : Librairie Droz, 1976. 405 p

3830. Krieken, P.J.van Hijacking and asylum. - Leiden : 1975. p. 3-30. Netherlands International Law Review. ; 22:1.

3831. Kwiatkowska-Czechowska, B. The problem of terrorism in the light of international law. - Warsaw : Polish Institute of International Affairs, 1977. p. 119-138. Studies on International Relations. ; 9.

3832. Laan-Bouma, R.van der * Wiersma, J. Terrorisme en burgerlijke grondrechten. 1978. p. 210-215. Civis Mundi. ; 17:5.

3833. Lador-Lederer, J.J. A legal approach to international terrorism. April 1974. p. 194-220. Israel Law Review. ; 9:2.

3834. Langemeijer, G.E. Terrorisme, uitlevering, asyl. March 1978. Socialisme en Democratie

3835. Lauterpacht, H. Revolutionary activities by private persons against foreign states. 1928. p. 105. American Journal of International Law. ; 22.

3836. Legros, P. The idea of terrorism in comparative law. - Rockville, Md. : National Criminal Justice Reference Service, Law Enforcement Assistance Administration, Department, 1979. p. 115-122.
In: M. Kravitz (ed.), International summaries. A collection of selected translations in law enforcement and criminal justice

3837. Linke, R. Internationaler Terrorismus als Rechtsproblem. 1976. p. 230-236. Oesterreichische Juristen-Zeitung. ; 31:9.

3838. Malawer, S.S. United States foreign policy and international law: the Jordanian civil war and air piracy. 1971. p. 31-40. International Problems. ; 10.

3839. Malik, S. Legal aspects of the problem of unlawful seizure of aircraft. 1969. p. 61-71. Indian Journal of International Law. ; 9.

3840. Marcuse, H. Ethics and revolution. - Englewood Cliffs, N.J. : Prentice Hall, 1971.

In: E. Kent (ed.), Revolution and the role of law

3841. Mayer-Tasch, P.C. Guerillakrieg und Voelkerrecht. - Baden-Baden : Nomos, 1972. 221 p

3842. McWhinney, E.W. * et al. Aerial piracy and international law. - Leiden : Sijthoff, 1971. 213 p
Also: Dobbs Ferry, N.Y.: Oceana Publ., 1971.

3843. McWhinney, E.W. The illegal diversion of aircraft and international law. - Leiden : Sijthoff, 1975. 123 p

3844. Mendelsohn, A.I. In-flight crime: the international and domestic picture under the Tokyo convention. 1967. p. 509-563. Virginia Law Review. ; 53.

3845. Meron, Th. Some legal aspects of Arab terrorists' claim to privileged combatancy. 1970. p. 47-85. Nordisk Tidaskrift for International Ret. ; 40:1-4.
Also: New York: Sabra, 1970.

3846. Meyrowitz, H. Status des guerrilleros dans le droit international. Oct. 1973. p. 875-923. Journal du droit international. ; 100.

3847. Moore, J.N. Terrorism and political crimes in international law. Nov. 1973. p. 87-111. American Journal of International Law. ; 67.

3848. Murphy, J.F. * (ed.) Legal aspects of international terrorism. 1984. p. 119-239. Terrorism. ; 7:2.
Theme issue.

3849. Nagel, W.H. Terrorisme. 1972. p. 135-156. Tijdschrift voor Sociale Wetenschappen. ; 17:2.

3850. Neier, A. Terror and the sense of justice. 25 March 1978. p. 326-327. Nation. ; 226.

3851. Panhuis, H.F.van Aircraft hijacking and international law. 1970. p. 1-22. Columbia Journal of Transnational Law. ; 9.

3852. Paust, J.J. Terrorism and the international law of war. 1974. p. 1-36. Military Law Review. ; 64.

3853. Peterson, E.A. Jurisdiction-construction of statute-aircraft piracy. 1964. p. 292-295. Journal of Air Law and Commerce. ; 30.

3854. Poulantzas, N.M. Hijacking or air piracy?. 1970. p. 566-574. Nederlands Juristenblad. ; 20.

3855. Poulantzas, N.M. Hijacking v. piracy: a substantial misunderstanding, not a quarrel over semantics. 1970. p. 80-90. Revue hellenique de droit international. ; 23:1-4.

3856. Poulantzas, N.M. Some problems of international law connected with urban guerrilla warfare: the kidnapping of members of diplomatic missions, consular offices and other foreign personnel. 1972. p. 137-167. Annales d'etudes internationales. ; 3.

3857. Richard, Ph. La Convention de Tokyo : Etude de la Convention de Tokyo relative aux infractions et a certaines autres actes survenant a bord des aeronefs. - Lausanne : Thonney-Dupraz, 1971. 240 p

3858. Rozakis, C.L. Terrorism and the internationally protected persons in the light of the I.L.C.'s draft articles. 1974. p. 32-72. The International and Comparative Law Quarterly. ; 23, 4th series:1.

3859. Rubin, A.P. Proceedings of the ILA International Law Association Committee on International Terrorism (August 1984). 1986. p. 379-412. Terrorism. ; 8:4.

3860. Saldana, I. Le terrorisme. 1936. p. 26-37. Revue internationale de droit penal. ; 13.

3861. Schlaeffer, C.V. American courts and modern terrorism : The politics of extradition. Winter 1981. p. 617-643. Journal of International Law and Politics. ; 13.

3862. Schnorr von Carolsfeld, L. Straftaten in Flugzeugen : Zugleich ein Beitrag zum deutschen internationalen Strafrecht. - Erlangen : Universitaetsbund, 1965. 69 p. Erlanger Forschungen. ; Reihe A, Bd. 18.

3863. Schornhorst, F.Th. The lawyer and the terrorist: another ethical dilemma. 1978. p. 679-702. Indiana Law Journal. ; 53:4.

3864. Seidl-Hohenveldern, I. Kombattantenstatus fuer Terroristen?. - Berlin : 1973. p. 81-88. Neue Zeitschrift fuer Wehrrecht. ; 15:3.

3865. Shubber, S. Aircraft hijacking under the Hague Convention 1970 - a new regime?. Oct. 1973. p. 687-726. International and Comparative Law Quarterly. ; 22.

3866. Shubber, S. Is hijacking of aircraft piracy in international law?. 1968. p. 193-204. British Yearbook of International Law. ; 43.

3867. Sofaer, A.D. Terrorism and the law. Summer 1986. p. 901-922. Foreign Affairs. ; 64.

3868. Stein, T. Die Auslieferungsausnahme bei politischen Delikten. - Berlin

* New York : Springer, 1983. 401 p

3869. Stevenson, J.R. International law and the export of terrorism. 1972. p. 716. Record of the Association of the Bar of the City of New York. ; 27.

3870. Tate, D. Law agencies braced for possible years of terror. 25 Jan. 1976. Rocky Mountain News

3871. Thompson, D.K. The evolution of the political offense exception in an age of modern political violence. Spring 1983. p. 315-341. Yale Journal of World Public Order. ; 9.

3872. Tomasevski, K. Some thoughts on constraints upon the approach of international law to international terrorism. 1980. p. 100-109. Yugoslav Review of International Law. ; 27:1.

3873. Tran, T. Terrorisme et le droit penal international contemporain. 1967. p. 11-25. Revue de droit international de sciences diplomatiques et politiques. ; 45.

3874. Vasilijeric, V.A. Essai de determination du terrorisme en tant que crime international. 1973. p. 169. Jugoslavenska Revija za Medunarodno Praro. ; 20.

3875. Villavicencio Terreros, F. Delitos contra la seguridad publica, delito de terrorismo. - 2nd. ed. - Lima : Tip Sesastor, 1983. 249 p

3876. Vucinic, M. The responsibility of states for acts of international terrorism. 1972. p. 11-12. Review of International Affairs. ; 23:536-537.

3877. Wilkinson, P. Terrorism and the rule of law. May-June 1985. p. 11-15. Harvard International Review. ; 7:6.

3878. Wilkinson, P. The laws of war and terrorism. - New York : Pergamon Press, 1982. p. 308-324.
In: D.C. Rapoport and Y. Alexander (eds.), The morality of terrorism: religious and secular justifications

3879. Wille, J. Die Verfolgung strafbarer Handlungen an Bord von Schiffen und Luftfahrzeugen. - Berlin : De Gruyter, 1974. 288 p

3880. Wurfel, S.W. Aircraft piracy : Crime or fun?. Spring 1980. p. 820-873. William and Mary Law Review. ; 78.

3881. Zivic, J. Die blockfreien Laender und das Problem des internationalen Terrorismus. 1973. p. 7-9. Internationale Politik. ; 24:547.

3882. _____ Airport security searches and the fourth amendment. 1971. p. 1039-1058. Columbia Law Review. ; 71.

3883. _____ Bestraffing gewapende overvallen en gijzelingen verzwaard. May 1975. p. 177. Tijdschrift voor de Politie. ; 37:5.

3884. _____ Changing rules for changing forms of warfare. Spring 1978. Law and Contemporary Problems. ; 42.
Whole issue.

3885. _____ International humanitarian and human rights law in non- international armed conflicts. Fall 1983. American National Red Cross - Washington College of Law Conference. American University Law Review. ; 33.
Whole issue.

3886. _____ Report of the ad hoc committee on international terrorism. 1970.
United Nations. ; A/9028.

3887. _____ The Abu Daoud affair. 1977. p. 539-582. Journal of International Law and Economics. ; 2:3.
Background information and documentation for analysis.

P. MASS COMMUNICATION ASPECTS OF TERRORISM

3888. Adams, W.C. Television coverage of international affairs. - Norwood, N.J. : Ablex, 1982.

3889. Adams, W.C. Television coverage of the Middle East. - Norwood, N.J. : Ablex, 1981.

3890. Adams, W.C. The Beirut hostages : ABC and CBS seize an opportunity. Aug.-Sept. 1985. p. 45-48. Public Opinion. ; 8.

3891. Alexander, Y. Communications aspects of international terrorism. - Tel Aviv : 1977. p. 55-60. International Problems. ; 16:1-2.

3892. Alexander, Y. Terrorism and the media : Some observations. 1980. p. 179-180. Terrorism. ; 3.

3893. Alexander, Y. Terrorism and the media in the Middle East. - New York : The John Jay Press, 1977.
In: Y. Alexander and S.M. Finger (eds.), Terrorism: interdisciplinary perspectives

3894. Alexander, Y. Terrorism and the media: some considerations. - Boulder, Colo. : Westview, 1979. p. 159-174. In: Y. Alexander, D. Carlton, and P. Wilkinson (eds.), Terrorism: theory and practice

3895. Alexander, Y. Terrorism, the media and the police. June 1978. Police Studies

3896. Alexander, Y. Terrorism, the media and the police. 1978. p. 101-113. Journal of International Affairs. ; 32.

3897. Alexander, Y. The role of communications in the Middle East conflict: ideological and religious aspects. - New York : Praeger, 1973.

3898. Altheide, D.L. Format and symbols in tv coverage of terrorism in the United States and Great Britain. 1986. ; Unpubl. paper

3899. Anable, D. Terrorism : Violence as theater. Jan. 1976. p. 1, 6. The Inter-Dependent. ; 3.

3900. Andel, W.M.van Media en gijzeling. 2 Aug. 1975. p. 384-386. Algemeen Politieblad. ; 124:16.

3901. Andison, F.S. TV violence and viewer aggression : A cumulation of study results 1965-1976. Fall 1977. p. 314-331. Public Opinion Quarterly. ; 41:3.

3902. Andrews, W. Pentagon says persistent media endanger hostages lives. 19 June 1985. p. 8. Washington Times

3903. Arieff, I. TV terrorists : The news media under siege. May 1977. p. 44-46. Videography

3904. Arlen, M.J. Reflections on terrorism and the media. June 1977. p. 12-21. More. ; 7.
Four articles on broadcasting coverage of ongoing crimes involving hostages.

3905. Asi, M.O. Arabs, Israelis and U.S. television networks : A content analysis of how ABC, CBS, and NBC reported the news between 1970-1979. Ohio University, 1981. ; Ph.D. dissertation

3906. Bailey, N.T. The mathematical theory of epidemics. - New York : Hafner, 1957.

3907. Ball, S. Methodological problems in assessing the impact of television programs. 1976. p. 8-17. Journal of Social Issues. ; 32.

3908. Bandura, A. * Ross, D. * Ross, S.A. Transmission of aggression through imitation of aggressive models. 1961. Journal of Abnormal and Social Psychology. ; 63.

3909. Barnes, J. Back to Beirut : Media pull out all the stops. 8 July 1985. p. 26. U.S. News and World Report

3910. Barnett, M. Rich news, poor news. - New York : Th.Y. Crowell, 1978. 244 p
pp. 98-113 are on terrorism and the media.

3911. Barton, R.L. * Gregg, R.B. Middle East conflict as a tv news scenario : A formal analysis. Spring 1982. p. 172-186. Journal of Communication. ; 32.

3912. Bassiouni, M.C. Media coverage of terrorism : The law and the public. Spring 1982. p. 128-143. Journal of Communication. ; 32.

3913. Bassiouni, M.C. Problems in media coverage of nonstate-sponsored terror-violence incidents. - Wilmington, Del. : Scholarly Resources, 1983. p. 177-200. In: L.A. Freedman and Y. Alexander (eds.), Perspectives on terrorism

3914. Bassiouni, M.C. Terrorism, law enforcement and the mass media : Perspectives, problems, proposals. 1981. p. 1-51. The Journal of Criminal Law and Criminology. ; 72:1.

3915. Bazalgette, C. * Paterson, R. Real entertainment : The Iranian embassy siege. 1980. p. 55-67. Screen Education. ; 37.
On British media and the siege in the Iranian embassy in London, 31 April 1980.

3916. Bechelloni, G. Il colpo di stato indiretta. Jan. 1978. Problemi dell' informazione
On Italian media and Moro kidnapping; reprinted in A. Silj (ed.), Brigate Rosse. Firenze: 1978, pp. 217-228.

3917. Bechelloni, G. Terrorismo, giovani, mass media : I limiti del modello liberale. 1977. p. 303-309. Problemi dell' informazione. ; 3.
On Italian media, terrorism and youthful dissidents.

3918. Bell, J.B. Terrorist scripts and live-action spectaculars. May 1978. p. 47-50. Columbia Journalism Review

3919. Bennett, J.R. Page one sensationalism and the Libyan 'hit team'. Spring 1983. p. 34-38. Newspaper Research Journal. ; 4.

3920. Berkowitz, L. * MacAubry, J. The contagion of criminal violence. 1971. p. 238-260. Sociometry. ; 34.

3921. Berkowitz, L. The contagion of violence : An S-R mediational analysis of some effects of observed aggression. - Lincoln : University of Nebraska, 1970. p. 95-135.
In: W.J. Arnold and M.M. Page (eds.), Nebraska symposium on motivation, 1970

3922. Blumler, J.G. Ulster on the small screen. 23 Dec. 1971. New Society

3923. Bolling, L.R. * (ed.) Reporters under fire : U.S. media coverage of conflicts in Lebanon and Central America. - Boulder, Colo. : Westview Press, 1985.

3924. Boyanowsky, E.O. * Newtson, D. * Walster, E. Film preferences following a murder. 1974. p. 32-43. Communications Research. ; 1.

3925. Bramstedt, E.K. Goebbels and national socialist propaganda 1925-1945. - East Lansing : Michigan State University Press, 1965.

3926. Brodhead, F. * Herman, E.S. The press, the K.G.B. and the Pope. 2 July 1983. p. 14-17. Nation. ; 237.

3927. Brousse, P. * Kropotkin, P.A. La propaganda par le fait. 5 August 1877. Bulletin de la Federation jurasienne

3928. Browne, D.R. The voices of Palestine : A broadcasting house divided. Spring 1975. p. 133-150. Middle East Journal. ; 29.

3929. Brunnen, A. Die Rolle des Mediums Fernsehen in Krisenzeiten : Zusammenfassung aktueller Ueberlegungen und Beschluesse. March 1975. p. 110-112. Fernseh-Informationen. ; 6.
On Lorenz kidnapping.

3930. Brustein, R. Revolution and social change: revolution as theatre. 1970. p. 3-9. Current. ; 118.

3931. Brustein, R. Revolution as theatre : Notes in the new radical style. - New York : Liveright, 1971.

3932. Cantor, M. Prime-time television : Content and control. - Beverly Hills, Calif. : Sage, 1980.

3933. Cantor, N. The age of protest. - London : Allen and Unwin, 1970.

3934. Carter, D. * Adler, R. * (eds.) Television as a social force : New approaches to TV criticism. - New York : Praeger, 1975.

3935. Catton jr., W.R. Militants and the media: partners in terrorism?. 1978. p. 703-715. Indiana Law Journal. ; 53:4.

3936. Chaffee, S.H. * Ward, L.S. * Tipton, L. Mass communication and political socialization. 1970. p. 647-659. Journalism Quarterly. ; 47.

3937. Chaffee, S.H. Television and adolescent aggressiveness. - Washington, D.C. : GPO, 1971.
In: G.A. Comstock and E.A. Rubinstein (eds.), Television and social behavior (Vol. 3)

3938. Chibnall, S. Law-and-order news : An analysis of crime reporting in the British press. - London : Tavistock Publ., 1977. 288 p
Also deals with news treatment of "Angry Brigade"

3939. Christian, S. Covering the sandinistas. March 1982. p. 32-38. Washington Journalism Review

3940. Clark, D.G. * Hutchinson, E.R. * (eds.) Mass media and the law, freedom and restraint. - New York : Wiley-Interscience, 1970.

3941. Clutterbuck, R.L. The media and political violence. - 2nd ed. - London : MacMillan, 1981. 191 p

3942. Cohen, S. * Young, J. * (eds.) The manufacture of news : Social problems, deviance and the mass media. - London : Constable, 1973.

3943. Collins, R. Terrorism and the mass media. Jan. 1982. p. 48-50. Intermedia. ; 10.

3944. Combs, J. * et al. * (eds.) Drama in life : The uses of communication in society. - New York : Hastings House, 1976.

3945. Combs, J.E. Dimensions of political dream. - Santa Monica, Calif. : Goodyear, 1984.

3946. Commer, K. Nicht mehr heiter, aber: weiter : Versuch einer subjektiven Bilanz nach der Fernseh-Olympiade. 14 Sept. 1972. p. 13-17. Funk-Korrespondenz. ; 37.
On Munich Olympic Games 1972 and Palestinian attack on Israeli athletes.

3947. Consoli, J. Covering terrorism. 2 Nov. 1985. p. 11. Editor and Publisher

3948. Cooke, G.E. News media perception and projection of the Castro rebellion; 1957-1958 : Some image theme affects in the foreign policy system. University of Maryland, 1969. ; Ph.D. dissertation

3949. Cooper, H.H.A. Terrorism and the media. - New York : John Jay Press, 1977. p. 141-156.
In: Y. Alexander and S.M. Finger (eds.), Terrorism: interdisciplinary perspectives

3950. Cooper, H.H.A. Terrorism and the media. Sept. 1976. Chitty's Law Journal. ; 24:7.

3951. Corsi, J.R. Terrorism as a desperate game : Fear, bargaining, and communication in the terrorist event. March 1981. p. 47-85. Journal of Conflict Resolution. ; 25.

3952. Cox, R. The media as a weapon. 1981. p. 297-300. Political Communication and Persuasion. ; 1.

3953. Cox, R. The sound of one hand clapping : A preliminary study of the Argentine press in a time of terror. - Washington, D.C. : Woodrow Wilson International Center for Scholars, 1980. Working paper no. 83 of the Latin American Program.

3954. Crozier, B. Television and conflict. - London : ISC, 1978.

3955. Crozier, B. Terrorism and the media. - London : IPI, 1980.

3956. Crozier, B. Terrorism and the media. - Washington, D.C. : American Legal Foundation, 1985.

3957. Czerniejevski, H.J. Guidelines for the coverage of terrorism. 1977. p. 21-23. Quill

3958. Davidson, W.P. Mass communication and conflict resolution. - New York : Praeger, 1974.

3959. Davis, H. * Walton, P. Death of a premier : Consensus and closure in international news. - New York : St. Martin's Press, 1983. p. 8-50. Language, Image, Media

3960. DeBoer, C. The polls : Terrorism and hijacking. Fall 1979. p. 410-418. Public Opinion Quarterly. ; 43.

3961. Debord, G. La societe du spectacle. - Paris : Ed. Champ Libre, 1971. Orig. 1967.

3962. Dijk, T.A.van Discourse analysis : Its development and applications to the structure of news. Spring 1983. p. 20-44. Journal of Communication. ; 33.

3963. Dimbleby, J. The BBC and Northern Ireland. Dec. 1971. New Statesman Article unsigned.

3964. Doyle, E.J. Propaganda by deed : The media's response to terrorism. June 1979. p. 40-41. Police Chief

3965. Drummond, W.J. * Zycher, A. Arafat's press agents. March 1976. p. 24, 26, 27, 30. Harper's Magazine On role of international press in Palestinian terrorist campaign.

3966. Duve, F. * Boell, H. * Staeck, K. * (eds.) Briefe zur Verteidigung der Republik. - Reinbek : Rowohlt Verlag, 1977.

3967. Ellinghaus, G. * Rager, G. Arbeitsmaterialien zu einer vergleichenden Untersuchung der Presseberichter-Stattung ueber die Entfuehrung des Berliner CDU- Vorsitzenden Peter Lorenz. May 1975. p. 1-10; 1-18. Funk Report. ; 11:7-8.

3968. Elliot, P. * Murdock, G. * Schlesinger, P. Terrorism and the state : A case study of the discourses of television. April 1983. p. 155-177. Media, Culture and Society. ; 5.

3969. Elliot, P. * Murdock, G. * Schlesinger, P. The state and 'terrorism' on British television. 73 p ; Paper presented at an international seminar on the representation of terrorism in television programmes, Florence, Festival dei Popoli, 6-7 December

3970. Epstein, E.C. The uses of terrorism: a study in media bias. 1977. p. 67-78. Stanford Journal of International Studies. ; 12.

3971. Ertl, E. Geiseldramen : Ueber den Unterhaltungswert der Gewalt. - Frankfurt a.M. : 1975. p. 4-6. Medium. ; 5:6.

3972. Faber-de Heer, T. * Leeuwen, W.van Voorlichting bij gijzelingen zo eerlijk en zo snel mogelijk. 1 Dec. 1976. p. 10-11. De Journalist. ; 27:23.

3973. Fabreguettes, P. De la complicite intellectuelle et des delits d'opinion; de la provocation et de l'apologie criminelles, de la propaganda anarchiste. - Paris : 1894.

3974. Feighan, E.F. After the hostage crisis : TV focuses on itself. 19 Aug. 1985. 19 p. New York Times

3975. Flanders, J.P. A review of research on imitative behavior. 1968. p. 316-337. Psychological Bulletin. ; 69.

3976. Fleming, M. Propaganda by the deed : Terrorism and anarchist theory in late nineteenth-century Europe. p. 1-23. Terrorism. ; 4:1-4.

3977. Francis, R. Broadcasting to a community in conflict - the experience in Northern Ireland. - London : BBC, 1977. 16 p A lecture given by the BBC controller, Northern Ireland.

3978. Francis, R. The BBC in Northern Ireland. 3 March 1977. Listener

3979. Friedlander, R.A. Terrorism and the media : A contemporary assessment. - Gaithersburg, Md. : IACP, 1981. 22 p

3980. Friendly, F.W. International terrorism and journalism : Remarks to the Association of Schools of Journalism and Mass Communication. - Memphis, Tenn. : 4 Aug. 1985.

3981. Frye, R.E. The diary of 'tango delta' : An insider's account of ABC's 'secret nations'. May 1981. p. 30-36.

Washington Journalism Review

3982. Gallasch, P.F. Informatoren oder Komplizen in den Funkhaeusern? : Terrorismus und elektronische Medien - Modellfall Geiselnahme Beilen. 14 Jan. 1976. p. 1-4. Funk-Korrespondenz. ; 3. On Dec. 1975 South Moluccan train incident.

3983. Gallines, P. * (ed.) Terrorism and the media : An international seminar held in Florence, Italy 1978. - London : The International Press Institute, 1980.

3984. Gamson, W.A. The strategy of social protest. - Homewood, Ill. : Dorsey, 1975. 217 p

3985. Ghareeb, E. * (ed.) Split vision : Tbe portrayal of Arabs in the American media. - Washington, D.C. : American-Arab Affairs Council, 1983.

3986. Gill, G.N. Press viewpoints in civil disorders and riots. April 1969. Police Chief. ; 36.

3987. Gladis, S.D. The hostage/terrorist situation and the media. Sept. 1979. p. 11-15. FBI Law Enforcement Bulletin. ; 48:9.

3988. Gonzales, L. The targeting of America : A special report on terrorism. May 1983. p. 88-92. Playboy

3989. Goranson, R.E. A review of recent literature on psychological effects of media portrayals of violence. - Washington, D.C. : GPO, 1969.
In: R.K. Baker and S.J. Ball (eds.), Violence and the media: A staff report to the National Commission on the Causes and Prevention of Violence

3990. Gordon, T.F. * Verna, M.E. Effects and processes of mass communication : A comprehensive bibliography, 1950-1975. - Beverly Hills, Calif. : Sage Publications, 1978.

3991. Graham, K. Terrorism and the media : Speech to the English-speaking Union of the Commonwealth. - London : 6 Dec. 1985.

3992. Grave, J. Quarante ans de propaganda anarchiste. - Paris : 1973.

3993. Greenberg, B.S. * Parker, E.B. * (eds.) The Kennedy assassination and the American public : Social communication in crisis. - Stanford, Calif. : 1965. 392 p

3994. Greenberg, B.S. Diffusion of news of the Kennedy assassination. 1964. p. 225-232. Public Opinion Quarterly. ; 28.

3995. Greer, H. Terrorism and the media : Myths, illusions, abstractions. Aug. 1982. p. 67-74. Encounter. ; 59.

3996. Gruen, G.E. Public opinion and terrorism. - New York City : June 1976. ; Paper presented to the Conference on international terrorism, sponsored by the Ralph Bunche Institute

3997. Gunther Moor, L.H.G. Gijzelingen in de media. 1976. p. 182-183. Delikt en Delinkwent. ; 3.

3998. Guttman, D. Killers and consumers : The terrorist and his audience. Autumn 1979. p. 517-526. Social Research. ; 46.

3999. Hall, P.C. Nachrichtensperre als publizistische Mitschuld. 1977. p. 2. Medium. ; 7:14.
BRD government, press and Schleyer kidnapping.

4000. Halloran, J.D. Mass communication : Symptom or cause of violence?. 1978. p. 816-833. International Social Science Journal. ; 30:4.

4001. Harms, L.S. * Richstad, J. Evolving perspectives in the right to communicate. - Honolulu : East-West Center, 1977.

4002. Hartland, P. Terror and the press : Politics and greed when lives are at stake, where is the difference?. Nov. 1977. p. 5-7. IPI Report. ; 26:10.

4003. Hartnagel, T.F. * Teevan, J.L. * McIntyre, J.J. Television violence and violent behavior. 1975. p. 341-351. Social Forces. ; 54.

4004. Havandjian, N.R. National differences in the press coverage of the Lebanese civil war. University of Texas, 1979. ; Ph.D. dissertation

4005. Havighurst, C.C. * (ed.) International of propaganda. - Dobbs Ferry, N.Y. : Oceana, 1967.

4006. Haye, Y.de la Petit traite des media en usages terroristes. - Grenoble : 1978. p. 117-125.
In: G. Lipovetsky (comp.), Territoires de la terreur. Silex. ; 10.
Analyzes news treatment of the Moro case based in 'Le Monde'.

4007. Herman, E.S. The use and abuse of terrorism : A comment. - Canada : Carleton University, Fall 1985. 15 p ; Symposium in media and terrorism

4008. Herman, V. * Laan-Bouma, R.van der Martyrs, murderers or something else? : Terrorism in the Netherlands, the United Kingdom and the Federal Republic of Germany. - Unpubl. manuscript. - Rotterdam : Erasmus University, 1979.
A comparative analysis of public opinion towards terrorist groups.

4009. Heron, P. Television's role in reporting Ulster violence. - Belfast :

1974. Harrangue: a political and social review. ; 2.

4010. Heumann, J. U.S. network television : Melodrama and the Iranian crisis. Summer-Fall 1980. p. 51-55. Middle East Review. ; 12.

4011. Hickey, N. Terrorism and television, Part I. 31 July 1976. p. 2-6. TV-guide

4012. Hickey, N. Terrorism and television, Part II. 7 Aug. 1976. p. 10-13. TV-guide

4013. Hickey, N. The battle for Northern Ireland : How TV tips the balance. 26 Sept. 1981. p. 8-9, 11-13, 16, 18-19, 22,. TV Guide. ; 29.

4014. Hill, F.B. Media diplomacy : Crisis management with an eye on the tv screen. May 1981. p. 23-27. Washington Journalism Review

4015. Hoar, W.P. The human cost of betrayal. p. 5-6, 9-10, 77, 79, 81, 83,. American Opinion. ; 20.
The terror in Indochina and the silence of the news media in the West.

4016. Hoffer, T.W. Broadcasting in an insurgency environment : USIA in Vietnam, 1965-1970. University of Wisconsin, 1972. ; Ph.D. dissertation

4017. Hofmann, G. Bemerkungen eines Bonner Journalisten zur Nachrichtenlenkung. 1977. p. 3-5. Medium. ; 7:11.
BRD government, press, and Schleyer kidnapping.

4018. Hooper, A. The military and the media. - Brookfield, Vt. : Gower, 1982.

4019. Huebner, H.W. WDR-Fernsehdirektor Huebner zur "Nachrichtensperre". 1977. p. 7-14. Hoerfunk, Fernsehen, Film. ; 27:10.
On press, government, and Schleyer kidnapping.

4020. Isaac, D. Entebbe televised. June 1977. p. 69-73. Midstream. ; 23:6.

4021. Jaehnig, W.B. Journalists and terrorism: captives of the libertarian tradition. 1978. p. 717-744. Indiana Law Journal. ; 53:4.

4022. Jannuzi, L. * et al. * (eds.) La pelle del d'urso : A chi serviva, chi se l'e venduta como e stata salvata. - Rome : Radio Radicale.,
On Italian media on Urso abduction.

4023. Jenkins, B.M. Talking to terrorists. - Santa Monica, Calif. : RAND, 1982. 15 p. RAND Paper Series. ; P-6750.

4024. Jenkins, B.M. The psychological implications of media-covered terrorism. - Santa Monica, Calif. : RAND, June 1981. 9 p. RAND Paper Series. ; P-6627.

4025. Johnpoll, B.K. Terrorism and the media in the U.S. - New York : The John Jay Press, 1977.
In: Y.Alexander and S.M. Finger (eds.), Terrorism: interdisciplinary perspectives

4026. Jones, J.B. * Miller, A.H. The media and terrorist activity : Resolving the first amendment dilemma. 1979. p. 70-81. Ohio Northern University Law Review. ; 6:1.

4027. Kaplan, R.M. Television violence and viewer aggression : A reeaxamination of the evidence. 1976. p. 35-70. Journal of Social Issues. ; 32:4.

4028. Karber, Ph.A. Newspaper coverage of domestic bombings: reporting patterns of American violence. - Gaithersburg, Md. : IACP, March 1973. Bomb Incident Bulletin

4029. Kelly, M.J. * Mitchell, Th.H. Transnational terrorism and the Western elite press. 1981. p. 269-296. Political Communication and Persuasion. ; 1:3.

4030. Kepplinger, H.M. * Aachenberg, M. * Fruehauf, H. Struktur und Funktion eines publizistischen Konfliktes : Die Auseinandersetzung von Heinrich Boells Artikel "Will Ulrike Gnade oder freies Geleit?". 1977. p. 14-34. Publizistik. ; 22:1.

4031. Kirkpatrick, J.J. * Kolakowski, L. Lost in terrorist theater. Oct. 1984. p. 43-47, 50-54, 56, 58. Harper's Magazine. ; 269.

4032. Knight, G. * Dean, T. Myth and the structure of news. Spring 1982. p. 144-162. Journal of Communication. ; 32.

4033. Kopkind, A. Publish and perish. April 1978. p. 12-21. More. ; 8.
Discusses the increase in incbdents of violence against journalists by the police and political extremists. Includes a list, by country, of journalists, publishers and news organizations which have been targets of "extra-legal" political violence since Jan. 1, 1977 (pp. 16-21).

4034. Kracauer, S. Hollywood's terror films: do they reflect an American state of mind?. 1946. p. 132-136. Commentary. ; 2.

4035. Krattenmaker, T.G. * Powe, L.A. Television violence : First amendment principles and social science theory. 1978. p. 1123-1134. Virginia Law Review. ; 64.

4036. Kucuk, E. Political terrorism as a means of psychological warfare and propaganda. August 1981. p. 76-88. Socialist Thought and Practice. ; 21.

4037. Lang, E. * Lang, K. Some political questions on collective violence and the news media. 1972. p. 93-111. The Journal of Social Issues. ; 28:1.

4038. Lapham, L.H. Assassin or celebrity. 22 Nov. 1975. p. 16-18. Harper's Magazine. ; 251.

4039. Laqueur, W. Terrorism makes a tremendous noise. Jan. 1978. p. 57-67. Across the Board. ; 15.

4040. Lasswell, H.D. World revolutionary propaganda. - Westport, Conn. : Greenwood Press, 1973. 200 p

4041. Latham, A. The bravest journalist in the world. 9 May 1978. p. 48-49, 51-54. Esquire. ; 89.
Freedom of expression can cost Italian journalists their lives. Arrigo Levi, the editor of La Stampa, braves the bullets.

4042. Lavoinne, Y. Presse et cohesion sociale : Le cas des prises d'otages!. 1979. p. 35-41. Revue francaise de communication

4043. Lawrence, J.S. * Timberg, B. News and mythic selectivity : Mayaguez, Entebbe, Mogadishu. Winter 1979. 82 p. Journal of American Culture. ; 29.

4044. Ledeen, M. The Bulgarian connection and the media. June 1983. p. 45-50. Commentary. ; 75.

4045. Leibstone, M. Terrorism and the media. - Gaithersburg, Md. : IACP, Nov. 1978. ; Paper

4046. Leibstone, M. Terrorism and the media. - Los Angeles : UCLA, March 1979. ; Paper presented to the Conference on moral implications of terrorism

4047. Levere, J. Guidelines for covering terrorists debated. 3 Dec. 1977. p. 15, p. 35. Editor and Publisher

4048. Levin, J. The hostages, the U.S. government and the press : Testimony before the House Foreign Affairs Committee's Subcommittee on Europe and the Middle East. - Washington, D.C. : 30 July 1985.

4049. Levy, R. Terrorism and the mass media. Oct.-Dec. 1985. p. 34-38. Military Intelligence

4050. Lewandowski, R. * Lohr, S. Buergerliche Presse, Gewalt gegen Links : Strategie der Gegenreform. - Starnberg : Raith, 1974. 187 p

4051. Lumley, B. * Schlesinger, Ph. The press, the state and its enemies : The Italian case. Nov. 1982. p. 603-626. Sociological Review. ; 30.

4052. Madden, P. Banned, censored and delayed : A chronology of some tv programmes dealing with Northern Ireland. - London : Campaign for Free Speech in Ireland, 1978.
In: The British media and Ireland

4053. Maloney, L.D. TV on trial : Is coverage a part of crisis?. 1 July 1985. p. 36. U.S. News and World Report

4054. Manchel, F. Terrors of the screen. - Englewood Cliffs, N.J. : Prentice-Hall, 1970. 122 p
On horror movies.

4055. Mark, R. * et al. Price press pays for voluntary suppression. International Press Institute, June 1976. p. 3-4. IPI Report. ; 25:6.

4056. Mark, R. Kidnapping, terrorism and the media in Britain. - New York : Crane, Russak, 1979. p. 76-86.
In: J. Shaw, E.F. Gueritz and A.E. Younger (eds.), Ten years of terrorism. Selected views
On media handling of terroristic incidents.

4057. Martin, L.J. International terrorism : A USIA approach. 1974. ; Presented to the USIA-State Department Conference on Terrorism

4058. Martin, L.J. Mass media and terrorism. ; Presented to the D.C. Psychological Association Annual Convention, Washington, D.C., 30 Nov. 1984

4059. Martin, L.J. Mass media and the threat of terrorism to democracy. ; Presented to the Conference of Criminal Justice Institute, Atlanta University, and State University of New York Institute for Studies in Internation

4060. Martin, L.J. Mass media treatment of terrorism. 1985. p. 127-146. Terrorism. ; 8.

4061. Martin, L.J. Terrorism and media : Middle East. ; Presented to the World Media Conference, Seoul, South Korea, 6 Oct. 1982

4062. Martin, L.J. Terrorism and the mass media. - Washington, D.C. : 27 June 1982. ; Presented to the International Society of Political Psychology Conference

4063. Martin, L.J. The media's role in international terrorism. 1985. p. 127-146. Terrorism. ; 8:2.

4064. Mattelart, A. * Mattelart, M. Information et etat d'exception. - Paris : Alain Moreau, 1979.
In: De l'usage des media en temps de crise

4065. Mazur, A. Bomb threats and the mass media : Evidence for a theory of suggestion. June 1982. p. 407-411. American Sociological Review. ; 47:3.

4066. McCann, E. The British press and Northern Ireland. - London : Constable, 1973. p. 242-261.
In: S. Cohen and J. Young (eds.), The manufacture of news. Social problems, deviance and the mass media

4067. McEwen, M.T. Psychological operations against terrorism : The unused weapon. Jan. 1986. p. 59-67. Military Review. ; 66.

4068. Meeske, M.D. Network television coverage of the Iranian hostage crisis. Winter 1982. p. 641-645. Journalism Quarterly. ; 59.

4069. Meeuwisse, E.Th.F. * Ploeg, H.M.van der Eens gegijzeld blijft gegijzeld? : De invloeden van perspublicaties op de gevolgen van gijzeling. - Amsterdam : 27 July 1979. p. 1-7. Intermediair. ; 15:30.
'Once a hostage always a hostage? The influences of presspublications on the consequences of having been a hostage.'

4070. Mendelson, H. Socio-psychological perspectives on the mass media and public anxiety. 1963. p. 511-516. Journalism Quarterly. ; 40.

4071. Mentzel, V. Gijzelingen : Films in beslag genomen, pers werken belemmerd. 7 July 1977. p. 28-29. De Journalist. ; 28:13/14.

4072. Methvin, E.H. Modern terrorism and the rise of megamedia in "The global village". March 1976. ; Unpubl. paper

4073. Methvin, E.H. Objectivity and the tactics of terrorists. - New York : Hastings House Publishers, 1975. p. 199-205.
In: J.C. Merrill and R.D. Barney (eds.), Ethics and the press. Readings in mass media reality

4074. Meyer, T.P. Some effects of real newsfilm violence on the behavior of viewers. 1971. p. 275-285. Journal of Broadcasting. ; 15.

4075. Mickolus, E.F. Assessing the degrees of error in public reporting of transnational terrorism. - Washington, D.C. : CIA, Office of political research, 1976.

4076. Midgley, S. * Rice, V. * (eds.) Terrorism and the media in the 1980s. - Washington, D.C. : The Media Institute, 1980.

4077. Midlarsky, M.I. Analyzing diffusion and contagion effects : The urban disorders of the 1960s. 1978. p. 996-1008. American Political Science Review. ; 72.

4078. Miller, A. * (ed.) Terrorism, the media and the law. - Dobbs Ferry, N.Y. : Transnational, 1982.

4079. Miller, A.H. * (ed.) Terrorism : The media and the law. USA Transnational Publishers, 1982.

4080. Miller, A.H. Terrorism and the media. 1979. p. 79-89. Terrorism. ; 3.

4081. Miller, B.H. The language component of terrorism strategy : A text-based, linguistic study of contemporary German terrorism. Georgetown University, 1983. ; Ph.D. dissertation

4082. Miller, C.M. An analysis of the American networks : Evening news coverage of the 'Iran crisis: Dateline Tehran, 5 Nov. 1979-15 Jan. 1980. North-Western University, 1982. ; Ph.D. diss
ertation

4083. Monaco, J. The mythologizing of citizen Patty. - New York : Delta Book, 1978. p. 65-78.
In: J. Monaco (ed.), Celebrity. The media as image makers

4084. Monday, M. What's wrong with our aim. 1977. p. 19-20. Quill

4085. Monk, R. The use of foreign mass media as an effective nonviolent strategy by participants in internal wars. ; Unpubl. paper, Sociology World Conference, Uppsala, 1978

4086. Moodie, M. The violent theater of the terrorist. Jan. 1978. p. 17-21. Defense and Foreign Affairs Digest. ; 6.

4087. Morsy, S. Politicization through mass information media : American images of the Arabs. Winter 1984. p. 91-97. Journal of Popular Culture. ; 17.

4088. Mosse, H.L. Terrorism and mass media. 1977. p. 2294-2296. New York State Journal of Medicine. ; 77.

4089. Mosse, H.L. The media and terrorism. - Westport, Conn. : Greenwood Press, 1978. p. 282-286.
In: M.H. Livingston et al. (ed.), International terrorism in the contemporary world

4090. Murty, B.S. Propaganda and world public order : The legal regulation of the ideological instrument of coercion. - New Haven : Yale University Press, 1968.

4091. Nelson, S. Reporting Ulster in the British press. Aug. 1977. Fortnight

4092. Nichols, J.S. News media in the

Nicaraguan revolution. - New York : Praeger, 1981.
In: T.W. Walker (ed.), Nicaragua in revolution. Praeger Special Studies

4093. Nimmo, D. * Combs, J.E. Mediated political realities. - New York : Longman, 1983.

4094. Nimmo, D. * Combs, J.E. Nightly horrors : Crisis coverage in television network news. - Knoxville : University of Tennessee Press, 1985.

4095. Nussbaum, H.von Das Verhaeltnis Politiker/Journalist hat sich veraendert : Ein Interview mit Horst Schaettle (ZDF) ueber die Nachrichtensperre der letzten Wochen. 5 Nov. 1977. p. 1-4. EPD/Kirche und Rundfunk. ; 86.
BRD: Schleyer kidnapping and news management.

4096. Padelford, E.A. The regional American press : An analysis of its reporting and commentary on the Arab-Israeli situation. American University, 1979. ; Ph.D. dissertation

4097. Paletz, D.L. * Ayanian, J.Z. * Fozzard, P.A. Terrorism on tv news : The I.R.A., the FALN, and the red brigades. - Norwood, N.Y. : Ablex, 1982.
In: W.C. Adams (ed.), Television coverage of international affairs

4098. Paletz, D.L. * Ayanian, J.Z. * Fozzard, P.A. The I.R.A., the Red Brigades, and the F.A.L.N. in the New York Times. Spring 1982. p. 162-272. Journal of Communication. ; 32.

4099. Palmerton, P.R. Terrorism and the media : A rhetorical critical analysis of the crisis in Iran. University of Minnesota, 1984. ; Ph.D. dissertation

4100. Parenti, M. Inventing reality. - New York : St. Martin's Press, 1986.

4101. Parenti, M. Soviet terrorists, Bulgarian pope killers, and other big lies. - New York : St. Martin's Press, 1986. p. 148-172.
In: Inventing reality

4102. Paust, J.J. International law and control of the media: terror, repression and the alternatives. 1978. p. 621-677. Indiana Law Journal. ; 53:4.

4103. Pontello, C. * (ed.) Terrorismo e informazione. - Roma : July 1978. p. 411-508 ; Papers of IPI conference on terrorism and the media in Florence, June 16-18, 1978. Affari Esteri. ; 10:39.
Contains case studies on U.K., Italy, BRD, USA, Japan, Spain and some general papers.

4104. Preston, J. Killing off the news in Guatemala. Jan.-Feb. 1982. p. 33-35. Columbia Journalism Review. ; 20.

4105. Rada, S.E. Transnational terrorism as public relations?. Fall 1985. p. 26-33. Public Relations Review. ; 11.

4106. Raucher, S.A. An analysis of sensationalism in network news coverage of violent events. Wayne State University, 1979. ; Ph.D. dissertation

4107. Redlick, A.S. The impact of transnational interactions on terrorism : A case study of the Quebec terrorist movement. Fletcher School of Law and Diplomacy, Tufts University, 1977. ; Ph.D. dissertation

4108. Redlick, A.S. The transnational flow of information as a cause of terrorism. - Boulder, Colo. : Westview, 1979. p. 73-95.
In: Y. Alexander, D. Carlton, and P. Wilkinson (eds.), Terrorism: theory and practice

4109. Said, E.W. Covering islam : How the media and the experts determine how we see the rest of the world. - New York : Pantheon, 1981.

4110. Said, E.W. U.S. coverage of the Iran crisis : An assessment. 1980. p. 62-70. Media Asia. ; 7.

4111. Salomone, F. Terrorism and the mass media. - Springfield, Ill. : Charles C. Thomas, 1975. p. 43-47.
In: M.C. Bassiouni (ed.), International terrorism and political crimes
Author works as journalist for 'Il tempo di Roma'.

4112. Saur, K.O. Die Katerstimmung nach der Nachrichtensperre. 17 Dec. 1977. p. 2-4. EPD/Kirche und Rundfunk. ; 98.
BRD: Schleyer case and press.

4113. Schang, G. * Rosenbaum, R. Now the urban guerrillas have a real problem. They're trying to make it in the magazine business. Nov. 1976. p. 16-21. More. ; 6.
Describes the efforts of the fugitive leaders of the Weather Underground to publish their magazine 'Osawatomie'.

4114. Schlesinger, Ph. * Murdock, G. * Elliott, Ph. Televising 'terrorism' : Political violence in popular culture. - London : Comedia Publishing, 1983.

4115. Schlesinger, Ph. "Terrorism", the media and the liberal democratic state. 1981. Social Research. ; 48:1.

4116. Schlesinger, Ph. Princes' Gate 1980 : The media politics of siege management. 1980. p. 29-54. Screen Education. ; 37.

4117. Schlesinger, Ph. Putting 'reality' together: BBC news. - London : Constable, 1978. 303 p pp. 205-243: the reporting of Northern Ireland.

4118. Schlesinger, Ph. The BBC and Northern Ireland. - London : Campaign for Free Speech on Ireland, 1979. 10 p
The British media and Ireland.

4119. Schmid, A.P. * Graaf, J.F.A.de Violence as communication : Insurgent terrorism and the Western news media. - London and Beverly Hills : Sage, 1982. 283 p

4120. Schmid, A.P. Terrorisme en de jacht op publiciteit. 4 Dec. 1981. p. 1-7, 13. Intermediair. ; 17:49.
Terrorism and the search for publicity.

4121. Schneider, P. Pressefreiheit und Staatssicherheit. - Mainz : Hase & Koehler, 1968. 211 p

4122. Schultz, E. Censorship is no solution to coverage of hostage situations. July 1977. p. 6-7. RTNDA Communicator

4123. Schwartz, D.A. How fast does news travel. 1973. p. 625-627. Public Opinion Quarterly. ; 37.

4124. Sheatsley, P.B. * Feldmand, J.J. Assassination of president J.F. Kennedy : A preliminary report on public reactions and behavior. 1964. p. 289-215. Public Opinion Quarterly. ; 28.

4125. Shipman, J.M. New York Times' coverage of the war in El Salvador. Winter 1983. p. 719-722. Journalism Quarterly. ; 60.

4126. Siegal, A. Canadian newspaper coverage of the FLQ crisis : A study of the impact of the press on politics. McGill University, 1974. ; Ph.D. dissertation

4127. Sincinski, A. Dallas and Warsaw : The impact of a major national political event on public opinion abroad. 1969. p. 190-196. Public Opinion Quarterly. ; 33.

4128. Smith, C.F. Reporting grief : Marine families review the press invasion. March 1984. p. 21-22. Washington Journalism Review

4129. Smith, D. Scenario reality: a new brand of terrorism. 30 March 1974. p. 392-394. The Nation

4130. Smith, D. Wounded knee: the media coup d'etat. 25 June 1973. The Nation

4131. Snider, M. * (ed.) Media and terrorism : The psychological impact. - Newton, Kansas : Mennonite Press, 1978. 51 p ; A seminar sponsored by Growth Associates, a division of Prairie View, Inc., 3-4 March 1978
5 papers by F.M. Ochberg, D. Anable and H. Siegel.

4132. Snyder, D. * Kelly, W.R. Conflict intensity, media sensitivity and the validity of newspaper data. 1977. p. 105-123. American Sociological Review. ; 42:1.

4133. Sorrentino, R.M. * Vidman, N. * Goodslad, M.S. Opinion change in a crisis; effects of the 1970 Canadian kidnapping crisis on political and ethnic attitudes. 1974. p. 199-218. Canadian Journal of Behavioural Science. ; 6:3.

4134. Stein, M.L. Police and press clash over terrorist reporting. 4 Nov. 1978. p. 111-122. Editor and Publisher

4135. Stephen, A. A reporter's life in Ulster. 29 Febr. 1976. Observer

4136. Stephen, A. Mason wants Ulster news black outs. 23 Jan. 1977. Observer

4137. Stern, J.Ch. News media relations during a major incident. Oct. 1976. p. 256-260. The Police Journal. ; 4.

4138. Stoil, M.J. * Brownell, J.R. Research design for a study of threat communication and audience perception of domestic terrorism. - New York : 1981. Political Communication and Persuasion. ; 1:2.

4139. Stolte, D. Das Fernsehen als Medium und Faktor in Krisenzeiten. 11 Jan. 1978. p. 1-3. Funk-Korrespondenz. ; 2.
BRD: Schleyer, Mogadishu and media.

4140. Taylor, E. The strategy of terror: Europe's inner front. - Boston : Houghton Mifflin, 1940.
On Nazi German propaganda strategy.

4141. Taylor, P. Reporting Northern Ireland. Nov. 1978. p. 3-11. Index on Censorship. ; 7:6.
Author is reporter for the Thames television 'This week' programme.

4142. Terraine, J. * Bell, M. * Walsh, R. Terrorism and the media. - New York : Crane, Russak, 1979. p. 87-108. In: J. Shaw, E.F. Gueritz and A.E. Younger (eds.), Ten years of terrorism

4143. Terry, H.A. Television and terrorism: professionalism not quite the answer. 1978. p. 745-777. Indiana Law Journal. ; 53:4.

4144. Thomson, O. Mass persuasion in history : An historical analysis of the development of propaganda techniques. - Edinburgh : Paul Harris Publ., 1977.

4145. Tobin, R.L. More violent than ever : Preoccupation with bad news in the mass media. 9 Nov. 1968. p. 79-80. Saturday Review

4146. Tolz, V. Soviet press treatment of terrorism. - New York : Radio Liberty Research, 1986. 6 p

4147. Turner, R.H. The public perception of protest. Dec. 1969. p. 815-831. American Sociological Review. ; 34.

4148. Uilenbroek, H. Discussienota op komst over afspraken voor 'perspauze'. 16 Febr. 1978. p. 13. De Journalist. ; 29:4.

4149. Vat, D. van der Terrorism and the media : Publicity is one of the aims of terrorism - should the media be prevented from providing it?. April 1982. p. 25-27. Index on Censorship. ; 11.

4150. Walker, J. Psychologist proposes terrorist news guides. 17 Sept. 1977. p. 12. Editor and Publisher

4151. Watson sr, F.M. Terrorist propaganda. - Gaithersburg, Md. : IACP, 1975. 54 p

4152. Weimann, G. The theater of terror : Effects of press coverage. Winter 1985. p. 38-45. Journal of Communication. ; 33.

4153. Weisman, J. When hostages' lives are at stake : Should a TV reporter push on or pull back. 26 Aug. 1978. p. 4-6. TV-Guide

4154. Weisman, J. Why American TV is so vulnerable to foreign propaganda. 12 June 1982. p. 4-6, 10, 12, 14, 16. TV guide. ; 30.

4155. Werf, H.van der 100 uur wereldnieuws op stoep Haags NOS-gebouw. 1 Oct. 1974. p. 10-11. De Journalist. ; 25:19.

4156. Westermeyer, J. On the epidemicity of amok violence. June 1973. p. 873-876. Archives of General Psychiatry. ; 28.

4157. Wijgaerts, D. Politiek terrorisme en massamedia : Een causaal verband?. May 1983. p. 167-180. Mens en Maatschappij. ; 58:2.

4158. Wilbur, H.B. The role of the mass media during a terrorist incident. April 1985. p. 20-23. FBI Law Enforcement Bulletin. ; 54.

4159. Wilkinson, P. Relationship between freedom of press and information and publicity given by the mass media. ; Paper presented at the Council of Europe conference on the defence of democracy against terrorism in Europe, November 1980

4160. Wilkinson, P. Terrorism and the media. June 1978. p. 2-6. Journalism Studies Review. ; 3.

4161. Wilkinson, P. Terrorism, the mass media and democracy. July 1981. p. 35-44. Contemporary Review

4162. Wilson, J.V. Police and the media. - Boston : 1975. 175 p

4163. Woerdemann, F. Was wird bei noch staerkerer Belastung sein? : Aktuelle Ueberlegungen zum Thema "Terrorismus und Medien". 23 Nov. 1977. p. 1-3. Funk-Korrespondenz. ; 47.

4164. Wurth-Hough, S. Network news coverage of terrorism : The early years. 1983. p. 403-422. Terrorism. ; 6:3.

4165. Yong, T. International terrorism and public opinion policy processes. July 1971. p. 147-159. Co-Existence. ; 8.

4166. Zeman, Z.A.B. Nazi propaganda. - London : Oxford University Press, 1973.

4167. Zoest, A.J.A.van * et al. De Haagse gijzeling in de Franse en in de Nederlandse pers. - Utrecht : Frans en Occitaans Instituut, 1975. 72 p ; Mimeo On Japanese Red Army occupation of French embassy in The Hague, 14-17 Sept. 1974, as reflected in the French en Dutch press.

4168. _____ Bericht aus Bonn : Die Entfuehrung von Peter Lorenz - Anfrage zu Vorgaengen im WDR. March 1975. p. 113-114. Fernseh-Informationen. ; 6.

4169. _____ Calls for a code on terrorist coverage. 22 July 1985. p. 36. Broadcasting

4170. _____ CBS ignores silence request. 4 Aug. 1974. The Huntsville Item. ; 124:182.

4171. _____ Closer look at network coverage of TWA flight 847. 5 Aug. 1985. p. 58. Broadcasting

4172. _____ De Haagse gijzeling in de Franse en in de Nederlandse pers. 72 p.
Doktoraalwerkgroep van het Frans en Occitaans Instituut, Utrecht
A comparison of French and Dutch newspaper reporting of the embassy occupation in 1974 by the Japanese Red Army.

4173. _____ Drie radio-uitzendingen over symposium 'Media en gijzeling'. - Den Haag : 1975. 18 p.
Ministerie van Justitie, Stafbureau Voorlichting
Three radiobroadcasts on a symposium 'media and acts of hostage taking'.

4174. _____ European terrorism and the media : Report on the one-day conference organized by the International Press Institute on Nov. 9, 1978, in

London. - London : IPI, 1978. 18 p

4175. _____ Evolution in hijack coverage : NBC's Tom Brokaw says reporting on Achile Lauro incident shows networks learned from mistakes in TWA flight 847 story. 22 July 1985. 36 p. Broadcasting

4176. _____ From Azeff to Agca : Misinformation and disinformation. Autumn-Winter 1983. p. 1-89. Survey. ;

27.

4177. _____ Guatemalan cover-up. Nov. 1978. p. 52-54. Index on Censorship. ; 7:6.
On 28 May 1978 incident at Panzo's and how Reuter distributed the unbelievable government version of the incident.

4178. _____ Many stations enact guidelines on involvement with terrorists. 24 Oct. 1977. Television/Radio. ; 25:7.

4179. _____ Media accused of creating terrorists. 14 May 1983. p. 116-132. Editor and Publisher

4180. _____ Media misreport N. Ireland. - Belfast : 1978. Belfast Workers Research Unit Bulletin. ; 6.

4181. _____ Media vigil for hostages of flight 847. 24 June 1985. p. 33. Broadcasting

4182. _____ Political violence and the role of the media : Some perspectives. 1980. p. 79-99. Political Communication and Persuasion. ; 1.

4183. _____ Terror in the news : Dramatic functions of press coverage. Spring 1982. p. 128-185. Journal of Communication. ; 32.

4184. _____ Terrorism : Police and press problems. ; Proceedings of a conference sponsored by the Oklahoma Publishing Company and the University of Oklahoma, Oklahoma City, April 1977

4185. _____ Terrorism : Police and press problems. 1979. p. 1-54. Terrorism

4186. _____ Terrorism and the media : Conference report. 1985. p. 185-190. Political Communication and Persuasion. ; 3.

4187. _____ Terrorism and the media : Legal response. 1978. p. 619-777. Indian

Law Journal. ; 53.

4188. _____ Terrorism and the media : A discussion. Oct. 1984. p. 47-58. Harper's

4189. _____ Terrorism and the media. 1979. 147 p. Terrorism. ; 2:1-2.
Whole issue, containing the proceedings of two conferences on the subject held in Oklahoma, April 1976 and New York, Nov. 1977.

4190. _____ Terrorists and hostage coverage. ; Proceedings of a conference sponsored by the Radio New Directors Association, Washington, D.C., Nov. 1977

4191. _____ The British media and Ireland. - London : 1978. 50 p. Campaign for Free Speech on Ireland

4192. _____ The media : Hindrance or help to hostages?. 1 July 1985. p. 27. Broadcasting

4193. _____
The media and terrorism : A seminar. - Chicago : Field Enterprises, 1977. 38 p.
Chicago Sun-Times and Chicago Daily News

4194. _____ The media, diplomacy, and terrorism in the Middle East. - Washington, D.C. : GPO, 1985. 152 p.
U.S. Congress. House. Committee on Foreign Affairs. Subcommittee on Europe and the Middle East ; Hearing 99th Cong., 1st sess. 30 July 1985

Q. THE ETIOLOGY OF TERRORISM

4195. Abdel-Malek, A. A critical survey of sociological literature of the causes of violence. - Paris : UNESCO, 1975. ; Mimeo

4196. Adamo, H. Vorgebliche und tatsaechliche Ursachen des Terrorismus. 1977. p. 1436-1448. Blaetter fuer deutsche und internationale Politik. ; 12.

4197. Adams, H.E. The origins of insurgency. University of Lancaster, 1970. ; Ph.D. dissertation

4198. Adolph jr, R.B. Terrorism : The causal factors. July-Sept. 1982. p. 49-57. Military Intelligence. ; 8.

4199. Ahlberg, R. Ursachen der Revolte : Analyse des studentischen Protests. - Muenchen : Urban.,

4200. Alexander, Y. * Gleason, J.M. * (eds.) Behavioral and quantitative perspectives on terrorism. - New York : Pergamon Press, 1981. 396 p

4201. Aya, R. Theories of revolution reconsidered : Contrasting models of collective violence. July 1979. p. 39-99. Theory and Society. ; 8:1.

4202. Backes, U. Ursachen des Linksterrorismus in der Bundesrepublik Deutschland. 1983. p. 493-509. Neue Politischer Literatur. ; 28.

4203. Baumann, M. Bommi : Wie alles anfing. - Munich : Trikont, 1975.
On the evolution of elements of the Berlin student movement towards terrorism; by an insider.

4204. Becker, H.S. Outsiders : Studies in the sociology of deviance. - New York : Free Press of Glencoe, 1963.

4205. Belson, W.S. Television and violence and the adolescent boy. - Farnborough, Hampshire : Saxon House, 1978.

4206. Benthem van den Bergh, G.van De staat van geweld : Hedendaags terrorisme in lange-termijn-perspektief. 1978. p. 483-499. De Gids. ; 140:8.

4207. Berkowitz, L. Studies of the contagion of violence. - New York : Harper & Row, 1973. p. 41-51.
In: H. Hirsch and D.C. Perry (eds.), Violence as politics. A series of original essays

4208. Bialer, S. * Sluzar, S. * (eds.) Radicalism in the contemporary age : Vol. 1: Sources of contemporary radicalism. - Boulder, Colo : Westview Press, 1977.

4209. Blok, A. Selbsthilfe and the monopoly of violence. 1977. p. 179-189.
In: Human figurations. Essays for Norbert Elias. Amsterdams Sociologisch Tijdschrift

4210. Bowen, D. * Marotti, L.H. Civil violence : A theoretical overview. - Cleveland, Ohio : Case Western Reserve Civil Violence Research Center, 1968.

4211. Braunschweig, P. Terrorismus als Signal : Ueber Ursachen von Terrorismus. - Bremen : 1973. p. 190-200. Junge Kirche. ; 34:4.

4212. Buehl, W.L. * (ed.) Konflikt und Konfliktsoziologie. - Muenchen : 1973.

4213. Burki, S.J. Social and economic determinants of political violence: a case study of the Punjab. 1971. p. 465-480. Middle East Journal. ; 25.

4214. Burnham, J. Roots of terrorism. 16 March 1974. National Review

4215. Buss, A.H. A psychology of aggression. - New York : Wiley, 1961.

4216. Cavalli, L. La citta divisa : Sociologia del conflitto e del consenso in ambiente urbano. - Milano : Giuffre, 1978.

4217. Charray, J.P. * et al. Terrorisme et culture : Pour une anthropologie strategique. - Paris : Fondation pour les Etudes de Defense Nationale, 1981. 213 p

4218. Collins, R. Three faces of cruelty: toward a comparative sociology of violence. 1974. Theory and Society. ; 1.

4219. Corning, P.A. * Corning, C.H. Toward a general theory of violent aggression. 1972. p. 7-35. Social Science Information. ; 11:3-4.

4220. Corning, P.A. Human violence : Some causes and implications. - San Francisco : W.H. Freeman and Co., 1973. p. 119-143.
In: C.R. Beitz and T.Herman (eds.), Peace and war

4221. Couzens, M. Reflections on the study of violence. 1971. p. 583-604. Law and Society Review. ; 5.

4222. Crenshaw, M. The causes of terrorism. July 1981. p. 379-399. Comparative Politics. ; 13:4.

4223. Crick, B. * Robson, W.A. * (eds.) Protest and discontent. - Harmondsworth : Penguin, 1970. 220 p

4224. Davies, D.M. Terrorism: motives and means. Sept. 1962. p. 19-21. Foreign Service Journal

4225. Davies, J.C. When men revolt and why: a reader in political violence and revolution. - New York : Free Press, 1971. 357 p

4226. Dijk, J.J.M.van Dominantiegedrag en geweld. - Nijmegen : Dekker & Van de Vegt, 1977. 165 p
Multidisciplinary vision on etiology of violence.

4227. Eckstein, H. * (ed.) Internal war: problems and approaches. - New York : Free Press, 1964. 339 p
Contains a.o.: The theoretical study of internal war.

4228. Eckstein, H. Internal war: the problem of anticipation. - Washington, D.C. : Smithsonian Institute, 1963.
In: S. de Solar Pool et al. (eds.), Social science research and national security: a report prepared by the research group in psychology and the social sciences

4229. Eckstein, H. On the etiology of internal war. 1965. p. 133-163. History and Theory. ; 4:2.

4230. Edelman, M. Political symbols, myths and language as factors in terrorism. ; Paper presented to the Conference on terrorism in the contemporary world, Glassboro State College, April 1976

4231. Elser, A. Bombs, beards and barricades : 150 years of youth revolt. - New York : Stein and Day, 1971.

4232. Epstein, S. * Taylor, S.P. Instigation to aggression as a function of defeat and perceived aggressive intent of the opponent. 1967. p. 265-289. Journal of Personality. ; 35.

4233. Feierabend, I.K. * Feierabend, R.L. * Gurr, T.R. * (eds.) Anger, violence, and politics: theories and research. - Englewood Cliffs, N.J. : Prentice-Hall, 1972.

4234. Feierabend, I.K. * Feierabend, R.L. * Nesvold, B.A. The comparative study of revolution and violence. April 1973. p. 393-424. Comparative Politics. ; 5:3.

4235. Ferrarotti, F. Alle radici della violenza. - Milano : Rizzoli, 1979.

4236. Field, W.S. * Sweets, W.H. * (eds.) Neural bases of violence and aggression. - St. Louis : Warren H. Green Inc., 1975.

4237. Firestone, J.M. Continuites in the theory of violence. 1974. p. 117-133. Journal of Conflict Resolution. ; 18.

4238. Flacks, R. The liberated generation: an exploration of the roots of student protest. 1967. p. 52. Journal of Social Issues. ; 23.

4239. Flanigan, W.H. * Fogelman, E. Patterns of political violence in comparative historical perspective. 1970. p. 1-20. Comparative Politics. ; 3:1.

4240. Forster, R. * Greene, J.P. * (eds.) Preconditions of revolution in early modern Europe. - Baltimore : John Hopkins Press, 1970. 214 p

4241. Frank, R.S. The prediction of political violence from objective and subjective social indicators. - Edinburgh : 1976. ; Paper presented to the International Psychoanalytical Congress

4242. Friedlander, R.A. Sowing the wind: rebellion and violence in theory and practice. 1976. p. 83-93. Denver Journal of International Law. ; 6. Analyzes background and causes of terrorism and discusses ways to control it.

4243. Friedlander, R.A. The origins of international terrorism : A micro legal-historical perspective. 1976. p. 49-61. Israel Yearbook of Human Rights. ; 6.

4244. Gagel, W. Terrorismus: Versuche zu seiner Erklaerung. 1978. Gegenwartskunde. ; 27:2.

4245. Galtung, J. A structural theory of aggression. 1964. p. 95-119. Journal of Peace Research. ; 2.

4246. Galtung, J. The specific contribution of peace research to the study of the causes of violence: typologies. - Paris : UNESCO, 1975. 21 p ; Mimeo

4247. Geissler, H. * (ed.) Der Weg in die Gewalt : Geistige und gesellschaftliche Ursachen des Terrorismus und seine Folgen. - Muenchen : Olzog-Verlag, 1978. 224 p
Wissenschaftliche Fachtagung der CDU am 29 und 30 Nov. 1977 in Bonn.

4248. Goldstone, J.A. Theories of revolution; the third generation. April 1980. p. 425-453. World Politics

4249. Greig, I. Subversion: propaganda, agitation and the spread of people's war. - London : T. Stacey, 1973.

4250. Gross, F. Social causation of individual political violence. - Glassboro, N.J. : Glassboro State College, April 1976. ; Paper presented to the Conference on terrorism in the contemporary world

4251. Grossarth-Maticek, R. Anfaenge anarchistischer Gewaltbereitschaft in der Bundesrepublik Deutschland. - Bonn : Hohwacht-Verlag, 1975. 80 p

4252. Gurr, T.R. * Guttenberg, Ch.R. The conditions of civil violence: first tests of a causal model. - Princeton, N.J. : Center of International Studies, 1970.

4253. Gurr, T.R. * Lichbach, M.I. A forecasting model for political conflict within nations. - Beverly Hills : Sage, 1979. p. 153-193.
In: J.D. Singer and M.D. Wallace (eds.), To augur well: early warning indications in world politics

4254. Gurr, T.R. * Lichbach, M.I. The conflict process : A self-generative model. March 1981. p. 3-29. Journal of Conflict Resolution. ; 21.

4255. Gurr, T.R. A causal model of civil strife: a comparative analysis using new indices. 1968. p. 1104. American Political Science Review. ; 62:4.

4256. Gurr, T.R. Civil strife in the modern world: a comparative study of its extent and causes. - Princeton, N.J. : 1969.

4257. Gurr, T.R. New error-compensated

measures for comparing nations: some correlates of civil violence. - Princeton, N.J. : Center for International Studies, 1966.

4258. Gurr, T.R. Sources of rebellion in western societies: some quantitative evidence. 1970. p. 128-144. Annals of the American Academy of Political and Social Science. ; 391.

4259. Gurr, T.R. Why men rebel. - Princeton, N.J. : Princeton University Press, 1970. 421 p

4260. Hacker, F.J. Materialien zum Thema Aggression. - Vienna : Molden, 1972.

4261. Hamilton, L.C. Ecology of terrorism: a historical and statistical study. - Boulder, Colo. : University of Colorado, 1978. ; Unpubl. Ph.D. dissertation

4262. Hammes, N. Ueberfaellig: die Erforschung der Ursachen des Terrorismus. 1979. p. 291-293. Kriminalistik. ; 6.

4263. Hartup, W.W. * Wit, J.de * (eds.) Determinants and origins of aggressive behavior. - Den Haag : Mouton, 1974.

4264. Hewitt, Chr. Majorities and minorities : A comparative survey of ethnic violence. 1977. p. 150-160. The Annals. ; 433.

4265. Hibbs jr., D.A. Mass political violence: a cross-national causal analysis. - New York : Wiley, 1973.
Investigation of psychological, socio-economic, and ideological hypotheses on causation.

4266. Hirsch, H. * Perry, D.C. * (eds.) Violence as politics : A series of original essays. - New York : Harper & Row, 1973. 262 p

4267. Hudson, M.C. Conditions of political violence and instability. - Beverly Hills : Sage, 1970. Professional Paper in Comparative Politics Series. ; No. 01-005.

4268. Hudson, M.C. Political protest and power transfers in crisis periods : Regional, structural, and environmental comparisons. 1971. Comparative Political Studies. ; 4:3.

4269. Ilfield jr, F.W. Overview of the causes and prevention of violence. June 1969. p. 675-689. Archives of General Psychiatry. ; 20:6.

4270. Jahn, E. Das Theorem der "strukturellen Gewalt" als eine angebliche geistige Ursache des Terrorismus. - Bonn : June 1979. p. 23-29. DGFK-Information. ; 79:1.
Etiology of terrorism; reply to Peter Graf Kielmansegg.

4271. Jubelius, W. Frauen und terror : Erklaerungen, Diffamierungen. June 1981. p. 247-255. Kriminalistik

4272. Karstedt-Henke, S. Soziale Bewegung und Terrorismus : Alltagstheorien und sozialwissenschaftliche Ansaetze zur Erklaerung des Terrorismus. - Frankfurt : 1980. p. 169-234.
In: E. Blankenburg (ed.), Politik und innere Sicherheit

4273. Kawa, R. Strategien der Verunsicherung : Die demokratische Linke im Faden-Kreuz der "Suche nach den geistigen Ursachen des Terrorismus". Jan. 1978. p. 107. Das Argument. ; 20.

4274. Kent, I. * Nicolls, W. The psychodynamics of terrorism. 1977. p. 1-8. Mental Health and Society. ; 4:1-2.
Sees etiology not in nature of terrorist but in legitimizing circumstances.

4275. Kerr, L. Youth gangs - a comparative historical analysis of their evolution from recreation to terror. April 1976. ; Paper presented to the Conference on terrorism in the contemporary world at Glassboro State College

4276. Kerscher, I. Sozial-wissenschaftliche Kriminalitaetstheorien. - Basel : Beltzverlag, 1977.

4277. Kielmansegg, P. Politikwissenschaft und Gewaltproblematik : Ueber die Gefahren des Verlustes an Wirklichkeit. - Bonn : June 1979. p. 20-23. DGFK-Informationen. ; 79:1.

4278. Knauss, P.R. * Strickland, D.A. Political disintegration and latent terror. - New York : Dekker, 1979. p. 77-117.
In: M. Stohl (ed.), The politics of terrorism

4279. Kuhn, H. Rebellion gegen die Freiheit : Ueber das Generationsproblem und die Jugendunruhen unserer Zeit. - Stuttgart : Kohlhammer, 1968. 78 p

4280. Legum, C. The rise of terrorism. Jan. 1973. p. 3-9. Current. ; 147.

4281. Leites, N. * Wolf jr., Ch. Rebellion and authority: an analytic essay on insurgent conflicts. - Chicago : Markham, Lieuwen, Edwin, 1970.

4282. Letman, S.T. Some sociological aspects of terror-violence in a colonial setting. - Springfield, Ill. : Thomas, 1975. p. 33-42.
In: M.C. Bassiouni (ed.), International terrorism and political crimes

4283. Lupsha, P.A. Explanation of political violence: some psychological theories versus indignation. Nov. 1971. p. 88-104. Politics and Society. ; 2.

4284. Lupsha, P.A. On theories of urban violence. March 1969. Urban Affairs Quarterly. ; 4.
Incomplete information.

4285. May, R.R. Power and innocence : A search for the sources of violence. - New York : Norton, 1972. 283 p

4286. Megargee, E.I. * Hokanson, J.E. * (eds.) The dynamics of aggression : Individual, group, and international analyses. - New York : Harper and Row, 1970. 271 p

4287. Mehden, F.R.von der Comparative political violence. - Englewood Cliffs, N.J. : Prentice-Hall, 1973.

4288. Mehnert, K. Twilight of the young: the radical movements of the 1960s and their legacy. - New York : Holt, Rinehart & Winston, 1978. 480 p
Explores the subject world-wide.

4289. Methvin, E.H. The rise of radicalism : The social psychology of messianic extremism. - New Rochelle, N.Y. : Arlington House, 1973.

4290. Meyer, T.P. Effects of viewing justified and unjustified real film violence on aggressive behavior. 1972. p. 21-29. Journal of Personality and Social Psychology. ; 23:1.

4291. Midlarsky, M.I. * Crenshaw, M. * Yoshida, F. Why violence spreads: the contagion of international terrorism. June 1980. p. 262-298. International Studies Quarterly. ; 24:2.

4292. Moore jr, B. Injustice: the social bases of obedience and revolt. - New York : M.E. Sharpe, 1978. 540 p

4293. Moscati, R. Violenza politica e giovani. 1977. p. 335-362. Rassegna italiana di sociologia. ; 18:3.

4294. Moyer, K. The psychobiology of aggression. - New York : Harper & Row, 1976.

4295. Muller, E.N. A test of a partial theory of potential for political violence. 1972. p. 928-959. The American Political Science Review. ; 66:3.

4296. Murphy, J.F. Legal aspects of international terrorism. - St. Paul, Mich. : West Pub. Co., 1980. 74 p

4297. Nesvold, B.A. A scalogram analysis of political violence. - Beverly Hills : Sage, 1970.
In: J.V. Gillespie and B.A. Nesvold (eds.), Macro-quantitative analysis conflict, development and democratization

4298. Nieburg, H.L. The uses of violence. March 1963. p. 43-54. Journal of Conflict Resolution. ; 7:1.

4299. O'Sullivan, N. * (ed.) Terrorism, ideology and revolution : The origins of modern political violence. - Lexington, Mass. : Lexington Books, 1986. 256 p
Also: Boulder, Colo.: Westviev Press.

4300. Oberschall, A. Theories of social conflict. 1978. p. 291-315. Annual Review of Sociology. ; 4.

4301. Oestreicher, P. The roots of terrorism : West Germany: a special case?. Jan. 1978. p. 75. Round Table. ; 269.

4302. Parsons, T. Certain primary sources and patterns of aggression in the social structure of the Western world. 1947. p. 167-181. Psychiatry. ; 10:2.
Also published in: L. Bryson, L. Finkelstein and R.M. MacIver (eds.), Conflicts of power in modern culture. Conference on science, philosophy and religion, 7th symposium, New York 1947.

4303. Parsons, T. Some reflections on the place of force in social process. - New York : Free Press, 1964. p. 33-70.
In: H. Eckstein (ed.), Internal war. Problems and approaches

4304. Paynton, C.T. * Blackey, R. Why revolution? : Theories and analyses. - Cambridge, Mass. : Schenkman Publishing Co., 1971.

4305. Pierre, A.J. An overview of the causes of and cures for international terrorism. 1975. ; Unpubl. paper, Convention of the International Studies Association

4306. Pitcher, B.L. * Hamblin, R.L. * Miller, J.L.L. The diffusion of collective violence. Febr. 1978. p. 23-35. American Sociological Review. ; 43:1.

4307. Possony, S.T. The genesis of terrorism. Jan. 1978. p. 36-38. Defense and Foreign Affairs Digest. ; 6.

4308. Pye, L.W. The roots of insurgency and the commencement of rebellions. - New York : Free Press, 1964. p. 157-179.
In: H. Eckstein (ed.), Internal war. Problems and approaches

4309. Rittberger, V. Ueber sozialwissenschaftliche Theorien der Revolution : Kritik und Versuch eines Neuansatzes. 1971. p. 492-529. Politische Vierteljahresschrift. ; 12:4.

4310. Rock, M. Anarchismus und Terror : Urspruenge und Strategien. - Trier : Spee-Verlag, 1977. 105 p

4311. Rose, Th. How violence occurs: a theory and review of the literature. - New York : Vintage Books, 1969.

In: Th. Rose and P. Jacobs (eds.), Violence in America

4312. Sanford, N. * Comstock, C. Sanctions for evil : Sources of social destructiveness. - San Francisco : 1971. 387 p

4313. Schroers, R. Der Partisan : Ein Beitrag zur politischen Antropologie. - Koeln : Kiepenheuer und Witsch, 1961.

4314. Schuck, J.R. Paths to violence : Toward a quantitative approach. - Chicago : Nelson Hall, 1976. p. 171-193. In: A.G. Neal (ed.), Violence in animal and human societies

4315. Schwind, H.D. * (ed.) Ursachen des Terrorismus in der BRD. - Berlin : Walter de Gruyter, 1978. 174 p Roots of terrorism in the German Federal Republic.

4316. Segre, D. * Adler, J.H. The ecology of terrorism. 1973. p. 17-24. Encounter. ; 40:2.

4317. Selg, H. * Mees, U. Menschliche Aggressivitaet. - Goettingen : Hogrefe, 1974.

4318. Short jr, J.F. * Wolfgang, M.E. * (eds.) Collective violence. - Chicago : Aldine, 1972. Readings in theory and research on violence as a group phenomenon, with analysis of the forms, sources, and meanings of riot and rebellion.

4319. Southwood, K. Riot and revolt: sociological theories of political violence. 1967. p. 1-75. Peace Research Reviews. ; 1:3.

4320. Spiegel, J.T. Theories of violence : An integrated approach. 1971. p. 77-90. International Journal of Group Tensions. ; 1:1.

4321. Steinmetz, S.K. * et al. Family as craddle of violence. 10 Sept. 1973. p. 50-56. Society

4322. Stone, L. Recent academic views of revolution. - New York : Random House, 1973. In: L. Kaplan (ed.), Revolutions. A comparative study from Cromwell to Castro

4323. Stonner, D.M. The study of aggression : Conclusions and prospects for the future. - New York : Academic Press, 1976. p. 235-260. In: R.G. Geen and E. O'Neal (eds.), Perspectives on aggression

4324. Storr, A. Human destructiveness. - London : Sussex University Press, 1972.

4325. Strauss, F.J. Die geistigen Urheber des Terrorismus. - Breitbrunn : 1977. p. 22-24. Deutschland-Magazin. ; 9:5.

4326. Tanter, R. * Midlarsky, M.I. A theory of revolution. 1967. p. 264. Journal of Conflict Resolution. ; 9.

4327. Targ, H.R. Societal structure and revolutionary terrorism: a preliminary investigation. - New York : Dekker, 1979. p. 119-143. In: M. Stohl (ed.), The politics of terrorism

4328. Venturi, F. Roots of revolution. - New York : Grosset & Dunlap, 1966.

4329. Vollrath, E. Die Erzeugung des Terrorismus : Betrachtungen zu einer deutschen Diskussion. 1979. p. 83-93. Die Politische Meinung. ; 24:183.

4330. Walzer, M. The revolution of the saints: a study in the origins of radical politics. - Cambridge, Mass. : Harvard University Press, 1965.

4331. Wassmund, H. Die Revolutionsforschung, ihr Stand und ihre Aspekte. 1976. Universitas. ; 31:4.

4332. Weil, H.M. Domestic and international violence: a forecasting approach. Dec. 1974. p. 477-485. Futures. ; 6.

4333. Weizsaecker, C.F.von Der heutige Terrorismus ist ein Krisensympton des heutigen Bewusstseins. - Zuerich : 25 Febr. 1978. p. 22-23, 28. Tagesanzeiger Magazin. ; 8.

4334. Werbik, H. Theorie der Gewalt : Eine neue Grundlage fuer die Aggressionsforschung. - Muenchen : UTB, 1974. 206 p

4335. West, D.J. * Wiles, P. * Stanwood, C. Research on violence. - London : University of Cambridge, Institute of Criminology.,

4336. Wilber, Ch.G. * (ed.) Contemporary violence: a multi-disciplinary examination. - Springfield, Ill. : Thomas, 1975.

4337. Wilkinson, D.Y. * (ed.) Social structure and assassination. - New Brunswick, N.J. : Transaction Books, 1976.

4338. Wilkinson, P. Social scientific theory and civil violence. - Boulder, Colo : Westview, 1979. p. 45-72. In: Y. Alexander, D. Carlton, and P. Wilkinson (eds.), Terrorism: theory and practice

4339. Wipfelder, H.J. Philosophie und Ursachen des Terrorismus. 1978. p. 287-293. Europaeische Wehrkunde. ; 32:6.

4340. Wolfgang, M.E. Youth and violence. - Washington, D.C. : 1970.

Possible explanation for violent behavior in youth and discussion ofsociety's responses to such behavior.

4341. Zimmermann, E. Soziologie der politischen Gewalt : Darstellung und Kritik vergleichender Agregatdaten-analysen aus den USA. - Stuttgart : F. Enke, 1977.

4342. Zinam, O. Terrorism and violence in the light of a theory of discontent and frustration. - Westport, Conn. : Greenwood Press, 1978. p. 240-268. In: M. Livingston et al. (eds.), International terrorism in the contemporary world

4343. _____ Combats etudiants dans le monde. - Paris : Editions du Seuil, 1968. 310 p. Collection "combats" On the worldwide student revolt.

4344. _____ Monkey-wrench politics: why terrorists emerge. 7 Nov. 1974. p. 4-8. Senior Scholastic. ; 105.

4345. _____ Narren, Traeumer und Verzweifelte : Westdeutsche Vergangenheits-Bewaeltigung: die Suche nach den Ursachen des Terrorismus. 17 April 1978. p. 113-129. Der Spiegel. ; 16.

4346. _____ Political terrorism, an indictment of imperialism. - Moscow : Progress Publishers, 1983. 278 p

4347. _____ Terrorism, origins, direction, and support. - Washington, D.C. : GPO, 1981. 92 p.
U.S. Congress. Senate. Committee on the Judiciary. Subcommittee on Security and Terrorism

4348. _____ The origins and fundamental causes of international terrorism. - New York : 2 Nov. 1972.
United Nations, General Assembly. ; Doc. A/C.6/418.

4349. _____ Universita, cultura, terrorismo. - Milano : F. Angeli, 1984. 297 p

4350. _____ Violence in America: the latest theories and research. Jan. 1974. p. 52-53. Todays Health. ; 52.

R. IDEOLOGIES AND DOCTRINES OF VIOLENCE AND VIOLENT LIBERATION

4351. Adler, H.G. * Voss, R.von * (eds.) Von der Legitimation der Gewalt : Widerstand und Terrorismus. - Stuttgart : Verlag Bonn Aktuell, 1977. 141 p

4352. Alexander, Y. * (ed.) Terrorism: moral aspects. - Boulder, Colo : Westview, 1980.

4353. Ali, T. The new revolutionaries: a handbook of the international radical left. - New York : William Morrow, 1969.

4354. Allemann, F.R. Realitaet und Utopie der Guerillas. - Stuttgart : 1974. p. 809-824. Merkur. ; 28:9.

4355. Apter, D.E. * Joll, J. * (eds.) Anarchism today. - London : MacMillan, 1971. 237 p

4356. Apter, D.E. Notes on the underground : Left violence and the national state. 1979. p. 155-172. Daedalus. ; 108:4.

4357. Arendt, H. Ideologie und Terror. - Muenchen : R. Piper, 1953.
In: Offener Horizont: Festschrift fuer Karl Jaspers

4358. Arendt, H. On violence. - Harmondsworth : Penguin, 1970. 106 p
Major theoretical work distinguishing, defining, and classifying various forms of private and official political violence.

4359. Arendt, H. Reflections on violence. 1969. p. 1-35. Journal of International Affairs. ; 23:1.

4360. Aron, R. History and the dialectic of violence: an analysis of Sartre's "Critique de la raison dialectique". - London : Blackwell, 1975.

4361. Bakunin, M. Gesammelte Werke. - 3 vols. - Berlin : 1921.

4362. Batalov, E.J. Philosophie der Rebellion : Kritik der Ideologie des Linksradikalismus. - East-Berlin : Verlag der Wissenschaften, 1975. 290 p

4363. Bell, J.B. On revolt: strategies of national liberation. - Cambridge, Mass. : Harvard University Press, 1976. 272 p

4364. Bell, J.B. The myth of the guerrilla: revolutionary theory and malpractice. - New York : Knopf, 1971.

4365. Bello, A. L'idea armata. - Roma : L'Opinione, 1981. 122 p

4366. Benjamin, W. Zur Kritik der Gewalt und andere Aufsatze. - Frankfort a.M. : Suhrkamp, 1965.

4367. Berki, R.N. Marcuse and the crisis of the new radicalism: from politics to religion?. - Gainsville, Florida : 1972.

p. 56-92. The Journal of Politics. ; 34:1.

4368. Berkman, A. Now and after: the A.B.C. of communist anarchism. - New York : Vanguard, 1929.

4369. Berkman, A. What is anarchist communism?. - New York : 1972.

4370. Berner, W. Der Evangelist des Castroismus-Guevarismus : Regis Debray und seine Guerilla-Doktrin. Wieso "Revolution in der Revolution"?. - Koeln : Kappe, 1969. 82 p

4371. Black, C.E. * Thornton, T.P. * (eds.) Communism and revolution : The strategic uses of political violence. - Princeton, N.J. : Princeton University Press, 1964. 467 p

4372. Black, C.E. * Thornton, T.P. Estrategias de violencia politica. - Buenos Aires : Editorial Torquel, 1968.

4373. Blackey, R. * Paynton, C. Revolution and the revolutionary ideal. - Cambridge, Mass. : Schenkmann Publishing Company, 1976.

4374. Blumenthal, M.D. * Kahn, R.L. * et al. Justifying violence - attitudes of American men. - Ann Arbor : University of Michigan Press, 1972.
Analyses particularly that violence employed on behalf of social change or social control.

4375. Blumenthal, M.D. More about justifying violence: methodological studies of attitudes and behavior. - Ann Arbor : University of Michigan Press, 1975.

4376. Boire, M.C. Terrorism reconsidered as punishment : Toward an evaluation of the acceptability of terrorism as a method of societal change or maintenance. Spring 1984. p. 45-134. Stanford Journal of International Law. ; 20.

4377. Bolaffi, A. Ideologia e technica del nuovo terrorismo. March 1978. Rinascita. ; 35:12.

4378. Bonino, M. Revolutionary theology comes of age. - London : 1975.

4379. Bories, A. * Brandis, F. * (eds.) Anarchismus: Theorie, Kritik, Utopie : Texte und Kommentare. - Frankfurt a.M. : Melzer, 1970. 450 p

4380. Bowles, R. * et al. Protest, violence and social change. - Toronto : Prentice-Hall, 1972.

4381. Broekman, J.M. Humanisme en terreur. Nov. 1969. p. 556-565. Wending. ; 24:9.

4382. Brueckner, P. Ueber die Gewalt : Sechs Aufsaetze zur Rolle der Gewalt in der Entstehung und Zerstoerung sozialer Systeme. - Berlin : 1978.

4383. Brugman, J. Zondaar of gelovige : De theologische achtergrond van het islamitische terrorism. March 1982. p. 19-24. Hollands Maandblad. ; 23:412. "Sinner or believer, the theological background of islamic terrorism"

4384. Buonarotti, F. Conspiration pour l'egalite dite de Baboeuf. - 2 vols. - Brussel : 1928.
Describes social consequences of Reign of Terror and background to the conspiracy of 1796.

4385. Burton, A.M. Revolutionary violence: the theories. - London : Cooper, 1977. 147 p

4386. Calvert, P. A study of revolution. - Oxford : Clarendon Press, 1970.

4387. Carmichael, S. * Hamilton, Ch.V. Black power. - New York : Random House, 1967.

4388. Carmichael, S. Stokeley speaks. - New York : 1971.

4389. Carr, E.H. Michael Bakunin. - London : 1961.

4390. Carre, O. L'ideologie palestinienne de resistance: analyse de textes 1964-1970. - Paris : Colin, 1972.

4391. Carter, A. The political theory of anarchism. - London : 1971.

4392. Caute, D. Fanon. - London : Fontana/Collins, 1970.

4393. Cavalli, L. Socialismo e violenza. 1977. p. 134-199. Citta e regione. ; 3:4.

4394. Chierici, M. Mordwaerts : Gewalt als Credo. - Aschaffenburg : Pattlock, 1976. 272 p
Orig.: Dopo caino.

4395. Claussen, D. Fetisch Gewalt : Zum historischen Funktionswechsel des Terrors. - Offenbach/M. : 1977. p. 14-19. Links. ; 93.

4396. Cohan, A.S. Theories of revolution : An introduction. - New York : Wiley, 1976. 228 p
Orig.: London: Nelson, 1975.

4397. Cohn-Bendit, G.D. Linksradikalismus - Gewaltkur gegen die Alterskrankheit des Kommunismus. - Reinbek : Rowohlt, 1968. 277 p

4398. Confino, M. Il catechismo del revoluzionario : Bakunin et l'affaire Necaev. - Roma : Adelphi, 1976. 266 p

4399. Confino, M. Violence dans la violence: le debat Bakounine-Necaev. -

Paris : 1973.

4400. Covert, L.A.S. A fantasy-theme analysis of the rhetoric of the Symbionese Liberation Army : Implications for bargaining with terrorists. University of Denver, 1984. ; Ph.D. dissertation

4401. Cranston, M.W. Sartre and violence. July 1967. Encounter

4402. Cranston, M.W. The new left: six critical essays on Che Guevara, Jean-Paul Sartre, Herbert Marcuse, Frantz Fanon, Black Power, R.D. Laing. - New York : The Library Press, 1971. 208 p

4403. Crespigny, A.de * Cronin, J. * (ed.) Ideologies of politics. - New York : Oxford University Press, 1975.

4404. Debray, R. Ensayos sobre America Latina. - Mexico City : Editores Eva, 1969.

4405. Debray, R. La critique des armes. - Paris : Le Seuil, 1974.

4406. Debray, R. La larga marcha de America Latina. - Mexico City : Editores Siglo 21, 1974.

4407. Debray, R. Las pruebas de fuego. - Mexico City : Editores Siglo 21, 1975.

4408. Debray, R. Prison writings. - New York : Random House, 1973.

4409. Debray, R. Strategy for revolution : Essays on Latin America. - New York : Monthly Review Press, 1970.

4410. Deppe, F. * (ed.) Auguste Blanqui : Instruktionen fuer den Aufstand. Aufsetze, Reden, Aufrufe. - Wien : Europa Verlag, 1968. 189 p

4411. Derrienic, J.P. Theory and ideologies of violence. 1972. p. 361-374. Journal of Peace Research. ; 9:4.

4412. Dolgoff, S. La anarquia segun Bakunin. - Barcelona : Tusquets, 1976. 471 p

4413. Draper, H. Karl Marx's theory of revolution. - 2 vols. - New York : Monthly Review Press, 1977.

4414. Draper, Th. Castroism, theory and practice. - New York : Praeger, 1965.

4415. Elliott, J.D. Writer-theoreticians of urban guerrilla warfare : Short essays in political science. - Washington D.C. : American Political Science Association, March 1975.

4416. Engel-Janosi, F. * et al. * (eds.) Gewalt und Gewaltlosigkeit : Probleme des 20. Jahrhunderts. - Muenchen : Oldenburg, 1977. 275 p

4417. Enthoven, F.B. Studie over het anarchisme van de daad. - Amsterdam : 1901.

4418. Fanon, F. The wretched of the earth. - New York : Grove, 1968.

4419. Fanon, F. Toward the African revolution. - New York : Monthly Review Press, 1967.

4420. Fleming, M. The anarchist way to socialism : Elisee reclus and nineteenth century European anarchism. - Ottawa : Rowman and Littlefield, 1979.

4421. Freund, M. Propheten der Revolution : Biografische Essays und Skizzen. - Bremen : Schuenemann, 1970. 223 p

4422. Friedrich, C.J. * (ed.) Revolution. - New York : Atherton, 1966.

4423. Friedrich, C.J. The anarchist controversy over violence. 1972. p. 167-177. Zeitschrift fuer Politik. ; 19:3.

4424. Friedrich, C.J. The pathology of politics; violence, betrayal, corruption, secrecy and propaganda. - New York : Harper & Row, 1972.

4425. Frignano, G. Teoria della guerra di popolo. - Milano : Libri rossi, 1977.

4426. Furet, F. Le catechisme revolutionnaire. 1971. p. 255-289. Annales/Economies Societes. Civilisations. ; 26.

4427. Gendzier, I.L. Frantz Fanon: a critical study. - London : Wildwood House Ltd., 1973. 300 p

4428. Gerassi, J. * (ed.) Towards revolution. - London : Weidenfeld and Nicholson, 1971.

4429. Gerassi, J. * (ed.) Venceremos! : The speeches and writings of Che Guevara. - London : Panther, 1968. 606 p Also: New York: Simon & Schuster, 1968.

4430. Giesmar, P. Fanon. - New York : Dial, 1971. 214 p

4431. Green, G. Terrorism: is it revolutionary?. - New York : Outlook Publications, 1970.

4432. Gregor, A.J. The fascist persuasion in radical politics. - Princeton, N.J. : Princeton University Press, 1974. 472 p

4433. Grundy, K.W. * Weinstein, M.A. The ideologies of violence. - Columbus, Ohio : Charles E. Merrill, 1974. 117 p Describes types of ideologies woven into violence by groups, explores the arguments used to justify violence in each type, and illustrates the application of these justifications in concrete political processes.

4434. Guerin, D. L'anarchisme. - Paris : 1965.

4435. Guerin, D. Ni dieu, ni maitre : Anthologie de l'anarchisme. - 4 vols. - Paris : Maspero, 1976.

4436. Guevara, E. (Che). Bolivianischer Tagebuch. - Muenchen : Trikont, 1968. 205 p
El diario de Che Guevara.

4437. Guillen, A. Desafio al Pentagono. - Montevideo : Ediciones Andes, 1969.

4438. Guillen, A. Teoria de la violencia. - Buenos Aires : 1965.

4439. Gurr, T.R. The revolution - social-change nexus: some old theories and new hypotheses. 1973. p. 359-392. Comparative Politics. ; 5:3.

4440. Gussejnow, A.A. * Weiler, N, Marxistisch-leninistische Ethik. - Berlin : Dietz Verlag, 1979.

4441. Gutierrez, G. A theology of revolution. - New York : 1973.

4442. Gutierrez, G. Theologie der Befreiung. - 5th ed. - Muenchen : Christian Kaiser Verlag, 1980.

4443. Haag, E.van den Political violence and civil disobedience. - New York : Harper & Row, 1972.

4444. Hachey, T. * (ed.) Voices of revolution; rebels and rhetoric. - Hinsdale, Ill. : Dryden Press, 1973.

4445. Halliday, F. An interview with Ghassan Kannafani on the PFLP and the September attack. May 1971. p. 47-57. New Left Review. ; 67.

4446. Hansen, E. Frantz Fanon: social and political thought. - Columbus : Ohio State University Press, 1976. 232 p

4447. Harich, W. Zur Kritik der revolutionaeren Ungeduld : Eine Abrechnung mit dem alten und dem neuen Anarchismus. - Basel : Edition etcetera, 1971. 117 p

4448. Harris, J. The marxist conception of violence. 1974. p. 192-220. Philosophy and Public Affairs. ; 3:2.

4449. Harris, J. The morality of terrorism. Spring 1983. Radical Philosophy

4450. Haskins, J. Revolutionaires: agents of change. - Philadelphia : Lippincott, 1971.

4451. Hazelip, A.Ch. Twelve tents of terrorism : An assessment of theory and practice. The Florida State University School of Criminology, 1980. 323 p ; Ph.D. dissertation

4452. Heinzen, K. Die (R)Evolution. - Biel : 1849.
Also reprinted under the title "Der Mord" (Murder) - "the most important ideological statement of early terrorism" in the view of W. Laqueur.

4453. Ho Chi-Minh. On revolution : Selected writings, 1920-1966. - London : Pall Mall Press, 1967. 389 p

4454. Hobe, K. Zur ideologischen Begruendung des Terrorismus : Ein Beitrag zur Auseinandersetzung mit der Gesellschaftkritik und der Revolutionstheorie des Terrorismus. - Bonn : 1979. 48 p

4455. Hobsbawn, E.J. Revolution und Revolte : Aufsaetze zum Kommunismus, Anarchismus und Umsturz im 20. Jahrhundert. - Frankfurt a.M. : Suhrkamp, 1977. 382 p

4456. Hodges, D.C. * (ed.) Philosophy of the urban guerilla : The revolutionary writings of Abraham Guillen. - New York : William Morrow and Co., 1973. 305 p

4457. Hodges, D.C. The legacy of Che Guevara : A documentary study. - London : Thames & Hudson, 1977. 216 p

4458. Holz, H.H. Die abenteuerlichen Rebellion : Buergerliche Protestbewegungen und ihre Widersprueche. - Neuwied : Luchterhand, 1977. 292 p. Philosophische Texte. ; Bd. 5.

4459. Holz, H.H. Hat der Terrorismus eine theoretische Basis?. 1978. p. 317-329. Blaetter fuer Deutsche und Internationale Politik. ; 3.
"Terrorismus ist die Theorielosigkeit par excellence" - useful, marxist theoretical position.

4460. Honderich, T. Violence for equality : Inquiries in political philosophy (incorporating three essays on political violence). - Harmondsworth : Penguin, 1980. 222 p
The first, third and fourth essays were first published as "Political violence" by Cornell University Press.

4461. Hook, S. Myth and fact in the marxist theory of revolution and violence. 1973. p. 271-290. Journal of the History of Ideas. ; 34:2.

4462. Hook, S. The ideology of violence. April 1970. p. 26-38. Encounter. ; 24.

4463. Horowitz, I.L. * (ed.) The anarchists. - New York : Dell Publishing, 1964.

4464. Jaeggi, U. * Papcke, S. Revolution und Theorie : Vol. 1: Materialien zum buergerlichen Revolutionsverstaendnis. - Frankfurt a.M. : Athenaeum Fischer, 1974.

4465. James, D. * (ed.) The complete Bolivian diaries of Che Guevara and other captured documents. - New York : Stein and Day, 1968. 330 p

4466. Joll, J. Anarchism - a living tradition. - London : MacMillan, 1971. In: D.E. Apter and J.Joll (eds.), Anarchism today

4467. Joll, J. The anarchists. - New York : Grossett & Dunlap, 1964.

4468. Kahn, L.R. The justification of violence: social problems and social solutions. 1972. p. 155-175. The Journal of Social Issues. ; 28:1.

4469. Kaminski, H.E. Bakounine: la vie d'un revolutionnaire. - Paris : 1938.

4470. Kaplan, L. * (ed.) Revolutions : A comparative study from Cromwell to Castro. - New York : Random House, 1973.

4471. Karasek, H. Propaganda und Tat : Drei Abhandlungen ueber den militanten Anarchismus. - Frankfurt : Verlag Freie Gesellschaft.,

4472. Kraemer-Badoni, R. Anarchismus: Geschichte und Gegenwart einer Utopie. - Molden : 1978. 288 p

4473. Kravchinski, S.M. La Russia sotteranea. - New ed. - Milano : 1896. Transl. as: Underground Russia. New York, 1883.

4474. Kroker, E.J.M. * (ed.) Die Gewalt in Politik, Religion und Gesellschaft. - Stuttgart : Kohlhammer, 1976. 248 p

4475. Kropotkin, P.A. L'anarchie - sa philosophie, son ideal. - Paris : 1912.

4476. Kropotkin, P.A. Memoirs of a revolutionist. - New York : Doubleday-Anchor Books, 1962.

4477. Kropotkin, P.A. Selected writings on anarchism and revolution. - London-Cambridge, Mass. : 1973.

4478. Laqueur, W. A reflection on violence. 1972. p. 3-10. Encounter. ; 30.

4479. Laqueur, W. The origins of guerrilla doctrine. 1975. p. 341-382. Journal of Contemporary History. ; 10:3.

4480. Lehning, A. * (ed.) Selected writings of Michael Bakunin. - New York : Grove Press, 1974. 288 p

4481. Lenin, W.I. Ueber den kleinbuergerlichen Revolutionarismus. - Moskau : APN-Verlag, 1974. 199 p

4482. Lenin, W.I. Was hat der Oekonomismus mit dem Terrorismus gemein?. - Berlin : 1970. In: Ausgewaehlte Werke, Bd. 1

4483. Lenk, K. Theorien der Revolution. - Muenchen : Fink, 1976. 208 p

4484. Lindner, C. Theorie der Revolution. - Muenchen : Wilhelm Goldman, 1972.

4485. Lussu, E. Theorie des Aufstandes. - Wien : 1974.

4486. Lutz, W. * Brent, H. * (eds.) On revolution : Eldridge Cleaver discusses revolution: an interview from exile. - Cambridge, Mass. : Winthrop, 1971.

4487. Mackay, J.H. Die Anarchisten. - Berlin : 1893.

4488. Mallin, J. * (ed.) Strategy for conquest : Communist documents on guerrilla warfare. - Coral Gables : University of Miami Press, 1970. 381 p

4489. Mandel, E. Revolutionaere Strategien im 20. Jahrhundert : Politische Essays. - Wien : 1978.

4490. Marcuse, H. Counterrevolution and revolt. - Boston : Beacon Press, 1972. 138 p

4491. Marcuse, H. One-dimensional man: studies in the ideology of advanced industrial society. - Boston : Beacon Press, 1964.

4492. Marighella, C. For the liberation of Brazil. - Harmondsworth : Penguin, 1972. 191 p

4493. Marighella, C. Teoria y accion revolucionaria. - 2nd ed. - Cuernavaca, Mexico : Editorial Diogenes, 1972. 135 p

4494. Marletti, C. Immagini publiche e ideologia del terrorismo. - Milano : F. Angeli editore, 1979. p. 181-238. In: L. Bonanate (ed.), Dimensioni del terrorismo politico

4495. Marshall, C.B. Morality and national wars of liberation. - Chicago : Precedent Publishing Inc., 1975. In: S.C. Sarkesian (ed.), Revolutionary guerrilla warfare

4496. Martic, M. Insurrection: five schools of revolutionary thought. - New York : Dunellen, 1975.

4497. Marx, K. * Engels, F. Ueber Anarchismus. - Berlin : Dietz, 1977. Ca. 500 p. Institut fuer Marxismus- Leninismus beim ZK der SED (ed.)

4498. Maschke, G. Kritik des Guerillero : Zur Theorie des Volkskrieges. - Frankfurt a.M. : S. Fischer Verlag, 1973. 125 p

4499. Massari, R. Marxismo e critica del terrorismo : Un analisi storica delle posizioni critiche del marxismo teorico e militante nei confronti dei fenomen terroristi. - Roma : Newton Compton, 1979. 304 p

4500. Matz, U. Das Gewaltproblem im Neomarxismus. - Stuttgart etc. : Kohlhammer, 1976. p. 59-79.
In: E.J.M. Kroker (ed.), Die Gewalt in Politik, Religion und Gesellschaft

4501. Matz, U. Politik und Gewalt : Zur Theorie des demokratischen Verfassungsstaates und der Revolution. - Freiburg-Muenchen : Verlag Karl Alber, 1975. 314 p

4502. Matz, U. Untersuchungen ueber die Gewalt und ihre Rechtfertigung in der Politik. - Munich : 1970. ; Mimeographed Habilitation thesis

4503. Mazrui, A.A. The contemporary case for violence. - London : IISS, 1971. Adelphi Papers. ; 82.

4504. Mazumdar, S.N. In search of a revolutionary ideology and a revolutionary programme : A study in the transition from national revolutionary terrorism to communism. - New Delhi : People's Publ. House, 1979. 309 p

4505. Mazzeti, G. Utopia e terrore : Le radici ideologiche delle violenga politica. - Florence : Le Monnier, 1981. 165 p

4506. McWilliams, W.C. On violence and legitimacy. 1970. p. 623-646. Yale Law Journal. ; 79.

4507. Miller, B.H. * Russell, Ch.A. The evolution of revolutionary warfare: from Mao to Marighella and Meinhof. - Stanford : Hoover, 1979. p. 185-199.
In: R.H. Kupperman and D.M. Trent (eds.), Terrorism

4508. Miller, M.A. Kropotkin. - Chicago : 1976.

4509. Mitchell, O.C. Terror as a neomarxian revolutionary mechanism in the Nazi- SA, 1932. - Wichita, Kan. : Wichita State University, 1965. 10 p

4510. Moreno, F.J. Legitimacy and violence. 1974. p. 93-103. Sociologia Internationalis. ; 12:1-2.

4511. Moreno, J. Che Guevara on guerrilla warfare. - New York : Mss Information Corporation, 1976.
In: K. Remmer and G. Merkx (eds.), New perspectives on Latin American political conflict and social change

4512. Morozov, N. Terroristicheskaya borba. - London : 1880.
"Terrorist struggle". An important Russian theoretical contribution;repr. in: F. Gross (ed.), Violence in politics. The Hague, Mouton, 1972, pp. 101-112.

4513. Most, J. Memoiren : Erlebtes, Erforschtes und Erdachtes. - 4 vols. - London : Slienger, 1977.
Orig. New York, 1903-1907.

4514. Most, J. The beast of property. - New Haven, Conn. : International Workingsman's Association Group, 1883.

4515. Moynihan, D.P. The totalitarian terrorists. 26 July 1976. p. 38-41. New York

4516. Muehlmann, W.E. Chiliasmus und Nativismus. - Berlin : Dietrich Reimer, 1971.

4517. Narr, W.D. Gewalt und Legitimitaet. 1973. p. 7-39. Leviathan. ; 1.

4518. Nechayev, S. Catechism of the revolutionist. - London : Alcove Press, 1974. p. 221-230.
In: M. Confino (ed.), Daughter of a revolutionist

4519. Nettlau, M. Der Anarchismus von Proudhon zu Kropotkin : Seine historische Entwicklung in den Jahren 1859-1880. - Berlin : 1927.

4520. Nettlau, M. Michael Bakunin: eine Biographie. - 3 vols. - London : 1896.

4521. Neuberg, A. (pseud.). Armed insurrection. - New York : St. Martin's Press, 1970.
First published in German in 1928; on Comintern's insurrectionary theory.

4522. Neumann, F. * (ed.) Politische Theorien und Ideologien. - 2nd ed. - Baden-Baden : Signal Verlag, 1977.

4523. Nomad, M. Aspects of revolt: a study in revolutionary theories and techniques. - New York : Bookman Associated, 1959.

4524. Nomad, M. Rebels and renegades. - New York : 1932.
On anarchist terrorism.

4525. Novak, D. Anarchism and individual terrorism. May 1954. p. 176-184. Canadian Journal of Economics. ; 20.

4526. Oberlaender, E. * (ed.) Der Anarchismus. - Olten-Freiburg : Walter, 1972. 479 p. Dokumente der Weltrevolution. ; 4.

4527. Papcke, S. Progressive Gewalt : Studien zum sozialen Widerstandsrecht. Die rolle der Gewalt am Beispiel revolutionaerer und restaurativer Ideen und Bewegungen. - Frankfurt/M. : Fischer, 1973. 544 p

4528. Parkin, F. Middle class radicalism.

- Manchester : Manchester University Press, 1968.

4529. Parrilli, R.E.F. Effects of castrismo and the guevarismo on leftish thought in Latin America. 1972. p. 69. Revista de derecho puertorriqueno. ; 12.

4530. Perlin, T.M. * (ed.) Contemporary anarchism. - New Brunswick : 1978.

4531. Pirou, G. George Sorel. - Paris : 1927.

4532. Pomeroy, W.J. * (ed.) Guerrilla warfare and marxism. - New York : International Publishers, 1973. 336 p

4533. Pouyan, A.P. On the necessity of armed struggle and a refutation of the theory of survival. - New York : 1975.

4534. Radek, K. Proletarische Diktatur und Terrorismus : Anti-Kautsky. - Wien : 1920.

4535. Ramm, H. The marxism of Regis Debray : Between Lenin and Guevara. - Lawrence : Regents Press of Kansas, 1978.

4536. Rammstedt, O.H. * (ed.) Anarchismus : Grundtexte zur Theorie und Praxis der Gewalt. - Koeln : Oplander, Westdeutsche Verlag, 1969. 168 p

4537. Rapoport, D.C. * Alexander, Y. * (eds.) The morality of terrorism : Religious and secular justifications. - New York : Pergamon, 1982.

4538. Rapoport, D.C. * Alexander, Y. * (eds.) The rationalization of terrorism. - Frederick, Md. : University Publications of America, 1982. 233 p

4539. Rapoport, D.C. Fear and trembling : Terrorism in three religious traditions. Sept. 1984. p. 658-677. American Political Science Review. ; 78.

4540. Rejai, M. The comparative study of revolutionary strategy. - New York : David McKay, 1977.

4541. Rejai, M. The strategy of political revolution. - New York : Doubleday & Co., 1973.

4542. Rendtorff, T. Politische Ethik und Christentum. - Munich : Kaiser, 1978. 67 p

4543. Risaliti, R. Violenza e terrore nel marxismo. 1970. p. 249-269. Vita Sociale

4544. Robespierre, M. Textes choisies. - 3 vols. 1956.

4545. Rocker, R. Johan Most. - Berlin : 1924.

4546. Rocker, R. The London years. - London : 1956.
On Johan Most.

4547. Rojo, R. My friend Che. - New York : Dial, 1969.

4548. Rubin, J. Do it! : Scenarios of the revolution. - New York : Simon and Schuster, 1970.
Rubin, together with Abbie Hoffman "created" the yippies as a fusionbetween the hippies and the New Left.

4549. Runkle, G. * Plecher, G.K. Is violence always wrong?. May 1976; Nov. 1977. p. 367-389; 1055-1063. Journal of Politics. ; 38; 39.

4550. Said, A.A. * Collier, D.M. Revolutionism. - Boston : Allyn & Bacon, 1971.

4551. Sarkesian, S.C. * (ed.) Revolutionary guerrilla warfare. - Chicago : Precedent Publishing, 1975. 623 p
Anthology containing work by both practitioners and scholars.

4552. Sartre, J.P. Der Intellektuelle und die Revolution. - Neuwied-Berlin : Luchterhand, 1971. 155 p

4553. Saxon, K. The poor man's James Bond. - Boulder, Colo : Paladin Press., 150 p
Guide to 'action'.

4554. Schack, H. Marx, Mao, Neomarxismus : Wandlungen einer Ideologie. - Frankfurt a.M. : Verlagsgesellschaft Athenaion, 1969.

4555. Schack, H. Volksbefreiung. Sozialrevolutionaere Ideologien der Gegenwart. - Frankfurt a.M. : Akademische Verlagsgesellschaft Athenion, 1971. 239 p

4556. Schickel, J. * (ed.) Guerilleros, Partisanen : Theorie und Praxis. - Muenchen : Carl Hanser Verlag, 1970. Reihe Hanser. ; 42.

4557. Shigenobu, F. My love, my revolution. 1974.
By the leader of the Japanese Red Army.

4558. Shulman, A.K. Red Emma speaks. - New York : Random House, 1972.

4559. Silber, I. * (ed.) Voices of national liberation : The revolutionary ideology of the "third world" as expressed by intellectuals and artists at the cultural congress of Havana, January 1968. - Brooklyn, N.Y. : Central Book Comp., 1970. 326 p

4560. Sinclair, A. Guevara. - London : William Collins, 1970.

4561. Sorel, G. Reflections on violence. - New York : MacMillan, 1961.
Orig. ed.: Reflexions sur la violence.

Paris: 1908.

4562. Spitzer, A.B. The revolutionary theories of Auguste Blanqui. - New York : Columbia University Press, 1957. 208 p

4563. Springer, Ph.B. * Truzzi, M. * (eds.) Revolutionaries on revolution. - Pacific Palisades : Goodyear, 1973.

4564. Stafford, D. From anarchism to reformism : A study of the political activities of Paul Brousse, 1870- 1890. - London : 1971.

4565. Stanley, J.L. * (ed.) From Georges Sorel : Essays in socialism and philosophy. - London : Oxford University Press, 1976. 398 p

4566. Stirner, M. Der Einzige und sein Eigentum. - Berlin : 1845.

4567. Stone, L. Theories of revolution. Jan. 1966. p. 159-176. World Politics. ; 18.

4568. Tinker, J.M. * Molnar, A.R. * LeNoir, J.D. * (eds.) Strategies of revolutionary warfare. - New Delhi : S. Chand & Co., 1969.

4569. Trotsky, L. Against individual terrorism. - New York : Pathfinder Press, 1974. 23 p
4 articles.

4570. Trotsky, L. Terrorism and communism: reply to Karl Kautsky. - Ann arbor, Mich. : Ann Arbor Paperbacks, 1961.

4571. Trotsky, L. The defence of terrorism. - London : Georg Allen and Unwin, 1921.

4572. Tucker, R.C. Marxian revolutionary ideas. - New York : W.W. Norton, 1969.
Including terrorism and violence.

4573. Vasale, C. Terrorismo e ideologia in Italia : Metamorfosi della rivoluzione. - Roma : A. Armando, 1980. 102 p

4574. Vizetelly, E.A. The anarchists. - New York : 1912.

4575. Waldmann, P. Strategien politischer Gewalt. - Stuttgart : Kohlhammer Verlag, 1977. 140 p

4576. Walter, E.V. Politiche della violenza: da Montesquieu ai terroristi. 1971. p. 7-30. Communita. ; 25:113.

4577. Wassmund, H. Revolutionstheorien : Eine Einfuehrung. - Muenchen : Beck, 1979.

4578. Weiner, Ph.P. * Fisher, J. * (eds.) Violence and aggression in the history of ideas. Rutgers University Press, 1974.

4579. Wilkinson, P. Fascism has never believed in waiting for a democratic mandate. ; Paper presented at the Council of Europe conference on the defence of democracy against terrorism in Europe, November 1980

4580. Winston, H. Zur Strategie des Befreiungskampfes der Afroamerikaner : Ein kritische Untersuchung neuer Theorien des Befreiungskampfes in den USA und in Afrika. - East-Berlin : Dietz, 1975. 302 p
Translation of: Strategy for a black agenda.

4581. Wittkop, J.F. Bakunin in Selbstzeugnissen und Bilddokumenten. - Reinbek : Rowohlt, 1974. 149 p

4582. Wolff, K.D. * (ed.) Tricontinental : Eine auswahl, 1967-1970. - Frankfurt a.M. : Maerz Verlag, 1970. 316 p

4583. Wolff, R.P. * Moore, B. * Marcuse, H. Kritik der reinen Toleranz. - Frankfurt : 1966.
Includes Marcuse's essay 'Repressive tolerance'

4584. Woodcock, G. * Avakumovic, L. The anarchist prince, Peter Kropotkin. - Schocken : 1971.

4585. Woodcock, G. Anarchism : A history of libertarian ideas and movements. - Harmondsworth : Penguin, 1977.

4586. Woods, J. New theories of revolution: a commentary on the views of Frantz Fanon, Regis Debray, and Herbert Marcuse. - New York : International Publishers, 1972. 415 p

4587. Yaari, E. Al-Fath's political thinking. Nov.-Dec. 1968. p. 20-33. New Outlook. ; 11.

4588. Zahn, G.C. Terrorism for peace and justice. 23 Oct. 1970. p. 84-85. Comm
onweal

4589. Zenker, E.V. Anarchism. - London : 1895.

4590. Zoccoli, H. Die Anarchie und die Anarchisten. - Leipzig : 1909.

4591. _____ Anarcho-Nihilism. 1970. p. 2-33. Economist. ; 237-6635.

4592. _____ Handbook for volunteers of the IRA, notes on guerrilla warfare. - Reprint. - Boulder, Colo. : Paladin, 1956.
IRA, General Headquarters

4593. _____ La ideologia politica del anarquismo espanol. - Madrid : Siglo XXI, 1976. 660 p

4594. _____ Materialien zur Revolution in Reden und Aufsaetzen, Briefen von F. Castro, Che Guevara, R. Debray. - Darmstadt : Melzer, 1968. 264 p

4595. _____ Prairie Fire: the politics of revolutionary anti-imperialism. - San Francisco : Prairie Fire Distribution Committee, 1974.
Weather Underground

4596. _____ Terrorism and marxism. Nov. 1972. p. 1-6. Monthly Review. ; 24.

4597. _____ Terrorism in Cyprus: the captured documents. - London : HMSO, 1956. ; Transcribed extracts issued by authority of the Secretary of State for the Colonies

4598. _____ Textes des prisonniers de la Fraction Armee Rouge et dernieres lettres d'Ulrike Meinhof. - Paris : Maspero, 1977. 244 p

S. COUNTERMEASURES AGAINST TERRORISM

S.1. General

4599. Alexander, J. Countering tomorrow's terrorism. July 1981. p. 45-50. United States Naval Institute Proceedings. ; 107.

4600. Alexander, Y. * Browne, M.A. * Nanes, A.S. * (eds.) Control of terrorism: international documents. - New York : Crane, Russak, 1979. 240 p

4601. Ashby, T. Winning the war against terrorism. - Washington, D.C. : Heritage Foundation, 1986. 9 p

4602. Atwater, J. Time to get tough with terrorists. April 1973. p. 89-93. Reader's Digest. ; 102.

4603. Bass, G.V. * Jenkins, B.M. * Kellen, K. * Ronfeldt, D.F. * Peterson, J.E. Options for U.S. policy on terrorism. - Santa Monica, Calif. : RAND, 1981. 13 p. RAND Paper Series. ; R-2764-RC.

4604. Becker, L.G. * Browne, M.A. * Cavanaugh, S. * Kaiser, F.M. Terrorism: information as a tool for control. - Washington, D.C. : Library of Congress: Congressional Research Service, 1978. 237 p

4605. Bell, J.B. A time of terror : How democratic societies respond to revolutionary violence. - New York : Basic Books, 1978. 292 p

4606. Bell, R.G. The U.S. response to terrorism against international civil aviation. 1976. p. 1326-1343. Orbis. ; 19:4.

4607. Ben Rafael, E. * Lissak, M. Social aspects of guerrilla and anti-guerrilla warfare. - Jerusalem : The Magnes Press, 1979.

4608. Berger, E. Dealing with Libya. 1986. p. 187-204. Washington Congressional Quarterly

4609. Berkers, W. Terreurbestrijding : Symptoombestrijding. - Nijmegen : Studiecentrum voor Vredesvraagstukken, 1979. 45 p ; Master's thesis in war and peace studies

4610. Berry, N.O. Dealing with terrorism. July 1984. p. 40-42. USA Today

4611. Bienen, H. * Gilpin, R. Economic sanctions as a response to terrorism. May 1980. p. 89-98. Journal of Strategic Studies. ; 3.

4612. Billstein, H. * Binder, S. Innere Sicherheit. - Hamburg : Landeszentrale fuer politische Bildung, 1976.

4613. Bishop jr, J.W. Can democracy defend itself against terrorism?. May 1978. p. 55-62. Commentary. ; 65.
British and Northern Ireland experience.

4614. Bobrow, D.B. Preparing for unwanted events : Instances of international political terrorism. p. 397-422. Terrorism. ; 1:3-4.

4615. Bodmer, D. Terrorismus - Bekaempfung. Nov. 1977. p. 683-686. Schweizerische Monatshefte. ; 57:8.

4616. Boe, E.E. * Church, R.M. * (eds.) Punishment : Issues and experiments. - New York : Appleton-Century-Crofts, 1968.

4617. Bourne, R. Terrorist incident management and jurisdictional issues : A canadian perspective. 1978. p. 307-313. Terrorism. ; 1:3-4.

4618. Brady, B.J. * Faul, D. * Murray, R. Internment, 1971-1975. - Dungannon : St. Patrich's Academy, 1975. 15 p
Roman catholic viewpoints on internment of suspected terrorists in Northern Ireland.

4619. Breit, J.M. * Clark, D.K. * Glover, J.H. * Smith, B.J. A summary report of research requirements for sensing and averting critical insurgent actions in an urban environment. - McLean, Va. : Research Analysis Corp., 1966.

4620. Bremer III, L.P. Terrorisme en democratie : De noodzaak van een strategie. 24 April 1986. p. 137-139. Sta Vast. ; 29:4.

4621. Browne, J.T. International terrorism: the American response. - Washington, D.C. : School of International Service, the American University, Dec. 1973.

4622. Brueckner, J.A. * Schmitt, H.Th. Verfassungsschutz und innere Sicherheit. - Wupperthal : Dt. Consulting Verlag, 1977. 383 p

4623. Buchheim, H. Der linksradikale Terrorismus : Voraussetzungen zu seiner Ueberwindung. 1977. Die politische Meinung. ; 22:170.

4624. Buckelew, A.H. Terrorism and the American response : An analysis of the mechanisms used by the government of the United States in dealing with national and international terrorism. - San Rafael, Calif. : Mira Academic Press, 1984. 161 p

4625. Burnham, J. The protracted conflict. 29 March 1974. National Review. ; 26.
On countermeasures against terrorism.

4626. Burton, J. Deviance, terrorism and war : The process of solving unsolved social and political problems. - Oxford : Martin Robertson, 1979. 240 p
Contains almost nothing on terrorism.

4627. Chalfont, A.G.J. Baron Terrorism and international security. 1982. p.309-323. Terrorism. ; 5:4.

4628. Chapman, B. The police state. - London : Pall Mall, 1970.

4629. Clark, L.S. The struggle to cure hijacking. Jan. 1973. p. 47-51. International Perspectives

4630. Clutterbuck, R.L. Management of the kidnap risk. 1981. p. 125-137. Terrorism. ; 5.

4631. Clutterbuck, R.L. Terrorism: a soldier's view. - New York : Crane, Russak, 1979. p. 56-75.
In: J. Shaw, E.F. Gueritz and A.E. Younger (eds.), Ten years of terrorism: collected views

4632. Cobler, S. Law, order and politics in West Germany. - Harmondsworth : Penguin, 1978.
Deals with anti-terrorist measures.

4633. Cole, R.B. Executive security : A corporate study to effective response to abduction and terrorism. - New York : John Wiley and Sons, 1980.

4634. Conley, M.C. The strategy of communist-directed insurgency and the conduct of counter-insurgency. 1969. p. 73-93. Naval War College Review. ; 21:9.
Central to achieve insurgent goals is the need for revolutionary forces to displace existing civil authority. To counteract this effort the central thrust of counterinsurgency must be socio-political rather than military.

4635. Conquest, R. Thwarting terrorism. Oct. 1976. p. 22-24. Alternative. ; 10.

4636. Constance, G.W. Obstacles that block U.S. efforts to control international terrorism. New School for Social Research, 1981. ; Ph.D. dissertation

4637. Cooper, H.H.A. Terrorism and the intelligence function. March 1976. p. 24. Chitty's Law Journal. ; 73:3.

4638. Copeland, M. Unmentionable uses of a C.I.A. counterterrorist activity. 14 Sept. 1973. p. 990-997. National Review. ; 25.
Contains information on the CIA's computerized anti-terrorist system"Octopus".

4639. Copeland, M. Without cloak or dagger : The truth about the new espionage. - New York : Simon & Schuster, 1970.

4640. Corves, E. International cooperation in the field of international political terrorism. 1978. p. 199-210. Terrorism. ; 1:2.

4641. Crozier, B. New dimensions of security in Europe. - London : ISC, May 1975. 56 p
Notes the new security threat posed by terrorists and suggests ways of combatting it.

4642. Crozier, B. Strategy of survival. - London : Temple Smith, 1978.

4643. Daeniker, G. Antiterror-Strategie: Fakten, Folgerungen, Forderungen, neue Wege der Terroristen-Bekampfung. - Stuttgart : Verlag Huber, 1978. 325 p

4644. Dailey, J.T. Some psychological contributions to defense against hijacking. Feb. 1975. p. 161-165. American Psychology. ; 30.

4645. Daly, J.Ch. * et al. Terrorism : What should be our response?. - Washington, D.C. : American Enterprise Institute, 1982. 25 p

4646. Davis, A. The industry response to terrorism. - New York : Praeger, 1979. In: Y. Alexander and R.A. Kilmarx (eds.), Political terrorism and business: the threat and response

4647. Dean, B. Organizational response to terrorist victimization: a case study of the Hanafi hostage-takings. - Montreal : ICCC, 1977. p. 119-127. In: R.D. Crelinsten (ed.), Dimensions of victimization in the context of terroristic acts

4648. Delmas, C. Terrorisme en de open samenleving. Dec. 1982. p. 12-17. NAVO Kroniek. ; 30:5.

4649. Derrienic, J.P. The nature of terrorism and the affective response. May-June 1975. p. 7-10. International Perspectives. ; 3.

4650. Dimitrijevic, V. Aircraft hijacking : Typology and prospects for prevention. 1972. p. 55-64. International Problems

4651. Dobson, Chr. * Payne, R. Counterattack : The battle against the terrorists. - New York : Facts on file, 1982. 198 p

4652. Dobson, Chr. * Payne, R. Private enterprise takes on terrorism. Jan. 1983. p. 34-41. Across the Board. ; 20.

4653. El-Amin, A.S. Concerted actions towards combating terrorism with special emphasis on air transport. - Ottawa : Canadian Theses on Microfiche Service, 1982.

4654. Ellenberg, E.S. International terrorism vs. democracy. - Koeln : 1972.

4655. Epstein, D.G. Combating campus terrorism. Jan. 1971. p. 46-47, 49. Police Chief. ; 38:1.

4656. Evans, E.H. Calling a truce to terror : The American response to international terrorism. - Westport, Conn. : Greenwood Press, 1979. 180 p Criticizes the depolitized U.S. approach which treats the matter in purely legal and humanitarian terms.

4657. Evelegh, R. Peacekeeping in a democratic society: the lessons of Northern Ireland. - London : C. Hurst, 1978. 174 p

4658. Farrell, W.R. The U.S. government response to terrorism : In search of an effective strategy. - Boulder, Colo. : Westview Press, 1982. 200 p

4659. Farrell, W.R. The United States government response to terrorism, 1972-1980 : An organizational perspective. University of Michigan, 1981. ; Ph.D. dissertation

4660. Fisk, R. Terrorism in the United Kingdom and the resultant spread of political power to the army. ; Paper presented at Glassboro State College, New Jersey, International symposium on terrorism in the contemporary world, April 26-28, 1976

4661. Flamigni, S. * et al. Sicurezza democratica e lotta alla criminalita : Atti del convegno organizatto dal centro studi per la riforma dello stato 25-26 febr. 1975. - Roma : Editori Riuniti, 1975.

4662. Fleckenstein, B. Zwoelf Thesen zur inneren Sicherheit und zum Problem des politischen Terrorismus. 1975. Weltkunde. ; 24:5.

4663. Fogel, L.J. Predictive antiterrorism. Decision Sciences, Inc., April 1977.

4664. Franceschini, A.M. Le norme antimafia : Affidamento e conduzione delle opere della pubblica amministrazione, subappalti e cottimi, iscrizione, sospensione, decadenze albo costruttori. - Milano : Pirola, 1984. 187 p

4665. Friedland, N. National responses to terrorism. 1983. p. 21-26. Social Science News Letter. ; 68.

4666. Friedlander, R.A. * (comp.) Terrorism : Documents of international and local control. - 4 vols. - Dobbs Ferry, N.Y. : Oceana Publications, 1979-1984.

4667. Friedlander, R.A. Terror - violence : Aspects of social control. - Dobbs Ferry, N.Y. : Oceana Publications, 1983. 299 p

4668. Friedlander, R.A. Terrorism: documents of international and local control, 1977-1978. - Dobbs Ferry, N.Y. : Oceana Publications, 1978.

4669. Friestad, D.E. A descriptive analysis of terrorist targets in a crime prevention through environmental design context. The Florida State University School of Criminology, 1978. ; Unpubl. Ph.D. dissertation

4670. Fulton, A.B. Countermeasures to combat terrorism at major events : A case study. - Washington, D.C. : Department of State, 1976. 66 p

4671. Fuqua, P.Q. Terrorism : The executive's guide to survival. - Houston : Gulf Publ., 1978. 158 p 1st ed. 1971.

4672. Furet, F. * Liniers, A. * Raynaud, Ph. Terrorisme et democratie. - Paris : Fayard, 1985. 226 p

4673. Gal-Or, N. International cooperation to suppress terrorism. - New York : St. Martin's Press, 1985. 390 p

4674. Gardiner, L. Report of a committee to consider, in the context of civil liberties and human rigths, measures to deal with terrorism in Northern

Ireland. - London : HMSO, 1975. 78 p

4675. Gavzer, B. The terrorists : How the free world can fight back. 20 May 1979. p. 4-7. Parade Magazine

4676. Genova, R. Missione antiterrorismo. - Milano : SugarCo., 1985. 222 p

4677. Genscher, H.D. Beitrag zur Verbesserung der inneren Sicherheit. Ansprache am 13.11.1972. 1972. p. 1885-1886. Bulletin. Presse- und Informationsamt der Bundesregierung. ; 158.

4678. Genscher, H.D. Massnahmen zum Schutz der inneren Sicherheit : Interview mit dem Z.D.F. am 10.9.1972. 1972. p. 1533-1534. Bulletin. Presse- und Informationsamt der Bundesregierung. ; 123.

4679. Genscher, H.D. Massnahmen zur Wahrung der inneren Sicherheit : Interview mit dem Saarlaend. Rundfunk am 8.10.72. 1972. p. 1705-1706. Bulletin. Presse- und Informationsamt der Bundesregierung. ; 141.

4680. Giehring, H. Die Reaktion des Gesetzgebers auf den Terrorismus. - Munich : 1979. p. 61-83. In: Jugend und Terrorismus. Ein Hearing des Bundesjungend-Kuratoriums

4681. Gilboa, E. The use of simulation in combatting terrorism. 1981. p. 265-279. Terrorism. ; 5:3.

4682. Glejdura, S. Lucha contra el terrorismo internacional. Jan. 1978. Revista de politica internacional. ; 155.

4683. Godfrey, D. Terrorism and banking. 1982. p. 353-361. Terrorism. ; 5:4.

4684. Godfrey, D. The response of the banking community. - New York : Praeger, 1979. p. 244-264. In: Y. Alexander and R.A. Kilmarx (eds.), Political terrorism and business: the threat and response

4685. Godson, R. * (ed.) Counterintelligence. - Washington, D.C. : National Strategy Information Center, distributed by Transaction Books, 1980. 339 p

4686. Goldie, L.F.E. Combatting international terrorism : The United Nations developments. 1979. p. 49-60. Naval War College Review. ; 31:3.

4687. Graves, C.A. The U.S. government's response to terrorism. - New York : Praeger, 1979. p. 293-306. In: Y. Alexander and R.A. Kilmarx (eds.), Political terrorism and business: the threat and response

4688. Green, L.C. Terrorism and its responses. 1985. p. 33-77. Terrorism. ; 8:1.

4689. Greisman, H.C. Terrorism and the closure of society: a social impact projection. July 1979. p. 135-146. Technological Forecasting and Social Change. ; 14.

4690. Grondona, M. Reconciling internal security and human rights. 1978. p. 3-16. International Security. ; 3.

4691. Gude, E. Alternative response to violence. - Chicago : Precedent Publication Inc., 1975. In: S.C. Sarkesian (ed.), Revolutionary guerrilla warfare

4692. Haakmat, A.R. De bestrijding van terreuracties : Juridische en polemologische visies vergeleken. 25 Nov. 1977. p. 9, 11, 13. Intermediair. ; 13:47.

4693. Henry, E. Stop terrorism. - Moscow : Novosti Press Agency, Publ. House, 1982. 200 p

4694. Henze, P.B. Coping with terrorism. Summer 1985. p. 307-323. Fletcher Forum. ; 9.

4695. Herold, H. Perspektiven der internationalen Fahnung nach Terroristen. April 1980. p. 165-171. Kriminalistik. ; 4.

4696. Hewitt, Chr. The effectiveness of anti-terrorist policies. - Lanham : University Press of America, 1984. 122 p

4697. Hoffacker, L. The U.S. government response to terrorism: a global approach. - Springfield, Ill. : Thomas, 1975. p. 537-545. In: M.C. Bassiouni (ed.), International terrorism and political crimes Also: Department of State Bulletin 70, 1974, pp. 274-278.

4698. Horchem, H.J. Die innere Sicherheit der Bundesrepublik Deutschland : Bedrohung und Abwehr. 1976. Beitraege zur Konfliktforschung. ; 6:4.

4699. Horchem, H.J. Terrorism and government response : The German experience. 1980. p. 43-55. Jerusalem Journal of International Relations. ; 4.

4700. Horchem, H.J. The German government response to terrorism. - New York : Praeger, 1979. p. 428-447. In Y. Alexander and R.A. Kilmarx (eds.), Political terrorism and business: the threat and response

4701. Horowitz, I.L. Can democracy cope with terrorism?. May 1977. p. 29-32, 34-37. Civil Liberties Review. ; 4.

4702. Hoveyda, F. The problem of international terrorism at the United Nations. 1977. p. 71-83. Terrorism. ; 1.

4703. Hubbard, J. * Fried, B. A weaponless defense : A law enforcement guide to non-violent control. - Springfield, Ill. : C.C. Thomas, 1979.

4704. Jacobson, Ph. Terrorists at large: the trouble with arresting hijackers is that governments keep letting them go. 6 Nov. 1977. p. C1-C4. Washington Post

4705. Janke, P. The response to terrorism. - New York : Crane, Russak, 1979. p. 22-38.
In: J. Shaw, E.F. Gueritz and A.E. Younger (eds.), Ten years of terrorism

4706. Jenkins, B.M. * Tanham, G. * Wainstein, E. * Sullivan, G. U.S. preparation for future low-level conflict : A report of a discussion, 19-20 Oct. 1976 RAND Corporation, Washington, D.C. - Santa Monica, Calif. : RAND, July 1977. RAND Paper. ; P. 5830.

4707. Jenkins, B.M. A strategy for combatting terrorism. - Santa Monica, Calif. : RAND, May 1981. 8 p. RAND Paper Series. ; P-6624.

4708. Jenkins, B.M. Combatting terrorism. - Santa Monica, Calif. : Rand Corp., 1981. 11 p

4709. Jenkins, B.M. Fighting terrorism : An enduring task. - Santa Monica, Calif. : RAND, 1981. 8 p

4710. Jenkins, B.M. The US response to terrorism : A policy dilemma. 1985. p. 39-45. Armed forces journal international. ; 122:9.

4711. Jenkins, B.M. Upgrading the fight against terrorism. 27 March 1977. Washington Post

4712. Jimlstad, L. Preventive measures against terrorists by the Swedish police. 1975. p. 1-6. Svensk Polis. ; 4.

4713. Kaiser, K. * Kreis, K.M. * (eds.) Sicherheitspolitik vor neuen Aufgaben. - Frankfurt/M. : Alfred Metzner Verlag, 1977. 447 p
Also deals with fight against terrorism.

4714. Karkashian, J.E. Dealing with international terrorism. 31 Oct. 1977. p. 605-609. Department of State Bulletin. ; 77.

4715. Kerr, D.M. Coping with terrorism. 1985. p. 113-126. Terrorism. ; 8:2.

4716. Kimche, J. Can Israel contain the Palestine revolution?. - London : ISC, 1971. 11 p. Conflict Studies. ; 13.

4717. Kittrie, N.N. New look at political offenses and terrorism. - Westport, Conn. : Greenwood Press, 1978. p. 354-375.
In: M.H. Livingston et al. (eds.), International terrorism in the contemporary world

4718. Kittrie, N.N. Reconciling the irreconcilable: the quest for international agreement over political crime and terrorism. - Boulder, Colo. : Westview Press, 1978. p. 208-236.
In: S.A. Banks (ed.), Yearbook of world affairs

4719. Koch, K. Enige opmerkingen over het terrorisme en de ontwikkeling naar een "sterke" staat. March 1978. p. 41-48. Transaktie. ; 7:1.

4720. Kogon, E. * (ed.) Terror und Gewaltkriminatitaet : Herausforderung fuer den Rechtsstaat. - Frankfurt a.M. : Aspekte Verlag., 1975. 114 p

4721. Kraus, D.M. Searching for hijackers : Constitutionality, costs and alternatives. Winter 1973. p. 383-420. University of Chicago Law Review. ; 60.

4722. Kupperman, R.H. Facing tomorrow's terrorist incident today. - Washington, D.C. : Law Enforcement Assistance Administration, Department of Justice, 1977.

4723. Kupperman, R.H. Treating the symptoms of terrorism: some principles of good hygiene. 1977. p. 35-49. Terrorism. ; 1.

4724. Lachica, E. Japan using diplomacy to fight terrorists. 10 March 1975. Washington Star-News

4725. Lacoste, I. Die Europaeische Terrorismus-Konvention : Eine Untersuchung des Europaeischen Uebereinkommens zur Bekaempfung des Terrorismus vom 27. Januar 1977 im Vergleich mit aehnlichen internationalen Abkommen und unter Beruecksichtigung des Schweizerischen Rechts. - Zuerich : 1982.

4726. Lagorio, L. Contro il terrorismo per la liberta. - Venezio : Marsillio, 1979. 89 p

4727. Legum, C. How to curb international terrorism. Jan. 1973. p. 3-9. Current History. ; 147.

4728. Leites, N. Understanding the next act. 1980. p. 1-47. Terrorism. ; 3.

4729. Lineberry, W.P. * (ed.) The struggle against terrorism. - New York : H.W. Wilson, 1977. 203 p

4730. Livingstone, N.C. * Arnold, T.E. * (eds.) Fighting back : Winning the war against terrorism. - Lexington, Mass. : Lexington Books, 1986. 288 p

4731. Lord Grey of Naunton. Political problems of terrorism and society. -

New York : Crane, Russak, 1979. p. 39-55.
In: J. Shaw, E.F. Gueritz and A.E. Younger (eds.), Ten years of terrorism

4732. Lynch, E.A. International terrorism : The search for a policy. 1986. p. 1-85. Terrorism. ; 9:1.

4733. Mahoney, H.T. After a terrorist attack - business as usual. March 1975. p. 16, 18, 19. Security Management. ; 19:1.

4734. Maihofer, W. Rechtsstaat gegen Terrorismus. 1976. Tribuene. ; 15:57.

4735. Martin, L.J. Violence, terrorism, non-violence : Vehicles of social control. - Westport, Conn. : Greenwood Press, 1978. p. 183-193.
In: J. Roucek (ed.), Social control for the 1980s, a handbook for order in a democratic society

4736. McClure, B. Corporate vulnerability and how to assess it. - New York : Praeger, 1979. p. 138-169.
In: Y. Alexander and R.A. Kilmarx (eds.), Political terrorism and business: the threat and response

4737. McEwen, M.T. * Sloan, S. Terrorism preparedness on the state and local level : An Oklahoma perspective. - Gaithersburg, Md. : IACP., 15 p

4738. Meachling, E. Security risks to energy production and trade : The problems of the Middle East. June 1982. p. 120-130. Energy Policy. ; 10.

4739. Meisel, J.H. Counterrevolution : How revolutions die. - New York : Atherton Press, 1966.

4740. Mensing, W. Zum "Offensivkonzept zur Bekaempfung des anarchistischen Terrorismus" der CDU/CSU. 1976. Aus Politik und Zeitgeschichte. ; 25.

4741. Merari, A. * (ed.) On terrorism and combating terrorism. - Frederick, Md. : University Publications of America - Jaffee Center for Strategic Studies, 1985. 188 p
Proceedings of an international seminar, Tel Aviv, 1979.

4742. Methvin, E.H. Domestic intelligence is our only curb on terrorism. Febr. 1976. p. 10-12. Human Events. ; 36.

4743. Mickolus, E.F. * Heyman, E.S. * Schlotter, J. Responding to terrorism: basic and applied research. - New York : Pergamon, 1980. p. 174-189.
In: R.H. Schultz jr and S. Sloan (eds.), Responding to the terrorist threat: security and crisis management

4744. Mickolus, E.F. Combatting international terrorism: a quantitative analysis. - New Haven, Conn. : Yale University, Department of Political Science, 1981. 600 p ; Ph.D. dissertation

4745. Milte, K.L. Prevention of terrorism through development of supra-national criminology. 1975. p. 519-538. Journal of International Law and Economics. ; 10:2-3.

4746. Moodie, M. * Bray, F.T.J. British policy options in Northern Ireland : Alternative routes to the cemetery?. Fall 1976. p. 3-14. Fletcher Forum. ; 1.

4747. Moore, K.C. Airport, aircraft and airline security. - Los Angeles : Security World Publishing, 1976. 374 p

4748. Munck, L.de Het internationale terrorisme en zijn bestrijding. - Leuven : Katholieke Universiteit, 1978. 154 p
Master thesis, dealing with U.N. approach to terrorism and its suppression.

4749. Murphy, J.F. International terrorism : From definition to measures toward suppression. - Milwaukee : Institute of World Affairs, University of Wisconsin, 1974. p. 14-29.
In: International terrorism. Proceedings of an intensive panel at the 15th annual convention of the International Studies Association

4750. Netanyahu, B. * (ed.) Terrorism : How the West can win. - New York : Farrar, Strauss, Giroux, 1986. 254 p

4751. Newhouse, J. The diplomatic round : A freemasonry of terrorism. 8 July 1985. p. 46-49, 51-63. New Yorker. ; 6.

4752. Nollau, G. Wie sicher ist die Bundesrepublik?. - Muenchen : 1976.

4753. Novogrod, J.C. Internal strife, self-determination and world order. - Springfield, Ill. : Thomas, 1975. p. 98-119.
In: M.C. Bassiouni (ed.), International terrorism and political crimes

4754. Oakley, R.B. Combatting international terrorism. - Washington, D.C. : U.S. Dept. of State, Bureau of Public Affairs, 1985. 7 p

4755. Oseth, J.M. Combatting terrorism : The dilemma of a decent nation. Spring 1985. p. 65-76. Parameters. ; 15.

4756. Pedersen, F.C. Comment - controlling international terrorism: an analysis of unilateral forces and proposals for multilateral cooperation. 1976. p. 209-250. University of Toledo Law Review. ; 8:1.

4757. Peijster, C.N. Politiek terrorisme en de verdediging van de demokratische rechtsstaat. Sept. 1978. p. 216-222. Civis Mundi. ; 5.

4758. Pierre, A.J. Coping with international terrorism. March-April 1976. p. 60-67. Survival. ; 18:2.

4759. Pop, J.M.M. Enkele juridische aspecten bij de bestrijding van terreuracties. 20 Dec. 1974. Intermediair. ; 51.

4760. Possony, S.T. Coping with terrorism. Feb. 1973. p. 6-7. Defense and Foreign Affairs Digest. ; 2.

4761. Quainton, A.C.E. Government policy and response in a terrorist crisis situation. Spring 1979. p. 442-452. Current Municipal Problems. ; 5.

4762. Quainton, A.C.E. Terrorism: do something! But what?. Sept. 1979. p. 60-64, 79. Dept. of State Bulletin. ; 79.

4763. Radliffe, J The insurance companies' response to terrorism. - New York : Praeger, 1979. p. 265-276.
In: Y. Alexander and R.A. Kilmarx (eds.), Political terrorism and business: the threat and response

4764. Reber, J.R. Threat analysis methodology. - Gaithersburg, Md. : IACP, 1976.

4765. Reinares-Nestares, F. * (ed.) Terrorismo y sociedad democratia. - Madrid : Akal, 1982. 185 p

4766. Rivers, G. The specialist. - New York : Stein and Day, 1985. 212 p

4767. Rivers, G. The war against the terrorists : How to win it. - New York : Stein and Day, 1986. 250 p

4768. Robertson, K. The state and security. - London : MacMillan, forthcoming.

4769. Rose, R.N. Preventive measures against terrorists by the Swedish police. - Washington, D.C. : Law Enforcement Assistance Administration, National Criminal Justice Reference Service., 1976. 7 p

4770. Rose-Smith, B. Police powers and terrorism legislation. - Vol. 1. - London : John Calder, 1979.
In: P. Hain (ed.), Policing the police

4771. Rosen, S.J. Measures against international terrorism. - New York : Wiley, 1975. p. 60-68.
In: D. Carlton and C. Schaerf (eds.), International terrorism and world security

4772. Rosenfield, S.B. Air piracy - is it time to relax our security?. - Buffalo, N.Y. : William S. Hein, 1974. p. 67-94.
In: J.S. Schultz and J.P. Thames (eds.), Criminal justice systems review

4773. Rosenthal, U. Terreurbestrijding in Nederland: vijf thema's. 1979. p. 251-265. Tijdschrift voor de Politie

4774. Rositzke, H. Terrorism. - New York : Reader's Digest Press, 1977. p. 111-117.
In: H. Rositzke, The CIA's secret operations: espionage, counterspionage and covert operations

4775. Roukis, S. * Montana, P.J. * (eds.) Managing terrorism: strategies for the corporate executive. - Westport, Conn. : Greenwood Press, 1982.

4776. Russell, A.L. Corporate and industrial security. - Houston : Gulf Publ. Co., 1980.

4777. Russell, Ch.A. * Banker jr., L.J. * Miller, B.H. Out-inventing the terrorist. - Boulder, Colo. : Westview, 1979. p. 3-42.
In: Y. Alexander, D. Carlton and P. Wilkinson (eds.), Terrorism: theory and practice

4778. Russell, Ch.A. * Miller, B.H. Terrorism, tactics and the corporate target. - New York : Praeger, 1979. p. 106-119.
In: Y. Alexander and R.A. Kilmarx (eds.), Political terrorism and business: the threat and response

4779. Sabetta, A.R. Transnational terror: causes and implications for response. 1977. p. 147-156. Stanford Journal of International Studies. ; 12:1.

4780. Salewski, W. * Lanz, P. Die neue Gewalt und wie man ihr begegnet. - Locarno : Droemer Knaur Verlag, 1978. 224 p
Salewski, a former police psychologist and adviser to the German government in matters of terrorism, Describes 'the new violence and how to cope with it'

4781. Schutter, B.de Prospective study of the mechanisms to repress terrorism. - Brussels : Institute of Sociology of the Free University of Brussels, 1974. p. 253-266.
In: Reflections on the definition and repression of terrorism

4782. Schwarz, H. Die Herausforderung des Terrorismus : Sicherheit nach innen und Freiheitsrechte. 1975. Die politische Meinung. ; 20:158.

4783. Shaw, E.D. * Hazelwood, L. * Hayes, R.E. * Harris, D.R. Analyzing threats from terrorism. - Washington : National Bureau of Standards, 1977. p. 3-27.
In: J.J. Kramer (ed.), The role of behavioral science in physical security. Proceedings of the Annual symposium held at the Defense Nuclear Agency, Washington, D.C., 29-30 April 1976. Special Publication. ; 480-24.

4784. Shaw, P.D. Extortion threats: analytic techniques and resources. 1975. p. 5-16. Assets Protection. ; 1:2.

4785. Shultz jr, R.H. * Sloan, S. * (eds.) Responding to the terrorist threat : Security and crisis management. - New York : Pergamon Press, 1980.

4786. Sirey, P.J.R. La repression internationale du terrorisme. 1937. p. 518-523. Affaires etrangeres. ; 7.

4787. Sjaastad, A.C. Deterrence of terrorism and attacks against off-shore oil installations in Northern Europe. - Jerusalem : Hebrew University Leonard Davis Institute for International Relations, 1979. p. 182-202.
In: Y. Evron (ed.), International violence: terrorism, surprise and control

4788. Sloan, S. International terrorism: academic quest, operational art and policy implications. 1978. p. 1-6. Journal of International Affairs. ; 32.

4789. Sloan, S. Simulating terrorism. - Norman : University of Oklahoma Press, 1981.

4790. Sloan, S. Simulating terrorism: from operational techniques to question of policy. 1978. p. 3-8. International Studies Notes. ; 5.

4791. Spjut, R.J. * Wilkinson, P. A review of [ten] counter-insurgency [and terrorism] theorists. 1978. p.54-64, 231-232. Political Quarterly. ; 49.

4792. Steiner, W. Anti-terrorism: the making of bureaucracy. 1978. p. 48-51. The Public Eye. ; 1:2.
Shows U.S. build up of anti- terrorist

measures following West-Germany's example.

4793. Sullivan, D.S. * Sattler, M.J. * (eds.) Revolutionary war : Western response. - New York : Columbia University, 1971.

4794. Sulzberger, C.L. The antiterrorist league. 14 April 1976. p. 39. New York Times

4795. Sweet, W. Anti-terrorism : New priority in foreign policy. 1981. p. 231-248. Washington Congressional Quarterly

4796. Tanter, R. * Kaufman, L. Terror and reprisal: process and choice. - Jerusalem : Hebrew University, Leonard Davis Institute for International Relations, 1979. p. 203-230.
In: Y. Evron (ed.), International violence: terrorism, surprise and control

4797. Terekhov, V. International terrorism and the fight against it. March 1974. p. 20-22. New Times (Moscow). ; 11.

4798. Tomasevski, K. The United Nations activities concerning the problem of terrorism. 1980. p. 61-76. Archives of Legal and Social Sciences. ; 66:1-2.
In Croatian, with English summary.

4799. Trent, D.M. A national policy to combat terrorism. Summer 1979. p. 41-53. Policy Review. ; 9.

4800. Tuckerman, A U.N.: new look for 1972: debate on terrorism. 2 Oct. 1972. p. 258. Nation

4801. Volpe, J. * Stewart, J.T. Aircraft hijacking : Some domestic internal responses. Winter 1971. p. 273-318. Kentucky Law Journal. ; 59.

4802. Vos, H.M. Elementen voor een anti-terrorisme-ethiek. Febr. 1976. p. 75-80. Algemeen Politieblad. ; 125:4.

4803. Wahl, J. Responses to terrorism: self-defense or reprisal?. June 1973. p. 28-33. International Problems. ; 5:1-2.

4804. Warbrick, C. The European Convention on Human Rights and the prevention of terrorism. Jan. 1983. p. 82-119. International and Comparative Law Quarterly. ; 32.

4805. Waterman, D.A. * Jenkins, B.M. Heuristic modeling using rulebased computer systems. - Santa Monica, Calif. : RAND, 1977. 53 p. RAND Paper. ; P-5811.

4806. Watson jr, F.M. Political terrorism: how to combat it. - New York : McKay, 1976.

4807. Waugh, W.L. Emergency managemen

and mass destruction terrorism : A policy framework. - Alexandria, Virg. : Triton Corporation, Aug. 1984. ; Report submitted to the Federal Emergency Management Agency

4808. Waugh, W.L. International terrorism : How nations respond to terrorists - a comparative policy analysis. - Chapel Hill, N.C. : Documentary Publications, 1982.

4809. Waugh, W.L. International terrorism: theories of response and national policies. University of Mississippi, 1980. ; Ph.D. dissertation

4810. Wermdalen, H. Foeretagen och terrorismen. - Stockholm : Foerfattares Bokmaskin, 1977. 94 p
On terrorism prevention for journalists.

4811. Whitehead, D. Attack on terror: the FBI against the Ku Klux Klan in Mississippi. - New York : Funk & Wagnalls, 1970. 321 p
Written with the help of the FBI.

4812. Wilferink, B.W. De internationale bestrijding van terrorisme. - Nijmegen : 1977.
In: Yearbook of Volkenrechtelijk Dispuut Robert Regout 1976/77

4813. Wilkinson, P. Proposals for government and international responses to terrorism. 1981. p. 161-193. Terrorism. ; 5:1-2.

4814. Wilkinson, P. State-sponsored international terrorism : The problems of response. July 1984. p. 292-298. The World Today. ; 40:7.

4815. Wilkinson, P. Terrorism versus liberal democracy: the problems of response. - London : ISC, 1976. Conflict Studies. ; 67.

4816. Wilkinson, P. Terrorism: the international response. - London : Chatham House, Jan. 1978. p. 5-13. The World Today. ; 34:1.

4817. Wise, Ch. * Sloan, S. Countering terrorism - United States and Israeli approach. 1977. p. 55-59. Middle East Review. ; 9:3.

4818. Wittke, Th. Terrorismusbekaempfung als rationale politische Entscheidung : Die Fallstudie Bundesrepublik. - Frankfurt a.M./Bern : Verlag Peter Lang, 1983. 308 p. Europaeische Hochschulschriften. Politikwissenschaft. ; 31:43.

4819. Wolf, J.B. Anti-terrorism : Protective security aspects. - Gaithersburg, Md. : IACP, 1981. Update Report. ; 7:4.

4820. Wolf, J.B. Antiterrorism: objectives and operations. - Gaithersburg, Md. : IACP, 1978.

4821. Wolf, J.B. Controlling political terrorism in a free society. - Gaithersburg, Md. : IACP, 1978. p. 165-180.
In: J.D. Elliot and L.K. Gibson (eds.), Contemporary terrorism: selected readings

4822. Wolf, J.B. Countering tomorrow's terrorism. Jan. 1982. p. 70. Proceedings of the United States Naval Institute

4823. Wolf, J.B. Crime prevention skills and non-verbal communications. Fall 1980. p. 7. Viewpoints: Victim/Witness Newsletter

4824. Wolf, J.B. Cycle of terror and counterterror. Nov/Dec 1973. p. 27-32. International Perspectives, a journal of the Department of External Affairs, Canada

4825. Wolf, J.B. Enhancement of the national mission by intelligence gathering. Fall 1979. p. 3. Association of Federal Investigators. ; 2:3.

4826. Wolf, J.B. Intelligence stupidity. Fall 1979. p. 9-12. TVI Journal. ; 1:1.

4827. Wolf, J.B. Strategic aspects of American anti-terrorist related intelligence activities. - Gaithersburg, Md. : IACP, 1979. Update Report. ; 5:6.

4828. Wolf, J.B. Target analysis : Part I: Techniques and practices of terrorist groups. - Gaithersburg, Md. : IACP., 17 p

4829. Wolf, J.B. Target analysis : Part II: the essential component of anti-terrorist operations. - Gaithersburg, Md. : IACP., 18 p

4830. Wolf, J.B. Unique encounter : Anti-terrorist intelligence. Febr. 1982. p. 14, 23. Law Enforcement Communications

4831. Wurth, P. La repression internationale du terrorisme. - Lausanne : Imprimerie de la Concorde, 1941. 139 p ; These

4832. Yallop, H.J. Protection against terrorism. - Chichester : Rose, 1980.

4833. Yoder, A. United Nations resolutions against international terrorism : The effectiviness of UN action against international terrorism: conclusions and comments. 1983. Terrorism. ; 6:4.

4834. Young, R. * Adams, J. Case for detention. - London : Bow Publications, 1974. 18 p
Argues for detention of terrorists without trial in Northern Ireland.

4835. _____ Combatting international and domestic terrorism. - Washington, D.C. : GPO, 1978. 119 p.
U.S. Congress, Senate. Committee on foreign relations

4836. _____ Controlling international terrorism: an analysis of unilateral force and proposals for multilateral cooperation. 1976. p. 209-250. University of Toledo Law Review. ; 8.

4837. _____ Curbing terrorism. Jan. 1978. p. 31-37. Atlas World Press Review. ; 25.

4838. _____ Der freiheitliche Rechtsstaat und seine Gegner, Mittel und Grenzen der Abwehr : Verteidigerbeschraenkungen in Terroristenverfahren, Nichtuebernahme von Verfassungsgegnern, Ansprachen und Diskussionsbeitrage auf der Juristenkonferenz vom 13 bis 15 Okt. 1978 in Berlin. - Karlsruhe : Muller, Juristischer Verlag, 1979. 173 p.
International Commission of Jurists, German section

4839. _____ Deutsche Massnahmen und Initiativen zur Terrorbekaempfung. -

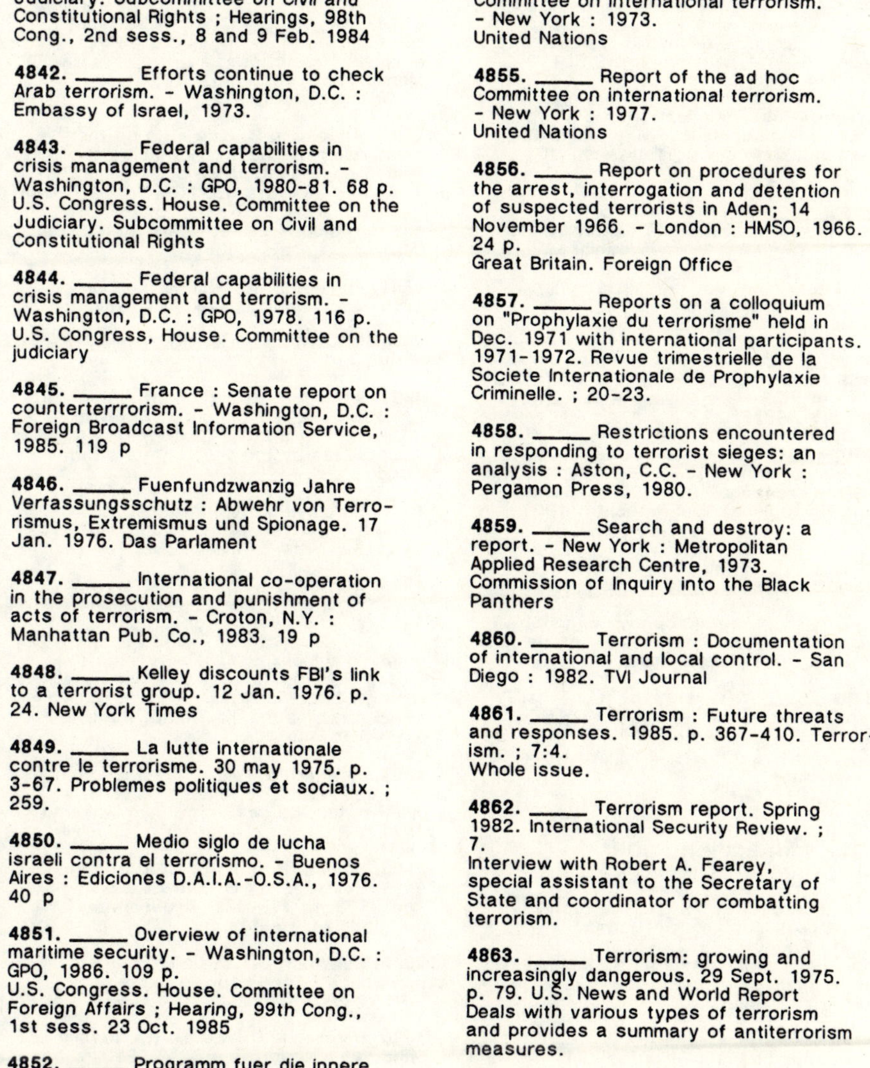

Hamburg : 1976. DPA-Hintergrund

4840. _____ Domestic security (Levi) guidelines. - Washington, D.C. : GPO, 1983. 587 p.
U.S. Congress. Senate. Committee on the Judiciary. Subcommittee on Security and Terrorism ; Hearings, 97th Cong., 2nd sess

4841. _____ Domestic security measures relating to terrorism. - Washington, D.C. : GPO, 1984. 138 p.
U.S. Congress. House. Committee on the Judiciary. Subcommittee on Civil and Constitutional Rights ; Hearings, 98th Cong., 2nd sess., 8 and 9 Feb. 1984

4842. _____ Efforts continue to check Arab terrorism. - Washington, D.C. : Embassy of Israel, 1973.

4843. _____ Federal capabilities in crisis management and terrorism. - Washington, D.C. : GPO, 1980-81. 68 p.
U.S. Congress. House. Committee on the Judiciary. Subcommittee on Civil and Constitutional Rights

4844. _____ Federal capabilities in crisis management and terrorism. - Washington, D.C. : GPO, 1978. 116 p.
U.S. Congress, House. Committee on the judiciary

4845. _____ France : Senate report on counterterrrorism. - Washington, D.C. : Foreign Broadcast Information Service, 1985. 119 p

4846. _____ Fuenfundzwanzig Jahre Verfassungsschutz : Abwehr von Terrorismus, Extremismus und Spionage. 17 Jan. 1976. Das Parlament

4847. _____ International co-operation in the prosecution and punishment of acts of terrorism. - Croton, N.Y. : Manhattan Pub. Co., 1983. 19 p

4848. _____ Kelley discounts FBI's link to a terrorist group. 12 Jan. 1976. p. 24. New York Times

4849. _____ La lutte internationale contre le terrorisme. 30 may 1975. p. 3-67. Problemes politiques et sociaux. ; 259.

4850. _____ Medio siglo de lucha israeli contra el terrorismo. - Buenos Aires : Ediciones D.A.I.A.-O.S.A., 1976. 40 p

4851. _____ Overview of international maritime security. - Washington, D.C. : GPO, 1986. 109 p.
U.S. Congress. House. Committee on Foreign Affairs ; Hearing, 99th Cong., 1st sess. 23 Oct. 1985

4852. _____ Programm fuer die innere Sicherheit in der Bundesrepublik Deutschland : Staendige Konferenz der Innenminister/-Senatoren des Bundes und der Laender, Febr. 1974. - Mainz : Krach, 1974. 28 p.
Innenministerium Rheinland-Pfalz

4853. _____ Public report of the Vice President's Task Force on Combatting Terrorism. - Washington, D.C. : GPO, 1986. 34 p.
Vice President's Task Force on Combatting Terrorism (U.S.)

4854. _____ Report of the ad hoc Committee on international terrorism. - New York : 1973.
United Nations

4855. _____ Report of the ad hoc Committee on international terrorism. - New York : 1977.
United Nations

4856. _____ Report on procedures for the arrest, interrogation and detention of suspected terrorists in Aden; 14 November 1966. - London : HMSO, 1966. 24 p.
Great Britain. Foreign Office

4857. _____ Reports on a colloquium on "Prophylaxie du terrorisme" held in Dec. 1971 with international participants. 1971-1972. Revue trimestrielle de la Societe Internationale de Prophylaxie Criminelle. ; 20-23.

4858. _____ Restrictions encountered in responding to terrorist sieges: an analysis : Aston, C.C. - New York : Pergamon Press, 1980.

4859. _____ Search and destroy: a report. - New York : Metropolitan Applied Research Centre, 1973.
Commission of Inquiry into the Black Panthers

4860. _____ Terrorism : Documentation of international and local control. - San Diego : 1982. TVI Journal

4861. _____ Terrorism : Future threats and responses. 1985. p. 367-410. Terrorism. ; 7:4.
Whole issue.

4862. _____ Terrorism report. Spring 1982. International Security Review. ; 7.
Interview with Robert A. Fearey, special assistant to the Secretary of State and coordinator for combatting terrorism.

4863. _____ Terrorism: growing and increasingly dangerous. 29 Sept. 1975. p. 79. U.S. News and World Report
Deals with various types of terrorism and provides a summary of antiterrorism measures.

4864. _____ Terrorisme. - Den Haag :

Ministerie van Justitie, 1975. p. 138-150. Justitiele Verkenningen. ; 4.

4865. _____ To counter international terrorism : Report to accompany S. 2236. - Washington, D.C. : GPO, 1978. 35 p.
U.S. Congress. Senate. Committee on Foreign Relations

4866. _____ U.S. action to combat terrorism. - Washington, D.C. : GPO, 1973.
U.S. Department of State. Bureau of public affairs. Office of media services

4867. _____ U.S. economic sanctions against Chile. - Washington, D.C. : GPO, 1981. 86 p.
U.S. Congress. House. Committee on Foreign Affairs. Subcommittee on International Economic Policy and Trade ; Hearing, 97th Cong., 1st sess., 10 March 1981,

4868. _____ U.S. efforts to deter hijacking : A presentation to foreign countries and airlines. - Washington, D.C. : GPO, 1970.
U.S. Department of Transportation. Federal aviation administration
Whole issue.

4869. _____ Una regione contro il terrorismo, 1969-1978 : Dati e cronache. - Torino : Consiglio regionate del Piemonte, 1979. 253 p

4870. _____ Una regione contro il terrorismo, anni 1979-1980 : Supplemento a dati e cronache 1969-1978. - Torino : Consiglio regionate del Piemonte, 1981. 30 p

4871. _____ United Nations cooperation against terrorism. 1983. Terrorism. ; 6:4.

4872. _____ Wen suchen wir denn eigentlich? : (Terroristenbekaempfung.). 1977. p. 26-33. Der Spiegel. ; 31:46.

4873. _____ West-Germany's political response to terrorism. - Washington, D.C. : GPO, 1978. 23 p.
U.S. Congress, Senate. Committee on the judiciary

S.1.1. Military and police

4874. Ackroyd, C. * et al. The technology of political control. - Harmondsworth : Penguin, 1977. 320 p
On British counter-insurgency techniques and technologies with special regard to Northern Ireland.

4875. Adkins jr, E.H. Protection of American industrial dignitaries and facilities overseas. July 1974. p. 14, 16, 55. Security Management. ; 18:3.

4876. Aguilera Peralta, G. Terror and violence as weapons of counterinsurgency in Guatemala. Spring and Summer 19. p. 91-113. Latin American Perspectives. ; 7.

4877. Alexander, Y * Nanes, A. * (eds.) Legislative responses to terrorism. - The Hague : Martinus Nijhoff, 1981.

4878. Alexander, Y. * Levine, H.M. Prepare for the next Entebbe. - Washington : Sept. 1977. Chitty's Law Journal. ; 25:7.

4879. Alon, H. Countering Palestinian terrorism in Israel : Toward a policy analysis of countermeasures. - Santa Monica, Calif : RAND, 1980. 271 p ; Ph.D. dissertation

4880. Anderson, R. Sidelights on the home rule movement. - London : 1907. Ireland and British police countermeasures against terrorists.

4881. Andrieux, L. Souvenirs d'un prefet de police. - Paris : 1885.

4882. Applegate, R. * (comp.) Kill or get killed. - Boulder, Colo. : Paladin Press, 1976.
A widely used book on suppression of unrest.

4883. Applegate, R. * (comp.) Riot-control : Material and techniques. - Stackpole : 1969.
Widely used by the police around the world.

4884. Barclay, C.N. Countermeasures against the urban guerrilla. Jan. 1972. p. 83-90. Military Review. ; 52:1.

4885. Barnett, R.W. The U.S. Navy's role in countering maritime terrorism. 1983. p. 469-480. Terrorism. ; 6:3.

4886. Beaumont, R.A. Military elite forces : Surrogate war, terrorism, and the new battlefield. March 1979. p. 17-29. Parameters, journal of the U.S. Army War College. ; 9.

4887. Blechmann, B.M. The consequences of Israeli reprisals : An assessment. - Washington, D.C. : Georgetown University, 1971. ; Ph.D. dissertation

4888. Boeles, P. Scherpschuttersteams, en wat de regering er mee wil. 25 April 1973. p. 478-482. Nederlands Juristenblad. ; 48:16.

4889. Bohanan, C.T.C. Counter-guerrilla operations : The Philippine experience. - New York : 1962.

4890. Bourret, J.C. Wie ein franzoesisches Sonderkommando die in Nov. 1979 besetzte Moskee in Mekka befreite. - Paris : Editions France Empire, 1981.

Cf. Der Spiegel, 22 June 1981, pp. 144ff; on French nerve gas attackagainst the occupants of the Holy Shrine in Mecca.

4891. Bowden, T. Men in the middle--the U.K. police. - London : ISC, 1976. Conflict Studies. ; 68.

4892. Bunyan, T. The history and practice of the political police in Britain. - London : Quartet Books, 1977.

4893. Chase, L.J. * (ed.) Bomb threats, bombings and civil disturbances: a guide for facility protection. - Corvallis, Oregon : Continuing Education Publications, 1971.

4894. Clutterbuck, R.L. Police and urban terrorism. July 1975. p. 204-214. Police Journal (England). ; 48.

4895. Cobb, J. Counterterrorism : Should the U.S. have bombed Qaddafi?. July-Aug. 1986. p. 37-40. Common Cause Magazine. ; 12.

4896. Cohen, E.A. Commandos and politicians : Elite military units in modern democracies (U.S., Britain, France, Israel). - Cambridge : Center for International Affairs, 1978. 136 p. Studies in International Affairs. ; 40.

4897. Cooper, H.H.A. Evaluating the terrorist threat : Principles of applied risk assessment. - Gaithersburg, Md. : IACP., 22 p

4898. Davidson, Ph.L. SWAT (Special Weapons and Tactics). - Springfield, Ill. : C.C. Thomas, 1979. 148 p

4899. Deerin, J.B. Frustrating duty for British troops : Northern Ireland's 'twilight war'. Dec. 1976. p. 14-21. Army. ; 26.

4900. Del Grosso, D.S. * Short, J.C. A concept for anti-terrorist operations. June 1979. p. 54-59. Marine Corps Gazette. ; 63.

4901. Dimitrijevic, V. Nova konvencija za zastitu bezbednosti civilnog vazduhoplovstva. 1971. p. 551-562. Anali pravnog fakulteta u Beogradu

4902. Dodd, N.L. The corporal's war: internal security operations in Northern Ireland. July 1976. p. 58-68. Military Review. ; 56.

4903. Doss, S.R. Defense planning for the 1980's and the changing international environment. - Washington, D.C. : 1975.

4904. Dupuy, T.N. Isolating the guerrilla : Vol. 3: Supporting case studies. - Washington, D.C. : Hist. Eval. and Res. Organization, 1 Febr. 1966.
Distribution limitation now removed.

4905. Elliott, J.D. Contemporary terrorism and the police response. Febr. 1978. p. 40-43. Police Chief. ; 45.

4906. Evans, E.H. American policy response to international terrorism : Problems of deterrance. Massachusetts Institute of Technology, 1977. ; Ph.D. dissertation

4907. Evans, R.D. Brazil: the road back from terrorism. - London : ISC, 1974. 18 p. Conflict Studies. ; 47.
Concentrating on the 1969-72 government repression of urban guerrillas.

4908. Faligot, R. Britain's military strategy in Ireland. - New York : Morrow, 1983.

4909. Fenello, M.J. Technical prevention of air piracy. Nov. 1971. p. 28-41. International Conciliation. ; 585.

4910. Fraser, C.A. Revolutionary warfare: basic principles of counterinsurgency. - Pretoria : 1968.

4911. Galula, D. Counterinsurgency warfare: theory and practice. - New York : Praeger, 1964.

4912. Gennaro, G.de La controguerriglia : Fattori di successo. 1966. p. 1327-1334. Rivista militar. ; 22:11.

4913. Geraghty, T. Who dares wins: : The story of the Special Air Services, 1950-1980. - London : Arms and Armour Press, 1980.
On British anti-terrorist unit S.A.S.

4914. Glick, E.B. Isolating the guerrilla : Some Latin American examples. Fall 1968. p. 873-886. Orbis. ; 12.

4915. Greene, T.N. * (ed.) The guerrilla: and how to fight him. - New York : Praeger, 1962.

4916. Greenwood, C. Police tactics in armed operations. - Boulder, Colo. : Paladin Press, 1979. 320 p

4917. Gregory, F. Protest and violence: the police response : A comparative analysis of democratic methods. - London : ISC, 1976. 15 p. Conflict Studies. ; 75.

4918. Haaren, L.van De overheid en het terrorisme. 16 June 1973. p. 279-282. Algemeen Politieblad. ; 122:12.

4919. Haber, E. Raid on Entebbe. - New York : Delacorte Press, 1977.

4920. Ham, G.Van Het moderne terrorisme en zijn bestrijdings-mogelijkheden. - Apeldoorn : Nederlandse Politie Akademie, 1979. 101 p

4921. Hermann, K. * Koch, P. Entscheidung in Mogadishu : Die 50 Tage nach Schleyers Entfuehrung. Dokumente, Bilder, Zeugen. - Hamburg : Gruner und Jahr, 1977. 248 p

4922. Hicks, R.D. Undercover operations and persuasion. - Springfield, Ill. : C.C. Thomas, 1973. 104 p

4923. Higham, R. * (ed.) Bayonets in the streets; the use of troops in civil disturbances. - Lawrence : University of Kansas Press, 1969.

4924. Hobsbawn, E.J. Pentagon's dilemma: Goliath and the guerrilla. 10 July 1975. p. 20-21. Nation

4925. Hoggart, S. The army PR men of Northern Ireland. Oct. 1973. New Society

4926. Hosmer, S.T. * Tanham, G.K. Countering covert aggression. - Santa Monica, Calif. : RAND, 1986. 28 p

4927. Hosmer, S.T. Viet Cong repression and its implications for the future. - Lexington : Heath Lexington Books, 1970.

4928. Jenkins, B.M. Soldiers versus gunmen : The challenge of urban guerilla warfare. - Santa Monica, Calif. : RAND, 1974.

4929. Kee, R.J. Algiers - 1957 : An approach to urban counter-insurgency. 1974. p. 73-84. Military Review. ; 54:4.

4930. Kelly, G.A. Revolutionary warfare and psychological action. Oct. 1960. p. 4-13. Military Review. ; 40.

4931. Kitson, F.R. Bunch of five. - London : Faber & Faber, 1977.
By counter-insurgency expert, describing his experience in Kenya, Malaya and Cyprus.

4932. Kitson, F.R. Low intensity operations: subversion, insurgency, peace-keeping. - London : Faber & Faber, 1971. 208 p
Author is a counter-insurgency expert and reviews various experiences during the decolonization of the British empire.

4933. Kobetz, R.W. * Cooper, H.H.A. Target terrorism: providing protective services. - Gaithersburg, Md. : IACP, 1978. 203 p

4934. Koch, P. * Hermann, K. Assault at Mogadishu. - London : Corgi Books, 1977.

4935. Krumm, K.H. Probleme der Organisation und Koordination der Terroristen-Bekaempfung in der Bundesrepublik. 1977. Aus Politik und Zeitgeschichte. ; 41.

4936. Kupperman, R.H. * et al. An overview of counter-terrorism technology. - Washington, D.C. : ACDA, Dec. 1977.
Classified report by the U.S. Arms Control and Disarmament Agency for the Cabinet committee to combat terrorism and the national securitycouncil staff.

4937. Laporte, M. Histoire de l'Okhrana. - Paris : 1935.

4938. Leibstone, M. * Evans, J. * Shriver, R. Countering terrorism on military installations. - MacLean, Va. : Science Applications, Inc., July 1978. ; Study prepared for the U.S. army

4939. Lenz, R.R. Explosives and bomb disposal guide. - Springfield, Ill. : C.C. Thomas, 1976. 320 p

4940. Livingstone, N.C. Fighting terrorism and "dirty little wars". March-April 1984. p. 4-16. Air University Review. ; 35.

4941. Longuet, J. * Zilber, G. Les dessous de la police russe. - Paris : 1909.

4942. Longuet, J. * Zilber, G. Terroristes et policiers. - Paris : 1909.

4943. Lopez, V.C. What the U.S. army should do about urban guerrilla warfare. - Springfield, Va. : National Technical Information Service, 1975. 36 p

4944. MacDonald, P.G. Stopping the clock : Bomb disposal in the world of terrorism. - London : Hale, 1977. 159 p

4945. McCuen, J.J. The art of counter-revolutionary war. - Harrisburg : Stockpole Books, 1966. 349 p

4946. McDowell, Ch.P. * Harlan, J.P. Police response to political crimes and acts of terrorism - some dimensions for consideration. - Toronto, Canada : American Society of Criminology, Annual meeting, 30. 18 p

4947. Meulen, J.S.van der * (ed.) De bestrijding van terrorisme : In het bijzonder de rol van de krijgsmacht daarbij. - The Hague : Stichting Volk en Verdediging, May 1979. 74 p. Kontaktbulletin. ; 15:30.
The fight against terrorism with particular emphasis on the role of the armed forces

4948. Meulen, J.S.van der Terrorisme en krijgsmacht. Sept. 1978. Civis Mundi

4949. Miller, A.H. Implications from the police experience. 1978. p. 125-146. Terrorism. ; 1:2.

4950. Moss, R. Counter terrorism. - London : 1972. 64 p. Economist Brief Books. ; 29.

Claims that there is a need for specially trained police unit to respond to terrorists.

4951. Motley, J.B. US strategy to counter domestic political terrorism. - Washington, D.C. : National Defense University Press, 1983. 136 p

4952. Moyer, F.A. Police guide to bomb search techniques. - Boulder, Colo. : Paladin Press., 200 p

4953. Nikolajewski, B. Asew. - Berlin : 1932.
On the Ochrana agent provocateur and Russian terrorism before World War I.

4954. O'Ballance, E. Goliath's war : Israeli operation LITANI, 15-21 March 1978. Dec. 1978. p. 34-40. Marine Corps gazette. ; 62.

4955. O'Ballance, E. Israeli counter-guerrilla measures. March 1972. Journal of the United Services Institute for Defence Studies. ; 117.

4956. Ofer, Y. Operation Thunder: the Entebbe raid : The Israeli's own story. - Harmondsworth : Penguin, 1976. 141 p

4957. Paget, J. Counter-insurgency campaigning. - London : Faber & Faber, 1967. 189 p

4958. Paret, P. French revolutionary warfare from Indo-China to Algeria. - London : Pall Mall, 1964.

4959. Paust, J.J. Entebbe and self-help: the Israeli response to terrorism. Jan. 1978. The Fletcher Forum. ; 2:1.

4960. Perkus, C. COINTELPRO: the FBI's secret war on political freedom. - New York : Monad Press, 1975.

4961. Phillips, Ch.D. Counterterror campaign - the road to success or failure. - Carlisle Barracks, Pa. : Army War College, Oct. 1975. 24 p

4962. Piekalkiewicz, J. Israels langer arm : Geschichte der israelischen Geheimdienste und Kommandounternehmen. - Frankfurt a.M. : Goverts, 1975. 407 p

4963. Price, D.L. Ulster-consensus and coercion : Part 2: Security force attrition tactics. Oct. 1974. p. 7-24. Conflict Studies. ; 50.

4964. Pustay, J.S. Counterinsurgency warfare. - New York : Free Press, 1965.

4965. Rabe, R. The police response to terrorism. - New York : Praeger, 1979. p. 307-330.
In: Y. Alexander and R.A. Kilmarx (eds.), Political terrorism and business: the threat and response

4966. Rapoport, D.C. The government is up in the air over combating terrorism. 26 Nov. 1977. p. 1853-1856. National Journal. ; 9.

4967. Roberts, K.E. Terrorism and the military response. - Carlisle Barracks, Pa. : Army War College Strategic Studies Institute, Oct. 1975. 23 p

4968. Ropelewski, R.R. Commandos thwart hijackers : The rescue of 85 hostages of Lufthansa 737 in Somalia. 24 Oct. 1977. p. 14-16. Aviation Week and Space Technology. ; 107.

4969. Rossani, O. Intervista sui rapimenti : Parla Pomarici. - Milano : Edizione Elle, 1977.
The Milan magistrate, Ferdinando Pomarici, who led many kidnapping investigations, offers hard-line advise on how to cope with the problem.

4970. Rouzitti, N. Rescuing nationals abroad through military coercion and intervention on grounds of humanity. - The Hague : Martinus Nijhoff, 1985.

4971. Schonborn, K. Dealing with violence : The challenge faced by police and other peace-keepers. - Springfield, Ill. : C.C. Thomas, 1975. 376 p

4972. Shani, J. Airborne raids : A potent weapon in countering transnational terrorism. March-April 1984. p. 41-55. Air University Review. ; 35.

4973. Shepherd, T.E. * et al. Exercise Europe (anti-terrorism in Belgium, West Germany, Italy and Holland) : 12th Senior Command Course. - Hampshire, Eng. : Bramskill Police College, 1975. 60 p

4974. Simpson, H.R. Organizing for counter-terrorism. Winter 1982. p. 28-33. Strategic Review. ; 10.

4975. Stevenson, W. 90 minutes at Entebbe. - New York : Bantam Books, 1976.

4976. Tanham, G. * Jenkins, B.M. * et al. United states preparation for future low-level conflict. 1978. p. 1-19. Conflict. ; 1:1.

4977. Terry, J.P. An appraisal of lawful military response to state-sponsored terrorism. May-June 1986. p. 59-68. Naval War College Review. ; 39.

4978. Thackrah, R. Army-police cooperation against terrorism. Jan.-March 1983. p. 41-53. Police Journal

4979. Thackrah, R. Army-police cooperation : A general assessment. 1982. p. 10-12. Police and Society Research Paper. ; 1:7.

4980. Thackrah, R. Evolution of police-public relations. Winter 1982-1983. p. 6-7. Police World. ; 27.

4981. Tinnin, D.B. Hit team. - Boston : Little, Brown & Co, 1976. 240 p
On Israeli counter-terrorism against alleged perpetrators of the Munich Olympics massacre.

4982. Tomkins, T.C. Military counter-measures to terrorism in the 1980s. - Santa Monica, Calif. : RAND, 1984. 38 p

4983. Tophoven, R. Der internationale Terrorismus : Herausforderung und Abwehr. 1977. p. 28-38. Aus Politik und Zeitgeschichte. ; 6.

4984. Tophoven, R. Die israelischen Konterguerillas : Israels Kampf gegen die Fedayin. 1974. p. 33-44. Wehrforschung. ; 2.

4985. Tophoven, R. GSG 9 - Kommando gegen Terrorismus. - Bonn : Wehr & Wissen, 1978. 96 p

4986. Tophoven, R. GSG 9 - Operation Mogadishu : Feuertaufe der Spezialeinheit. 1977. p. 13-17. Wehrtechnik. ; 11.

4987. Tophoven, R. Zahal in Entebbe : Anmerkungen zur Psyche einer Armee. 1977. Wehrwissenschaftliche Rundschau. ; 1.

4988. Vasilyev, A.T. The Okhrana. - London : 1930.

4989. Wegener, W. Bekaempfung des Terrorismus durch Spezialeinheiten im Rahmen des Sicherheitskonzept der BRD. 1977. p. 6-10. Loyal. ; 9:11.

4990. Wilkinson, P. Adaptation for the struggle against terrorism of international co-operation between the police and security services. ; Paper presented at the Council of Europe conference on the defence of democracy against terrorism in Europe, November 1980

4991. Williamson, T. Counterstrike Entebbe. - London : Collins, 1976. 184 p

4992. Wolf, J.B. Anti-terrorism and West German police operations. - Gaithersburg, Md. : IACP, 1978. Update Report. ; 4:4.

4993. Wolf, J.B. Anti-terrorism: operations and controls in a free society. p. 35-41. Police Studies. ; 1:3.

4994. Wolf, J.B. Anti-terrorism: technological, corporate and personal considerations. - Gaithersburg, Md. : IACP, 1980. Update Report. ; 6:2.

4995. Wolf, J.B. Counter-terrorism and open societies. Nov. 1977-Feb. 1978. Counterforce

4996. Wolf, J.B. Enforcement terrorism. 1981. p. 45-54. Police Studies. ; 3:4.

4997. Wolf, J.B. Intelligence operations and terrorism. - Gaithersburg, Md. : IACP, 1981. Update Report. ; 7:1.

4998. Wolf, J.B. Police intelligence - focus for counter-terrorist operations. Jan.-March 1976. p. 19-27. The Police Journal. ; 49:1.

4999. Wolf, J.B. Prison, courts and terrorism : The American and West German experience. July 1977. p. 211-230. The Police Journal. ; 51:3.

5000. Wolf, J.B. Urban terrorist operations. Oct. 1976. p. 227-284. The Police Journal. ; 49:4.

5001. _____ Advisor handbook for counterinsurgency. - Boulder, Colo. : Paladin Enterprises, 1977. 210 p.
U.S. Army

5002. _____ Aftermath of the Achille Lauro incident. - Washington, D.C. : GPO, 1986. 74 p.
U.S. Congress. House. Committee on Foreign Affairs. Subcommittee on International Operations ; Hearing and markup, 99th Cong., 1st sess. on H. Con. Res. 228

5003. _____ Aids to the detection of explosives : A brief review of equipment for searching out letter bombs and other explosive devices. Febr. 1975. p. 48-49, 61. Security Gazette. ; 17:2.

5004. _____ Anti-terrorism program. - Springfield, Ill. : 1977.
Illinois State Police Academy

5005. _____ California - nuclear blackmail or nuclear threat : Emergency response plan. - Sacramento, Calif. : 1976. 40 p.
California Office of Emergency Services
An officials' guide to emergency procedures.

5006. _____ Colloque sur la prophylaxie du terrorisme. Jan. 1971. p. 74. Revue internationale de criminologie et de police technique. ; 25:1.

5007. _____ Counterguerrilla operations. - Boulder, Colo. : Paladin Enterprises, 1965.
U.S. Army

5008. _____ Department of Defense guidance document on protection of MAAG/MSN/MILGP personnel and installations against terrorism. - Fort Bragg, N.C. : U.S. Army Institute for Military Assistance, April 1975. 116 p.
U.S. Army Institute

5009. _____ Fatal error: murder of A. Bouchiki by Israeli killers. 6 Aug. 1973.

p. 31-32. Time. ; 102.

5010. _____ Is the U.S. next?. 22 May 1977. p. 38-39. Newsweek

5011. _____ Revolutionary warfare and counter-insurgency. - Pretoria : Institute for Strategic Studies, University of Pretoria, 1984. 47 p

5012. _____ State-sponsored terrorism: the threat and possible countermeasures : Conference report. 1986. p. 253-313. Terrorism. ; 8:3.

5013. _____ Terrorism in the 80's : A workshop. March 1985. p. 130-141. Police Chief. ; 52.

5014. _____ The army line on Northern Ireland. June 1979. p. 97-98. State Research Bulletin. ; 12.

S.1.2. Legal

5015. Andrews, J. The European convention on the suppression of terrorism. 1977. p. 323-326. European Law Review. ; 2.

5016. Aston, C.C. International legislation against political terrorism. March 1980.
In: A. Martin (ed.), Political terrorism: a United Nations Association special report

5017. Aston, C.C. The UN convention against the taking of hostages: realistic or rhetoric?. Dec. 1980. p. 139-160. Terrorism. ; 5:1-2.

5018. Bassiouni, M.C. International extradition and world public order. - Dobbs Ferry : Oceana, 1974.

5019. Bassiouni, M.C. The political offense exception in extradition law and practice. - Springfield, Ill. : Thomas, 1975. p. 398-447.
In: M.C. Bassiouni (ed.), International terrorism and political crimes

5020. Baxter, R.R. The Geneva conventions of 1949 and wars of national liberation. - Springfield, Ill. : Thomas, 1975. p. 120-132.
In: M.C. Bassiouni (ed.), International terrorism and political crimes

5021. Bekes, I. The legal problems of hijacking and taking of hostages. - Westport, Conn. : Greenwood Press, 1978. p. 346-353.
In: M.H. Livingston et al (eds.), International terrorism in the contemporary world

5022. Bennett, W.T. U.S. initiatives in the United Nations to combat international terrorism. 1973. p. 752-760. International Lawyer. ; 7:4.

5023. Bennett, W.T. U.S. outlines principles for work of ad hoc committee on terrorism. 3 Sept. 1973. p. 337-339. Department of State Bulletin

5024. Bennett, W.T. U.S. votes against U.N. General Assembly resolution calling for study of terrorism. 22 Jan. 1973. p. 81-94. Department of State Bulletin

5025. Bik, R.G.C. Het Europees verdrag tot bestrijding van terrorisme, 27 januari 1977. - Apeldoorn : Febr. 1978. 47 p ; Skriptie Nederlandse Politie Akademie

5026. Blishchenko, I.P. * Zhdanov, N.V. Combating terrorism by international law. 1976. p. 81-96. Soviet Law and Government. ; 14:3.

5027. Blum, Y.Z. State response to acts of terrorism. 1976. p. 223-237. German Yearbook of International Law

5028. Bopp, A. Moderner Kleinkrieg und Kriegsgefangenenrecht. - Wuerzburg : 1970. ; Dissertation

5029. Boyle, R.P. International action to combat aircraft hijacking. 1972. p. 460-473. Lawyer of the Americas. ; 4.

5030. Brach, R.S. The inter-American convention on the kidnapping of diplomats. 1971. p. 392-412. Columbia Journal of Transnational Law. ; 10.

5031. Brady, J.A. The threat of terrorism to democracy : A criminal justice response. 1986. p. 205-211. Terrorism. ; 8:3.

5032. Brandt, W. Internationale Massnahme gegen Terror und Gewalt : Feststellungen vor dem Bundeskabinett, 31.10.1972. 1972. p. 1817-1818. Bulletin. Presse- und Informationsamt der Bundesregierung. ; 153.

5033. Caloyanni, M.A. Le terrorisme et la creation d'une cour repressive internationale. 1935. p. 46ff. Revue de droit international. ; 15.

5034. Caradon, L. * Bathurst, M. * Van Straubenzee, W.R. International law and international terrorism. - New York : Crane, Russak, 1979. p. 147-169.
In: J. Shaw, E.F. Gueritz and A.E. Younger (eds.), Ten years of terrorism: collected views

5035. Chelazzi, G. La dissociazione del terrorismo : (artt. 4 e 5 d.L. 15 dicembre 1979, n. 625, convertito con modeficazioni nella L. 6 febbrairo 1980 n. 15). - Milano : Giuffre, 1981.

5036. Child, R.B. Concepts of political

prisonerhood. 1974. p. 1-33. New England Journal on Prison Law. ; 1.

5037. Dershowitz, A.M. Terrorism and preventive detention: the case of Israel. Dec. 1970. p. 3-14. Commentary. ; 50:6.

5038. Dewar, M. Internal security weapons and equipment of the world. - New York : Charles Scriber's Sons, 1979.
On repression technology.

5039. Diplock, L. Report of the Commission to consider legal procedures to deal with terrorist activities in Northern Ireland. - London : HMSO, 1972. 42 p

5040. Dominguez, C.H. La nueva guerra y el nuevo derecho : Ensayo para una estrategia juridica contrasubversiva. - 2 vols. - Buenos Aires : Circulo Militar, 1980. 951 p

5041. Donnedieu de Vabres, H. La repression internationale du terrorisme : Les conventions de Geneve. 1938. p. 37-74. Revue de droit international et de legislation comparee. ; 19.

5042. Dumas, J. De l'urgence d'un accord international contre les actes de terrorisme. 1935. p. 281-287, 343-348. La paix par le droit. ; 45.

5043. Dumas, J. Du fondement juridique de l'entraide internationale pour la repression du terrorisme. 1935. p. 609-640. Revue de droit international et de legislation comparee. ; 16.

5044. Elwin, G. Swedish anti-terrorist legislation. - Amsterdam : July 1977. p. 289-301. Contemporary Crises. ; 1.

5045. Emanuelli, C. Les moyens de prevention et de sanction en cas d'action illicite contre l'aviation civile internationale. - Paris : Pedone, 1974. 160 p

5046. Eustathiades, C. La Cour Penale Internationale pour la repression du terrorisme et le probleme de la responsabilite internationale des etats. 1936. p. 385-415. Revue generale de droit international public. ; 43.

5047. Evans, A.E. Aircraft hijacking: its cause and cure. 1969. p. 695-710. American Journal of International Law. ; 63.

5048. Evans, A.E. Aircraft hijacking: what is being done. Oct. 1973. p. 641-671. American Journal of International Law. ; 67.

5049. Falk, R. Legal order in a violent world. - Princeton, N.J. : Princeton University Press, 1968.

5050. Feraud, H.J. La convention de Montreal du 23 septembre 1971 pour la repression d'actes illicites diriges contre la securite de l'aviation civile. 1972. p. 1-29. Revue de science criminelle et de droit penal compare. ; 1.

5051. Fields jr, L. Terrorism: summary of applicable U.S. and international law. - New York : Praeger, 1979. p. 277-292. In: Y. Alexander and R.A. Kilmarx (eds.), Political terrorism and business: the threat and response

5052. Finger, S.M. The United Nations response to terrorism. - New York : Praeger, 1979. p. 428-490. In: Y. Alexander and R.A. Kilmarx (eds.), Political terrorism and business: the threat and response

5053. Fitzgerald, G.F. Offences and certain other acts committed on board aircraft: the Tokyo convention of 1963. 1964. p. 191-204. Canadian Yearbook of International Law. ; 2.

5054. Fitzgerald, G.F. Toward legal suppression of acts against civil aviation. 1971. p. 42-78. International Conciliation. ; 585.

5055. Franck, Th.M. * Lockwood, B.B. Preliminary thoughts towards an international convention on terrorism. 1974. p. 69-90. American Journal of International Law. ; 68:1.

5056. Franck, Th.M. International legal action concerning terrorism. 1978. p. 187-197. Terrorism. ; 1:2.

5057. Friedlander, R.A. Coping with terrorism: what is to be done?. - Boulder, Colo. : Westview, 1979. p. 231-245. In: Y. Alexander, D. Carlton and P. Wilkinson (eds.), Terrorism: theory and practice

5058. Friedlander, R.A. Terrorism and political violence : Do the ends justify the means?. - Westport, Conn. : Greenwood Press, 1978. p. 316-324. In: M.H. Livingston et al. (eds.), International terrorism in the contemporary world

5059. Friedlander, R.A. Terrorism: what's behind our passive acceptance of transnational mugging?. 1975. p. 10-71. Barrister. ; 2.

5060. Gaynes, J.B. Bringing the terrorist to justice : A domestic law approach. 1978. p. 71-84. Cornell International Law Journal. ; 11:1.
On international extradiction of political offenders.

5061. Gilbert, G.S. Terrorism and the political offence exemption reappraised. Oct. 1985. p. 695-723. International and Comparitive Law Quarterly. ; 34:4.

5062. Ginzburg, N. La lutte contre le terrorisme. 1935. p. 878-889. Revue de droit penal et de criminologie et archives internationales de medecine legale. ; 15.

5063. Goldberg, A.J. The murder in St. James's Square : What diplomatic immunity for terrorists?. Nov. 1984. p. 67-70. Encounter. ; 64:4.

5064. Golsong, H. The European convention on the suppression of terrorism: provocation or instrument of peace?. 1977. p. 5-7. Forward in Europe. ; 1.

5065. Green, L.C. International law and the suppression of terrorism. 1975. p. 129-163. Malaya Law Review. ; 17.

5066. Green, L.C. The legalization of terrorism. - Boulder, Colo. : Westview, 1979. p. 175-197.
In: Y. Alexander, D. Carlton, P. Wilkinson (eds.), Terrorism: theory and practice

5067. Hirano, R. Convention on offences and certain other acts committed on board aircraft of 1963. 1964. p. 44-52. Japanese Annual of International Law. ; 8.

5068. Hirsch, A.I. * Otis, D. Aircraft piracy and extradition. 1970. p. 392-419. New York Law Forum. ; 16.

5069. Holden, A. How much use is our anti-terrorist law?. 2 Nov. 1975. p. 6. Sunday Times

5070. Hruska, R.L. Aircraft piracy amendments of 1972 : Remarks in the senate. 15 Febr. 1973. p. S1183-S1186. Congressional Record (daily ed.). ; 119.

5071. Ingraham, B. Political crime in Europe: a comparative study of France, Germany, and England. - Berkeley : University of California Press, 1979.

5072. Jack, H.A. Terrorism: another U.N. failure. 20 Oct. 1973. p. 282-285. America

5073. Janke, P. International drive to curb terrorism : An enlarged reference book, 1976-77. - London : ISC, 1977.
In: The Annual of Power and Conflict

5074. Jenkins, B.M. Columbia's bold gamble for peace. - Santa Monica, Calif. : RAND, 1981. 21 p
On amputy policy of President Bekucur.

5075. Keijzer, N. Het Europees verdrag tot bestrijding van terrorisme. - Deventer : Kluwer, 1979. 36 p

5076. Khairallah, D. Insurrection under international law. - Beirut : Librairie du Liban, 1973.

5077. Klughardt, W. Die Gesetzgebung zur Bekampfung des Terrorismus aus strarechtlich-soziologischer Sicht. - Muenchen : Florentz, 1984. 411 p

5078. Kos-Rabcewicz Zubkowski, L. Essential features of an international criminal court. - Westport, Conn. : Greenwood Press, 1978. p. 333-340.
In: M.H. Livingston et al. (eds.), International terrorism in the contemporary world

5079. Kos-Rabcewicz Zubkowski, L. The creation of an international criminal court. - Springfield, Ill. : Thomas, 1975. p. 519-536.
In: M.C. Bassiouni (ed.), International terrorism and political crimes

5080. Kuhn, T.M. Terrorism in international law. University of South Africa, 1980. ; L.L.D. dissertation

5081. Kutner, L. Constructive notice: a proposal to end international terrorism. 1973. p. 325-350. New York Law Forum. ; 19.

5082. Lahey, K. * Sang, L.M. Control of terrorism through a broader interpretation of article 3 of the four Geneva conventions of 1949. - Springfield, Ill. : Thomas, 1975. p. 191-200.
In: M.C. Bassiouni (ed.), International terrorism and political crimes

5083. Laudi, M. I casi di non punibilita dei terroristi "pentiti". - Milano : Giuffre, 1983. 415 p

5084. Laudi, M. Terroristi "pentits" e liberazione condizionale : Artt. 8 e 9 l 29 maggio 1982 n. 304. - Milano : Giuffre, 1984. 173 p

5085. Leaute, J. Terrorist incidents and legislation in France. - Lexington, Mass. : Heath Lexington Books, 1978.
In: R.D. Crelinsten, D. Laberge-Altmejd, and D. Szabo (eds.), Terrorism and criminal justice: an international perspective

5086. Legros, P. La notion de terrorisme en droit compare. - Brussels : Editions de l'Universite de Bruxelles, 1974. p. 229-239.
In: Reflexions sur la definition et la repression du terrorisme

5087. Lissitzyn, O.J. International control of aerial hijacking: the role of values and interests. 1971. p. 80-86. Proceedings of the American Society of International Law

5088. Litvine, M. Aircraft security and the repression of terrorism. Oct. 1976. p. 50-60. Revue de droit penal et de criminologie. ; 1.

5089. Lockwood, B.B. Modern American convention on the prevention and punishment of serious forms of violence, with appendices. - Washington, D.C. : American Bar Association, 1983. 17 p

5090. Lopez Gutierrez, J.J. Should the Tokyo convention of 1963 be ratified?. 1965. p. 1-21. Journal of Air Law and Commerce. ; 31.

5091. Loy, F.E. Some international approaches to dealing with hijacking of aircraft. 1970. p. 444-452. International Lawyer. ; 4.

5092. Maddalena, M. * G. Conso Le circostanze attenuanti per i terroristi pentiti : Artt. 2 e 3 l. 29 maggio 1982, n. 304. - Milano : Giuffre, 1984. 372 p

5093. Mallison jr, W.T. * Mallison, S.V. An international law appraisal of the juridical characteristics of the resistance of the people of Palestine : The struggle for human rights. - Springfield, Ill. : Thomas, 1975. p. 173-190.
In: M.C. Bassiouni (ed.), International terrorism and political crimes

5094. Mallison jr, W.T. * Mallison, S.V. The concept of public purpose terror in international law : Doctrines and sanctions to reduce the destruction of human and material values. - Springfield, Ill. : Thomas, 1975. p. 67-85.
In: M.C. Bassiouni (ed.), International terrorism and political crimes

5095. Malmborg, K.E. New developments in the law of international aviation: the control of aerial hijacking. 1971. p. 75-80. Proceedings of the American Society of International Law

5096. Mankiewicz, R.H. The 1970 Hague convention. 1971. p. 195-210. Journal of Air Law and Commerce. ; 37.

5097. Maul, H. Gesetz gegen Terrorismus und Rechtsstaat. 1977. Deutsche Richterzeitung. ; 55:7.

5098. McKeithen, R.L.S. Prospects for the preventing of aircraft hijacking through law. 1970. p. 61-80. Columbia Journal of Transnational Law. ; 9:1.

5099. McMahon, J.P. Air hijacking: extradition as a deterrent. 1970. p. 1135-1152. Georgetown Law Journal. ; 58.

5100. Meyer, A. Der Begriff "Terrorismus" im Lichte der Eroerterungen auf dem fuenften Kongress der Vereinigten Nationen betr. die Verhuentung von Verbrechen und die Behandlung von Verbrechern in Genf, 1. bis 12.9.1975. 1976. p. 223-233. Zeitschrift fuer Luftrecht und Weltraumrechtsfragen. ; 25:3.

5101. Meyers, L. Europees verdrag tot bestrijding van terrorisme. July 1977. p. 321-327. Tijdschrift voor de Politie. ; 39:7-8.

5102. Mickolus, E.F. Multilateral legal efforts to combat terrorism: diagnosis and prognosis. 1979. p. 13-51. Ohio Northern University Law Review. ; 6.

5103. Migliorino, L. International terrorism in the United Nations debates. 1976. p. 102-121. Italian Yearbook of International Law. ; 2.

5104. Mok, M.R. De strijd tegen de luchtpiraterij. 1973. p. 837, 839. Nederlands Juristenblad

5105. Mok, M.R. Het Europees verdrag tot bestrijding van het terrorisme. 16 July 1977. p. 665-671. Nederlands Juristenblad. ; 22.

5106. Moore, J.N. Toward legal restraints on international terrorism. 1973. p. 88-94. American Journal of International Law. ; 67:5.

5107. Munck, L.de * (ed.) Het internationaal politiek terrorisme. 1979. 76 p. KIB Vizier. ; 2:2-3.

5108. Murphy, J.F. International legal controls of international terrorism: performance aand prospects. April 1975. p. 444. Illinois Bar Journal. ; 3.

5109. Murphy, J.F. Prof. Gross's comments on international terrorism and international criminal jurisdiction. April 1974. p. 306-308. American Journal of International Law. ; 68:2.

5110. Murphy, J.F. Punishing international terrorists : The legal framework for policy initiatives. - Totowa, N.J. : Rowman & Allanheld, 1985. 142 p

5111. Murphy, J. United Nations proposals on the control and repression of terrorism. - Springfield, Ill. : Thomas, 1975. p. 493-506.
In: M.C. Bassiouni (ed.), International terrorism and political crimes

5112. Nagel, W.H. Het Europees verdrag over de bestrijding van terrorisme van 27 januari 1977. 24 Sept. 1977. Nederlands Juristenblad. ; 32.

5113. Panzera, A.F. Postal terrorism and international law. 1975. p. 762-765. Revista di diritto internazionale. ; 48.

5114. Paust, J.J. A survey of possible legal responses to international terrorism: prevention, punishment and cooperative action. 1975. p. 431-469. Georgia Journal of International and Comparative Law. ; 5.

5115. Paust, J.J. Approach to decision with regard to terrorism. Spring 1978. p. 397-403. Akron Law Review. ; 7.

5116. Paust, J.J. Responses to terrorism: a prologue to decision concerning private measures of sanction. 1977. p. 79-130. Stanford Journal of International Studies. ; 12.

5117. Pella, V.V. La repression des crimes contre la personnalite de l'etat. 1930. p. 677-831. Recueil des Cours de l'Academie de Droit International de La Haye. ; 3.

5118. Pella, V.V. La repression du terrorisme et la creation d'une cour internationale. 1939. p. 785. Nouvelle revue de droit international prive. ; 5:6.

5119. Pella, V.V. Les conventions de Geneve pour la prevention et la repression du terrorisme et pour la creation de la Cour Penale Internationale. 1938. p. 409-453. Revue de droit penal et de criminologie et archives internationales de medicine legale. ; 18.

5120. Pels, M. Europees verdrag en bestrijding van terrorisme. Sept. 1977. p. 19-24. Kriminologenkrant. ; 28.

5121. Philipp, O.M. Internationale Massnahmen zur Bekaempfung von Handlungen gegen die Sicherheit der Zivilluftfahrt. - Berlin : Duncker und Humbolt, 1977. 154 p

5122. Poulantzas, N.M. The Hague convention for the suppression of unlawful seizure of aircraft [16 Dec. 1970]. 1971. p. 25-75. Nederlands Tijdschrift voor Internationaal Recht. ; 18:1.

5123. Pulsifer, R. * Boyle, R. The Tokyo convention on offences and certain other acts committed on board aircraft. 1964. p. 305-354. Journal of Air Law and Commerce. ; 20.

5124. Radvanyi, M. Anti-terrorist legislation in the Federal Republic of Germany. - Washington, D.C. : Library of Congress, Law Library., 1979. 140 p

5125. Rafat, A. Control of aircraft hijacking: the law of international civil aviation. 1971. p. 143-156. World Affairs. ; 134.

5126. Riggle, R. Affaire Abou Daoud : Some problems of extraditing an international terrorist. Spring 1978. p. 333-350. International Lawyer. ; 12.

5127. Rogers, W.P. U.S. and Cuba reach agreement on hijacking. 5 March 1973. p. 260-262. Department of State Bulletin

5128. Roux, J.A. Le projet de convention internationale pour la repression des crimes presentant un danger public. 1935. p. 99-130. Revue Internationale de Droit Penal. ; 12.

5129. Rovine, A.W. The contemporary international legal attack on terrorism. 1973. p. 3-38. Israel Yearbook on Human Rights. ; 3.

5130. Roxin, C. Strafprozessordnung : Gerichtsverfassungs-Vorschriften. Mit den neuen Bestimmungen zur Bekaempfung des Terrorismus. 1976. DTV-Beck Texte. ; 580.

5131. Rubin, A.P. Terrorism and social control. 1979. p. 60-69. Ohio Northern University Law Review. ; 6.

5132. Rumpf, H. Voelkerrechtliche Probleme des Terrorismus. 1985. p. 383-388. Aussenpolitik. ; 36:4.

5133. Samuels, A. Crimes committed on board aircraft: Tokyo Convention Act, 1967. 1967. p. 271-277. British Yearbook of International Law. ; 42.

5134. Schloesing, E. La repression internationale du terrorisme. April 1973. p. 50. Revue politique et parlementaire. ; 841.

5135. Schwarzenberger, G. Terrorists, hijackers, guerrilleros, and mercenaries. 1971. p. 257-282. Current Legal Problems. ; 24.

5136. Shearer, I.A. Extradition in international law. - Manchester : Manchester University Press, 1971. 283 p

5137. Smith, C.L. Probable necessity of an international prison in solving aircraft hijacking. 1971. p. 269-278. International Lawyer. ; 5.

5138. Sofaer, A.D. Fighting terrorism through law. Oct. 1985. p. 38-42. Dept. of State Bulletin. ; 85.

5139. Sofaer, A.D. The U.S.-U.K. Supplementary Extradition Treaty. 1986. p. 327-343. Terrorism. ; 8:4.

5140. Stein, T. Die europaeische Konvention zur Bekaempfung des Terrorismus. 1977. p. 668-684. Zeitschrift fuer auslaendisches oeffentliches Recht und Voelkerrecht. ; 37:3-4.

5141. Stratton, J.G. The terrorist act of hostage-taking : Considerations of law enforcement. June 1978. p. 123-134. Journal of Police Science and Administration

5142. Stratton, J.G. The terrorist act of hostage-taking: a view of violence and the perpetrators. March 1978. p. 1-9. Journal of Police Science and Administration. ; 6:1.

5143. Street, H. The Prevention of Terrorism (temporary provisions) Act 1974. April 1975. p. 192-199. Criminal Law Review

5144. Sundberg, J.W.F. Antiterrorist legislation in Sweden. - Westport, Conn. : Greenwood Press, 1978. p. 111-121. In: M.H. Livingston et al. (eds.), International terrorism in the contemporary world

5145. Sundberg, J.W.F. The wisdom of treaty making: a glance at the machinery behind the production of law-making treaties and a case study of the Hague hijacking conference of 1970. 1972. p. 285-306. Scandinavian Studies in Law

5146. Taulbee, J.L. Retaliation and irregular warfare in contemporary international law. - Chicago : Jan. 1973. p. 195-204. International Lawyer. ; 7.

5147. Tharp, P.S. The laws of war as a potential legal regime for the control of terrorist activities. 1978. p. 91-100. Journal of International Affairs. ; 32.

5148. Thornton, T.P. Terrorism and the death penalty. 11 Dec. 1976. p. 410-412. America

5149. Tiewul, S.A. Terrorism: a step towards international control. 1973. p. 585. Harvard International Law Journal. ; 14.

5150. Vinke, H. * Witt, G.W. * (eds.) Die Anti-Terror-Debatten im Parlament : Protokolle 1974-1978. - Reinbek : Rowohlt, 1978.

5151. Weis, P. Asylum and terrorism. Dec. 1977. p. 37-43. International Commission of Jurists Review

5152. White, G.M.E. The Hague convention for the suppression of unlawful seizure of aircraft. 1971. p. 38-45. International Commission of Jurists Review. ; 6.

5153. Wilkinson, P. Problems of establishing a European judicial area. ; Paper presented at the Council of Europe conference on the defence of democracy against terrorism in Europe, November 1980

5154. Williams, M. * Chatterjee, S.J. Suggesting remedies for international terrorism : Use of available international means. - London : Nov. 1976. p. 1069-1093. International Relations. ; 5:4.

5155. Wood, M. The convention on the prevention and punishment of crimes against internationally protected persons, including diplomatic agents. 1974. p. 791. International and Comparative Law Quarterly

5156. Yamamoto, S. The Japanese enactment for the suppression of unlawful seizure of aircraft and international law. 1971. p. 70-80. Japanese Annual of International Law. ; 15.

5157. Zotiades, G.B. The international criminal prosecution of persons charged with an unlawful seizure of aircraft. 1970. p. 12-37. Revue hellenique de droit international. ; 23:1-4.

5158. ______ A study of the applicability of the laws of war to guerrillas and those individuals who advocate guerrilla warfare and subversion. - Washington, D.C. : U.S. Army, Office of the Judge Advocate General, 1972.

5159. ______ Aircraft hijacking convention : Hearings. - 92nd Cong., 1st sess. - Washington, D.C. : GPO, 1971. 99 p. U.S. Congress, House, Committee on Foreign Relations

5160. ______ Amendments to the Freedom of Information Act. - Washington, D.C. : GPO, 1985. 175 p.
U.S. Congress. Senate. Committee on the Judiciary. Subcommittee on the Constitution

5161. ______ American draft convention on terrorism. 1973. Survival. ; 15:1.

5162. ______ An act to combat international terrorism : Hearings. - Washington D.C. : GPO, 1978. 1190 p.
U.S.Congress, Senate. Committee on governmental affairs ; 95th Congr., 2nd sess

5163. ______ Anti-hijacking act of 1971 : Hearings. - 92nd Cong., 2nd sess. - Washington, D.C. : GPO, 1972. 144 p. U.S. Congress, House, Committee on Foreign Affairs, Subcommittee on Aviation

5164. ______ Approaches to the problem of international terrorism. 1975. p. 483-538. Journal of International Law and Economics. ; 10:2-3.

5165. ______ Bills to authorize prosecution of terrorists and others who attack U.S. government employees and citizens abroad. - Washington, D.C. : GPO, 1986.
U.S. Congress. Senate. Committee on the Judiciary ; Hearing, 99th Cong., 1st sess on S. 1373, S. 1429 and S. 1508. 30 July 1985

5166. ______ Causes and preventions of international terrorism : Comments of member states on the question of the protection and inviolability of diplomatic agents and other persons entitled to special protection under international law. Nov. 1972.
United Nations. United Nations Study. ; A/C 6/418, Corr. 1 Add. 1.

5167. ______ Chile : Legislacion sobre seguridad del estado, control de armas y terrorismo. - Santiago de Chile : Editorial Juridica de Chile, 1985. 192 p

5168. _____ Convention for the suppression of the unlawful seizure of aircraft, The Hague, 16 Dec. 1970. 2 Nov. 1972.
United Nations. United Natons Study. ; A/C 6/418 Annex 3.

5169. _____ Convention for the suppression of unlawful acts against the safety of civil aviation, Montreal, 23 Sept. 1971. 2 Nov. 1972.
United Nations. United Nations Study. ; A/C 6/418 Annex 4.

5170. _____ Convention on offenses and certain other acts committed on board aircraft, Tokyo, 14 Sept. 1963. 2 Nov. 1972.
United Nations. United Nations Study. ; A/C 6/418 Annex 2.

5171. _____ Convention on the prevention and punishment of crimes against internationally protected persons, including diplomatic agents. 1973. p. 91-95.
United Nations. Department of State Bulletin. ; 70.

5172. _____ Convention to prevent and punish the acts of terrorism taking the form of crimes against persons and related extortions that are of international significance. - Washington, D.C. : Pan American Union, 2 Febr. 1971. Serie Sobre Tratatos

5173. _____ Convention to prevent and punish acts of terrorism : Note. 1971. p. 898. American Journal of International Law. ; 65.

5174. _____ Convention to prevent and punish the acts of terrorism taking the form of crimes against persons and related extortion that are of international significance. 22 Febr. 1971. Department of State Bulletin. ; 64:1652.

5175. _____ Current foreign policy: role of international law in combating terrorism. - Washington, D.C. : GPO, 1973.
U.S. Department of State

5176. _____ Der Buerger ruft nach haerteren Strafen : Sondergesetze fuer Terroristen - Todesstrafe fuer Geiselnehmer?. 1977. p. 26-33. Der Spiegel. ; 31:39.

5177. _____ Documenti: convenzione europea sulla repressione del terrorismo : Strasburgo, 10 november 1976. April 1977. Rivista di studi politici internazionali. ; 44:2.

5178. _____ Draft convention for the prevention and punishment of certain acts of international terrorism. 1972. p. 431. Department of State Bulletin. ; 67.

5179. _____ Draft protocol on terrorism. 1970. p. 1177.
Inter-American judicial committee. International Legal Materials. ; 9.

5180. _____ European convention on the suppression of terrorism. - Strasbourg : 27 Jan. 1977. 9 p.
Council of Europe. European Treaty Series. ; 90.

5181. _____ Explanatory report on the European convention on the suppression of terrorism. - Strasbourg : 1977. 30 p.
Council of Europe

5182. _____ General assembly resolution on terrorism: final text and member votes. 18 Dec. 1972.
United Nations. U.N. A/res. ; 3034 (xxvii).

5183. _____ Hijacking accord between the United States and Cuba : Hearings. - 93rd Cong., 1st sess. - Washington, D.C. : GPO, 1973. 18 p.
U.S. Congress, House, Committee on Foreign Affairs, Subcommittee on Inter-American Affairs

5184. _____ Implementing international conventions against terrorism : Report together with dissenting views to accompany H.R. 15552. - Washington, D.C. : GPO, 1976. 16 p.
U.S. Congress, House. Committee on the judiciary ; 94th Congr., 2nd sess

5185. _____ Internationale verdragen tegen terrorisme. 7 Feb. 1986. p. 6-8. Atlantisch Nieuws. ; 1:2.

5186. _____ Law enforcement faces the revolutionary-guerrilla criminal. Dec. 1970. p. 20-22, 28. FBI Law Enforcement Bulletin. ; 39:12.

5187. _____ League of Nations convention for the prevention and punishment of terrorism, Geneva, 16 Nov. 1937. 2 Nov. 1972.
United Nations. United Nations Study. ; A/C 6/418 Annex 1.

5188. _____ Legal committee report on the terrorism issue. 16 Dec. 1972. United Nations. ; A/8069.

5189. _____ Legislation to combat international terrorism : 98th Congress. - Washington, D.C. : GPO, 1984. 461 p.
U.S. Congress. House. Committee on Foreign Affairs. Subcommittee on International Security and Scientific Affairs ; Hearings and markup before the Subcommittees on International Security and Scientific Affairs and on International Operations, House of Representati

5190. _____ Legislative initiatives to curb domestic and international terrorism. - Washington, D.C. : GPO, 1984. 194 p.
U.S. Congress. Senate. Committee on

the Judiciary. Subcommittee on Security and Terrorism

5191. _____ Measures for protecting public order : Especially against terrorists. Nov. 1975. p. 705-722. Rivista di polizia. ; 28:11.
Article, in Italian, analysing the application of laws for combatting terrorism.

5192. _____ Omnibus antiterrorism act of 1979. - Washington, D.C. : GPO, 1979. 448 p.
U.S. Congress. Senate. Committee on Governmental Affairs

5193. _____ President Nixon establishes Cabinet committee to combat terrorism. 1972. p. 475-480. Department of State Bulletin. ; 67.

5194. _____ Problems of protecting civilians under international law in the Middle East conflict. - Washington, D.C. : GPO, 1974.
U.S. Congress, House. Committee on foreign affairs

5195. _____ Proceedings of the international conference on the repression of terrorism, Geneva, Nov. 1st-16th, 1937. - Geneva : 1938. 218 p.
League of Nations

5196. _____ Prohibition against the Training or Support of Terrorist Organization Act of 1984. - Washington, D.C. : GPO, 1984. 75 p.
U.S. Congress. House. Committee on the Judiciary. Subcommittee on Civil and Constitutional Rights ; Hearing, 98th Cong., 2nd sess. on H.R. 5613. 2 Aug. 1984

5197. _____ Regering over gijzeling; beklemmende vragen van recht en gerechtigheid. 12 Oct. 1974. p. 1113. Nederlands Juristenblad. ; 49:34.

5198. _____ Report on legislative responses to international terrorism. 1985. p. 147-163. Terrorism. ; 8:2.

5199. _____ State responsibility to deter, prevent or suppress skyjacking activities in their territory, 1970. 25 Nov. 1970.
United Nations. U.N. A/res. ; 2645 (xxv).

5200. _____ Terror in the modern age : The vision of literature, the response of law. May 1983. p. 109-213. Human Rights Quarterly. ; 5.

5201. _____ Terrorism legislation. - Washington, D.C. : GPO, 1984. 42 p.
U.S. Congress. House. Committee on the Judiciary. Subcommittee on Crime ; Hearing, 98th Cong., 2nd sess. on H.R. 5612, H.R. 5689, and H.R. 5690. 26 Sept. 1984

5202. _____ Terrorism: the proposed U.S. draft convention. 1973. p. 430. Georgia Journal of International and Comparative Law. ; 3.

5203. _____ The Antiterrorism and Foreign Mercenary Act. - Washington, D.C.; : GPO, 1983. 79 p.
U.S. Congress. Senate. Committee on the Judiciary. Subcommittee on Security and Terrorism

5204. _____ The Central American counterterrorism act of 1985. - Washington, D.C. : GPO, 1986. 321 p.
U.S. Congress. House. Committee on Foreign Affairs ; Hearings, 24 Oct.-19 Nov. 1985

5205. _____ The convention for the prevention and punishment of terrorism. 1938. p. 214. British Yearbook of International Law. ; 19.

5206. _____ The Cuban hijacking law (September 16, 1969). Nov. 1969. p. 1175-1177. International Legal Materials. ; 8.

5207. _____ The I.C.A.O. and Arab terrorist operations : A record of resolutions. - Jerusalem : 1973.
Israel Ministry for Foreign Affairs

5208. _____ The role of international law in combatting terrorism. Jan. 1973. p. 1-7. Current Foreign Policy

5209. _____ The terrorism act of South Africa. June 1968. p. 28-34. Bulletin of the International Commission of Jurists

5210. _____ Victims of Terrorism Compensation Act. - Washington, D.C. : GPO, 1986. 106 p.
U.S. Congress. House. Committee on Foreign Affairs. Subcommittee on International Operations ; Markup, 99th Cong., 1st sess. on H.R. 2851. 8, 29 Oct. 1985

5211. _____ Wetgeving inzake terreur : Beknopt rechtsvergelijkend onderzoek op het gebied van de wetgeving betreffende de preventie of bestrijding van terreur in een aantal westerse democratieen. - Nijmegen, : Katholieke Universiteit, 1976. 53 p

S.1.3. Hostage saving measures

5212. Beall, D. Hostage negotations. 1976. p. 30-39. Military Police Law Enforcement Journal. ; 111.

5213. Ben-Porat, Y. * Haber, E. * Schiff, Z. Entebbe rescue. - New York : Delacorte Press, 1976. 347 p

5214. Bennett, J.P. * Saaty, T.L. Terrorism: patterns for negotiations : Three case studies through hierarchies and holarchies. The Wharton School, University of Pennsylvania, Aug. 1977.

5215. Blacksten, R. Appendix: hostage games. - Arlington, Virg. : Ketron, 1974.
In: R. Blacksten and R. Engler, Hostage studies
A game theory approach.

5216. Bolz jr, F.A. Detective bureau hostage negotiating team. - New York : N.Y. City Police Department, 1975.

5217. Bolz, F. * Hershey, E. Hostage cop. - New York : Rawson Wade, 1979.
Study of a policeman who negotiates with terrorists for hostages.

5218. Connelly, S. Staying alive as a hostage. 29 April 1979. p. 12-19. Cincinnati Inquirer Magazine

5219. Cooper, H.H.A. Hostage negotiations : Options and alternatives. - Gaithersburg, Md. : IACP., 65 p

5220. Cooper, H.H.A. Hostage rescue operations: denouement at Algeria and Mogadishu compared. March 1978. p. 91-103. Chitty's Law Journal. ; 26.

5221. Cooper, H.H.A. Kidnapping : How to avoid it, how to survive it. - Gaithersburg, Md. : IACP., 19 p

5222. Crelinsten, R.D. * Laberge-Altmejd, D. * (eds.) Hostage taking: problems of prevention and control. - Montreal : ICCC, 1976.
Final report on management training seminar.

5223. Culley, J.A. Defusing human bombs; hostage negotiations. 1974. p. 10-14. FBI Law Enforcement Bulletin. ; 43:10.

5224. Doan, G.G. Hostage negotiator's manual. - Dublin, Calif. : Police Press, 1977.

5225. Foxley-Norris, C. Entebbe and after. 19 July 1976. p. 397-401. Army Quarterly. ; 81.

5226. Friedland, N. Hostage negotiations : Dilemma's about policy. - Wilmington, Del. : Scholarly Resources, 1983.
In: L.Z. Freedman and Y. Alexander (eds.), Perspectives on Terrorism

5227. Gallagher, R. * Rosenberg, Ch. Hostage negotiations for police : Officer reference. - Schiller Park, Ill. : MTI Teleprograms, 1977.

5228. Gelb, B. A cool-headed cop who saves hostages. 17 April 1977. p. 30-33, 39-91. New York Times Magazine

5229. Hastings, M. Yoni : Hero of Entebbe. - New York : Dial Press, 1979.
Deals with Col. Jonathan Netanjahu.

5230. Jenkins, B.M. Terrorist seize hostages in Arcadia - Laconia commandos on alert : A scenario for stimulation in negotiating with terrorists holding hostages. - Santa Monica, Calif. : RAND, 1979. 9 p. RAND Paper. ; P-6339.

5231. Johnson, T.A. Role for the behavioral scientist in hostage-negotiation incidents. Oct. 1978. p. 797-803. Journal of Forensic Sciences. ; 23.

5232. Kobetz, R.W. * Cooper, H.H.A. Hostage rescue operations and teaching the unteachable. June 1979. p. 24-27. Police Chief

5233. Kobetz, R.W. * Goldaber, I. Checklist for tactics and negotiation techniques in hostage incident responses. - Gaithersburg, Md. : IACP, 1975.
Author has been assistent director with the International Association of Chiefs of Police since 1968.

5234. Kobetz, R.W. Hostage incidents: the new police priority. March 1975. Police Chief. ; 45.

5235. Kobetz, R.W. Hostages: tactics and negotiation techniques.

5236. Laingen, B. Diplomats and terrorism : A former hostage looks at the need for physical safety and multilateral accords. Sept. 1981. p. 19-21. Foreign Service Journal. ; 58.

5237. Maher, G.F. Hostage : A police approach to a contemporary crisis. - Springfield, Ill. : Charles C. Thomas, 1977. 90 p

5238. Maher, G.F. Organizing a team for hostage negotiation. June 1976. p. 61-62. Police Chief. ; 43:6.
Discusses Nassau County, N.J., police training methods.

5239. McClure, B. Hostage survival. 1978. p. 21-48. Conflict. ; 1.

5240. Menarchik, E.D. The politics of the Israeli rescue operation at Entebbe : Crisis resolution between state and terrorist organizations. The George Washington University., 1983. ; Ph.D. dissertation

5241. Mickolus, E.F. Negotiating for hostages: a policy dilemma. 1976. p. 1309-1325. Orbis. ; 19:4.
Reprinted in: J.D. Elliott and L. Gibson (eds.), Contemporary terrorism: selected readings. Gaithersburg, Md.: IACP, 1978, pp. 207-221.

5242. Miller, A.H. Negotiations for hostages: implications from the police experience. 1978. p. 125-146. Terrorism. ; 1.

5243. Miller, A.H. SWAT (Special Weapons and Tactics) - the practical link in hostage negotiations. - New York : Praeger, 1979. p. 331-356. In: Y. Alexander and R.A. Kilmarx (eds.), Political terrorism and business : the threat and response

5244. Miller, A.H. Terrorism and hostage negotiations. - Boulder, Colo : Westview Press, 1980. 134 p

5245. Needham, J.P. Standing operating procedures : Hostage situations. - Fort Leavenworth, Kansas : U.S. Army Command and Staff College, 1977. 43 p

5246. Needham, J.P Neutralization of prison hostage situations. - Huntsville, Texas : Institute of Contemporary Corrections and the Behavioral Sciences, Sam Houston State University., 1977. 48 p

5247. Pieczenik, S.R. Hostage negotiations with terrorists. - Cambridge : Massachusetts Institute of Technology, 1982. ; Ph.D. dissertation

5248. Reber, J.R. * Singer, L.W. * Watson, F.M. Hostage survival. Aug. 1978. p. 46-50. Security Management

5249. Schlossberg, H. * Freeman, L. Psychologist with a gun. - New York : Coward, McCann & Geoghegan, 1974. On New York City Police Department's hostage negotiations team.

5250. Schroeder, F.L. * (comp.) Der Muenchner Bankraub. - Berlin-New York : De Gruyter, 1972. 164 p. Aktuelle Dokumente
On police and hostages.

5251. Silverstein, M.E. Emergency medical preparedness. 1977. p. 51-69. Terrorism. ; 1:1.
On terrorism victims.

5252. Smith, S. Political preferences and bureaucratic position : The case of the American hostage rescue mission. Winter 1984-85. p. 9-25. International Affairs. ; 61:1.

5253. Strentz, Th. Law inforcement policy and ego defences of the hostage. April 1979. p. 2-12. FBI Law enforcement Bulletin

5254. Waugh, W.L. Political skyjackings and hostage safety : An exploratory analysis. Spring 1983. p. 27-48. Southeastern Political Review. ; 11.

5255. Wilkinson, P. Admissiability of negotations between organs of the democratic states and terrorists. ; Paper presented at the Council of Europe conference on the defence of democracy against terrorism in Europe, November 1980

5256. Winkates, J.E. Hostage rescue in hostile environments: lessons learned from the Son Tay, Mayaguez and Entebbe missions. - New York : Praeger, 1979. p. 357-427.
In: Y. Alexander and R.A. Kilmarx (eds.), Political terrorism and business, the threat and response

5257. Wolf, J.B. Hostage extraction: a comparative analysis of the options. - Gaithersburg, Md. : IACP, 1980. 22 p

5258. Zartman, I.W. * (ed.) The 50 percent solution : How to bargain successfully with hijackers, strikers, bosses, oil magnates, Arabs, Russians, and other worthy opponents in this modern world. - Garden City, N.Y. : Anchor Press, 1975.

5259. _____ Hostage negotiation - training key no. 235. - Gaithersburg, Md. : 1976. 5 p.
IACP

5260. _____ Hostage negotiations. Oct. 1974. p. 10-14. FBI Law Enforcement Bulletin. ; 43:10.
On the New York City hostage negotiating team.

5261. _____ Patient sieges: dealing with hostage-takers. 1976. p. 21-27. Assets Protection. ; 1:3.
Hostage-taking incidents in the Netherlands, Great Britain, USA and Ireland recounted; reviews methods used by governments in dealing with hostage situations.

5262. _____ Terroristic activity : Hearings. Part 5: Hostage defense measures. - Washington, D.C. : GPO, 1975. p. 261-317.
U.S. Congress, Senate. Committee on the judiciary ; 94th Congr., 1st sess., July 25 1975

S.1.4. Protecting individuals against terrorism

5263. Adams, R.J. * et al. Street survival : Tactics for armed encounters. - Evanston, Ill. : Calibre Press, 1980. 416 p
Designed for police and security officers.

5264. Alexander, Y. * Kilmarx, R.A. * (eds.) Political terrorism and business : The threat and response. - New York : Praeger, 1979. 345 p

5265. Bassiouni, M.C. Protection of diplomats under islamic law. July 1980.

p. 609-633. The American Journal of International Law. ; 74:3.

5266. Bilek, A.J. Prevention of terroristic crimes : Security guidelines for business, industry and other organizations. - Washington, D.C. : GPO, May 1976.

5267. Busuttil, J.J. The Bonn Declaration on International Terrorism : A non-binding international agreement on aircraft hijacking. July 1982. p. 474-487. International and comparative law quarterly. ; 31.

5268. Clark, J.M. Emergency and high-speed driving techniques. - Houston, Texas : Gulf Publ. Co., 1976. 140 p

5269. Cunningham, W.C. * Gross, Ph.J. * (eds.) Prevention of terrorism: security guidelines for business and other organizations. - McLean, Virg. : Hallcrest, June 1978. 98 p

5270. Cunnliff, R.E. * McCoy, K.B. Safeguards against terrorism : A handbook for U.S. military personnel and families. - Maxwell Air Force Base, Ala. : Air University, 1973. 52 p

5271. Ellenberg, E.S. Western democracies vs. terrorism : A study of ineffectiveness. - Cologne : 1974.

5272. Fisher, A. Security for business and industry. - Englewood Cliffs, N.J. : Prentice-Hall, 1979.
Basic security manual.

5273. Friedland, N. Desensitizing the public to terrorist attacks : Methods and dilemma's. University Publications of America., In press.
In: A. Merari (ed.), On terrorism and combating terrorism

5274. Grodsky, M. Protection of dignitaries. 4 Oct. 1972. p. 1-6. International Police Academy Review. ; 6:4.

5275. Hamer, J. Protection of diplomats. 3 Oct. 1973. p. 759-776. Editorial Research Reports. ; 7.

5276. Hoffmann, P. Die Sicherheit des Diktators. - Muenchen : Piper, 1977. 328 p
On security precautions taken to protect Hitler's life.

5277. Jenkins, B.M. * (ed.) Terrorism and personal protection. - Boston : Butterworth Publ., 1985. 451 p

5278. Juillard, P. Les enlevements de diplomates. - Paris : Centre National de la Recherche Scientifique, 1972. p. 205-231. Annuaire francais de droit international. ; 17.

5279. Leibstone, M. Terror and its survival : Discussions about manipulable operational conditions which have favored the political terrorist. - Gaithersburg, Md. : IACP., 15 p

5280. McGuire, E.P. Safeguarding executives against kidnapping and extortion. - London : June 1974. The Conference Board Record

5281. Michal, E. Diplomatic protection. June 1981. p. 23-25, 40. Foreign Service Journal

5282. Monday, M. * Profitt, J. Protecting yourself from terrorism. - Phoenix, Arizona : Joseph Davidson Co., 1978.

5283. Nathan, J.A. The new feudalism. Spring 1981. p. 156-166. Foreign Policy. ; 42.
Private security firms.

5284. Pike, E.A. Protection against bombs and incendiaries : For business, industrial and educational institutions. - Springfield, Ill. : C.C. Thomas, 1973. 92 p

5285. Purnell, S.W. The problems of U.S. businesses operating abroad in terrorist environments. - Santa Monica, Calif. : Rand, 1981. 103 p

5286. Rayne, F. Executive protection and terrorism. Oct. 1975. p. 220-225. Top Security. ; 1:6.

5287. Reber, J.R. Executive protection manual. - Schiller Park, Ill. : Motorola Teleprograms, 1978. 289 p

5288. Scotti, A.J. Executive safety and international terrorism. - Englewood Cliffs, N.J. : Prentice-Hall, 1986. 220 p

5289. Selth, A. The terrorist threat to diplomacy : An Australian perspective. - Canberra : Strategic and Defence Studies Centre, 1986.

5290. Shaw, P. Terrorism and executive protection. 1976. p. 8-13. Asset Protection. ; 1:4.

5291. Siljander, R.P. Terrorist attacks : A protective service guide for executives, bodyguards and policemen. - Springfield, Ill. : Thomas, 1980. 328 p

5292. Walsh, E.A. * (ed.) Diplomats and terrorists : What works, what doesn't. A symposium. - Washington, D.C. : School of Foreign Service, 1982. 69 p

5293. Wilson, J.V. * Fuqua, P. Terrorism - the executive's guide to survival : Basic manual for counter-terrorist measures. - Houston, Texas : Gulf Publications, Nov. 1977.

5294. _____ Ambush attacks : A risk reduction manual for police. - Gaithersburg, Md. : 1974. 97 p.
IACP

5295. _____ Deterring aircraft terrorist attacks and compensating victims. May 1977. p. 1134-1165. University of Pennsylvania Law Review. ; 125.

5296. _____ Diplomatic security in Beirut. - Washington, D.C. : GPO, 1985. 31 p.
U.S. Congress. House. Committee on Foreign Affairs. Subcommittee on Europe and the Middle East ; Hearing before the Subcommittees on Europe and the Middle East and on International Operations of the Committee on Foreign Affairs, House of Represe

5297. _____ Diplomatic security. - Washington, D.C. : GPO, 1985. 100 p.
U.S. Congress. House. Committee on Foreign Affairs ; Hearings, 99th Cong., 1st sess., 16 and 24 July 1985

5298. _____ Executive protection handbook. - Miami, Florida : 1973. 26 p.
Burns International Investigation Bureau

5299. _____ FAA's civil aviation security program. - Washington, D.C. : GPO, 1985. 36 p.
U.S. Congress. House. Committee on Government Operations, Government Activities and Transportation Subcommittee ; Hearing, 99th Cong, 1st sess. 27 June 1985

5300. _____ Impact of international terrorism on travel. - Washington, D.C. : GPO, 1986. 432 p.
U.S. Congress. House. Committee on Foreign Affairs. Subcommittee on Arms Control, International Security and Science ; Joint hearings before the Subcommittees on Arms Control, International Security and Science and on International Operations of the Committee on Fore

5301. _____ Measures to prevent international terrorism which endangers or take innocent human lives or jeopardizes fundamental freedoms, and study of the underlying causes of those forms of terrorism and acts of violence which lie in misery, frustration grie. - New York : 1981. 20 p.
United Nations, Secretary General 1972-1981 (Waldheim)

5302. _____ Personnel security : Precautions against acts of terrorism. - Washington, D.C. : June 1978.
U.S. Army

5303. _____ Physical security. - Washington, D.C. : GPO, 1979. 513 p.
U.S. Department of the Army

5304. _____ Protective security review report : Unclassified version. - Canberra : Australian Government Publication Service, 1979. 360 p

5305. _____ Securitech: the international guide to security equipment. UNISAF Publications Ltd, 32-6 Dudley Road, Tunbridge Wells, Kent, England., Published annually.

5306. _____ Security procedures at U.S. embassies : Hearings before the Subcommittees on International Operations and on Asian and Pacific Affairs of the Committee on Foreign Affairs, House of Representatives. - 96th Cong. - Washington, D.C. : GPO, 1980. 240 p.
U.S. Congress. House. Committee on Foreign Affairs. Subcommitte on International Operations

S.1.5. Countermeasures against regime terrorism

5307. Aleff, E. * Reinter, J. * Zipfel, F. Terror und Widerstand 1933-1945 : Dokumente aus Deutschland und dem besetzten Europa. - Berlin : Colloquium Verlag, 1966. 234 p

5308. Berman, H.J. The struggle of Soviet jurists against a return to stalinist terror. June 1963. p. 314-320. Slavic Review. ; 22.

5309. Blankenburg, E. * (ed.) Politik der inneren Sicherheit. - Frankfurt a.M. : Suhrkamp, 1980. 239 p
On anti-terrorism in the German Federal Republic.

5310. Cowan, L. Children of the resistance : The young ones who defied the naziterror. - London : Frewin, 1968. 191 p

5311. Fogelson, M.R. Violence as protest. - New York : Doubleday, 1971.

5312. Foot, M.R.D. Resistance : An analysis of European resistance to nazism, 1940-1945. - London : Eyre Methuen, 1976. 346 p

5313. Hoffmann, P. Problems of resistance : National socialist Germany. Maine State University, 1975.
In: F.H. Wittell and H. Locke (eds.), The German church struggle and the holocaust

5314. Mallison, S.V. * Mallison jr, W.T. Control of state terror through the application of the international humanitarian law of armed conflict. 16 p ;
Paper presented to the international symposium on terrorism in the contemporary world, Glassboro, N.J., April 26-28, 1976

5315. _____ Torture: how to make the international convention effective : A draft optional paper. - Geneva : 1980. 60 p.
International Commission of Jurists. * Swiss Committee against Torture

S.1.6. Critiques of state countermeasures against insurgent terrorism

5316. Bakker-Schut, P.A. Politieke justitie in de Bondsrepubliek Duitsland. 15 Febr. 1975. p. 203-212. Nederlands Juristenblad. ; 50:7.

5317. Balbus, I.D. The dialectics of legal repression: black rebels before the American criminal courts. - New Brunswick, N.J. : Transaction Books, 1976. 269 p

5318. Basten, T. Von der Reform des politischen Strafrechts bis zu den Anti-Terror-Gesetzen. - Koeln : Pahl-Rugenstein, 1983. 348 p

5319. Berry, S. The prevention of terrorism act: legalized terror. - Cotton Garden London : Socialist Workers, Printers and Publishers, 1977. 15 p

5320. Blank, M. * et al. Wohin treibt der Rechtsstaat?. - Koeln : Pahl Rugenstein, 1977.
On German anti-terrorist measures.

5321. Boell, H. * Wallraff, G. Berichte zur Gesinnungslage der Nation/Bericht zur Gesinnungslage des Staatsschutzes. - Reinbek : Rowohlt, 1977.

5322. Bonner, D. Emergency powers in peacetime. - London : Sweet & Maxwell, 1985. 295 p

5323. Brady, B.J. * Faul, D. * Murray, R. British army terror. - West Belfast : Sept. 1970.

5324. Brueckner, P. * et al. 1984 schon heute, oder wer hat Angst vorm Verfassungsschutz?. - Frankfurt a.M. : Verlag Neue Kritik, 1976. 132 p

5325. Brueckner, P. * Krovoza, A. Staatsfeinde : Innerstaatliche Feinderklaerung in der BRD. - Berlin : Wagenbach, 1972. 115 p

5326. Buchholtz, H.Chr. * Zabern, T.von * (eds.) Dokumentation ueber die Art der Fahndungsmassnahmen im Zusammenhang mit der Lorentz-Entfuehrung. - Berlin : 1975. 65 p ; Ed. im Auftrage der Internationalen Liga fuer Menschenrechte, Sektion West-Berlin, und der Humanistischen Union, Landesverband Berlin

5327. Carmichael, D.J.C. Of beasts, gods, and civilized men : The justification of terrorism and of counterterrorist measures. 1982. p. 1-26. Terrorism. ; 6:1.

5328. Connell, D. U.K.: the prevention of terrorism act. 1980. Index on Censorship. ; 3.

5329. Dahs, H. Das "Anti-Terroristen-Gesetz" - eine Niederlage des Rechtsstaates. 1976. Neue Juridische Wochenschrift. ; 29:47.

5330. Donahue, D.E. Human rights in Northern Ireland : Ireland versus the United Kingdom. Summer 1980. p. 377-432. Boston College International and Comparative Law Review. ; 3.

5331. Dupont, F. La securite contre les libertes : Le modele ouest-allemand modele pour l'Europe. - Paris : EDI, 1970. 301 p
On the growing state surveillance of citizens in the German Federal Republic and its implications for Europe.

5332. Enzensberger, H.M. * Michel, K.M. Folter in der BRD. - Berlin : Rotbuch Verlag, 1973. Kursbuch. ; 32.

5333. Faul, D. * Murray, R. * (comp.) British army and special branch RUC brutalities, Dec. 1971- Febr. 1972. - Dungannon : St. Patrick's Academy, 1972. 78 p

5334. Faul, D. * Murray, R. The RUC: the black and blue book. - Dungannon : St. Patrick's Academy, 1975. 108 p
Roman Catholic viewpoints on alleged brutality by Royal Ulster Constabulary special branch 1971-1972.

5335. Faul, D. S.A.S. terrorism. - Dungannon : 1976.
Roman Catholic viewpoints on alleged brutality by Royal Ulster Constabulary 1969-1975 against suspected terrorists.

5336. Fillet, H. Uitsluiting van verdedigers in de Bondsrepubliek Duitsland. Sept. 1975. p. 525-536. Ars Aequi

5337. Font, H. Yo fui torturado y secuestrado por una democracia. - Madrid : Editorial Finhaxel, 1983. 192 p

5338. Freund, W.S. Am Rande des Terrors. 1977. p. 366-380. Die Dritte Welt. ; 4.
West Germany; effect of anti- terrorism measures on intellectual climate.

5339. Frostmann, H.M. International political terrorism and the approaching emergence of the authoritarian state. 1981. 146 p

5340. Gollwitzer, H. * Menne, A. Les nouvelles restrictions aux libertes en Allemagne de l'Ouest. March 1978. Le monde diplomatique

5341. Haasbroek, N. * et al. Brochure naar aanleiding van de radioserie van Nico Haasbroek over de Rote Armee Fraktion door de VPRO-radio uitgezonden in 6 afleveringen van 5 augustus tot en met 23 september <1977>. - Hilversum : Het Gooi, 1977. 49 p

5342. Hansen, K.H. Gegen Terror - fuer mehr Demokratie. 1978. ; Unpublished On German anti-terrorist legislation by SPD member of parliament.

5343. Heldmann, H.H. Die neue Ordnung unserer Sicherheit oder: die Gewoehnung an den Polizeistaat. - Weinheim : 1973. p. 103-112. Vorgaenge. ; 12:2.

5344. Horowitz, I.L. Civil liberties dangers in antiterrorist policies. March 1977. p. 25-32. Civil Liberties Review

5345. Horowitz, I.L. Transnational terrorism, civil liberties, and social science. - New York : John Jay Press, 1977. p. 283-297.
In: S.M. Finger and Y. Alexander (eds.), Terrorism: interdisciplinary perspectives

5346. Klare, M.T. Operation Phoenix and the failure and pacification in South Vietnam. May 1973. p. 21-27. Liberation. ; 17:9.

5347. Koch, P. * Oltmanns, R. SOS Freiheit in Deutschland. - Hamburg : Gruner & Jahr, 1979. 272 p

5348. Lehning, A. * Wielek, H. * Bakker-Schut, P.H. Duitsland: voorbeeld of waarschuwing : West-duitsland een politiestaat of de geschiedenis herhaalt zich. - Baarn : Wereldvenster, 1976. 83 p

5349. Lowry, D.R. Draconian powers: the new British approach to pretrial detention of suspected terrorists. 1977. p. 185-222. Columbia Human Rights Law Review. ; 9.

5350. Lowry, D.R. Ill-treatment, brutality and torture: some thoughts upon the "treatment" of Irish political prisoners. 1973. p. 553. DePaul Law Review. ; 22.

5351. Lowry, D.R. Terrorism and human rights : Counter-insurgency and necessity at common law. Oct. 1977. p. 49-89. Notre Dame lawyer. ; 53.

5352. Mack, A. Terrorism and the left. p. 18-31. Arena. ; 51.

5353. Mahler, H. Wie westberliner Staatsanwaelte den Landfrieden wieder herstellen und das Recht brechen : Eine dokumentarische Studie ueber die praktische Verwirklichung des Gleichheits-Grundsatzes in Westberlin.

5354. McGuffin, J. The Guinea pigs. - Harmondsworth : Penguin, 1974.
On torture in Northern Ireland by the British.

5355. Meulen, J.S.van der Anti-terrorisme wetten in de BRD. Nov. 1977. p. 54-57. Wetenschap en Samenleving. ; 77:9-10.
Plus various other related articles, also on Italy.

5356. Nicolas, E. * Tongeren, P.van * et al. Repressie in Nederland. - Amsterdam : Van Gennep, 1980. 264 p

5357. O'Boyle, M. Torture and emergency power under the European convention on human rights : Ireland vs. the United Kingdom. Oct. 1977. p. 674-706. American Journal of International Law. ; 71:4.

5358. Palermo, I. Condanna preventiva : Cronaca di un clamoroso caso giudiziario che si vuol dimenticare, il 7 aprile. - Napoli : T. Pironti, 1982. 161 p

5359. Rauch, E. The compatability of the Detention of Terrorists Order (Northern Ireland) with the European convention for the protection of human rights. 1973. p. 1. New York University Journal of International Law and Politics. ; 6.

5360. Rueter, C.F. Een "Lex Baader-Meinhof"?. June 1975. p. 327-350. Delikt en delinkwent

5361. Ruthven, M. Torture : The grand conspiracy. - London : Weidenfeld & Nicolson, 1978. 342 p

5362. Schlesinger, Ph. On the shape and scope of counter-insurgency thought. - London : Croom Helm, 1978. p. 98-127.
In: G. Littlejohn et al. (eds.), Power and the state

5363. Scorer, C. * Hewitt, P. The prevention of terrorism act : The case for repeal. - London : National Council for Civil Liberties, 1981.

5364. Scorer, C. The prevention of terrorism's acts 1974-1976: a report on the operation of the law. - London : National Council for Civil Liberties, 1976. 39 p

5365. Shackleton, E.A.A. Review of the operation on the prevention of terrorism : Temporary provision acts 1974 and 1976. - London : HMSO, 1978. 88 p

5366. Sonnemann, U. * (ed.) Der misshandelte Rechtsstaat in Erfahrung und Urteil bundesdeutscher Schriftsteller, Rechtsanwaelte und Richter. - Koeln : 1977.

5367. Taylor, P. Beating the terrorist? : Interrogation in Omagh, Gough and Castlereagh. - Harmondsworth : Penguin, 1980.

5368. Weiss, P. Joe McCarthy is alive and well and living in West Germany: terror and counter-terror in the Federal Republic. 1976. p. 61-88. New

York University Journal of International Law and Politics. ; 9.

5369. Wildhorn, S. * et al. Intelligence constraints of the 1970s and domestic terrorism. - 2 vols. - Santa Monica, Calif. : RAND, 1982. 179 pp.; 155 p

5370. Wright, S. An assessment of the new technologies of repression. - Abridged. - Amsterdam : Swets & Zeitlinger, 1977. p. 133-166.
In: M. Hoefnagels (ed.), Repression and repressive violence

5371. _____ "Bommi" Baumann. Wie alles anfing : Beslagnahmt. Diskussion ueber das Buch: "Wie alles anfing". - Muenchen : Trikont, 1976. 35 p

5372. _____ Anti-Terror-Gesetze; Russell-Tribunal. - Frankfurt a.M. : Unterbezirksausschuss d. Frankfurter Jungsozialisten, 1978. 47 p

5373. _____ Civil war in Rhodesia : Abduction, torture and death in the counterinsurgency campaign. - Salisbury : 1976. 102 p.
Catholic Commission for Justice and Peace in Rhodesia

5374. _____ Derechos humanos y ley antiterrorista. - Lima, Peru : Servicios Populares, 1982. 51 p

5375. _____ Europees verdrag tegen terrorisme : Dokumentatie. - Amsterdam : 1979. 63 p.
Komitee voor de Rechtsstaat. * (ed.)

5376. _____ FBI counterintelligence programs : Hearings. - Washington, D.C. : GPO, 1974. 47 p.
U.S. Congress, House. Committee on the judiciary ; 93rd. Cong., 2nd sess
On COINTELPRO operations against "extremists".

5377. _____ Hat sich die Republik verandert?. - Bonn : Arbeitsstab Offentlichkeitsarbeit gegen Terrorismus im Bundesministerium des Innern, 1978. 285 p

5378. _____ Het Europees verdrag ter bestrijding van het terrorisme: een kwestie van vertrouwen? : Bijzonder nummer van Nederlands Juristencomite voor de Mensenrechten. Dec. 1977. 35 p

5379. _____ Informatiebulletin Repressie. - Utrecht : MJC, 1977.
Medisch Juridisch Comite voor Politieke Gevangenen * Rood Verzetsfront
On European convention to fight terrorism.

5380. _____ Konterrevolution in der BRD : Ein Handbuch zur Entwicklung der inneren Sicherheit. - Zuerich : Eco-Verlag, 1976. 119 p.
Internationales Arbeiterarchiv

5381. _____ Nach Schleyer - Sonderkommandos in der BRD : Zugiger Ausbau der neuen Gestapo. - Hamburg : Reents, 1978. 236 p.
Kommunistenbund
Documents activities of state security organs. This book has been confiscated under p. 88a of the penal code.

5382. _____ Report of an aid mission to Northern Ireland 28 November - 6 December 1977. - London : 1978. 72 p.
Amnesty International

5383. _____ Terreur. - Utrecht : Vredesopbouw, Oct. 1977. 24 p
On the European convention against terrorism and the Dutch antiterrorist legislation (W.H. Nagel) and the Dutch commission nonviolent conflict resolution (H.W. Tromp).

5384. _____ Uruguay, seguridad nacional y carceles politicas. - Madrid : IEPALA, 1984. 167 p

5385. _____ Zwartboek Assen, september 1977. - Rotterdam : Ordeman, 1977.
Landelijk Comite Zuid-Molukken
On the trial of the De Punt train hijackers and a police weapon search in South Moluccan communities.

T. SPECIAL FORMS OF TERRORISM

T.1.1. Assassination

5386. Abrahamsen, D. The murdering mind. - New York : Harper Colophon, 1973. 245 p

5387. Agirre, J. Operation Ogro: the execution of admiral Luis Carrero Blanco. - New York : Quadrangle, 1975. 196 p
A journalist interviews the four ETA members who killed the Spanish chief of government, Carrero Blanco, on Dec. 20, 1973. - the original edition: Operacion Ogro. Como y por que ejecutamos a Carrero Blanco, was published in Paris, Ed. Ruedo Iberico, 1974.

5388. Bebel, A. Attentate und Socialdemokratie. - Berlin : 1905.

5389. Bell, J.B. Assassin!. - New York : St. Martin's Press, 1979. 310 p

5390. Bornstein, J. The politics of murder. - New York : William Sloine Associates, 1950.

5391. Bremer, A.H. An assassin's diary. - New York : Harper's Magazine Press, 1973.

5392. Camellion, R. Assassination : Theory and practice. - Boulder, Colo. : Paladin Enterprises, 1977. 161 p

5393. Cassidy, W.L. Planned political assassinations : An introductory overview. - Gaithersburg, Md. : IACP., 29 p

5394. Charters, D. Assassination and sabotage revived : Toward a redefinition of terrorism. ; Paper for the 1986 terrorism conference at the University of Aberdeen

5395. Clague, P. Iron spearhead : The true story of a communist killer squad in Singapore. - Singapore : Heinemann Educational Books, 1980. 153 p

5396. Crotty, W.J. * (ed.) Assassination and the political order. - New York : Harper & Row, 1971. 562 p

5397. Crotty, W.J. Presidential assassinations. - New Brunswick, N.J. : Transaction Books, 1973. p. 189-213.
In: J.F. Short (ed.), Modern criminals

5398. Demaret, P. * Plume, Chr. Target De Gaulle. - New York : Dial, 1975.

5399. Dinges, J. * Landau, S. Assassination on Embassy Row. - New York : Pantheon Books, 1980. 411 p
Leftist account of the assassination of Orlando Letelier.

5400. Donoghue, M.A. Assassination : Murder in politics. - Canoga Park, Calif. : Major Books, 1979.

5401. Donovan, R.J. The assassins. - New York : Harper, 1952.

5402. Duncan, E. Terrorist attacks on US official personnel abroad. April 1981. p. 34-37. Department of State Bulletin. ; 81.

5403. Ellis, A. * Gullo, J. Murder and assassination. - New York : Stuart Lyle, 1971.

5404. Fine, S. Anarchism and the assassination of McKinley. July 1955. p. 777-799. American Historical Review. ; 60.

5405. Ford, F.L. Political murder : From tyrannicide to terrorism. - Cambridge, Mass. : Harvard University Press, 1985. 440 p

5406. Gribble, L. Hands of terror: notable assassinations of the 20th century. - London : Frederik Miller, 1960.

5407. Gross, F. Political assassination. - Westport, Conn. : Greenwood Press, 1978. p. 307-315.
In: M. Livingston et al. (eds.), International terrorism in the contemporary world

5408. Havens, M.C. * Leiden, C. * Schmitt, K.M. The politics of assassination. - Englewood Cliffs, N.J. : Prentice-Hall, 1970.
Revised ed.: Assassination and terrorism: their modern dimensions, 1975.

5409. Henze, P.B. Origins of the plot to kill the Pope. Autumn 1983. p. 3-20. Washington Quarterly. ; 6.

5410. Herzog, W. Barthou. - Zuerich : 1938.

5411. Horowitz, I.L. Assassination. - New York : Harper and Row, 1972.

5412. Howard, D.R. Political assassinations : Towards an analysis of political crime. 1977. Series SSS

5413. Hurwood, B.J. Society and the assassin: a background book on political murder. - New York : Parent's Magazine Press, 1970. 240 p

5414. Hyams, E. Killing no murder: a study of assassination as a political means. - London : Nelson, 1970.

5415. Jenkins, B.M. Diplomats on the front line. - Santa Monica, Calif. : RAND, 1982. 11 p. RAND Paper Series. ; P-6749.

5416. Joesten, J. De Gaulle and his murders. - Isle of Man : Times Press, 1964.

5417. Kelly, J.B. Assassination in wartime. Oct. 1965. p. 101. Military Law Review. ; 30.

5418. Kirkham, J.F. * Levy, S. * Crotty, W.J. Assassination and political violence : A staff report to the National commission on the causes and prevention of violence. - New York : Bantam, 1970. 580 p
Orig. Washington, D.C.: GPO, 1969.

5419. Lacasagne, A. l'Assassinat du president Carnot. - Paris-Lyon : 1894.

5420. Laney, R.B. Political assassination: the history of an idea. - Ann Arbor, Mich. : University Microfilms, 1966.

5421. Lerner, M. Assassination. - New York : 1933.
In: Encyclopedia of the social sciences

5422. Levy, S.G. Political assassination and the theory of reduced alternatives. 1971. p. 75-92. Peace Research Society Papers. ; 17.

5423. Lewis, P. Old soldiers never die : Alexander Haig assassination attempt. July 1979. p. 18-19. MacLeans. ; 42.

5424. Liman, P. Der politische Mord im Wandel der Geschichte : Eine historisch-psychologische Studie. - Berlin : 1912.

5425. Marshall, J. The twentieth century vehme: terror by assassination. June 1945. p. 421-425. Blackwood's Magazine. ; 257.

5426. McConnell, B. The history of assassination. - London : Frewin, 1969.

5427. McKinley, J. Assassination in America. - New York : Harper and Row, 1976.
Historical account of the (attempted) murders of 12 national figures.

5428. Melady, T.P. * Kikoski, J.F. The attempted assassination of the Pope. Winter 1985. p. 775-801. Orbis. ; 28.

5429. Middendorff, W. Der politische Mord. - Wiesbaden : 1968.

5430. Milicevic, V. Der Koenigsmord von Marseille. - Bad Godesberg : 1959.

5431. Miller, T. Assassination please almanac. - Chicago, Ill. : Contemporary Books, 1977.
Facts about assassinations.

5432. Mindt, R. Assassins and murderers: a comparison. Febr. 1976. p. 2-17. Monatsschrift fuer Kriminologie und Strafrechtsreform. ; 59.

5433. Perez, F.H. Terrorist target : The diplomat. - Washington, D.C. : US Department of State, Bureau of Public Affairs, 1982. 4 p. Current Policy. ; 402.

5434. Plat, W. Attentate : Eine Sozialgeschichte des politischen Mordes. - Dusseldorf/Wien : 1982.

5435. Raper, A. The tragedy of lynching. - Chapel Hill : University of North Carolina Press, 1933.

5436. Rapoport, D.C. Assassination and terrorism. - Toronto : Canadian Broadcasting System, 1971. 88 p

5437. Remak, J. Sarajevo. - London : 1959.

5438. Scherer, J.L. The plot to kill the Pope. 1985. p. 351-365. Terrorism. ; 7:4.

5439. Schorr, D. The assassins. 13 Oct. 1977. p. 14-22. New York Review of Books. ; 24:16.

5440. Snitch, T.H. Assassinations and political violence 1968-1978 : An events data approach. - Washington, D.C. : American University, 1980. ; Mimeo

5441. Snitch, T.H. Terrorism and political assassinations : A transnational assessment, 1968-80. 1982. p. 54-68. The Annals. ; 463.

5442. Sparrow, J.G. The great assassins. - New York : Arco, 1969. 207 p
Sketches major assassinations in history.

5443. Taylor, R.L. * Weisz, A.E. American presidential assassination. - Boston : Little, Brown & Co., 1970. p. 291-307. In: D.N. Daniels, M.F. Gigula and F.M. Ochberg (eds.), Violence and the struggle for existence

5444. Tessendorf, K.C. Kill the tsar. - New York : Atheneum, 1986. 128 p

5445. Truby, J.D. How terrorists kill: the complete terrorist arsenal. - Boulder, Colo. : Paladin, 1978. 87 p

5446. Whittier, Ch.H. Assassination in theory and practice: a historical survey of the religious and philosophical background of the doctrine of tyrannicide. - Washington, D.C. : Library of Congress, Congressional Research Service, 12 April 1978.

5447. Wilde, H. Der politische Mord. - Bayreuth : 1962.

5448. Wilkinson, D.Y. Political assassins and status incongruence: a sociological interpretation. 1970. p. 400-412. British Journal of Sociology. ; 21:4.

5449. Wilson, C. Encyclopedia of modern murder, 1962-82. - New York : Putman, 1985. 279 p

5450. Zentner, Chr. Den Dolch im Gewande : Politischer Mord durch 2 Jahrtausende. - Muenchen : Suedwest Verlag, 1968. 223 p

5451. _____ Alleged assassination plots involving foreign leaders : An interim report. - Washington, D.C. : GPO, 1975. 349 p.
U.S. Congress, Senate. Committee on governmental operations for intelligence activity ; 94th. Cong., 1st session. ; 94-465.
On Congo, Cuba, Dominican Republic, Vietnam, Chile, involvement of CIA.

5452. _____ Background documentation relating to the assassinations of ambassador Cleo A. Noel jr. and George Curtis Moore. - Washington, D.C. : 1973.
U.S. Department of State, Bureau of Public Affairs

5453. _____ Implementation of the Helsinki accords : The assassination attempt on Pope John Paul II. - Washington, D.C. : GPO, 1983. 29 p.
U.S. Congress. Commission on Security and Cooperation in Europe ; Hearing, 97th Cong., 2nd sess., 23 Sept. 1982

5454. _____ Report. - 6 vols. - New Delhi : 1970.
Commission of Inquiry into the conspiracy to murder Mahatma Gandhi

5455. _____ The lost significance of Shiran's case. - Los Angeles : 1969.
Organization of Arab Students
On the murder of Robert Kennedy.

T.1.2. Bombing

5456. Ariel, D. Explosion!. - Tel Aviv : Olive Books, 1972.

5457. Bennett, R.K. Brotherhood of the bomb. Dec. 1970. p. 102-106. Reader's Digest

5458. Brodie, T.G. Bombs and bombings : A handbook to detection, disposal and investigation for police and fire departments. - Springfield, Ill. : Thomas, 1975.

5459. Clutterbuck, R.L. Bombs in Britain. Jan. 1975. p. 279-290. Army Quarterly. ; 55.

5460. Gibson, B. The Birmingham bombs. - Chichester : Rose, 1976. 164 p

5461. Harris, F. The bomb. - Chicago : 1963. ; Reissue
Orig. New York, 1920.

5462. Ikle, F.C. The social impact of bomb destruction. - Norman : University of Oklahoma Press, 1958.

5463. Karber, Ph.A. Insurgency without revolution: terrorist bombings in the United States. ; Paper presented before the annual convention of the American Sociological Association, Sept. 1972

5464. Lewald, Ch.E. Fundamentals of incendiarism for raiders and saboteurs, and for planning measures. - Washington, D.C. : Research Analysis Corporation, 1956.

5465. MacDonald, J.M. Bombers and firesetters. - Springfield, Ill. : Thomas, 1977.

5466. Packe, M.St.J. The bombs of Orsini. - London : 1957.
French 19th century terrorism.

5467. Powell, W. The anarchist cookbook. - New York : Lyle Stuart, 1971. 160 p

5468. Stoffel, J. Explosives and homemade bombs. - 2nd ed. - Springfield, Ill. : Thomas, 1973. 324 p

5469. Styles, G. Bombs have no pity. - London : Luscombe, 1975.

5470. Styles, G. The car bomb. - London : April 1975. p. 93-97. Journal of the Forensic Science Society

5471. _____ Behind the terror bombings. 30 March 1970. p. 15. U.S. News & World Report

5472. _____ Beirut tragedy: "a new crowd in town" and Beirut casualties : Care and identification. - Washington, D.C. : GPO, 1983. 14 p.
U.S. Congress. House. Delegation to Beirut ; Report together with supplemental views of the Delegation to Beirut of the Committee on Armed Services and Committee on Veterans' Affairs, House of

5473. _____ Bomb plots: warning on terror war. 26 Oct. 1970. p. 36. U.S. News & World Report

5474. _____ Bomb research center. - New York : 8 Dec. 1971. Morning Telegraph

5475. _____ Bomb summary : A comprehensive report of incidents involving explosive and incendiary devices in the nation. - Washington, D.C. : U.S. Department of Justice, 1972.
FBI. FBI Uniform Crime Reports

5476. _____ Bomb threats. Oct. 1974. p. 21. Environment

5477. _____ Bomb threats against U.S. airports, 1974. - Washington, D.C. : 1975.
U.S. Department of Transportation, Civil Aviation Security Service

5478. _____ Bombing incidents - 1972. April 1972. p. 21. FBI Law Enforcement Bulletin

5479. _____ Boobytraps. - Boulder, Colo. : Paladin Press, 1979. 133 p.
U.S. Department of the Army

5480. _____ Death comes in small parcels. Dec. 1971. p. 56. Economist

5481. _____ Explosives and demolitions. - Boulder, Colo. : Paladin Enterprises, 1967.
U.S. Department of the Army

5482. _____ How Israelis started the terror by post. - London : 24 Sept. 1962. p. 3-11. The Sunday Times

5483. _____ Improvised munitions/black books. - 2 vols. - Boulder, Colo. : Paladin Press, 1979.

Frankfort Arsenal

5484. _____ Letter bombs : How to recognize them. 14 Dec. 1973. p. 15-16. TIG Brief. ; 25.

5485. _____ New Arab terror - murder by mail. 2 Oct. 1972. p. 31. Newsweek

5486. _____ New way to war on innocents: Swissair crash. 9 March 1970. p. 32. Newsweek. ; 75.

5487. _____ Report. - Washington, D.C. : GPO, 1983.
DOD Commission on Beirut International Airport Terrorism Act, Oct. 23, 1983

5488. _____ Terror through the mails: the bombs posted in Amsterdam leave a trail that stretches back to the core of the Palestine guerrilla movement. 23 Sept. 1972. p. 15-16. Economist

5489. _____ Terrorist explosive handbook : Vol.1: the Irish Republican Army. - Boulder, Colo. : Paladin Press., 31 p
Described as a concise up-to-date intelligence report on IRA bombings.

5490. _____ Terroristic activity. Hearings : Part 7: terrorist bombings and law enforcement intelligence. - Washington, D.C. : GPO, 1976. p. 497-605.
U.S. Congress, Senate. Committee on the judiciary ; 94th Cong., 1st sess
Mostly on Weather Underground, with many documents.

5491. _____ The U.S. Embassy bombing in Beirut. - Washington, D.C. : GPO, 1983. 25 p.
U.S. Congress. House. Committee on Foreign Affairs. Subcommittee on International Operations ; Hearing before the Committee on Foreign Affairs and its Subcommittees on International Operations and on Europe and the Middle East of the House of

T.1.3. Hijacking and hostage taking

5492. Aggarwala, N. Political aspects of hijacking. 1971. p. 7-27. International Conciliation. ; 585.

5493. Alix, E.K. Ransom kidnapping in America, 1874-1974 : The creation of a capital crime. - Carbondale : Southern Illinois University Press, 1978.

5494. Andel, W.M.van Gijzelingsdrama vraagt om politieke en principiele bezinning. 19 Oct. 1974. Nederlandse Gedachten

5495. Arenberg, G. Hostage. - Washington, D.C. : American Police Academy, 1974.

5496. Arey, J.A. The sky pirates. - New York : Scribner's, 1972. 418 p
Appendix A, pp. 314-414, includes inventary of skyjackings, 1930-1972.

5497. Aston, C.C. Governments to ransom: the emergence of political hostage- taking as a form of crisis. - Westport, Conn. : Greenwood Press, 1982.

5498. Aston, C.C. Hostage-taking: an overview. - London : MacMillan Press, 1980.
In: D. Carlton and C. Schaerf (eds.), The age of terror

5499. Aston, C.C. Political hostage taking in Western Europe. - New York : Pergamon, 1980.
In: S. Sloan and R. Schultz (eds.), Responding to the terrorist threat: prevention and control

5500. Atala, Ch. Le "hijacking" aerien ou la maitrise illicite d'aeronef hier, aujourd'hui, demain. - Ottawa : 1973. 119 p

5501. Baccelli, G.R. Pirateria aerea: realta effettiva e disciplina giuridica. 1970. p. 150-160. Diretto aereo. ; 9:35.

5502. Baldwin, D.A. Bargaining with airline hijackers. - New York : Doubleday, 1976. p. 404-429.
In: W. Zartman (ed.), The 50 percent solution

5503. Blacksten, R. * Engler, R. Hostage studies. - Arlington : Ketron, 1974.
Offers theoretical models of political kidnappings based on game anddecision-making theories.

5504. Blair, E. Odyssey of terror. - Nashville : Broadman Press, 1977. 316 p
On hijacking.

5505. Bolz jr, F.A. Hostage confrontation and rescue. - Stanford, Calif. : Hoover, 1979. p. 393-404.
In: R.H. Kupperman and D.M. Trent (eds.), Terrorism

5506. Bongert, Y. * Kellens, G. * Leaute, J. * Schaub, S. * Grebing, G. * Lafon, J. * Taillanter, R.le Taking hostages. - Paris : Neret, 1975. 84 p

5507. Brenchley, F. Living with terrorism : The problem of air piracy. - London : ISC, 1986. 17 p. Conflict Studies. ; 184.

5508. Bristow, A.P. Preliminary [statistical] research on hostage situations. March 1977. p. 73-77. Law and Order. ; 25:3.

5509. Burris, J.B. A study of aerial hijacking. - Maxwell Air Force Base, Ala. : Air Command and Staff College, Air University, 1972. 39 p

5510. Cassidy, W.L. Political kidnapping. - Boulder, Colo. : Sycamore Island Books, 1978. 47 p

5511. Clyne, P. An anatomy of skyjacking. - London : Abelard-Shuman, 1973. 200 p
Categorizes six categories of skyjackers.

5512. Cocca, A.A. Hacia una tipificacion del delito de apoderamiento de aeronave en vuelo. 1969. p. 279-286. Terceras Jornadas

5513. Connolly, C. Herrema. Siege at Monastervin. - Dublin : Olympic Press, 1977. 114 p
On IRA kidnapping of Dutch industrialist.

5514. Cooper, H.H.A. Pacta sunt servanda: good faith negotiations with hostage takers. - Gaithersburg, Md. : IACP, 1977.

5515. Cooper, H.H.A. The hostage-takers. - Boulder, Colo. : Paladin Press, 1981. 100 p

5516. Cramer, Ch. * Harris, J. Hostage. - London : John Clare, 1982. 213 p
By two BBC TV newsmen taken hostage in the Iranian Embassy in Londonon 30 April 1980.

5517. Crelinsten, R.D. * Szabo, D. Hostage taking. - Lexington, Mass. : Lexington Books, 1979. 160 p

5518. Dalia, A.A. I sequestri di persona a scopo di estorsione, terrorismo od eversione. - Milano : Giuffre, 1980. 219 p

5519. Eisenkolb, G. Das Kommando "Muenchen Schalom". - Wien : Molden, 1976. 316 p
Olympic Games 1972 incident.

5520. Elten, J.A. Flugzeug entfuehrt. - Muenchen : Goldman, 1972.

5521. Evans, A.E. Aerial hijacking. - Springfield, Ill. : Charles C. Thomas, 1974.
In: M.C. Bassiouni (ed.), International terrorism and political crimes

5522. Fariello, A. The phenomenon of hostage-taking: the Italian experience. - Lexington, Mass. : Lexington Books, 1979. p. 97-103.
In: R.D. Crelinsten and D. Szabo (eds.), Hostage-taking

5523. Fitzgerald, B.D. The analytical foundations of extortionate terrorism. 1978. p. 347-362. Terrorism. ; 1.

5524. Frackers, W. Organizational aspects of hostage-taking prevention and control in the Netherlands. - Lexington, Mass. : Lexington Books, 1979. p. 105-118.
In: R.D. Crelinsten and D. Szabo (eds.), Hostage-taking

5525. Hassel, C.V. * et al. Hostage-taking : Problems of prevention and control. - Montreal : ICCC, Oct. 1976.

5526. Hassel, C.V. The hostage situation: exploring the motivation and cause. Sept. 1975. p. 55-58. Police Chief. ; 42.

5527. Hawkins, G. Skyjacking. June 1975. p. 157-168. Australian Journal of Forensic Sciences. ; 7.

5528. Horvitz, J. Arab terrorism and international aviation. 1976. p. 145-154. Chitty's Law Journal. ; 24.

5529. Hubbard, D.G. Winning back the sky. - New York : W.W. Norton, 1986. 140 p

5530. Hughes, E. Terror on train 734; hostages taken by South Moluccan guerrillas. Aug. 1976. p. 64-69. Reader's Digest. ; 109.

5531. Jack, H.A. Hostages, hijacking and the Security Council. - New York : World Conference on Religion and Peace, 1976.

5532. Jacobson, P.M. From piracy on the high seas to piracy in the high skies: a study of aircraft hijacking. 1972. p. 161-187. Cornell International Law Journal. ; 5.

5533. Jenkins, B.M. * Johnson, J. * Ronfeldt, D. Numbered lives: some statistical observations from seventy-seven international hostage episodes. 1978. p. 71-111. Conflict. ; 1.

5534. Jenkins, B.M. Hostage survival: some preliminary observations. - Santa Monica, Calif. : RAND, April 1976. 16 p. RAND Paper. ; P-5627.

5535. Jenkins, B.M. Hostages and their captors: friends and lovers. - Santa Monica, Calif. : RAND, Oct. 1975. RAND Paper. ; P-5519.

5536. Kissinger, H.A. Hijacking, terrorism and war. 8 Sept. 1975. p. 360-361. Department of State Bulletin. ; 73.

5537. Kupperman, R.H. * Wilcox, R.H. * Smith, H.A. Crisis management: some opportunities. - Stanford, Calif. : Hoover, 1979. p. 224-243.
In: R.H. Kupperman and D.M. Trent (eds.), Terrorism

5538. Kwok, M.L. * Peterson, R.E. Political kidnapping: 1968-1973. 1974. Journal of Contemporary Revolutions. ; 6.

5539. Landes, W.M. An economic study of the U.S. aircraft hijacking, 1961-1976.

April 1978. p. 1-32. Journal of Law and Economics. ; 21.

5540. Lehmann, W. Boeing 727 entfuhrt : Ein Tatsachenbericht. - Berlin : Verlag Neues Leben, 1975. 159 p

5541. Loman, M. Train of terror. - Old Tappan, N.J. : Revell Co, 1978. 63 p
Memoirs of a Dutch hostage in train-hijacking.

5542. Marks, J.M. Hijacked. - Nashville : T. Nelson, 1973. 167 p

5543. McClintock, M.C. Skyjacking : Its domestic, civil and criminal ramifications. Winter 1973. p. 29-80. Journal of Air Law and Commerce. ; 39.

5544. McFadden, R.D. * Treaster, J. * Carroll, H. No hiding place : The New York Times inside report on the hostage crisis. - New York : Times Books, 1981.

5545. McGinley, G.P. The Achille Lauro affair - implications for international law. Summer 1985. p. 691-738. Tennessee Law Review. ; 52.

5546. Meyer, A. Internationale Luftfahrtabkommen : Band 4: Luftpiraterie - Begriff, Tatbestaende, Bekaempfung. - Koeln : Carl Heymanns Verlag, 1972. 245 p

5547. Miller, A.H. Hostage negotiations and the concept of transference. - Boulder, Colo. : Westview, 1979. p. 137-158.
In: Y. Alexander, D. Carlton and P. Wilkinson (eds.), Terrorism: theory and practice

5548. Miron, M.S. * Goldstein, A.P. Hostage. - Kalamazoo : Behaviordelia, 1978. 190 p

5549. Montreuil, J. La prise d'otages. Jan. 1974. p. 15-25. Revue internationale de criminologie et de police technique. ; 27:1.

5550. O'Donnell, J.J. Skyjacking : Problems and potential solutions. - Villanova, Pa. : Villanova University Press, 1973.

5551. Oren, U. Ninety-nine days in Damascus: the story of professor Shlomo Samueloff and the hijack of TWA flight 840 to Damascus. - London : Weidenfeld and Nicolson, 1970.

5552. Pepper, C.B. Kidnapped! : Seventeen days of terror. - New York : Harmony Books, 1978. 150 p
On a 1977 kidnapping, Milan, Italy.

5553. Phillips, D. Skyjack : The story of air piracy. - London : Harrap, 1973.

5554. Quandt, R.E. Some statistical characterizations of aircraft hijacking. 1974. p. 115-123. Accident Analysis and Prevention. ; 6.

5555. Reitsma, O. * Labeur, C. De gijzeling : Honderd uren machtloze kracht. - Amsterdam : Bonaventura, 1974. 160 p
Sept. 13, 1974 Japanese Red Army action against French embassy in Amsterdam.

5556. Rich, E. Flying scared: why we are being skyjacked and how to put a stop to it. - New York : Stein and Day, 1972.

5557. Salewski, W. Conduct and negotiations in hostage situations. 1977. Schriftenreihe der Polizei-Fuehrungsakademie. ; 4.
Also in: J.J. Kramer (ed.), International summaries: a collection of selected translations in law enforcement and criminal justice, vol. 3. Washington, D.C.: U.S. Department of Justice, National Criminal Justice Reference Service, 1979, pp. 98-104.

5558. Samuels, J.M. Hostage situations. - Gaithersburg, Md. : IACP., 18 p

5559. Sato, B. Hijack. - Los Angeles : Gateway Publications, 1975. 196 p

5560. Shelhoup, K.G. Extradition and political asylum as applied to aircraft piracy. Claremont Graduate School, 1979. ; Ph.D.dissertation

5561. Shepard, I.M. Air piracy: the role of the International Federation of Airline Pilots Associations. 1970. p. 79-91. Cornell International Law Journal. ; 3.

5562. Simon, D.W. * Rhone, R.S. * Perillo, M. Simulation of the seizure of heads of state. - Madison, N.J. : Drew University Department of Political Science., Jan. 1977. ; Mimeo

5563. Sloan, S. * Kearney, R. An analysis of a simulated terrorist incident. June 1977. p. 57-59. Police Chief. ; 44.

5564. Sloan, S. * Kearney, R. * Wise, Ch. Learning about terrorism: analysis, simulations, and future directions. 1978. p. 315-329. Terrorism. ; 1.

5565. Snow, P. * Phillips, D. The Arab hijack war. - New York : Ballantine, 1970. 176 p
Concentrates on the Sept. 1970 Dawson Field incident and the Jordanian civil war triggered off by it. Also published as: Leila's hijack war. London: Pan Books, 1971.

5566. Souchon, H. Hostage-taking: its evolution and significance. June-July 1976. p. 168-173. International Criminal Police Review. ; 299.

5567. Stech, F.J. Terrorism and threat communication. - Bethesda : Analytic Support Center, May 1978. ; Mimeo

5568. Stephen, J.E. Going south: air piracy and unlawful interference with air commerce. 1970. p. 433-443. International Lawyer. ; 4.

5569. Sundberg, J. Operation Leo : Description and analysis of a European terrorist operation. 1981. p. 197-232. Terrorism. ; 5:3.
On Stockholm seizure of West German embassy, 1976.

5570. Sundberg, J.W.F. Lawful and unlawful seizure of aircraft. 1978. p. 423-440. Terrorism. ; 1.

5571. Turi, R.T. * et al. Descriptive study of aircraft hijackings. - Huntsville, Texas : Institute of Contemporary Corrections and the Behavioral Sciences, 1972. 171 p. Criminal Justice Monographs. ; 3:5.

5572. Whelton, Ch. Skyjack. - New York : Tower Publications, 1970.

5573. White, E.T. Terrorism in civil aviation : A perennial world problem. - Maxwell Air Force Base, Ala. : Air Command and Staff College, Air University, 1974. 59 p

5574. _____ Aircraft hijacking : Hearings. - 91st Cong., 2nd sess. - Washington, D.C. : GPO, 1970. 199 p.
U.S. Congress, House, Committe on Foreign Affairs

5575. _____ Aircraft piracy - international terrorism : Hearings. - 96th Cong., 1st sess. - Washington, D.C. : GPO, 1979. 437 p.
U.S. Congress, House, Committee on Public Works and Transportation, Subcommittee on Aviation

5576. _____ Aviation safety and aircraft piracy. - Washington, D.C. : GPO, 1970. 488 p.
U.S. Congress, House. Committee on interstate and foreign commerce

5577. _____ Domestic and foreign aircraft hijackings [1931-1979]. - Washington, D.C. : 1979. 77 p.
U.S. Department of Transportation, Federal Aviation Administration

5578. _____ Domestic and foreign aircraft hijackings, as of July 1, 1976. - Washington, D.C. : 1976. 61 p.
U.S. Department of Transportation. Federal aviation administration
Updated version of 1 Jan. 1977, 63 pp.

5579. _____ Extortion. 1975. Asset Protection. ; 1.
Entire issue.

5580. _____ Hijack reference data. - Washington, D.C. : GPO, 1970. 29 p.
U.S. Department of Transportation, Federal Aviation Administration

5581. _____ Hijacking statistics : U.S. registered airport, 1961 - April 1975. - Washington, D.C. : 1975. 18 p.
U.S. Department of Transportation. Federal aviation administration

5582. _____ Hostage-negotiation response. - Gaithersburg, Md. : Professional Standards Division of the IACP, 1976. Training Key. ; No. 235.

5583. _____ On Attica : Official report. - New York : Bantam Books, 1972.
New York State Special Commission
On Sept. 1971 hostage taking incident in a New York prison.

5584. _____ Skyjacking : Hearing. - Washington, D.C. : GPO, 1970. 26 p.
U.S. Congress, Senate. Committee on finance ; 91st Cong., 2nd sess., 6 Oct 1970

5585. _____ Soviet airliner hijacked to Turkey. 1970. p. 6-7. Current Digest of the Soviet Press. ; 22.

5586. _____ The events of September 28 and 29, 1973 : A documentary report. - Vienna : 1973. 92 p.
Federal Chancellery of Austria
On the terrorist attack on a train carrying Soviet jews.

T.1.4. Kidnapping

5587. Alves, M.M. Kidnapped diplomats: Greek tragedy on a Latin stage. 1970. p. 311-314. Commonweal. ; 92.

5588. Arnau, F. Menschenraub : Alexander P. Katjepow, Berthold Jacob, Jesus de Galindez, Ben Bella, Adolf Eichmann, Antoine Argoud, Mehdi Ben Barka, Moise Tschombe, Komponist Isang Yun und andere. - Muenchen : 1968. 232 p

5589. Baumann, C.E. The diplomatic kidnappings: a revolutionary tactic of urban terrorism. - The Hague : Martinus Nijhoff, 1973. 182 p
22 cases of diplomatic kidnappings from the period 1968-1971 are discussed.

5590. Clutterbuck, R.L. Kidnapping. Oct. 1974. p. 529-534. Army Quarterly. ; 104.

5591. Cox, R.V. Deadly pursuit. - Harrisburg, Pa. : Cameron House, 1977.

5592. Fawcett, J.E.S. Kidnappings versus government protection. Sept. 1970. p. 359-362. World Today. ; 26.

5593. Geyer, G.A. The blood of Guatemala. 8 July 1968. p. 8-11. The Nation
On kidnapping of archbishop Mario Casariego.

5594. Hamilton, L.C. Political kidnapping. - Boulder : University of Colorado, 1976. ; Unpubl. paper

5595. Hunt, D. On the spot. - London : Peter Davies, 1975.
British ambassador to Brazil on diplonappers.

5596. Jenkins, B.M. Terrorism and kidnapping. June 1974. 10 p

5597. Mangham, W.D. Kidnapping for political ends. 1971. Seaford House Papers

5598. Melo, A.L. Le inviolabilidad diplomatica y el caso del embajador Von Spreti. 1970. p. 147-156. Revista de derecho internacional y ciencias diplomaticas. ; 19:37-38.

5599. Messick, H. * Goldblatt, B. Kidnapping: the illustrated history. - New York : Dial, 1974. 206 p
Journalistic treatment of major kidnappings.

5600. Middendorff, W. Menschenraub, Flugzeug-Entfuehrungen, Geiselnahme, Kidnapping : Historische und moderne Erscheinungsformen. - Bielefeld : Gieseking, 1972. 62 p

5601. Middendorff, W. New developments in the taking of hostages and kidnapping. - Washington, D.C. : National Criminal Justice Reference Service, 1975.
Offers a typology of kidnappers and takers of hostages, discusses personality of terrorist.

5602. Miller, G. 83 hours till dawn. - Garden City, N.Y. : Doubleday, 1971.

5603. Miller, G. Kidnapped at Chowchilla. - Plainfield, N.J. : Logos International, 1977. 181 p

5604. Moorehead, C. Fortune's hostages : A study of kidnapping in the world today. - London : Hamish Hamilton, 1980. 256 p
Traces historical antecedents of contemporary kidnapping wave.

5605. Najmuddin, D. Kidnapping of diplomatic personnel. Febr. 1973. p. 18, 20, 22, 23. Police Chief. ; 40:2.

5606. Navarro Olmedo, F. El secuestro de 60 milliones de dolares : El golpe maestro de los "Montoneros" victoria guerrillera en Argentina. - Mexico, D.F. : Editorial Posada, 1976. 151 p
On the kidnapping of Jorge and Juan Born, 19 Sept. 1974 in Argentina.

5607. O'Mara, R. New terror in Latin America: snatching the diplomats. 1970. p. 518-519. Nation. ; 210:17.

5608. Rose, R.N. New developments in the taking of hostages and kidnapping - a summary. - Washington, D.C. : Law Inforcement Assistance Administration, National Criminal Justice Reference Service, 1975. 9 p

5609. Sponsler, T.H. International kidnapping. Jan. 1971. p. 25-52. International Lawyer. ; 5.

5610. Stechel, I. Terrorist kidnapping of diplomatic personnel. Spring 1972. p. 189-217. Cornell Unternational Law Journal. ; 5.

5611. Tuchman, B. Perdicaris alive or Raisuli dead. Aug. 1959. American Heritage. ; 10:5.
On 1904 incident involving Morocco and USA.

5612. Vayrynen, R. Some aspects of theory and strategy of kidnapping. 1971. p. 3-21. Instant Research on Peace and Violence. ; 1:1.

5613. Vidal, D. Wave of abductions in Columbia creates climate of insecurity. 26 June 1978. p. A-6. New York Times

5614. _____ Die Entfuehrung aus unserer Sicht.
Bewegung 2 Juni 1975
On kidnapping of Peter Lorenz.

5615. _____ Kidnapping incidents. Dec. 1967. p. 24-33. Bulletin of the International Commission of Jurists

5616. _____ Political kidnappings. - Gaithersburg, Md. : 31 p.
IACP

5617. _____ Political kidnappings, 1968-1973. - Washington, D.C. : GPO, 1973. 54 p.
U.S. Congress, House. Committee on internal security ; 93rd Cong., 1st sess., 1 Aug. 1973

T.1.5. Nuclear terrorism

5618. Alexander, Y. * Ebinger, Ch. Political terrorism and energy : The threat and response. - New York : 1982.

5619. Bass, G. * Jenkins, B.M. * Keller, K. * Reinstedt, R. Motivations, capabilities and possible actions of potential criminal adversaries of U.S. nuclear programs. - Santa Monica, Calif. : RAND, 1982.

5620. Bass, G.V. A review of recent trends in international terrorism and nuclear incidents abroad. - Santa Monica, Calif. : Rand, 1983. 73 p

5621. Beckman, R.L. International terrorism : The nuclear dimension. 1986. p. 351-378. Terrorism. ; 8:4.

5622. Berard, S.P. Nuclear terrorism : More myth than reality. 1985. p. 30-36. Air University Review. ; 36:5.

5623. Beres, L.R. Apocalypse. - Chicago : University of Chicago Press, 1980.

5624. Beres, L.R. International terrorism and world order: the nuclear threat. 1977. p. 131-146. Stanford Journal of International Studies. ; 12.

5625. Beres, L.R. Terrorism and global security: the nuclear threat. - Boulder, Colo. : Westview Press, 1979. 225 p

5626. Beres, L.R. Terrorism and international security: the nuclear threat. March 1978. p. 73-89. Chitty's Law Journal. ; 26.

5627. Beres, L.R. Terrorism and nuclear threat in the Middle East. Jan. 1976. p. 27-29. Current History. ; 70:412.

5628. Beres, L.R. The nuclear threat of terrorism. 1976. p. 53-66. International Journal of Group Tensions. ; 6:1-2.

5629. Beres, L.R. The threat of nuclear terrorism in the Middle East. Jan. 1976. p. 1-15. Current History. ; 70:412.

5630. Beres, L.R. The threat of Palestinian nuclear terrorism in the Middle East. 1976. p. 48-56. International Problems. ; 15.

5631. Berkowitz, B.J. * et al. Superviolence: the civil threat of mass destruction weapons. - Santa Barbara, Calif. : ADCON Corporation, 1972.

5632. Berry, N.O. How Israel can avoid a nuclear threat. 30 April 1985. The Des Moines Register

5633. Billington, G.R. Nuclear terrorism. - Maxwell Air Force Base, Ala. : Air War College, Air University, 1975. 46 p

5634. Blair, B.G. * Brewer, G.D. The terrorist threat to world nuclear programs. Sept. 1977. p. 379-403. Journal of Conflict Resolution. ; 21:3.

5635. Blair, B.G. A proposal for analyzing the terrorist threat to U.S. nuclear programs. Yale University, 1976. ; Unpubl. manuscript

5636. Buchanan, J.R. * (ed.) Safeguards against the theft or diversion of nuclear materials. 1974. p. 513-619. Nuclear Safety. ; 15.

5637. Burnham, S. The threat to licensed nuclear facilities. - McLean, Va. : MITRE Corporation, 1975. 223 p. MITRE Technical Report. ; MTR-7022.

5638. Chester, C.V. Estimates of threats to the public from terrorist acts against nuclear facilities. Nov. 1976. p. 659-665. Nuclear Safety. ; 17.

5639. Clark, R.P. Coping with nuclear terrorism: the assessment of countermeasures. - Washington, D.C. : Brookings Institution, 1977.

5640. Cohen, B.L. The potentialities of terrorism. June 1976. p. 34-35. Bulletin of the Atomic Scientists. ; 32:6.

5641. Coleman, J.P. International safeguards against non-government nuclear theft: a study of legal inadequacies. 1976. p. 493-513. International Lawyer. ; 10.

5642. Comey, D.D. The perfect Trojan horse : The threat of nuclear terrorism. June 1976. p. 33-34. Bulletin of the Atomic Scientists. ; 32:6.

5643. Compert, D.C. * et al. Nuclear weapons and world politics : Alternatives for the future. - New York : McGraw-Hill, 1977. 370 p

5644. Corwin, A.J. Survey of terrorist capabilities, the threat to nuclear resources, and some recommended improvements for defensive security posture. - Wright Patterson Air Force Base, Ohio : U.S. Air Force Institute of Technology, 1977. 177 p. Report. ; AFIT-CI-77-66.

5645. Crenshaw, M. Defining future threats: terrorist and nuclear proliferation. - New York : John Jay Press, 1977. In: S.M. Finger and Y. Alexander (eds.), Terrorism: interdisciplinary perspectives

5646. Crenshaw, M. Incentives for terrorism. ; Paper presented to the Defense Nuclear Agency's 10th Annual symposium on the role of the behavioral sciences in physical security, Springfield, Virg

5647. DeNike, L.D. Radioactive malevolence. Febr. 1974. p. 16-20. Science and Public Affairs

5648. Douglas, J.H. The great nuclear power debate 1: a summary. Jan. 1976. p. 44-45. Science News. ; 109:3.

5649. Dumas, L.J. National security in the nuclear age. May 1976. p. 24-35. Bulletin of the Atomic Scientists. ; 32:5.

5650. Dunn, L.A. * Bracken, P. * Smernoff, B.J. Routes to nuclear weapons: aspects of purchase or theft. - Croton-on-Hudson, N.Y. : Hudson Institute,

April 1977.

5651. Flood, M. * White, R.G. Nuclear prospects. 1976.
Pamphlet on possibilities of nuclear terrorism in the United Kingdom.

5652. Flood, M. Nuclear sabotage. Oct. 1976. p. 29-36. Bulletin of the Atomic Scientists. ; 32.

5653. Frank, F. Nuclear terrorism and the escalation of international conflict. Fall 1976. p. 12-27. Naval War College Review. ; 29.

5654. Friedlander, R.A. The ultimate nightmare : What if terrorists go nuclear?. Fall 1982. p. 1-11. Denver Journal of International Law and Policy. ; 12.

5655. Gallois, P. The balance of terror. - Boston : Houghton Mifflin, 1961.

5656. Hirsch, D. * Murphy, S. * Ramberg, B. Protecting reactors from terrorists. March 1986. p. 22-25. Bulletin of the Atomic Scientists. ; 42:3.

5657. Hoffman, B. * et al. A reassessment of potential adversaries to U.S. nuclear programs. - Santa Monica, Calif. : RAND, 1986. 29 p

5658. Hoffman, B. Terrorism in the United States and the potential threat to nuclear facilities. - Santa Monica, Calif. : RAND, 1986. 56 p

5659. Ingram, T.H. Nuclear hijacking now within the grasp of any bright lunatic. Jan. 1973. p. 20-28. Washington Monthly. ; 4.

5660. Janke, P. Nuclear terrorism. - Boulder, Colo. : Westview Press, 1977. p. 103-112.
In: Royal United Service Institution for Defence Studies (ed.), RUSI and Brassey's defence yearbook 1977- 78

5661. Jenkins, B.M. * Krofcheck, J. The potential nuclear non-state adversary. ; Report prepared for the congress of the U.S. Office of Technology Assessment, May 1977

5662. Jenkins, B.M. * Rubin, A.P. New vulnerabilities and the acquisition of new weapons by nongovernment groups. - Washington, D.C. : American Society of International Law, 1977.
In: A.E. Evans and J.F. Murphy (eds.), Legal aspects of international terrorism

5663. Jenkins, B.M. International cooperation in locating and recovering stolen materials. 1983. p. 561-575. Terrorism. ; 6:4.

5664. Jenkins, B.M. Nuclear terrorism and its consequences. July 1980. p. 5-16. Society

5665. Jenkins, B.M. Terrorism and the nuclear safeguards issue. - Santa Monica, Calif. : RAND, 1976. 7 p. RAND Paper. ; P-5611.

5666. Jenkins, B.M. Terrorism and the nuclear safeguards issue. - Santa Monica, Calif. : RAND, Jan. 1975. RAND Paper. ; P-5339.

5667. Jenkins, B.M. The consequences of nuclear terrorism. - Santa Monica, Calif. : RAND, 1979.

5668. Jenkins, B.M. The impact of nuclear terrorism. - Santa Monica, Calif. : RAND, 1978.

5669. Jenkins, B.M. The potential for nuclear terrorism. - Santa Monica, Calif. : RAND, May 1977. 9 p. RAND Paper. ; P-5876.

5670. Jenkins, B.M. Will terrorists go nuclear?. - Santa Monica, Calif. : RAND, Nov. 1975. 12 p. RAND Paper. ; P-5339.

5671. Jungk, R. De atoomstaat. - Amsterdam : Elsevier, 1978. 176 p

5672. Karber, Ph.A. * et al. Draft working paper B: analysis of the terrorist threat to the commercial nuclear industry : Summary of findings. - Vienna, Va. : BDM Corporation, 1975. ; BDM/W-75-176-TR.

5673. Karber, Ph.A. * et al. Draft working paper C: analysis of the terrorist threat to the commercial nuclear industry : Supporting appendices. - Vienna, Va. : BDM Corporation, 1975. ; BDM/W-75-176-TR.

5674. Karber, Ph.A. * Mengel, R.W. * Novotny, E.J.S. A behavioral analysis of the terrorist threat to nuclear installations. Sandia Laboratories, July 1974. ; Unpubl. manuscript prepared for the U.S. Atomic Energy Commission

5675. Karber, Ph.A. * Mengel, R.W. * Greisman, H.C. * Newman, G.S. * Novotny, E.J.S. * Whitley, A.G. Analysis of the terrorist threat to the commercial nuclear industry : Report submitted to the special safeguards study, Nuclear Regulatory Commission, in response to contract no. AT(49-24)- 0131. - Vienna, Va. : BDM Corporation, 1975. 414 p. ; BDM/75-176-TR.

5676. Kinderman, E.M. * et al. The unconventional nuclear threat. - Stanford, Calif. : Stanford Research Institute, Menlo Park, 1969.

5677. Kinderman, E.M. Plutonium: home made bombs?. - Washington, D.C. : GPO, 1975. p. 25-26.
In: U.S. Senate committee on government operations (ed.), Peaceful nuclear

exports and weapons proliferation

5678. Krieger, D.M. Nuclear power: a Trojan horse for terrorists. - Cambridge : MIT Press for the Stockholm International Peace Research Institute, 1974. p. 187-200.
In: B. Jasani (ed.), Nuclear proliferation problems

5679. Krieger, D.M. Terrorists and nuclear technology: the danger is great; the question is not whether the worst will happen, but where and how. June 1975. p. 28-34. Bulletin of the Atomic Scientists. ; 31:6.

5680. Krieger, D.M. What happens if..? : Terrorists, revolutionaries, and nuclear weapons. 1977. p. 44-57. The Annals of the American Academy of Political and Social Science. ; 430.

5681. Kuipers, M. Nucleair terrorisme. - Groningen : Polemologisch Instituut., 28 p ; Unpubl. paper

5682. Kupperman, R.H. * et al. Mass destruction terrorism study. - Washington, D.C. : ACDA, Sept. 1975.
Classified report by the U.S. Arms Control and Disarmament Agency for the Cabinet committee to combat terrorism and the National SecurityCouncil Staff.

5683. Kupperman, R.H. Nuclear terrorism: armchair pastime or genuine threat?. Summer 1978. p. 19-26. Jerusalem Journal of International Relations. ; 3.

5684. Leon, P.de * Jenkins, B. * Keller, K. * Krofcheck, J. Attributes of potential criminal adversaries to U.S. nuclear programs. - Santa Monica, Calif. : RAND Corporation, Febr. 1978. ; R-2223-SL.Re
printed in: U.S. Congress, Senate, Committee on governmental affairs, An act to combat international terrorism, 1978.

5685. Lovins, A.B. * Lovins, L.H. Energy policies for resilience and national security. 1982

5686. Mabry jr, R.C. Nuclear theft: real and imagined dangers. March 1976. 144 p ; Master's thesis
The study investigates the availability of fissionable material, vulnerable portions of the nuclear fuel cycles, weapon construction, andthe regulations regarding the protection of fissionable material.

5687. Matson, E.K. Terrorists armed with nuclear weapons. - Maxwell Air Force Base, Ala. : Air Command and Staff College, Air University, May 1976. 50 p

5688. McPhee, J. The curve of binding energy. - New York : Farrar, Straus and Giroux, 1974. 170 p

5689. Meguire, P.G. * Kramer, J.J. Psychological deterrents to nuclear theft: a preliminary literature review and bibliography. - Gaithersburg, Md. : National Bureau of Standards, March 1976. ; NBSIR 76-1007.

5690. Mengel, R.W. Terrorism and new technologies of destruction: an overview of the potential risk. - Vienna, Va. : BDM Corporation, 25 May 1976. ; Report prepared for the National advisory committee task force on disorder and terrorism. ; BDM/W-76-044-TR.

5691. Mengel, R.W. The impact of nuclear terrorism on the military's role in society. - Westport, Conn. : Greenwood Press, 1978. p. 402-414.
In: M.H. Livingston et al. (eds.), International terrorism in the contemporary world

5692. Meyer, W. * Loyalka, S.K. * Nelson, W.E. * Williams, R.W. The homemade nuclear bomb syndrome. July 1977. Nuclear Safety

5693. Motley, J.B. The US ICBM force : A high-value terrorist target. - Fairfax, Virg. : National Institute for Public Policy, forthcoming.

5694. Mullen, R.K. Mass destruction and terrorism. 1978. p. 63-89. Journal of international affairs. ; 32.

5695. Mullen, R.K. The international clandestine nuclear threat. - Santa Barbara, Calif. : Mission Research Corporation, June 1975.

5696. Norman, L. Our nuclear weapon sites; next target of terrorists?. June 1977. p. 28-31. Army. ; 27.

5697. Norton, A.R. * Greenberg, M.H. * (eds.) Studies in nuclear terrorism. - Boston : G.K. Hall & Co., 1979.

5698. Norton, A.R. Nuclear terrorism and the Middle East. April 1976. p. 3-11. Military Review. ; 56.

5699. Norton, A.R. Terrorists, atoms and the future: understanding the threat. May-June 1979. p. 30-50. Naval War College Review

5700. Norton, A.R. Understanding the nuclear terrorism problem. - Gaithersburg, Md. : IACP, 1979.

5701. Pajak, R.F. Nuclear proliferation in the Middle East : Implications for the superpowers. - Washington, D.C. : National Defense University Press, 1982. 117 p

5702. Phillips, J.A. * Michaelis, D. Mushroom: the story of the A-bomb kid. - New York : Morrow, 1978. 287 p

5703. Phillips, J.A. The fundamentals of atomic bomb design : An assessment of the problems and possibilities confronting a terrorist group or non-nuclear nations attempting to design a crude PU-239 fission bomb. Princeton University, 1976. ; Junior thesis

5704. Ponte, L. Who is arming the new terrorists?. April 1977. p. 34-124. Playgirl

5705. Ramberg, B. Nuclear plants - military hostages. March 1986. p. 17-21. Bulletin of the Atomic Scientists. ; 42:3.

5706. Ramberg, B. Nuclear power plants as weapons for the enemy : An unrecognized peril. - Berkeley : University of California Press, 1984.

5707. Rosenbaum, D.M. Nuclear terror. 1977. p. 140-161. International Security. ; 1.
Repr. in: J.D. Elliott and L.K. Gibson (eds.), Contemporary terrorism: selected readings. Gaithersburg, Md.: IACP, 1978, pp. 129-147.

5708. Salmore, B. * Simon, D. Nuclear terrorism in perspective. July 1980. p. 21-23. Society

5709. Schelling, Th. C. The terrorist use of nuclear weapons. - Los Angeles : Center for International and Strategic Affairs, 1981. 23 p

5710. Schelling, Th.C. Thinking about nuclear terrorism. Spring 1982. p. 61-77. International Security. ; 6.

5711. Schelling, Th.C. Who will have the bomb. 1976. p. 77-91. International Security. ; 1.

5712. Scott, D. Terrorism: the nuclear threat. - Washington, D.C. : Citizens Energy Project, 1981.

5713. Shapley, D. Plutonium: reactor proliferation threatens a nuclear black market. 9 April 1971. p. 143-146. Science

5714. Taylor, T. Magnets for terrorists : Weapons grade uranium in university research reactors. April 1984. p. 3-6. Critical Mass Bulletin. ; 1.

5715. Taylor, Th.B. * Colligan, D. Nuclear terrorism: a threat of the future. Aug. 1974. p. 12-17. Science Digest

5716. Taylor, Th.B. * VanCleave, W.R. * Kinderman, E.M. Preliminary survey of non-national nuclear threats. - Stanford, Calif. : Stanford Research Institute, Sept. 1968. Technical Note. ; SSC-TN-520-83.

5717. Watson jr, F.M. Terrorists and the homemade 'A' bomb. - Gaithersburg, Md. : IACP., 23 p

5718. White, A. The terror of balance : Deterrence , rearmament and the illusion of security. - London : Menard, 1983. 36 p

5719. Willrich, M. * Taylor, Th.B. Nuclear theft. July-Aug. 1974. p. 186-191. Survival. ; 16.

5720. Willrich, M. * Taylor, Th.B. Nuclear theft: risks and safeguards. - Cambridge, Mass. : Ballinger Press, 1974. 252 p

5721. Willrich, M. Nongovernmental nuclear weapon proliferation. - Stockholm : SIPRI Almqvist and Wiksell, 1974.
In: B. Jasani (ed.), Nuclear proliferation problems

5722. Willrich, M. Terrorists keep out! : Problem of safe-guarding nuclear materials. May 1975. p. 12-16. Bulletin of the Atomic Scientists. ; 31:5.

5723. Woods, G.D. The possible criminal use of atomic or biological materials. June 1975. p. 113-123. Australian and New Zealand Journal of Criminology. ; 8
:2.

5724. Zofka, Z. Denkbare Motive und moegliche Aktionsformen eines nuklear Terrorismus. - Essen : Auge, 1981. 107 p
'Thinkable motives and possible forms of action of nuclear terrorism'.

5725. _____ Austria seeks atom guerrilla. 23 April 1974. p. A-18. Washington Post

5726. _____ Effects of nuclear war. - Washington, D.C. : Office of Technology Assessment, 1979. 151 p
Contains description of a hypothetical 1 kt. terrorist explosion in a major city.

5727. _____ Exports of nuclear materials and technology. - Washington, D.C. : GPO, 1974.
U.S. Congress, Senate. Committee on banking, housing, and urban affairs

5728. _____ Nuclear blackmail or nuclear threat : Emergency response plan. - Sacramento, Calif. : 1976. 40 p.
California Office of Emergency Services

5729. _____ Nuclear theft and terrorism : Discussion group report. - Muscatine, Iowa : Stanley Foundation, Oct. 1975. p. 33-40.
In: Sixteenth Strategy for Peace Conference Report

5730. _____ Peaceful nuclear exports and weapons proliferation: a compendium. - Washington, D.C. : GPO, 1975.

U.S.Congress, Senate. Committee on government operations

5731. _____ Psychosocial aspects of nuclear developments. - Washington, D.C. : 1982. 96 p.
American Psychiatric Association. Task Force on Psychosocial Aspects of Nuclear Developments

5732. _____ Report. - Washington, D.C. : Nuclear Control Institute, 1986. 33 p.
International Task Force on Prevention of Nuclear Terrorism

5733. _____ The terrorist and sabotage threat to U.S. nuclear programs : Phase one final report. - Dunn Loring, Virg. : HERO, Aug. 1974.
Historical Evaluation and Research Organization

T.1.6. Other forms of terrorism

5734. Baron, D.P. The increasing vulnerability of computers to terrorist attack. - London : Foreign Affairs Research Institute, 1978. 10 p

5735. Clark, R.C. Technological terrorism. - New York : Devin-Adair Co., 1978.

5736. Cobler, S. Die Gefahr geht von den Menschen aus : Die vorverlegte Staatsschutz. - Berlin : 1976.

5737. Hurwitz, E. Terrorists and chemical/biological weapons. 1982. p. 36-40. Naval War College Review. ; 35:3.

5738. Hurwood, B.J. Torture through the ages. Paperback Library, 1969.

5739. Kupperman, R.H. * et al. The near-term potential for serious acts of terrorism. - Washington, D.C. : ACDA, April 1976.
Classified report by the U.S. Arms Control and Disarmament Agency for the Cabinet committee to combat terrorism and the National Security Council Staff.

5740. Lea, H.Ch. A history of the Inquisition of Spain. - New York : 1906.

5741. Lea, H.Ch. A history of the Inquisition of the Middle Ages. - New York : 1906.

5742. Leibstone, M. Corporation terror : Violence and the business community. - Gaithersburg, Md. : IACP., 21 p

5743. Livingstone, N.C. * Douglass jr, J.D. CBW: the poor man's atomic bomb. - Cambridge, Mass. : Institute for Foreign Policy Analysis, 1984. 36 p

5744. Livingstone, N.C. Vulnerability of chemical plants to terrorism : An examination. 21 Oct. 1985. p. 7-13. Chemical and Engineering News. ; 63.

5745. Naquet, P.V. Torture : Cancer of democracy. - Harmondsworth : Penguin, 1963.

5746. Newhouser, C.R. Mail bombs. - Gaithersburg, Md. : IACP., 32 p

5747. Peters, E. Torture. - Basil Blackwell : 1985. 202 p

5748. Robinson, D. * (ed.) The dirty wars : Guerrilla actions and other forms of unconventional warfare. - New York : Delacorte, 1968. 356 p

5749. Scott, G.R. History of torture. - London : Sphere Books, 1971. 328 p
1st ed. 1967.

5750. Shue, H. Torture. 1978. p. 124-143. Philosophy and Public Affairs. ; 7:2.

5751. Stephens, M.M. The oil and natural gas industries: a potential target of terrorists. - Stanford, Calif. : Hoover, 1979. p. 200-223.
In: R.H. Kupperman and D.M. Trent (eds.), Terrorism

5752. Tichy, W. Poisons, antidotes and anecdotes. - New York : Sterling Publishing Co., 1977. 192 p
Poisoning as a potential terrorist weapon.

5753. Verin, J. Torture and hostage-taking. - New York : United Nations Social Defense Research Institute, 1971. 8 p

5754. _____ Incendiaries. - Boulder, Colo. : Paladin Enterprises, 1975.
U.S. Army

5755. _____ Incendiaries. - Boulder, Colo. : Paladin Press, 1979. 150 p.
U.S. Department of the Army

5756. _____ The phenomenon of torture. - Washington, D.C. : GPO, 1984. 296 p.
U.S. Congress. House. Committee on Foreign Affairs

5757. _____ Unconventional warfare devices and techniques. - Boulder, Colo. : Paladin Enterprises, 1965. 234 p.
U.S. Army

5758. _____ Unconventional warfare devices and techniques. - Boulder, Colo. : Paladin Press, 1979. 234 p.
U.S. Department of the Army

U. VARIA AND RELATED STUDIES

5759. Adams, J. The financing of terror. - New York : Simon and Schuster, 1986.

5760. Alcock, N. * Quittner, J. The prediction of civil violence to the year 2001. - Ontario : Canadian Peace Research Institute, 1977. ; Unpubl. manuscript

5761. Backman, E.L. * Finlay, D.J. Student protest : A crossnational study. Sept. 1973. p. 3-46. Youth and Society. ; 5:1.

5762. Ben-Dak, D. * (ed.) The future of collective violence : Societal and international perspectives. - Lund : Studentlitteratur, 1974. 251 p

5763. Berger, A.A. Television as an instrument of terror : Essays on media, popular culture and everyday life. - New Brunswick, N.J. : Transaction Books, 1980. 214 p

5764. Bracken, P. * Shubik, M. Strategic war : What are the questions and who should ask them?. 1982. p. 155-179. Technology in Society. ; 4.

5765. Brown, L.A. Diffusion patterns and location : A conceptual framework and bibliography. - Philadelphia : Regional Science Research Institute, 1968.

5766. Buckley jr, W.F. Dance of the terrorists. 1974. National Review. ; 26. On U.N. debate on terrorism.

5767. Chapman, R. * Chapman, M.L. The crimson web of terror. - Boulder, Colo. : Paladin Press, 1980. 160 p
By CIA veteran.

5768. Colin, J.P. Les etats et la violence.

Jan. 1978. p. 87-114. Politique etrangere. ; 1.

5769. Crozier, B. A theory of conflict. - New York : Scribners, 1974. 245 p
Also: London: Hamish Hamilton, 1974.

5770. Curle, A. Mystics and militants : A study of awareness, identity and social action. - London : Tavistock, 1972.

5771. Demaitre, E. Terrorism and the intellectuals. 17 April 1973. p. 12660-12662. Congressional Record. ; 119.
Reprinted from the Washington Sunday Star, 15 April 1973.

5772. Dimitrijevic, V. Medjunarodni terorizam. 1980. p. 23-44. Arhiv za pravne i drustvene nauke

5773. Dimitrijevic, V. Sta je medjunarodni terorizam. 1979. p. 55-67. Jugoslovenska revija za medjunarodno pravo

5774. Dimitrijevic, V. Terorizam u unutrasnoj i medjunarodnoj politici. - Beograd : Radnicka stampa, 1981. 220 p

5775. Eayrs, J. Diplomacy and its discontents. - Toronto : University of Toronto Press, 1971.

5776. Eckhardt, W. * Koehler, G. Structural and armed violence in the 20th century : Magnitudes and trends. 1980. p. 347-375. International Interactions. ; 6:4.

5777. Ellsburg, D. The theory and practice of blackmail. - Urbana, Ill. : University of Illinois Press, 1975.
In: O. Young (ed.), Bargaining

5778. Fach, W. * Degen, U. * (eds.) Politische Legitimitaet. - Frankfurt a.M. : Campus Verlag, 1978.

5779. Friedrich, C.J. Pathologie der Politik. - Frankfurt a.M. : Herder & Herder, 1973.

5780. Galtung, J. Gewalt, Frieden und Friedensforschung. - Frankfurt a.M. : Suhrkamp, 1972.
In: D. Senghaas (ed.), Kritische Friedensforschung

5781. Gurr, T.R. Comparative studies of political conflict and change : Cross national datasets. - Ann Arbor, Mich. : Inter-University Consortium for Political and Social Research, 1978. 194 p

5782. Gurr, T.R. Group protest and policy responses : New cross-national perspectives. Jan.-Febr. 1983. p. 283-416

American Behavioral Scientist. ; 26.

5783. Gurr, T.R. On the political consequences of scarcity and economic decline. March 1985. p. 51-75. International Studies Quarterly. ; 29.

5784. Gusfield, J.R. Mass society and extremist politics. 1962. p. 19-30. American Social Review. ; 32.

5785. Hamilton, M.P. Terrorism: its ethical implications for the future. Dec. 1977. p. 351-354. The Futurist. ; 11:6.

5786. Holmes, R.L. Violence and nonviolence. - New York : David McKay, 1971.
In: J.A. Shaffer (ed.), Violence: award-winning essays in the Council for Philosophical Studies competition

5787. Hunter, E.L. Huurmoordenaar Carlos : De gevreesde terroristenleider. - Amsterdam : Teleboek, 1976.

5788. Huntington, S.P. Remarks on the meanings of stability in the modern era. - Boulder, Colo. : Westview Press, 1977. p. 269-282.
In: S. Bialer and S. Sluzar (eds.), Radicalism in the contemporary age. Vol. 3. Strategies of contemporary radicalism

5789. Inglehart, R. The silent revolution : Changing values and political styles among Western publics. - Princeton : Princeton University Press, 1977.

5790. Israel, G. Ou mene le terrorisme?. 1968. Les nouveaux chiers. ; 13/14.

5791. Kamp, A. * Quittner, J. Cycles foresee the future of international violence. - Ontario : Canadian Peace Research Institute, 1977. ; Unpubl. manuschript

5792. Karagueuzian, D. Blow it up!. - Boston : Gambit, 1971.

5793. Kwitny, J. The terrorists : Thriving black market puts military weapons into amateurs' hands; small arms abound; legal export shipments can and do go away. 11 Jan. 1977. Wall Street Journal. ; 189:1.

5794. Laqueur, W. Diversities of violence and the current world system. - London : IISS, 1971. p. 9-16.
In: Civil violence and the international system. Adelphi Papers. ; 82-83.

5795. Levitt, E.E. The psychology of anxiety. - Indianapolis : Bobbs-Merrill, 1967.

5796. Lewis, F. The anatomy of terror. 18 Nov. 1956. p. 67. New York Times

5797. Lipset, S.M. Rebellion in the university. - London : Routledge and Kegan Paul, 1972.

5798. McMaster, D. Forecasting political violence. - Syracuse : University of New Mexico Press, 1979.

5799. Melman, B. The terrorist in fiction. July 1980. Journal of Contemporary History. ; 15:3.

5800. Morton, M.J. The terrors of ideological politics. - Cleveland : The Press of Case Western Reserve University, 1972. 192 p

5801. Newman, G.R. Understanding violence. - New York : Harper & Row, 1979.

5802. Novotny, E.J.S. * Karber, Ph.A. Organized terror and politics. - Washington, D.C. : 1973.
In: American Political Science Association (ed.), Short essays in political science

5803. O'Brien, C.C. Liberty and terrorism. 1977. p. 56-67. International Security. ; 2.

5804. Reenen, P.van Overheidsgeweld : Een sociologische studie van de dynamiek van het geweldsmonopolie. - Alphen aan den Rijn : Samsom, 1979.

5805. Revel, J.F. Comment les democraties finissent. - Paris : 1983.

5806. Roeling, B.V.A. * et al. Politiek geweld. - Utrecht : Vredesopbouw, 1978. 112 p
7 articles on different aspects of violence based on lectures given in Fall 1977 at the Rijksuniversiteit Utrecht.

5807. Russett, B.M. Who are the terrorists?. July 1980. p. 16. Society

5808. Schelling, Th.C. Arms and influence. - New Haven, Conn. : Yale University Press, 1966.
Discusses 'coercive bargaining' which is relevant in the conteet of terrorism.

5809. Schwarz, U. Die Angst in der Politik. - Dusseldorf-Wien : 1967. 244 p

5810. Steedly, H.R. * Foley, J.W. The success of protest groups : Multivariate analyses. 1979. p. 1-15. Social Science Research. ; 8:1.

5811. Strauss, H. Revolutionary types. 1973. p. 307. Journal of Conflict Resolution. ; 14.

5812. Taylor, Ch.L. * Hudson, M.C. World handbook of political and social indicators. - 2nd ed. - New Haven, Conn. : Yale University Press, 1972.

5813. Taylor, D.L. The dimensions of the effectiveness of terrorism. 1979. ; Unpubl. paper, Annual meeting of the North Central Sociological Association

5814. Taylor, E. The terrorists. 1973. p. 58-64. Horizon

5815. Troch, E. Vier miljard gijzelaars : Wereldpolitiek 1945 tot heden. - Antwerpen : Standaard, 1977. 338 p

5816. Turk, A.T. Social dynamics of terrorism. Sept. 1982. p. 119-128. Annals of the American Academy of Political and Social Science. ; 463.

5817. Vestdijk, S. Het wezen van de angst. - Amsterdam : De Bezige Bij, 1979. 700 p

5818. Wallace, M.D. * Varseveld, G.van Violence as a technique of social change : Toward emperical measurement. University of Manitoba, June 1970. ; Paper presented at the Annual meeting of the Canadian Research and Education Association

5819. Welch, C.E. * Taintor, M.B. Revolution and political change. - Belmont, Calif. : Duxbury Press, 1972.

5820. Willmer, A. Terrorism and social criticism. Summer 1981. Telos. ; 48.

5821. Wimmer, E. Antimonopolistische Demokratie und Sozialismus. - Wien : Globus Verlag, 1974. 66 p
pp. 49-56: Ueber den Terrorismus.

5822. Young, O. Bargaining. - Urbana, Ill. : University of Illinois Press, 1975.

5823. Zald, M.N. * McCarthy, J.D. * (eds.) The dynamics of social movements : Resource mobilization, social control, and tactics. - Cambridge, Mass. : Winthrop Publishers, 1979.

5824. Zwieback, B. Civility and disobedience. - London : Cambridge University Press, 1975.

5825. _____ Dossier politiek terrorisme. - Amsterdam : Sept. 1979. 't Kan anders. ; 2:6-7.
Transcript of a symposium held in June 1979 by a workgroup for ecology, pacifism and socialism.

5826. _____ Drugs and terrorism. - Washington, D.C. : GPO, 1984. 120 p. U.S. Congress. Senate. Committee on Labor and Human Resources. Subcommittee on Alcoholism and Drug Abuse

5827. _____ Getting away with murder. 4 Nov. 1972. p. 15-16. Economist

5828. _____ PvdA en terrorisme. 1973. p. 156-169. Socialisme en Democratie. ; 30:3.
Reactions by P.J. Kapteyn, A.van der Leeuw, Relus ter Beek on AlfredMozer: De gedesintegreerde internationale. (Socialisme en Democratie 29:10, Oct. 1972, pp. 454-456.). With a reply by Alfred Mozer.

5829. _____ PvdA en terrorisme. 1972. p. 565-568. Socialisme en Democratie. ; 29:12.
Reactions by A.J.F.Koebben, J.S.Wijne, J.J.van der Lee on Alfred Mozer: De gedesintegreerde Internationale (Socialisme en Democratie 29:10, pp. 454-456. Oct. 1972).

5830. _____ Terrorist acts against United Nations missions. 1971. p. 61. United Nations Chronicle. ; 8.

5831. _____ When tradition comes to the aid of terrorism. 17 March 1973. p. 23. Economist

AUTHOR INDEX TO BIBLIOGRAPHY ON TERRORISM

Lakos, A. ; 31, 32, 33, 34.
Lall, D. ; 578.
Lallemand, R. ; 381.
Lamberg, R.F. ; 836, 2483, 2484, 2653.
Lamberg, V.B.de ; 2485.
Lambrick, H.T. ; 2211.
Lampert, D.E. ; 846.
Landau, E. ; 1916, 2934.
Landau, J.M. ; 2155.
Landau, S. ; 2645, 5399.
Landazabal Reyes, F. ; 2486.
Landazabal, R.F. ; 382, 2487.
Landes, W.M. ; 5539.
Landis, F. ; 566.
Landorf, S. ; 1234.
Laney, R.B. ; 5420.
Lang, D. ; 3403.
Lang, E. ; 4037.
Lang, K. ; 4037.
Langemann, H. ; 3596.
Langemeijer, G.E. ; 3834.
Langer, F. ; 1933.
Langguth, A.J. ; 623.
Langguth, G. ; 976, 1081, 1082, 1083.
Lanz, P. ; 4780.
Lapham, L.H. ; 4038.
Laporte, M. ; 4937.
Laquain, A. ; 882.
Laqueur, W. ; 172, 173, 383, 384, 385, 386, 387, 388, 389, 390, 391, 837, 1882, 2990, 3679, 4039, 4478, 4479, 5794.
Lara, P. ; 2654.
Larsson, J.E. ; 1767.
Larteguy, J. ; 392, 2488, 2489.
Lasch, Chr. ; 2794.
Laschi, R. ; 3598.
Lasky, M.J. ; 1084.
Lassiera, R. ; 1253.
Lasswell, H.D, ; 3248.
Lasswell, H.D. ; 393, 4040.
Latey, M. ; 3680.
Latham, A. ; 4041.
Latouche, D. ; 2699.
Laudi, M. ; 5083, 5084.
Laurendeau, M. ; 2700.
Laurent, F. ; 1235.
Laurent, R. ; 2991.
Laushey, D.M. ; 2212, 2213.
Lauterpacht, H. ; 3835.
Lavin, M.M. ; 2786.
Lavoinne, Y. ; 4042.
Lawrence, J.S. ; 4043.
Lawrence, R. ; 2795.
Lazarus, R. ; 3404.
LeNoir, J.D. ; 4568.
Lea, H.Ch. ; 5740, 5741.
Leach, E.R. ; 174.
Leakey, L.S.M. ; 2380.
Leaute, J. ; 3597, 5085, 5506.
Leber, J.R. ; 2992.
Lebjaoui, M. ; 2349, 2350.
Lebow, R.N. ; 1359, 1360.
Ledeen, M. ; 1528, 4044.
Ledeen, M.A. ; 1527.
Lederer, H. ; 838.
Lee, A.M. ; 1361, 1362, 1363.
Leeuwen, W.van ; 3972.
Lefebvre, G. ; 1236, 1237.
Leff, A. ; 394.
Leggett, G.H. ; 624.
Legros, P. ; 3836, 5086.
Legum, C. ; 2312, 2412, 4280, 4727.
Lehane, D. ; 1328.
Lehman, A.S. ; 555.
Lehmann, W. ; 5540.
Lehnert, D. ; 1080.
Lehning, A. ; 4480, 5348.
Leibstone, M. ; 2041, 4045, 4046, 4938, 5279, 5742.
Leichter, O. ; 2993.
Leiden, C. ; 395, 5408.
Leigh, I. ; 2381.
Leirgner, G. ; 3406.
Leiser, B.M. ; 839.
Leites, N. ; 4281, 4728.
Lejeune, A. ; 2413.
Leloup, J.J.H. ; 3525.
Lenin, W.I. ; 4481, 4482.
Lenk, K. ; 4483.
Lennhoff, E. ; 3249.
Lens, S. ; 2796.
Lentner, H.H. ; 396.
Lenz, R.R. ; 4939.
Leon, P.de ; 5684.
Leonard, L.L. ; 2994.
Leonhard, W. ; 625.
Leoni Houssay, L.A. ; 2995.
Lerner, D. ; 3248.
Lerner, M. ; 2797, 5421.
Lersch, P. ; 1085.
Lesch, A.M. ; 2069.
Lespart, M. ; 1854.
Letamendia, F. ; 1655.
Letman, S.T. ; 4282.
Leurdijk, D.A. ; 840.
Levasseur, G. ; 2952.
Leventhal, H. ; 3405.
Levere, J. ; 4047.
Levergeois, P. ; 1238.
Levi, G. ; 2490.
Levin, J. ; 4048.
Levine, H.M. ; 4878.
Levine, I.D. ; 3250.
Levitt, E.E. ; 5795.
Levy, R. ; 4049.
Levy, S. ; 5418.
Levy, S.G. ; 5422.
Levytsky, B. ; 626, 627, 628.
Lewald, Ch.E. ; 5464.
Lewandowski, R. ; 4050.
Lewis, B. ; 2042, 2156.
Lewis, F. ; 5796.
Lewis, G.K. ; 2798.
Lewis, J.D. ; 159.
Lewis, P. ; 5423.
Lewis, T.J. ; 396.
Lichbach, M.I. ; 4253, 4254.
Lichter, S.R. ; 3526, 3527.
Lida, C.E. ; 1656.
Lieberson, G. ; 1364.
Liebert, R. ; 3528.
Lifton, R.J. ; 3787.
Lijphart, A. ; 1365.
Lilienthal, A.M. ; 2043.
Lillich, R.B. ; 2996, 2997.
Lily, C. ; 315.
Lima, D. M.de ; 2547.
Liman, P. ; 5424.
Lincoln, A. ; 3406.
Lindner, C. ; 4484.
Lindroth, K. ; 3407.
Lineberry, W.P. ; 4729.
Liniers, A. ; 4672.
Linke, R. ; 3837.
Linz, J.J. ; 629.
Lipovetsky, G. ; 397.

CORPORATE AUTHOR INDEX

TITLE INDEX TO BIBLIOGRAPHY ON TERRORISM WHERE NO AUTHOR WAS MENTIONED (25 characters)

List of abbreviations

ACDA - U.S. Arms Control and Disarmament Agency, Washington, D.C.
CIA - U.S. Central Intelligence Agency, Washington, D.C.
FAA - Federal Aviation Administration, U.S. Department of Transportation, Washington, D.C.
GPO - Government Printing Office, Washington, D.C.
GPV - Gereformeerd Politiek Verbond (Reformed Political Union), Dordrecht, The Netherlands.
HMSO - Her Majesty's Stationary Office, London.
IACP - International Association of Chiefs of Police, Gaithersburg. Md.
ICCC - International Centre for Comparative Criminology, Montreal, Canada.
IDAF - International Defence and Aid Fund, London.
IISS - International Institute for Strategic Studies, London.
IPI - International Press Institute, London.
IPRA - International Peace Research Association.
ISC - Institute for the Study of Power and Conflict, London.
MIT - Massachusets Institute of Technology, Cambridge, Mass.
NACLA - North American Congress on Latin America, New York.
NIVV - Nederlands Instituut voor Vredesvraagstukken (Dutch Institute for Questions of Peace).
NKVD - Predecessor of the Russian KGB (until 1946).
RGPO - Rhodesian Governmental Printing Office, Salisbury.
RUSI - Royal United Services Institute for Defence Studies.
SORO - Special Operations Research Office, American University, Washington, D.C.

WORLD DIRECTORY OF TERRORIST AND OTHER ORGANIZATIONS ASSOCIATED WITH GUERRILLA WARFARE, POLITICAL VIOLENCE, AND PROTEST

A. J. Jongman, in collaboration with A. P. Schmid

INTRODUCTION

Since 1980, a data-gathering effort in the broad field of political violence has been carried out at the Polemological Institute of Groningen State University. Its core consists of a systematic coding of all instances of violence reported in the Paris-based *International Herald Tribune*. The instances of violence coded from this main source range from political suicides to interstate wars, from terrorist acts to guerrilla operations. In addition, attention is given to extranormal repressive acts of violence by government actors, whether these be the armed forces, the police, or secret services.

This is an area which has been relatively neglected by the terrorism research community. Given the magnitude and near-ubiquity of illegitimate state violence, this uneven distribution of attention cannot be justified. Consider the following comparison: One of the most extensive data bases on terrorism, from *Risk International*, recorded for the period 1970-1983 a total of 18,727 domestic and international terrorist incidents in which a total of 28,110 people were killed and another 18,925 people were injured. In the first global survey of episodes of massive state repression which have occurred since World War II, B. Harff and T. R. Gurr recorded forty-two episodes of state-sponsored mass murder in which an estimated 10 million people died. Eighteen of the forty-two cases occurred in the context of civil wars and rebellions. Although the time periods as well as other aspects of the two data sets are not equal, this juxtaposition indicates that far more people are killed in state-sponsored violence than in antistate terrorism.

Fortunately, extranormal state violence is finally beginning to receive the attention it deserves. In recent years, a number of studies have been published to define the concepts of state violence (Stohl and Lopez, 1984), to reveal international networks of the secret police (Plate and Darvi, 1983, and Herman, 1982), and to improve the data bases (Stohl and Lopez, 1986). The activities of human rights organizations have also contributed to the growing attention to the subject of state violence. Reports of church organizations and national human rights organizations, the annual reports of Amnesty International, the *Country Reports on Human Rights Practices* of the U.S. State Department, and the U.N./ECOSOC reports on disappearances, summary executions, and torture have resulted in a growing awareness of state violence and a demand for better and more detailed information.

In the discipline of international relations, the "cobweb model" has become polular in recent years. In this model, the interdependent relationships between actors (state and non-state) in networks play a central role. As a means of identifying the networks of actors having in common the use of political violence, a list of actors is a first necessity. It is hoped that the present directory, which includes state actors and state-supported actors along with non-state actors in a single list of perpetrators of political violence, serves the needs of those interested in such networks.

There are a number of changes in the present directory. Contrary to the list included in the 1984 edition of this *Research Guide*, the present list excludes victim groups which do not engage in violence themselves. The list has been updated from 1983 to the spring of 1987. The number of sources has been increased and the list has been cross-checked with other directories. New sources for the updated list include specialized literature in scientific journals, Dutch newspapers (*NRC Handelsblad*, *Volkskrant*, and *Trouw*), weeklies (*Time* magazine, *Newsweek*, *The Economist*, *Der Spiegel*, and *Jane's Defence Weekly*), and monthlies (*South Africa Now*, *New African*, *AfricAsia*, *Arabia*, and the *Middle East Review*), and the *Knipselkrant* of the Red Resistance Front (RFF), a weekly collection of press clippings from the international press.

As a result both of better coverage and of increases in political violence, the number of recorded actors has doubled since 1983, from about 1,500 to about 3,000 groups, parties, movements, and organizations. It is, to our knowledge, the most complete list on political violence presently available in the open literature.

Since 1983, an attempt has been made to standardize the information with the help of a codesheet based on Waterman and Jenkins (1977). However, the information included in the present list is based largely on a card index and clippings archive. The practice of coding has shown that information on all included variables is available for only a limited number of actors, and then only by combining a large number of different sources. The standard sheet contains the following variables:

1. Source;
2. Date;
3. Page;
4. Column;
5. Name (the full proper name in English and in the original language);
6. Acronym;
7. Nationality (country of origin or primary base);
8. Year of establishment;
9. Year of dissolution;
10. Objective (the strategic objectives of the group);
11. Action frequency (the approximate number of incidents perpetrated per year);
12. Past incidents (the names of past incidents instigated by the group);
13. Affiliations (names of allied groups);
14. Stage of development (stages 1 to 5 allowed);
15. Ethnic composition (major nationality or ethnic composition represented in the group);
16. Supporters (groups, sectors, and organizations that aid and abet the group);
17. Level of sophistication (in terms of planning and execution);

18. Tactics (the typical types of events perpetrated by the group);

19. Type (characterization of the goal of the group);

20. Targets (the types of objects or persons typically attacked);

21. Membership (the number of active and passive members);

22. Headquarter location (where the decision makers are located);

23. Territory of operations (the territorial area over which the group spreads its operations);

24. Level of support (extent of support for the group, e.g., local, regional);

25. Type of support (expressions of support for the group);

26. Finances (available budget and means of financing activities);

27. Leadership (names of most important leaders);

28. Educational composition (what kind of education the group members have).

The most controversial variables are supporters, affiliations, level of sophistication, finances, action frequency, and membership. Information in the sources on these six variables is scarce and disputed. In many cases, the information in the public sources is based on accusations, rumor, or disinformation.

Global data bases tend to concentrate on international or transnational terrorist incidents and to neglect domestic terrorism. They also tend to include different sets of activities. To illustrate: The *Risk International* global data base recorded a total of 18,727 terrorist incidents for the 1970-1983 period. However, one group alone, the Shining Path organization in Peru, claimed to have been responsible for 30,000 domestic terrorist incidents in the 1980-September 1986 period. The Peruvian government, on the other hand, recorded 13,000 incidents. Obviously, different activities must have been counted. It must be kept in mind too that the parties involved in a conflict tend to upgrade or downgrade such numbers.

There is no standardized way of presenting information on terrorist activities in the literature. The larger data bases tend to concentrate on specific sets of clearly defined activities. However, terrorists do not confine themselves to sets of activities defined a priori by researchers, and they have shown considerable inventiveness in developing new methods in their struggle. The media tend to concentrate on particular activities and to use certain thresholds such as the extensiveness of the damage caused, the number of casualties, and the importance of the victims as criteria for coverage.

Some organizations use rather primitive homemade weapons and explosives while others use state-of-the-art weapons from the armories of the big powers or surplusses dumped on the black market. In many cases, it is unclear how the organizations obtain their weapons. The supply of new sophisticated weapons like the Stinger or the Redeye missiles can significantly affect the outcome of a conflict.

The ethnic composition of the organization plays an important role in many African and Asian countries. A Doeschot and Jongman (1985) survey of ethnic conflict showed that during the 1980-April 1982 period ethnic conflicts were reported in ninety-two states and twelve dependent territories involving at least 259 separate ethnic groups.

The membership figures for an organization change constantly in time. In the literature, distinctions are made between hard-core fighters and supporters, and between armed and unarmed, trained and untrained, and active and passive members. In the present list, the date is mentioned for membership estimates, when available. Since the conflict parties tend to upgrade or downgrade figures, the source of the figures is also given, when available.

The basic criterion for inclusion of antistate groups in the list was the reported fact that a group engaged in violent activities for political purposes. The violent activities can range from *threats* to damage particular material objects or to harm people, to actually damaging material objects or harming people. The circumstances in which the violence occurs can vary from civil wars to low-intensity conflict and election campaigns. There are several indications for labeling an actor "terrorist," "guerrilla," or otherwise violent. These can be accusations by other persons, groups, or governments that an actor is plotting an act of political violence. Indicators for planning an act of violence can be preparatory activities, arms caches, acquisition of arms, recruitment, or training activities. An actor can publish political manifestos in which he announces plans for overthrowing a government or other specified goals.

As a general guideline, the clear intention or the actual perpetration of a violent act have been used as criteria for inclusion.

A great number of vigilante groups have been included. In the context of some civil wars, these vigilante-type groups are armed and supported by the official armed forces and can play a significant role in extranormal violence. In the context of counterinsurgency programs in some countries, governments have established village militias. Although they are mainly intended for defensive roles they sometimes engaged in gross human rights violations and are therefore included in the directory.

Commandos of an organization who have operated under different names have been included under separate entries. In a number of cases, the political and the military branches of an organization have been listed separately.

The inclusion of an actor in our list does not automatically indicate that he is presently engaging in politically motivated violence. In our list there are several examples of terrorist organizations that abandoned violence and operate now as normal political parties.

A general criterion for inclusion of state actors was that the actor engaged in gross human rights violations, including arbitrary arrests, illegal detention, disappearances, torture, assassinations, or summary executions. The direct opponents of non-state terrorists are the antiterrorism or counterinsurgency units of the government. The high number of terrorist incidents in a number of countries has resulted in the proliferation of such units. Although they do not necessarily all engage in extralegal violent activities, they were included in the present list. Some countries which experienced high levels of terrorism in the 1970s now export their knowledge to other conflict-ridden countries. In some cases, the newly established units engage themselves in terrorist activities. Another group of actors are the secret services. In a number of cases, they engaged in violent covert activities which match or surpass those of non-state terrorist actors.

Our original 1983 list was compared with those of Banks, Crozier, Mickolus, and Monday. The Mickolus list is highly Western-oriented and underrepresents Africa and Asia. This thirteen-page list is concerned mainly with transnational actors, excluding many internally operating national groups. Given the author's former association with the U.S. Central Intelligence Agency, it is arguably biased in its coverage in favor of anti-U.S. and left-wing manifestations of violence. A similar imbalance can be found in the *Annuals of Power and Conflict* issued by the London-based Institute for the Study of Conflict. The ISC annuals (publication ceased in 1982) concentrate on organizations threatening the security of state power on a country-by-country basis. While these two lists are preoccupied with insurgency and terrorism, a third one by Mark Monday in a special edition of *TVI Journal* (vol. 2, 1981) is broader. Basing himself on a CIA list and extending it, Monday covers "insurgency and dissent," by which he means "all acts other than voting or lobbying, aimed at the personnel, structure or decision making process of a government with the intent of decisively altering any of these--usually for a redistribution of advantage or power, whether political, social or economic." Insofar as the Monday list includes nonviolent *actors* it is broader than the one presented here. Monday's list, which is a mere name list, is very extensive. For Italy, for instance, he has many more names of "terrorist" groups than our list has. However, most of these names appear to be different cover names for a much smaller number of organizations. The present directory limits itself to the most important country groups, including, however, in the case of Italy, the Mafia, which cannot be considered to be a purely criminal and nonpolitical organization.

Apart from checking our list against those of Monday, Mickolus, and the ISC, we have also consulted Arthur S. Banks and W. Overstreet (eds.), *Political Handbook of the World* (New York, 1981). The *Handbook* lists the official and illegal political parties of the countries of the world. Our list is less broad, concentrating only on those parties which have a military or underground wing or which were involved in election-time violence.

From the above it should be clear that our list is *not* a mere directory of "terrorist" movements. Entry of a non-state actor means that he engaged in violence according to the sources on which the list was based. Characterization of an organization as "terrorist," "guerrilla," or "protest" movement has been made on the basis of evidence and comments from sources in the public domain which were judged to be credible enough to be incorporated. However, we cannot guarantee that our sources cannot be wrong. Some of the groups might never have existed (being cover names) or might no longer exist. In recent years loosely organized groups with generic names have used fantasy names and we have included these without being sure whether the members of these fantasy groups belong to one or another concrete organization.

A note of caution about our use of the terms "movements," "organizations," "groups," and "parties" is required. The term "party" is used for political parties as well as in the sense of "party to a conflict." The term "group" refers in common parlance to a number of people, a part, class, or layer of the population. More scientific usage attributes characteristics like "we-feeling," joint actions, common goals, and a relatively long existence in time to groups. It is questionable whether many terrorist groups would meet this last criterion. The term "group" is therefore used loosely here. In social science jargon, "movements" usually stand somewhere between groups and organizations in terms of coherence, division of labor, planning, and direction. In the present list, however, the term "movement," like the terms "group," "party," and "organization," is not meant to indicate a particular structure of the entity in question. Given the life cycles of such entities, these can at various stages be any of the four.

While updating the 1983 list we also consulted several other directories, including Janke (1982), Degenhardt (1983), Keegan (1983), Dobson and Payne (1986), and Rosie (1986). Repeatedly we utilized information from these sources when our own data were insufficient. The Janke directory concentrates on the most important terrorist and guerrilla organizations, presenting them by nation. The national sections also contain useful introductions and bibliographies. The Degenhardt directory is broader in scope and includes also extraparliamentary and illegal political movements, exile organizations, and governments in exile that have not resorted to political violence (in some cases these are just paper organizations). He also offers short introductions with basic information on the countries and presents the actors not only by nation but also by issue and by ideology. For a number of actors, the Janke and Degenhardt directories present far more extensive histories and more detailed information than the present directory. The Keegan study is not a directory of organizations but a study of the development of national armies in the world. It contains useful sections on the role, commitment, deployment, and recent operations of each national army and its direct opponents in armed conflicts. The Dobson and Payne dictionary is mainly an alphabetical list of spies, but it also includes a section on countries with a selection of a number of secret services and intelligence organizations. The Rosie directory concentrates on the most recent actors, persons, and activities that have been widely publicized in the media, and the level of media attention seems to have been an important criterion for the inclusion of particular groups, organizations, incidents, and persons. They are presented in alphabetical order. We have not been able to consult the Andrade (1985) study with 177 entries providing detailed information on the police and paramilitary forces in the world and their role in maintaining internal security.

Our directory is structured on a country-by-country basis; in each case the actors are enumerated alphabetically. Where a group acts without a country of its own--like the exile Armenians and Croatians--the country "occupying" their homeland is usually taken as category. Exceptions to this rule (which places the Armenians under Turkey and the Croatians under Yugoslavia) are made in a number of cases, such as Namibia, Western Sahara, Northern Ireland, and Palestine. Although many governments engage in political violence at home and abroad, these are not listed here directly. Instead, agencies of these governments which engaged in violence are listed under their official or cover names. It is worth emphasizing that this list is much less thorough with regard to extralegal state violence than with regard to violence directed against states. There are many explanations for this: the deeper cover of state agencies, the structure of media reporting, and censorship are among them.

Needless to say, the present list, while fairly up-to-date (the last entries were made in June 1987), is far from being complete and thorough. Given the limitations imposed by the sources, and given the nature of the subject matter (acts of violence are increasingly committed under false names to confuse the opponents or the public or both), such a list has to be used with great caution by researchers. Errors, omissions, corrections, comments, and additions should be communicated to Dr. A. J. Jongman, Polemological Institute of the State University of Groningen, Heresingel 13, Groningen, The Netherlands. It is our intention to periodically improve and update the information contained in this list so that this directory can gradually evolve into a more authoritative research instrument.

LITERATURE REFERRED TO

Amnesty International. *Annual Report 1980, 1981, 1982, 1983, 1984, 1985.* London: Amnesty International.

J. Andrade. *World Police and Paramilitary Forces.* London: Macmillan, 1985 (272 pp.).

A. S. Banks and W. Overstreet (eds.). *Political Handbook of the World.* New York: McGraw-Hill, 1981.

H. W. Degenhardt and H. J. Day. *Political Dissent: An International Guide to Dissent: Extra-parliamentary, Guerrilla and Illegal Political Movements.* Harlow, Essex: Longman Group, 1983.

C. Dobson and R. Payne. *The Dictionary of Espionage.* London: Grafton Books, 1986 (423 pp.).

R. Doeschot and A. J. Jongman. "Peoples in Conflict with States." In G. Fisher (ed.), *Armament-Development-Human Rights-Disarmament.* Paris: Faculté de Droit, Université René Descartes, 1985, pp. 373-400.

B. Harff and T. R. Gurr. "Toward an Empirical Theory of Genocides and Politicides: Identification and Measurement of Cases since 1945." Paper presented to the 28th Annual Convention of the International Studies Association, Washington, D.C., April 15, 1987.

E. Herman. *The Real Terror Network: Terrorism in Fact and Propaganda.* Boston: South End Press, 1982 (252 pp.).

P. Janke. *World Directory of Guerrilla and Terrorist Organizations: From 1945 to the Present.* Hassocks: Harvester Books, 1983 (537 pp.).

A. J. Jongman and H. Tromp. "War, Conflict and Political Violence: A Description of Five Data Collection Projects." In *UNESCO Yearbook on Peace and Conflict Studies 1982.* Westport, CT: Greenwood Press, 1983, pp. 164-192.

J. Keegan. *World Armies.* 2d ed. London: Macmillan Publishers, 1983 (688 pp.).

E. F. Mickolus. "List of Organizations and Acronyms." In *Transnational Terrorism: A Chronology of Events, 1968-1979.* London: Aldwych Press, 1980.

M. Monday. *TVI Journal Special Edition* 2 (1981).

T. Plate and A. Darvi. *The Secret Police: The Terrifying Inside Story of an International Network.* Abacus, 1983 (448 pp.).

G. Rosie. *The Directory of International Terrorism.* Edinburgh: Mainstream Publishing, 1986 (310 pp.).

M. Stohl and G. A. Lopez (eds.). *The State as Terrorist: The Dynamics of Governmental Violence and Repression.* Westport, CT: Greenwood Press, 1984 (202 pp.).

U.S. Congress. *Country Reports on Human Rights Practices, 1980, 1981, 1982, 1983, 1984, 1985, 1986.* Report(s) submitted to the Committee on Foreign Affairs, U.S. House of Representatives, and the Committee on Foreign Relations, U.S. Senate. Washington, D.C.: U.S. Department of State.

D. A. Waterman and B. M. Jenkins. *Heuristic Modeling: Using Rule Based Computer Systems.* Santa Monica, CA: Rand, 1977.

OVERVIEW OF COUNTRIES AND TERRITORIES LISTED

OVERVIEW OF COUNTRIES AND TERRITORIES LISTED

AFGHANISTAN

* Afghan Islamic and Nationalist Revolutionary Council
Umbrella organization which was established to unify the several guerrilla factions. Most of these unification attempts failed because of leadership struggles.

* Afghan Nation
(Afghan Mellat)
Social democratic guerrilla faction led by Gholam Mohammad Farhad (a former mayor of Kabul) and Chamshuhuda Sjams. It is mainly concentrated on Pushtun.

* Afghan National Liberation Front (ANLF)One of the guerrilla factions which was established on March 12, 1979. It called for a jihad (holy war) against the Kabul regime. It is led by Imam Seghbatullah Mujjaddedi. It has been a member of several umbrella organizations. Together with Harakat and NIFA it has formed a 'moderate' alliance sometimes known as Islamic Unity (not to be confused with the Islamic Unity party).

* Against Oppression and Tyranny
(Setem-i-Melli)
Guerrilla faction which split off from the DPPA. It is active in the northern part of the country and is led by Taher Badakshi. It expressed opposition to Pushtun domination, especially in areas inhabited by ethnic minorities such as Tadjiks in Badakshan province who are Shia moslems. Members of the group were held responsible for the Feb.14, 1979, assassination of the US ambassador in Kabul.

* Akhgar
Small pro-Albanian guerrilla faction that broke away from Eternal Flame.

* Alliance of Islamic Fighters
(Hedadia Mujaheddin Islami Afghanistan)
A guerrilla faction which was established in May 1979. It is mainly based on Hazara and is led by Wali Beg. Its strength was estimated at about 5,000 in 1979.

* Badakshan National Minority Front
A nationalist movement in Badakshan province.

* Eternal Flame (Shola-e-Jawed) Sama Tendency
A small guerrilla faction.

* Eternal Flame (Shola-e-Jawed) Raha'i tendency
A small pro-Chinese guerrilla faction.

* Ghazni National Minority Front
A nationalist movement based in Ghazni.

* Hazarat Jat
An informal coalition of predominantly Shi'ite Persian-speaking groups in central Afghanistan including NASR, a Shi'ite organization known to be funded by Iran. It maintains a loose affiliation to NIFA.

* Hazara National Minority Front
A nationalist movement based in Hazara which claims to run its own autonomous administration.

* Islamic Afghan Society
(Jamiaat-i-Islami Afghanistan)
One of the main Peshawar based guerrilla factions. It is supported by the Tadjiks and is strongly influenced by fundamentalist young intellectuals. It is led by professor Ustad Burhanuddin Rabbani. Its field commander is Ahmad Shad Massoud. It has trained more than 5,000 men in modern guerrilla warfare and operates a special guerrilla warfare academy. It operates in the Panjshir valley which is run like a semi-autonomous state with a resistance council that operates its own financial office to collect taxes, an office to deal with information and propaganda and a defense office to coordinate guerrilla activities.

* Islamic Alliance of Afghan Mujaheddin
(Ittihad-e-Islami Mujahideen) (IAAM)
Umbrella organization which was established in May 1985. It consists of four Islamic parties and three nationalist groups seeking international recognition as the official voice of the Afghan resistance. To overcome the sensitive leadership issue it has a rotating leadership. The first president was Ghulam Abdur Rasoul Sayaf. Total strength is estimated at 90,000 fighters. It called for joint military and political action. In January 1987 it accepted a proposal to establish an interim government. In May 1987 it announced plans for the election of a council that would appoint the members of the interim government when the Soviet troops have left the country. The elections will be held in the liberated areas of Afghanistan and the refugee camps in Iran and Pakistan. The 'fundamentalists' wanted the head of government to be chosen from among the seven party leaders. The 'nationalists' wanted the post to be open to any Afghan Muslim, including the exiled King Zahir Shah, who has lived in Rome since he was deposed in 1973 but is said to be willing to return.

* Islamic Alliance for the Liberation of Afghanistan (IALA)
Umbrella organization of several guerrilla factions which was established on Jan.27, 1980. It was formed at an extraordinary meeting of the Foreign Ministers of the Organization of the Islamic Conference in Islamabad (Pakistan) by representatives of five Afghan guerrilla organizations. It had moral and political support of the Islamic nations. It was led by Professor Ghulam Abdur Rasoul Sayaf. It was dissolved on Apr.22, 1981.

* Islamic Movement of Afghanistan
(Mahaz Melli Islami Afghanistan)
One of the main guerrilla factions. Its strength is estimated at about 8,000 fighters.

* Islamic Movement Organization of Afghanistan
(Harakata Islami Afghanistan)
Small Shi'ite group outside the seven-party alliance led by Ayatollah Mohammed Assef Mohseni of Qandahar. It has influence in the north and west of Afghanistan and is significant for its efforts to forge closer ties between resistance parties and their military commanders.

* Islamic Party of Afghanistan (Hezb-i-Islam)
(Hekmatyar faction)
Well armed and organized Peshawar based guerrilla faction. It stayed out of the paper federation known as the Islamic Alliance. It had started as an armed insurgent movement in 1974 when it joined a clandestine effort by the former Pakistani government of prime minister Zulfikar Ali Bhutto to destabilize the Kabul regime. It emphasizes its own variety of a strict Sunni interpretation of Islam. Its leader, Gulbuddin Hekmatyar, was accused of striving for political hegemony over other guerrilla groups. He has been accused of liquidating his political enemies. The party has diffuse support within Afghanistan and is a very significant political and military force. Its membership tends to be young and educated.

* Islamic Party of Afghanistan (Hezb-i-Islam) (Younes Khales faction) One the main Peshawar based guerrilla factions which broke away from Hekmatyar's party. It is more traditionalist than fundamentalist. It is concentrated on Pushtun. Its strength is estimated at about 8,000 fighters. While it lacks an effective political organization, it is successful militarily- as proven by Commander Jalaludin Hakani in Pakhtia province and Abdul Haq in and around Kabul.

* Islamic Unity of Mujaheddin of Afghanistan
Umbrella organization of six guerrilla factions which was established on July 7, 1981. The members include the Islamic Front of Afghanistan, the Afghan National Liberation Front and the Movement for the Islamic Revolution.

* Kunar National Minority Front
A nationalist movement based in Kunar.

* Moslem Brotherhood
(Ikhwan-i-Musalamin)
In September 1978 the government of Afghanistan was reported to have declared a jihad (holy war) against the Brotherhood which received aid from several Arab countries.

* Movement for the Islamic Revolution
(Harakat-i-Inquilabi-i-Islami)
One of the main Peshawar based guerrilla factions. It is traditionalist, close to the fundamentalists and is led by Maulvi Mohammed Nabi. Its strength is estimated at 25,000 fighters. Headquarters is located at Meshad. It has influence on the Front of Nimruz. It is particularly strong in central and north-east Afghanistan-although its influence there may have eclipsed by the military successes of Massoud of Jamiat-i-Islami. The party is tribal and valley-based, and suffers from disorganization. Its commanders tend to be educated Mullahs but they lack conventional military training. It has been responsible for some spectacular ambushes of convoys on the Kabul-Qandahar road.

* Movement of Islamic Revolution (MIR)
Guerrilla faction which was formed after the 1978 coup as an alliance of two Moslem extremist groups, opposed to the Taraki regime. Differences within the movement's leadership weakened its capacity to appeal to a broader range of traditional interests.

* National Fatherland Front
A broad alliance of political parties, mass organizations and tribal bodies, formed at a congress on June 15, 1981 with the object of promoting national unity under the guidance of the PDPA. The front failed because of dissension between its two main factions.

* National Front of Militant Combatants
(Jebheye Mobarizin Mujahid-i-Afghanistan)
Internal based guerrilla faction. Several leftists organizations are operating within this front and in individual capacities within various regional fronts. It staged the Balu Hisan mutiny in the Kabul garrison in August 1979.

* National Intelligence Service
(Khedmat-e-Etala'at-e-Daulat) (KHAD)
Governmental intelligence service which has been involved in severe human rights violations. It operates under the direct control of the Soviet KGB and is trained by East German instructors. It was led by Dr.Najibullah from 1979 to May 1986. Since then he replaced Babrak Karmal. It has an estimated 25,000 agents and has tens of thousands of paid informers. It has an extensive network of prisons and interrogation centers and has executed guerrillas which had been taken prisoner without a trial. Agents have infiltrated guerrilla factions and it allegedly has been involved in a bombing campaign on Pakistani territory.

* National Islamic Front for Afghanistan (NIFA)
One of the Peshawar based guerrilla factions. It is led by Pir Sayed Ahmed-al-Gailani, the descendant of a Sufi saint. Although it is based on heriditary leadership and formerly promoted a return of the monarchy, the party supports the concept of Afghanistan as a democratic nation. It has deep organizational problems and has not proved to be effective militarily-despite having a number of senior western-trained Afghan Army officers. Recently its fortunes appear to have risen, possibly due to intense lobbying in Washington by their spokesman and military commander, General Abdul Rahim Wardak.

* National United Front of Afghanistan (Djebh-e-Melli)
Extreme leftwing group which in 1981 was reported to be based inside Afghanistan.

* Nuristan National Minority Front
A nationalist movement which claimed to run its own autonomous administration. It is led by Mohammed Anwar Amin.

* Organization for the Liberation of the Afghan People (SORKHA)
Small pro-Chinese guerrilla faction which broke away from Eternal Flame.

* Organisation for the Liberation of Afghanistan
(Sazman-e-Azadbaksh Mardom-e-Afghanistan)
(SAMA)
One of the internal based guerrilla factions which is linked to a number of internal fronts. It is most

active in Kabul and other urban centers.

* Partisans of National Liberation of Afghanistan (Front of Nimruz)
Nationalist guerrilla faction which was established in December 1979. It rejects dependence on any foreign power and is led by Gol Mohammed Rahimi. It is concentrated on the Baluchi and its strength is estimated at about 1,000 fighters. It has liberated almost all of the province and introduced a number of programs to improve agriculture, education and the health situation.

* People's Democratic Party of Afghanistan (Khalq faction) (Masses) (PDPA)
One of the two factions of the communist government party which has been involved in a fratricidal struggle with the rival Parcham faction.

* People's Democratic Party of Afghanistan (Parcham faction) (Banner) (PDPA)
Government party which was established in 1965. Political withdrawal in 1973 following Khalq defiance of a Soviet directive to support the Daoud regime. The two factions were reunited in 1977 but most prominent Parcham members were purged in the wake of an abortive coup on August 7, 1978. Babrak Karmal attempted to reunite the two factions within both government and party. In 1986 he was replaced by General Najibullah, the former head of the national intelligence service. It had 60,000 members by the end of 1979. Since then membership had decreased to 20,000.

* Revolutionary Council of the Islamic Union of Afghanistan
(Schurai Enqelabe Itifaq Islami Afghanistan) (RCIUA)
A guerrilla faction led by Sia Nassari Chan, who has the American nationality. It operates in the Baluchi area and is the largest organization in Hazarajat.

* Revolutionary Groups of the Afghan Peoples (Grohe Inquilabi Khalqhaie Afghanistan)
One of the internally based guerrilla factions, extremely active in anti- Soviet resistance, particularly in various rural areas.

* Sepha-i-Pasdaran
A pro-Khomeini guerrilla faction based in Hazarajat eager to spread the Islamic revolution. It allegedly has ties with the Iranian Revolutionary Guard.

* Those Who Have Sworn to Fight for Islam (Teiman Atahad-Islami)
Guerrilla faction which was established on Aug.11, 1979. It was formed among refugees in Peshawar by a merger of four groups, the Afghan National Liberation Front, the Islamic Afghan Association, the Movement for Islamic Revolution and the faction of the Islamic Party led by Yunes Khales. Its declared objective is the establishment of an Islamic republic of Afghanistan.

* Victory
(Sazman-i-Nasr)
Small pro-Khomeini guerrilla faction based in Hazarajat. It wants to spread the Islamic revolution of Ayatollah Khomeini. It recrutes members among Hazara's who work in Iran. It has attacked other guerrilla fronts.

ALBANIA

* HDP
An Albanian Croatian organization which is seeking independence for Croatia and the return of Albanian territory under Yugoslav control. It attacked Yugoslav embassy personnel in Brussels in 1981.

* National Liberation Army (NLA)
A group of followers of King Leka which still claims the Albanese throne. It has been alleged that the NLA staged a small scale invasion in October 1982. It was reported that the group was totally eliminated by the Albanian army.

* Sigurimi
Albania's secret police which has been largely responsible for maintaining Albania's isolation.

ALGERIA

* Berber Cultural Movement
Berber movement that has protested the Arabization program of the government. Berber student protests led to violent riots in 1980 after which the government announced measures designed to appease the militant Berbers who want to keep alive their distinct language (Kabyle) and culture.

* Front of Socialist Forces (FFS)
Opposition movement formed in February 1964. It was led by Dr.Hocine Aït Ahmed who announced that the movement was resuming the armed struggle against the Ben Bella regime. In this attempt it failed. Dr.Hocine Aït Ahmed escaped from prison in 1966. The FFS has been linked with the Berber agitation against the government's Arabization measures.

* Moslem Fundamentalists
A group which has support under students in Algiers. Fundamentalists have been arrested and charged with subversion and forming an organization aimed at destabilizing the state.

* National Liberation Army
(Armeé de Libération Nationale) (ALN)

Military wing of the FLN which was established in 1954. It fought a bloody independence war against the French. By 1962 it had 150,000 lightly armed men. Most of them were stationed along the frontiers with Tunesia and Morocco and were not involved in the fighting. The actual fighting was done by a fluctuating number of irregular 'internal' members of the ALN organized in six regional commands. Only some 10,000 of the 50,000-60,000 men who had fought in the internal forces oncorporated into the Armée Nationale Populaire (ANP) as it was renamed in 1962 while the remainder (most of them Berbers) were demobilized.

* National Liberation Front
(Front de Libération Nationale) (FLN)
Liberation movement in the fifties which gained independence. It was established in 1954 and was led by Ben Bella and Colonel Houari Boumedienne. In 1961 it had 5,000 fighters inside Algeria and 25,000 waiting to infiltrate from Tunesia. In 1958 it set up an Algerian government in exile in Cairo. It had links with Egypt, Morocco, Tunesia and Syria. France withdrew in 1962 after which the FLN emerged as the sole political movement in Algeria.

* Revolutionary Committee for Unity and Action
(Comité Revolutionnaire pour l'Unité et l'Action) (CRUA)
A group of young militant Algerians led by Ben Bella who took up arms against French colonial rule. It was renamed FLN in 1954.

* Secret Organisation
(Organisation Secrète) (OS)
Clandestine paramilitary organization established as a breakaway of the non-violent Movement for the Triumph of Democratic Liberties (MTDC) in 1947. The forerunner of the FLN was led by Ahmed Ben Bella. French police uprooted the organization in 1950.

* Soldiers of the Algerian Opposition
Group which was held responsible for the bombing of three Algerian embassies in Europe in 1975.

ANGOLA

* Armed Forces for the Liberation of Angola (FALA)
Armed wing of the UNITA guerrilla movement. UNITA claimed to have 60,000 men, 26,000 regular forces and 34,000 guerrillas. The former are organized in regular batallions of 900 to 1,500 men, more mobile batallions of 300 to 500 men and special troops, small units of up to 45 men. The guerrilla forces are organized in compact columns of 150 to 180 men. They have lighter weapons and less firepower. In its conventional campaigns it has been supported by South Africa. The guerrilla forces, however, play a decisive role. Tribal support as well as permanent military pressure throughout the country depends on them.

* Liberation Front of the Enclave Cabinda
(Frente de Libertacao do Enclave de Cabinda) (FLEC)
Set up in 1963 as a separate liberation movement of the enclave Cabinda by Zaire and France. It was supported by the local Fiote tribe and was led by Enrique N'Zita Tiago and Francisco Xauter Lubota. Its strength was estimated at 7,000 fighters. In 1977 it formed a provisional government with Enrique N'Zita Tiago as head of state. He died in 1979 in a clash with Cuban forces. In 1979 it claimed that it held 30 percent of the territory of Cabinda. Half the enclave's population (150,000) had fled to Zaire since 1975. In January 1979 Luizi Ballu, a FLEC member responsible for foreign affairs, assumed leadership of the movement.

* Military Command for the Liberation of Cabinda
(Comando Militar para a Libertacao de Cabinda) (CMLC)
In an attempt to restructure FLEC this organization broke away in 1977. It was led by Marcelino Tumbi and Luis Matos Fernandu.

* Military Council of Angolan Resistance
(Conselho Militar de Resistencia Angolana) (COMIRA)
Established in August 1980 to replace the FLNA. The council was said to have been formed on request of the United States government as a counterrevolutionary movement capable of coordinating and organizing subversive action in northern Angola, replacing the 'demoralized' FLNA. It also had links with Zaire.

* Movement for the Liberation of Cabinda
(Movimiento para a Libertacao de Cabinda) (Molica)
A FLEC offshoot led by Joao da Costa.

* National Front for the Liberation of Angola
(Frente Nacional de Libertacao de Angola) (FLNA)
One of the three guerrilla movements in the independence war against the Portuguese which was established on March 27, 1962 by a merger of UPA and ALAZO. It formed a Revolutionary Government in Exile (GRAE) and was led by Holden Roberto. It had between 4,000 and 7,000 men under arms plus at least that many men who acted as support groups. Since February 1976 it has been involved in guerrilla warfare against the MPLA government. It is supported by the Bakongo and Kimbundu. By mid 1981 Holden Roberto was reported to have been replaced by Paulo Tuba and Hendrik Vaal Neto. Holden Roberto sought political

asylum in France. Its activities are limited to hit-and-run guerrilla tactics. In 1984 the government announced that several hundred guerrillas had surrendered.It has been supported by the United States, Zaire, South Africa, China and North Korea.

* National Union of Total Independence of Angola (Uniao Nacional para a Independencia Total de Angola) (UNITA)
One of the three original liberation movements which is now involved in a guerrilla war against the MPLA government. It was established on May 13, 1966 and is led by Jonas Savimbi (president) and Miguel N'Zau Puna (secretary-general). It claimed to have 60,000 men under arms. It is supported by the Ovimbundu, Bailundo and Chokwe and is based in the central and southern Ovimbundu regions. It has established an agricultural and industrial base. In recent years it shifted tactics from hit-and-run guerrilla warfare to more conventional warfare. For money, weapons, instructors and direct support in combat it relies on the support of South Africa, United States, Ivory Coast, Senegal, Saudi Arabia, France, Zambia and Morocco. After the battle of Mavinga, which was a turning point in the conflict, UNITA activity has generally dropped in intensity. It has not recovered from the losses which it suffered of the order of 2,000 men. American deliveries of arms via Zaire have resulted in an increase in UNITA's capacity for sabotage. So far there have been no reports of Stinger missiles used in action. In collaboration or coordination with specialized South African units it has carried out a number of sizable operations. Anti-personnel mines are laid on tracks and paths, on river banks and at the edge of manioc fields, resulting in a growing number of deaths and injuries among civilians and soldiers.

* Popular Liberation Movement of Angola-Labour Party
(Movimiento Popular de Libertacao de Angola-Partido de Trabacho) (MPLA)
A Soviet-backed liberation movement which was established in December 1956 by a merger of Vamos Escobrir, PLUA and MINA. It provided the primary resistance to Portuguese colonial rule and is mainly based on the Lunda people. In 1961 an all out struggle began and in 1975 independence was reached. After independence it has been involved in a guerrilla war with the FLNA and UNITA. The guerrilla forces were dissolved and reorganized in the Angolan Army. The armed forces consist of the People's Armed Forces for the Liberation of Angola (FAPLA) (80.000 men), the Popular Defense organization (ODP) and the Border Guard troops (TGTA). It is supported by Cuba, the Soviet Union, Hungary and East Germany. It allows the Namibian guerrilla movement SWAPO to launch operations from Angolan territory. This has led to a number of South African hot pursuit operations and outright invasions.

* Popular Movement for the Liberation of Cabinda (Movimiento Popular de Libertacao de Cabinda) (MPLC)
Movement set up in June 1979 as a progressive but not anti-Western faction by the Armed Forces of Liberation of Cabinda (FALC). It is headed by Major Vicente Balenda.

ARGENTINA

* Argentine Anti Communist Alliance
(Alianza Anticomunista Argentina) (AAA)
A terrorist organization established in October 1973, predominantly made up of police and security force agents. There appeared to be no organization nationwide, nor even within a city. Between 1974 and 1975 the murders escalated at an alarming rate. Targets were mainly leftist journalists, academics, trade union officials, students, lawyers, priests, doctors, engineers and politicians. José López Rega, its principal instigator had for many years been a close adviser of General Péron and his wife Isabel. He left Argentina in July 1975. After the introduction of military rule in March 1976 AAA activities declined.

* Argentine National Intelligence Agency (CNI)
Security organization of the government which has been involved in the disappearance of about 9,000 people in the 1974-1978 period and in other grave violations of basic human rights.

* Argentinian National Socialist Front
(Frente Nacional Socialista Argentina) (FNSA)
Rightwing anti-semitic organization which was held responsible for bomb explosions at several synagogues in Buenos Aires in August 1976.

* Armed Forces of Liberation
(Fuerzas Armadas de Liberación) (FAL)
Terrorist organization which was established in 1969 and operated out of Buenos Aires. It was pro-Cuban but was variously described as Trotskyite, Castroite and Maoist Peronist. Many members went to ERP which superseded FAL around 1970. It targeted banks, military posts and foreign firms until 1973.

* Commando Cisneros
A group which claimed responsibility for a bomb attack on a ship of Shell in the harbor of Buenos Aires in 1984. The police denied the attack and said that it was an accident.

* Fifth of April

(Cinco del Abril)
Obscure left-wing group held responsible for a bomb attack on June 8, 1980.

* Free Argentina
A group which has been involved in kidnappings and murders of critics of the government.

* Montoneros
Leftwing Peronist urban guerrilla group which was established in 1970. From 1975 on it acted as the armed branch of the PPA seeking a 'socialist revolution'. In September 1976 the group announced that it would return to clandestinity, using arson, sabotage, assassination and bombings to promote a 'popular war'. Its strength increased from 350 to 5,000 at its peak with another 15,000 active sympathizers. It lost 1,600 followers in 1976 and a further 500 in 1977. By 1978 it was defeated by the government. Fidel Castro permitted the group to relocate its headquarters in Cuba. In December 1981 its leader Mario Eduardo Firmenich publicly called on the movement to abandon all attempts to pursue armed struggle so as to concentrate on political action. In May 1987, he was sentenced to life in prison for his involvement in the murder of a businessman and a driver in 1974. Other important leaders were Rodolfo Galimberti, Fernando Vaca Narvaja and Juan Gelman.

* National Liberation Army
(Ejército de Liberación Nacional) (ELN)
Minor guerrilla group active in the 1960s. After the death of Che Guevara nothing more was heard of the group.

* October 17 Montoneros
(Montoneros 17 de Octubre)
Dissident faction of the Peronist Montoneros movement which emerged in April 1980 and is led by Miguel Bossano. It is committed to insurrection and is named after the 1945 mass rally which started the Peronist movement.

* People's Guerrilla Army
(Ejército Guerrillero del Pueblo) (EGP)
Cuban-backed rural guerrilla movement established in 1963. Its main leaders, including Jorge Masetti, were captured by the Argentinian armed forces. The movement had little impact. Some members escaped and later reappeared in other organizations.

* People's Revolutionary Army
(Ejercito Revolucionario del Pueblo) (ERP)
Pro-Cuban guerrilla movement established in May 1969. It acted as the armed branch of the Workers Revolutionary Party. It was expected to become an 'army of the masses' to embody a so-called national liberation organization. It linked urban terrorist tactics with a working class movement. It was organized on a cellular basis but came closer to becoming a guerrilla army than other terrorist groups. It was at its height in 1975, but by 1977 it was eradicated. Many members fled into exile, some were hired as assassins. An ERP hit team murdered the exiled Nicaraguan dictator Somoza in Paraguay in September 1980. Its leaders Roberto Santucho and José Urteaga were both killed in 1976. Via the Junta Coordinadora Revolucionario (JCR) it had contacts with ELN (Bolivia), MIR (Chile) and the MLN (Uruguay).

* People's Revolutionary Army/ August 22 (ERP)
A Trotskyite guerrilla movement which broke away from ERP and joined the left-wing Peronists.

* Peronist Armed Forces
(Fuerzas Armadas Peronistas) (FAP)
Small Peronist and pro-Cuban guerrilla movement which was established in the 1950s. It began to operate in 1969 in a series of urban crimes in Buenos Aires and carried out bomb attacks and bank raids in 1971. It targeted the military government of general Lanusse and multinational companies. It discussed unification with FAL. Later it consulted and planned with FAR and the Montoneros. By 1975 nothing more was heard of the FAP. Some members joined the Montoneros.

* Red Brigades of Worker Power
(Brigadas Rojas del Poder Obrero) (BRPO)
Trotskyite terrorist group which emerged in 1976 in response to AAA activities. It was said to consist of former militants from FAL. The group was uprooted by the government in 1976.

* Revolutionary Armed Forces
(Fuerzas Armadas Revolucionarias) (FAR)
Pro-Cuban rural guerrilla movement established in 1967. Originally it was set up to aid Che Guevara in Bolivia. In 1971 it tried to unify extremist movements into a common front. It was led by Roberto Quieto and Fernando Vaca Narvaja. It was involved in crimes and theft and targeted the military, police posts and banks. It was grouped alongside the Montoneros and FAP in an umbrella organization known as the Armed Peronist Organizations (OAP) and was encouraged by Cuba. Activities slackened after the general elections of March 1973. In October 1973 FAR joined the Montoneros.

* Rightist Terrorist Cell
A 15-member group made up of former agents from military, security and intelligence services. Several members also were linked to the AAA. Its activities were directly linked to the trial of military junta members after Raul Antonio Gughialminetti was accused as its leader. He was a

former security and intelligence agent attached to the government palace who continued in official service during the first three months of Mr.Alfonsin's government. He also reportedly served as a trainer to Nicaraguan anti-government rebels in Honduras.

AUSTRALIA

* Australian League of Rights
A neo-nazi group which was established in 1970 by Donald A.Martin. It operates as a propaganda front and has tried to influence opinion leaders and key figures in the Australian establishment. It preaches anti-semitism and a nazi-style conspiracy.

* Australian National Front (ANF)
A right-wing extremist group modelled after the British National Front in terms of policies and methods.

* Greek-Bulgarian-Armenian Front
Obscure group which claimed responsibility for a car bomb attack in front of the Turkish consulate in Melbourne (Australia) on Nov.23, 1986. Several Armenians were arrested.

AUSTRIA

* Foreigners Stop Movement
(Ausländer Halt Bewegung) (AUS)
Extremist movement with neo-nazi tendencies. Its militant nucleus is made up of members of the forbidden neo-nazi Kameradschaft Babenberg. Its actions are directed against immigrants.

* Kobra
Anti-terrorist unit of the government.

* Kranich
Anti-terrorist unit of the government.

* Nordland National Alliance
(Nationalistischer Bund Nordland)
A fascist group.

BAHREIN

* Islamic Front for the Liberation of Bahrein
(Al Jabihah al-Islamiyah Litahrir al-Bahrein) (IFLB)
This group was largely trained and financed by Tehran, entering Bahrein directly from Iran. Its mission was to sabotage key installations around the country and assassinate leading officials in a bid to topple the government. In 1981 the Iranian chargé d'affaires in the capital of Al Manamah was declared persona non grata and expelled from Bahrein for using a diplomatic pouch to bring arms and explosives for a force of 60 Shi'ite terrorists. In 1983, 73 people were charged in a trial with involvement in the plot (60 Bahrainis, 11 Saudi Arabians, one Kuwaiti and one Omani).

BANGLA DESH

* Awami League

A major force in the struggle for independence in 1971. Although formally disbanded in 1975 it remained the best politically organized political group in the country and served as the nucleus of the Democratic United Front (DUF). During 1980 and 1981 there was a severe leadership struggle between a pro-Moscow and a pro-Indian faction. The election of Hasine Wajed was considered as a pro-Indian lobby victory against the stronger pro-Moscow group.

* Communist Party of Bangla Desh (CPB)
Party that sprang from the Communist Party of Pakistan. One of its factions engaged in guerrilla operations during the struggle for independence. It resurfaced in the late 1970s without a military wing.

* East Bengal Communist Party (EBCP)
Pro-Chinese guerrilla faction which advocated independence for East Bengal (later Bangla Desh). It was led by Abdul Matin Alauddin Ahmed and worked closely with the Mukhti Bahini. The party was dismantled during General Ziaur Rahman's regime in the mid-seventies.

* East Bengal Communist Party-Marxist-Leninist (EBCP-ML)
Minor guerrilla faction established in 1971 as a result of a split in the EPCP(ML). It was based in the Noakhali-Chittagong region and fought against both Mukhti Bahini and Pakistani armed forces. It reportedly continued an underground existence in the 1980s.

* East Bengal Proletarian Party
(Purba Bangla Sharbohara) (PBSB)
Minor guerrilla faction established in 1971. It was led by Siraj Sikder and reached its peak in 1974. After independence it reorganized its guerrilla bands and identified the Mujibur Rahman government (1972-1975) as its new enemy. It attacked police posts throughout the country and sometimes broke open government warehouses to distribute food to the hungry. It faded in the late 1970's as a result of repression.

* East Bengal Workers' Movement (see East Bengal Proletarian Party) (EBWM)
This party was established on Jan.8, 1968 at a conference in Dacca by a group under leadership of Siraj Sikder. On June 3, 1971 it was

abolished when Sikder formed the EBSP. The party was influenced by Mao's teachings and the Naxalbari movement in West Bengal. It started its activities with wall writings in 1968. In 1970 it used bomb attacks and in the mid-1970s it began guerrilla warfare in the remotest rural areas. In 1971 it decided to form a national liberation front together with various progressive parties. It was the first organization that declared East Bengal a colony of Pakistan and that called for a national liberation struggle against the Pakistani ruling class. It advocated a national democratic revolution through armed struggle under the leadership of the proletarian party the CP).

* East Pakistan Communist Party Marxist-Leninist (EPCP-ML)
Maoist group active during the war of independence. It was reported to have continued its activities as an underground urban subversive group in the early 1980s.

* Freedom Fighters Mukhti Fouj (or Mukhti Bahini)

Guerrilla organization which sprang from the EBSP and Awami League. The Awami League rejected a proposal by EBSP to cooperate against the Pakistani Army, and killed EBSP guerrillas. The EBSP called on the people to fight against the Awami League, the Indian Army and the Pakistani Army. Its strength was estimated at 30,000 in 1971. The resistance took three forms. Conventional warfare with two brigades based in the Indian border territories Assam and Tripura. Guerrilla resistance exemplified by the commanders Taher and Ziaddin. And thirdly, a loosely organized guerrilla resistance involving thousands of civilians which operating without a formal command structure, initiated hundreds of guerrilla attacks on Pakistani forces. On Dec.16, 1971, Bangla Desh became an independent state after an Indian intervention.

* Liberation Force (Kader Bahini)
Guerrilla movement active in the early 1970s. It was led by Abdul Kader Siddiqui. It is based on the Garo people in the Mymensingh district. Early in 1976 the strength of the movement was estimated at between 500 and 3,500 men. In 1981 the force was said to consist of about 1,000 'deserters' from the army and police. India allegedly supplied arms.

* National Liberation Front of East Bengal (Purbo Banglar Jatio Mukti Front) (PBJMF)
Liberation movement which was formed on Apr.20, 1973 by Siraj Sikder to challenge the Awami League government. Siraj Sikder was arrested Jan.1, 1975 and the day after killed by the Rakkhi Bahini. The Sarbohara Party gradually lost its cohesion and because of ideological and personal conflicts became divided into three factions.

* National Socialist Party (Jatiyo Samajtantrik Dal) (JSD)
Maoist party formed in the 1960s. In July 1972 it founded its armed wing, the People's Revolutionay Army and at about the same time a clandestine organization within the army, the RSO. Its aim was a socialist revolution. It was led by Major J.A.Jalil. A coup and countercoup in 1975 led to a thorough purge of the army and the banning of JSD. Thousandes were arrested. Major Jalil was imprisoned and Colonel Abu Taher, head of the PRA, was executed.

* Parbottya Chattyram Jana Sarghati Samity (PCJSS)
Minority movement of the Bhuddist Chakma people which is based in the Chitta Gong Hill Tracts. It strives for a greater autonomy and protection as recognised under the constitution. It cooperated with insurgents in the Indian states Tripura and Mizoram.

* Party of the Disinherited of East Bengal
Group which has been active in the Jessore and Faridpur districts. It has murdered a number of landlords and distributed their crops among landless peasants.

* Peace Fighters (Shanti Bahini)
A collective name for rebel groups operating in the Chitta Gong Hill Tracts since 1974. It probably has 2,000 to 3,000 full time fighters. They retaliate against the atrocities perpetrated by the Bangla Desh army by staging sporadic ambushes and occasional battles. They also attacked lowland Moslem settlers and kidnapped foreigners. It has a formal relationship with Indians in the state of Tripura. It is led by Manabendra Lama and wants to restore tribal autonomy. It received substantial Indian arms and ammunition in 1975 and 1977. It resists the construction of a hydroelectric dam and the exploitation of the Islamic Bengal population. Rivaling factions unified in 1986 which will possible lead to a intensification of the war. The government has been accused of a genocidal policy. Amnesty International estimated that at least 6,500 people have been killed since 1974.

* People's Revolutionary Army (Biplopi Gono Bahini) (BGB)
Military wing of the JSD established in July 1972. It was led by Colonel Abu Taher who was executed on July 21, 1976. It concentrated on building up a peasant para-military force to challenge the police and the army. The group was uprooted during the Ziaur Rachman regime.

* Revolutionary Soldiers' Organization
(Biplopi Shainik Sangtha) (BSS)
Maoist JSD members were able to penetrate and to radicalize large sections of the armed forces. In November 1975 BSS members mutinied. In a counter coup the BSS was purged and thousands were executed. After a right-wing coup in November 1975, it surfaced again and issued 12 revolutionary demands.

* Temporary Managing Committee
(Asthayee Parichalona Committee) (APC)
Temporary committee of the communist party formed in March 1976 under the leadership of Arif and Zianuddin. In July 1977 Arif and Rana the Secretary and a Central Committee member respectively, were arrested by the police, so Zianuddin became the acting Secretary of the party. After Arif and Rana were released from jail in mid-1978, they advocated the line of an open mass party. For this reason the party ousted them and elected Zianuddin as the new secretary. In 1981 the party chalked out a program for national democratic revolution and a national front. By the end of 1983 the name was changed to Bangladesher Sarbohara Party. It is now trying to overthrow the military regime through armed struggle, but it has only a weak organizational basis. It has established some hold in several subdistricts.

<u>BELGIUM</u>

* Black Lebanon
(Zwart Libanon)
Terrorist group which claimed responsibility for a machine gun attack on Sep.12, 1982 in front of the synagogue in Brussels.

* Black March
(Zwarte Maart)
Terrorist group which was responsible for an attack on the airport at Zaventem on April 16, 1979.

* Commando Andreas Baader
One of three groups which claimed responsibility for an unsuccessful attempt on the life of Alexander Haig, NATO Supreme Commander in Europe, in June 1979. It is named after the West German terrorist who died in the Stammheim prison in October 1977.

* DIANE
One of the anti-terrorist units of the Belgian government.

* Direct Action (Belgian Section)
Possible offshoot of the French Action Directe terrorist group. It claimed responsibility for a bomb attack at the synagogue in Antwerp in October 1981. The Belgian authorities, however, attributed the action to a Palestinian splinter group.

* European Front of Belgian Solidarity
(Europees Front van Belgische Solidariteit) (EFBS)
Group which claimed responsibility for a bomb attack in 1984 on the liberal study center Paul Heymans at Elsene. The letter was signed by 'Delta Command'.

* Fighting Christian Cells
(Cellules Chretiennes Combattantes) (CCC)
Probably a copycat group which claimed responsibility for a bomb attack on a court building in Luik on Dec.6, 1985.

* Fighting Communist Cells
(Cellules Communistes Combattantes) (CCC)
Terrorist group which surfaced in 1984 but which had already contacts with the German RAF for eights years. It has been responsible for 27 bomb attacks in the October 1984-December 1985 period. It supposedly consisted of four to five cells of four to five members. A reconnaissance cell to visit the targets and make photographs, a logistics cell to build the explosives, an ideological cell to plan the attacks and to write the action declarations and finally an executive cell. The group targeted multinational companies particularly those linked with the arms industry, and NATO facilities. Five possible members have been arrested. These are Pierre Carette, Bertrand Sassaoye, Didier Chevolet, Pascal Vandegeerde and Pierre Vos. In January 1986 the police discovered the headquarters of the group. It had links with the Red Line Collective, Direct Action, RAF and FRAP.

* Flemish Militant Order
(Vlaamse Militanten Orde) (VMO)
An extreme nationalist movement which calls for a Flemish republic. It was led by Armand 'Bert' Erikson. It was banned by the government on May 23, 1983, as an illegal para-military organization. Militant action is directed against French speaking groups in various disputed linguistic areas, in particular in the district of Voeren (Fourons) which was in 1962 transferred from the (Walloon) province of Liège to the (Flemish) province of Limburg. The transfer was opposed by militant Walloons. The group did reportedly have contacts with the UVF in Northern Ireland in 1983. Several members reportedly visited Ulster to be trained in the use of explosives.

* Gang of Nijvel
(Bende van Nijvel, 'Les Tueurs Fous du Brabant')
Criminal gang which has been responsible for a

number of bloody raids on supermarkets, restaurants, a taxi company and a textile firm in which a total of 20 people were killed. The name stands for three more or less autonomously operating cells. It was allegedly led by a former policeman, Michel Cocu. Other possible members are Jean Claude Estiévenart, Michel Baudet, Kasi Bouaroudj, Adrien Vittorio, Serge Papadopoulos and Philippe De Staercke.

* Interforce Antiterrorist Groups
(Groupes des Interforces Anti-terroristes) (GIA)
Anti terrorist unit of the Belgian government which was established in September 1982 after a terrorist attack in Brussels. It became operational in 1984. It functions as an umbrella organization of several government agencies with a budget of 20 million BF. Its tasks are to inform the government about possible terrorist attacks, to suggest measures against terrorist attacks and to advise the government during hijackings and acts of hostage taking.

* Julien Lahaut Brigade
One of three groups which claimed responsibility for an attack on the life of General Alexander Haig on June 25, 1979. It is named after a leading member of the Communist Party in Belgium who was assassinated in Belgium after the outbreak of World War II.

* National Front for the Liberation of Belgium
(Nationaal Front ter Bevrijding van België) (NFLB)
A right-wing group which has claimed responsibility for the murder of a Moroccan. It was also responsible for a false bomb alarm in the mosque at Oudegem.

* Peace Conquerors
(Vredesveroveraars)
Group which claimed responsibility for a bomb attack on the chemical company Bayer in revenge of the chaining of the Greenpeace Ship Sirius. Greenpeace has denied any connection with the attack and has suggested that it could have been an action of the French secret service. The group also claimed responsibility for an attack on the Frankfurt airport. In a letter it demanded a world free of nuclear weapons, nuclear energy and the dismantling of all American military bases.

* Red Line Collective
(Ligne Rouge Kollektief)
Extreme left-wing printing office which has been linked to activities of the CCC, AD and the FRAP.

* Revolutionary Front for Proletarian Action (FRAP)
A group wich has been responsible for two bomb attacks in Belgium in 1985. In January 1986 the police arrested Luc van Acker, who probably was the explosives expert of the group.

* Special Investigations Brigade
(Bijzondere Opsporings Brigade) (BOB)
Belgian security service.

* Terror Group X
Group which was reported to consist of criminals and extreme rightist militants including at least one police informer. The last was said to be the same man who infiltrated as editor of the magazine 'Pour'. The group planned a number of bomb attacks which were never executed due to the Bologna bloodbath. Pierre Carette, who has been arrested for involvement in CCC attacks, was said to have been a member of the group.

* Vengeance and Liberty
(Vengeance et Liberté)
One of three groups that claimed responsibility for an attack on the life of General Alexander Haig on June 25, 1979.

* Flemish Militant Order- Odal
(Vlaamse Militanten Order- Odal) (VMO-Odal)
Most active and violent neo-nazi group in Belgium. It was established after the VMO was banned as an illegal para-military organization on May 23, 1983. Until June 1985, it was led by Bert Erikson. Its present leader is Jef Eggermont. The group has strong ties with the Flemish Bloc. It functions as an 'order service' for this party. Members have been involved in anti-immigration actions.

* Westland New Post (WNP)
Neo nazi group with alleged ties with the Belgian security service. It was established as an information gathering organization in 1980 and has branches in France and Germany. It is headed by Michel Libert who calls himself Wagner von Graffenberg and Paul Latinus who was found hanged in his apartment. It is estimated to have 260 members and reportedly had a secret police section modelled on the Gestapo. The State Security Service was involved in the training of members in infiltration techniques and shadowing. During a shadowing exercise F.Vermeulen, a suspected Russian agent was murdered. The Belgian section reportedly is dependent of a headquarters in Köln, from where several sections are led including one in the United States. In all these countries there allegedly are strong ties to official security services.

* Youth Front
(Front de la Jeunesse)
Neo nazi front which has an illegal private militia. On May 14, 1981 the government declared it to be a paramilitary organization. It is led by Francis

Dossogne, a former army captain who commanded a para-regiment. He was excluded from the active cadre but later reinstalled in an important position.

BELIZE

* Anti Communist Society (ACS)
Organization which was established in 1980. It is suspected of engineering attacks against leftists and persons with pro-Guatemalan leanings. It is led by Santiago Perdomo, a former trade minister.

* Belize Action Movement (BAM)
Extremist faction of the United Democratic Party, the official opposition, led by Odinga Lumumba. The movement unsuccessfully called for the holding of a referendum on the question of independence. Public safety regulations were introduced after clashes between BAM members and the police in 1981.

BENIN

* Front for the Liberation and Rahabilitation of Dahomey (FLRD)
Illegal organization which was established in France after the military takeover on Oct.26, 1972, bringing to power the left-wing military regime which is still in office. The aim of the FLRD has been to return to a democratic government in Benin. An invasion by some 100 armed men (about 40 of them white) who arrived at Cotenou airport on Jan.15, 1977 was specifically attributed to the FLRD. In 1979 a revolutionary court condemned to death in absentia a total of 100 persons alleged to have been involved in the invasion. The group included 62 European mercenaries.

BOLIVIA

* Che Guevara Brigade
This group claimed responsibility for the assassination in Paris on May 11, 1976 of General Joaguin Zentena Anaya, then Bolivian ambassador to France. He had been a local commander of the forces which had killed Che Guevara in October 1967. French press reports claimed that the general had been murdered by the Bolivian secret service because leading exiles had charged him with forming a new government.

* Death Squad
(Esquadron de la Muerte)
Right-wing terrorist organization. Activities increased considerably in 1980, especially after the coup.

* The Engaged of Death
(Los Novios de la Muerte)
International neo-fascist organization that operated as a death squad. According to a contract between the ex-Nazi Klaus Barbie and Colonel Luis Gomez Arce, then head of the military intelligence service, Barbie was appointed to lieutenant-colonel in active service to form army elite units for special operations. This led to the establishment of the death squad that was strengthened with European neo-Nazis, like Stefano della Chiaie. The group played an important role in the coup d'état of Garcia Meza and Gomez Arce. The government brought to power later became known for its involvement in the trade of cocaine. Members of the death squad also were active in the drugtraffic.

* Movement of Revolutionary Left
(Movimiento de Izquierda Revolucionaria) (MIR)
Social democratic movement which surfaced in August 1971 at the San Andrés University campus of La Paz. It has been responsible for occasional violent activities in the late 1970s and early 1980s. Jose Reyes Carvajal, one of its main leaders was killed in June 1980. It has been banned since July 17, 1980. It aimed at the political organization of the people and concentrated on radicalising Christian opinion within the Catholic church.

* National Liberation Army
(Ejercito de Liberacion Nacional) (ELN)
Pro-Cuban rural guerrilla movement which was established in 1967. It was led by Che Guevara. He went to rural Bolivia to start revolution in South America. In October 1967 he was executed after being captured and became a cult figure in the Western world. In 1969 attempts were made to resusciate ELN as an urban group. It committed a number of terrorist acts. In July 1970 the group claimed it had returned to the mountains. Oswaldo Chato Peredo was captured after which the rural bases collapsed. After 1970 the ELN continued to exist in La Paz and Cochabamba as a small urban nucleus. Close contacts with priests and nuns widened ELN appeal. After its network was discovered activities decreased.

* People's Command
Group which claimed responsibility for a bomb attack on the US embassy.

* Revolutionary Anti-Imperialist Front
(Frente Anti-imperialista Revolucionario)
An organization based in Cuba which was stated to have organized the escape from Bolivia of numerous left-wing activists after the advent to power of President Hugo Banzer Suárez in August 1972.

* Special Security Service
(Servicio Especial de Seguridad) (SES)

Security service of the government which was established shortly after the July 1980 coup. It has been involved in torture and political killings. Many of its members had no police training. In October 1981 it was replaced by the Directorate of State Intelligence which has been less active than SES.

* State Intelligence Department
(Departemento de Inteligencia del Estado) (DIE)
Intelligence service of the government which replaced the SES.

* Underground Revolutionary Leftist Movement
Movement which emerged in 1981.

BRAZIL

* Ala (Red Wing)
Group that broke away from the PCdoB in 1966. Police broke up the group in 1969. Surviving members joined the ALN, VAR-Palmares and VPR.

* 21st of April Revolutionary Movement (MR-21)
Name adopted by a group of militants connected with the journalist Flávio Tavares. Between July and August 1967, in the midst of plans for initiating military training with the objective of launching a guerrilla movement in the interior of Minas Gerais, the group was disbanded by the government.

* Araguaia Guerrilla Forces
As of 1966 members of the Communist Party of Brazil (PCdoB) installed themselves on the left bank the Araguaia River in northern Brazil. From April 1972 to January 1975, in three separate campaigns, government forces tried to eliminate the Araguaia guerrilla movement. Prolonged warfare resulted in deaths on both sides. Ultimately, the guerrillas were defeated. Some of them were taken prisoner and were charged, tried and sentenced under the National Security Law. Approximately 60 militants of PCdoB were killed in combat. The location of their burial site is unknown to this day despite the fact that their bodies were identified by government forces.

* Armed Revolutionary Vanguard- Palmares
(VanguardaArmadaRevolucionaria)(VAR-Palmares)
Organization which was established in April 1969 by a merger of the National Liberation Commando (COLINA) and the Revolutionary Popular Vanguard (VPR). Militants split on the question of whether to pursue armed struggle or whether to concentrate upon building a mass party. Advocates of the former reverted to calling themselves the VPR, the latter became VAR-Palmares, which has been responsible for hijacking an aircraft to Cuba in January 1970. In Rio de Janeiro one faction withdrew from the parent organization and formed the VAR-Palmares Dissidence, later renamed Unified Group. Those who called for an end of armed actions turned instead to organizing urban workers in 'Workers' Unions'. Others persisted upon preparing for armed struggle in rural areas. From 1971 on, VAR-Palmares began to disintegrate.

* Brazilean Anti-Communist Alliance
(Alianca Anticomunista Brasileira) (AAB)
A right-wing terrorist organization which has been involved in car bombs and telephone threats. It has directed its actions against the press association and churchmen charged with left-wing tendencies.

* Brazilean Communist Party
(Partido Comunista Brasileiro) (PCB)
Party which was established on Mar.25, 1922. It was led by Luis Carlos Prestes, who remained its secretary-general until March 1980. In the 1960s, the PCB stuck to a strategy of peaceful transition to socialism. This was the principal reason who so many militants split from the party and formed other clandestine parties. After the 1964 coup it reverted to illegality. The orthodox wing of the party rejected the armed struggle and allied itself with the officially permitted opposition party, the Brazilean Democratic Movement, in order to participate legally in the Congress. As a result, this PCB faction was relatively protected from the repression unleashed after 1968. A general attack against the PCB, was launched only after 1974. In successive waves of detentions, hundreds of members and important leaders were imprisoned, tortured and killed throughout the country. L.C.Prestes returned from exile in 1979. During the 7th Congress in 1982 the federal police arrested the entire central committee and about 80 ordinary members. All but seven were released.

* Caparaó Guerrilla
Minor guerrilla group that sprang from the National Revolutionary Movement. Its activities mounted to no more than a sequence of military training exercises carried out in the vicinity of a mountain called the Pico das Bandeiras, in Minas Gerais. All the members of the group were detained for interrogation in March 1967, and one of them, Milton Soares de Castro, was killed. When militants involved in the 'Caparaó Guerrilla began to be released from prison, during the second half of 1969, they initiated a new organization. It was first known as the Independence or Death Movement and later became known as National Armed Resistance.

* Comando Delta
A right-wing death squad.

* Comando Herzog

A right-wing death squad.

* Communist Party of Brazil
(Partido Comunista do Brasil) (PCdoB)
Maoist breakaway from the main Moscow-line PCB formed in 1961. Its leaders were Joao Amazonas, Mauricio Grabois, Pedro Pomar. The party openly advocated armed struggle in Brazil, in cooperation with other Marxist guerrilla groups. For the PCdoB, the most important stage of the revolutionary struggle would take place in rural areas. The struggle would be waged by means of a war supported from its inception by strong popular participation, particularly among peasants. It criticized other groups for giving to little importance to the participation of the 'masses' in the revolutionary struggle. Internal disagreement culminated in the formation of two dissident groups: the Red Flank in Sao Paulo and the center-south of the country, and the Revolutionary Communist Party in the north-east. Both groups were formed in 1966-67. From the end of 1966 on the PCdoB devoted itself to relocating party members to the Araguaia region in the state of Pará, This region was chosen as the most likely site of a future 'popular army'. In April 1972, security organs detected their presence. Large numbers of army troops engaged in successive siege operations against the militants. When the battles began the party constituted itself as the Araguaia Guerrillas Forces. In the end the government troops won a clear military victory. Two splinter groups of the Red Flank appeared in the 1967-1970 period. They were known as the Tiradentes Revolutionary Movement (MRT) and the Marxist Revolutionary Movement (MRM). During a raid by security forces in Sao Paulo on Dec.16, 1976, three members of the party's central committee, among them Pedro Pomar, were killed and six others were arrested. The party remained illegal, although some members were allowed to return from exile under a 1979 government amnesty. In the 1980s no more violent activities were reported.

* Communist Revolutionary Movement
(Movimiento Comunista Revolucionário) (MCR)
In 1970, a small group of militants left the Communist Workers' Party (POC) and created the MCR. The group executed a few joint armed actions with the VPR.

* Death Squad
(Escudrao da Morte)
A right-wing terrorist organization founded in 1961 by policemen who wished to avenge the death of one of their collegues at the hands of a criminal. It was lead by Sergio Paranhos Fleury (head of police of Sao Paulo) who died on May 1, 1979, in an accident. By 1970 its members were estimated to have killed 1,000 of more alleged criminals and other 'undesirables', marking their victims with a skull and crossbones. The murdering continued in the 1970s and 1980s. Only a few policemen have been sentenced on murder charges.

* Democratic Resistance or Nationalist Democratic Popular Resistance
In mid-1969 a former army soldier named Eduardo Leite, known as 'Bacuri' withdrew from the VPR. He formed a small dissident group called Democratic Resistance, which existed for only one year. It perpetrated armed actions in Sao Paulo, collaborating with the ALN, the VPR, and the MRT in a combined 'front'. Bacuri himself was captured in August 1970, in Rio de Janeiro, by Sao Paulo policeman Fleury and by agents of Rio's Navy Information Center. By that time, Bacuri was a member of the ALN. He was subjected to prolonged tortures until December of that year, when he appeared on the list of prisoners to be freed in exchange for the safe return of the kidnapped Swiss ambassador. Instead of releasing Bacuri, security agents executed him. After the murder, they released a public version of the events, claiming that he had been killed during a shootout.

* Departemento de Operacoes de Informacoes-Coordencao da Defensa Interna (DOI-CODI)
Main office of the military intelligence service which has links with paramilitary groups. It operated a number of clandestine prisons and engaged in human rights abuses.

* Departemento de Orden Politica Social (DOPS)
Police service that engaged in torture.

* Garimpeiros
A private defence force of the gold company Gold Amazon. Armed with automatic weapons they force Indians from their homeland.

* Groups of Eleven
(Grupos de Onze) (G-11)
Secret organization consisting of 11-member cells. It was led by the leftist deputy and former governor of Rio Grande de Sul state, Leonel Brizola. When the military seized power in 1964, Brizola fled to Uruguay. Presumably due to its earlier activities, the second wave of Brazilean political violence in the 1960s found support in the Rio Grande do Sul. The PCB was thought to be responsible for a number of actions of the organization.

* Lieutenant Mendes
(Tenente Mendes)
A right-wing terrorist group which directed its actions against left-wing newspapers. It was active in 1980 and has been involved in bombings and

assassinations.

* 26th of March Revolutionary Movement (MR-26)
A minor guerrilla group headed by Colonel Jefferson Cardim Osório, tried to unleash an armed movement in the Três Passos and Tenente Portela regions in March 1965. It was defeated in a few days. Those militants who had not been captured organized the 26th of March Revolutionary Movement in honor of those who had fought with Osório and who remained in prison after suffering tortures. The MR-26 was also involved in a few armed actions in the city of Porto Alegre. In 1969, after several of its members were captured, the group was disbanded.

* Movement of Revolutionary Action (MRA)
This group represented military personnel who were held in the Lemos Brito Penitentiary in Rio de Janeiro. These individuals had been prosecuted and condemned in military courts for their involvement in the Association of Navy and Marine Personnel in Brazil and in the 'Sergeants Uprising' in 1963. In brief, they represented those forces within the military that had been loyal to the Goulart government. In May 1969 the group made a spectacular escape from the penitentiary, eluding authorities who pursued them for several days in the mountains around Angra dos Reis on the Rio coast. The group carried out several armed actions in the city of Rio, but almost all members were captured in August of that year. Those who escaped became members of other urban guerrilla organizations.

* National Intelligence Service (SNI)
Intelligence service of the government which was established after the 1964 coup. It has been led for five years by president Figueiredo and has been involved in scandals and murder.

* National Liberating Alliance
(Alianca Libertadora Nacional) (ALN)
Pro-Cuban urban guerrilla movement set up in 1968 by dissidents of the pro-Moscow PCB. Its activities decreased after the death of its leaders. Carlos Marighella died in a gun battle with police in Sao Paulo in 1969. The murder was engineered by civilian police chief Sérgio Paranhas Fleury, a notorious torturer. Joachim Camara Ferreira was abducted in Sao Paulo and killed under torture by the same police chief on a secluded farm that operated as a clandestine repression center. The security forces uncovered its links and many members were jailed or fled into exile in the 1969-1971 period. It advocated demoralization of the government by persistent terrorist actions in the cities and a concentrated attacks upon the economy by targeting foreign and national companies. It has been involved in bank raids, kidnappings, sabotage of transport and oil pipelines and the destruction of food supplies. It had contacts with MR-8 and VPR. The ALN fell apart in several splinter organizations, including the Movement of Popular Liberation (MPL), Marx, Mao, Marighella and Guevara (M3G), and the Front for the Liberation of the North East.

* National Liberation Commando
(Comando da Libertacao Nacional) (COLINA)
A Marxist-Leninist faction which sprang from the majority of POLOP militants in Minas Gerais in 1967. It supported armed revolution, alongside the Revolutionary Popular Vanguard (VPR). As it was hit by a number of arrests, it merged with the VPR in April 1969. The result of the merger was a new organization, VAR-Palmares, named in honor of a historic rebel slave settlement. From 1968 on, COLINA engaged in armed actions to obtain funds that would be used to create a 'strategic area' in the rural region of Brazil.

* National Liberation Front
(Frente de Liberacion Nacional) (FLN)
Group that emerged in 1969. It incorporated some survivors of the MR-26. It lasted one year only, executing some urban guerrilla operations in Rio Grande do Sul and Rio de Janeiro in conjunction with other groups. Its leader, Joaquim Pires Cerveira, was imprisoned in April 1970. In June 1970, when the German ambassador was abducted, Cerveira was among those prisoners for whom the ambassdor was exchanged. He was banished from Brazil upon his release from prison. Three years later he was arrested by security agents when he and other exiles tried to reenter the country. To this day he remains on the list of 'disappeared political prisoners'.

* National Revolutionary Movement
(Movimiento Nacionalista Revolucionário) (MNR)
Minor rural guerrilla group active in the late 1960s. It was joined by the pro-Chinese PCdoB and Popular Action (AP). It had in its ranks a nucleus of former members of the armed services.

* New Fatherland Phalange
(Falange Patria Nova) (FPN)
Extreme right-wing guerrilla group which emerged in August 1980. It carried out many bomb attacks.

* Operacao Bandierantes (OBAN)
A death squad which emerged in 1969, formed by army, navy and police officers. It was very active in Sao Paulo.

* Popular Revolutionary Vanguard
(Vanguardia Popular Revolucionaria) (VPR)
Pro-Cuban guerrilla movement which emerged from Workers' Politics (POLOP) in March 1968. It was

led by Carlos Lamarca (killed by security forces in 1971) and by Joao Quartim. The VPR joined with the COLINA group in July 1969, forming the VAR-Palmares. In September of the same year, Lamarca took the VPR out of VAR-Palmares and determined to concentrate activities upon the countryside. Despite successive waves of imprisonments of militants, the VPR kept up a strong rythm of armed actions from 1968 to 1971, mainly in Sao Paulo and Rio. Beginning in 1971, the VPR rapidly disintegrated. The death blow occurred in 1973, when police infiltrator 'Cabo Anselmo' supervised the killing of the remaining militants, who were trying to restructure the organization in the Recife region. It had links with the ALN and the PLO. Since the death of its leaders activities have decreased. Arrests of suspected members continued until 1978. In 1979 it was reported that a number of VPR members were receiving guerrilla training in camps of the PLO.

* Popular Action
(Acao Popular) (AP)
Group which was established in 1962. It consisted of young and radical church-minded people who saw the resort to violence as the only means of achieving social justice. In its basic document written in 1963, the AP proposed to struggle for a just society. The group condemned both capitalism and existing socialist countries. It was most influential among students but also penetrated worker and peasant circles. After the 1964 coup the AP suffered the full impact of repression. During a period in which it redefined its principles it was gradually taken over by a Maoist faction. In practice, however, the AP was never involved in guerrilla actions. In 1968, an internal struggle took place that resulted in the formation of a new dissident group, the Workers' Revolutionary Party (PRT). The PRT executed some armed actions but broke up in 1971. AP after being attacked by the repressive organs became the Marxist- Leninist Popular Action of Brazil (APML) and merged with the PCdoB in 1972. From 1973, a group that had rejected the incorporation with the PCdoB in 1972, became better known as the Socialist AP. The latter suffered harsh repression by the security organs.

* Revolutionary Communist Party of Brazil
(Partido Comunista Revolucionario do Brasil) (PCBR)
Maoist party which broke away from the PCB in March 1967. Its founders included Mario Alves de Souza Vieira, Carlos Marighella, and Apolonia de Carvalho who was released from detention in March 1970 in exchange for the release of the West German ambassador kidnapped by the VPR. It was formally constituted as a party in Rio in April 1968. The strategy of the PCBR for taking power was similar to that of the ALN, especially in choosing rural areas as the most important staging ground for the struggle toward a 'popular revolutionary government'. After April 1969, the PCBR dedicated itself to armed activities in urban centers, primarily for the purpose of promoting revolutionary propaganda. The intensification of the repression during the second half of the year drove the party underground. After their first attack on a bank in Rio de Janeiro, half of the group's Central Committee was imprisoned. Mario Alves was brutally murdered with a series of tortures that included the scraping of his skin with a steel brush and the medieval torment of impalement. Between 1970-1972 the PCBR practiced urban guerrilla warfare. At the beginning of 1973, members of the last designated Central Committee of that phase of the organization were killed in Rio when the DOI-CODI of the First Army set fire to a car of the organization in which some of the militants were present.

* Revolutionary Movement 8 October
(Movimiento Revolucionario do Octubre 8) (MR-8)
Revolutionary movement which was established in 1968. The name commemorates the death of Che Chevara on Oct.8, 1967. It consisted of Marxist-Leninists who broke with the orthodox communist movement. It operated in Paraná and had links with radical student circles in the Federal University of Rio de Janeiro and with the ALN. After the MR-8 abducted the American ambassador Elbrick in September 1969, it suffered its first wave of violent reprisals. It continued to carry out armed operations in Rio throughout 1970. In 1971, as a result of the break-up of the VPR, a group of former VPR-militants, including leader captain Carlos Lamarca, requested admission into the MR-8. It was as a member of MR-8 that he was killed in an ambush. His death which occurred only after a prolonged nation-wide search by the authorities, was a serious blow to the armed struggle. The MR-8 was dismantled in 1972, when virtually all its surviving members fled to Chile. In subsequent years, however, the organization was rebuilt. It resurfaced in other Brazilean states, after members had repudiated armed struggle and adopted political positions that differed substantially from their former views.

* Revolutionary Tiradentes Movement
(Movimiento Revolucionario Tiradentes) (MRT)
Urban guerrilla group which had been active in 1970 and 1971. One of its founders, José de Carvalho, was killed by police in Sao Paulo on Apr.5, 1971. On Apr.15, 1971, police announced the death of Dimas Antonio Cassemiro and another MRT member.

* Rota

A death squad which has operated in Sao Paulo.

* Socialist Convergence
(Convergenca Socialista) (CS)
Small Trotskyite group which was said to be involved in the April 1982 riots in Sao Paulo. Several members were detained.

* Union of Democratic Ruralists (UDR)
Ultra rightist organization of rich landowners which was established in July 1986. Together with other landed interests it is combatting land reform proposals. It has close links with military officials in the intelligence service (SNI), the military command in Brasilia and the National Security Council. It has between 1,200 and 5,000 members. The organization is led by Plinio Junquiera and Ronaldo Caiado and has $ 250.000 at its disposal. It finances armed resistance against land occupations.

* Vanguard of the Commando of Communist Hunters
(Vanguarda do Comando de Cacu aos Comunistas) (CCC)
Anti communist death squad which is held responsible for hundreds of assassinations in the early 1980s.

* White Hand (Rio de Janeiro)
A death squad which operated in Rio de Janeiro.

BRUNEI

* Brunei People's Party
(Parti Ra'ayat Brunei) (PRB)
Banned organization which was established in 1959 and which operates from Malaysia. It is led by A.M.N.Azahari. In December 1962, the North Borneo Liberation Army linked with the PRB carried out a revolt with the object of preventing Brunei's entry into the then proposed Federation of Malaysia. The revolt was repressed with the help of a British Task Force. It subsequently operated from exile in Malaysia, with the use of facilities in Sarawak (East Malaysia). At the UN the PRB has petitioned for the right of the people of Brunei to self-determination and independence.

* North Kalimantan National Army
(Tentera Nasional Kalimantan Utara) (TNKU)
The military wing of the PRB.

BULGARIA

* Dazjavna Sigurnost
Bulgarian security service.

* Social Democratic Union (SDU)
Munich (West Germany) based social democratic group which was accused of being linked with the Bulgarian secret service. Stefan Tabakov (chairman of the exiled Social Democratic Party) alleged that the Union's vice-chairman had hired a Bulgarian to make an attempt on his (Tabakov's) life on the model of the murder of Georgi Markov, a Bulgarian employee of the BBC who was killed in London in Sep.1978.

BURMA

* Arakan Liberation Front (ALF)
A small guerrilla movement which was established in 1974 by Khaing Mo Lin to form a cohesive organization of Moslem Arakanese which periodically had revolted against Rangoon. The movement suffered serious losses in the mid 1970s and did not recover from the death of its leader in June 1977. It superseded a Moslem Mujahid movement which had conducted guerrilla operations in 1952-1954. By 1961 it had been reduced to insignificance.

* Arakan Communists 'Red Flag' (ACRF)
A group which demanded the establishment of a 'Republic of Arakan' with the right to secede from the Union of Burma. It had unsuccessfully talks on the restoration of peace with the Revolutionary Council, which were broken off on Nov.18, 1963, because the council could not accede to the communists' demand.

* Burmese Communist Party (Red Flags)
Trotskyite party which was formed in 1946 as a result of a split in the BCP. It conducted its own guerrilla operations but by 1961 its strength was officially estimated at no more than about 500 men with this number declining further, as two of its leaders had surrendered.

* Burmese Communist Party (White Flags) (BCP)
One of the oldest insurgent groups which has operated underground since 1948. It did not become a significant factor in the Shan state insurgencies until 1967. Peng Chia'a-fa is its key military commander. It operates in areas that accounts for nearly half of Burma's opium production. It drew heavily on the Akha, Lisu, Lahu and Wa minorities and its strength is estimated at 8,000 to 15,000 fighters. It appealed to other insurgent forces to form alliances. Since China's aid levels dropped sharply in 1980, it moved more deeply into the opium trade. It developed its own narcotics production and sales capability. Secret negotiations with the government failed in 1981. Since then the BCP has resumed miltary action, albeit not on the scale of the late 1970's. It demanded that its armed units be included in Burma's armed forces, two seats in the State Defence Council and recognition of the territories it holds as autonomous regions.

• Chinese Irregular Forces (CIF)
The 3rd and 5th CIF are remnants, now in the third generation, of KMT divisions which retreated into Burma in 1949-50. Their presence in the triangle has involved thorny diplomatic problems for Burma, Thailand, the US and Taiwan. Both CIF forces were loosely supervised by the Thai Army Supreme Command, which hired some of their soldiers for security operations in Chiang Rai and Nan Provinces. Thai Prime Minister Prem Tidsalunon dissolved the relationships between the Thai Army and the CIF in 1981. Thai narcotics suppression forces have actively targetted the CIF in recent years, particularly their refining complex in Piag Luang. Nevertheless, the 3rd CIF remains a significant force on the Thai-Burmese border and an important link in the Golden Triangle opium economy.

• Chin National Organisation (CNO)
Minor guerrilla group which has been striving for Chin autonomy.

• Federal National Democratic Front (FNDF)
Front formed by five insurgent organizations of national minorities, the KNU, KNPP, NMSP, SSPP and ACP with the object of overthrowing 'Ne Win's one party military dictatorship' which had come to power in 1962, and establishing in Burma a federal union based on national self determination. By 1976 the FNDF was said to have been joined by four other organizations. It superseded the earlier NDUF. It was established on May 27, 1975 and is led by Mahn Ba Zan and Bo Mya.

• Kachin Independence Army (KIA)
Ethnic guerrilla group which conducted guerrilla operations before the military coup in 1962. Its strength is estimated at 4,000 to 5,000 fighters. It operates in Kachin state and in northern Shan State supporting the political KIO. It maintains a small base in Tham Ngop, Thailand, to handle its external trade affairs. It has an off-on relationship with the BCP. It controls significant opium producing areas and was once a primary operator of opium caravans to the border.
Its role has diminished in recent years.

• Kachin Independence Organisation (KIO)
Kachin separatist group that signed an alliance with the BCP in 1976. Its strength is estimated at 1,500 fighters. In October 1980, KIO forswore independence and committed itself instead to national revolution.

• Karenni National Liberation Army (KNLA)
Armed wing of the KNU which is striving for an autonomous Karen republic. It is led by General Bo Mya and its strength was estimated at 4,000 armed men and a militia of 1,000 men in 1983. It operates south of the Shan States. It is involved in traditional guerrilla tactics but in October 1980 and January 1981 it deployed larger units. It is relatively well armed despite the absence of external backers, thanks to an illegal arms market and theft from the Burmese army.

• Karenni National Progressive Party (KNPP)
Small guerrilla faction which has been active in the 1950s. It has also been involved in narcotics trafficking and was a member of the NDUF. It operates in the southern Shan State and northern Kayah State on the southern boundary of the Golden Triangle. From time to time it ran its own refineries but it has never developed enough infrastructure within the regional trafficking system to make it a key narcotics organization.

• Karen National Union (KNU)
Organization which became active in 1949. It is striving for an autonomous state. It is led by General Bo Mya and Mahu Ngwe Aung. Its strength was estimated at 5,000 to 8,000 fighters in late 1982. It has been a member of the illegal NDUF coalition. Since its collapse in 1963 the KNU has offered a dogged resistance in the east, without substantial impact. In recent years it has been involved in several large scale operations and attacks on ferries and trains.

• Kayah New Land Revolutionary Council (KNLRC)
A local and small guerrilla faction in Kayah state which fought together with the SSNLO and the BCP against government forces in 1981.

• Lahu State Army (LSA)
Small guerrilla faction led by Chau Erh, son of the Lahu 'Man Good'. His control over Lahu has been challenged since 1979 by A Bi, a leader of pro-Communist Lahu who split from the BCP. Its strength is estimated at 300 to 400 fighters. It has provided protection for narcotics' refiners in the Doi Lang area. Doi Lang, one of the primary concentrations of heroin refineries on the Thai-Burmese border, has been at the center of conflict for most of the 1980s. Both the SUA and BCP have tried to control the Doi Lang area. At the same time, Doi Lang has been attacked numerous times by Burmese army troops and Thai narcotics suppression forces. The Lahu must continually forge new alliances to maintain their presence in this thriving drug center.

• Mon National Liberation Army
Ethnic guerrilla organization led by General Taw Mon. It is reported to have 3,000 members.

• National Liberation Front (NLF)
Formed in June 1970 under an agreement signed by

U Nu, the KNU and Mon rebel leaders. It aimed at the restoration of democracy in Burma and the establishment of a federal form of government under which the national minorities would enjoy complete autonomy, including the right to control their own police force and armed militia. It was led by General Bo Let Ya. By September 1973 the NLF's strenght was estimated at less than 1,000 men.

* New Mon State Party (NMSP)
Mon guerrilla faction established in 1940s. It aimed at greater Mon autonomy from Rangoon and fought during the 1950s and 1960s. It largely disappeared by the end of the next decade. It was a member of the NDUF and FNDF.

* Nom Suk Han
One of the oldest groupings under the leadership of Sao Noi. It broke up and the nucleus of 90 men, many of them nationalistic students, joined 140 Shan deserters from the Burmese army. Together they were to constitute the basis of the future Shan State Independence Army.

* Paluang National Liberation Organization (PNLO)
Guerrilla movement based in the Taunggyi area. It is thought to have 1,500 armed followers.

* Parliamentary Democratic Party (PDP)
Guerrilla faction established in 1962. It was led by former Prime Minister U Nu. It engaged in small-scale guerrilla raids and minor bomb attacks.

* Patriotic Liberation Army (PLA)
Military wing of the Parliamentary Democratic Party. Its strength was estimated from 1,200 in October 1970 to 3,000-5,000 in August 1971. It operated in the Thai border area and called for an insurrection in 1972. In October 1972, 500 PLA supporters had been arrested in various cities. Since then activities ceased.

* People's Patriotic Party (PPP)
Party which superseded the PDP in 1975. It was led by Bo Let Ya and U Thwin. Factions which had seceded from the PDP were the Union Solidarity Party led by Tin Maung Win and the Anti Fascist People's Unity Party led by Bo Hmu Aung and Kyaw Din. Three smaller underground factions were called the Kawthulay Insurgents, the Mon Patriotic Group and the Expatriate Faction.

* Self Defense Militias
(Ka Kwei Yei) (KKY)
Confronted with a Chinese backed Burmese Communist insurgency, Rangoon deputized 50 warlord armies as mobile militias in 1967. They were given patents by the central government to engage in smuggling including opium, in return for their commitment to fight Burmese Communist insurgents. They were outlawed in 1971-1973. Some returned to the government camp while others moved deeply into narcotics trafficking, a thriving industry as the war escalated in Vietnam. Two heads Chan Shee Fu, alias Khun Sa and Lo Hsin Han, became at its dissolution in 1973 the 'opium kings'. Lo Hsin Han, sentenced to death and liberated in 1980 reconstituted, with the help of Birmans a new militia destined to fight Shan nationalists and communist guerrillas.

* Shan National Army (SNA)
A small guerrilla faction of 500 fighters led by Duan Shiwen, a former Kuomintang general.

* Shan State Army (SSA)
Largest ethnic guerrilla organization which dates back from the 1957 Shan rebellion. It is the military arm of the SSPP. Since 1959 it was called SSIA and in 1964 it changed to the SSA. Hso Lane assumed leadership in 1964. It has 8,000 fighters of which 3,500 are well armed. It is based on the Wa and Paluang people and operates on the Thai border east of the Salween River. It has been engaged in a struggle for supremacy in the Shan region with SURA since 1972. It broke its links with the BCP in 1977, but finding itself short of arms settled for a compromise whereby the BCP was permitted to use the enclave as a staging post in exchange for continued supplies. The Pa-o, Lahu and Paluang have created their own armed groups.

* Shan State Army Eastern (SSAE)
One of the guerrilla factions. Its strength is estimated at 10,000 armed insurgents. It is supported by a village militia of 30,000 men.

* Shan State Independence Army (SSIA)
Guerrilla movement which appeared in 1959. Until 1964 it was led by Pi Sai Luang. After his resignation and retirement the guerrillas changed their name in SSA.

* Shan State Nationalities Liberation Organization (SSNLO)
Guerrilla organization which undertook combined guerrilla operations with units of the People's Army of the BCP and also the Kayah New Land Revolutionary Council in 1981. It is led by Tha Kalei and is dominated by the Pa-o people. It has tried to control narcotics trafficking in the South Central Shan State through taxation of opium passing through the refineries. Some SSNLO leaders have particpated in refining consortia.

* Shan State Progress Party (SSPP)
A political party supported by Shan and Paluang. It is the principal Shan insurgent organization led by Hso Lane. It has grown through a myriad

permutations and alliances with other insurgent or narcotics trafficking organizations. The party shapes the military organization, political officers hold positions in the SSA and have the exclusive right to sit in committees, something their military counterparts do not. Its central committee is based in the district of Kyaukme.

* Shan State Voluntary Force
(Lo Hsing Han Organization) (SSVF)
Lo's Kokang KKY was a major power in the Golden triangle from 1967, when Royal Lao Government generals lost a major battle for control of opium, until 1973 when he was captured by the Thai and extradicted to Burma. During this period Lo was loosely allied with Jimmy Yang, former Sawbwa of Kokang, and his New Shan State Army. His younger brother, Lo Hsing Min, attempted to fashion the remnants of the Lo Organization into the Shan State Revolutionary Army. Without Lo's leadership it remained a second-rate trafficking organization dependent on alliances with other groups. In June 1980 Lo was released from jail, and the SSRA came back to Burma under a general amnesty order. Since then Lo has reformed his group as the SSVF to fight the BCP. Should support from Rangoon be inadequate to maintain his force, he could return to the opium business. He is believed to be a leader capable of challenging Chang Chi-fu.

* Shan State People's Freedom League (SSPFL)
A faction of younger Shan leaders who allied themselves with the Burman socialist leaders. The 1962 coup by the Burmese military and the radical, revolutionary program of socialist unity which it proposed, propelled the reactionary group into active insurgency. The SSPFL, on the other hand was torn apart by the coup. The SSPFL leader U Tun Aye, joined force with the military government, and became the ranking Shan member of the Burmese Socialist Program Party. He also became chairman of the new Revolutionary Government's Shan State Affairs Council. The difficulty for the Shan insurgent leaders was that there were so many alliance possibilities and that there was so little common agreement on either goals or organization. For Shan leaders with aspirations for greater power, this inability to forge a unified movement among the Shan meant going beyond the Shan community for allies, whether they were other ethnic insurgents, warlord organizations, or other groups.

* Shan United Army (SUA)
Most important drug traffic organization which emerged from the Loi Maw KKY, one of the two largest militias. Since 1975 it has sought to extend its operations in the Thai-Burmese border area. Chang Chi-fu (or Khun Sa) has 5,000 to 8,000 men under his command. He emerged as the undisputed king of the Golden triangle. It has maintained close ties in the past with senior Thai military officers and politicians, the Thai Supreme Command and with an intelligence bureau of Taiwan. Until displaced by Thai military action in 1982, it operated out of the fortified village of Ban Hin Taek in Thailand. It also has bases along the border in Lao Lo Chai, a key refining complex, and in Mae Suya in Mae Hong Son province. The old KKY base area in Loi Maw remains a SUA strongpoint and the principal source of its opium. Bases are now located deeper into the Burmese side of the border.

* Shan United Revolutionary Army (SURA)
Small Shan based guerrilla group. Previously it was called the Tan Gyan .Ka Kwei Yei. It was established in 1969 and is led by Moh Heng. Its strength is estimated at 2,000-3,000 guerrillas and 8,000 trained reservists. It was strongly anti-communist and was equipped with US-made weapons. After an open conflict with the SSA, it has been closely allied with the 3rd CIF. Today it has re-organized as the T'si Independence Army. It continues to maintain its role in both refining and trafficking drugs.

* Thailand Revolutionary Council (TRC)
On March 3, 1985 rivalling chiefs Moh Heng and Khun Sa signed a treaty in which they declare to fuse their respective forces to constitute an enlarged TRC which marked the definitive rupture with the KMT. Moh Heng became president and Khun Sa controlled the army and the finances.

* United Pa-o Organization
Small communist Pa-o guerrilla group. Its strength is estimated at 300 regular soldiers and an armed militia of 500 men. It operates alongside the BCP on the borders of the Shan and Karen states, west of Mong Mah.

* Wa National Army (WNA)
A company size force commanded by Ma Ha San which once was a party of the SSA. It broke away to become a separate force in 1975-1976 following the SSA's alliance with the BCP. Like the Lahu, the Wa have sought to capitalize on their alliances as a way of preserving Wa organization. They have never been able to build their own narcotics trafficking group but have usually linked their forces with one of the powerful warlord armies.

BURUNDI

* Inyenzi
Tutsi terrorist organization which was established in 1961 by Tutsi exiles after the assassination of the Crown Prince in October 1961. Its aim was to overthrow the Rwandan government and restore monarchical rule. On Nov.25, 1965 it launched its

first invasion which was successfully countered by Burundi.

• Revolutionary Youth Rwagasore (JRR)
Organization which is led by Nanga Yivuza.

CAMEROON

• Army of the Black People of Cameroon
On July 10, 1980, an anonymous caller claiming to speak for this organization accepted responsibility for a bomb attack on the Paris office of the German Federal Railways. He declared that the attack marked the start of an offensive against German imperialism in Africa.

• Mixed Mobile Brigade (BMM)
Paramilitary police which has been responsible for routine beatings and ill-treatment of suspects held in custody.

• Union of Cameronian Peoples
(Union des Populations Camerounaises) (UPC)
Clandestine party based in Paris which was banned when it was regarded as communist led and responsible for riots in May 1955. After 1956 it split into a Marxist wing led by Félix Moumié and a nationalist wing led by Ruben Um Nyobé, who led a rebellion inside Cameroon but was killed by security forces in September 1958. Dr.Moumié planned to launch a guerrilla war in Cameroon with troops trained in China and Nkrumah's Chinese-run guerrilla school. He died on Nov.3, 1960, in Geneva after he alleged that he was poisoned by the 'Red Hand', a French organization engaged in counter-terrorist activities against the Algerian nationalists. In the post-independence period UPC was held responsible for protracted unrest until 1970.

CANADA

• Babbar Khalsa Organization (BKO)
A radical Sikh underground group which has been active under Indian immigrants. In 1985, two Sikhs, Lal Singh and Ammand Singh, have been named in connection with a bomb explosion in a plane on the Narita-airport in Tokyo, in which two people were killed. Their names have also been mentioned in connection with a bomb attack on an Indian Airways Boeing 747 that crashed near Ireland, killing 329 persons. The latter attack has been claimed by several groups.

• Canadian Knights of the Ku Klux Klan
White supremacist group which has been involved in militant actions. It is led by James McQuirter ('grand wizard' and national director). Mary Ann McGuire, described as a 'grand titan' in the Canadian Klan was arrested in Dominica on April 29, 1981, in connection with a proposed invasion of the island by US and Canadian mercenaries.

• Direct Action
Terrorist group which claimed responsibility for bomb attacks at the Hydro Electric Substation in British Columbia and at a factory of Litton Systems (which produces guidance systems for cruise missiles) in Toronto in 1982.

• Quebec Liberation Front
(Front de Libération du Quebec) (FLQ)
Urban terrorist group which was responsible for more than 200 bomb attacks in the 1964-1969 period. Activities reached a peak in 1970. It broke away from the Réseau de Résistance which had begun to stockpile arms for an eventual campaign. It operated in small independent cells without a central command and targeted public buildings, post boxes and telephone booths. Its tactics developed from molotov cocktail attacks, to kidnappings, bank raids and finally to political murder. Its aims were a complete separation of the province of Quebec, an end to English-language 'colonial domination' of Quebec and a transition to a socialist economy. By 1969 the authorities were convinced that they faced an organized subversive movement which planned eventual armed insurrection. It proclaimed the War Measures Act and arrested 250 suspects. Since then its separatist aspirations were channeled into legitimate political paths through the Parti Quebecois.

• Western Guard
Xenophobic paramilitary organization which has a small group of followers. Formerly it was known as the Edmund Burke Society.

• Wimmin's Fire Brigade
Militant feminist group which has claimed responsibility for several cases of arson at pornography video shops in November 1982.

CANARY ISLANDS

• Movement for Self-Determination and Independence for the Canary Islands Archipelago (MPAIAC)
Independence movement which has been active since 1961. It has been the personal creation of Antonio Cubillo, who left the islands after receiving two jail sentences for his part in labour disputes in 1962. Since 1976 it has been involved in a campaign of 'armed propaganda'. In 1977 armed struggle began. Its aims are the creation of an independent Canary Islands republic to be called the Guanch Republic with limited autonomy for each of the seven main islands. Two other aims are election of a national assembly by universal suffrage and restoration of the Guanch language. It has been involved in bomb attacks in 1977 in

Tenerife, Las Palmas and La Laguna. A bomb attack in the metro of Madrid was its first action on the main land. It has engaged in extortion and kidnapping for ransom. No incidents were recorded in the early 1980's. The movement had links with POLISARIO.

CAPE VERDE

* Independent and Democratic Union of Cape Verde
(Uniao Caboverdiana Independente e Democrática) (UCID)
Clandestine opposition movement that was opposed to the ruling PAIGC's policy of eventual union between Cape Verde and Guinea Bissau, on the grounds that such union would extend Soviet influence in the region. Since independence of Cape Verde UCID's influence declined. Members were linked to a rebellion on San Antao island against the implementation of the land reform during August 1981.

CENTRAL AFRICAN REPUBLIC

* Movement for the Liberation of the Central African People
(Mouvement pour la Libération du Peuple Centreafriain) (MLPC)
Opposition movement established in Paris in 1979. It was led by Ange Patasse, a former prime minister (Sept.1976-July 1978). The movement called for the resignation of President Dacko and the establishment of a national council charged with setting up a 'provisional government of national unity'.

* Movement for the National Liberation of Central Africa
(Mouvement Centreafricain de Libération Nationale) (MCLN)
Pro-Lybian movement which emerged in July 1981 and is led by Rodolphe Idi Lala. It was officially banned in July 18, 1981. It has been responsible for a grenade explosion in a Bangui cinema. It threatened to commit further acts of violence unless President Dacko formed a unity government comprising all political parties and also arranged for repatriation of the French troops stationed in the republic. It had links with the OPF.

* Oubangian Liberation Front
(Front de Libération Oubanguienne) (FLO)
Front set up on Sep.11, 1979 to overthrow Emperor Bokassa. It was led by General Sylvestre Bangui, former ambassador to France. He announced (in Paris) the formation of a provisional government in exile, the Republic of Oubangui, with the aim to overthrow the Emperor, drafting a new constitution and holding elections to a new national assembly within 18 months. The front had links with the FPO and the MLPC.

CHAD

* Armed Forces of the North
(Forces Armées du Nord) (FAN)
A faction of the northern Moslem opposition movement FROLINAT which was established in 1978. It had an estimated 3,000 to 8,000 armed men and was led by Hissene Habré. It took part in the government of national unity in Nov.1979, but fell out with its rivals in early 1980. In fierce fighting in the capital it was eventually beaten by the forces loyal to Goukouni Oueddei who drew upon Libyan reinforcements. Habré retreated to Sudan where his forces were re-equipped and trained to a high standard. After Libyan withdrawal he reoccupied those towns previously under FAN control. In mid-1982 he replaced Goukouni Oueddei and also reached an accord with the south.

* Armed Forces of the West (FAO)
One of the smaller guerrilla factions led by Mussa Medela.

* Chadian Armed Forces
(Forces Armées du Tchad) (FAT)
Guerrilla faction which was established in 1975 and which represented the rump of the Chadian armed forces. It was led by Abdelkader Kamougué, a former chief of the gendarmerie. It was based in the populous negroid south and had no representation in the capital. It was opposed to Libyan interventionism and even considered partition, opting for separatism. A large part of FAT forces defected to the FAN. In December 1982 FAN and FAT reportedly had combined to form a new national army.

* Chadian Democratic Front (FDT)
Opposition group which claimed to offer an alternative to Hissene Habré and Goukouni Oueddei. It is a coalition of four pre-existing opposition groups and claimed to represent 80 percent of the country. Jean Alingué, its leader and a former ambassador to Washington and Paris, said that he receives support from France and the United States. It associated itself with the struggle of the Codos in the south and the rebels in the center and center-east of the country.

* Chadian Liberation Front (FLT)
Front which emerged in the 1960s in opposition to the Tombalbaye regime. It is an orthodox moslem movement striving for an independent state in northern Chad. It merged with the UNT (Chadian National Union) into FROLINA. After three years the FLT retreated and FROLINA changed its name to FROLINAT. It operated out of Sudan.

* Chadian National Liberation Front (fundamental) (FROLINAT)
One of the FROLINAT factions which still existed in 1982. It emerged after a split in the FROLINAT in 1972. The nationalist movement led by Bibikir Ismail is opposed to neo-colonialism.

* Chadian National Liberation Front (original) (FROLINAT)
A nationalist movement opposed to neo-colonialism. It was established in 1966 by a merger of the FLT and the UNT. It was first called FROLINA but later changed its name to FROLINAT. In 1972 the latter split into a 'fundamental' and an 'original' faction. The original faction is led by A.Saddick and had links with Algeria and Libya.

* Chadian National Union
(Union Nationale Tchadienne) (UNT)
A leading Marxist opposition organization during the Tombalbaye regime. It merged with the FLT into FROLINA.

* Codos
Anti-government commandos which operate in the south. In 1985 Hissene Habré declared that several thousand codos were operating in the south of Chad, destabilizing that area so effectively that all normal activity came to a virtual halt.

* Common Action Front
(Front d'Action Commune) (FAC)
A guerrilla faction that broke away from the FROLINAT in 1980. It was led by Ahmat Acyl, who died in an accident in July 1982. Prior to becoming the FAC the group was known as Vulcan Force. It took part in the government of national unity in February 1979 and was involved in subsequent fighting in 1980 when that agreement broke down. It supported Libyan intervention in 1981.

* Democratic Revolutionary Council (CDR)
One of the numerous factions of the FROLINAT, also known as the New Vulcan Army. It was led by Acheikh Ibn Oumar. It had its base in the extreme north of the country and partly also in the south-east.

* First Army (also Vulcan Force)
One of the guerrilla factions which was active in the 1970s. It was led by Ahmat Acyl and was later renamed Common Action Front (FAC).

* Idriss Miskine Group
Group which claimed responsibility for a bomb attack on an airplane in N'Djamena in March 1984.

* National Integrated Army (ANI)
National army which was formed by integrating several guerrilla factions.

* National Patriotic Movement
(Mouvement National Patriotique) (MNP)
A politico-military front which was formed in July 1981 to resist Libyan expansionism. It is led by Doungou Kimto and has links with FAO, FROLINAT Fundamental and MPLT.

* National Peace Government (NPG)
The Chadian National United Government (GUNT) was overthrown by forces of Hissene Habré in June 1982. In reaction the NPG was established. Its formation on Oct.28, 1982, at Bardei was announced in Libya. It was stated to have been the result of a meeting in Algiers early in October of eight of the eleven factions which had composed the GUNT. Its objective was the overthrow of the Hissene Habré regime and the restoration of peace. It formed a National Liberation Army which reportedly fought several successful battles against the forces of Hissene Habré's government in January and May 1983.

* Popular Armed Forces
(Forces Armées Populaires) (FAP)
One of the armed factions consisting of the Second Army and the FROLINAT Original. It was led by Goukouni Oueddei until 1982. In May 1981 it announced a merger with FAO, CDR and First Army to form the National Council of the Revolution (CNR) and the National Integrated Army (ANI). Goukouni Oueddei presided over the government of national unity set up in November 1979. The FAN attempted a coup in early 1980. Libyan troops intervened in support of Oueddei. He complied with Libya's request to bring about a merger between the two countries. Confronted with opposition within and outside the country he eventually negotiated a withdrawal in November 1981. Habré took advantage of the withdrawal and defeated the forces of Oueddei.

* Popular Front for the Liberation of Chad
(Front Populaire pour la Libération du Tchad) (FPLT)
One of the armed factions which was established in 1979 and was led by Awad Moukhtar Nasser. It represented Sudanese interests. By 1982 the Sudanese interest was represented by Hissene Habré's FAN, with the consequent decline of the FPLT.

* Popular Movement for the Liberation of Chad (also Third Army) (Mouvement populair pour la Libération du Tchad) (MPLT)
One of the armed factions which was established in 1978. It was led by Abubakar Abderaman until his death in 1979. It represented Nigerian interests

and operated from islands in Lake Chad. It influenced events in Kanem province.

* Second Army
Guerrilla faction which was active in the north during the 1970s. It was based on the Tubu people and was led by Hissene Habré.

CHILE

* National Information Center
(Central National de Informaciones) (CNI)
Military intelligence agency established in 1978, replacing DINA. It had less power than DINA, and was principally concerned with gathering information for security purposes.

* Commando of Avengers of Humberto Tapia Barraza
A group which claimed responsibility for the killings of two left-wing members in Santiago in July 1981.

* Commando for Avenging Martyrs
(Comando Vengadores de Mártires) (COVEMA)
Right-wing group which has been active from July 1980 onwards. It is believed to consist of members of the Servicio de Investigaciones. It has been involved in kidnappings of journalists connected with church radio stations and of six students. One of them died of wounds inflicted by the kidnappers.

* Commando Carevic
Clandestine anti-communist association which caused a series of deaths in June 1979.

* Commandos of the People's Resistance
Clandestine organization which emerged in 1980. It is believed to be an offshoot of the MIR and has claimed responsibility for a number of bomb explosions.

* Commando Salvador Allende
A militia linked with the Movement of Revolutionary Left (MIR).

* Communist Party of Chile
(Partido Comunista Chileno) (PCC)
Party which was founded in 1912 and is led by Luis Corvalan. It was part of the Popular Unity Alliance. In 1971 it set up a Revolutionary Workers' Front which established 'anti-fascist brigades' in the factories. In 1972 it criticized the 'sectarian extremism' of the MIR which had alienated middle sectors of the population, and it emphasized that the correct strategy was to devide the opposition by attracting progressive sections of the PDC. After the banning by the junta it claimed that 'communal struggle' was being prepared for the overthrow of the military regime. It coordinated its anti-junta activities in exile within the framework of the Popular Unity Alliance. In 1985 it called for an armed struggle as the only means to overthrow the Pinochet regime.

* Death Squads
(Escuadrones de la Muerte)
Right-wing clandestine groups which have been responsible for assassinations and disappearances of left-wing people. The Roman Catholic Church reported in 1985 an alarming wave of kidnapping and torture cases, many of them involving young people from church-based social action groups. The abductions have been carried out by armed men in civilian clothes in a style reminiscent of death squads in Central America. Human rights officials in the church suspect that the operations are executed with the participation of the security forces.

* Directorate of National Intelligence
(Direccíon de Intelligencia Nacional) (DINA)
Intelligence agency established in 1974. It carried out assassinations on the orders of the military junta. It has been responsible for the murder of Chilean ambassador Orlando Letelier and Ronnie K.Moffitt, an American associate, in the United States in 1976. The United States has asked the Chilean government to expel two Chilean officers wanted in the 1976 murder. Washington charged General Manuel Contréras Sepulveda and Lt.Col.Pedro Espinoza, who were officers in 1976, as accessories in the assassination. The government declared that the agency was dissolved in Aug.1978. It was replaced by a new military intelligence agency called the CNI.

* Fatherland and Liberty
(Patria y Libertad) (PL)
Neo fascist para-military movement established in 1970. It was led by Pablo Rodriguez and Walter Roberto Thieme and has been involved in anti state arson and sabotage attacks. In mid-1973 the government cracked down on the organization following an attack upon the life of General Prats Gonzalez.

* FM-7
Small guerrilla group linked to the Movement of Revolutionary Left.

* Javier Carrerera Popular Resistance Commando
(Comando de Resistencia Popular Javier Carrera) (CRP)
Small guerrilla group which is thought to be an offshoot of the MIR. It carried out two operations in April 1980.

* Junta for Revolutionary Coordination (JRC)
An international subversive movement which

includes revolutionary groups from Argentina, Chile, Bolivia and Uruguay.

* Lantaro Youth Movement (LYM)
Small terrorist group active in 1985.

* Manuel Rodriquez Revolutionary Front
(Frente Revolucionario Manuel Rodriquez) (FRMR)
Guerrilla group which was established in 1983 and named after a popular Chilean guerrillero Manuel Rodriguez who fought against Spanish colonial rule. Some said it is the armed wing of the Communist party. The FRMR disdains any organizational links with political parties. It aims at the overthrow of the Pinochet regime. Previous estimates had put its strength at 1,000 to 2,000 fighters. Arms discoveries in 1986 suggest it already has about 4,000 members or hoped to expand to that number. The discovery of the arsenals were greated by widespread disbelief that government officials launched a public counter attack against sceptics, arrested a magazine editor for an article calling the arsenals phoney, and displayed some of the 50 tons of captured arms for the entire diplomatic corps. Still large sections of the society scoffed at the arsenals as a state propaganda fantasy. Long-sceptical journalists and diplomats, on the other hand have concluded that at least a fraction of the arms were in fact destined for the FPMR. The group consists of representatives of many parties who are convinced that the Pinochet regime should be overthrown by violent means. It has been involved in kidnappings, economic sabotage, assassinations and hundreds of bombings and bus burnings. An attempt to assassinate General Pinochet failed.

* Movement of Revolutionary Left
(Movimiento de la Izquierda Revolucionaria) (MIR)
Extreme left-wing group which emerged in 1967 when several ultra left-wing students at the University of Concepcion started to raid banks. The student body was transformed into a group employing violence, murder and intimidation for political ends. Its most important members were Andres Pascal Allende, Luciano Cruz and Miguel Enriquez. It had 3,000 acting members and thousands of sympathizers. It contributed to the formation of a para-military militia in the 1970s. It was not strong enough to wage armed struggle after the coup in 1973. In the 1980s occasional terrorist incidents were committed in its name. A 1981 communiqué said that the MIR leadership had joined with exiled leaders of the Popular Union formation in signing a declaration of unity providing for joint opposition to the Pinochet regime. The Chilean Communist Party labeled MIR action as mere adventurism. Members received training in Cuba.

* People's Organized Vanguard
(Vanguardia Organizada del Pueblo) (VOP)
Miniscule ultra-leftist group which was set up in 1968/69 and led by Ismael Villegas, a former Minister. It has been responsible for the 1971 murder of the Christian Democratic leader Pérez Zujovic.

* Popular Militias
(Milicias Populares) (MP)
Overall title for a number of leftist groups predominantly urban such as Commando Salvador Allende or Popular Resistance Militia which are all linked to the MIR and have been involved in a number of killings.

* Popular Nationalist Movement
(Movimiento Nacionalista Popular) (MNP)
Right-wing movement which emerged in 1980. It is led by Robert Thieme, a former military officer. It operates in Temuco in the south and has some support from dissident farmers. In October 1982 Thieme mounted an unsuccessful coup attempt against the Pinochet regime, claiming that the latter had betrayed the 'nationalist revolution' in Chile.

* Popular Unity
(Unidad Popular) (UP)
An electoral alliance of left-wing parties which led to the election of the Socialist Dr.Salvador Allende Gossens as president on Nov.4, 1970. The Allende government was overthrown by the military on Sep.11, 1973, on which day President Allende committed suicide. A secretariat was set up in Rome which disseminated news of persecution and repression. It claimed that more than 3,000 officers and men of the armed forces loyal to Allende had been executed. In 1974 it called for the formation of an 'anti-fascist front' in order to end 'illegal detention, torture and summary executions' and to regain democratic rights. It joined an alliance to oppose the Pinochet regime.

* Radical Party
(Partido Radical) (RP)
Chile's main reformist party which was founded in 1906. It has been strongly anti-communist in the 1940s and 1950s. It later gravitated to the left in 1969 and joined the Popular Action alliance. It is led by Anselmo Sule and has its main strength among white-collar workers and public officials. It has been banned by the junta. Since then it has co-ordinated its efforts to overthrow the Pinochet regime with the Popular Unity Alliance. The party was weakened by breakaways of elements opposed to its espousal of Marxism in 1971.

* Roger Vergara Command
Rightist terrorist group named after the director of the school of the intelligence service of the army,

Roger Vergara who was assassinated in July 1980.

• September Eleven Command
Group which claimed responsibility for the deaths of four leftists in 1986 saying they were killed to avenge the assassination attempt against President Pinochet.

• Unified Popular Action Movement
(Movimiento de Accion Popular Unitario) (MAPU)
One of the constituent parties of the Popular Unity Alliance. It is led by Jaime Anselmo Cuevas Hormazábal and was banned by the military junta. Since then it has coordinated its anti-junta activities within the Popular Unity Alliance.

• Unified Socialist Base (USB)
Small terrorist group active in 1985.

• White Guard
(Guardia Blanca)
Armed force set up in rural Chile by landowners to protect themselves in the early 1970s from armed land seizures organized by the Movement of the Revolutionary Left.

CHINA, PEOPLE's REPUBLIC of

• Chinese Communist Party (CCP)
Party founded in 1921. It spread quickly in the cities and among students. Initially it placed its faith in urban insurrection but when this was put down in 1927 it turned its attention to the peasantry. After a civil war against the Kuomintang Mao Tse Tung proclaimed the People's Republic of China on Oct.1, 1949. After a split with the Soviet Union it supported foreign communist movements hostile to Moscow. Its present leader, Deng Xiaoping launched a crime suppression campaign in the fall of 1983 which continued in 1985, although on a lesser scale. The authorities claimed that the campaign had reduced the crime rate by 30 percent. An estimated 5,000-10,000 persons have been executed. Some of those executed in 1985 were charged with 'counter revolutionary crimes' (usually espionage).

• Chinese National United Front (CNUF)
Underground organization which is opposed to the pragmatic policies of Deng Xiaoping. It advocates the re-establishment of the ultra-leftist policies of the Cultural Revolution. Its leaders are Zhang Sanyi, Qiu Liangqing and Ren Yuanqing. They rose to power during the violence of the Cultural Revolution. After their dismissal they formed CNUF. In July 1984, 18 members have been jailed.

• Emperor's Group
Organization which was banned in 1953. In 1984 two members were executed for having revived the group and having recruited hundreds of members.

• Nationalist Party of China
(Chung-Kuo-min-tang) (KMT)
Nationalist movement that has been involved in a war with the Japanese and the Communists. It was led by Sun Yat Sen until 1925 and by Chiang Kai-Chek until 1975. In 1949 the nationalists were beaten by the communists and the remnants of the force retreated to Formosa (Taiwan), where they set up a government under US protection. It is now the ruling party of Taiwan. The Taiwan government has consistently rejected overtures from Beijing for negotiations on peaceful reunification, detailed proposals for which have been put forward from time to time by Chinese government spokesmen. Parts of the KMT fled into Thailand and Burma where they have been involved in counterinsurgency operations and drugtrafficking.

• Red Guards
Collective name for young leftist radicals who participated in the violent upheavals accompanying the Cultural Revolution (1966-1967) in China. The armed forces and youth organizations were used by Mao Tse Tung to purge the party and to keep control until his death in 1976. In their intimidation of rightist elements, the Red Guards operated independently and outside the constraints of law and order. In January 1967 Lin Piao, defense minister, described the country as in a state of civil war. They were disbanded after the Party's 9th Congress 1969. The Red Guards served as a revolutionary model for many young leftists throughout the world. An estimated 100 million people were reported to have suffered somehow from the reign of terror by the Red Guard. Prosecutors who confined themselves to cases they could document came to an estimated 34,000 deaths and 700,000 persecutions.

• Xinjiang Dissidents
Internal opposition group of the Uighur minority. According to unofficial reports there have been armed clashes between (Moslem) Uighurs and Chinese officials and soldiers in April 1980, apparently caused by Uighur resentment against mass immigration of Chinese into the region. Ethnic tension surfaced again in 1981 as a result of renewed demands for self-rule. They seek greater religious freedom and fiscal autonomy from Beijing and less control by the Chinese. The frictions exploded into a number of violent incidents. Students from the region have protested in Beijing in 1985 against nuclear tests in their region. Other demands were democratic election of officials of ethnic minorities to replace Han Chinese, an end to coercive family planning and better education.

COLOMBIA

* Anti Kidnap Group
(Movimiento Anti Secuestro) (MAS)
Rightist paramilitary group which emerged in December 1981. It operates as the most active death squad and has been accused of killing at least 300 leftists and union members. Carlos Lehder, a cocaine king, is suspected of having established the group to halt the kidnappings for ransom by the guerrillas. It changed quickly into a force which directed its violent offensive against anything it considered leftish. The group was said to include members of the police and the army in its ranks. A published list of 163 persons which were involved included 59 names of military personnel in active service, including two colonels. At certain nights in 1986 more than 20 people were shot and killed from cars or from motorcycles.

* April 19 Movement
(Movimiento 19 Abril) (M-19)
Guerrilla group which was established in 1974. It is named after the date on which ex-President General Gustavo Rojas Pinilla, the leader of ANAPO had been defeated in presidential elections in 1970. The group rejected the claim to be the armed wing of ANAPO. On Aug.28, 1978, it declared war on the right-wing government of president J.C.Turbay Ayala. By 1981 it was the second strongest guerrilla force. Its leader Ivan Marino Ospina was killed by government forces on Aug.28, 1985. In 1981 it split into two factions, one favouring a legal political role while the other faction (CNB) called for a continuation of the struggle. It has about 2,000 armed fighters and operates in the principal cities with autonomous cells. Membership declined from 1,750 in 1985 to 550 in 1986. It has been involved in kidnappings, acts of hostage taking, bomb attacks, occupations, hijackings and bank raids and has targeted foreign consulates, the national palace and multinational companies. In the 1974-1986 period it collected a total sum of 714 million pesos in ransom money.

* Armed Revolutionary Forces of Columbia
(Fuerzas Armadas Revolucionarias de Colombia) (FARC)
Pro-Moscow guerrilla organization which was established in April 1966. It originated in Marquetalia. It is the largest and most powerful guerrilla organization in Colombia with an estimated 3,000-3,500 armed fighters and a support network of 7,000-8,000 people. It has 27 fronts in the country. The number of active fighters increased from 1,500 in 1983, to 3,050 in 1985 and 3,640 in 1986. One of its leaders, Manuel Marulanda Vélez was killed in 1970. The organization has been involved in kidnappings, armed attacks, ambushes and occupations. It has targeted the police, the army, US businesses and villages. It aims at the establishment of a 'people's government'. In guerrilla action it attacked the nerve centers of the country. The new movement also embraced labour strikes and student demonstrations as part of the struggle.

* Bandera Negra
One of the 40 active death squads that has targeted ex-convicts. It always leaves a miniature black flag in the main wound of the victim.

* Batallion America (BA)
Guerrilla organization which emerged at the end of 1985. It is an international fighting force formed by M-19. The BA has recruits from the Sandinists, and from El Salvador, Panama, Ecuador, Peru, Bolivia and Colombia itself. Although it has proclaimed its existence, so far it has mounted no significant operations.

* Cobras
A death squad which has been responsible for a mass execution of 20 alleged criminals in Cali.

* Commando Quintin Lame
Small Indian guerrilla group active in the El Cauca region. It is named after the legendary Indian leader Manuel Quintin Lame, who led the Paez and Guambiano Indians in their struggle against the land tax (terraje) they had to pay to landowners. The Paez and Guambiano Indians, which number about 200,000, established the armed self-defense force after several Indian leaders were killed by FARC. Since 1979 FARC guerrillas have killed more than 100 Indians. The Indian group has links with the Ricardo Franco group.

* Communist Party of Columbia Marxist-Leninist
(Partido Comunista de Colombia Marxista-Leninista) (PCC-ML)
Breakaway from the pro-Soviet PCC in July 1965. It advocated a prolonged revolutionary war according to the doctrine of Mao and supported Castro's Cuba. It set up the FPL and later the EPL which as a guerrilla group was active in the early 1980s. It was led by Pedro Léon Arboleda, who died in a shoot-out with the police in July 1975. It had fewer than a 1,000 members in the early 1980s and chose to remain underground.

* Deathsquads of Vigilance
Vigilant death squads which have operated under a number of exótic names and have been involved in assassinations and disappearances. They have targeted criminals, beggars and homosexuals. The Attorney General of Colombia said that 344 persons had disappeared during the first 11 months of 1985

compared with 150 in 1984. Of those reported in 1985, 71 had been released safely, 67 had been found dead and the remaining 206 were still missing. The Permanent Committee for the Defense of Human Rights has asserted that during the year ending July 1985 , 644 people were killed by the armed forces, police, secret agents, paramilitary groups or unknown persons.

* Fatherland and Order
(Patria y Orden)
Extreme right-wing paramilitary group. During 1980 it claimed several hundred lives. It continued its activities unabated during 1981.

* Green Commandos
Vigilant death squad active in 1986. It operates in Cali and has targeted criminals, beggars and homosexuals.

* Guerrillas of the Marguetalia Region
Guerrilla movement active in the Marquetalia during the 1948-1953 'Violencia' period when an independent republic was declared.

* International Coordinating Committee (ICC)
An international committee that was organized in November 1985, to pool information and to intensify the battle against governments in South America. The groups represented in the committee were said to include M-19; the Farabundo Marti National Liberation Front, the umbrella organization for five insurgent groups fighting in El Salvador; Alfaro Vive of Ecuador; the Tupac Amaru Revolutionary Movement of Peru; the Red Banner of Venezuela, and perhaps two other groups according to US military sources. Colombian officials say the coordinating committee also includes representatives from the pro-Cuban National Liberation Army and Quintin Lame.

* Justiciero Implacable
One of the 40 active death squads in Colombia that has targeted thiefs. They are shot from driving motorcycles in the street.

* National Coordination of Bases
(Coordinadora Nacional de Bases) (CNB)
M-19 faction which in 1981 rejected peaceful negotiation and the amnesty (which specifically excluded all those guilty of murder, kidnapping and extortion) and called for the continuation of the armed struggle.

* National Guerrilla Coordination
Organization in which six guerrilla groups are cooperating, including M-19, PLA, NLA, Quintin Lame, RWP and PL.

* National Latin Civil Movement
(Movimiento Civico Latino Nacional) (MCLN)
Right-wing movement established by the neo nazi and cocaine warlord Carlos Enrique Lehder Rivas to 'wage war against the US-Colombian extradition treaty'. He portrays himself as a visionary revolutionary.

* National Liberation Army
(Ejército de Liberación Nacional) (ELN)
Rural guerrilla group which was established on July 4, 1964. Its first action was recorded in January 1965. It fought for a democratic revolutionary front of workers, peasants, intellectuals, students and progressive sectors of the middle class. By September 1980 it was reduced to less than 40 active members. It increased its activities again in 1981. The number of active members increased from 430 in 1983, to 520 in 1984, to 1,040 in 1986. An attempt to set up an urban network was foiled by security forces. Until 1976 it was led by Fabio Vašquez Castano. Since then its leaders were Nicolas Rodriquez Bautista and Fr.Manuel Pérez Martinez ('Poliarco'). It cooperated cloosely with FARC and had links with Cuba. A new amnesty offer, made by President Betancur and effective from November 1982 was accepted by a number of ELN guerrillas. It has been involved in kidnappings, ambushes, town occupations and bank raids and has targeted the police and the army.

* Operation Carlos Toledo Plata
A merger of five guerrilla groups which were active in 1981. It included FARC, ELN, MAO, EPL and M-19.

* Patriotic Liberation Front
(Frente Patriotica de Liberacion) (FPL)
Guerrilla faction which emerged in Bogota in October 1979. It was set up by PCC-ML.

* Patriotic Union (PU)
Political arm of the FARC which was established in March 1985. FARC promised to reject the use of armed violence and to operate as a normal political party. The step can be seen as a first success of the Betancur government to pacify the country. In 1984 it signed a cease fire agreement with the government which went into action on May 28. The party is led by Jaime Pardo Leal. It aims at revolutionary changes and the establishment of a people's democracy and is supported by the small communist party.

* Pedro Leon Abroleda Brigade (PLAB)
Marxist guerrilla group thought to be an offshoot of the PLA. It was reported to have about 300 active fighters in September 1980.

* Peoples Revolutionary Organization (ORP)
In November 1982 this group claimed responsibility for the assassination of Gloria Lara de Echeverry

(the wife of a former President of Congress). She had been kidnapped on June, 23, 1982. Her father, Oliveiro Lara Borrero, had been assassinated in Huila in 1975.

* Popular Forces of Guerrilla Action
(Fuerzas Populares de Accion Guerillera) (FPAG)
Small guerrilla faction which emerged in 1977 in southern Colombia.

* Popular Liberation Army
(Ejército Popular de Liberación) (EPL)
Pro-Beijing guerrilla faction which was established in late 1967 by the PCC-ML. It has been active in the early 1980s and was involved in sabotage, kidnappings, armed attacks, bank robberies and bomb attacks. It had about 60 active members in September 1980. Since then the number of active members increased from 220 in 1983, to 350 in 1985, to 700 in 1986. It carried out armed attacks on the army. Important leaders were Bernardo Ferreira Crandet (who died in a clash with the army), Pedro Vásquez Rendón (disposed of by Pedro León Arboleda), Gonzalo González Mantilla, Libardo Mora Toro. The last two were replaced by Francisco Carvallo. He lost control in 1977. EPL has been mainly active in rural areas; yet failed to develop an effective rural campaign. Collaboration with other groups (ELN, M-19) contributed to ideological dissension. In the 1980s the group retained influence in the big cities despite arrests.

* Pure Law
Vigilant death squad which has been active in 1986. It operated in the Cali area and has targeted criminals, beggars and homosexuals.

* The Revenger Without a Name
Vigilant death squad which has been active in 1986. It operated in the Cali area and targeted criminals, beggars and homosexuals.

* Ricardo Franco Front (RFF)
Small guerrilla faction led by Commander Javier Delgado (José Fedor Rey). It is an offshoot of the FARC which refused to negotiate with the government. It had an estimated 40 members in February 1986. Delgado is held responsible for the killing of many of his own members. A mass grave of 164 tortured, burned and mutilated corpses was found. Delgado said these were army infiltrators who tried to destroy the organization from within. M-19 broke relations with the RFF over the incident. The RFF relieved Delgado of his command and said he would be tried for 'arbitrary detentions, torture and homicide'.

* September 14 Workers Self Defense Command
(Comando de Auto Defensa Obrera 14 de Septiembre) (CAOS)
Trotskyite guerrilla group which was established in February 1978. It operated as a MAO commando and was responsible for the killing of Rafael Pardo Buelvas, who had been Minister of the Interior at the time of a 24-hour general strike on Sep.14, 1974, which had led to widespread clashes and the death of about 18 people.

* Special Anti Narcotics Unit (SANU)
A paramilitary force which employs 1,700 top army and police recruits. It has been involved in search-and-destroy missions across Colombia's drug producing zones.

* United Front for Guerrilla Action
(Fuerzas Unidas Para la Accion Guerrillera) (FUPAG)
A unified action front of several guerrilla movements established in March 1979. It is led by Lazaro Pineda Guerra. Its total strength was estimated at 1,800 men. It was dismantled by the police and has been inactive.

* Workers' Self-Defense Movement
(Movimiento de Autodefensa Obrera) (MAO)
Movement which was established in 1978 by Armando López Suárez ('Coleta'). He was arrested in May 1980 together with Oscar Mateus Puerto ('Julian'). It operated as the urban branch of the pro-Chinese PLA in September 1978. Its strength was estimated at 20 active members (August 1980). It has been involved in assassinations and armed attacks. By mid-1981 MAO guerrillas were again active in several areas.

* Workers' Students' and Peasants' Movement
(Movimiento de Obreros, Estudiantes y Campesinos) (MOEC)
Minor movement which has been active in the 1960s. It was established in January 1960 and advocated an ultra-leftist political line, independent of the PCC. Its leaders were Antonio Larotta (killed May 1961) and Federico Arango (also killed). The movement engaged in a brief guerrilla campaign in the Valle de Cauca region.

COMOROS

* Democratic Front (DF)
Communist dominated group which has been involved in a coup attempt in March 1985. The group of two dozen Comoran soldiers and civilians attempted to assassinate the mercenary officers of the Presidential Guard, as well as certain senior members of the Abdallah regime. The action led to the arrest of about 200 military and civilian personal and to the detention of about 80 persons.

* Movement for a Democratic Comores Republic (Union pour une République Démocratique des Comores) (URDC)
Movement which was established in August 1981. It is led by Mouzaoir Abdallah (a former Foreign Minister) who had been under house arrest for three years. He fled the country in June 1981. On Nov.7, 1981 he was arrested and accused of being engaged in subversive activities. On May 19, 1982 he was given a suspended two-year prison sentence, but was pardoned on May 28.

CONGO BRAZZAVILLE

* Armed Patriotic Group of the Congo (Groupe Patriotique Armé du Congo) (GPAC)
Clandestine organization which claimed responsibility for a bomb attack in a Brazzaville cinema in 1982. The group wanted clarification of the May 18, 1977, murder of President Ngougabi and also of the imprisonment of President Joachim Yhombi Opango in 1979 after he had relinguished power to Col.Sassou-Nguesso. It also has been involved in an armed attack on the first secretary of the Congolese embassy in Brussels on Jan.29, 1980, and a bomb attack at the Congolese embassy on Feb.20, 1983.

* State Security Organization (DGSE)
This organization has been accused of torture.

COSTA RICA

* Carlos Aguero Echeverria Commando
A small guerrilla cell of the MRP which has been responsible for an RPG attack on a van used by Marine Guards at the US embassy in March 1981. Members confessed to having been trained in Cuba. It was named after a Costa Rican opponent of the Somoza regime in Nicaragua.

* The Family
Popular name of a terrorist group which emerged in March 1981. It reportedly was preparing to mount a terror campaign designed to destabilize Costa Rica, to support efforts to eliminate anti-Sandinist rebels operating out of Costa Rica, and to influence the upcoming presidential campaign in the US.

* Free Costa Rica Movement (MCRL)
Ultra rightist paramilitary movement which has been involved in an attack on the Nicaraguan embassy on June 12, 1985. It has been involved in intimidation tactics and has targeted democratic institutions in the country.

* El Gallito
Left-wing group backed by Cuba which has been responsible for the killing of policemen in 1981.

* Organization for National Emergencies
Paramilitary organization to fight terrorism which was established in 1983.

* People's Revolutionary Movement (Movimiento Revolucionario del Pueblo) (MRP)
Cuban-backed terrorist group which has been responsible for attacks in San José, including a RPG attack on a van used by Marine Guards at the US embassy in March 1981.

* Tupamaro
Uruguayan guerrilla group which was believed to train Costa Rican students in the early 1980s.

CUBA

* Alpha 66
US-based anti-Castro group. It was set up by 66 Cuban refugees in Miami in 1962 with the aim to overthrow the Castro regime. It has been involved in several attempted landings in Cuba. Andrés Nazario Sargen acted as its secretary-general and Humberto Pérez Alvarado as its chief of military operations.

* Communist Party of Cuba (PCC)
A direct descendent of Fidel Castro's guerrilla army and the July 26 Movement which constituted the personal political following during the anti-Batista period. Fidel Castro Ruz still acts as its first secretary. The organizational revolution began in 1961 with the formation of the Integrated Revolutionary Organization (ORI) which included the Popular Socialist Party, July 26 Movement and the Revolutionary Directorate. The ORI was transformed into the United Party of the Cuban Socialist Revolution in 1963. In 1965 the latter was renamed Communist Party.

* El Condor
Anti-Castro Cuban exile group. It claimed responsibility for an explosion of a Cuban airliner off Barbados on Oct.6, 1976, in which 73 persons (including 57 Cubans) were killed.

* Coordination of United Revolutionary Organizations (CORU)
Terrorist group which was founded in 1975 in Chile. Its aim was to undermine all links between Cuba and other American states. Orlando Bosch, its founder, has been responsible for several bomb attacks.

* Cuban Intelligence Agency (Directorate of General Intelligence) (DGI)
Main intelligence service of Cuba. According to some sources the Department of State Security (DSE) is the 'new' DGI. G-2 is the branch of the overall intelligence service responsible for

controlling internal subversion.

• Cuban National Revolutionary Council (CNRC)
US-based anti-Castro group formed in New York in 1961. It is led by Dr.José Miro Cardona, first prime minister in Castro's government, and called on the Cuban people to overthrow the Castro regime. It strongly denied that it was backed by the CIA.

• Cuban Nationalist Movement
(Movimiento Nacionalista Cubano) (MNC)
US based movement. Three members, Alvin Ross Díaz, Guillermo Novo Sampol and Ignacio Novo Sampol, were sentenced in Washington in 1979, for complicity in the 1976, murder of Orlando Letelier (a former Chilean ambassador and former minister under President Allende in Chile) and Ronnie K.Moffitt, an American associate.

• Cuban Power
(El Poder Cubano)
Group which has frequently attacked offices of countries and private firms doing business with Cuba.

• Independence and Democracy for Cuba
Anti-Castro group led by Mr.Matos, a former head of Castro's military forces. He reportedly has been seen with anti-Sandinist forces inside Nicaragua.

• July 26 Revolutionary Movement
Guerrilla movement named after the attack on the Moncada barracks in Santiago de Cuba on July 26, 1956. Led by Fidel Castro it succeeded in the overthrow of the Batista regime after a three year guerrilla war in which 1,000 to 2,500 people were killed. During the war its strength grew from 12 to 2,000 fighters.

• Omega Seven
US based terrorist group of Cuban exiles. Originally it was called Cuban Nationalist Action. In 1963 the name was changed to Cuban Nationalist Movement. After the 1976 murder of Orlando Letelier (a Chilean diplomat) in Washington the MNC set up Omega-7. According to the FBI it is the most dangerous terrorist group in the US. It has been responsible for a number of murders, armed attacks and bomb attacks. It has targeted newspapers, diplomatic missions at the UN, air travel agencies and commercial companies. Eduardo Arocena, its alleged leader,
was arrested on July 22, 1983. He is held responsible for at least two murders and 30 bombings in the last seven years. Omega-7 was said to have no more than 15 active members.

• Organization for the Liberation of Cuba
(Organizacion para la Liberacion de Cuba) (OPLC)
Miami-based exile group. The Reagan administration was reported to tolerate the existence of camps for clandestine training in guerrilla warfare.

• Youths of the Star Anti-Castro force which received training in the US. It is led by Jorge Gonzales.

CYPRUS

• Commander Nemo of Force Majeure
A group that has been responsible for a plot to blackmail the nation for $ 15 million in May 1987. Five suspects have been accused of threatening to poison thousands of people with deadly dioxin gas. The threat to release the dioxin was received in the form of a 13-page document sent to the presidential palace. The extortionists had threatened to release the gas near the capital, Nicosia. Four suspects were arrested in London, in an operation code-named 'Drifter'. The Scotland Yard operation was initiated on the request of the Republic of Cyprus. Four suspects were identified as Panos Koupparis, his wife Kika, and his two brothers Jason and Andreas. A fifth suspect, Thekla Andreou Hallouma, was arrested in Nicosia.

• National Organization of Cypriot Fighters
(Ethniki Organosis Kyprion Agoniston) (EOKA)
Nationalist organization which specifically rejected all contact with Marxist-Leninist organizations or movements. It advocated an armed struggle to oust the British from Cyprus and to bring about a union (enosis) with Greece. Led by George Grivas it launched a guerrilla campaign in April 1955 which reached a peak in the end of 1956 with 416 actions in one month. It had about 200 to 350 hardcore fighters and about 750 armed sympathizers. It tried to organize the population and set up a clandestine youth organization (ANE) and a covert civilian front (PEKA). After 1956 actions decreased and in 1959, it accepted a course leading to independence in 1960. Grivas disbanded EOKA and returned to Greece.

• National Front
(Ethniki Parataxis)
Greek-Cypriot nationalist organization active in 1969 which sought to impose union with Greece upon the Cypriot people. It has been involved in armed attacks and bombings. It targeted police posts, British military buildings, British vehicles, President Makarios and ministers. The campaign was not supported by the Greek government. When General Grivas arrived on the island it was succeeded by EOKA-B.

• National Organization of Cypriot Fighters
(Ethniki Organosis Kypriakou Agoniston) (EOKA-B)
Guerrilla force which emerged in September 1971. General Grivas returned secretly from Greece to

give support to the terrorist activities of the National Front. He used a network identical to the original EOKA organization and penetrated the National Guard and police. Its strength was estimated at 3,000 fighters. It has been involved in kidnappings, bombings, raids on police stations and gunsmiths, and theft of explosives. After the February 1973 elections it embarked upon a campaign of terrorism. It played a crucial role in the coup of July 15, 1974, when Makarios was temporarily ousted from power. Nicos Sampson, a former EOKA-terrorist who had joined EOKA-B became at Greek instigation a short-lived president, but was subsequently arrested for his role and jailed in 1976. It did not develop an offensive terrorist capacity against Turkish occupation of northern Cyprus and in 1978 its dissolution was announced.

DENMARK

* BZ Brigade
A squatters' organization in Copenhagen which has been involved in violent riots.

* Danish National Socialist Alliance (DNSA)
Extreme right-wing organization which has attracted only minimal support on the right-wing fringe. In 1980 it was reported to have links with similar groups in Europe, Australia, Canada and Latin America. It has been involved in the painting of swastikas on the El Al office in Copenhagen and attacking the head of the office.

* The Green Jackets
Right-wing extremist group which has been responsible for clashes with immigrants in 1985. Members of the group have killed a taxidriver.

* "Revolutionary Army" Group
Group which had plans to assassinate the Danish royal family and leading politicians and to overthrow parliament. It hoped to finance its plans with money from the sale of drugs. In 1980, 16 members of the group were arrested.

DJIBOUTI

* African Popular League for the Independence (Ligue Populaire Africaine pour l'Independence) (LPAI)
Party led by Hasan Gouled. In December 1975 France dropped its anti-Somali, anti-independence policy and announced that the territory would be granted full independence, and then immediately shifted its support from the Afar parties to the main Issa party, LPAI. Leading LPAI members were released from jail or allowed to return from exile. After a referendum the country became independent on June 27, 1977, with Hasan Gouled as president. The new government proved entirely willing to sign a military agreement with France which left it all its naval facilities and indeed retained almost the entire French garrison in the country.

* Popular Movement for Liberation (MPL)
A group which has been involved in kidnappings of foreigners, demanding the release of political prisoners and better political representation for the Afar. After an attack on the French military followed by the arrest of 600 Afars the government dissolved the group in December 1977. In 1981 the party was outlawed again, following community violence. Several members have been charged with offenses against state security.

* Troops of Revolutionaries and Resisters
Group that claimed responsibility for a bomb attack on a café in Djibouti on Mar.22, 1987. Eleven people were killed in the attack. The café was frequently visited by French military. A captured Tunesian, Adouani Hamouda Hassan, said he was recruited in Damascus.

DOMINICA

* The Rastafarians (also known as Dreads)
Black cult which originated in Kingston (Jamaica). It is named after the former Ethiopian emperor Haile Selassi (whose original name was Ras Tafari). It advocates the return of the Blacks in the Americas to Africa, the use of natural food, the cultivation and smoking of marijuana and the playing of music. Desmond Trotter acts as its spiritual leader. In 1974 the Dominican Labour Party government of P.R.John passed the Dread Act under which Rastafarians could be shot on site. Trotter was condemned to death in 1976 but after riots in 1979 he was released following the removal of P.R.John from office. Members of the Dominican Defense Force have traded weapons for marijuana supplied by the Dreads. The Defense Force was disbanded in 1981 after two coup attempts. The police are now the nation's only security force. In 1981 the government uncovered a plot prepared in a Dread stronghold in the mountains.

DOMINICAN REPUBLIC

* Dominican Popular Movement
(Movimiento Popular Dominicano) (MPD)
Movement which originated in the 1950s. It has been more important outside the country as a focus for exiles than inside the Republic as a revolutionary nucleus. Members had ideological disputes with rival ultra-leftists, especially with members of the pro-Chinese Communist Party (PACOREDO). In January 1971 the hostility led to the deaths of as many as 40 extremists. It has

been involved in kidnappings and has been held responsible for fomenting rebellion with Cuban backing.

* Movement of the Revolutionary Left
(Movimiento de la Izquierda Revolucionaria) (MIR)
Group which emerged in 1979 and which was led by Fernando Paniagua and Enrique Vásquez. It claimed that a previously unknown group, the Armed Forces of National Liberation, had joined it. Nothing further was heard of it in the early 1980s.

* Pedro Santa Patriotic Front
Obscure group which claimed responsibility for a grenade attack carried out on June 18, 1982, on the premises of the central electoral tribunal, where five people were killed and at least 20 were injured. Three former colonels and a number of civilians were subsequently arrested on suspicion of having been involved in the incident.

* Revolutionary Movement 14 June
(Movimiento Revolucionario 14 de Junio) (MR-14)
Pro-Cuban guerrilla group which was established in November 1963. It was named after the date of landing of a group of exiles in June 1959 with the aim of overthrowing the regime of President Trujillo. One of its leaders, Amaury Germán Aristy, was killed in a streetfight in 1972. He was behind an uprising in April 1965 led by Colonel Francisco Caamano Deno, who for a time held the capital Santa Domingo, before US intervention quelled the rebellion. It split into numerous factions in the early 1970s. At least one, the Red Line of June 14 Movement, retained something of the original leading sections and has been involved in kidnappings. In February 1973, Caamano landed with ten men on Caracoles beach and died in the first clash with the military.

* Socialist Party
Small extremist splinter group. Its members allegedly received military instructions from Cuba.

* Social Workers Movement
Small extremist splintergroup. Its members allegedly received military instructions from Cuba.

* Trinitarian National Liberation Movement
(Movimiento de Liberación Nacional de los Trinitarios) (MLNT)
Urban terrorist group active in the late 1970s. Some sources say it is a group of common bank robbers which from 1982 on have cloaked their criminal activities with leftist slogans. It is led by Juan Bautista Castillo Pujols. In 1981 Panama granted political asylum to a Trinitarian leader, Lorenzo Mejia Frias.

ECUADOR

* Alfaro Vive Carajo (AVC)
Guerrilla group which emerged in 1983 when it stole the statue and the sword of general Eloy Alfaro. He was a liberal general who led a revolution against the conservatives in the 19th century. It has done little to explain its political philosophy. It has demonstrated logistical profiency but has failed to kindle popular support. It is estimated to have about 200 members and has been involved in bank robbings, assassinations of policemen and spectacular jail breaks. Its terror tactics have been condemned by the Ecuadorean left. The violence has intensified in 1985. AVC is believed to have contacts with M-19 and other Latin American extremists.

* Death Squad
A sort of AAA, like the Argentine right-wing terrorist organization.

* Garcia Moreno Also Lives
(Garcia Moreno Tambien Vive)
A group that has been established in reaction to Alfaro Vive Carajo (AVC). The name refers to a conservative 19th century president.

* Montoneros Patria Libre
Organization which on May 21, 1986, kidnapped Enrique Echeverria, a member of the Tribunal for Constitutional Guarantees. The organization is believed to be a radical offshoot of the AVC. It is unclear whether it is a right-wing or a left-wing organization. Through inexperience the left has been infiltrated by the right and the secret services.

* Tradition, Family and Property
(Tradicion, Familia, Propriedad)
A reactionary group, a copy of the Argentine model, which allegedly has an armed wing.

EGYPT

* Arab Egypt Liberation Front
Group which claimed responsibility for an explosion on a US jet fighter on Aug.23, 1980.

* The Coptic Orthodox Church
The largest Christian church in Egypt. Hostility between Moslems and Copts has led to numerous clashes resulting in casualties. Pope Shenouda III and other Coptic clergy have been accused of seeking the partion of Egypt and to set up a Christian state with Asyut as its capital. The charge was strongly denied by Coptic leaders. In 1981 more than 1,500 people were arrested and Pope Shenouda himself was placed under restriction. His temporal powers were transferred to a five-member committee appointed by the

government, although he remained the spiritual leader of the Copts. In January 1985 he was released again.

* Egyptian Communist Workers' Party (ECWP)
An offshoot of the ECP. It was said to have links with the ruling National Liberation Front, later the Yemen Socialist Party of Southern Yemen and with the Palestinian Rejectionist Front led by the PFLP of G.Habash. In 1977, the party reportedly was dismantled.

* Egyptian National Front
(Jabhat al-Wataniya al-Misriya) (ENF)
Organiziation set up in Damascus in March 1980 by General Saad Eddine Shazli, a former chief of staff. It was opposed to the politics of President Sadat and had offices in Syria, Libya, Algeria and Lebanon. Shazli later lived in exile in Algeria and offered his military services to the PLO. It defined its aim as being to uniting all opposition forces for the overthrow of the Sadat regime. It had links with Libya.

* Egyptian Revolution
Terrorist group of which it is not known whether it really exists or functions as a cover for a foreign intelligence service. It calls itself a Nasserite movement and threatened to kill all Israelis in Egypt. Some say its members are Egyptians who are not to be sought under Moslem fundamentalists. Others said it had a leftist-nationalistic character. It is reported to have links with Abu Nidal and the Arab Nationalist Command. It claimed credit for the hijacking of an Egypt Air jet to Malta in November 1985 which resulted in the death of 60 passengers when Egyptian security forces stormed the plane.

* Egypt of Abrahim
Group which has been responsible for the murder of two Israelis in Cairo on Mar.26, 1981.

* Front for the Liberation of Egypt
Organization which was officially announced on May 27, 1978. It was alleged that it was financed by Libya to carry out a campaign against the Egyptian government through press and radio. President Sadat had accused Colonel Kadhafi, of having promoted sabotage operations in Egypt. Similar claims were made by the Egyptian government in subsequent years.

* Holy War
(Al Jihad)
Extremist Moslem fundamentalist group banned by the government. It is one of the fundamentalist factions which adopted the use of violence in the latter years of President Sadat's rule to change the nature of Egyptian society. It was very active in 1981 when it promoted attacks on the Christian Coptic community. Five of its members were sentenced to death in April 1982 for their involvement in the death of President Sadat in 1981. It is headed by Mohammed Abdel-Salam Faraq. In December 1986 four officers and 29 others were arrested and charged with plotting the overthrow of the government of Hosni Mubarak. Dr.Abdul Rahman, a blind teacher of theology and spiritual leader, has spent three years in prison without having been convicted of any offense.

* Moslem Brotherhood
(Majallat al-Ikhwan al-Musalamin)
Moslem fundamentalist organization which was established in 1928 by Hassan al Banna. It fights against what is seen as a Western attack on the Islamic traditions. It became one of the two mass parties in Egypt. It engaged in political violence in the late 1940s. Until Nasser's death in 1970 it remained underground. It numbered 40,000 in the 1940s. The society spread abroad to many countries including Morocco, Sudan, Iraq, Syria, Jordan, Yemen and Saudi Arabia. In the 1950s it had a terrorist wing known as the Secret Organ. Its most recent leader, Omar el Telmessani died in 1986. He had replaced Hassan el Hodeiby in 1954. In recent elections it has sought a coalition with the New Wafd party. It gained control over two smaller opposition parties.

* The Organization
(Tanzim)
Islamic fundamentalist group that first emerged in 1974 when it fomented an uprising at a technical academy run by the armed services. Since then it has been involved in riots on several occasions. An Egyptian secret service (Mukhabarat) report identified 280 Tanzim members. Seventy-three came from the Cairo area, 67 from Giza and 37 from Asyut, a southern town where riots erupted after the assassination of Sadat. About 250 of the Tanzim members are under 30. Most are literate; 123 are students. They come for the most part from lower-middle class families. The leaders, however, come from the upper class. One of them was Abbud al-Zomor, an army intelligence officer who joined Tanzim and plotted the assassination of Sadat. Its civilian leader, Muhammed Abdel Salam Farag was jailed for conspiring to kill Sadat. Tanzim's constitution calls on Moslems to fight a holy war against the 'atheistic' government of Egypt, on the ground that it does not conform to Islamic law. After this is done, Jerusalem must be recaptured in a holy war against Israel.

* Repentance and Holy Flight
(Al Takfir Wal Hijira)
Group which broke away from the clandestine Islamic Liberation party which operated in many Arab countries. It was founded by Shukri Ahmed

Mustafa in 1971. He was executed in 1977. In Egypt the group was charged with an attempted coup in 1974 after an attack on the Military Technical College. It rejects all modern Western innovations and advocates an Iranian-style Islamic republic. It was thought to have participated in the food riots of 1977 and has an estimated strength of 3,000 to 5,000. It has been involved in kidnappings, assassinations and bomb attacks. It claimed responsibility for the murder of President Sadat declaring that he deserved to be put to death because he made concessions to Islam's three main external enemies: atheistic Communism, the West and particularly Zionism. Its present spokesman is Omar Mohammed Abdel Rahman (a mufti or official interpreter of Islamic law). It is highly organized and spread horizontally and vertically throughout Egyptian society.

* Revolutionary Stream Group
Forty-four members of this group were arrested on Dec.12, 1986, during a secret convention in the Gizo-district. The group intended to 'change the basic systems and constitution and enforce Communism by force'. The members of the group were arrested for plotting a coup d'état. Some of them were reported to be professors.

* Storm
(Saiqa)
Specialist anti-terror unit formed in 1975 on the personal order of President Anwar Sadat. It is trained specifically to deal with hijackings and other hostage-type situations. Egypt has a total of 1,000 troops trained in general counter-insurgency operations, with an estimated 250 belonging to the Saiqa unit. It is believed to have received training in the early years of its existence from Soviet special forces and more recently from US Green Beret troops. It is led by Major General Kamal Attia and its slogan is 'be clandestine, daring and use surprise. Strike at night rather than in the day'. In a badly organized rescue operation of a hijacked plane in Malta 60 passengers of Egypt Air were killed on Nov.24, 1985.

* Those Escaped from Hellfire
Breakaway group from the fundamentalist Takfir Wal Hijira movement. It has claimed responsibility for several assassinations in 1987. Targets included Abu Basha, a former minister of the interior, and Makram Mohammed, chief editor of the weekly Al Mussawar. In August 1987, Nabawi Ismael, a former minister of the interior, was injured in an attempt to assassinate him.

EL SALVADOR

* Anti Communist Commando for the Salvation of the University
Rightist death squad which has been responsible for the kidnapping of Hugo Francisco Carrillo, a professor in international relations, on Nov.18, 1983.

* Anti Communist Political Front
(Frente Politico Anticomunista) (FPA)
Militia which emerged in May 1979. It has been active in attacks on alleged left-wing leaders.

* Armed Forces of National Resistance
(Fuerzas Armadas de Resistencia Nacional) (FARN)
Guerrilla faction which was formed in 1975 by a group of ERP dissidents led by Roque Dalton Garcia. Ideologically it has been the most conciliatory and nationalistic of the guerrilla organizations and the most hostile to Soviet and Cuban influence. It considers itself a Marxist-Leninist proletarian army. Later is was described as the armed branch of FAPU. The group aimed at the foundation of a vanguard party and the building up of a revolutionary armed force on the basis of a guerrilla army. Its strength increased from 800 fighters in 1980 to 2,000 in 1984. It has been involved in kidnappings and has targeted foreign businesses and multinational companies. One of its leaders, Ernesto Jovel, was killed in Sep.1980. Its present leader is Eduardo Sancho Castaneda (Ferman Cienfuegos). It joined the FMLN in 1982.

* Civil Defense Patrols
(Brigadas de Defensa Civil) (BDC)
Local defense patrols which have been implicated in the arbitrary arrest, torture, 'disappearance' and extra judicial execution of people from a wide-cross section of Salvadorean society. In 1985 violations appeared to be more selectively directed against people suspected of opposition to the government or of being sympathetic to the opposition.

* Clara Elizabeth Ramirez Front (CERF)
Small urban guerrilla movement which split off from the FPL in December 1983.

* Communist Party of El Salvador
(Partido Comunista de El Salvador) (PCES)
Pro-Moscow party founded by Farabundo Marti, who was shot dead in the 1932 uprising which was put down by the military. It agreed to embrace armed struggle at its 7th Congress in 1979. It has been illegal for most of the time. Its leaders are Jorge Shafik Handal, Jaime Barrios and Victor Montes. Its fighting forces are insignificant but it carries considerable weight in the councils of the FMLN because of Handal's close ties with the Soviet Union and the International Communist Movement. The party argued that a revolutionary vanguard should emerge from an eventual unity of

all the revolutionary organizations. The National Democratic Union has served since 1977 as its legal front.

* Death Squad
General name for rightist groups which have been involved in assassinations of leftists. By late 1983 death squads committed an average of 800 killings per month. Death squad assassinations declined dramatically after 1984 when the United States brought their leaders under F.B.I. surveillance and encouraged the Duarte regime to conduct their own investigations.

* Eastern Anti Guerrilla Bloc
(Bloque Antiguerillero del Oriente) (BAGO)
Right-wing guerrilla group which emerged in September 1980. It has been responsible for a number of killings and bomb attacks.

* Falange
A paramilitary organization with links to the military and the '14 families'.

* Farabundo Marti Popular Forces of Liberation
(Fuerzas Populares de Libéracion Farabundi Marti) (FPL-FM)
Pro-Cuban guerrilla movement named after a former PCES secretary-general, who died at the onset of a peasant revolt in 1932. Its leader Salvador Cayetano Carpio committed suicide in 1983 and was replaced by Salvador Guerra Firma. It moved to the foreground of political violence in 1977. In 1978 it emerged as the most active guerrilla force. It has been involved in sabotage, kidnappings, assassinations and bomb attacks. It targeted sugar cane crops, radio stations and US interests. In 1980 the FPL played a prominent role in coordinating the activities of the revolutionary forces. Together with other groups it set up the Coordinating Committee for the Movement of Popular Unity. From this body stemmed the FMLN, which was controlled by the DRU. Although the FPL preserved its own structure in 1981 it acted increasingly as part of the FMLN.

* Farabundo Marti Front for National Liberation (FMLN)
Main guerrilla faction in El Salvador headed by a unifying revolutionary directorate (DRU) formed in May 1980 with the object of launching a 'final offensive' against the government. The stated aim was to create a 'proletarian unity party' which would form the basis of a 'people's state' after a guerrilla victory. Its main components are: CP, FPL, BPR, FARN, FAPU, ERP and LP-28. It has a strength of about 4,000 to 6,000 fighters with another 5,000 to 30,000 reservists. Until 1983, it was led by Cayetano Carpio. It has been involved in economic sabotage, traffic stoppages, use of land mines, assasinations and kidnappings. After suffering on the battlefield it has increasingly resorted to terrorist tactics. A change in counterinsurgency strategy has weakened the guerrillas in 1985.

* Mardequeo Cruz Command (MCC)
A commando of the PRTC which engaged in urban terrorism, particularly in 1985.

* Maximiliano Hernandez Martinez Anti Communist Alliance
Group named after President Martinez who was in power in 1931-1944 and under whose regime the 1932 peasant rebellion was suppressed. It claimed responsibility for the murder of six leaders of the FDR in November 1980. It issued death threats and is believed to have links to the National Guard. It targeted Christian Democrats and Catholic activists.

* National Democratic Organization
(Organizacion Democratica Nacional) (ORDEN)
Organization set up in 1968 as a part-time militia. By the late 1970s it had degenerated into a murderous organization, responsible for indiscriminate killing of left-wing suspects both rural and urban. In the rural areas especially, the organization had many thousands of members. Estimates put its size between 30,000-60,000. In November 1979 it was officially banned by the government. Some activity continued in 1980.

* National Police
Police force which has been accused of severe human rights violations in recent years.

* Organization for the Liberation from Communism
(Organizacion para la Liberacion del Comunismo) (OLC)
Right-wing paramilitary group which emerged in early 1980. It has been involved in assassinations and bomb attacks.

* Pedro Pablo Castillo Front (PPCF)
A commando of the PCES which was responsible for the kidnapping of the daughter of President Duarte. It operated more or less independently.

* People's Armed Revolutionary Forces
(Fuerzas Revolucionarias Armadas del Pueblo) (FRAP)
Armed branch of the Workers' Revolutionary Organization which first emerged in 1977. It has been involved in murders and kidnappings in the 1970s. It did not join the Coordinating Committee for the Movement of Popular Unity, nor did it become a part of the FMLN. By 1981 little was heard of either FRAP or the ORT.

* People's Revolutionary Army

(Ejército Revolucionario del Pueblo) (ERP)
One of the left-wing guerrilla movements organized like an army. Its origins go back to 1971 but it first emerged in 1973. It is said to be the armed branch of the LP-28. It has a Marxist-Leninist ideology and is pro-Cuban. Led by Joaquin Villalobos it has an estimated 800 fighters (1980). During 1975 it expanded its terrorist activities to include guerrilla attacks on small towns. In May 1975 a split occurred, the deserters founded FARN. ERP retained its own strategy aimed at mass insurrection for which it has propagated armed self-defense by its militants, especially in urban areas. It has been involved in bank raids, kidnappings, assassinations, bomb attacks and small scale guerrilla operations. It has targeted government and business premises, radio stations, the army and police. It formed part of the FLMN and joined the DRU in May 1980.

* Popular Leagues of February 28
(Ligas Populares 28 de Febrero) (LP-28)
The ERP set up this mass organization in 1979. The name refers to the date of a mass confrontation with the military in 1977 following fraudulent elections. It was not a guerrilla group nor was it involved in terrorist acts. Members and spokesmen were targeted by the security forces and the ultra-rightist paramilitary death squads. In a later stage it moved to outright political violence. Members were said to have been involved in bomb attacks, occupations and violent clashes with the security forces. It has an estimated 10,000 members.

* Popular Liberation Army
(Ejército Popular de Liberación) (EPL)
Offshoot of the FPL which was formed in November 1979. Its leader Humberto Mendozo was killed in 1980.

* Popular Revolutionary Bloc
(Bloque Popular Revolucionario) (BPR)
Marxist-Leninist formation founded in 1975 by the FPL. It stands for a revolutionary socialist society independent of Soviet influence. It proclaimed the thesis of a prolonged people's war. It is led by Juan Chacon (killed in November 1980), Facundo Guardado and José Ricardo Mena and has an estimated 40,000 members or sympathizers. It sought to provide one body which could unite the various peasant, labour and student organizations of the left. It acted as a mass movement favorable to the terrorist and guerrilla campaigns waged by the violent factions. Although founded as a non-violent movement, it soon engaged in acts of violence. In the conflict which followed Archbishop Romero's death, the BPR was overshadowed by the FMLN. It embraced the Salvadorean Christian Peasants' Federation, the Agricultural Workers Union, ANDES, FUR-31, UR-19, the Slum Dwellers Union and the Trade Union Coordinating Committee.

* Raphael Antonio Arce Zablah Brigade
One of the guerrilla factions.

* Revolutionary Action of Secondary School Students
(Accion Revolucionaria de Estudiantes Secundarios) (ARDES)
Direct action leftist student group.

* Revolutionary Co-ordination of the Masses
(Coordinacion Revolucionaria de las Masas) (CRM)
Formed on Jan.10, 1980, as a 'revolutionary alliance' of three major left-wing organizations, BPR, LP-28 and FAPU. Other participants were the Communist Party and the UDN. At the end of February 1980 the alliance announced as its aims the overthrow of the current government; the installation of a 'democratic revolutionary government'; and the nationalization of the means of productions, the banking and financial system and foreign trade. It also wanted the creation of a new army and the investigation of cases of missing persons dating back to 1972.

* Revolutionary Democratic Front
(Frente Democratico Revolucionaria) (FDR)
Front set up in January 1981 as the political arm of the FMLN. It is led by Guillermo Ungo and is comprised of the FSD, MNR, MPSC, several trade union, student, and professional organizations, BPR, FAPU, LP-28, MPL and UDN. On January 14, 1981, the FDR formally announced that it had formed a seven member diplomatic commission which would seek to establish a 'democratic revolutionary government'. Its main leaders were killed in November 1980. FDR leaders repeatedly called for a dialogue with the new government of El Salvador while making it clear that the guerrilla war would continue until a satisfactory agreement for a return to full democracy has been achieved.

* Revolutionary Party of Central American Workers
(Partido Revolucionario de Trabajadores de America Central) (PRTC)
Small guerrilla group which emerged in September 1976. It is said to be the military wing of a group known as the Liberation Leagues. It is led by Roberto Roca and had an estimated 300 armed members in 1984. It has been involved in kidnappings, occupations, armed attacks and arson.

* Salvadorean Christian Peasants Federation
(Federación de Campesinos Cristianos Salvadorenos) (FECCAS)
Organization which was actively involved in demonstrations for the release of political

prisoners in 1977. It was declared illegal on the grounds that it had 'communist' links which it denied. It declared that it was campaigning for fair wages, the right to organize and the radical transformation of the Salvadorean society to construct a new society where there is no misery, hunger, repression of exploitation of one group by another. It accused vigilantes belonging to Orden for having murdered peasants and evicted villagers from their homes. It has been involved in occupations of plantations for wage increases and formed part of the BPR and the FDR. It has an estimated 7,000 members and was backed by the church.

* Salvadorean Anti-communist Army
(Ejército Salvadoreno Anticomunista) (ESA)
Right-wing death squad which emerged in 1980. It has been held responsible for numerous acts of persecution directed notably against teachers, priests, monks and nuns. It also was responsible for the dynamiting of the print shop of the University of El Salvador on June 29, 1980.

* Special Command of the Domingo Monterrosa Barrios Brigade
A death squad.

* S-2 Intelligence Unit of the Treasury Police
Police unit which was dissolved in 1984 when its 100 agents were sent to combat positions at isolated parts of the country in the east. It was disbanded because of reports of illegal action by some S-2 agents and as a way to improve the image of the Treasury Police.

* Treasury Police
(Policía de Hacienda)
Police unit which has been accused of continuing human rights violations, including extra judicial executions, 'disappearances' and torture.

* Unified Revolutionary Directorate (DRU)
Guerrilla alliance of the FPL, ERP, FARN, PCES, FAPU, BPR, LP-28 guerrilla groups. It was led by Cayetano Carpio who committed suicide in 1983. It controlled the activities of the FMLN and was the principal force behind the civil war which gradually engulfed El Salvador following the murder in March 1980 of Archbishop Oscar Romero. Since then the war has claimed already more than 65,000 deaths. Fidel Castro helped the DRU organize during meetings in Havana in December 1979 and May 1980. It reportedly received arms from Vietnam, Ethiopia, the PLO, Cuba and Eastern Europe.

* Union of White Guerrillas
(Union de Guerilleros Blancos) (UGB)
A self-styled death squad which emerged in 1976. It has been held responsible for killing a number of individuals, including Jesuit priests, teachers and union members believed to be associated with left-wing terrorists.

* Unified Popular Action Front
(Frente de Acción Popular Unificada) (FAPU)
Mass movement which was established in 1974 as an alternative to the BPR. It was reportedly close to FARN and claimed to have 40,000 members or sympathizers. With a more distinctly Marxist orientation it attracted much support from young people in the capital as a direct action pressure group. It participated in the Coordinating Committee for the Movement of Popular Unity. It has been involved in bomb attacks and occupations of buildings and has targeted schools, the headquarters of the ICRC and the Mexican embassy. Neither the BPR nor the FAPU is known to have engaged in overt guerrilla activity.

* University Revolutionary Front
(Frente Universitario Revolucionario) (FUR 30)
Student branch of the BPR which has been active since 1980. In 1980 it took 60 people hostage at the Jesuit University of Central America in San Salvador.

* Urban Paramilitary Police Unit
In 1985 authorities created an urban paramilitary police force unit to fight increased attempts by leftist guerrillas to bring the war to the capital. The unit to be trained by US military experts will be part of the Treasury Police, an agency linked in the past to right-wing death squads. The US Congress has barred foreign aid for police training but it was said that the restriction did not apply in this case because the Treasury Police unit would have 'no regular line law enforcement responsibility'. The unit would report to the army chief of staff.

* Workers Revolutionary Organization
(Organization Revolutionaria de Trabajadores) (ORT)
Marxist-Leninist party which had an armed branch (FRAP). It has been active in the mid-1970s. By 1981 little was heard of either the FRAP or the ORT.

ETHIOPIA

* Afar Liberation Front (ALF)
Guerrilla movement of the Afar people who first fought the forces of Haile Selassi because his government condemned the Afar to a perpetual nomadic existence. It demanded autonomy in the tribal area and wanted exemption from the land reform and new taxes decreed by the military regime. It also was opposed to the expropriation of

their grazing areas for capital intensive agriculture. Thousands of Afar-nomads died in the early 1970s when they were driven from their traditional grounds. It had an estimated strength of 5,000 to 6,000 fighters and operated in southern Eritrea and western Wollo. After the independence of Djibouti (1977) the government resisted an Afar demand that 6,000 men of the ALF be brought to Djibouti and enlisted in the army. It declared that it would be prepared to assimilate between 700 to 1000 Afar fighters into the army. The ALF has been involved in armed attacks, sabotage and guerrilla warfare and has targeted troops and militia men. It cooperated with Eritrean secessionists. Military effectiveness diminished after an Ethiopian attack in early 1980. The front is led by Sultan Ali Mirah who lives in Saudi Arabia.

* Afar National Liberation Movement (ANLM)
Marxist guerrilla movement with the aim of autonomy for the Afar people. It operated in southern Eritrea and eastern Wollo. It cooperated with PMAC against the ALF and the traditional tribal leadership. For years the local men in power on the district level have been members of the ANLM.

* Anouak/ Komo Resistance Movement
Both the Anouak and the Komo peoples had their their own shortlived resistance groups which cooperated with the Oromos.

* Eritrean Democratic Movement, Falcool (anarchists) (EDM)
Guerrilla faction which emerged in 1982. It is led by Himy Tedla Bairr, son of the president of Eritrea during the early years of the federation.

* Eritrean Liberation Front (ELF)
Ten years after its foundation in 1961, the ELF spawned an organization named the Forces of the Peoples Liberation (FPL) under the leadership of Osman Saleh Sabbe. In 1977 the FPL changed its name to the EPLF, leaving Osman Saleh Sabbe to lead the FPL under the name of the ELF. After its withdrawal to Sudan in 1981, the ELF broke into three disputing factions. When the faction led by Sabbe agreed to unification, the leader of his military wing, Mohammed Saeed Noud, broke with him.

* Eritrean Liberation Front (ELF-PLF)
Guerrilla movement that broke away from the EPLF in 1976. It is a moderate nationalist, anti-Marxist movement aimed at the independence of Eritrea. It is led by Osman Saleh Sabbe and had an estimated 5,000 fighters in 1977. By 1982 it had lost many supporters after in-fighting with other factions in 1981. It now has a small combat force and is more effective at propaganda abroad than fighting in Eritrea. It has been supported by Sudan, Egypt, Saudi Arabia and other conservative Arab states. In May 1980 the ELF-PLF had split in two factions when a group led by Osman Agyp, based in Iraq, broke away in opposing the leadership of Osman Saleh Sabbe, based in Egypt and Dubai. On Nov.15, 1980, Osman Agyp was assasinated by an unknown assailant. Shortly after the murder the Sudanese government expelled the Cuban chargé d'affaires in Khartoum.

* Eritrean Liberation Front-General Command (ELF-GC)
Small guerrilla faction formed in August 1969. It broke away from the ELF.

* Eritrean Liberation Front-Revolutionary Council (ELF-RC)
Marxist oriented Moslem secessionist guerrilla movement which was set up in 1958. It was led by Ahmed Muhammad Nasser until 1981. Since then Abdullah Idris took over command. Its strength increased from 2,500 in 1970, to 5,000-10,000 in 1974 and 22,000 in 1977. From 1969 on there was a shift to a more socialist commitment. The isolated terrorist incidents in the early 1970s grew out to a systematic guerrilla campaign. In 1977 it was engaged in full-scale warfare with the government forces. It also battled with the rival EPLF in 1981. Ideological splits occurred in 1970 and 1975. It set up an alternative administrative system. By 1978 it was hard hit by Ethiopian offensives and numerous defections to the EPLF. It has been supported by the PLO, Syria, Sudan, Saudi Arabia, Kuwait, Iraq, Somalia, South Yemen, Libya, China and the Soviet Union. In 1983 it joined the ELF-PLF.

* Eritrean Liberation Front-United Organization (ELF-UO)
Predominantly Moslem umbrella organization of three guerrilla organizations, PLF, ELF-RC and ELF-GC, established in January 1985. It has a 15-member executive committee (3x5 representatives) and is led by Osman Saleh Sabbe. United they equal in military strength the largest guerrilla organization of the EPLF which has refused to take part in the unity efforts. It was practically dissolved 19 months after its establishment.

* Eritrean Peoples Liberation Front
(Hisbouwi Gumbar Harret Eritrea) (EPLF)
Largest and most effective of the Eritrean secessionist movements established in 1970. It fights for a national democratic revolution without ethnic or religious discrimination, a state at the service of the people and an independent nation which would be nobody's satellite. Its strength increased to 8,000 fighters in the field and a militia of 10,000 to 15,000 in 1982. It has been

prisoners in 1977. It was declared illegal on the grounds that it had 'communist' links which it denied. It declared that it was campaigning for fair wages, the right to organize and the radical transformation of the Salvadorean society to construct a new society where there is no misery, hunger, repression of exploitation of one group by another. It accused vigilantes belonging to Orden for having murdered peasants and evicted villagers from their homes. It has been involved in occupations of plantations for wage increases and formed part of the BPR and the FDR. It has an estimated 7,000 members and was backed by the church.

* Salvadorean Anti-communist Army
(Ejército Salvadoreno Anticomunista) (ESA)
Right-wing death squad which emerged in 1980. It has been held responsible for numerous acts of persecution directed notably against teachers, priests, monks and nuns. It also was responsible for the dynamiting of the print shop of the University of El Salvador on June 29, 1980.

* Special Command of the Domingo Monterrosa Barrios Brigade
A death squad.

* S-2 Intelligence Unit of the Treasury Police
Police unit which was dissolved in 1984 when its 100 agents were sent to combat positions at isolated parts of the country in the east. It was disbanded because of reports of illegal action by some S-2 agents and as a way to improve the image of the Treasury Police.

* Treasury Police
(Policía de Hacienda)
Police unit which has been accused of continuing human rights violations, including extra judicial executions, 'disappearances' and torture.

* Unified Revolutionary Directorate (DRU)
Guerrilla alliance of the FPL, ERP, FARN, PCES, FAPU, BPR, LP-28 guerrilla groups. It was led by Cayetano Carpio who committed suicide in 1983. It controlled the activities of the FMLN and was the principal force behind the civil war which gradually engulfed El Salvador following the murder in March 1980 of Archbishop Oscar Romero. Since then the war has claimed already more than 65,000 deaths. Fidel Castro helped the DRU organize during meetings in Havana in December 1979 and May 1980. It reportedly received arms from Vietnam, Ethiopia, the PLO, Cuba and Eastern Europe.

* Union of White Guerrillas
(Union de Guerilleros Blancos) (UGB)
A self-styled death squad which emerged in 1976. It has been held responsible for killing a number of individuals, including Jesuit priests, teachers and union members believed to be associated with left-wing terrorists.

* Unified Popular Action Front
(Frente de Acción Popular Unificada) (FAPU)
Mass movement which was established in 1974 as an alternative to the BPR. It was reportedly close to FARN and claimed to have 40,000 members or sympathizers. With a more distinctly Marxist orientation it attracted much support from young people in the capital as a direct action pressure group. It participated in the Coordinating Committee for the Movement of Popular Unity. It has been involved in bomb attacks and occupations of buildings and has targeted schools, the headquarters of the ICRC and the Mexican embassy. Neither the BPR nor the FAPU is known to have engaged in overt guerrilla activity.

* University Revolutionary Front
(Frente Universitario Revolucionario) (FUR 30)
Student branch of the BPR which has been active since 1980. In 1980 it took 60 people hostage at the Jesuit University of Central America in San Salvador.

* Urban Paramilitary Police Unit
In 1985 authorities created an urban paramilitary police force unit to fight increased attempts by leftist guerrillas to bring the war to the capital. The unit to be trained by US military experts will be part of the Treasury Police, an agency linked in the past to right-wing death squads. The US Congress has barred foreign aid for police training but it was said that the restriction did not apply in this case because the Treasury Police unit would have 'no regular line law enforcement responsibility'. The unit would report to the army chief of staff.

* Workers Revolutionary Organization
(Organization Revolutionaria de Trabajadores) (ORT)
Marxist-Leninist party which had an armed branch (FRAP). It has been active in the mid-1970s. By 1981 little was heard of either the FRAP or the ORT.

ETHIOPIA

* Afar Liberation Front (ALF)
Guerrilla movement of the Afar people who first fought the forces of Haile Selassi because his government condemned the Afar to a perpetual nomadic existence. It demanded autonomy in the tribal area and wanted exemption from the land reform and new taxes decreed by the military regime. It also was opposed to the expropriation of

them might have been summarily executed. It had its headquarters in London and reportedly received CIA support for propaganda and resistance tactics. It reportedly receives an estimated yearly sum of $ 500,000 of the United States.

* Ethiopian People's Democratic Movement (EPDM)
A multi-national organization established in early 1983. It has been active in northern Wollo. The EPDM has been known for joint military operations with the TPLF.

* Islamic Front for the Liberation of Eritrea (IFLE)
Minor Moslem guerrilla organization established in 1981.

* Gambela Peoples Liberation Front (GPLF)
Revolutionary movement that was established in 1980. It fights against the DERG with the aim to liberate the Gambela-region. It is based on the Anuak people. It lacks a strong leadership and program since its founders were killed. The Nilotics are negro people despised by the Ethiopians and they suffered the consequences of Mengistu's villagization and resettlement programs too. In the mainly Nilotic-inhabited Gambela, more than 50,000 family heads from the north have been resettled. The rebellion started there too, and the OLF is providing training and arms to the GPLF which has just begun to operate. The resistance to enforced villagization, the resentment against heavy taxation imposed by the government, the fear of being conscripted into the army are the main motivating factors for those who join the rebels.

* Kebelle
Urban dwellers' association defence guards. They have been used by the DERG in the 'Red Terror' campaign.

* Marxist All-Ethiopian Socialist Movement (MAESON)
Political organization of the Derg which was established in August 1968. It consisted of intellectuals who took the line that a people's revolution could emanate from a military takeover and who therefore gave critical support to the DERG. The organization sprang from the World Union of Ethiopian Students and was divided in two factions. The Regimguzo (the long road) faction emphasized the maintenance of a broad front and the formation of cadres. The Atcherguzo (the short road) faction wanted to start immediately with an armed struggle. On Aug.19, 1976, the MAESON-leadership went underground. After elimination of the MAESON, DERG-supporters were placed on the leading positions of the existing structures. In April 1977, however, some 50 of its members decided to change to 'revolutionary opposition' to the Derg because they opposed the exclusively pro-Soviet line taken by the regime. From July 1977 onwards the MAESON which had played a leading role in the elimination of the EPRP was itself discarded by the regime and many of its leading members went into hiding. Several of them joined the Seded. Nowadays it still exists underground in the cities.

* Marxist-Leninist League of Tigray (MLLT)
Party established on July 12-25, 1985. The league supports the idea of a unified Ethiopian party but with national sections. The MLLT is aimed at the formation of a broad tactical front (of all democratic, anti-imperialist forces of the several nationalities) against the major enemy of the moment: the DERG and the Soviet Union; and a strategic front against the three strategic enemies: imperialism, feodalism and bureaucratic imperialism.

* Ministry of State and Public Security
Ministry which has secretly sentenced to death prisoners without any recognized form of trial and without any opportunity for prisoners to submit defence or appeal. Those sentenced to death in this way were reportedly summarily executed. The ministry has several interrogation and torture centers. In 1985, 15 alleged members of the EPLF and up to 40 longterm political detainees were executed in this way.

* Moslem Pioneers Organization (MPO)
Moslem organization established in 1981. It is headed by Hamid Turkey. It is aimed at the unification of the Eritrean Moslems and raising their religious and national awareness. It operates from the countries of asylum. The fact that there are no significant ideological differences between the MPO and IFLE may result in their unification. The major challenge facing them is to establish a military presence inside Eritrea.

* Oromo Liberation Front (OLF)
Nationalist movement established in 1973. It aims at autonomy for the Oromo region or establishment of an independent state (Oromia). The Oromos call it Finfine. In the 1960s the resistance against the Amhara reached a new stage under Wako Guto. The armed struggle began in 1963. In 1965 almost all of Bale was under control of the resistance. With Israeli, American and British support the emperor was able to suppress the insurrection. The Oromo-guerrillas joined the WSLF. From this organization sprang the SALF which was supported by Somalia. The Oromos disliked the idea of a Greater Somalia which included the eastern Oromo-areas. For that reason they established their own organization in 1973, the OLF. Somalia demanded a merger between SALF and the OLF, as a condition for support to

the OLF. In March 1980 four topleaders of the OLF were murdered by WSLF members. Relations with Somalia deteriorated and in 1982 the OLF was forced to close its offices in Somalia. It has some 3,000 well-trained fighters and a militia of 10,000 men. It claims to conduct a struggle through self-reliance. Assistance remains a mystery. It was trained by the EPLF and had links with Somalia and Syria. It has operated in northern Bale, Sidamo, Arsi, southern Shewa and Hararghe provinces. The front was less active militarily in the early 1980s than other separatist groups. In the early 1980s the first OLF fighters began to operate in the west trying to build a guerrilla force, and received training and weapons from the EPLF. Now the OLF is largely self-sufficient and mans its own training camps inside Ethiopia. In a few years the rebels were able to build up a sizable force , structured in companies of 90-120 men, divided in 30-45 strong platoons and 9-15 men squads. Dispersed and mobile guerrilla forces are permanently operating deep in the interior of the country, relying upon the local population for food, supplies and intelligence. In early 1987 it was described as one of the fastest spreading guerrilla fronts. It is potentially the most dangerous of the armed opposition, because the Oromos (Galla) to whom its revolutionary appeal is aimed is the largest ethnic group in Ethiopia (35-40 percent of the population). The enforced resettlement and villagization policies of the government have led to large streams of refugees to Sudan (30,000) and Somalia (500,000).

* Popular Liberation Forces-Revolutionary Council (PLF-RC)
Guerrilla faction that broke away from the ELF-PLF in 1980. It was first headed by Abu Bakr Gimma and later by Abdulkadir Gailani.

* Popular Liberation Forces (PLF)
A more radical guerrilla movement than the ELF. It asserted that Ethiopia and Eritrea were two separate countries. In the latter part of 1974 the ELF and PLF intensified their military activities and greatly increased their influence in the countryside. Early 1975 the two movements reached agreement on the formation of a common front, and thereafter the two organizations gradually coalesced into a unitary movement based on non-Marxist principles. By 1981 the EPLF claimed to have demolished the ELF-PLF having been forced to retreat across the border into the Sudan. The PLF had links with Libya.

* Provisional Military Administrative Council (PMAC) (DERG)
A council that was established on Sep.15, 1974. It was headed by General Aman Andom. He resisted the policy of summary executions. On Apr.23, 1974, he was killed during an attempt to arrest him. On Apr.20, 1976, a political agreement was signed between the DERG and MAESON. Its program of a national-democratic revolution rejected feodalism, imperialism and bureaucrátic capitalism. In an armed clash on Feb.3, 1977, all major opponents of Mengistu were killed, including Teferi Bante, Senay Likke, Alemayehu Haile and Mogus Wolde. Since then the council is headed by Lt.Col.Mengistu Haile Mariam who acts as head of state and chairman of the council of ministers. On Feb.4, 1977, he announced his 'Red Terror Campaign'. The EPRP itself claimed in Khartoum on Jan.30, 1978, that during the previous three years the PMAC has 'assassinated' 3,500 persons and that in Addis Ababa alone about 8,000 had been arrested and deported to the countryside. Human rights groups have reported 30,000 deaths in the 'Red Terror' campaign during the 1974-1978 period. The headquarters of the council is used as interrogation center.

* Public Security Organization
(Hizb Dehninet)
Government organization which has been involved in torture and ill-treatment of prisoners inAddis Ababa, Asmara, Mekelle, Harar, Gondar and other places.

* Revolutionary Flame
(Abyotowi-Seded)
A movement that was controlled by the DERG. A number of alleged EPRP attacks against MAESON were in fact the work of Revolutionary Flame.

* Sidamo Liberation Movement (SLM)
Guerrilla movement which operated in Sidamo province. It was established in 1981 and is led by Emmanuel Dubale. Until 1981 the Sidamo's were organized in the Somali-Abo Liberation Front (SALF). More than 600 civilians reportedly were killed by the army in November 1981 out of revenge for an SLM attack on a military convoy. Nothing has been reported recently about the SLM in the south, which was reportedly destroyed by a major DERG offensive in 1983.

* Somali Abo Liberation Front (SALF)
Guerrilla movement which emerged in the course of the 1977 Ogaden war. The Somali and Oromo nationalists both aim at the union with Somalia or the creation of a separate state for the Abo people. Waku Guto led the front in 1980 which operated in the Bale, Sidamo and Arsi provinces in the south where it controlled much of the countryside. It had links with the WSLF and Somalia.

* Stranglers
Government assassination squad which operated in

Eritrea.

* Tigray Peoples Liberation Front (TPLF)
Guerrilla movement which was formed in February 1975 under the auspices of the EPLF. It sprang from the Tigrayan National Organization (TNO). In 1976, the DERG organized a farmers march to Eritrea. It resulted in a defeat for the regime and 20,000 Tigrayans deserted and returned to the countryside with their weapons. It was badly mauled in the 1978 Ethiopian offensive, but continued guerrilla activities with small forces in close cooperation with EPLF and carried on separate battles with EPRA and EDU. It mounted a guerrilla campaign in 1979 and by August 70 percent of Tigray province was said to be under TPLF control. In its operations in western Tigray around the Amba Alagi Pass, near Makale and Maichew it has targeted the army. It has been involved in ambushes and attacks on small garrisons. Since 1980, the Ethiopian army has doubled its presence from 20,000 to 40,000 men and stepped up its offensives. The guerrillas operate in small mobile units and engage in blitz-attacks and short occupations of minor towns. According to the TPLF 8,000 civilians were killed in the 1975-1980 period. Another 15,000 were imprisoned. During the army offensives harvests were destroyed. The program of the TPLF is that of a national-democratic revolution within an autonomous Tigray or a union with an independent Eritrea. A new dimension of socialist revolution was brought to the nationalist rebellion as young militants sought to overturn the established social order. In the liberated areas the TPLF introduced a totally new administrative structure. It reportedly had links with Sudan, Syria and Somalia. In early 1985, an estimated 200,000 Tigrayan refugees were reported reported to be in Sudan. In December 1986, TPLF forces in conjunction with their allies of the EPDM were able to attack for the first time, a brigade-size garrison in Sokota (Welo region).

* Western Somali Liberation Front (WSLF)
Guerrilla faction which emerged in 1974. It held its first congress in 1975. Its aim was to implement self-determination for the Somalis living in Ethiopia. It claimed all territory east of the line running from Moyale, on the Kenyan border to El Adde. In mid-1977 the WSLF was backed up by Somali forces many of whom resigned their commission to join what they viewed as a liberation war. The front is led by Abdullah Hassan Mohamoud Dubed and Abd An-Nasir Sheik Adam. It had links with the SALF, the OLF and Somalia. The WSLF cause foundered in 1978 as the Ethiopian government employed a large number of Cuban troops and Soviet and East German advisers to plan a counter strategy which in March pushed the Somalis out of the Ogaden. Yet in the course of 1979 and 1980 it became increasingly clear that the Ethiopians were unable to close the Somali border and consequently to prevent infiltrations to cross it. From rural bases the guerrillas carried out ambushes. Within the WSLF there is a growing trend to obtain a greater autonomy for the Ogaden within an Ethiopian federation. In early 1987 the WSLF suffered from a severe internal crisis and hardly existed as an active organization.

FINLAND

* Patriotic People's Front (PPF)
Organization banned by the government in November 1977. Its leader, Pekka Siitoin, was sentenced to five years in prison for arson at two Communist newspapers in 1978 and for heading an illegal political organization. Five others were also sentenced.

* Vidkun Quisling
A fascist group.

FRANCE

* Action Autonomy (AA)
Autonomist group which claimed responsibility for a bomb explosion at the state broadcasting station in Toulouse on Dec.23, 1982.

* Action for French Corsica
(Action pour la Corse Francaise) (ACV)
Corsican anti-separatist movement active in February 1977.

* Action for the Rebirth of Corsica
(Action pour la Renaissance de la Corse) (ARC)
The parent body of Corsican autonomist sentiment led by Max and Edmond Siméoni. The Aleria siege in August 1975 in which 50 ARC members faced hundreds of police radicalized the autonomist movement. Dr.Edmond Siméoni received a five-year prison term and the ARC was banned. It has been replaced in 1976 by a cluster of organizations, the Corsican Revolutionary Action, the Association of Corsican Patriots and the Corsican National Liberation Front.

* A Diaspora
Clandestine Corsican group striving for autonomy, established in 1983. It is led by Lucien Felli and Jean Francois Ferrandi.

* Anger of the Legions
(Colère des Légions)
Obscure group, one of several extremist organizations (of both the right and the left) which claimed responsibility for a raid on a military arms depot near Toulouse in November 1981. Police recovered most of the weapons in

early 1982.

* Angry Farmers Movement
(Mouvement des Paysans en Colère) (AFM)
Movement responsible for the bombing of the Hotel Salon de Provence on July 13, 1980.

* Anti Corsican French Committee
(Comité Anti Corse Francais) (CACF)
Corsican separatist group active in September 1976.

* Anti Italian Corsican Front
(Front Corse Anti-Italiens) (FCAI)
Corsican anti-separatist movement active in the Nov.1975-Jul.1976 period. Previously it was called FBAI.

* Anti Italian League
(Ligue Anti-Italienne) (LAI)
Corsican anti-separatist movement active in January 1976. It has been responsible for one attack.

* Armed Nuclei for Popular Autonomy
(Noyaux Armeés pour l'Autonomie Populaire) (NAPAP)
Leftist terrorist group which was established in 1977. It sprang from Gauche Proletarienne and was striving for workers' autonomy. It targeted big industries and companies like Citroen, Renault, Simca and Chrysler. In 1977 the guard who had shot and killed the Maoist Pierre Overney, was murdered in front of the gate of the Renault factory. By 1980 no further actions were reported. Militants still active had joined Direct Action.

* Association of Corsican Patriots
(Associo di Patrioti Corsi) (APC)
Corsican separatist organization established in January 1976 when it succeeded ARC. It is led by Marcel Bartoli. By 1978 most APC members had joined the UPC, a new legal autonomist body. It remained less militant than the other separatist organizations in the early 1980s.

* Autonomous Coordination of the Rebels in Open Struggle against Security
(Coordination Autonome des Révoltés en Lutte Ouverte contre le Sécurité) (CALLS)
Group which has been responsible for a bomb attack on the Centre de Traitement de la Direction des Services Financieres de l'EDF in Toulouse.

* Autonomous Fighters against Capitalism (AFC)
Autonomous group which claimed responsibility for a bomb attack on the Ministry of Finance in Paris on Feb.27, 1979.

* Autonomous Group for Radical Action against Capital (AGRAC)
Autonomous group which claimed responsibility for a series of attacks on fashionable shops in Paris and other cities. Other targets were parking meters, many hundreds of which were destroyed in Paris alone in the early months of 1979.

* Autonomous Intervention Groups
(Les Groupes d'Intervention Autonomes) (GIA)
Revolutionary anarchist organization.

* Autonomous January 22 Group
Autonomous group whose members forcibly invaded and ransacked the Paris flat of a public prosecutor in revenge for the passing of prison sentences (on Jan.22) on four young autonomists.

* Autonomous Movement (AM)
Generic name for several cells of young extremists influenced by anarchist ideas, active in 1979. Small groups of autonomists also took part in industrial disturbances in early 1979, including clashes between police and workers in the northern steeltown of Denain and in Longwy. The groups have been involved in bomb attacks and shootings. Targets include bank premises, parking meters, the Finance Ministry and broadcasting offices.

* Autonomous Revolutionary Action (ARA)
Autonomous group which claimed responsibility for a bomb attack on a Paris electricity office on Mar.19, 1980.

* Autonomous Revolutionary Brigades (ARB)
Autonomous group which claimed responsibility for the Feb.1, 1980, fatal shooting of Joseph Fontanet, a former centrist cabinet minister under president De Gaulle and Pompidou, in Paris.

* Basque Justice
(Eazkal Zuzentasuna) (EZ)
Basque nationalist group which has been active since the late 1970s. Militants were motivated by growing unemployment and attacked the tourist industry for inhibiting industrialization. It has been involved in bomb attacks and armed attacks. Targets included a train and the tourist industry.

* Black War (BW)
Terrorist group which has been responsible for a bomb attack on an office of the European Labour Party on Apr.7, 1986.

* Black Wolves Alsatian Combat Group
(Elsässische Kampfgruppe Schwarze Wölfe) (EKSW)
(also Rat der Frankreich-Deutschen)
Small right-wing militant group which claimed responsibility for three bomb attacks in 1981, two of them on a Cross of Lorraine Monument at Thann commemorating Alsation resistance to the German Nazis during World War II. Thirteen

suspected activists were detained in October 1981, including three Germans. Six were subsequently brought to trial.

* Bonifacian Revolutionary Front
(Front Révolutionnaire Bonifacien) (FRB)
Corsican separatist group active in September 1976.

* Breakers (or Incontrolables)
(Les Casseurs)
Group of persons which frequently emerged during the supposedly peaceful student demonstrations in Paris in 1986, turning them into episodes of vandalism and provoking violent confrontations with the police. They took a leading role in the fighting by smashing windows and helping set cars on fire. They were dressed for the party, usually masked, often wearing motorcycle helmets and sometimes carrying iron bars. Much of the French press and many students believed that they were mainly agents provocateurs from the far right who often were working with the police. Their goal was to discredit the students and encourage support for the government's law-and-order policies among ordinary people. The government denied any responsibility suggesting instead that anarchists and other leftist fringe groups were responsible for the violence and property damage.

* Breton Republican Army
(Front de Libération de la Bretagne-Armeé Republicaine Bretonne) (FLB-ARB)
Nationalist Breton movement which was established in June 1966. It is more autonomist than separatist. The 1972 attempts to turn it into a socialist movement led to a split. Important leaders were Yann Fouéré, Yann Puillandre, Dr.Gourves and Father Le Breton. In 1976 the FLB issued a 'declaration of war'. The indecision over ideology and over whether or not to embrace separatism caused the movement to split in 1977. The group attempted to embrace the ecology movement by adopting an anti-nuclear power stance. Most of its members were in jail. Those in prison were granted an amnesty in May 1981. It has been involved in bomb attacks and theft and has attacked government buildings, police barracks, industrial companies, naval posts, the gendarmerie, a nuclear power station and the Palace de Versailles. In the early 1970s it had been infiltrated by DST agents.

* Breton Republican Party
(Strolled Pobl Breiz) (SPB)
Breton autonomist movement which was established in 1980. It propagates the idea of eventual independence for Brittany, on the model of Ireland's achievement of independence. It is led by Jean Pierre Le Mat. In April 1982 three members of the party were detained.

* Bulagne Anti Italian Front
(Front de Bulagne Anti-Italiens) (FBAI)
Corsican anti-separatist movement active in October 1975.

* Charles Martel Group
(Club Charles Martel) (CMG)
Rightist anti-immigrant group which first appeared in 1978. It is named after the Frankish King who in the battle of Tours in 732 stopped the Arabian advance into Europe. It has a record of violence against North African property in France. It had its origins in the forces which opposed the granting of independence to Algeria in 1962. It has been responsible for a bomb attack on the Algerian consulate in May 1980.

* Christian Revolution against Jewish Enemies
Palestinian group which planned a bomb attack on a Jewish synagogue in Paris in 1986. See St.Peter Resistance Command.

* Ciro Rizzato Combat Unit
(Unité Combattante Ciro Rizzato)
Direct Action commando named after a member of Prima Linea who was killed in a hold up in Oct.1983 in Villiers. It has been active in July 1984 when it attacked the Surveillance Industrielle de l'Armement (SIAR) and the Ministry of Industry.

* Civic Action Service
(Service d'Action Civique) (SAC)
A secretive rightist counter-terrorist group which was established in 1958 as the unofficial security arm of the Gaullist movement. It is led by Pierre Debizet and has 10,000 active members. It was banned by the government on Jul.28, 1982, because its actions were based on violence and practices close to gangsterism. J.Massié, a regional head was murdered in 1981, because of alleged ties with the underworld. The movement acquired a status of extra legal security force in the early 1960s when it recruited old resistance fighters as well as underground figures to wage a deadly underground war against the OAS which opposed De Gaulle's policy to negotiate and withdraw from Algeria. Up to 15 percent of the movement are police officers. It had activated a well-prepared plan to go fully underground in the event of a left-wing victory in the 1981 presidential and parliamentary elections.

* Collective of Autonomous Groupings (CAG)
Autonomous group which claimed responsibility for eight bomb explosions at bank premises in the Paris area during the night of April 10-11, 1979.

* Communist· Anti Nuclear Front
Group which has been responsible for five bomb attacks in Paris on June 27, 1980.

* Committee for Corsican Independence

(Comité pour l'Indépendance de la Corse) (CIC)
Corsican separatist group active in 1962.

* Commitee for the French People
(Comité pour le Peuple Francais) (CFP)
Extreme right-wing organization led by Thierry Colombo. He was sentenced to four years in prison on May 22, 1981, after being convicted of non-denunciation of criminals in connection with the murder in May 1976 of an extreme rightwinger.

* Committee for the Liquidation or Deterrence of Computers
(Comité Liquidant ou Détournant les Ordinateurs) (CLODO)
Anarchist group which has attacked a number of computer companies in 1980 and 1981 including Philips Informatique (Toulouse), Honeywell-Bull (Toulouse), International Computers Ltd.(Toulouse) and the Institute for Business Administration (Toulouse). It re-emerged in 1983 when it claimed responsibility for three bomb explosions at a government computer center in Toulouse on Jan.28.

* Commando Llamado of Jesus Christ
See St.Peter Resistance Commando.

* Committees of National Liberation
(Cumitati di Libérazione Nasiunale) (CNC)
Corsican separatist group active in January 1976.

* Committee of Solidarity with Arab and Middle East Political Prisoners (CSPPA)
Middle East terrorist group which has been responsible for a bombing campaign in Paris in Sep.1986 that took nine lives and wounded 160 persons. Its first attack was in December 1985. It demanded the release of several people held in French prisons on charges of terrorism. Among them was George Ibrahim Abdallah a suspected Lebanese terrorist leader. In the attacks, meant to kill and maim as many people as possible, it used penthrite bombs.

* Committee for the Study and the Defense of the Corsican Interests
(Comité d'Etude et de Défense des Interets de la Corse) (CEDIC)
Clandestine Corsican group striving for autonomy which was established Apr.28, 1964. It was led by Max Simeoni and Marc-Paul Seta.

* Communist Youth Movement, Marxist-Leninist
(Union des Jeunesses Communistes, Marxistes-Léninistes) (UJC-ML)
Maoist group which was active on the streets of Paris in the events of May 1968.

* Confrontation
(Faire Front)
Group which in 1973 replaced New Order as the principal activist ultra-rightist group in France. It has been responsible for occasional bomb attacks on ultra-leftist newspapers, and Soviet Bloc targets in Paris.

* Consulta
The political arm of the FLNC which was banned on Sep.28, 1983.

* Consulta de la Jeunesse Nationaliste (CGNC)
Clandestine Corsican group striving for autonomy, established on July 31, 1976. It was led by Léonard Battesti and was dissolved in April 1977.

* Corsican Front
(Front Corsu) (FC)
Clandestine Corsican party which comprised the hardcore of ARC who did not recognize itself in the new movement. It was established in March 1976 and was led by Vincent Stagnara.

* Corsican Movement for Socialism
(Mouvement Corse pour le Socialisme) (MCS)
Clandestine Corsican party striving for autonomy which was formed after a split in the PS. It is led by Charles Santani and Admiral Sanguinetti.

* Corsican National Liberation Front
(Front de Libération Nationale de la Corse) (FLNC)
Autonomist front established in 1976 by members of the FPLC and Ghjustizia Paolina. It has accused the French government of colonizing the island. The Council of National Committees is generally viewed as the political wing of the front which has an estimated 30 active guerrillas an another 200 members. In the summer of 1982 it stepped up its campaign mainly against security forces and the property of non-Corsican residents. It also collects a revolutionary tax. The government outlawed the front on Jan.5, 1983. On the political level the FLNC appeared to moderate its demands, when at the end of January 1983 it declared itself ready to accept 'association' between an independent Corsica and the French Republic. In March 1986, it stepped up its bombing campaign on the mainland where it attacked the Ministry of Finance and the Palace of Justice. On the island the attacks were mainly directed at property. It reportedly had links with the IRA and the PLO.

* Corsican Party for Progress
(Parti Corse pour le Progrès) (PCP)
Clandestine Corsican party striving for autonomy which was established Aug.12, 1970. It was led by Dominique Alfonsi.

* Corsican Party for Socialism
(Parti Corse pour le Socialisme) (PCS)
Clandestine Corsican party striving for autonomy.

It broke away from the PPC in June 1974 and was dissolved in 1977.

* Corsican Peasant Front for Liberation
(Frente Paesanu Corsu di Liberazione) (FPCL)
Clandestine separatist organization active in the early 1970s. It demanded the creation of a sovereign state of Corsica and the withdrawal of recently established French mainland farmers. It claimed to be a genuine national liberation movement fighting French imperialism. It has been responsible for bomb attacks but refrained from murder and assassination. Many members joined the FLNC.

* Corsican Regionalist Action
(Action Régionalist Corse) (ARC)
Clandestine Corsican group striving for autonomy, established on Sep.3, 1967.

* Corsican Regionalist Front
(Front Régionaliste Corse) (FRC)
Clandestine Corsican group striving for autonomy which was established on Jul.31, 1966.

* Corsican Revolutionary Action
(Action Révolutionnaire Corse) (ARC)
Organization which was established in July 1976 and intended to advance the cause of the Corsican people. It was led by Max Simeoni. It has been responsible for several bomb attacks. By 1981 the ARC appeared to be defunct.

* Corsican Revolutionary Front
(Front Révolutionnaire Corse) (FRC)
Corsican separatist front active in September 1975. It has been responsible for two attacks in Ghisonaccia.

* Corsican Guerrillas and Partisans
(Franc Tireurs et Partisans Corses) (FTPC)
Organization which was established in March 1981 by former members of the National Front of Corsica to carry on the tradition of Pasqualini Paoli (1725-1807) the founder of Corsican nationalism and the head of a Corsican Republic in 1775-69. It has been responsible for arson at the Total oil depot in Chateauroux on Mar.14, 1981, as well as several acts of violence in mainland France.

* Corsican Revolutionary Brigades
(Brigades Révolutionaires Corses) (BRC)
Corsican separatist group active in January 1983.

* Delta Organization (DO)
Active anti-semitic organization which was established in 1977. It sprang from the OAS and claimed responsibility for the murder of Henry Curiel, the founder of the Egyptian Communist Party, and Laid Sebai. It consisted of no more than a handful of individuals. It took its name from a commando group formed during the Algerian war of independence under the leadership of Roger Degueldre, a former lieutenant with the French paratroops. It has been responsible for a parcel bomb sent to the director of Le Monde and was one of several extremist organizations which claimed responsibility for a raid on a military weapon depot in Toulouse in November 1981.

* Direct Action
(Action Directe) (AD)
Extreme left-wing terrorist group which was established in May 1979. It sprang from GARI and NAPAP and developed into two factions, an international wing which has directed its actions against NATO and US imperialism and a national wing which directs its actions against more symbolic targets linked to the foreign policy of the French government. The international wing has a dozen members and the internal wing has several dozen members. At least 36 members have been arrested. After an amnesty of the government in 1981 it reorganized. It started to operate in small cells, recruited Turkish and North African immigrants and changed its themes. The government banned the organization on Aug.18, 1982. At the end of 1984 it again changed its strategy and started with assassinations. Together with the Belgian CCC and the German RAF it started an offensive against NATO military targets. It also had contacts with the Italian Red Brigades. Leaders are J.M.Rouillan and M.Frerot.

* Directorate for Territorial Security
(Direction de la Sûreté du Territoire) (DST)
Internal security service with the task of tracking foreign spies. It is largely composed of ex-police officers and since 1981 it is headed by Yves Bonnet. To its customary duty of detecting and arresting spies in France, new tasks of countersubversion and counterterrorism were added in the 1970s as Paris became a center of political violence. The service keeps a large number of dossiers, and now uses a computer to replace its system of card indexes. It also employs the resources of the Renseignements Généraux, another police service which keeps track of foreigners, political and trade union militants.

* Documentation Service and Contra Espionage
(Service de Documentation et Contre Espionage) (SDECE)
French secret service established in the 1940s. Since 1982 it changed its name into DGSE. It has been involved in a great number of secret operations in the 1940s and 1950s. In 1948 it kidnapped the top-Nazi O.Skorzeny from an American prison in the German city of Darmstadt.

In the 1950s it was involved in operations against the Viet Minh in Indo-China. In the Algerian war agents were involved in murder and sabotage and psychological warfare. In 1956 it hijacked the plane of FLN-leader Ben Bella after an unsuccesful attempt to kill him with a car bomb in Cairo. Since 1962 it operated in sub-Saharan Africa. Operations included the supply of weapons to insurgents in Biafra and an attempt to topple the government of Ahmed Sekou Touré in Guinea. Until 1970 it was headed by Jean Foccart and until 1981 by Alexandre de Marenches.

* Elizabeth van Dijck Commando
Direct Action commando named after a member of the RAF who was killed in Nuremberg in 1978. It has been responsible for the assassination of R.Audran, an official of the Ministry of Defense, on Jan.26, 1985.

* Enbata Galerne
Basque nationalist organization which was established in 1953 as a student association in Bordeaux. It is named after a sea wind from the north-west. It took up the struggle for national liberation in 1972. After a government ban militants went underground and began a violent campaign which continued into the early 1980s. Members act within a variety of clandestine groups, the two most active being Iparretarrak and Hordago. Enbata itself did not act as a terrorist group.

* Etienne Bandera Group
Group named after an Ukrainian nationalist who was murdered in 1959. It has been involved in attacks on Soviet embassy vehicles and demanded recognition of the "rebirth of the Ukraine."

* European Nationalist Fasces
(Faisceaux Nationalistes Européens) (FNE)
Neo-fascist group which succeeded FANE in late 1980 when FANE was banned. It is led by Henry-Robert Petit. It has been involved in arson attacks on synagogues and attacks on Jews.

* Fascist Party of Revolutionary Action
(Parti Fasciste d'Action Révolutionnaire) (PFAR)
Obscure party which claimed responsibility for planting a bomb at a Paris court house on May 11, 1980. The bomb was defused before it could explode.

* Federation for European Nationalist Action
(Fédération d'Action Nationale et Europeénne) (FANE)
Propaganda organization specialized in anti-semitism which was set up in 1966. It is an amalgamation of two former factions of the extreme right-wing Occident Movement, which was itself banned in 1968. It has about 200 members and is led by Marc Fredericksen. It has been involved in attacks on left-wing and Jewish targets. Following the banning by the government on Sep.3, 1980, it regrouped under a different name, Faisceaux Nationalistes Européens.

* French Resurrection
(France Résurrection) (FR)
Group which appeared on Jan.9, 1983, when it announced reprisal actions against Corsicans living in the area of Paris. It published a hit list of four alleged members of the FLNC and their addresses in the Paris area and declared that they will be the first to pay if the continentals living in Corsica are attacked again.

* Free France Corsica
(France-Corse Libre) (FCL)
Corsican anti-separatist movement active in the Oct.-Nov.1976 period. It has been responsible for one attack.

* French National Liberation Front
(Front de Libération Nationale Francais) (FLNF)
Anti-Jewish, anti-Black and anti-Arab group which appeared in 1978. It claimed responsibility for a bomb attack at the Pompidou center in Paris in 1980.

* French Command against the North African Invasion (FCNAI)
French racist group which claimed responsibility for two bomb attacks, one on an immigrant district in Marseille in May 1986, and one on a bar in Toulon.

* French Revolutionary Brigades
(Brigades Révolutionnaires Francaises) (BRF)
Right-wing group which appeared in 1982. It has been responsible for the kidnapping of the left-wing writer Jean Edern Hallier and a bomb attack on the apartment of Régis Debray. Conditions for Hallier's release were listed as the dismissal of Communist ministers from the government, cancellation of natural gas contracts with the Soviet Union, the allocation of national aid to the 'resistance of the Afghan people' and the resignation of Gaston Defferre as Minister of the Interior. None of the demands were taken seriously by the government and Hallier reappeared on May 4.

* Front of the Corsican People
(Front du Peuple Corse) (FPC)
Clandestine Corsican party striving for autonomy which sprang from a merger of PPCA, FC, PCS and CGNC. It annouced the constitution of a Fronte Nazionalistu in April 1977.

* General Directorate for External Security (Direction Générale de la Sécurité Extérieure) (DGSE)
Governmental security agency which has been responsible for the bomb attack on the Rainbow Warrior, flagship of the environmentalist group Greenpeace, in New Zealand in July 1985. The action reportedly was intended to prevent that Greenpeace would discover a new runway on the island of Hao in the Muroroa Atoll. The Dutch photographer Fernando Peirera was killed in the attack. The original plan was to blow up the ship at sea. Defense Minister C.Hernu was eventually forced to resign. Admiral P.Lacoste, head of the secret service, was dismissed. In July 1986 France and New Zealand settled their dispute over the act of sabotage. As part of the deal New Zealand agreed to turn over two French intelligence agents imprisoned for their part in the sabotage. In return, France apologized formally for the sabotage, paid $ 7 milllion in damages to New Zealand and promised an end to its obstruction of New Zealand exports.

* Ghjiustizia Corsa (GC)
Corsican separatist group active in the period of November 1974 to September 1975. It has been responsible for two attacks.

* Ghjiustizia Francèsa e Corsu (GFC)
Corsican anti-separatist movement active in November 1975. It has been responsible for one attack at Picanale.

* Ghjiustizia Sampiero (GS)
Corsican separatist group active in May-June 1974. It has been responsible for two attacks in Bastelica.

* Ghjustizia Paolina
Extremist separatist faction in Corsica within the FLNC which was created in 1974. It split from the FLNC in 1982 and has been responsible for the bomb attack on the Calvi townhall on Feb.14, 1982.

* Group Bakunin-Gdansk-Paris-Guatemala-El Salvador (GBGPGS)
Anarchist group which emerged in 1980s. It was opposed to the policy of the Socialist-led government (which came to power in mid-1981) of maintaining trading links with South Africa and of continuing to sell armaments to 'repressive third world regimes'. It has targeted US-owned multinational companies in France, offices of firms trading with Eastern Europe and Latin America, Polish and Soviet trading organizations and South African business premises.

* Groupement de Commandos Mixtes Aeroportes (GCMA)
French anti-guerrilla unit in Vietnam in the 1950s led by colonel Roger Trinquier. It attempted to mobilize the local mountain population (the Meo) againt the Viet Minh. Activities included guerrilla, antiguerrilla, infiltration, penetration, psychological warfare, reconnaissance, organization of the maquis, pacification, sabotage of lines of communication, kidnappings and executions in the Viet Minh zone.

* Honour of the Police (Honneur de la Police)
Group which has been responsible for the 1979 assassination of P.Goldman and the 1980 arson attack on the apartment of Mr.H.Noguères. In the early 1980s allegations were made by the two main French police trade unions and other organizations that the memberships of various extreme right-wing movements included a substantial number of serving police officers. It was believed that the existence of right-wing sympathies in the upper echelon of the police forces had effectively sabotaged official investigations into anti-Jewish actions and other attacks attributed to the extreme right.

* Hordago (Je Tiens)
Basque nationalist group which was established in 1978. It called for a halt to 'cultural oppression' and the influx of summer tourists. It has been responsible for bomb attacks on a tourist center and official buildings. Activities ceased in the early 1980s.

* Interior Front (IF)
Group which claimed responsibility for a bomb attack on the National Employment Agency at Issy-Moulineaux in April 1984.

* Internationalist Communists (IC)
French terrorist group which has signed pamphlets together with the Belgian CCC.

* Intervention Group of the National Gendarmerie (Groupe d'Intervention de la Gendarmerie Nationale) (GIGN)
French anti-riot and anti-terrorist force of the Gendarmerie Nationale. It was established in 1972 and consists of a force of 54 men (four officers and 50 NCO's). There are three squads, one of which is always on duty. Like the West German GSG-9 and the British SAS the GIGN constantly practice ways of storming buildings, trains, ships and aircraft to release hostages and deal with terrorists and/or criminals. It was headed by Mr.Prouteau and subsequently by Mr.Baril. It played a role in Corsica, Saudi Arabia and Djibouti.

* Iparretarrak

(Those from the North)
Revolutionary socialist national liberation organization established in 1973. The French Basque organization turned to violence in 1976. It has been responsible for more than 100 attacks, mainly on tourist targets and the police. It allegedly killed three French policemen in 1982 and 1983. The group renewed its bombing campaign in 1986 to protest the expulsion of Basque refugees suspected of belonging to ETA. The government outlawed the group in July 1987.

* Jacques Mesrine Group (JMG)
Terrorist group named after France's most-sought criminal jailbreaker killed by police in 1979. It claimed responsibility for a bomb attack on a train in May 1981.

* Jewish Brigades (JB)
Group which attacked a political associate of Marc Fredericksen in October 1980. In a telephone call it said that it had carried out the attack as a warning to neo-Nazis and that they could not act with impunity.

* Lahouari Farid Benchellalo Combat Unit
Direct Action commando named after a French activist who died in jail in Helsinki in January 1982. It claimed responsibility for bomb attacks on the Ministry of Industry, the Defense Ministry and the Atlantic Institute on July 15, 1984.

* Lebanese Armed Revolutionary Fractions
(Fractions Révolutionaire Armées Libanaises) (FRAL)
Marxist Maronite Christian terrorist organization. Many members came from the village of Kabbayat in northern Lebanon. It wants to show that not all Lebanese Maronites favor Israel and that it is dedicated to the Palestinian cause.It is led by George Ibrahim Abdallah who was arrested in October 1984 in Lyon. In 1983 activities peaked when the entire Abdallah family was in France, including Salem, Joseph, George, Maurice and Robert, possibly with the exception of Emile. George Ibrahim Abdallah once was an important member of the 'foreign operations' branch of the PFLP. It also was alleged to have contacts with DA, the CCC, the RAF and ASALA. It has been responsible for a number of assassinations in Europe. Victims were Western, an Israeli and a US diplomat. In the fall of 1986 the CSPPA launched a bombing campaign and demanded Abdallah's release.

* Liberation Front of Brittany for National Liberation and Socialism
(Front de Libération de la Bretagne pour la Libĕration Nationale et Socialism) (FLB-LNS)
Breton organization which split off from the FLB in March 1973. It has been responsible for bomb attacks and had links with Basques organizations. The government banned the organization on Jan.30, 1974, but activities continued. Most known FLB-LNS activists had been brought to trial in the late 1970s. The French authorities are confident that the organization had effectively ceased to exist.

* Libertary Internationalist Communist Student Workers Party
(Parti Ouvrier Libertaire Internationaliste Communiste Etudiante) (POLICE)
Group which has been responsible for an attack on a police post.

* Loic Lefèvre Commando
Direct Action commando named after a man who was shot and killed by the police. It has been responsible for a bomb attack on a building of the police in Paris in July 1986.

* Mario Tuti Commando
A Delta commando named after an activist of the extreme right-wing Armed Revolutionary Nuclei (NAR) of Italy with which Delta was believed to have links. The group attacked the Paris home of Rosette Curiel, the widow of Henry Curiel, on July 13, 1980.

* March 22 Movement
(Mouvement 22 Mars)
A Paris-based student organization active in the 1968 revolt. It was led by Daniel Cohn Bendit. He was hostile to 'established communism'. French authorities refused his right of residence and he returned to the Federal Republic of Germany where he became active in the Green politics.

* The Mongoose
(La Mangouste)
Obscure group which claimed responsibility for three bomb explosions at left-wing premises in Toulouse in early May 1981. The targets were the printers of the anarchist review Basta, the studio of radio Barberouge and the local headquarters of the Revolutionary Communist League.

* M-10 Movement
(Mouvement M-10) (M-10)
Obscure group which claimed responsibility for the bomb attack on Mr.Peyrefitte on Dec.15, 1986. An anonymous telephone caller said the attack was an act of revenge for the death of the student Malik Oussekine during demonstrations in Paris.

* National Armenian Movement
(Mouvement Nationale Armenienne) (MNA)
Armenian umbrella organization which has its seat in Paris. It functions as a coordinator of numerous Armenian organizations in France. Its relationship with ASALA has been ambivalent and can be

compared with the relation of Sinn Fein to the IRA in Northern Ireland. Its leader Ara Toranian has been arrested in 1984. It demands independence for Armenia and the official recognition of the genocide of 1.5 million Armenians.

* Nationalist Information and Action Committee
(Comité d'Information et d'Action Nationaliste) (CIAN)
Clandestine Corsican group striving for autonomy, formed on the island of Rousse.

* National Front
(Front National) (FN)
Extreme rightist movement which was established in 1972 as an umbrella organization of several rightist nationalist movements. Among the founders were Pierre Bousquet, Alain Robert, Francois Brigneau, Roger Holeindre and Francois Duprat. The organization is led by Jean Marie Le Pen. The front gained nearly 11 percent in the June 1984 elections. During the election campaign a member of FN murdered Philippe Brocard, a member of the Socialist Party when he removed a FN election poster from space reserved for the Socialist Party.

* National Liberation Army of Corsica
(Armée de Libération Nationale de la Corse) (ALNC)
Corsican separatist group active in July 1983.

* National Savoyard Front (NSF)
Group which has been responsible for an attack on a cable chair lift on the Mont Blanc in July 1978.

* National Socialist Movement
(Mouvement National Socialiste) (MNS)
Right-wing group which has been responsible for anti-Jewish attacks in the early 1980s.

* National Youth Front
(Front National de la Jeunesse) (FNJ)
Front which claimed that a commando of its members had been responsible for a bomb explosion on the Paris-Moscow express train on Apr.26, 1980.

* New Action Front Against the Independence and Autonomy of Corsica (Front d'Action Nouvelle Contre l'Indépendence et l'Autonomie) (FRANCIA)
Corsican anti-separatist movement which was active in the April 1977-January 1981 period. It acted as a counterforce to Corsican terrorism. It was believed to recruit among the pied noirs. It was led by Yannick Leonelle who was arrested in 1980. Attacks were directed at property of Corsican nationalists who were regarded as posing a threat to the island's status as an integral part of France.

* New Nazi Front
(Nouvelle Front Nazi) (NFN)
Believed to be one of the successor groups of the FANE created after the banning of the latter in September 1980.

* New Order
(Ordre Nouveau) (NO)
Right-wing group which was established in 1969. It was banned in June 1973. Almost immediately after its demise it was replaced by Confrontation. Sympathizers oppose immigration, especially of Arabs from Northern Africa.

* Order and New Justice
(Ordre et Justice Nouvelle) (ONJ)
Neo-Nazi group which claimed responsibility for a bomb attack on left-wing printing offices in Marseille on Aug.11, 1980.

* Party of the Corsican People for Autonomy
(Parti du Peuple Corse pour l'Autonomie) (PPCA)
Clandestine Corsican party which sprang from a merger of the PPC and the PCP in October 1974. It was led by Dominique Alfonsi.

* Party of the Corsican People
(Parti du Peuple Corse) (PPC)
Clandestine Corsican party striving for autonomy which was established in 1980. It is led by Dominique Alfonsi and Jean Pierre Arrighi.

* Peiper Vengeance Group
A clandestine group named after a former German SS officer. It has claimed responsibility for numerous bombings and other assaults on Jewish and Moslem premises in France.

* Pessah
Jewish anti Nazi group. It announced in 1981 that it planned to place bombs at neo-nazi centers throughout Paris.

* Pierre Overney Commando
Direct Action commando named after a leftist worker who was killed by a company security guard during a demonstration near Paris. It has been responsible for the assassination of George Besse, chairman of Renault, on Nov.17, 1986.

* Proletarian Left
(Gauche Proletarienne) (PL)
Maoist group established in 1968. It has been involved in a number of kidnappings and bomb attacks. It did not go underground arguing that priority should be given to the organization of the masses.

* RAID
Special commando unit of the police established by Robert Broussard. It acted for the first time in public during a hostage situation in Nantes in

September 1985.

• Red Brigade of Occitania
(Brigade Rouge d'Occitanie) (BROC)
Clandestine Occitanian group which claimed responsibility for attacks on military targets in Larzac in 1973 and 1974. The attacks apparently were in protest against expropriations of land for extensions to the military camp.

• Red Hand
A French organization that engaged in counterterrorist activities against Algerian nationalists. It reportedly has been involved in the Nov.3, 1960 poisoning in Geneva of Dr.Felix Moumié, a leader of the Cameronian UPC.

• Red Poster
(l'Affiche Rouge)
Group which claimed responsibility for a number of attacks on targets in the Lyon area in mid-1982.

• Refugee Aid Committee (RAC)
Basque group which has destroyed French property in 1986 in retaliation for the deportation of alleged Basque terrorists to Spain.

• For Resolute Anti Militarist Actions
(Pour des Actions Résolument Anti-militaristes) (PARA)
Anti-militarist group which has been responsible for the Apr.18, 1980, bombing of the headquarters of a para-regiment which simultaneously acts as counterinsurgency unit.

• Revolutionary Collective (RC)
Group which has been responsible for a bomb attack on the courthouse in Tours on May 26, 1980.

• Revolutionary Communist Youth
(Jeunesse Communiste Révolutionnaire) (JCR)
Trotskyite group active during the 1968 revolt in Paris.

• Revolutionary Coordination Group (RCG)
Autonomous group which claimed responsibility for a series of bomb explosions in Paris and in Toulouse.

• Revolutionary Internationalist Action Group
(Group d'Actions Révolutionaires Internationaliste) (GARI)
Group of exiled Spanish anarchists active in the early 1970s. The developments in Franco's Spain were the direct reason for its acts. It was fighting against the Franco dictatorship, against capital, against the state and for the liberation of Spain, Europe and the world. It never had more than 100 members. After a series of arrests the group was dissolved. Some members joined Direct Action.

• Revolutionary Nationalist Movement
(Mouvement Nationaliste Révolutionnaire) (RNM)
Right-wing group led by Jean Gilles Malliarkis. It claimed responsibility for a bomb explosion in Paris on Oct.5, 1980, as a protest against the 'foreign invasion'.

• Secret Army of the Pacific People-European Command (SAPP-EC)
Group which has been involved in actions against French nuclear reactors and nuclear transports since 1974.

• Secret Army Organization
(Organisation de l'Armée Secrète) (OAS)
Organization which was established in 1960. It consisted of European settlers ('colons') in Algeria who resisted General De Gaulle's policy shift towards self-determination. It had active support of certain sections of the French security forces and was led by Jean Jacques Susini. It failed in an attempt to seize power in April 1961. Prior to that date the OAS had turned to terrorism not only in Algeria but also in France. In 1962 it tried to set up a National Council of French Resistance. Divided leadership caused the organization to break up after 200 officers were arrested and its leaders sentenced to death or imprisonment. It has been responsible for the death of hundreds of Algerian Arabs and many Europeans. A well-known operator was Roger Degueldre who was obsessed by the idea that Algeria must remain French. The cutting edge of the OAS were Degueldre's 'Deltas' which the authorities tried to attack by a special undercover anti-terror unit.

• Self Defense against All Powers
(Autodefense contre tous les Pouvoirs)
Group which has attacked US businesses in France in 1980. Since then it has not been active.
• Revolutionary Internationalist Solidarity Group
(Groupe de Solidarité Rèvolutionaire Internationaliste) (GSRI)
Revolutionary anarchist organization.

• S.O.S. France
Anti-immigrant organization founded by Claude Noblia (ex National Front).

• Special Staff to Coordinate Information and Action against Terrorism
A special anti-terrorism group established in August 1982. It stands completely outside the police hierarchy and has 15 members.

• Stop the Priests
Group which claimed responsibility for the Aug.12, 1983, bomb attack on the statue of Pontius Pilatus,

a day in advance of a visit of the Pope. It said the attack was directed against 'the director general of the Vatican multinational organization' and announced more actions.

* St.Peter's Resistance Command (or Llamado Command of Jesus Christ) French police arrested two Portuguese and an Egyptian in January 1986, for having planned an attack on a Jewish synagogue. They said the action was planned and paid by the Libyan embassy in Madrid and that the group was led by the Syrian Faried Hazan and the Jordanian Hanna Joude. The two were allegedly released on the condition that they would infiltrate the Libyan embassy in Madrid. The Spanish weekly Cambio 16 said that DGSE 'controlled and manipulated' the group. In May 1986, Spain announced the arrest of the two men, three Lebanese, four Spaniards and a Portuguese for plotting attacks against American interests in Western Europe.

* Superman
Anti-nuclear group which bombed the hydro-electric installation in Malause on July 16, 1980.

* The Survivors of the Genocide in Cambodia (SGC)
Group which left its name on the door of an apartment in Paris where four Cambodians were killed in March 1985. The police believed it was a revenge attack directed at the Khmer Rouge. One of the victims was the chemist Try Meng Huot, former deputy-director of a re-education camp during the regime of Pol Pot. In circles of Cambodian refugees it was alleged that he was responsible for the execution of about 30 intellectuals.

* U Cumunu
Clandestine Corsican group striving for autonomy which was established in March 1978. It was led by Dominique Cervoni.

* Union Corse (UC)
Clandestine Corsican group striving for autonomy which was established in 1960. It was led by Dominique Alfonsi, Charles Santani and Gisèle Poli.

* Union of the Fatherland
(Unione di a Patria) (UP)
Clandestine Corsican party striving for autonomy. It issued the 'Castellare Appeal' on Jan.7, 1973. It was led by Jacques Martini and Gisèle Poli.

* We Shall Blow Everything Up
(Farem Tot Petar)
Occitanian group which was responsible for 15 explosions carried out in 1974-75. At the time it expressed support for the Corsican and other separatist movements which it regarded as allies in the opposition to the centralized French state.

* Yann Kel Kernaleguen Group
Group which claimed responsibility for an unsuccessful attempt to place a mortar shell on a railway line at Ingrandes station on Aug.7, 1982. It took its name from that of a young Breton activist who was killed in September 1976 when a bomb exploded while still in his possession.

* Youth Action Group
(Groupe d'Action Jeunesse)
Anti-semitic group which claimed responsibility for a molotov cocktail attack on the Paris office of a pacifist movement on June 15, 1981. In a message it declared itself to be 'against cosmopolitanism and internationalism'.

* Zionist Militant Resistance (ZMR)
Group which bombed Libyan embassy buildings in Paris on May 6, 1980.

FRENCH GUYANA

* Guyana National Liberation Front
(Front National de Libération Guyanais) (FLNG)
Liberation front led by Raymand Charlotte. It has been responsible for bomb attacks on the Kourou space station on Apr.20, 1980, and on a police building in Cayenne.

FRENCH POLYNESIA

* The Ancestors Blood
Anti-French terrorist group with which the legal pro-independence Te Taata Tahiti Tiama party ledCharlie Ching was suspected of having co-operated in 1978-79.

* Maohi Republic Provisional Government (MRPG)
Small pro-independence movement which came to prominence in 1982.

GABON

* Directorate for Counter Intelligence and Military Security
(Direction de Contre-ingérence et de la Sécurité Militaire) (DCISM)
Governmental security agency which reportedly has been involved in torturing of political prisoners.

* Movement for National Recovery
(Mouvement de Redressement National) (MORENA)
Clandestine opposition party advocating a multi-party system. Several members detained in the Libreville prison on political charges reportedly have been mistreated or kept in degrading

circumstances.

* Research Brigade
(Brigade de Recherche)
Section of the National Gendarmerie which reportedly has been torturing political prisoners.

GAMBIA

* Movement for Justice in Africa (MOJA)
Movement which has been declared an 'unlawful society' and was charged of 'possessing firearms and ammunition'.

GERMAN FEDERAL REPUBLIC

* Aktion Christian Klar
Group which claimed responsibility for a bomb attack on the Herti-Department store in Dortmund in March 1985. It later turned out that the attack was a hoax by four students who did not have any links with known terrorist groups. They said they wanted to experience a big bang.

* Adolf Eichmann Command
(Kommando Adolf Eichmann)
Right-wing terrorist group.

* Andreas Baader Commando
RAF commando named after one of its principal founders.

* Anti Fascist Action Ruhr Area
(Antifascistische Aktion Ruhrgebiet) (AAR)
Spontaneous group which set fire to a transport bus of the local FAP, the organization which succeeded ANS, on March 10, 1985. In a letter it said that the anti-fascist struggle is part of the anti-imperialist struggle.

* Anti Fascist Commando Siegbert and Lotte Rotholz
A group which claimed responsibility for an arson attack on one of the main centers of the FAP in Niedersachsen on July 25, 1987.

* Arab Revolutionary Organization
One of several unknown groups which claimed responsibility for the bomb attack on the Frankfurt airport on June 21, 1985.

* Armed Secret Execution Organisation (ASEO)
Organization which claimed responsibility for a bomb attack on Radio Free Europe and Radio Liberty on Feb.28, 1981. The letter was written in Polish.

* Autonomous Destruction Society for Illusions
(Autonome Abrissgemeinschaft für Potemkinsche Dörfer)
Group that claimed responsibility for an arson attack on the Berlin underground on Apr.21, 1987. The attack caused extensive damage.

* Autonomists
(Autonomen)
Generic name for anarchists who reject any ideology. Their actions are directed against the state which they want to destroy in a 'permanent struggle'. Autonomous groups have operated under fantasy names and have been involved in bomb attacks and arson. Targets are linked to various themes, from disarmament, to ecology to DNA research. See also Guerrilla Diffusa.

* Avanti Dillettanti (AD)
Spontaneous group which has been responsible for a series of arson attacks in department stores in Göttingen and an arson attack at the Beton-Mischmaschinen of the TGB company in Schwandorf on July 21, 1986.

* Avanti Militanti Group
(Gruppe Avanti Militanti) (GAM)
Group which caused 250,000 DM damage to banks and department stores in the center of Göttingen on Nov.24, 1986. In a declaration the acts were portrayed as a protest to the massive presence of security forces in recent times.

* Bad Mannered Children
Spontaneous group which has been active in 1986.

* Black Bloc
(Schwarzer Block)
Left-wing group which was active from May 1980 onwards. It was suspected of supporting the RAF and of arson and bomb attacks. Twenty alleged members of the group were arrested in the Frankfurt area on July 28, 1981.

* Black Forest Combat Group
(Kampfgruppe Schwarzwald) (KS)
Right-wing group founded by Ottfried Hepp.

* Border Protection Group Nine
(Grenzschutz Gruppe Neun) (GSG-9)
Elite anti-terrorist federal squad formed in 1972 following the police debacle of the Munich Olympics attacks. It is headed by Ulrich Wegener and its headquarters is located in Hangelaar near Cologne. Like the British SAS, GSG-9 personnel are trained to use a wide variety of weapons and explosives and communication systems. It is organized into six units of approximately 30 men each. There is a command group, four 'action groups' and a 'back up group'. All four action groups have identical capabilities. Members are volunteers from the borderguard and must have an IQ of at least 110. Nine out of ten candidates are

eliminated in the six month training course. It has been involved in the Jul.25, 1978, bomb attack at the Celle prison in order to place a criminal as infiltrator in the terrorist scene.

* Brigades for the Liberation of the Turkish People (BLTP)
Group which claimed responsibility for an attack on the Turkish consulate in Stuttgart on Oct.31, 1983. It said it was opposed to the military government in Turkey and that the attack was meant as a protest against the elections in Turkey.

* Brunswick Group
(Braunschweig Gruppe) (BG)
Members of this neo-Nazi group engaged in preparations for explosions.

* Bugs Bunny and the Mudkillers
(Bugs Bunny und die Baggerkiller)
Group which claimed responsibility for an arson attack on a vehicle of the Plunk company on June 30, 1986. Damage was estimated at 180.000 DM.

* Children of the Economic Miracle
(Wirtschaftwunderkinder)
Spontaneous group which claimed responsibility for a bomb attack on an administrative office of the Hannover-Messe in Hannover on June 2, 1985. One of the perpetrators, Franz Jürgen Pemöller died in the attack.

* Commando of the Little Girls from the Suburb
(Kommando der kleinen Mädchen aus der Vorstadt) (KKMV)
Group which has been responsible for a series of arson attacks on department stores in Göttingen on Mar.17, 1986.

* Comradeship of National Activists
(Kameradschaft Nationaler Aktivisten) (KNA)
Right-wing organization which was established in the fall of 1982. It is led by Arndt Heinz Marx and has about 30 members.

* Conservative Action
Neo-Nazi youth group in Hamburg.

* Crespo Cepa Gallende Commando
RAF commando named after a member of the Spanish GRAPO who was killed by the police. The commando claimed responsibility for an attack on a border control facility in Heimerzheim in August 1986.

* Defense Sport Group-Hoffmann
(Wehrsport Gruppe Hoffmann) (WGH)
Neo-Nazi organization which was established in 1974. It is led by Karl Heinz Hoffmann. It wants to destroy the existing social structure in Germany and to replace it by an authoritarian 'Führer' state. It has about 80 active members and about 400 sympathizers. Since Hoffmann's arrest and the outlawing of the group, 25 similar paramilitary organizations, made up of many of his adherents, have sprouted around the country. It has been involved in the bomb explosion in Munich on Sep.26, 1980, in which 13 people were killed and 200 were wounded. It also has been involved in attacks on left-wing students and the assassination of Shlomo Levin, a Jewish publisher, and his female companion. Members have received training in Palestinian camps in Lebanon. The organization was banned on Jan.30, 1980. It has cooperated with the Armenian ASALA in a bomb attack on the French Orly airport. It has close links with KDS, WJ and ANS.

* Diffused Guerrilla
(Guerrilla Diffusa) (GD)
Generic name used by young people living in squatting communities of the larger West German cities. They are particularly active in West Berlin and Frankfurt. Sympathizers were characterized by an interest in ecology, opposition to development of nuclear power and the practice of an alternative life-style. They also have a shared hostility towards the establishment in general and formed a recruiting pool for Revolutionary Cells in the early 1980s. German law enforcement statistics refer to a yearly average of 1,500 acts of violence from leftists of which some 80 percent fall into the category of GD and RZ. Annual damage estimates now rank into the tens of millions of German Marks. Authorities fear some groups and cells will cross the borderline to terrorist murders.

* Disturb the Economic Summit
(Stört den Weltwirtschaftgipfel) (SWG)
Group which claimed responsibility for a bomb attack on a building of the Siemens company in Düsseldorf on Apr.23, 1985.

* Edelweiss Pirates to build up a Bavarian Guerrilla

(Edelweiss Piraten zum Aufbau einer Bayerischen Guerrilla) (EPABG)
Group which claimed responsibility for a bomb attack on an electric power pylon near the nuclear plant at Gundremmingen on June 28, 1986.

* European Labor Party (ELP)
Political group established in 1974 which is bitterly opposed to the Soviet Union. It is led by Lyndon LaRouche and has about 1,800 members. It operates in Sweden, Denmark, Italy, France and Belgium. It has mounted apparently well-funded campaigns attacking communism and urging support for European unification and nuclear power. It wants neutral Sweden to join NATO. In Sweden the party

made strong personal attacks against the late Olaf Palme with posters portraying him as a devil and comparing him to Hitler. Former members have declared that the party was led as a religious sect and that members who wanted to leave the party were threatened and brainwashed.

* Fedayin of the Imperial Iranian Monarchy (FIIM)
Iranian monarchist group which claimed responsibility for an attack on the Melli Bank in Frankfurt/M on Feb.6, 1985, and for an attack on an Iran Air Office on June 5, 1984.

* Federal Intelligence Service
(Bundes Nachrichtendienst) (BND)
The West German equivalent of the American CIA and the British MI6. It was established in April 1956 when the Gehlen organization was brought under government control. The Gehlen organization had itself been assisted by the Americans after the Second World War. It possessed unique archives collected by Gehlen as Hitler's masterspy on the Eastern Front. The function of the BND was laid down as 'to gather information on other countries which will be of importance in the shaping of foreign policy'. In practice the BND went further than that, and in the early days indulged in sabotage and subversion behind the Iron Curtain. After Gehlen's retirement the old SS and Abwehr men were removed and the organization was transformed into a modern intelligence gathering operation relying more on electronics and analysis. It cooperates closely with the CIA, MI6 and MOSSAD.

* Fiery Rats
(Feurigen Ratten) (FR)
Group which claimed responsibility for an arson attack on a local administration office of the Bundeswehr on July 1, 1986.

* Fight the War Commando
(Kommando Krieg dem Krieg) (KKK)
Group which claimed responsibility for an attack on vehicles of the US Army in Stuttgart on Sep.8, 1985.

* Fight Work, Sabotage All Day
(Kampf der Arbeit, alle Tage Sabotage)
Group which claimed responsibility for an attack on the power circuit of the German Railways and a power station in the Freiburg northern industrial area in December 1986.

* Fighting Unit August 13, 1986
Group which claimed responsibility for a bomb attack on the American owned branch of the Westinghouse Co. in Wuppertal on Aug.13, 1986. The attack was labelled as a protest to US business ties to South Africa and Morocco.

* Fighting Unit for the Construction of the Anti Imperialist Front
Group which claimed responsibility for an attack on a radio transmission tower of the American Forces Network in Mönchengladbach on Aug.17, 1985. It is suspected to be a Revolutionary Cell.

* Fighting Unit Christos Tsoutsouvis
Group possibly linked to the RAF which is named after a Greek citizen who was killed in a gun battle with the police in Athens in May 1985. The group claimed responsibility for a bomb attack on a building of the Office for the Protection of the Constitution in Cologne on Sep.8, 1986.

* Fighting Unit Hind Alameh
Possibly a RAF commando named after a female member of the Palestinian group that hijacked a Lufthansa flight to Mogadishu (Somalia) in 1977. The commando claimed responsibility for a bomb attack on an IBM office in Heidelberg on Nov.16, 1986.

* Fighting Unit Johannes Thimme
Group which claimed responsibility for a bomb attack on a NATO fuel pipeline near Dinklage on Oct.5, 1985.

* Fighting Unit Mustafa Aktas (Celal)
RAF commando named after a Kurd (a PKK member) who fought in Lebanon with the Palestinians and was murdered in Paris on Dec.25, 1985. The commando claimed responsibility for the bomb attack on the building of the Friedrich Ebert Stiftung in Bad Münster-Eifel on Dec.23, 1986.

* Fighting Unit Phillip Müller
BKA officials arrested a man in Bielefeld who wanted to plant a bomb at building of the Siemens company. In his apartment they found a declaration which said: We have been responsible for the attack at the office of Siemens AG Bielefeld on Dec.9, 1986. It was signed by the Fighting Unit K.E.P.Müller. P.Müller was a demonstrator who was killed during a demonstration against rearmament in 1952.

* Fighting Unit Rolando Ulalia
RAF commando named after a Filipino labour union leader who was murdered in November 1986. The commando claimed responsibility for a bomb attack on the DEG-Deutsche Finanzierungsgesellschaft in Entwicklungsländern in Cologne on Dec.21, 1986.

* Fighting Unit Sheban Atlouf
Group possibly linked to the RAF which claimed responsibility for a bomb attack on the Fraunhofer Institute for laser technology in Aachen on Aug.24, 1986.

* Fighting Unit Ulrike Meinhof (RZ)
RZ commando named after one of the principal RAF leaders who committed suicide in prison. The commando claimed responsibility for an attack on an electric power pylon near Herlikofen on Oct.14, 1986.

* Front for the Protection against Left and Right (FPLR)
Group which threatened to poison all SPD politicians on July 27, 1983. It demanded a ransom of one million DM within two days. The threat letter contained 3,8 grams of arsenicum.

* Furious Youth 1986
(Zorniger Jugend 86)
Group which claimed responsibility for the sabotage of an underground electric power cable near a construction site in Gorleben on July 7, 1986.

* George Jackson Commando
Cooperative RAF/DA commando named after a black American activist who was known in the beginning of the 1970s as one of the 'Soledad brothers' and who was killed on Aug.21, 1971, in the US prison of San Quentin. The commando claimed responsibility for a bomb attack on a US Airforce Base in Frankfurt on Aug.10, 1985. It denounced the base as a link in the chain for wars in the Third World.

* German Action Groups
(Deutsche Aktionsgruppen) (DA)
Right-wing organization led by Raimund Hörnle. On Sep.4, 1980, he confessed to having prepared bombs for several attacks and he himself had thrown a molotov cocktail at a Hamburg hostel for Vietnamese refugees, two of whom were killed. On June 28, 1981, four members of the group were sentenced, including R.Hörnle, Sybille Vorderbrügge, Manfred Roeder and Dr.Heinz Colditz. Several other bomb attacks obviously also directed against foreigners took place in various locatilities during 1980.

* German Action Front
(Deutsche Aktionsfront) (DA)
Group which claimed responsibility for causing five explosions between Feb.2 and Aug.17, 1980. One of these targeted an exhibition at Auschwitz.

* German People's Union
(Deutsche Volksunion) (DPU)
Neo-Nazi and anti-semitic organization led by Dr.Gerhard Frey and Erwin Arlt. It has about 1,000 members in Bavaria alone. In total it has about 12,000 members. It has two subsidiary organizations, Aktion Deutsche Einheit and the Volksbewegung für Generalamnestie.

* German Socialist Student Association
(Sozialistischer Deutscher Studentenbund) (SDS)
In 1961, the SDS cut all its original links with the Socialist Party (SDP). It gained prominence at the Free University of West Berlin in the mid-1960s. It promoted the struggle to reform university education. Led by Rudi Dutschke, SDS students were behind serious rioting in 1967 when the Shah of Iran visited Berlin. The death of Benno Ohnesorg, a student shot by police in the demonstration, transformed the situation into a nationwide student revolt, which included highschool pupils. Rudi Dutschke was himself shot in the head by a young worker in West Berlin in March 1968.

* German Workers' Youth
(Deutsche Arbeiterjugend) (DAJ)
Anti-semitic group. A police raid on the homes of 17 suspected members of the group on Dec.8, 1982, led to the seizure of ammunition, parts of uniforms and neo-Nazi literature.

* Get Rid of the Shit Command
(Kommando hau weg die Scheisse)
Group which has claimed responsibility for an arson attack on the premises of Daimler-Benz on Mar.5, 1986.

* God Willing
(Inshallah)
Arab group directed against Western imperialism. It was one the groups which claimed responsibility for the bomb attack on the La Belle discothek in Berlin on Apr.5, 1986. Libyan and Syrian involvement has been alleged. Two American servicemen and one Turkish woman were killed and more than 100 others were wounded.

* Group of March 6
Leftist group which claimed responsibility for bomb explosions at the Paris offices of several West German newspapers, in particular those of the Axel Springer group (which has been the target of RAF attacks on other occasions) and on radio stations on Mar.6, 1975.

* Gudrun Enslin Commando
RAF commando which claimed responsibility for an attack with a Soviet-made anti-tank grenade on the car of General Frederick Kroesen, US Ground Forces Commander in Europe, in Heidelberg on Sep.5, 1981.

* Guerrilla Front Upper Bavaria-Commando Munich Bogenhausen
(Guerrilla Front Oberbayern-Kommando München Bogenhausen) (GFOKMB)
Group which claimed responsibility for an arson attack on a building of the German Bank in

Munich in 1986.

* Haag-Mayer Group
RAF group which was formed in 1976 around the legal office of Siegfried Haag with the object to restructure the RAF at the end of the first phase of the RAF's operations marked by the suicides (?) in prison of its leading figures. The principal aim of the group appeared to be the release of imprisoned RAF members and revenge for the deaths of others, rather than the achievement of a political revolution. Most of the founding members were said to have received training at a PFLP camp in Southern Yemen in 1976. The Hamburg section of the group was held responsible for the assassination of Dr.Jürgen Ponto, chief executive of the Dresdener Bank, on July 30, 1977. Leading members were Roland Mayer and Günter Sonnenberg.

* Hepp/Kexel Group
Right-wing terrorist group which claimed responsibility for a number of bomb attacks on American objects in 1985. Previously these attacks were ascribed to the Revolutionary Cells. On Mar.15, 1985 five members were convicted for three murder attempts and five bank raids. Walther Kexel who was sentenced to 14 years in prison, committed suicide. Odfried Hepp was arrested in Paris on Apr.8, 1985. He was suspected of illegal weapon deals with the Palestinian PLF.

* Holger Meins Commando
Commando named after one of the first leaders of the RAF who died in prison as a result of a hungerstrike on Nov.9, 1974. It has been involved in several bomb attacks and the attack on the West German embassy in Stockholm on Apr.24, 1975. On that occasion the military and the economic attachés were killed. An accidental explosion set the building on fire and killed one member of the commando, while the other five were arrested by the police, with all remaining hostages escaping alive. The name also has been used by two agent provocateurs of GSG-9 who placed a bomb at the prison in Celle on July 24, 1978, in an attempt to liberate Sigurd Debus. Anonymous telephone callers claimed responsibility for the bomb attack on the Berlin disco on Apr.5, 1986 and the assassination of Olaf Palme (1986) in the name of this commando.

* Horst Wessel Fighting League (Kampfbund Horst Wessel)
Right-wing organization.

* Illegal Militant Combat Unit Jonas Thimme
Group which claimed responsibility for bomb attacks on the offices of the Internationalen Schiffahrts Studiengesellschaft (ISS) and the Project Management Office (PMO) in Hamburg on Apr.4, 1985. The group claimed that the two companies were involved in the planning of the NATO-frigate 90.

* Ingrid Schubert Commando of the Revolutionary Front of Western Europe
RAF commando named after a former RAF member. The commando claimed responsibility for the assassination of Gerold von Braunmühl, director of the political section of the German Foreign Ministry on Oct.11, 1986. The attack led to fears that the RAF would try to kill leading politicians during the general election campaign in January 1987. No attacks occurred.

* June 2 Movement
(Bewegung 2.Juni)
Leftist terrorist group named after the date of the death of Benno Ohnesorg, a student who was shot by police during a protest demonstration against a visit by the Shah of Iran in West Berlin in 1967. It was formed by members of the RAF in 1973. Members were drawn from the anarchist Black Cells and Black Help. It had a core of about 20 members and was led by Ralph Reinders. It has been involved in bank robberies, abductions, and bomb attacks. On Feb.27, 1975, Peter Lorenz, the chairman of the CDU in West Berlin, was kidnapped by the group. They threatened to kill Lorenz unless all their demands were fulfilled, in particular the immediate release of all persons arrested in connection with demonstrations following the death of Holger Meins and also the release of six RAF members. Horst Mahler refused. The other five were granted political asylum in the Republic of Southern Yemen and P.Lorenz was released. Survivors joined the RAF.

* Mara Cagal Commando
RAF commando named after the wife of Renato Curcio, one of the founders of the Italian Red Brigades, who was killed by the police in a razzia in 1975. The commando claimed responsibility for the bomb attack on K.H.Beckurts, the director of Siemens, on July 10, 1986. Authorities considered the attack as an attempt of the RAF to forge links with the anti-nuclear movement which enjoys broader popular support.

* Michael Knoll-Willy Peter Stoll Commando
A RAF commando.

* Mutual Support Society of Former Waffen SS Soldiers
(Hilfsgemeinschaft auf Gegenseitigkeit der Soldaten der ehemaligen Waffen-SS e.V.) (HIAG)
Right-wing group established in 1951 with the ostensible aim to investigate the fate of lost comrades. During its meetings it keeps alive its traditions. At the Nuremberg Tribunal the Waffen SS was convicted as a criminal organization. Before and during the Second World War the Waffen SS

was established within the SS (Schutz Staffel), headed by the Reichsführer SS (Himmler). The Waffen SS guarded concentration camps and numerous members have been convicted as mass murderers and sadistic hangmen. In countries occupied by Germany, the Waffen SS was involved in the enforced employment of workers needed for its war industry. It was specialized in 'punitive' actions against civilian populations, like Lidice (Czechoslovakia) and Oradour (France).

* National Democratic Party
(National demokratische Partei Deutschlands) (NPD)
Right-wing party which was established in November 1964. It defends the crimes of the national-socialist regimes and pledges for the restoration of the 'Greater Germany'. Members of the NPD and the youth section JN have participated in numerous attacks on anti-fascists. Some members have openly shown sympathy with fascist gangs. In 1978 the Verwaltungsgerichtshof in Munich ruled that the organization was not unconstitutional. In 1985 a demonstrator, Günther Sare, was killed during an anti-NPD demonstration. His death led to violent riots in 15 German cities. The party is led by Mr.Mussgnug and has about 6,100 members.

* National Front
(Nationalistische Front) (NF)
Right-wing organization which sprang from the cell which called itself Nationale Front/ Bund Sozial Revolutionärer Nationalisten. It changed its name to Nationalistische Front in 1984. Members came from VSBD/PdA and its youth organization Junge Front (JF). It described itself as 'part of the worldwide movement of the liberation nationalists to beat international imperialism'. Its goal is a unified Germany on the basis of the 'modern nationalism'. It calls for a struggle against US and Soviet imperialism and wants to free the country of foreigners. It is led by Bernhard Pauli and has several dozen members.

* National Socialist Action Front
(Aktionsgemeinschaft Nationaler Sozialisten) (ANS)
Right-wing organization which first appeared in Hamburg on Nov.26, 1977. It sprang from the Freizeitverein Hansa. It is led by Michael Kuhnen, a former army lieutenant, who was arrested in 1978. Thereafter Christian Worch took a leading role until his arrest on bombing charges in March 1980. The group has been involved in bank robberies and theft of arms at the base of a Dutch Army unit in Germany. After ANS was banned by the government many members entered the Freiheitlichen Deutschen Arbeiterpartei (FAP). The group does have contacts with skinheads and has been involved in attacks on foreigners. In 1971 the organization accepted CDU money for a promise not to partake in elections in Berlin. Shortly after the money was paid stickers were put on SDP election posters with the text 'away with the socialists'.

* National Socialist German Workers Party
(National Sozialistische Deutsche Arbeiter Partei-Auslandsorganization) (NSDAP-AO)
Right-wing organization which was established in 1970 as NSDAP. Since 1974 it is called NSDAP-AO. It is led Gary Rex Lauck, an American, who stayed in the FRG to build up the organization. He was expelled in 1974 by the Hamburg senator of internal affairs. He keeps contacts with militant neo-Nazi groups in several European countries. The party has a mailorder service in the United States for fascist material. It has links with the French Faisceaux Nationalistes Européens.

* Organization of Former SS Members
(Organisation der Ehemaligen SS-Angehörigen) (ODESSA)
Organization which was established by Colonel Otto Skorzeny and Hans Ulrich Rudel to assure an escape route for representatives of the Nazi regime. An important escape route ran through Italy and the harbour of Bari.

* Office for the Protection of the Constitution
(Bundesamt für Verfassungsschutz) (BfV)
Organization which was established in September 1950 as West Germany's counter espionage service. Its function is to provide a defense against espionage, sabotage and sedition, and its efforts are directed mainly against infiltration by communist agents, although in later years it has been forced to shift its attention to the urban terrorists and their international allies. It does this by classic counter-espionage techniques of infiltration and close surveillance. It also uses a computer whose databanks are filled with information about communist agents and terrorists. According to the office there are 200,000 'political extremists' in the country which are considered as a danger for democracy and public order. They include 22,100 rightists, 61,300 leftists and 116,000 foreigners. In 1986 it said it had identified 45 sabotage groups. It has made use of criminals to infiltrate the terrorist scene.

* Partisans of the Night
(Partisanen der Nacht)
Group which claimed responsibility for an unsuccessful attack on a US military facility, the headquarters for winter exercises in Erlensee near Hanau on Jan.6, 1985.

* Patsy O'Hara Commando
RAF commando named after an IRA hungerstriker who died in May 1981. The commando claimed

responsibility for the assassination of Ernst Zimmermann, of the MTU company, on Feb.1, 1985.

* Peace Conquerors (PC)
Ecologist and pacifist group which claimed responsibility for a bomb attack on the Bayer company on June 23, 1985, and a bomb attack in Frankfurt. With the attack it wanted to protest the dumping of chemical waste in the North Sea.

* People's Socialist Group
(Volkssozialistische Gruppe) (VSG)
Right-wing organization. The alleged leader of the organization, Frank Schubert, had been expelled as unreliable from the People's Socialist Movement of Germany (VSBD). He was involved in numerous violent actions. When he tried to smuggle arms and ammunition from Switzerland to Germany on Dec.24, 1980, he killed two Swiss borderguards and thereupon committed suicide.

* People's Socialist Movement of Germany/Workers Party (Volkssozialistische Bewegung Deutschlands/Partei der Arbeit) (VSBD/PdA)
Right-wing organization which was established in 1971 as the Party of Labour, as an offshoot of the National Democratic Party of Germany (NPD). In 1975 it adopted its extended name. It has a youth group known as Junge Front. Its leader, Friedhelm Busse, was reported to have secretly visited France to meet members of FANE with a view of creating a European nazi umbrella organization for the various neo-Nazi movements in France, Belgium, Austria, Britain, Switzerland as well as Germany. The organization was officially banned on Jan.27, 1982. It has about 50 paying members and about 1000 supporters. On Oct.21, 1981, two alleged members of the party were killed and three others including the chairman were arrested while attempting to carry out a bank raid near Munich. Four other members were arrested in Belgium on Oct.22.

* Petra Schelm Commando
Group which claimed responsibility for a bomb attack on the headquarters of the 5th Army Corps of the US Forces in Frankfurt and Berlin on May 11, 1972.

* Pigs in Space
(Schweine ins Weltall)
Group which claimed responsibility for an arson attack on a building of the Hochtief company in Siegen on May 31, 1986.

* Progressive Garden Dwarfs
(Progressive Gartenzwerge) (PG)
Anti-nuclear energy group which claimed responsibility for the sabotage of electric power pylons in 1986.

* Proletarian Initiative and Offensive for Western Europe as War Zone
(Proletarische Initiative und Offensive für West Europa als Kriegsabschnitt (PIOWK)
Group which claimed responsibility for a bomb attack on a NATO pipeline on Nov.11, 1985.

* Puig Antich-Ulrike Meinhof Commando
RAF commando named after a member of the left-wing Iberian Liberation Movement (MIL) who was executed in Barcelona on Mar.2, 1974 for the killing of a policeman and involvement in a bank robbery despite widespread protests against his death sentence. The commando claimed responsibility for a bomb explosion at a nuclear power station construction site at Fessenheim (Alsace) on May 3, 1975. It also claimed responsibility for bomb explosions at various offices of Swedish companies in Paris and at the West German consulate in Nice on May 21, 1975.

* Red Army Faction
(Rote Armee Fraktion) (RAF)
Left-wing terrorist group which was established in 1968. It took its name from the Japanese Red Army. Its history can be traced back to the Sozialistischer Deutscher Studentenbund (SDS). Extra parliamentary opposition in the form of non-violent demonstrations escalated from arson to bomb attacks, kidnappings and assassinations. Targets included US property, Israeli airlines, German magistrates, school buildings and administrative offices and US targets in Germany. In 1977 a new generation of adherents replaced the imprisoned founders. This generation displayed more careful planning, a wider variety of tactics, better logistics and greater brutality than their forebears. Authorities distinguish four levels: the commando level (about 20-30), the level of illegal militants (about 20), the legal level (about 200-300) and the 31 imprisoned members. In the end of 1984 it attempted to establish a European front against imperialism with AD (France) and the CCC (Belgium).

* Red Help
(Rote Hilfe) (RH)
RAF support group active in the early 1970s.

* Red Morning
(Roter Morgen) (RM)
Left-wing terrorist group. After Dr.Jürgen Ponto, chief executive of the Dresdener Bank, had been fatally wounded at his home in Oberursel on July 30, 1977, this group claimed responsibility for his death on July 31, adding that further killings would follow unless, 'all political prisoners of war' in the FRG were released immediately. The chief federal prosecutor, Kurt Rebmann, stated on Aug.10, 1977, that links had been established

between the assassinations of Dr.Buback on June 24, 1977 and Dr.Ponto and that they were part of a plot worked out by the Haag-Mayer group.

* Red Panthers (RP)
Group which was comprised of former RAF members who planned attacks on military installations.

* Revolutionary Autonomous Commando
(Revolutionärer Autonomes Kommando)
Group that claimed responsibility for an arson attack on government buildings in Schwaben on Apr.13, 1987.

* Revolutionary Cells
(Revolutionaire Zellen) (RZ)
Offshoot of the RAF, founded in 1973. Its aim was to establish autonomously organised nuclei in factories and universities so as to build up a 'revolutionary counter power'. Authorities estimate that there are about 50 to 100 groups with an overall total of 300 to 500 members. They do not adopt a clandestine existence with false identities but continue their normal lifes whilst practizing what they termed Diffused Guerrilla. The groups operate independently. There is no hierarchical structure, communication between the cells is arranged via delegates. Every attack must have 'the sympathy of the people' and the operations must be kept on a simple easy-to-copy base to demonstrate that resistance is feasible. It wants to create a 'new consiciousness of justice and injustice' and to mobilize 'all victims of an inhuman society', such as anti-nuclear militants, squatters, prisoners and other social outcasts. In 1984 the organization reorganized.

* Revolutionary Homeworker
(Revolutionaire Heimwerker) (RH)
Anti-nuclear energy group which has claimed responsibility for the sabotage of electric power pylons in 1986.

* Revolutionary Viruses
Youth organization of the Revolutionary Cells that claimed responsibility for an arson attack in Berlin on July 8, 1987, in which 6,000 files of foreigners were destroyed.

* Rote Zora
Female branch of the RZ active since 1983. It claimed responsibility for a bomb attack on the Max Planck Institute in Cologne (Müngersdorf) on Aug.21, 1985. It said the institute was involved in genetic technology research to assure a worldwide 'control of agriculture by some multinational companies'. It also claimed responsibility for a bomb attack on the Technology Park of the University of Heidelberg on Apr.13, 1985. The attack was directed at the 'Gesellschaft zur Förderung molekular biologischer Forschung in Heidelberg e.V.

* Rudolph Hess Restitution Commando (RHRC)
Group which has been responsible for a bomb attack on the Spandau prison in Berlin on Oct.23, 1986. It demands the release of Rudolph Hess.

* Ruhr Area Defence Sport Group
(Wehrsportgrupppe Ruhrgebiet) (WR)
Two members of this right-wing organization received prison sentences for various offenses including armed robbery, theft and violation of arms control legislation.

* Sawing Cells
(Sägende Zellen) (SZ)
Anti-nuclear energy group which claimed responsibility for the sabotage of electric power pylons in 1986.

* Schlageter Defence Sport Group
(Wehsportgruppe Schlageter) (WSGS)
Right-wing organization which was said to have been formed by Kay-Uwe Bergmann, Steffen Dupper and Ottfried Hepp in November 1980. All three disappeared, apparently having left for Lebanon, after Hepp had been found to be connected with the perpetration of the Munich bomb attack on Sep.26, 1980, and had also be named as founder of a Black Forest Combat Group.

* Siegfried Hausner Commando
RAF commando named after a member of the Holger Meins commando who died after being wounded by Swedish police in connection with the attack on the West German embassy in Stockholm on Apr.24, 1975. The commando claimed responsibility for the abduction of Hans Martin Schleyer, president of the Federal Union of German Industry and the German Employers' Association. On Oct.17 a skyjacked West German airliner flew to Mogadishu (Somalia) where it was stormed by GSG-9, assisted by SAS. Three of the kidnappers were killed and a fourth was wounded. A few hours after the storming of the airliner, A.Baader, G.Enslin and J.C.Raspe were all found dead in their cells at Stammheim prison. On Oct.19 the dead body of Dr.Schleyer was found in Mulhouse (Alsace). The controversial suicide of the three RAF leaders marked the end of the 1st phase of RAF activities which had failed to evoke a general mobilization of revolutionary forces.

* Sigurd Debus Command
RAF commando named after an imprisoned RAF member who had died as a result of a hunger strike on Apr.6, 1981. The commando has claimed responsibility for two explosions at the US Air

Force base at Ramstein on Aug.31, 1981. In a statement issued in 1981 the commando listed among its aims the ending of the 'lack of perspective, alienation, dehumanization of labour and the destruction of living standards by the nuclear and chemical industries and by concrete'.

* Skinheads
Generic name for right-wing youths which have been involved in violent acts, including the murder of foreigners. Neo-Nazi groups have tried to exploit them during rallies and demonstrations.

* Socialists Patients Collective
(Sozialistisches Patientenkollektiv) (SPK)
Anti psychiatry group therapy unit based on the belief that the patient's illness stemmed from capitalism. Working groups of the SPK included one in making explosives, another for radio transmission and a third for judo/karate. A number of student members of the SPK became active RAF and June 2 Movement members. Dr.Wolfgang Huber who formed the unit, was sentenced to seven years in prison for forming a criminal association. It was succeeded by the People's Red University Information center.

* Spezialeinsatzkommandos (SEK)
West German Länder (state) police special units which are modelled closely on the federal government's GSG-9 force. Most SEK's contain 40-60 members who are specially equipped and trained to cope with terrorists, violent criminals and riots.

* Support Organization for National Political Prisoners and their Relatives
(Hilfsorganization für Nationale Politische Gefangene und derer Angehörige)(HNG)
One of the bigger neo-Nazi organizations led by Christa Goerth. It gives financial support to 30 imprisoned rightist extremists including Manfred Roeder and Michael Kuhnen. It has links with neo-Nazis in Belgium and Austria.

* Throw Down the Pylon
(Kipp den Masten)
Anti-nuclear energy group which claimed responsibility for the sabotage of electric power pylons in 1986.

* Turn Off Directly
(Sofortabschalter)
Anti-nuclear energy group which claimed responsibility for the sabotage of electric power pylons in 1986.

* Ulrike Meinhof Commando
RAF commando named after one of its first members who committed suicide in prison on May 9, 1976. The commando claimed responsibility for the killing of Dr.Siegfried Buback, Chief Federal Prosecutor, and his bodyguard and chauffeur in Karlsruhe on Apr.7, 1977. Mr.Buback had been responsible for the co-ordination of measures against espionage and terrorism in the FRG. Three persons suspected of involvement in the assassination of Dr.Buback were Knut Folkerts, Christian Klar and Günter Sonnenberg, all of whom had joined the Haag-Mayer group in 1976.

* The Unbearables
(Die Unausstehlichen)
Group which claimed responsibility for a bomb attack on the 'Haus des Einzelhandels' in Hannover on May 17, 1985.

* Waltraud Boock Liberation Group
RAF group named after a member of the Haag-Mayer group who had been arrested on Dec.13, 1976. It claimed responsibility for two bomb attacks in Austria. Hans Georg Wagner was killed and another member of the group, Peter Hörmann was seriously injured in a bomb explosion in Vienna on Jan.28, 1977.

* Wilfried Boese Command
(Kommando Wilfried Boese)
Terrorist group which claimed responsibility for an attack on the Genetik Institut in Cologne on Oct.7, 1985.

* Working Circle to get rid of the Ruling Class
(Arbeitskreis zur Abschaffung der herschenden Klasse)
Group which claimed responsibility for an attack on the AEG research center in Frankfurt on June 11, 1986.

* Working Society Pissnelken
(Arbeitsgemeinschaft Pissnelken)
Group which claimed responsibility for an arson attack on the Sand und Kieswerk of the Hochtief company in Essen in March 1986.

GHANA

* Ghanaian Democratic Movement
Opposition party which stands for an anti-imperialist democratic policy. Leaders of the New Democratic Movement, a group of Christian intellectuals (CAGA), and a number of leading Ghanaians have criticized the new line of the Provisional National Defence Council (PNDC) which has been in power since 1981. Three members were arrested in New York in December 1985. They were accused of buying missiles, grenades launchers, anti-tank artillery and other weapons.

* Provisional National Defence Council (PNDC)
Council which governs Ghana after a military coup

by Jerry Rawlings on Dec.31, 1981. The council was expanded to 10 members and now includes in addition to the chairman (the lone survivor of the seven original members) two military officers and seven civilians. A network of Committees for the Defense of the Revolution (CDR) is designed as a channel to transmit government policies to the citizens and citizens concerns to the government. There have been several attempts to topple the government. At least six people were executed in 1985. Banned political organizations have called the council an 'intrument of terror' which had violated human rights and destroyed the freedom of the press.

GREECE

* Anti Militarist Struggle
(Antistratiotiki Pali) (AP)
Group which claimed responsibility for the assassination of George Athanassiades, publisher of the conservative daily, Evening Press and president of the Union of Owners of Athens newspapers, on Mar.19, 1983. He had written about soldiers who had participated in disguise in anti-American demonstrations.

* Autonomous Resistance Group
(Aftonomos Antistasi) (AA)
Leftist group which has been responsible for a bomb attack on a factory of Nestlé's subsidiary in Athens in 1981. It also has been involved in a bomb attack on cars of the Soviet trade mission.

* Blue Archers
(Galazios Toxotis) (GT)
Right-wing group that claimed responsibility for an outbreak of fires outside Athens in 1981. It demanded the release of imprisoned members of the former Greek junta.

* Central Intelligence Agency (KYP)
Greek security police which has been responsible for most of the torturings. Many of the torturers are still on active service. In 1985 the Greek government arrested suspected terrorists. The most important, Daniel Kristallis, worked for the KYP. He said he also worked for four other intelligence services. From hearings and talks with the press it appeared that he himself had placed bombs and had been responsible for explosions. Thereafter, he cashed money from his employer for information about the attacks. Opposition parties have pressed for a reorganization of the service with a better parliamentary control.

* Greek National Socialist Struggle
Group which claimed responsibility for a fire at Jewish owned shops in Saloniki in 1983.

* Iconoclast-Nihilists
Obscure left-wing group.

* June 1978 Organization
Breakaway group of the November 17 Revolutionary Organization that claimed responsibility for the assassination of a convicted torturer, Babalis (member of the secret police under the military regime in 1964-1974) on Jan.31, 1979. The group has been responsible for winter murders. Every winter at least one person is assassinated. In 1980 the victim was a commander of the police. Earlier targets included a CIA agent.

* Martyrs of Issam Sartawi
Group which has been responsible for bomb attacks on a private school of Libyan embassy personnel and the Syrian embassy in Athens on Mar.17, 1983. Issam Sartawi was a moderate PLO official who was murdered.

* May First Group
This group claimed responsibility for an armed attack on George Raftopoulos, a labour union official on June 29, 1987.

* National Front (NF)
Group which claimed responsibility for the Feb.2, 1985 bomb attack on Bobby's Bar in Glyfada which was frequented by US soldiers and airmen stationed at the Hellenikon Air Base. Seventy-eight visitors, including 70 Americans were injured in the attack. An anonymous telephone caller said the act was not directed against Greeks but against Americans held responsible for the occupation of Cyprus. Greek authorities said the attack probably had no political background. It could have been an act of revenge. According to Cypriote sources an organization with the name National Front was formed in 1968, as predecessor to EOKA-B, a Greek-Cypriote terror group which operated on the island.

* New October 1980 Revolutionary Organisation
(Epanastatiki Organosi 80 Oktvri) (EO80O)
Small left-wing terrorist group which emerged in 1980. It has been responsible for arson attacks on two Athens department stores. It took its name from the month in which Greece re-entered the military structure of the North Atlantic Treaty Organization (NATO).

* New Order (NO)
Right-wing organization which in 1974 obtained recognition as political party. It was reported to have carried out a number of subversive activities in 1975-1976. It was affiliated to the Italian Ordine Nuovo (banned in Italy in 1973). During the 1967-1974 period the military used the organization to intimidate opponents.

* November 17 Revolutionary Organisation (Epanastatiki Organosi 17 Noemvri) (EO17N)
Leftist terrorist organization which first surfaced in 1975 and which has been responsible for at least ten assassinations. It is named after the date of an insurrection at the Polytechnical Highschool against the regime of the colonels in 1973. Victims include Richard Welch (CIA station chief), Evangelos Mallios (former police officer), Nikos Momferratos (Greek publisher), Captain George Tsantes (US Naval officer), R.H.Judd (US Army sergeant) and Dimitris Angelopoulos (steel magnate). The attacks are perfectly prepared. The group has selected less spectacular targets, has made use of the same weapon (a .45 mm pistol) in all the attacks, manifests have been written in advance and have been written on the same typewriter. Greek authorities believe the attacks are prepared by the group but executed by professional foreign killers. On Nov.28, 1985, the group has been responsible for a bomb attack on a bus carrying police agents. So far nine members of the group have been arrested.

* Organization for National Recovery (Organismos Ethnikis Anorthosoos) (OEA)
Right-wing group which emerged in the late 1970s glorifying the period of military rule of the junta (1967-1974). Its violent activities caused minimal damage and made little public impact. It claimed responsibility for the detonation of tens of explosive devices in Athens on Dec.17, 1978.

* Organization for the Struggle against the State (OSS)
Group which claimed responsibility for the assassination of George Theofanopoulos, the public prosecutor, in Athens on Apr.1, 1985.

* Peoples Power (PP)
Terrorist group led, according to Greek authorities, by Zyrinis.

* People's Revolutionary Struggle (Epanastatikos Laikos Agonas) (ELA)
Offshoot of the November 17 Revolutionary Organization that emerged in 1979. It has been responsible for a number of bomb explosions. Targets included the US ambassador's residence and US multinational companies. In 1985 police raided 17 houses in Athens and arrested 52 persons.

* Popular Front Action (PFA)
Established as an offshoot of a Marxist-Leninist People's Power Group. Some of the ten members arrested on Feb.15, 1980, were said to have been trained in Lebanon by the Popular Front for the Liberation of Palestine (PFLP) and to have planned attacks on various targets, including the US embassy in Athens and the US ambassador's residence.

* Rapid Units for Domestic Security (TEA)
Civil defense forces established in 1951 to improve internal security. In 1970 its new task became to defend the countryside against communist and anarchist actions. In 1982 it was decided to disarm the force and to reduce it to one tenth of its strength. It will be maintained in border areas. Weapons will only be handed out during exercises and during mobilisation.

* Revolutionary Anti-Capitalist Initiative (RACI)
Group which claimed responsibility for arson attacks in Athens in 1981.

* Revolutionary Group of International Solidarity Christos Kassimis (RGISCK)
Group, probably an offshoot of ELA, which claimed responsibility for blowing up the statue of President Truman as a welcome to Minister Shultz 'the representative of US imperialism'. It is named after Christos Kassimis who was killed by the police in 1977 when he placed a bomb at buildings of the West German AEG company in Piraeus. He was suspected of having contacts with the Baader-Meinhof group. The group announced an 'unlimited and prolonged war' against US military presence in Europe. 'Any basis, any vehicle, any US facility will be a target.' On Mar.2, 1985 a bomb was found and defused outside the West German embassy in Athens. In a letter the group expressed full support for the demands of the jailed suspects in West Germany.

* Revolutionary Left (RL)
Group that has been responsible for car bombs and arson attacks in the early 1980s.

* Revolutionary Nucleus (Epanastatikos Pyrenas) (EP)
Leftist group which carried out an attack on an Athens store in 1981.

* Revolutionary Party of the Left (RPL)
Group which claimed responsibility for a bomb attack on a bus in Athens on Nov.1, 1985.

* Secret Yellow Organization of Air Force Officers (SYOATO)
Group which has been responsible for bomb attacks. It demanded the resignation of General Nicos Kouris.

GRENADA

* Mongoose Gang
Secret police of Prime Minister Gairy. One of its

victims, killed in 1974, was the father of Gairy's successor, Maurice Bishop.

* New Jewel Movement
(Joint Effort for Wealth, Education and Liberty) (NJM)
Party formed in 1973 by a merger of the Joint Endeavor for Welfare, Education and Liberation (JEWEL) with the Master Assembly for the People. The party overthrew the Gairy government in March 1979. Though the NJM initially called for adoption of a number of radical programs, including nationalization of foreign owned banks, its policies were more moderate. The NJM's experiment in Caribbean-style Marxism-Leninism collapsed as a result of a power struggle between the party's two wings. The final split in the People's Revolutionary Government between the Bishop's Castroite wing and the Stalinist Coard faction occurred at a central committee meeting on Oct.12, 1983. Bishop was expelled from the NJM and placed under house arrest. On Oct.19 a large crowd of supporters freed Bishop and carried him to Fort Rupert. A PRA unit counter-attacked, killing and wounding nearly 200 civilians before capturing Bishop and six of his senior colleagues, who were summarily executed. On Oct.25 US forces intervened.

* People's Action Group (PAG)
An alliance of smaller right-wing groupings which was established in 1979. It was led by Winston Whyte. It included members of the UPP and two members of a faction of the Rastafarian sect who were hostile to the PRG. These two and Mr.Whyte were, with others, arrested on Oct.15, 1979, for plotting against the PRG.

* People's Revolutionary Army (PRA)
After the March 1979 coup 'Internationalist Workers' from the USSR, Cuba, East Germany and North Korea arrived in Grenada to arm and train the PRA, organize a state security apparatus and infiltrate government ministries.

GUADELOUPE

* Camus
Pro-independence group that has ransacked government offices in Point-à-Pitre.

* Caribbean Revolutionary Alliance
(Alliance Révolutionnaire Caraibe) (ARC)
Terrorist group which has been responsible for at least 60 bomb attacks and numerous cases of arson. Targets included hotels, department stores, automobile clubs, banks, prison, restaurants, offices of Air France, police stations and tax offices. The group threatened to carry the struggle against colonialism to France itself. In November 1984, French authorities arrested Luc Reinette, the alleged leader of the group. In March 1985, 60 more French police were flown in to bolster security after a bomb attack.

* Committee against Genocide of Blacks by Substitution
(Comitè contre le Genocide des Noirs par Substitution) (CGNS)
Group which claimed responsibility for starting a fire in the car park of Point-à-Pitre on July 30, 1982. Activities are directed against French 'settler' presence in Guadeloupe.

* Guadeloupe Liberation Army (GLA)
Pro-independence group which was widely believed to be the armed wing of the UPLG. On Jan.8, 1981, it announced that it would continue its campaigns against French 'capitalism and socialism' both on the island and in metropolitan France. It also warned that no compromise or truce should or can be envisaged irrespective of the colour of successive governments in France. It has been responsible for bomb attacks. Its leader, Luc Reinette, formed his own party in 1982.

* Metro Clandestine Committee of Resisters
(Comité Clandestin des Résistants Mètro) (CCRM)
Obsuce extremist group that has attacked advocators of independence.

* Movement for the Unification of National Liberation Forces of Guadeloupe
(Mouvement pour l'Unification des Forces de Libération de la Guadeloupe) (MUFLING)
Pro-independence alliance established in January 1982. It is headed by Rosan Mounien. Member organizations are: Popular Union for the Liberation of Guadeloupe (ULPG), Union Générale des Travailleurs de la Guadeloupe (UGTG), Union des Paysans Pauvres de la Guadeloupe (UPPG), Syndicat Général de l'Education en Guadeloupe (SGEG), Syndicat des Instituteurs Professeurs et Agent de Guadeloupe (SIPAG), Associations Générale des Etudiants Guadeloupéens (AGEG), Union Nationale des Elèves et Etudiants de Guadeloupe (UNEEG) and Chrétiens pour la Libération du Peuple Guadeloupéen (CLPG).

* National Liberation Army
(Armée de Liberation Nationale) (ALN)
Group which claimed responsibility for an arson attack in Point-à-Pitre on Apr.7, 1982.

* Popular Movement for the Independence of Guadeloupe
(Mouvement Populaire pour la Guadeloupe Indépendante) (MPGI)
Militant pro-independence movement which was established in June 1982. It is headed by Luc Reinette. It has been responsible for bomb attacks.

• Popular Union for the Liberation of Guadeloupe (Union Populaire pour la Libération de la Guadeloupe) (UPLG)
Pro-independence organization which succeeded the earlier Groupe d'Organization Nationale Guedeloupéenne (GONG) in 1978. It is led by Theodor Francois. It was initially believed that the GLA was the armed wing of the UPLG but the latter dissociated itself publicly during 1980 from the GLA's violent actions and claimed that the attacks attributed to the GLA were in fact 'police provocations' designed to discredit the independence movement. It tries to unite all organizations which are fighting for independence with the aim to establish a national liberation front. The aim of the front is a national-democratic people's revolution. In July 1985 barricades were erected and for five days Point-à-Pitre was blocked from the rest of the country. The people's movement involved in the actions was organized by the UPLG and 20 other organizations.

GUATEMALA

• Anticommunist Council of Guatemala
(Consejo Anti Comunista de Guatemala) (CODEG)
Anti-communist vigilante group which degenerated into a death squad. As a semi-official organ it was given carte blanche to use the most extreme methods in eradicating 'communist sympathizers' and extracting intelligence from the local peasantry.

• Armed Action Force
(Fuerza de Acción Armada) (FAA)
Right-wing paramilitary group formed in the 1978-1979 period that has been responsible for political murders.

• Armed People's Organized Youth
(Juventud Organizada del Pueblo en Armas) (JOPA)
Anti-communist execution squad that emerged in 1980.

• Augusto Cesar Sandino Front (ACSF)
EGP guerrilla front which operated in Quiche province in 1985.

• Band of the Hawks
(Banda de los Halcones)
Extreme right-wing group.

• Band of Vultures
(Banda de los Buitres)
Extreme right-wing group.

• The Centurians
(Los Centuriones)
Extreme right-wing group.

• Christians for Respect for Life
Group that has been responsible for the 1982 kidnapping of a nephew of President Rios Montt. The victim was freed by security forces.

• Civil Defense Militias
(Patrulas de Defensa Civil) (PDC)
Paramilitary civil patrols which operate under army supervision. The militias were established under President Rios Montt to isolate the guerrillas. They were present in 850 villages with a total membership of 300,000. The surviving local population is put in strategic model villages in which they are under total control of the army. The patrols have been involved in human rights abuses.

• Commander Ernesto Guevara Front
EGP guerrilla front which operated in the Huehuetenango province in 1985.

• Committee of Peasant Unity (CUC)
Large farmers federation which emerged in 1978. It is not a guerrilla movement but a social mass movement that said it necessarily had to use violence. In the beginning it fought the struggle of a labour union following the rules of the law. It mainly has been active under ladinos. Pablo Ceto is one of its 12 leaders.

• Commando of the Popular Forces of People
(Comando de las Fuerzas del Pueblo) (CFP)
Left-wing group that announced in 1981 that it was ready for armed action against the government.

• Democratic Renewal Movement (MRD)
Right-wing movement that does not abhor violence. In March 1987 it published a death list with the names of 25 well-known Guatemalans, including politicians and professors. They were called 'communist infiltrators'.

• Edgar Ibarra Guerrilla Front (EIGF)
Guerrilla force active in the 1960s led by Ricardo Ramirez. It formed the second front of the FAR. It fought in the arid hills of the Sierra las Minas and became one of the continent's strongest guerrilla forces. Under a new agreement in 1965 the front would furnish the combatants and the Communist Party the organization structure. From this alliance the second FAR was born. After a military reverse, the remains went to ORPA.

• Eye for an Eye
(Ojo por Ojo)
Anti-communist death squad.

• Guatemalan Committee of Patriotic Unity
(Comite Guatemalteco de Unidad Patriotica) (CGUP)

Political umbrella organization of several opposition parties and movements which was established on Feb.16, 1982. Members are the DFR, FP-31, FUR, CUC, PSD and 26 prominent Guatemalan exiles of various political affiliations. Luis Cardozo y Aragon is head of the coordinating committee. It endorsed the basic program of the Guatemalan National Revolutionary Unity (URNG) and stated that it had no direct link with the guerrillas. It denounced the Mar.7, 1982, elections as a farce.

* Guatemalan Labour Party
(Partido Guatemalteco de los Trabajadores) (PGT)
Party founded in September 1949 as the Communist Party of Guatemala (after having previously been known as Democratic Vanguard of Guatemala). In 1954 the party was outlawed. From then on it worked underground. Since 1961 it conducted an armed struggle. At its second Congress in December 1962 it adopted the name of Guatemalan Labour Party. In 1969 the party adopted a new program aiming at a 'socialist revolution'. After the murder of all members of the party's central committee during the 1972-74 period, the majority reverted to armed struggle and participated in the formation of the FAR. By 1980 PGT guerrillas were active in Guatemala City and areas south and west of it. In Feb.1982 the guerrilla faction of the PGT joined the URNG. It was led by Isias de Léon in 1980.

* Guatemalan National Revolutionary Unity
(Unidad Revolucionaria Nacional Guatemalteca) (URNG)
Union formed on Feb.8, 1982 by four guerrilla organizations. The four organizations, EGP, ORPA, FAR and PGT have a total of 6,000 men and women under arms. The formation is modelled after the FDR (El Salvador) and NDF (Nicaragua). It intended to pursue a 'popular revolutionary war'.

* Guatemalan Secret Service (G-2)
Secret service housed in the Polytechnical Institute. Equipped with Israeli computers it collects information which is given to the police. The information is used to identify, track and murder political opponents. The characteristics young, intellectual and Indian are very important for the target selection. There is a labour division between the normal police (responsible for road blockades) the riot police SWAT (responsible for house searches) and a sort of super SWAT (the BROE) who actually takes care of the victims.

* Guatemalan Workers' Militia
(Milicias Obreras Guatemaltecas) (MOG)
Extreme right-wing organization founded in March 1978 in opposition to the alleged 'marxist' tendencies of vice-president Villagrán Kramer. In has been active during 1980.

* Guerrilla Army of the Poor
(Ejército Guerrillero de los Pobres) (EGP)
Guerrilla organization which emerged in the early 1970s. By the end of 1976 it controlled certain areas in the country's northern mountains. It has mainly been active among landless peasants but operated also in Guatemala City. By 1982 it was the most active politically violent group. Its strength was estimated at about 750 men. It was led by Valentin Ramos (killed in 1976) and by Cesar Montes. It has been involved in bomb attacks, kidnappings of industrialists and sabotage. In 1980-1981 the EGP operated largely in the northern highlands and also in and around Guatemala City. It has considerable influence among the Indian population and has repeatedly occupied villages temporarily. Such action has led to punitive raids by the army in which large numbers of people have been killed. The EGP is a member of the URNG.

* The Hawk of Justice
Death squad which was active in the 1960s.

* Ho Chi Minh Front
EGP guerrilla front which operated in Quiché province in 1985.

* Independent Armed Revolutionary Movement
(Movimiento Independista Revolucionario Armado) (MIRA)

* January 31 Popular Front
(Frente Popular 31 de Enero) (FP'31)
Umbrella opposition front named after the date of the 1980 attack on the Spanish embassy in Guatemala City by peasants. It was established in January 1981. Its component parties were: Federation of Guatemalan Workers (FTG), Committee of Peasant Unity (CUC), Felipe Antonio Garcia Revolutionary Workers Nuclei, Trinidad Gómez Hernández Settlers Coordinating Body, Vicente Menchu Revolutionary Christians and Ruben Garcia Revolutionary Student Front. It wants to overthrow the existing regime and to establish a revolutionary, popular and democratic government.

* King's Band
(Banda del Rey)
Extreme right-wing group.

* League for the Extermination of the Indian Race

Right-wing death squad which was established in August 1981.

* Military Police
(Policia Militar Ambulante)
Police service that reportedly engaged in

intimidation, threats and illegal arrests of people, particularly in the rural areas.

* National Anti Communist Organisation (NACO)
Right-wing death squad active in the early 1960s. During the peak years of counterinsurgency (1966-1968) the death squads multiplied. They adopted flamboyant names like Eye for an Eye, Purple Rose and Hawk of Justice. They mutilated their victims and boasted of their exploits in apocalyptic communiqués. Publication of death lists and victims' photos added to a national psychosis of terror.

* National Liberation Movement
(Movimiento de Liberacion Nacional) (MLN)
Movement which called itself 'the party of organized violence' and claimed to maintain a 3,000 man paramilitary force. The origins of the right-wing MLN date back to the 'Liberation Movement' headed by Carlos Castillo Armas which deposed the Arbenz government in 1954. It retained its anti-communist orientation and favors close ties to the catholic Church. It formed an alliance with the Institutional Democratic Party to support the successful candidacies of Colonel Arana in 1970 and General Langerud in 1974, but broke with General Langerud to endorse the 1978 candicady of Colonel Enrique Peralta Azurdia, leader of the small National Reconstruction and Action Party. The movement is led by Mario Sandoval Alarcon, a former vice-president.

* New Anti-Terrorist Organization
(Nueva Organización Antiterrorista) (NOA)
Anti-communist death squad. It emerged in 1982 and announced publicly that it would cut off the tongue and left hand of its enemies.

* North-Eastern Anti-Communist Front
(Frente Anticomunista del Nororiente) (FANO)
Extreme right-wing organization established on May 8, 1980.

* Order of Death
(Organizacion de la Muerte)
Right-wing paramilitary group formed in the 1978-79 period.

* Organization Zero
(Organización Cero) (OC)
Extreme right-wing paramilitary organization formed in the 1978-1979 period.

* People's Revolutionary Movement-Ixim
(Movimiento Revolucionario del Pueblo-Ixim) (MRP)
Movement that has been responsible for the kidnapping of the daughter of Dr.Roberto Suazo Córdova, the President of Honduras on Dec.14, 1982. She was released after the Guatemalan government permitted the publication of an MRP manifesto in local newspapers and in newspapers in Mexico and Central America.

* Popular Resistance Committee (PRC)
Small left-wing group which emerged in 1981 claiming responsibility for the murder of San Carlos University's rector in December.

* Purple Rose
Extreme right-wing death squad.

* Rebel Armed Forces
(Fuerzas Armadas Rebeldes) (FAR)
Guerrilla organization which was established in December 1962. It superseded the November 13 Revolutionary Organization (MR-13) which had arisen out of a rebellion led by Luis Turcios Lima (died in 1966) Marco Antonio Yon Sosa (killed in May 1970) and Luis Trejo Esquivel. In 1972 it was reorganized with the aim of constituting a mass party. By 1967 the foco theory was replaced by the 'prolonged popular war' model. By 1980 it operated in northern areas and also near Lake Izabál, in eastern Guatemala. In February 1982 the FAR joined the URNG.

* Revolutionary Armed Forces
(Fuerzas Armadas Revolucionarias) (FAR)
Guerrilla faction that was founded in 1968. It was conceived as the armed branch of the PGT, an orthodox Marxist-Leninist party loyal to Moscow. In 1985 it operated in the western jungles of Petén.

* Revolutionary Movement Alejandro de Leon 13 November
(Movimiento Revolucionario Alejandro de León 13 Noviembre) (MR-13)
Guerrilla group established in Feb.1962. It was led by Yon Sosa and Turcios Lima who joined forces with the PGT to form the united Rebel Armed Forces (FAR). It consisted of young nationalist officers. It did not recover from the counterinsurgency operations led by Colonel Arana Osorio in 1967, and the death of its leader, Yon Sosa, in May 1970.

* Revolutionary Organization of the People in Arms
(Organización Revolucionario del Pueblo en Armas) (ORPA)
The FAR's switch to urban work brought a sharp reaction from many of its members working to win Indian support in the departments of San Marcos and Quezaltenango. From the dispute a new guerrilla nucleus emerged, 95 percent of its original members Indians. The group remained for eight years in the mountains of the Sierra Madre slowly expanding its strength without firing a single shot. It announced itself in September 1979

as a political and military movement to be built up secretly. First in rural areas and later among all sections of the people. It is anti-racist and stands for the development of the indigenous people's culture. In July 1981 security forces destroyed ORPA bases in the capital. ORPA guerrillas operated in joint operations with the EGP, FAR and PGT. In February 1982 it joined the URNG. In 1985 it operated in the south and southwest of Lake Atitlan and the San Marcos province.

* Revolutionary Unity Front (FUR)
Social democratic organization which went underground in 1978 when its leader Manuel Colom Argueta was assassinated. It is the successor of the former Revolutionary Democratic Union (URD) founded by Francisco Villagrán Kramer as a left-wing breakaway from the Revolutionary Party.

* Secret Anti Communist Army
(Ejército Segredo Anti-comunista) (ESA)
Right-wing death squad established in 1976. It has been responsible for thousands of political killings. It targeted politicians and officials as well as trade unionists and student leaders. ESA was believed to be linked to the extreme right-wing National Liberation Movement (NLM) led by Mario Sandoval Alarcón, who was vice-president of Guatemala in 1974-1978. According to a statement made in Panama on Sep.1, 1980, by an agent of the EGP, Elias Bonaharo, ESA was directed by the President, the Prime Minister and a number of generals.

* September 15 Liberty
(Libertad 15 de Septiembre) (LS-15)
Extreme right-wing organization.

* The Shadow
(La Sombra)
Extreme right-wing organization.

* Southern Anti-Communist Commando
(Commando Anti-Communista del Sur) (CADS)
Right-wing death squad established in May 1980.

* Special Investigations and Drugs Squad (BIEN)
On its creation in 1986, the Cerezo government stated that it would not carry out illegal detentions, nor would its members be dressed in civilian clothing. However, events have contradicted such assurances.

* Technical Investigations Department (DIT)
Special military unit which has jurisdiction over investigations of homicides, robberies and thefts. It had about 600 members. It has been held responsible for the disappearance of thousands of Guatemalans and had links with death squads. For that reason the government disssolved it on Feb.5, 1986.

* The Thunderbolt
(El Rayo)
Extreme right-wing organization.

* Twelfth of April Revolutionary Movement
(Movimiento Revolucionario 12 Abril) (MR-12A)
Student movement active in the early 1960s. Members joined the Rebel Armed Forces (FAR). It engaged in armed resistance to the military government of Colonel Peralta Azurdia (1963-1966). It withdrew from the FAR in 1965.

* Twentieth of October Front
(Frente 20 Octubre) (F-20-O)
Minor guerrilla front active in the early 1960s. It was founded by Lt.Col.Paz Tejada. A coup attempt was suppressed by the security forces.

* Voluntary Defense Force
(Frente Voluntario de Defensa) (FVD)
Small left-wing guerrilla group which emerged in July 1980.

* White Hand
(Movimiento de Acción Nacionalista Organizada) (MANO)
Paramilitary organization which has its origins in the counterinsurgency campaign of the late 1960s. It has been active since 1970 when its headquarters were said to be in the police building in Guatemala City. The White Hand was reported to be linked to General Carlos Manuel Arana Osorio, the President of Guatemala (1970-1974) and leading member of the National Liberation Movement (MLN).

* Workers Revolutionary Party of Central America
(Partido Revolucionario de Trabajadores de America Central) (PRTC)
Organization which emerged in El Salvador in September 1979. It has been responsible for one attack in Guatemala in 1980 but operated predominantly in El Salvador.

* Yuxa Shona Front
(Frente Yuxa Shona) (FYS)
Marxist-Leninist group established in March 1980. It was named after a survivor of the siege at the Spanish embassy by peasants on Jan.31, 1980.

* Zacapa Panthers (ZP)
Organization which beginning in 1966 spearheaded a wave of terror which reportedly left more than 3,000 peasants dead.

GUINEA

* Guinea Union of Senegal
(Union des Guinéens au Sénégal) (UGS)

External opposition group which on Feb.20, 1977, signed a declaration on a joint action program with three other Guinean opposition movements. However, following the conclusion of a treaty of friendship and co-operation between Guinea and Senegal on May 7, 1978, and the failure of a conspiracy against President Sekou Touré in August 1979 (in which Senegal based Guinean exiles were reported to have been involved) the activities of the UGS were severely restricted.

* National Liberation Front of Guinea
(Front de Libération Nationale de Guineé) (FLNG)
External opposition group based in Paris. It reportedly has branches in Senegal and Ivory Coast.

* Organization of Guinean Unity
(Organisation de l'Unité Guinéenne) (OUG)
External opposition group based primarily in Ivory Coast. It is led by Ibrahima Kaké. During a visit to Paris by President Sekou Touré on Sep.16-20, 1982, five Guineans attempted to kidnap Ibrahima Kaké, but French police prevented them from doing so.

* Patriotic Front (PF)
Active service wing of the Group of Guineans in Exile. It has been involved in attacks on President Sekou Touré.

* Rally of External Guineans
(Rassemblement des Guinéens à l'Exterieur) (RGE)
The RGE, as the principal organization of Guineans in exile, claimed in Sep.1971 to have several thousand members in the Congo, the Ivory Coast, Liberia, Senegal, Sierra Leone and several European countries. It declared at the same time that it would use force to overthrow President Sekou Touré. On Feb.20, 1977 the RGE signed a declaration on a joint action program with three other Guinean opposition movements. The RGE is led by Siriadou Diallo.

* Unified Guinea Liberation Organization
(Organisation Unifiée de Libération de la Guinée) (OULG)
On Jan.2, 1978, the OULG stated a letter to President Giscard d'Estaing of France (who was then planning a visit to Guinea) that a change of regime in Guinea was 'not only possible but inevitable' and expressed the hope that the French government would give 'active, direct and discrete support' to 'the current stage' of the OULG struggle. On Feb.20, 1977 the OULG signed a declaration on a joint action program with three other Guinean opposition movements.

GUINEA BISSAU

* African Party for the Independence of Guinea and Cape Verde
(Partido Africano da Independencia da Guiné Portuguesa e das Illias de Cabo Verde) (PAIGC)
Guerrilla movement which, after a non-violent stage, adopted armed struggle in 1959 when Portuguese troops fired on rioting dockers. Sabotage acts followed but a more important development was the creation of a rural guerrilla force known as the Revolutionary Armed Forces of the People. It received aid from the OAU and sent militants abroad for training to the Soviet Union and Cuba. It was led by Amilcar Cabral and had an estimated 7,000 fighters in 1972. In 1973 Amilcar Cabral was murdered. Aristides Pereira took over the leadership of the movement, with Luis Cabral heading the armed forces. In September 1973 it announced an independent state of Guinea Bissau. Portugal granted independence in 1974. PAIGC became the ruling party and formed the government. PAIGC losses in the war were less than 1,000. Portuguese losses were 1,084 killed and 6,000 wounded.

* Front for the Liberation and Independence of Guinea
(Frente da Luta pela Independencia Nacional da Guiné-'Portuguesa') (FLING)
National liberation movement recognized by Senegal in May 1964 on an equal footing with the PAIGC. In May 1965, the council of ministers of the OAU recognized the PAIGC as the only liberation movement of Guinea Bissau and decided to give no further aid to the FLING. It was led by Benjamin Pinto Bull. After independence, FLING remained in existence as a party in exile (based in Paris and Senegal) opposed to the PAIGC's policy of ultimate union between Guinea Bissau and the Cape Verde Islands.

* Local Armed Forces
(Forcas Armadas Locales) (FAL)
Village militia of the guerrillas during the war of independence.

* Popular Revolutionary Armed Forces
(Forces Armeés Révolutionnaires du Peuple) (FARP)
Rural guerrilla movement which fought for independence. It operated as the armed wing of the PAIGC. It had an estimated 7,000 fighters in 1972. It inflicted upon the Portuguese enemy some 300 casualties a year. Toward the end of the struggle deaths were running at more than 1,000 every year.

GUYANA

* House of Israel (HI)
Black supremacist sect which has acted as a pro-government death squad. It was headed by David Hill (also known as Edward Emmanuel Washington).

It has been held responsible for acts of violence which led to the death of the deputy editor and a photographer of The Catholic Standard (a newspaper which had been critical of the government's human rights record) in Georgetown in July 1979. The Working People's Alliance (WPA) regarded the House of Israel as 'mainly a pseudo-military arm' of the PNC, since it had earlier been involved in strike-breaking and harassment of critics of the government.

* Peoples Temple (PT)
Religious sect which under the influence of its leader Rev.Jim Jones, was involved in a collective suicide at Jonestown which left more than 900 men, women and children dead.

* Working People's Alliance (WPA)
Small radical opposition group led by Black Power activist Dr.Walter Rodney. Cuban military advisers have provided guerrilla training outside Guyana. Some of its members were sentenced to imprisonment others were not allowed to leave the country, and several were murdered. Those killed included Dr.Walter Rodney, who died in a car bomb explosion in June 1980. He was one of the Caribbean region's leading radical historians and founder of the 'New Left' movement in Commonwealth Caribbean politics.

HAITI

* Autonomous Center of Haitian Workers (Centrale Autonome des Travailleurs Haitiens) (CATH)
Labour federation led by Yves Antoines Richard which worked underground. Several members have been murdered by the Tonton Macoutes. After the overthrow of 'Baby Doc' Duvalier on Feb.7, 1986, it became legal as an umbrella federation.

* Council for the National Liberation of Haiti (CNLH)
Exile organization, led by Roland Magloire, the nephew of former president Paul Magloire (1950-56) that was involved in an attempt to invade Haiti from Florida on Mar.16, 1982, when a part of his force was arrested by US coast guards.

* Hector Riobe Brigade (HRB)
Group which is named after a government opponent who was killed in 1963 in a clash with the forces of Duvalier. It is comprised of Haitian exiles based in Miami. One of its members, Jean-Claude Jean Louis reportedly followed a training course in a Palestinian camp in Lebanon. The group has been responsible for several air attacks, bomb explosions and threats.

* High Secret State Police
Police force which was established in the 1960s by F.Duvalier. It has been accused of hundreds of disappearances and deaths by torture. It was renamed the Permanent Investigation Commission for the Dessaline Barracks. It was dissolved in January 1986.

* Leopard Corps
Elite anti-subversion unit.

* National Haitian Popular Party (NHPP)
Party led by Bernard Sansaricq. In late 1981 the President Duvalier's yacht was said to have been hijacked and there followed numerous arrests of political and trade union figures. An invasion attempt co-ordinated by B.Sansaricq (who was allegedly involved in two earlier invasion attempts in 1964 and in 1968) was launched from the British Turks and Caicos Islands on Jan.9, 1982. Twelve people died in the unsuccessful invasion.

* National Security Volunteers (Tonton Macoutes) (VSN)
Sort of people's militia bigger than the Haitian army which acted as a security force loyal to Duvalier. It had an estimated 15,000 members. It has been involved in raiding homes and violently breaking up public meetings. After the overthrow of Duvalier on Feb.7, 1986, its power vis-á-vis the military decreased but the Tonton Macoutes were not disarmed and continued to harass and murder people. In August 1987, remnants of the force were involved in a massacre of several hundred people.

* Union of Democratic and Patriotic Forces (Union des Forces Patriotiques et Démocratiques) (UFPD)
Umbrella opposition organization with headquarters in Paris. It was represented at the continental conference of solidarity with the people of Haiti, held in Panama in September 1981. It called for a general strike and uprising against the 'bloodthirsty, corrupt, illegal regime of Duvalier which is directed against the people.'

* United Front for the National Liberation of Haiti (UFNLH)
Organization which reportedly formed a government in exile on Feb.2, 1986 on the request of 'regional leaders'. It is seeking the restoration of democracy in Haiti.

HONDURAS

* Anti Communist Combat Army (ELA)
Army which was founded in 1979. It had close ties with the MHM Brigade (El Salvador). It claimed to have 400 members in 1984 and also claimed to have infiltrated their spies in the universities and labor unions. It has murdered several labor unionists as

well as Marxist university professors. The group gets 'unofficial help' from the Honduran military.

* Anti Subversive Police Corps
(Cuerpo de Policia Anti Subversivo)
Security unit also known as 'Cobras'.

* Cinchoneros Popular Liberation Movement
(Movimiento de la Liberación Popular Cinchonero) (MLPC)
Offshoot of the pro-Soviet Communist Party, established in 1978. It is named after a nickname given to peasant hero Serapio Romero who was executed in 1865 for refusing to pay tax to the church. Its political wing is the Revolutionary People's Union (URP). It has been involved in a hijacking (Mar.1981), bomb attacks (Sep.1981) and the occupation of the chamber of commerce building in San Pedro (Sep.1982). It demanded the release of eleven detained Salvadoreans and two Hondurans. Other demands were a protest against joint US-Honduras military maneuvers, repeal of anti-terrorist legislation, expulsion of military advisers from the US, Argentina, Chile and Israel and the release of 57 political prisoners.

* Civil Defense Committees
(Comités de Defensa Civil) (CDC)
Civil defense like groups consisting of ex-military and large landowners which have been established by former General Alvarez to establish a national repression network in support of the army.

* Honduran Army
The Honduran Army high command maintained a network of secret jails, special interrogators and kidnapping teams who detained and killed nearly 200 suspected leftists between 1980 and 1984. The US CIA had access to the secret army jails and to the written reports summarizing the interrogation of suspected leftists. In May 1987, Florencio Caballero, a former Honduran Army interrogator gave a detailed account of how army and police units were authorized to organize death squads that seized, interrogated and killed suspected leftists in Honduras. Argentine and Chilean trainers taught the Honduran Army kidnapping and 'elimination' techniques. The program all but eliminated radical leftist activity in the country.

* Lorenzo Zalaya Popular Revolutionary Forces
(Fuerzas Populares Revolucionarias Lorenzo Zelaya) (FPRLZ)
Anti-Soviet communist group which on Sep.23, 1981, shot and wounded two US military advisers in Tegucigalpa. In 1982 the FPR was reported to have carried out a number of bomb attacks and occupations of buildings in the capital.
* Martyrs of the Talanguera
Left-wing group which emerged in February 1981. It has been involved in several bombings.
* Morazanista National Liberation Front
(Frente Moranista para la Liberacion Nacional) (FMLN)
Liberation front which was established in September 1979. It derives its name from Francisco Morazán, a 19th century military leader. It aims at a land reform and the establishment of a people's government.

* Peasant Alliance of National Organizations of Honduras
(Alianza Campesina de Organizaciones Nacional de Honduras) (ALCONH)
Revolutionary peasant alliance established in October 1980, under the leadership of Reyes Rodrigues Arevalo.

* Peoples' Guerrilla Command (PGC)
Minor guerrilla group established in April 1980. It is headed by José Alberto Munguia Vélez and José Antonio Montalvan Munguia.

* Public Security Forces
(Fuerzas de Seguridad Publica) (FUSEP)
Secret military police.

* Revolutionary University Force (FUR)
A group which was involved in training students in the use of weapons and kidnap techniques.

* Revolutionary People's Union
(Unión Revolucionario del Pueblo) (URP)
Guerrilla group established in September 1979 by defectors from the Communist Party. It was led by Tomas Native and Fidel Martinez who died in June 1981 when gunmen attacked their office. On Oct.2, 1980 it announced the start of its 'armed struggle'. It was active mainly in the northern part of the country and was said to be in sympathy with the Popular Revolutionary Bloc (BPR) of El Salvador.

* Special Troops for Jungle and Night Operations
(Tropas Especiales para Operaciones de Selva y Nocturnas) (TESON)
A new anti-terrorist force.

* Urban Operations Command (UAC)
US trained anti-terrorist squad with a strength of 40 men. At times they have been portrayed as members of a regular internal security force called the Cobras. The training was carried out by US Special Forces personnel in collaboration with the CIA and was conducted in secret at the Honduran Army's Special Forces Command at La Venta.
* White Hand
(Mano Blanco) (MB)
Para-military organization targeting left-wing groups. It was said to have links with similar groups in neigboring countries.

* Workers' Revolutionary Party of Central America (Partido Revolucionario de Trabajadores de América Central) (PRTC)
Trotskyist group that emerged in 1980. The PRTC was held responsible for the kidnapping of an executive working for the US multinational Texaco. It was active in student circles and opposed the presence of foreign capital in the country as well as military agreements with the United States.

HONG KONG

* Triad Organizations
(14-K, Wo Shing Wo, Shui Fong, Wo On Lok)
Brotherhoods operating mafia-like networks of crime. About 35 triads have been identified in Hong Kong.
* The Vagabonds
An association of clandestine immigrants from the People's Republic of China. It is anti-communist and manipulated by the Taiwan secret services.

ICELAND

* Sea Shepherd Conservation Society (SSCS)
Breakaway group from the environmentalist organization Greenpeace. It allegedly sunk two whaling ships in the harbor of Reykjavik in January 1987. The group is led by Paul Watson.

INDIA

* Akali Religious Party
(Shiromani Akali Dal) (SAD)
Party whose influence is confined primarily to Punjab, where it campaigns against excessive federal influence in Sikh affairs. It is led by Jathedar Jagdev and Singh Talwandi.

* Akal Takht (AT)
Sikh militants wish to dismantle the building opposite to the Golden Temple in Amritsar in which Sikh high priests have their seats, and rebuild it.

* All Assam People's Struggle Council
(Gana Sangram Parishad) (GSP)
Organization that has been hostile to Moslems who fled from Eastern Pakistan in 1971 when that territory seceded from Pakistan and became Bangla Desh.

* All India Communist Party (AICP)
A small section of the CPI opposed to the CPI's surrender to the CPM-M out of electoral opportunism. It was established in the fall of 1980 and is led by Roza Deshpande. It regarded Mrs.Gandhi as the representative of the progressives which Moscow wanted Indian communists to befriend. Its ideological position is in fact close to Moscow but it is not recognized by the Soviet Union which favours the CPI.

* All India Forward Bloc (AIFB)
A leftist party confined primarily to Bengal. It is led by Hemanta Kumar Bose and R.K.Haldulkar. Its program calls for land reform and nationalization of key sectors of the economy.

* All India Sikh Students Federation (AISSF)
Student federation which was banned until Apr.4, 1985. It has mounted a campaign of terror to enforce the strict tenets of their religion. Militant Sikhs, whose religion forbids the use of alcohol and tobacco, have burned cigarette shops and liquor stores in rural areas and have killed some offenders. It has three apparent objectives: 1) To win the sympathies of the moderate majority of Punjab's Sikhs; 2) To increase pressure on Barnala. They would like the chief minister to resign and turn over control of the Akali Dal to more sympathetic leaders; 3) To nudge New Delhi into acceding to their demand for making Punjab into a separate Sikh nation. In the September 1985- April 1987 period an estimated 1,800 people died in the conflict.

* All Nagaland Communist Party (ANCP)
Maoist party established in 1979. It was suspected of having links with several ethnic guerrilla organizations in Burma.

* Amra Bengali
(We Bengalis) (WB)
Bengali organization that resisted moves to return to local tribesmen land taken by the Bengali immigrants. The dispute led to communal violence in the late 1970s.

* Army of Tripura People's Liberation Organization (ATPLO)
Separatist organization formed in 1982 by young extremists who had participated in the tribal rising of 1980 before going underground. In the latter part of 1982 the ATPLO was thought to be responsible for a series of attacks on policemen in northern Tripura and for the seizing of substantial quantities of arms and ammunition from government forces. It is led by Vijaya Hrankale, Chuni Koloi and Binanda Jamatiya. Its strength is estimated at 350 men. It is striving for an independent Tripura.
* Asom Gana Parishad (AGP)
Xenophobic Assamese political party established prior to the 1985 elections. It is led by Prafula Kkmar Mahanta.

* Assam for the Assamese Movement
Movement opposed to the Bengali immigrants in Assam.

• Bansropar Sah
Naxalite movement named after its leader. See Naxalites.

• Black Cats
Special security unit of the government. It was formed after the assassination of Indira Gandhi.

• Center of Indian Communists (CIC)
Dissident members of the CPI(ML) formed the 4th Communist party in India in December 1974. It rejected the right-wing opportunism of the CPI, the left-wing opportunism of the CPI(M) and the adventurism of the CPM(ML). It declared that it would follow the Chinese party's line in ideological struggles while taking local conditions into account in applying it. It defined its aims as the establishment of a people's government by organizing an armed revolution by workers and peasants.

• Communist Party of India (CPI)
Though the CPI-M took with it the majority of the CPI members when it broke away in 1964, most of the party bureaucracy legislative representatives and trade unionists remained in the CPI. Loyal to the international goals of the Soviet Union, the CPI favours large scale urban, capital intensive industrialization and 'democratic socialism'.

• Communist Party of India-Marxist (CPI-M)
Pro-Chinese party which led a peasant revolt in the Darjeeling district of West Bengal in 1967. The Naxalite movement started in Siliguri where the CPI-M committee called for the arming of peasants and setting up of rural bases in preparation for armed struggle. The CPI-M, however, expelled the leaders of the revolt, which was suppressed by the Indian Army in August 1967.

• Communist Party of India-Marxist Leninist (Krishak Mukti Samiti) (CPI-ML)
Communist party established on Apr.22, 1969, as a new 'truly revolutionary party'. Its program was to liberate the rural areas through revolutionary armed agrarian revolution; to encircle the cities; and finally to liberate the cities and thus complete the overthrow throughout the country. It decided to build up a strong People's Liberation Army and to create 'innumerable points of guerrilla struggle throughout the countryside to form 'red bases through annihilation of class enemies'. It was officially supported by the Chinese Communist Party. The CPI(ML), led by S.N.Singh, which rejected terrorism, advocated a combination of legal and illegal activities and also participation in mass movements launched by other left-wing parties. It was officially banned from July 4, 1975, until Mar.22, 1977. A document issued in December 1982 offered an analysis of the experiences of the Naxalites. One cause of its setbacks was the one-sided emphasis on armed struggle and neglect of other forms of struggle.

• Dalit Panthers (DP)
Movement modelled after the US Black Panther Movement which took its name from the word dalit (meaning 'oppressed'). It was set up in 1972 by Raja Dhale to defend the interests of the Harijans (untouchables). Its members were involved in clashes with caste Hindus. The movement spread to Gujarat where upper cast militants objected to the reservation of government jobs and university places for Harijans and launched an agitation campaign which led to riots. It was also active in encouraging conversions of Harijans to Islam (as a means of escaping the caste system).

• Dal Khalsa (DK)
Sikh youth organization of the National Council of Khalistan established by Dr.Jagjit Singh in 1979. It seeks secession and the establishment of an independent Khalistan. It engaged in hijackings, desecrations and riots. After serious Sikh-Hindu rioting in April 1982, the government banned the organization, then led by Gajendra Singh.

• Damdani Taksal (DT)
Extremist Sikh organization striving for a seminary to propagate Sikh fundamentalism.

• Dashmesh Regiment ("Followers of the 10th Guru") (DR)
Group which claimed responsibility for the assassination of V.N.Tiwari, a Hindu member of parliament in the Punjabi capital of Chandigarh on Apr.3, 1984. The group also claimed also responsibility for two other killings, of Harbans Lal Khanna and of R.Chander, a newspaper editor who had written that Punjab state had become 'a slaughterhouse'.

• Devendra Majhi
Naxalite movement named after its leader. See Naxalites.

• Dravidian Progressive Federation (Dravida Munnetra Kazha) (DMK)
An anti-Brahmin regional party dedicated to the promotion of Tamil interests. It opposes the retention of Hindi as an official language and seeks more autonomy for the states. It is led by Dr.Muthuvel Karananidhi Era Sezhian.

• Gurkha National Liberation Front (GNLF)
Gurkha activist organization active in West Bengal since 1980. It contends that the Gurkha population is ignored economically and politically. It is seeking to create an autonomous Ghurkaland,

India's 24th state. Communists and Ghurka's have repeatedly clashed since May 1986 in Darjeeling near the border with Nepal. The front is led by Subash Gheising. His demands have lurched between secession and statehood, and his targets between Delhi and Calcutta. The Bengal Marxists, while denouncing separatism are offering the Ghurkas local autonomy. Mr.Gandhi denounces the Marxists and their solution but has nothing else to offer.

* Indian Peoples Front (IPF)
A coalition of far left groups active in Bihar with an estimated membership of 400,000. Its aims are enforcement of land reform; minimum wage laws; impartial treatment from the police; and no rigging of elections.

* Jamaat-i-Tulaba
Student wing of Jamaat-i-Islami (a pro-Pakistani political party) that advocates an Iranian-type revolution in Kashmir. In the early 1980s, members engaged in attacks on police stations and Hindus.

* Jammu Kashmir Liberation Front (JKLF)
Separatist nationalist movement working for the independence of the state of Kashmir from the Republic of India. The JKLF was responsible for the assassination of the Indian diplomat Ravindra Mhatre in Birmingham (England) in February 1984. Two members were later tried and convicted of his murder. On Sep.6, 1985, six members of the front were arrested by British police under the Prevention of Terrorism Act. They included Amanulah Khan, head of the front in Britain who was arrested at the organization's headquarters in Luton, Bedfordshire. The front has 18 branches in Azad Kashmir, the Middle East, Europe and the US and a good number of sympathizers in the Indian-held part of Kashmir.

* Kannamani
'Annihilationist' group which has been active in Tamil Nadu. Its leader was killed on Dec.28, 1980. The group is held responsible for several murders and armed robberies.

* Khalistan Armed Police (KAP)
Sikh terrorist group which has been responsible for a massacre of bus passengers in December 1986. It is reportedly led by Manjit Singh Kaljala.

* Khalistan Commando Force (KCF)
The largest of 17 Sikh groups fighting for an independent Sikh state in the Punjab. On Apr.1, 1987, the group announced 13 commandments. Violators of the commandments have been murdered. The group has been involved in a violent campaign against Hindus. It has been responsible for the assassination attempt on police inspector J.F.Ribeiro on Oct.3, 1986, and has targeted haircutters, butchers, owners of liquor stores and sellers of cigarettes and women's underwear. More than 1,000 people have been killed since early 1986.

* Mizo National Front (MNF)
Guerrilla movement established in 1959. It demands the secession of the contiguous Mizo areas of India, East Pakistan and Burma to form an independent state. It was led by Laldenga who was replaced by Biakchunga in 1978. In 1966 the MNF launched a revolt which was repressed by Indian army units. By 1969 half the Mizo population was settled in 'protected villages'. At the end of 1971 guerrilla activity subsided. Since then terrorist and guerrilla activities have continued on a small scale. In 1978 a conflict developed between the moderate and extremist elements of the MNF. Laldenga was expelled from the movement but was readmitted in January 1979. In July 1979 it was declared an illegal organization. On June 25, 1980, Laldenga stated that the MNF had agreed on a cease-fire. It suspended military activities but did not surrender its arms and continued to collect 'taxes'. On June 30, 1986, the government signed an accord with the MNF.

* Naga Federal Army (NFA)
Separatist guerrilla organization active in Nagaland in the 1970s. Several hundred members were reported to have received training in China.

* Nagaland Federal Government (NFG)
One of the larger separatist guerrilla movements operating in Nagaland during the 1970s. Activities decreased after a counterinsurgency campaign in which one of its leader was captured and its headquarters destroyed.

* National Council of Khalistan (NCK)
Sikh organization established in 1972. It is striving for an independent Sikh state (Khalistan) and is led by Balbir Singh Sandu. From its headquarters in the Golden Temple in Amritsar it issued Khalistan passports, postage stamps and currency notes. A youth organization, the Dal Khalsa was founded in 1979. It has been involved in assassinations, bomb attacks, riots, fights with Hindus, arson and slaugthering of cattle in front of Hindu temples. It was officially banned on May 1, 1982.

* Nationalist Socialist Council of Nagaland (NSCN)
A Maoist breakaway faction of the Naga separatist movement established in 1978. It was reported to have seized control of Naga rebel forces in Burma. In 1980 NSCN followers clashed with Nagaland guerrillas led by A.Z.Phizo. In early 1982 the NSCN cooperated with the People's Liberation Army active in Manipur. In late 1982 it was reported to

be in disarray following the surrender of several of its leading members.

* National Union of Selfless Servers (Rashtriya Swayan Sewak Sangh) (RSSS)
Paramilitary Hindu organization that repeatedly has engaged in communal violence. According to its principles, Indian nationality is founded on Hinduism. Consequently Moslems, Christians and Communists are considered as 'internal threats'.

* Naxalite Movement
Communist movement in West Bengal named after the village Naxalbari near Darjeeling who murdered landlords and exhorted peasants to occupy their land in the late 1960s. During the 1970s between 10,000 and 20,000 Naxalites were reported to have launched a 'cultural revolution' on the Chinese model. In February 1979, guerrilla activities were reported to have intensified in West Bengal, Andhra Pradesh, Bihar, Punjab and Kerala and to have spread to Uttar Pradesh, Maharashtra, Tamil Nadu and Assam. Total strength was estimated at 15,000. In 1982 the CPI(ML) urged as the theoretical basis of the movement the upholding of both armed struggle and all other forms of struggle complementary to it, as well as the upholding of the Proletarian revolutionary line of Charu Mazumdar. A 'red army' has grown to rival the caste armies. It has taken over some 100 villages in 1985 and 1986. The police and the caste armies dare not enter them.

* Path of Bliss (Ananda Marg) (AM)
Fanatical Hindu religious and political movement which was founded in 1955 and is striving for a new world order. It resorted to terrorism as a result of the life imprisonment of its founder Prabhat Ranjan' Sarkar (alias Anand Murtiji) who was convicted of murder. He developed a 'progressive utility' theory and is regarded by his followers as an incarnation of God. It combined the worship of Kali (the Hindu goddess of destruction) with extreme right-wing views. It claimed to have 1.9 million members in India and 400,000 members abroad by the late 1970s. Members have been involved in assassinations and bomb and grenade attacks on Indian diplomats abroad. A number of former members of the sect have been murdered.

* Peasants and Workers Party of India (Bharatiye Krishi Kamghar Paksha) (BKKP)
A Marxist party whose influence is confined primarily to Maharashtra. In addition to nationalization of the means of production, the party advocates a redrawing of state boundaries on an exclusive language base. It is led by Dajiba Desai.

* People's Liberation Army (PLA)
A Maoist guerrilla organization operating mainly in Manipur but advocating independence for the whole north-east region of India. Its first commander in chief is Biseswar Singh. Many members are from the Meteis tribal people of the plains of Manipur, many of whom have rejected Hinduism as a faith identified with New Delhi's cultural domination. They were held responsible for destroying temples and images. It has been involved in armed robberies of banks and government offices. It cooperated with the National Socialist Council of Nagaland in an ambush of an army convoy on Feb.19, 1982. Kunj Behari Singh who replaced Biseswar Singh (who was arrested on July 6, 1981) was killed on Apr.13, 1982, together with eight other PLA members.

* People's Revolutionary Party of Kungleipak (PREPAK)
Secessionist guerrilla organization which has been active in Manipur. In 1980 it split into two factions. The first was led by Maipak Sharma and Leishabi Singh as commander (who was killed in a battle with police on July 23, 1980). Rajkumar Tulachandra Singh led the second faction. He was captured by government forces in February 1980 and later issued a statement calling for suspension of insurgent operations. His own followers expelled him from the organization. It is believed that guerrillas were trained by China in Tibet.

* People's War
Naxalite faction in Andhra Pradesh which was involved in fighting in a village on April 20, 1981, when thirteen tribesmen and one policeman were killed.

* Research and Development Wing (RAW)
Indian intelligence service.

* Revolutionary Army of Kuneipak (RAK)
Small secessionist guerrilla movement active in Manipur. It has been responsible for shootings and ambushes in the early 1980s. It is supported by China and has financed its activities by bank robberies.

* Revolutionary Government of Manipur (RGM)
A minuscule left-wing group held responsible for several attacks in the late 1970s. Targets included banks and police stations.

* Revolutionary Youth and Students' Federation (RYSF)
Small revolutionary youth movement, influenced by the Naxalites and active in Uttar Pradesh in the late 1970s. It attacked police stations.

* Shiv Sena
Hindu group which appeared in Punjab in 1984. It has 30,000 members armed with the trishul tridents, symbols of Shiva, destroyer of evil. It went openly paramilitary in 1986. It plans eventually to outgun such militant Sikh groups as the Babbar Khalsa and the ultras in the AISSF. It has no connection with the Bombay organization of the same name.

* Sikh League
Sikh separatist organization established in late 1981. It is led by Sukhjinder Singh, a former education minister of Punjab, who had been expelled from the Akali Dal, the main Sikh political party.

* Tamil Liberation Army (TLA)
Indian Tamil secessionist group that operates in the South Arcost district of Tamil Nadu. It has about 60-70 members. It claimed to have blown up a bridge south of Madras on Mar.15, 1987. An hour after the explosion, the Rockfort Express passenger train plunged from the bridge, killing at least 25 persons and injuring more than 200 others.

* Tripura Sena
Separatist and anti-Bengali organization which is thought to be an extremist faction of the Tripura Tribal Youth Organization. It is led by Vijoy Rankal. It has been responsible for acts of terrorism and shootouts with the police. A tribal rising resulted in the murder of up to 2,000 Bengalis on June 6-10, 1980. The army was called in to restore order. Over 200,000 people became homeless and had to be accommodated in government relief camps. About 40,000 tribal people were said to have fled to the forest to evade arrest. Bands of separatists operated from the Chitta Gong Hill tracts area into border areas of Tripura in the early 1980s.

* Tripura Tribal Youth Organization
(Tripura Upajaty Yuba Samiti) (TUYS)
Cultural and social organization of the hill youth. Tripura radicals function under the cover of the TUYS. By 1978 the radicals had formed a secret group, the Tripura National Volunteers, without knowledge of the TUYS leadership and began sending volunteers for guerrilla training in the Chitta Gong Hill Tracts where the Mizo had regained their sanctuaries. It has links with the Mizo National Front. By 1979 the Chakma, Mizo, Tripura insurgencies had converged.

* United Liberation Army (ULA)
Its formation was announced in April 1980 with the objective to fight for the independence of the seven northern states.

* United Minorities Front (UMF)
Front consisting of Moslem Bengali from lower Assam.

* Universal Proutist Revolutionary Front (UPRF)
Organization which name is derived from the 'progressive utility' theory developed by P.R.Sarkar. It is generally regarded as the political wing of the Anand Marg sect (Path of Eternal Bliss). It claimed responsibility for a terrorist campaign in favour of the release from life imprisonment of the Anand Marg leader, P.R.Sarkar, involving attacks on Indian diplomats in Australia. It also threatened to blow up an Air India airliner which in fact exploded in the air off Bombay in January 1978.

INDONESIA

* Abode of Islam
(Dar-ul-Islam)
Movement aiming at the violent overthrow of the secular republic and its replacement by an Islamic state. Although banned it was active from the early 1950s. Revolts organized by it broke out in South Celebes in 1951 and in Atjeh in 1953. In November 1981 the Dar-ul-Islam leader Daud Baruah was reported to be under house arrest in Jakarta, but in Atjeh the movement continued to run a parallel administration as the effective government of the the province. In late 1981 militant Moslems in Banda Aceh launched a series of violent attacks on the local Chinese community. Government troops were sent from Jakarta to quell the disturbances.

* Anti Communist Revolutionary Movement (MRAC)
Supporters of the Democratic Union of Timor (UDT) fled to West Timor and were included in this movement which launched a counter attack against FRETILIN on Oct.9, 1975.

* Association of Wild Children
(Gabungan Anak Liar) (GAL)
Criminal youth gangs alienated from Indonesian society and adhering to a kind of subterranean cult of outlaw nihilism. Indonesians also call them the 'wild bunch' or 'gali,gali'.

* A-1
Military intelligence unit which has been involved in torturing.

* Communist Party of Indonesia
(Partai Kumunis Indonesia) (PKI)
Communist party established in May 1920, which was involved in an unsuccessful rising against Dutch rule in 1926-27, whereafter it went underground. In the 1930s, it took part in the establishment of an anti-fascist front which during the Second World War opposed the Japanese forces.

After the proclamation of Indonesia's national independence on Aug.17, 1945, the PKI took part in the government. In September 1948, the government was overthrown in a right-wing coup which led to the killing of PKI leaders. The Dutch returned temporarily until Dec.27, 1949, when sovereignty was transferred to the Republic of the United States of Indonesia. The PKI was reconstituted. In 1965 the party led the September 30 Movement. A new military regime suppressed the CPI and alleged sympathizers. Several hundred thousand people died. It nevertheless claimed to have reconstituted itself in the 1960s and 1970s. In the May 1982 elections 40,000 ex-detainees who had been adherents of the PKI were denied voting rights.

* Democratic Union of Timor
(Uniao Democratica de Timor) (UDT)
One of three independence movements which emerged in East Timor in 1974. It envisaged eventual independence but hoped to maintain Timor's historic links with Portugal. It was led by Lopez Cruz and Costa Mousinho (mayor of Dili). It represented those professional, merchant and tribal interests that lived well under Portuguese rule. The UDT staged a coup in August 1975. Its forces seized the police headquarters, the radio station and the airport. Thus strengthened, the UDT demanded immediate independence from Portugal. Fighting ensued between the UDT allied with APODETI and FRETILIN. Despite evidence of Indonesian backing for UDT, FRETILIN proved a stronger force on the streets. To prevent a FRETILIN seizure of power, Indonesia invaded East Timor in December 1975.

* Free Aceh Movement
(Gerakin Aceh Merdeka) (GAM)
Movement which was established in 1976. It was influenced by the Islamic fundamentalist ideology of the Abode of Islam. Its aim was independence for Atjeh (Aceh) in northern Sumatra.It launched a small scale secessionist terrorist campaign which was continued into the early 1980s. Its leader, Hasan de Tiro, was said to have been killed in October 1980.

* Holy War Commando
(Jihad Kommando)
Militant Moslem group active around the general elections in 1977. Contemporary extremists, while all variously falling under the government's uniquitous Jihad Kommando label, represent in fact at least four separate factions advocating the creation of an islamic state in Indonesia. It has been held responsible for a number of acts of violence. In April 1979 the security forces arrested the group's leader Warman and charged him with murder.

* Indonesian Islamic Revolutionary Council (IMRON)
Radical Indonesian Moslem group which is striving for an orthodox-Moslem state. Number two of the organization, Salman Hafidz was convicted for 'subversive activities' and executed in 1983. It appeared to be the political counterpart of the Holy War Command.

* Jemaah Imran
Moslem Brotherhood of about 300 members led by Imran Mohammed Zein, who has been sentenced to death and executed. He and about 25-30 hard core followers have had at least two violent confrontations with other Moslems over religious issues, one of which allegedly led to the death of a religious rival. Imran is suspected to be behind the March 28, 1981, hijacking in which seven people were killed. Besides the hijacking, the group has been involved in an attack on a police post in West Java on June 11, 1981, in which three policemen were killed.

* Kopassus
Special army unit which has been involved in torturing.

* Melanesian Socialist Party (MSP)
Underground political movement in Papua New Guinea offering the Soviet Union a communist foothold in the country in exchange for money and arms. Government sources believed the new party was formed out of an earlier one, the Christian Democratic Alliance, an exile group also based in Papua New Guinea.

* Moslim National Liberation Front for Aceh (NLFA)
Insurgent movement in northern Sumatra led by Hasan di Toro. The majority of the leaders of the movement are doctors, lawyers or engineers. See Free Aceh Movement.

* Mysterious Killers
(Penembak Misterius) (PETRUS)
Officially sanctioned 'hit' teams of soldiers and policemen which have been responsible for the death of between 4,000 and 8,500 people, mainly ex-prisoners. The teams were established to reduce the crime rate. The targets, at least in the early weeks of 1983 when the campaign reportedly began, were active local criminals, ex-convicts and recidivists who in many cases apparently had been able to prey on their communities with impunity for years.

* Operational Command for the Restoration of Security and Order
(Komando Operasi Pemulihan Keamanan dan

Ketertiban) (KOPKAMTIB)
Command which was established on Oct.3, 1965. Its principal duty was to protect security and order after the revolt of 1965. It conducted a countrywide campaign of repression against suspected communists and other left-wing elements. According to Amnesty International 500,000 persons had been killed and 700,000 arrested after the 1965 coup attempt. In October 1977, Amnesty International estimated that there were at least 55,000 and probably 100,000 political prisoners (known as 'tapols'), many of them having been held without trial since 1965.

* Papua Independent Movement
(Organisasi Papua Merdeka) (OPM)
Liberation movement founded by exiled Papuans in 1963 when Irian Jaya (formerly Dutch New Guinea and known as West Irian until 1973) was incorporated into Indonesia. It is led by Elkie Bemei and 'Brig.Gen.' Seth Rumkorem. In 1976 the insurgents claimed to control a number of 'liberated zones'. It claimed to control an armed force of 10,000 men and was believed to be responsible for a rebellion in April-May 1977. It was crushed by Indonesian troops. In April 1978 it was reported that over 5,000 guerrillas and civilians as well as over 3,500 Indonesians had been killed in the fighting since the beginning of 1976. Military activities decreased and the OPM is estimated to have been reduced to a few hundred fighters.

* Pemuda Ansor
Anti-communist youth organization which operated as Moslem murder squads in East Java during the massacres in 1965. Swept up by islamic fanaticism they first killed known communists but later went into the villages and town districts at night. In many cases, the whole male population of entire villages was killed. Sometimes women and children were included as well to be sure that nobody could take revenge in the future. Cut off heads were put on stakes and on walls. For several weeks, hundreds of maimed bodies floated in the rivers of Solo and Brantas. The elimination squads were established and trained before the Untung-putsch.

* Popular Democratic Association of Timorese
(Associacao da Popular Democratica dos Timorenses) (APODETI)
Indonesia-backed political associations which emerged after the Lisbon coup in 1974. It favoured the transformation of East Timor into an autonomous province of Indonesia. After the August 1975 coup, APODETI allied itself with the UDT in the subsequent fighting against leftist FRETILIN forces.

* Pusat Komando Tertinggi Badan Pertahanan Perdjuangan Kemerdekaan Maluku di Maluku
Secessionist movement active on the South Moluccans. It is striving for an independent Tanah Air Maluku. Markus Josef Jantje Wattisoumahu acts as its general coordinator. The movement has called on South Moluccans in the Netherlands to form a new government in exile, named Cabinet Nunusaku. The name Nunusaku refers to a former kingdom.

* Red Berets
(KomandoPasukanSandiYudha)(KOPASSANDHA)
Para commando units supervised by military intelligence chief Lt.Gen.Benny Murdani.

* Revolutionary Front for the Independence of East Timor
(Frente Revolucionaria Timorense de Libertacao e Independencia) (FRETILIN)
Organization which was established on May 20, 1974. It superseded the Timorese Social Democratic Association (ASDF). Its aim is full independence for East Timor. The front was opposed by the other political parties formed in East Timor in 1974 and soon a civil war erupted. By Sep.8, 1975, it claimed to have gained complete control of East Timor. On Nov.28, 1975, it proclaimed the Democratic Republic of East Timor. On Dec.7, 1975, the Indonesian forces began to occupy the territory and formally incorporated it into Indonesia on Aug.17, 1976. To break the insurgency, Indonesia resorted to use of defoliants, napalm and heavy bombing. Survivors were driven back into the mountains and efforts were made to starve them out. Casualty estimates vary from 100,000 to 250,000 since 1975. In 1982 five members of the old leadership rebuilt the organization from scratch. It now claims to have about 4,000 fighters.

* September 30 Movement
(GerakanSeptemberTigapulahGestapu)(GESTAPU)
Movement that staged a coup attempt on Sep.30, 1965. The elements of the Indonesian Communist Party in concert with elements of the Indonesian military were led by Lt.Col.Untung. The coup was staged to prevent a planned right-wing coup. The young officers attempt was defeated, however, and right-wing generals led by General Suharto installed a military regime. In reaction about 500,000 people in Jakarta and parts of Java have been massacred by usually military supervised youth groups, often Moslem in orientation, by village guards and other vigilante units. PKI and front group members, real or suspected party sympathizers, and many with not the slightest connection either to the coup attempt or the PKI but instead targets of various personal dislikes, vendettas and rumours, were murdered.

* United Democratic Party

(Partido Democratico Unido) (PDU)
Party in East Timor which advocated union with Indonesia. APODETI joined the PDU in seeking integration with Indonesia.

IRAN

* Ahmad Madani Group
A paramilitary unit based in eastern Turkey of 6,000 to 8,000 mostly Iranian exiles but also Kurds, commanded by Rear Admiral Ahmad Madani. He was commander in chief of the Iranian Navy under the Shah. He is generally described as neither an islamic revolutionary nor a monarchist and tries to project the image of a strongman. The CIA reportedly backed the group with money and arms.

* Al Amal al-Islami
Movement which has been involved in terrorist activities. It is believed to have operated under the name Islamic Jihad. It depends directly on the Supreme Council of the Iranian Islamic Revolution. It is led by Mohammed Taki al-Moudarissi and is based in Tehran. It is a multinational movement with members from Iran, Iraq, Bahrein, northern Africa and some sub-Saharan countries.

* Arab Front for the Liberation of Ahvaz (AFLA)
Iraqi-backed separatist movement established in 1981. It is led by Sayyid Hashim Sayyid Adnan.
* Arabistan Liberation Front (ALF)
Arab organization which has been responsible for acts of sabotage in Khuzestan province in 1979 and 1980. It is fighting the Tehran government for local autonomy or full independence.

* Arab Political and Cultural Organization (APCO)
Arab organization which is striving for greater autonomy for the Khuzestan province. It was formed in 1979 by various political and cultural societies and is led by Shaikh Mohammed Taher Shobeir Khaghani. Although Khomeini made some concessions clashes were reported between Khaghani followers and the Revolutionary Guards.

* Arab Popular Movement of Arabistan (APMA)
Arab movement fighting for autonomy for Khuzestan, 'within the framework of a democratic Iranian state'.

* Armed Movement for the Liberation of Iran (AMLI)
Movement which claimed to represent the monarchist opposition to the Tehran regime. It was established in 1979 and is based in Paris. It is led by Princess Azzadeh, a niece of the late Shah, and was supported by Princess Ashraf, the late Shah's twin sister.

* Ashraf Dehghani
Banned Marxist group, several members of which have been executed.

* Association for the Defense of the Liberty and Sovereignty of the Iranian Nation
New Iranian opposition group which was established in May 1986. It is led by Mehdi Bazargan, former prime-minister. The central council of the group is composed of at least seven former politicians of Bazargan's cabinet. The association operates 'within the system' and supports the Islamic revolution and the constitution.

* Azadegan Movement (AM)
Paramilitary unit of about 2,000 men commanded by General Bahram Aryana, the former chief of staff of the Iranian army under the Shah. In 1981, members the movement seized the Tabarzin, one of three French-built Iranian gunboats sailing past the Spanish port of Cadiz. The seajackers were offered political asylum in France. The nationalist movement maintained close ties with Shahpur Bakhtiar. The CIA reportedly backed the unit with money and arms.

* Azerbaijani Autonomist Movement (AAM)
Ethnic movement striving for greater autonomy for Azerbaijan. The Azerbaijanis, variously estimated at between 5,000,000 and 10,000,000 people, are forming the largest ethnic majority group in Iran. They were mainly Shi'ite moslems acknowledging as their spiritual leader Ayatollah Kazem Shariat Madari. Many of them had taken an active part in religious opposition to the Shah's regime and played an important part in the Islamic Revolution. Ayatollah Shariat Madari, however, rejected the supremacy of Ayatollah Khomeini and the involvement of the clergy in the running of the country. In this he. was supported by the (Azerbaijani) Moslem People's Republican Party (MPRP) led by Abdelhassan Rostamkani. On Dec.5, 1979, a rebellion broke out in Qom which spread to Tabriz.

* Baluchi Autonomist Movement (BAM)
Ethnic guerrilla movement led by Mowlawi Abdul-Aziz Mollazadeh. In Iran's south-eastern province of Baluchistan Sistans and Baluchis form the majority of the 550,000 inhabitants and are predominantly Sunni moslems. They speak their own language. The Sistans, numbering about 110,000, are mainly Shi'ite Moslems and enjoy a higher standard of living than the Baluchis. Baluchi demands for limited autonomy within Iran and economic concessions have been largely ignored.

* Baluchi Liberation Front (BLF)
Baluchi guerrilla movement established in 1964 and led by Jumma Khan, a graduate from Karachi University. He operated from Dubai. In 1965, Mir

Abdi Khan of the Sardaizai tribe joined the front and from the Gulf States mobilized support among Baluchi exiles for an armed struggle against the Shah regime. The Baluchis were trained in Iraq. Resistance weakened when Mir Abdi Khan made peace with the Shah in 1975. Iraq ceased to aid the Baluchis in return for Iran's agreement not to aid the Kurds.

* Baluch Pesh Merga
(Baluch Volunteer Force) (BVF)
Baluchi guerrilla group organized by Amanullah Barakzai. It is opposed to the Khomeini regime. It worked alongside the Vahdat Baluch (United Baluch), seeking to unite tribal resistance with urban nationalists against Tehran.

* Black Wednesday
(Chaharshanbeh-e-Siah)
Arab organization which claimed responsibility for a bomb explosion at the Abadan refinery on June 14, 1979, and a pipeline explosion on July 10, 1979.

* The Call
(al-Dawa)
Organization which was established in 1959 and is led by Mohammed Mehdi al-Asefi. It is believed to have operated under the name Islamic Jihad and depends directly on the Supreme Council of the Iranian Islamic Revolution.

* Communist Party of Iran
(Hezb-e-Komunist-e-Iran) (HKI)
An small group organized in early 1979 as an alternative to the pro-Soviet posture of Tudeh. It is led by Azaryun.

* Committee for Safeguarding the Islamic Revolution
Group which claimed responsibility for a bomb attack on a factory in Italy on Aug.7, 1980. The factory exported nuclear technology to Iraq.

* Fighters
(Razmandegan)
Left-wing group whose supporters engaged in street violence in the early 1980s.

* Fighters of the Forests
(Jangali)
Maoist organization of the Iranian Communist League which tried to conquer the city of Amol on Jan.24-25, 1982.

* Forghan Group
(Grouh-e-Forghan) (GF)
Marxist Moslem underground organization formed in 1979. It is opposed to the political role assumed by the Moslem clergy and is led by Akbar Goudarzi. It follows the teachings of the late Dr.Ali Shariati who died in 1977. It assassinated several leading members of the islamic regime and a West German businessman.

* Front for the Liberation of Iran (FLI)
Group which advocates the Ayatollah's overthrow and since 1983 called for restoration of the Iranian monarchy. Its headquarters is located in Paris and it is led by Ali Amini, a former prime-minister. Since 1982 it reportedly received CIA money.

* Global Islamic Movement (GIM)
Organization which is in charge of exporting the Islamic revolution. It was led by Mr.Hashemi.

* Group of the Martyr
Group of six Iranian Arabs who seized the Iranian embassy in London on Apr.30. 1980, taking 26 hostages and demanding that in return for their release 91 Arabs imprisoned in Iran should be set free. After the six had killed two of the hostages, members of the British SAS penetrated the embassy, killing five of the Arabs and seizing the sixth, who was sentenced to life imprisonment on Jan.22, 1981.

* Guardians of the Islamic Revolution
Group that claimed responsibility for a car bomb attack on July 19, 1987, that wounded Mr.Amirhussein Amir-Parviz, the head of the London office of the Iranian National Movement. The group announced there would be further attacks against monarchists.

* Hojatieh
A radical religious group which takes credit for initially influencing the official campaign against the 450,000 Baha'i in Iran and which advocates a more fundamentalist interpretation of Islam than that of Ayatollah Khomeini.

* Iranian National Council of Resistance (INCR)
Council set up in 1981 by ex-president Abolhassan Bani-Sadr and Massoud Rajavi, the leader of the Mujahideen Khalq upon arriving in Paris on July 29, 1981. On June 10, 1981, Ayatollah Khomeini ordered Bani-Sadr to be dismissed as commander in chief of the armed forces. On June 12, 1981, he attacked the rule of the IRP as having 'worsened the condition of country day by day' and Parliament thereupon, on June 21 declared him incompetent. The following day he was formally dismissed as president. He disappeared from public life until his arrival in Paris. In November 1981 the Kurdish Democratic Party of Iran joined the INCR. Bani Sadr terminated his cooperation with the council in 1984 and in 1985 the PDKI left the council as a result of several differences, including the nature of relations with Iraq.

* Iran Liberation Movement (ILM)

Founded in 1961 by Mehdi Bazargan as splinter group of the National Front. From it split a number of Maoist militants who formed the guerrilla group, People's Mujahideen, in 1965. Dr.Bazargan later became prime-minister under the Ayatollah Khomeini's Islamic Republic until his fall in November 1979.

* Iranian People's Strugglers, Holy Warriors (Mujahideen-e-Khalq)
A militant splinter of the ILM which was established in 1965. It launched its armed struggle in 1971. It advocates a non-Marxist democratic socialism based on Islam. Following the fall of the Shah, the Mujahideen, numbering tens of thousands, opposed the pretensions of the ruling IRP and under their exiled leader, Massoud Rajavi, joined other groups in a resistance council. It developed into the most active opposition group in Iran since 1982. It has carried out repeated attacks and assassinations of government leaders. Since 1981 it has been systematically persecuted. In 1986 its headquarters was moved from Paris to Iraq. It has a hardcore of 700 militants of whom 200 have received training in urban guerrilla warfare by the PFLP. It has an armed strength of 20,000 to 25,000 man and has half a million supporters. It claimed to have killed more than 15,000 opponents and Revolutionary Guards. Thousands of cells operate in Iran.

* Islamic Arab Front for the Liberation of Baluchistan (IAFLB)
Baluchi front set up by Sheikh Mohammed Bin Hassan Al-Mohammed in Bahrein in 1980. He tried to rally the 350,000 Baluchi living in the Gulf States behind an independent Baluchistan.

* Islamic Republican Party
(Hezb-e-Jomhori-e-Islami) (IRP)
Essentially a ruling party by late 1979. It is led by a group described as fanatically loyal to Ayatollah Khomeini. It is supported by the masses of Shi'ite believers who compose the lower and lower-middle class of the Iranian society.

* Islamic Revolutionary Guards Corps
(Pasdarans) (IRGC)
A formation dedicated to protect the Islamic Revolution that ousted Shah Reza Pahlavi in 1979. It operates as a regular army of 400,000 man. It trained a variety of foreign liberation movements, primarily Arab Shiites in Islamic ideology, organization and paramilitary use of weapons and explosives. It has a training camp in a former army installation near the city of Isfahan. It is estimated that three million Moslem combatants, including a great number of school pupils, have been trained and sent to the fronts by the IRGC. It plays a dual role in both internal security and in the war with Iraq.

* Kurdish Democratic Party of Iran
(Hezb Democrat Kurdistan) (KDPI)
Kurdish guerrilla organization which was established in 1945. It is striving for an independent Kurdish state and is led by Dr.Abdel Rahman Qasemlu. The party was originally formed as an illegal organization out of an Association for the Resurrection of Kurdistan, but was practically liquidated when a Kurdish rebellion in Iran was crushed in 1966-67. Dr.Qasemlu returned from exile in February 1979. It stepped up its guerrilla war and in 1980 more than 1,000 Kurds and 500 government forces died. After the outbreak of the war between Iran and Iraq in September 1980 KDPI leaders initially declared that they would not hinder the Iranian war effort against Iraq. In fact they intensified the struggle and were reported to receive aid from Iraq. By mid-1982 it was estimated that a third of the Iranian army (including several thousand Pasdarans) was fighting in Kurdistan. Its strength in 1982 was 12,000 Pesh Mergas and 60,000 armed peasants. It cooperated with the Mujahideen Khalq.

* Kurdish Sunni Moslem Movement (KSMM)
Kurdish movement which incorporates various leftwing Kurdish groups, notably the Marxist-Leninist Komaleh faction which on June 8, 1980, rejected any negotiations about a cease fire. The movement is seeking a social revolution in Iran. Shaikh Ezzedin Hosseini was the acknowledged leader of the Kurdish Sunni community and as such opposed to the domination of the state by the Shi'ite clergy.

* Martyrs of the Islamic Revolution
An Iran-directed terrorist cell. A hijacking of an Saudi Arabian airliner in Madrid in July 1985 was pre-empted. It was controlled by an operative at the Iranian embassy who maintained direct contact with terrorists who had entered Spain from Syria to conduct the hijacking. The group had already conducted bombings against Iraqi and French diplomatic facilities in Spain.

* Mobilization
(Bassijis)
Paramilitary volunteer force which in 1984 was said to number one million nationwide.

* Muslim People's Republican Party
(Hezb-e-Jomhori-e-Khalq-e-Mosalman) (MPRP)
Party in Azerbaijan which rejected the supremacy of the clergy in ruling the country. It was established by followers of the opposition religious leader Ayatollah Shariat Madari. It favors a strong secular government within the context of the Islamic Republic. It is led by Abdelhassan Rostamkhani. On Jan.11, 1980, Revolutionary Guards

seized the headquarters of the MPRP in Tabriz. Several members were summarily tried on various charges, including 'subversion with guns' and 'waging war on God and his messenger' and were executed. A.Rostamkhani and another member were executed for their involvement in the rebellion in Qom in December 1979.

* Movement for the Liberation of Iran (MLI)
Movement which was opposed to the regime of the Shah in the 1970s. It advocated a democratic, non-socialist islamic state not ruled by the clergy. It was led by Mehdi Bazargan. Its founder died in the prisons of the Shah. From it sprang the Mujahideen Khalq.

* Mujahideen
Organization which has been involved in terrorist activities. It is believed to have operated under the name of Islamic Jihad and depends directly on the Supreme Council of the Iranian Islamic Revolution (SCIIR). It appeared in 1980 and is run by Aziz al Hakim, the brother of Mohammed Bakr al Hakim, the leader the SCIIR.

* National Democratic Front
(Jebhe-e-Democratic-e-Melli) (JDM)
A leftwing secular party which was established in 1979. It accused Ayatollah Khomeini of attempting to establish a religious dictatorship. It is led by Hedatollah Matine-Daftari, grandson of Dr.Mohammed Mossadeq. In 1981, Matine-Daftari left Iran for Paris, where he announced his support for the National Council of Resistance.

* National Equality Party (NEP)
External opposition movement based in Turkey. It was established in August 1980. It is headed by General Moukhtar Karabagh. It claimed responsibility for bomb attacks in Tehran in the early 1980s.

* National Information and Security Organization
(Sazman-e Etelaat va Amniate Kechvar) (SAVAK)
The intelligence service of the late Shah of Iran, created in 1956 with the help of the CIA and the MOSSAD. It was controlled in its early years by the powerful leader General Teymur Bakhtiar and reached out beyond Iran to intimidate and kill students and dissidents in exile. Its agents even killed their former leader Bakhtiar after he had been dismissed for plotting against the Shah. According to Western sources it had a full time staff of 30,000 men plus a much larger number of part time spies, informers and messengers. The excesses of SAVAK agents who tortured everyone who fell into their hands were one of the major causes of the Iranian revolution. When that took place the hated Komiteh building, SAVAK's headquarters, was wrecked, its files thrown into the streets and instruments of torture burned. General Nematollah Nassiri was the third and last head of the SAVAK.

* National Islamic Liberation Front (NILF)
* National Resistance Movement of Iran (NRMI)
External opposition movement established in France on Aug.8, 1980 by Dr.Shahput Bakhtiari, a former prime-minister. On May 13, 1979, Ayatollah Khalkhali, then head of Iran's Revolutionary Courts declared that Dr.Bakhtiari was among those former prime-ministers on whom sentences had been passed under 'religious laws'. On June 10 and July 12, 1980, the Iran government announced that a conspiracy by military men to restore Mr.Bakhtiari to power had been uncovered. Some 300 persons were arrested in this connection. By Sep.3, 1980, a total of 96 of them, including two generals, had been executed. In Paris, Dr.Bakhtiari escaped an assassination attempt on July 18, 1980, when three persons were killed and one injured. He denied on Sep.26, 1980, that he had formed a government in exile and that he had armed supporters waiting to invade Iran.

* Nationalist and Revolutionary Front of Iran (NRFI)
External opposition movement which was established in Paris in April 1982. It is led by Mozzafar Firouz, nephew of the late Dr.Mossadeq, Amir Bahman Samsam Bakhtiari (a leader of the Bakhtiari tribe), Professor Fariborz Nozari and general Jahangir Qaderi (member of the general staff and of the Imperial Guard under the Shah).

* Organization of Marxist Leninists
(Sazman-e-Tudeh-e-Iran) (STI)
Maoist offshoot of the Tudeh party.

* Organization of Revolutionary Brigades (ORB)
Group which claimed responsibility for bomb attacks on two restaurants in Kuwait. It is regarded as part of the Shi'ite Islamic Jihad.

* Organization Struggling for the Freedom of the Working Class
(Sazmane Peykar da Rahe Azadieh Tabaqe Kargar)

Small pro-Chinese communist formation which has actively opposed the Khomeini regime. In May 1982 the Iranian security authorities claimed to have smashed its entire leadership in a series of raids in the southern town of Bandar Abbas. Arrested members of the group who recanted their beliefs were reportedly often forced to join the firing squads for their former colleagues.

* PARS Group
The authorities accused the group of having links with Dr.Shahput Bakhtiar, the leader of the

National Resistance Movement then living in France, and with certain members of the late Shah's family. The group claimed responsibility for a bomb explosion outside a Revolutionary Guards barracks in Tehran on Feb.22, 1982.

* Party of God
(Hezbollah)
Fundamentalist group which actively supported the Islamic Republic in the streets of Tehran and other cities, where militants clashed with leftist opposition elements in 1981/1982. It was founded in 1973 by Ayatollah Mahmoud Ghaffani who secretly organized the revolution against the Shah from Qom. He was imprisoned by the SAVAK and tortured to death. His son Hadi inherited the party which then had less than hundred members. After the Islamic Revolution in February 1979 Imam Khomeini resurrected the party. In 1982 he ordered all Islamic fighting groups to melt with Hezbollah under the slogan 'only one party, the party of Allah, only one leader, Ruhollah'. In the same year Hezbollah was established in Lebanon by sheikhs and mullahs who had close contacts with Ayatollah Khomeini. See Lebanon.

* Party of the Masses
(Hezb-e-Tudeh)
Orthodox pro-Soviet communist party of Iran which was founded in 1941 after the Allied invasion of Persia. It is led by Noureddin Kianouri. It was declared illegal in 1949 and again in 1953. In 1965 the party was divided into three factions (with a pro-Soviet, Maoist and Castroite orientation). The pro-Soviet faction remained the official Tudeh. It adopted a new program in 1973 with the object of uniting all democratic forces. Its support for the new Islamic regime waned as the latter became more committed to clerical fundamentalism. The party was dissolved by the government on Mar.5, 1983.

* Party of Toilers
(Hezb-e-Kumelah)
Kurdish Marxist-Leninist guerrilla group striving for a socialist and democratic Iran in which national and ethnic minorities have self-rule. It was founded by Illekansadeh. Its strength is variously estimated at 1,800 (1982), 8,000 to 10,000 (1983), 2,000 (1984). Its spiritual leader is Sheikh Azedin Husseini.

* People's Sacrificers
(Fedayeen-e-Khalq)
Militant Marxist guerrilla movement which has been responsible for numerous acts of violence committed under the Shah's regime with the purpose of hastening its overthrow. It split from the pro-Soviet Tudeh party in 1963 under the leadership of Bijan Jazani. It drew support from student circles and was active in the cities. It supported the Islamic Revolution in its early stages but later clashed with Revolutionary Guards. In 1980 the movement split into three factions. These were the Fedayeen Guerrillas, Minority (Aqaliyyat) and Majority (Aksariyyat). After the outbreak of the war with Iraq the movement initially strongly supported the Iranian war effort. However, by mid-1981, elements aligned to the Communist Tudeh party formed the predominant political current, which accordingly came to echo Tudeh's opposition to the war. It was decimated by the Islamic Revolutionary Guards in 1982.

* Popular Front for the Liberation of the Gulf
Members of this front reportedly are trained in Iran, South Yemen and Libya. It has about 600 recruits. Training in Iran takes place in a camp in the northwest of Iran which is in the hands of a highranking Ayatollah. Its task is to destabilize conservative regimes in the Gulf.

* Popular Front for the Liberation of Ahwaz
(Jabhat Tahrir Ahvaz) (PFLA)
In 1975 the PFLA became known as the Ahvaz National Front. Following the 1975 Algiers agreement with Iran, Iraq withdrew its support. On occasions the front launched armed actions against the Shah's regime. A Marxist-Leninist splinter known as the Revolutionary Democratic Movement for the Liberation of Arabistan broke away in the mid-1970s. After the fall of the Shah Iraq continued its support for the front.

* Revolutionary Democratic Liberation Movement of Arabistan
Organization which has been active in the 1970s. It advocated greater autonomy for the Arabs.

* Supreme Council of the Iranian Islamic Revolution (SCIIR)
Organization which wants to install a Khomeini-style regime in Iraq and the propagation of the Moslem faith. It was established in 1981 and is headed by Hojatoteslam Mohammed Bakr al-Hakim. All the logistics are reportedly provided by Syria, including arms, training and money. It controls four movements, Amal, Al-Dawa, al Amal al-Islami and the Mujahideen which have been involved in terrorist attacks under the cover of Islamic Jihad.

* Toilers
(Ranjbaran)
Maoist organization which claimed to be the sole genuinely communist group. It was led by a number of US educated individuals such as the physicist Iraj Farhumand who was executed in February 1982, after six months of imprisonment.

* Tupamaros

Iraqi oriented urban terrorist movement which appeared in Gilan province and carried out assassinations and provoked wild-cat strikes. It had an estimated strength of 130 to 200 in 1971.

* Turkoman Autonomists
The predominantly Sunni moslem Turkomans in the north-east are striving for greater autonomy. Unrest broke out after seizure by Turkomans of disputed land, mainly farmed by absentee landlords. They were also angered by the intransigence of the Islamic regime with regard to the Turkoman demands. In fighting which broke out on March 26, 1979, Turkoman rebels were supported by the Fedayeen-e-Khalq. The government said the rebellion was the result of large-scale aid from the Soviet Union. This was denied by the rebels who rejected a cease fire offer. Army units said to be assisted by Mujahideen Khalq guerrillas forced the rebels to hand over their weapons at local mosques.

* Union of National Front Forces
(Jebhe-e-Melli)
A secular anti-regime movement which was established in 1977. One of its founders, Dr.Shahpur Bakhtiar, was formally expelled upon designation as prime-minister by the Shah in late 1978. Another founder, Dr.Karim Sanjabi, resigned as foreign minister of the Islamic Republic in April 1979 to protest a lack of authority according to Prime Minister Bazargan. The union was led by Dr.Karim Sanjabi and Dariush Foruhar.

* Union of Communists
Small pro-Chinese formation which has actively opposed the Khomeini regime. By mid-1982 Iranian authorities were claiming to have virtually destroyed it as a significant force.

IRAQ

* Arab Baath Socialist Party
(Hizb al-Baath al-Arabi al-Ishtiraki)
A long established Arab nationalist movement with branches in Syria and Arab countries. It is the principal component of the National Front. Its leadership is identical with that of the Revolutionary Command Council, Saddam Hussein (President of the Republic and regional secretary-general of the party) and 'Izzat Ibrahim al-Duri.

* Arab Socialist Movement (ASM)
Although not organized in a party or group of their own, Baathists opposed to the Iraqi Baath Arab Socialist Party have generally been either in sympathy with or directly linked to the Baath Party of Syria. Several members linked with a reported plot in 1979 were executed. The plot was said to have been aided by Syria with the object of removing the dominance of President Saddam Hussein's family, promoting union between Syria and Iraq and ending suppression of dissident members of Iraqi's Shi'ite community.

* The Call
(al Dawa al Islamiya)
Fundamentalist group promoting religious upheaval in Iraq and calling for a social revolution. It has been aligned with the Iranian Islamic Revolution. Ayatollah Bakr al-Sadr (executed in 1980), acted as its spiritual leader. In 1980, 40,000 Shi'ite Moslems were deported to Iran. Several thousand have been executed. Iranian support is said to have taken the form of training Iraqi exiles near Damascus (ostensibly to aid Palestinians in Lebanon) and their infiltration into Iraq. The group engaged in assassinations, car bomb attacks and acts of sabotage.

* Iraqi Communist Party
(al-Hizb al-Shy'i al-Iraqi) (ICP)
Pro-Soviet party which was founded in 1934. It was severely repressed in 1963 and many of its members were executed. It was led by Aziz Mohammed. After coming to power in 1968, the Iraqi Baath party took steps to achieve reconciliation with the ICP. However, from 1975 onwards the Baath party began to impose restrictions on the ICP. Several members were tried for forming secret cells in the armed forces. The party opposed the government's anti-Syrian propaganda and called for a more realistic autonomy for the Kurds in Iraq (whom a number of communists were said to have joined in renewed fighting against government forces). In March 1979 it terminated the membership of the National Progressive Front. During the Iran-Iraq war the ICP sided with Iran and in particular looked to Syria as an ally in its fight against the Saddam Hussein regime.

* Iraqi Vanguard Movement
A left-wing front aided by Syria.

* Islamic Action Organization (IAO)
A pro-Iranian fundamentalist group which has claimed responsibility for bomb attacks in 1983.

* Islamic Revolution of Iraq
(Sairi)
Organization which was established in 1983 in Tehran to coordinate activities of several Iraqi opposition groups. It is headed by Hakim Bakr.

* Kurdistan Democratic Party
(al-Hizb al-Dimuqraati al-Kurd) (KDP)
Kurdish party founded in 1946. It was originally led by Mullah Mustafa Barzani who led the struggle for autonomy of the Kurds in Iraq, for over 30 years. This struggle came to a temporary

end in 1975 after the Shah of Iran had ceased to support the Kurds and had concluded a treaty with the government of Iraq. Barzani died in exile in the US on Mar.1, 1979. In 1977 the DPK resumed the armed struggle against Iraqi government forces. Since mid-1979 the struggle intensified. The government deported Kurds from the mountainous northern border area where some 5,000 Pesh Mergas were fighting. In 1986 it claimed to have 10,000 guerrillas and a militia of similar size. It is supported by Iran, Libya and Syria. The government concluded an agreement with Turkey to crush Kurdish guerrilla activities. It is led by Massoud Barzani. In November 1986 a cooperation accord was signed with the PUK which meant an end to the rivalry and conflicts between the two parties.

* Kurdistan Democratic Party (Provisional Leadership) (KDP)
Iraqi government forces took the Kurdish Democratic Party headquarters at Galala in April 1975. Barzani fled to Iran before emigrating to the USA. After 1979, his sons, Idriss and Massoud, inherited the KDP leadership and reverted to traditional guerrilla warfare tactics. The party was known as the KDP (Provisional Leadership) and counted on 7,000 armed men. A late 1979 congress failed to resolve differences between the party's 'traditionalist' and 'intellectual' factions. Idris Barzani, the traditionalist, died on January 31, 1987. Before his death he succeeded in signing a cooperation accord with the Patriotic Union of Kurdistan (PUK).

* Kurdistan Revolutionary Party (KRP)
A party which originated as a secessionist offshoot of the original Kurdish Democratic Party and in 1974 joined the National Progressive Front along with the neo-KDP and another offshoot, the Progressive Kurdistan Movement. At a conference in January 1978, KRP members remaining in Baghdad reiterated their support for the National Front.

* Kurdish Socialist Party (BASSOK)
Offshoot of the Democratic Party of Kurdistan that engaged in armed resistance against the government forces in Kurdistan. It is led by Dr.Mahmoud Othman and Rasoul Hamand. In November 1980 BASSOK had joined with other Iraqi opposition groups to establish the Damascus-based National Democratic and Pan-Arab Front of forces seeking to overthrow the Saddam Hussein regime.

* The Listening Post
(Al Mukharabat)
Iraq's secret service which was established soon after the Baath Party seized power in July 1968. It controls all aspects of political, military and economic life and carries out intelligence and violent operations abroad. Hit teams have murdered opponents of President Saddam Hussein. One such murder was reported in London in July 1978, when General Abdul Razzak al-Naif, former Prime Minister of Iraq, was assassinated outside the Intercontinental Hotel. The assassination group is known as Al Hunain. The service is commanded by Brigadier Khalil al-Wazir. It also carried out military and technical espionage on behalf of the Soviet Union. Iraq security officers were sent for training at KGB and GRU schools in the Soviet Union. The Soviets supplied the Iraqis with modern espionage and interrogation equipment. The service also engaged in repression of the Kurds. In October 1985, 300 Kurdish children were imprisoned. Hundred of them were executed in early 1987. Relatives of the children have confirmed that the dead bodies showed signs of torture.

* Mahlis Ulema
Iraqi opposition group run from Iran by Mehdi Hakim's brother Bakr.
* Martyr Abu Jafar Group
Iraqi opposition group.

* Mujaheddin
Iraqi opposition group led by exile Mehdi Hakim. It has claimed responsibility for bomb attacks in Karachi (Pakistan) on French targets in February 1983, to protest against increasing French military aid to the Ba'athist regime. The targets included offices of Air France and of the Alliance Francaise and the residence of the French consul.

* National Democratic and Pan-Arabic Front (Al-Jabham al-Wataniyah al-Qawmiyah ad-Dimuqratiyah fi al-Iraq)
Set up in Damascus (Syria) on Nov.12, 1980, by eight Iraqi opposition groups. Each member of the front was to retain its own ideological political organizational independence and independent activities. Its aim was stated to be the overthrow of the existing 'dictatorial regime' in Iraq and to establish a national coalition government which would achieve democracy for Iraq and self-rule for Kurdistan within the framework of Iraqi national sovereignty. The group has been involved in assassinations of Sunni Baathists and sabotage of rail links and ammunition depots near Basra.

* National Front for the Liberation of Iraq (NFLI)
Coalition of dissident groups, brought together by Syria and which had an interest in toppling the Iraqi President Saddam Hussein. It was set up in London in 1980 and is headed by General Mustafa Hasan Al Naqib. It included major Kurdish groups, the Call, dissident Baath party factions and the

Iraqi Communist Party.

* Patriotic Union of Kurdistan (PUK)
Kurdish party which was established in July 1975 by a merger of a Kurdistan National Party, the Socialist Movement of Kurdistan and an Association of Marxist-Leninists of Kurdistan. It is headed by Jalal Talabani and has been involved in sporadic attacks on government forces, partly from Iranian territory, in support of its demand for complete autonomy for Kurdistan. Its headquarters is located in Damascus and it is supported by Iran, Libya and Syria. In the end of the 1970s the PUK was in conflict with the Democratic Party of Kurdistan and in Oct.1978 the PUK claimed in Stockholm that the DPK had executed three PUK members a year earlier. It claimed to have 8,000 Pesh Mergas and a volunteer militia of 5,000 men. Since it joined an alliance with the Kurdish Democratic Party in November 1986, it has stepped up its activities and attacked oil installations in Kirkuk. Since then the government has stepped up army operations against the Kurds, including the alleged use of chemical weapons in bombardments on the villages of Balisan, Haledan, Jargalu, Kanitu, Awaje and Chinare. It also deported thousands of Kurds in the oil-rich area around Kirkuk and Khanaqin to the south.

* Popular Liberation Army of Iraq
Offshoot of the Communist Party which emerged in 1964.

* The Rafidein Movement-Vanguards of Hezbollah in Iraq
Obscure group which issued a warning not to proceed with the meeting of the Islamic Conference Organization in Kuwait in January 1987. It threatened with terrorist attacks.

* Supreme Council of the Islamic Revolution of Iraq (SCIRI)
Iraqi Shi'ite group opposed to the prosecution of the war with Iran. It was established in November 1982, and is led by Hojatoteslam Seyyed Mohammed Bakr Hakim, an exiled Iraqi religious leader. The group provides humanitarian assistance to refugees and recruits Iraqi refugees for Khomeini's Revolutionary Guards and plays a role as a kind of parent organization for four operational terrorist groups. Dawa is one of them. The council has links with the Islamic Amal faction in Lebanon. Seyyed Mohammed Bakr Hakim is also secretary general of the Combatant Ulema Society.

* Those Who Face Death
(Pesh Mergas)
Armed wing of the Democratic Party of Kurdistan. Its strength was estimated at 20,000 in the 1960s and at 50,000 in the 1970s.

* Unified Socialist Party of Kurdistan (USPK)
Syria-supported Kurdish nationalist splintergroup which emerged in 1979. The group sprang to prominence in January 1981, when it kidnapped a number of West German technicians. Until Aug.1981 Dr.Magmoud Osman led the USPK.

* Volunteers of the Peoples Army of Iraq (VPAI)
Volunteer force established to fight on the front in the war with Iran. It has developed into a real military force. The volunteers are trained in two periods of a month. About 100,000 are permanently stationed at the front. It has an estimated total strength of 500,000. It is headed by Taha Yassin Ramadhan, the number two of the Saddam Hussein regime. Originally it was a militia of militants and 'spearpoint' of the Ba'ath party. They are armed with light weapons. A large number of Egyptians who live in Iraq have become member of the People's Army.

ISRAEL

* The Avengers
Unofficial murder squad of the MOSSAD for revenge actions.

* Center for Political Planning and Research (CPPR)
This is the smallest branch of Israeli intelligence and part of the Foreign Ministry. It was extended after the intelligence failure in the October war but is still a relatively small research department. Its main function is to provide political analysis based on intelligence 'raw material' collected by the Mossad and Military Intelligence. Arie Levin was mentioned in the press as a successor to Yitzhak Oron as the new Director of the center.

* Defense Organization
(Haganah) (DO)
Underground Jewish defense organization founded in Jerusalem and Jaffna during unrest in Palestine. They were active before the armed rebellion of 1936-39. During the Second World War, the British military used the men involved for unconventional warfare in Syria, where the units were known as Palmach. They numbered some 80,000 including soldiers, activists and reservists and in 1944 became the Jewish Brigade Group. In the reserve troops (Mishmaar Haam) women were in the majority. After the war the group was disbanded, whereupon Haganah revived as a clandestine body involved in guerrilla sabotage operations. It favoured the establishment of the state of Israel. In the war with the Arabs after the British had withdrawn, it formed the backbone of the Israeli army in 1947 and 1948.

* Family of Jihad

Major Arab resistance movement which is closely allied with the Moslem Brotherhood in Israel. Israeli security forces broke up the movement and charged members with conspiracy to conduct guerrilla operations in collaboration with Al Fatah.

* Fighters for the Freedom of Israel (Stern gang) (Lohame Herut Israel) (LHI)
A breakaway faction from the IZL led by Abraham Stern. He would not observe the truce between IZL and the British on the outbreak of the war with Germany. He inspired and led terrorist attacks against the British in Palestine, and against more moderate Jews who opposed the use of terrorism to gain political objectives. Its strength was estimated at a few hundred to about 1,000 in 1947. Stern was succeeded by David Friedman Yellin in 1942. Up to 1943 no more than a handful of Jews, Arabs and British policemen died at the hands of the gang. But thereafter isolated attacks were escalated into a campaign of murder. Many were rounded up and deported. Others joined the Haganah.

* General Staff Reconnaissance Unit (Sayaret Matkal) (SM)
The Israeli government's elite anti-terrorist force which has been responsible for many of Israel's counter terrorist operations. The Sayaret Matkal is answerable directly to the chief of military intelligence and is never mentioned by name in Israeli military communiqués. The unit is known colloquially as 'Ha Yehida' (The Unit) and its members as 'Ha Hevreh' (The Guys). Members also operate undercover in the streets of Beirut and in rural Lebanon. The unit's emphasizes speed, decisiveness and the art of the pre-emptive strike.

* Group 101 (or 1001)
Unofficial murder squad of the MOSSAD for revenge attacks.

* Institution for Intelligence and Special Services (Le Aliyah Beth) (MOSSAD)
The largest and most aggressive of Israel's intelligence gathering and special operations services. It is Israel's external espionage organization with agents in most parts of the world. It employs 1,500-2,000 men and women of whom 500 are officers. It was officially constituted in 1951 under the leadership of Isser Harel and was built on the intelligence arm of the pre-war Haganah. The other two main arms of the Israel secret service are the Shin Beth and the Aman. According to press reports its present head is Nahum Adnoni. The new organization was considerably helped by the CIA with up-to-date training methods and with the latest equipment. It has a comprehensive disinformation department and works closely with Western security services. The Mossad has a total of eight departments, the most important of which are Collection, Operational Planning and Co-ordination, and Political Action and Liaison. It has a virtual monopoly on the collection of intelligence outside Israel, with the exception of certain military targets which are the concern of the Military Intelligence. The Political Action and Liaison department has functioned for many years as something like a second Foreign Ministry. It can call on a special army unit (General Staff Reconnaisance Unit, Sayaret Matkal) for back up in its operations. Because it regards itself as being constantly involved in a struggle for survival it has never hesitated to use assassination as a tactic.

* International Security and Defense Systems (ISDS)
Private anti-terror company which has a government license. It is headed by Leo Gleser. Its export of technology and knowledge is estimated at 100 million dollars yearly. Israeli anti-terror specialists have worked in El Salvador and Guatemala. They helped install an electronic data system for the police in Guatemala and trained secret service employees in anti-guerrilla techniques and interrogation techniques. Israeli anti-terror trainers are good friends with General Stroessner in Paraguay, General Pinochet in Chile and General Mobutu in Zaire. Other customers of the company are Singapore, Taiwan and South Africa. Two dozen anti-terror specialists were sent to Sri Lanka in 1984. Following protests of Arab countries they were sent back. In a cooperative effort Israeli specialists together with the German GSG-9 train a Saudi Arabian anti-terror unit.

* Jewish Defense League (JDL)
Extreme right-wing organization which was established in New York in 1968. It is led by Rabbi Meir Kahane. It conducts counter-terrorist operations against militant Palestinians. It advocates the removal from the occupied West Bank and Gaza Strip of the Arab inhabitants. Members of the League engaged in bomb attacks and was held responsible for acts of vandalism against the property of Christian churches in Jerusalem. It was strongly opposed to the Israeli withdrawal from Sinai under the 1979 peace treaty with Egypt.

* Jewish Underground (JU)
Militant anti-Arab terror group. Israel convicted 25 members of anti-Arab bomb attacks in 1984.

* July Unit
Unofficial murder squad of the MOSSAD for revenge attacks.

* Kach Movement (KM)
Tiny extremist party headed by Rabbi Meir Kahane.

It has been involved in unauthorized settlements on the West Bank. It inserted a full-page advertisement in every major Israeli newspaper, advocating the expulsion of all Arabs from Israel as a 'stage' in the establishment of a 'Greater Israel'. Its methods include disturbing political meetings and beating up activists of moderate and left-inclined parties.

* Massada
Unofficial murder squad of the MOSSAD for revenge attacks.

* Military Intelligence
('Ama'n)
With 7,000 people, of whom only about 500 are officers, the Military Intelligence is more a Photoint, Elint and Sigint organization than any other branch of the community. The technical means of collection belong to it as do most of the documentation and more surprisingly most of the production of intelligence. Maj.Gen.Ehud Barak is head of the Military Intelligence.

* National Military Organization
(Irgun Zevai Leumi) (IZL)
Terrorist organization which was established in 1937 by David Raziel. The IZL responded to Arab attacks upon Jews with offensive actions and started a general terrorist campaign against the Arab population. After 1941, the IZL was led by Menachim Begin. The organization used violence as well as psychological warfare to wage its struggle. It had about 1,000 active fighters and about 6,000 supporters. In 1944 Begin operated alongside the Stern Gang in attacking British rule in Palestine by launching raids on government offices. His campaign found support from the US Hebrew Committee of National Liberation. Many IZl members joined the Israeli army in 1948, and its supporters established the right-wing Herut party.

* Naturei Carta (NC)
Anti-Zionist group whose members believe Jews do not have the right to establish a state until the appearance of the Messiah. It is led by Rabbi Moshe Hirsh. In October 1980 this orthodox sect (which claimed to have 5,000 followers in Jerusalem alone), distributed leaflets urging members of the orthodox community to resist state tax collection and even to murder tax collectors. In March 1981 hundreds of members were involved in street battles with police in Jerusalem.

* Rebirth Movement
(Tenuat Hathiya Tehiya) (THT)
Organization which was established in October 1979 by members of a number of right-wing groups that continue to exist outside the party structure. The party advocates formal annexation of the Gaza Strip, the West Bank and the Golan heights, without their inhabitants becoming Israeli citizens. It is led by Yuval Ne'eman, Geula Cohen and Moshe Shamir.

* Redemption of Israel
In 1978, ten members of this small organization were charged in Jerusalem with plotting to overthrow the government and to replace it with one functioning in strict accordance with Jewish religious law, and also with planning to commit murder and arson against Arabs in East Jerusalem with 'intent to incite hatred'. It was led by Yoel Lerner and Armand Azran.

* Security Department
(Sherut Habitachon) (Shin Beth)
Israeli counter-intelligence service which is responsible for Israel itself and the occupied territories. It has about 1,000 employees. It is belived to have eight departments responsible for information on subversive elements in the Israeli society, radical political movements, foreign delegation, terrorist activities and the occupied territories as well as for the training and protection of Israeli installations. Its head, Avraham Shalom reportedly has been involved in the murder April 1984 of two detained Palestinian terrorists. The case led to a big scandal in Israel. Sixteen months after the murder an inquiry commission was installed. According to press reports Shin Beth officials were forced to give false statements and to embezzle evidence material. It likes to operate through the civilian and military police wherever possible, making no arrests and remaining deep in the background. Following the official IDF withdrawal from south Lebanon in June 1985, an unofficial Israeli presence of up to a 1,000 members of the IDF and Shin Beth, assisted by the SLA, continued to control the 'security zone'. Shin Beth assisted running a prison in the town of Khiam. There have been reports of ill-treatment and torture of prisoners.

* Terror against Terror (TNT)
Jewish group which has been responsible for attacks against Arab targets including handgrenades on mosques.

* Wrath of God (WOG)
Name given to the assassination squads set up by the Israeli MOSSAD following the Munich Olympics attack in October 1972. Between October 1972 and November 1974 MOSSAD WOG teams are believed to have killed at least 12 Arabs (most of them Palestinians) believed by the Israelis to have been involved in the terror campaign against Israel. In July 1973 a MOSSAD team killed an innocent man in Lillehammer (Norway). The six members of the team were tried by Norwegian authorities.

• 007 Squad/Skymarshal
Israeli airliners all carry members of the 007 squad who have orders to fight it out in mid air if an El Al plane is attacked. In February 1969 Mordechai Rachamin killed one of three Arab gunmen during the Zurich airport attack. In September 1970 another EL Al Skymarshall shot dead an American-born hijacker (a PFLP member).

ITALY

• Alfa
During the funeral of General Franco (1975) in Spain General Pinochet of Chile had contacts with this right-wing Italian movement which was prepared to murder Chilean opposition leaders in exile in Europe on orders of the general.

• Anna Maria Ludmann Column
Red Brigades column which had been active in Venetia. Five members were captured in connection with the kidnapping of Brig.Gen. James L.Dozier, a US army staff officer and deputy commander of NATO land forces Southern Europe, on Dec.17, 1981. The BR issued several communiqués and on Dec.22 they announced that he had been found guilty by a 'people's court' and would be killed. However, on Jan.28, 1982, police freed the general unhurt and arrested the five BR members who were holding him in an apartment in Padua. The police action constituted the first occasion on which Italian police had succeeded in freeing a hostage seized by the BR.

• Anti-fascist Nuclei
(Nuclei Antifascisti)
On March 21, 1980, this small group bombed the offices of the Italian Social Movement (MSI) in Rome.

• Anti-fascist Proletarian Movement
Group which claimed responsibility for bomb attacks on four neighborhood offices of the Italian neo-fascist party on Jan.24, 1981.

• Anti-fascist Territorial Groups
(Gruppi Antifascisti Territoriali) (GAT)
Leftist group which claimed responsibility for the arson of a Rome movie theater on Jan.12, 1985, where a meeting of the rightist but lawful MSI was planned for the following day. The attack was also claimed by the rightist NAR.

• Anti-imperialist International Brigade
This group claimed responsibility for the detonation of a car rigged with explosives next to the US embassy on June 9, 1987, and fired rockets at the American and British compounds in Rome while leaders of seven industrialized countries met in Venice.

• Armed Communist Squads
(Squadri Armati Comunisti) (SAC)
Small left-wing terrorist group active in the early 1980s. It killed a state prosecutor in Salerno on March 16, 1980.

• Armed Communist Union (ACU)
One of the two wings of the renewed Red Brigades. One member was involved in a shootout with the police in Rome on Jan.22, 1987. He was possibly on his way for an attack on police judge Caselli.

• Armed Nazi Squad
(Squadre Nazi Armate) (SNA)
Neo-Nazi group which was responsible for the fire bombing of the home of a Jewish community leader in Livorno on Feb.17, 1980.

• Armed Nuclei for Territorial Alternative Power
Fascist group which shot dead two young MSI members in Rome in 1978. The attack led to riots and fighting between extremists of the left and right in the streets of the capital because leftist extremists were blamed for the attack.

• Armed and Organized Proletarian Group
(Gruppo Armato Organizzato Proletario) (GAOP)
On May 6, 1980, this small left-wing group shot and wounded two guards in Rome.

• Armed Patrols for Communism
(Ronde Armati per il Comunismo) (RAC)
Members of this left-wing group were responsible for the bombing of a labour exchange at Rovigo (south of Padua) on Feb.7, 1980.

• Armed Proletarian Power
(Potere Proletario Armato) (PPA)
This offshoot of the BR was responsible for attacking Germana Stefani, a physician employed at a woman's prison in Rome in December 1982 and for killing a woman warder at the same prison on Jan.28, 1983. Germana Stefani was overpowered in the lobby of her building and forced into her apartment, where she was 'tried' and 'sentenced' under an impromptu red banner. She was then led to an isolated area forced into the trunk of a stolen car and 'executed' with a pistol. Her task at the Rome's Rebibbia Prison was to check packages addressed to the inmates.

• Armed Proletarian Nuclei
(Nuclei Armati Proletari) (NAP)
Left-wing terrorist organization originating in Italian prisons in the late 1960s. Major prison uprisings occurred in Turin and Milan in 1969. Its first actions were reported in 1974. By January 1977 it was held responsible for 30 political crimes

which included the kidnapping of Guido De Martino, a socialist leader in Naples. Many members were arrested by the police in 1977, after which the movement was largely absorbed by the BR. It was believed to have formed a central command with the BR and it later claimed responsibility, together with the BR, for the murder of a prison guard in Udine on June 6, 1978. It probably numbered less than 100 activists; most members were only loosely attached to the organization.

* Armed Radical Groups for Communism
(Gruppi Armati Radicali per il Comunismo) (GARC)
Left-wing terrorist group responsible for bomb attacks in the late 1970s.

* Armed Revolutionary Nuclei
(Nuclei Armati Rivoluzionari) (NAR)
Neo-fascist organization which has been responsible for major bomb explosions and for the killing of a number of its political opponents. Among its actions figured a bomb explosion damaging the Capitol in Rome on Apr.20, 1979; a bomb attack on the regina Coeli prison in Rome on May 14, 1979; and an explosion at the Bologna railway station on Aug.2, 1980, when 85 persons were killed and 194 injured. The Bologna attack was reportedly carried out 'in honour of Mario Tutti, a right-wing extremist serving a life sentence for murdering a policeman and also charged with involvement in an explosion on a Rome-Munich express on Aug.5, 1974. The NAR later denied any involvement in the Bologna railway station explosion. Other targets of the group included members of the Workers Autonomy group, an office of the Communist Party, a policeman and a deputy public prosecutor. It surfaced again in 1985.

* Association for the Protection of Italians
Obscure right-wing group active in the late 1970s. It engaged in several bomb explosions in Bolzano province (South Tirol) in 1979. The group is committed to the use of violence to maintain the Italian status of the predominantly German-speaking South Tirol (ceded to Italy by Austria in 1919, and now part of the autonomous region of Trentino-Alto Adige).

* Autonomists
Generic name for groups which, between 1974 and 1977, sprang up in northern and central Italy. Since the early 1970s the Italian university system had been suffering from virtual collapse. The number of students grew to over a million (the Rome University served four times the number of students it was built for), and the prospects for jobs after graduation shrank dramatically. Autonomia found fertile soil among these discontended youths confined to universities which were described as 'social parking lots' as well as among workers hard hit by a declining economy. They also took root among the 'metropolitan spontaneists' and frichettoni(freaks) of the counterculture. What bound this groups was a repudiation of the work ethic, of alienated labor, and of the PCI's separation, of the revolutionary process. They called for the destruction of all power, beginning with the state.

* Ayatollah Hadi Khosraw-Shahi network
Press accounts reported that a network of politico-religious fanatics had been organized in Rome under the Iranian Ayatollah Hadi Khosraw-Shahi to carry out anti-Western subversive and possibly terrorist activity. This network reportedly included various foreign nationals, to wit Pakistanis, Tunesians, and Turks, and appeared to be modeled after one already operating in France.

* Black Order
(Ordine Nero) (ON)
This group was established in 1974 as a successor to the New Order organization which was banned in November 1973. It probably numbered some 300 loosely affiliated individuals. It did have no proper structure nor did it have contacts abroad. It has been involved in bloody bomb attacks including Brescia on May 28, 1974, (8 killed, 95 injured), Rome-Munich express train on Aug.5, 1974, (12 killed, 48 injured). The group seems to have been dormant since the mid-1970s. Mario Affatigato, a former leader of the group , was extradited from France to Italy on Sep.7, 1980, being suspected of involvement in the Bologna station explosion of Aug.2, 1980, attributed to the NAR. Its military leader, Pierluigi Concutelli, was convicted in Florence in 1978 of the 1976 murder of judge Vittorio Occorsio, who had been responsible for the dissolution of New Order in 1973. When on Aug.10, 1983, a bomb failed to derail the Milan-Palermo train, ON was again cited as likely to be responsible.

* Camorra
The power of organized crime embodied in the Mafia of Sicily and the Camorra of Naples, has manifested itself in numerous assassinations of opponents, including representatives of the state. The most significant of these murders has been that of General Carlo Alberto Dalla Chiesa (and his wife) in Palermo on Sept.3, 1982. The general had been co-ordinator of anti-terrorist measures since 1978 and had since May 1982, been directing operations against the Mafia. In the eight months before his death 103 murders were attributed to the Mafia. Official statistics gave the total number of Mafia killings in Palermo in 1982 as 151, while those attributed to the Camorra in Naples in the same year were given as 265. The strength of the hardcore of the Camorra was estimated at 5,000

man. In November 1985, 475 members went on trial. A 8,000-page report was prepared on the criminal activities of the Mafiosi which has been dubbed 'the encyclopedia of Mafia crimes'.

* Central Bureau for General Investigations and Special Operations
(Ufficio Centrale per le Indagini Generali e le Operazioni Speciali) (UCIGOS)
Agency set up by the Interior Ministry. Manned by State Police officers, the UCIGOS is responsible for the conduct of counter-terrorist operations. These operations are executed through the police headquarters at the provincial level, called Division for General Investigations and Special Operations (DIGOS) in the main centers and UIGOS where the U stands for Ufficio (Office) in smaller centers. UCIGOS was later renamed 'Central Directorate of the Prevention Police' (DCPP).

* Central Directorate of the Prevention Police
(Direzione Centrale della Polizia di Prevenzione) (DCPP)
Operative arm of the counter-terrorist organization, previously called UCIGOS. It is divided into two services, the General Investigations Service and the Special Operations Service. The agency has in a short time gained very specialized experience of counter-terrorism. It works together with the territorial structure of the Carabinieri.

* Central Special Operations Cells
(Nuclei per le Operazioni Centrali Speciali) (NOCS)
Highly specialized intervention groups of the police.

* Communist Fighting Nuclei
(Nuclei Combattenti Comunisti) (NCC)
A group under this name claimed responsibility for a bomb explosion which, on Jan.3, 1982, shattered the outside wall of the prison at Rovigo enabling three women of the Front Line and one of the Red Brigades to escape. More than 30 members received prison sentences after being convicted for attempted homicide, kidnapping, robbery, bombing attacks and violation of arms regulations.

* Communist Group for Internationalism
Group which has been responsible for attacks on the Honduran embassy and the Italy-US cultural exchange center in 1984.

* Communist Group for Proletarian Internationalism

Left-wing group active in the early 1980s. It engaged in attacks on embassies and newspaper offices.

* Communist Nucleus
(Nucleo Comunista) (NC)
Left-wing group that claimed responsibility for bomb attacks on a prison under construction near Pesaro in 1982.

* Compagne Organizzate per il Contropotere Femministe
Group which attacked the embassy of Taiwan in February 1981. It demanded the release of the widow of Mao, mistaking the embassy for the one of the People's Republic of China.

* Compass Card
(Rosa dei Venti) (RV)
Right-wing movement supported by some members of the armed forces. It was investigated by the authorities in late 1973, when a list of some 2,000 persons was found whom the movement allegedly planned to assassinate after a coup.

* Communist Patrols for Counter-power
(Ronde Comunisti per Contrapotere) (RCC)
Members of this group were responsible for bombing police barracks in Rome on Apr.4, 1980.

* Confidential Matters Office
(Ufficio Affari Riservati) (UFR)
Organization of the Interior Ministry for counter terrorist action which was transformed into the Inspectorate for Anti-terrorist Action. It later was succeeded by SISDE.

* Continuous Struggle
(Lotta Continua) (LC)
Maoist group which held its first national Congress in 1979. It had existed for a decade on the local level and attracted considerable attention through the columns of its own publication. Its leaders wére Guido Vale, Francesco Tolin and Pier Paolo Pasolini. Some of its members were involved in acts of violence mainly directed against rightists. Targets included the office of the Italian Social Movement in Turin.

* Division for General Investigations and Special Operations
(Divisione per le Investigazioni Generali e le Operazioni Speciali) (DIGOS) See UCIGOS.

* Executive Committee for Intelligence and Security Services
(Comitato Executivo per i Servizi di Informazione e Sicurezza) (CESIS)
Special committee coordinated by the Prime Minister's Office which controls the SISDE and SISMI intelligence agencies.

* Front Position
(Prima Posizione) (PP)
Group claiming responsibility for killing a

Carabinieri officer in Milan on Jul.16, 1982.

* Front Line
(Prima Linea) (PL)
Group which was established in November 1976 as one of the groups of 'organized autonomists' outside the three major union federations, with a largely working class membership. It was led by Sergio Segio (arrested Jan.15, 1983) and Corrado Alunni (a leading BR figure) and had up to 100 hardcore members. There was no recognized leadership, each unit or cell operated on its own. The attacks were aimed at 'the military and political institutions of the state and to sabotage the regular functioning of the capitalist machinery'. It targeted industrialists, a university professor, magistrates, judges, policemen, a public prosecutor and a business school. It adopted popular local causes to deepen its roots in society. By Feb.6, 1982, the police claimed to have 'neutralized' 15 PL bases in various parts of the country. It announced its self-dissolution in April 1983.

* Front Line Armed Nucleus
(Nucleo Armato dalla Prima Linea) (NAPL)
Left-wing terrorist group active in the early 1980s.

* Inspectorate for Anti-Terrorist Action
Ispettore per l'Azione contro il Terrorismo) (IAT)
Organization of the Ministry of the Interior for counter terrorist action. It was succeeded by SISDE.

* Italian Fighters for Alto Adige
Right-wing movement active in 1979 and 1980. It engaged in bomb explosions and arson attacks. It demanded the restoration of an Italian war memorial which was said to have been destroyed by militant (German-speaking) South Tiroleans.

* Italian Social Movement
(Movimiento Sociale Italiano) (MSI)
Right-wing party led by Giorgio Almirante which in the past had lent cover to violence committed by fringe groups. It spawned a whole cluster of fascist secret societies to mount a terrorist campaign against the democratic institutions of the Republic and against the communists of the PCI and the neo-Marxist terrorist groups of the extreme left. It attempted to become a normal political party. MSI's party offices have served as 'base camps' for groups of young fascist thugs roaming the streets in search of left-wingers to be beaten up. They mounted 'revenge' attacks following the death of a member of the security forces in the 1969-1974 period. By 1974 the violence of fascist terrorist groups lost momentum when their leaders lost contacts with their former protectors in the security forces. The initiative in political violence switched to the Red Brigades and other left-wing groups. The right did not regain the initiative until 1980.

* Ludwig Group
(Gruppe Ludwig)
By February 1983 two members of this Neo-Nazi group, Marco Furlan and Wolfgang Abel, had committed eight to ten murders, including three priests. The victims were stabbed, burned or assaulted with a hammer and a hatchet. All of them were either social deviants (gypsies, drug addicts, homosexuals and prostitutes) or 'unworthy' clergymen. The first murders took place in the Veneto region and in the municipality of Trento. After each incident a leaflet was distributed in Italian in runic characters explaining the reasons for the latest murder. In May 1983 the group extended its sphere of action. It claimed responsibility for the burning of the Milan movie theater 'Eros' resulting in the death of six spectators. Responsibility claims were also issued by Ludwig for the arson of two porno centers in Amsterdam and Munich in December 1983 and January 1984 respectively. Furlan and Abel went on trial in December 1986 and are facing life sentences.

* Mafia
('Onerata Societa')
Criminal organization principally based in Sicily, with branches in other parts of the country and gangs which operate independently. Since 1977 it has changed its strategy and tactics. It started to kill anybody who formed a threat to the organization including policemen, journalists, politicians and magistrates. Also the character of the organization changed. The rivalling clans which were involved in small scale extortion developed into syndicates concentrating on drug traffic and illegal arms trade. In recent years the authories have stepped up law enforment activities and have made use of reduced sentences in return for information. One of the most well-known 'pentiti' is mafia leader Tomasso Buscetta, who was extradited from Brazil to Italy. In a 3,000-page statement he explained in which activities the Mafia has been involved in recent years. On the basis of his statement several hundred members of the mafia including many leaders have been arrested and tried.

* March 28 Brigade
Red Brigades column which has been responsible for the assassination of Walter Tobagi, a journalist of Corriere della Sera in Milan, on May 28, 1980. Tobagi was co-author of a book on the psychology of terrorism and had, after police had killed four BR suspects on March 28, 1980, written a newspaper article on the 'disintegrating myth of the (Genoa) column of the BR'. On Sep.9, 1980, all

members were arrested.

* Marksmen
(Schuetzen)
Secret organization which has been involved in terrorist attacks in Alto Adige (South Tirol), including a bomb attack on a post office in June 1986.

* Movement for Armed Proletarian Power
Small left-wing organization which has been active in Rome.

* Mussolini Action Squads
(Squadre d'Azione Mussolini) (SAM)
Secret right-wing society which was established in the early 1970s. It repeatedly claimed responsibility for bomb attacks on offices of left-wing organizations before 1974. It also engaged in street violence and murdered magistrates. Groups which acted alongside the SAM were Phoenix (La Fenice), Year Zero (Anno Zero), National Vanguard (Avanguardia Nazionale) and Young Italy (Giovine Italia). It was not clear which group has been responsible for the bomb attack during a public rally against fascism in Brescia (Lombardy) in May 1974. Eight people died and 95 were injured in the attack.

* National Front
(Fronte Nazionale) (FN)
Group which allegedly has been involved in a plot to overthrow the Republic between 1969 and 1972. It was led by Prince Junio Valerio Borghese who died in Spain in August 1974. In September 1975 the attorney-general proposed charges to be brought against 84 people, for trying to seize power in 1970 in an operation known as 'Tora, Tora'.

* National Vanguard
(Avangardia Nazionale) (AN)
Neo-fascist group which was formed in 1959 by Stefano della Chiaie. It has been accused by the Minister of Interior on Aug.13, 1974 of trying to create chaos. One of the group's leading members, Pier Luigi Concutelli, confessed of having murdered judge Vittorio Occorsi in Rome on July 10, 1976. Before 1974 it has been involved in bomb attacks on offices of left-wing groups. On Dec.7, 1970, the AN was involved in what was suspected to be a coup d'état attempt against the Italian government when they forced their way into the Ministry of Interior and seized 200 machine guns. The 'coup' was called off by its leader Prince Valerio Borghese. The AN has contacts with numerous other right-wing groups in Greece, Spain, Portugal and France and has tried to establish a right-wing terrorist international, the 'Black Orchestra'. The group has been involved in the attack on the Bologna railway station in 1980 in which 85 people were killed and more than 200 were injured.

* N'drangheta
Organized crime organization in Calabria. Giuseppe Piromalli, the 'charismatic leader' of the organization went on trial in June 1986 together with 109 other members. They were charged with 27 murders, five kidnappings, 16 murder attempts and extortion. Seventeen defendents were sentenced to life in prison. The others received prison sentences of up to 61 years or were acquitted. In the 1979-1980 period 100 deaths, 150 unsuccessful attacks and 200 bomb attacks have been recorded. With the October 1985 murder of Paolo de Stefano, an important N'drangheta leader in Reggio di Calabria gang killings increased significantly. The murder ended a 'pax mafiosi' and produced a general breakdown of the underworld's own rules and regulations. During 1986, a total of 112 killings were reported in the Calabria region. Small towns with broad beaches have been used as points of entry for herion that was then shipped to the industrial cities of Northern Italy.

* New Armed Partisans for Communism
Group which claimed responsibility for bombing a national television transmitter in Trent that caused a blackout. In a leaflet it said: 'against the disinformation of national radio-television, against those who prepare war and the armaments race...against dismissals and unemployment; for the mobilization of the masses, for the proletarian cause, from Trent to Sicily, resistance now and forever.'

* New Order
(Ordine Nuovo) (ON)
Right-wing organization founded by Tino Rauti, a journalist and former member of the Italian Social Movement. The organization was banned on Nov.23, 1973, after 30 of its members had been sentenced to prison terms on charges of trying to reconstitute the Fascist Party and belonging to the New Order. It had some 600 members in a dozen cities. Membership ranged from lawyers and businessmen to students and workers, mostly under 30 years old. There was no structure to the organization which was led by Giorgio Almirante. It has been involved in the attack on the Bologna railway station in 1980 in which 85 people were killed and more than 200 were wounded.

* New Organized Camorra
(Nuova Camorra Organizzata) (NOC)
In February 1985, 252 people went on trial, accused of being a member of this organization. In the summer of 1984 640 people were arrested in a national action. Most of them were being suspected of being a member of the gang which is headed by

Raffaele Cutolo. The gang, together with the Mafia, has been the significant force behind the drug traffic in Italy. More than 700 people were killed in clashes which Cutolo started in 1980 with other groups within the Camorra to gain the leading role in the drugs and cigarette trade. The trials were held in a specially-built heavily guarded bunker in the Poggioreale prison in Naples.

* Nuclei of Territorial Communists
(Nuclei Comunisti Territoriali)
A member of this group killed a janitor at the Fiat plant in Turin on Jan.31, 1980. In connection with arson at the Lancia works and the killing of a nightwatch in January 1980, a group of 25 suspected members of the group were arrested in Turin on Feb.6, 1982.

* October 22 Group
(Circulo XXII Ottobre)
A group which emerged from the 1968 student revolt. It attracted mainly former members of the PCI. The reason for the defection was the pragmatic and less doctrinaire approach to politics which Enrico Berlinguer, the PCI leader had introduced. Amongst the better known names were Rinaldi Fiorani, Silvio Malagoli and Mario Rossi. The group engaged in kidnappings and bank robberies. It cooperated with the Partisan Action Groups. Most members were caught and imprisoned. Others joined the Red Brigades.

* Organized Comrades for Proletarian Liberation
(Compagni Organizati per la Liberazione Proletaria) (COLP)
Group which was established in the early 1980s by PL members Sergio Segio and Susanna Ronconi, to free prison inmates committed to the 'armed struggle'. It is the principal element of the Italo-French terrorist connection.

* Organization of Fighting Communists
(Organizzazione Comunista Combattente) (OCC)
Group active in 1980, attacking in particular a politician in Milan on Feb.10.

* Partisan Action Groups
(Gruppi d'Azione Partigiana) (GAP)
Members of this organization were officially held responsible for a number of acts of violence, notably against NATO installations and also against political opponents, and for the murder of the Bolivian consul-general in Hamburg in 1971. Giangiacomo Feltrinelli, a publisher whose dead body had been found on Mar.15, 1972, near a power-line pylon to which explosives were attached, was said to have been an active member of the GAP. Incriminating material, found on Apr.15, 1972, indicated that Feltrinelli had been involved in organizing a network of left-wing 'resistance centers' against a possible rightwing coup. However, all charges against persons suspected of involvement in the conspiracy were dropped in 1973. After Feltrinelli's death members of the GAP probably joined other groups, excluding the Red Brigades. They engaged in arson attacks.

* Proletarians for Communism
(Proletari per il Comunismo) (PC)
Group believed to be connected to the Red Brigades. On Jan.2, 1984, bystander Stanislao Ceresio, an employee of the State Railroad Administration, was killed in Portici (Naples), when the automobile of prison guard Giuseppe Montelone exploded. Responsibility for the car bombing was claimed by the PC.

* Propaganda Two
Propaganda Due (P-2)
One of about 550 Free Masonic Lodges in Italy. It became known in March 1981 when the police revealed a list of 931 alleged members and other documents showing that the lodge had been involved in large-scale crimes but also in right-wing terrorist activities in the late 1960s and 1970s, including a bomb explosion in Milan in 1969 and the bomb attack at the Bologna railway station in 1980. The lodge was headed by Lucio Gelli (Grand Master). In a report to the government by a Milan magistrate in May 1981 it was stated that the P-2 lodge is a secret sect which has combined business and politics with the intention of destroying the constitutional order of the country and transforming the parliamentary system into a presidential system. A total of 22 members, including a former head of the secret service (SID), were charged with political conspiracy and activities against the state.

* Proletarian Squadron
(Squadre Proletari) (SP)
Members of this group reportedly killed, on Dec.11, 1980, a Christian Democratic mayor accused of having misappropriated earthquake relief funds.

* Red Brigades-Fighting Communist Party
(Brigate Rosse-Partito Comunista Combatente) (BR-PCC)
Breakaway of the Red Brigades formed in 1982. The group assumed responsibility for an attempt to murder a professor of labour law in Rome on May 3, 1983. Together with another RB faction, the Union of Fighting Communists, it is estimated to have 150 members. The two factions have tried to make contact with environmentalist groups and the peace movement. By concentrating on an anti-NATO and anti-Starwars program they also attempted to open a road to a possible cooperation with the West German RAF and the French AD.

* Red Brigades

(Brigate Rosse) (RB)
Marxist-Leninist urban guerrilla organization modelled on the Tupamaros in Uruguay which was established in 1969. Its most important leaders were Renato Curcio (jailed since 1976), Margharita Cagol (killed in 1975 in a shootout) and Alberto Franceschini (chief ideologue). It operates in 'columns' in cities or regions and has a cell structure. It had an estimated membership of 500 activists with a further 10,000 supporters. It has been been involved in arson, kidnapping, kneecapping, assassinations and bank robberies. At least 50 people have been killed. Since the abduction of General Dozier in 1982, at least 340 members have been arrested. The original aim was to create a revolutionary situation and a revolutionary consciousness among the masses by demonstrating the feasibility of armed struggle; the return of the Communist Party to a radical opposition was part of this goal. The Red Brigades as such do not exist any longer. It split in two factions, the Party of Fighting Communists and the Union of Fighting Communists, which continue the political and 'terror-technical' tradition of the Red Brigades. In raids on leftwing bookshops in several Italian cities in February 1987, the police captured what were believed the political manifestos of both groups.

* Red Squad Organized Campaign
(Squadra Rossa Campagni Organizzati) (SRCO)
Left-wing terrorist group that killed an employee of a right-wing newspaper in 1980.

* Revolutionary Action Movement
(Movimiento d'Azione Rivoluzionaria) (MAR)
Right-wing organization led by Carlo Fumagalli who was jailed in 1978. In the north of the country MAR ran paramilitary training camps for young men. In 1974, Carlo Fumagalli and 21 MAR members were arrested after the discovery of an arms smuggling ring linking subversive right-wing movements in Milan and Brescia regions. The MAR was accused of having planned to set up, in collaboration with the Compass Card group, a fascist republic in Italy. The organization had sought and gained funds through ransoms.

* Revolutionary Action
(Azione Rivoluzionaria) (AR)
Small left-wing group active in 1980. It was led by professor Gianfranco Faina.

* Revolutionary Fascist Nuclei
(Nuclei Fascisti Rivoluzionari) (NFR)
Right-wing terrorist group active in 1980. It has been responsible for the murder of the president of the Sicilian Regional Council in Palermo.

* Revolutionary Mass Organisations
(Organismi di Massa Rivoluzionari) (OMR)
Left-wing group active in 1983. Four members have been charged with robbery and illegal possession of arms.

* Sardinian Action Party
(Partido Sardo d'Azione Psd'Az) (PSAP)
Party in Sardinia seeking independence from Italy.

* Sardinian Armed Movement
(Movimiento Armato Sardo) (MAS)
Party in Sardinia; its goals include the selling of military installations on the island to the highest bidder; an insular economy based principally on tourism; and eventually Sardinian independence. It also proposed the punishment of those who destroy or undermine 'the morality, proper way of living and noble traditions' of Sard society and warned that it would 'restore justice' where abuses are not cured. It has been responsible for six murders in 1983. It is led by Annino Mele.

* Sardinian Independentist Front
(Fronte Independista Sardo) (FIS)
Sardinian party striving for independence. It is led by Bainzu Piliu. Members of the group were arrested on charges of planning sabotage at Cagliari airport, the NATO base at Decimannu and refineries, as well as the abduction of a US officer. Those arrested included several members of the Sardinian Action Party.

* Sardinian Independist Party
(Partidu Independista Sardu) (PARIS)
In January 1984, the party demanded from the US government a payment of $ 5 billion as rear rent for the submarine base at La Maddalena. It remains to be seen whether this demand will be backed by violence.

* Service for Intelligence and Democratic Security
(Servizio Informazioni Sicurezza Democratica) (SISDE)
Secret intelligence and security service of the Ministry of the Interior. It is controlled by the Prime Minister's Office through a special committee called CESIS. It is headed by General G.Grassini (a member of P-2). It is the oldest service formed as a direct consequence of the terrorist wave of the 1970s. Manned exclusively by civilians, it is the principal counter-terrorist intelligence service.

* Servizio Informazioni Difensa (SID)
Italian secret service. According to a statement of General Ambrogio Viviani, the service helped Libyan leader Moammar Qadhafi to stay in power. The service supplied weapons and foiled a plot to overthrow the Libyan leader. It also helped to organize a Libyan secret service and sent experts

to organize a modern army. One of its former heads provided passports for imprisoned terrorists sentenced for involvement in bomb attacks.

* Service for Military Intelligence and Security
(Servizio Informazioni Sicurezza Militare) (SISMI)
Military intelligence service of the Defense Ministry which is headed by General G.Santorito (a member of P-2). It is controlled by the Prime Minister's Office through a special committee called CESIS. Two former members, General Petro Musumeci and Francesco Pazienza, were sentenced in 1985 to nine years in prison and two and a half years in prison, respectively for crimes such as embezzlement of government money, theft of explosives, betrayal of state secrets and abuse of power. Pazienza has been mentioned in connection with the Banco Ambrosiano scandal, the murder attack on Pope John Paul II, the death of Roberto Calvi and the bloody bomb attack on the Bologna railway station. In a 1986 SISMI report it was said that the number of terrorist attacks in Italy has decreased in 1984 and 1985, to 85 and 64, respectively. The number of casualties was 20 in both years. The level of the 'traditional' criminality of organizations like the Camorro, Mafia, N'drangheta remained high. In the first three months of 1986 71 persons were killed while in the same period of 1985 77 people were killed.

* South Tirol Liberation Committee
(Befreiungsausschuss Südtirol) (BAS)
Organization favouring the return of South Tirol to Austria. It has been responsible for a large number of violent acts in the period 1963-1971. From 1980 onwards the aims of the committee were pursued by a group calling itself 'Tirol'.

* Special Intervention Groups
(Gruppi d'Intervento Speciale) (GIS)
Highly specialized intervention groups which were established in 1980 by the State Police. They are similar to the West German GSG-9 and the British SAS.

* Territorial Antifascist Squad
(Squadre Antifascisti Territoriali) (SAT)
Left-wing terrorist group active in 1980. It has been responsible for a bomb attack on a fascist newspaper office in Rome.

* Third Position
(Terza Posizione)
Group which presented itself as one of the so-called 'organized autonomists' (outside the three trade union federations) with a largely working-class membership. It advocated indiscriminate attacks on 'all enemies of the working class'. It was led by Roberto Fiore and G.Adinolfi who were reported to be hiding in England.

* Tirol
Group of German-speaking Tiroleans that has called for full self-determination for South Tirol. It has been responsible for a number of explosions in the early 1980s. Targets included power pylons and cars registered in other parts of Italy.

* Union of Fighting Communists
(Unita Combattenti Comunisti) (UCC)
Antonio Campesi, the group's leader and seven other members were arrested in Milan on Feb.18, 1980. Police believed that the group was an offshoot of the Red Brigades. On Feb.21, 1986, the group claimed responsibility for the armed attack on Antonio da Empoli, an economic adviser of Prime Minister Bettino Craxi. One of the attackers, a woman suspected as Red Brigades member, was killed in the attack. The group is also held responsible for the murders of the economist, Ezio Tarantelli, of the ex-mayor of Florence, Lando Conti, and of the air force general, Licio Georgeri in April 1987. On Feb.14, 1987, the group raided a mail-van and captured a sum of money equal to one million dollars. The structure of the group differs from the one of the Red Brigades. It is believed to have less firepower.

* Union for the Protection of Tyrol (UPT)
(Tiroler Schutzbund)
In German -speaking Tirol region of Alto Adige in Italy, members of the Tiroler Schutzbund have exploded a number of bombs without loss of life. Ethnically and geographically the region naturally forms a part of Austria rather than Italy. The population is particularly fearful of the influence on government of the Italian PCI and there is little doubt that disturbances of serious nature would arise were the PCI to assume state power.

* Walter Alasia Column
Offshoot of the Red Brigades established in 1980. It was responsible for the abduction of Renzo Sandrucci, an Alfa Romeo executive on June 10, 1981. After a claim by the police that it had been broken up it reappeared in 1983. After the imprisonment of Aurore Betti, the group's historic leader, he was succeeded by Nicolo Di Maria in 1981.

* Workers Autonomy Movement
(Autonomia Operaio) (AUTOP)
Illegal left-wing organization established as a successor to Workers' Power. A well-known member was Professor Toni Negri, a teacher of political science at Padua University. The organization was said to have links with the Red Brigades.

* Worker Power
(Potero Operaio) (PO)
In 1968 Professor Negri working at the University of Padua broke with the PCI. He called for a

'revolution from below' and embraced as the new agent of this revolutionary change the growing number of students, radicals, marginalized youth, and semi-employed workers of northern Italy. By the early 1970s it boasted 4,000 members and 1,000 militants. It dissolved in the summer of 1973. Two opposing lines had developed within the movement. One, led by Franco Piperno and Oreste Scalzone, wanted to organize PO along the strict lines of Leninist centralism and to guide the movement toward imminent insurrection. On the other hand, Negri advocated the dissolving of the organization into loosely connected groups of students and workers who would claim 'autonomy' or independence not only from capitalist society but from the PCI and the unions as well. These would go 'among the people' to create mass support for a future revolution.

* Workers Brigades (BO)
(Brigate Operaie)
In the Rome subway on Feb.9, 1985, a bag containing incendiary bottles seriously damaged an empty wagon. Had the explosion taken place a few minutes earlier or later, passengers would have been hurt. BO claimed responsibility for the attack. A leaflet stated: 'This is not an act of violence, but an act of love against the daily exploitation of the labor force from the hinterland to the material places of its exploitation. This is not a protest but a precise act of war.' A few terrorist actions had been perpetrated in Como in 1981 under the name of the Workers Brigades.

* Workers' Vanguard
(Avanguardia Operaia) (AO)
Movement which emerged in Italy as part of the New Left in 1971. Its members were drawn from the PCI, but even more from Maoist and Trotskyist groups. By the early 1970s it had some 30,000 adherents, many in the south. It did not advocate terrorism, but supported a more thorough-going revolutionary approach to politics. It was active amongst both workers and students and played an active role in the mobilization of street demonstrations.

* Year Zero
(Anno Zero) (AZ)
Neo-fascist groups active in the early 1970s.

* Young Italy
(Giovane Italia) (GI)
Right-wing group that engaged in acts of violence against leftists in the early 1970s.

* Youth Front
(Fronte dalla Gioventu) (FG)
Right-wing group that has been responsible for bomb attacks on offices of left-wing organizations in the early 1970s.

JAMAICA

* Jamaica Defense Force (JDF)
The Chief of Staff of the JDF said in December 1980 that the military were preparing to deal with possible 'threats to Jamaica's economic recovery' including 'industrial sabotage' and 'guerrilla or radical political activity'. He gave no names of organizations engaged in such activities. The 1980 election campaign was marked by unprecedented political violence, with the total of fatal shootings being given as 638.

JAPAN

* Battle Flag Mainstream Faction
(Senki-ha)
Extreme left-wing group which split off from Kyosando (radical communist alliance) in 1958. For years it concentrated on increasing its membership. Only after cooperation with the protest movement against the Narita airport it began an armed struggle. It has been very active in 1983 and 1984 with attacks on US military bases. It is opposed to the US-Japanese security treaty.

* Black Helmet
(Kuro Heru)
Group which has been responsible for the 1971 bomb attack on a police station in the Tokyo Shinjuku shopping district. It shared a bomb factory north-east of Tokyo with the Red Army.

* Cabinet Research Office
(Naicho)
Most important of four intelligence agencies in Japan. It is the Prime Minister's own security service and has a staff of less than 100 men. Up to two thirds of the Naicho budget is spent on commissioning reports from private institutions and journalists. First steps to the establishment of a central agency were taken in 1971 to work in cooperation with the United States in collecting and analyzing information from the outside world about political as well as military developments.

* Commune Minokamo
Leftist radical group which is striving for the overthrow of the existing societal order. It also rejects discrimination of minority groups. It was reportedly involved in a bomb attack in March 1976 in which two people were killed and 95 injured. Katsuhisa Omoni was convicted although he did not plead guilty.

* Defence Youth League
A member of this fascist group tried to stab Prime Minister Ohira outside his official residence,

injuring two bodyguards in December 1978. The attacker, Sumio Hirose, claimed to be inspired by the ideals of Yukio Mishima.

* East-Asia Anti-Japanese Armed Front (EAAJAF)
This left-wing urban terrorist group denounced 'Japanese imperialists' for occupying Hokkaido Island (the most northerly of Japan's four main islands) and demanded that this island should be returned to the original inhabitants, the Ainu. The front also claimed to fight for the rights of the Okinawa, Korean, Taiwanese, Baraku (social outcasts) and other Asian peoples. It has been responsible for numerous bomb attacks. Among the targets were Mitsubishi Heavy Industries headquarters (1974), Mitsui trading company (1975), the Korean Research Institute (1975) and government buildings in Sapporo (1976). In a trial of four members of the front two were sentenced to death on Nov.12, 1980, for their involvement in an attack on Aug.30, 1974, and for conspiring to assassinate the Emperor Hirohito in 1974. ('Operation Rainbow')

* Fangs of the Earth
Left-wing cell thought to be part of the East-Asia Anti Japanese Armed Front. Its policy was to attack offices of large business companies said to be exploiting underdeveloped Asian nations. The targets included the Tansei Construction Co.'s head quarter on Dec.12, 1974, and the computer room of Mitsui Products Co.'s main office on Oct.14, 1974.

* Fourth (Trotskyist) International-Japanese Section
Left-wing organization which played a leading role among the political groups which from 1971 onwards actively opposed the construction and opening of a new international airport at Narita. Demonstrations by local farmers, left-wing student groups and environmentalists led to several years delay in the completion of the airport. The months preceding and following the official opening of the airport on May 20, 1978, were characterized by violent riots.

* Hidaka Commando Unit
Unit which has been responsible for a hijacking on Sep.28, 1977. It was named after a comrade who died in prison in Jordan. The unit consisted of five men, Osamu Maruoka (Shigenobu's husband and leader of the unit), Norio Sadaki, Kazuo Tohira, Kunio Bando and Jun Nishikawa. All of them had been released by the Japanese government because of the Kuala Lumpur operation in August 1975.

* Ichiwa-kai
Gangster federation which in 1984 split from the Yamaguchi-gumi because it did not agree with the installation of Masahisa Takenaka as Kumi-Cho ('Godfather'). Although it had 6,000 members just after the split, membership later decreased to 2,800.

* Japanese Red Army, or Arab Red Army, or Army of the Red Star (Sekigunha, Rengo Sekigun or Nippon Sekigun) (JRA)
Terrorist group which has not been known to carry out any actions since it hijacked a JAL plane in September 1977. Its leaders are believed to be living in the Bekaa Valley in Lebanon. On Mar.19, 1981, it made public its first official communiqué in four years, in Beirut. It was led by Fusako Shigenobu ('Samira'). See United Red Army.

* Kansai's Regional Revolutionary Army (KRRA)
An anonymous telephone caller claimed that this group launched a bomb campaign to protest the visit of the US Enterprise to Sasebo in March 1983.

* Middle Core Faction
(Chukaku-ha)
Marxist breakaway faction from the National Federation of Students' Organizations established in 1960 to oppose the security treaty concluded between the US and Japan. Members of the faction were repeatedly involved in violent clashes with members of the rival Revolutionary Marxist faction. Chukaku-ha was involved in protest demonstrations against a visit to Okinawa by the crown prince and princess in 1975. It has been responsible for attacks on facilities of the Self-Defence Force, the Imperial Palace in Tokyo, the headquarters of the Liberal Democratic Party, and the commuter railway network in Osaka. It stepped up activities in 1985. Over the years it is believed to have been responsible for 100 deaths, mainly radicals of rival groups. It is estimated to have 5,000 members with a revolutionary army of 200. Five hundred members have been arrested in the May 1985-May 1986 period.

* The Mystery Man with 21 Faces
(Kaijin 21-Menso)
Mysterious group which in 1985 sent threat letters to food factories in an attempt to extort money. It threatened to poison food with cyanide. The name seemed to be a reference to 'Kaijin 20-Menso', a series of mystery books and television dramas for children that were popular 30 years ago.

* Okinawa Liberation League (OLL)
Group that expressed its opposition to the rule of the Imperial family and 'the imperialist bourgeoisie' of Japan over Okinawa (the largest of the Ryukyu islands) and the use of the island as a military base and terminal station for oil storage.

* Radical Revolutionary Workers Association

(Kakurokyo)
Left-wing radical group which has been active in 1985. It is one of the groups which claimed to have fired home-made missiles at the Akasaka and Togu palaces in Tokyo in April 1986. It tried to disturb an economic summit and the celebration of the 85th birthday of the emperor.

* Revenge Against Communism Corps
Ultra-nationalist group which has claimed responsibility for a shotgun attack ('divine punishment') in which a Japanese newspaper reporter was killed on May 3, 1987. Another journalist was injured. The group annouced that it would continue to murder people.

* Revolutionary Army of Kansai (RAK)
Group which claimed responsibility for two bomb attacks in Osaka on Feb.1, 1984.

* Revolutionary Marxist Faction
(Kakumaru-ha)
A breakaway group from the National Federation of Students' Organization which has been involved in violent clashes with the rival Middle Core Faction.

* Scorpion
Left-wing cell thought to be part of the East-Asia Anti-Japanese Armed Front which was active in the 1970s. Its policy was to attack the offices of large business companies said to be exploiting underdeveloped Asian nations. On Dec.23, 1974, it attacked the Kajima Construction company's headquarters. During World War II, Kajima used slave labor conscripted from Korea, China and Formosa in the war industries in Japan. It forced 986 Chinese prisoners of war to work in the Hanaoka agency of Akita province, and was responsible for the massacre of 418 of them through starvation, lynching, torture and other means of execution. The Chinese prisoners responded by launching an uprising which ended in failure and the further massacre of half of them.

* Shibayama Alliance
A group that has been opposed to the building and expansion of the Tokyo airport at Narita for 17 years. It broke into factions because of differences over strategy in March 1983.

* Shield Society
(Tatenokai)
Extreme right-wing organization established in 1967 which had been disbanded after the suicide of its leader, the well-known writer Yukio Mishima. It had about 100 members and its aim was to restore the ideals of the Samurai and to overturn the democratic 'Peace Constitution' imposed on Japan after World War II. It tried to restore the cult of the God-Emperor. On November 25, 1970, Yukio Mishima committed suicide (seppuku) in the Army Headquarters in Tokyo in front of the soldiers after an emotional speech.

* Showa Restoration League (SRL)
A right-wing group which still deifies the emperor despite his renunciation of divinity six months after the surrender of Japan in 1945. In1978 it tried to prevent a performance of a play in which Emperor Hirohito was displayed as a weak and tragic figure. The performance was cancelled after fighting broke out.

* Sons of the Occupied Territory (SOT)
Group which has been responsible for the hijacking of a Japanese Jumbo airliner after it left Amsterdam bound for Tokyo on July 20, 1973. The members of the group were Osamu Maruoka (Sekigun), three Arabs and a girl , a Christian Iraqi, Katie George Thomas. The hijacking became a disaster when Katie was killed while she accidentally exploded a grenade. She was the only one who knew the action plan.

* United Red Army
(Rengo Sekigun) (URA)
Leftist terrorist organization formed in 1969 by a merger of the Red Army Faction (which was an offshoot of the Trotskyist Communist League) and the Keihin Joint Struggle Committee. It agitated against the US-Japan Security Treaty and launched an armed struggle campaign for revolution. It was led by Miss Fusako Shigenobu. In February 1972 it militants 'executed' 14 alleged 'deviationists'. Its major operations were: the hijacking of JAL airliners (1970, 1973, 1977); the massacre at the Lod airport (1972); an attack on a Shell oil refinery in Singapore (1974); the occupation of the French embassy in The Hague (1974); the seizure of the US consulate and Swedish embassy in Kuala Lumpur (1975); the seizure of a bus in Nagasaki (1977). It was estimated to have 30 members and more than 100 sympathizers. In 1977 it was reported to have formed the United World Revolutionary Force in cooperation with other groups. In 1982 it announced that it had abandoned terrorism. Members were trained in Lebanon.

* VZ 58
In 1974 French police started to trawl through the Japanese community in Paris. They picked up hundred people for questioning and eight were deported. They included Mariko Yamamoto, a salesgirl at a Japanese department store. She was one of Fusako Shigenobu's (Red Army) closest associates. In her flat the police found a coded notebook with the addresses of some fifty safehouses in European cities. She was a key member of the the ten-member unit which called

itself VZ-58, the type of the assault rifle used in the Lod masscre.

* Wolf
(Okami)
Left-wing cell active in the 1970s thought to be part of the East-Asia Anti-Japanese Armed Front. Its policy was to attack the offices of large business companies said to be exploiting underdeveloped Asian nations. One of the attacks was directed at the main office of the Mitsubishi Heavy Industry on Aug.30, 1974. On Nov.12, 1979, Daidoji Masashi and Kataoka Toshiaki were sentenced to death.

* Yakuza
Largest confederation of Japanese gangsters. On Feb.8, 1987, its leadership decided to end its feud with an upstart rival over the question who should be the Godfather of the Japanese underworld. An estimated 108,000 members operate openly in Japan. The old godfathers prospered by peddling amphetamines, loan-sharking, gambling, smuggling, controlling prostitutes and 'protecting' people. The modern gang leader, more interested in money than in power, will smuggle heroin and weapons. Crime is spreading abroad. Across the Pacific, alliances are made with local gangs in Hawaii and on the American mainland. Yakuza have been active in Los Angeles and San Francisco buying import-export business, real estate, oil leases, night clubs, restaurants, gift shops and tour agencies. It is feared that the group may be moving into US heroin sales.

* Yamaguchi-gumi
Gangster federation which has been involved in clashes with a rival organization. The feud between the Yamaguchi-gumi and Ichiwa-kai began with the death (of old age) in 1981 of Kazuo Taoka who had ruled the Yamaguchi-gumi for 35 years. In 1984 Mr.Mashisa Takenaka was chosen as his successor. His main rival Mr.Hiroshi Yamamoto refused to be number two. He broke away to form the Ichiwa-kai, taking half of the 13,000 gangsters and most of the weapons. In 1985 Ichiwa-kai members fatally wounded Takenaka and two associates in Osaka where his mistress lived. The feud grew violent and spilled into the streets. In fights since June 1986 at least 25 people were killed and more than 70 yakuza were injured in more than 300 armed fights. Almost every yakuza now has a gun. Ten years ago there were practically no guns in Japan. Experts expect the conflict will last about two to three years.

* Youth League for the Overthrow of the Yalta and Potsdam Structure Group that has been responsible for taking hostage about a dozen leaders of the Federation of Economic Organizations (Keidanren) in Tokyo in 1977. It denounced big business for 'poisoning Japan's post-war society and its landscape' and also for corruption. Two members of the four man group had been members of the Shield Society. The league is opposed to the Allied decisions arrived at during the Yalta and Potsdam conferences in 1945 which it regarded as having destroyed Japan's political independence.

JORDAN

* Department of General Intelligence
(Da'irat al-Mukhabarat al-'Amma) (DMA)
Largest intelligence service in Jordan which carried out arrests for political reasons in recent years. Seventy such arrests were reportedly made during 1985. Six of those were tried, 14 were released and the others reportedly detained without trial. There were persistent reports that persons held incommunicado were subjected to torture and ill-treatment.

* Front for Syrian Struggle
Group which has been responsible for attacks on Jordanian diplomats in 1983.

* Jordanian Moslem Brotherhood (JMB)
Members of the Moslem Brotherhood found asylum in Jordan at the time of the movement's suppression by President Nasser of Egypt. It is represented in Amman by a spokesman of its international organization (while its headquarters have remained in Egypt) who stated that nobody in Jordan was perturbed by the movement. Nevertheless, the MB has supported the Iranian revolution whereas the Jordanian government has backed Iraq in its war with Iran. On several occasions it has extradited MB members to Syria where they were wanted on criminal charges.

* Jordanian Revolutionary Movement (JRM)
Movement which is supported by Syria.

* People's Militia
King Hussein reportedly ordered the creation of a new military force in 1982, charged specially with defending against Palestinian terrorism and Israeli inspired acts of sabotage. It will be composed of Bedouins and former regular army troops whose loyalty to Hussein is unquestioned.

* Yarmak
Jordanian volunteer corps which reportedly supported Iraq in its war with Iran.

KAMPUCHEA

* Army of Nationalist Sihanoukists (ANS)
On Jan.4, 1986, the two non-Communist groups, the

KPNLF and the ANS, reached agreement on the establishment of a joint military command with General Sak Sutsakhan, KPNLF C-in-C of the joint military command, and General Teap Ben of the ANS, Deputy C-in-C.

* Communist Party of Kampuchea (CPK)
(Parti Communiste du Kampuchea-PCK/ Kanapak Kumunist Kampuchea)
Pro-Chinese party that originated from the formation in February 1951 of the Kampuchean People's Revolutionary Party (KPRP) which was taken over by the Maoist faction led by Pol Pot in 1960 and renamed. The party came to power in April 1975 when its armed wing (the Red Khmers) overthrew the right-wing Lon Nol regime but was itself overthrown at the end of 1978 by Vietnamese-backed communists, which established the KPRP as a pro-Soviet ruling party on attaining power. Thereafter the exiled CPK-led government of Democratic Kampuchea continued to regard itself as the legitimate government of the country (and was recognized as such by most UN members) while at the same time seeking to overthrow the new regime by force.

* Confederation of Khmer Nationalists (CNK)
Nationalist opposition movement set up by Prince Norodom Sihanouk at a conference held on Sep.28, 1979, in Pyongyang, the capital of North Korea where he was then living in exile. The conference was attended by 38 representatives of refugee groups. Several groups later withdrew. A successor organization of the CNK was the National United Front for an Independent National, Peaceful and Cooperative Kampuchea.

* Free Khmer
(Khmer Serei)
The term Khmer Serei has been used for different groups of non-communist organizations in Kampuchea. After the overthrow of the government in 1975, Free Khmers fighting against the Red Khmer government were active in the areas on the border with Thailand. In 1979 the term Khmer Serei was applied to several movements opposed to both the Vietnamese and the Red Khmer. These included the KPNLAF, the KPNLF, MOULINAKA, LNGK and the NLM. The total strength of these groups was believed to be not more than 6,000 men. Fighting occurred between rival Free Khmer groups, who disagreed partly over their attitude to the Red Khmers and partly over distribution of food supplied by international relief organizations.

* General Association of Khmers Abroad (AGKE)
An organization established by Son Sann to coordinate activities abroad. Former members of the Democratic Party of Kampuchea joined the organization, including Sim Var, Chkeam Vam and Than Ouk.

* Independence
(Sereika)
Organization established in January 1979 with the aim of opposing both the PRK government and the Red Khmers. It formed a provisonal government led by Hem Kroesna.

* Kampuchean National United Front for National Salvation
(Ranakse Samakki Sangkroh Cheat Kampuchea) (KNUFNS)
Front which was set up in December 1978, shortly after signing a friendship treaty with the Soviet Union in which pro-Vietnamese Khmers were paramount. On Christmas Day 1978 Vietnam launched an invasion of Kampuchea, took Phnom Penh on Jan.7, 1979, and two days later Hanoi announced the victory of its forces. The KNUFNS group, led by Heng Samrin, Chea Sim and Pen Sovan, arrived in the baggage train of the Vietnamese Army and set up a regime. The new regime was promptly recognized by Vietnam and a number of Soviet-bloc countries. The KNUFNS ran the pro-Vietnamese government of the People's Republic of Kampuchea. Subsequently small PRK forces fought alongside Vietnamese units against the Khmer Rouge and Khmer Serei.

* Khleang Meoung (KM)
Pro-Sihanouk resistance movement which joined ANS in the summer of 1981. It was led by Tuon Chay.

* Khmer People's National Liberation Front (KPNLF)
Front established in 1979, as a democratic and non-communist movement with the object of uniting all non-communist resistance to the Vietnamese-backed regime. It is headed by Son Sann, a former Prime Minister. By 1981 the front claimed to control 9,000 armed men (other estimates ranged from 3,000 to 6,000), and to have received arms from China. It has an armed wing, the FANLPK, under General Dien Del, operating in the west close to the Thai border. Son Sann pursued the possibility of forming a coalition with the Khmer Rouge and MOULINAKA and reached a tentative agreement in June 1982 to form a coalition government in exile.

* National Liberation Government of Kampuchea (NLGK)
This government is in fact a small Khmer Serei guerrilla force, operating to the West on the Thai border and north of Highway 5. It was formed on Oct.3, 1979, under the leadership of Van Saren. It had an army of several thousand men. Its seat is Camp 004 near the border village of Ban Non Mak

Moon. It was reported to terrorize refugees.

* National Armed Liberation Forces of the Khmer People
(Forces Armeés Nationales de Libération du Peuple Khmer) (FANLPK)
The military wing of Son Sann's KPNLF organization which was formed in March 1979 by General Dien Del, a former officer in Lon Nol's army. It is the strongest of the Khmer Serei forces numbering some 3,000 men, although it claimed to have 10,000 men. It is said to receive aid from Singapore.

* The Nationalists
(Neak Cheat Niyum)
Nationalist group led by Vann Sao Yuth. The group is said to have its headquarters in Thailand.

* National Liberation Movement of Kampuchea
(Mouvement de la Libération Nationale du Kampuchea) (MOULINAKA)
One of the active guerrilla movements established in August 1979. Originally it was led by Kong Sileah, a supporter of Prince Norodom Sihanouk who had political disagreements with General Dien Del, leader of the FANLPK. In 1980 MOULINAKA units were involved in clashes with Free Khmers. After the death of Kong Sileah on Aug.16, 1980, MOULINAKA agreed to co-operate with the KPNLF of Son Sann. On Dec.1, 1980, it was reported that the first joint military operation by MOULINAKA and the Red Khmer's had been launched on Nov.28. In June 1982 it came to an agreement with Son Sann's KPNLF and the Khmer Rouge to work together in a new coalition government in exile under Prince Sihanouk.

* National United Front for an Independent, National, Peaceful, and Cooperative Kampuchea (FUNCINPEC)
Party which was announced on Mar.25, 1982, by Prince Norodom Sihanouk. It apparently replaced the Confederation of Khmer Nationalists.

* National United Front of Kampuchea
(Front Uni National du Kampuchea) (FUNK)
This group was formed in March 1970 under the nominal leadership of Prince Norodom Sihanouk to fight against the recently installed pro-US regime of General Lon Nol. The Khmer Rouge dominated the organization. In May 1970 the coalition formed the Royal National Union Government of Kampuchea which was immediately recognized by China and North Vietnam. It formally came to power in April 1975, but was progressively discarded by the Khmer Rouge, the real rulers of the country.

Oddar Tus (OT)
Pro-Sihanouk resistance movement which joined the ANS in the summer of 1981.

* People's Revolutionary Party of Kampuchea (PRPK)
Official government party since the occupation of Kampuchea by Vietnam. It is headed by General Pen Sovan (secretary-general) and Heng Samrin (president of the revolutionary council).

* Red Khmer
(Khmer Rouge)
Armed branch of the Communist Party of Kampuchea. It is the strongest of the active guerrilla movements and has an estimated strength of 20,000 to 35,000 armed men. The leading cadres of the Communist Party of Kampuchea, Saloth Sar (Pol Pot), Ieng Sary and Son Sen took to the jungle in 1962. All had been educated in France. The other CPK leaders, Khieu Samphan, Hu Nim and Hou Yuon, fleeing Prince Sihanouk's bloody repression of the Battambang peasant uprising, joined them in 1965. It probably numbered no more than 4,000 men in the 1960s. After the civil war the Red Khmer assumed power in 1975. The CPK thereupon carried out the most radical communist policy program ever implemented anywhere, involving the forcible removal of the country's urban population to the rural areas and mass executions of alleged reactionaries. Fatality estimates vary from 500,000 to 2,500,000. Since the Vietnamese invasion in 1978 the Chinese promised full support and by 1980 aid was clearly forthcoming, including weapons and ammunition. In recent years it has cooperated with two other guerrilla movements in a coalition.

* Resistance Coalition Government of Democratic Kampuchea
Alliance of three active guerrilla organizations.

* Serika National Liberation Movement (SNLM)
Movement which was established in 1979. It was regarded as a Free Khmer group and was led by In Sakhan. In July 1980 it lost control of a camp at Nong Samet to the forces of Mitr Don, the leader of another Free Khmer group. On Apr.15, 1981, In Sakhan announced his support for the MOULINAKA movement.

* S-21 Special Section
Unit of the Pol Pot government which was responsible for the extermination of 20,000 political prisoners at the Tuol Sleng prison in the 1970s.

KENYA

* Association of Kenyan Freedom Fighters
(Muungano Wa Wazalendo Wa Kenya) (Mwakenya)
A political organization which emerged in 1980.

President Daniel Arap Moi said it advocates 'evil against the state'. Between 30 and 50 persons have been arrested and sentenced to prison terms in 1986. Most of them were intellectuals. Others are students, teachers and officials. Ngugi wa Thiongo'o has been mentioned in the press as the brain behind the organization which reportedly wants to establish a communist system in Kenya. It has been involved in sabotage of a railway line in 1986.

* Land Freedom Army (LFA)
A liberation movement active in the 1950s. It was largely based on the Kikuyu people of Jomo Kenyatta.

* Mau Mau
Terror organization active in 1950s. In the late 1940s the Mau Mau knitted its gangs in the tradition of the Kikuyu Association. By 1952 the society was deemed to have thousands of members. Firearms were stolen from police posts or armories. Food and arms were purchased with money raised by intimidation. Revenues were also used to bribe. Activities covered onlu about one-sixth of the country's territory. The activities did not develop into guerrilla warfare. Terrorism was used to drive white men from Kikuyu lands. After 1952 the campaign intensified. The death and execution of Dedan Kimathi effectively ended the resistance. In all 11,000 Mau Mau, 167 security forces and under 2000 civilians had been killed.

* Northern Frontier District Liberation Front (NFDLF)
Front which was set up in 1981. Its origins go back to the mid-1960s, when Somali irredentists caused the Kenyan army to preserve Kenyan sovereignty. Abd al Qadir Sheikh Hussein, Ali Abdullah and Sheikh Abd al Rahman transformed the shifta bandits into the NFDLF. Once constituted as a movement representatives toured Arab capitals in search for funds. In 1983 the NFDLF claimed that some 720 people had been killed and 500 houses destroyed in security operations. Somali eyewitnesses spoke of at least three lorry loads of bodies being taken out of the town and a minimum of 100 dying in Garissa alone in November 1980. On Feb.10, 1984 government forces operated in the Wajir district.In its 1985 report Amnesty International said it received disturbing reports of the arrest, torture and killing of a large number of people of Somali ethnic origin. Estimates of the number of deaths ranged from several hundred to 1,400.

* People's Redemption Council (PRC)
An organization of members of the Kenyan Air Force attempted to carry out a '1st August Revolution' in 1982 aimed at overthrowing the government of President Arap Moi. The attempt was rapidly suppressed by loyal sections of the armed forces and was accompanied by widespread looting. The Air Force itself was officially disbanded in order to be replaced by a new one. Nairobi University was closed down and President Moi announced on Oct.20 that it would be restructured before being reopened. According to a government statement made in early September 1982, 160 people had died as a result of the attempted coup.

* Shifta Bandits
The colonial boundaries imposed from Europe in Africa led to a dispute in the north-east frontier district of Kenya, where ethnic Somalis found themselves governed by southern Kikuyu. Known as shiftas, those who took up arms were aided and abetted from Somalia which never renounced its claim to the area. Despite diplomatic agreements the problem persisted. In 1982 the Northern Frontier District Liberation Front was active.

KOREA (SOUTH)

* Agency for National Security Planning (NSP)The South Korean Intelligence Agency (KCIA) was renamed Agency for National Security Planning in January 1981. A government spokesman explained that the change had been been introduced because the KCIA had been guilty of 'absurdities and irrational practices' in the past.

* Anti Communist Bureau of the National Police
Section of the national police which has been involved in torture.

* Constituting Assembly Group (CAG)
In February 1987 the authorities announced to have dismembered this organization which was said to prepare for an armed uprising to establish a communist state. The police arrested 32 members of the organization which consisted of former students and activists of the labour movement. The arrested people were accused of violating the national security law which forbids any communist activity (the maximum punishment being the death sentence).

* Council for Freedom and Unification (CFU)
Paramilitary movement supported by North Korea.

* Korean Central Intelligence Agency (KCIA)
Korean intelligence organization which was modelled on the US CIA by its creator Kim Jong Pil. It has been involved in human rights abuses. It was renamed in January 1981 the Agency for National Security Planning. Prior to the name change the KCIA had an estimated permanent staff of about 30,000 agents, not counting so-called

'outside agents'. For years KCIA agents roamed the United States more or less at will, shadowing their exiles. Korean residents on the West Coast were so intimidated by KCIA reprisals that they refused to inform American police authorities that the agents were extorting money from them like mafia goons.

* Korean Christian Action Organization (KCAO)
Inter-denominational body that has been prominent in a growth of anti-US sentiments among a small but growing minority of the population, arising mainly from a belief that US support for President Chun constitutes an obstacle to the development of democracy in South Korea. When it called for the withdrawal of the US ambassador in 1982, several leaders of the KCAO were briefly detained. Dissidents were suspected of an arson attack on the US cultural center in the southern city of Pusan on Mar.18, 1982. After police investigations several thousand people were detained for questioning. The principal suspects, Kim Hyong Jang and Moon Bu Shik were both sentenced to death.

* Kwangju Citizens' Committee
This committee of religious leaders, professors and students, was formed to negotiate with the local martial law commander in Kwangju, on the demand made by a mass movement which had erupted in a popular rising on May 19, 1980. The revolt had its origins in a student protest which had begun in March 1980 and had led to the extension of martial law throughout the country on May 17, the banning of all political activities and the arrest of many anti-government politicians. On May 27 tanks and infantry quelled the rising. The Committee stated later that 261 dead bodies had been found of which 100 had not been identified. Officially it was stated that 144 civilians, 27 soldiers and four policemen were killed, and those arrested numbered 1,740 of which 1,010 had been released. On Oct.25, 1980, five alleged participants in the revolt were sentenced to death. Other unofficial fatality figures vary from 1,000 to 2,000.

* Minmintu
Student group which has sought confrontations with the police to dramatize their cause.

* National Security Bureau (NSB)
Agency which reportedly has been involved in torture.

* Security Service of the Army
Service which reportedly has been involved in torture.

* United Minjung Movement for Democracy and Unification
Umbrella organization made up of almost two dozen political groups opposing the government. It was banned by the government on Nov.9, 1986. It is headed by Moon Ik Hwan who was arrested in June 1980.

KUWAIT

* Forces of the Prophet Mohammed
On June 7, 1987, this obscure group threatened to kill Kuwaiti leaders if the emirate carries out death sentences passed down against six Kuwaiti Shi'ite Moslems accused of sabotaging Kuwaiti oil fields.

* Moslem Fundamentalists
Sporadic political opposition has come from Moslem fundamentalists, especially under the influence of the Shi'ite Islamic Revolution in Iran. Between 20 and 30 percent of Kuwaiti citizens are thought to be Shi'ites.

LAOS

* Ethnics Liberation Organization of Laos (ELOL)
Laotian resistance organization led by Pa Kao Her. It is a member of the Democratic International.

* Laos Front for National Reconstruction
A front which was formed as successor of the Lao Patriotic Front in 1979. It is headed by Souphanouvong.

* Laos Patriotic Front
(Neo Lao Hak Xat) (NLHX)
In 1950 a conference of Laotian communist exiles in Vietnam, proclaimed a liberation government of the Pathet Lao. Prince Souphanouvong became prime minister and a People's Liberation Army was set up. In 1953 the Vietminh army gained control of two northern provinces and handed them to the Pathet Lao administration. In 1962, following the breakdown of the Geneva agreement the Pathet Lao reverted to armed struggle. Gradually the Pathet Lao forces came to dominate most of the country. A cease-fire was negotiated in 1973, which paved the way for fresh negotiations for a new government of national union involving communist participation. This government was formed on Apr.5, 1974. The name of the Patriotic Front was in February 1979 changed to Lao Front for National Reconstruction.

* Lao People's Revolutionary Party
(Phak Pasason Pativat Lao) (LPRP)
This party was the communist core of the Lao Front for National Reconstruction which was prior to the communist takeover known as the People's Party of Laos (Phak Pasason Lao). It is led by Kaysone Phomvihan (secretary-general).

* Lao Socialist Party (LSP)

An anti-Vietnamese party led in the late 1970s by General Kong Lae.

* Laos United Liberation Front (LULF)
Guerrilla organization with an estimated strength of approximately 4,000 fighters. Individual units are operating under one command and are comprised of the hill peoples of H'mong, Lao Tung, Lahu, Yao, Liu and Lao. Many of the cadres are veterans of the clandestine war waged by the United States in Laos against the North Vietnamese in the 1950s and 1960s. The ranks were reported to be trained, armed and equipped by the People's Republic of China at Szemao in Yunnan province.

* Meo Tribesmen
Meo (i.e.barbarian) tribesmen who call themselves H'mong or 'free men' maintain a guerrilla resistance against the LPRP-regime since 1975. In 1980 General Vang Pao (who had commanded a Meo force financed by the US CIA until 1975) claimed that at least 40,000 tribesmen had died in Laos since Vietnamese and Pathet Lao forces began a post liberation crackdown against H'mong holdouts in central Laos. There have been allegations that the Vietnamese have used chemical weapons against the tribesmen.

* Lao National Liberation Front (LNLF)
This organization conducted guerrilla operations in southern Laos in 1980. It is mainly composed op soldiers and officials of the pre-1975 government. In the Champassak and Savannaket provinces it successfully recruited rural militiamen. LNLF units varying in size from 10 to 50, and operate with little coordination. It is largely armed by supplies captured from government and Vietnamese forces. The LNLF allegedly uses Thai territory as a safe haven, and in the 1980s there was some evidence of Khmer Rouge support.

* Royal Lao Democratic Government (RLDG)
General Phoumi Nosavan (the former right-wing deputy premier who had fled into exile after an abortive coup attempt in 1965) announced on Aug.18, 1982, the formation of an anti-communist and anti-Vietnamese 'Royal Lao Democratic Government' in Bangkok. He subsequently claimed on Oct.23 that this 'government' had been established in southern Laos with himself as head of government, minister of defense and C.-in-C of the 'Army of Lao Liberation'. His proclaimed goal is to overthrow the existing communist regime and to expel the Vietnamese. He cooperates with guerrilla forces currently fighting the Vietnamese backed regime in Kampuchea.

* State of Laos Defectors
(Pathet Lao)
Liberation movement which brought an end to the monarchy in 1975. Since then insurgent activity within Laos has been limited. Pathet Lao defectors opposed to the influx of Vietnamese appear to be operating in small bands. They have an estimated strength of 2,000 to 3,000 men.

* United National Front for the Liberation of Laos (LPNLUF)
Front formed in 1980 by four anti-Vietnamese movements representing righ-wing forces, neutralists and tribal people opposed to the LPRP regime. The LPNLUF aims at expelling the Vietnamese from Laos, dissolving the present government in Vientiane and holding a general election. In 1982 a 'liberation government' was to be installed. The front was led by Sisouk Na Champassak and Phoumi Nosavan. The 40,000 men allegedly receive Chinese training and support. Training is also reportedly provided by the Khmer Rouge.

LEBANON

* Al Amal
(Hope)
Founded in 1979 as the military wing of the polical movement of the deprived Shiite Moslem community, led by Nabbih Berri. The Moslem community is led by Shaikh Muhammed Maudi Shams ad-Din, and Sadr ad-Din as Sadr. Under the influence of the Islamic revolution and after the disappearance of the spiritual leader, Imam Moussa Sadr, at the end of a visit to Libya in August 1978, Amal became militant. In 1982 Amal adopted Ayatollah Ruhollah Khomeini as Imam of all Moslems. It has been involved in fighting with the Arab Liberation Front (1980), pro-Iraqi Lebanese and Palestinians (June 1980 and March 1981), the Lebanese Communist Party and the Organization of Communist Action in Lebanon (August 1981). In 1982 Amal's forces had 30,000 fighters which made them second only to the Falangists. It began to create a regular army in 1985 when it received 50 tanks from Syria in 1985.

* Amal Group (not to be confused with Amal of N.Berri)
Group led by Hussein Musawi which split from Amal in 1982. It is believed to have operated under the name Islamic Jihad and depends directly on the Supreme Council of the Iranian Islamic Revolution. Other representatives are Sadek Musawi, an Iranian, and Dakhani, an Iraqi, who also controls the Iranian Revolutionary Guards in Baalbek.

* Arab Cavalry or Pink Panthers Militia (AC)
Militia loyal to Colonel Rifaat al-Assad. They are called Pink Panthers because of their raspberry-red fatigue uniforms. It is the military branch of the Arab Democratic Party supported by Syria. It has

been involved in battles with the Islamic Union Movement in June 1983.

* Arab Commando Cells -Omar Mukhtar Forces
Pro-Libyan group which in a telephone call claimed responsibility for the kidnapping of two US citizens in 1986. It also claimed responsibility for a rocket propelled grenade attack on the residence of the British ambassador in Beirut in April 1986.

* Arab Democratic Party (ADP)
Party which appeared in 1981. It is mainly comprised of Syrian immigrants (Alawites) concentrated in Tripoli. Its military branch, the Pink Panthers is supported by Damascus and is headed by Rifaat al Assad, the brother of President Hafez al Assad.

* Arab Nationalists Movement
(al-Harakiyines al-Wataniyah al-'Arab) (HWA)
Marxist-oriented Palestinian organization founded in 1948 by the George Habash and Hani al-Hindi. It is also based in Jordan and is one of several Palestinian groups operating in Lebanon.

* Arab Revolutionary Brigades
(Wahdat al-Thawra al-Arabiya) (ARB)
According to their self-description 'a world pan-Arab movement whose objective is to free Arabs and to restore their dignity, and to fight in association with their friends in all organizations throughout the world.' It is considered as part of the Islamic Jihad and has claimed responsibility for several attacks including a bomb attack in Kuwait, the murder of the Kuwaiti journalist Ahmed Jarallah and the blowing up of an airplane in September 1983 above Abu Dhabi. In April 1982 it also claimed responsibility for the murder of an Israeli diplomat in Paris.

* Arab Socialist Action Party
(Hizb al-Amal al-Ishtiraki al-Arabi) (ASAP)
Formed in 1972 by George Habash the ASAP played a leading role in the Lebanese civil war of 1975-76. It was conceived as the Lebanese counterpart of the Popular Front for the Liberation of Palestina (PFLP).

* Arab Socialist Renaissance Party
(Munazzamat Hizb al-Baath) (MHB)
Al Baath was divided into competing factions as a result of the Syrian intervention in 1976 (two were reconciled in 1978). The pro-Iraqi faction was led by Abd al Majid Rafi'i, the pro-Syrian faction by Asim Qansu. The pro-Syrian group's ceased after the Syrian interventian.

* Arab Socialist Union (ASU)
Small leftist party consisting of several factions. The ASU was one of the groups which claimed responsibility for the bomb attack on the US embassy in Beirut on Apr.19, 1983, which killed 64 persons.

* Armenian Revolutionary Federation
(Parti Dashnak)
A right-wing Armenian group originally allied with Maronite groups in 1958. Like other Armenian organizations, it remained politicallly neutral in the civil war. Fighting between Armenians and rightists, including Falangists, broke out in Beirut during 1979. The federation is led by Khatchig Babikian.

* Black Flags (BF)
Shiite group involved in the kidnapping of Spanish diplomats in 1986.

* Black Mountain Cats of the People
On July 16, 1987, this obscure group announced to start a struggle against the 'dollar mafia that is starving out the people'. The next day a bomb exploded at an exchange office in Beirut.

* The Call of Jesus Christ
International terrorist organization fighting for 'the freedom of Palestinians from Zionist domination.' It was founded by Feisal Joudi and first emerged in Lebanon in 1978. Attacks have been reported in Lisbon, Paris, and Madrid. It reportedly received orders from Libya and had contacts with Triple A (Argentina). In May 1986 Spanish authorities arrested ten members including four Spaniards and a Portuguese. The Spanish were believed to have been hired for executing an attack. The organization offered an equivalent of 20,000 Dutch guilders for attacks on offices of Air France in Lisbon and the Bank of America in Madrid.

* Committee for the Islamic Revolution (CIR)
Committeee headed by Ayatollah Hussein Montazeri (a possible successor to Ayatollah Khomeini) which strongly supports fundamentalist movements in Lebanon and other countries.

* Democratic Alliance (DA)
An alliance critical of Yasser Arafat but indendent of Syria and Libya. It emerged in 1983. Like Al Fatah it has publicly renounced terrorism outside the borders of Israel and the occupied territories.

* Egypt the Arab
(Misr Aruba)
A tiny Egyptian opposition group that operates in southern Lebanon. It claimed responsibility for a suicide attack in 1985.

* The Forces of Nasser
(Quwwat Nasir) (QN)
Militia belonging to the Nasserite organization-The Correctionist Movement, a breakaway group

from the Nasserite Organization of the Toiling People's Forces. It is led by Isam Arab and had an estimated strength of less than 5,000 fighters.

* Free Christian Army (FCA)
Christian militia supported by Israel which began to form a regular army in 1986. It succeeded the Lebanese Forces and is led by Samir Geaga.

* Free Islamic Revolutionary Movement (FIRM)
Possibly a split off from the pro-Iranian Amal. FIRM has been held responsible for the the attacks on the French and US headquarters of the Multi National Force on Oct.23, 1983 (241 Americans and 58 French troops were killed). Some reports said it proclaimed an Iranian free state in northern Lebanon with Baalbek as its center. It supports a greater Syria policy as well as a return of Palestina to the Palestinians and the freing of Lebanon from imperialism. It also wants to strengthen the Islamic Revolution in the whole world. Its spiritual leader is Sheikh Sobhi, imam of the Shiite mosque of Brital near Baalbek. Two important training camps are at Ras el-Ain and Janta near Baalbek.

* Free Lebanese Army
(Jaish Lubnan al-Hur) (FLA)
In May 1980, Major Saad Haddad (died Jan.14, 1984) merged Christian militia groups with Israeli support into the FLA in southern Lebanon. Haddad's forces clashed with Palestinian guerrilla units as well as UN forces which had been stationed in the south since 1976. The FLA formed a buffer zone between Israel and parts of Lebanon under Syrian influence. In 1984 Haddad was succeeded by General Antoine Lahd. The militia consisted of 500 regulars, a village militia of 1,000 men and 2,000 part timers.

* Front of Justice and Vengeance (FJV)
Group which claimed responsibility for the assassination of Colonel Goutierre, a French military attaché, on Sep.18, 1986.

* Front for the Liberation of Lebanon of Foreigners (FLLF)
A group of this name claimed responsibility for planting two car bombs in West Beirut on Feb.23, 1982, as well as for a bomb attack in Damascus on Nov.29, 1981, when at least 90 people were killed and over 135 injured. In another attack on Feb.18, 1982, it bombed the Ministry of Information, including the office of Al Baath newspaper in Damascus. The name of the group and the choice of the targets led many to believe that the FLLF was part of Haddad's militia in the south or simply a cover name for Israeli intelligence operations. Others suspected a Syrian attempt to eliminate the Fatah leadership.

* Front for the Liberation of Lebanon
(Jabhat Tahrir Lubnan) (FLL)
Group which in 1980 claimed responsibility for an attempt on the life of Greek Orthodox Archbishop Maximum Hakim and for a shooting incident at Rome airport.

* The Giants Brigade
(Liwa al-Marada)
Christian militia of Soleiman Frangié, President of Lebanon 1970-1976, centered around Zghorta (northern Lebanon). His reconcialiation with a leading Sunni Moslem, Rashid Karami, angered the rival Christian Phalangists. On June 13, 1978, Phalangist forces killed the ex-President's eldest son Tony, the latter's wife and his daughter, at Ehden. Followers of Soleiman Frangiè's organized the Marada militia, and fought back against the Phalangists, attacking in particular the family of their leader, Pierre Gemayel.

* Green Cells
Group which threatened to attack Swiss targets unless a Lebanese hijacker is released from a Geneva jail or if he is extradited to France. The hijacker was arrested on July 24, 1987, after commandeering an Air Afrique flight en route from Brazzaville (Congo) to Paris.

* Group 219 FA
Group which claimed responsibility for a bomb attack on the British Bank of the Middle East in West Beirut in April 1986.

* Guardians of the Cedars
(Hurras al-Arz)
Extreme right-wing group based in the Christian heartland in the mountains north of Beirut. It was active during the civil war 1975-76. It was led by Etienne Saqr, while the writer, Said Aql, was its ideologue. In 1979 it clashed with the Tiger militia. It was active in the conflict of 1982 at the time of the Israeli invasion of Lebanon. Influential leaders hold intelligence and security jobs. Several hundred of them were trained in Israel. One of its objectives is to liquidate the Palestinian presence in Lebanon.

* Hezbollah
See Party of God.

* Holy Fighters for Freedom
Obscure group that claimed responsibility for the kidnapping of two West Germans, Rudolf Cordes and Adolf Schmidt, in January 1987.

* Imam Hussein Fedayeen
Group which is comprised of several dozen members led by Abdullah Mussavi, known as Abu

Haidar. It operated in Beirut in 1985.

* Independent Movement for the Liberation of the Kidnapped (IMLK)
Group which claimed responsibility for the kidnapping of Lebanese Christians on June 16, 1986. It demanded the release of at least 2,200 kidnapped Moslems in Lebanon.

* Independent Nasserite Movement
(Harakat al- Nasiriyun al Mustaqallin) (al-Morabitoun) (INM)
Movement which was founded in 1958 as a socialist party opposed to the Chamoun government. It was the largest of at least 13 extant Nasserite groups in Lebanon. It has never been an exclusively Moslem organization, although its main support came from from the Sunni urban poor. The INM was part of the National Movement in Lebanon during the 1975-76 civil war. Its militia was called the Morabitoun.

* Islamic Holy War
(Jihad Islami) (JI)
Pro-Iranian fundamentalist organization which first surfaced on Apr.18, 1983. It possibly is a front name for the Party of God (Hezbollah). Very few members have been identified. Lebanese and US officials have said that there may actually be no such group and that the name may be used by many individual attackers or small independent groups. Arab intelligence specialists said the name is used by several loosely connected terrorist cells that have ties to Iran and Syria but are capable of operating independently. Characteristic are its suicide attacks. Among the acts for which responsibility was claimed figure the attacks on the French Army and the marine headquarters in 1983. In the eyes of the perpetrators they are committing a justified act assuring them a place in heaven.

* Islamic Unification Movement
(Tawheed) (IUM)
Islamic fundamentalist organization led by Sheik Saeed Shaaban.The group's influence from 1983 to September 1985 brought a foretaste of islamic rule imposed by the force of arms and religious fervor. Shops selling alcohol were dynamited as were women's beauty shops run by male hairdressers. Christian parochial schools were asked to offer Koranic teachings and women were warned against appearing in public without headdress or long sleeves. In 1984 the fundamentalists cracked down on on Lebanese communists in Tripoli, killing at least 50 and driving them out of the city along with other leftist parties. In December 1986 more than 200 members were reportedly massacred in the city of Tripoli in a Syrian-backed sweep into the slum of Tabbaneh. The massacre occurred after clandestine preparations for a plot to seize control of a part of the city in a surprise offensive on New Year's eve had touched off a wave of arrests.

* Islamic Jihad for the Liberation of Palestine (IJLP)
Group which claimed responsibility for the Jan.24, 1987, kidnapping of four professors of the Beirut University College. It is believed that the name is a cover for the Party of God (Hezbollah).

* Islamic Resistance (IR)
The Islamic Resistance is an alliance of both Shiite and Sunni Moslem fundamentalists dominated by Hezbollah. It has been attacking the Israeli troops who remain in Lebanon in a buffer zone along the border. It is one of four organizations that claimed responsibility for the Sep.8, 1986, attack on the Istanbul synagogue. The group is attracting more and more young militants away from Amal. It is especially antagonistic to France, first because of an accident and second because of the Gulf War.The accident occurred in August 1986 when French troops from UNIFIL shot a Shia leader. He was an Amal official but Hezbollah took offence.

* Islamic Liberation Organization (ILO)
A terrorist group which has claimed responsibility for the kidnapping of four Soviet embassy officials in 1985.

* Kata'eb
See Lebanese Phalangist Party.

* Khaibar Brigades
Group which has been responsible for the kidnapping of Westerners in 1985.

* Lebanese Army
The Lebanese army broke into four separate forces during the course of the civil war. The army now has 12 brigades divided by sect. The army commander is still a Maronite Catholic Christian who heads a military council that includes officers represententing the five other main sects. Christian brigades are assigned to Christian areas, Moslem units to Moslem districts. The army has a strength of 37,000 men with Moslems making up the majority of the rank and file. In the office corps Christians outnumber Moslems.

* Lebanese Armed Revolutionary Factions (LARF)
Terrorist organization with an estimated hardcore of 18 men. It is almost a small family company of the Abdallah family from the village Kubajjat, an enclave of Maronite Christians. George Ibrahim Abdallah, the presumed leader, first engaged himself with the SSP and later the PFLP. He financed his activities with money from bank raids and drugtrade. As cadre of the PFLP he came to

know members of the RAF and AD in Europe who received training in PFLP camps. In the late 1970s he established LARF, first as an PFLP splinter, later independent. In 1980 he went to Europe to set up a terror network.At the end of 1983 the group greatly expanded its logistical network by establishing bases in Italy and setting up new safehouses in France. Operatives enrolled in language institutes or universities to establish a legal presence in Europe. The Paris, Madrid, Rome bases were usually apartments in working-class suburbs near the airports. George Ibrahim Abdallah was arrested in France and subsequently tried in February 1987. He received a life sentence. France fears a new wave a attacks to gain his release after a campaign of terror in September 1986, cost more than 10 lives and produced more than 160 injured.

* Lebanese Communist Party
(al-Hizb al-Shuyu'i al-Lubani/Parti Communiste Libanais) (LCP)
Party formed in 1924 which has its own militia, the Popular Guard. The LCP began its activities by fighting against the French occupation of Lebanon (under the League of Nations mandate). In 1975 it joined the alliance of pro-Palestinian Moslem leftists in the struggle against the Christians. It had a militia of about 1,000 men, 200 of whom died in the conflict, mostly in Beirut. It wants to establish a national democratic regime to open the road to transition to socialism. It was transformed into a predominantly Moslem organization actively engaged in promoting Palestinian resistance and anti-Israeli and anti-US actions.

* Lebanese Phalangist Party
(Hizb al Kataeb al Lubnaniya) (HKL)
The military arm of the Phalangist party which was established in 1936 as a right-wing Maronite Christian formation led by Pierre Gemayel. It forms a leading party in the country's long-running inter-communal strife. A particular object of Phalangist hostility is the PLO, which is accused of forging an alliance with leftist Moslem groups intent on overthrowing Lebanon's established order. Following the June 1982 Israeli invasion of Lebanon it co-operated closely with the Israelis in actions to eliminate the military presence of the PLO from Beirut. Immediately after the assasination of President elect Bashir Gemayel on Sep.14, 1982, its units purged the Chatila and Sabra refugee camps of PLO guerrillas. In the operation an estimated 500 to 1,200 civilians were massacred.

* Lebanese Fighting Force (LFF)
Militia which was established in March 1983. It split off from the Phalange militia to protest the traditionalist policy of the Phalange and the strong influence of President Gemayel.

* Lebanese Forces (LF)
Christian miltia. It is one of the three dominant militias which began to form a regular army in 1986. It is led by Samir Geaga who reportedly is streamlining his 8,000 militiamen into a regular force of 5,000. It operates a military academy in the village of Ghorta and reportedly received M1 'Super Sherman' tanks and other armor from Israel. It was renamed Free Christian Army.

* Lebanese National Movement (LNM)
Left-wing Moslem alliance emerging after an agreement concluded on Sep.12, 1977, by Walid Jumblatt, the Druze chairman of the PSP, with the pro-Syrian Baath party organization in Lebanon. Units of the movement were regularly clashing with Christian militias.

* Lebanese National Resistance Front (LNRF)
Initiative of three Marxist groups: the Lebanese Communist Party, Organization of Communist Action and the Arab Socialist Union. Other members of this braod coalition were the Shia Hezbollah group, the Shia Amal movement, the Syrian Social National Party, a few Druze socialists and a growing number of Palestinians from camps near Tyre and Sidon. Its objectives are to force a complete Israeli withdrawal and to eliminate the SLA in the south. This battle in the border zone has intensified since 1984. Operations are carefully planned. Until 1985 1471 operations were executed of which 89 percent by the Resistance Front and 11 percent by the Islamic Resistance. The front has claimed responsibility for an attack on the Israeli headquarters in Tyrus in which 74 military were allegedly killed.

* Lebanese Red Brigades (LRB)
Responsibility for the killing of Louis Delamare, the French ambassador in Beirut on Sep.4, 1981, was claimed by the LRB.

* Martyr Nabil Hamdash Unit
One of the groups which claimed responsibility for the Feb.14, 1984 killing in Italy of Leamon R. Hunt, the American director-general of the Multinational Observer Force in the Sinai. It was generally believed that the Italian Red Brigades were responsible for the killing.

* Martyrs of Sabra and Chatila
Group which claimed responsibility for the attack on the US embassy in Beirut on Apr.19, 1983.

* Mikdad
One of the many violent groups that is linked to Hezbollah.

* Militia of Chakr el Berjaouri
Militia which has been responsible for attacks on Amal and the 6th Brigade of the Lebanese Army (predominantly Shiites).

* Movement of the Disinherited
(Harakat al-Mahrumin) (HM)
This political arm of Amal was led by Imam Musa al-Sadr, the spiritual leader of landless Shiites in Beirut. Since 1976 it is pro-Syrian. Presently it is anti-Palestinian.

* National Forces of West Beirut
Group responsible for attacks on Amal and the 6th Brigade of the Lebanese Army (predominantly Shiites).

* National Guard
A group of about 50 or so young men have been given pistols by Israel and roam the streets 'protecting the people'. It is led by Mr.Abdallah Nasser, who is said to be a major in the MOSSAD. The Guard is said to be a group controlled by Israel to control the Palestinians in Sidon.

* National Liberation Militia (also known as Tigers Militia)
(Numur al-Ahrar) (NLM)
Right-wing Christian militia representing the interests of Camille Chamoun's National Liberal Party. Supported militarily by Israel and diplomatically by France in the 1970s. In 1980 they were beaten by the Phalangists. Tiger militants were nonetheless active in the 1980s.

* National Liberal Party
Hizb al-Wataniyah al-Ahrar/Parti National Liberal) (NLP)
A right-wing Maronite grouping founded in 1958. It has refused to consider any coalition with Moslem groups that would involve the Palestinians. It has repeatedly called for the withdrawal of Syrian and other Arab troops from Lebanon and has insisted that a federal system is the only way to preserve the country's unity. It was led by Camille Chamoun and had its own militia, the Tigers, led by his son Dory Chamoun.

* National Movement
(Harakat al-Wataniya)
A leftist coalition founded in 1972 by Kamal Jumblatt, the Druze leader, consisting of the Progressive Socialist Party, Independent Nasserite Movement, Lebanese Communist Party, Organization of Communist Action, the Syrian Social Nationalist Party, the Arab Socialist Baath Party, the Union of the Forces of the Working People-Corrective Movement, Oct.24 Democratic Socialist Movement, the National Christian Front and the Populist Nasserite Organization.

* National Syrian Socialist Party (NSSP)
Terrorist group allegedly run by the Syrian intelligence service and East European agents. The 'party' is made up almost entirely of Lebanese Christian communists from Dhur Sheir, a small Lebanese village. It has agents in several EEC countries and in Egypt. Its men are highly trained, and equipped with the most advanced guerrilla weapons. Its agents placed the bomb that exploded aboard a TWA airliner and tried to put a bomb aboard an El Al airliner at London airport.

* National Union Front (NUF)
Coalition of 11 political groups and militias, numbering 25,000 fighters, led by Amal and the Progressive Socialist Party.

* 24th of October Democratic Socialist Movement
A local Sunni Moslem militia in Tripoli, strongly pro-Palestinian and leftist. It fought the Zghartan Liberation Army and later the Syrians. It was led by Faruq al-Muqaddam and had an estimated strength of 2,500 fighters.

* Organization of the Baath Party (OBP)
Asim Quansu led the leftist OBP in the Lebanese civil conflict of 1975-76 when it supported first Kamal Jumblat in the National Movement and later the Nationalist Front.

* Organization of Black Tigers-People's Forces (OBT-PF)
This group claimed responsibility for a rocket propelled grenade attack on the Central Bank in Beirut on November 19, 1986. It threatened to kill bank directors and speculators in foreign currency. 'We will execute anybody who contributes to the poverty of the people.'

* Organization of Communist Action in Lebanon
(Munazzamat al-Amal al-Shuyu'i) (OCAL)
Left-wing group led by Muhsein Ibrahim. It was founded in 1970 by a merger of the Movement of Lebanese Socialists and the Socialist Lebanon. Members consists of Maronite, Catholic and Sunni Moslem workers and students in Beirut and the bekaa, as well as in the south.

* Organization for the Defense of the Free People
Obscure group which claimed responsibility for the kidnapping of the American journalist, Charles Glass, in Beirut on June 17, 1987. Authorities believed the real kidnappers have to be sought in circles of the Iranian Hizb Allah movement.

* Organization of Holy Struggle
This organization claimed responsibility for planting two car bombs in West Beirut on Feb.23, 1982, (for which the Front for the Liberation of

Lebanon from Foreigners also claimed responsibility). A spokesman for the organization described the attack as the start of a fierce war against Syrian forces 'in reply to the extermination to which our beloved families in Tripoli were subjected.' This was a reference to fighting on Feb.19-21, 1982, between Alawite and Sunni Moslems in the northern city of Tripoli, involving the Syrian backed Arab Democratic Party and the (Sunni) Popular Resistance Movement, said to be backed by al Fatah.

* Organization for the Oppressed on Earth (OSE)
Fundamentalist Shiite group, possibly a front name for the Party of God. It has taken hostage at least twelve Jews in southern Lebanon in response to the Israeli invasion. Eight of them have been murdered as 'Zionist spies'. One of the last victims was the 80-year old Yehuda Benesti.

* Organization of the People in Rising
In November 1986 this group threatened, in the name of hungry children, to attack anybody trying to make the people poorer. The group said to execute its threat within 48 hours unless drastic measures were taken to solve the economic crisis.

* Organization of the Poor of All Sects
Group which has been active in November 1986.

* Organization of Revolutionaries of the North (ORN)
This organization, believed to be closely associated with the Phalangist militia and opposed to Soleiman Frangié, claimed on Oct.10, 1979 to have assassinated five Frangié followers whom it had abducted on Oct.9.

* Party of God
(Hizb Allah, Hezbullah, Hezbollah)
Shi'ite fundamentalist organization founded by Sheikh Mohammed Hussein Fadlallah, an Iran-trained priest (mullah). He incorporated the Al Dawa sect into his party. It emerged in February 1985 with the publication of a 48-page manifesto outlining its position. It had about 3,000 fighters at its disposal in the Bekaa Valley in September 1983. In 1985 estimates ran up to 5,000. UNIFIL is considered an obstacle to the future holy war that it says must be launched from Lebanon to 'liberate Jerusalem'.
It has also attacked Israeli troops in southern Lebanon and its Christian militia allies. It is believed that its operational wing operates under the names: Jihad Islami, Organization of Revolutionary Justice and Organization of the Oppressed on Earth. Investigation of the major truck bombings in Lebanon that destroyed US and French military headquarters in October 1983, appears to indicate a joint operation between Palestinian and Shi'ite Moslem terrorists with backing from Iran and Syria. Ayatollah Khomeini is reported to spend anywhere from $ 15 million to $ 50 million a year to finance Hizb Allah activities.

* Partisans of God
(Ansar Allah)
In January 1987 this unknown terrorist group treatened with attacks on Italian targets if Italy did not free two imprisoned Lebanese. It threatened to kill the Italian Minister of Justice and the involved prison director, to blow up the Italian embassy in Beirut and to kidnap and torture any Itanian civilian in the world.

* People's Army (PA)
A group of 3,500 men which began to form a regular army in 1986. It reportedly received 120 T-54 tanks from Syria and Libya manned by Druze soldiers of the Progressive Socialist Party, headed by Walid Jumblat

* People's Resistance Movement (PRM)
Leftist organization operating in Tripoli. It is headed by Khalil Akkawi.

* Popular Arab Liberation Front (MPLA)
Palestinian terrorist organization led by Naji Alush.

* Populist Nasserite Organization
(Tanzim a-Nasari al-Jamahiri) (TNJ)
Local militia in Sidon led by Mustafa Saad. It had an estimated strength of 1,000 fighters. It fought as part of the National Movement in the civil war 1975-76.

* Popular Guard (PG)
The militia of the Lebanese Communist Party which is drawn mainly from the underprivileged Shi'ite community. It has an estimated strength of about 2,000 to 3,000 men.

* Progressive Vanguards
(Tali'a Taqqadamiya) (TT)
A pro-Syrian militia led by Muhammed Zakariya 'Itani which fought within the Nationalist Front during the civil war 1975-75.

* Progressive Socialist Party
(al-Hizb al-Taqaddami al-Ishtiraki/Parti Socialiste Progressiste) (PSP)
Moslem party led by the Druze Kamal Jumblat (assassinated Mar.16, 1977). Kamal was succeeded by his son Walid.

* Rawwad al Islah Militia (RIM)
Militia headed by Saib Salaam, a former Prime Minister (1970-73).

* Revolutionary Islamic Movement (RIM)
Extremist Shi'ite organization which threatened to disturb the Islamic summit in Kuwait in January

1987.

* Revolutionary Islamic Organisation
(Tanzim al-Islami al-Thawri) (TIT)
Pro-Iraqi group active in 1980 in Beirut where it claimed responsibility for the assassination of the Lebanese Shia leader, Hassan Shirazi.

* Revolutionary Justice Organization (RJO)
Pro-Iranian group which has claimed responsibility for the kidnapping of a French television crew in 1986. It also issued a warning not to proceed with the meeting of the Islamic Conference Organization in Kuwait in February 1987.

* Revolutionary Organization of Socialist Moslems (ROSM)
Terrorist organization which has threatened attacks in Italy, Great Britain and Spain. It has claimed responsibility for the assassination of P.Norris, Britain's deputy high commissioner in Bombay, on Dec.27, 1984, and a bomb attack on a British Airways office in Rome on Sep.25, 1985.

* Revolutionary Work Organization (RWO)
Previously unheard-of group which claimed responsibility for blowing up an Iraqi Airways airliner in Saudi Arabia on Dec.25, 1986. It threatened to carry out more attacks against Iraqi intesrests unless three of their comrades were not released within the next 72 hours.

* September Martyrs Brigade (SMB)
Dissident PLO faction which advocated armed struggle against Israel in June 1983.

* Shi'ite High Council (SHC)
A religious organization of the Shi'ite community in West Beirut led by Sheikh Mohammed Chamseddine. It is fundamentally anti-Israel. Chamseddine clashes often with Nabbih Berri of Amal, advocating more radical approaches.

* Siffine Islamic Organization (SIO)
Poosibly a Shi'ite faction which has been responsible for the kidnapping of M.Brian, a French teacher, in April 1986.

* Sixth of February Movement
A Lebanese Sunni militia headed by Chaker Berjaoui.

* Soldiers of God
(Jundullah)
A Lebanese Sunni Moslem fundamentalist organization that has some links to Tawheed, a Sunni group that dominates the northern city of Tripoli under its self-styled emir, or prince Saeed Shabaan. The group is known to have operated in Tripoli, Beirut and Sidon. It is one of the four organizations that claimed responsibility for the Sep.6, 1986 attack on the Istanbul synagogue.

* Sons of Imam Moussa Sadr (SIMS)
Name of a group of 12 Shi'ites, apparently supporters of Amal, who seized a Kuwaiti aircraft at Beirut airport on Feb.24, 1982, demanding that it should be taken to Tehran. This was the eighth hijacking meant to secure the release from alleged captivity of the Imam Moussa Sadr. On Feb.25 the hijackers surrendered to Lebanese army units, freeing the 125 passengers. The hijackers were not detained. Their leader had led six other hijackings without ever being prosecuted.

Southern Lebanese Army (SLA)
Christian militia in southern Lebanon which is trained, financed and armed by Israel. At least 300 Israeli soldiers are stationed permanently on Lebanese territory for 'advise'. Its strength decreased from 2,500 to 1,800 in January 1987 as a result of desertion. It has frequently been involved in clashes with the UNIFIL peacekeeping forces. The Irish and Nepalese battalions in UNIFIL are the SLA's favorite targets.

* Standard Bearers of Imam As Sadr Organization (SBISO)
Group led by Sheikh Mohammed and Mehdi Shamseddine, both deputies for the missing Imam Moussa Sadr.

* The Student Association (SO)
Organization established in the mid-1970s by Moussa Sadr among highschool and university students in Beirut. It seceded from Amal and is composed of several dozen members in Beirut and southern Lebanon. A small militant faction also operates under the leadership of Sheikh Muhammed Hussein Fadlallah.

* Sunni Resistance
Group which has been responsible for attacks on Amal and the predominantly Shi'ite 6th Brigade of the Lebanese Army.

* Syrian Peace Keeping Forces
Syrian army which intervened in the Lebanese civil war in 1976. Since then an estimated 22,000 to 30,000 soldiers have been stationed in Lebanon. In February 1987 a special elite force of 7,000 soldiers entered Beirut to restore public order.

* Syrian Social Nationalist Party
(Hizb al-Suri al Qaumi al-Ijtimi) (SSNP)
This party which was established in 1932. Until 1970 it was a right-wing party. Then it adopted a nationalist secular and reformist line, attracting Greek orthodox, Shiite, Druze, Maronite and Sunni support. It supported the Palestinian cause. Its objective is a 'greater Syria' embracing Iraq,

Jordan, Lebanon, Syria and Palestine. It split in two factions in 1974, one led by Abdallah Saada and the other by George Keneizeh and Issam Mahayri. They were reunited in 1978.

* Takhrir Party
A terrorist group opposed to the Moslem Brotherhood. It joined Fatah in 1981.

* Organization
(Tanzim)
Maronite militia which was active in the civil war 1975-76 as part of the Conservative Lebanese Front. It was set up by Fuad Shamali.

* Tigers Militia (TM)
Christian militia loyal to the National Liberal Party of former President Camille Chamoun; second in strength to the Phalangists until 1980. It was led by Dany Chamoun. The NLP represents the conservative Christian establishment.

* Union of the Forces of the Toiling People-Corrective Movement
(Itihad Qawa al-Shaab al-Amal al-Harakat al-Tashihiya)
Leftist Nasserite movement with its own militia Quwwat Nasir, led by Isam al-Arab.

* Vengeance Organization for the Martyrs of Islam
One of two groups that claimed responsibility for the bomb attack that killed Mr.Karami, to avenge Syrian attacks on Moslem militants in Tripoli.

* The Victory Division
(Firqat al-Nasser) (FN)
A Nasserite group led by Najah Wakim and Kamal Shatila which fought the Phalangist in the Beirut area but did not resist the Syrians. The political party associated with it was the Nasserite Organization Union of the Toiling People's Forces. Its strength was estimated at about 5,000 men.

* The Vigilant
(al Mourabitoun)
Moslem militia of the Independent Nasserite Movement led by Ibrahim Qulailat. It was a strongly pro-Palestinian force which with 2,000 fighters was the biggest leftist militia in Beirut during the civil war in the mid-1970s. It has been involved in fighting with the Tiger militia (1978), the Syrian National Socialist Party (November 1980), the Phalangist Christian militia (April 1981) and Kurdish activists (June 1981). It reportedly used Libyan military equipment and included some 300 Libyans.

* Youth of Free Beirut
Group which claimed responsibility for a bomb attack on a bank on Jan.11, 1985, as a warning to Druze leader Walid Jumblat.

* Zahla Bloc
(Tajammu al-Zahli)
A regional organization led by Ilyas al-Harawi, the Maronite deputy for Zahla. The bloc had its own militia in the Lebanese civil war 1975-76.

* Zghartan Liberation Army (also known as Giants Brigade)
(Jaish al-Tahrir al-Zghartawi) (ZLA)
Militia of supporters of Soleiman Frangié which fought with the Phalange in 1978 against Palestinians in and around Tripoli. The militia was commanded by Soleiman Frangié's son Tony. The latter was assassinated in mid-June 1978.

LESOTHO

* Basutoland Congress Party (BCP)
This party was founded in 1952 as the National Basutoland Congress. It is led by Ntsu Mokhele. In 1973 the BCP split. One section accepted seats in an appointed Assembly. The other remaining under the leadership of Mokhele was involved in an unsuccessful attempt to overthrow the government in 1974. It has an armed wing, the Lesotho Liberation Army.

* Communist Party of Lesotho (CPL)
Party founded in May 1962, mainly by migrants working in the Republic of South Africa. It was banned in February 1970 for its part in national liberation front.

* Koeeoko
Pro-government death squad.

* Lesotho Liberation Army (LLA)
In 1979-80 heavy fighting occurred in parts of Lesotho. Ntsu Mokhele, its leader claimed that the LLA had 65 Libyan-trained guerrillas and 500-1,000 other men in training in secret mountain camps. During 1981 and 1982 it intensified its operations which included laying of landmines, bomb attacks mortar and machine attacks. Targets included Leribe airport, policemen, leading politicians, petroleum installations, Hilton Hotel, the US cultural center, an electricity substation, and the West German ambassador's car.

LIBERIA

* Liberian Action Party (LAP)
Opposition party led by exiled General T.Quiwonkpa which made a coup attempt on Nov.12, 1985. Western diplomats estimated some 1,500 people were killed in revenge attacks by government forces. They reportedly killed 200 soldiers in the Barclai garrison where T.Quiwonkpa had strong

support. A few days after the coup a government army unit headed by Colonel Harrison Pennue went to the Nimba area where more than 500 Ghio (Quiwonkpa's people) were reportedly killed in a punitive attack.

* People's Redemption Council of the Armed Forces (PRC)
Military council which assumed power on Apr.12, 1980. It is led by Master Sergeant (later C.-in-C.) Samuel K.Doe. Several attempted counter coups were reported in April-May 1980, following which two further attempts to overthrow the PRC government were made in May and August 1981. In connection with the May 1981 attempt 13 men were condemned to death by a special court-martial board and executed in June, while the August 1981 plot resulted in the execution of five leading members of the PRC (including its co-chairman and deputy head of state).

* Revolutionary Action Committee (REACT)
A political science professor, two colonels and a student leader were arrested for security reasons in August 1984. An official statement said they had planned to force Mr.Doe to resign by using a series of bomb attacks and to install a Socialist government 'with the aid of foreign countries, including three African states.' In a demonstration at Monrovia University in August troops opened fire on the protesters. A REACT leaflet said 16 people were killed. The regime claimed that 102 demonstrators had been injured but none fatally.

LIBYA

* Allied Leadership of the Revolutionary Forces of Arab Nations
A cooperative organization of 22 revolutionary movements in the world which was established in 1984. It adopted a resolution which said that it would form a suicide force to strike at American targets throughout the world if the United States attacked Libya and other Arab nations. The organization was headed by Colonel Moammer Qadhafi.

* April Seven Organization
Terrorist organization which wants to overtrow the regime of Colonel Qadhafi. It claimed responsility for bomb attacks on Libyan targets in Athens on Oct.8, 1985. The organization is named after the day anti-Qadhafi rebels were executed in 1977.

* Front for the Liberation of Eastern Sahara
A Tuareg-based organization supported by Libya. Qadhafi began to claim they were being persecuted in many countries and declared his intention to defend them.

* General People's Congress of the Socialist People's Libyan Arab Jamhitirah ('State of the Masses')
Calls for the physical liquidation of political opponents by this ruling organ were renewed throughout 1985. On March 2, it reiterated the 'stand of the the Basic People's Congresses concerning the pursuit and physical liquidation of the stray dogs' and called for a response to states which protected the fugitives, including 'backing hostile and opposition movements' within such states. On Sep.3, 1985, Colonel Qadhafi said those sentenced to death 'have the right to return to the Jamahiriya with total freedom and without being subjected to any punishment for acts committed against their homeland' provided that they declare their repentance'. He added however, that 'those who prefer to stay abroad and work against the interests of their homeland will be pursued and punished.' He singled out members of the Moslem Brotherhood and the Islamic Liberation Party. In 1985 there have been reports of at least four coup attempts with subsequent arrests and punishments.

* Huni Group
This group is made up of several dissident organizations led by Abdel Monem al-Huni who once served as Libyan Foreign Minister and the head of counter-intelligence.

* Islamic Liberation Party
In 1973 members of this illegal organization were arrested and accused of membership of an illegal organization which had as its goal the overthrow of the government and which had criticized the government in its publications. In April 1983 a member was hanged.

* Libyan Baathist Party
One of the founders of this party, Amer Taher Dgaies, died in police custody on Feb.27, 1980. His funeral on the following day led to anti-Qadhafi demonstrations by several thousand people in Tripoli.

* Libyan Democratic Movement
Movement established in 1977 by exiled opponents of the Qadhafi regime abroad. Its members have been subject of an assassination campaign by Qadhafi's 'revolutionary committees'.

* Libyan Liberation Organization (LLO)
Opposition organization led by Abdul Hamid Bakoush. Qadhafi plotted to assassinate Bakoush in Egypt in 1985, but the scheme failed when the Egyptians pretended Bakoush had been killed. When Qadhafi triumphantly broadcast that the assassination had been successful, they produced the former Libyan Prime Minister and those hired

to kill him.

• Libyan National Association (LNA)
Libyan opposition group organized in late 1980 among exiles in Cairo. It is led by Mustafa al-Barki.

• Libyan National Democratic Movement
Libyan opposition group led by Mohmoud Suleyman Magrebi who served as Prime Minister of Libya for five months in 1969.

• Libyan Revolutionary Committees
On Apr.27, 1980, all Libyans living abroad (some 100,000) were ordered to return to Libya by June 11, 1980. The price of non-compliance was declared to be death. Libyans were subsequently assassinated in Britain, Italy, the FRG, Greece and Lebanon. At home revolutionary committees have been involved in torturing and ill-treatment of people held in custody.

• Libyan Revolutionary Officers (LRO)
Group which has been involved in summarily executions including one on Nov.24, 1985, of Hassan Ishkal, a prominent Libyan official and Nov.26, 1985, his cousin al-Burran Ishkal. In a radio broadcast on Nov.21, 1985 it was stated that the officers declared themselves 'members of the revolutionary committees' and pledged to turn themselves into 'suicide squads which will destroy everything'. Among their stated aim was the continuation of the pursuit of the stray dogs, the dogs of the CIA and their liquidation.'

• Libyan Students Militia
This militia took ten employees of German companies hostage in April 1983, to demand the release of a friend of the Qadhafi regime in the Federal Republic of Germany.

• National Front for the Salvation of Libya
(Al Jabah al-Wataniyah li inqedh Libya)
Libyan opposition group established on Oct.7, 1981, to 'liberate Libya and safe it from Qadhafi's rule; to find the democratic alternative; and to unite all nationalist elements inside and outside Libya in an integral program of action and struggle in order to replace the existing regime by a constitutional elected government.' It is headed by Dr.Muhammed Yusuf al Magariaf. The front claimed to have contacts with high-ranking Libyan officials and support within Libya's armed forces. It reportedly received assistance from Saudi Arabia and the US CIA. It has been involved in the attempted coup near Qadhafi's barracks in May 1984 and organized an unsuccessful uprising in early 1985.

• Revolutionary Council of the Prophet of God
Obscure opposition group which operates inside Libya.

• Revolutionary Guards
Governmental security organization; many of its members come from Colonel Qadhafi's tribe in Sirte. It is armed with light weapons and has an estimated strength of 2,000 to 3,000 men. Members have installed themselves as watchdogs at almost every army post and barracks even at Bab el-Azziziya installation which is Colonel's Qadhafi's base.

• Salvation Army for the Liberation of Sudan (SALS)
Reports in 1981 indicated that Colonel Qadhafi was seeking a coup in Sudan. He had organized a 'salvation army' and was recruiting Sudanese workers and other refugees in Libya to join training camps. There are tens of thousands of Sudanese living and working in Libya.

• The Volcano
(Al Borkan)
Libyan opposition group which claimed responsibility for the attack on the Libyan ambassador, Ammar El Taggazy in Rome on Jan.21, 1984. It also claimed responsibility for the murder of the Libyan press attaché Magkjun Farg on Jan.13, 1985.

LUXEMBURG

• Struggling Ecological Movement
(Strijdende Ecologische Beweging)
Group which claimed responsibility for blowing up two electric power pylons in May 9, 1985.

• Unknown Group
A group which is believed to be behind at least 14 attacks in Luxemburg since 1984. Most attacks occurred at weekends or during the night. Targets were electric power pylons, the electricity company Cegedel, radar installations at the Findel airport, the European Common Market building, the Palace of Justice, a customs office, a gas company, underground telephone lines, the Olympic swimmingpool, a police office and a telephone exchange building. The police believed the attacks had a criminal background.
The Cegedel company received an extortion letter in which the group demanded an equivalent of 900,000 Dutch guilders.

MADAGASCAR

• Democratic Movement for the Renovation of Madagascar (Mouvement Démocratique de Rénovation Malgache) (MDRM)
Insurrectionary nationalist movement which emerged in the French colony of Madagascar in

1947. The MDRM insurrection was launched on March 29, 1947, with concerted attacks on military depots, railway stations and telegraph communications mainly in the east of the island. The MDRM were banned by the French Cabinet on May 10, 1947, although two of their members had been elected to the French Chamber of Deputies. In September 1958 the people of Madagascar voted to set up an independent Malagasy Republic ending 62 years of French colonial rule. Casualty estimates for the emergency period vary from 11,000 to 80,000 dead.

* Kung Fu Sect
Group led by Pierre Misael Andrianarijaona (killed Aug.2, 1985) which rejected the leftist nationalist state ideology and called for a new social order based on the religion and rules of Kung Fu. It became popular in the early 1970s through Bruce Lee movies. It had an estimated 10,000 supporters. The group terrorized the capital and repeatedly was involved in clashes with the government militia Youth Consciousness (TTS) which was trained by North Koreans. In August 1984 the government responded to the vigilant activities of the group and attacked its headquarters. Some Kung Fu members were shot on sight. In December 1984 a riot with government sponsored youth groups escalated. The official casualty count was 20 dead, 31 wounded and 208 arrested, but there were credible reports that approximately 50 people were killed and 300 arrested.

* Madagascar for the Malagasy Party
(Madagasikara Otronin'ny Malagasy) (MONIMA)
Party which has been associated with manifestations of political dissent in recent years. Frequent demonstrations and disturbances by students and unemployed young people discontented with the Ratsiraka regime have often taken the Monima leader, Monja Jaona, as a rallying figure, Jaona has frequently attacked what he describes as the repressive approach of the security authorities to such dissent. In 1982 Jaona accused the Army and police of carrying out 'massacres' in various localities in southern Madagascar.

MALI

* Committee for the Defence of Democratic Liberties in Mali
(Comité de Défense des Libertés Democratiques au Mali) (CDLDM)
Exile organization opposed to the existing military regime in Mali and attempting to present a united anti-government front. Its headquarters is located in Paris.

* Front for the Liberation of the Central and Arab Desert (FLCAD)
Revolutionary movement which held its founding conference in 1979. It organized a widespread underground movement by organizing masses of people, ideologically guiding them and by establishing a monetary fund. This was done in order to enable the payment of 10 million French Francs for the release of the leader Ziad Ben Taher, who found refuge in Algeria. Ben Bella extradited him to the Mali government which jailed him in 1963 and did not free him until 1979. Camps and offices were opened in Libya in coordination with Algeria. It's primary aim is the liberation of the central Arab desert from the colonization of Mali and Niger, reuniting it and to establish a free and democratic state.

* Malian National Union of Pupils and Students
(Union Nationale des Elèves et Etudiants du Mali) (UNEEM)
Forbidden breakaway group from the youth movement of the ruling UDPM. In 1980 at least 18 persons had been shot, stabbed or tortured to death by security forces. On July 10, 1981, clemency was granted by the President to all persons involved in the 1979-1980 student unrest.

MALAWI

* Congress for the Second Republic (CSR)
Organization headed by M.W.Kanyama Chiume, a former minister of external affairs (until Sep.7, 1964). In May 1976, President Banda announced the arrest of a group of agents who had, he said, been sent by Chiume and had confessed that their mission had been to assassinate him.

* Malawi Freedom Movement (MAFREMO)
Exile group which was founded in 1977 in Dar es Salam. It is headed by Orton Chirwa. Its aim is restoring 'democracy justice and liberty' in Malawi. Orton Chirwa, a former Justice minister, has attempted to unite all exiled Malawi political groups and announced in March 1981 to have started a guerrilla training program, but no evidence had emerged that armed conflict was pursued in Malawi.

* Murder Squad
Murder squad which has been active in 1983. It reportedly is most likely part of the traffic section of the police which either bumps off victims with lorries or pumps intoxication gas into the intended victim's car so that he crashes after a social evening or a meeting.

* Socialist League of Malawi (LESOMA)
Exile grouping which was established in Maputo (Mozambique). It was headed by Dr.Attati Mpakati (or Mphakathi). It claimed to receive support from

Cuba and the Soviet Union. In 1980 Lesoma was said to have formed a People's Liberation Army of Malawi, but no activities have been recorded.

* Young Pioneers
Mr.Banda's youth league which reportedly is trained by Israel. It has been involved in the murder and torture of dissidents. They were reported to be roaming about villages and ransacking homes in towns beating any suspect or anyone who did not have a Malawi Congess Party membership card.

MALAYSIA

* Asal Group
Communist guerrilla group which worked with aborigines based at Ulu Perak and in Ule Kelantan. In 1981 the unit reportedly broke up and dispersed.

* Communist Party of Malaysia (CPM)
Established in 1930, the CPM was banned in 1948, after taking part in an armed insurrection. The insurgency was suppressed (with the help of British, Australian and New Zealand forces) in 1960. The insurrection had resulted in the death of more than 11,000 persons. The party was headed by Chin Peng. It initially had some 15,000 men in the field, largely ethnic Chinese. It was supported by the People's Republic of China. From 1966 onwards a Malayan National Liberation Army (MLNA) organized by the CPM carried on guerrilla activities near Malaysia's border with Thailand. In 1986 the CPM was estimated to have 1,500 fighters. Leaders, old men in their 60s and 70s, abandoned trying to 'liberate' their homeland across the border. Thailand urged Malaysia to grant an amnesty.

* Communist Party of Malaysia-Marxist Leninist (CPM-ML)
Party which emerged in 1970 as a splinter group from the CPM, from which it differed in advocating the use of urban guerrilla warfare rather than reliance on the rural areas, as practized by the Maoist CPM. Following a purge of the CPM in which 200 members were executed to counter an infiltration threat, elements of the CPM 8th Regiment and the 2d District of the 12th Regiment formed the CPM-RF and CPM-ML. The latter group organized in the Thai salient of Betong, but did not until 1974 become known as an organization. It had some 500 members in the early 1980s. It concentrated its activities in urban areas, demoralizing the population and undermining foreign investment. Police infiltration and use of informers reduced the movement to a relatively insignificant rural unit operating in the distant Betong salient.

* Communist Party of Malaysia-Revolutionary Faction (CPM-RF)
Party which seceded from the CPM in 1970 mainly because of the latter's Maoist policy of using rural areas to encircle the cities, a policy which the CPM-RF considered unworkable in Malaysia, where a majority of the population were Malays. It tried to recruit followers among the Chinese population in the towns and to conduct urban guerrilla warfare. Its operating ground was the Sadao district of Thailand on Malaysia's north-west frontier. It set up an underground support unit, the Malayan People's Liberation Front (MPLF) but it had very little effect. At the outset it numbered some 500 men. Security force action reduced the figure to less than 150 in 1982.

* Crypto
Described by the authorities as a 'deviant Islamic cult'. Nine leaders of this group were arrested under the Internal Security Act on May 27, 1982.

* Dakwah (Missionary) Moslem Movement
Moslem movement involved in violent clashes with police in South Jahore in August 1980. The Dakwah movement advocated the destruction of symbols of modern or Western life, such as television sets and the exclusion of women from higher education being regarded as contrary to the Koran.

* Imbo
Group claiming responsibility for an assassination attempt on the Soviet ambassador in Kuala Lumpur in 1983, in protest against the Soviet occupation of Afghanistan.

* Malayan Islamic Youth Organization (Abim)
Moslem fundamentalist group clashing with the government in 1980-1981, after harassing non-Moslems, in particular Indians and Chinese. It has an estimated 35,000 members and is led by Datuk Asri Muda.

* Malayan National Liberation Army (MNLA)
Guerrilla organization of the Communist Party of Malaysia (CPM) which has been active since 1966. It has been renamed Malayan People's Army in 1982 and is led by Chin Peng. Its strength increased from 1,000 in 1968, to 1,400 in 1973, and to 2,400 to 3,000 in the 1979-1980 period. According to a statement of the police on Oct.28, 1981, there were only about 230 insurgents still operating in the jungles of Pahang, Perak and Kelentang. It has been involved in grenade, rocket and bomb attacks,
assassinations and ambushes. It has targeted police and army facilities and personnel, roadbuilding projects and the Kuala Lumpur airbase. The MNLA consists of three units: the 8th, 12th and 10th regiments. Armed groups in the jungle have links

to the outside world through cells in the towns.

* Malayan National Liberation League (MNLL)
Support unit for the Malayan National Liberation Army. It was established in 1965 in Djakarta (Indonesia).

* Malayan Peoples' Army
(Tentara Rakyat Malaya) (TRM)
On June 20, 1982, the Malayan National Liberation Army has been renamed the Malayan People's Army.

* Malayan National Liberation Front (MPLF)
Support unit of the Communist Party of Malaysia-Revolutionary Front.

* Malayan Races Liberation Army (MRLA)
Military wing of the Malayan People's Anti-Japanese Army guerrilla organization which has been involved in an insurrection (1948 to 1960). A mix of political incentives and security force measures broke the back of the insurgency which resulted in the death of more than 11,000 people, including 2,500 civilians. The guerrillas were deprived of contact with the population through protected villages, whilst plans for independence were accelerated. It was renamed Malayan National Liberation Army in 1965.

* National Revolutionary Front
(Barisan Revolusi Nasional) (BRN)
A splinter group of the parent Communist Party of Malaysia (CPM).

* North Kalimantan Communist Party (NKCP)
This party, operating through its armed wing the PARAKU, was closely allied to the CPM and was in 1980 said to have some 100 fighters active in the first division of Sarawak. They were restricted to the area near Kuching where they maintained relations with the CPM. The party was led by Bong Chee Chok.

* North Kalimantan People's Guerrilla Forces
(Pasokan Rakyat Kalimantan Utara) (PARAKU)
Armed wing of the North Kalimantan Communist Party which fought a low level guerrilla war in the 1950s and 1960s. By the late 1960s the campaign failed and the guerrillas were driven back to operate only in the remotest jungle areas. It had an estimated strength of 600 to 700 fighters in 1971. It was closely allied to the Communist Party of Malaysia and was most active in the Sarawak's first division.

* Pan Malayan Islamic Party (PMIP)
In November 1985, 18 people were killed in fighting in the state of Kedah. A police force of 200 men stormed a barricaded holdout of the fundamentalist leader Ibrahim Mahmood who was defended by 400 Moslems. He was sought for 'extremist missionary activities'. A total of 159 Moslems were arrested.

* Sarawak People's Guerrilla Forces
(Pergerakan Guerilja Rakyat) (PGRS)
During the 1950s communist organizations were active in Sarawak working through the Sarawak Communist Organization. From the start the SCO opposed Sarawak's joining the Malaysian Federation opting for the creation of an independent communist state. The two principal Marxist-Leninist organizations, the PARAKU and the PGRS took up arms, supported by Indonesia. By the late 1960s this campaign had failed and the guerrillas were driven back to operate only in remote jungle areas.

MARTINIQUE

* Armed Liberation Group of Martinique
(Groupe de Liberation Armèe de la Martinique) (GLAM)
This group, said to be an offshoot of the GLA of Guadeloupe, claimed responsibility for attacks carried out in December 1980, including one on the headquarters of French television in Martinique.

* Martinique Independence Movement
(Mouvement Indépendantiste Martiniquais or La Parole au Peuple) (MIM)
Organization led by Alfred Marie-Jeanne (mayor of the town of Rivière-Pilote) which is striving for independence. He declared in March 1980: 'It is not through elections that we will take power, but we shall use the conseil général and the mayor's offices to help our struggle for revolutionary unity in the Caribbean. We do receive help from other countries (including Cuba and the Soviet Union)... Our revolution embraces all solutions, including armed struggle.' There have been signs of dissension within the MIM.

MAURETANIA

* Alliance for Democratic Mauretania (ADM)
Paris-based opposition front sympathetic to former President Ould Daddah of Mauretania who was overthrown in July 1978. Its coup attempt was foiled on Mar.16, 1981. It resulted in the death of 28 people, including 13 civilians. A total of 60 persons were arrested. The alliance was led by Lt.Col.Mohammed Ould Ba Ould Abdel-Kadir and Lt.Col. Ahmed Salem Ould Sidi (executed Mar.26, 1981).

* El Hor
Banned organization of the black Arab-speaking Haratin people who form one third of the population. Leaders are exiled in France.

* Islamic Party
(Parti Islamique) (PI)
Opposition movement led by Lt.Col.Muhammad Abdel-Kadir who has been involved in an attempted coup in March 1981.

* Mauretanian Democratic Union
(Union Démocratique Mauretanienne) (UDM)
Union which was established in Senegal to join forces of Black Africans (making up about one third of Mauretania's population) and the half-caste Haratines (almost equal in number to the Black Africans) to confront the country's dominant Arab Berbers.

* Organization of Mauretanian Nationalists (ONAM)
Group which claimed responsibility for the death of Mohammed Khomsi, a Libyan political refugee. He was found strangled in a Rome Hotel on Sep.20, 1984. The claim was not deemed credible by the investigators.

* Walfougi Front
Armed Front for the Self Determination of the Black African Population of the southern Mauretanian Regions of Walo, Fouta and Guidimalia (or Walfougi Front) established in 1979. It criticized the military government of Mauretania; it opposed the imposition of Arabic as the main language; it called for the continued use of French and numerous tribal languages; it called for an even distribution of posts in the administration between the country's ethnic communities; and finally it supported secession of the southern half of Western Sahara to the Saharan Arab Democratic Republic (SADR).

MEXICO

* The Falcons
(Los Halcones)
Right-wing group responsible for an attack on left-wing students on June 10, 1971. A student committee claimed that the group had killed 25 students and that 62 others had disappeared. The group was banned in June 1971.

* Federal Directorate of Security
(Direccion Federal de Seguridad) (DFS)
This security force repeatedly has been in the news in connection with arbitrary arrests and torturing of political prisoners. After the earthquake tortured bodies, including those of children, were discovered under the collapsed building of the state-attorney in Mexico-City. In 1985 the name of the service was changed into National Service for Research and Security (DISN). In May 1985, more than 400 agents who were suspected of involvement in drug trafficking or other corrupt activities have been dismissed or resigned.

* International Commando Simon Bolivar
Group which placed a bomb in a car near the US embassy in Mexico City in April 1986.

* Investigation Department for the Prevention of Delinguency (Departemento de Investigacion de Prevencion de la Delincuencia) (DIPD)
Secret service of the general directorate of the police in Mexico-City which has been involved in human rights violations. It operated under the name Brigada Blanca. It was officially dissolved in January 1983 and its agents were transferred to other police units.

* Judicial State Police Force
Members of this police force in the state of Jabisco, functioned as a private army for narcotics traffickers in Guadalajara, performing personal errands and acting as bodyguards in return for money and cocaine.

* Los Lacandones
Left-wing, university-based urban terrorist group active in the early 1970s. It was reportedly led by Rigoberto Lorence, a journalist who founded the Zapatista Urban Front (FUZ).

* Latin American Anti-Communist Confederation (CAL)
An umbrella group for the Latin American death squad network with the purpose to intimidate suspected leftists and to deter movements that threaten the status quo. Its methods include kidnapping, assassination, secret pacts, intrigue, terrorism and blackmail. The US columnist, Jack Anderson suggested the possibility of a Murder Incorporated germinated by the CIA.

* Movement of Revolutionary Action
(Movimiento de Accion Revolucionaria) (MAR)
Small terrorist movement active in the early 1970s. Some of the sixty members had received education and training in the Soviet Union and North Korea.

* National Confederation of Peasants
(Confederacion Nacional Campesina) (CNC)
An official farmers federation that is affiliated to the ruling PRI. Members of this federation have repeatedly been involved in the killing of members of independent peasant organizations and rural trade unions in the context of land disputes. The CNC attributes fatalities in its ranks to members of independent unions, encouraged by leftist political activists. Others, however, suggest that for the most part CNC members who have been killed were victims of internal CNC struggles.

* National Patriotic Anticommunist Front (Frente Patriotica Anti-comunista Nacional) (FPAN)
A paramilitary group.

* National Revolutionary Civic Association (Associación Civica Nacional Revolucionaria) (ACNR)
Urban middle class group, led by Genero Vásquez Rojas from 1968-1971 which attempted to set up a rural guerrilla base among peasants in Atoyac mountains of Guerro state in south-west Mexico. After the arrest of several prominent members in 1971, nothing further was heard of the group.

* Los Negros
A 2,000 men strong anti-guerrilla force whose existence was revealed in March 1980 by the paper Uno Mas Uno.

* Party of the Poor
(Partido de los Pobros)
Guerrilla movement established in 1967 and led by Lucio Cabanas, a former school teacher and member of the Communist party. It did not long survive the death of its leader on Dec.2, 1974, by the security forces.

* People's Revolutionary Armed Forces
(Fuerzas Revolutionarias Armadas del Pueblo) (FRAP)
Group which has been responsible for a number of kidnappings in 1973 and 1974 including two US-consuls. In FRAP statements published in newspapers and broadcast on radio on television it called on the people to overthrow the government by armed struggle. After the capture in 1976, of the reported leader, Ramón Campana López was captured by police in Jalisco state, the group lost momentum. In September 1977 the FRAP joined the September 23 Communist League in urban bombings of government and party buildings in Mexico City, Oaxaca and Guadalajara. No incidents were reported since 1978.

* People's Union
(Unión del Pueblo) (UP)
A small Leninist group which arose out of the student revolt of 1968 in Mexico and remained active for a decade. It was led by José Maria Ortiz Vides, a Guatemalan who had previously been trained in Cuba. Most members were arrested in October 1972. The rump joined forces with the September 23 Communist League in 1975. It resurfaced in 1977 but has been less active in 1978.

* Pistoleros
Generic name for gunmen acting on behalf of the large landowners (caciques) with the implicit or overt support of local military commanders and local state and federal authorities. They have been involved in acts of violence against civilians.

* Red Faction of the Workers Revolutionary Party (RF-WRP)
Six Argentines and a Mexican kidnapped the daughter of an industrialist, B.Madero Garza, on Oct.23, 1981. The kidnappers were arrested when they tried to collect the ransom of US $ 1.6 million. According to the police, two kidnappers belonged to the RF-WRP, a group which was held responsible for the assassination of President Somoza (Nicaragua).

* Revolutionary Action Movement
(Movimiento de Accion Revolucionario) (MAR)
Urban guerrilla group active in 1971 in Mexico City. It consisted of about 60 men and women. Its founders were educated at Patrice Lumumba University in Moscow. Subsequently they were sent to North Korea for military training before returning to Mexico in 1966/67. It has been involved in armed assaults, bank robberies and the kidnapping of the Mexican director of civil aviation. A campaign of sabotage was prevented by police action which uncovered the network. This led to the expulsion of five Soviet embassy staff in March 1971 and the recalling of the Mexican ambassador from Moscow.

* September 23 Communist League
(Liga Comunista 23 de Septiembre)
This Marxist-Leninist group was said to be the urban guerrilla group of the Poor People Party. It started urban terrorist activities in Mexico in 1974. Some of its members had belonged to the Revolutionary Action Movement. It has been involved in kidnappings, assassinations, armed attacks, bank robberies and bombings of government buildings, banks, police stations, and telephone booths. In August 1978 its second leader, Carlos Jiménez Sarmiento was killed. The group was rolled up by the police in February 1981.

* Los Tecos
Extreme right-wing paramilitary group which reportedly terrorized the university of Guadalajara.

* Triqui Movement for Unity and Struggle
(Movimiento de Unificacion y Lucha Triqui) (MULT)
Organization of the Triqui people (about 15,000) which has been established in 1981. According to MULT hundreds of people have lost their lives during the last five years and a number of MULT leaders have been murdered. The organization attempts to organize agriculture in a cooperative way and wants to execute the 1973 presidential decision which means that the Triqui people have a right to communal land. Local authorities have

been involved in 'disappearances', arbitrary arrests, torturing, and the setting afire of houses and forests.

* Unified Socialist Party of Mexico (PSUM)
A coalition of five left-wing groups which was established on Nov.8, 1981. On Feb.27, 1985, Alejandro Cardenas Peralta, a PSUM member, was killed in Oaxaca. The PSUM accused an agent of the State Attorney General and two agents of the State Judicial Police in Oaxaca of having carried out the murder. Other allegations are that his opposition to a tourist project which would have entailed expropriation of communal land was a factor in his murder.

* White Brigade
(Brigada Blanca) (BB)
Right-wing militia, allegedly supported by members of the secret service of the general directorate of the police of Mexico-City (DIPD), that has claimed responsibility for nearly 500 hundred kidnappings of people considered to have been involved in left-wing activities or to have left-wing sympathies. It was said to have been active since 1976. In 1980 the existence of the White Brigade was officially denied. It had a secret detention center (Campo Militar Numero Uno) in a suburb of Mexico-City where it tortured prisoners. It served the interests of landowners and company directors.

* Zapatista Urban Front
(Frente Urbano Zapatista) (FUZ)
Urban terrorist group active in Mexico City around 1971/72. It was named after after the revolutionary hero, Emiliano Zapata (1877-1919). Its leader, Francisco Urango López, was arrested in January 1972. Group members received training from individuals trained in North Korea or in China.

MOROCCO

* August 16 Movement
(Mouvement du 16 Aout)
Movement of liberal officers named after the date of an armed attack on a Boeing aircraft in 1972. It is believed to have been involved in a plot against King Hassan II.

* Forward Movement
(Ilal Amam)
Left-wing organization which surfaced in 1974 when a large number of persons were arrested. Ilal Amam, the March 23 Group and Al Moutakalinine (Rally) were planning to be merged into a Marxist-Leninist front with a 'Red Army'. Their goal was a people's democratic republic to be headed by Abraham Serfaty, an anti-Zionist Jewish engineer and former member of the Moroccan Communist Party. On Feb.15, 1977, a total of 176 of the arrested persons were sentenced to terms of imprisonment, including Serfaty. In late 1985 more than 40 individuals, including students, lawyers and doctors were arrested in several cities, allegedly in connection with the distribution of a leaflet by the illegal left-wing group. There were reports of ill treatment and torture of detainees.

* Frontistes
Two hundred members of this socialist group were detained in the 1974-1976 period and charged with being member of an illegal society and to have conspired against the internal security of the state.

* Holy War
(Al Jihad)
Seventy-one members of Al Jihad, a section of the Islamic Movement were sentenced for plotting against the regime of King Hassan II. The leaders were sentenced to death.

* Islamic Youth
Banned organization which was reportedly led by Abdelkrim Motei and the Algerian security service. The purpose of the organiztion was to destabilize the government of King Hassan II by organizing attacks and by spreading unrest. Three members confessed to have brought weapons and explosives to Morocco from Algeria where they had received military training.

* Moroccan Patriotic Front
(Frente Patriotico Moroqui) (FPM)
Organization which stands for the restoration of Moroccan sovereignty over the cities of Ceuta and Melilla. Members were responsible for several bomb attacks in the Spanish enclave in late 1978 and early 1979 in protest against Spain's insistence on these cities' status as part of the Kingdom of Spain.

MOZAMBIQUE

* Dragons of Death
Former Portuguese commandos which were active in 1974.

* Free Africa Movement
(Movimiento da Africa Livre) (FAM)
Terrorist organization which was established in 1965. It operated from Malawi and was led by Amos Sumane. It was supported by Rhodesia (now Zimbabwe) and has been involved in acts of sabotage in the Niassa and Zambezi provinces. In 1981 four terrorists were comdemned to death for killing policemen, soldiers and peasants inside Mozambique.

* Mozambique Liberation Front
(Frente da Libertacao de Mocambique)

(FRELIMO)Liberation movement which was established in 1962 by a merger of three smaller movements. It was led by Dr.Eduardo Mondlane (murdered on Feb.3, 1969) and developed into a well-organized guerrilla movement. After Mondlane's death, Samora Machel and Marcellino Dos Santos became the principal leaders. FRELIMO had its headquarters and its training camps in Tanzania. During the last stage of the war an estimated 7-8,000 guerrillas operated inside Mozambique. The Lisbon coup in 1974 caused Portugal to withdraw from Africa. After independence on June 25, 1975 FRELIMO, led by President Samora Machel, became a 'vanguard party'. The total number of casualties of the independence struggle was estimated at 30,000 deaths. Machel was killed in October 1986 in a plane crash widely attributed to South African sabotage.

* Mozambique Resistance Movement
(Movimiento da Resistencia Mocambicana) (MRM)
Guerrilla movement which emerged in 1976 and became fully active in late 1978-79. It members were drawn from dissident Mozambicans, trained in Rhodesia by former disaffected FRELIMO guerrillas and seasoned Portuguese fighters. It was led by Andrew Matade Matsangai and had about 1,000 fighters. It was established by the Rhodesian secret service. After Rhodesian independence in 1980 South Africa took over the foreign support role. The purpose of the organization was to destabilize Mozambique so that it could not be used as a guerrilla base for attacks on South Africa and Zimbabwe. The guerrilla movement has been involved in a campaign to sabotage railway and power lines. Associated with MRM were Miguel Murrupa, Mateus Gwengere and Joao Mario Tudele, Afonso Dhlakama and Andreas Shimango. Its principal spokesman was Domingo Arouca. It was restructured in 1980 and renamed RENAMO.

* Mozambique National Resistence
(Resistencia Nacional Mocambicana) (RENAMO)
Guerrilla movement which has been active since 1976. Until 1980 it was known as MNR. In February 1980 all MNR men still in Rhodesia were sent to South Africa which set up a MNR training camp in Transvaal and rebuild the organization under a new commander, Afonso Dhlakama. By 1982 it was active in seven of the eleven provinces of Mozambique. Armed bands of up to 200 men sweep through the countryside burning villages and mutilating and killing civilians. It has an estimated 5,000 fighters although its own claims reach up to 17,000. It is not considered a nationalist movement and has no political base or deep roots among the Mozambican people nor a coherent political program. Its economic sabotage campaign has paralyzed the country's economy. Thousands of civilians have lost their lives in recent years and the economic sabotage has worsened a food crisis. The guerrillas have been responsible for numerous massacres of civilians. Mercenaries of several nations are reported to fight along RENAMO.

* Revolutionary Committee of Mozambique
(ComitêRevolucionáriodeMocambique)(COREMO)
Small guerrilla organization which was formed in 1965 by dissidents from FRELIMO. It was led by Paulo Gumane. A number of its members had undergone guerrilla training in China. Nothing more was heard of their guerrilla activities after 1972.

* United Mozambique Front
(Frente Unido Mocambiquena) (FUMO)
Organization which was formed in the latter days of Portuguese colonial rule by Portuguese business elements with a view to protecting their interests in an independent Mozambique. During 1980 FUMO, then based in Portugal, was reported to be making efforts among emigrés from Mozambique to set up forces to fight the FRELIMO regime. FUMO leaders refused, however, to cooperate in any way with the Mozambican National Resistance (RENAMO). Joao Khan acts as its president.

* United Rhombezia African National Union (URANU)
A secessionist group which has been active in 1986.

NAMIBIA

* Caprivi African National Union (CANU)
Organization led by Mishahe Muyongo which seeks independence for the Caprivi Strip. It merged with SWAPO. On Aug.6, 1980, Muyongo, acting vice president of SWAPO, announced in Lusaka (Zambia) that he would reassert the separate existence of the CANU, which had been one of SWAPO's constituent parties. The Zambian government did not allow CANU to be established in Zambia, and it was officially alleged in Windhoek that numerous Caprivians were being detained in Zambia.

* People's Liberation Army of Namibia (PLAN)
Armed branch of SWAPO which has an estimated strength of 8,500 fighters. About 1,500 are believed to de deployed in the war in Namibia. Sam Nujoma acts as its commander-in-chief. Training is provided mainly in Angola by Cubans, and since 1978 by East Germans as well. A few recruits are sent to Cuba. Much of SWAPO's military activity took place inside Angola against guerrillas of the South African-backed UNITA. SWAPO rarely operates in big units inside Namibia confining its actions for the most part to hit and run raids across the border.

* South West African People's Organization (SWAPO)

Main guerrilla organization in Namibia which was founded in 1960 when it replaced the Ovamboland People's Party. It has an estimated 7,000 to 10,000 guerrillas of which 1,500 are assigned to operations in Namibia. Others are in camps in Angola, Zambia and Botswana. It is headed by Sam Nujoma who also acts as Commander in Chief. The armed struggle began in 1966 and was intensified in 1974 and again in 1986. The number of incidents in 1986 was three times higher than the total for the previous ten years. It employs the classic guerrilla tactic of surprise attacks and ambushes followed by a quick withdrawal and the dispersal of forces. The South African Defense Force (SADF) has used counter-insurgency measures, such as mass arrest; interrogation and intimidation of local people; the creation of a 'free fire' zone; the invasion of neighboring countries where the guerrilla bases are located; the recruitment of local forces; attempts to win hearts and minds; and the deployment of 'reaction' units.

* South West Africa Territory Force (SWATF)
Established on Aug.1, 1980, as the basis of a future independent South West African defence force. It is made up mainly of South African Army units bases in South West Africa. In 1987 the SWATF provided 60 percent of the troops in combat operations and about 40 percent of the total military strength. The SWATF remains a part of the SADF. It is largely a militia force with a mobilization strength of around 22,000 and has three main components, a Standing Force, a reaction Force and an Area Force. The Area Force (a counter insurgency force of some 26 units) is a territorial force with responsibility for internal security operations. The policy of South Africa is to reduce the deployment of the SADF in SWA as the SWATF and the SWA Police have expanded their ability to handle the situation.

* South West Africa Police's Counterinsurgency Unit
(Teeninsurgensie Eenheid) (SWAPCU)
South African counterinsurgency unit, previously called Koevoet. In 1986, it reportedly killed over 2,500 insurgents in some 800 contacts with own losses of 100 killed and about 400 injured. It is comprised of three units, one each in Kaokoland, Ovamboland and Kavango. Each unit has several platoon-sized fighting groups and a small special investigation team which also handles supporting special and covert operations. Its headquarters is located at Oshakati.

NEPAL

* Anti Chinese Khampa Guerrillas
Tibetans which settled in Nepal in the early 1970s and which took up arms against Nepal's sovereignty.

* Communist Party of Nepal (CPN)
The party was declared illegal on Jan.25, 1952, on the ground that it had been involved in an attempted revolt with other left-wing groups, including dissidents of the Nepalese Congress Party. On Apr.15, 1956, the ban on the party was lifted after it had given a written assurance that it would conduct its activities peacefully and constitutionally and that it acknowledged the King as the constitutional head of state. In 1968 pro-Chinese Communists led by Gopal Parsai were said to be engaged in guerrilla warfare in the Jhapha district (south-east Nepal) , where they cooperated closely with the naxalites of India, responsible for the 1967 Naxalbari revolt. Gopal Parsai was reportedly arrested in late 1968. In January 1973 members of the Maoist faction of the party fled to West Bengal.

* Nepali Congress Party (NCP)
The NCP was founded in Calcutta in 1946 under the leadership of Bisheswar Prasad Koirala (who had been active in the Indian Congress Party and its struggle for Indian independence). In 1947 the left wing of the NCP broke away to form the Nepali Democratic Congress founded by Mahendra Bikram Shan (a member of the Nepali royal family). On Sep.29, 1950, it was announced in Katmandu that NCP supporters had plotted to assassinate the prime Minister, and in November-December 1950, NCP followers were involved in a revolt against the government which induced the latter to introduce constitutional reforms. The state of emergency imposed by the king ended in April 1963 with the introduction of a system of indirect representation. Since then there have been short periods in which the NCP has been involved in acts of terrorism, including 1973-74 and in 1977. In May 1985 it called for a campaign of civil disobedience for the restoration of parliamentary democracy.

* Peoples Front
(Janwadi Morcha) (JM)
Front which was established in 1976 and is based in Uttar Pradesh. It is led by Ramrajo Prsad Singh, a former member of parliament. It is striving for the establishment of a democratic republic, economic equality and the abolishment of private property. Members of the front are trained in guerrilla warfare. In June 1985 it claimed responsibility for a number of bomb attacks.

* United Liberation Army or Torchbearers
(Samyukta Mukti Bahini) (SMB)
Obscure group which claimed responsibility for a number of bomb attacks in June 1985. The name refers to its banner showing a hand with a torch

symbolizing freedom.

NETHERLANDS

* The Activists of March 29
(De Aktievoerders van 29 Maart)
One of two anti-fascist groups which claimed responsibility for the events at Kedichem on Mar.29, 1986, when a meeting of the right-wing Center Party at the Cosmopolite Hotel was broken up. The hotel was attacked by about 200 activists throwing smoke bombs and incendiary devices. A secretary fell from a window and one of her legs had to be amputated. More than 70 people were arrested.

* AGIT
Anti-nuclear action group which has claimed responsiblity for a minor bomb attack at the IJselcentrale in Zwolle on Nov.1, 1985. Several weeks later it claimed responsibility for an arson attack at a Mercedes Benz garage also in Zwolle with an estimated damage of 1,5 million Dutch guilders. The latter attack was a protest against involvement of Mercedes in weapon deliveries to South Africa.

* Aid Oldelft to get rid of its Military Image
(Help Oldelft van haar Militaire Imago af)
Anti-militarist action group which placed minor bombs at a building of the Delft Electronics Products (DEP) in Roden on May 16, 1985. Twenty minutes after the announcement of the attack two fire bombs exploded which caused minor damage. The Oldelft company produces nightvision products which have been exported to Chile and South Africa.

* Amsterdam People's Resistance
(Amsterdams Volksverzet) (AVV)
Surinam organization which has organized activities against the regime of Desi Bouterse.

* Anti Terror Team
(Anti-terreur Team)
Anti-terror unit of the Dutch police which has been established in January 1987 after a series of harsher actions of anti-apartheid groups, which included arson attacks on three big warehouses of the SHV company and Shell petrol filling stations. The unit (which is called the section) is comprised of 12 persons, six of the state police and six of the Central Detective Information Service (CRI). Their task is to observe persons suspected of terrorist activities. The section is added to the Observation group West I (The Hague).

* Atom Free State
(Atoomvrijstaat)
Anti-militarist action group which has tried to delay the construction of the cruise missile base at Woensdrecht by buying pieces of land in the neighborhood of the base. The land has been financed by 4,500 'passport holders' and 1,500 supporters, who bought obligations of 100 Dutch guilders. Protection of the base has cost the Dutch state already 30 million Dutch guilders, which excludes additional costs for the deployments of the state police. A total of 3,000 'incidents' have been recorded which vary from large scale demonstrations and blockades to minor sabotage actions. The activists developed into a sort of construction police and have recorded the activities of the companies involved in the construction which are officially secret. These companies have been subjected to minor sabotage actions and threat letters.

* Autonomists
(Autonomen)
Generic name for individuals who regularly clashed with police and Mobile Units during or at the end of demonstrations. During the visit of the Pope in 1985 autonomists distributed posters with a call to liquidate the Pope, while others desecrated graves of priests.

* Burn Down Apartheid
Anti-apartheid action group which has been responsible for the arson of five Shell petrol filling stations in Amsterdam, Amstelveen, Marssum and Emmen on June 16, 1986. Damage was estimated at one million Dutch guilders.

* Citizens of Amsterdam Opposing Racism
(Amsterdammers tegen Racisme)
Loosely organized group with links to the squatters movement and action world. Minor groups which operate under fantasy names like 'Commando Crash and Carry' or 'Pyromaniacs against Apartheid' have staged actions against companies with links to South Africa. The legal anti-apartheid groups have denounced the harsher actions of these groups.

* Citizen League of the Netherlands
(Burgerbond Nederland)
Anti-apartheid action group which has claimed responsibility for the arson of a villa in Berg en Dal. The owner of the villa, John Deuss, was said to be involved in oil deliveries to South Africa.

* Council for the Liberation of Surinam
(Raad voor de Bevrijding van Suriname) (RBS)
Surinam resistance group established in January 1983 with the aim of overthrowing the regime of Desi Bouterse. It was led by Henk Chin a Sen, a former prime minister. He was replaced by Glenn Tjong-Akiet in March 1986. With the new leader it no longer excluded violent activities against the Bouterse regime. In 1984 Tjong-Akiet had prepared an invasion from French Guyana. The plot was

discovered by French Guyanan authorities and the group, which included American mercenaries, was expelled. Inspired by events in Haiti and the Philippines, the council announced it would develop a strategy of a people's insurrection. On its second Congress in March 1986 suggestions were made for a directed mobilization of resistance in Surinam. Within a year three murder and three bomb attacks have been recorded in direct relation to the Surinam resistance in the Netherlands. A tragic climax was the attack in Rijswijk on Mar.7, 1985. Three members of an amateur pop group were, in what has been suggested to be a case of mistaken identity, executed in a building of the organization. The murder has not been solved. It has been sugested that the perpetrators belonged to a death squad controlled by the military regime of Surinam.

* Domestic Security Service
(Binnenlandse Veiligheidsdienst) (BVD)
In 1985 the Dutch security service spoke of a rising trend in right-wing extremism and violent activism of the hardcore of the squatters movement with an anarchist character. The service collects information on persons which might be involved in terrorist activities. In the beginning of 1987 the five Dutch security services were reorganized into three services, the Domestic Security Service (BVD), the Central Detective Information Service (CRI) and one military service (previously three).

* Federation of Turkish Societies in the Netherlands
(Federatie van Turkse Verenigingen in Nederland)
Possibly a front organization for the Turkish Grey Wolves. It is reportedly led by Cengiz Ozdemir and Mustafa Bac.

* Free South Moluccan Youth Movement
(Vrije Zuid Molukse Jongeren) (Pemuda Masjarakat) (VZJ)
Organization set up by South Moluccans (of whom some 15,000 had been brought to the Netherlands in 1951) after the collapse of the Republic of the South Moluccas (Republik Maluku Selatan, RMS) proclaimed in April 1950. South Moluccans continued their resistance to the Indonesian government until the leader of the RMS was arrested in 1963, and executed in 1966. 'President' Chr.Soumoukil was succeeded by Ir.Jan Alvares Manusama as leader of the Government of the South Moluccan Republic in Exile. Certain South Moluccans in the Netherlands pursued their aim of restoring the RMS and to further their aim, resorted to acts of violence, including the setting of fire to the Indonesian embassy in the Hague (1966), temporary occupation of the Indonesian ambassador's residence (1970), hijacking of a train (1975), occupation of the Indonesian consulate in Amsterdam (1975), hijacking of a train and a hostaging of a school (1977).
In 1986 the Dutch government and the South Moluccan community signed a definitive 'peace treaty'. Political issues like the acknowledgement of the right of self-determination of the Independent South Moluccan Republic (RMS) no longer were included in the dialogue. J.A.Manusama said it was of no use to continue to press for recognition on this issue. At this point RMS-leaders said they prefer to cooperate with other secessionist movements in Indonesia (Timor, Atjeh) and the young island republics in the west of the Pacific. When supporters of the RMS ideal raised a flag in the South Moluccas on Apr.25, 1986, tens of them were arrested and mistreated by the Indonesian government. The arrests in Indonesia led to a demonstration in The Hague. Minor groups within the South Moluccan community that do not agree with Manusama sometimes established their own governments in exile. One such group is the Lawa Mena Hau Lala established in 1983. It was headed by Demi Malawau until December 1986. Since then it is headed by Arie Salempessy. On the request of the Pusat Komando Tertinggi on the South Moluccans it established the Cabinet Nanusaku. The standpoint of this group is that the resistance in the South Moluccans will not succeed without a political unity of the South Moluccans in the Netherlands and those in the rest of the world. The group coordinates support for the South Moluccans in Indonesia from abroad.
In June 1987, an unknown group, the 'Gerakun Maloekoe 11 Joeni', claimed responsibility for a number of fake bombs in trains, in commemoration of the Moluccans who died during the train hijacking in 1977.

* Life Tree Consortium
(Consortium de Levensboom)
A circle of friends around Mrs.Florrie Rost van Tonningen-Heuvel which was established in July 1984. She was married to Meinoud Rost van Tonningen, who was the president of the Dutch bank during the occupation by the Nazis in the Second World War. The circle propagates the old German national socialist NSB ideals. Prominent members are H.Heringa (NVU), J.Kruls (Northern League), W.Zeilmaker, F.Zoetmulder (NVU), C.van Rijn (Viking Youth), F.Naebout (Moon Sect) and S.de Beukelaar (Voorpost). The villa of Mrs.Rost van Tonningen is used as a meeting center for neo-Nazis. She has been convicted for the distribution of anti-semitic literature. Infiltrated anti-fascists found out that the group was involved in death threats and intimidation.

* Makmur
Surinam organization which assists and controls Surinam refugees. It is led by Paul Somohardjo and

is based in Rotterdam. In a police raid in August 1985 weapons were discovered. There have been reports that the organization repeatedly has been involved in preparations for armed resistance against the regime of Desi Bouterse.

* Militant Autonomists Front
(Militant Autonomen Front) (MAF)
After the riots in connection with the eviction of the Lucky Luyk, a squatted building in Amsterdam, in late 1982, this action group claimed responsibility for three minor bomb attacks. Targets were an underground (Metro) railway carriage, an office of the City Housing Service and an office of the Labour Party (Partij van de Arbeid).

* National Youth Front
(Nationaal Jeugdfront) (NJF)
Right-wing organization which has been responsible for two bomb attacks on offices of the Pacifist Socialist Party (PSP) in Tilburg on May 13 and 16, 1983. It has also been involved in the distribution of racist pamphlets. After a quarrel it has severed links with the Dutch People's Union (NVU). In March 1980 it joined the Bund Europa which is aimed at the unification of the right-wing radicals of Germany, Flanders and the Netherlands.

* Nightshade
(Nachtschade)
Anti-apartheid action group which claimed responsibility for a series of acts of sabotage on Shell petrol filling stations at Amstelveen (twice), Zoetermeer (three times), Breukelen, Someren, Kesteren, Jutphaas, Nieuwegein, Deil and De Bilt on May 12, 1986. According to the group Shell circumvents an international oil embargo and plays a vital role in the supply of oil to South Africa. The group demanded an immediate end to the export of oil to South Africa. It considered the sabotage as an effective means to put Shell under pressure. The group said to have no contacts with another group called Even More Nightshade.

* Northern Terror Front
(Noordelijk Terreurfront) (NTF)
Obscure minor action group which claimed responsibility for three molotov cocktail attacks in Groningen in early 1985. Targets included the main office of the police (Jan.23), a recruitment office of the Ministry of Defense (Jan.29) and a building of the Technical Service of the State Police (Feb.1). The group claimed the attacks by telephone and announced further attacks on 'Nato objects and its accomplices'. Nothing further was heard of the group.

* Northern League (NL)
Right-wing party led by Max Lewin. It has been involved in propaganda activities for the colonels regime in Greece and the White regime in Rhodesia (now Zimbabwe) in the 1960s. It has been responsible for the first violent action of the extreme right. On Feb.14, 1975, police arrested three men near an underground (Metro) station under construction in the Bijlmermeer. They made an attempt to place explosives. At the time local authorities erroneously blamed the left-wing action group Nieuwmarkt for this right-wing provocation.

* Onkruit
Anti-militarist action group which sprang from a loosely organized group of conscientious objectors. They started with open public confrontations during the 'open days' of the military and discussed their actions in the media. It developed into small autonomous groups which advocated harsher resistance, like occupations, theft, sabotage and destruction, without announcing their activities. It had an estimated 15 to 100 members in 15 city groups. Conscientious objectors have become a minority. Other members come from the squatters movement, anti-nuclear movement and women movement. Activities are prepared in secret but have publicity as its goal. Members have publicly declared they do not want an underground armed struggle. It prefers 'liberating' government documents and confrontational activities. It has published material which explained the operational methods of the Dutch intelligence services and the police and Dutch war preparations in peace time. It also stole war time medical supplies which were sent to Nicaragua and Eritrea.

* Pan Turkish Organization (PTO)
Group which claimed responsibility for a parcel bomb at a Bulgarian travel agency in Amsterdam on Mar.27, 1985. In a pamphlet sent to international news agencies, the group said it would continue with attacks. About 800,000 Turks live in Bulgaria. Bulgarian authorities have engaged in a Bulgarization campaign in which reportedly several hundred Turks were reportedly killed and thousands detained.

* Pyromaniacs against Apartheid
(Pyromanen tegen Apartheid)
Anti-apartheid action group which claimed responsibility for an arson attack on the villa of John Deuss, an oil trader, in January 1986.

* Red Action Front
(Rood Actie Front) (RAF)
Group which claimed responsibility for molotov cocktail attacks on M.Leerling and H.Knoop in May/June 1982. Three members of the group were arrested on July 5, 1982.

* Red Help

(Rode Hulp) (RH)
Members and sympathizers of Red Youth set up Red Help in 1973 to agitate for the release of two collegues from jail- Lucien van Hoesel and Geert Flokstra. The principal organizers included Henk Wubben, Willem Oskam, Evert van den Berg, Roel Koopmans and Joost van Steenis. In jail, Lucien van Hoesel came into contact with Adri Eeken and his wife, who were active on behalf of the Palestinian cause. The contact was extended once van Hoesel had been released in November 1974. In July, 1976, ten RH members were able to visit South Yemen for three weeks' training under the auspices of the Popular Front for the Liberation of Palestine (PFLP). In return RH agreed to carry out a terrorist attack at Tel Aviv airport, but the Israelis preempted the attack by arresting two members, Ludwina Jansen and Marius Nieuwburg. The incident discredited RH, which was disbanded in December 1976.

* Red Resistance Front
(Rood Verzets Front) (RVF)
Left-wing action group which sprang from Red Help in 1977. It was set up by Adri Eeken and his wife, Ciska Brakenhof. The purpose of the new organization was to lend support to the German RAF. During the first years of its existence it indulged in little more than painting graffitti on public buildings, sit-ins and non-violent occupations. In 1979 two members of the group tried to steal blank passports. It had about 100 members. The group publishes a two-weekly 'Press Clippings Magazine' (Knipselkrant) which contains pressclippings (from 175 dailies and weeklies), action declarations, strategy papers and scientific journal articles on terrorism, counter-insurgency, secret service activities, squatting, imperialism, fascism and anti-militarism. Originally it was meant for its own members but now it is available from left-wing bookshops in the Netherlands, Belgium and West Germany, and functions as a communication medium for leftwing action groups. In the summer of 1986 Dutch authorities detained one of the producers. He was released after two weeks for lack of evidence for the charges brought against him. In the Netherlands there is no law, like in West Germany (129a) to ban publications advocating violence.

* Red Revolutionary Front
(Rood Revolutionair Front) (RRF)
Group of three men from The Hague responsible for nine attacks since the fall of 1984. The targets included a police station, a Texaco petrol filling station, an energy company building (GEB), an office of the Christian employers, an office of the Atlantic Commission, an office of Neratom, an office of the European Political Cooperation, an office of Shell, all in The Hague, and an office of American Express in Rotterdam. The three were arrested in December 1986 and tried in March 1987.

* Red Youth
(Rode Jeugd) (RJ)
A maoist splinter group of the Communist Party of the Netherlands established in 1966, influenced by the Brazilean urban guerrilla leader Carlos Marighela. It tried to transform street demonstrations into battles with the Dutch police. It was established in 1966. Its biggest and most violent section was in Eindhoven. RJ activists took to throwing fire and smoke bombs, and in 1972 attacked a Holiday Inn in Utrecht and the Philips corporation in Rotterdam and Eindhoven. The latter attacks were undertaken under the name of the Revolutionary People's Organization of the Netherlands. Others were perpetrated under the name of Red People's Resistance. Members supported the armed resistance in Greece and Portugal. They rejected the idea of going underground like the West German RAF for fear of losing all contacts with the left-wing movement. The group was disbanded in November 1974. Prominent members were Lucien van Hoesel, Aat van Wijk, Joost van Steenis and Ger Flokstra.

* Revolutionary Anti Racist Action
(Revolutionaire Anti Racistische Aktie) (RARA)
Anti-apartheid action group which has claimed responsibility for a series of arson attacks. They include the fire at the Makro shopping center in Duivendrecht on Sep.17, 1985, the fire at the Makro in Duiven and Duivendrecht on Dec.18, 1986, and the fire at the main office of the Royal Packing Industry Van Leer BV in Amsterdam on July 9, 1986. The fire in Duivendrecht caused extensive damage estimated at between 20 and 30 million Dutch guilders. The actions at the Makro were a protest against the owner of Makro , the HSV company which has extensive interests in South Africa. The group declared the actions were in sympathy with the liberation struggle in South Africa, 'a struggle against the regime in Pretoria which is regarded as a part of the imperialist system, the worldwide network of political and business interests that has kept in power the apartheid regime and will continue to do so until it has created an alternative'. The Dutch Minister of the Interior used the word 'terrorists' in connection with these arsonists attacks.

* Revolutionary Cells- Commando Tupac Amaru
Anti-militarist action group which claimed responsibility for a bomb attack on the office of a concrete company, the Dutch Concrete Group (HBG), in Rijswijk on Sep.7, 1986. The company was accused of being involved in the construction of the cruise missile base in Woensdrecht and

blamed for investments in South Africa.

* Revolutionary Cells, Into the Blue
(Revolutinaire Cellen, Ins Blaue Hinein)
Action group which claimed responsibility for two minor bombs at the Olympic Games Foundation and at Teleport in Sloterwijk (Amsterdam) on Aug.21, 1986. The actions were a protest against the plans of the authorities and business to organize the Olympic Games in Amsterdam.

* Society for the Call of Islam
(Al Dawa Al Islamia)
A religious society which has been established after the Libyan revolution in 1969. Its aim is to spread the Islamic revolution around the world by building mosques. It is a Libyan governmental institution. It has been accused of injecting politics in the mosques under the cover of social and cultural activities. A Dutch section was established in 1982 and is headed by Mohammed Benchamach. The society has been named by other Moroccan organizations in connection with the murder of Rachid Zibouh on May 24, 1985, which has increased tensions within the Moroccan community in the Netherlands.

* Society of Moroccan Workers and Traders
(Amicales des Ouvriers et Commercants Marocains)

Organization which has been established in 1972 in Morocco. It operates abroad to control Moroccan communities and to prevent that Moroccans join labour unions in the countries of residence and to prevent the establishment of radical organizations which would strengthen political consciousness. In practice Amicales members function as informers for Moroccan agencies. It has tried to increase its influence on the Moroccans in the Netherlands and has been accused of intimidation. As a cover for its activities it has set up several front organizations like the Democratic Alliance of Moroccans, the Democratic Union of Moroccans, the Moroccan Federation of Parents, sport federations, mosque societies and the Society of Moroccan Teachers. Persons who do not sympathize with Amicales are not allowed to return to Morocco or only after long delays.

* Squatters Movement
(Kraakbeweging)
According to the late Minister of Internal Affairs, K.Rietkerk, the Dutch Domestic Security Service (BVD) has prevented violent actions of the hardcore of the squatters movement. Knowledge of the planned actions enabled the authorized agencies to pre-empt the actions. The movement has repeatedly been involved in violent clashes with the police and the Mobile Units. The death of Hans Kok in police custody on Oct.15, 1985, resulted in severe intimidation campaigns of both sides. Squatters claimed that 20,000 people are illegally housed in Amsterdam and that the movement contained 5,000 activists in the city. For the Netherlands as a whole, the figures would probably have to be doubled. Squatters operate in most university towns, including Amsterdam, Utrecht, Nijmegen and Groningen. The movement functions as a reservoir for a whole range of action groups which have operated under fantasy names during various events.

* Terrorists Social Security Service
(Terroristen Sociale Dienst) (TSD)
Group which claimed responsibility for the arson attack on the building of the Social Security Service in Winterswijk on Mar.7, 1987. The attack was claimed by telephone. The group claimed to be an extremist breakaway from the Revolutionary Anti Racist Action (RARA).

NEW CALEDONIA

* Independence Front
(Front Indépendiste)
Broad pro-independence coalition which was established on June 4, 1979. It is comprised of UC, PALIKA, FULF, UPM, PSC. It is directed against imperialism and capitalism and demands land redistribution in favour of the local population. At a 1983 roundtable conference a final communiqué stressed the necessity to work out a statute of progressive internal autonomy, as a transitory step towards the independence of New Caledonia. The statute provides for a state commission which will prepare a referendum on the right of self-determination to be held in 1989. Because the Kanak people are a minority the FI proposed to change the election corps by giving more extensive voting rights to the Kanak people. The rejection of the proposal by the French government resulted in a radicalization of the Kanak and the establishment of the Front for Kanak National Liberation and Socialism (FLNKS) in 1984.

* Kanak Liberation Party
(Parti de Libération Canaque) (PALIKA)
A pro-independence movement led by Nidouish Naisseline which has been associated with various acts of violence, including disturbances during a demonstration on July 13, 1980. It emerged in the late 1970s demanding independence for New Caledonia and land redistribution in favour of natives. It established a presence in the expatriate Kanak community in France, and in October 1981 carried out two bomb attacks on nightspots in Paris. Two waiters were injured in an attack on a restaurant. The term 'Kanak' is local and was used in a derogatory manner by Europeans to denote their superiority over natives.

* Kanak Socialist National Liberation Front
(Front de Libération National Kanak Socialiste) (FLNKS)
A broad pro-independence coalition which has been established on Sep.22-24, 1984, after a French rejection of a proposal to extend voting rights for the Kanak people in a referendum on self-determination. A violent campaign led to a state of emergency whereupon France moved in several thousand troops. In 1985 more than 20 people were killed in violent incidents. The FLNKS boycotted the November 1984 election which was accompanied by violence. After the installation of a local government, the FLNKS started an active struggle. The mining town Thio was occupied and barricades separated the town from the rest of the country. Harbour activities were paralyzed, vehicles were captured and Europeans were disarmed. On Dec.1, the FLNKS installed a provisional government for a future state Kanaky. On Dec.4, 6,000 French troops arrived on the island. The most militant leaders, Eloi Machoro and Marcel Nonnaro, were summarily executed by members of the Groupe d'Intervention de la Gendarmerie (GIGN) on Jan.12, 1985. Security forces and colonists plundered tribes. Fifteen militants were killed and hundreds were injured. More than 100 people were imprisoned. The July 1987 referendum, which the Chirac government has said will offer a choice between independence and autonomy within France, replaces a Socialist plan to move New Caledonia toward independence in association with France. Details of the referendum will be in the draft law to be submitted to the National Assembly. The outcome of the referendum is clear because the Kanaks form 43 percent of the population and the voting behaviour of the non-Melanesian population can be predicted. Supporters of the independence movement have announced that they will boycot the referendum. They also have warned the French government that they will transfer allegiance to a 'provisional government' under their own control.

* Movement for Order and Peace
(Mouvement pour l'Ordre et la Paix) (MOP)
This movement was founded in 1979 by Europeans in opposition to extremist Melanesian pro-independence elements. Early in January 1980 an off-duty police inspector (who according to pro-independence sources was a MOP member) shot and killed a Melanesian youth. This led to increased unrest among the pro-independence Melanesians.

* Secret Action Committee
(Comité d'Action Secrète) (CAS)
European group which has been involved in violent acts directed against Melanesians.

* Socialist Kanak Liberation
(Libération Kanake Socialiste) (LKS)
Nidoish Naisseline, the leader of this movement, declared after the assassination of the secretary-general of the Caledonian Union in September 1981 that his group would continue to struggle for independence until victory. He alleged that 'fascist groups' were threatening the lives of pro-independence representatives. On Nov.10, 1981, the LKS put demands to the French high commissioner for initiating the process of decolonization, the dissolution of extreme right-wing movements and the requisition of all weapons.

NICARAGUA

* Anti Communist Armed Forces
(Fuerzas Armadas Anticomunistas) (FARAC)
A right-wing militia which has been active in 1980. Seven members of FARAC were sentenced to prison terms on Aug.20, 1980.

* Anti Terror Brigade (BECAT)
Anti-terror brigade which has been accused of arresting boys in the street. After a few weeks the dead bodies of the boys were returned with the comment that they had been with the guerrillas and had died in the struggle.

* Armed Democratic Forces
(Fuerzas Armadas Democraticas) (FAD)
Right-wing Somocist militia active in 1980. It was led by Carlos Garcia Solorzano, former head of the National Security Office under president Somoza. He was arrested with several other FAD members on May 9, 1980. On Aug.25 of that year he was sentenced to 14 years in prison. The reputed commander of the FAD, Lt.Col.Bernadino Larios (a former National Guard under the Somoza regime, who had been appointed Minister of Defence in the first Sandinista Government) was arrested on Sep.19, 1980, and charged with conspiring to assassinate members of the Sandinista directorate. On Oct.31, he was sentenced to seven years in prison. At the time of his arrest he alleged that the FAD had received aid from Jorge Salazar Arguello, the head of the landowners' organization, who was shot dead on Nov.17, 1980, by police who regarded him as the leader in an anti-government plot. A Spanish diplomat said to be connected with the FAD was expelled from Nicaragua on Oct.10, 1980.

* Authentic Sandinist
(Sandinist Autentica) (AS)
Small guerrilla movement which emerged after the August 1978 offensive.

* Comites de Defensa Sandinista (CDS)
Clandestine civilian organizations on town district

level with the tasks to defend the Sandinist revolution; to organize the people; to contribute to the social and economic reconstruction; and to consolidate a mass organization. Fifteen CDS form a district committee. These district committees are intermediaries between the people and the ministries. They also have a vigilance function; incidents reportedly were few and trivial.

* Communist Party of Nicaragua
(Partido Comunista de Nicaragua) (PCN)
This pro-Chinese faction broke away in 1967 from the original Communist Party founded in 1939 (still in existence as the Nicaraguan Socialist Party, which is pro-Soviet and part of the Sandinista-led Patriotic Front for the Revolution, FPR). On Oct.20, 1981, its leader, E.Altamirano, was arrested and charged with violating laws under the economic and social emergency declared on Sep.9 of that year after the PCN had, on Oct.6, published a document on 'the serious economic crisis and the deviation of the Sandinista revolution.' While the PCN has retained its legal status, D.Ortega Saavedra, the co-ordinator of the junta, accused the PCN of promoting strikes and carrying out 'organized and systematic sabotage' against the national economy.

* Democratic Nicaraguan Forces
(Fuerzas Democratica de Nicaragua) (FDN)
Armed organization founded on Nov.27, 1981. Its proclaimed aim was 'to liberate our people from Marxist totalitarianism'. Its political leader is Adolfo Calero and its military leader is H.Bermudez, a former officer of the National Guard under Somoza. It has an estimated 15,000 to 25,000 men under arms which operate from Honduras where it has developed a network of military bases and refugee camps in the Las Vegas Salient. US officials said they plan the contras to expand to 30,000 and to create a 'traditional conventional army'. The 14 FDN regional commands (each has roughly 750-800 combatants organized into two to four task forces) are organized into some 52 separate task forces or equivalent commands, each having 60 to 700 personnel. It engaged in a campaign of economic sabotage and moved from hit-and-run attacks to multi task force operations. It is manipulated by the US CIA which is waging a 'covert' war against the Sandinist regime. Already 30,000 people have been killed in this war.

* Miskito and Rama Indian Movement (MISURASATA)
This group, representing the English speaking Black community and the Miskito, Sumo and Rama Indians in the east coast province of Zelaya (the Mosquito Coast) was represented in the Council of State by Steadman Fagoth Müller. The latter was arrested (with about 70 others) in February 1981 and accused of having been a security agent for President Somoza, while two others were charged with fomenting a separatist plot. The arrests were followed by protest demonstrations which led to clashes. S.Fagoth Müller, having been released provisionally, fled to Honduras on May 11, 1981. On May 21 it was reported that many other Miskito Indians had left Nicaragua. In December 1982 the MISURASATA group led by Brooklyn Rivera joined forces with ARDE.

* MISURA
Anti-government organization set up by the Miskito indians of north-east Nicaragua. MISURA, like the other Miskito organizations, claim they are being harassed and persecuted by Nicaragua's left-wing Sandinista government, and that an estimated 50,000 Miskito people have been forced to flee to other parts of Nicaragua and into neighbouring Honduras. Despite the existence of a 'peace' faction inside MISURA, it voted to abandon negotiations with the Sandinistas in September 1985, and joined the Nicaraguan Opposition Union, an alliance of right-wing Contra guerrilla groups. In early 1986 it was renamed KISAN. It is led by Steadman Fagoth Müller.

* National Army of Liberation
(Ejercito Nacional de Liberacion) (ENL)
Somocist group which operated from Honduras in the early 1980s. It is composed of former National Guards under President Somoza. Late in 1980 it claimed to control 4,000-6,000 armed men inside Nicaragua and several hundred elsewhere. It has also claimed to favour elections, free enterprise and respect for human rights, and to have influence with the autonomist MISURASATA organization on Nicaragua's east coast. The ENL operated independently of the Nicaraguan Democratic Union (UDN) and the Nicaraguan Armed Revolutionary Forces (FARN). It was led by Pedro Ortega (Juan Carlos). It was reported that about 600 men received military training in the United States.

* National Guard
(Guardia Nacional) (GN)
This security force has been involved in a systematic terror campaign during the regime of Somozo. It had an estimated membership of 15,000. After the overthrow of Somoza in 1979 many members joined guerrilla groups with the aim to overthrow to Sandinist regime.

* Nicaraguan Armed Revolutionary Forces
(Fuerzas Armadas Revolucionarias Nicaraga) (FARN)
The armed wing of the right-wing Nicaraguan Democratic Union which carried out a number of attacks in 1980. It claimed to have 2,000 members. In March 1981 it claimed that a 600-man 'freedom

force' was waiting in Honduras and would soon be joined by 'thousands of supporters' from Guatemala and Miami (Florida) to carry out an insurrection to 'liberate' Nicaragua with the help of the Governments of El Salvador and Guatemala. Daniel Ortega Saavedra alleged on April 19, 1981, that invaders from Honduras had conducted attacks in which they had killed more than 60 Nicaraguans. However, an open conflict between Honduras and Nicaragua was avoided through talks between Honduras and Nicaragua between Daniel Ortega Saavedra and President Paz Garcia of Honduras at a border post on May 13, 1981.

* Nicaraguan Coast Indian Unity (KISAN)
Miskito Indian organization which has been involved in armed activities against the Sandinist government. It was previously called MISURA. It has an estimated strenght of about 2,000 to 3,000 men. Its goal for 1987 was to block Nicaragua's access to all sea and river ports on the Atlantic with sabotage operations and powerboat ambushes. At least 38 guerrillas were reported to have received training since February 1986 with the Honduran 5th Battalion. KISAN leaders said they hoped some fighters will get US training by the US Army Special Forces or the CIA in the use of underwater explosives and SAM-7 anti-aircraft missiles. In April 1987, Steadman Fagoth Müller announced that his group was suspending military operations because of continued disunity in the anti-Sandinist movement. As part of an effort to find a new strategy, he and another Indian leader, Brooklyn Rivera, called a 'general assembly' of delegates from about 250 Indian communities in Nicaragua.

* Nicaraguan Democratic Union
(Unidad Democratica Nacional) (UDN)
The UDN was formed by conservative businessmen; its leader had actively opposed the Somoza regime and had recognized the FSLN, at the time of the overthrow of that regime, as leader of the revolutionary process. Since then it has criticized the Sandinists for its undemocratic style of governing. Edmundo Chamorro Rapaciolli claimed in late 1980 that the UDN and its armed wing, the Nicaraguan Revolutionary Armed Forces (FARN), were fighting not for a return to a right-wing dictatorship but for democracy. They would therefore not accept into their ranks former National Guards who wished to revert to the old ways. On Aug.25, 1981, E.Chamorro was sentenced in absentia with 25 others (of whom only about half were present in court) to prison terms of up to 25 years and the confiscation of their property for subversive activities. In December 1982 the UDN joined ARDE.

* Nicaraguan Democratic Union Assembly
(Asamblea Nicaraguense de Unidad Democratica) (ANUDE)
Opposition group which was formed in September 1982. Its founders included José Davila, a leader of the exiled section of the Social Christian Party. He was quoted as saying that ANUDE had offices in Costa Rica, Venezuela and Europe and maintained links with the military forces in Honduras; that one of its aims was to foster the creation of a united opposition front; and that in his view only violence would remove the Sandinistas. While ANUDE was said to represent right-wing elements who had opposed the Somoza regime, it appeared at the same time to maintain links with Somocist groups.

* Nicaraguan International Rescue from Communism (SINC)
Five members of this right-wing group hijacked a Costa Rican aircraft with 22 persons on board at San José airport on Oct.29, 1981. The hijackers demanded the release of seven members of SINC who had been imprisoned in December 1980, after attacks on the left-wing Radio Noticias del Continente transmitter, the transmissions of which were suspended by the Costa Rican Government on Feb.20, 1981. The government eventually agreed to the release of the seven prisoners. One of them reportedly has chosen to remain in prison. The other six, and the five hijackers, were flown to El Salvador, where they were arrested. In November 1981 it was announced that they were all to be returned to Costa Rica, where the hijackers were to face trial.

* Nicaraguan Workers' Centre
(Central de Trabajadores de Nicaragua) (CTN)
Authorities have accused CTN officials of maintaining contact with former union leaders who had left the country and played a prominent role in armed opposition groups. Several members and leaders have been detained and held incommunicado.

* Opposition Bloc of the South (BOS)
Guerrilla movement which was established in 1986. For unclear reasons it refused to cooperate with UNO, a guerrilla alliance finally established after many efforts and severe pressure from the United States.

* Phoenix Battalion (PB)
A one-man operation by Sam Nesley Hall. He described himself as a self-employed military adviser and counter terrorist. He said he was teaching commando tactics to anti-Sandinist Miskito Indians in Central America. He was arrested by the Sandinists and accused of carrying out espionage and gathering military intelligence data of interest to the US government. He was

reportedly linked to a private group in Flint City, Alabama, called Civilian Military Assistance (CMA), which was organized to supply and assist anti-communist forces in Central America.

* Popular Antisomocist Militias
(Milicias Populares Antisomocistas) (MILPA)
Armed units of the PCN (M-L).

* Proletarian Tendency
(Tendencia Proletaria) (PT)
One of three factions within the FSLN which advocated a general people's insurrection. It reportedly did not have guerrilla units but members were reported to have been involved in bank raids. Its most important leaders were Jaime Wheelock, who became Minister of Landreform in the Sandinist government, and Lea Lopez de Guido, who became Minister of Social Affairs.

* Protracted Popular Warfare
(Guerra Popular Prolongato) (GPP)
The faction within the FSLN farthest to the left after the split in 1975. It advocated a prolonged people's war. Guerrilla units should stay in the mountains to expand its base. After the fall of Somozo the cadre was convinced that an American intervention would take place within a few months. It tried to consolidate its power by a moderate stance in order to postpone this intervention as long as possible. The faction was led by Tomas Borge, now Minister of Interior.

* Revolutionary Democratic Alliance
(Allianza Democratica Revolucionaria) (ARDE)
This organization was formed in San José (Costa Rica) in December 1982 by representatives of four groups: 1) The Sandinist Revolutionary Front (FRS) led by Eden Pastora Gomez, who had on July 7, 1981, resigned as Deputy Minister of Defence and head of the Sandinista people's militia; 2) the Nicaraguan Democratic Movement (MDN) led by Alfonso Robelo Callejas; 3) the MISURATA led by Brooklyn Rivera; and 4) the Nicaraguan Democratic Union (UDN) with its armed wing, the Nicaraguan Armed Revolutionary Forces (FARN). ARDE operated from Costa Rican territory against the Sandinist regime. In May 1986, Eden Pastora resigned as military leader because six other leaders wanted to join UNO to get more American aid. He was replaced by Fernando (El Negro) Chamorro. Alfonso Robelo acted as its political leader. The organization split into two main groups: one consisted of those who continued to support Pastora (about 700 men), the other of a smaller band of 100 devoted anti-Sandinistas.

* Revolutionary Sandinist Front
(Frente Revolucionario Sandino) (FRS)
Breakaway guerrilla group from ARDE led by Eden Pastora Gomez.

* Sandinist National Liberation Front
(Frente Sandinista de Liberación Nacional) (FSLN)
Guerrilla movement named after General Augusto César Sandino, who, having opposed US rule for six years, was treacherously murdered in 1934 by supporters of the Somoza family. The organization was founded in 1958 by Carlos Fonseca Amador (died in clash with security forces in 1976). It was not very successful in the early 1970s and split into three factions in 1977, Proletarian Tendency, Prolonged War and Third Line. The two columns led by Carlos Aguero and Victor Manuel Tirado Lopéz developed into a guerrilla force of 1,500 fighters by the end of 1978. In 1979 the Sandinistas succeeded in overthrowing the Somoza regime, due to a new unity between the three factions, improved military performance, and of US pressure on Somoza and the National Guard to relinguish power and seek exile. The human cost of the war had been 50,000 dead, 100,000 wounded, 40,000 orphaned and one fifth of the population homeless. Physical damage was estimated to amount $ 2 billion.

* State Security Service
(Direccion General de Seguridad del Estado) (DGSE)
State security service which has been involved in arrests without warrant. Amnesty International wrote a letter to President Daniel Ortega in 1985 to outline its concern about the detention of prisoners of conscience under state of emergency powers and interrogation procedures of the DGSE.

* Task Force Jane Patrick
Armed group which operates from Honduras. It is commanded by Gerardo Martinez and has an estimated strength of 800 men.

* Third Line or Insurrectionists
(Terceristas or Insurreccionales)
Of of three factions within the FSLN which emerged after a split in 1977. It was the most moderate faction identified with social democracy. Its most important representatives were Eden Pastora and Daniel Ortega. It dropped all ideological elements from its platform and succeeded in winning a broad spectrum of support from peasants to wealthy upperclass intellectuals. It repeatedly broke agreements with the other factions and called for a popular insurrection. It favoured military attacks on towns, and was accused of compromising revolutionary orthodoxy for the sake of attracting reformists to the FSLN. At that time, Costa Rica provided a model for a future post-Somoza Nicaragua.

* United Nicaraguan Opposition
(Union Nacional de Opposicion) (UNO)
An alliance of several guerrilla factions designed

to give political direction to the fight against the Sandinists. It was established in Miami (Florida) in August 1985. Spokesmen for the alliance were Alfonso Robelo Callejas, Adolfo Calero Portocalero and Arturo José Cruz. Its present secretary-general is Leonardo Somarriba. Financial, military and ideological clashes led to a split in January 1987 and Arturo Cruz resigned. Cruz and Robelo have advocated a two-track strategic emphasizing the political struggle. They have criticized the Somocist leadership of the Contras and said that UNO has not succeeded in convincing the world of its democratic intentions. The FDN, led by Calero, and manipulated by the US CIA, is advocating a military struggle. In May 1987, Nicaraguan rebel leaders agreed to merge the largest US-backed insurgent army with rival Costa Rica-based forces in the guerrilla war against Nicaragua's leftist government. The new political and military alliance has been named the Nicaraguan Resistance. The alliance called for a radical restructuring of the movement, including the unification of fighting forces into a single 'national army'. A key provision of the accord was that a new seven-member civilian directorate would be granted full control of the military. The agreement to join forces was planned to be ratified in Miami by a new 54-member political assembly. The plan brings together the United Nicaraguan Opposition and the Southern Opposition Bloc. UNO's supporters concede that the contra's attachment to their Miami base makes them look like American puppets, which is one reason why Washington wants to move UNO and its staff back to central America.

* Workers' Front
(Frente Obrero) (FO)
The armed members of the left-wing FO (which was affiliated to the (pro-Chinese) Communist party) had before 1979 formed the People's Anti-Somocist Militias (MILPAS). The Sandinista government, however, claimed that the FO and MILPAS were threatening production and provoking unrest in some areas by inciting workers to strike and take possession of land. By October 1979 some 70 FO members were reported to be under arrest; on Jan.25, 1980, the Government closed down the daily El Pueblo, the mouthpiece of the FO; and on April 10, 1980, a member of the junta declared that neither the FO nor the Communist Party would be allowed to participate in the Council of State.

NIGER

* Niger Popular Liberation Front (NPLF)
Front which reportedly has been involved in commando raids into Niger. Members include M.M.Abdoulaye Diori, son of Hamani Diori (former head of state) and Kamed Moussa (former head of the cabinet of General Kountché at the ministry of defense). They were exiled in Libya in August 1981. The front has operated from Libya.

NIGERIA

* Squad Eight Organization (SEO)
A new organization which emerged in 1985. It claimed to be behind the deaths of prominent Lagosians, including prominent businessmen and public servants. In a letter it said that they were not merely armed robbers, but an urban guerrilla organization. Their declared objective was 'to deliver the oppressed and put a check to wealthy Nigerians who recklessly flaunt their ill-gotten gains to the consternation of the poor masses.'

* Yen Izala
This sect of dissident Moslem fundamentalists was led by Alhaji Mohammadu Marwa (alias Maitatsine) , who originally came from northern Cameroon and who preached a revolutionary version of Islam which rejected the prohet Mohammed as a Moslem leader; the sect opposed all official authority and demanded absolute loyalty to Mahammadu Marwa as its leader. It is believed to have some 3,000 members. The sect was responsible for serious riots in Kano (northern Nigeria) between Dec.18 and 31, 1980, which were forcibly suppressed by the Nigerian army. According to an official inquiry, a total of 4,177 persons lost their lives in the riots. These included the leader and numerous other members of the sect and also large number of civilians killed as 'infidels' by members of the sect and of other civilians killed by police or army action. In 1981 and 1982 renewed riots were reported. The sect was officially banned on Nov.18, 1982. In March 1987 Moslems attacked Christians in an orchestrated campaign.

NORTHERN IRELAND

* Anti-Sinn Fein Societies (AFSS)
Terror group which had declared its aim to be the killing of two Sinn Fein members for every British soldier that died in the struggle.

* Catholic Reaction Power (CRP)
Group which claimed responsibility for an attack on a Protestant church on Nov.20, 1983.

* Cuman na mBan
Female wing of the Provisional IRA. The women tried to date British soldiers and lure them to their homes to spend the night with them. When the soldiers agreed they were murdered.

* Defense Intelligence Staff (DIS)
The largest intelligence service in Northern Ireland

which has 90 departments and operates via a system of Field Intelligence Officers. The axis DIS-SAS is the pivot of the military repression in Northern Ireland.

* Fianna Na h'Eireann
Youth wing of the Provisional IRA, whose members assist PIRA in gathering intelligence, act as look outs and transport weapons.

* Irish National Liberation Army (INLA)
Terrorist organization which was established in December 1974 when it broke away from the Official IRA. It is considered to be the military wing of the IRSP. Through armed actions it intends to force a British withdrawal from Northern Ireland, in order to reunite with the south. Its membership is variously estimated from no more than four dozen to up to 200. Its headquarter is located in Dublin. It was led by Dominic McGlinchey ('Mad Dog') who was sentenced to ten years in prison in 1984. He was replaced by Gerard Steenson ('Dr.Death') who was murdered in March 1987 following his release from prison in December 1986. It has been involved in bomb attacks and assassinations and targeted Protestant paramilitaries, security forces, British military installations in Germany and loyalist politicians. In March 1979, INLA claimed responsibility for the murder of Airey Neave, the opposition spokesman on Northern Ireland, in the House of Commons. In early 1987, it has been involved in a bloody internal feud after the establishment of a dissident IPLO faction. Already 12 people have been killed in the feud.

* Irish Republican Army (IRA)
Terrorist organization founded in 1914 or 1916. It has been involved in violent campaigns against the British authorities in Northern Ireland, in 1916, in 1919-1921, in 1923-29, in 1939, from 1956 to 1962 and between 1969 and 1972. In 1969 it split into two factions, the Official IRA and the Provisional IRA. The Official IRA has adopted constitutional methods. Those disagreeing with the truce of May 1972 seceded to form the Irish Republican Socialist Party (IRSP) and its armed wing, the Irish National Liberation Army (INLA). The Official IRA was led by the Marxist-Leninist Cathal Goulding (born in 1922) in the late 1960s. Presently he is supporting the (Republican) Workers' Party (formerly known as Official Sinn Fein), which campaigns north and south of the border without attracting significant electoral support. The Official IRA has declared an indefinite cease-fire without excluding actions 'to defend the people'. In recent years some bank and post office robberies have been attributed to the Official IRA. The Workers' Party has denied that it has obtained funds from this source.

* Irish People's Liberation Organization (IPLO)
INLA splinter which has been responsible for killing several INLA members in an internal feud in early 1987.

* Irish Republican Socialist Party (IRSP)
Formed in December 1974 after a split in official Sinn Fein, the Marxist IRSP has sought to advance a distinctive republican socialist strategy. It acts as a political front for INLA and has faced intense repression in Northern Ireland, the Republic and Britain. It has also suffered in a murderous feud with the Official IRA in which several members, including its former leader Seamus Costello (Oct.1977) were assassinated.

* Loyal Citizens of Ulster (LCU)
Strong arm force that lent support to Ian Paisley's political arm in the late 1960s. It was led by Ronald Bunting, a former British army officer. Members of the group were prominent in street violence.

* Military Intelligence, Department Five (MI-5)
British security service which belongs to the Ministry of Interior. It was established in 1909 and had 2,000 employees in 1980. Its main task is to track East Bloc agents. It has six main departments: counter espionage, protection, counter sabotage, counter subversion, scientific research and logistical support and register. In 1961 it had already 2,000,000 people on filing cards.

* Military Intelligence, Department Six
or Secret Intelligence Service (MI-6)
This British intelligence service has been active in Northern Ireland in tracking IRA militants and in research into the channels through which arms reach Northern Ireland. It also has shown an interest into the activities of East Bloc embassies, the Irish Communist party and the Arab cultural centers. One of its aims is to block any possible foreign support for the Irish republicans. Reportedly, it had execution lists of IRA members. Since 1972 it has allegedly been involved in assassinations and letter bombs.

* Military Reconnaissance Forces
(also Military Reaction Forces) (MRF)
Autonomous SAS intervention groups each consisting of two to three men of Irish background. They organized pseudo groups to infiltrate the enemy. In 1974 the authorities admitted that the MRF was comprised of 'SAS elements'. Members have been involved in at least 17 executions in the 1976-1978 period.

* Ourselves Alone
(Sinn Fein) (SF)
Established in 1905 under British rule, Sinn Fein fought for the independence of Ireland. After the

political success of 1922, Sinn Fein has continued to fight for a 'democratic socialist republic' in north and south. In 1970, it split into the Workers' Party, which is Marxist in outlook, and the Provisional Sinn Fein. It has been the political wing of the OIRA and, since the 1970s the PIRA in Northern Ireland. In the south it is presently led by Ruairi O'Bradaigh, in the north Gerry Adams is Vice-President of the Provisonal Sinn Fein. Since Sinn Fein candidates did poorly in the February 1987 election, Ulster has been plagued by an escalating campaign of IRA violence.

* People's Democracy (PD)
Revolutionary splintergroup which emerged in October 1968 at Queens University, Belfast. It staged a civil rights march in January 1969 against the discrimination of of the Roman Catholic minority. It came under the influence of the Trotskyist Young Socialist Alliance, which advocated world revolution. It was sympathetic to PIRA and the IRSP.

* People's Liberation Army (PLA)
An armed group with leanings to the IRSP.

* Protestant Action Force (PAF)
Loyalist paramilitary gang responsible for a campaign of sectarian assaults, bombings and murders in the eighties. It is largely made up of Ulster Defense Regiment members who pick out nationalists for harassment while in uniform and attack them when off-duty. In November and December 1983 a dozen UDR members in County Armagh were arrested in connection with the PAF's murder of a Catholic man. The name has been used by Ulster Defense Association and the Ulster Volunteer Force. It claimed responsibility by telephone for a shooting on Mar.9, 1983, and announced a campaign against 'Republican Murder Squads'.

* Provisional Irish Republican Army (PIRA)
Terrorist organization which emerged from a split in IRA in 1969. On the political level it has operated through the Provisional Sinn Fein. It has an estimated 350 to 400 hardcore members. Important leaders have been John Stephenson (Sean MacStiofain), Rory O'Brady (Ruairi O'Bradaigh), Leo Martin, Billy McKee, Seamus Twomey and Francis Card (Prionnsias MacAirt), who together formed the Provisional Army Council. The Provos reorganized the organization from a brigade to a cell structure. It has been involved in sectarian murders, bank raids, nail bombs, fire bombs, letter bombs, parcel bombs, car bombs, kneecappings, sniping, tarring and feathering. It has targeted soldiers, policemen, judges, civil servants and random individuals, not only in Northern Ireland but also in the United Kingdom and West Germany. Its goal in the 1970s was to unite the north with the south into a 32-county island of Ireland, which would be republican and socialist. Adopting a non-aligned posture, the 'New Ireland' would neither form part of the European Economic Community nor would it belong to NATO. On the economic front, PIRA advocated the nationalization of key industries and severe limitations on foreign investments, largely, it appeared for nationalist reasons. Political violence in Northern Ireland has been more frequent than anywhere else (except Turkey) in Europe since the late 1960s. Figures listed for the 1969-1982 period include a total of 7,521 bombings (which killed 608 people). Also 1,000 kneecappings have been recorded. In the August 1969- December 1984 period a total of 2,412 people died and more than 25,000 were injured in the violence. The figures refer to all, not just PIRA violence.
In early 1987, PIRA allegedly received large quantities of plastic explosives, weapons and money from Libya. The military support supplied by Colonel Qadhafi is considered to be an important reason for the increase in violent attacks since Sinn Fein candidates did poorly in the February 1987 election. More than 20 RUC stations have been attacked and the police reported being fired upon virtually every day. The so-called Semtex-bombs provided by Libya which are produced in eastern Europe, are far more effective than those produced by the IRA itself. They have been used in the early 1987 letter bomb campaign and in the attacks on the airforce base in West Germany and on Sir Maurice Gibson and his wife.

* Red Hand Commandos (RHC)
A loyalist paramilitary group involved in sectarian assassinations in 1972 and 1973 set up by John McKeague (killed in 1982) set up in mid-1972. It was banned in 1973 at the same time as another UDA front, the Ulster Freedom Fighters. In 1974 the RHC issued a statement that for every Protestant killed in the border areas of Fermanagh and South Tyrone four Roman Catholics would be shot.

* Royal Ulster Constabulary (RUC)
Largely Protestant, civilian police force formed in 1922. It has been a favorite target of Republican terrorists, suffering 214 fatalities since 1969. The most serious single incident was the Newry police station attack in February 1985 which killed nine RUC officers. Since a reorganization in 1970 its strength increased steadily from 3,500 to 8,000 regulars and 5,000 reservists. In the last 16 years the RUC has charged almost 8,000 people with terrorist offenses. In recent years the RUC has been heavily criticized for their extensive use of 'supergrass' informers, usually terrorists who have been 'turned' in exchange for immunity from

prosecution. After a series of shooting incidents in 1982 (in which six people were killed) the RUC was accused of operating a 'shoot-to-kill' policy against suspected Republicans. In May 1987 Northern Ireland Minister Tom King unveiled new security measures for the province that include adding 500 new RUC officers and calling up 600 members of the part-time UDR for a month of duty. He also hinted that the elite SAS will play a greater role in fighting terrorism.

* Shankhill Defence Association (SDA)
Vigilante group set up in 1969 as a Belfast community association. Its protestant members patrolled the upper Shankhill. Members intimidated Catholics forcing them to move from a predominantly Protestant area to a Catholic one. As answer to the SDA terror tactics, the Official IRA, the British troops entered the struggle.

* Special Air Service Regiment (SAS)
British elite anti terror unit which has been involved in the British ruthless undercover operations in Northern Ireland. It was established in 1941 when it served as an action branch of the intelligence services. It recruits from other army units. The 23th Reserve regiment has been involved in an unsuccessful coup attempt against Colonel Qadhafi (Libya) in 1970. Since 1972 the presence of SAS members has been camouflaged as 'support by detached advisers'. In many places in the world ex-SAS members have been involved in mercenary raids. In early 1987 Northern Ireland Minister Tom King hinted that the SAS will play a greater role in fighting terrorism.

* Tara
Loyalist paramilitary group. By some authors it is considered to be a spook organization.

* The Third Force (TF)
Plans for the establishment of this force were revealed by the Rev.Ian Paisley, the leader of the Democratic Unionist Party, at a rally at Newtonards on Nov.23, 1981. Dr.Paisley had earlier said that, in view of official plans to set up an Anglo-Irish Inter Governmental Council and of the British Government's refusal to establish a third security force (in addition to the Army and the police), Ulster Unionist would make the province of Northern Ireland ungovernable and would demonstrate that such a third force was already in existence. The Newtonards rally was attended by Unionist supporters in paramilitary uniform, but estimates of numbers involved in the parade of the 'Third Force' varied between 5,000 and 15,000.

* Ulster Army Council (UAC)
Co-ordinating body of Northern Ireland's paramilitary groups, including UDA, UVF, USC, LDV, RHC, set up in late 1973 to organise Protestant resistance to British government policy. The UAC organized the Ulster Workers' strike of 1974 which brought down the Stormont assembly.

* Ulster Citizen Army (UCA)
Secret faction within the Ulster Defence Association led by Tommy Herron (killed in September 1973 by the SAS). The UCA had in 1972 announced a war against the presence of the British Army in the Shankhill district. Its name referred to a workersmilitia led by James Connolly which had been active in 1916.

* Ulster Defense Association (UDA)
Largest Protestant paramilitary group founded in 1971 as a coalition of local 'defence associations'. Its strength is variously estimated as between 5,000 and 11,000. Membership peaked in 1972 when it was reported to have 40,000 members. It claimed that it could mobilize 50,000 men should civil war break out. From the start it was faction ridden and had links with several other Protestant paramilitary groups. The membership of the UDA overlaps with that of the RUC and the British Army's Ulster Defence regiment. Its involvement in the campaign of sectarian murders is beyond dispute , but the UDA remains a legal organization. Many of its members have been imprisoned on charges of murder and other firearm offenses. It has also been involved in bomb attacks. The bombs were placed in hotels or known meeting places of the IRA. The UDA manned the Protestants' barricades of 1972.

* Ulster Defence Regiment (UDR)
Military force raised in Northern Ireland after 1970. The UDR has over 7,000 members (2,500 of whom full-time soldiers of the British Army). There are also 700-800 women UDR members (known as 'Greenfinches'). The percentage of Catholics in the UDR has declined after PIRA and INLA attacks.

* Ulster Freedom Fighters (UFF)
Protestant paramilitary group which operated under the aegis of the Ulster Defence Association, although the latter has on occasion disowned it. In 1973 members of the UFF claimed responsibility for killing two young Catholics, and also for several bombings, in the Belfast area. Late in June 1973 the UFF accepted responsibility for the murder of a Catholic ex-senator and former election agent for the leader of the Social Democratic and Labour Party. The UFF were officially banned on Nov.12, 1973, but nevertheless continued to be involved in assassinations both in the Republic and in Northern Ireland. In particular the UFF accepted responsibility for killing the (Protestant) Fine Gael Senator Billy Fox at Clones on Mar.11, 1974, for which five alleged members of the PIRA were

sentenced in Dublin on June 7 of that year to penal servitude for life. It may have numbered several dozen regulars.

• Ulster Protestant Action Group (UPAG)
A grouping of this name claimed responsibility for the killing of a number of Catholics, mainly in Belfast, between Sep.16 and Nov.28, 1974.

• Ulster Resistance (UR)
Organization of Protestant hardliners whose establishment was announced on Nov.11, 1986. It is dedicated to abolishing the British-Irish agreement. It would seek to mobilize the men of Ulster into an organized and disciplined force. It was unclear whether the new organization would use violence in its campaign.

• Ulster United Loyalist Front (UULF)
Rival Protestant groups said they had joined forces in a new organization to resist any attempt by Britain to give the Irish Republic a voice in administering Northern Ireland. Its backers said it eventually would unite 750,000 Protestants. It was organized in Portadawn on Aug.7, 1985, at a meeting attended by 650 Protestant leaders. The closing of the ranks byProtestant politicians and paramilitary groups followed reports from Dublin and London that the two governments were near an agreement giving Dublin a role in monitoring Northern Ireland's minority Roman Catholic community.

• Ulster Volunteer Force (UVF)
Founded in 1966, the UVF consists of militant working-class Protestant loyalists. On May 21, 1966 the UVF declared a war against the IRA. Since then it has been involved in assassinations and sabotage. In the early 1970s it numbered some 1,500 men. In 1983, 14 senior organizers of the UVF were jailed after one UVF member 'talked' to the police.

NORWAY

• National Freedom Party (NFP)
Neo Nazi party which has been held responsible for a series of crimes and a bomb attack on a mosque of the Ahmadia sect on June 15, 1985. The bomb attack was claimed by telephone in the name of the Norwegian National Socialist Front. The telephone caller threatened with more attacks on foreign institutions. In 1986 Jan Odegaard, the leader of the party, was sentenced to three years in prison, for being the spiritual father of a series of crimes in the summer of 1985. Ole Kristian Brastad was sentenced to five years in prison for three armed robberies and involvement in the bomb attack.

• Norwegian German Army (NGA)
Neo Nazi group led by Espen Lund (an army sergeant). Together with two other members of the group, Johnny Olsen (a member of Vigilant) and Jon Charles Hoff, he was charged with murdering two of their comrades on Feb.21-22, 1981, in order to prevent them from revealing to the police a large theft of weapons (from a Home Guard depot) and details of their secret organization. Lund was said to have stated that he had been recruited by the Odessa organization (a German organization of former SS members); that Odessa had at least 50 members in the Norwegian Army; and that their aim was to train members in sabotage and guerrilla warfare with the ultimate aim of a rightwing takeover in Norway. On Jan.26, 1982, the court sentenced Lund and Olsen to 18 years in prison, and Hoff to 12 years. Investigating other thefts of weapons and explosives, .the police subsequently arrested several other suspected members of Nazi organizations.

• Vigilante
Members of this right-wing group were responsible for attacks on left-wing demonstrators, in particular at May Day celebrations in 1979-1982. In March 1981 the police found a large depot of explosives believed to have been assembled by Vigilante members north of Oslo. The group co-operated with the Norwegian German Army.

PAKISTAN

• Baluchistan Liberation Front (BLF)
Socialist separatist group active since 1976. In the 1980s it was led by Mir Hazar Ramkhani.

• Baluch People's Liberation Front
(Baluch Awami Azadi Mahaiz) (BPLF)
Armed Baluch group active since 1973. It is seeking the creation of an independent state of Baluchistan (one of Pakistan's four provinces). It was supported by Iraq and subsequently by the Soviet Union. The latter transferred weapons and equipment from a progressive-oriented BPLF-faction to a tribal-oriented faction. As part of a reorientation the Soviets maintain direct links with the tribal leaders, Ataullah Mengal who resides in exile in London but whose brother, Mehrullah Mengal, is the military commander of the Mengal tribe. The Soviets have established training camps through which several thousand Baluchis have passed since the Soviet army occupied Afghanistan in 1979. Although the violence has been reduced experts said that the potential for renewed activity remains.

• Baluch Students' Organization (BSO)
Separatist militant movement founded in 1967. Khair Jan Baluch, the BSO president, organized a

guerrilla group during the 1973-1977 insurgency. After 1979 small groups were training for guerrilla warfare in the hills.

* Baluch Students' Organisation-Awami (BSO-Awami)
A militant dissident faction which in 1972 split from the original BSO. It was reckoned in the early 1980s to enjoy a membership of 2,000 in all major Baluch teaching establishments. It supported the armed struggle waged by the Baluch People's Liberation Front, although it remained a separate organization.

* Field Intelligence Unit (FIU)
Over 600 Sikh insurgents were reportedly being trained in camps established by the Pakistani military authorities in the northern frontier area of Pakistan, including Kashmir, according to Indian claims. Pakistan's Field Intelligence Unit (FIU) is charged with supervising training at six camps in the area. Earlier in August 1985, the Indian Minister of State for External Affairs, Khurshid Alam Khan, said that although Pakistan had denied giving assistance to insurgents in the Punjab, 'facts are, however, contrary and their reply is not satisfactory'.

* God's Army
(Jondollah)
One of the organizations that claimed responsibility for the seizure of a Panam jet in Karachi in 1986.

* Jamaat-i-Islami
Extreme right-wing and ultra-orthodox Islamic party advocating the establishment of an Islamic state in Pakistan. Its youth wing, the Jamiat-i-Talaba (JIT) has been involved in violent disturbances at universities.

* Jama'at-i-Ulema-i-Pakistan
Progressive Islamic fundamentalist party established by left-wing mullahs in 1968. The party had an armed 'Thundersquad' which has been involved in actions against left-wing student movements.

* Jamiat-i-Talaba (JIT)
Militant youth wing of the Islamic fundamentalist Jamaat-i-Islami. It has been in conflict with other student groups in a struggle for control of the universities. The organization's leader, Shabbir Ahmed, was arrested in April 1982, for arms possession.

* Kashmir National Liberation Front (KNLF)
Secular separatist party founded by the journalist Maqbool Ahmed Butt. He reportedly was awaiting execution in Delhi's Tihar jail in 1982. The party is led by Amanullah Kahn, who believes in guerrilla tactics to win independence.

* Muhajir People's Movement
(Muhajir Qaumi Movement) (MQM)
Organization of the Islamic Muhajir minority which has been involved in violent riots with the Pathan people in late 1986 and early 1987 which resulted in several hundred dead. It has been engaged in a campaign for the termination of a quota system for government jobs and enrollment in primary and secondary schools. The Urdu speaking Islamic Mujahirs came as refugees from India (Uttar Pradesh) in 1947. They are striving for the recognition of a fifth nationality, along the Punjabis, Baluchis, Pathans and Sindhis.

* National Awami Party (NAP)
The aim of this party based on peasant and labour interests, is secession of the Baluchistan and North West Frontier Provinces. Following a rebellion in Baluchistan in 1973-74 (when the NAP had its own militia) the NAP was declared illegal on Feb.10, 1975. The NAP attempted to bring about the secession of the NWFP and Baluchistan through insurrection, terrorism and sabotage. The party was led by Khan Abdul Wali Khan.

* National Democratic Party (NDP)
The NDP was formed in 1976 as a successor to the banned National Awami Party. It was reported in May 1982 that the entire NDP leadership had been arrested at a meeting in Lahore.

* Pakistan Liberation Army (PLA)
Founded in 1979 by Murtaza Bhutto, son of the former prime minister. Its headquarters are located in Kabul. In the course of 1980 the PLA claimed responsibility for numerous acts of terrorism and sabotage. At his mother's request, Murtaza Bhutto dissolved the PLA in 1981.

* The Sword
(Al Zulfikar)
Successor movement of the PLA established in February 1981 by the late Z.A.Bhutto's eldest son, Murtaza Bhutto. It has offices in Tripoli and Kabul. The movement has been linked to bombings, student riots, and strikes by doctors and lawyers. In March 1981 Al Zulfikar members hijacked a Pakistani aircraft and killed a Pakistani diplomat. The hijackers also said that the organization was responsible for the bomb which exploded prematurely before the Pope celebrated mass in the Karachi stadium on Feb.16. They took responsibility for a fire which destroyed a Pakistani DC-10 in its hangar in early January. The movement is armed with weapons stolen from police outposts or smuggled in from Afghanistan.

* Pakistan People's Party (PPP)
The PPP described its policy as one of Islamic

socialism, democracy and independence in foreign affairs. It was established by Zulfikar Ali Bhutto in 1967. On Sep.3, 1977, he was arrested on a charge of conspiracy to murder: he was found guilty and sentenced to death, with four other men, on Mar.18, 1978. General Zia stated on Sep.6 that Z.A.Bhutto had been 'running this country on more or less Gestapo lines, misusing funds, blackmailing people, detaining them illegally, and even perhaps ordering people to be killed.' The arrest of Z.A.Bhutto was followed by demonstrations in his favour, in particular in Punjab and Sind. The former Prime Minister was hanged in April 1979.

* Parari
Guerrilla movement which emerged in the 1960s. It was established by Sher Mohammed Marri. Its local part-time volunteers, ambushed convoys, sabotaged trains and raided Pakistani military encampments. Fighting continued until 1969, when a ceasefire was negotiated. Some members then formed the BPLF.

* Pathan Tribesmen
In December 1985 Pakistani troops put down a revolt by Pathan tribesmen in the Khyber Pass. The Afghan-backed tribesmen were accused of arms and drug trading had been removed by force in three days of fighting.

* Plebiscite Front (PF)
Organization which has been active in Azad Kashmir and stands for an independent Kasmir. It was founded in 1955 and reportdly has a military alliance with the National Liberation Front. It is led by A.Ansari.

* Popular Front for Armed Resistance (PFAR)
Tribal Baluch separatist organization active in guerrilla warfare since 1973. The PFAR also carried out bomb attacks in the cities. In 1974 Z.A.Bhutto claimed that the insurgency in Baluchistan was over and announced a pardon for over 5,000 guerrillas who had been captured or had surrendered. Unofficial sources reported that the fighting had claimed the lives of at least 3,300 soldiers and a further 5,300 Baluch guerrillas. Guerrilla warfare continued and in 1976 some 20,000 guerrillas opposed six army divisions. Mr.Bhutto's overthrow by the army in July 1977, has led to a substantial decrease in the intensity of the fighting in Baluchistan.

PALESTINE

* Abu Nidal Group
Militant Palestinian faction which broke away from Al Fatah in 1973. It is led by Sabri Khalil al-Banna (Abu Nidal) and has an estimated 300 to 500 agents. Abu Nidal has attempted to kill Yasser Arafat several times. Abu Nidal was sentenced to death in absentia by the PLO. He received support from Iraq, Syria and Libya. His headquarters moved from Baghdad to Damascus and from Damascus to Baghdad where it was expelled again in November 1983. The group has operated under various names, including Fatah Revolutionary Council, Arab Revolutionary Brigades, Black June, Al Asifa and Revolutionary Organization of Socialist Moslems. Infiltration appeared to be impossible because of the small separately operating cells. It has reportedly been responsible for more than 100 attacks, including assassinations, bomb attacks and hijackings. It has targeted moderate PLO representatives, Egyptians, Jordanians, British, European Jews and Israeli diplomats. It has set up networks in Madrid, Rome, Vienna, Paris and Athens and has been the only Palestinian organization operating in Eastern Europe, raiding targets in Bucharest, Belgrade and Warsaw. According to a DFLP official the group received a total of $ 1,2 billion dollars from Libya over a ten-year period. Syria reportedly betrayed the identities of 20 members of the Abu Nidal group to European governments and Jordan to show its right intentions. In 1987 Abu Nidal's state supporters forced him to an attempt to reconcile with El Fatah at the 18th meeting of the PNC in Algiers in April 1987.

* Action Organization for the Liberation of Palestine (AOLP)
Palestinian group which attacked Munich airport in February 1970.

* Al Fatah Uprising
Syrian supported Palestinian faction which broke away from Fatah in 1983. It has about 5,000 members and is led by Abu Musa. It has been responsible for a series of bombings in Jerusalem and the West Bank in 1984 and 1985. Its headquarters is located in Damascus.

* Ali Abu Taouk Unit
A PLO group which claimed responsibility for an explosion outside the Damascus Gate of Jerusalem's Old City on Feb.22, 1987. Twelve policemen and five others were injured.

* Al-Seeir
Breakaway group from Al Fatah. Mrs.Khouloud Moghrabi, one of its members, was sentenced on May 15, 1979, to 12 years imprisonment for conspiring to murder the Iraqi ambassador in London.

* Anti Arafat PLF
Palestinian faction which in 1983 broke away from the PLF in protest over Abul Abbas' growing ties to Yasser Arafat. It is led by Talaat Yacoub and

has an estimated 100 members. Its headquarters is located in Damascus and it is supported by Syria.

* Anti Imperialist Brigades (AIB)
Group which claimed responsibility for the bomb attack on the British embassy in Beirut on July 11, 1986.

* Arab Guerrilla Cells (AGC)
Palestinian terrorist group possibly linked to Abu Nidal which claimed responsibility for the December 1985 attacks on Rome and Vienna airports. In a type-written statement in Arabic it said that 'by adopting the road of sacrifice and martyrdom and by the death of all members of the two units in Rome and Vienna, we hereby declare the birth of a revolutionary and suicidal group. Having decided to die, we have also decided to kill as many imperialists and Zionist killers as possible'.

* Arab Liberation Front
(Jabhat al-Tahrir al-Arabiya) (ALF)
Founded in April 1969 by Iraq as a counterweight to the Syrian-backed Al-Saiqa. In 1978 and 1980 it was involved in raids against targets in Israel and subsequently also in clashes with (Shi'ite Moslem) Amal forces and with Israeli troops. Its leader, Dr.Abdel Wahab Kayyale, was assassinated in Beirut in December 1981. He was succeeded by Abdel Rahim Ahmad. It has been involved in terrorist actions in Western Europe. It had an estimated 500 members and was a member of the 'rejectionist' front within the PLO. Presently it is inactive.

* Arab Nationalist Command (ANC)
Arab umbrella organization which was established in March 1984. Its constitution declares 'resistance to all reactionary projects of surrender'. Its 20 or more member organizations, including 'Egypt's Revolution' retain a wide degree of autonomy.

* Arab Nationalist Youth Organization for the Liberation of Palestine (ANYOLP)
Breakaway group of the PFLP (1972). It was responsible for an attack on the Israeli ambassador in Nicosia (Cyprus) in April 1973 and for a number of hijacking operations in 1973-75 at a time when Al Fatah had officially abandoned such operations. It has supported the PLO's 'rejectionist' wing.

* Arab Revolutionary Army-Palestine Commando (ARA-PC)
Name under which a group claimed responsibility for the poisoning of Israeli oranges exported to Western Europe in 1978.

* Arab Revolutionary Brigades (ARB)
Beirut-based pan-Aranic terrorist group which has been involved in attacks on Jordanians. One attempt against King Hussein involved two three-member units equipped with heat-seeking shoulder-fired SAM missiles, who planned to shoot down his official aircraft during a flight between Amman and Aqaba. A defecting Libyan diplomat who revealed the operation to Jordanian authorities had been instructed by Tripoli to cooperate with the assassins. Several bombings targeting diplomatic and commercial facilities have been successfully carried out in Amman in 1985. The organization also claimed resonsibility for the hijacking of a Saudi airliner over the Persian Gulf in 1984.

* Arab Revolutionary Cells-Ezzedin al-Kassam Unit
Possibly a pro-Libyan Palestinian group which has been responsible for the bomb attack on a TWA Boeing 727 in Athens on Apr.2, 1986. Ezzedin Kassam was hanged by the British for leading a Palestinian revolt against the British Mandate in 1936. The name has been used frequently by terrorist factions linked to Abu Nidal.

* Arab Revolutionary Committees in Lebanon
Arab group which distributed a statement to the media in Beirut in January 1986, saying that the consequences of aggression against Libya 'will be suicide missions in the heart of Washington and inside occupied Palestine'. The organization which was set up in 1985 with Libyan help, also expressed support for the attacks in Rome and Vienna, saying they were ' a true expression of the sentiment of all revolutionaries in the Arab world.'

* Arab Revolutionary Organization (ARO)
Terrorist group which claimed responsibility for the June 1985 bomb attack in Frankfurt. The group accused the West German secret service of forcing Arabs who live in West Germany to commit murder attacks on revolutionary leaders in the Middle East.

* Black June Organization
(Munadamat Huzairan al-Aswad) (BJO)
In June 1976, the Palestinian-backed Lebanese Moslem leftists were defeated by the combined forces of the Syrians and the Lebanese Christians. The BJO is led by Sabri al-Banna (Abu Nidal) and was believed to have an estimated 500 members. BJO was opposed to the PLO's conciliatory line, and was responsible for a series of assassinations in 1978, when PLO representatives in London (Said Hammami), Kuwait (Ali Yassin), Paris (Izz ad-Din Qalaq) and in Istanbul were murdered. The BJO again resorted to terrorism in Europe in the early 1980s, when it attacked the congregation of a Vienna synagogue and a pro-Israeli Austrian. In 1982 its assassination attempt on the Israeli ambassador in London, Shlomo Argov, was taken as a protest to invade Lebanon.

• Black September Organization
(Munadamat Aylul al-Aswad) (BSO)
Cover name for certain Al Fatah operations. The name refers to the bloody events in Jordan in September 1970 when King Hussein cracked down on Palestinian organizations, driving them into exile. Black September was set up by two Fatah officials, Abu Daoud and Ali Hassan Salameh. The group has been responsible for the Munich Olympics attack in 1972, several assassinations, bomb attacks and armed attacks on embassies and on airports. Its operations had ceased in December 1974 as a result of a Fatah decision to suspend terrorist operations. In 1984 its rebirth was announced in a declaration which was distributed in Rome, probably by members of the Abu Nidal group. On Mar.22, 1985, it claimed responsibility for simultaneous attacks on offices of the Royal Jordanian airlines in Athens, Rome and Nicosia. On Sep.3, 1985, it claimed responsibility for a bomb attack on a hotel in Glyfada (Greece) to put pressure on the Greek government to release an arrested Palestinian.

• Black September-June Organization (BSJO)
A combination of the Black September and Black June organizations and the group led by Abu Nidal. It claimed responsibility for the killing of a Minister of State for Foreign Affairs of the United Arab Emirates in Abu Dhabi on Oct.25, 1977. The assassin, who was said to have been supported by the Iraqi regime, was executed on Nov.16, 1977.

• Commando of the Martyr Kamal Adwan
Terrorist group which claimed responsibility for a bomb attack in Jerusalem on Oct.16, 1986.

• Commando Mohammed Boudia (CMB)
Terrorist group led by Mohammed Boudia who had been active in the FLN in Algeria. He was the leader of the European section of the PFLP in the 1969-1973 period. The Israel secret service (Wrath of God) killed him in 1973. He was replaced by Carlos (Ilich Ramirez Sanchez). The group cooperated with the June 2 Movement, Black September, the Japanese Revolutionary Army and Turkish and Italian organizations.

• Commando Naharya (CN)
Unit of the Palestinian Liberation Front (PLF) responsible for the seajacking of the Italian cruise ship Achille Lauro in Oct.1985.

• Commando of the Palestinian Martyr Moudher Abu-Ghazala
Palestinian group responsible for a bomb attack on a military bus in Haifa on Feb.1, 1987. Nine persons were injured in the attack.

• Democratic Alliance (DA)
An alliance of Palestinian groups which has been established in 1983. It has been critical of Arafat but independent of Syria and Libya. Like Al Fatah it has publicly renounced terrorism outside the borders of Israel and the occupied territories.

• Democratic Front for the Liberation of Palestine
(Jabhat al-Dimuqratiya li Tahrir Falistin) (DFLP)
Left-wing Palestinian group which split from the PFLP in 1969. It is led by Nayef Hawatmeh. The DFLP rejected the PFLP's policy of staging terrorist attacks outside the 'occupied territories'. Its goal is a 'democratic Palestine State' within which Jews and Arabs would have equal rights. The PFLP was responsible for the Ma'alot massacre on May 15, 1974 during which 22 Israeli children were killed. It has an estimated strength of about 900 to 1,100 men.

• Eagles of the Palestine Revolution or Red Eagles
(El Nisr)
Unit of the Syrian-based Al Saiqa organization which has been responsible for the hijacking of a Moscow to Vienna Express (Chopin Express) train carrying Soviet Jews emigrating to Israel on Sep.28/29, 1973. The group demanded that the Austrian government close down the Schonau transit camp which was being used by the Jewish Agency to receive Soviet Jews on their way to the West (normally Israel). The Austrian government acceded to the terrorists demand.

• Egyptian Liberation Organization (ELO)
Name adopted by four terrorists involved in the Egypt Air hijacking to Luqa airport, Malta in November 1985. The ELO is thought to be one of the many noms de guerre of the Abu Nidal organization. It was the bloodiest hijack in aviation history in which 57 people died, most of them when Egyptian commandos stormed the airliner. Following a brief gun battle between Egyptian Skymarshals the fuselage of the aircraft was punctured and the Boeing was forced to make an emergency landing. The hijackers threatened to kill hostages every hour on the hour until the Maltese allowed the jet to be refuelled. Five people were shot, one of them died. Fearing that they would systematically kill all the passengers the Egyptian commando unit stormed the aircraft. The operation failed to take the hijackers by surprise. Grenades were thrown, a gun battle ensued, and the rear of the aircraft caught fire. Of the 57 people who died, eight were killed by grenade fragments, seven by bullet wounds and the rest from the effects of fire.

• Al Fatah
See Movement for the National Liberation of Palestine.

* Fatah Reform Movement (FRM)
Breakaway group led by Abu Zaim to oppose the policies and management style of Yasser Arafat. Abu Zaim was Mr.Arafat's chief of security and intelligence in the official Fatah movement from 1976 to 1985. Since then he claimed to head the 'real' Fatah and planned to call a National Assembly of the movement in late 1986 to have himself democratically confirmed as commmander in place of Mr.Arafat. Forty-one of 55 military men with seats in Fatah's National assembly have sided with Abu Zaim; more than 400 entitled to attend some larger congress backed the breakaway movement. Its headquarters is located in Damascus.

* Al Fatah-Revolutionary Council
Palestinian terrorist group which is led by Abu Nidal. Its stated aim is the destruction of Israel. It has about 4,800 supporters with a hardcore of 300 men. During the last 12 years it has been responsible for more than 100 attacks (35 in 1985) which resulted in 181 deaths and more than 200 people injured. Its headquarters is said to be in Libya. The targets include a number of PLO moderates, Ali Yasin (1978), Said Hammami (1978), Ezzedine Kalak (1978), Naim Khader (1981), Majed Abu Shra (1981), Issam Sartawi (1983) and Aziz Shehadah (1985). At different times it was supported by Syria, Iraq and Libya.

* Fifteenth of May Arab Movement for the Liberation of Palestine
Terrorist group of radical Palestinians named after the day Arab states began their struggle against the new Israeli state in 1948. It was established in 1979 when it broke away from the PFLP-GC. It was reported to have about 70 members and specialized in attacks on airliners. It has been responsible for an attack on a Jumbo jet of Panam airlines near Hawai on Aug.15, 1982; and also has been mentioned in connection with an attack on a TWA Boeing 727 in Greece on Apr.2, 1986. The group is suspected of having developed an undetectable suitcase bomb which in some cases was placed by Western women. It is led by Husayn Mohammed al-Umari (Abu Ibrahim). It established a secret network in Kuwait, Lebanon and Western Europe and received financial and military support from Iraq. Sometimes it has been described as the arm of the Iraqi military intelligence. Its headquarters is located in Baghdad and the group was reportedly suppressed by mid-1984.

* Force 17
After the attack on the Olympic Games in Munich (1972) Yasser Arafat took new security measures. A special group of security agents could reach him directly via the telephone number 17. Since then the unit was called Force 17. It developed into one of the elite units of the PLO. Originally consisting of 10 members, Force 17 grew to 1,500 men. The Israelis believe it was behind the Larnaca Marina attack in Cyprus in September 1985. Some Force 17 detachments are believed to be specially trained in mine laying, shore landings, and underwater sabotage. Western intelligence believe there are Force 17 groups or cells all over Western Europe. The force is commanded by Abu Tayeb and reportedly moved a forward based section from Amman (Jordan) to Cairo (Egypt) in an attempt to mend relations between Arafat and President Mubarak.

* Heroes of Return
(Abtal al-Anda)
Heroes of return was founded in Lebanon by the PLO. It rivalled Fatah for a time, until it merged in December 1967 with the Popular Front for the Liberation of Palestine (PFLP). It was led by Fayez Abdul Rahmin Jaber (killed in the Entebbe raid) who was also one of the founding fathers of the PFLP. Jaber was head of the PFLP's internal security and was then appointed commander of special operations 'in the external sphere' that is outside Israel.

* International Fighting Front (IFF)
One of four organizations that claimed responsibility for the Sep.6, 1986 attack on the Istanbul Synagogue (Turkey).

* Movement of Arab Nationalists
(Harakat al-Qaumiyyin al-Arab) (MAN)
Pan-Arab movement founded by future Palestinian guerrilla activists such as Naif Hawatmeh and George Habbash. It split up after the 1967 Arab defeat. Local liberation groups were set up in South Yemen, Oman and Lebanon.

* Movement for the National Liberation of Palestine ('Conquest') (Harakat al-Tahir al-Hatani al-Falastini) (Al Fatah)
Fatah was established in the years 1959-1962. It has been led since 1964 by Yasser Arafat who also became chairman of the PLO. In a key document ('The seven points', January 1969) Fatah describes itself as 'the expression of the Palestinian people and of its will to free its land from Zionist colonization in order to recover its national identity.' It is estimated to keep 10,000 to 15,000 men under arms. In 1970 the Palestinians were driven from Jordania to Lebanon. In 1982 they were driven out of Lebanon into exile in Syria, Iraq, Tunesia and Yemen. Since then large numbers have returned to the Lebanon. It emphasized the armed struggle, together with all other means to achieve national liberation for the Palestinians. It called for Israeli withdrawal from the occupied territories of the West Bank and Gaza, and implementation of the UN resolutions recognizing

the Palestinians' right to repatriation and the formation of an independent state. The Jordan-PLO accord of Feb.11, 1985 proposed: 1) Land in exchange for peace as cited in the UN resolutions including the security council resolutions; 2) The Palestinian people's right to self-determination, to be exercised within the framework of an Arab confederation established between Jordan and Palestine; 3) A solution to the Palestinian refugee problem in accordance with UN resolutions; 4) Solving all aspects of the Palestine Peace negotiations within the framework of an international conference, attended by the five permanent members of the UN security council and all parties to the conflict including the PLO-as part of a joint Jordanian-Palestinian delegation. This accord was abrogated by the PLO in May 1987.

* National Arab Youth Organization for the Liberation of Palestine (NAYOLP)
Group which claimed responsibility for a bomb attack on a TWA-airliner on Sep.8, 1974. The bomb exploded with 88 passengers aboard. Abu Nidal was one of the leaders of the group which was established by Libya.

* National Palestinian Council (NPC)
A body in which most Palestinian guerrilla movements are represented. They have 94 elected seats out of a total of 426. The distribution of the seats of the guerrilla organizations in 1983 was: Fatah (33), Saiqa (12), PFLP (12), DFLP (12), LAF (9), PFLP-GC (8), PSF (4) and PLF (4). The Central Council of the PLO (55 members) takes care of the daily execution of the adopted resolutions. During its 18th meeting in Algiers in April 1987 the several factions reconciled to support the idea of an international conference. It stuck to the idea of a confederation of two states, a Jordanian and a Palestinian. Security Council resolution 242 remained unacceptable unless a paragraph on Palestinian rights on self-determination is added.

* National Palestinian Salvation Front (NPSF)
A hardline anti-Arafat umbrella group which rejects the idea of talks with Israel but would accept a Palestinian state in the West Bank and Gaza. It was set up by Syria to rival the PLO. Syria is determined to defeat any Middle Eastern initiative that does not include Damascus in the negotiations. It is comprised of the PFLP (G.Habash), PFLP-GC (Ahmed Jibril), Saiqa, PSF and a faction led by Sayed Musa (also Abu Musa). It was established in 1984. Ahmed Jibril acted as its spokesman. In April 1987 the six groups announced they would dissolve the NPSF and attend the meeting of the PNC in Algiers.

* Organization for Arab Armed Struggle (OAS)
Organization which has been responsible for bomb attacks in France. One of its members was Ilich Ramirez Sanchez ('Carlos'). It surfaced following the murder of Michel Moukarbal, one of its founders, and two policemen in Paris. Carlos killed Moukarbal because he suspected him to be a police informer.

* Organization of the Struggle against World Imperialism (SAWIO)
Group which claimed responsibility for the hijacking of a West German Lufthansa airliner on Oct.13, 1977. See Popular Front for the Liberation of Palestine-Special Operations. (PFLP-SO)

* Palestinian Arab Revolutionary Committees (PARC)
Palestinian terrorist organization based in t[illegible]e Bekaa Valley. The organization. Libya was re[illegible]d to fund and arm the group which is lead by [illegible]ad el-Khumsi.

* Palestine Armed Struggle Command (Qiyadat al-Kifah al-Mussalah) (PASC)
The PLO set up PASC in 1969 to act as a joint military coordinating body. Defacto, it replaced the Palestine Coordinating Council. By 1980, however, the PASC had been reduced to acting as an arbiter in factional disputes. In 1981 its commander was Mustafa Dib Khalil (Abu Ta'an).

* Palestine Liberation Army (Jaish Tahrir Falistin) (PLA)
The PLA was set up in 1964 as the conventional armed forces of the PLO. Its commander-in-chief is the PLO chairman, Yasser Arafat. Most PLA forces were in Syria in 1980, having acted alongside the Syrian armed forces in the Lebanese civil war of 1975-76. The organization's chief of staff in 1981 was Brigadier General Tariq Khadra. He no longer recognized Mr.Arafat as head of the PLO in October 1983. The PLA has 20,000 troops attached to the armies of Syria, Egypt and Iraq.

* Palestinian Liberation Front (PLF) (Jabhad Tahrir Falistin)
A breakaway group from the PFLP-GC in eastern and southern Lebanon. In August 1978 over 180 people died in a bomb explosion which destroyed the PLF's headquarters in Beirut. It is known for its daring raids into Israel. Four of its members raided Nahariya in northern Israel on Apr.22, 1979-allegedly to emphasize the front's rejection of the March 1979 Egyptian-Israeli peace treaty. The PLF is part of the 'rejectionist front' within the PLO and numbered 200 members. It split in three factions in 1982. A pro-Syrian faction is headed by Talaat Yaaqub. The smallest pro-Libyan faction is headed by Abdel Fatah Ghanem and the pro-Iraqi faction is headed by Mohammed (Abu) Abbas. The

latter has been responsible for the Achille Lauro hijacking on October 7, 1985.

* Palestine Liberation Organization
(Munadamat Tahrir Falistin) (PLO)
The main political body of the Palestinian people founded in 1964. The PLO has been recognized by the Arab nations as 'the sole legitimate representative of the Palestinian people.' The PLO is led since 1969 by Yasser Arafat who enjoys the support of a majority of the Palestinians. The PLO is made up of a number of components the largest and most powerful of which is the military wing Fatah. The PLO is currently based in Iraq and Yemen after having been expelled from Tunesia in 1985 after an Israeli bombing raid on their headquarters. Three years previously, in the autumn of 1982, the PLO were driven out of Lebanon by the Israeli invasion of June 1982 and its 12,000 fighters scattered around eight Arab countries. During 'Operation Peace for Galilea' the PLO lost 2400 fighters. In the total operation more than 18,000 people died, mostly civilians, including many Palestinians, while 30,000 people were injured. Since then fighters have trickled back to Lebanon where they have engaged in heavy fighting with Lebanese factions including Amal. By the end of 1984 it was concluded that some 2,000 to 2,500 PLO members were in training camps in and around Beirut. Although the invasion succeeded in undermining the PLO's political infrastructure and in severely weakening Arafat's power, it did not result in a major decline in attacks on Israeli- and Jewish targets when compared to the immediate pre-invasion period.

* Palestine National Front in Occupied Territories
(Jabhat al-Wataniya al-Falestiniya fi al-Aradi al-Muhtala) (PNF)
According to Israeli sources the PNF-formed in 1974- was the first serious resistance group formed on the occupied West Bank since 1967, its core being the Jordanian Communist Party. Its strength was estimated to be 100 to 500 armed men. Its aim was to establish a Marxist-Leninist regime. Muhammad Abd al-Mohsen (Abu Maizer), Dr.Walid Qamhawi and Abd al-Jawad Saleh represented the PNF in the executive committee of the PLO. Its effectiveness as a guerrilla movement was contained by Israel's countermeasures by the late 1970s.

* Palestine Popular Struggle Front
(Jabhat al-Kifah al-Shaabi al-Falistini) (PPSF)
The PPSF had its origins in the commando force of the Palestine Liberation Army (PLA). It is led by Bahjat Abu Garbiyyah and Dr.Samir Ghusha. The front was dedicated to attacks inside Israel and the occupied territories.

* Palestinian Revenge Organization (PRO)
One of four organizations that claimed responsibility for the Sep.6, 1986, attack on the Istanbul synagogue (Turkey).

* Partisans of Right and Freedom (PRF)
Group which claimed responsibility for a bomb attack on the Paris City Hall on Sep.8, 1986.

* Popular Arab Liberation Front (MPLA)
Palestinian terrorist organization established in 1979 after a split with the Abu Nidal faction. It is led by Naji Alush and maintains contacts with Fatah and the Habash front.

* Popular Front for the Liberation of Palestine
(al-Jabha al-Sha'biyyah li Tahrir Falastin) (PFLP)
A Marxist-Leninist organization founded by Dr.George Habash in December 1967. Its goal was the elimination of the Israeli state. It suffered from internal disputes that gave rise to factions. Among the most prominent were the PFLP-GC, OAP and the PDFLP. It numbers some 800 men (1986) stationed in Lebanon. The PFLP was the first of the Arab groups to use aerial hijacking as a military tactic. Beginning in July 1968 the PFLP's 'external operations' branch led by Wadi Haddad organized some of the most spectacular terrorist operations in the post-war history, including the Zurich airport attack in 1969, the Dawson's field hijackings in September 1970, and the Lufthansa hijacking to Mogadishu airport, Somalia in 1977. The PFLP are also thought to have engineered the OPEC attack, Vienna in December 1975.

* Popular Front for the Liberation of Palestine-General Command
(Jabhat al-Shaabiya li Tahrir Falistin al-Qiyadat al-Ama) (PFLP-GC)
An offshoot of the PFLP which emerged in October 1968, shortly after the PFLP had been formed. Led by an ex-Syrian army officer called Ahmed Jibril (Abu Jihad) the PFLP-GC joined the Iraqi backed Rejectionist Front which opposed (sometimes violently) the policies of the mainstream PLO. In 1977 the PFLP-GC split when Jibril's second in command Abu Abbas formed the PLF. The PFLP-GC were blamed for a massive explosion in Beirut in August 1978 which destroyed the headquarters of Abu Abbas organization, killing some 200 people in the process. Jibril's PFLP-GC are now a hardline 'physical force' of about 500 men based in Lebanon. It has been responsible for bomb attacks and armed assaults. They included the blowing-up of a Swiss airliner in February 1970 (47 deaths), an attack on an Israeli schoolbus in May 1970 (12 children and several adults died), the killing of 18 Israelis (12 children and five women) at Kiryat Shemona in April 1974.

* Popular Front for the Liberation of Palestine-Special Operations (PFLP-SO)
This Baghdad-based organization was formed in 1975, as a splinter of the PFLP. On Oct.27, 1977, it was reported to have claimed responsibility for the hijacking of a West German Lufthansa airliner. Among other acts of which the front claimed responsibility was an attack on an El Al(Israeli airline) bus in London on Aug.20,1978. The group was led by Wadi Haddad (died of cancer in 1978). He has been replaced by Salim Abu Salim (Abu Muhammad). The group has an estimated strength of 100 men. Its military chief is Zaki Hilo and Sadki el-Atri (Abu Faras) is in charge of recruitment. It reportedly has branches in Iraq, Kuwait, Algeria, South Yemen, Lebanon, Cyprus, Yugoslavia and Bulgaria.

* Rejectionist Front
(Jabhat al-Rafud)
In 1974 the Palestine Liberation Organization (PLO) moderated its armed activities and political claims on UN resolution 242. In reaction, a number of extreme sections of Palestinian opinion formed a Front Rejecting Capitalist Solutions, which became known as the Rejectionist Front. It included the PFLP, PFLP-GC, ALF, PPSF and the PLF. In 1977 the PFLP-GC was expelled from the Front, but the group continued to follow rejectionist policies. Libya, Iraq and Syria supported the Rejection Front. The front reconciled with the mainstream PLO at the April 1987 PNC meeting in Algiers.

* Revolutionary Brigades for the Liberation of the Borderstrip (RBLBS)
Palestinian group which threatened the UN peace keeping forces in southern Lebanon in September 1986. They demanded Israel to withdraw from southern Lebanon within a month. A deadline of Oct.3 was set for implementation of Security Council resolution 425 of 1978.

* Revolutionary Organization of Socialist Moslems (ROSM)
Name by which the Abu Nidal organization claimed responsibility for a series of attacks on British individuals and institutions in Greece, Lebanon, India and Italy since March 1984. It warned the British to 'stop their aggressive attacks' and to 'release all Moslem freedom fighters from British imperialist jails.' The campaign was probably directed at the release from jail of two Palestinians involved in the assault on the Israeli ambassador Shlomo Argov in London in June 1982.

* The Secret Army for the Liberation of Palestine (SALP)
Eight members of this group linked to Abu Nidal and George Habash were arrested in Greece on Jan.1, 1986. Unofficial sources said that the group had plans to attack the PLO and that they belonged to the Abu Nidal group. The arrest came a few days following the announcement that Greece and the PLO would cooperate in the struggle against terrorism. The men were released because no evidence was found that they were planning or had planned violent actions.

* Thunderbolt or Vanguards of the Popular Liberation War (Al Saiqa)
The military wing of the pro-Syrian Palestinian organization known as The Vanguards of the Popular War of Liberation (The Vanguards). It was established in 1968. Close connections with the ruling Ba'ath party in Syria have made the organization vulnerable to Syrian internal disputes. From time to time the Syrian military has purged Saiqa of its leadership and replaced it with Syrian appointees. In 1970 the Syrians installed a veteran Ba'athist called Zuhair Muhsin to lead Saiqa but he was assassinated in Cannes in July 1979. Saiqa units played an active part in the civil war in Lebanon. It is now led by Issam al Qadi and has an estimated strength of 1,000 to 2,000 men stationed in eastern and northern Lebanon and Syria.

PANAMA

* F-7
Paramilitary force that served to repress political opponents during the presidential election in 1984. The leader of the unit was killed under mysterious circumstances.

* F-8
Unknown group which has been responsible for the death of Mr.Spadafora, a former deputy minister of health. His decapitated body stuffed in old US mail bag was found on Sep.15, 1985, in Costa Rica near the Panamanian border. The dead body had a symbol into it that read'F-8'. It was speculated that F-8 might be the name of a new army unit or death squad. Public demands for an investigation led to a military coup. Mr.Spadafora, a medical doctor, had in the the 1970s joined Eden Pastora Gomez, in having recruited more than 300 Panamanians to help overthrow A.Somoza in Nicaragua. Later he became an adviser of the Miskito Indian rebels fighting the Sandinist government. Another victim of F-8 was Dr.Mauro Zuniga, the head of an umbrella opposition group, National Civil Coordinating Committee (COCINA). He was abducted at gunpoint from a restaurant on Aug.21, 1985. His body, badly beaten but alive, was found along the roadside in Chiriqui province.

PARAGUAY

* First of March Organisation or Politico-Military

Organisation (Organización 1 Marzo, or Organización Politico-Militar) (OPM)
Guerrilla group formed by radical Catholic students in 1974 who had links with the Argentinian ERP. In April 1976 the police raided its headquarters in Asuncion. Five policemen and 30 guerrillas were killed in the shooting. The leaders of the group, Juan Carlos de Costa and Mario Schaerer, were wounded and died in custody. Over 1,500 suspects were detained. The remaining members escaped to Argentina.

* Police Investigations Department
(Departemento de Investigaciones de la Policia) (DIPC)
Police force which has been involved in torture and illegal deprivation of liberty.

* Popular Colorado Movement
(Movimiento Popular Colorado) (MOPOCO)
A dissident faction of the Colorado Party led by Dr.Enrique Riera. He was detained for short periods in 1985 and was sent to internal exile. His banishment was lifted in October 1985. A decade before, another leader, named as Dr.Goiburu, was accused of plotting to kill President Stroessner and to abduct ministers and other office bearers of the regime. The plot planned for January 1975, was was said to be supported by the (Argentinian) People's Revolutionary Army (ERP). Some MOPOCO members were kidnapped in Brazil. Dr.Goiburu escaped a kidnap attempt in Argentina.

PERU

* Civil Guard
A government force accused of torture.

* Communist Party of Peru/ Red Flag
(Partido Comunista Peruano/ Bandera Roja)
In 1982 Red Flag was led by Lawyer Saturnino Paredes, who in 1964 had headed a pro-Chinese faction which broke with the Moscow-line of the Peruvian Communist Party. Members started a paper, Red Flag, which advocated armed struggle. From this group split a further faction known as Red Fatherland in 1967, and in 1970 Shining Path split from Red Flag. Although Red Flag advocates the armed struggle it is acccused by Shining Path of collaborating with the government. Its main front organizations are the Peasant Confederation of Peru (CCP) and the Popular Democrat Front (FDP).

* Farmers Confederation of Peru
(Conféderación Campesina del Peru) (CCP)
Organization of the Indian highland farmers which has been accused by the government of being a terrorist organization.

* Front of the Revolutionary Left
(Frente Izquierda Revolucionaria) (FIR)
Small Trotskyite organization set up in the city of Cuzco in December 1961. Principal organizers were Hugo Blanco, the Argentinian, Arturo 'Che' Pereyra and the Spaniard, José Martorell. It had some 60 urban members and has been involved in two bank robberies. Hugo Blanco was captured on May 29, 1963. He was subsequently pardoned and became a senator.

* Investigative Police
Police force which involved in torture.

* Movement of Revolutionary Left
(Movimiento de la Izquierda Revolucionaria) (MIR)
The MIR sprang from a rebel faction of the American Popular Revolutionary Alliance (APRA) in June 1962. Its leader, Luis de la Puente Uceda, obtained Castro's help for his objectives. Two rural foci were active in the mid-1960s. The actions lasted no longer than six months as the groups were eliminated by the army. Leaders who survived were released in 1970 and began to resume activities in the early 1970s.

* National Liberation Army
(Ejercito de Liberación Nacional) (ELN)
One of several Peruvian guerrilla organizations which had been active in the 1960s. It was established in 1962 and was led by Juan Pablo Chang Navarro. In a manifesto issued in 1965 the ELN proclaimed that, for the liberation of the country's workers and peasants, it would pursue both armed struggle and a 'policy of unity'. However, guerrilla operations begun in September 1965 were successfully suppressed by the army by December of that year, with the remaining guerrillas withdrawing into Ecuador. Its leader Hector Béjar was captured in February 1966. A reorganized ELN appeared in September 1980 under the leadership of Juan Pablo Chang Navarro, but its operations appear to have remained insignificant.

* Peasant Patrols
(Rondas Campesinas)
Illegal quasi paramilitary peasant pressure group which has been very active in 1980 in land occupations in the Sierra Region. When the Minister of the Interior in the newly-appointed government refused to legalize the patrols, they decided in September 1980 to declare the Chota province (in north-western Peru) an 'independent zone'. Their activities were not a serious challenge to the authorities.

* Runa Huanuchiq Runa
(People which kill other people) (RHR)
Paramilitary farmers militias which have defended

themselves with axes, spades, stone slings and cudgels against Senderistas, Sinchis and collaborators.

* Peruvian Communist Party
(Partido Comunista del Peru) (PCP)
The political arm of the Shining Path guerrilla organization. It appealed to the heritage of the Inca's which have been praised for their 'advanced working methods' and their 'independent development model'. It also appealed to the long tradition of resistance against the Spanish conquistadores. It is mainly based on the Pakra and Chanca tribes in Ayacucho province. Its ideologue is Abimael Guzman who succeeded in a synthesis of the concept of a rural revolution and the Indian myth of the Panchacuti ('the revolution of the world').

* Puka Llacta
Guerrilla organization which reportedly operated in the highland of Puno.

* Red Earth
(Tierra Roja)
Trotskyite group which temporarily seized a radio station in 1981.

* Red Fatherland
(Patria Roja) (PR)
Maoist group split from the (Pro-Soviet) Peruvian Communist Party. On Mar.2, 1982, 150 members stormed a prison in Ayacucho freeing about 250 prisoners, including 54 guerrillas.

* Revolutionary Movement Tupac Amaru (MRTA)
(Movimiento Revolucionario Tupac Amaru)
Castroite urban guerrilla group whose leaders reportedly have been tied to Cuba and Nicaragua. Allied with Shining Path, it operates in northern departments of La Libertad, Cajamarca, Jaen, Lambayeque and Amazonas. Tupac Amaru refers to a freedom fighter who was put to death in the eighteenth century. Unlike the Shining Path the organization does not indulge in a secret semi-religious violence cult. It is more open and has better propagandistic qualities. It has raided supermarkets and handed out the booty in poor districts in Lima. The result of these activities has been that it has been more successful in the recruitment of supporters. It also gained more support under the most leftwing sectors of United Left.

* Revolutionary Peoples Commandos (CRP)
An offshoot of MRTA which has been active in 1985 and 1986 causing disruption and damaging property but apparently causing few fatalities. It possibly was responsible for an attack on a train in which eight people were killed and another 35 were injured.

* Shining Path
(Sendoro Luminoso) (SL)
Guerrilla organization founded in 1970 when a faction led by Abimael Guzmán split from the Peruvian Communist Party Red Flag group. It gained major public attention since 1980. Its guerrilla campaign and the government's counter-action have cost more than 10,000 lives. Up to 2,000 more have disappeared after being abducted by security forces. The name refers to a statement from Peru's first prominent Marxist, José Carlos Mariatequi that 'Marxism-Leninism will open the shining path to revolution'. Its core leaders are former students at the Ayacucho university, familiar with the area, and knowledgeable of the local Indian language Quechua. It has an estimated 2,000 guerrillas. World revolution is to be achieved through a prolonged popular war in the countryside, eventually encircling the cities. After a May 1983 government counterinsurgency offensive in Ayacucho the movement was dispersed and its overall composition may have shifted in an urban direction. It has engaged in ruthless assassinations, bomb attacks and sabotage. In the rebels' new emphasis on political operations, they have stepped up efforts to infiltrate union and civic groups. They said to have carried out 30,000 actions through June 1986, affecting all but two of the country's 25 provinces. More than half of these actions are reported to have taken place since mid-1984. The government lists a total of 13,100 attacks through September 1986. A purge within the organization began before a rebellion in three Lima jails on June 19, 1986 that ended with the killing of up to 270 Sendero prisoners in an operation led by the armed forces. The loss of its prison bases weakened the organization and may have prolonged internal upheaval. It also has to compete with Tupac Amaru for gaining support of the far left sectors of society. Therefore it concentrated attacks on Lima and distributed public justifications. Renewed attacks in 1987 (average of 80 per month) showed that a reorganization was complete. The Senderistas have few connections abroad, although it signed an agreement in May 1987, with Spanish Marxist-Leninist Maoists to stimulate the 'proletarian world revolution'. Their money comes largely from 'protecting' drugtraffickers. They steal their arms and ammunition from the security forces, and their dynamite from mines.

* Sinchis
Special counter-terrorist troops which have been trained by the United States. The name refers to the Quechua word for 'warrior'. About 1,500 men operated in the province of Ayacucho. In their killing and plundering they equal the Senderistas.

The unit has engaged in extra-judicial executions since mid-January 1983.

* Tawanttinsuyo Liberation Front (TLF)
This front was established on Sep.15, 1981, by representatives of Indians from Bolivia, Ecuador and Peru. Named after the region of the former Inca empire centered on Peru, the Front was aimed at regaining sovereignty over that region. The front is led by Aurelio Turpo Choquehuanca.

PHILIPPINES

* April Six Liberation Movement
The movement claimed responsibility for bomb explosions in Manila on Aug.22, Sep.12 (when five persons were killed and 10 injured) and Oct.4, 1980.

* Bangsa Moro Army (BMA)
The military wing of the MNLF which is entrenched in the Sulu archipelago. At its height the BMA numbered 20,000 to 30,000 armed rebels. Through effective police actions and diplomatic negotiations with the backers of the MNLF, the rebellion has subsided and now the MNLF may not have more than 2,000 armed regulars in Mindanao.

* Bangsa Moro Liberation Organization (BMLO)
Splinter group of the MNLF, established in 1977 which was prepared to negotiate with the Marcus government. It was led by Rashid Lucman and Salipada Pendatun, two former politicians. It had about 28 armed men but it never developed a military capability. In 1981 Lucman agreed to ally with Misuari under the latter leadership. Pendatun accepted the government amnesty offer and retired from politics. There have been reports that the BMLO might have been a Marcos sponsored body, aimed to split the rebel camp.

* Barracudas
A private army linked to a leading Moslem, Ali Dimaparo, a supporter of former President Marcos. It has been responsible for the kidnapping of a Presbyterian missionary.

* Caca
A civil guard, like Risen Masses, active on the island of Cebu in Cebu City.

* Charismatic Movement of the Philippines (CMP)
Movement headed by Rev.Arnold Buenafe (shot on Mar.25, 1981) that pursuaded rather than intimidated villagers to confess what they knew about their neighbors. The CMP's converts mostly illiterates lured with promises of supernatural powers have willingly-albeit suspectingly- obliged. It has operated between Magpet in the north of Cotabato province and Davao City. Its main function has been to observe NPA movements in strategic areas where rebel bases are likely to be set up. It also has put armed men on strategic NPA pathways with orders to kill armed men entering their respective areas and to confiscate arms for their own use.

* Christian Liberation Army (CLA)
Christian army which has been build up in Mindanao following the signature of the Tripoli agreement in 1976 which provides for the independence for the whole of Mindanao.

* Christian People's Army
The alleged leader of this group, Innocencio Espinoso ('Big Boy'), was killed, with three other members of the group, in a gun battle in Negros Occidental province on Jan.18, 1980 when three further members were captured.

* The Church of Jaweh
Fanatic religious group which has been used in counter-insurgency operations. It operated in Mindanao.

* Civil Home Defense Force (CDHF)
A government militia which had been established during the Marcos regime. It has a strength of 70,000 men. It has been accused of human rights violations. President Aquino ordered its dissolution in March 1987. She wanted to integrate the force in a national police force under civilian control.

* Cordillera People's Liberation Army (CPLA)
Small tribal insurgent group led by the Catholic priest Rev.Conrado Balweg. It has an estimated strength of 50 to 100 men and operates in the Cordillera mountains. On Sep.14, 1986, it signed an agreement to cease hostilities and to set up negotiating panels.

* Crusade of the World Army (CWA)
Fanatic religious group which has been used in counter-insurgency operations. It is led by Anang Frank who has the status of God for his supporters. The group emerged in 1984 and operated in Mindanao.

* Democratic Mission Church (DMC)
Fanatic religious group opposing smoking, drinking and gambling. It has been responsible for numerous massacres.

* Followers of Rizal
Fanatic religious group which has been used in counter-insurgency operations. It operated in Mindanao. The name refers to a national hero of the Philippines.

* Four K's Sect (KKKK)

A sect which emerged in 1978. It is based in Siayan and reportedly took part in two multiple murders. Its supreme chief is Ruben Ecleo with Potentiano Marindaque as his deputy. It is said to have much the same beliefs as Rock Christ.

* Goons
Generic name for squads on which local powerful men rely to intimidate the people or to commit murders. Particularly the Marcos government party KBL, made use of goon squads for intimidation, terror and murder.

* Guardians
A military brotherhood whose members have been involved in the unsuccessful January 1987 coup. Members occupied the broadcasting building in Manila. Later in March a captain was sought for involvement in a bomb attack on the Military Academy meant for President Aquino. Four people died in the explosion. The bomb accidentally exploded as a result of the activities of a mine clearing squad.

* Hardcore
Group accused of plotting to assassinate President Marcos. Its alleged leader, prof.Ali Macaraya, was arrested in June 1981.

* Haring Gahum Sect
A sect affilated with Rock Christ which had been formed into small groups and trained by the army for counter-insurgency operations.

* Jihad Brigade
Group that claimed responsibility for an attack on the Joint US Military Advisory Group in Quezon City on Apr.27, 1987.

* Jihad fi Sabililah
During a demonstration on the Edsa Avenue in Manilla on May 24, 1987, this group announced a plan to murder 12 members of the government and members of President Aquino.

* Light a Fire Movement (or Third Force) (LFM)
A loosely organized grouping of predominantly middle class and Roman Catholic radicals. It was strongly opposed to both communism and the 15-year old authoritarian regime of President Marcos. It has been responsible for a wave of bombings and a series of fires in Manila that injured more than 30 people and killed one US visitor. The movement was led by Eduardo Olaguer.

* Lord of the Sacred Heart
Fanatical religious sect which has been involved in counter-insurgency operations. Members are dubbed 'Tadtad' (Philippine word for chop) because of a ritual in which they repel machete blows and because they chop up their enemies. In Cebu province more than 2,000 Tadtads have gone on the offensive since February 1987 when communists attacked a cultist village, taking two lives. Members believe they are invulnerable to bullets.

* Lost Command Group
A group of military renegades loosely affiliated with the AFP and involved in fighting with the NPA. Its task was to liquidate opposition in critical areas so as to avoid direct military involvement in operations which might bring accusations of brutality from foreign governments. It also provided mercenaries hired by politicians and businessmen whose interests are threatened.

* Mindanao Independence Movement (MIM)
A Moslem Independence Movement founded by Datu Udtog Matalam in Pagalongan in May 1968. Many MIM members were active in the MNLF, its armed branch, fighting for a separate Moslem republic in the south.

* Mindanao's People's Democratic Movement (MPDM)
Formed in March 1986 by Ali Dimaporo, a Moslem and the former governor of Lanao del Sur province and Ruben Canoy, a Christian, who was Mr.Marcos' information undersecretary in the 1970s. The two stated they would tap all forces opposing the government including secessionist Moslem rebels, and consider the possibility of establishing independence in Mindanao if harassment by the Aquino administration would continue.

* Moro National Liberation Front-Reformist Group (MNLF-RG)
A front which had been formed in 1982 by former field commander and vice chairman Dimasankay Pundato. It rejected Misuari's leadership and called for autonomy instead of independence.

* Moro Islamic Patriotic Front (MIPF)
Moslem resistance organization active in Mindanao which is striving for independence.

* Moro Islamic National Liberation Front (MILF)
One of the main guerrilla organizations in the south which split off from the MNLF in 1984. The fundamentalist Hasim Salamat advocated a different policy than the policy of chairman Nur Misuari. It has been involved in severe clashes with the Philippine army in January 1987. It did not agree with the accord on self-rule between the Aquino administration and the MNLF led by Nur Misuari. It claimed to have 200,000 guerrillas 75,000 of which permanently armed. Other sources said the front has no more than 3,000 armed fighters. It said it would not abide by any peace agreement unless it were included in the peace talks. The front has been supported by Saudi Arabia.

* Moro National Liberation Front (MNLF)
The main guerrilla organization in the southern Philippines which was established in 1968. Since 1972 it has been involved in an armed insurrection in which more than 60,000 people have been killed. At its height it had an estimated 50,000 fighters. Late 1986 it was estimated to have 6,000 armed rebels with 12,000 in reserve. Its military arm is the Bangsa Moro Army which is operating in five of Mindanao's 12 provinces. President Aquino has named her brother-in-law Agapito Aquino as her representative who will meet with MNLF leaders led by Nur Misuari to negotiate peace. It demands an immediate autonomy over 13 southern provinces and a referendum on the autonomy of 10 other provinces. Nur Misuari threatened with the destruction of all foreign plantations in the south if the government does not agree. Earlier the MNLF was reported to have split into three factions: 1) the main faction led by Nur Misuari; 2) another faction led by Hashim Salamat, supported by Egypt; 3) a minor faction supported by Saudi Arabia. The faction of Nur Misuari has been supported by Libya and Iran. In April 1987, the MNLF agreed to cooperate with the NDF in the southern Philippines.

* Movement for Free Philippines (MFP)
Raul Manglapus, a former Christian Democrat senator, was one of a group of right-wing opposition members who had set up a government-in-exile in the United States and who were influencing foreign governments' relations with the Philippines. Following an explosion at a conference attended by President Marcos and the US ambassador, on Oct.19, 1980, the President ordered the arrest of Manglapus, whose movement was accused of this and other bombings.

* Movement for an Independent Negros
A group of rebellious landowners resisting a landreform program signed into law by President Aquino in 1987. It said it had assembled an armed force of about 300 men to fight the government. Sources in the group said the landlords were also planning to sabotage government installations as part of a campaign to stall the reforms. The group urged landowners to take money out of the banks, stop paying taxes and servicing loans and ignore government calls to surrender titles.

* National Democratic Front (NDF)
A coalition of 12 mass organizations including the banned Communist Party and the New People's Army, which was formed in 1973 with the aim of overthrowing the Marcos' government. It built up an extensive underground in the towns and cities among workers, students and low income professionals. Its international office in Utrecht (the Netherlands) still spreads information on the situation in the Philippines. Dutch authorities declared that the NDF operated within the boundaries of the Dutch law.

* National Intelligence and Security Authority (NISA)
NISA has been described as a secret organization which was the strong arm of the Marcos dictatorship. Agents were infiltrated in all government agencies and were active in the countryside to track dissidents and alleged subversives. It was led by Fabian Ver, former chief of staff of the armed forces of the Philippines. It had an estimated strength of 15,000 men. President Aquino dissolved the service and replaced it by a smaller one which only has an advisory task.

* National Movement for Freedom and Democracy (NMFD)
Under the NMFD umbrella, some 1,300 Filipino farmers have organized themselves into a so-called Citizen's Anti-Communist Army, supplying the military with information on rebel activity and conducting security patrols. The farmers' arsenal consists of pre-World War II Garand rifles, home-made guns with water-pipe barrels and primitive pistols.

* National People's Democratic Socialist Party (NPDSP)
This party had an armed wing called the Sandigan Filipino National Liberation Army. A Philippine Minister of Defence (Ponce Enrile) described the party in November 1978 as a 'third force' underground movement which was winning a broad following among students, intellectuals and labour groups. The NPA was responsible for armed encounters with government forces in some areas of the central southern Philippines.

* Nationalist Youth Organization (Kabataang Makabayan) (KM)
The KM was a youth front operated by the Maoist faction of the Communist Party of the Philippines in the late 1960s. It was active in street disturbances. In the early 1970s it had more than 100,000 supporters. Despite Maoist ideology its activities were largely restricted to the cities. It was crushed by the introduction of martial law in 1972. Some KM militants fled to Mindanao and offered the MNLF collaboration. KM viewed the problem of the south as essentially one of class conflict and discounted the Islamic factor. The MNLF leadership felt it would lose support by associating with Maoists and turned down collaboration.

* The New Apostolian Church (NAC)
Fanatic religious group in Mindanao which has been used in counter-insurgency operations.

• New Israel
Fanatic religious group in Mindanao which has been used in counter-insurgency operations.

• New People's Army
(Bagong Hukbong Bayan) (NPA)
An ideological division in the Communist Party of the Philippines (PKP) resulted in the formation of the Communist Party of the Philippines-Marxist-Leninist (CPP-ML) as a rival to the pro-Soviet and Maoist factions. In March 1969 it founded an armed wing, The New People's Army, which engaged in rural guerrilla activities since the early 1970s. It operated mainly from sanctuaries on Luzon, Mindanao, Samar and Negros. Rodolfo Salas acts as its president and Rafael Baylosis as its secretary. The number of regular NPA fighters reached in 1986 a total of 24,430, according to Pentagon figures. The insurgency has expanded its presence and influence to 8,496 of the country's barangays. In 1985 NPA guerrillas were reported to be killing AFP soldiers of a rate of more than 100 per month. The authorities have seriously underestimated the rebels' motivation to keep fighting since the overthrow of the Marcos regime in early 1986. President Ronald Reagan has issued a secret intelligence finding authorizing the US CIA to step up assistance to the Philippine Army. More than 60,000 people have already been killed in the conflict.

• Paramilitary Force of Surrendered Rebels
A unit which has been used in counter-insurgency operations.

• People's Anti-Japanese Resistance Army
(Hukbong Bayan Laban Sa Hapon-Hukbalahap) (Huks)
A resistance movement with the aim to fight against the Japanese occupation during the Second World War. It had been established by the Communist Party of the Philippines in March 1942. It was led by Luis Taruc and recruited among the peasantry who held grievances against money lenders and absentee landlords. After the Japanese withdrawal the Huks attempted to set up a 'People's Democratic Government'.
General MacArthur disbanded the organization and had Taruc arrested. After the war the movement resurfaced as the People's Liberation Army (HMB).

• People's Liberation Army
(Hukbong Mapagpalaya ng Bayan) (HMB)
After the Second World War the Philippine Communist Party set up the People's Liberation Army. Recruits consisted of former Huks who had hidden their weapons in the countryside. Their aim was the overthrow of the Manila government by waging rural guerrillla warfare. It had an estimated strength of 10,000 fighters supported by 200,000 local sympathizers. The HMB lacked weapons, training, outside contacts, logistics, and a central command system. Ramon Magsaysay crushed the insurgents in the early 1950s in exemplary counter-insurgency operations. Luis Taruc, the commander of the Huks surrendered in September 1954. An estimated 9,000 people were killed including 5,000 civilians during the rebellion.

• Philippine Communist Party
(Partido Komunista ng Pilipinas) (PKP)
Originally founded in 1930, the PKP was split in 1968 when the Maoist faction broke away from the pro-Soviet wing and set up as its military arm, the New People's Army. Whereas the pró-Soviet PKP achieved legal recognition in October 1974, the pro-Chinese faction continued its underground activities and set up a front organization called the National Democratic Front. The leader of the front, Sixto Carlos, went underground in 1972. He was arrested in April 1979 when he was accused of being a member of the NPA. Intelligence sources believe the PKP, which has a mass base of 50-100,000, is split into three factions and instead of taking up arms against the authorities, is concentrating on infiltrating government agencies and labour unions. They claim that the government has not grasped the extent of this infiltration and influence in practically every sector of society. Through a front called Partido Ng Bayan, the party geared up to contest local and congressional elections expected in 1987.

• Philippine Liberation Movement (PLM)
The existence of this movement was announced on Feb.18, 1982, when the Philippine authorities accused it of being linked with the NPA, of being responsible for the killing of six policemen and of intending to assassinate President Marcos.

• The Philippine World Mission (PWM)
Fanatic religious sect in Mindanao which has been used in counter-insurgency operations. Its members do believe that Mindanao is the promised land.

• Presidential Security Commando (PSC)
Security service under the Marcos regime which has been dissolved by the Aquino administration. It had a strength of 15,000 men.

• The Rats
(Ilaga)
Fanatic religious sect in Mindanao which has been used in counter-insurgency operations. It appeared in 1970 and. was commanded by 'Commander Toothpick' (because of his skinny appearance). It has been involved in a campaign of terror against Mindanao Moslems, cutting an ear off all their victims as a mark of their brutal work. It has been

used by the military to conduct operations which would have brought criticism if they had been mounted by the AFP.

* Reform the Armed Forces (RAM)
Movement within the army which has been involved in three coup plans to overthrow the Aquino regime. It has about 700 to 800 members. among colonels and junior officers. As its core were young officers who had been recruited by Mr.Enrile as his personal security force, led by army Colonel Gregorio Honasan. During the four-day February 1987 revolt, they did not fire a shot but they engaged in a campaign of propaganda, disinformation and psychological warfare with their opponents. In early 1987 the RAM officers have spread reports of their plans and have let it be known that they are importing weapons and training special strike forces.

* The Remains of God
Fanatic religious group in Mindanao which has been used in counter-insurgency operations.

* Risen Masses
(Alsa Masa)
Local anti-communist vigilant group in the city of Agdao. It has a strength of several thousand men and is led by Rolando Cagay. It said it had restored peace in Agdao and ended terrorism by wiping out the Communists' network of control. 'Core' members of the Agdao group were former Communist guerrillas, including assassins. In Agdao many of the core members of Alsa Masa were former gangsters, some of whom had been used by police intelligence as informers and undercover agents in the Agdao communist network. The group was employing some of the methods used by Communists. One was to establish a network of informers including children to guard against leftist infiltration of the community. Alsa Masa killed 104 NPA members in the first two weeks of March 1987.

* Rock Christ Sect
Fanatic religious group in Mindanao which has been used in counter-insurgency operations. It claimed to have a membership of 600 of which 20 are reported to be armed. It consists of members of the Tingol clan and is based in the Osmena town. Basically it is an animistic sect with a thin overlay of Christianity. Members believe their chiefs have healing powers and that incantation of their special prayer, known as Orasyon, shields them from danger. The sect's high priests are reputed to be rich landlords and farmers. It has been responsible for brutal murders.

* Rural Reformist Movement (RRM)
Movement which has engaged in a terror campaign around the town of Calinan in March/April 1981. A manifesto issued on Feb.13, 1981, stated RRM's objectives as 'support to the Marcos' program for good government'. It is commanded by Commander Alitaptap ('Firefly'). A 30-man team visited villagers to seek recruits and to ask where abouts of NPA members in the area. Those who refused to help were branded subversives and became targets for liquidation. Some sources claimed that RRM was controlled by the National Intelligence and Security Authority (NISA). Many of those who were forced to join the RRM were members of the Gawilan and Libayo tribes.

* Sandigan Army (SA)
Church guerrilla organization that was organized in 1978. It was encouraged by the government to undermine the NPA's link with some church people. See NPDSP.

* Secret Marshal Corps
Special government unit which has been used for killing criminals during the Marcos regime.

* Sparrows
NPA liquidation units which have targeted pro-government provincial officials and policemen. During 1983 and 1984 they killed at least 70 policemen. They operate on motorcycles. The Sparrows stepped up activities in Manila in early 1987.

* The Tiger
(El Tigre)
Group of planters in Negros who have declared a war on President Aquino's land reform program. It emerged in April 1987, when it claimed responsibility for a bomb attack on the house of the bishop of Negros, Antonio Fortich.

* United People for Peace (NAKASAKA)
Anti-communist civil guard established in March 1987. It operates in Mindanao. To channel the vigilante trend toward non-violent methods, President Aquino has approved a plan for special Nakasaka, patrols in virtually every village in the country. Armed only with machetes and organized to raise alarm with bells, gangs or horns, the patrols are supposed to deny rebels the free movement, food supplies and mass political support they need to survive.

* Upside Down
(Tiwarik)
According to statements from military intelligence, this group had plans for a plot. Members of the group planned to occupy radio and television stations near the military headquarters. By hostaging foreign teachers and students they hoped to put pressure on President Aquino to resign.

POLAND

* Anti Solidarity Organization
Group which first surfaced in February 1983 when it announced its formation with leaflets criticizing the government for its 'ineffective suppression' of Solidarity. It has threatened with attacks.

* Armed Forces of the Underground Poland
This group emerged on Feb.18, 1982, when a policeman was killed in Warsaw and nine members of the group (including a Roman Catholic priest) were arrested. Eight of those arrested were sentenced to imprisonment for terms of from two to 25 years on Sep.9, 1982. No details on the composition and aims of the group were disclosed.

* Direct Action
(Akcja Bezposrednia) (AB)
Obscure group which claimed responsibility for a bomb attack on the headquarters of the party in Gdynia on Feb.29, 1987. It distributed pamphlets in which it criticized the Polish regime, Solidarity and its leadership and the church. Leaders of the Polish opposition considered the action to be a provocation of the secret police.

* Motorised Units of the Citizens' Militia
(Zmotoryzowane Oddzialy Milicji Obywatelskiej) (ZOMO)
Mobile police units which have been used in the suppression of labour unrest. They were established in 1956 following labour unrest in Poznan. Membership was estimated at 10,000 men in 1981. They have been responsible for the death of at least 60 persons since December 1981. Dissidents have mentioned numbers twice as high. It can be compared with a regular army as it uses helicopters, APC's, artillery, parachute and pioneer units in the suppression of disorders. They also engaged in psychological warfare, including the distribution of compromising photographs of L.Walesa. It used a variety of new riot control techniques, including paralysing gasses fired by handweapons and reflectors on APC's which set afire the clothes of demonstrators.

* Polish Home Army of Resistance
Name used by four hostage-takers who occupied the Polish embassy in Bern (Switzerland) on Sep.6, 1982, threatening to blow the building up-including themselves and 13 hostages-unless the Polish authorities lifted the state of martial law in Poland. The incident was ended on Sep.9, when Swiss anti-riot police stormed the embassy and arrested four men, the hostages being freed without injury. Solidarity spokesmen in Poland disclaimed any connection with the group and described the incident as a possible 'provocation' by the Polish authorities.

* Sluzba Bezpieczenstwa (SB)
Polish political police which belongs to the Ministry of Internal Affairs. The military intelligence service belongs to the Ministry of Defence. The civilian apparatus has four sections: 1) Foreign intelligence, foreign operations; 2) counter espionage; 3) counter subversion; 4) Church affairs and national minorities. It has engaged in human rights violations including torture. According to the Polish Helsinki committee, police violence during the 1982-1985 period had caused the death of 72 persons. Many of them died under mysterious circumstances. More than 5,400 people have been arrested for political reasons.

POLYNESIA

* The Ancestors' Blood
(Te Toto Tupana)
This organization was described as an anti-French terrorist group with which the (legal) pro-independence Te Taata Tahiti Tiama party, led by Charlie Ching, was suspected of having co-operated in 1978-79.

* Maohi Republic Provisional Government
(Gouvernement Provisoire de la Republique Maohi)

This small pro-independence movement came to prominence when its leader, Mai Tetua and 40 of his followers were arrested on Aug.15, 1982, after two local policemen had been briefly held and ill-treated by members of this group. The latter abductions had been carried out after the police had stopped a uniformed group of the movement's members and confiscated their banners. On Aug.17 Tetua and 16 others were charged with premediated violence against representatives of public order and other offences.

PUERTO RICO

* Armed Forces of National Liberation
(Fuerzas Armadas de Liberacion Nacional) (FALN)
A Puerto Rican separatist group active since 1974 mainly in New York and Chicago. In the early 1980s it began to attack US military installations on the island. It defended its actions as justifiable 'armed struggle' in defiance of colonial 'repression' dating back to American occupation of the former Spanish colony in 1898. It is estimated to have no more than 50 members, ten of whom were jailed in 1980. It is led by Carlos Alberto Torres. In the course of their campaign the FALN exploded almost 200 bombs, killing four people and injuring more than 50. Targets included the offices of the FBI, Gulf Oil, the Chrysler Corporation, various banks and also the famous Fraunces Tavern in Manhattan. In September 1985 another 13 members were detained. Three members, Alejandrina Torres,

Alberto Rodriquez and Edwin Cortés, were convicted of seditious conspiracy and were sentenced to 35 years in prison. A fourth member, Jose Luis Rodriquez was convicted of conspiracy but was given a suspended sentence and released. William Morales is the object of an international campaign demanding that he not be extradited back to the United States from Mexico. Nine countries have offered political asylum.

* Boricua Popular Army (or Machete Wielders) (Ejercito Popular Boricua (or Los Macheteros) (EPB)
The EPB emerged in Puerto Rico in August 1978 as a small separatist group. It targeted the police and the military as representatives of US domination. Boricua refers to the rural inland islander in Puerto Rico. The US authorities claimed to have smashed the Macheteros. On Aug.30, 1985, when 300 FBI agents descended on Puerto Rico. The agents raided 38 homes and offices, seizing thousands of papers, destroying other property and arresting 11 independistas. The prisoners were hooded and shackled and quickly removed to the United States in military aircraft. The group had been responsible for the ambush of a navy bus at Sabena Seca in December 1979, the destruction of 10 US aircraft at Base Muniz on Jan.11, 1981 and the $ 7 million theft of a Wells Fargo truck in Hartford, Connecticut. On Oct.27, 1986, two bombs exploded at military bases in Puerto Rico. Eight others were discovered and defused. The bombings were claimed as a joint action by the EPB-Macheteros, the OVRP and the FARP, in response to the planned logging of El Yunque rain forest and the proposed training of the Nicaraguan contras in Puerto Rico.

* Organization of Volunteers for the Puerto Rican Revolution (Organizacion de Voluntarios para la Revolucion Puertorriquena) (OVPP)
One of the armed clandestine organizations in Puerto Rico which emerged in 1978. It claimed to have stolen explosives from a public works warehouse at Manati, Puerto Rico. Since then it has been involved in several armed attacks and bomb explosions on US army recruiting offices. The attacks were part of a broader campaign to stop the conscription of Puerto Rican youth into the US military. It placed posters in highschools with the message: 'Be all that you can be: become a combatant for independence.'

* Puerto Rican Nationalist Party
(Partido Nacionalista Puertorriqueno) (PNP)
Party founded in 1928 by Dr.Pedro Albizu Campos. In an insurrection attempt carried out on Oct.30, 1950, 27 people were killed and 51 injured. An attempt on the life of President H.S.Truman was made on Nov.1, 1950, whereby a White House guard was killed. On Mar.1, 1954, PNP gunmen shot and wounded five members of the House of Representatives in Washington, D.C.

* Puerto Rican Armed Resistance Movement (Movimiento de Resistencia Armada Puertorriquena) (MRAP)
An offshoot of the Armed Forces of the National Liberation which claimed responsibility for numerous bomb attacks in recent years. On May 16-17, 1981, a young airport employee was killed on the Panam terminal at Kennedy Airport, New York.

* Puerto Rican Movement of National Liberation (Movimiento de Liberacion Puertorriqueno) (MLN-PR)
A FALN support group led by Julio and Andres Ayala. It supports national liberation for Puerto Rican and Mexican-Chicano peoples. It called for armed struggle to take back Mexican territories captured by 'US imperalist wars'.

* Puerto Rican National Revolutionary Front (FRN-PR)
This organization claimed responsibility for a series of bombings in Puerto Rico on Jan.6, 1986. The targets were US Post offices and Selective Service registration centers. It is the youngest of six armed clandestine groups fighting for Puerto Rican independence.

* Revolutionary Action Movement
(Movimiento de Accion Revolucionaria) (MAR)
Minor separatist group which operated intermittently during the late 1970s in Puerto Rico, especially in the San Juan area. Other such minor groups included the so-called Revolutionary Commandos of the People (CRP) and the Organization of Volunteers for the Puerto Rican Revolution (OVRP).

PORTUGAL

* Armed Forces Movement/Military Revolutionary Council
Opposition movement within the army which staged a coup against Dr.Marcello Caetano, successor to Salazar, who had applied a form of fascist-corporatist dictatorship to the country 'to serve the nation from the government'.

* Armed Revolutionary Action
(Accao Revolucionaria Armada) (ARA)
The Portuguese Communist Party (PCP) formed ARA initially mainly for propaganda purposes to show the ultra-left in Portugal that the PCP was also activist. In May 1973, the ARA central command suspended its bombing campaign. After the April 1974 military coup, the legalized PCP

reactivated ARA, in response to the attempted coup by General Spinola in 1975. ARA was formed out of a PCP militia. A coup attempt by ARA and other PCP forces in 1975 failed.

* Autonomous Revolutionary Groups (GAR)
Terrorist group which split off from FP-25. On Apr.10, 1985 it exploded a bomb at a government housing office to protest government plans to lift a 50-year rent freeze. It also has been responsible for a bomb attack on an office of Iberia in December 1985.

* Front for the Liberation of the Azores
(Frente Libertacao dos Acores) (FLA)
Separatist movement which emerged after the revolutionary events in 1974. The islanders reacted strongly against the left. On Oct.10, 1975, the FLA informed the United Nations that the islanders would have no part in any system other than a democratic one, and rejected the revolutionary course of events which culminated in the unsuccessful coup led by the PCP in November 1975. Armed backing came from local military units which called themselves Azorean Patriots in the Garrisons (PAG). The movement was supported by Azorean emigrants in the United States, Canada and Brazil. The FLA was apparently led by Jose de Alemida and Manuel Bento.

* International Police for the Defense of the State
(Policia Internacionale de Defensa da Estada) (PIDE)
Political police and secret service during the Salazar regime.

* League of Union and Revolutionary Action
(Liga de Uniao e Accao Revolucionária) (LUAR)
A small group which was founded by Herminio da Palma Inácio in 1966, following the murder on the Portuguese opposition leader General Delgado. During the late 1960s it has been involved in handful of violent actions aimed at drawing attention to the lack of liberty under the Salazarist regime. After the revolutionary events in 1974 LUAR was actively engaged in street violence in the capital, although it never adopted terrorist tactics. LUAR militants numbered perhaps 2,000.

* Liberation Front for Madeira
(Frente Libertacao Arquipelago de Madeira) (FLAMA)
Anti-communist movement which emerged in 1975 as a reaction to the left-wing politics of ultra-leftist groups and parties which sought to seize power through armed action. It advocated the separation of Madeira from Portugal and a possible federation of Madeira with the Azores and the (Spanish) Canary Islands. In August 1975 members of the movement were involved in a number of bomb attacks, in particular on the property of its (left-wing) political opponents. After the Portuguese government had granted Madeira a regional government and assembly, violence ceased.

* Reorganization Movement of the Party of the Proletariat
(Movimiento Reorganizado do Partido do Proletario) (MRPP)
Maoist movement led by José Luis Saldanha Sanches and Arnaldo Matos. It emerged in 1974 following the collapse of the Salazar regime. It was one of the groups responsible for political violence in the capital. MRPP supporters were involved in clashes with the police and with conservatives political supporters. Activities ceased in the late 1970s.

* New Order
(Ordem Novo) (ON)
Organization established by ultra-rightist officers in May 1981. Colonel Gilberto Santos e Castro, the founder the group, had links with the Spanish ultra-rightist leader, Blas Pinar, who led New Force. New Order favoured a return to the corporatist state of Salazar and Primo de Rivera.

* Peoples Forces of April 25
(Forcas Populares do 25 Abril) (FP-25)
Small left-wing group which took its name from the date of the 1974 revolution which overthrew the Caetano regime. It sprang from LUAR and the Revolutionary Brigades. From 1980 onwards, members of the group have been involved in bank raids, bombings and extortion. It has targeted industrialists, landowners, NATO installations and banks. Following a phase of armed propaganda it started with an operative phase in 1983. It has been responsible for at least 70 attacks in which twelve people died. In 1984 it murdered the industrialist R.Baptista de Cunha de Canha e Sa and attacked the US embassy. In 1985 it targeted a West German airbase in Beja, the US embassy, a NATO headquarters and a NATO squadron anchored in the Tagus River and French, West German and British businesses and homes. It was led by Joao Carlos de Macedo Correia who was arrested in August 1984. In 1985 a total of 72 alleged members of the group went on trial. Lt.Col.Otelo Saraiva de Carvalho was convicted of running a secret leftist terrorist group that sought to overthrow democracy. He was given a maximum 20-years prison sentence. The organization known as 'Global Project' sought to 'subvert the normal functioning of the institutions of this democratic state consecrated in the constitution'. Global Project was in fact a guerrilla group called FP-25. See also OUT.

* Popular Unity Force

(Forca de Unidade Popular) (FUP)
Major Otelo Saraiva de Carvalho, one of the figureheads of the 1974 military coup, established the FUP in 1980. It did not participate in the 1985 election. Its aim is to unite all leftist forces, expand the consciousness of the workers and finally the violent overthrow of the regime within a period of ten to fifteen years. It established an armed civilian structure (ECA) which Otelo considered to be the embryo of a future revolutionary army. According to the Portugese police ECA and FP-25 are two names for the same organization.

* Proletarian Revolutionary Party
(Partido Proletariano Revolucionario) (PPR)
After the revolution in 1974, this party took part in political life through violent activities. Among the party's members who unsuccessfully contested the 1980 parlimentary elections from prison were two of its founders, Dr.Isabel do Carmo and Carlos Melo Antunes. They had been arrested in 1978 for their complicity in a series of bank robberies and the murder of a policeman carried out by the party's military wing, the Revolutionary Brigades.

* United Workers' Organisation
(Organizacao Unida dos Trabalhadores) (OUT)
Otelo Saraiva de Carvalho merged two small groups on the ultra-left of Portuguese politics, the Popular Socialist Front and the Revolutionary Party of the Proletariat, in 1978 into OUT. Nothing was heard of the group after Carvalho had founded Popular Unity Force (FUP) in 1980. During a trial in 1985 Otelo Saraiva de Carvalho was suspected of being the leader of the FP-25. A day before the trial on July 19, 1985, one of the main witnesses, Jose Rosa Barradas was murdered. Carvalho is suspected of being the brain behind the formation of an armed movement with the aim to 'prevent the return of fascism'.

* Workers' and Peasants' Alliance
(Alianca Operária e Campenesa) (AOC)
Maoist organization which emerged after the April 1974 revolution in Lisbon. It was led by Carlos Guisote, a trade union official.The new government banned the movement in 1975 after its involvement in street violence.

* Zionist Action Group (ZAG)
Group which has claimed responsibility for attacks on offices of Air France and Lufthansa in Lissabon.

RUMANIA

* Securitate
Rumanian secret police that engaged in torture, harassment, intimidation and beating up of political opponents of the regime, particularly Transylvania.

SAUDI ARABIA

* Anti Terrorism Squad
Saudi Arabia is to set up an elite anti-terrorist squad under the guidance of Ulrich Wegener, now head of the Federal Border Guard, but best known as commander of GSG-9, West Germany's anti-terrorist organization. Wegener is being given two years official leave by the West German government to work with the Saudis. A small number of West German officers in cooperation with advisers from an Israeli security company are expected to be involved in the training, scheduled to start in 1987.

* Moslem Revolutionary Movement in the Arabian Peninsula
Religious sect founded in 1974 numbering several hundred members. It was led by Mohammed ibn Abdullah al-Qatani ('Mahdi') and Juhayman bin Mohammed bin Seif al-Oteiba. Its goal was the recognition of Mohammed al-Qatani as the expected 'Mahdi'. On Nov.20, 1979, some 200 members took over the Grand Mosque in Mecca. The siege was ended on Nov.29 after a gas attack by French specialists.

SENEGAL

* Movement of the Democratic Forces of the Casamance
(Mouvement des Forces Démocratiques de la Casamance) (MFDC)
Separatist movement which has called for the independence of the region of the lower Casamance in 1982. Violent disturbances broke out in the Casamance area after the trial in December 1983 of some 40 advocates of autonomy. On December 18, thousands of Diola, the majority women, marched to Ziguinchor. They were armed with old rifles, machetes and bows and arrows. In streetfighting six policemen and 17 demonstrators were killed. The real number of deaths might be higher. Unofficial estimates range up to 300 deaths.

SEYCHELLES

* Movement for Resistance
(Mouvement pour la Résistance)
Seychelles exile organization based in Britain. Its aim is to restore the pre-1977 democratic regime of ex-President Mancham.

* Seychelles National Movement (SNM)
Sechelles exile movement which has been involved in a coup attempt by white mercenaries to overthrow the René regime in November 1981. Its

leader, Gerard Hoareau, has been assassinated in London on Nov.29, 1985. James Mancham, a former president, accused President Albert René of having organized the assassination.

SINGAPORE

* Singapore People's Liberation Organization (SPLO)
In 1982, ten members of this 'Moslem extremist' organization had been arrested for attempting to overthrow the government. Its leader, Zainul Abiddin bin Mohammed Shah, was said to be a member of the Workers' Party of Singapore.

SOMALIA

* Democratic Front for the Liberation of Somalia (DFLS)
Somali guerrilla organization led by Abd Rahman Aidid Ahmad who joined the DFSS in 1981.

* Democratic Front for the Salvation of Somalia (DFSS)
The DFSS was set up in October 1981 by representatives of the Somali Salvation Front (FOSAS) the Democratic Front for the Liberation of Somalia (DFLS) and the Somali Workers' Party (SWP). It claimed major victories on the battlefield against President Siad Barre's regime. It had an estimated 8,000 to 10,000 men and is based on the Mijertein and Hawiyah people. Outside support was provided by Ethiopia and Libya. An 11-member executive committee included Col.Abdullahi Yusuf Ahmad (chairman), Said Jana Husayn (vice chairman), Abder Rahman Aidid Ahmad (secretary for information). The smaller Marxist parties retreated from the coalition in 1983. Internal clashes were reported and several hundred members returned to Somalia and made use of an amnesty arrangement. Since then its military significance has declined, although it still exists.

* Ogaden Liberation Front
Guerrilla organization active in the Ogaden in the 1960s. Ethiopia reacted with a war against Somalia in 1964. Since then the Somali government has limited the activities of the front.

* Ogaden National Liberation Front (ONLF)
Guerrilla organization that broke away from the WSLF. It resisted the Ethiopian-Somali negotiations.

* Somali Abo Liberation Front (SALF)
Small guerrilla organization based on the Somali Abo people. It is striving for a Somalia for the Oromo.

* Somali National Movement (SNM)
The SNM was founded in London in 1981 by Somali intellectuals, mullahs and businessmen exiled in Europe and the United States, most of them Issaq from northern Somalia opposed to President Siad Barre's regime. The leadership is pro-Western and has good contacts with Saudi Arabia. It is aimed at the overthrow of the government. It began guerrilla operations inside Somalia during 1982. In October 1982 it was announced that the DFSS and the SNM has established a joint military committee. Siad Barre is inclined to give up his claims on the Ogaden. This has led to fears that the SNM would control the local administration in the Ogaden, to the disadvantage of the Ogadeni. Severe conflicts have been reported between the Issaq and the Ogadeni. This could lead to a separatist movement of the Issaq in Somalia. In February 1987 the SNM attacked Somali towns. The unrest amounted to a people's insurrection aiming at the separation of the north. The SNM is financially supported by the thousands of Issaq exiled in Arab countries.

* Somali Popular Liberation Front (SPLF)
A small guerrilla movement that broke away from the SSDF in 1983. Little is known about the movement.

* Somali Salvation Front
(Front de Salut Somalien) (FOSAS)
In 1979 the FOSAS replaced a Somali Democratic Action Front established in 1976. It is based on the Mijertein people which had been dominant in Somalia's government until General Siad Barre came to power in 1969. It was armed by Libya and attacked the Somali Army from March 1980 onwards. It claimed to have 10,000 active members. Its aim is the overthrow of the Barre regime and the establishment of a non-aligned democratic state. Its leader, Colonel Abdullah Yusuf Ahmad, became chairman of the DFSS. In the end of 1985, Abdullah Yusuf Ahmed was imprisoned by Ethiopia and replaced with Mohamed Abshir. Ethiopia hopes he will be more inclined to a merger with the SNM.

* Somali Workers' Party (SWP)
Organization that joined the Somali Democratic Salvation Front (DFSS) in October 1981 with a view to waging armed struggle against the regime of President Siad Barre. The SWP is led by Sa'id Jama Husayn.

SOUTH AFRICA

* African National Congress (ANC)
Principal black nationalist liberation organization in South Africa. It was established as a non-violent organization in 1912. It abandoned its non-violent policy in 1961, as a result of the shooting

at Sharpeville on Mar.21, 1960, when police killed 69 blacks and wounded 180 during a protest demonstration against the pass laws. Subsequently it followed a policy of 'controlled sabotage' by its armed branch, Umkhonto We Sizwe. It has 8,000 to 10,000 fighters outside the country. Another 1,000 to 2,000 fighters operate inside South Africa. Its 1955 Freedom Charter calls for setting up a unitary South African government by universal franchise and with a socialist economic system. In recent years it has stepped up activities Reported incidents: 1980:20, 1981:55, 1985:136, 1986: 124 (1st ½ year). Targets included an oilstorage depot, military facilities, shopping centers, government buildings, railways, electricity supplies and the nuclear power plant near Cape Town. It has at least five training camps in Angola (Quibaxe, Pango, Malanja, Vienna and Caxito) where it also has an economic infrastructure. Its main headquarters is located in Lusaka (Zambia) from where it operates as a government in exile. It is led by Nelson Mandela (imprisoned president), Oliver Tambo (acting president) and Alfred Nzo (sec.-gen.)

* African Resistance Movement (ARM)
Predominantly white movement, established in 1962 as the National Council of Liberation. The ARM was held responsible for a number of bomb explosions in 1964. One of its members, Fredrick John Harris was sentenced to death while others succeeded in fleeing the country.

* African Resistance Movement
(Afrikaner Weerstandsbeweging) (AWB)
Ultra-rightwing movement established in 1973 with the aim of maintaining White supremacy in South Africa. The AWB is organized on paramilitary lines and uses emblems reminiscent of fascist movements. It is led by Eugene Terreblanche and has a hardcore of 5,000 members. Headquarters is located in Heidelberg (Transvaal). It speaks of establishing an Afrikaner fatherland based on the historical boundaries of the old Afrikaner republics of the Transvaal and Orange Free State. In 1980 it registered as the Witvolk party in the hope to use it as an umbrella to unite the extreme right. Two members were sentenced for a plan to spread syphilis in Sun City by releasing infected rats. Other members have been convicted for illegal arms possession.

* A-Team
A vigilant black gang which has been responsible for black-on-black violence. It emerged in 1986 in the Chesterville township in Durban. It has attacked UDF supporters, trade unionists and students.

* Azanian National Youth Unit
Black organization which resists the UDF. Coloured and Asians are not allowed to become members.

* Azania People's Liberation Army (APLA)
Armed branch of the PAC. Until January 1979 it was led by Lancelot Dube (Eddie Phiri) who died in a car accident. It has been responsible for a handgrenade attack on the exercise area of a police school, killing one person and injuring 64 others.

* Azanian People's Organization (AZAPO)
An offshoot of the ANC that was launched in Roodepoort in May 1978. The aim was to organize black workers in industrial struggle against the white regime. AZAPO has been accused by other black groups of acting as agents provocateurs in the black townships, inciting black youngsters to futile and often fatal assaults on the country's powerful security forces. Several of its early leaders have been detained, including Mkabela of Soweto, Lybon Mabosa and Curtis Nkondo. In 1986 Saths Cooper was named as its president.

* Black People's Convention (BPC)
The BCP was established in 1972 and is led by Sipho Buthelezi. After the Soweto riots on June 16, 1976 (which led to the death of 176 persons and injury to 1,228 others), several leaders and members received banning orders. The movement retained its influence among younger Black people who were opposed to the ANC.

* Bureau of State Security (BOSS)
South African intelligence agency which has carried out its war against opponents of apartheid wherever they could be found. BOSS sent parcel bombs to Black 'Freedom Fighters' in African bases, burgled the offices of anti-apartheid groups in London, including Amnesty International, and carried out a systematic campaign of disinformation. Much of its work involved infiltrating groups supporting workers in South Africa. Prime Minister P.W.Botha restructured the service in 1978 and its leader General Hendrik van den Bergh was retired. It was renamed the National Intelligence Service. It appeared that the changes were largely cosmetic.

* Comrades
Loosely organized youth groups which have been responsible for much of the killing in the townships in recent years. Until January 1987 more than 650 necklacings have been recorded. Ranging in age from about 14 to 22, they are typically poor, uneducated and overflowing with rage. The primary object of their wrath is anyone suspected of collaborating with the government. The victim's 'crime' can be trivial or wholly non-existent. Even payment of rent for government-owned housing can

be a capital offense. So intimidating have the comrades become that in many parts of South Africa they can terrify township residents simply by holding up boxes of matches. When they are not carrying out spontaneous attacks they may hold kangaroo 'people's courts' that are designed to intimidate the public. In a typical court session, young toughs drag the accused forward, inform him or her of the charge and then pronounce and execute the sentence.

* Crowbar
(Koevoet)
A police unit with an estimated 2,000 to 3,000 members which has been involved in counterinsurgency operations in Namibia. The members wear insurgent uniforms to seek out guerrilla sympathizers and use AK-47 machine guns. They pay children to inform against their parents and they are paid bounty money for insurgents killed (100 to 300 Rand per dead guerrilla). It has been renamed 'Teeninsurgensie Eenheid'. In 1986, the South African police was looking for an excuse to ban any public activity by SWAPO. On Nov.30, 1986, the Koevoet forces tried to stir up incidents in Katatura by infiltrating the ranks of demonstrators with plainclothes elements armed with blunt instruments. The 'regular' Koevoet units were sent into action against the crowd with the result of 20 wounded and two dead, including a two-year-old child and one of SWAPO's leaders, Emmanuel Shifidi. The latter was freed in 1985, after 20 years in prison, of which 18 were spent on Robben Island.

* Fathers
In the Crossroads squatter camp near Cape Town, community leaders known as 'fathers', have organized patrol groups called vigilants. Frequent clashes with the Comrades have claimed dozens of lives on both sides and destroyed thousands of shanties. In Soweto, the city council has called for the formation of vigilante bands to stamp out 'political renegades' and protect local citizens. Many vigilants are middle-class people who are willing to strike back at the Comrades to protect their property and the positions they have achieved. They include shopkeepers, taxi owners, police officers and town councilors.

* Fire Watch
White national militia established by the Afrikaner Resistance Movement (AWB).

* Green Berets
Black gang which has been responsible for black-on-black violence.

* The Intimidators
(Mabangalala)
A black gang which has been responsible for black-on-black violence.

* Mbokhoto
The plans of the government of Simon Skhosana in Kwandebele to become 'independent' resulted in an insurrection. Skhosana personnally organized the 'Mbokhoto', a group responsible for a terror campaign in the area. Conflicts between this group and young radicals led to the death of at least 100 people.

* National Cultural Liberation Movement
(Inkatha Yenkululeko Yesizwe) ('Impis')
Zulu-based political party established in 1975. It is led by Gatsha Buthelezi. Its youth brigade has been responsible for black-on-black violence.

* National Security Management System (NSMS)
An elaborate network of security committees, set up to counter activism in the black townships, established as a shadow administration under the state of emergency. It was established in 1979 and is led by Lt.Gen.Pieter van Westhuizen. It has more than 500 regional and local committees all over the country.

* Pan-Africanist Congress of Azania (PAC)
The PAC broke away from the parent body of South African black nationalism, the African National Congress, in 1959 over a disagreement on whether or not to adopt a multi-racial approach to the South African problem. In 1960 it opted for a non-violent political campaign against the pass laws. It had a military arm 'Alone, for Africans Only (POQO)' which was activated when PAC was banned. In 1964 the PAC adopted the name of PAC of Azania- Azania being an African name for South Africa. Its leadership adopted a protracted revolutionary struggle doctrine along the lines advocated by the Chinese. China took up the PAC cause and provided guerrilla training and facilities in Tanzania. Since 1981 it has been led by John Nyati Pokela. PAC leadership has always been in dispute.

* PW Freedom Fighters
(PW Vrijheidsvegters) (PWV)
Right-wing terrorist group which announced its existence in a telephone call to the press in January 1986. It said that it intends to respond to ANC acts of terrorism on the basis of 'an eye for eye' and will hit at 'soft targets' every time the ANC does so. It claims to have some 100 members with military and police experience and to also have informers in various left-wing organizations, including the ANC itself. Nothing more was heard of the group.

* Republican Union of Africans

(Republikeinse Afrikaner Unie) (RAU)
A strong arm force which has murdered Mr.Smit, an 'enlightened' candidate for the National Party.

* South African Communist Party (SACP)
A Communist Party of South Africa (CPSA) was established in Cape Town in July 1921 by a merger of several Marxist groups. Originally a white party, it soon accepted members of other races. In 1953 it was renamed as the South African Communist Party, led by a central committee based in London. A number of Communists served on the ANC's national executive. The party is led by Yusuf Dadoo.

* South African Youth Revolutionary Council (SAYRC)
An organization of Black youths who fled South Africa after uprisings in 1976 and 1977 in Soweto. It surfaced first in Nigeria. There have been reports that it received funds from the PLO and that it was ready to consider terrorist tactics.

* Spear of the Nation
(Umkhonto We Zizwe) (UWZ)
The military arm of the African National Congress set up in 1961 by Nelson Mandela. It is now led by Joe Modise. It has an estimated strength of 8,000 to 10,000 guerrillas, most of whom are based in camps in Angola and Tanzania. Members have received training in the Soviet Union, East Germany, Cuba, Angola, North Korea, and Bulgaria. In recent years it has developed a four-pronged strategy: rural terrorism against white farmers, industrial sabotage, attacks on African policemen and politicians in the black 'townships', and urban terrorism in South African cities. Between 1977 and 1983 Umkhonto activists staged more than 200 incidents including industrial sabotage, assassinations, and attempted assassinations, bombings in city-centers, shooting incidents at police stations and a variety of pamphlet bombings. It operates in groups rarely more than a dozen strong. At best they manage to stage occasional hit-and-run raids inside the country. Within most black townships and large cities, there are small ANC cells complete with arms caches, safe houses and communication lines to Zambia.

* United Democratic Front (UDF)
A broad opposition coalition formed in August 1983 to oppose a new constitution offering persons of Indian and mixed racial descent limited parliamentary representation, but excluding the black majority of 23 miliion within South Africa's traditional borders. It is headed by Mrs.Albertina Sisulu and Mr.Archie Gumede. It claimed to have a following of 2 million people from about 700 church, community, student and trade union groups. The government considers the UDF as a political front organization of the banned ANC. The UDF has always denied any link with the ANC. As a result of the continuing repression, it is feared that the UDF might abandon its non-violent principles. Of some 24,000 people detained in 1986, at least three quarters were members of the UDF or its affiliates. Most of the UDF's leaders have been charged with high treason. Hostility between Inkatha and the UDF is deepening.

* Vigilantes
(Kabasas)
Black strongarm forces which have been involved in an orchestrated terror campaign against the United Democratic Front since 1986. They attacked in large groups, sometimes 1,500 men, and received active support from the so-called 'instant cops', young police agents which have been trained in three weeks. Vigilantes have been responsible for numerous killings of UDF activists. They have also killed at least 39 COSATU members in retaliation for strikes. The transition period between the two emergencies was the beginning of the period of the activities of the vigilantes, including the cutting off of fingers, cutting of tendons or stabbing of eyes.

* Warriors
(Amabutho)
A vigilant group which sometimes operates in traditional Zulu tribal gear. Its members are mostly avowed supporters of Chief Gatsha Buthelezi's Inkatha Movement.

* White Commando
(Wit Kommando)
Ultra-right white vigilante movement founded in 1980. The movement attacked the property of whites suspected of selling out the country to Marxist forces. It was broken up by the government in 1981.

SOVIET UNION

* Action Front for the Liberation of the Baltic Countries
This group claimed responsibility for bomb attacks made in Paris on the Soviet embassy on Apr.5, 1977 and on the offices of two Soviet organizations seven days later.

* Chief Intelligence Directorate
(Glavnoye Razvedyvatelnoye Upravleniye) (GRU)
The GRU is the military counterpart of the KGB. Its chief function is to acquire military intelligence. This it does legally through the military attaché system and illegally through espionage cells which are distinct and separate from the KGB. It is estimated to number around 5,000 operatives. Its present director is General Petr Ivanovich Ivashutin. The service is divided

into four main divisions - operations, information, training and auxiliary. It is also subdivided into 24 geographical units. The service is subordinate to the KGB, with the latter having the power to investigate its members. One of the GRU's operating arms are the so-called Spetnaz troops, the Soviet Union's special forces who are trained in subversion, infiltration, sabotage and assassination. See separate entry. GRU is reputedly responsible for the training of foreign terrorists mainly at the Sanprobal Military Academy in the Crimea and the Higher Infantry School in Odessa. It operates its own global network of agents independent of the KGB although there is an area of averlap between the two agencies at the higher levels of the Soviet bureaucracy.

* Committee for State Security
(Komitet Gosudarstvennoi Bezopastnosti) (KGB)
The Soviet Union's internal-security and intelligence gathering bureaucracy which operates both within the Soviet Union and throughout the world. Since its creation in 1917 the state security apparatus has been known as the Cheka, the GPU, the OGPU, the NKVD, the NKGB, the MVD-MGB, before becoming the KGB in March 1954. Its headquarters is in Moscow. The First Chief Directorate is responsible for foreign operations, the second CD is responsible for internal security and surveillance, while the Fifth CD tries to control religious, ethnic and polical dissent. Department V or the Executive Action Department of the First Chief Directorate is believed to be responsible for training the KGB's assassination squads. Educated guesses put the strength of the apparat in the Soviet Union at around 1,750,000 while the agents in the field abroad, including diplomats, journalists, Aeroflot personnel and co-opted members serving on international bodies, are estimated to amount to some 300,000, with another 100,000 deployed mainly in the Eastern European countries.

* Georgian Rebels
According to Georgian nationalists, Vladimir Zhvaniya was, on Feb.4, 1977, reported to have been condemned to death for having planted bombs at three government buildings. He was executed on Jan.13, 1978. In 1984 three persons went on trial on charges of membership of a 'National Liberation Organization of Georgia'.

* Resistance International
New worldwide anti-communist organization of exiled dissidents from the Soviet Union, Poland, Czechoslovakia, Afghanistan, Laos, Vietnam, China, Cuba and Nicaragua, established in Paris in May 1983. It was announced by the dissident Soviet scientist Vladimir Bukovsky and the Cuban poet Armando Valladares. It advocates a 'counter offensive against Soviet imperialism' and announced that it will support 'resistance groups in totalitarian states'. It wants to show that pacifism and reconciliation via concessions are no road to peace.

* Spetsialnoje Naznatsjenie
(Spetsnaz)
The Soviet special forces also known as reydoviki (raiders) reputed to number around 30,000 (although some sources say 15,000) are specially trained in infiltration, sabotage, assassination and other 'behind the lines' operations. They are reputed to have spearheaded the invasions of Czechoslovakia (1968) and Afghanistan (1979) and to have been heavily involved in the campaign against the Polish trade union movement. Spetsnaz troops also have a counter-insurgency role, and are reported to have been used to some effect against the Moslem rebels in Afghanistan. They are controlled by the Soviet military intelligence (GRU). Operating in units of between three and 10 their role is to sabotage important military and industrial installations such as power stations, missile bases, airfields, communication centres, gas and oil pipelines and gas processing plants. In the West they are referred to as 'diversionary troops' since one of their primary tasks is to create confusion and panic deep behind NATO lines by such means as sabotage and the attack of key mobile headquarters. They have the further task of providing detailed information on NATO targets for Soviet missile and air strikes. They wear Western uniforms and speak Western languages to facilitate these tasks. Many precautions are taken to cover up its strength, organization and function, deployment and even the very fact of its existence. All candidates undergo a preliminary loyalty check and upon entry have to sign an official secrets act. The Spetsnaz agents actually form 'sleeping' agent networks which would be brought into action only in the event of war.

* Ukrainian Liberation Front (ULF)
Group which carried out a bomb attack on the Luxemburg offices of Aeroflot on Nov.11, 1980.

* Ukranian Dissidents
Ukrainian group which has been held responsible for the Moscow subway explosion in 1977.

SPAIN

* Almond Trees
(Almendros)
This name was adopted by a group of officers of the armed forces and civilians who were believed to have planned a right-wing coup for the spring of 1981. Members of the group were among those arrested after an attempted coup of Feb.23, 1981,

by Lt.Col.Antonio Tejero Molinas, allegedly supported by high-ranking military officers. Some of the military leaders associated with the February 1981 coup attempt were also implicated in a further right-wing plot to seize power on the eve of the general elections of Oct.28, 1982.

* Apostolic Anti-Communist Alliance
(Alianza Apostolica Anticomunista) (AAA)
A para-military right-wing group which operated principally in the Basque country against left-wing separatist violence from ETA in the early 1980s. It operated in different cities under the name of Benito Mussolini Commando, Adolf Hitler Commando and so forth. Members were sheltered and encouraged by the fascist old-guard and the emigré Nazi community in Spain. It was held responsible for assassination attempts of ETA leaders in the Basque region and in France. It was also active against purely left-wing activities in the labour movement. Its most notorious action was the assassination of four liberal lawyers in broad daylight in Madrid on Jan.24, 1977. In September 1977 it killed two people when it bombed a left-wing newspaper office. Members of the group viewed themselves as defenders of Spanish national unity, and as such attacked not only ETA, but also bombed the Catalan centre in Madrid, and the Barcelona newspaper offices of El Papus. On Sep.28, 1978, the AAA announced its intention to to execute the Prime Minister, the Ministers of Interior and Defence and other 'agents of freemasonry separatism and Marxism'.

* Anti-Terrorism ETA
(Antiterrorismo ETA) (ATE)
As a reaction to the left-wing separatist violence of ETA a clandestine group emerged in April 1975. It sought out Basque terrorists in France and murdered them. It also bombed meeting places for separatists. Several hundred such actions have been recorded.

* Anti-Fascist and Revolutionary Patriotic Front
(Frente Revolucionario Antifascista y Patriotico) (FRAP)
Left-wing (Maoist) group which has been active in the 1970s. The group was set up by the maoist Communist Party of Spain-Marxist Leninist (PCE-ML) in 1973. FRAP sought to overturn the Franco regime by violence and by doing so to strike a blow at United States 'imperialism'. It wanted to establish a 'popular democratic and federal republic' and to create 'an army in the service of the people'. Ideological infighting caused it to split in 1976. It began its campaign of terror in 1975, specifically targetting the security forces. Other activities included bank robberies and bomb attacks. Before the end of the year the government had arrested more than 100 activists. When a number of FRAP terrorists were sentenced to death on Sep.12, 1975 for killing a policeman in Madrid, the sentences raised an international protest. Thereafter FRAP was more active in crowds and demonstrations. The group was defunct by 1980.

* Anti-terrorist Liberation Group
(Gruppos Antiterroristas de Libéracion) (GAL)
Spanish death squad which has been involved in attacks on ETA members in France. It allegedly has intelligence support in France, possibly from members of some special security force. France has denied the allegations. Spanish officers or former policemen were also involved. Since it emerged in 1983 it has killed more than 30 alleged ETA members. Some reports say that GAL is formed by contract killers from the French underworld and supplied by the intelligence services with information on the whereabouts of ETA members. Tactics include car bombs and armed assaults in the street or on cafés. In a French State Televison documentary it was alleged that a Spanish general and officials of the Spanish Ministry of Interior were the founders of GAL.

* Autonomous Anti-capitalist Commandos
(Comandos Autonomos Anticapitalistas) (CAA)
Breakway group from ETA which has been active in the north of Spain. It was established in 1976 but first came to the fore in 1978. It targeted police, army, companies, banks, youth courts, UDC politicians, local employers societies, and labour unions.

* Catalan Red Liberation Army (CRLA)
Group which claimed responsibility for a car bombing in Barcelona on Mar.27, 1987. One Spanish civil guard was killed and 15 people were injured.

* Catalan Liberation Front
(Front d'Alliberament Català) (FAC)
Small Catalan organization which has been active in and around Barcelona in the early and late 1970s. It perpetrated a number of terrorist acts including bomb attacks on television and radio stations and a railway station. Its stated aim was the independence of a united Catalonia. FAC claimed responsibility for the murder of two policemen in Barcelona in January 1979.

* Catalan Socialist Party for National Liberation (CSPNL)
Group which has attacked US businesses. It has not been active in recent years.

* Centro Superior de Información de la Defensa (CESID)
The Spanish intelligence service established in 1977, when Spain became a democracy after the

death of Franco. It covers both internal and external affairs. Most of the CESID staff came from the earlier military intelligence under General Franco, and most of its operatives are still ex-army officers. Under Franco there were no less than eight secret services, and the police kept extensive political files. Prime Minister Suarez ordered the destruction of these files.

* Civil Guard
(Guardia Civil)
Spanish police force which has been involved in torturing and maltreatment of prisoners held under the 'anti-terrorism law'. It also has killed Basque militants. In November 1985 Mikel Zabaltza, a bus driver suspected of ties with ETA, was found drowned in a river with his hands tied on his back. The discovery of his dead body led to violent riots. Members of the Guardia Civil have also been involved in 'shootouts' with ETA members which later appeared to have been summarily executions. In the six year period (1977-1982) about 720 to 980 prisoners, 20 percent of the total being held, were tortured. Several innocent persons have died in prison as a result of torture.

*Ertzantza
Autonomous Basque police that gradually replaces the Guardia Civil and the Policia Nacional.

* First of October Anti-fascist Resistance Group
(Grupo de Resistencia Antifascista Primero de Octubre) (GRAPO)
Left-wing urban terrorist group that took its name from the killing of four Spanish police officers on Oct.1, 1975 in response to the execution of five left-wing terrorists. It sprang from the Stalinist Organization of Maxist Leninist Spaniards (OMLE) that was established in Galicia in 1968. In 1975 the Reconstituted Spanish Communist Party (PCE(R)) was established and GRAPO acted as its military wing. In 1983, it demanded: 1) total amnesty and the abolition of repressive laws; 2) the purge of fascist elements from judicial police and other state agencies; 3) political and union freedoms without limitations, improvement of living conditions, self-determination for several nationalities; 4) dismantling of US bases and retreat from NATO; 5) dissolution of the parliament, free elections and formation of a real democratic constitution. It financed its activities by extortion and bank robberies. It also has been involved in assassinations, bomb attacks and armed assaults. It is thought to have been behind at least one attempt to kill King Juan Carlos. The group had an estimated membership of 300 (1979). Women played an important role in the group. Targets included police and military personnel and judges, the French Lycée, US Cultural Institute, Lufthansa offices. By the start of 1979 52 members were in prison. In a new wave of arrests 17 members were arrested in 1985, including Mercedes Padrós Corominas, its alleged leader. At least 17 of its members and leaders were killed in police shoot outs, including Carlos Delgado de Codex (Apr.20, 1979), Cerdán Calixto (Sep.1981) and Juan Martínez Luna (Dec.1982). It mainly operated in Madrid, Barcelona and Sevilla. In July 1984, GRAPO exploded bombs in five cities in a coordinated offensive targeting an optician's office, a municipal tax office, a courthouse, a bank, and a shipyard. GRAPO has also given operational support to ETA.

* Freedom for the Basque Homeland
(Euskadi ta Askatasuna) (ETA)
Basque terrorist organization which has been fighting for more than 25 years for an independent Basque homeland. ETA's actions began in the 1960s with little more than the painting of graffiti on walls and the attempts to bomb regime monuments and government buildings. The first death occurred in 1968. In December 1973 it assassinated Prime Minister Admiral Carrero Blanco. So far 530 people have been died in the violence, 40 of whom in 1986. Most of killings took place after 1977 mainly in the cities of San Sebastian, Madrid and Bilbao. The victims were high-ranking military officers, senior judges, and government officials, but also journalists and workers. ETA has been successful in stopping the construction of a nuclear reactor at Lemoniz. More than 250 ETA attacks caused damage amounting to two billion pesetas. The technical leader of the project was also murdered. Formed in 1959 as a breakaway of the Basque Nationalist Party (PNV), ETA split in 1966 into ETA-Zarra (old ETA) and ETA-Berri (young ETA). Four years later ETA-Zarra subdivided into ETA-5 and ETA-6 with the latter abandoning the armed struggle. A few years later ETA-5 split into ETA-7 and ETA-8. The main line of division is the one between a romantic nationalist faction with the aim to create an independent Basque country if necessary with violent means (ETA-M) and a faction for which nationalism is a means to create a socialist society. The former is strongly anti-Spanish, the latter seeks cooperation with the working class in other parts of Spain. Of all the ETA subgroups, ETA-M is the most seasoned and effective. At the peak of its activities ETA had about 1,000 members. According to Spanish intelligence (1984) it has a hardcore of 225 persons, a support organization of 200 persons in the French Basque country, and about 300-400 persons who incidentally have contacts with ETA in the French Basque country. It has about 20 commandos with a total of 90 trained terrorists.

* Freedom for the Basque Homeland-Military
(Euzkadi ta Askatasuna-Militar) (ETA-M)
Hardline breakaway group of ETA established in

1979. In 1980 the violent leadership came from men and women outside the country in France , principally Domingo Iturbe Abasolo (died in early 1987), Francisco Mugica Garmendia, Juan Angel Ochoantesana Badiola and Juan Lorenzo Santiago Lasa Michelena. It enjoyed a certain freedom of movement across the French frontier until the mid-1980s when France started to extradite ETA members to Spain. It financed its activities with a 'tax' levied on small firms and industrialists. People's Unity (Herri Batasuna) acts as its political front. It is prepared to negotiate when five demands are fulfilled. These are: 1) a general amnesty; 2) a retreat of the Spanish repressive apparatus from the Basque country; 3) improvement of living conditions; 4) democratic freedoms including the legalization of all political parties; 5) a true autonomy statute (four provinces, recognition of the Basque language, an army and local armed forces under Basque control and recognition of the right of self-determination). It is strongly anti-Spanish and advocates international proletarian solidarity. It denied to have logistic or organizational links with other foreign movements or states. It engaged in kidnappings, extortions, bomb attacks, armed assaults and car bomb attacks. In July 1985 it killed Vice Admiral F.Escrigas Estrada, one of Spain's top anti-terrorist experts.

* Freedom for the Basque Homeland-PM
(Euzkadi ta Askatasuna-Polimilis) (ETA-PM)
Section of ETA favoring a political solution after a split within ETA in 1979. The Party for the Basque Revolution (Euskal Iraultzako Alderdia) acted as its political front. In 1982, a minority faction of ETA-PM said that it halted all terrorist action and will henceforth fight peacefully for its political ideals. The decision involved about a quarter of ETA-PM, covering approximately 40 refugees and exiles in France and about 20 militants jailed in Spain. At its 1982 assembly the majority (ETA-8) determined to resume violent action under Jesus Abrisketa Korta.

* Free Land
(Terra Lliure) (TL)
Catalan nationalist movement which emerged in 1980. It demanded equal rights for the Spanish and Catalan languages in Catalonia. It claimed responsibility for blowing up an electrical installation (which was to be used by a nuclear plant in Tarragona province) on Aug.18, 1980. It also exploded a number of small devices in Barcelanoa, Tarragona, Valencia and Alicante. Since 1982 it has been responsible for numerous bomb attacks.

* Special Operations Group
(Grupo Especiale Para los Operaciones) (GEO)
Governmental anti-terrorist unit of the police that has operated in France to kidnap ETA members. In 1983 four of its members were arrested by France. The unit has 58 members and is led by Captain Ernesto Garcia Quijada. Most of its members come from the Spanish security service and the Civil Guard. The unit has been trained by the British SAS.

* Iberian Liberation Movement
(Movimiento Ibërico de Liberacion) (MIL)
Catalan anarchist group which has sought to maintain the long Spanish tradition of support for anarchist concepts. One of its leaders, Puig Antich, was executed in 1974.

* International Revolutionary Action Groups
(Grupos de Acción Revolucionaria Internacionalista) (GARI)
A small Spanish anarchist group active in the early 1970s. It largely disappeared after the death of General Franco in November 1975. The group engaged in kidnappings, minor bomb explosions and acts of sabotage. Targets included Spanish consulates in the Netherlands and Belgium. French police arrested half a dozen members in September 1974, including the French Catalan, Jean Marc Rouillan who later became an important leader of Direct Action (see separate entry under France).

* Iraultza
The name of this anti-capitalist Basque group refers to the Basque word meaning revolution. It was established in 1982. The group is believed to be responsible for bomb attacks on businesses and companies associated with the United States in the Basque country in 1983. Actions are directed at bad labour conditions and arbitrariness of the employers.

* Islamic Jihad
Eighteen people were killed and another 82 persons were wounded in an explosion at the El Descado restaurant in Madrid on Apr.14, 1985. The restaurant was frequently visited by US military personnel of the nearby Torrejon air base. An anonymous telephone called claimed responsibility for the attack in the name of Islamic Jihad.

* Moroccan Patriotic Front
(Frente Patriótico Maroqui) (FPM)
This organization stands for the restoration of Moroccan sovereignty over the cities Ceuta and Melilla. It has been involved in minor bomb attacks on cafés and a hotel in 1978 and 1979.

* National Revolutionary Youth (NRY)
Neo-Nazi group allegedly led by Juan Rubio Gomez. At least one of its members was suspected of involvement in the murder of a Communist in Madrid on Apr.29, 1979, while others were arrested

after the police had found an arms cache.

* New Force
(Fuerza Nueva) (FN)
Right-wing organization which was formed in the mid-1970s. It sought the return to an authoritarian regime. It is led by Blas Pinar, a prominent lawyer and politician. Members have been involved in confrontations with with left-wing elements, one of the latter being killed in Madrid suburb on Feb.10, 1980. The organization recruited supporters in the Civil Guard and the military.

* Octavos
Splinter group of ETA which announced new attacks on June 17, 1986. The announcement came after a truce in which most members decided to give up the armed struggle.

* Organization of the Oppressed
In an anonymous telephone call from Beirut this organization claimed responsibility for two bomb attacks on travel agencies in Madrid on July 2, 1985. The first bomb exploded in a building housing an office of Trans World Airlines and British Airways. One person was killed and 27 others were injured. The second bomb exploded at the nearby office of the Jordanian ALIA agency. Five people were lightly injured. Simultaneously bombs exploded in Rome and Athens. The attacks appeared to be a retaliation for the conviction of two shi'ites. They were sentenced to 23 years in prison. The attacks were also a response to the US announcement to attack the centers of international terrorism.

* Red Guerrillas
(Guerrilleros Rojos) (GR)
Group which has claimed responsibility for a series of attacks on cars of French tourists north of Barcelona on June 27, 1979. The attacks were accompanied by demands for the release of a militant Basque arrested in France on June 2, 1977, on suspicion of involvement in the kidnapping and murder in May-June 1977 of an industrialist and former Mayor of Bilbao by the Bereziak wing of ETA.

* Rural Anti-terrorist Units
(Unidades Antiterroristas Rurales) (UAR)
Units for rural counterinsurgency operations which have been trained by the British SAS.

* Spanish Basque Batallion
(Batalon Vasco Espagnol) (BVE)
Right-wing para-military group which emerged in 1980. It was active in Durango, Berriz and Hernani, small towns in the Spanish Basque country, where it attacked separatist bars. On occasions ETA suspects were targeted, particularly in the French Basque country, where they had sought refuge or where they planned attacks in Spain. During 1980 alone the BVE was responsible for 16 political killings (out of a total of 126 for the whole of Spain).

* Spanish Catalonian Battalion (SCB)
Previously unknown right-wing group which claimed on Mar.1, 1981, to have abducted a famous football player on the ground that his club (FC Barcelona) was a separatist organization and should not be allowed to become Spain's football champion.

* Spanish Circle of Friends of Europe
(Circulo Espanol de Amigos de Europa) (CEDADE)
Neo-fascist group which was founded in Barcelona in 1965. It was led by Jorge Mota and had close contacts with .neo-Nazi organizations all over Europe. It includes among its members German and Italian exiles (i.e. former leading Fascists and Nazis) and veterans of the Blue Division (the Spanish unit which served on the Nazi side in World War II). It has become a forum and a source of propaganda and encouragements for fascists from other countries. It claimed to have 2,500 supporters including a 200-man strongarm force, called Sicherheitsdienst (SD).

* Spanish Liberation Army (SLA)
Group which has been responsible for attacks on left-wing organizations and public buildings and also for bank robberies. Police announced in 1980 that 12 of its members had been arrested and the group had been dismantled.

* Spanish National Action
(Acción Nacional Espagnola) (ANE)
Right-wing terrorist organization which emerged in the 1970s in the Basque country in reaction to the activities of ETA. The ANE have been responsible for a number of killings of alleged ETA members in Spain and in France, and bomb attacks in Bilbao and San Sebastian. Activities diminished in the early 1980s.

* United International Secret and Revolutionary Cells (UISRC)
Members of this group claimed responsibility for a bomb explosion at the Cuban national airline office in Madrid on Oct.27, 1976.

* Warriors of Christ the King
(Guerrilleros de Cristo Rey) (GCR)
Organization that emerged in the late 1960s. Its enemies were 'the adversaries of the Church of Spain, principally the progressives, the heretical and subversive Christian movements'. In 1975 it embarked on reprisals against members of the Basque separatist ETA and their families. Mariano Sanchez Corvisa, the organization's alleged leader, was thought to have cooperated with Italian right-

wing extremists. On Sep.28, 1977 the organization joined the AAA and the Anti-terrorist Organization against ETA in forming a 'committee for patriotic justice' with the object of 'executing' opponents. Little was heard of them since then.

SRI LANKA

*Civil Defense Force
The membership of this civil defence force is planned to increase from 12,000 to 20,000 men in 1987. It was established by the government to support the police. It consists of young villagers checked on loyality. They are given a three to four months of training and are lightly armed. Their main task is to defend the villages and improve the alarm system. In 1986 members of this force repeatedly attacked Tamil-villagers in retaliation for Tamil attacks on Sinhalese civilians.

*Criminal Investigation Department (CID)
Police unit that has engaged in killings of young Tamils in 1985.

* Ealam People's Revolutionary Liberation Front (EPRLF)
One of the active guerrilla organizations in Sri Lanka. It was formed by Tamil students in the mid-1970s. Its members are better educated that the Tigers and are more ideological, espousing a Marxist-Leninist line. It reportedly has links with Palestinian organizations.

* Ealam Revolutionary Communist Party (ERCP)
Group which emerged in 1986. It claimed responsibility for the sabotage of a dam which resulted in the death of 200 people. Another 40,000 people became homeless.

* Eelam National Liberation Front (ENLF)
Umbrella organization of three Tamil guerrilla organizations (TELO, EROS and EPRLF) which emerged in 1984. The LTTE joined the organization as a fourth group in April 1985. Together it can field 10,000 fighters. It has training camps in the northern jungles. Leaders received training in Palestinian camps in Lebanon. Activities are financed with money from bank robberies and from Tamil communities all over the world. Since its formation in April 1984, there has been constant bickering and occasional bloody clashes between the various Tamil groups, out of which the Tamil Tigers have emerged as the most powerful organization. The long-standing hostility between the Hindu Tamils and Buddhist Sinhalese flared into guerrilla warfare and terrorism in 1983 when Tamil activists decided their future lay in an independent Tamil state carved out of Sri Lanka. The conflict has already claimed between 6,000 and 16,000 lives, mostly civilians.

* Liberation Tigers of Tamil Eelam (LTTE)
The largest and most aggressive Tamil guerrilla organization which is fighting for an independent Tamil state. It was established in 1972 and is led by Vellupilai Prabhakaran who went underground in south India in October 1985 after the Indian government issued deportation orders against him. It had 30 armed members in 1983. Now the organization can field 2,500 trained guerrillas and 5,000 untrained recruits. It has not followed traditional military structures and has developed a home-made system, consisting of a Military Office (two basic units) and a Political Office (29 political divisions). It lacks heavy firepower and great emphasis is placed on home-made weapons (particularly mortars). Over two dozen different rifles and machine guns are in current use. It has engaged in armed raids on police stations, post offices and military outposts. Its members are well-trained and disciplined. They do not drink and do not smoke. They wear cyanide capsules to commit suicide when they are captured by the security forces. Its strategy it to eliminate rival guerrilla groups and to establish supremacy in Jaffna. It enjoys safe havens in the predominantly Tamil Indian state of Tamil Nadu. It is striving for an 'international socialism adapted to Sri Lankan circumstances' and a 'state led by nationalist movement in which all inhabitants participate'. However, in August 1987, LTTE, appeared preprared to accept a compromise imposed by India, which fell short of autonomy.

* People's Liberation Front
(Janatha Vimukhti Peramuna) (JVP)
An outlawed Maoist organization that was responsible for the terrorist attacks and attempted overthrow of the government in 1971. The insurgency broke out on Apr.5-6, 1971, when JVP squads attacked some 90 police stations. By the end of April the insurgency had been broken with Soviet, Chinese and Western assistance. An estimated 10,000 people were killed and many thousands were detained. The front regained legal status following the lifting of the state of emergency on Feb.16, 1977. Since 1977 the JVP has not generally resorted to force, although members of its youth movement were held responsble for bomb attacks on the opposition leader, Mrs.Bandanaraike, on Aug.12, 1981. In the 1983 the government outlawed the organization because of evidence that it helped instigate the bloody anti-Tamil riots that year. Its leader, Rohan Wijerwee, went underground in 1985. The front claimed responsbility for a bomb attack on the central telegraph office in Colombo on May 7, 1986. In May 1987, the JVP was reported to be back on the stage. It led anti-Tamil demonstrations in

university campuses and has welcomed Sri Lankan army deserters in its ranks. According to some reports it has stolen 70 machine guns from Sri Lankan army barracks. Many JVP youths received military training in jungle camps. On Apr.11, 1987, it attacked an army camp.

* People's Liberation Organization of Tamil Ealam (PLOTE)
Tamil guerrilla organization which is regarded as something of a mystery. It has training camps and bases in Tamil Nadu (India) and is led by Uma Maheswaran. It condems hit-and-run tactics. Its stated aim is to work with the Sinhalese left to foment an island-wide Communist revolution. It has been most violent against its own members. Scores of PLOTE dissidents and deserters have been murdered.

* Revolutionary Ealam Organization (EROS)
Marxist-Leninist Tamil guerrilla organization which was formed by Tamil students in the mid-1970s in London. It reportedly has links with Palestinian groups. It has about 700 members and is led by Edward Ratnasabapaty.

* Sinhalese Vigilantes Squads (Lions)
Sinhalese groups which have been involved in violent activities directed against Tamils.

* Special Task Force
Members of this taskforce established in 1985 are trained by the Israeli Mossad, Pakistani advisers and employees of the KMS, a private British company specialized in counter-terrorism. They receive a three-month course. Former prisoners who are unemployed have been recruited. The force has been involved in operations in which hundreds of Tamil civilians have been murdered. It also engaged in intimidation and retaliation attacks. At least 1,400 members have received training in Pakistan. This country also supplied weapons and military equipment. According to press reports 60 British mercenaries left Sri Lanka after complaints that forces trained by them had used extremely violent methods against the Tamil population.

* Tamil Ealam Liberation Organization (TELO)
Tamil guerrilla organization which is led by Sri Sabaratnam. It has about 3,000 ill-trained fighters.

* Tamil United Liberation Front (TULF)
The TULF was initially organized as the Tamil Liberation Front (Tamil Vimukhti Peramuna-TVP) in May 1976 by a number of Tamil groups, including the Federal Party (ITAK), the National Liberation Front (JVP), the Tamil Congress, the Moslem United Front, and the Ceylon Workers' Congress. It is the most moderate and constitutional of the Tamil separatist organizations. It wants to unite the northern and eastern provinces to create one Tamil province which should have greater autonomy. It rejects armed struggle. It is led by Appapillai Amirthalingam, F.R.P.Suriyapperuma and G.G.Ponnambalam. Two of its senior members, V.Dharmalimgam and A.Alaslasundram, were shot dead by the LTTE guerrillas in September 1985 after being kidnapped from their homes. The two men were killed in an attempt by Tamil Tigers to prevent them signing a devolution pact with the Sri Lankan government.

* United Front of Eelam Liberation (UFEL)
Umbrella organization of four guerrilla organizations (EROS, EPRLF, TELO and LTTE) that emerged in 1984. It strives for an independent, socialist blockfree Tamil state. With the threat of closing the offices and centers, India forced the organization to the negotiating table. In June 1985 it formulated seven conditions for a truce. These were: 1) opening of the prohibited zones for fishermen and Tamils; 2) free traffic of persons; 3) abolition of the rationing of food, fuel and other goods; 4) abolition of the curfew, 5) no settlements in Tamil areas; 6) no more military violence against Tamils; 7) amnesty for political prisoners.

<u>SUDAN</u>

* ANSAR Movement
In July 1985 it was reported that around 3,500 rebels from the ANSAR movement began returning home from training camps in Ethiopia.The return of the men followed a visit to Addis Ababa by Wali Al Din Al Hadi, son of the former leader of the ANSAR sect. Following the coup on Apr.6 which toppled Numeiri, Al Hadi had promised to call his supporters home. The Ansari's (two to three million) were involved in an insurrection in 1971 that was suppressed by the Numeiri regime at a cost of an estimated 12,000 lives.

* Anyanya II
A former rebel movement based on the Nuer people which has been acting as a pro-army militia against the SPLA. It has engaged in guerrilla activity in the south since February-March 1983 when it broke away from the SPLA. Most guerrillas are former government soldiers from garrisons in three southern towns that mutinied in May 1983. The government accused Libya and Ethiopia of sheltering and supplying the movement and says most of the rebels are Marxists. It is pro-Western and advocates a total separation of the south.

* Any Anya
Sudanese guerrilla organization active in the south in the late 1960s. The name refers to a word for snake poison. It was formed in September 1963 in the south at a meeting organized by J.Oduho. At

first it lacked firearms and military discipline. In 1963 Emilio Tafeng. established training camps across the southern borders in Zaire and Uganda and waged an intermittent war of sabotage and ambush against government forces. It was predominantly a tribal movement. It had an estimated strength of 10,000 men in 1968. A quarter of them were armed. In August 1971 Joseph Lagu captured the leadership from Tafeng and became military and political head of a new Southern Sudan Liberation Movement with headquarters in the Immatong mountains. Throughout 1970 and 1971 the government suffered greater casualties. In March 1972 President Numeiry ordered a ceasefire when Anya Anya dropped its opposition in return for southern autonomy. Their numbers (12,000) were absorbed in the police and armed forces. The conflict claimed an estimated 300,000 lives in the 1963-1972 period.

* Islamic Brigade
Irregular mercenary groups of Libyans, Syrians, Chadians and some Sudanese.

* Marahlin Militia
An Arab militia supported by the government that engaged in counter-insurgency operations in the south against the SPLA. It has been responsible for a massacre in the village of el-Dhaein in the province of Darfur in March 1987. According to reports of the SPLA more than 1,000 Dinkas were killed. The authorities confirmed the massacre but said there were several hundred deaths. The government ordered an investigation.

* Messerya Militia
Nomadic ethnic group of the Messerya people in Darfur and Kordofan that has been armed and supported by the army to create an aggressive militia whose main targets have been civilians. Messerya and Anyanya II militias are cooperating to step up their pressure on Dinka civilians in early 1987. Evidence of this has been seen in the push by the Messerya against the Dinka in Bahr El Ghazal, including the assassination of four out of five district chiefs, which has forced people and cattle to move south and west. This brings them into greater contact with Nuer civilians and attempts are being made by the Anyanya II to undermine the fairly peaceful working relationship chiefs on both sides have built up.

* Movement of Revolutionary Committee (MRC)
Organization whose objectives are similar to those of the Libyan 'Green Revolution'. It is aimed at establishing popular congresses and instigating people to assume full authorities. It is led by Abdalla Zakaria.

* National Islamic Front (NIF)
A Moslem coalition which includes the Moslem Brotherhood. It is a well-armed political party in northern Sudan which is held responsible for a number of bloody election riots. It has support under students and the army and is led by Hassan al Turabi. It receives financial support from Islamic banks and Saudi Arabia.

* Noba Mountain Front (NMF)
A front which operated from Ethiopia. It is trained by Libya and has an estimated strength of several hundred men.

* Rigazat Militia
Nomadic ethnic group of the Rigazat people that has been armed and supported by the army to create an aggressive militia whose main target has been civilians.

* Southern Sudan Liberation Front (SSLF)
Front which was established in 1971. It included most of the southern leaders in exile and for the first time military and political activities were united under one authority.

* Sudan African Liberation Front (SALF)
Aggrey Jaden set up SALF as a splinter group from the Sudan African National Union in 1965. Jaden subsequently became vice-president of the Azania Liberation Front (ALF), only to be expelled after which he set up the Southern Sudan Provisional Government, which had links with Any Anya.

* Sudan African National Union (SANU)
Southern Sudanese political movement set up in the early 1960s and led by William Deng, a former Assistant District Commissioner. He sought a peaceful means to establish a separate non-Moslem southern Sudan. In 1965 SANU rejected federal autonomy offered by Khartoum; but Deng favoured negotiation and remained in the Sudan as head of the internal SANU. He was assassinated by the army in May 1968.

* Sudanese Socialist Popular Front
(Al-Jabhah ash-Shabiyah al-Ishtirakiyah as-Sudaniyah) (SSPF)
Pro-Libyan front backed by Colonel Qadhafi, the Libyan leader. The front is led by Mahgoub Elfil.

* Sudanese National Front (SNF)
The SNF was set up in 1969 by exiled members of the center and right-wing parties of the pre-1969 regime. It was led by Dr.Sadiq el-Mahdi. Under a national reconcialition agreement subsequently signed in London on Apr.12, 1978, it was provided that the SNF would be abolished and their arms and equipment were to be handed over to the Sudanese armed forces. Some of the SNF leaders were admitted to the central committee of the

ruling Sudanese Socialist Union. Others did not accept the agreement and continued its opposition to President Numeiry's regime.

* Sudanese People Liberation Army (SPLA)
Military arm of the Sudanese People's Liberation Movement. It emerged in 1983 and is led by Colonel John Garang. It seeks to unite the disadvantaged peoples of Sudan's southeast and west against Arabic-speaking Moslem northerners, who have controlled the nation's political and economic life since independence was achieved in 1956. It demands are: 1) abolition of the Islamic Law (sharia); 2) a constitution not based on religion; 3) a federal status for the south; 4) more investments in the south. It has an estimated strength of about 15,000 fighters, the majority coming from the Dinka people. It has pursued a strategy of isolating southern towns by ambushing truck convoys and steamers on the West Nile , the country's main transportation artery. Analysts believe Mr.Garang's goal is to reduce food supplies to the towns, force the civilian population to flee, and then starve out army garrisons. However, instead of fleeing to the bush, many civilians have streamed into the towns to search for food and escape the fighting. Since 1983 an estimated 10,000 people have been killed in the fighting. Libyan aid has been stopped since the 1985 coup. Tacit but increasing diplomatic support is being given to the SPLA by Uganda, Zaire and Kenya, including treatment of wounded fighters in Kenyan hospitals according to claims in the press.

SURINAM

* Action Committee to Restore Democracy in Surinam
(Actie Comité Herstel Democratie Suriname) (ACHDS)
Committee based in the Netherlands which advocates the violent overthrow of the Bouterse regime. It is led by Rob Wormer and has a crisis center in Amsterdam-Osdorp. It claimed that 80 percent of the Surinam people in the Netherlands supported its aim. After a visit to Surinam in May 1983, Wormer decided to stop his resistance against the Bouterse regime.

* Away with the Dictatorship in Surinam
(Weg met de Dictatuur in Suriname)
Group which claimed responsibility for an arson attack on a radio transmitter on Oct.28, 1983.

* Collective Resistance
(Collectief Verzet) (CR)
Group of Surinam people which occupied the Surinam embassy in the Netherlands in January 1984.

* Council for the Liberation of Surinam
(Raad voor de Bevrijding van Suriname) (RBS)
Surinam opposition movement in the Netherlands which was established on Jan.5, 1983. It was led by Chin a Sen, an ex-President and ex-prime minister. Since March 1986, it is led by Glenn Tjong Akiet. On its second Congress in 1986 it changed its policy. From now on it would no longer refrain from violent resistance against the Bouterse regime. There have been several attempts to unite the resistance against the Bouterse regime and to coordinate the support for the Jungle Commando of Ronnie Brunswijk. On its March 1986 congress it proposed a directed mobilization of the resistance and to create a massive people's movement against the Bouterse regime.

* Death Squad
Special commando unit which reportedly has operated as a death squad in Paramaribo in 1986. It has an estimated strength of about 200 men and is comprised of military and military police personnel. The unit has also operated in eastern Surinam where it has targeted Maroons and bush negros.

* February 25 Movement
The political arm of the military led by Desi Bouterse. It has no plans to participate in the planned elections. In May 1987, it announced plans to establish the New Democratic Party Surinam (NDPS) in June 1987. The aim of the reorganization is to improve contacts between the leadership and the members of the party. Its main political leaders are Chas Mijnals, Frank Playfair and Ernie Brunings. All ethnic groups in Surinam will be represented in the leadership of the new party. The present prime-minister Jules Wijdembosch has been mentioned as future chairman of the party.

* Jungle Command (JC)
Surinam guerrilla organization engaged in an armed struggle against the Bouterse regime since 1986. It is led by Ronnie Brunswijk and has an estimated strength of about 200 armed and 600 unarmed men. It is based on the Maroon people. Experts on the Surinam's varied and disunited Maroon clans say many in the tribal population of roughly 50,000 support the revolt. A power struggle developed between the tribal Aucan and the Saramaccan factions. Brunswijk belongs to the Aucans. Another line of division is the one between the Hindustanis and the bush negros. The Hindustanis reportedly signed an accord with the foreign mercenaries. The commando has engaged in acts of sabotage, including bridges, roads, the electricity supply and the strategic bauxiet mining complex (Suralco). Several hundred people have died in the fighting which escalated in late 1986. Mercenaries of several nationalities (Britain, Belgium, France) have

operated with the command. Surinam support organizations in the Netherlands have attempted to raise money in several countries for more weapons. Means of communication are lacking. For that reason small rebel groups (10 to 20 man strong) operate independently without a central command. Independent groups have used the name of the Jungle Command without having direct links with it. In 1987, the commando received small handweapons via Dr.John, of the US private organization 'Soldier of Fortune'.

* League of Surinam Patriots
(Liga van Surinaamse Patriotten) (LSP)
Organization of Surinam groups in the Netherlands which support the revolution of Desi Bouterse. It was established in January 1983 and held its first congress on Feb.27, 1983. It has between 500 and 1,000 members. Leaders are Ludwig van Mulier and Waldy Breedveld. The latter was arrested in connection with the Rijswijk murder but it turned out that he had nothing to do with it. Members mainly come from the young Surinam subproletariat.

* Maroon Resistance Organization (MRO)
Surinam organization that has tried to contact ultra-conservative and anti-communist organizations in the United States to raise funds for the armed struggle of the Jungle Command of Ronnie Brunswijk. The organization was an initiative of Mr.Chin a Sen, Dr.Jozefzoon and Mr.Wijngaarde. Ronnie Brunswijk reportedly had contacts with US General John Singlaub. The organization wants more heavy weapons.

* Moederbond
Largest of the right-wing unions in Surinam which staged a strike at Paramaribo airport on Oct.28, 1982, in protest against the delay in restoring democratic civilian rule in Surinam. Together with four other trade union groupings it called for a general strike which was widely observed. On Nov.4 the government agreed to implement a timetable for the restoration of parliamentary democracy, starting with the election of a constituent assembly to draft a constitution. It also agreed to release the chairman of the Moederbond, Cyriel Daal. However, on Dec.7, 1982, severe disturbances broke out in Paramaribo, where the Moederbond headquarters and the offices of a newspaper were burned down, apparently by pro-government forces. These events were followed by the proclamation of martial law on Dec.8 and an announcement that an attempted coup had been foiled. On the following day it became known that 17 opposition figures had been executed, among them Cyriel Daal. Bouterse participated personnally in the massacre.

* National Military Council (NMC)
The NMC led by Sgt.-Maj. (later Lt.-Col.) Desi Bouterse has ruled the Republic of Surinam since February 1980. It succeeded in foiling several attempts by army officers to overthrow it, and on Nov.27, 1981, it set up a 'Revolutionary Front' including 'political parties, progressive organizations and other sectors'. On Mar.31, 1982, a mainly civilian government was set up. However, as a result of a confrontation between the government and the country's trade unions in October-December 1982 the NMC on Dec.8 declared a state of martial law, dismissed the government and destroyed the headquarters of the opposition media and of the largest right-wing trade union, the Moederbond. Lt.Col.Bouterse stated on Dec.20 that he intended to form a 'truly revolutionary government', and he added on Dec.30 that there would 'never again' be a parliamentary democracy in Surinam of the type in existence until February 1980. In March 1987, the National Assembly approved a draft for a new constitution in which the power of the military has been limited. Within a period of six months the Surinam population will speak out in a referendum on a concept constitution. General free and secret elections will be held before Mar.31, 1988.
The NMC maintained contacts with Cuba until the Grenada invasion. Later it turned to Libya.

* National Resistance Council
The faction ridden Surinam resistance united itself in this umbrella organization at a secret meeting in Rotterdam (Netherlands) in April 1987. Michel van Rey, military adviser of the Jungle Command, accomplished his mission with a formal accord after several groups had come to a provisional agreement on Stoelmans Island.

* Pendawa Lima-Fighters for Justice
(Pendawa Lima-Strijders voor Rechtvaardigheid) (PL-SVR)
Militant political organization led by Paul Somohardjo, a former member of parliament. A Dutch section was established in May 1986. Although it is mainly based on the Javanese people it wants to be a multiracial party. It has made attempts to raise money for the violent overthrow of the Bouterse regime. It has an agreement of cooperation with the Amsterdam People's Resistance (AVV) and supports the Jungle Command of Ronnie Brunswijk. P.Somohardjo was arrested after the police discovered an arms cache in Rotterdam in 1985.

* Surinam National Liberation Army (SNLA)
Organization that was established on December 1, 1986. It advocates the overthrow of the military dictatorship of Bouterse and the establishment of a third republic. Henk Chin a Sen and Dr.E.Jozefzoon would acts as its political coordinators and Michel

van Rey as its military coordinator.

SWEDEN

* Nordic State Party
(Nordiska Rikspartiet) (NRP)
Neo-Nazi group that engaged in intimidation of immigrants and the destruction of their property.

SWITZERLAND

* Autonomous Cells
(Autonome Zellen) (AZ)
Group which has claimed responsibility for several minor attacks in 1985. Most of them were arson attacks. Targets included the Palladium theater in Geneva, a Swiss train, army trucks and a police station.

* Coordination of Anti Nuclear Energy Saboteurs
Anti-nuclear energy action group that has been involved in cases of arson and minor acts of sabotage during the 1970s. Targets included facilities and construction equipment related to nuclear power plants, representatives of the nuclear lobby and power pylons.

* European New Order
(Europäische Neu-Ordnung) (ENO)
Neo-Nazi party based in Lausanne. It defends an Arian race society.
It is sometimes referred to as New Social Order. The movement was, in 1980, reported to have links with other, mainly neo-Nazi, organizations in various countries of Europe and elsewhere.

* International Revolutionary Organization (IRO)
Two members of this group, Bruno Brequet (Swiss) and Magdalena Kaupp (West German) were arrested by Swiss authorities.

* Movement of the Discontented
Loosely organized group of youths which has been involved in violent clashes in Zurich.

SYRIA

* Air Force Intelligence (AFI)
One of the half dozen Syrian security agencies which has been linked to international terrorist attacks. It is led by General Mohammed al-Kholi.

* Arab Communist Organization (ACO)
In 1975, fourteen members of this organization were sentenced for a series of acts of sabotage, including the bombing of Egyptian, Jordanian and US diplomatic of information offices.

* Defense Units
(Saraya al-Difa an-al-Thawra)
A 10,000 praetorian guard responsible for the protection of Damascus and other cities and the security of the regime itself. It is headed by Colonel Rifaat al-Assad and is made up almost exclusively of Alawites. Colonel Rifaat al-Assad was declared persona non-grata and went into exile. The force has been involved in executions of members of the Moslem Brotherhood.

* Fighting Vanguard
(Talia al-Mukatila)
Military wing of the Moslem Brotherhood. It adheres closely to the Brotherhood's original goal of an Islamic state by a Holy War, without considering the possibility of any compromise. It split from Saadeddin in December 1981 and refused to join the National Alliance. It is led by Adnan Okla. Its methods include the use of all possible means except those prohibited by the Koran such as violence against innocents.

* Islamic Front (IF)
Front established in January 1981 consisting of the political wing of the Moslem Brotherhood, the Islamic Liberation Party and various Sufi groups under the overall leadership of Ali Bayanouni.

* Moslem Brotherhood
(Majallat al-Ikhwan al-Musalamin) Deriving from the historic movement originally founded in Egypt (in 1928), the Syrian offshoot of the Moslem Brotherhood has in recent years been engaged in a bloody struggle with the regime of President Assad. It advocated the use of violence where necessary to achieve its aims-which were the establishment of an Islamic state and the end of colonial rule. The movement split in two factions in 1981, one led by Adnan Saadeddin and the other by Adnan Okla. The political violence practised by the movement included a terrorist campaign of bombings and assassinations against the ruling Alawite community. Targets included Soviet advisers and army cadets. In the early 1980s, widespread unrest was reported from Aleppo, Homs and Hama. Following an attempted assassination attempt on President Assad on June 26, 1980, a law was accepted instituting the death penalty for membership of the Brotherhood, with the proviso that those who left it within a month would be pardoned. In February 1982 an armed insurrection broke out in Hama. Security forces completely destroyed the inner city and reportedly killed an estimated 20-40,000 people, mostly civilians.

* Movement of October 17 for the Liberation of the Syrian People
Organization which has been responsible for bomb attacks on buses on Apr.16, 1986. Its stated aim was 'the liberation of the Syrian people from President Assad who supports Khomeini against the

sons of the Arab nation in Iraq'.

* National Alliance Charter for the Liberation of Syria
Broad opposition alliance established in 1982 by political and religious groups. The aim of the Alliance is the violent overthrow of the Assad government and its replacement by a constitutional, elective system. Islam would be the country's religion and the Sharia (Islamic law) would be the basis of legislation, but the rights of the non-moslems would be protected. The alliance is backed by Iraq.

* National Front for the Liberation of Arab Syria (Jabhat Tahrir Suria al-Arabiya)
A dissident faction of Syrian Baathists sponsored by Iraq and led by Akram al-Hourani. Other members include General Amin al-Hafiz, General Hamud Suwaidani, Shibli al-Aysami and Mahmud al-Shufi.

* National Salvation Command (NSC)
Dissident Baathist group which claimed responsibility for bomb explosions at the Prime Minister's offices in Damascus on Aug.17, 1981, and at the Baath party's headquarters (also in Damascus) on Sep.12; the latter explosion resulted in the death of about 43 persons working at the party's headquarters.

* Regional Command of the Arab Socialist Renaissance Party
(Hizb al-Baath al-'Arabi al-Ishtiraki)
The Baath Party is the Syrian branch of an international political movement that emerged in 1940 and remains active in Iraq and other Arab countries. The contemporary party dates from a 1953 merger of the Arab Resurrectionist Party, founded in 1947 by Michel Aflak and Salah al-Din Bitar, and the Syrian Socialist Party founded in 1950 by Akram al-Hurani. In 1963 the leftwing of the movement was separated from the right-wing 'historic' Baath party of Iraq. It is led by Hafiz al-Assad (President of the Republic and Secretary General of the Party). The regime was accused of an 'impossible degree of repression' in 1979 and of having imprisoned 'former presidents, prime ministers and army officers by the hundreds'. Dissident groups of the party have engaged in terrorist acts. See National Salvation Command and Vanguard of the Arab Revolution.

* Syrian Intelligence Service
A service which reportedly has been involved in sabotage operations in Egypt.

* Vanguard of the Arab Revolution
This group claimed on Feb.8-9, 1981, to have been involved in heavy fighting with Syrian army units in Aleppo when attempting to storm a prison in order to release Salah Jadid, a former Syrian chief of staff and senior Baath party member. The group also claimed to have 'executed' a Syrian secret agent in Kuwait 'in revenge for the execution of Salah al-Bitar'. Bitar was assassinated in Paris on July 21, 1980, in the course of an 'assassination campaign' against external opposition members by the Assad regime.

TAIWAN

* Taiwan Independence Movement (TIM)
Non-communist opposition movement resisting the Kuomintang domination of Taiwan. It has been effectively crushed in Taiwan itself. It continues its activities among exiles in Japan (where it has some 10,000 members) and in the United States. In the 1970s it was responsible for anti-American and anti-government bombings in the United States and Taiwan.

* United Bamboo Gang (UBG)
Taiwan's largest underworld gang. It leader Chen Chi-li has been convicted of the political killing on Oct.15, 1984, of a Chinese-American journalist who had frequently criticized the Taiwanese government.

TANZANIA

* Tanzanian Youth Democracy Movement (TYDM)
Established in 1979, this opposition movement led by Moussa Membar, claimed to have 3,000 members. Its goal is a return to democracy. Five members of the movement hijacked a Tanzanian airliner on an internal flight on Feb.28, 1982, and diverted it to Stansted (Essex, England), where the five men surrendered.

THAILAND

* Armed Forces of the National Liberation of the People (AFNLP)
Guerrilla organization established on Dec.31, 1968. From a force of about 2,000 men it developed into a force of more than 8,000 guerrillas in 1975. Since then membership decreased to 920 in 1984, 200 in the north, 200 in the northeast, 120 in the center and 400 in the south.

* Armed Forces of the Thai Peoples Revolution (AFTPR)
Armed wing of the PCS, established on the basis of the 121st battalion of the PCT. It had an estimated strenght of 200 to 300 armed men stationed in two camps in Laos, Khammouane and Savanaket.

* Asia 88
Small group, believed to be split off the Communist

Party of Thailand. It first emerged in 1982, when it was regarded as backed by Laos. From its headquarters and training center in Laos' Pak Se province it dispatched infiltrators into the north-east of Thailand.

* Committee for the Coordination of Patriotic and Democracy Loving Forces (CCPDF)
The CCPDF was formed in 1977 by the Communist Party of Thailand (CPT) and former members of the Socialist Party and the United Socialist Front. It was led by Udom Sisuwan. After the invasion of Kampuchea it split into a pro-Chinese and a pro-Vietnamese faction. The latter, led by Thoetphun Chaidi, sought refuge in Laos in 1979. The former CCPDF changed its name to North East Association for the Liberation of Thailand (NEALT).

* Communist Party of Malaya (CPM)
Maoist party, mainly Chinese from Malaysia who had entered southern Thailand in the early 1970s. It developed into a force of 3,500 guerrillas by 1975. Since then the number dwindled to an estimated 2,500 in 1978 and 1,300 in early 1987. Since 1976 Thai and Malaysian troops have organized several joint operations against the Malaysian guerrillas. It was reported that the CPM headquarters had been captured. In March 1987 114 guerrillas surrendered and another 800 surrendered in April 1987. They accepted Thailand's offer of amnesty on the condition that they not be sent back to Malaysia. The Thai government is to set up villages for the defectors along the border and provide each with farmland.

* Communist Party of Thailand
(Phak Communist Haeng Pratesthai) (CPT)
Established in 1952, the pro-Chinese CPT, supported by Meo tribesmen, began guerrilla activities in 1965. In 1969 it set up a military wing, the Thai People's Liberation Armed Force (TPLAF). It reached an estimated peak strength of 12,000 members following the 1976 coup. An amnesty and rehabilitation program reduced the CPT to an armed force of about 600 members. The party is led by Udom Sismuan.

* Communist Terrorist Organization (CTO)
An organization comprising CPM activists driven north of the Malaysian border. It numbered about 2,000 to 3,000 men in 1980. It was weakened by internecine feuds.

* Green Star
Pro-Vietnamese and pro-Soviet Thai guerrilla movement that broke away from the Communist Party of Thailand. It was said to have training camps in Laos in 1983.

* Internal Security Operations Command (ISOC)
Counter insurgency unit that replaced the Special Operations Command. It was restructured in early 1987. It was given an enlarged role likely to reduce that of the National Assembly.

* Islamic Brotherhood Party
(Persatuan Pemuda Rakyat Islam) (PAPERI)
A party set up by the CPM's 12th Regiment. It appeals to Malays and Pattani Moslems still reluctant to break with traditional Islam.

* Kuomintang Veterans
About 12,000 Kuomintang veterans went to Thailand in the late 1940s. Three thousand of them live in Mae Salong. By the 1980s the power of the warlords was waning as their armies became domesticized.

* Mujahideen Pattani
(Barisan Bersatu Mujahideen Pattani) (BBMP)
This separatist group based across the border in Kelantan State (Malaysia) was said to be operating in southern Thailand in early 1987.

* Muslim Seperatist Movement
A Moslem separatist movement in southern Thailand led by Datuk Mohammed Asri, a former Malaysian minister.

* National Revolutionary Front
(Barisan Revolusi Nasional) (BRN)
Obscure splintergroup of the Communist Party of Malaysia which emerged in the 1960s. It is committed to Marxism-Leninism, but largely devoted its activities to an attempt to wrest control of the lucrative extortion racket in the Betong Salient, where the CPM enjoyed a monopoly. It seeks the establishment of an independent Islamic and socialist state in Thailand's four southern provinces of Pattani, Narathiwat, Yala and Satan. It is led by Ustaz Abdul Karim ibn Haji Hasan, an Islamic teacher. Its military chief is Jehku Baka. It was said to have 2,300 armed men operating in Yala's Bannang Sata district in 1981. It was also said to be working closely with PULO in the jungle and mountain ranges of Pattani and Narathiwat.

* New Force
(Nawapol or Nawaphon)
Extreme right-wing Buddhist movement which was reported to have 500,000 members in the mid-1970s. It was said to be supported by wealthy businessmen and politicians and to have links with the National Security Council and Thai military intelligence. The movement is led by Dr.Watama Keovimal. In 1976 members of New Force were involved in violent action against left-wing students at Thammasat University (Bangkok), which led to the death of about 40 of them and to the

military coup.

* New Party
(Phak Mai)
Pro-Vietnamese Communist party formed in 1978/79 by Thoetphum Chaidi who had sought refuge in Laos after the split of the Communist Party of Thailand (CPT). By November 1979 the New Party was reported to be divided into a pro-Soviet, a pro-Chinese and a non-aligned faction. The party, numbering between 200 and 1,000 members, was reported to have been dissolved in September 1982.

* Pattani National Liberation Front
(Barisan Nasional Pembebasan Pattani) (BNPP)
Thai Moslem separatist organization founded in 1947, also known as National Liberation Front of Pattani. Its objectives are to liberate the homeland of the Moslem people of Pattani from the Thai colonialists; to reestablish as independent and sovereign the islamic state of Pattani; to uphold and protect Islam as well as the Malay-Moslem race, culture, traditions and customs; to support and work closely with the Moslem and Arab countries for advancement of Moslems all over the world and for world peace. It wants to regain the independence it lost to the Thais in the early 19th century when it was an independent kingdom. Since the death of its leader Tengku Jalal Nasae in 1977, the group appears to have declined. It has an estimated strength of 50 armed men. Its present leaders are Badril Hamdan (political head) and Bapa Idris (military commander).

* Pattani Islamic Nationalities' Revolutionary Party

(Phak Patiwat Phaochon Islam Pattani) (PPPIP)
A minor separatist guerrilla organization headed by Amin Tomina. It is believed to maintain contacts with some Arab countries. It seeks the secession of the five southern provinces of Yala, Songkhala, Pattani, Narathiwat and Sata. Favorite targets of assassinations are pro-government Moslem leaders.

* Pattani United Liberation Organization
(Petubohan Persatuan Pembebasan Pattani) (PULO)
Moslem secessionist movement founded in 1960. PULO fights for independence for three southern provinces, Pattani, Yala and Narithawat, which have been annexed by Thailand (then Siam) in the 19th century. Its political leader is Tengku Bira Kotanila (alias Kabir Abdul Rahman), who heads the unofficial government in exile of the 'Republic of Pattani'. Its military leader is Sama-eh Thanam. Its activities included bombings, arson attacks and kidnappings. In 1980 it had an estimated 3,000 to 4,000 armed men. PULO claims about 20,000 members. It is supported by several Middle Eastern countries, including Syria. Its headquarters is located in the Budoh hills.

* Ranger Units
Counterinsurgency units which took over tasks from the army in 1982. The units consisted of civilian volunteers recruited from communist infiltrated areas. In four years the Ranger force grew to about 160 companies totalling 13,000 men. The strategy of using guerrilla tactics to counter a similar guerrilla warfare approach used by the CPT, was devised by of Maj.Gen.Chaowalit Yongchaiyuth.

* Red Gaur Movement
(Krathing Daeng) (RGM)
Extreme right-wing organization formed in 1973 from technical college students, led by Maj.Gen.Sudsai Hasdin. It was involved in numerous acts of violence against members of the left-wing National Student's Centre during the election campaign of February-April 1976. Red Gaurs were involved in the storming of the university on Oct.6, 1976. Red Gaurs practised widespread intimidation, and assassinated peasant and labour leaders. They also acted as guards for civilian construction crews building roads through communist areas. The organization's leader was appointed as minister attached to the Prime Minister's office in 1981.

* Shan United Army (SUA)
Private army of Khun Sa (Chang Shi Fu) involved in heroin trafficking and related activities. It also strives for independence for the Shan people of eastern Burma.

* Socialist Party (SP)
Until 1976 this party used constitutional and parliamentary methods. After the military takeover this was no longer possible. In late 1976 the socialists joined the guerrilla forces of the Communist Party Thailand and the Committee for the Coordination of Patriotic and Democracy-loving Forces. The party is led by Colonel Somkid Srisangkom.

* Thai Moslems People's Liberation Armed Forces (TMPLAF)
Organization formed in August 1977 as an armed wing of the Communist Party of Thailand (CPT).

* Thai People's Liberation Armed Forces (TPLAF)
Military wing of the Communist Party if Thailand established in 1969. Its targets include government officials, provincial chiefs, road construction and timber workers. TPLAF activities expanded in 1976 when dissident urban students joined the insurgents. For two years their activities posed a serious threat to the government. As a result of Vietnam's invasion in Kampuchea in 1978 the TPLAF lost its safe havens in Laos and Kampuchea. By the early 1980s it had an estimated strenght of 13,000. A government amnesty policy

resulted in a decrease of activities.

* Way of God
(Sabil-Illah Movement)
Small fanatical Moslem fundamentalist sect which struggles for the independence of Thailand's southern provinces. Members have engaged in urban terrorism. On June 24, 1977, a bomb exploded at Bangkok airport.

TUNESIA

* Habib Dhaoui Group
An Islamic Jihad group that claimed responsibility for bomb attacks on four hotels in Sousse and Monastir on August 2, 1987. The group said the attacks were in retaliation for the execution of Habib Dhaoui in 1986, who was convicted for bomb attacks on police stations. During the trial he said that he belonged to the Islamic Jihad. The authorities believe that the Islamic Trend Movement has been responsible for the bomb attacks.

* Islamic Trend Movement
(Mouvement de la Tendance Islamique) (ITM)
Fundamentalist movement established in 1981 and led by Rachid Ghannouchi and Abdel Fatah Mourou. Violent incidents at a number of colleges and schools during February 1981 were officially attributed to activists of the newly formed MTI. On July 11-18, 1981 large-scale arrests took place among Moslem fundamentalists. Many members of the movement have fled to France. In March 1987, several MTI leaders were arrested and charged with instigating violent demonstrations of fundamentalist students. The group is held responsible for bomb attacks on hotels in Sousse and Monastir in August 1987.

* Popular Revolutionary Movement
(Mouvement Populaire Révolutionnaire) (MPR)
Tunesian authorities announced in November 1982 that about 10 'terrorists' belonging to this organization had been arrested as they were 'preparing criminal acts against certain institutions in the capital and its suburbs'.

* Progressive Nationalist Front for the Liberation of Tunesia
(Front Nationaliste Progressiste pour la Libération de la Tunesie) (FNPLT)
Illegal party led by Mahvez Saadawi. It is comprised of the Union Socialiste Arabe de la Tunesie (of Nasserites), the Mouvement Socialiste (of Baathists) and Youssefists (named after the late Salah Ben Youssef (murdered in the Federal Republic of Germany in 1961). It has been involved in several plots against President Bourguiba in the 1950s and 1960s. It has been inactive since 1979 when a number of persons were sentenced to prison terms for membership of the FNPLT.

* Tunisian Armed Resistance
(Résistance Armée Tunisienne) (RAT)
Military organization of Tunisians working in Libya. On Jan.28, 1981, the movement claimed responsibility for an attack launched on the previous day by some 50 armed men from Algerian territory against the Tunisian town of Gafsa. Those involved in the attack reportedly were part of a force of 7,000 volunteer soldiers and terrorists trained in 20 Libyan camps and recruited from Egypt, Tunesia, Algeria, Morocco, Mali, Niger, Chad, Guinea, Senegal and the Ivory Coast and also from the Philippines, Pakistan, South Korea and including some members of the Irish Republican Army (IRA).

TURKEY

* Akincilar
Fanatic religious youth association.

* Alevi Moslem Sect
Shiite group involved in political clashes with Sunni groups in 1978 at Kharamanmaras. A further riot at Corum led to the imposition of a curfew on May 28, 1980.

* Armenian Liberation Army (ALA)
Armenian terrorist group striving for the restoration of autonomy for the Armenian areas of eastern Turkey. In 1979, it claimed responsibility for two bombs placed at Istanbul international airport on May 6; for three bomb attacks on Turkish institutions in Paris on July 8 of that year; and also for attacks on the Turkish consulate-general in Geneva on Aug.23 and on the Turkish airlines office in Frankfurt (West Germany) on Aug.27.

* Armenian Liberation Movement
(Mouvement de Libération Arménienne) (ALM)
Organization of Armenians in France in support of the Armenian Secret Army for the Liberation of Armenia (ASALA).

* Armenian Secret Army for the Liberation of Armenia (ASALA)
Left-wing Armenian exile organization. ASALA seeks to revenge the Armenian genocide of 1915-22. Its ultimate goal is a 'united Armenia with a democratic, socialist and revolutionary government'. It was established in 1975, the 60th anniversary of the massacre. Together with the Justice Commandos of the Armenian Genocide, ASALA has been responsible for some 200 attacks in which 120 people were killed and hundreds of others were injured. Terrorist incidents were recorded in North

America, Asia, Europe and Australia. Most incidents took place in France (37), Switzerland (25), Italy (20), Lebanon (17), Turkey (14) and Spain (11). Other countries in which incidents were recorded were: Iran (10), Belgium (6), United Kingdom (5), Denmark (4), Canada (4), Greece (4), West Germany (4), Austria (3), Netherlands (2), Portugal (2), Australia (1), Iraq (1), Soviet Union (1), Bulgaria (1) and Yugoslavia (1). Activities peaked in 1981 and since then the number of incidents decreased to the pre-1979 level. Until 1979 less than 10 incidents were recorded, 1979 (29), 1980 (38), 1981 (47), 1982 (26), 1983 (13) and 1984 (6). The majority of the incidents were bomb attacks. The main targets have been Turkish diplomats and institutions in more than eleven countries. Activities are financed with money from robberies, extortion and drugtraffic. It has connections with Palestinian and European terrorist groups and Libyan and Syrian secret services. Its operational capability was significantly weakened as a result of the Israeli invasion in Lebanon in mid-1982. A militant faction in the Middle East and Greece wanted to continue with violent attacks. A more moderate faction in Europe advocated more selective attacks against Turkey. The latter faction was called ASALA-RM and was led by Monte Melkonian (alias Dimitriu Georgiu) and Ara Toranian. It wants to mobilize Armenians for a political struggle and to cooperate with other liberation movements, particularly the Kurds. The split resulted in factional murders. The organization re-emerged in 1986 which might be a sign that the differences between the two factions were settled. Its most militant leader, Hagop Hagopian (pseud.), refused to abandon the use of terror. He left ASALA's homebase, the 250,000 Armenians in Beirut, and set up his own headqurters in the Bekaa Valley. The Armenian movement used a variety of names to create the impression that its goals are supported by many like-minded groups and to confuse intelligence agencies. The 'people's movements for ASALA' in France, Canada, United Kingdom, India and the United States act as support organizations. ASALA reportedly had links with the PFLP (Lebanon), the Red Brigades (Italy) and Direct Action (France).

* Army for the Protection of Turkey's International Rights (APTIR)
This group is fighting the ASALA. It engaged in threats on French diplomats to force them to a crackdown on Armenian militants.

* Confederation of Nationalist Trade Unions (Milliyctci Isciler Sendikalari Konfederasyonu) (MISK)
Right-wing trade union organization led by Faruk Akinci. On July 17, 1979, he was given a prison sentence for taking part in a bomb attack, in which two persons were killed. The confederation was banned on Sep.12, 1980 when the military took state power.

* Federation of Turkish Revolutionary Youth (Türkiye Devrimci Genclik Dernekleri Federasyonu) (Dev Genc)
Left-wing terrorist organization set up by Atilla, an Ankara university student, in 1968. It engaged in bank robberies and attacks on US military personnel in the early 1970s.

* General Revolutionary Command Armenia (GRCA)
Umbrella organization whose directives synchronize operations undertaken by the Armenian Army for the Liberation of Armenia; the Commando of Armenian Avengers; the Justice Commandos for Armenian Genocide; the Boldikian Commando; the Kurken Menikian Commando; and the Armenian Revolutionary Army.

* Great Ideal Society
(Buyuk Ulku Dernegi)
A group linked with the National Action Party which has been responsible for acts of violence in the late 1970s.

* Grey Wolves
(Bozkurtlar)
Neo-fascist Turkish terrorist group active in Turkey and Western Europe. Members are drawn from the youth wing of the National Action Party (NAP) led by Col.Alparslan Turkes. The NAP has an extensive European network with more than 129 branches in major European centers. It has an estimated 3,000 hardcore activists. Turkish authorities accused the organization in 1981 of carrying out 694 murders in the years 1974 to 1980. Most of their victims were prominent Turkish left-wingers such as labour leaders, liberal journalists, academics and politicians. One of the Grey Wolves assassins is Mehmet Ali Agca, the young Turk who tried to assassinate Pope John Paul II on May 13, 1981. He has been sentenced to life imprisonment by an Italian court on July 22, 1981.

* Halk Der
Part of Devrimci Sol which is believed to act as front organization for the extremist activities the Revolutionary Left. It has been active in West Germany from where it supports members in Turkey in their armed struggle against the ruling regime. The West German government banned the organization.

* Hizb-i-Islam
A society of Moslem Kurds in Iran, Iraq, Syria and Turkey which reportedly received support from Libya, Syria and the Soviet Union. The movement

was believed to be a breakaway from the older Hizb-üt Tahrir which has the aim of uniting all Moslems under one caliph. It has been involved in armed clashes in Hakkari.

* Idealist Heart Youth Movement
Right-wing terrorist group.

* Idealistic Path
(Ulku Yolu)
Youth organization which has been responsible for political killings before the military takeover of Sep.12, 1980. On Jan.23, 1981, it was reported that 87 of the organization's members had been arrested at Bursa on charges of involvement in 30 murders during the past two years, and that warrants of arrest had been issued against 113 others. On Mar.19, 1981, it was announced that another 57 members had been arrested. In December 1985 a military court sentenced seven members to death. Fifty 86 members received prison sentences ranging from one to 36 years.

* June 9 Organization
Armenian group formed to exert pressure on the Swiss authorities to release Mardiros Jamkodjian, arrested for the murder of a Turkish consular employee in Geneva on June 9, 1981. It claimed responsibility for a number of explosions in 1981 targeting the Swissair office in Tehran, the Swiss Bundeshaus building in Berne, the Zürich international airport, a department store in Lausanne, Geneva's main railway station, a Swissair office in Copenhagen, a Swiss precision instruments office in Los Angeles and the Palace of Justice and other Swiss obkects.

* Justice Commandos of the Armenian Genocide (JCAG)
Right-wing nationalist Armenian terrorist organization with bases in the United States, Canada and the Near East. It was established in reaction to ASALA. Its long-term goal is an independent non-communist Armenia and compensation from the Turkish government for the crimes committed against the Armenian people. Its targets were Turkish diplomats in various countries, including the Turkish ambassdor to the Holy See (1977), the Turkish consul-general in Sydney (1980), the Turkish consulate-general in Los Angeles (1980) the Turkish diplomatic mission at the UN in New York (1980), a Turkish diplomat in Copenhagen (1981), the Turkish consulate-general in Los Angeles (1981), and the Turkish consul-general in Los Angeles (1982).

* Kawa
Left-wing Kurdish separatist organization. Several hundred members have been arrested in 1981.

* Kurdish Democratic Party (KDP)
Clandestine secessionist organization involved in assassinations between 1977 and 1980.

* Kurdish National Liberation Front (KNLF)
A spokesman of this front stated in March 1986 that the front had killed at least 24 Turkish soldiers in clashes in eastern Turkey.

* Kurdish Workers Party
(Patiya Karkeren Kurdistan) (PKK)
Kurdish secessionist movement established in 1974 and led by Abdullah Ocalan. In 1980 the party was held responsible for 200 murders as well as hold ups and kidnappings in eastern Turkey. More than 2,000 alleged members were arrested and later tried. In August 1984 the PKK launched an offensive after it joined a coalition with the Iraqi KDP of Bazargan. Since then more than 600 people have been killed, including 344 civilians. In March 1987 Turkey deployed 150,000 troops on the border with Syria, Iraq and Iran and stepped up activities against the Kurds, including bombing raids on Iraqi territory. According to Turkish intelligence Kurdish guerrillas are trained and armed by Syria. In recent years the PKK also has murdered defectors in other European countries, including Enver Ata (Uppsala, 1984) and Cetin Gungör (Stockholm, 1985) in Sweden, and others in West Germany (1986), the Netherlands (1987), Denmark, France and Switzerland. The party organ announced that all those cooperating with colonialists, imperialists and their collaborators would be liquidated.

* Leftist Liberation Army of Turkish Workers and Farmers (LLATWF)
Left-wing organization of Turkish workers and farmers which claimed responsibility for several murders in the violent years preceding the 1980 coup.

* Liberation
(Rizgari)
Secret Kurdish organization. Alleged members have been imprisoned and tortured.

* Marxist Leninist Armed Propaganda Unit
(Marksist Leninist Propaganda Silahli Birligi) (MLAPU)
Left-wing group established by Turkish students in the early 1970s in Paris. It was said to be the 'hit squad' of the Turkish People's Liberation Party. It was trained by Palestinian guerrillas in the Middle East. Targets included US servicemen and the manager of the Israeli El Al office in Istanbul. The MLAPU had contacts with European terrorist groups in Germany and Italy. One of its leaders, Zeki Yumurtaci, was assassinated in Istanbul on Sep.17, 1980.

* Milli Istihbarat Teskilati (MIT)
Turkish secret service which has special teams (Mehmets) operating abroad to murder Armenians. In the Netherlands, Nubar Yalimian reportedly was murdered by such a team.

* Moslem Brotherhood Union (MBU)
Islamic fundamentalist movement seeking the establishment of a state based on the rule of Koranic law. It has targeted left-wing terrorists as well as others.

* National Action Party
(Millyetci Hareket Partisi) (MHP)
Right-wing party established in 1948 and led by Col.Alparslan Türkes. It claimed a membership of over 300,000 in 1980. It is the political home of para-military groups such as the Grey Wolves, the Federation of Turkish Democratic Idealist Associations and the Great Ideal Society. It aspired to establish a fascist dictatorship in Turkey by forceful means, according to an indictment by Turkish martial law prosecutors. Its affiliates were actively engaged in the widespread political terrorism that tormented Turkey until the September 1980 coup. By August 1981 nearly 600 party activists were on trial, for many of whom, included Col.Türkes himself, the military prosecutor demanded the death penalty.

* National Salvation Party
(Milli Selamet Partisi) (NSP)
Islamic party founded in October 1972. It is a direct descendant of the National Order Party which was banned in 1971 by order of the constitutional Court for using religion for political purposes. The party was led by Necmettin Erbakan. It was held responsible in 1980 by the military for provoking political violence.

* New Armenian Resistance Group (NAR)
Armenian group which has been responsible for bombings in Belgium, France, Italy and Switzerland. The main targets were Soviet, British and Israeli travel agencies. It has been active until October 1980 when ASALA was convulsed by a power struggle.

* October Third Organization
Armenian group which took its name from the date of arrest of two ASALA members in Geneva. Following their arrest, the group attacked numerous Swiss targets to compel the Swiss authorities to release them (which happened in 1981).

* Orly Organization
Armenian group which took its name from Orly airport (Paris) where the French authorities, arrested a member of the ASALA on Nov.11, 1981. The group claimed responsibility for two attacks on the Air France office and the French Cultural center in Beirut on Nov.15, 1981, and for explosions at the Gare de l'Est in Paris on Nov.16, at the Air France office in Tehran on Nov.21, 1981, and again in Paris on Jan.16, 1982. It was widely believed that ASALA had directed its activities to bring about the release of the arrested (which was taking place).

* Pan Turkish Organization (PTO)
Organization which claimed responsibility for a bomb attack on the Bulgarian travel agency in Amsterdam (Netherlands). The attack was in retaliation against the Bulgarization campaign of the Turkish minority in Bulgaria.

* Partizan
Faction of the Maoist Turkish Communist Party, M-L. Fifty-one alleged members were on Jan.8, 1981, reported to have been arrested for killing six people, including a policeman, and for committing armed robberies and bombings. On Dec.6, 1981, two members (together with two security men) were killed in a shoot-out at Tunceli. Reso Yalim, a member of the underground group, possibly has been murdered by the Turkish secret service (MIT) in the Netherlands in November 1982.

* Progressive Youth Association (PYO)
Organization established to repel the commandos of the National Action Party after 1975. One PYO member was part of a team which hijacked a Turkish airliner to Bulgaria in May 1981, demanding the release of 47 political prisoners.

* Red Armenian Army (RAA)
Armenian group which has been responsible for the attack on the Turkish consul in the Netherlands on July 21, 1982.

* Resistance Front against Fascism (FKBDC)
Coalition of eight socialist or marxist oriented parties established in July 1982. In its program it was said that the fall of the fascist military dictatorship has to be accomplished by a prolonged armed struggle by a united left. Dev Yol and the PKK are members of the front.

* Revolutionary Left
(Devrimci Sol)
Left-wing terrorist group which broke away from Revolutionary Path in 1978. Its members waged an assassination campaign against the National Action Party. After September 1980, hundreds of Dev-Sol members were arrested and went on trial for killings, bomb attacks, robberies, extortions and other crimes with the aim of 'setting up a Marxist-Leninist social order'. Edip Erhan Eranil, the alleged Dev-Sol leader for the Ankara region, was arrested in Burgas (Bulgaria) after an

unsuccessful attempt to hijack a Turkish airliner on May 24, 1981. According to government sources Dev Sol co-operated with the PFLP of George Habash.

* Revolutionary Path Organization
(Devrimci Yol) (Dev Yol)
One of the major left-wing groups involved in the political violence between left and right which resulted in more than 5000 deaths in the late 1970s. The group broke away from the TPLA in 1975. In 1978 some of its members created a further split by founding the terrorist Revolutionary Left (Dev Sol). Since the Sep.1980 coup hundreds of members have been arrested and convicted in mass trials. In 1981 the headquarters of Dev Yol is believed to have been set up in Paris. Its six-member committee is reportedly headed by Gulten Cayan, whose husband Mahir Cayan, had been the leader of Dev Genc and the founder of the TPLA.

* Revolutionary Trade Unions' Federation
(Devrimci Isci Sendikalari Konfederasyonu) (DISK)
Established in 1967 and led by Abdullah Bastürk. It has about 400,000 members in 1980. After the September 1980 coup DISK's activities were suspended and many its members were arrested and tried. In December 1986 a mass trial ended. According to the verdict 28 affiliated syndicats have to be dissolved. Of the 1477 defendants 1166 were acquitted. Seven leaders including chairman Abdullah Bastürk were sentenced to prison for ten years. Cetin Uygur, the leader of the miners union, was charged with links to the terrorist organization Dev Yol and was sentenced to prison for 15 years.

* Revolutionary Vanguard of the People (RVP)
Armed group which formed part of the Front of the Liberation Party of the Turkish People. After the military takeover the prosecutor demanded the death penalty for 25 members of the group on charges of 'armed insurrection'.

* Socialist Party of Turkish Kurdistan
Marxist-Leninist group struggling for an independent Kurdistan. The party also operated under the name of Socialist Party of Iraqi Kurdistan. After the September 1980 coup several members have been detained.

* Suisse XV
Armenian group responsible for attacks on targets in Switzerland, including a match factory in Nyon on Jan.13, and a funicular at Crans-Montana on Jan.20, 1982. The actions served to bring about the release of Mardiros Jamkodjian, the murderer of a Turkish consular employee in Geneva.

* Turkish Communist Party, Marxist-Leninist (TKP-ML)
Maoist party founded by Ibrahim Kaypakkaya in 1973. The party also founded a 'Turkish Revolutionary Peasants' Liberation Army'. Kaypakkaya died in custody following the military takeover of September 1980.

* Turkish Communist Party
(Türkiye Komünist Partisi) (TKP)
Party established on Sep.10, 1920. After it was banned in 1923 it continued underground activities. Since World War II its headquarters are located in East Berlin. Following the military takeover in September 1980, hundreds of alleged party members were arrested.

* Turkish Communist Workers' Party (TKEP)
After the military takeover of 1980, a number of TKEP members were given death sentences for acts of political violence.

* Turkish Islamic Army (TIA)
Right-wing group which took responsibility for the July 22, 1980, assassination of Kemal Türkler, chairman of the Confederation of Revolutionary Trade Unions of Turkey (DISK).

* Turkish People's Liberation Party (TPLP or TKHP)
After September 1980 many members of this party were given death and prison sentences for involvement in murders and other crimes and for planning a coup to set up a Marxist-Leninist regime.

* Turkish People's Liberation Army
(Türk Halk Kurtulus Ordusu) (TPLA)
Left-wing terrorist organization established in 1970 under the leadership of Deniz Gezmis. It engaged in bank raids, kidnappings and murders. Denis Gezmis was arrested in 1971 and condemned to death. A political amnesty in 1974 allowed the TPLA to re-emerge in 1975, with training and arms provided by Palestinian groups. Its members attacked police posts, banks, right-wing newspaper offices and conservative party headquarters. The military coup of 1980 curtailed TPLA violence sharply.

* Turkish Security Forces
After a wave of political violence costing more than 5,000 lives, the military intervened onSep.12, 1980. While a total of 33,000 acts of political and religious violence occurred between December 1978 and September 1980, the three years following the coup showed a total of 7,500 violent acts. This decline was brought about by drastic repression. Over 66,000 people were detained for suspected terrorist activities, of whom over 8,000 had

received prison sentences by the end of 1982, with a further 18,000 in detention awaiting trial. Huge quantities of illegally held arms were seized, including 40,000 rifles and half a million handguns. By 1982 deaths from terrorism were reduced to an average of three per week. Demokrat Turkiye reported in September 1982 that the generals' regime had resulted in 170,000 arrests, 593 people killed in razzias, 125 people tortured, 21 people 'officially' executed and 4522 death sentences. Under pressure of Western countries the Turkish government promised to restore democracy. There have been continuous reports of repression and human rights violations. In November 1985 there were 15,569 political prisoners, including members of political parties, union members, writers, journalists, academics, Kurds and members of religious groups. Many prisoners have been tortured. According to official figures more than 600 policemen and military personnel have been sentenced to prison terms on charges of torturing. More than 5,000 complaints have been submitted. In 1985 Amnesty International presented a list of 100 names of persons who were assumed of having died in custody after torture.

* Turkish Workers' Peasant Party
(Türkiye Isci Köylü Partisi) (TWPP)
Maoist formation established in January 1978 under the leadership of Dogu Perincek.

* Turkish Labour Party
(Türkiye Isci Partisi) (TIP)
Left-wing socialist party founded in 1961 and led by Ms.Behice Boran. In 1971 the party was banned but re-emerged in 1975. In late February 1981, Behice Boran was deprived of her Turkish citizenship.

* Turkish Mafia
Bekir Celenk, one of the godfathers of the Turkish mafia was mentioned as one of the key figures in the plot to murder pope John Paul II. He fled to Bulgaria in 1980 where he was arrested by Bulgarian authorities in 1982. He reportedly had connections with the Bulgarian secret service and was involved in illegal arms deals.

* Turkish People's Liberation Front
(Türk Halk Kurtulus Cephesi) (TPLF)
Left-wing terrorist group set up by Mahir Cayan in the early 1970s. Members received training in Syria. launched an attack in which Cayan and nine collegues died. The hostages had been killed before the shoot-out. The TPLF suffered from splits, but it survived nonetheless as a vigorous violent faction in the late 1970s. Its activities were curtailed by the Sep.12, 1980 coup.

* Warriors of the Turkish People's Liberation Front
(WTPLF)
Terrorist group led by Omer Faruk Aydin. On Dec.17, 1980, the front's leader and five other members were arrested on suspicion of involvement in 35 political murders within three years, including the killing of a US serviceman on May 11, 1979. On Jan.7, 1981, four members were arrested in Antalya province for killing a US sergeant on Apr.12, 1979. Of a 'liberation faction' of this organization, ten leaders and over 200 active supporters were arrested later, as announced on Feb.13, 1981.

* Yaya Kashakan Suicide Squad
This group of four men, formed within the armenian Secret Army for the Liberation of Armenia (ASALA), attacked the Turkish consulate-general in Paris on Sep.24, 1981, killed a guard and took 51 persons as hostages pending the fulfillment of a demand for the release of alleged Armenian political prisoners in Turkey. Turkish authorities refused to negotiate with the attackers. On Sep.25 the French police stormed the building concerned, setting all the hostages free and arresting the four attackers, who were subsequently charged.

UGANDA

* Democratic Party (DP)
Nationalist party formed in 1954 under the leadership of Paul Ssemogerere. It advocates a policy of equality and social responsibility and has large Catholic support. It is based on the Baganda people. In 1980 it reportedly was training guerrillas in Kenya. In october 1986, a wave of arrests was reported, including David Lwanga, Andrew Kayyira and Evaristo Nyanzi. They were all associated with the DP or the army's 35 Battalion, made up exclusively of former UFA and FEDEMU fighters. The wave of arrests followed the discovery of a secret meeting of members of the 35 Battalion at the Colline Hotel, 20 kilometers from the capital, at which the government says a coup plot was being discussed. Some days later, the detainees appeared before a Kampala magistrate's court to be charged with treason.

* Falcon Star
Former British army men working for this British security company reportedly have been involved in training a new security force in Uganda in 1981.

* Federal Democratic Movement of Uganda (FEDEMU)
One of Uganda's guerrilla organizations which grew out of the UFF. Its military arm is the Federal Democratic Army. It was led by David Lwanga, Minister of Environment until his imprisonment in October 1986. In July 1985, it launched an operation called Opapex intended to liquidate what

it claimed was the 'government machinery for killing innocent civilians'. It called upon civilians to avoid any places in Kampala and other towns frequented by government personnel and officials. In January 1986, one of its leaders, G.Nkwanga was shot and killed.

* Force Obote Back (FOBA)
Guerrilla movement fighting for the return of Milton Obote. In June 1986 it was reported to store arms in the north of the country.
It is based on the Iteso people. In April 1987 it was reported to engage in systematic attacks on NRA convoys.

* Former Ugandan National Army (FUNA)
A guerrilla force of about 9,000 fighters, composed mainly of former Idi Amin soldiers. They have returned from Zaire and Sudan. The force is commanded by Idi Amin's old chief of staff, major General Isaac Lumago. It waged a sporadic and ineffectual resistance war against President Obote and his UNLA.

* Front for the National Salvation (FRONASA)
A guerrilla faction established by Yuweri Museveni. It was based on the Banyankole people.

* Karamojong and Turkana Cattle Raiders
Tribes with a long tradition of cattle raiding with primitive weapons. They acquired automatic weapons during the 1979 ouster of Amin. Since then they have been responsible for numerous massacres in the tribal areas on the eastern border. In 1984 Karamojong raiders took advantage of the death of major General Oyite Ojok, the Ugandan Army Chief of Staff, who kept a farm in the Karamojong area. They stole his cattle then set an ambush that reportedly killed more than 100 local militiamen pursuing them.

* Military Intelligence and Security (MIS)
Security organization set up under the Obote regime to deal with the guerrillas. It was divided in an Acholi and a Langi tribe faction. The Langi faction was called the Crack Unit. It kidnapped and murdered Ugandan exiles, particularly in Kenya.

* Movement of the Holy Spirit
More than 400 members of this obscure guerrilla group were killed by government forces in August 1987, when a group of 750 guerrillas attacked a train station in Soroti. Earlier government forces killed 200 members of the group. The group was reported to be led by Alice Lakwena, a priestess who said she was inspired by the spirits.

* National Resistance Army (NRA)
Military wing of the NRM under the leadership of Yuweri Museveni, the Minister of Defense and acting President under the interim regime of president Binaisa. The goal of the NRA was the overthrow of the Obote regime. Starting with 26 guerrillas it developed into a well-disciplined guerrilla army of 10,000 to 15,000 fighters (including 3,000 orphaned children under the age of 16). In early 1986 the army reached Kampala and succeeded in overthrowing the Okello government. During the For the first time in the history of post-colonial Africa a guerrilla movement supported by the population overthrew a corrupt and illegal military regime. Museveni improved the human rights situation and established a broadly based government. In the last stage of the struggle the NRA was able to employ brigade and battalion strength units in mobile warfare. Until 1982 the NRA had received arms from Libya. Since then, the guerrillas did not receive weapons from outside Uganda. Many of the NRA commanders were FRELIMO and Tanzanian trained and fought in the war which ousted Idi Amin. Only after it captured a large weapon depot, it had enough ammunition and reserves to sustain a longer offensive. In late 1986 fighting continued in the north between the NRA and remnants of the government army and former Amin soldiers. Some Acholi claimed a new 'Luwero triangle' had been created in the square between the towns of Gulu, Kitgun, Kalongo and Paranga. The NRA has yet to win the 'hearts-and-the minds' of the local population in the north.

* National Resistance Movement (NRM)
The NRM formed the political wing of the National Resistance Army whose goal it was to overthrow Obote. It was led by Professor Yusufu K.Lule and Yuweri Museveni. It was created on May 2, 1981, by a merger of the PRA, UFM, UFF, UNLFTW and ULG. It had support from the Baganda, Banyankole and Bantu people.

* National Security Service (NSS)(GS)(NASA)
Secret police organization under the Obote regime responsible for extensive human rights violations. It changed its name to General Service (GS) and later to NASA. It had its own academy in Cape Town Villas. Tony Masaba, a former agent of NASA, estimated the number of deaths under the Obote regime at 500,000. From his personal experiences he believed that UNLA government troops have been responsible for 50 percent of the deaths, the guerrillas for 40 percent and hunger and disease for eight percent. The remaining two percent of the total number of deaths were killed by NASA and other security organizations.

* People's Revolutionary Army (PRA)
Guerrilla organization led by Yuweri Museveni. It changed its name to National Resistance Army (NRA).

* Presidential Escort Intelligence Unit
Security organization under the Obote regime responsible for human rights violations.

* Rescue Pentagon
Group which claimed to have 1,000 armed fighters and reportedly to have been trained by five US trained commandos and Tanzanian instructors. It first emerged in August 1985.

* Special Brigade
Government unit set up under the Obote regime to deal specifically with guerrillas. Its headquarters were located in Katikamu.

* Uganda Freedom Fighters (UFF)
One of the Ugandan guerrilla organizations which joined the NRM.

* Uganda Freedom Movement (UFM)
Guerrilla organization based on the Baganda people and established in June 1979. It announced an armed struggle against the Obote regime on Feb.9, 1981. It had a joint leadership of B.K.Kirya, Dr.Andrew K.Kayiira (a former Interior Minister) nd Dr.Arnold Bisase. It attacked police posts in and around Kampala. Occasionally it did stop the passage of all goods on roads into the capital. It merged with NRM-NRA and UNRF to form the Ugandan Popular Front on Jan.7, 1982.

* Uganda National Liberation Front (UNLF)
A coalition of 22 externally based opposition groups established in Moshi (Tanzania) in March 1979. It was aimed at the overthrow of Idi Amin and pressed for the return of ex-President Obote. Idi Amin was toppled in April 1979 by the Tanzanian armed forces, which remained in Uganda until 1981.

* Uganda National Liberation Army (UNLA)
Force of 3,000 men from the Acholi and Langi peoples in the north. In early 1986, the UNLA was routed by the NRA headed by Yuweri Museveni, before fleeing to southern Sudan.

* Uganda National Rescue Front (UNRF)
A guerrilla organization composed of three groups of remnants from Amin's army predominantly from Kakwa and Aringa peoples, and groups led by former UPC secretary-general Felix Onama and former Amin Finance Minister Brig.Moses Ali. It had a collective strenght of 4,000 to 5,000 fighters and waged a sporadic and ineffectual resistance war against President Milton Obote and his UNLA. It operated mainly in the Western Nile districts. Prominent members were Maj.Gen.Isaac Lumago, Col.Emilio Mondo and Col.Christopher Mawadiri. The UNRF signed an agreement with the NRA and UFM in 1981.

* Ugandese Patriotic Movement (UPM)
The UPM was established as a political party in June 1980 with a view to contesting the general elections of Dec.10, 1980. It was led by Yuweri Museveni. It threatened to overthrow Militon Obote's regime by force. Yuweri Museveni went into hiding and set up his own guerrilla organization, first known as People's Revolutionary Army and later as the National Resistance Army.

* Uganda People's Democratic Movement (UPDM)
In 1986 UNLA and ex-Amin commandos met in Khartoum and Juba and formed this anti-Museveni resistance force. It said it expected to be able to recruit from some 5,000 UNLA soldiers (mainly from the Acholi people) and up to 15,000 Amin troops (mostly from West Nile) who are in exile in Sudan. Some members of FUNA and UNRF who refused to follow their leaders to Kampala, were said to have joined the front. In October 1986, someone identifying himself as John Okello had told the BBC that a rebel organization calling itself the UPDM was waging war against the NRM, claiming that it was undemocratic. Okello said that the UPDM wanted talks with the government leading to their inclusion in the administration in Kampala, a demand immediately rejected by the NRM, which said it refused to include 'criminal elements and killers' in its coalition. The NRM also hinted that the rebels were being supported by external forces who wanted to see a weak administration in a country which would bend to foreign demands. Its military wing is called the Ugand People's Democratic Army.

* Uganda Popular Front (UPF)
Common front formed in 1982 by all Ugandan exile groups except the Ugandan National Liberation front (UNLF). The declared aim of the UPF was to co-ordinate all opposition groups and to overthrow the Obote government by force.

* Uganda People's Congress (UPC)
Party led by Milton Obote. It is based on the Langi people. The UPC gained much support from the protestant electorate. It was reported to have murdered candidates of the Democratic Party and to have formed an armed force based on the northern peoples with the help of Tanzania.

<u>UNITED KINGDOM</u> (for Northern Ireland see separate entry)

* Angry Brigade
Anarchist student group responsible for 19 bomb and machine gun attacks, mainly in the London area. The attacks were not designed to cause the loss of life. Targets included a fashionable clothes store in Kensington, the Miss World contest at the

Albert Hall, a London Territorial Army center, a police computer at Tintagel House and the homes of the London Metropolitan Police commissioner and attorney general. In August 1971 the Stoke Newington eight were arrested. A year later, four of them, Anna Mendelson, Hilary Greek, John Barker and Jim Greenfield, were sentenced to ten years in prison each in 1972. The name 'Angry Brigade' was again used in recent years. Responsibility was claimed in the name of the group for bomb attacks on a prison officers' training college in Wakefield (Nov.1982), a Conservative Party's headquarters in Leeds (Jan.1983) and a building housing British Airways and American Express in London (Apr.1986). In a pamphlet it announced that it had become angry again and that it was prepared to defend itself 'against the provocations of a virulently anti-working class State and its multi-national manipulators...'. It also declared that 'The social revolution will not be built on the corpses of the old rulers or their functionaries; it can only be built by people taking control of their own lives, asserting their independence, their rejection of the State, of power politics, of authoritarian life-styles and the competitive values of consumerism forced on us from birth to death'. It rejected the 'mindless terror' of other groups like the R.A.F, Red Brigades, P.L.O or 'any other authoritarian group committed to a struggle for power or control of the State at the expense of the man and woman in the street'.

* Animal Liberation Front (ALF)
Animal welfare group formed in 1976 under the alleged leadership of Ronald Lee. It has engaged in raids to rescue animals and raids on fur shops and fur farms, bomb letters and poisoning threats (cyanide in candy bars and cigarettes). In 1984 five times as many actions were recorded as in 1983. On Feb.5, 1987, ten members of the group were sentenced to imprisonment on charges of arson and criminal damaging. Ronald Lee was sentenced to 10 years in prison.

* Animal Rights Militia (ARM)
Animal welfare group which broke away from the Animal Liberation front (ALF). It raided breeding and animal research establishments. In January 1986 ARM planted car bombs on the vehicles of Peter Savage, sales director of an animal importing and breeding firm, and Brian Meldrum, head of a psychiatric research team. Other targets were Alan Armitage, director of a research laboratory and professor Ted Evans, head of a university neuro-science unit. Warnings were given and none of the bombs exploded. In 1982 the group had directed a bomb letter to Mrs.Margaret Thatcher.

* Anti-Nazi League
Left-wing organization formed in 1975 to counter the extreme right-wing movements. It was sponsored by the Socialist Workers' Party as well as others and played an important part in opposing the election campaign of the National Front during the 1979 general elections. Members organized counter-marches to those planned by the NF, often seeking confrontation in the streets. One of the worst examples was that of Southall (London) in April 1979, when one man died and scores of police and demonstrators were injured.

* Army for Freeing Scotland (AFS)
Scottish group of three men which has been responsible for placing bombs in Glasgow in June and September 1975.

* Army of Gael
(Armach Nan Gaidheal) (ANG)
Scottish nationalist group which claimed responsibility for starting a fire on Nov.24, 1982, at a location in Edinburgh where the Prime Minister Margaret Thatcher was scheduled to address Scottish Conservatives.

* Army of the Provisional Government of Scotland ('Tartan Army')
Scottish nationalist organization which emerged in 1973. Its aim was to free Scotland of its 'British yoke' by revolutionary means. The organization was variously known as 'the 100 Organization', the 'APG', the 'Border Clan' and the 'Tartan Army'. It claimed responsibility for sabotage attacks on an oil pipeline on Sep.1, 1973, on the Clyde tunnel, and on the railway line near Dunbarton East station. Eight of the organization's members were, in April and May 1975, sentenced to imprisonment for up to 12 years.

* British Movement (BM)
Anti-immigration and anti-semitic organization formed in 1968 by Colin Jordan. The BM was by 1980 organized in some 25 branches. It has claimed a membership of 4,000. It encourages military training and has its own Leader Guard which has a reputation for violence. The BM has also been reported as having provided mercenary units for foreign wars.

* Column 88
Right-wing organization formed in 1970. (The 8 refers to the eighth letter of the alphabet, standing for Heil Hitler). Membership is said to be highly selective. The group has carried out a number of attacks on left-wing bookshops. It is said to have contacts with terrorist right-wing groups in Italy and Belgium, as well as with Palestinian groups.

* College for the Welsh People's Movement

(Mudidad Coeg I'r Cymry)
Group which claimed responsibility for damaging a computer at the University College of Wales in Aberystwyth in protest against the College authorities' refusal to increase Welsh language education.

* Free Wales Army
(Mudiad Amddiffyn Cymru) (MAC)
Welsh nationalist group which claimed responsibility for a number of arson attacks against English holiday homes in Wales in 1980. It has also been responsible for a fire-bomb attack on the Conservative Party office in Cardiff on Mar.28, 1980.

* KMS
London security organization run by David Walker, an ex-SAS major, and James Johnson, an Ex-Guards officer. The organization has been hired by the British government on several occasions. It has recruited mercenaries for its operations abroad. In 1985 KMS sent a team of 100 men to Sri Lanka with the tacit support of the British government to assist in the struggle against Tamil insurgents. In 1986 an agent of KMS was moved to a base in Honduras to help train and to fly missions for the contras. KMS' biggest contract was to help keep the Sultan of Oman in power.

* League of St. George (LSG)
Right-wing organization established in 1974 by former members of the Union Movement of Sir Oswald Mosley. The League acts as an umbrella organization of fascist movements in Europe.

* Makhno's Secret Army (MSA)
Anarchist group which has been involved in attacks against Soviet targets.

* Movement for the Defense of Wales
(Cadwyr Cymru) (CC)
Welsh group (also operating under the names Sons of Glendower and the Workers' Army of the Welsh Republic) which has been involved in a number of arson attacks in 1980 against English holiday homes in Wales and against Conservative Party premises in Cardiff and Shotton (Clwyd). Only occasional incidents were recorded in the early 1980s. A handful of militants were jailed in November 1981 for arson.

* National Front (NF)
Xenophobic organization formed in 1967 out of a merger of the Racial Preservation Society, the British National Party and the Greater Britain Movement. It has several thousand supporters led by Colin Jordan, John Tyndall, and Martin Webster. It has engaged in street violence. Several members were sent to jail.

* National Socialist Movement (NSM)
Breakaway group of the British National Party formed by Colin Jordan and John Tyndall. It was later joined by Martin Webster. In 1982 Colin Jordan was proclaimed 'World Führer' of a World Union of National Socialists.

* Scottish National Liberation Army (SNLA)
Small Scottish extremist group responsible for parcel bombs sent to British government ministers. Like the other Scottish groups which have emerged over the past 15 years the SNLA want to see the Treaty of Union of 1707 between Scotland and England revoked, and an independent Scotland re-established.

* Second of April Organization
Nationalist group named after the day of the attack on the Falkland Islands. It has claimed responsibility for a bomb letter sent to Mrs.Margaret Thatcher and an attack on the headquarters of the US Navy in London in March 1982.

* Skinheads
Loosely organized youths gangs that have been exploited by right-wing organizations in street violence.

* Spearhead
The paramilitary wing of the British National Party.

* Special Advisory Service (SAS)
Security company supervised by the US CIA, British MI-6 and the French SDECE. Its aim was to recruit mercenaries to fight the A.Neto regime in Angola. It was established in 1975 and was headed by Leslie Aspin, a journalist who worked for MI-6.

* Special Air Service Regiment (SAS)
Elite, Army unit trained for undercover operations and anti-terrorist action. It was founded in July 1941 by Lt.Col.David Sterling of the Scots Guards. After 1945 SAS squadrons were sent to Malaya, Kenya, Borneo, Yemen, Aden, Oman, Northern Ireland and the Falkland campaign. SAS troopers are trained to work in 16-man 'troops' each divided into four-man sub-units. Since 1972 the SAS formed Counter Revolutionary Warfare (CRW) teams.

* SS Wotan 71
Right-wing terrorist group that emerged in 1976. It has operated under various names (Adolf Hitler Commando, the Iron Guard and the Knights of the Iron Cross) against minorities and the property of left-wing organizations. Its principal organizers

have been named as David Wilson and Michael Noonan (a former head of the Leader Guard of the British Movement).

• Stirling GB-75
A private militia which was specially trained for clearing occupied factories. It was headed by David Sterling, who in 1978 had been involved in the recruitment of mercenaries to fight in Zimbabwe and South Africa. It reportedly had close contacts with the SAS.

• Watchguard
Recruitment office for mercenaries headed by David Sterling. It has been involved in a British attempt to overthrow the regime of Col.Qadhafi in Libya in 1970. The operation code-named Hilton was planned to be executed by the 23st SAS. The operation included an attack of the prison in Tripoli, the release of the old guard of the Idriss regime and the overthrow of Qadhafi. It failed after a first reconnaissance commando was captured by the Italian secret service. The Foreign Office assured that it had no responsibility for the operation. Umar al-Shalhi, a royalist Libyan politician and 'some SAS veterans' were blamed for the operation. Since then Col.Qadhafi has supported the IRA.

• Welsh Language Society
(Cymdeithas yr laith Cymraeg)
Welsh organization established in 1962 which campaigned for a separate Welsh television channel and for increased use of the Welsh language in radio broadcasts. Some members of the society burnt cottages owned as second homes by English people. Between December 1979 and the end of 1982 there were more than 60 arson incidents against second homes in Wales owned by non-residents of Wales. Damage was also done to television relay stations in Avon, Somerset ans Sussex during 1980 as part of a campaign for a Welsh television channel. Its present chairman is Karl Davies.

UNITED STATES

• Animal Liberation Front (ALF)
Animal welfare group which has been involved in attacks on medical and pharmaceutical laboratories.

• Armed Resistance Unit (ARU)
Terrorist group which emerged in April 1983. It has claimed responsibility for three attacks in solidarity with the revolutionary struggles of the peoples of Central America and the Caribbean. Targets were the National War College at Fort Mc.Nair and the Navy Yard's Computer Operations Complex in Washington, D.C. This was followed by the bombing of the US Capitol Building on July 11. This was meant as protest against US invasions of Grenada and in Lebanon. Perhaps the group is identical with the UFF.

• Army Intelligence Support Activity (AISA)
The Pentagon allegedly had set up a secret unit for intelligence and covert operations. The unit was established in 1980 and conducted clandestine operations without a presidential finding.

• Army of God
Anti-abortion groups have since March 1982 been responsible for 42 bombings, and more than 150 'acts of vandalism' on abortion clinics all over the United States. In addition to bombing and vandalism of abortion clinics anti-abortionists have perpetrated one kidnapping (1982) and have fired a shot through the window of Supreme Court Justice Harry Blackman's home in March 1985. Anti-abortion terror groups have been operating under a number of names including The Army of God, God's Army and the Armies of the Living God. Behind these attacks stand fundamentalist Christians frustrated by the failure of conventional lobbying to halt abortion. So far, no one has been seriously injured, and most clinics have been attacked when they were empty. A nationwide investigation has failed to uncover evidence that the attacks are the work of an organized group. The anti-abortion movement reportedly is increasingly attracting persons from the fringes of the Identity movement. The Posse Comitatus, for instance, has stated that abortion is part of a global conspiracy 'masterminded' by the Jews.

• Aryan Nations Church (ANC)
Right-wing American 'umbrella' organization linking like-minded groups such as the Christian Identity Movement, The Order, The Covenant, The Sword and the Arm of the Lord (CSA), the Ku Klux Klan and Posse Comitatus. It was founded in 1974 by Christian fundamentalist Richard Girnt Butler. Through a computerised 'bulletin board' known as the Arayan Liberty Net the Aryan Nations have forged contacts with most of the right-wing groups in the US and Canada. It has branches in 18 states and it has an estimated 40-500 active and 6,000 passive members united by a doctrine called Identity. They believe that Aryans, or whites of north European stock, are the true nation of Israel. They regard modern America as hopeless degenerate and overrun by inferior races, and have threatened white-supremacist violence. It has discussed plans for a 'sanctuary', a separate nation for them and their kind, in Idaho, Washington, Montana and Wyoming. As group it has not engaged in violent acts, though members of associated groups have been involved in bombings, assassinations and armed robbery. Its sources of economic support are donations, contributions and

money obtained through bank and armored car robberies and counterfeiting operations staged by The Order.

* Bible Camp of the Life Science Church
Extreme right-wing sect which has a paramilitary compound. Members donate their possessions to the church to avoid taxes and have maintained that because the church owns their weapons they cannot be prosecuted on any charges of illegal possession of fire arms.

* Black Liberation Army (BLA)
Believed to be a breakaway group of the Black Panther Party which engaged in the killing of policemen since it emerged in 1971. The group had about 100 members in the early 1970s. Joanne Chesimard, a reputed BLA leader, was sentenced to life imprisonment for the murder of a New Jersey state trooper in 1973 but escaped from prison on Nov.2, 1979. Marilyn Buch, who was described as the only White member of the BLA, was one of eight persons charged with involvement in the robbery organized by the Weather Underground on Oct.20, 1981, although she had not been captured.

* Black Moslem Movement (BMM) or Nation of Islam
Racist, ascetic, anti-white Moslem sect, formally known as the Nation of Islam, was founded in Detroit by W.D.Fard, who claimed to have come from Mecca but who eventually disappeared. He was succeeded as leader of the sect by Elijah Poole (or Elijah Muhammed), who advocated complete separation for negroes in a closed economic society to be established in two or three states of the USA. The organization became increasingly conservative after 1964 and took no further part in the civil rights movement but engaged in developing its business interests. It established mosques and its membership was estimated at several hundred thousands. Dissident young members of the movement, who opposed these developments, were responsible for a clash with police on Jan.10, 1972, leading to the death of two policemen and two Negroes. The emergence of the charismatic Malcolm X created tensions and eventually a split. Eliyah Mohammed and his followers were blamed (but never convicted) for the assassination of Malcom X in New York in 1965.

* Black Panther Party (BPP)
Black power movement established in Oakland, California, in October 1966, by Huey.P.Newton and Bobby Seale. It first advocated only defensive violence but grew increasingly violent after the assassination in 1968 of the black leader Martin Luther King. It engaged in gunfights, bomb attacks and acts of sabotage. In May 1971 it renounced violent tactics to work 'within the system'. Many leading party members were imprisoned or shot by the police, or went into exile. The party alleged at the end of 1969 that 28 Black Panthers had been killed by the police (which put the figure at 10). BPP leaders included Eldridge Cleaver, Stokely Carmichael, David Hilliard and Rap Brown. At its peak it had an estimated 2,000 members.

* Central Intelligence Agency (CIA)
Principal foreign intelligence-gathering organization of the United States of America. Based at Langley, Virginia, but with 'stations' and outposts throughout the world, the CIA is one of the biggest intelligence bureaucracies in the world. It has an estimated full-time staff of 18,000 to 20,000. William Webster (head of the FBI) replaced William Casey as its head in 1987. Its clandestine activities are the responsibility of the Operations Directorate. What used to be called 'covert operations' are now known as 'special activities'. There has been a sharp expansion of covert activities under the Reagan administration. Since 1979 the expansion meant at least a fivefold increase to over 50 continuing operations. About half of these are said to be in central America with a large percentage in Africa. In recent years the CIA has operated in Iran, Afghanistan, Nicaragua, Guatemala, El Salvador, Surinam and Mauritius, Philippines and Honduras. CIA personnel trained anti-terrorist units of foreign governments as part of the Reagan administration's stepped-up policy of combatting terrorism around the world. The training has been conducted in about a dozen of countries, including Lebanon and Honduras. Repeatedly US-trained anti-terrorist forces engaged in terrorist acts and human rights violations. In the past, CIA counter-insurgency activities like 'Operation Phoenix' (South Vietnam, 1968-1971) have resulted in large numbers of casualties.

* Civilian Military Assistance (CMA)
In 1983 four right-wing members of the Alabama National Guard, formed this group to supply and assist anti-Communist forces in Central America. One of the founders, Dana Parker, a Huntsville police detective, was killed on Sep.1, 1984, when the helicopter they had flown across the Honduran border was shot down by Nicaraguan soldiers. Thomas Vincent Posey acts as its national director. The group has about 1,000 members in Alabama, Tennessee and Missisippi, many of them are Vietnam veterans. In 1985 it raised $ 4 million for the contras in Nicaragua. In 1986 it reportedly sent $ 200.000 in non-lethal equipment to the FLNA of Holden Roberto in Angola.

* Committee 208
In 1986 the Washington Post reported that a secret governmental working group had been established

to coordinate clandestine and paramilitary sabotage projects in anti-Western countries in the Third World. The group is named after the building where its meetings are held. The group consists of representatives of the White House, the Ministry of Foreign Affairs, the Pentagon and the CIA. According to the Washington Post, the CIA has a budget of $ 25 billion dollar annually for secret military interventions. Countries where the CIA is reported to have operated recently are Afghanistan, Nicaragua, Angola, Iran, Lebanon, Ethiopia, Liberia, Chad, Surinam, Mauritius.

* Coordination of United Revolutionary Organizations
(Coordinacion de Organizaciones Revolucionarias Unidas) (CORU)
Florida-based umbrella organization for right-wing Cuban exiles in the United States founded in June 1976 by Orlando Bosch Avila. Among the groups supposedly represented were Cuban Action, Cuban National Liberation Front, the Bay of Pigs Veterans' Association and the National Cuban Movement. Members attacked Cuban government interests in Miami, Washington, New York and Puerto Rico. The worst incident was the explosion of a bomb on a Cuban airliner in mid-flight in October 1976, killing 73 persons. The group also attacked Venezuelan and Mexican government property.

* The Covenant, The Sword, The Arm of the Lord (CSA)
Anti-semitic white supremacist organization founded by Jim Ellison. He organized a paramilitary camp near the Bull Shoals Lake in Arkansas where he is living together with 100 heavily armed disciples and their families. Ellison called his church 'Zarephath Horeb', the name of a biblical purging place. The group engaged in bombings, arson, and vandalism. In April 1985 police arrested four men in the Mountain Camp where they discovered many weapons and explosives.

* Croation Liberation Fighters (CLF)
Underground group of Croatian exiles who support a free an independent Croation state and the break up of Yugoslavia. It has been active in 1980.

* Crusade for Justice
Chicano movement in the southwest involved in the supply of explosives for Puerto Rican FALN bombing operations in the midwest and northeastern states.

* Delta Force
Anti-terrorist unit of the United States Army. It is closely modelled on the British Army's Special Air Services (SAS) regiment. Delta Force was set up by Colonel Charles Beckwith in 1977. Presently it numbers about 800 men from the Army Special Operations Forces (SOF), a special helicopter unit from the 101st Air Assault Division, Navy Seals, and Marine reconnaissance teams. Air Force special operation units from the 23rd Air Force at Eglin AFB in Florida support the Fort Bragg-based counter-terrorist unit. Delta has been involved in operations in Tehran, Grenada, the Meditteranean, and according to some sources, in support of the Nicaraguan Contra guerrillas on the Nicaragua/Honduras border. The force is built on four-man patrols each member of which has a special skill. Like the SAS, Delta Force specialises in Close Quarter Battle (CQB) training, the solving of hostage-taking situations, and resolving the hijacking of aircraft, trains, ships and buildings. Delta Force is based at Fort Bragg in North Carolina but has an advance unit in Europe. The unit is also assigned to gathering information on tactics and operations of other anti-terrorist groups.

* Democratic International (DI)
An alliance of four anti-Soviet insurgent movements from Africa, Asia and Central America established in Jamba (Angola) in June 1985. The conference in Jamba was organized by a US lobbying group called Citizens for America led by L.E.Lehrman, a millionaire Republican who ran unsuccessfully for governor of New York in 1982. An accord was signed by Dastagir Wardak of the Afghan Mujahideen, Pa Kao Her of the Ethnic Liberation Organizations of Laos, Adolfo Calero of the Nicaraguan FDN and Jonas Savimbi of the Angolan UNITA. It was unclear in which areas the organizations were going to co-operate. It was not the first attempt to unite the anti-communist resistance. In 1984 17 organizations participated in the International Conference for the Resistance in Occupied Areas led by Pierre Vilmarest in Paris. The organizations talked about mutual exchanges of troops and weapons. It was reported that the Afghan Mujahideen had supplied weapons to the MNR in Mozambique.

* European Labor Party (ELP)
An organization founded in 1974 by Helga Zepp-La Rouche, the wife of Lyndon H.La Rouche. It developed into a worldwide movement with branches in West Germany, Sweden, Denmark, Italy and France. It supports European unification, a strong US-European alliance and the nuclear power industry. It is stridently anti-communist in its public statement and it frequently criticizes the Soviet Union. Its membership is variously reported as ranging from several hundred up to 2,000. It advocates strong measures against the sale and use of illegal drugs and calls for the swift development of the Third World. It published a book on the Greens in West Germany to justify a demand that

the party be legally banned because of purported communist and terrorist connections. It made a 180-degree reorientation from 'Soviet friendly' to 'Soviet hostile'. It has an international network of correspondents for its publication Executive Intelligence Review. An alleged member of the party is sought by the Swedish police in connection with the assassination of Olaf Palme (Sweden). See also NDPC.

* Federal Bureau of Investigation (FBI)
The main internal security arm of the United States. It was set up in 1908. It has 9,100 specialized agents and a budget of $ 1,2 billion a year. It is based in Washington with 'field offices' around the country. The FBI spent most of its resources fighting organized crime. During World War II were given an anti-espionage and internal security role. As the main Federal agency responsible for combating internal terrorism, the FBI has developed Special Weapons and Tactics (SWAT) teams which operate through a special command-and-control centre. In 1978 William Webster took command of the agency. Under him the FBI has expanded while dramatically shifting the focus of its investigations. It now concentrates on white-collar crime, corruption by public officials and espionage. The FBI also intensified drug investigations, an area largely ignored under Mr.Hoover. In recent years it attempted to broaden the scope of the National Terrorism Research Analysis Center, begun in 1980. The center analyzes incidents, finds patterns between groups and assesses their threats. The number of terrorist incidents in the US has declined dramatically in recent years from 1977 (100), 1980 (29), 1981 (42), 1982 (51), 1983 (31), 1984 (8). The decline was the result of FBI arrests of members of terrorist groups including Armenian, Croatian and Puerto Rican groups. In 1983 the FBI was given important new powers to investigate groups that might turn to terrorism. In 1987, W.S.Sessions replaced W.Webster, who became head of the C.I.A.

* Freedom Flotilla Refugees (FFR)
A group of Cuban refugees wishing to return home. Individuals have been involved in a number of hijackings.

* FUQRA
A Moslem sect which has attempted to eliminate rival Moslem groups, such as the Ahmaddiya Movement of Islam (AMI), in order to purify their Islam. It engaged in assassinations, molotov cocktail attacks and arson in 1983 and 1985.

* George Jackson Brigade (GJB)
Group named after a black writer killed in August 1971, during a prison riot in San Quentin jail. The group engaged in bank robberies and bombings in the states of Oregon and Washington in the mid-1970s.

* Inter American Defense Force (IADF)
Cuban exile group dedicated to the armed overthrow of the governments of Nicaragua, Cuba and Panama. In 1981, 800 exiles have been trained in a camp near the Florida Everglades. Hector Fabian was named as one of the group's leaders. J.Gonzalez ('Bombadillo' or 'Light Bulb') acted as military commander. It said that it was financed by Panamanian and Cuban exile groups and fund-raising efforts by Nicaraguans.

* Islamic Guerrilla of America (IGA)
Group which reportedly had been involved in the 1980 Bethesda, Maryland, murder of Ali Akbar Tabatabai, a former Iranian diplomat.

* Jewish Armed Resistance (JAR)
Breakaway group of the Jewish Defense League which reportedly has been responsible for an attack on two members of the PLO on June 18, 1982.

* Jewish Defense League (JDL)
Right-wing Jewish group established in September 1968 by Rabbi Meir Kahane in New York City. Members consider violence necessary to protect Jewish rights and support Israel. It claimed to have an estimated 13,000 members and is led by Irv Rubin. It has branches in eight US cities and seven countries. It has been responsible for several assassinations and bomb attacks. On Oct.11, 1985, a bomb exploded at the office of the American-Arab Anti-Discrimination Committee in Santa Ana, California, killing one person and wounding seven others. Other targets were connected with the Soviet Union and former Nazis. The JDL broke up in 1978/79 in the Jewish Armed Resistance, Jewish Action Movement and the New Jewish Defense League.

* Jewish Direct Action (JDA)
A Jewish group which emerged on Feb.23, 1984, with the explosion of three bombs at the Soviet residential complex in the Bronx.

* John Birch Society (JBS)
Established by Robert H. W. Welch in 1958, this right-wing organization had about 100,000 members in 1960s but now has shrunken to half that number. The organization was widely denounced in the 1960s as conspirational, fascist, anti-semitic and un-American, then virtually ignored for years. R.H.Welch resigned as leader in 1983 and died two years later. In 1985 it reportedly mounted a recruiting campaign. The Society opposes the Civil Rights Act of 1964, US membership of the UN and NATO, and all exchanges with the Soviet Union.

* Joint Terrorist Task Force (JTTF)

Elite force of FBI and local police 'red squad' agents. The unit operates in many cities and has recently received a multi-million dollar funding for expanding its operations coast-to-coast. It even operates outside the United States.

* Ku Klux Klan (KKK)
White-supremacist organization established in 1865 in the southern states. It is dedicated to 'defending' White America against the advance of blacks and other 'inferior' races. James Ferrands was installed as Imperial Wizard on Sep.1, 1986. National membership declined from an estimated 10-12,000 in 1981 to 6-7,000 in 1986. The Klan has a long history of terrorism and violence, mainly against blacks, but also against Jews, Roman Catholics, homosexuals and left-wingers. It has para-military training camps in Seabrook. In recent years the Klan has developed links (and overlapping membership) with other right-wing organizations such as Aryan Nations, the Posse Comitatus and the Order. It also tried to recruit the hard-pressed farmers of the Middle West by blaming the agricultural crisis of the 1980s on 'bankers and Zionists operating through the Federal Reserve System' and warning that 'the Jew plan is to steal your land'. It advocates the initiation of a race war with the eventual goal of establishing a 'white Christian republic'.

* Land and Freedom
(Tierra y Liberdad)
Movement of Mexican Americans (Chicanos) aimed at the mobilization of the Chicanos as part of a Third World Liberation Front with other revolutionary minorities in the United States. It seeks to gain control, by electoral means, of regions where Chicanos are in the majority; to recover land of which they have been expropriated; to boycott 'Anglo-American' businesses; and to form Chicano political parties and armed groups to organize 'counterviolence' and to carry out 'revolutionary justice' on 'collaborationists, accommodationists and agents', who play a 'neo-colonialist' role.

* Legion of Doom
A highschool vigilant group at Fort Worth, Texas, which has been active in 1985. The group, believed to have nine or 10 members is suspected of multiple pipe bombings, fire bombings, possessing unlawful weapons, criminal terrorist threats and cruelty to animals. Pets had been slaughtered and their blood smeared on automobiles as a warning to their owners. Students and others received warnings marked with swastikas.

* Mafia or Cosa Nostra
For more than three decades, five major organized-crime syndicates in the New York area, collectively called the Mafia or La Cosa Nostra, have been active. The leaders of the five groups were indicted in 1985 for being members of a 'commission' that federal prosecutors say governs the group's participation in such illegal activities as narcotics trafficking, loan sharking, gambling, labor racketeering, automobile theft, truck hijacking and extortion. The five families are the Gambino family (250 core members), the Genovese family (200 members), the Colombo familiy (115 members), the Bonanno family (195 members) and the Luchese family (100 members). In April 1986 a federal commission said that the mafia remained a dominant force in an underworld that makes $ 100 billion a year. In early 1987 the Mafia was said to be a dying organization. A leading federal prosecutor said that it will cease to be a major threat within the next ten years. The decline was attributed to the rigorous prosecution under strengthened racketeering laws and the shifting demographics that have made it difficult for Mafia leaders to recruit new members from an upwardly mobile Italian-American community. This would not mean the end of organized crime. Twenty to 25 other organizations drawing their members from various racial and ethnic groups have emerged in recent years.

* May 19 Coalition (or May 19th Communist Organization)
Marxist-Leninist group established in 1978. A breakaway from the Weather Underground-linked Prairie Fire Organizing Committee. It perceived its mission as the development and strengthening of links between political and militant blacks and Hispanics and their white ideological counterparts. It has largely become the above ground political support apparatus of the RATF and the BLA. May 19th cadres functioned as couriers for the RATF and BLA running a communications network among the imprisoned terrorists and their peers outside. It has 34 members including David Gilbert, Janet Clark, Katherine Boudin.

* Ministry of Christ Church
Right-wing supremacist group, known to its adherents as the religious spearhead of the Identity Movement. It is closely linked to Posse Comitatus. It teaches that all Jews are children of Satan and should be exterminated. It is headed by Rev.Potter Gale of Mariposa, California, a retired US army colonel and expert in guerrilla warfare.

* Minutemen
Right-wing organization established in 1959 and led by Robert Bolivar DePugh. It was organized in secret groups of from five to 15 members and claimed in 1961 to have about 25,000 members. While fervently anti-communist, it also held Jews, Blacks and the government in Washington

responsible for all misery. In 1966, police discovered large arms caches and arrested 20 members.

• Naval Investigative Service (NIS)
US Navy agency established on Aug.8, 1985. It is mainly concerned with counterespionage and terrorism. It is headed by commander Cathal L.Flyn and its headquarters are located in Suitland, Maryland. It has three directorates, naval investigations, counter-intelligence and security.

• National Democratic Policy Committee (NDPC)
Neo-Nazi organization which spreads complot theories in which Jews play a central role. It has a hardcore of 300 members supported by several thousand militants and is led by Lyndon H.La Rouche. It has a security guard which has developed paramilitary activities. Intimidation is its major weapon including telephone threats and the killing and maiming of pets. It has infiltrated the Democratic Party.

• National Security Agency (NSA)
Intelligence organization responsible for all forms of signals and electronic espionage, established by President Truman in 1952. Its main task is decyphering messages projected by all forms of sophisticated communications. Headquarters are at Fort Meade, Maryland. Some 70,000 people work for the organization. NSA has become the most important source of intelligence in the United States. It has the capability to intercept every form of communication, and its staff regularly monitor the outpourings of neutrals, as well as of friend and foe. NSA works in close co-operation with the British Goverment's Communications Headquarters at Cheltenham, which is in control of similar though less extensive operations in Britain.

• National Security Council (NSC)
The most powerful group in the United States dealing with intelligence matters. It is a policy-making body under the direct control of the President, and is composed of senior members of the government, the armed forces and the intelligence community. It was founded in December 1947 under the National Security Act which was passed to reorganize America's intelligence services in the light of Russian aggression in Europe. However, in 1955 the NSC formed a group known as 5412 Committee which was given responsibility of approving all covert operations considered important or sensitive enough to warrant the President's approval. This committee has undergone changes over the years, and has been variously called the Special Committee, the 303 Committee, and currently the Forty Committee. After 'Irangate' the NSC was completely reorganized in 1987 under Frank Carlucci.

• National Socialist (Nazi) Party of America
Small neo-Nazi party. In 1981, six members were tried for plotting terrorist bombing attacks at Greeensboro (North Carolina) in 1980.

• New African Freedom Fighters (NAFF)
Black and White militant group linked to the above ground Republic of New Africa (RNA).

• New World Liberation Front (NWLF)
Small extremist group based in California, active in the mid-1970s. According to the FBI, between 1974 and 1978 the NWLF was responsible for almost 100 bombings in the San Francisco Bay area against banks, business premises and police stations. The NWLF also exploded a pipe bomb outside a nuclear power plant in Oregon. The activities of the NWLF ended in September 1979 when the NWLF leader was arrested. NWLF units have operated under diverse names including Emiliano Zapata Unit, Environmental Assault Unit, Eugene Kuhn Unit, Jonathan Jackson-Sam Melville Unit, Lucio Cabanas Unit, Tom Hicks-Bill Blizzard Unit, Tom Hicks Unit, Unit II and Unit III of the Peoples Forces.

• Office for Combatting Terrorism (OCT)
Special unit of the American State Department, set up in 1972 after the Munich Olympics attack, presently headed by Paul Bremer. Made up of senior officials from a number of US government agencies (including State, Defence, Justice, Treasury and the CIA) the OCT coordinates the American government's campaign against internal and external terrorism. It works from the Operations Centre in Washington DC and is responsible to the National Security Council. It is one of the few agencies that publish an annual survey of recorded international terrorist incidents. During 1985 a total of 782 incidents were recorded in which more than 800 people were killed and another 1,200 people were injured. During 1986 the total rose to 848 incidents, including seven hijackings & attempted hijackings, 82 acts of hostage taking and kidnapping, 164 arson attacks, 183 shootings and 412 bombings. The 1986 total figures showed a big drop in the number of attacks conducted outside the Middle East by Middle Eastern groups.

• The Order (or Silent Brotherhood)
American neo-Nazi white supremacist organization founded in 1982 by Robert Matthews (killed in 1984). It developed into a paramilitary group with a sophisticated armoury, and has staged a number of armed robberies which netted $ 4 million. The group takes its philosophy from an apocalyptic novel by the American writer William Pierce called The Turner Diaries in which a right-wing terrorist group (also called the Order) stage a coup d'etat in the US, takes over the nuclear arsenal and

bombs Israel out of existence. The group has declared its intention to make the US a 'white Christian society' and regard the Jews as an evil influence which must be rooted out. Investigatiors have gradually uncovered links between the Order and such groups as the KKK, the American Nazis, the Posse Comitatus, the Covenant, the Sword and the Arm of the Lord. In June 1984, a Jewish talk-show host, Alan Berg was assassinated in Denver. Bruce Pierce and Randolf Duey were sentenced to 100 years in prison. Pierce was held responsible for the murder of Alan Berg. All 24 known members of the group are dead or imprisoned.

* Organisation of Afro-American Unity (OAAU)
Organization formed by Malcolm X (a former member of the BMM) in 1964. He was shot to death by three (black) gunmen in Harlem on Feb.21, 1965. Elijah Muhammed and the Nation of Islam were widely blamed for his death, although their complicity in the murder was never proved. The OAAU promoted the idea that black Americans should identify with the Third World's coloured minorities. It was opposed to the US policy in Vietnam. The organization advocated a right for blacks of 'retaliatory violence', or 'armed self-defense'.

* Pagan International (PI)
A private company specialised in fighting action groups. It is known as a kind of mini-CIA that works via a lobbying and information system to discredit and stigmatise opponents. It divides activists in three categories, radicals, romantics and realists. The policy of the company is to stigmatise the radicals by revealing left-wing connections and to corrupt the realists. The company works for multi-national companies.

* Posse Comitatus (PC)
Group, also known as the Citizens Law Enforcement Research Committee, founded by Henry Lamont Beach in Portland, Oregon in 1973. PC advocates forming a cell in each county to help county sheriffs, the only legitimate law enforcement authority, to fight federal and state officials. PC opposes the graduated income tax and the federal courts. It reportedly has a hardcore of 2,500 members and is supported by another 10,000 sympathizers. Headquarters are located in Tigerton, Wisconsin. Chapters are present in almost every state. It has engaged in bombings, shootings, resisting arrest and guerrilla/paramilitary terrorist training. It is led by Jim Wickstrom. A defector, James Thimme and Luke Stice, the son of another defector, were murdered by the PC. The five-year old Luke was used as a target during paramilitary training. The majority of its members come from Oregon, Montana, Minnesota, Illinois, Kansas and North Dakota. The organization has links with the KKK and the Life Science Bible Church.

* Prairie Fire Organization Committee (PFOC)
Above ground support organization for the Weather Underground.

* Raza Unida Party (RUP)
Chicano movement in the southwest that has been involved in the supply of explosives for Puerto Rican FALN bombing operations in the midwest and northeastern states.

* Red Guerrilla Resistance (RGR)
Terrorist group which has claimed responsibility for several bomb attacks. It is opposed to Israeli and US policies and South African apartheid. It bombed the Israeli Airçraft Industry office in New York City on Apr.5, 1984. Another device was detonated at the Officer's Club at the Washington Naval Yard on Apr.20, 1984. This attack was dedicated to Carroll Ishee, a North American who died fighting alongside the FMLN guerrilla organization in El Salvador. On Sep.26, 1984, a bomb was placed in the building housing the South African consulate in New York City. On Feb.25, 1985, a bomb exploded at the Police Benevolent Association of the New York City Police. The attack was in commemoration of the 20th anniversary of the Malcolm X assassination and to support a demand of Black communities across the country to stop 'killer cops'.

* Revolutionary Armed Task Force (RATF)
An alliance of the Weather Underground and the BLA which is believed to have emerged in 1979 after BLA leader Joanne Chesimard's escape from prison. It has fewer than 50 active members. A network appears to extend across the United States. The existing groups share arms and intelligence, provide safehouses and assist in the planning and execution of operations including prison escapes. The group is highly disciplined and its limited membership makes it virtually impossible to infiltrate. The New York cell is thought to have accumulated an estimated $ 1 million form bank robberies between 1976 and 1981. The money was used for safe houses, food, and other living expenses, as well as weapons and drugs. Susan Rosenberg and Tim Blunk were arrested in Clerry Hill, New Jersey, on Nov.29, 1984. They were sentenced May 20, 1985, for the maximum penalty of 55 years.

* Revolutionary Fighting Group (RFG)
The RFG claimed to have planted a bomb at an FBI building on Staten Island on Jan.29, 1982. It is believed that the RFG is a pseudonym for the Revolutionary Armed Task Force (RATF).

* Sam Melville-Jonathan Jackson Unit
A group which has been responsible for several

bombings and the murder of a state trooper in 1981. See UFF.

* Special Operations Command (SOCOM)
US Army unconventional force headed by Maj.Gen.Leroy N.Suddath Jr. Its headquarters are located at Fort Bragg, North Carolina. The force includes the ranger regiments, special forces unconventional warfare trainers and behind-the-line saboteurs, a psychological warfare group, a civilian affairs battalion and an expanding special aviation unit. From 1982 to 1990, the SOCOM is planned to rise from $ 250 million to about $ 700 million. Manpower will increase from 6,900 to 13,900. Its current manpower is 4,800 soldiers in Special Forces; 1,500 soldiers in three Ranger battalions; 800 in the Psychological warfare group; 250 in the civil affairs battalion; and roughly 800 men in the aviation section. About one-third are stationed at Fort Bragg.

* Students for a Democratic Society (SDS)
Parent body from which several violent factions emerged in the late 1960s. Under Carl Davidson the SDS had some 40,000 supporters by 1968. SDS members turned to direct action, e.g. at Columbia University, where it occupied buildings. Mark Rudd, a future Weatherman, was one the leaders. The New Left SDS broke up into factions. The most notable was the Revolutionary Youth Movement (RYM) which gave rise to the violent Weatherman Faction. Other factions to emerge from the splintering in 1969 were the October League, Revolutionary Union, and the New American Movement. During the 1970s, the New Year's Gang, the Red Guerrillla Family and the Venceremos Brigades emerged as new splintergroups.

* Student' Non-Violent Co-ordinating Committee (SNCC)
Originally the SNCC, founded in 1960 as a bi-racial student organization, advocated the attainment of racial integration through non-violent means; any of its members was liable to be expelled. However, after the election of Stokely Carmichael as its chairman in 1966, the SNCC repudiated non-violence, replaced integration by 'Black Power' as its aim it adopted a black panther as its emblem and advocated 'guerrilla warfare in the streets'. In May 1967 Carmichael was replaced by Hubert ('Rap') Brown.

* Symbionese Liberation Army (SLA)
Left-wing California-based terrorist group formed by Donald DeFreeze in July 1973. The group achieved notoriety after kidnapping newspaper heiress Patricia Hearst in February 1974 and then converting her to their cause. The SLA were responsible for bombing attacks and armed robberies in California. The group consisted of three independently operating teams. Six members of the SLA, including Donald DeFreeze died on May 17, 1974, in a shoot-out with the police. The remaining members were rounded up by the police.

* Unification Church of the Reverend Sun Myung Moon
Anti-communist sect linked to the South Korean intelligence service (KCIA).

* United Freedom Front (UFF)
Left-wing terrorist group which operated in the New York area. In May 1986 eight members of the group, five men and three women, were charged with conspiracy to overthrow the American government, 19 bomb attacks, ten bank robberies, three murders and an attempt to murder in the 1975-1984 period. The bomb attacks were on courts, banks, companies (military contractors) and military installations. The group financed its activities with bank raids. One of the arrested men was Raymond Luc Levasseur, a member of the Sam Melville-Jonathan Jackson Unit, who was wanted for the 1981 murder of a New Jersey state trooper. The Sam Melville-Jonathan Jackson Unit and the UFF are now believed to have been the same group. The attacks were part of a campaign against the US military machine and in solidarity and support for the people in Central America and South Africa.

* United States Council for World Freedom (USCWF)
An organization based in Phoenix (Arizona). It is an affiliate of the World Anti-Communist League which has provided aid to rebel forces trying to overthrow leftist governments in Angola, Mozambique, Ethiopia, Cambodia and Nicaragua. General Singlaub is a former chairman of the world league and currently a member of its board of directors.

* Weather Underground
Revolutionary left-wing movement founded in June 1969 as an offshoot of the Students for a Democratic Society (SDS). It had 300 members in late 1969. About 40 went underground in 1970. Its five-member central committee included Katherine Boudin, Cathlyn Platt Wilkerson, Bernadine Dohrn, Jeffrey Carl Jones and William B.Ayers. In October 1969 some 200 members staged riots in Chicago ('days of rage'). Between 1970 and 1975 Weatherpeople were responsible for at least 20 bombings. Thirty-seven members were identified as still being active in the Weather Underground. On Oct.20, 1981, four alleged members of the movement were arrested, among them two leading women, Judith A.Clark and Katherine Boudin.

* White Patriot Party (WPP)
Until 1985 this right-wing organization was known

as the Confederate Knights of the Ku Klux Klan. The group espouses anti-semitic and anti-black doctrines. It claims to have 4,400 members and supporters. Members receive weapons training and wear military fatigue. A small number of Marines stationed at Camp Lejeune and soldiers at Fort Bragg are said to be supporting the WPP.

* World Anti-Communist League (WACL)
Right-wing organization founded in Taiwan in 1967. It has close links with the Unification Church (known as the 'Moonies'). Based in the US, the league is run by retired US general John K.Singlaub. It specilises in raising money for anti-communist groups operating around the world, mainly in Latin America, Africa and South-East Asia. In recent years Singlaub and the WACL have raised more than $ 20 million dollars to help Contra guerrillas in Nicaragua. In 1985 it agreed to support anti-government rebels operating in Angola, Afghanistan, Mozambique and Indo-China. WACL support is thought to have been given to the right-wing death squads which operated in Argentina, Uruguay, El Salvador and Chile.

* World Union of National Socialists (WUNS)
Right-wing organization established in 1962 with the aim of combating the 'Judeo-Communist international'. It was led by the self-proclaimed 'Führer' Lincoln Rockwell, an American Nazi who later was murdered.

URUGUAY

* Anti Subversive Operations Coordinating Organization (OCOA)
An organization which reportedly was sent on assassination missions to Europe.

* Commando Caza Tupamaros (CCT)
A commando with alleged links to the military. In February 1972 it started with a wave of bomb attacks on representatives of Frente Amplio. On Apr.15, 1972, martial law was declared. It operated as a death squad in 1974. Its leader, Armando A-costa y Lura (former minister of education) was killed by the Tupamaros.

* Defense Intelligence Service (SID)
Some of its members were reportedly sent to Europe with assassination assignments.

* Gaudicio Nunez (GN)
A right-wing commando which in September 1985 claimed responsibility for the death of a Tupamaro. The dead body was found in a river with the hands tied on the back and a suitcase with filled stones tied around his waist.

* National Liberation Movement, Tupamaros (Movimiento de Liberaci6n Nacional) (MLN)
Left-wing revolutionary urban terrorist group formed in 1963. It was suppressed by the Uruguayan security forces in the early 1970s. The name Tupamaros refers to Tupac Amaru, a Peruvian Indian leader who was killed in the 18th century. At its peak strenghth in 1971 it was estimated to have about 6,000 members. It recruited at every level of society. Its principal leaders were Raul Sendic, Julio Angel Marenales Saenz, Gabino Falero Montes de Oca, Jorge Amilcar Manera Lluveras and Heraclio Jesus Rodrigues Recalde. In the late 1960s it engaged in raids on banks, businesses and arsenals. In the early 1970s it began killing policemen and soldiers and also engaged in bomb attacks and kidnappings. It was urban-based and operated mainly in Montevideo where it developed an extensive subversive network. In 1972 the military took power. About 7,000 alleged Tupamaro's were imprisoned, 200 had been killed and 2,000 fled the country. Many of those imprisoned were tortured. In 1985 Raul Sendic re-established the organization as a legal political party.

* Party for the Victory of the People (Partido por la Victoria del Pueblo) (PVP)
The PVP was an independent opposition party distinct from the Frente Amplio. On Oct.29, 1976, the security forces announced that the party had been planning the assassination of members of the Uruguayan regime. Uruguayan exile groups, however, asserted that many of those arrested under this charge had earlier been kidnapped in Argentina.

* Raoul Sendic International Brigade
Organization which has been responsible for the assassination in Paris on Dec.19, 1974, of Col.Ramon Trabal (Uruguayan military attaché). The attack was revenged by the killing of five former Tupamaros and by the arrest of numerous persons, the rearrest of hundreds of provisionally released political prisoners as well as by sanctions against university staff and the press in Uruguay.

VANUATU

* Nagriamel Movement
Secessionist movement which has been involved in a revolt in May 1980. Some 800 supporters captured the British district commissioner and some of his officials and police, occupied the police station and cut off all communications with Port Vila. Jimmy Stevens, its leader, announced the formation of a six-member 'Provisional Government of the independent state of Vemerana' with himself as 'Prime Minister'. The revolt was suppressed by a joint Anglo-French force of 200 men and some 150 troops from Papua New Guinea, with Australian support. Jimmy Stevens was sentenced to 14½ years

imprisonment and 550 others were convicted as well. French nationals were said to have instigated the secession.

VENEZUELA

* Argimirio Gabaldon Revolutionary Command
Terrorist group responsible for the kidnapping of William F.Niehous (general manager in Venezuela of the US Owens-Illinois glass firm and its world president), Feb.27, 1976. W.F.Niehous was, according to official reports, rescued on June 30, 1979, and according to other sources, released as a result of government concessions such as the pardoning of Douglas Bravo of the Armed Forces of National Liberation.

* Armed Forces of National Liberation
(Fuerzas Armadas de Liberación Nacional) (FALN)
Left-wing guerrilla organization active between 1963 and 1977, which was linked to the Venezuelan Communist Party (PCV). It engaged in sabotage, arson, abductions and armed attacks. In 1967 the PCV rejected the armed path it had originally encouraged. Cuba continued support until Soviet pressure compelled Castro to abandon the FALN. Consequently, FALN activities greatly declined after 1972. In 1979 Douglas Bravo, one of the main leaders, accepted a government amnesty. He distanced himself from the armed struggle and turned to legal activities.

* International Movement of the Proletariat
(Movimiento Internacional del Proletariado) (MIP)
Members of this Movement hijacked a Venezuelan airliner on Nov.6, 1980, diverting it to Havana in protest against the acquittal by a Venezuelan court of four men accused of placing a bomb on a Cuban airliner in 1976, which killed 73 persons.

* Movement of the Revolutionary Left
(Movimiento de la Izquierda Revolucionaria) (MIR)
Left-wing terrorist organization active in the early 1960s. It was led by Américo Martín and Alberto Rangel. In January 1970 a Committee of Revolutionary Integration was set up by members of a breakaway group of the MIR, called Red Banner and the FALN leader, Douglas Bravo. It engaged in kidnappings and bank raids. The MIR was legalised as a party in 1973 and participated in the electoral process.

* Ramón Emeterio Betance Commando
(Commando Ramón Emeterio Betance) (CREB)
Extreme left-wing group, named after a 19th century Puerto Rican nationalist. It claimed responsibility for hijacking three Venezuelan airliners, and their diversion to Havana on Dec.7, 1981. On arrival in the Cuban capital, all the hijackers were taken into custody. The hijackers had demanded the release of 23 alleged political detainees in Venezuela and payment of $ 10,000,000. They had also appealed for solidarity with the guerrillas of El Salvador and distributed leaflets on behalf of a group called Manuel Rojas Luzardo International Commandos, said to be a branch of Red Flag organization.

* Red Flag
(Bandera Roja)
Small Marxist-Leninist guerrilla organization that broke away from the FALN. It engaged in armed attacks until 1978. Its leaders, the brothers Carlos and Argenis Betancourt were both arrested in 1977. The group resurfaced in September 1980 when it seized weapons in a raid in Valencia. Gabriel Puerte Aponte, the group's leader, was captured in Caracas on Apr.9, 1982. The BR was reported to have 100 members in 1987 and to have been revived by the Colombian M-19 organization. It was said to have extorted money from oil companies.

* Zero Point
(Punto Cero)
Small Marxist urban guerrilla group active in the 1970s.

VIETNAM

* HX-47
A group that opposes the present regime with sabotage and armed attacks. It operates on the border with Cambodia and is led by a former major of the army under the old regime.

* League for the Independence of Vietnam
(Vietnam Doc Lap Dong Minh Hoi) (Vietminh)
Coalition of Vietnamese nationalist groups founded in 1941 which drove the French colonial regime out of Indo China. Its dominating force was the Indo China Communist Party (ICP) led by Nguyen Al Quoc (better known as Ho Chi Minh). As the Japanese surrendered on Aug.13, 1945, the Vietminh called for an insurrection and pressed ahead to form their own government in Hanoi on Aug.29, 1945. Some 10,000 people died in the bloody August revolt. As French control was reestablished, the Vietminh turned its attention to destroying rival Vietnamese nationalist movements. By December 1946 these elements no longer had any influence. Talks with the French failed and the Vietminh embarked upon the first Indo-Chinese war. In 1951 the Vietminh organization was formally dissolved and replaced by the ICP.

* National Front for the Liberation of South Vietnam
(Mat Tran Dan Toc Giai Phong Mien Nam Viet Nam) (Viet Cong)

The Viet Cong ('Vietnamese Communist') was also known as the National Liberation Front (NLF). The Communist-led guerrilla organization was established in 1961, as a result of a decision taken in September 1960 by the ruling party of North Vietnam, the Vietnam Workers' (Lao Dong) Party. Its first secretary-general was Nguyen Van Hieu. It envisaged a 'broad national democratic administration'. By 1966 it had 50,000 fighters and some 100,000 part-time soldiers. With the Tet (New Year) offensive in early 1968, the Viet Cong assisted by North Vietnam, attempted a transition from guerrilla to regular warfare, although it subsequently reverted to the former. It gained a victory in April 1975, thanks to overwhelmingly conventional attacks by the North Vietnamese allies.

* National Front for the Liberation of the Central Highlands (NFLCH)
Resistance movement active in 1981. It was said to have its own provincial government (the 'Dega') inside Vietnam; to be composed of Rhade tribes from Dac Lac province and of other Vietnamese, Kampuchea and Lao hill tribes. It is supported by China.
* National Salvation Front (NSF)
Underground organization set up by officers and officials of the former South Vietnamese regime and by Chinese 'reactionary capitalists' in 1975. Several members were tried for plotting murders of government officials, hoarding weapons, and organizing armed groups.

* National United Front for the Liberation of Vietnam (NUFLV)
California-based resistance organization. In 1985, it claimed to have united 38 resistance groups within Vietnam, mainly members of the former South Vietnamese army, with a total of 10,000 'resistance soldiers' ready to fight. The front is led by Hoang Co Minh, a retired admiral. It has trained and organized armed propaganda groups and has secretly sent them to work 'in appropriate areas' in preparation for an eventual rising of the Vietnamese people which will occur before 1990, according to Hoang Co Minh.

* Secret Armed Group (SAG)
Group that was reported to operate on the Chinese-Vietnamese border. In August 1980, it reportedly captured the well-known Pak Bo cave where Ho Chi Minh previously had his headquarters.

* United Front for the Struggle of Oppressed Races
(Front Uni pour la Lutte des Races Opprimeés) (FULRO)
Anti-communist front set up as by tribal people of the Central Highlands of Vietnam. These Montagnards demand autonomy for the 12 northern provinces of South Vietnam. Until 1975 it was supported by the US. Since 1979 it has been supported by China. Guerrilla activities have been limited to the Central Highlands.

* Vietnamese Resistance Movement (VRM)
Vietnamese resistance organization aimed at disrupting or overthrowing the Communist regime in Hanoi. It has an infrastructure in South Vietnam to support such underground operations and has links with the Kampuchean KPNLF.

<u>WESTERN SAHARA</u>

* Association of People from Sahara (AOSARIO)
Moroccan organization active in the Western Sahara in 1980. Its aim was to counteract Polisario guerrilla operations in the former Spanish Sahara.

* Liberation Front of the Sahara under Spanish Domination
(Front de Liberation du Sahara sous Domination Espagnole) (FLSDE)
Guerrilla organization established in 1967. It preceded Morehob and changed its name in 1972.

* Liberation Movement of Saquiet el-Hamra and Rio de Oro
Liberation organization established in December 1967. Its leader, Sid Brahim Bassiri, was imprisoned in Spain in 1970.

* Liberation Movement for Western Sahara
Liberation organization emerging in December 1981. Its secretary-general, Sidahmed Mohammed Larosi, said it had been clandestinely active in Saharan refugee camps in Algeria since 1975.

* Liberation and Unity Front
(Front de Liberation et de l'Unité) (FLU)
Guerrilla organization established in 1974 under pressure of Morocco. It had a core of exile Sahraouis. However, the majority was comprised of members of the Moroccan army. It had bases on the Moroccan side of the border.

* Movement of August 21
(Mouvement du 21 Aout)
This organization first emerged in Morocco in 1973. It was led by Mohammed Abdu.

* Movement for the Liberation of the Sahara
(Mouvement pour la Libération du Sahara) (MLS)
National liberation movement established in 1968 by sons of tribal heads studying in Rabat. In the beginning it was unclear whether they advocated complete independence or a kind of unification with Morocco. In June 1970 they proclaimed

independence.

* Organization for the Liberation of Saquiet el-Hamra and Oued el-Dahab (OSLHOD)
From this organization sprang MOREHOB, led by Edouard Moha (probably a false name).

* Party of National Sahraouis Unity
(Partido de Unidad Nacional Sarauis) (PUNS)
Independence movement established in October 1974, under pressure of Spain. In 1975, its secretary-general Henna uld er Rachid fled with the money to the FLU in Morocco. When it was visited by a UN-commission it discredited itself by not being able to show its rank and file.

* Popular Front for the Liberation of Saguia el Hamra and Rio de Oro
(Frente Popular de Liberacion de Saguiet el-Hamra y Rio de Oro) (POLISARIO)
Guerrilla movement established in February 1970. Its armed struggle began on May 20, 1973, with attacks on Spanish military bases. Since 1976, it is led by Mohammed Abdelaziz, Ibrahim Hakim and Ibrahim Ghamli. General Franco promised the West Sahara to Morocco and Mauretania in 1975. Polisario, in turn, announced the creation of a Saharan Arab Democratic Republic (SADR). In 1979 Mauretania withdrew from the territory after a peace agreement with Polisario had been concluded. However, Morocco annexed this part of the territory as well. In January 1980 it could count on the backing of 36 countries. The Algerian support is vital for Polisario. Libya and the Soviet Union have also assisted the Polisario Front. Its strength dwindled from about 6,000 well-trained fighters to about 3,000 in May 1986. It operates with 12-man commandos based on a traditional cell structure. Morocco has established a number of 'defense walls' with a total length of 2,500 km. against the hit-and-run attacks of Polisario. The walls enabled the army to set up a hermetic defense line behind which forces could move without detection and from which it could through radar and sensors, detect and destroy insurgents. Rabat has between 80,000 and 100,000 soldiers in Western Sahara including units stationed permanently along the wall and mobile back up forces to support any point under attack. Building and defending the walls costs $ 400 million a year, but Moroccan officers say their casualties have dropped from 40 per month to one or two per month. Since the conflict began an estimated 10,000 people have been killed. After several quiet years Polisario stepped up activities again in early 1987. It attacked several outposts and reportedly killed several hundred Moroccan soldiers.

* Revolutionary Movement of the Blue People
(Mouvement Revolutionnaire des Hommes Bleus)
(MOREHOB)
This organization was established as the Front de Liberation du Sahara sous Domination Espagnole (FLSDE) in 1967. Since April 1973 it operated from Algiers. In 1975/76 it split into the Frente Polisario and the FLU, a pro-Moroccan organization. The latter was led by Edouard Moha, probably a false name. His aim was the expulsion of the Spanish occupier with the help of the neigboring African states and to establish a Greater Magreb.

* Sahraouis Popular Liberation Army
(Armée Populaire de Libération Sahraoui) (ALPS)
Guerrilla organization active in the mid-1970s. It was responsible for daily attacks during 1976 and 1977 in the occupied Western Sahara, South Morocco and Mauretania.

<u>YEMEN, NORTH</u> (YEMEN ARAB REPUBLIC)

* Islamic Front (IF)
Organization of tribes in remote mountain regions supported and financed by Saudi Arabia to oppose North Yemen's proposed merger with South Yemen. Its leader, Shaikh Abdullah Bin Hussein al-Ahmar, made an unsuccessful insurrection attempt aimed at the establishment of a strict Moslem regime in North Yemen in mid-1977.

* National Democratic Front
(Jabhat al-Wataniya al-Dimukratiya) (NDF)
Organization of North Yemeni tribesmen, established in 1977 in South Yemen. Armed attacks have been reported from February 1977 until 1979. Reports of alleged Cuban and Soviet involvement led the US government to order a naval taskforce to the Arabian peninsula. The US government also decided to step up arms deliveries and to send military advisers to North Yemen. Sporadic clashes between the NDF and North Yemeni troops have since then been reported. In January 1981 it was claimed that an offensive by North Yemeni government forces had defeated the NDF and had forced it to withdraw to South Yemen. More than 1,000 people died in 1981 alone. Severe fighting between government forces based in Sana'a and the NDF broke out in the spring of 1982 and continued throughout the first half of the year. At one point the rebels, who were reported to have obtained some new recruits from the powerful Bakil confederation of tribesmen, were said to be controlling large parts of central North Yemen as well as more southernly areas around the border with South Yemen. However, by the autumn the fighting appeared to have died somewhat after President saleh promised to hold free elections in the country in 1983.

* National Liberation Army (NLA)

Several men claiming to be members of this group were among 13 South Yemenis sentenced in Aden on Apr.7, 1982 (12 of them to death and the other to 15 years in prison) for 'plotting' to sabotage South Yemen's economic and oil installations after being allegedly trained by the US Central Intelligence Agency (CIA) in Saudi Arabia and having brought explosives into the country. Of the death sentences, two were commuted to 15 years' imprisonment, where as the other 10 were carried out on Apr.22, 1982.

* Party of Popular Yemenite Unity (PPYU)
Most active opposition force in the Yemen Arab Republic. It reportedly received weapons via South Yemen and had guerrillas crossing the frontier from that country. It allegedly had close links with the Yemen Socialist Party (YSP), the sole legal party of South Yemen. Three of the PPYU's leaders, named as Yehua el-Chami, Mohammed Kassem el Thawr and Jarallah Omar, were said to be members of the YSP's political bureau.

YEMEN, SOUTH (PEOPLE's DEMOCRATIC REPUBLIC OF YEMEN)

* Front for the Liberation of Occupied South Yemen
(Jabhat al-Tahrir al-Janubi al-Yaman) (FLOSY)
Liberation front established in January 1966 by a merger of the Organization of the Occupied South and the National front for the Liberation of the Occupied South. Backed by Egypt it favoured a nationalist government which would supercede the traditional authority of the local tribal leaders in South Arabia. It engaged in the killing of leading communists and trade unionists. Clashes between FLOSY and NLF in 1967 resulted in a victory of the rival liberation movement to which the British transferred power in 1968. After independence FLOSY claimed responsibility for disturbances in South Yemen. Its sponsor was Saudi Arabia after Egypt had ceased support.

* National Grouping of Patriotic Forces (NGPF)
Opposition group established in March 1980 in Baghdad (Iraq) under the leadership of Abdul Qawee Mackawee, a former FLOSY-leader. Its objectives are to bring together all 'progressive national and patriotic forces' opposed to what it calls 'the puppet fascist regime' in South Yemen. It has vowed to fight 'all forms of foreign presence in South Yemen', to liberate the country from 'the authority of the secessionists and their overlords' and to unify the two Yemens.

* National Liberation Front
(Jabhat al-Tahrir al-Qaumia) (NLF)
A nationalist front established in June 1963 against Britis presence. Rural operations began in October 1963 in the mountains of Radfan. The urban campaign was initiated in August 1964, when attacks began on British military installations. The NLF had contacts with Palestinian exiles, particularly George Habash. In 1967 Britain transferred power and the NLF proclaimed the People's Republic of Yemen. In 1970 the name was changed to People's Democratic Republic of Yemen, in accordance with Marxist-Leninist usage.

* National Unification Army (NUA)
Ten members of this right-wing organization were sentenced to death on Mar.31, 1982, for sabotage with outside help.

* Yemen Socialist Party (YSP)
This Marxist-Leninist vanguard party was formed on Oct.11, 1978. Its secretary-general was 'Abd al-Fattah Isma'il. He was overthrown by his 'faithful' friends, Ali Nasser and Ali Antar on Apr.21, 1980. He went into exile to the Soviet Union. Ali Nasser became president. In 1985 Isma'il returned from the Soviet Union and started again political activities. In early 1986, a bloody civil war broke out between several factions of the party. Casualty estimates range up to 13,000 deaths. Many poltical, military and union leaders were killed. Ali Nasser Mohammed was forced to leave the country. A collective leadership was established with Abu Bakr al-Attas as president. It is unclear whether 'Abd al-Fattah Isma'il was killed in the war or whether he is still alive, probably in the Soviet Union. About 30,000 South Yemenites fled to the Northern Yemen from where resistance operations are organized.

YUGOSLAVIA

* Albanian Independence Movement (AIM)
Albanikos and other Albanian ethnics in Kosovo have pressured Belgrade to make Kosovo a republic. The ultimate goal is a separate republic united with Albania. It engaged in strikes, sabotage and threats to Serbs. There were student disturbances in 1968, demonstrations in the provincial capital Pristina in 1976, and a number of riots some of the worst occurring in 1981. In that year mass demonstrations caused extensive damage to public and private property. Eight demonstrators and a policemen had been killed and 257 persons injured. On Apr.3 the government declared a state of emergency. The demonstrators had demanded a full republican status for Kosovo. More then 1,000 people went on trial charged with nationalism.

* Albanian Marxist-Leninist Communist Party (AMLCP)
It was alledged in 1981 that the riots in Pristina(Kosovo) had been provoked by this clandestine party. Its aims were said to be the

overthrow of the constitutional order in Yugoslavia and the proclamation of an Albanian republic.

* Chetniks
Serbian exile movement, consisting of adherents of the late General Draja Mihailovic, who had during World War II opposed Josip Broz Tito. In the 1970s several members have been sentenced to varying terms of imprisonment. In Western Europe, the Chetniks were organized in the Ravnagora movement, one of whose leaders (Borivoje Blagojevic) was assassinated in Brussels on Mar.8, 1975. Other Serbian nationalists murdered in Brussels included the editor of Vascrc Spoije on May 13, 1975, and two other alleged Serbian royalists, found killed on Aug.11, 1976. In 1985 a pro-Chetnik group was disbanded in Yugoslavia. Six persons were arrested and tried. Its alleged leader, Risto Radovic, was given a prison sentence.

* Committee for the Area Around Jur
Eight persons of Albanian origin charged to be members of this nationalist and secessionist organization were sentenced to terms of imprisonment in April 1986.

* Cominformist Congress (CC)
Organization of pro-Soviet communists who opposed the 1948 break between Yugoslavia and the Soviet Union-controlled Cominform. In 1975 the Cominformists were said to have formed nine secret organizations working in Yugoslavia, committing acts of terrorism and being supported by subversive groups in various countries (notably Australia, Canada, France, FRG, Sweden and the USSR). A Communist Party of Yugoslavia was reported to have been established at a secret conference during 1974. Its program contained a condemnation of President Tito for having 'betrayed' the original Communist party of Yugoslavia. It allegedly has been involved in the spring 1981 disturbances in Kosovo.

* Croatian Revolutionary Brotherhood
(Hrvatsko Revolucionarno Bratsvo) (HRB)
Croation exile group which was banned in the FRG in 1968. A group of 19 members of this organization, trained in Australia and Austria, entered Yugoslavia in July 1972. In a clash with security forces 15 of the infiltrators and 15 security forces were killed. Three of the remaining attackers were sentenced to death in Sarajevo on Mar.17, 1973, and a fourth had his death sentence commuted to imprisonment for 20 years.

* Croatian Liberation Fighters (CLF)
Croatian underground movement aimed at a free and independent Croatia. It engaged in terrorist activities in the United States in 1980. It has been responsible for bomb attacks on a Yugoslav bank in New York and on the house of a Yugoslav chargé d'affaires in Washington.

* Croat National Congress
(Hrvatsko Narodno Vijecé) (HNV)
Umbrella organization of nationalist Croatian exiles with headquarters in New York. In 1985 it established a Croatian Information Center to inform the public about the cultural tradition and the unbroken will to establish an independent state. It also has offices in Cologne (West Germany). It has served as a support base for Croatian terrorists.

* Croatian National Resistance
(Hrvatski Narodni Odbor) (HNO)
Croatian exile organization mainly active in the Federal Republic of Germany, Australia and the United States. The anti-communist nationalist group is dedicated to achieving independence for Croatia. In the United States members have been convicted for murder, arson, bombings and extortion. Its leader, Stjepan Bilandzic, was on June 25, 1964, given a 3½-year prison sentence for his involvement in an attack on the Yugoslav trade mission in Bad Godesberg on Nov.29, 1962. On May 25, 1978, he was again arrested, and with others, accused of various crimes against the Yugoslav state. It had an estimated membership of several hundred.

* Croatian State forming Movement (HDP)
Croatian organization that propagates violence inside and outside Yugoslavia as a legitimate means to reach its goals.

* Drina
Croatian terrorist unit of the HNO, banned by the Federal Republic of Germany on June 9, 1976. It targeted Yugoslav institutions and representatives.

* Hrvatska Revolucja (HR)
Croatian exile organization in Sweden. Several persons were arrested in December 1981 when an arms cache was discovered.

* Mother Croatia
(Matica Hrvatska) (MH)
Croatian nationalist movement founded in the 1840s as a cultural organization. In the early 1970s it was accused of threatening the unity of Yugoslavia. President Tito said that it was organized by a 'so-called revolutionary committee of 50' which had infiltrated the Croatian League of Communists. The accusations led to a purge and reorganization of the Croatian party and state leadership. MH was said to have contacts with émigré groups in various countries. It was also said hat it had set up 36 branches abroad and that its membership included Ustashi members.

* Ravnagora Movement

Anti-communist Croatian organization. Two Yugoslavs were sentenced to prison for 12 years on charges of the Mar.10, 1986, murder of a Yugoslav and wounding another in the Netherlands. The action was part of a power struggle in the Yugoslav organized crime. Dutch authorities feared a possible move to free the two perpetrators.

* Rebel Croat Revolutionary Organisation
(Ustasa Hrvatska Revolucionarna Organizacija) (UHRO)
Fascist terrorist organization active since the interwar years. Its goal, an independent Croate State, was realized in the period 1941-1945 when Ante Pavelic was the 'Führer'. It was one of the most cruel regimes of Europe, killing more than 700,000 Serbians. After the Second World War the Ustasha leadership fled to Argentina and, together with Croatian exiles in other countries, continued to oppose the Tito regime in third countries as well as at home. It engaged in hijackings, armed assaults, assassinations and bomb attacks on Yugoslav targets and representatives. In 1985 45 members of the organization went on trial.

* Red Front
General Franjo Herlevic, Federal Secretary for Internal Affairs, claimed in an interview on May 13, 1981, to have 'concrete evidence' of the pursuit of pan-Albanian goals in Yugoslavia by official representatives of the Albanian government and of the existence of a clandestine 'Red Front' closely linked with the ruling Albanian Party of Labour and with the Albanian intelligence services.

* Sluzba Drzavne Bezbednosti (SDB)
Yugoslav security service previously called UDBA. In 1966 it was renamed SDB. Until 1966 it was led by Mr.Rancovic. The service engaged in killing Yugoslav exiles, mainly in West Germany. Targets were members of the Info-Bureau (former Stalinist partisans), Cominformists and Ustasjis (Croatian exiles).

* United Croats of West Germany
(Ujedinjeni Hrvati Njemaske) (UHNJ)
Croatian exile organization aiming at the violent overthrow of the Yugoslav government.

* World League of Croatian Youth
(Svetska Liga Hrvatske Omladine) (SLHO)
Croation youth organization in support of the Croatian Liberation Movement.

* Yugoslav Security Police (LCY)
In August-September 1966 it was officially disclosed that in dealing with Albaninans accused of secessionist activities the security police in what was then the Kosovo-Metohija (or Kosmet) autonomous region had been guilty of irregularities involving the murder and torture of a number of Albanians. As a result of the disclosures the LCY was restructured.

ZAIRE

* Action Movement for the Resurrection of Congo
(Mouvement d'Action pour la Résurrection du Congo) (MARC)
Opposition movement founded in Belgium under the leadership of Monguya Mbenge in 1974. It was held responsible for planning a coup d'etat for February 1978. In this connection its founder, Kanyonga Mobateli, as well as Monguya Mbenge (a former governor of Shabà province) and two other MARC members, were sentenced to death in absentia on Mar.16, 1978. Kanyonga Mobateli was shot and killed by an unidentified person in 1978.

* Congolese Front for the Restoration of Democracy
(Front Congolais pour le Rétablissement de la Démocratie) (FCRD)
Umbrella organization established in Brussels in October 1982 as an alliance of opposition groups. It is led by Nguza Karl I Bond.

* Congolese National Liberation Front
(Front de Libération Nationale du Congo) (FLNC)
Front set up in Paris in 1963 by former gendarmes from Katanga. Led by Lt.Gen. Nathaniel Mbumba the front was said to number between 5,000 and 7,000 in 1977. It has been involved in two invasions of the province of Shaba (formerly Katanga) in 1977 and 1978. In July 1980 it joined the Council for the Liberation of the Congo-Kinshasa. Presently it consists of about 3,000 dissidents in camps in Zambia and Angola lacking major foreign support.

* Congo National Movement-Lumumba
(MouvementNationalduCongo-Lumumba) (MNC-L)
Zairan exile opposition group based in Belgium. Its leader, Paul Roger Mokede, was expelled from Brussels to Paris in May 1978.

* Council for the Liberation of Congo-Kinshasa
(Conseil pour la Libération du Congo-Kinshasa) (CLC)
The CLC was established in Brussels in July 1980 as a merger of various exile groups in opposition to the Mobutu regime. The declared aim of the CLC is the restoration of democracy and fundamental human rights in Zaire. Bernardin Mungul Diaka, a former minister of education, acted as its president. Member parties of the organization were: 1) the National front for the Liberation of the Congo; 2) the National Movement for Union and Reconciliation in Zaire (MNUR); 3) the People's Revolutionary Party (PRP); 4) the

Congolese Socialist Party; 5) the Congolese Progressive Students.

• Kamanyola
Special elite unit of President Mobutu established in 1974 after he had visited China and North Korea. It is trained by North Korean instructors. About 800 soldiers reportedly deserted following mutual murders of instructors and soldiers.

• Marxist Revolutionary Party of Congo Kinshasa (PRMC)
Radical party established in 1972, by Emmanuel Kasbassu-Balenga and Kibwe - Tcha-Malenge. Its armed branch, the Red People's Army, captured large areas in the east of the country.

• Military Security and Intelligence Service (Service de Renseignement et de Securité Militaires) (SRSM)
Government agency which engaged in torturing of people held in communicado without benifit of a trial. It is led by Col.Bolozi Gbudu Tanakpma. The agency is known as G2 in Kinshasa, T2 at provisional headquarters and S2 in the field.

• National Documentation Center
(Agence Nationale de Documentation) (AND)
Government security service that engaged in torture.

• National Movement for Unity and Reconciliation in Zaire
(Mouvement National pour l'Union et la Réconciliation au Zaire) (MNUR)
Zairan opposition movement established in Brussels in 1978 by Mbeka Makosso, a former Minister of Economy and ambassador to Iran. In 1980 it joined the opposition Council for the Liberation of Congo-Kinshasa.

• National Research and Investigation Centre
(Centre National de Recherches et d'Investigations) (CNRI)
Government agency responsible for internal security.

• People's Revolutionary Party
(Parti Revolutionaire de Peuple Zairois) (PRP)
Internal resistance movement which since 1967, has held guerrilla strongholds in the Fizi Baraka area. Since 1969 its armed branch, the Forces Armeés Populaires (FAP) operated in Kivu and Shaba. It had a strength of about 3,000 fighters. Its leaders were Laurent Kabila, Gabriel Yumu, Kashimu and Gaston Soumalot. In 1980 the PRP joined the Council for the Liberation of the Congo-Kinshasa.

• Zairan Army
In 1985, arrests made by the army were associated with a pattern of torture, brutal treatment and extra-judicial execution. Arbitrary arrests by soldiers were reported in southeast Kivu, mostly of traders and young men who were accused of being 'Gaddafistas' (supporters of the Libyan Col.Gaddafi), apparently solely because they frequently travelled away from home. Throughout 1985 continued instability affected the region along Lake Tanganyika in Eastern Zaire, from Uvira in Kivu region down to Moba, with rebel attacks against Kalemie and once more again in May, Moba itself, which had been a rebel target in 1984. There is credible evidence that both government forces and the insurgents carried out a number of summary executions early in the year. There are reports that at least 100 people have disappeared from the Kalemie-Moba area as a result of military reprisals.

ZIMBABWE

• Central Intelligence Organization (CIO)
Security organization which has engaged in torture.

• Front for the Liberation of Zimbabwe (FROLIZI)
Minor guerrilla organization active in the 1970s. It broke away from ZAPU in October 1971 under the leadership of Chikerema.

• Grey's Scouts
Counter-insurgency force used in the protracted war against African insurgents in the 1960s and 1970s. The mixed (black and white) unit comprised around 300 skilled horsemen and trackers who patrolled the borders between Rhodesia (now Zimbabwe) and her African neighbors.

• Gukurahundi
A special security unit for internal unrest trained by North Korean instructors.

• Matabele Brigade
In 1983, Eddison Munangagwa, the Minister of State for Defense, said that he was convinced that South Africa has already recruited 1,000 former ZIPRA guerrillas to form a Matabele Brigade. He claimed that they are being trained at a military camp at Letaba in the Northern Transvaal near the Phalaborwa Camp where RNM units are said to have been trained in the past. He also said the brigade was being outfitted in uniforms similar to those of the Zimbabwe national army. South Africa denied these allegations.

• Patriotic Front (PF)
In 1976 two Rhodesian liberation movements, the Zimbabwe African People's Union (ZAPU) and the Zimbabwe African National Union (ZANU) agreed to negotiate with the Rhodesian government. They attended as the Patriotic Front. The two movements maintained separate identities and

military forces. After the Lancaster Agreements of December 1979 the two parties drifted apart contesting each other in elections. J.Nkomo, the ZAPU leader, retained the label of the Patriotic Front. ZANU under the leadership of R.Mugabe won the elections. The rivalry between the two parties led to bloody clashes in Matabele land in the early 1980s.

* Rhodesian Special Air Service (RSAS)
Rhodesia's main anti-terrorist unit in the civil war between 1966 and 1980. The RSAS were used as a counter-terror force inside Rhodesia and for 'search-and-destroy' missions into Angola and Zambia. The all-white unit was disbanded in 1980, and many of its members joined the South African Defence Force (SADF).

* Selous Scouts
Anti-terrorist force active under the Ian Smith regime. It was named after the legendary white hunter Frederick Selous. At any one time the unit had no more than 700 Scouts. Of this number less than 25 were American by nationality. The scouts enlisted black troops (some of them ex-terrorists). The unit was commanded by Ron Reid-Daley, one-time member of the British Army's Special Air Services (SAS). The Selous Scouts specialised in tracking and 'hot pursuit' anti-terrorist operations, often across the borders of Zambia and Angola. After the civil war most members left for South Africa.

* Super-ZAPU
Group of insurgents which in 1986 was reported to be active in the Ndebele area.

* Zimbabwe African National Liberation Army (ZANLA)
The military arm of the Zimbabwe African National Union (ZANU) led by Robert Mugabe who later became President of Zimbabwe. It operated out of bases in Mozambique and recruited mainly from the Shona people. It had training camps in Tanzania and Mozambique and was supported by the 'front-line' states. ZANLA never mounted an effective military challenge to the Rhodesian regime. Its leader emerged as a clear winner in the December 1979 elections. Since Zimbabwean independence in April 1980 tensions between the two communities (Shona and Ndebele) have been growing, and there have been a number of armed clashes, and rumours of massacres of Ndbele civilians by Shona soldiers.

* Zimbabwe African National Union (ZANU)
The ruling party in Zimbabwe following the elections of February 1980. It was established in 1963 under the leadership of Ndabaningi Sithole. Robert Mugabe took over the leadership in 1975. It opted early for guerrilla warfare and operated through its armed branch, the Zimbabwe African National Liberation Army (ZANLA) which developed into an army of 10,000 fighters in 1979 and 20,000 in 1980 under the command of Dumiso Dabengwa. During the war it targeted white farms, trains, road traffic, hotels, urban targets, mission schools. After independence ZANLA fighters were integrated into a new national army alongside ZIPRA recruits, to whom they were generally hostile, by 1982. An estimated 30,000 people died in the war.

* Zimbabwe African People's Union (ZAPU)
Party established in 1961 under the leadership of Joshua Nkomo, a father figure of Zimbabwean nationalism. Its armed branch was the Zimbabwe Peoples Revolutionary Army (ZIPRA) which started an armed struggle in 1967. Supported by the Soviet union it operated from Zambia and Botswana. Several members of its cadre received training in the Soviet Union and Cuba. It recruited mainly from the Ndebele speaking peoples in the West. By 1978 it had a strenght of about 1,250 and in the last year of the conflict had about 3,000 fighters. Parts of the force were integrated in a new national army in 1981. Others returned to the bush as dissident ZAPU terrorists. The greatest difficulty arises in the refugee camps across the border with Botswana. There, a few of the people who formerly followed Mr.Nkomo have accepted guns and training from the South Africans, who claimed that Mr.Mugabe provides bases for attacks across their border. South Africa backed bands, have in recent years been accused by Zimbabwe's government of several atrocities.

* Zimbabwe's People's Revolutionary Army (ZIPRA)
The military arm of the Zimbabwe African People's Union (ZAPU), the mainly Ndebele party led by Joshua Nkomo. It spent many years waging a hit-and-run terrorist war against the forces of the Rhodesian regime. Internal unrest which has persisted since 1980 has been due mainly to a conflict between ZANU-PF and PF-ZAPU and their respective former armed forces, ZANLA and ZIPRA. Clashes between the two armies led to the death of hundreds of people in 1980-82 and also to the periodoc renewal of regulations under an Emergency Powers Act of 1965. In early 1982 large quantities of arms were discovered in Matabeleland. They had been hidden in caches by guerrillas loyal to Joshua Nkomo in preparation for a military coup. Senior military advisers to Nkomo, as well as former ZIPRA members said to have undergone military training in Matabeleland, were arrested during March 1982. The Fifth Brigade (trained by North Korean instructors) intervened early in 1983. The unit terrorized the Ndebele people in Matabeleland. The International Federation of Human Rights estimated the number of people killed at 1,500-3,000. In 1985, Mr.Nkomo said that

almost 300 people disppeared in Matabeleland. The release of Dumiso Dabengwa in December 1986 signalled an impending announcement that the long-feuding major parties have agreed to a unification plan. Mr.Mugabe's goal is to make Zimbabwe a one-party state.